Directory of Unpublished
Experimental Mental Measures

VOLUME 9

BERT A. GOLDMAN
DAVID F. MITCHELL

Series Editors: Bert A. Goldman and David F. Mitchell

American Psychological Association, Washington, DC

Published by
American Psychological Association
750 First Street, NE
Washington, DC 20002
www.apa.org

To order
APA Order Department
P.O. Box 92984
Washington, DC 20090-2984
Tel: (800) 374-2721; Direct: (202) 336-5510
Fax: (202) 336-5502; TDD/TTY: (202) 336-6123
Online: www.apa.org/books/
E-mail: order@apa.org

In the U.K., Europe, Africa, and the Middle East, copies may be ordered from
American Psychological Association
3 Henrietta Street
Covent Garden, London
WC2E 8LU England

Typeset by Shepherd, Incorporated, Dubuque, IA

Printer: Port City Press, Baltimore, MD
Cover Designer: Minker Design, Bethesda, MD
Technical/Production Editor: Devon Bourexis

Printed in the United States of America
First Edition

Contents

■ ■ ■

Preface

Purpose: The *Directory of Unpublished Experimental Mental Measures, Volume 9,* enables researchers to determine what types of noncommercial experimental test instruments are currently in use by providing ready access to information about recently developed or recently used experimental measurement scales. The instruments are not evaluated, but the information given about each test should make it possible for researchers to make a preliminary judgment of their usefulness. It does not provide all necessary information for researchers contemplating the use of a particular instrument. It does describe basic test properties and in most cases identifies additional sources from which technical information concerning an instrument can be obtained.

Development: Thirty-four relevant professional journals available to the authors were examined. The following list includes those journals that in the judgment of the authors contained instruments of value to researchers in education, psychology, and sociology. Foreign journals were not surveyed for use in this directory. Measures published only in dissertations were excluded as a matter of expediency and because the microfilm abstracts generally contain minimal information.

American Journal of Sociology
Brain and Language
The Career Development Quarterly
Child Development
Child Study Journal
Educational and Psychological Measurement
Educational Research Quarterly
Gifted Child Quarterly
Journal of Applied Psychology
Journal of College Student Development
Journal of Consulting and Clinical Psychology
Journal of Counseling Psychology
The Journal of Creative Behavior
Journal of Educational Psychology
The Journal of Educational Research
The Journal of Experimental Education
The Journal of General Psychology
Journal of Marriage and Family
Journal of Occupational Psychology
Journal of Personality Assessment
Journal of Psychopathology and Behavioral Assessment
Journal of Research and Development in Education
Journal of Research in Personality
Journal of School Psychology

The Journal of Social Psychology
Journal of Vocational Behavior
Measurement and Evaluation in Counseling and Development
Perceptual and Motor Skills
Personnel Psychology
Professional School Counseling
Psychological Reports
Research in Higher Education
Social Psychology Quarterly
Sociology of Education

Volume 9 lists tests described in the 2001 through 2005 issues of the journals. An attempt was made to omit commercially published standardized tests, task-type activities such as memory word lists used in serial learning research, and achievement tests developed for a single, isolated course of study. Readers should not assume that the instruments described herein form a representative sample of the universe of unpublished experimental mental measures.

Organization: The following is a brief description of each of the 24 categories under which the authors grouped the measures of Volume 9.

Achievement: Measures learning and/or comprehension in specific areas. Also includes tests of memory and tests of spatial ability.

Adjustment—Educational: Measures academic satisfaction. Also includes tests of school anxiety and teacher–student relationships.

Adjustment—Psychological: Evaluates conditions and levels of adjustment along the psychological dimension, including, for example, tests of mood, fear of death, anxiety, and depression.

Adjustment—Social: Evaluates aspects of interactions with others. Also includes tests of alienation, conformity, need for social approval, and social desirability as well as instruments for assessing interpersonal attraction and sensitivity, acculturation, and racial and ethnic identity.

Adjustment—Vocational: Identifies burnout, vocational maturity, job-related stress, job frustration, job satisfaction, and so forth.

Aptitude: Predicts success in given activities.

Attitude: Measures reaction to and beliefs about a variety of experiences and objects.

Behavior: Measures general and specific types of activities such as classroom behavior; leader behavior; alcohol, eating, and drug-use behavior; and abusive and violent behavior.

Communication: Evaluates information exchange. Also includes tests of self-disclosure, leader–member exchange, and feedback.

Concept Meaning: Measures understanding of words and other concepts. Also includes tests of conceptual structure and style and information processing.

Creativity: Measures ability to reorganize data or information into unique configurations. Also includes tests of divergent thinking.

Development: Measures emerging characteristics, primarily for preschool ages. Also includes tests of cognitive and moral development.

Family: Measures intrafamily relations. Also includes tests of marital satisfaction, nurturance, and parental interest.

Institutional Information: Evaluates institutions and their functioning, community and involvement satisfaction, and organizational climate. Also includes job characteristics and distributive and procedural justice.

Motivation: Measures goal strength. Also includes measures of curiosity and need to achieve.

Perception: Determines how one sees self and other objects. Also includes tests dealing with empathy, imagery, locus of control, self-concept, self-esteem, and time. Also includes role conflict.

Personality: Measures general personal attributes. Also includes biographical information, defense mechanisms, and temperament.

Preference: Identifies choices. Also includes tests of preference for objects, taste preference, and sex-role preference.

Problem Solving and Reasoning: Measures general ability to reason through a number of alternative solutions, to generate such solutions to problems, and so forth.

Status: Identifies a hierarchy of acceptability.

Trait Measurement: Identifies and evaluates unitary traits. Also includes tests of anger, authoritarianism, blame, cheating, and narcissism.

Values: Measures worth one ascribes to an object or activity. Also includes tests of moral, philosophical, political, and religious values.

Vocational Evaluation: Evaluates a person for a specific position. Also includes client–therapist working alliance and mentoring.

Vocational Interest: Measures interest in specific occupations and vocations as well as interest in general categories of activity. Also includes organizational commitment and career commitment.

The choice of the category under which each test was grouped was determined by the purpose of the test and/or its apparent content. Three facts are always listed: test name, purpose, and source. In addition, at least four of the following facts (starred in the list below) had to be present in the source in order for the test to be listed in the directory: number of items, time required, format, reliability, validity, or related research. Readers should note that if no information was given for any one of the starred facts, the heading was not included in the entry. For example, if no information about validity was given in the source, validity was not listed in the test entry. A minimum of four starred items listed below was required to include a test.

Test Name

The name of the test listed in the directory was usually given by the author of the paper in which it was found. When a name was not given in the source, one was created for it by the authors of the directory.

Purpose

The general purpose of each scale was usually stated in the source or was suggested by its name. When available, additional detail about the test's purpose is given.

Description

Number of items: The number of items in a scale as stated in the source.

Time required: Few scales are administered under a time constraint. When they are, the time requirements are specified here.

Format: The description of the format of the scales varied widely in the sources. The authors of the directory have presented the essential characteristics of the format, such as general type (Likert, true–false, checklist, and semantic differential). Less common formats are briefly described in additional detail as needed.

Statistics

Reliability: When available, reliabilities and the Ns on which they were based are reported. Commonly reported reliabilities are alpha, split-half, item–total, and K-R 20.

Validity: When available, validity data are reported. The authors have also included correlations with other tests and group difference information that help define the characteristic being measured by the test.

Source

Author

Title

Journal (includes date of publication, volume, and page number)

Related Research

The purpose of this section is to provide additional information about the test. In some cases the original source of the test is given. If an existing test was revised for use with a special population, the original version may be cited. In other cases, a publication that offered additional technical information is listed.

Readers should note that the numbers within the index refer to test numbers, not page numbers.

The authors thank Doris Deal for her accurate and timely typing of much of the manuscript. Thanks also to Nathan Richardson, Jonathan Anderson, and Rebecca Finch for typing early entries in Volume 9. Special appreciation is expressed to Richard Allen for doing the complex and time-consuming final sorting and processing of the entries included in this volume. Their efforts made it possible to finish the manuscript on schedule. Furthermore, the authors wish to thank the American Psychological Association for continuing the publication of the directories.

Bert A. Goldman
David F. Mitchell

Directory of Unpublished
Experimental Mental Measures

CHAPTER 1
Achievement

10210

Test Name: ACADEMIC ACHIEVEMENT SCALE

Purpose: To enable teachers to assess academic achievement in reading, writing, and mathematics.

Number of Items: 3

Format: Responses are made on a 5-point scale ranging from 1 (*for under the mean*) to 5 (*for above the mean*).

Validity: Correlations with other variables ranged from .43 to .72. Test–retest reliability was .69.

Author: Guay, F., et al.

Article: Academic self-concept and academic achievement: Developmental perspectives on their causal ordering.

Journal: *Journal of Educational Psychology*, March 2003, *95*(1), 124–136.

Related Research: Frentz, C., et al. (1991). Popular, controversial, neglected and rejected adolescents: Contrasts of social competence and achievement difference. *Journal of School Psychology, 29*, 109–120.

10211

Test Name: AIDS RISK KNOWLEDGE TEST

Purpose: To measure knowledge of AIDS risk.

Number of Items: 40

Format: A true–false format is used. All items are presented.

Reliability: Spearman–Brown split-half reliability was .73. Test–retest reliability was .84. K-R 20 reliability was .74.

Author: Demmer, C., and Caroleo, O.

Article: College students' perceptions of advances in HIV treatment and the need for safer sex practices.

Journal: *Psychological Reports*, April 2001, *88*, 431–442.

Related Research: Kelly, J. A., et al. (1998). Implications of HIV treatment advances for behavioral research on AIDS: Protease inhibitors and new challenges in HIV secondary prevention. *Health Psychology, 17*, 310–319.

10212

Test Name: ASSESSING EMOTIONS SCALE

Purpose: To measure emotional intelligence.

Number of Items: 33

Format: Scales range from 1 (*strongly disagree*) to 5 (*strongly agree*). Sample items are presented.

Reliability: Alpha coefficients exceeded .86.

Author: Schutte, N. S., et al.

Article: Emotional intelligence and interpersonal relations.

Journal: *The Journal of Social Psychology*, August 2001, *141*, 523–536.

Related Research: Schutte, N. S., et al. (1988). Development and validation of a measure of emotional intelligence. *Personality and Individual Differences, 25*, 167–177.

10213

Test Name: CANTONESE ORAL CLOZE TASK

Purpose: To measure syntactic processing of Chinese.

Number of Items: 17 + 2 training items.

Format: The child is told to replace one word missing in each sentence.

Reliability: Split-half (Spearman–Brown) reliability was .83.

Validity: Correlations with other variables ranged from −.27 to .65.

Author: Gottardo, A., et al.

Article: Factors related to English reading performance in children with Chinese as a first language: More evidence of cross-language transfer of phonological processing.

Journal: *Journal of Educational Psychology*, September 2001, *93*, 530–542.

Related Research: So, D., & Siegel, L. S. (1997). Learning to read Chinese: Semantic, syntactic, phonological and working memory skills in normally achieving and poor Chinese readers. *Reading and Writing: An Interdisciplinary Journal, 9*, 1–21.

10214

Test Name: CHILDREN RHYME DETECTION TASK

Purpose: To measure Chinese rhyme detection.

Number of Items: 15 + 2 training items.

Format: The child indicates one of three words that does not rhyme with the other two.

Reliability: Split-half reliability (Spearman–Brown) was .62.

Validity: Correlations with other variables from −.24 to .59.

Author: Gottardo, A., et al.

Article: Factors related to English reading performance in children with Chinese as a first language: More evidence of cross-language transfer of phonological processing.

Journal: *Journal of Educational Psychology*, September 2001, *93*, 530–542.

Related Research: So, D., & Siegel, L. S. (1997). Learning to read Chinese: Semantic, syntactic, phonological and working memory skills in normally achieving and poor Chinese readers. *Reading and Writing: An Interdisciplinary Journal, 9*, 1–21.

10215

Test Name: CHILDREN'S COMPETENCY SCALE

Purpose: To measure children's abilities by parent report.

Number of Items: 14

Format: Item responses range from 1 (*very little*) to 5 (*clearly above average*). All items are presented.

Reliability: Reliability coefficients ranged from .78 to .88.

Validity: Correlations between scales averaged .60.

Author: Raety, H.

Article: A measure of parents' assessments of their children's abilities.

Journal: *Psychological Reports*, December 2004, *95*, Part 1, 957–963.

10216

Test Name: CHILDREN'S NONWORD REPETITION TEST

Purpose: To assess the child's ability to report unfamiliar nonwords.

Number of Items: 40

Format: Includes two-, three-, four-, and five-syllable items. Examples are presented.

Reliability: Split-half reliability was .66.

Validity: Correlations with other variables ranged from .01 to .49.

Author: Griffiths, Y. M., and Snowling, M. J.

Article: Predictors of exception word and nonword reading in dyslexic children: The severity hypothesis.

Journal: *Journal of Educational Psychology*, March 2002, *94*, 34–43.

Related Research: Gathercole, S. E., et al. (1994). The Children's Test of Nonword Repetition: A test of phonological working memory. *Memory, 2*, 103–127.

10217

Test Name: CHINESE ORTHOGRAPHIC LEGALITY TASK

Purpose: To measure Chinese orthographic processing.

Number of Items: 16

Format: Children are asked which word in pairs of not real words looked the most real.

Reliability: Split-half (Spearman–Brown) reliability was .56.

Validity: Correlations with other variables ranged from −.11 to .32.

Author: Gottardo, A. et al.

Article: Factors related to English reading performance in children with Chinese as a first language: More evidence of cross-language transfer of phonological processing.

Journal: *Journal of Educational Psychology*, September 2001, *93*, 530–542.

10218

Test Name: CHINESE PSEUDOWORD REPETITION MEASURE

Purpose: To measure Chinese pseudoword repetition.

Number of Items: 18

Format: Children are told they will hear some made-up words. They are to repeat them.

Reliability: Spearman–Brown reliability was .36.

Validity: Correlations with other variables ranged from −.23 to .30.

Author: Gottardo, A., et al.

Article: Factors related to English reading performance in children with Chinese as a first language: More evidence of cross-language transfer of phonological processing.

Journal: *Journal of Educational Psychology*, September 2001, *93*, 530–542.

10219

Test Name: CHINESE READING ABILITY TASK

Purpose: To measure ability to read Chinese.

Number of Items: 61

Format: Includes one- and two-character words.

Reliability: Internal consistency was .98.

Validity: Correlations with other variables ranged from −.46 to .63.

Author: McBride-Chang, C., and Kail, R. V.

Article: Cross-cultural similarities in the predictors of reading acquisition.

Journal: *Child Development*, September/October 2002, *73*, 1392–1407.

Related Research: Ho, C. S.-H., & Bryant, P. (1997). Phonological skills are important in learning to read Chinese. *Developmental Psychology, 33*, 946–951.

10220

Test Name: CHINESE TONE DETECTION TASK

Purpose: To assess linguistic processing at a syllabic level.

Number of Items: 15 + 2 training items.

Format: The child indicates which of three words has a different tone than the other two.

Reliability: Split-half reliability (Spearman–Brown) was .61.

Validity: Correlations with other variables ranged from −.34 to .50.

Author: Gottardo, A., et al.

Article: Factors related to English reading performance in children with Chinese as a first language: More evidence of cross-language transfer of phonological processing.

Journal: *Journal of Educational Psychology*, September 2001, *93*, 530–542.

Related Research: So, D., & Siegel, L. S. (1997). Learning to read Chinese: Semantic, syntactic, phonological and working memory

skills in normally achieving and poor Chinese readers. *Reading and Writing: An Interdisciplinary Journal, 9*, 1–21.

10221

Test Name: COMPUTER UNDERSTANDING AND EXPERIENCE SCALE

Purpose: To measure general computer experience.

Number of Items: 12

Format: A sample item is given.

Reliability: Coefficient alpha was .86.

Validity: Correlations with other variables ranged from −.18 to .70.

Author: Potosky, D., and Bobko, P.

Article: Selection testing via the internet: Practical considerations and exploratory empirical findings.

Journal: *Personnel Psychology*, Winter 2004, *57*, 1003–1034.

Related Research: Potosky, D., & Bobko, P. (1998). The Computer Understanding and Experience (CUE) Scale: A self-report measure of computer experience. *Computers in Human Behavior, 14*, 337–348.

10222

Test Name: CONCEPT MAPPING

Purpose: To measure concept mapping.

Number of Items: 1

Time Required: 20 minutes

Format: Abilities scored in concept mapping are propositions, hierarchies, cross-links, and examples. The item is given.

Validity: Correlations with other variables ranged from −.22 to .60.

Author: Yeh, Y.-C.

Article: Seventh graders' academic achievement, creativity, and ability

to construct a cross-domain concept map—A brain function perspective.

Journal: *The Journal of Creative Behavior*, Second Quarter 2004, *38*(2), 125–144.

Related Research: McClure, J. R., et al. (1999). Concept map assessment of classroom learning: Reliability, validity, and logistical practicality. *Journal of Research in Science Teaching, 36*, 475–492. Novak, J. D., & Gowim, D. B. (1984). *Learning how to learn.* Cambridge, England: Cambridge University Press.

10223

Test Name: CONCEPTS ABOUT PRINT TEST

Purpose: To measure emerging knowledge about print.

Number of Items: 24

Reliability: Coefficient alpha was .83.

Validity: Correlations with other variables ranged from −.34 to .63.

Author: Samuelsson, S., et al.

Article: Environmental and genetic influences on prereading skills in Australia, Scandanavia, and the United States.

Journal: *Journal of Educational Psychology*, November 2005, *97*, 705–722.

Related Research: Clay, M. (1975). *The early detection of reading difficulties: A diagnostic survey.* Auckland, New Zealand: Heineman.

10224

Test Name: CURRICULUM-BASED MEASUREMENT COMPUTATION TEST

Purpose: To measure first graders' computation ability.

Number of Items: 25

Time Required: 5 minutes

Format: A one-page test.

Reliability: Coefficient alpha was .95.

Validity: Correlations with other variables ranged from −.29 to .66 ($N = 272$).

Author: Fuchs, L. S., et al.

Article: The prevention, identification, and cognitive determinants of math difficulty.

Journal: *Journal of Educational Psychology*, August 2005, *97*, 493–513.

Related Research: Fuchs, L. S., et al. (1990). *Curriculum-based math computation and concepts/applications.* (Available from L. S. Fuchs, 328 Peabody, Vanderbilt University, Nashville, TN 37203)

10225

Test Name: ENGLISH AND DUTCH NONWORD READING SKILL TEST

Purpose: To measure English and Dutch nonword reading skills including accuracy and speed for children 6- to 11-years-old.

Number of Items: 60

Format: For both English and Dutch, there are 30 nonwords consisting of 5 monosyllabic three-letter strings, 15 monosyllabic four-letter strings, and 10 bisyllabic six-letter strings. All nonwords are presented.

Reliability: Alpha coefficients for accuracy were .91 (English) and .81 (Dutch). Split-half reliabilities for reaction time were .94 (English) and .96 (Dutch).

Validity: Correlations with other variables ranged from −.70 to .78.

Author: Patel, T. K., et al.

Article: A cross-linguistic comparison of children learning to read in English and Dutch.

Journal: *Journal of Educational Psychology*, December 2004, *96*, 785–797.

Related Research: Castles, A., & Coltheart, M. (1993). Varieties of developmental dyslexia. *Cognition, 47*, 149–180.

10226

Test Name: ENGLISH AND DUTCH REGULAR WORD READING SKILL TEST

Purpose: To measure English and Dutch regular word reading skill including accuracy and speed for children 6- to 11-years old.

Number of Items: 60

Format: Includes both English and Dutch word lists containing half monosyllabic and half bisyllabic words. All words are given.

Reliability: Alpha coefficients for accuracy were .94 (English) and .66 (Dutch). Split-half reliabilities for reaction time were .86 (English) and .66 (Dutch).

Validity: Correlations with other variables ranged from −.59 to .78.

Author: Patel, T. K., et al.

Article: A cross-linguistic comparison of children learning to read in English and Dutch.

Journal: *Journal of Educational Psychology*, December 2004, *96*, 785–797.

Related Research: Castles, A., & Coltheart, M. (1993). Varieties of developmental dyslexia. *Cognition, 47*, 149–180.

10227

Test Name: EXCEPTION WORD READING SCALE

Purpose: To measure exception word reading skill.

Number of Items: 44

Format: Includes high-frequency and low-frequency items. Examples are presented.

Reliability: Coefficient alpha was .89.

Validity: Correlations with other variables ranged from −.07 to .80.

Author: Griffiths, Y. M., and Snowling, M. J.

Article: Predictors of exception word and nonword reading in dyslexic children: The severity hypothesis.

Journal: *Journal of Educational Psychology*, March 2002, *94*, 34–43.

Related Research: Manis, F. R., et al. (1996). On the basis of two subtypes of developmental dyslexia. *Cognition, 58*, 157–195.

10228

Test Name: EXPOSITORY TEXT COMPREHENSION TEST

Purpose: To evaluate students' initial text comprehension abilities.

Number of Items: 25

Format: An additional 19-item multiple-choice test is provided for posttesting.

Reliability: K-R 20 reliability was .86. Pretest–posttest reliability was .77.

Author: Chang, K.-E., et al.

Article: The effect of concept mapping to enhance test comprehension and summarization.

Journal: *The Journal of Experimental Education*, Fall 2002, *71*, 5–33.

Related Research: Lin, C. S., & Su, Y. F. (1991). *The effect of metacognition training to enhance the metacognitive abilities and reading comprehension of sixth grade students* (technical report, NSC78-0301-H003-12). National

Science Council, Republic
of China.

10229

Test Name: FASHION
INNOVATIVENESS SCALE

Purpose: To measure how
knowledgeable a consumer is about
current fashions.

Number of Items: 6

Format: All items are presented in
English and Korean.

Reliability: Composite reliability
was .89.

Validity: Correlations with other
variables ranged from −.26 to .13.

Author: Goldsmith, R. E., et al.

Article: Price sensitivity and
innovativeness for fashion among
Korean consumers.

Journal: *The Journal of Social
Psychology*, October 2005, *145*,
501–508.

10230

Test Name: FIRST-GRADE
CONCEPTS/APPLICATIONS
TEST

Purpose: To measure typical first-
grade concepts/applications ability.

Number of Items: 25

Time Required: 15 seconds for 20
items and 30 seconds for 5 items.

Format: Includes numeration,
concepts, geometry, measurement,
applied computation,
charts/graphs, and word problems.

Reliability: Coefficient alpha was .92.

Validity: Correlations with other
variables ranged from −.32 to .59
($N = 272$).

Author: Fuchs, L. S., et al.

Article: The prevention,
identification, and cognitive
determinants of math difficulty.

Journal: *Journal of Educational
Psychology*, August 2005, *97*,
493–513.

Related Research: Fuchs, L. S.,
et al. (1990). *Curriculum-based
math computation and concepts/
applications*. (Available from L. S.
Fuchs, 328 Peabody, Vanderbilt
University, Nashville, TN 37203)

10231

Test Name: FRUIT AND
VEGETABLE KNOWLEDGE
SCALE

Purpose: To measure knowledge,
barrier, benefits, and consumption
of fruits and vegetables.

Number of Items: 17

Format: Various 5-point scales are
used. Each is described.

Reliability: Alpha coefficients
ranged from .74 to .81 across
subscales.

Author: Peltzer, K., and
Promitussananon, S.

Article: Knowledge, barriers, and
benefits of fruit and vegetable
consumption and lay conceptions
of nutrition among rural and
semi-urban Black South Africans.

Journal: *Psychological Reports*,
June 2004, *94*, Part 1, 976–982.

Related Research: Hagdrup, N. A.,
et al. (1998). Fruit and vegetable
consumption in Missouri:
Knowledge, barriers and benefits.
*American Journal of Health
Behavior*, *22*, 90–100.

10232

Test Name: HIV/AIDS
KNOWLEDGE AND ATTITUDES
SCALES

Purpose: To measure knowledge of
HIV/AIDS and attitudes about
HIV/AIDS.

Number of Items: 60

Format: Five-point scales range
from *very likely* or *strongly agree*
to *definitely not possible* or *strongly
disagree*.

Reliability: Reliability coefficients
ranged from .78 to .89.

Author: Costin, A. C., et al.

Article: HIV/AIDS knowledge and
beliefs among preservice and in-
service school counselors.

Journal: *Professional School
Counseling*, October 2002, *6*(1),
79–85.

Related Research: Koch, P. B., &
Singer, M. D. (1988). HIV/AIDS
Knowledge and Attitudes Scales for
teachers. In C. Davis, et al. (Eds.),
*Handbook of sexuality-related
measures* (pp. 317–320). Thousand
Oaks, CA: Sage.

10233

Test Name: HIV/AIDS
KNOWLEDGE INVENTORY

Purpose: To measure HIV/AIDS
knowledge.

Number of Items: 12

Format: A true–false format is used.
All items are presented.

Reliability: K-R 20 reliability was
.74. Item–total correlations ranged
from .18 to .46.

Author: Yancey, E. M., et al.

Article: HIV/AIDS knowledge scale
in relation to HIV risks among
African-American women.

Journal: *Psychological Reports*,
June 2003, *92*, Part 1, 991–996.

Related Research: Longshore, D.,
et al. (1992). AIDS knowledge and
attitudes among injection drug users:
The issue of reliability. *AIDS
Education and Prevention*, *4*, 29–50.

10234

Test Name: HIV KNOWLEDGE
QUESTIONNAIRE

Purpose: To measure knowledge about transmission and prevention of HIV.

Number of Items: 45

Format: A true–false format is used.

Reliability: Coefficient alpha was .87.

Author: Carey, M. P., et al.

Article: Reducing HIV-risk behavior among adults receiving outpatient psychiatric treatment: Results from a randomized controlled trial.

Journal: *Journal of Consulting and Clinical Psychology*, April 2004, *72*, 252–268.

Related Research: Carey, M. P., et al. (1997). The HIV-knowledge questionnaire: Development and evaluation of a reliable, valid, and practical self-administered questionnaire. *AIDS and Behavior*, *1*, 61–74.

10235

Test Name: HIV KNOWLEDGE TEST

Purpose: To measure knowledge of the HIV disease process, types of treatments and transmission risks.

Number of Items: 16

Format: A yes–no format is used. Sample items are presented.

Reliability: K-R 20 reliability was .78.

Author: Benotsch, E. G., et al.

Article: HIV–AIDS patients' evaluation of health information on the internet: The digital divide and vulnerability to fraudulent claims.

Journal: *Journal of Consulting and Clinical Psychology*, December 2004, *72*, 1004–1011.

Related Research: Kalichman, S. C., et al. (2002). Internet use among people living with HIV/AIDS association of internet use, health

behaviors, and health status. *AIDS Education and Prevention*, *14*, 51–61.

10236

Test Name: KNOWLEDGE ABOUT AIDS TRANSMISSION SCALE

Purpose: To measure knowledge about AIDS transmission.

Number of Items: 12

Format: Item responses are anchored by 1 (*definitely yes*) and 5 (*definitely no*). A sample item is presented.

Reliability: Cronbach's alpha was .74.

Author: Hayes, R. A., et al.

Article: Stigma directed toward chronic illness is resistant to change through education and exposure.

Journal: *Psychological Reports*, June 2002, *90*, Part 2, 1161–1173.

Related Research: Herek, G. M., & Glunt, E. K. (1991). AIDS-related attitudes in the United States: A preliminary conceptualization. *The Journal of Sex Research*, *28*, 99–123.

10237

Test Name: KNOWLEDGE OF NUTRITIONAL CONCEPTS TEST

Purpose: To measure knowledge of nutritional concepts.

Number of Items: 7

Format: Multiple-choice, curriculum-based test.

Reliability: Test–retest (2 weeks) reliability was .64.

Author: Blom-Hoffman, J., et al.

Article: Promoting healthy food consumption among young children: Evaluation of a multicomponent nutrition education program.

Journal: *Journal of School Psychology*, January/February 2004, *42*, 45–60.

Related Research: Auld, G. W., et al. (1998). Outcomes from a school-based nutrition education program using resource teachers and cross-disciplinary models. *Journal of Nutrition Education*, *30*, 268–280.

10238

Test Name: KNOWLEDGE OF TRANSMISSION OF AIDS

Purpose: To measure knowledge of the ways AIDS can be transmitted.

Number of Items: 37

Format: A true–false format is used. All items are presented.

Reliability: Alpha was .98.

Validity: Correlations with other variables ranged from .05 to .25.

Author: Thompson, K. L., et al.

Article: Psychological predictors of sexual behaviors related to AIDS transmission.

Journal: *Psychological Reports*, February 2001, *88*, 51–67.

Related Research: Gray, L. A. (1993). *Survey on HIV/AIDS: Oregon State University students*. Unpublished manuscript, Oregon State University Counselor Education Program.

10239

Test Name: MEMORY CHARACTERISTICS QUESTIONNAIRE

Purpose: To assess memory characteristics such as memory clarity, affective memory, reexperiencing memory, memory control, and nonvisual sensory, memory.

Number of Items: 45

Format: Various 7-point scales are used.

Reliability: Alpha coefficients ranged from .61 to .89 across subscales.

Author: Koss, M. P., et al.

Article: Cognitive mediation of rape's mental, physical, and social health impact: Tests of four models in cross-sectional data.

Journal: *Journal of Consulting and Clinical Psychology*, August 2002, *70*, 926–941.

Related Research: Koss, M. P., et al. (1996). Traumatic memory characteristics: A cross-validated mediational model of response to rape among employed women. *Journal of Abnormal Psychology*, *105*, 421–432.

10240

Test Name: MENTAL ROTATIONS TEST

Purpose: To assess controllability of mental imagery.

Number of Items: 20

Time Required: 5 minutes for each half.

Format: A two-part, timed, paper and pencil test.

Reliability: Test–retest reliability was .88. Kuder–Richardson reliability was .90.

Author: McIntyre, T., et al.

Article: Is controllability of imagery related to canoe–slalom performance?

Journal: *Perceptual and Motor Skills*, June 2002, *94*, Part 2, 1245–1250.

Related Research: Vandenberg, S. G., & Kuse, A. R. (1978). Mental rotations, a group test of three-dimensional spatial visualization. *Perceptual and Motor Skills*, *47*, 599–604.

10241

Test Name: MORPHOLOGICAL RELATEDNESS TEST

Purpose: To measure morphological knowledge.

Number of Items: 12

Format: Each item consists of pairs and the child decides if the second word is derived from the first. Examples are given.

Validity: Correlations with other variables ranged from –.20 to .39.

Author: Nagy, W., et al.

Article: Relationship of morphology and other language skills to literacy skills in at-risk second-grade readers and at-risk fourth-grade writers.

Journal: *Journal of Educational Psychology*, December 2003, *95*, 730–742.

Related Research: Mahony, D., et al. (2000). Reading ability and sensitivity to morphological relations. *Reading and Writing: An Interdisciplinary Journal*, *12*, 191–218.

10242

Test Name: NONWORD READING TEST

Purpose: To measure component reading skills.

Number of Items: 32

Format: Includes two groups of nonwords: 24 were monosyllabic nonwords and 8 were two-syllable nonwords. Examples are given.

Reliability: Coefficient alpha was .87

Author: Griffiths, Y. M., and Snowling, M. J.

Article: Predictors of exception word and nonword reading in dyslexic children: The severity hypothesis.

Journal: *Journal of Educational Psychology*, March 2002, *94*, 34–43.

Related Research: Manis, F. R., et al. (1996). On the basis of two subtypes of developmental dyslexia.

Cognition, *58*, 157–195. Castles, A., & Coltheart, M. (1993). Varieties of developmental dyslexia. *Cognition*, *47*, 149–180.

10243

Test Name: ORAL CLOZE TASK

Purpose: To measure syntactic processing in English.

Number of Items: 12 + 2 training items.

Format: Administered orally requiring an oral one-word response. Examples are presented.

Reliability: Split-half reliability (Spearman–Brown) was .56.

Validity: Correlations with other ranged from –.15 to .46.

Author: Gottardo, A., et al.

Article: Factors related to English reading performance in children with Chinese as a first language: More evidence of cross-language transfer of phonological processing.

Journal: *Journal of Educational Psychology*, September 2001, *93*, 530–542.

Related Research: Siegel, L. S., & Ryan, E. (1988). Development of grammatical-sensitivity, phonological, and short-term memory skills in normally achieving and learning disabled children. *Developmental Psychology*, *24*, 28–37.

10244

Test Name: ORTHOGRAPHIC LEGALITY TASK

Purpose: To measure orthographic processing.

Number of Items: 17 + 1 training item.

Format: The child is asked which one of two pseudowords looked more like it could be a word. An example is given.

Reliability: Split-half reliability (Spearman–Brown) was .37.

Validity: Correlations with other variables ranged from −.26 to .34.

Author: Gottardo, A., et al.

Article: Factors related to English reading performance in children with Chinese as a first language: More evidence of cross-language transfer of phonological processing.

Journal: *Journal of Educational Psychology*, September 2001, *93*, 530–542.

Related Research: Siegel, L. S., et al. (1995). Research report: Evidence for superior orthographic skills in dyslexics. *Psychological Science, 6*, 250–254.

10245

Test Name: PARENT REPORT OF CHILDREN'S ABILITIES

Purpose: To assess 2-year-olds' nonverbal performance.

Format: Includes two sections: Standard cognitive tasks, including design copying, match to sample, block building, and imitative actions; and parent's report on specific behaviors.

Reliability: Alpha coefficients were .75 and .83.

Validity: Multiple correlation between the two components and the Bayley index was .55.

Author: Eley, T. C., et al.

Article: Longitudinal analysis of the genetic and environmental influences on components of cognitive delay in preschoolers.

Journal: *Journal of Educational Psychology*, December 2001, *93*, 698–707.

Related Research: Saudino, K. J., et al. (1998). The validity of parent-based assessment of the cognitive abilities of two-year-olds. *British*

Journal of Developmental Psychology, 16, 349–363.

10246

Test Name: PAST-TENSE PRODUCTION TASK

Purpose: To measure children's production of past-tense forms.

Number of Items: 52

Format: Items were "regular" and "irregular."

Reliability: Interrater reliability was 99.8% and 99.9%.

Author: Marchman, V. A., et al.

Article: Productive use of the English past tense in children with focal brain injury and specific language impairment.

Journal: *Brain and Language*, February 2004, *88*, 202–214.

Related Research: Marchman, V. A., et al. (1999). Morphological productivity in children with normal language and SLI: A study of the English past tense. *Journal of Speech, Language, and Hearing Research, 42*, 206–219.

10247

Test Name: PHONEME AWARENESS TESTS

Purpose: To measure phoneme awareness.

Format: Includes two tests: phoneme identity and phoneme segmentation.

Reliability: Alpha coefficients ranged from .78 to .88.

Validity: Correlations with other variables ranged from .33 to .74.

Author: Walton, P. D., et al.

Article: Teaching rime analogy or letter recoding reading strategies to prereaders: Effects on prereading skills and word reading.

Journal: *Journal of Educational Psychology*, March 2001, *93*, 160–180.

Related Research: Yopp, H. K. (1988). The validity and reliability of phonemic awareness tests. *Reading Research Quarterly, 23*, 159–176.

10248

Test Name: PHONEME DELETION TASK

Purpose: To measure phonemic deletion skill.

Number of Items: 24

Format: Includes three subsets of nonwords. Examples are presented.

Reliability: Coefficient alpha was .83.

Validity: Correlations with other variables ranged from −.09 to .71

Author: Griffiths, Y. M., and Snowling, M. J.

Article: Predictors of exception word and nonword reading in dyslexic children: The severity hypothesis.

Journal: *Journal of Educational Psychology*, March 2002, *94*, 34–43.

Related Research: McDougall, S., et al. (1994). Learning to read: The role of short-term memory and phonological skills. *Journal of Experimental Child Psychology, 58*, 112–123.

10249

Test Name: PHONEME DETECTION MEASURE

Purpose: To measure phonological processing.

Number of Items: 15 + 3 training items.

Format: The child reports which of three words begins with a sound that differs from the beginning sound of the other two words. An example is presented.

Reliability: Split-half (Spearman–Brown) reliability was .73.

Validity: Correlations with other variables ranged from –.27 to .45.

Author: Gottardo, A., et al.

Article: Factors related to English reading performance in children with Chinese as a first language: More evidence of cross-language transfer of phonological processing.

Journal: *Journal of Educational Psychology*, September 2001, *93*, 530–542.

Related Research: Bradley, L., & Bryant, P. E. (1983). Categorizing sounds and learning to read: A casual connection. *Nature, 301*, 419–421. Stanovich, K. E., et al. (1984). Assessing phonological awareness in kindergarten children: Issues of task comparability. *Journal of Experimental Child Psychology, 38*, 125–190.

10250

Test Name: PRINT EXPOSURE MEASURES

Purpose: To measure print exposure.

Number of Items: 80

Format: Includes two measures: Author Recognition and Title Recognition. Each includes 25 actual name and foils.

Reliability: Alpha coefficients were .75 (Author Recognition) and .49 (Title Recognition).

Author: Griffiths, Y. M., and Snowling, M. J.

Article: Predictors of exception word and nonword reading in dyslexic children: The severity hypothesis.

Journal: *Journal of Educational Psychology*, March 2002, *94*, 34–43.

Related Research: Cunningham, A. E., & Stanovich, K. E. (1990). Tracking the unique effects of print exposure and orthographic skills in children—A quick measure of reading experience. *Journal of Educational Psychology, 82*, 733–740.

10251

Test Name: PSEUDOWORD PHONEME DELETION TASK

Purpose: To measure phonological processing.

Number of Items: 30 + 3 training items.

Format: After reporting a pseudoword the child is requested to delete certain phonemes. Examples are presented.

Reliability: Split-half (Spearman–Brown) reliability was .86.

Validity: Correlations with other variables ranged from –.34 to .59.

Author: Gottardo, A., et al.

Article: Factors related to English reading performance in children with Chinese as a first language: More evidence of cross-language transfer of phonological processing.

Journal: *Journal of Educational Psychology*, September 2001, *93*, 530–542.

Related Research: Wade-Woolley, L. (1999). First language influences on second language word reading: All roads lead to Rome. *Language Learning, 49*, 447–471.

10252

Test Name: PSY OA

Purpose: To assess students' knowledge of the basic facts and concepts presented in introductory psychology.

Number of Items: 20

Format: Multiple-choice assessment includes four answer options.

Reliability: K-R 20 reliability coefficients were .29 and .71.

Validity: Correlations with other variables ranged from .45 to .85.

Author: Napoli, A. R., and Raymond, L. A.

Article: How reliable are our assessment data?: A comparison of the reliability of data produced in graded and ungraded conditions.

Journal: *Research in Higher Education*, December 2004, *45*, 921–929.

10253

Test Name: REY–OSTERRIETH COMPLEX FIGURE TEST

Purpose: To measure perceptual organization and visual memory.

Number of Items: One complex figure

Format: Includes two conditions: Immediate recall and delayed recall. The item is presented.

Reliability: Interjudge reliability was 90%.

Author: Winner, E., et al.

Article: Dyslexia and visual–spatial talents: Compensation vs. deficit model.

Journal: *Brain and Language*, February 2001, *76*, 81–110.

Related Research: Osterrieth, P. A. (1944). Le test de copie d'une figure complexe. *Archives de Psychologie, 30*, 206–356.

10254

Test Name: RHYME DETECTION TASK

Purpose: To measure phonological processing skill.

Number of Items: 15 + 3 training items.

Format: The child reports which of these words does not rhyme with the other two. An example is presented.

Reliability: Split-half (Spearman–Brown) reliability was .43.

Validity: Correlations with other variables ranged from –.17 to .43.

Author: Gottardo, A., et al.

Article: Factors related to English reading performance in children with Chinese as a first language: More evidence of cross-language transfer of phonological processing.

Journal: *Journal of Educational Psychology*, September 2001, *93*, 530–542.

Related Research: Bradley, L., & Bryant, P. E. (1983). Categorizing sounds and learning to read: A casual connection. *Nature*, *301*, 419–421. Stanovich, K. E., et al. (1984). Assessing phonological awareness in kindergarten children: Issues of task comparability. *Journal of Experimental Child Psychology*, *38*, 175–190.

10255

Test Name: RHYME FLUENCY TASK

Purpose: To measure rhyme fluency.

Number of Items: 6

Time Required: 60 seconds per item.

Format: The child provides words orally to rhyme with each target word. All target words are given.

Reliability: Coefficient alpha was .91.

Validity: Correlations with other variables ranged from –.06 to .44.

Author: Griffiths, Y. M., and Snowling, M. J.

Article: Predictors of exception word and nonword reading in

dyslexic children: The severity hypothesis.

Journal: *Journal of Educational Psychology*, March 2002, *94*, 34–43.

Related Research: Muter, V., et al. (1998). Segmentation, not rhyming, predicts early progress in learning to read. *Journal of Experimental Child Psychology*, *71*, 3–27.

10256

Test Name: RHYME RECOGNITION TEST

Purpose: To measure rhyme recognition.

Number of Items: 10

Format: A three-choice, multiple-choice test to identify which one of three orally presented words rhymes with the target word. An example is given.

Reliability: Coefficient alpha was .75.

Author: Hindson, B., et al.

Article: Assessment and early instruction of preschool children at risk for reading disability.

Journal: *Journal of Educational Psychology*, November 2005, *97*(4), 687–704.

Related Research: Byrne, B., & Fielding-Barnsley, R. (1991). Evaluation of a program to teach phonemic awareness to young children. *Journal of Educational Psychology*, *83*, 451–455.

10257

Test Name: RHYMING TASK

Purpose: To measure rhyming.

Number of Items: 12

Format: 30 seconds (for rhyme generations).

Reliability: Includes two parts: rhyme oddity and rhyme generation. All items are presented.

Coefficient alpha was .78 (rhyme oddity).

Validity: Correlations with other variables ranged from .33 to .43 ($N = 127$).

Author: Walton, P. D., et al.

Article: Teaching rime analogy or letter recoding reading strategies to prereaders: Effects on prereading skills and word reading.

Journal: *Journal of Educational Psychology*, March 2001, *93*, 160–180.

Related Research: Bradley, L., & Bryant, P. E. (1983). Categorizing sounds and learning to read: A casual connection. *Nature*, *301*, 419–421.

10258

Test Name: SEVENTH-GRADE MATHEMATICS MEASURE

Purpose: To measure some aspects of seventh-grade mathematics.

Number of Items: 22

Format: Includes basic arithmetic skills, decimals, fractions, and simple algebra.

Reliability: Alpha coefficients were .77 and .80.

Validity: Correlations with other variables ranged from .08 to .64.

Author: Klassen, R. M.

Article: A cross-cultural investigation of the efficacy beliefs of South Asian immigrant and Anglo Canadian nonimmigrant early adolescents.

Journal: *Journal of Educational Psychology*, December 2004, *96*, 731–742.

10259

Test Name: SPECIAL EDUCATION KNOWLEDGE TEST

Purpose: To assess one's knowledge of special education.

Number of Items: 25

Format: Includes two sections: factual knowledge; pedagogical understanding and decision-making. Four-choice, multiple-choice format was used. Examples are presented.

Reliability: Coefficient alpha was .69.

Author: Alexander, P. A., et al.

Article: Modeling domain learning: Profiles from the field of special education.

Journal: *Journal of Educational Psychology*, September 2004, *96*, 545–557.

Related Research: Hardman, M. L., et al. (1998). *Human exceptionality: Society, school, and family* (6th ed.). Boston: Allyn & Bacon.

10260

Test Name: SUFFIX CHOICE TEST

Purpose: To measure morphological understanding of how suffixes in lexical items signal grammatical information in sentence context.

Number of Items: 14

Format: Items are grouped into three tasks. Examples are given.

Validity: Correlations with other variables ranged from –.28 to .51.

Author: Nagy, W., et al.

Article: Relationship of morphology and other language skills to literacy skills in at-risk second-grade readers and at-risk fourth-grade writers.

Journal: *Journal of Educational Psychology*, December 2003, *95*, 730–742.

Related Research: Berninger, V., et al. (2001). Processes underlying timing and fluency: Efficacy,

automaticity, coordination, and morphological awareness. In M. Wolf (ed.), *Dyslexia, Fluency, and the Brain* (pp. 383–414). Baltimore: York Press.

10261

Test Name: SURVEY OF ELEMENTARY EDUCATION STUDENTS' READING INSTRUCTIONAL BELIEFS

Purpose: To measure reading instruction beliefs: meaningful comprehension, word recognition, and comprehension skills.

Number of Items: 21

Time Required: 20 minutes

Format: Responses are anchored by 1 (*almost always*) and 5 (*almost never*).

Reliability: Internal consistency measures ranged from .47 to .78 across subscales. Total internal consistency was .83.

Author: Knudson, R. E., and Maxson, S.

Article: Use of the Survey of Elementary Education Students' Reading Instructional Beliefs.

Journal: *Psychological Reports*, April 2001, *88*, 451–455.

Related Research: Knudson, R. E., & Anderson, K. (2000). *A factor analytic approach to preservice teachers' beliefs about teaching reading*. Paper presented at the Annual Meeting of the Educational Research Association, New Orleans, LA.

10262

Test Name: SYLLABLE DELETION TASK

Purpose: To measure phonological awareness.

Number of Items: 25

Format: Consists of two-syllable compound words and three-syllable

phrases. Also includes analogous Chinese words. Examples are given.

Reliability: Internal consistencies were .96 and .97.

Validity: Correlations with other variables ranged from –.47 to .63.

Author: McBride-Chang, C., and Kail, R. V.

Article: Cross-cultural similarities in the predictors of reading acquisition.

Journal: *Child Development*, September/October 2002, *73*, 1392–1407.

Related Research: Goswami, U., & Bryant, P. (1990). *Phonological skills and learning to read*. Hove, England: Erlbaum.

10263

Test Name: TACIT KNOWLEDGE TEST

Purpose: To measure tacit knowledge in an academic environment.

Number of Items: 116

Format: Includes 12 situations representing typical academic scenarios. Responses are made on a 7-point scale ranging from 1 (*extremely bad*) to 7 (*extremely good*).

Reliability: Coefficient alpha was .89.

Validity: Correlations with other variables ranged from –.10 to .41.

Author: Edwards, W. R., and Schleicher, D. J.

Article: On selecting psychology graduate students: Validity evidence for a test of tacit knowledge.

Journal: *Journal of Educational Psychology*, September 2004, *96*, 592–602.

Related Research: Wagner, R. K., & Sternberg, R. J. (1985). Practical intelligence in real world pursuits: The role of tacit knowledge.

Journal of Personality and Social Psychology, 49, 436–458.

10264

Test Name: TACTICAL SKILLS INVENTORY FOR SPORTS— DUTCH VERSION

Purpose: To measure tactical skills in sports.

Number of Items: 34

Format: Includes four scales: Positioning and Deciding, Knowing About Ball Actions, Knowing About Others, and Acting in Changing Situations. Responses are made on 6-point scales. All items are presented.

Reliability: Alpha coefficients ranged from .72 to .91.

Author: Elferink-Gemser, M. T., et al.

Article: Development of the Tactical Skills Inventory for Sports.

Journal: *Perceptual and Motor Skills,* December 2004, *99,* Part 1, 883–895.

Related Research: Smith, R. E., et al. (1995). Development and

validation of a multidimensional measure of sport-specific psychological skills: The Athletic Coping Skills Inventory—28. *Journal of Sport and Exercise Psychology, 17,* 370–398.

10265

Test Name: TEST OF INTEGRATED PROCESS SKILLS

Purpose: To measure students' integration of scientific research methods.

Number of Items: 36

Format: A correct–incorrect format is used.

Reliability: Alphas ranged from .71 to .89.

Author: Onwuegbuzie, A. J.

Article: Correlation between scores on integration of scientific knowledge and achievement in a course in educational research methods.

Journal: *Psychological Reports,* April 2001, *88,* 517–520.

Related Research: Downing, J. E., et al. (1997). *Science process skills*

and attitudes of preservice teachers. Paper presented at the Mid-South Education Research Association, Memphis, TN [ERIC Document Reproduction Service No. ED 416 191].

10266

Test Name: TEST OF PHYSICS KNOWLEDGE

Purpose: To measure prior physics knowledge.

Number of Items: 10

Format: Responses are multiple-choice. Sample items are presented.

Reliability: Coefficient alpha was .72.

Validity: Correlations with other variables ranged from –.09 to .45.

Author: Ziegler, A., et al.

Article: Predictors of learned helplessness among average and mildly gifted girls and boys attending initial high school physics instruction in Germany.

Journal: *Gifted Child Quarterly,* Winter 2005, *49,* 7–18.

CHAPTER 2
Adjustment—Educational

10267

Test Name: ACADEMIC CAPABILITY BELIEFS SCALE

Purpose: To measure academic capability beliefs.

Number of Items: 10

Format: Sample items are presented.

Reliability: Coefficient alpha was .68.

Validity: Correlation with other variables ranged from −.46 to .42.

Author: Juang, L., and Vondracek, F. W.

Article: Developmental patterns of adolescent capability beliefs: A person approach.

Journal: *Journal of Vocational Behavior*, August 2001, *59*, 34–52.

Related Research: Juang, L. P., et al. (2000). *Report on the validation of the Academic Capability Beliefs Scale.* Unpublished manuscript.

10268

Test Name: ACADEMIC CLASSROOM COMMUNITY SCALE

Purpose: To measure students' feelings of community in the classroom.

Number of Items: 4

Format: Responses are made on a 6-point scale ranging from 1 (*strongly disagree*) to 6 (*strongly agree*). All items are presented.

Reliability: Coefficient alpha was .82.

Validity: Correlations with other variables ranged form .21 to .55.

Author: Summers, J. J., et al.

Article: Evaluating collaborative learning and community.

Journal: *The Journal of Experimental Education*, Spring 2005, *73*, 165–188.

10269

Test Name: ACADEMIC CONTROL SCALE

Purpose: To measure perceived influence on academic achievement outcomes.

Number of Items: 8

Format: Responses are made on a 5-point scale ranging from 1 (*strongly disagree*) to 5 (*strongly agree*). All items are presented.

Reliability: Coefficient alpha .80.

Validity: Correlations with other variables ranged from −.29 to .46.

Author: Perry, R. P., et al.

Article: Academic control and action control in the achievement of college students: A longitudinal field study.

Journal: *Journal of Educational Psychology*, December 2001, *93*, 776–789.

10270

Test Name: ACADEMIC DEFENSIVE PESSIMISM QUESTIONNAIRE

Purpose: To measure the use of pessimism or strategic optimism in academic situations.

Number of Items: 9

Format: Scales range from 1 (*not at all true of me*) to 7 (*very true of me*).

Reliability: Coefficient alpha was .74. Test–retest reliabilities were .73 (6 weeks) and .55 (3 weeks).

Validity: Correlations with other variables ranged from .35 to .40.

Author: Norem, J. K., and Illingworth, K. S. S.

Article: Mood and performance among defensive pessimists and strategic optimists.

Journal: *Journal of Research in Personality*, August 2004, *38*, 351–366.

Related Research: Norem J. K. (2001). Defensive pessimism, optimism, and pessimism. In E. C. Chang (Ed), *Optimism & Pessimism: Implications for theory, research, and practice* (pp. 77–100). Washington, DC: American Psychological Association.

10271

Test Name: ACADEMIC EXPECTATIONS SCALE

Purpose: To measure expectations for future academic performance.

Number of Items: 4

Format: Responses are made on a 5-point scale ranging from 1 (*strongly agree*) to 5 (*strongly disagree*).

Reliability: Alpha coefficients were .76 to .77.

Validity: Correlations with other variables ranged from −.29 to .43.

Author: Chemers, M. M., et al.

Article: Academic self-efficacy and first-year college student performance and adjustment.

Journal: *Journal of Educational Psychology*, March 2001, *93*, 55–64.

10272

Test Name: ACADEMIC HELPLESSNESS SCALE

Purpose: To assess persistence versus helpless behavior.

Number of Items: 12

Format: Teachers rated students' tendency toward helpless behavior concerning schoolwork, students' academic effort, and students' academic performance. Five-point and 7-point scales are used.

Validity: Correlations with other variables ranged from –.50 to .72.

Author: Rudolph, K. D., et al.

Article: Negotiating the transition to middle school: The role of self-regulatory processes.

Journal: *Child Development*, May/June 2001, *72*, 929–946.

Related Research: Nolen-Hoeksema, S., et al. (1992). Predictors and consequences of childhood depressive symptoms: A 5-year longitudinal study. *Journal of Abnormal Psychology*, *101*, 405–422.

10273

Test Name: ACADEMIC INTEGRATION SCALE

Purpose: To assess the degree to which students are academically integrated as college students.

Number of Items: 3

Format: Scales range from 1 (*not at all like me*) to 5 (*very much like me*). All items are presented.

Reliability: Alpha coefficients ranged from .75 to .78.

Validity: Correlations between subscales ranged from –.53 to .31.

Author: Rice, K. G., and Dellwo, J. P.

Article: Within-semester stability and adjustment correlates of the Multidimensional Perfectionism Scale.

Journal: *Measurement and Evaluation in Counseling and Development*, October 2001, *34*, 146–156.

Related Research: Cabrera, A. F., et al. (1993). Structural equation modeling test of an integrated model of strident retention. *Journal of Higher Education*, *64*, 123–139.

10274

Test Name: ADJUSTMENT QUESTIONNAIRE

Purpose: To assess how well the student has adjusted to the university environment in general.

Number of Items: 18

Format: Responses are made on a 5-point scale ranging from *not at all true of me* to *very much true of me*.

Reliability: Coefficient alpha was .89.

Author: Beyers, W., and Goossens, L.

Article: Concurrent and predictive validity of the Student Adaptation to College Questionnaire in a sample of European freshman students.

Journal: *Educational and Psychological Measurement*, June 2002, *62*, 527–538.

Related Research: Vlaander, G. P., & van Rooijen, L. (1981). Nieune gegevens over de Aanpassingsvragenlyst [New data about the Adjustment Questionnaire]. *Tijdschrift voor Onderwijsresearch*, *6*, 33–37.

10275

Test Name: ADJUSTMENT TO SCHOOL SCALE

Purpose: To measure students' adjustment to school by teacher report.

Number of Items: 8

Format: Teachers rate students on a scale ranging from 1 (*low*) to 5 (*high*). All items are described.

Reliability: Coefficient alpha was .80.

Author: Eshel, Y., et al.

Article: Reciprocated and unreciprocated dyadic peer preferences and academic achievement of Israeli and immigrant students: A longitudinal study.

Journal: *The Journal of Social Psychology*, December 2003, *143*, 746–762.

Related Research: Smilanski, S., & Sarid, M. (1977). *Sulam histaglut leveit hasefer hatichon* [High School Adjustment Scale]. Jerusalem: Szold Institute.

10276

Test Name: AVOIDANCE OF HELP-SEEKING SCALE

Purpose: To identify instances when a student needs help but does not seek it.

Number of Items: 9

Format: Responses are made on an 8-point scale. All items are presented.

Validity: Correlations with other variables ranged from –.44 to .35 (*n* = 314).

Author: Pajares, F., et al.

Article: Psychometric analysis of computer science help-seeking scales.

Journal: *Educational and Psychological Measurement*, June 2004, *64*, 496–513.

Related Research: Ryan, A. M., & Pintrich, P. R. (1997). "Should I ask for help?" The role of motivation and attitudes in adolescents help seeking in math class. *Journal of Educational Psychology, 89,* 329–341.

10277

Test Name: BASIC CONFIDENCE SCALES

Purpose: To measure confidence in either activities or school subjects.

Number of Items: 60

Format: Includes six basic confidence scales: Mathematics, Science, Writing, Using Technology, Leadership, and Cultural Sensitivity. Responses are made on a 5-point scale ranging from 1 (*no confidence at all*) to 5 (*complete confidence*). Examples are given.

Reliability: Alpha coefficients ranged from .80 to .94.

Validity: Correlations with the Career Decision Self-Efficacy Scale—Short Form ranged from .35 to .59.

Author: Paulsen, A. M., and Betz, N. E.

Article: Basic confidence predictors of career decision-making self-efficacy.

Journal: *The Career Development Quarterly,* June 2004, *52,* 354–362.

Related Research: Betz, N. E., et al. (2003). The Expanded Skills Confidence Inventory: Measuring basic domains of vocational activity. *Journal of Vocational Behavior, 67,* 76–100.

10278

Test Name: BRIEF COLLEGE STUDENT HASSLES SCALE

Purpose: To reflect hassles experienced by students in a variety of areas.

Number of Items: 20

Format: Includes such areas as school, social, future security, work, financial, environmental, household, family, and personal appearance. Responses are made on a 7-point scale ranging from 1 (*no hassle, not at all persistent*) to 7 (*extremely persistent, high frequency and/or duration*).

Reliability: Coefficient alpha was .81.

Author: Pett, M. A., and Johnson, M. J. M.

Article: Development and psychometric evaluation of the Revised University Student Hassles Scale.

Journal: *Educational and Psychological Measurement,* December 2005, *65,* 984–1010.

Related Research: Blankstein, K. R., & Flett, G. L. (1992). Specificity in the assessment of daily hassles: Hassles, locus of control, and adjustment in college students. *Canadian Journal of Behavioral Science, 24,* 382–398.

10279

Test Name: CHILDREN'S ACADEMIC ENGAGEMENT SCALE

Purpose: To assess the degree to which students pursue academic challenges, work independently in the classroom, accept the teacher's authority, and behave responsibly.

Number of Items: 6

Format: Responses are made on a 3-point scale, including *doesn't apply, applies sometimes,* and *certainly applies.*

Reliability: Alpha coefficients were .85 and .87.

Author: Valeski, T. N., and Stipek, D. J.

Article: Young children's findings about school.

Journal: *Child Development,* July/August 2001, *72,* 1198–1213.

Related Research: Birch, S., and Ladd, G. (1998). Children's interpersonal behaviors and the teacher–child relationship. *Developmental Psychology, 34,* 934–946.

10280

Test Name: CHILDREN'S SCHOOL ADJUSTMENT SCALE

Purpose: To enable parents to provide an estimate of children's school adjustment.

Number of Items: 5

Format: Responses are made on an 11-point scale ranging from 0 (*not very well*) to 10 (*extremely well*). Examples are presented.

Reliability: Coefficient alpha was .75.

Validity: Correlations with other variables ranged from −.35 to .53.

Author: Mantzicopoulos, P.

Article: Flunking kindergarten after Head Start: An inquiry into the contribution of contextual and individual variables.

Journal: *Journal of Educational Psychology,* June 2003, *95,* 268–278.

Related Research: Ramey, C., & Ramey, S. L. (1993). *The family interview.* Birmingham, AL: Civitan International Research Center.

10281

Test Name: CHINESE SOCIAL COPING QUESTIONNAIRE—17

Purpose: To assess the social coping strategies of gifted students in their response to being gifted.

Number of Items: 17

Format: Includes six factors: denying giftedness, attempting avoidance, discounting popularity, valuing peer acceptance, prizing conformity, and involvement in activities. Responses are made on a 5-point scale ranging from 1 (*strongly disagree*) to 5 (*strongly agree*). All items are presented.

Reliability: Alpha coefficients ranged from .57 to .84 ($n = 527$).

Validity: Correlations with psychological symptoms ranged from −.27 to .24 ($n = 264$).

Author: Chan, D. W.

Article: Social coping and psychological distress among Chinese gifted students in Hong Kong.

Journal: *Gifted Child Quarterly*, Winter 2004, *48*, 30–41.

Related Research: Swiatek, M. A. (2001). Social coping among gifted high school students and its relationship to self-concept. *Journal of Youth and Adolescence*, *30*, 19–39.

10282

Test Name: CLASS ENJOYMENT SCALE

Purpose: To measure how much a student enjoys a class.

Number of Items: 8

Format: Scales range from 1 (*strongly agree*) to 5 (*strongly disagree*). A sample item is presented.

Reliability: Coefficient alpha was .91.

Validity: Correlations with other variables ranged from −.12 to .35.

Author: Lee, F. K., et al.

Article: Personality and the goal-striving process: The influence of achievement goal patterns, goal level, and mental focus on performance and enjoyment.

Journal: *Journal of Applied Psychology*, April 2003, *88*, 256–265.

10283

Test Name: COLLEGE DISTRESS INVENTORY—MODIFIED

Purpose: To assess physical and psychological health.

Number of Items: 23

Format: Includes five factors: sleep difficulties, depression/anxiety, physical symptoms, overeating, and agitation. Responses as made on a 6-point scale ranging from *never* to *always*. Examples are presented.

Reliability: Alpha coefficients ranged from .83 to .93.

Validity: Correlations with other variables ranged from −.22 to .73.

Author: Torres, J. B., and Solberg, V. S.

Article: Role of self-efficacy, stress, social integration, and family support in Latino college student persistence and health.

Journal: *Journal of Vocational Behavior*, August 2001, *59*, 53–63.

Related Research: Ryan, N. E., et al. (1994, August). Racial/ethnic, gender, and within group differences in college distress. In V. S. Solberg (Chair), *Recommendation for designing culturally relevant persistence programming*. Symposium conducted at the 102nd annual Convention of the American Psychological Association, Los Angeles, CA.

10284

Test Name: COLLEGE STRESS INVENTORY

Purpose: To measure academic stress.

Number of Items: 21

Format: Responses are made on a 5-point scale ranging from 1 (*never*) to 5 (*always*). Sample items are presented.

Reliability: Coefficient alpha was .89.

Validity: Correlations with other variables ranged from −.27 to .73.

Author: Torres, J. B., and Solberg, V. S.

Article: Role of self-efficacy, stress, social integration, and family support in Latino college student persistence and health.

Journal: *Journal of Vocational Behavior*, August 2001, *59*, 53–63.

Related Research: Solberg, V. S., et al. (1993). Development of the College Stress Inventory for use with Hispanic populations: A confirmatory analytic approach. *Hispanic Journal of Behavioral Sciences*, *15*, 490–497.

10285

Test Name: COMPUTER ANXIETY SCALE

Purpose: To measure computer anxiety.

Number of Items: 6

Format: Responses are made on a 6-point Likert-type scale ranging from *strongly disagree* to *strongly agree*. All items are presented.

Reliability: Test–retest (3 weeks) reliability coefficient was .87. Alpha coefficients were .76 and .78.

Validity: Correlations with other variables ranged from −.01 to −.46.

Author: Lester, D., et al.

Article: A short computer anxiety scale.

Journal: *Perceptual and Motor Skills*, June 2005, *100*, Part 2, 964–968.

10286

Test Name: COUNSELING NEEDS QUESTIONNAIRE

Purpose: To assess counseling needs of elementary school students by student report.

Number of Items: 46

Format: Scales ranged from *strongly disagree* to *strongly agree*.

Reliability: Coefficient alpha was .93.

Validity: Correlations with self-concept were low and therefore unrelated to perceived needs.

Author: Thompson, D. W., et al.

Article: Development of an instrument to assess the counseling needs of elementary school students.

Journal: *Professional School Counseling*, October 2003, 7(1), 35–39.

10287

Test Name: COURSE-RELATED ANXIETY SCALE

Purpose: To assess students' academic performance in course anxiety.

Number of Items: 6

Format: Responses are made on a 5-point scale ranging from 1 (*not at all true*) to 5 (*completely true*).

Reliability: Coefficients alpha was .81. Test–retest (5 months) reliability was .61.

Validity: Correlation with other variables ranged from –.48 to .38.

Author: Perry, R. P., et al.

Article: Academic control and action control in the achievement of college students: A longitudinal field study.

Journal: *Journal of Educational Psychology*, December 2001, *93*, 776–789.

Related Research: Pekrun, R. (1993). Facets of students' academic motivation: A longitudinal expectancy-value approach. In M. Maehr & P. Pintrich (Eds.), *Advances in motivation and achievement* (Vol. 8, pp. 139–189). Greenwich, CT: JAI Press.

10288

Test Name: COURSE-RELATED BOREDOM SCALE

Purpose: To assess college students' course boredom.

Number of Items: 6

Format: Responses are made on a 5-point scale ranging from 1 (*not at all true*) to 5 (*completely true*).

Reliability: Coefficient alpha was .90. Test–retest (5 months) reliability was .68.

Validity: Correlations with other variables ranged from –.37 to .63.

Author: Perry, R. P., et al.

Article: Academic control and action control in the achievement of college students: A longitudinal field study.

Journal: *Journal of Educational Psychology*, December 2001, *93*, 776–789.

Related Research: Pekrun, R. (1993). Facets of students' academic motivations: A longitudinal expectancy-value approach. In M. Maehr & P. Pintrich (Eds.), *Advances in motivation and achievement* (Vol. 8, pp. 139–189). Greenwich, CT: JAI Press.

10289

Test Name: DOMAIN IDENTIFICATION MEASURE

Purpose: To measure identification in the domains of mathematics and English.

Number of Items: 16

Format: Includes two domains: Mathematics and English. Five-point response scales are used. All items are presented.

Reliability: Alpha coefficients were .90 and .93. Test–retest reliability coefficients were .56 and 89.

Validity: Correlation with math performance was .32.

Author: Smith, J. L., and White, P. H.

Article: Development of the Domain Identification Measure: A tool for investigating stereotypic threat effects.

Journal: *Educational and Psychological Measurement*, December 2001, *61*, 1040–1057.

10290

Test Name: EDUCATIONAL AND CAREER ANXIETY QUESTIONNAIRE

Purpose: To measure educational and career anxiety.

Number of Items: 20

Format: A yes–no format is used.

Reliability: Test–retest reliability was .82 (2 weeks).

Author: Salimi, S.-H., et al.

Article: Association of parental self-esteem and expectations with adolescents' anxiety about career and education.

Journal: *Psychological Reports*, June 2005, *96*, Part 1, 569–578.

Related Research: Bahrami-Ehsan, H. (2003). [Relationships between religious orientation, anxiety and self-concept]. [*Journal of Psychology*], *24*, 336–347.

10291

Test Name: EDUCATIONAL REQUIREMENTS—STRENGTH SCALE

Purpose: To assess one's confidence in completing the educational requirements for 15 technical–scientific fields.

Number of Items: 15

Format: Scales range from 1 (*completely unsure*) to 10 (*completely sure*).

Reliability: Coefficient alpha was .93.

Author: Scott, A. B., and Mallinckrodt, B.

Article: Parental emotional support, science self-efficacy, and choice of science major in undergraduate women.

Journal: *The Career Development Quarterly*, March 2005, *53*, 263–273.

Related Research: Lent, R. W. (1984). Relation of self-efficacy expectations to academic achievement and persistence. *Journal of Counseling Psychology*, *31*, 356–362.

10292

Test Name: EXECUTIVE HELP-SEEKING SCALE

Purpose: To assess a child's executive help seeking.

Number of Items: 10

Format: Includes two sources of help: From the Teacher and From Students. Responses are made on an 8-point scale. All items are presented.

Validity: Correlations with other variables ranged from –.73 to .35 ($n = 314$).

Author: Pajares, F., et al.

Article: Psychometric analysis of computer science help-seeking scales.

Journal: *Educational and Psychological Measurement*, June 2004, *64*, 496–513.

Related Research: Nelson-Le Gall, S. (1981). Help-seeking: An understudied problem-solving skill in children. *Developmental Review*, *1*, 224–246.

10293

Test Name: FEAR OF ACADEMIC FAILURE SCALE

Purpose: To measure fear of academic failure.

Number of Items: 6

Format: Responses are made on an 11-point scale ranging from 0 (*not true at all*) to 10 (*very true*). Examples are given.

Reliability: Internal consistency reliability coefficients were .63 and .68.

Validity: Correlations with other variables ranged from –.04 to .58.

Author: Klassen, R. M.

Article: A cross-cultural investigation of the efficacy beliefs of South Asian immigrant and Anglo Canadian nonimmigrant early adolescents.

Journal: *Journal of Educational Psychology*, December 2004, *96*, 731–742.

Related Research: Eaton, M. J., & Dembo, M. H. (1997). Differences in the motivation beliefs of Asian American and non-Asian students. *Journal of Educational Psychology*, *89*, 433–440.

10294

Test Name: GENERAL LIFE SATISFACTION AND COLLEGE SATISFACTION SCALES

Purpose: To measure general life satisfaction and college satisfaction.

Number of Items: 22

Format: Includes 15 general life satisfaction items and 7 college satisfaction items. Responses are made on a 7-point scale ranging from 1 (*very dissatisfied*) to 7 (*very satisfied*). All items are presented.

Reliability: Alpha coefficients were .84 and .86.

Validity: Correlations with other variables ranged from –.20 to .60.

Author: Lounsbury, J. W., et al.

Article: An investigation of broad and narrow personality traits in relation to general and domain-specific life satisfaction of college students.

Journal: *Research in Higher Education*, September 2005, *46*, 707–729.

Related Research: Andrews, F. M., & Withey, S. B. (1976). *Social indicators of well-being*. New York: Plenum Press.

10295

Test Name: HELPLESSNESS SCALE—ADAPTED

Purpose: To assess domain-specific helplessness as an emotional state adapted for mathematics.

Number of Items: 3

Format: Responses are made on a 6-point Likert-type scale ranging from 1 (*absolutely disagree*) to 6 (*agree completely*). All items are presented.

Reliability: Coefficient alpha was .69.

Author: Dresel, M., et al.

Article: Nothing more than dimensions? Evidence for a surplus meaning of specific attributions.

Journal: *The Journal of Educational Research*, September/October 2005, *99*, 31–44.

Related Research: Breitkopf, L. (1985). Zur Validität und Nützlichkeit der Ailflosigkeitsskala HIS in klinischpsychologisdren und medizinpsychologischen Untersuchugen [The validity and usefulness of the Helplessness Scale in psychological investigations conducted in the clinical and medical fields]. *Diagnostics*, *31*, 324–332.

10296

Test Name: IDENTIFICATION WITH SCHOOL QUESTIONNAIRE

Purpose: To assess the degree to which students value school and school-related outcomes.

Number of Items: 16

Format: Responses are made on a 4-point Likert scale ranging from 1 (*strongly agree*) to 4 (*strongly disagree*). Examples are given.

Reliability: Alpha coefficients ranged from .75 to .84.

Validity: Correlations with other variables ranged from −.19 to .41.

Author: Kenny, M. E., and Bledsoe, M.

Article: Contributions of the relational context to career adaptability among urban adolescents.

Journal: *Journal of Vocational Behavior*, April 2005, *66*, 257–272.

Related Research: Voelkl, K. E. (1997). Identification with school. *American Journal of Education*, *105*, 294–318.

10297

Test Name: INFLUENCE OF OTHERS ON ACADEMIC AND CAREER DECISION-MAKING SCALE

Purpose: To assess the types and amount of influence and support from others in making academic and career decisions.

Number of Items: 15

Format: Scales range from 1 (*strongly disagree*) to 5 (*strongly agree*). Sample items are presented.

Reliability: Alpha coefficients ranged from .85 to .94.

Author: Nauta, M. M., et al.

Article: Interpersonal influences on students' academic and career decisions: The impact of sexual orientation.

Journal: *The Career Development Quarterly*, June 2001, *49*, 352–362.

Related Research: Nauta, M. M., & Kokaly, M. L. (2001). Assessing role model influences on students' academic and vocational decisions. *Journal of Career Assessment, 9*, 81–99.

10298

Test Name: INSTITUTIONAL INTEGRATION SCALE—REVISED

Purpose: To measure five facets of college student academic and social integration.

Number of Items: 34

Format: Includes five subscales: Peer-Group Interactions, Interactions With Faculty, Faculty Concern for Student Development and Teaching, Academic and Intellectual Development, and Institutional and Goal Commitment.

Reliability: Alpha coefficients ranged from .76 to .89.

Author: French, B. F., and Oakes, W.

Article: Reliability and validity evidence for the Institutional Integration Scale.

Journal: *Educational and Psychological Measurement*, February 2004, *64*, 88–98.

Related Research: Pascarella, E. T., & Terenzini, P. T. (1980). Predicting persistence and voluntary dropout decisions from a theoretical model. *Journal of Higher Education, 51*, 60–75.

10299

Test Name: INSTRUMENTAL HELP SEEKING SCALE

Purpose: To assess instrumental help seeking.

Number of Items: 10

Format: Includes two sources of help: From the Teacher and From Fellow Students. Responses are made on an 8-point scale. All items are presented.

Validity: Correlations with other variables ranged from −.73 to .59 (*n* = 314).

Author: Pajares, F., et al.

Article: Psychometric analysis of computer science help-seeking scales.

Journal: *Educational and Psychological Measurement*, June 2004, *64*, 496–513.

Related Research: Nelson-Le Gall, S. (1981). Help-seeking: An understudied problem-solving skill in children. *Developmental Review, 1*, 224–246.

10300

Test Name: INTENTION FOR PRIMARY SCHOOL PHYSICAL EDUCATION MORAL BEHAVIOR SCALE

Purpose: To measure intent to engage in moral behavior in primary school physical education classes.

Number of Items: 5

Format: Responses are made on a 7-point scale ranging from 1 (*unlikely*) to 7 (*likely*). All items are presented.

Reliability: Alpha coefficients ranged from .79 to .92.

Validity: Correlations with other variables ranged from .37 to .67.

Author: Tsorbatzoudis, H., and Emmanouilidou, M.

Article: Predicting moral behavior in physical education classes: An application of the theory of planned behavior.

Journal: *Perceptual and Motor Skills*, June 2005, *100*, Part 2, 1055–1065.

10301

Test Name: INTEREST IN MATHEMATICS SCALE

Purpose: To measure interest in mathematics.

Number of Items: 8

Format: Scales range from 1 (*not at all true*) to 5 (*very true*). Sample items are presented in English.

Reliability: Coefficient alpha was .93.

Author: Keller, C.

Article: Effect of teachers' stereotyping on students' stereotyping of mathematics as a male domain.

Journal: *The Journal of Social Psychology*, April 2001, *141*, 165–173.

Related Research: Schiefele, U., et al. (1993). Der Fragebogen zum Studieninteresse (FSI) [Questionnaire on Subject Interests]. *Diagnostics*, *39*, 335–351.

10302

Test Name: INVENTORY OF COLLEGE STUDENTS' RECENT LIFE EXPERIENCES

Purpose: To identify concerns of college students.

Number of Items: 49

Format: Includes seven factors: developmental and academic challenges, time pressures, academic alienation, romantic problems, assorted annoyances, general social mistreatment, and friendship problems. Responses are made on a 4-point scale ranging from *not at all part of my life* to *very much part of my life*.

Reliability: Alpha coefficients ranged from .47 to .89.

Author: Pett, M. A., and Johnson, M. J. M.

Article: Development and psychometric evaluation of the Revised University Student Hassles Scale.

Journal: *Educational and Psychological Measurement*, December 2005, *65*, 984–1010.

Related Research: Osman, A., et al. (1994). Validation of the Inventory of College Students' Recent Life Experiences in an American college sample. *Journal of Clinical Psychology*, *50*, 856–863.

10303

Test Name: LEARNING EXPERIENCES QUESTIONNAIRE

Purpose: To measure learning experiences

Number of Items: 120

Format: Responses are made on a 6-point Likert-type scale ranging from 1 (*strongly disagree*) to 6 (*strongly agree*). Examples are given.

Reliability: Alpha coefficients ranged from .72 to .89 ($N = 222$).

Author: Schaub, M., and Tokar, D. M.

Article: The role of personality and learning experiences in social–cognitive career theory.

Journal: *Journal of Vocational Behavior*, April 2005, *66*, 304–325.

Related Research: Schaub, M. (2004). Social cognitive career theory: Examining the mediating role of sociocognitive variables in the relation of personality to vocational interests. *Dissertation Abstracts International Section A: Humanities and Social Sciences*, *64*(7–A), 2463. (UMI No. AAT 3098455)

10304

Test Name: MATH ANXIETY RATING SCALE—REVISED

Purpose: To measure anxiety in math-related situations.

Number of Items: 24

Format: Includes two subscales: Learning Math Anxiety and Math Evaluation Anxiety. Responses are made on a 5-point scale ranging from 0 (*no anxiety*) to 4 (*high anxiety*). All items are presented.

Reliability: Coefficient alpha was .98.

Validity: Correlations with other variables ranged from .30 to .39.

Author: Hopko, D. R.

Article: Confirmatory factor analysis of the Math Anxiety Rating Scale—Revised.

Journal: *Educational and Psychological Measurement*, April 2003, *63*, 336–351.

Related Research: Plake, B. S., & Parker, C. S. (1982). The development and validation of a revised version of the Mathematics Anxiety Rating Scale. *Educational and Psychological Measurement*, *42*, 551–557.

10305

Test Name: MATHEMATICS ANXIETY RATING SCALE

Purpose: To assess self-reported anxiety toward mathematical content and performance.

Number of Items: 98

Format: Responses are made on a 5-point scale ranging from 1 (*none at all*) to 5 (*very much*).

Reliability: Alpha coefficients ranged from .55 to .99. Test–retest (2 weeks) coefficients ranged from .78 to .95. Test–retest (7 weeks) was .85.

Validity: Correlation with the Differential Aptitude Test was –.64.

Author: Capraro, M. M., et al.

Article: Measurement error of scores on the Mathematics Anxiety Rating Scale across studies.

Journal: *Educational and Psychological Measurement*, June 2001, *61*, 373–386.

Related Research: Richardson, F., & Suinn, R. (1972). The Mathematics Anxiety Rating Scale: Psychometric data. *Journal of Counseling Psychology*, *19*, 551–554.

10306

Test Name: MATHEMATICS ANXIETY RATING SCALE

Purpose: To measure mathematics anxiety.

Number of Items: 30

Format: All items are presented.

Reliability: Coefficient alpha was .96. Test–retest reliability (1 week) was .90.

Validity: Correlations with other variables ranged from −.41 to .74.

Author: Suinn, R. M., and Winston, E. H.

Article: The Mathematics Anxiety Rating Scale, a brief version: Psychometric data.

Journal: *Psychological Reports*, February 2003, *92*, 167–173.

Related Research: Richardson, F., & Suinn, R. M. (1972). The Mathematics Anxiety Rating Scale: Psychometric data. *Journal of Counseling Psychology, 19,* 138–149.

10307

Test Name: MATHEMATICS ANXIETY SCALE

Purpose: To measure anxiety, dread, and nervousness related to doing mathematics.

Number of Items: 12

Format: Five-point scales are anchored by 1 (*strongly disagree*) and 5 (*strongly agree*).

Reliability: Coefficient alpha was .96.

Author: Alkhateeb, H. M., and Taha, N.

Article: Mathematics self-concept and mathematics anxiety of undergraduate majors in education.

Journal: *Psychological Reports*, December 2002, *91*, Part 2, 1273–1275.

Related Research: Fennema, E., & Sherman, J. (1976). *Fennema–Sherman Mathematics Attitudes Scales: Instruments*

designed to measure attitudes toward the learning of mathematics by females and males (Ms. No. 1225). *JSAS Catalog of Selected Documents in Psychology, 6,* 31.

10308

Test Name: MATHEMATICS ANXIETY SCALE FOR CHILDREN

Purpose: To identify mathematics anxiety in children.

Number of Items: 22

Format: Rating scales range from 1 (*not nervous*) to 4 (*very, very nervous*). All items are presented.

Reliability: Coefficient alpha was .92.

Validity: Correlations with other variables ranged from −.21 to .53.

Author: Beasley, T. M., et al.

Article: A confirmatory factor analysis of the Mathematics Anxiety Scale for Children.

Journal: *Measurement and Evaluation in Counseling and Development*, April 2001, *34*, 14–26.

Related Research: Chiu, L. H., & Henry, L. L. (1996). Development and validation of the Mathematics Anxiety Scale for Children. *Measurement and Evaluation in Counseling and Development, 23,* 121–127.

10309

Test Name: MINORITY STATUS STRESS

Purpose: To measure minority college student-specific stressors as well as general college student role stressors.

Number of Items: 37

Format: Includes five subscales: Social Climate, Interracial, Racism

and Discrimination Within Group, and Achievement. Responses are made on a 6-point scale ranging from 0 (*does not apply*) to 5 (*extremely stressful*).

Reliability: Alpha coefficients ranged from .63 to .93.

Validity: Correlations with other variables ranged from −.31 to .58.

Author: Liang, C. T. H., et al.

Article: The Asian American Racism-Related Stress Inventory: Development, factor analysis, reliability, and validity.

Journal: *Journal of Counseling Psychology*, January 2004, *51*, 103–114.

Related Research: Smedley, B. D., et al. (1993). Minority-status stresses and the college adjustment of ethnic minority freshmen. *Journal of Higher Education, 64,* 434–452.

10310

Test Name: MULTIDIMENSIONAL RESEARCH BURNOUT SCALE

Purpose: To measure burnout in an academic setting.

Number of Items: 8

Format: Item responses range from 1 (*strongly disagree*) to 5 (*strongly agree*). All items are presented.

Reliability: Alpha coefficients ranged from .74 to .80.

Author: Singh, S. N., et al.

Article: Research burnout: A refined multidimensional scale.

Journal: *Psychological Reports*, December 2004, *95*, Part 2, 1253–1263.

Related Research: Singh, S. N., & Bush, R. F. (1997). Research burnout in tenured marketing professors: An empirical investigation. *Journal of Marketing Education, 20,* 4–15.

10311

Test Name: MULTIPLE ASPECTS OF STUDENT ADAPTATION SCALES

Purpose: To enable teachers to rate multiple aspects of student adaptation.

Number of Items: 32

Format: Includes four scales: Academic Skills, Academic Effort, Aggression, and Prosocial Engagement. Responses are made on a 5-point scale ranging from 1 (*strongly disagree*) to 5 (*strongly agree*). Examples are given.

Reliability: Alpha coefficients ranged from .91 to .93.

Validity: Correlations with other variables ranged from −.32 to .56.

Author: Guest, S. D., et al.

Article: Peer academic reputation in elementary school: Associations with changes in self-concept and academic skills.

Journal: *Journal of Educational Psychology*, August 2005, 97, 337–346.

Related Research: Conduct Problems Prevention Research Group (1999). Initial impact of the Fast Track Prevention Trial for Conduct Problems: I. The high-risk sample. *Journal of Consulting and Clinical Psychology, 67,* 631–647.

10312

Test Name: ORIENTATIONS TO LEARNING SCALES

Purpose: To measure openness to learning, learning for self-understanding, internal locus of control for academic success, and preference for higher order activities.

Number of Items: 16

Format: Scales range from 1 (*strongly disagree*) to 5 (*strongly agree*). All items are presented.

Reliability: Alpha coefficients ranged from .62 to .84 across subscales.

Validity: Average correlations with other variables ranged from .12 to .30.

Author: Wolniak, G. C., et al.

Article: Effects of intercollegiate athletic participation on male orientations to learning.

Journal: *Journal of College Student Development*, November/December 2001, 42, 604–624.

10313

Test Name: PEER BELIEF INVENTORY

Purpose: To measure children's perceptions of the social dispositions of their schoolmates.

Number of Items: 10

Format: Includes two parts: the extent to which children view their schoolmates as prosocial and perceptions of peers' antisocial characteristics. Responses are made on a 5-point scale ranging from 1 (*not very true*) to 5 (*very true*).

Reliability: All alpha coefficients were greater than .80.

Author: Troop-Gordon, W., and Ladd, G. W.

Article: Trajectories of peer victimization and perceptions of the self and schoolmates: Precursors to internalizing and externalizing problems.

Journal: *Child Development*, September/October 2005, 76, 1072–1091.

Related Research: Rabiner, D. L., et al. (1993). Children's beliefs about familiar and unfamiliar peers in relation to their sociometric status. *Developmental Psychology, 29*, 236–243.

10314

Test Name: PEER BELIEFS SCALE

Purpose: To assess the degree to which a student believes that friends and classmates feel that school is important.

Number of Items: 6

Format: Responses are made on a 4-point Likert scale ranging from 1 (*strongly agree*) to 4 (*strongly disagree*). Examples are given.

Reliability: Alpha coefficients were .62 and .69.

Validity: Correlations with other variables ranged from −.23 to .38.

Author: Kenny, M. E., and Bledsoe, M.

Article: Contributions of the relational context to career adaptability among urban adolescents.

Journal: *Journal of Vocational Behavior*, April 2005, 66, 257–272.

Related Research: Radziwon, C. D. (2003). The effect of peers' beliefs on 8th grade students' identification with school. *Journal of Research in Childhood Education, 17*, 236–249.

10315

Test Name: PEER NOMINATION OF ACADEMIC COMPETENCE SCALE

Purpose: To measure peers' assessments of classmates' social and academic competence.

Number of Items: 10

Format: A paired-item format is used by which classmates are given positive and negative nominations.

Validity: Correlations with other variables ranged from .11 to .38.

Author: Vandiver, T.

Article: Children's social competence, academic competence, and aggressiveness as related to ability to make judgments of fairness.

Journal: *Psychological Reports*, August 2001, *89*, 111–121.

Related Research: Cole, D. A. (1991). Change in self-perceived competence as a function of peer and teacher evaluation. *Developmental Psychology, 27*, 682–688.

10316

Test Name: PERSONAL–EMOTIONAL ADJUSTMENT SUBSCALE

Purpose: To measure emotional adjustment to college.

Number of Items: 15

Format: Scales range from 1 (*applies very closely to me*) to 9 (*doesn't apply to me at all*).

Reliability: Coefficient alpha was .84.

Author: Rice, K. G., and Lapsley, D. K.

Article: Perfectionism, coping, and emotional adjustment.

Journal: *Journal of College Student Development*, March/April 2001, *42*, 157–168.

Related Research: Baker, R. W., & Siryk, B. (1986). Exploratory intervention with a scale measuring adjustment to college. *Journal of Counseling Psychology, 33*, 31–38.

10317

Test Name: PERSONAL PROBLEM INVENTORY— ADAPTED

Purpose: To assess problems commonly reported by college students.

Number of Items: 32

Format: Includes concern for each problem and willingness to seek counseling for each problem. Responses are made on 5-point scales.

Reliability: Alpha coefficients ranged from .89 to .97.

Validity: Correlations with other variables ranged from −.48 to .49.

Author: Liao, H.-Y., et al.

Article: A test of Cramer's (1999) help-seeking model and acculturation effects with Asian and Asian American college students.

Journal: *Journal of Counseling Psychology*, July 2005, *52*, 400–411.

Related Research: Gim, R. H., et al. (1990). Asian American acculturation, severity of concerns, and willingness to see a counselor. *Journal of Counseling Psychology, 37*, 281–285.

10318

Test Name: PHYSICAL EDUCATION STATE ANXIETY SCALE

Purpose: To measure state anxiety for school physical education.

Number of Items: 18

Format: Includes three subscales: Somatic Anxiety, Worry, and Cognitive Processes. Responses are made on a 5-point scale ranging from 1 (*not at all*) to 5 (*very much*). All items are presented.

Reliability: Alpha coefficients ranged from .79 to .83.

Author: Barkoukis, V., et al.

Article: The development of a Physical Education State Anxiety Scale: A preliminary study.

Journal: *Perceptual and Motor Skills*, February 2005, *100*, 118–128.

Related Research: Tsorbatzoudis, H., et al. (2001). Preliminary study on the psychometric properties of Academic Motivation Scale. *Hellenic Journal of Psychology, 8*, 526–537.

10319

Test Name: POSITIVE AFFECT TOWARD SCHOOL SCALE

Purpose: To measure positive affect toward school.

Number of Items: 11

Format: Scales range from 1 (*strongly disagree*) to 5 (*strongly agree*). Sample items are presented.

Reliability: Alpha coefficients ranged from .75 to .78.

Validity: Correlations with other variables ranged from −.27 to .27.

Author: Oyserman, D., et al.

Article: Possible selves as roadmaps.

Journal: *Journal of Research in Personality*, April 2004, *38*, 130–149.

Related Research: Arroyo, C., & Zigler, E. (1995). Racial identity, academic achievement, and the psychological well being of economically disadvantaged adolescents. *Journal of Personality and Social Psychology, 69*, 903–914.

10320

Test Name: POSITIVE AND NEGATIVE EVENTS CHECKLIST

Purpose: To measure positive and negative events among college students.

Number of Items: 20

Format: Responses are made on 5-point scales anchored by *less than average* and *more than average*.

Reliability: Coefficient alpha was .58. Test–retest reliability (1 week) was .70. Subscale alphas ranged from .60 (negative events) to .62 (positive events).

Author: Lee, D. Y., et al.

Article: Self and other ratings of Canadian and Korean groups of mental health professionals and their clients.

Journal: *Psychological Reports,* April 2002, *90,* 667–676.

Related Research: Weinstein, H. D. (1980). Unrealistic optimism about future life events. *Journal of Personality and Social Psychology, 39,* 806–820.

10321

Test Name: PREOCCUPATION WITH FAILURE SCALE

Purpose: To measure preoccupation with failure.

Number of Items: 12

Format: Forced choice.

Reliability: Alpha coefficients ranged from .70 to .77.

Validity: Correlations with other variables ranged from −.03 to .13.

Author: Perry, R. P., et al.

Article: Perceived academic control and failure in college students: A three-year study of scholastic attainment.

Journal: *Research in Higher Education,* August 2005, *46,* 535–569.

Related Research: Kuhl, J. (1994). A theory of action and state orientation. In J. Kuhl & J. Beckmann (Eds.), *Volition and personality* (pp. 9–46). Seattle, WA: Hogfre and Huber.

10322

Test Name: REACTIONS TO TESTS

Purpose: To measure dispositional test anxiety.

Number of Items: 40

Format: Responses are made on 4-point rating scales. An example is given.

Validity: Correlations with other variables ranged from −.35 to .50.

Author: Diaz, R. J., et al.

Article: Cognition, anxiety, and prediction of performance in 1st year law students.

Journal: *Journal of Educational Psychology,* June 2001, *93,* 420–429.

Related Research: Sarason, I. G. (1984). Stress, anxiety, and cognitive interference: Reactions to Texts. *Journal of Personality and Social Psychology, 46,* 929–938.

10323

Test Name: RESEARCH ANXIETY RATING SCALE

Purpose: To assess anxiety experienced by students in research methodology courses.

Number of Items: 45

Format: Responses are made on a 5-point Likert-format response scale.

Reliability: Coefficient alphas were .84 and .94.

Validity: Correlations with other variables ranged from −.51 to .53.

Author: Onwuegbuzie, A. J.

Article: Modeling statistics achievement among graduate students.

Journal: *Educational and Psychological Measurement,* December 2003, *63,* 1020–1038.

Related Research: Onwuegbuzie, A. J. (1996). *Development of the Research Anxiety Rating Scale.* Unpublished manuscript, University of Central Arkansas, Conway.

10324

Test Name: REVISED UNIVERSITY STUDENT HASSLES SCALE

Purpose: To identify university student hassles.

Number of Items: 57

Format: Includes 11 subscales: Time Pressures, Financial Constraints, Race/Ethnicity, Gender Issues, Friendships, Traffic, Religion, Safety, Employment, Physical Appearance, and Parental Expectations. Responses are made on a 5-point scale ranging from 0 (*did not occur*) to 4 (*always occurred*).

Reliability: Alpha coefficients ranged from .73 to .94.

Validity: Correlations with other variables ranged from −.03 to .50.

Author: Pett, M. A., and Johnson, M. J. M.

Article: Development and psychometric evaluation of the Revised University Student Hassles Scale.

Journal: *Educational and Psychological Measurement,* December 2005, *65,* 984–1010.

10325

Test Name: SATISFACTION WITH COLLEGE QUESTIONNAIRE

Purpose: To measure satisfaction with college.

Number of Items: 30

Format: Likert-type response categories are used. All items and response categories are presented.

Reliability: Alpha was .80.

Author: Landrum, E. R., et al.

Article: Satisfaction with college by traditional and nontraditional college students.

Journal: *Psychological Reports,* December 2001, *89,* 740–746.

Related Research: Greenland, A. (1992). Tracing adult student satisfaction in a large traditional university. *Continuing Higher Education Review, 56,* 8–22.

10326

Test Name: SCHOOL CONNECTEDNESS SCALE

Purpose: To assess a student's integration and feelings of belonging to school.

Number of Items: 4

Format: Responses are made on a 5-point Likert-type scale ranging from 1 (*strongly disagree*) to 5 (*strongly agree*). All items are presented.

Reliability: Alpha coefficients were .71 and .72.

Author: Akos, P., and Galassi, J. P.

Article: Gender and race as variables in psychosocial adjustment to middle and high school.

Journal: *The Journal of Educational Research,* November/December 2004, *98,* 102–108.

Related Research: National Longitudinal Study of Adolescent Health (1998). *Codebooks.* Retrieved June 19, 2002, from *http://www.cpc.unc.edu/addhealth/codebooks.html*

10327

Test Name: SCHOOL ENGAGEMENT MEASURE

Purpose: To measure school engagement.

Number of Items: 8

Format: Responses are made on a 7-point scale. Examples are presented.

Reliability: Coefficient alpha was .77.

Validity: Correlations with other variables ranged from –.25 to .39.

Author: Kenny, M. E., et al.

Article: The role of perceived barriers and relational support in the educational and vocational lives of urban high school students.

Journal: *Journal of Counseling Psychology,* April 2003, *50,* 142–155.

Related Research: Dornbusch, S. M., & Steinberg, L. (1990). *Measures of School Engagement.* Unpublished manuscript, Temple University, Philadelphia.

10328

Test Name: SCHOOL FAILURE TOLERANCE SCALE

Purpose: To assess students' willingness to persevere in difficult and challenging learning situations.

Format: Includes three subscales: Negative Feelings After Failure, Preference for Difficult Tasks, and Proactive Behaviors After Failure. Responses are made on a 5-point Likert-type scale ranging from 1 (*strongly agree*) to 5 (*strongly disagree*). An example is given.

Reliability: Alpha coefficients ranged from .78 to .86.

Validity: Correlations with other variables ranged from –.17 to .38.

Author: Mergendoller, J. R., et al.

Article: Comparing problem-based learning and traditional instruction in high school economics.

Journal: *The Journal of Educational Research,* July/August 2000, *93,* 374–382.

Related Research: Clifford, M. M. (1991). Risk taking: Theoretical, empirical, and educational considerations. *Educational Psychologist, 26,* 263–297.

10329

Test Name: SCHOOL-RELATED HASSLES SCALE

Purpose: To measure frustration and stress.

Number of Items: 12

Format: Scales range from 0 (*no frustration or stress*) to 3 (*high level of frustration or stress*).

Reliability: Coefficient alpha was .78.

Validity: Correlations with other variables ranged from .03 to .12.

Author: Fenzel, L. M.

Article: Multivariate analysis of predictors of heavy episodic drinking and drinking-related problems among college students.

Journal: *Journal of College Student Development,* March/April 2005, *46,* 126–140.

Related Research: Kohn, P. M., et al. (1990). The Inventory of College Students' Recent Life Experiences: A decontaminated hassles scale for a special population. *Journal of Behavioral Medicine, 6,* 619–630.

10330

Test Name: SENSE OF SCHOOL BELONGING SCALE

Purpose: To assess students' psychological sense of school belonging.

Number of Items: 5 and 8

Format: Sample items are presented.

Reliability: Alpha coefficients ranged from .80 to .82.

Validity: Correlations with other variables ranged from .10 to .58 ($n = 599$).

Author: Anderman, L. H.

Article: Academic and social perceptions as predictors of change in middle school students' sense of school belonging.

Journal: *The Journal of Experimental Education*, Fall 2003, 72, 5–22.

Related Research: Goodenow, C. (1993). The psychological sense of school membership among adolescents: Scale development and educational correlates. *Psychology in the Schools*, 30, 79–90.

10331

Test Name: SENSE OF SCHOOL MEMBERSHIP SCALE

Purpose: To assess a student's perceived belonging to the school environment.

Number of Items: 17

Format: Scales range from 1 (*not at all true*) to 5 (*completely true*). A sample item is presented.

Reliability: Coefficient alpha was .86.

Author: Vinokurov, A., et al.

Article: Acculturative hassles and immigrant adolescents: A life–domain assessment for Soviet Jewish refugees.

Journal: *The Journal of Social Psychology*, August 2002, 142, 425–445.

Related Research: Goodenow, C. (1993). The Psychological Sense of School Membership among adolescents: Scale development and educational correlates. *Psychology in the Schools*, 30, 79–90.

10332

Test Name: SITUATION-SPECIFIC SELF-STEREOTYPING SCALE

Purpose: To assess the extent to which a person identifies with others in a university setting.

Number of Items: 4

Format: Scales range from 1 (*not at all*) to 4 (*very much*). All items are presented.

Reliability: Coefficient alpha was .83.

Author: DeCremer, D.

Article: Relations of self-esteem concerns, group identifications, and self-stereotyping to in-group favoritism.

Journal: *The Journal of Social Psychology*, June 2001, 141, 389–400.

Related Research: Verkuyten, M., & Nekuee, S. (1999). In-group bias: The effect of self-stereotyping, identification and group threat. *European Journal of Social Psychology*, 29, 411–418.

10333

Test Name: SOCIAL CONNECTEDNESS SCALE—MODIFIED

Purpose: To measure connectedness to the campus.

Number of Items: 12

Format: Responses are made on a 6-point Likert-type scale ranging from 1 (*strongly disagree*) to 6 (*strongly agree*). All items are presented.

Reliability: Alpha coefficients were .90 and .92.

Validity: Correlations with other variables ranged form .16 to .55.

Author: Summers, J. J., et al.

Article: Evaluating collaborative learning and community.

Journal: *The Journal of Experimental Education*, Spring 2005, 73, 165–188.

Related Research: Lee, R.-M., & Robbins, S. B. (1995). Measuring belongingness: The Social Connectedness and the Social Assurance scales. *Journal of Counseling Psychology*, 42, 232–241.

10334

Test Name: SOCIAL INTEGRATION AND PERSISTENCE INTENTIONS MEASURE

Purpose: To measure college student social integration and persistence intentions.

Number of Items: 17

Format: Includes indexes of Social Integration and Persistence.

Reliability: Alpha coefficients were .73 and .84.

Validity: Correlations with other variables ranged from –.20 to .49.

Author: Torres, J. B., and Solberg, V. S.

Article: Role of self-efficacy, stress, social integration, and family support in Latino college student persistence and health.

Journal: *Journal of Vocational Behavior*, August 2001, 59, 53–63.

Related Research: Tinto, V. (1987). *Leaving college: Rethinking the causes and cures of student retention*. Chicago: University of Chicago Press.

10335

Test Name: STATISTICAL ANXIETY RATING SCALE

Purpose: To measure statistics anxiety.

Number of Items: 51

Format: All items are presented.

Reliability: Alpha coefficients ranged from .47 to .93 across subscales and across subjects in different areas of study.

Validity: Correlations with performance variables ranged from –.28 to –.21.

Author: Mji, A., and Onwuegbuzie, A. J.

Article: Evidence of score reliability and validity of the Statistical Anxiety Rating Scale among Technikon students in South Africa.

Journal: *Measurement and Evaluation in Counseling and Development*, January 2004, *36*, 238–251.

Related Research: Cruise, R. J., & Wilkins, E. M. (1980). *STARS: Statistical Anxiety Rating Scale.* Unpublished manuscript, Andrews University, Berrien Springs, MI.

10336

Test Name: STUDENT ADAPTATION TO COLLEGE QUESTIONNAIRE

Purpose: To measure students' adjustment to college.

Number of Items: 67

Format: Scales range from 1 (*applies very closely to me*) to 9 (*doesn't apply to me at all*).

Reliability: Alpha coefficients ranged from .82 to .94 across subscales.

Validity: Correlations with other variables ranged from −.15 to .56.

Author: Hinderlie, H. H., and Kenny, M.

Article: Attachment, social support, and college adjustment among Black students at predominately White universities.

Journal: *Journal of College Student Development*, May/June 2002, *43*, 327–340.

Related Research: Baker, R., & Siryk, B. (1984). Measuring adjustment to college. *Journal of Counseling Psychology, 33,* 179–189.

10337

Test Name: STUDENT ADJUSTMENT PROBLEMS INVENTORY

Purpose: To assess adjustment problems of Chinese secondary students.

Number of Items: 18

Format: Includes six problem dimensions/domains: relationship/ability concerns, unchallenging schoolwork, intense involvement, concerns for being different, parental expectations, and perfectionism. Responses are made on a 5-point scale ranging from 1 (*not at all descriptive*) to 5 (*very descriptive*). All items are presented.

Reliability: Alpha coefficients ranged from .58 to .74.

Author: Chan, D. W.

Article: Assessing adjustment problems of gifted students in Hong Kong: The development of the Student Adjustment Problems Inventory.

Journal: *Gifted Child Quarterly*, Spring 2003, *47*, 107–117.

Related Research: Chan, D. W. (1999). Reversing underachievement: Can we tap unfulfilled talents in Hong Kong? *Educational Research Journal, 14,* 177–190.

10338

Test Name: STUDENT COURSE ENGAGEMENT QUESTIONNAIRE

Purpose: To measure student engagement.

Number of Items: 23

Format: Includes four factors: skills engagement, emotional engagement, participation/interaction engagement, and performance engagement. All items are presented.

Reliability: Alpha coefficients ranged from .76 to .82.

Author: Handelsman, M. M., et al.

Article: A measure of college student course engagement.

Journal: *The Journal of Educational Research,* January/February 2005, *98*, 184–191.

Related Research: National Survey of Student Engagement (2002). *2002 Overview.* Bloomington: Indiana University Center for Postsecondary Research and Planning.

10339

Test Name: STUDENT–FACULTY AND STUDENT–PEER INTERACTIONS SURVEY

Purpose: To identify a student's interactions with faculty and peers.

Number of Items: 4

Format: A yes–no format is used.

Reliability: Alpha coefficients were .64 (student–faculty) and .81 (student–peer).

Validity: Correlations with other variables ranged from −.32 to .46 ($n = 50$).

Author: Weidman, J. C., and Stein, E. L.

Article: Socialization of doctoral students to academic norms.

Journal: *Research in Higher Education,* December 2003, *44*, 641–656.

Related Research: Trow, M. (Ed.) (1975). *Teachers and students: Aspects of American higher education.* New York: McGraw-Hill.

10340

Test Name: STUDENT HASSLES SCALE

Purpose: To measure student stressors experienced at college.

Number of Items: 55

Format: Scales range from 1 (*not at all part of my life*) to 4 (*very much a part of my life*).

Reliability: Coefficient alpha was .91.

Author: Pritchard, M. E., and Wilson, G. S.

Article: Using emotional and social factors to predict student success.

Journal: *Journal of College Student Development*, January/February 2003, *44*, 18–28.

Related Research: Kohn, P. M., et al. (1990). The Inventory of College Students' Recent Life Experiences: A decontaminated hassles scale for a special population. *Journal of Behavioral Medicine, 13*, 619–630.

10341

Test Name: STUDENT QUESTIONNAIRE

Purpose: To provide intervention outcome measures.

Number of Items: 16

Format: Includes two scales: Bullying Inventory and Life in School Checklist.

Reliability: Alpha coefficients were .81 to .82.

Author: Stevens, V., et al.

Article: Implementation process of the Flemish antibullying intervention and relation with program effectiveness.

Journal: *Journal of School Psychology*, July/August, 2001, *39*, 303–317.

Related Research: Stevens, V., et al. (2000). Bullying in Flemish schools: An evaluation of antibullying intervention in primary and secondary schools. *British Journal of Educational Psychology, 70*, 195–210.

10342

Test Name: STUDENT READINESS INVENTORY

Purpose: To provide psychosocial and academic-related skill factors that predict academic performance and retention.

Number of Items: 95

Format: Includes 10 factors: general determination, academic discipline, goal striving, commitment to college, study skills, communication skills, social activity, social connection, academic self-confidence, and emotional control. Responses are made on a 6-point Likert-type scale ranging from 1 (*strongly disagree*) to 6 (*strongly agree*). Sample items are presented.

Reliability: Alpha coefficients ranged from .72 to .87.

Validity: Correlations with other variables ranged from –.15 to .32.

Author: Le, H., et al.

Article: Motivational and skills, social, and self-management predictors of college outcomes: Constructing the Student Readiness Inventory.

Journal: *Educational and Psychological Measurement*, June 2005, *65*, 482–508.

10343

Test Name: STUDENT ROLE MANAGEMENT SCALE

Purpose: To assess the management of the student role.

Number of Items: 10

Format: Scales range from 0 (*no confidence*) to 9 (*complete confidence*). Sample items are presented.

Reliability: Internal reliability was .94.

Validity: Correlations with other variables ranged from –.24 to .69.

Author: Quimby, J. L., and O'Brien, K. M.

Article: Predictors of student and career decision-making self-efficacy among nontraditional college women.

Journal: *The Career Development Quarterly*, June 2004, *52*, 323–339.

Related Research: Lefcourt, L. A. (1995). *The Self-Efficacy Expectations for Role Management measure (SEERM) and its relationship with role salience, role conflict, and coping strategies.* Unpublished master's thesis, University of Illinois, Urbana–Champaign.

10344

Test Name: STUDENT SOCIAL ATTRIBUTION SCALE—REVISED

Purpose: To assess causal attributions for social success and failure in school-related situations.

Number of Items: 30

Format: Includes eight subscales: Success Ability, Success Effort, Success Chance, Success Task Difficulty, Failure Ability, Failure Effort, Failure Chance, and Failure Task Difficulty.

Reliability: Alpha coefficients ranged from .76 to .93. Test–retest (2 weeks) reliability coefficients ranged from .74 to .84.

Validity: Correlations with other variables ranged from –.83 to .78.

Author: Bein, S. K., and Bell, S. M.

Article: Social self-concept, social attributions, and peer relationships in fourth, fifth, and sixth graders who are gifted compared to high achievers.

Journal: *Gifted Child Quarterly*, Summer 2004, *48*, 167–178.

Related Research: Bain, S. K., & Reese, L. (2002). *Test–retest reliability for the Student Social Attribution Scale.* Unpublished manuscript.

10345

Test Name: STUDENT–TEACHER RELATIONSHIP SCALE—TWO SUBSCALES

Purpose: To assess conflictual teacher–child relationships and teacher–child closeness.

Number of Items: 23

Format: Includes two subscales: Conflictual Teacher–Child Relationships and Teacher–Child Closeness. Sample items are presented.

Reliability: Alpha coefficients >.89.

Author: Ladd, G. W., and Burgess, K. B.

Article: Do relational risks and protective factors moderate the linkages between childhood aggression and early psychological and school adjustment?

Journal: *Child Development,* September/October 2001, 72, 1579–1601.

Related Research: Pianta, R. C., et al. (1995). The first two years of school: Teacher–child relationships and deflections in children's classroom adjustment. *Development and Psychopathology,* 7, 295–312.

10346

Test Name: STUDENT UNREST INVENTORY

Purpose: To measure students' perception of the factors influencing student unrest.

Number of Items: 28

Format: Four-point Likert scales range from *strongly agree* to *strongly disagree.*

Reliability: Split-half reliability was .86.

Author: Aluede, O. O.

Article: Factors influencing student unrest in tertiary institutions in Edo State of Nigeria.

Journal: *Educational Research Quarterly,* March 2001, 24, 10–26.

Related Research: Aluede, O. O. (2000). An analysis of the attitude of university students toward campus unrest. *The Progress of Education,* 74, 154–160.

10347

Test Name: SURVEY OF ACADEMIC ORIENTATIONS

Purpose: To provide an early warning system to detect at-risk students.

Number of Items: 36

Format: Includes six orientations: Structure Dependence, Creative Expression, Reading for Pleasure, Academic Efficacy, Academic Apathy, and Mistrust of Instructors. Responses are made on a 5-point Likert-type scale ranging from 1 (*strongly disagree*) to 5 (*strongly agree*). Sample items are presented.

Reliability: Alpha coefficients ranged from .59 to .86.

Validity: Correlations with other variables ranged from –.17 to .31.

Author: Beck, H. P., and Davidson, W. D.

Article: Establishing an early warning system: Predicting low grades in college students from survey of academic orientation scores.

Journal: *Research in Higher Education,* December 2001, 42, 709–723.

Related Research: Davidson, W. B., et al. (1999). Development

and validation scores on a measure of academic orientations in college students. *Educational and Psychological Measurement,* 59, 678–693.

10348

Test Name: TEACHER–CHILD RATING SCALE

Purpose: To enable teachers to rate each child in their class on school-related social competence.

Number of Items: 20

Format: Responses are made on a 5-point scale ranging from 1 (*not at all*) to 5 (*very well*). Examples are given.

Reliability: Internal consistency was .91.

Author: Chen, X., et al.

Article: The peer group as a context: Mediating and moderating effects on relations between academic achievement and social functioning in Chinese children.

Journal: *Child Development,* May/June 2003, 74, 710–727.

Related Research: Hightower, A. D., et al. (1986). The Teacher–Child Rating Scale: A brief objective measure of elementary children's school problem behaviors and competencies. *School Psychology Review,* 15, 393–409.

10349

Test Name: TEACHER RATING SCALE OF STUDENTS' CLASSROOM ENGAGEMENT

Purpose: To assess student engagement versus disaffection.

Number of Items: 5

Format: Responses are made on a 4-point scale ranging from 1 (*not at all true*) to 4 (*very true*).

Reliability: Alpha coefficients were .81 and .88.

Author: Murry, C., and Malmgren, K.

Article: Implementing a teacher–student relationship program in a high-poverty urban school: Effects on social, emotional, and academic adjustment and lessons learned.

Journal: *Journal of School Psychology*, March/April 2005, *43*, 137–152.

Related Research: Connell, J. P., & Wellborn, J. G. (1991). Competence, autonomy, and relatedness: A motivational analysis of self-system processes. M. R. Gunnar, & L. A. Sroufe (Eds.), *Self-processes in development: Minnesota Symposium on Child Psychology* (Vol. 23, pp. 43–77). Hillside, NJ: Erlbaum.

10350

Test Name: TEACHER RELATIONSHIP INVENTORY

Purpose: To enable teachers to indicate their level of support or conflict in their relationships with individual students.

Number of Items: 22

Format: Includes three factors: support, intimacy, and conflict. Examples are given.

Reliability: Internal consistency coefficients were .60 and .92.

Validity: Correlations with other variables ranged from –.20 to .49.

Author: Hughes, J. N., et al.

Article: Relationship influences on teachers' perceptions of academic competence in academically at-risk minority and majority first grade students.

Journal: *Journal of School Psychology*, October 2005, *43*, 303–320.

Related Research: Hughes, J. N., et al. (2001). Further evidence of the developmental significance of the student–teacher relationship. *Journal of School Psychology, 39*, 289–302.

10351

Test Name: TEACHER–STUDENT RELATIONSHIP SCALE

Purpose: To assess students' perceptions of their relationships with teachers.

Number of Items: 4

Format: Scales range from 1 (*strongly disagree*) to 5 (*strongly agree*). All items are presented.

Reliability: Coefficient alpha was .74.

Validity: Correlations with other variables ranged from –.33 to .51.

Author: Lapan, R. T., et al.

Article: Helping seventh graders be safe and successful: A statewide study of the impact of comprehensive guidance and counseling programs.

Journal: *Professional School Counseling*, February 2003, *6*(3), 186–197.

10352

Test Name: TEST ANXIETY INVENTORY—SHORT VERSION

Purpose: To measure test anxiety.

Number of Items: 5

Format: All items are presented.

Reliability: Coefficient alpha was .87.

Validity: Correlations with other versions of the scale ranged from .17 to .69.

Author: Taylor, J., and Deane, F. P.

Article: Development of a short form of the Test Anxiety Inventory (TAI).

Journal: *The Journal of General Psychology*, April 2002, *129*, 127–136.

Related Research: Marteau, T. M., & Bekker, H. (1992). The development of a six-item short form of the Speilberger State–Trait Anxiety Inventory (STAI). *British Journal of Clinical Psychology, 31*, 301–305.

10353

Test Name: TEST ANXIETY SCALE—ADAPTED

Purpose: To measure test anxiety.

Number of Items: 21

Format: Includes four components: test–irrelevant thinking, worry, tension, and bodily reactions.

Reliability: Alpha coefficients ranged from .69 to .86.

Author: Matters, G., and Burnett, P. C.

Article: Psychological predictors of the propensity to omit short-response items on a high-stakes achievement test.

Journal: *Educational and Psychological Measurement*, April 2003, *63*, 239–256.

Related Research: Sarason, I. G. (1972). Experimental approaches to test anxiety: Attention and the uses of information. In C. D. Spielberger (Ed.), *Anxiety: Current trends in theory and research* (Vol. 2). New York: Academic Press.

10354

Test Name: UNIVERSITY SATISFACTION AND ADJUSTMENT SCALE

Purpose: To measure satisfaction with academic progress and intention to continue at the university.

Number of Items: 8

Format: Responses are made on a 5-point scale ranging from 1 (*strongly agree*) to 5 (*strongly disagree*). Examples are given.

Reliability: Coefficient alpha was .78.

Validity: Correlations with other variables ranged from –.26 to .20.

Author: Chemers, M. M., et al.

Article: Academic self-efficacy and first-year college student performance and adjustment.

Journal: *Journal of Educational Psychology*, March 2001, *93*, 55–64.

Related Research: Pascarella, E. T., & Terenzini, P. (1980). Predicting freshman persistence and voluntary dropout decision from a theoretical model. *Journal of Higher Education*, *51*, 60–75.

10355

Test Name: UNIVERSITY STUDENT HASSLES SCALE

Purpose: To measure university student hassles.

Number of Items: 35

Format: Includes five factors: personal conflicts, time demands, financial concerns, household tasks, and environmental issues. Responses are made on a 4-point scale ranging from 0 (*not at all severe*) to 3 (*extremely severe*).

Reliability: Alpha coefficients ranged from .64 to .91.

Author: Pett, M. A., and Johnson, M. J. M.

Article: Development and psychometric evaluation of the Revised University Student Hassles Scale.

Journal: *Educational and Psychological Measurement*, December 2005, *65*, 984–1010.

Related Research: Kanner, A. D., et al. (1981). Comparison of two modes of stress measurement: Daily hassles and uplifts versus major life events. *Journal of Behavioral Medicine*, *4*, 1–38.

10356

Test Name: WRITING APPREHENSION TEST

Purpose: To assess how much individuals associate writing with apprehension, anxiety, and failure.

Number of Items: 26

Format: Responses are made on a 5-point scale.

Reliability: Alpha coefficients were .94 and .96.

Author: Omwuegbuzie, A. J., & Collins, K. M. T.

Article: Writing apprehension and academic procrastination among graduate students.

Journal: *Perceptual and Motor Skills*, April 2001, *92*, 560–562.

Related Research: Daly, J. A., & Miller, M. D. (1975). The empirical development of an instrument to measure writing apprehension. *Research in the Teaching of English*, *9*, 242–249.

10357

Test Name: YOUNG CHILDREN'S APPRAISALS OF TEACHER SUPPORT—CONFLICT SUBSCALE

Purpose: To assess the child's perceptions of negativity and conflict in his or her interactions with the teacher.

Number of Items: 9

Format: Examples are given.

Reliability: Coefficient alpha was .75.

Validity: Correlations with other variables ranged from –.24 to .24.

Author: Mantzicopoulos, P.

Article: Conflict relationships between kindergarten children and their teachers: Associations with child and classroom context variables.

Journal: *Journal of School Psychology*, November 2005, *43*, 425–442.

Related Research: Mantzicopoulos, P., & Neuharth-Pritchett, S. (2003). Development and validation of a measure to assess Head Start children's appraisals of teacher support. *Journal of School Psychology*, *41*, 431–451.

CHAPTER 3
Adjustment—Psychological

10358

Test Name: ABBREVIATED ACCEPTABILITY RATING PROFILE

Purpose: To measure acceptance of interventions.

Number of Items: 8

Format: Scales range from 1 (*strongly disagree*) to 6 (*strongly agree*).

Reliability: Coefficient alpha was .94.

Author: Carter, S. L.

Article: College students' acceptance of potential treatments for ADHD.

Journal: *Psychological Reports*, August 2005, 97, 258–264.

Related Research: Tarnowski, K. J., & Simonian, S. J. (1992). Assessing treatment acceptance: The Abbreviated Acceptability Rating Profile. *Journal of Behavior Therapy and Experimental Psychiatry, 23*, 101–106.

10359

Test Name: ACCEPTANCE OF DISABILITY (ILLNESS) SCALE

Purpose: To measure acceptance of disability and illness.

Number of Items: 9

Format: Response scales range from 1 (*strongly agree*) to 5 (*strongly disagree*). Sample items are presented.

Reliability: Coefficient alpha was .74.

Validity: Correlations with other variables ranged from –.59 to .74.

Author: Abraído-Lanza, A. F., et al.

Article: En las manos de Dios [In God's hands]: Religious and other forms of coping among Latinos with arthritis.

Journal: *Journal of Consulting and Clinical Psychology,* February 2004, 72, 91–102.

Related Research: Linkowski, D. C. (1971). A scale to measure acceptance of disability. *Rehabilitation Counseling Bulletin, 14*, 236–244.

10360

Test Name: ACTIVATION–DEACTIVATION ADJECTIVE CHECKLIST

Purpose: To measure energy, tiredness, tension, and relaxation.

Number of Items: 20

Format: Includes four constructs: energy, tiredness, tension, and relaxation. Responses are made on a 4-point scale ranging from 0 (*slightly or not at all*) to 3 (*definitely*).

Reliability: Alpha coefficients were .62 and .80.

Validity: Correlations with other variables ranged from –.42 to .65.

Author: Huelsman, T. J., et al.

Article: Measurement of dispositional affect: Construct validity and convergence with a circumplex model of affect.

Journal: *Educational and Psychological Measurement,* August 2003, 63, 655–673.

Related Research: Thayer, R. E. (1989). *The biopsychology of mood and arousal.* New York: Oxford University Press.

10361

Test Name: ACUTE PANIC INVENTORY—CAMBODIAN VERSION

Purpose: To assess subjective responses to a challenge procedure.

Number of Items: 17

Format: Three-point Likert scales are used.

Validity: Correlations with other variables ranged from –.10 to .39.

Author: Hinton, D., et al.

Article: The psychophysiology of orthostatic panic in Cambodian refugees attending a psychiatric clinic.

Journal: *Journal of Psychopathology and Behavioral Assessment,* March 2004, 26, 1–13.

Related Research: Wiedemann, K., et al. (2001). Anxiolytic effects of atrial natriuretic peptide on cholecystokinin tetrapeptide-induced panic attacks. *Archives of General Psychiatry, 58*, 371–377.

10362

Test Name: ADDICTION RECOVERY SCALE

Purpose: To assess endorsement of the philosophy and behaviors advocated in 12-step programs.

Number of Items: 40

Format: Five-point rating scales are used. Sample items are presented.

Reliability: Coefficient alpha was .82. Test–retest reliability was .87.

Validity: Correlations with other variables ranged from −.31 to .39.

Author: Crits-Christoph, P., et al.

Article: Mediators of outcome of psychosocial treatments for cocaine dependence.

Journal: *Journal of Consulting and Clinical Psychology*, October 2003, *71*, 918–925.

10363

Test Name: ADOLESCENT CONCERNS SCALE—TURKISH VERSION

Purpose: To measure stress in adolescents.

Number of Items: 40

Format: Response scales are anchored by 0 (*never*) and 4 (*always*).

Reliability: Internal reliability was .86.

Author: Oğul, M., and Gençöz, T.

Article: Roles of perceived control and coping strategies on depressive and anxiety symptoms of Turkish adolescents.

Journal: *Psychological Reports*, December 2003, *93*, Part 1, 659–672.

Related Research: Sahin, N., & Sahin, N. H. (1995). Dimensions of concerns: The case of Turkish adolescents. *Journal of Adolescence, 18*, 49–69.

10364

Test Name: ADULT ATTACHMENT SCALE—REVISED

Purpose: To provide indicator variables for the latent attachment constructs of anxiety and avoidance.

Number of Items: 18

Format: Includes three subscales: Close, Depend, and Anxiety. Responses are made on a 7-point scale ranging from 1 (*not at all like me*) to 7 (*very much like me*). Examples are given.

Reliability: Alpha coefficients were .83 to .89.

Author: Mohr, J. J., and Fassinger, R. E.

Article: Self-acceptance and self-disclosure of sexual orientation in lesbian, gay and bisexual adults: An attachment perspective.

Journal: *Journal of Counseling Psychology*, October 2003, *50*, 482–495.

Related Research: Collins, N. L. (1996). Working models of attachment: Implications for explanation, emotion and behavior. *Journal of Personality and Social Psychology, 71*, 810–832.

10365

Test Name: AFFECT AND AROUSAL SCALES

Purpose: To measure positive and negative affect and hyperarousal in children.

Number of Items: 27

Format: Scales range from 0 (*never true*) to 3 (*always true*).

Reliability: Coefficient alpha for the negative affect subscale was .77.

Author: Higa, C. K., et al.

Article: Psychometric properties and clinical utility of the School Refusal Assessment Scale in a multiethnic sample.

Journal: *Journal of Psychopathology and Behavioral Assessment*, December 2002, *24*, 247–258.

Related Research: Chorpita, B. F., et al. (2000). Assessment of symptoms of *DSM–IV* anxiety and depression in children: A revised Child Anxiety and Depression Scale. *Behavior Research and Therapy, 38*, 835–855.

10366

Test Name: AFFECT BALANCE SCALE

Purpose: To measure positive and negative affectivity and their balance.

Number of Items: 10

Format: Scales range from 0 (*never*) to 2 (*often*).

Reliability: Alpha coefficients ranged from .55 to .73.

Validity: Correlations with depression (Zung Scale) ranged from −.59 to −.53.

Author: O'Rourke, N., and Cappeliez, P.

Article: Marital satisfaction and marital aggrandizement among older adults: Analysis of gender invariance.

Journal: *Measurement and Evaluation in Counseling and Development*, July 2001, *34*, 66–79.

Related Research: Brodburn, N. M. (1969). *The structure of psychological well-being*. Chicago: Aldine.

10367

Test Name: AFFECT INTENSITY MEASURE

Purpose: To measure affect intensity.

Number of Items: 40

Format: Responses are made on a 6-point Likert-type scale. Examples are presented.

Reliability: Coefficient alpha was .87. Test–retest reliabilities were .80 to .81.

Validity: Correlations with other variables ranged from −.08 to .41.

Author: Fortunato, V. J., and Goldblatt, A. M.

Article: Construct validation of a Revised Strain-Free Negative Affectivity Scale.

Journal: *Education and Psychological Measurement*, February 2002, *62*(1), 45–63.

Related Research: Larsen, R. J., and Diener, E. (1987). Affect intensity as an individual difference characteristic: A review. *Journal of Research in Personality, 21*, 1–39.

10368

Test Name: AFFECTIVE COMMITMENT SCALE

Purpose: To measure affective commitment.

Number of Items: 8

Format: Responses are made on a 7-point scale ranging from 1 (*strongly disagree*) to 7 (*strongly agree*). Sample items are presented.

Validity: Correlations with other variables ranged from −.47 to .68 (*n* = 311).

Author: Hochwarter, W. A., et al.

Article: Perceived organizational support as a mediator of the relationship between politics perceptions and work outcomes.

Journal: *Journal of Vocational Behavior*, December 2003, *63*, 438–456.

Related Research: Allen, N., & Meyer, J. (1990). The measurement and antecedents of affective, continuance, and normative commitment to the organization. *Journal of Occupational Psychology, 63*, 1–17.

10369

Test Name: AFFECTIVE CONTROL SCALE

Purpose: To measure fear of losing control of one's emotions.

Number of Items: 42

Reliability: Various reliability coefficients ranged from .66 to .91.

Validity: Correlations with other variables ranged from .08 to .54.

Author: Beck, J. G., and Davila, J.

Article: Development of an interview for anxiety-relevant interpersonal styles: Preliminary support for convergent and discriminant validity.

Journal: *Journal of Psychopathology and Behavioral Assessment*, March 2003, *25*, 1–9.

Related Research: Williams, K. E., et al. (1997). Are emotions frightening? An extension of the fear of fear construct. *Behavior Research and Theory, 35*, 239–248.

10370

Test Name: AFFECTIVE DISPOSITION SCALE

Purpose: To measure affective disposition.

Number of Items: 18

Format: Responses are either 1 (*satisfied*), 2 (*not satisfied*), or 3 (*neutral*). Examples are provided.

Reliability: Coefficient alpha was .73.

Validity: Correlations with other variables ranged from −.23 to .34.

Author: Zickar, M. J., et al.

Article: Job attitudes of workers with two jobs.

Journal: *Journal of Vocational Behavior*, February 2004, *64*, 222–235.

Related Research: Judge, T. A., & Bretz, R. D. (1993). Report on an alternative measure of affective disposition. *Educational and Psychological Measurement, 53*, 1095–1104.

10371

Test Name: AFFECTIVE EXPERIENCES SCALES

Purpose: To assess students' positive affect and anxiety.

Number of Items: 8

Format: Includes two scales: Positive Affect and Anxiety. Examples are given.

Reliability: Alpha coefficients were .79 and .91.

Validity: Correlations with other variables ranged from −.43 to .70.

Author: Ryan, A. M., et al.

Article: Differential profiles of students identified by their teacher as having avoidant, appropriate, or dependent help-seeking tendencies in the classroom.

Journal: *Journal of Educational Psychology*, May 2005, *97*, 275–285.

Related Research: Pintrich, P. R. (2000). Multiple goals, multiple pathways: The role of goal orientation in learning and achievement. *Journal of Educational Psychology, 92*, 544–555. Pintrich, P. R., et al. (1993). Reliability and predictive validity of the Motivated Strategies for Learning Questionnaire (MSLQ). *Educational and Psychological Measurement, 53*, 801–813.

10372

Test Name: AFFECTIVE WELL-BEING SCALE

Purpose: To measure affective well-being.

Number of Items: 12

Format: Includes two dimensions: Anxiety–Comfort and Depression–Enthusiasm. Responses are made on a 6-point scale ranging from 1 (*never*) to 6 (*all of the time*).

Reliability: Alpha coefficients ranged from .80 to .85.

Validity: Correlations with other variables ranged from .55 to .65.

Author: Conway, N., and Briner, R. B.

Article: Full-time versus part-time employees: Understanding the links between work status, the psychological contract, and attitudes.

Journal: *Journal of Vocational Behavior,* October 2002, *61,* 279–301.

Related Research: Warr, P. (1990). The measurement of well-being and other aspects of mental health. *Journal of Occupational Psychology, 63,* 193–210.

10373

Test Name: AIR TRAVEL STRESS SCALE

Purpose: To assess air travel stress.

Number of Items: 22

Format: Includes three factors: air travel anxiety, air travel anger, and airline/airport trust. Responses are made on a 6-point scale ranging from 0 (*completely disagree*) to 5 (*completely agree*). All items are presented.

Reliability: Test–retest reliabilities (6 to 7 weeks) ranged from .81 to .87.

Validity: Correlations with other variables ranged from −.39 to .63.

Author: Bricker, J. B.

Article: Development and evaluation of the Air Travel Stress Scale.

Journal: *Journal of Counseling Psychology,* October 2005, *52,* 615–628.

10374

Test Name: ALCOHOL USE DISORDER IDENTIFICATION TEST

Purpose: To measure alcohol use.

Number of Items: 10

Format: Four-point rating scales are used.

Reliability: Coefficient alpha was .80.

Author: Amodei, N., et al.

Article: Interview versus self-answer methods of assessing health and emotional functioning in primary care patients.

Journal: *Psychological Reports,* June 2003, *92,* Part 1, 937–948.

Related Research: Fleming, M. F., et al. (1991). The Alcohol Use Disorders Identification Test (AUDIT) in a college sample. *International Journal of Addictions, 26,* 1173–1185.

10375

Test Name: AMERICAN FEAR SURVEY FOR CHILDREN

Purpose: To measure fear among children's fear of death and danger, fear of the unknown, school–social stress fears, animal fears, and criticism–failure fear.

Number of Items: 98

Format: Response categories are *not scared, scared,* and *very scared.* All items are presented.

Reliability: Alpha coefficients ranged from .70 to .96.

Author: Burnham, J. J.

Article: Fears of children in the United States: An examination of the American Fear Survey Schedule with 20 new contemporary fear items.

Journal: *Measurement and Evaluation in Counseling and Development,* July 2005, *38,* 78–91.

Related Research: Burnham, J. J. (1995). *Validation of the Fear Survey Schedule for Children and Adolescents (FSSL–II) in the United States.* Unpublished doctoral dissertation, Auburn University, Auburn, AL.

10376

Test Name: ANXIETY ABOUT CREDIT CARD DEBT SCALE

Purpose: To measure college students' anxiety about credit card debt.

Number of Items: 3

Format: Scales range from *strongly disagree* to *strongly agree.* A sample item is presented.

Reliability: Coefficient alpha was .64.

Author: Pinto, M. B., et al.

Article: College student performance and credit card usage.

Journal: *Journal of College Student Development,* January/February 2001, *42,* 49–58.

Related Research: Pinto, M. B., et al. (2000). Materialism and credit card usage by college students. *Psychological Reports, 86,* 643–652.

10377

Test Name: ANXIETY CONTROL QUESTIONNAIRE

Purpose: To assess perceived control over anxiety-related events.

Number of Items: 30

Format: Scales range from 0 (*strongly disagree*) to 5 (*strongly agree*).

Reliability: Coefficient alpha was .87.

Validity: Correlations with other variables ranged from −.51 to .16.

Author: Zvolensky, M. J., et al.

Article: Incremental validity of perceived control dimensions in the differential prediction of interpretive biases for threat.

Journal: *Journal of Psychopathology and Behavioral Assessment,* June 2001, *23,* 75–83.

Related Research: Rapee, R. M., et al. (1996). Measurement of perceived control over anxiety-related events. *Behavior Therapy,* *27,* 279–293.

10378

Test Name: ANXIETY IN SELECTION INTERVIEWS MEASURE

Purpose: To provide a multidimensional measure of interview anxiety.

Number of Items: 30

Format: Includes five factors: communication anxiety, appearance anxiety, social anxiety, performance anxiety, and behavioral anxiety. Responses are made on a 5-point scale ranging from 1 (*strongly disagree*) to 5 (*strongly agree*). All items are presented.

Reliability: Alpha coefficients ranged from .69 to .92.

Validity: Correlations with other variables ranged from −.32 to .54.

Author: McCarthy, J., and Goffin, R.

Article: Measuring job interview anxiety: Beyond weak knees and sweaty palms.

Journal: *Personnel Psychology,* Autumn 2004, *57,* 607–637.

10379

Test Name: ANXIETY INTRUSIVENESS RATING SCALE

Purpose: To assess the extent to which anxiety causes impairment in each of twelve life domains which define lifestyle, involvement, and intimacy aspects of life.

Number of Items: 12

Format: Rating scales range from one to seven.

Reliability: Alpha coefficients ranged from the .80s to the .90s.

Validity: Correlations with other variables ranged from .25 to .62.

Author: Bieling, P. J., et al.

Article: Factor structure of the Wellness Intrusiveness Rating Scale in patients diagnosed with anxiety disorders.

Journal: *Journal of Psychopathology and Behavioral Assessment,* December 2001, *23,* 223–230.

Related Research: Devins, G. M. (1994). Illness intrusiveness and the psychological impact of lifestyle disruptions in chronic life-threatening disease. *Advances in Renal Replacement Therapy, 1,* 251–263.

10380

Test Name: ANXIETY RATING SCALE

Purpose: To measure anxiety.

Number of Items: 3

Format: Responses to each item are made on two 7-point scales. Each item is presented.

Reliability: Alpha coefficients ranged from .79 to .90.

Author: Chell, B. J., et al.

Article: Manipulated stress and dispositional reinvestment in a wall-volley task: An investigation into controlled processing.

Journal: *Perceptual and Motor Skills,* October 2003, *97,* 435–448.

Related Research: Cox, R. H., et al. (1996). Validity of the MRF and ARS Competitive State Anxiety Rating Scale for volleyball and basketball. *Research Quarterly for Exercise and Sport, 67,* 52–67.

10381

Test Name: ANXIETY SCALES

Purpose: To measure anxiety.

Number of Items: 9

Format: Scales range from 1 (*absolutely*) to 9 (*absolutely not*).

Reliability: Alpha coefficients ranged from .83 to .90.

Validity: Correlations with other variables ranged from .10 to .31.

Author: Klibert, J. J., et al.

Article: Adaptive and maladaptive aspects of self-oriented versus socially prescribed perfectionism.

Journal: *Journal of College Student Development,* March/April 2005, *46,* 141–156.

Related Research: Costello, C. G., & Comrey, A. L. (1967). Scales for measuring depression and anxiety. *The Journal of Psychology, 66,* 303–313.

10382

Test Name: ANXIETY SENSITIVITY INDEX

Purpose: To assess tendency to fear anxiety-related bodily sensations.

Number of Items: 16

Format: Scales range from 0 (*very little*) to 4 (*very much*).

Validity: Correlations with other variables ranged from .20 to .50.

Author: Carleton, R. N., et al.

Article: Fear of physical harm: Factor structure and psychometric properties of the Injury/Illness Sensitivity Index.

Journal: *Journal of Psychopathology and Behavioral Assessment,* December 2005, *27,* 235–242.

Related Research: Reiss, S., & McNally, R. J. (1985). The expectancy model of fear. In S. Reiss & R. R. Bootzin (Eds.), *Theoretical Issues in Behavior Research and Therapy* (pp. 107–121), New York: Academic Press.

10383

Test Name: APPLICATION STRESS SCALE

Purpose: To measure application stress.

Number of Items: 7

Format: Responses are made on a 4-point scale ranging from 1 (*no problem for me*) to 4 (*very stressful*). Examples are given.

Reliability: Coefficient alpha was .73.

Validity: Correlations with other variables ranged form −.33 to .17 (*n* = 391).

Author: Pinquart, M., et al.

Article: Self-efficacy and successful school-to-work transition: A longitudinal study.

Journal: *Journal of Vocational Behavior*, December 2003, *63*, 329–346.

10384

Test Name: APPROACH AND AVOIDANT COPING SCALES

Purpose: To measure approach and avoidant coping.

Number of Items: 34

Format: Response categories range from 1 (*not at all*) to 5 (*very much*). Sample items are presented.

Reliability: Alpha coefficients averaged .91 (*approach*) and .84 (*avoidant*) over four time periods.

Author: Frazier, P., et al.

Article: Correlates of levels and patterns of positive life changes following sexual assault.

Journal: *Journal of Consulting and Clinical Psychology*, February 2004, *72*, 19–30.

Related Research: Tobin, D. L., et al. (1984). *Users Manual for the Coping Strategies Inventory*. Athens: Ohio University Press.

10385

Test Name: ARABIC SCALE OF OPTIMISM AND PESSIMISM

Purpose: To measure optimism and pessimism.

Number of Items: 30

Format: Items are anchored by 1 (*no*) and 5 (*very much*). Sample items are presented.

Reliability: Coefficient alphas ranged from .91 to .95.

Validity: Correlations with other variables ranged from −.35 to .33.

Author: Al-Mashaan, O. S.

Article: Associations among job satisfaction, optimism, pessimism, and psychosomatic symptoms for employees in the government sector in Kuwait.

Journal: *Psychological Reports*, August 2003, *93*, 17–25.

Related Research: Abdel-Khalek, A. M. (1996). [*Manual for the Arab Scale of Optimism and Pessimism*]. Alexandria, Egypt: Dar Al-Maarifa Al-Jamiiyah. [in Arabic]

10386

Test Name: ATHLETIC COPING SKILLS INVENTORY—28

Purpose: To measure athletic coping skills.

Number of Items: 28

Format: Includes seven subscales: Coping With Adversity, Peaking Under Pressure, Goal Setting/Mental Preparation, Concentration, Freedom From Worry, Confidence or Achievement Motivation, and Coachability. Responses are made on a 4-point scale ranging from 1 (*almost never*) to 4 (*almost always*).

Reliability: Alpha coefficients ranged from .62 to .86.

Validity: Correlations with other variables ranged from −.85 to .83.

Author: Cresswell, S., and Hodge, K.

Article: Coping skills: Role of trait sport confidence and trait anxiety.

Journal: *Perceptual and Motor Skills*, April 2004, *98*, 433–438.

Related Research: Smith, R. E., et al. (1995). Development and validation of a multidimensional measure of sport-specific psychological skills: The Athletic Coping Skills Inventory—28. *Journal of Sport and Exercise Psychology, 17*, 379–398.

10387

Test Name: ATTENTION TO BODY SHAPE SCALE

Purpose: To measure one's preoccupation with the shape of one's body.

Number of Items: 7

Format: Responses are made on a 5-point scale ranging from 1 (*definitely disagree*) to 5 (*definitely agree*). An example is given.

Reliability: Internal consistency ranged from .70 to .82.

Author: Cameron, E. M., and Ferraro, F. R.

Article: Body satisfaction in college women after brief exposure to magazine images.

Journal: *Perceptual and Motor Skills*, June 2004, *98*, Part 1, 1093–1099.

Related Research: Beebe, D. W. (1995). The Attention to Body Shape Scale: A new measure of body focus. *Journal of Personality Assessment, 65*, 486–501.

10388

Test Name: AUTOMATIC THOUGHTS QUESTIONNAIRE

Purpose: To measure depression.

Number of Items: 30-, 15-, and 8-item versions.

Format: Responses are made on a 5-point scale ranging from 1 (*not at all*) to 5 (*all the time*). All items are presented.

Reliability: Alpha coefficients ranged from .92 to .98.

Author: Netemeyer, R. G., et al.

Article: Psychometric properties of shortened versions of the Automatic Thoughts Questionnaire.

Journal: *Educational and Psychological Measurement,* February 2002, *62,* 111–129.

Related Research: Hollon, S. D., & Kendall, P. C. (1980). Cognitive self-statements in depression: Development of an Automatic Thoughts Questionnaire. *Cognitive Therapy and Research, 4,* 383–395.

10389

Test Name: AUTOMATIC THOUGHTS QUESTIONNAIRE— NEGATIVE

Purpose: To measure the frequency of negative automatic thoughts related to depression.

Number of Items: 30

Format: Sample items are presented.

Reliability: Alpha coefficients ranged from .95 to .97.

Author: Rohan, K. J., et al.

Article: Cognitive–behavioral factors in seasonal affective disorder.

Journal: *Journal of Consulting and Clinical Psychology,* February 2003, *71,* 22–30.

Related Research: Hollon, S. D., & Kendall, P. C. (1980). Cognitive self-statements in depression: Development of an Automatic Thoughts Questionnaire. *Cognitive Therapy and Research, 3,* 383–395.

10390

Test Name: AUTOMATIC THOUGHTS QUESTIONNAIRE— POSITIVE

Purpose: To measure the frequency of positive self-statements.

Number of Items: 30

Format: Item responses range from 1 (*not at all*) to 5 (*all the time*).

Reliability: Coefficient alpha was reported to be as high as .95.

Author: Dozois, D. J. A., et al.

Article: Normative data on cognitive measures of depression.

Journal: *Journal of Consulting and Clinical Psychology,* February 2003, *71,* 71–81.

Related Research: Ingram, R. E., et al. (1995). Psychometric properties of the Positive Automatic Thoughts Questionnaire. *Psychological Assessment, 7,* 495–507.

10391

Test Name: AUTOMATIC THOUGHTS QUESTIONNAIRES

Purpose: To measure both positive and negative automatic thoughts.

Number of Items: 60

Format: Includes two scales: Positive and Negative Automatic Thoughts.

Reliability: Alpha coefficients were .95 and .96.

Validity: Correlation with other variables ranged from –.52 to .75.

Author: Dozois, D. J. A.

Article: The psychometric characteristics of the Hamilton Depression Inventory.

Journal: *Journal of Personality Assessment,* February 2003, *80,* 31–40.

Related Research: Hollon S. D., & Kendall, P. C. (1980). Cognitive self-statements in depression: Development of an Automatic Thoughts Questionnaire. *Cognitive Therapy and Research, 4,* 383–395. Ingram, R. E., & Wisnicki, K. S. (1988). Assessment of positive automatic cognition. *Journal of Consulting and Clinical Psychology, 56,* 898–902.

10392

Test Name: BALANCED INVENTORY OF DESIRABLE RESPONDING

Purpose: To measure defensiveness as self-deception and other-deception.

Number of Items: 40

Reliability: Coefficient alpha was .84.

Validity: The correlation between the two deception subscales was .44.

Author: Burns, J. W., et al.

Article: A fourth empirically derived cluster of chronic pain patients based on the Multidimensional Pain Inventory: Evidence for repression within the dysfunctional group.

Journal: *Journal of Consulting and Clinical Psychology,* August 2001, *69,* 663–673.

Related Research: Paulhus, D. L. (1984). Two-component models of socially desirable responding. *Journal of Personality and Social Psychology, 46,* 598–609.

10393

Test Name: BASIC PSYCHOLOGICAL NEEDS SATISFACTION SCALE— GENERAL VERSION

Purpose: To measure satisfaction of psychological needs.

Number of Items: 21

Format: Includes three psychological needs: autonomy, competence, and relatedness. Responses are made on a 7-point scale ranging from 1 (*not true at all*) to 7 (*very true*).

Reliability: Alpha coefficients ranged from .68 to .90.

Validity: Correlations with other variables ranged from −.25 to −.72 (*N* = 299).

Author: Wei, M., et al.

Article: Adult attachment, shame, depression, and loneliness: The mediation role of basic psychological needs satisfaction.

Journal: *Journal of Counseling Psychology*, October 2005, *52*, 591–601.

Related Research: Ilardi, B. C., et al. (1993). Employee and supervisor ratings of motivation: Main effects and discrepancies associated with job satisfaction and adjustment in a factory setting. *Journal of Applied Social Psychology, 23*, 1789–1805.

10394

Test Name: BECH–RAFAELSEN MANIA RATING SCALE

Purpose: To assess a range of mania-related symptoms by interview.

Number of Items: 11

Format: Specific anchors (5-point) follow each response option.

Reliability: Coefficient alpha was .88.

Validity: Correlations with other variables ranged from −.37 to .56.

Author: Meyer, B.

Article: Coping with severe mental illness: Relations of the brief COPE with symptoms, functioning, and well-being.

Journal: *Journal of Psychopathology and Behavioral Assessment*, December 2001, *23*, 265–277.

Related Research: Bech, P., et al. (1979). The Bech–Rafaelsen Mania Scale and the Hamilton Depression Scale: Evaluation of homogeneity and interobserver reliability. *Acta Psychiatrica Scandinavica, 130*, 330–351.

10395

Test Name: BECK HOPELESSNESS SCALE

Purpose: To measure hopelessness.

Number of Items: 20

Format: A true–false format is used.

Reliability: Coefficient alpha was .39.

Validity: Correlations with other variables ranged from −.40 to .65.

Author: Johnson, J. G., et al.

Article: Hopelessness as a mediator of the association between social support and depressive symptoms: Findings of a study of men with HIV.

Journal: *Journal of Consulting and Clinical Psychology*, December 2001, *69*, 1056–1060.

Related Research: Beck, A. T., et al. (1974). The measurement of pessimism: The Hopelessness Scale. *Journal of Consulting and Clinical Psychology, 42*, 861–865.

10396

Test Name: BEHAVIOR AND SYMPTOM IDENTIFICATION SCALE

Purpose: To measure relation to self–others, depression–anxiety, daily living–role functioning, impulsive–addictive behavior, and psychosis.

Number of Items: 32

Format: Item response scales are anchored by 0 (*no difficulty*) and 4 (*extreme difficulty*).

Reliability: Alpha reliabilities ranged from .62 to .95.

Author: Uttaro, T., and González, A.

Article: Psychometric properties of the Behavior and Symptom Identification Scale administered in a crisis residential mental health treatment setting.

Journal: *Psychological Reports*, October 2002, *91*, 439–443.

Related Research: Eisen, S. V. (1995). Assessment of subjective distress by patients' self-report versus structured interview. *Psychological Reports, 76*, 35–39.

10397

Test Name: BEHAVIORAL ACTIVATION AND INHIBITION SYSTEM SCALES

Purpose: To assess bipolar disorder sensitivities including negative affect, anxiety and fear, or positive affect when faced with incentives.

Number of Items: 20

Format: Sample items are presented.

Reliability: Alpha coefficients ranged from the .67 to .81 across subscales. Test–retest reliabilities ranged from .44 to .49 (11 months).

Author: Meyer, B., et al.

Article: Responsiveness to threat and incentive in bipolar disorder: Relations of the BIS/BAS scales with symptoms.

Journal: *Journal of Psychopathology and Behavioral Assessment*, September 2001, *23*, 133–143.

Related Research: Carver, C. S., & White, T. L. (1994). Behavioral inhibition, behavioral activation, and affective responses to impending reward and punishment: The BIS/BAS Scales. *Journal of Personality and Social Psychology, 67*, 319–333.

10398

Test Name: BIRLESON'S DEPRESSION INVENTORY–REVISED

Purpose: To measure depression.

Number of Items: 16

Format: Responses are made on a 3-point scale ranging from 0 (*most*) to 2 (*never*).

Reliability: Coefficient alpha was .51.

Author: Dybdahl, R.

Article: Children and mothers in war: An outcome study of a psychosocial intervention program.

Journal: *Child Development*, July/August 2001, 72, 1214–1230.

Related Research: Birleson, P. (1981). The validity of depressive disorder in childhood and the development of a self-rating scale: A research report. *Journal of Child Psychology and Psychiatry, 22,* 73–88.

10399

Test Name: BIS/BAS SCALES—DUTCH VERSION

Purpose: To assess worry, reward, drive, and fun as neurophysiological regulatory systems.

Number of Items: 20

Format: All items are presented in English.

Reliability: Alpha coefficients ranged from .59 to .79.

Validity: Correlations with other variables ranged from −.46 to .58.

Author: Franken, I. H. A., et al.

Article: Psychometric properties of the Dutch BIS/BAS Scales.

Journal: *Journal of Psychopathology and Behavioral Assessment*, March 2005, 27, 25–30.

Related Research: Carver, C. S., & White, T. L. (1994). Behavioral inhibition, behavioral activation, and affective responses to impending reward and punishment: The BIS/BAS Scales. *Journal of Personality and Social Psychology, 67,* 319–333.

10400

Test Name: BODY ESTEEM SCALE

Purpose: To measure constructs representing body esteem.

Number of Items: 32

Format: Includes three subscales: Weight Concern, Physical Condition, and Sexual Attractiveness. Responses are made on a 5-point scale ranging from 1 (*have strong negative feelings*) to 5 (*have strong positive feelings*).

Reliability: Internal consistency values ranged from .78 to .87. Test–retest (6 weeks) reliabilities ranged from .82 to .91. Test–retest (12 weeks) reliabilities ranged from .78 to .88.

Author: Annesi, J. J.

Article: Relations of body esteem factors with exercise session attendance in women initiating a physical activity program.

Journal: *Perceptual and Motor Skills*, June 2005, *100*, Part 2, 995–1003.

Related Research: Franzoi, S., & Shields, S. A. (1984). The Body Esteem Scale: Multidimensional structure and sex differences in a college population. *Journal of Personality Assessment, 48,* 173–180.

10401

Test Name: BODY ESTEEM SCALE—MODIFIED

Purpose: To measure sexual attractiveness, weight concern, and physical condition.

Number of Items: 35

Format: Five-point rating scales are used.

Reliability: Alpha coefficients ranged from .82 to .91.

Author: Basow, S. A., and Willis, J.

Article: Perceptions of body hair on white women: Effects of labeling.

Journal: *Psychological Reports*, December 2001, *89*, 571–576.

Related Research: Franzoi, S. L., & Shields, S. A. (1984). The Body Esteem Scale: A multidimensional structure and sex differences in a college population. *Journal of Personality Assessment, 48,* 173–178.

10402

Test Name: BODY IMAGE IDEALS QUESTIONNAIRE

Purpose: To assess the difference between self-perceived body attributes and idealized attributes.

Number of Items: 22

Format: Four-point scales are used to measure perceptions and ideals.

Reliability: Alpha coefficients ranged from .81 to .87.

Validity: Correlations with other variables ranged from −.13 to .47.

Author: Kimmel, S. B., and Mahalik, J. R.

Article: Body image concerns of gay men: The roles of minority stress and conformity to masculine norms.

Journal: *Journal of Consulting and Clinical Psychology*, December 2005, 73, 1185–1190.

Related Research: Cash, T., & Szymanski, M. (1965). The development and validation of the Body-Image Ideals Questionnaire. *Journal of Personality Assessment, 64,* 466–477.

10403

Test Name: BODY IMAGE QUESTIONNAIRE

Purpose: To measure body image.

Number of Items: 20

Format: Responses are made on a 3-point responses scale ranging from 1 (*agree*) to 3 (*disagree*). Examples are presented.

Reliability: Test–retest reliability coefficients were .96 and .97.

Author: Duncan, M. J., et al.

Article: Test–retest stability of body-image scores in a sample of 12- to 14-year-olds.

Journal: *Perceptual and Motor Skills*, December 2002, *95*, Part 1, 1007–1012.

Related Research: Huddy, D. C., et al. (1993). Relationships between body image and percent body fat among college male varsity athletes and nonathletes. *Perceptual and Motor Skills*, *77*, 851–857.

10404

Test Name: BODY IMAGE SATISFACTION QUESTIONNAIRE

Purpose: To assess one's satisfaction with various parts of the body.

Number of Items: 17

Format: Responses are made on a 5-point scale ranging from 1 (*dissatisfied*) to 5 (*satisfied*).

Reliability: Alpha coefficients ranged from .19 to .90.

Author: Sherblom, P. R., and Rust, D. M.

Article: Body image, figure rating, and body mass index of girls enrolled in health, physical education, or athletics classes.

Journal: *Perceptual and Motor Skills*, October 2004, *99*, 473–482.

Related Research: Rauste-von Wright, M. (1988). Body image satisfaction in adolescent girls and boys. *Journal of Youth and Adolescence*, *18*, 71–83.

10405

Test Name: BODY SHAME SUBSCALE

Purpose: To measure how much a woman feels like a "bad person" when she believes that her body

does not achieve cultural body standards.

Number of Items: 8

Format: Responses are made on a 7-point Likert-type scale ranging from 1 (*strongly disagree*) to 7 (*strongly agree*). Examples are presented.

Reliability: Alpha coefficients ranged from .70 to .84. Test–retest (2 weeks) reliability was .84.

Validity: Correlations with other variables ranged from .16 to .59.

Author: Moradi, B., et al.

Article: Roles of sexual objectification experiences and internalization of standards of beauty in eating disorder symptomatology: A test and extension of objectification theory.

Journal: *Journal of Counseling Psychology*, July 2005, *52*, 420–428.

Related Research: McKinley, N. M., & Hyde, J. S. (1996). The Objectified Body Consciousness Scale: Development and validation. *Psychology of Women Quarterly*, *20*, 181–215.

10406

Test Name: BODY SHAPE QUESTIONNAIRE—REVISED

Purpose: To measure the strength or salience of negative body image attitudes.

Number of Items: 10

Format: Responses are made on a 6-point scale ranging from 1 (*never*) to 6 (*always*).

Reliability: Internal consistency reliability was .96.

Validity: Correlations with other variables ranged from –.26 to .82.

Author: Tylka, T. L., and Subich, L. M.

Article: Examining a multidimensional model of eating disorder symptomatology among college women.

Journal: *Journal of Counseling Psychology*, July 2004, *51*, 314–328.

Related Research: Mazzeo, S. E. (1999). Modification of an existing measure of body image preoccupation and its relationship to disordered eating in female college students. *Journal of Counseling Psychology*, *46*, 42–50.

10407

Test Name: BODY SURVEILLANCE SUBSCALE

Purpose: To measure how much a woman thinks of her body in terms of how it looks rather than how it feels.

Number of Items: 8

Format: Responses are made on a 7-point Likert-type scale ranging from 1 (*strongly disagree*) to 7 (*strongly agree*).

Reliability: Alpha coefficients ranged from .76 to .89. Test–retest (2 weeks) reliability was .79.

Validity: Correlations with other variables ranged from .27 to .54.

Author: Moradi, B., et al.

Article: Roles of sexual objectification experiences and internalization of standards of beauty in eating disorder symptomatology: A test and extension of objectification theory.

Journal: *Journal of Counseling Psychology*, July 2005, *52*, 420–428.

Related Research: McKinley, N. M., & Hyde, J. S. (1996). The Objectified Body Consciousness Scale: Development and validation. *Psychology of Women Quarterly*, *20*, 181–215.

10408

Test Name: BOREDOM PRONENESS SCALE

Purpose: To measure the propensity to becoming bored.

Number of Items: 28

Format: Scales range from 1 (*high disagreement*) to 7 (*high agreement*).

Reliability: Alpha coefficients exceeded .79.

Author: Wallace, J. G., et al.

Article: The cognitive failures questionnaire revisited: Dimensions and correlates.

Journal: *The Journal of General Psychology*, July 2002, *129*, 238–256.

Related Research: Vodanovich, S. J., & Kass, S. J. (1990). A factor analytic study of the Boredom Proneness Scale. *Journal of Personality Assessment*, 55, 115–123.

10409

Test Name: BRIEF COPE

Purpose: To assess adaptive and maladaptive coping strategies.

Number of Items: 28

Format: Scales range from 1 (*I haven't been doing this at all*) to 4 (*I've been doing this a lot*). Sample items are presented.

Reliability: Alpha coefficients ranged from .57 to .81.

Validity: Correlations with other variables ranged from –.55 to .62.

Author: Meyer, B.

Article: Coping with severe mental illness: Relations of the Brief COPE with symptoms, functioning, and well-being.

Journal: *Journal of Psychopathology and Behavioral Assessment*, December 2001, *23*, 265–277.

Related Research: Carver, C. S. (1997). You want to measure coping but your protocol's too long: Consider the Brief COPE. *International Journal of Behavioral Medicine, 4*, 92–100.

10410

Test Name: BRIEF FEAR OF NEGATIVE EVALUATION

Purpose: To measure the degree to which people are concerned about being perceived and evaluated negatively by others.

Number of Items: 12

Format: Responses are made on a 5-point scale ranging from 1 (*not at all characteristic of me*) to 5 (*extremely characteristic of me*).

Reliability: Alpha coefficients were .90 and .91.

Validity: Correlations with other variables ranged from –.48 to .69 (*n* = 425).

Author: Wei, M., et al.

Article: Adult attachment, depressive symptoms, and validation from self versus others.

Journal: *Journal of Counseling Psychology*, July 2005, *52*, 368–377.

Related Research: Leary, M. R. (1983). A brief version of the Fear of Negative Evaluation Scale. *Personality and Social Psychology Bulletin, 9*, 371–375.

10411

Test Name: BRIEF MOOD INTROSPECTION SURVEY

Purpose: To measure current mood.

Number of Items: 16

Format: Adjective rating scales range from 1 (*definitely do not feel*) to 4 (*definitely feel*). Sample adjectives are presented.

Reliability: Alpha coefficients were .72 (positive affect) and .82 (negative affect).

Author: Norem, J. K., and Illingworth, K. S. S.

Article: Mood and performance among defensive pessimists and strategic optimists.

Journal: *Journal of Research in Personality*, August 2004, *38*, 351–366.

Related Research: Meyer, J. D., & Gasche, Y. N. (1988). The experience and metaexperience of mood. *Journal of Personality and Social Psychology, 55*, 102–111.

10412

Test Name: BRIEF PSYCHIATRIC RATING SCALE

Purpose: To measure the severity of mental illness.

Number of Items: 16

Format: Item responses range from 1 (*not present*) to 7 (*extremely severe*).

Reliability: Internal reliability was .86.

Author: Gray, N. S., et al.

Article: Prediction of violence and self-harm in mentally disordered offenders: A prospective study of the efficacy of the HCR–20, PCL–R and psychiatric symptomatology.

Journal: *Journal of Consulting and Clinical Psychology*, June 2003, *71*, 443–451.

Related Research: Overall, J. E., & Gorham, D. R. (1962). The brief psychiatric rating scale. *Psychological Reports, 10*, 799–812.

10413

Test Name: BRITISH COLUMBIA MAJOR DEPRESSION INVENTORY

Purpose: To measure depression.

Number of Items: 16

Format: Five-point scales range from 1 (*very mild problem*) to 5 (*very severe problem*). All items are presented.

Reliability: Alpha coefficients ranged from .83 to .86.

Author: Iverson, G. L., and Remick, R.

Article: Diagnostic accuracy of the British Columbia Major Depression Inventory.

Journal: *Psychological Reports*, December 2004, *95*, Part 1, 1241–1247.

Related Research: Iverson, G. L. (2001). Psychometric properties of the British Columbia Major Depression Inventory. *Canadian Psychology, 42*, 49.

10414

Test Name: BRUNEL MOOD SCALE

Purpose: To measure mood before competition.

Number of Items: 24

Format: Includes six subscales: Anger, Confusion, Depression, Fatigue, Tension, and Vigor. Responses are made on a 5-point scale ranging from 0 (*not at all*) to 4 (*extremely*).

Reliability: Alpha coefficients ranged from .70 to .85.

Author: Fazackerley, R., et al.

Article: Confirmatory factor analysis of the Brunel Mood Scale for use with waterskiing competition.

Journal: *Perceptual and Motor Skills*, October 2003, *97*, 657–661.

Related Research: Terry, P. C., et al. (1999). Development and validation of a mood measure for adolescents: The POMS–A. *Journal of Sports Sciences, 17*, 861–872.

10415

Test Name: BULIMIA TEST— REVISED

Purpose: To assess disordered eating.

Number of Items: 28

Format: Responses are made on a 1 to 5 scale.

Reliability: Test–retest (2 months) reliability was .95.

Validity: Correlations with other variables ranged from –.17 to .79.

Author: Mazzeo, S. E., and Espelage, D. L.

Article: Association between childhood physical and emotional abuse and disordered eating behavior in female undergraduates: An investigation of the mediating role of alexithymia and depression.

Journal: *Journal of Counseling Psychology*, January 2002, *49*, 86–100.

Related Research: Thelen, M. H., et al. (1991). A revision of the Bulimia Test: The BULIT–R. *Psychological Assessment, 3*, 119–124.

10416

Test Name: CANCER-SPECIFIC DISTRESS SCALE

Purpose: To measure distress associated with breast cancer and its treatment.

Number of Items: 15

Format: A 4-point Likert format is used.

Reliability: Alpha coefficients ranged from .89 to .91.

Author: Manne, S. L., et al.

Article: Couple-focused group intervention for women with early stage breast cancer.

Journal: *Journal of Consulting and Clinical Psychology*, August 2005, *73*, 634–646.

Related Research: Baider, L., et al. (2003). Effect of age on coping and psychological distress in women diagnosed with breast cancer. *Critical Reviews in Oncology/Hematology, 46*, 5–16.

10417

Test Name: CARDIAC DEPRESSION SCALE

Purpose: To measure depression in cardiac patients.

Number of Items: 26

Reliability: Coefficient alpha was .91.

Validity: The correlation with the Beck Depression Inventory was .73.

Author: Evon, D. M., and Burns, J. W.

Article: Process and outcome in cardiac rehabilitation: An examination of cross-lagged effects.

Journal: *Journal of Consulting and Clinical Psychology*, August 2004, *72*, 605–616.

Related Research: Hare, D. L., & Davis, C. R. (1996). Cardiac depression scale: Validation of a new depression scale for cardiac patients. *Journal of Psychosomatic Research, 40*, 379–386.

10418

Test Name: CAREER IDENTITY SALIENCE SCALE

Purpose: To measure how central career is to life satisfaction.

Number of Items: 5

Format: Scales range from 1 (*strongly disagree*) to 5 (*strongly agree*). A sample item is presented.

Reliability: Coefficient alpha was .75.

Validity: Correlations with other variables ranged from –.25 to .08.

Author: Major, V. S., et al.

Article: Work time, work interference with family, and psychological distress.

Journal: *Journal of Applied Psychology*, June 2002, *87*, 427–436.

Related Research: Lobel, S. A., & St. Clair, L. (1992). Effects of family responsibilities, gender, and career identity salience on performance outcomes. *Academy of Management Journal, 35*, 1057–1069.

10419

Test Name: CATASTROPHIZING SUBSCALE

Purpose: To measure catastrophizing about pain.

Number of Items: 6

Format: Sample items are presented.

Reliability: Coefficient alpha was .89.

Validity: Correlations with other variables ranged from −.30 to .62.

Author: Burns, J. W., et al.

Article: Do changes in cognitive factors influence outcome following multidisciplinary treatment for chronic pain? A cross-lagged panel analysis.

Journal: *Journal of Consulting and Clinical Psychology*, February 2003, *71*, 81–91.

Related Research: Rosentiel, A. K., & Keefe, F. J. (1983). The use of coping strategies in chronic low back pain patients: Relationship to patient characteristics and current adjustment. *Pain, 17*, 33–44.

10420

Test Name: CENTER FOR EPIDEMIOLOGICAL STUDIES—DEPRESSION SCALE

Purpose: To assess parents' depressive symptoms.

Number of Items: 20

Format: Responses are made on a scale ranging from 0 (*less than one day*) to 4 (*five days*).

Reliability: Alpha coefficients ranged from .85 to .92.

Validity: Correlations with other variables ranged from −.27 to .61.

Author: Schudlich, T. D. D. R., and Cummings, E. M.

Article: Parental dysphoria and children's internalizing symptoms: Marital conflict styles as mediators of risk.

Journal: *Child Development*, November/December 2003, *74*, 1663–1681.

Related Research: Radloff, L. S. (1977). The CES–D Scale: A self-report depression scale for research in the general population. *Applied Psychological Measurement, 1*, 385–401.

10421

Test Name: CENTER FOR EPIDEMIOLOGY STUDIES DEPRESSION SCALE FOR CHILDREN

Purpose: To measure symptoms common to depression.

Number of Items: 19

Format: Scales range from 0 (*never*) to 3 (*most of the time*).

Reliability: Coefficient alpha was .86.

Author: Gerard, J. M., and Buehler, C.

Article: Cumulative environmental risk and youth problem behavior.

Journal: *Journal of Marriage and Family*, August 2004, *66*, 702–720.

Related Research: Tally, S., et al. (2000, April). *Cross-cultural measurement equivalency of the CES–D in five adolescent populations.* Poster session presented at the biennial meeting of the Society for Research on Adolescence, Chicago, IL.

10422

Test Name: CES—DEPRESSION SCALE (PORTUGUESE VERSION)

Purpose: To measure depression.

Number of Items: 20

Format: All items are presented in English.

Reliability: Coefficient alpha was .85.

Validity: Four factors were extracted. Factor intercorrelations ranged from −.33 to .27.

Author: da Silveira, D. X., and Jorge, M. R.

Article: Reliability and factor structure of the Brazilian version of the Center for Epidemiologic Studies—Depression.

Journal: *Psychological Reports*, December 2002, *91*, Part 1, 865–874.

10423

Test Name: CHALLENGE AND THREAT AFFECT MEASURE

Purpose: To measure challenge and threat affect.

Format: Responses are made on a 5-point scale ranging from 0 (*not at all*) to 4 (*very much*).

Reliability: Alpha coefficients were .67 (challenge affect) and .82 (threat affect).

Validity: Correlations with other variables ranged from −.34 to .79.

Author: McGregor, H. A., and Elliot, A. J.

Article: Achievement goals as predictors of achievement-relevant processes prior to task engagement.

Journal: *Journal of Educational Psychology*, June 2002, *94*, 381–395.

Related Research: Folkman, S., & Lazarus, R. (1985). If it changes it must be a process: Study of emotion and coping during three stages of a college examination. *Journal of Personality and Social Psychology, 48,* 150–170.

10424

Test Name: CHILD AND ADOLESCENT SCALE OF IRRATIONALITY

Purpose: To assess irrational beliefs.

Number of Items: 28

Format: Item anchors are 1 (*not true*) and 4 (*true*). Sample items are presented.

Reliability: Coefficient alpha was .83. Test–retest reliability was .83 (3 weeks).

Author: Lee, D. Y., and Sohn, N. H.

Article: Adolescents' peer-rated mental health, peer acceptance, and irrational beliefs.

Journal: *Psychological Reports,* June 2004, *94,* Part 2, 1114–1148.

Related Research: Bernard, M. E., & Cronan, F. (1999). The Child and Adolescent Scale of Irrationality: Validation data and mental health correlates. *Journal of Cognitive Psychology, 13,* 121–132.

10425

Test Name: CHILD BEHAVIOR CHECKLIST DEPRESSION SCALE

Purpose: To measure depressive symptoms.

Number of Items: 6

Format: Responses are made on a 3-point scale ranging from 0 (*not true*) to 2 (*often true*). Items are presented.

Reliability: Alpha coefficients ranged from .72 to .84.

Author: Gazelle, H., and Ladd, G. W.

Article: Anxious solitude and peer exclusion: A diathesis–stress model of internalizing trajectories in childhood.

Journal: *Child Development,* January/February 2003, *74,* 257–278.

Related Research: Clarke, G. N., et al. (1992). A self- and parent-report measure of adolescent depression: The Child Behavior Checklist Depression Scale (CBCL–D). *Behavioral Assessment, 14,* 443–463.

10426

Test Name: CHILD BEHAVIOR CHECKLIST—YOUTH SELF-REPORT DEPRESSION VERSION

Purpose: To measure depression.

Number of Items: 13

Format: Response scales range from 0 (*not true*) to 2 (*very or often true*).

Reliability: Alpha coefficients ranged from .72 to .82.

Validity: Correlations with another depression measure ranged from .24 to .47.

Author: Garber, J., et al.

Article: Developmental trajectories of adolescents' depressive symptoms.

Journal: *Journal of Consulting and Clinical Psychology,* February 2002, *70,* 79–95.

Related Research: Clarke, G. N., et al. (1992). A self- and parent-report measure of adolescent depression. *Behavioral Assessment, 14,* 443–463.

10427

Test Name: CHILD PTSD REACTION INDEX

Purpose: To measure PTSD in school-aged children and adolescents.

Number of Items: 20

Format: Scales range from 0 (*none*) to 4 (*most of the time*).

Reliability: Coefficient alpha was .88.

Author: Ceballo, R., et al.

Article: Inner-city children's exposure to community violence: How much do parents know?

Journal: *Journal of Marriage and Family,* November 2001, *63,* 927–940.

Related Research: Pynoos, R. S., & Nader, K. (1993). *Child PTSD Reaction Index.* Unpublished text, University of California at Los Angeles.

10428

Test Name: CHILDHOOD ANXIETY SENSITIVITY INDEX

Purpose: To measure the tendency to view anxiety-related bodily sensations as dangerous.

Number of Items: 18

Format: Scales range from *none* to *a lot*.

Reliability: Coefficient alpha was .87.

Validity: Total score correlations with other variables ranged from .03 to .19.

Author: Tsao, J. C. I., et al.

Article: Parent and child anxiety sensitivity: Relationship in a nonclinical sample.

Journal: *Journal of Psychopathology and Behavioral Assessment,* December 2005, *27,* 259–268.

Related Research: Silverman, W. K., et al. (1991). Child Anxiety Sensitivity Index. *Journal of Child Psychology, 20,* 162–168.

10429

Test Name: CHILDHOOD DEPRESSION INVENTORY— CHINESE VERSION

Purpose: To measure children's depression.

Number of Items: 27

Format: Items are scored 0, 1, or 2.

Reliability: Internal reliabilities ranged from .84 to .87.

Validity: Correlations with other variables ranged from –.45 to .37.

Author: Chen, X., et al.

Article: Social functioning and adjustment in Chinese children: The imprint of historical time.

Journal: *Child Development*, January/February 2005, *76*, 182–195.

Related Research: Chen, X., & Li, B. (2000). Depressed mood in Chinese children: Developmental significance for social and school adjustment. *International Journal of Behavioral Development, 24*, 472–479.

10430

Test Name: CHILDREN'S ANXIETY SCALE

Purpose: To measure symptoms of social phobia, panic disorder, separation anxiety disorder, and generalized anxiety disorder.

Number of Items: 20

Format: Item responses are anchored by 0 (*never*) and 3 (*always*). Sample items are presented.

Reliability: Alpha reliabilities ranged from .74 and .80.

Validity: Correlations with other variables ranged from –.29 to –.02.

Author: Muris, P., and Meesters, C.

Article: Symptoms of anxiety disorders and teacher-reported school functioning of normal children.

Journal: *Psychological Reports*, October 2002, *91*, 588–590.

Related Research: Spence, S. H. (1998). A measure of anxiety

symptoms among children. *Behavior Research and Therapy, 36*, 545–566.

10431

Test Name: CHILDREN'S ANXIETY SCALE—REVISED

Purpose: To assess panic disorder, social phobia, separation anxiety, generalized anxiety disorder and obsessive–compulsive disorder.

Number of Items: 37

Format: Scales range from 0 (*never*) to 3 (*always*). Sample items are presented.

Reliability: Alpha coefficients ranged from .70 to .94.

Author: Muris, P., and Meesters, C.

Article: Attachment, behavioral inhibitions, and anxiety disorders symptoms in normal adolescents.

Journal: *Journal of Psychopathology and Behavioral Assessment*, June 2002, *24*, 97–106.

Related Research: Spence, S. H. (1998). A measure of anxiety symptoms among children. *Behavior Research and Therapy, 36*, 545–566.

10432

Test Name: CHILDREN'S DEPRESSION INVENTORY— TURKISH VERSION

Purpose: To measure depressive symptoms in children.

Number of Items: 27

Format: Forced-choice format.

Reliability: Coefficient alpha was .80. Test–retest reliability was .77.

Author: Oĝul, M., and Gençöz, T.

Article: Roles of perceived control and coping strategies on depressive and anxiety symptoms of Turkish adolescents.

Journal: *Psychological Reports*, December 2003, *93*, Part 1, 659–672.

Related Research: Kovacs, M. (1981). Rating scales to assess depression in school-aged children. *Acta Paedopsychiatria, 46*, 305–315.

10433

Test Name: CHILDREN'S DEPRESSIVE INVENTORY— MODIFIED

Purpose: To assess depressive symptomatology in children.

Number of Items: 16

Format: Includes cognitive, affective, and behavioral symptoms of depression. Responses are made by selecting one of three statements scored on a 0 to 2 scale. An example is given.

Reliability: Alpha coefficients ranged from .84 to .89.

Author: Fredriksen, K., et al.

Article: Sleepless in Chicago: Tracking the effects of adolescent sleep loss during the middle school years.

Journal: *Child Development*, January/February 2004, *75*, 84–95.

Related Research: Kovacs, M. (1980). Affective disorders in children and adolescents. *American Psychologist, 44*, 209–215.

10434

Test Name: CHILDREN'S FANTASY INVENTORY— AGGRESSIVE FANTASIES SUBSCALE

Purpose: To assess aggressive fantasies.

Number of Items: 6

Format: Responses are made on a 3-point scale of *no, a little,* and *a lot.* An example is given.

Reliability: Coefficient alpha was .66.

Author: Guerra, N. G., et al.

Article: Community violence exposure, social cognition, and aggression among urban elementary school children.

Journal: *Child Development*, September/October 2003, *74*, 1561–1576.

Related Research: Rosenfeld, E., et al. (1982). Measuring patterns of fantasy behavior in children. *Journal of Personality and Social Psychology, 42*, 347–366.

10435

Test Name: CHILDREN'S SOMATIZATION INVENTORY

Purpose: To assess the occurrence of somatization symptoms in children and adolescents.

Number of Items: 35

Format: Item anchors are 1 (*not at all*) and 4 (*a whole lot*). Sample items are presented.

Reliability: Coefficient alpha was .91.

Author: Muris, P., and Meesters, C.

Article: Children's somatization symptoms: Correlations with trait anxiety, anxiety sensitivity, and learning experiences.

Journal: *Psychological Reports*, June 2004, *94*, Part 2, 1269–1275.

Related Research: Garber, J., et al. (1991). Somatization symptoms in a community sample of children and adolescents: Further validation of the Children's Somatization Inventory. *Psychological Assessment, 3*, 588–595.

10436

Test Name: CHILDREN'S SOMATIZATION INVENTORY— ABBREVIATED VERSION

Purpose: To assess somatic symptoms such as headache and nausea.

Number of Items: 6

Format: All items are presented.

Reliability: Alpha coefficients ranged from .74 to .83.

Validity: Correlation with the full scale was .47.

Author: Walker, L. S., et al.

Article: The relation of daily stressors to somatic and emotional symptoms in children with and without recurrent abdominal pain.

Journal: *Journal of Consulting and Clinical Psychology*, February 2001, *69*, 85–91.

Related Research: Garber, J., et al. (1991). Somatization symptoms in a community sample of children and adolescents: Further validation of the Children's Somatization Inventory. *Psychological Assessment, 3*, 588–595.

10437

Test Name: CHINESE HAPPINESS INVENTORY

Purpose: To measure happiness.

Number of Items: 13

Format: Each of 13 types of happiness is followed by four statements that correspond to a subjective level of happiness. All items are presented.

Reliability: Alpha coefficients exceeded .92.

Validity: Correlations with other variables ranged from −.09 to .35.

Author: Lu, L., et al.

Article: Cultural values and happiness: An East–West dialogue.

Journal: *The Journal of Social Psychology*, August 2001, *141*, 477–493.

Related Research: Lu, L., & Shih, J. B. (1997). Personality and happiness: Is mental health a mediator? *Personality and Individual Differences, 25*, 195–207.

10438

Test Name: CLINICAL OUTCOMES IN ROUTINE EVALUATION—OUTCOME MEASURE

Purpose: To measure subjective well-being, problems, functioning, and risk.

Number of Items: 34

Reliability: Alpha coefficients ranged from .75 to .90. Test–retest reliabilities ranged from .64 to .91.

Validity: Correlations with other variables ranged from .39 to .78.

Author: Barkham, M., et al.

Article: Service profiling and outcomes benchmarking using the CORE–OM: Toward practice-based evidence in the psychological therapies.

Journal: *Journal of Consulting and Clinical Psychology*, April 2001, *69*, 184–196.

Related Research: Evans, C., et al. (2000). Clinical outcomes in routine evaluation: The CORE–OM. *Journal of Mental Health, 9*, 247–255.

10439

Test Name: CLINICIAN ADMINISTERED PTSD SCALE— CAMBODIAN VERSION

Purpose: To assess the frequency and intensity of PTSD symptoms.

Number of Items: 17

Format: Scales range from 1 (*mild, somewhat more realistic than just thinking about the event*) to 4 (*complete dissociation with no awareness of surroundings*). A sample item is presented in English.

Validity: Correlations with other variables ranged from −.15 to .76.

Author: Hinton, D., et al.

Article: The psychophysiology of orthostatic panic in Cambodian refugees attending a psychiatric clinic.

Journal: *Journal of Psychopathology and Behavioral Assessment*, March 2004, *26*, 1–13.

Related Research: Weathers, F. W., et al. (2001). Clinician administered PTSD scale: A review of the first ten years of research. *Depression and Anxiety, 13*, 132–156.

10440

Test Name: COGNITIVE APPRAISALS SCALE

Purpose: To assess cognitive appraisals regarding confidence in coping with negative emotions and behavior during conflicts with romantic partners.

Number of Items: 10

Format: Includes two subscales: Confidence in Emotions and Behavior. Responses are made on a 5-point scale ranging from 1 (*strongly disagree*) to 5 (*strongly agree*). Sample items are presented.

Reliability: Alpha coefficients were .63 and .72.

Validity: Correlations with other variables ranged from –.30 to .01.

Author: Creasey, G., & Hesson-McInnis, M.

Article: Affective responses, cognitive appraisals, and conflict tactics in late adolescent romantic relationships: Association with attachment orientations.

Journal: *Journal of Counseling Psychology*, January 2001, *48*, 85–96.

10441

Test Name: COGNITIVE ERROR QUESTIONNAIRE

Purpose: To measure catastrophizing, overgeneralization, personalization, and selective abstraction.

Number of Items: 48

Format: Respondents rate 48 vignettes on a 5-point scale that indicates how similar the thought is to one they have had.

Reliability: Internal consistency reliabilities ranged from .76 to .92.

Validity: Correlations with other variables ranged from .29 to .60.

Author: Dozois, D. J. A., et al.

Article: Normative data on cognitive measures of depression.

Journal: *Journal of Consulting and Clinical Psychology*, February 2003, *71*, 71–81.

Related Research: Lefebvre, M. F. (1981). Cognitive distortion and cognitive errors in depressed psychiatric and low back pain patients. *Journal of Consulting and Clinical Psychology, 49*, 517–525.

10442

Test Name: COGNITIVE FAILURES QUESTIONNAIRE

Purpose: To assess failures in memory, perception, and motor function by self-report.

Number of Items: 25

Format: Scales range from 0 (*never*) to 4 (*always*). All items are presented.

Reliability: Coefficient alpha was .91 for the total scale. Subscales alpha coefficients ranged from .76 to .86.

Validity: Correlations with other variables ranged from –.64 to .62.

Author: Wallace, J. G., et al.

Article: The cognitive failures questionnaire revisited: Dimensions and correlates.

Journal: *The Journal of General Psychology*, July 2002, *129*, 238–256.

Related Research: Broadbent, D. E., et al. (1982). The Cognitive Failures Questionnaire (CFQ) and its correlates. *British Journal of Clinical Psychology, 21*, 1–16.

10443

Test Name: COGNITIVE SYMPTOMS ACUTE STRESS SCALE

Purpose: To measure cognitive difficulties in situations of stress.

Number of Items: 6

Format: Scales range from 1 (*not at all*) to 4 (*very much so*). All items are presented.

Reliability: Alpha coefficients ranged from .38 to .67.

Author: Gohm, C. L., et al.

Article: Personality in extreme situations: Thinking (or not) under acute stress.

Journal: *Journal of Research in Personality*, September 2001, *35*, 388–399.

Related Research: Bauman, M. R., et al. (April, 1998). *Can "thinking positive" help performance? Cognitive resource allocation on a complex task under time pressure.* Paper presented at the 70th annual meeting of the Midwestern Psychological Association, Chicago, IL.

10444

Test Name: COLORADO SYMPTOM INDEX

Purpose: To assess psychiatric symptomatology.

Number of Items: 14

Format: Scales range from 1 (*never*) to 5 (*at least everyday*).

Reliability: Coefficient alpha was .90.

Author: Oyserman, D., et al.

Article: Positive parenting among African American mothers with a serious mental illness.

Journal: *Journal of Marriage and Family*, February 2002, *64*, 65–77.

Related Research: Shern, D., et al. (1994). Client outcomes II: Longitudinal client data from the Colorado Treatment Outcome

Study. *Milbank Quarterly, 72,* 123–148.

10445

Test Name: COMPETENCE AND PSYCHOLOGICAL SYMPTOMS SCALE

Purpose: To measure psychological health.

Number of Items: 15

Format: Scales are anchored by 1 (*very seldom*) and 5 (*very often*).

Reliability: Alpha coefficients were .75 (competence) and .88 (symptoms).

Validity: Correlations with other variables ranged from –.66 to .58.

Author: Toppinen-Tanner, S., and Kalimo, R.

Article: Psychological symptoms and competence at three organizational levels of industrial design: The main and moderating role of sense of coherence.

Journal: *Psychological Reports,* April 2003, *92,* 667–682.

Related Research: Elo, A.-L., et al. (1992). *OSQ, Occupational Stress Questionnaire: Users instructions* [Reviews 9]. Helsinki, Finland: Institute of Occupational Health.

10446

Test Name: COMPETITIVE STATE ANXIETY INVENTORY—2

Purpose: To measure both intensity and direction of precompetitive anxiety.

Number of Items: 27

Format: Includes three subscales: Cognitive Anxiety, Somatic Anxiety, and Self-Confidence. Sample items are presented.

Reliability: Alpha coefficients ranged from .79 to .90.

Author: Smith, D., et al.

Article: Social desirability bias and direction modified Competitive State Anxiety Inventory—2.

Journal: *Perceptual and Motor Skills,* December 2002, *95,* Part 1, 945–952.

Related Research: Martens, R., et al. (1990). Development and validation of the Competitive State Anxiety Inventory (CSAI–2). In R. Martens, et al. (Eds.), *Competitive anxiety in sport* (pp. 117–190). Champaign, IL: Human Kinetics.

10447

Test Name: COMPUTER ANXIETY RATING SCALE

Purpose: To measure anxiety and apprehension associated with computer tasks.

Number of Items: 20

Format: Responses are made on a 5-point Likert-type scale ranging from 1 (*strongly disagree*) to 5 (*strongly agree*).

Reliability: Coefficient alpha was .87. Test–retest (4 weeks) reliability was .70.

Validity: Correlations with other variables ranged from .27 to .45.

Author: Hopko, D. R.

Article: Confirmatory factor analysis of the Math Anxiety Rating Scale—Revised.

Journal: *Educational and Psychological Measurement,* April 2003, *63,* 336–351.

Related Research: Heinssen, R. K., Jr., et al. (1987). Assessing computer anxiety: Development and validation of the Computer Anxiety Rating Scale. *Computers in Human Behavior, 3,* 49–59.

10448

Test Name: COMPUTER ANXIETY SCALE

Purpose: To measure individuals' perceptions of their anxiety in different situations related to computers.

Number of Items: 20

Format: Includes two factors: general computer anxiety and equipment. Responses are made on a 5-point scale ranging from *not at all* to *very much*. All items are presented.

Reliability: Reliability coefficients were .93 and .97.

Author: Marcoulides, G. A., et al.

Article: Examining the psychological impact of computer technology: An updated cross-cultural study.

Journal: *Educational and Psychological Measurement,* April 2004, *64,* 311–318.

Related Research: Marcoulides, G. A. (1989). Measuring computer anxiety: The Computer Anxiety Scale. *Educational and Psychological Measurement, 49,* 733–739.

10449

Test Name: COMPUTERIZED ASSESSMENT SYSTEM FOR PSYCHOTHERAPY EVALUATION AND RESEARCH—35

Purpose: To assess 62 target complaints.

Number of Items: 35

Format: Includes seven subscales: Somatic Complaints, Depression, Agitation, Hyperactivated Attachments, Anxiety, Substance Abuse, and Suicidal Ideation.

Reliability: Alpha coefficients ranged from .62 to greater than .70.

Author: Snell, M. N., et al.

Article: Predicting counseling center clients' response to counseling: A 1-year follow-up.

Journal: *Journal of Counseling Psychology,* October 2001, *48,* 463–473.

Related Research: Mallinckrodt, B., et al. (2001). *Dimensions of presenting symptoms in a computerized intake assessment of counseling center clients.*

Unpublished manuscript, University of Missouri.

10450

Test Name: CONFIDENCE MEASURE

Purpose: To assess a subject's confidence in the correctness of responses to stimuli.

Number of Items: 40 (but may vary).

Format: For each stimulus subjects indicate their confidence in their response on a scale ranging from 1 (*completely uncertain*) to 4 (*completely certain*).

Reliability: Coefficient alpha was .96.

Author: Bar-Tal, Y., et al.

Article: A test of the overconfidence phenomenon using audio signals.

Journal: *The Journal of General Psychology*, April 2001, *128*, 76–80.

Related Research: Soll, J. B. (1996). Determinants of overconfidence and miscalibration: The role of random error and ecological structure. *Organizational Behavior and Human Decision Processes*, 65, 138–147.

10451

Test Name: CONSERVATION OF RESOURCES EVALUATION

Purpose: To measure stress in terms of threatened loss of resources.

Number of Items: 53

Format: Three point scales range from *no threat of loss* to *great threat of loss*.

Validity: Correlations with other variables ranged from –.23 to .35.

Author: Hobfoll, S. E., et al.

Article: The impact of perceived child physical and sexual abuse history on Native American women's psychological well being and AIDS risk.

Journal: *Journal of Consulting and Clinical Psychology*, February 2002, *70*, 252–257.

Related Research: Hobfoll, S. E., & Lilly, R. S. (1993). Resource conservation as a strategy for community psychology. *Journal of Community Psychology*, 21, 128–148.

10452

Test Name: COPE

Purpose: To assess coping.

Number of Items: 60

Format: Item responses are anchored by *I usually don't do this at all* and *I usually do this a lot*.

Reliability: Alpha coefficients ranged from .45 to .92 across subscales. Test–retest reliabilities ranged from .46 to .86.

Author: Nelson, H. G., et al.

Article: Stress, coping, and success among graduate students in clinical psychology.

Journal: *Psychological Reports*, June 2001, *88*, Part 1, 759–767.

Related Research: Carver, C. S., et al. (1989). Assessing coping strategies: A theoretically based approach. *Journal of Personality and Social Psychology*, 56, 267–283.

10453

Test Name: COPE (COPING STYLES QUESTIONNAIRE)

Purpose: To measure coping in 13 dimensions.

Number of Items: 52

Format: Scales range from 0 (*never*) to 4 (*very often*).

Reliability: Alpha coefficients ranged from .67 to .94 across subscales.

Author: Bishop, G. D., et al.

Article: The relationship between coping and personality among police officers in Singapore.

Journal: *Journal of Research in Personality*, September 2001, *35*, 353–374.

Related Research: Carver, C. S., et al. (1989). Assessing coping strategies: A theoretically based approach. *Journal of Personality and Social Psychology*, 56, 267–283.

10454

Test Name: COPE INVENTORY

Purpose: To assess five general coping styles.

Number of Items: 27

Format: Includes five scales: Substance Abuse, Venting, Acceptance, Positive Reframing, and Active Coping. Responses are made on a 4-point scale ranging from 1 (*I usually do not do this at all*) to 4 (*I usually do this a lot*).

Reliability: Alpha coefficients ranged from .58 to .93.

Validity: Correlations with other variables ranged from –.25 to .24.

Author: Bricker, J. B.

Article: Development and evaluation of the Air Travel Stress Scale.

Journal: *Journal of Counseling Psychology*, October 2005, *52*, 615–628.

Related Research: Carver, C. S., et al. (1989). Assessing coping strategies: A theoretically based approach. *Journal of Personality and Social Psychology*, 56, 267–283.

10455

Test Name: COPE INVENTORY

Purpose: To assess coping styles.

Number of Items: 53

Format: Includes 14 subscales: Active Coping, Planning, Suppressing Competing Activities, Restrain Coping, Seeking Social

Support for Instrumental Reasons, Seeking Support for Emotional Reasons, Positive Interpretations and Growth, Acceptance, Turning to Religion, Focusing on the Venting of Emotion, Denial, Behavioral Disengagement, Mental Disengagement, and Alcohol–Drug Disengagement.

Reliability: Alpha coefficients ranged from .51 to .92.

Author: O'Connor, R. C., and O'Connor, D. B.

Article: Predicting hopelessness and psychological distress: The role of perfectionism and coping.

Journal: *Journal of Counseling Psychology*, July 2003, *50*, 362–372.

Related Research: Carver, C. S., et al. (1989). Assessing coping strategies: A theoretically based approach. *Journal of Personality and Social Psychology, 56,* 267–283.

10456

Test Name: COPE—REVISED

Purpose: To assess the different ways people respond to stress.

Number of Items: 28

Format: Each item is rated on a 4-point scale ranging from 1 (*I haven't been doing this at all*) to 4 (*I've been doing this a lot*).

Reliability: Alpha coefficients were .76 and .78.

Author: Lee, R. M., & Liu, H.-T. T.

Article: Coping with intergenerational family conflict: Comparison of Asian American, Hispanic, and European American college students.

Journal: *Journal of Counseling Psychology*, October 2001, *48*, 410–419.

Related Research: Carver, C. S. (1997). You want to measure coping but your protocol's too long: Consider the Brief COPE.

International Journal of Behavioral Medicine, 4, 92–100.

10457

Test Name: COPING HUMOR SCALE

Purpose: To measure how much subjects use humor to deal with stress.

Number of Items: 7

Format: A Likert format is used.

Reliability: Cronbach's alpha was .57.

Validity: Correlation with empathic concern was .18.

Author: Hampes, W. P.

Article: Relation between humor and empathic concern.

Journal: *Psychological Reports*, February 2001, *88*, 241–244.

Related Research: Martin, R. A., & Lefcourt, H. M. (1993). Sense of humor as a moderator of relation between stressors and moods. *Journal of Personality and Social Psychology, 47*, 145–155.

10458

Test Name: COPING INVENTORY

Purpose: To measure problem-focused coping, emotion-focused coping, and dysfunctional coping.

Number of Items: 51

Format: Scales range from 1 (*I usually don't do this*) to 4 (*I usually do this a lot*).

Reliability: Subscale alphas ranged from .81 to .83.

Author: Rice, K. G., and Lapsley, D. K.

Article: Perfectionism, coping, and emotional adjustment.

Journal: *Journal of College Student Development*, March/April 2001, *42*, 157–168.

Related Research: Carver, C. S., et al. (1989). Assessing coping strategies: A theoretically based approach. *Journal of Personality and Social Psychology, 56,* 267–283.

10459

Test Name: COPING MEASURE

Purpose: To measure religious coping, passive coping, and active coping.

Number of Items: 16

Format: All items are presented.

Reliability: Alpha coefficients ranged from .64 to .84 across subscales.

Validity: Correlations with other variables ranged from –.59 to .43.

Author: Abraído-Lanza, A. F., et al.

Article: En las manos de Dios [In God's hands]: Religious and other forms of coping among Latinos with arthritis.

Journal: *Journal of Consulting and Clinical Psychology*, February 2004, *72*, 91–102

Related Research: Rosenstiel, A. K., & Keefe, F. J. (1983). The use of coping strategies in low back pain patients: Relationship to patient characteristics and current adjustment. *Pain, 17*, 33–40.

10460

Test Name: COPING RESPONSES INVENTORY

Purpose: To assess coping response styles as approach and avoidance.

Number of Items: 48

Format: Scales range from 1 (*not at all*) to 4 (*fairly often*). Sample items are presented.

Reliability: Alpha coefficients ranged from .73 to .87 across subscales.

Author: Gable, S. L., et al.

Article: Evidence for bivariate systems: An empirical test of appetition and aversion across domains.

Journal: *Journal of Research in Personality*, October 2003, *37*, 349–372.

Related Research: Moos, R. H. (1997). Coping Responses Inventory: A measure of approach and avoidance coping skills. In C. P. Zalaquett & R. J. Wood (Eds.), *Evaluating stress: A book of resources* (pp. 51–65). Lanham, MD: Scarecrow Education.

10461

Test Name: COPING RESPONSES INVENTORY— SPANISH YOUTH FORM

Purpose: To assess coping strategies.

Format: Scales range from 0 (*not at all*) to 3 (*fairly often*).

Reliability: Alpha coefficients ranged from .40 to .63 across subscales.

Validity: Correlations with other variables ranged from .04 to .34.

Author: Forns, M., et al.

Article: Psychometric properties of the Spanish Version of the Moos Coping Response Inventory for youth.

Journal: *Psychological Reports*, December 2005, *97*, 777–789.

10462

Test Name: COPING STRATEGIES INVENTORY

Purpose: To measure coping strategies.

Number of Items: 16

Format: Four-point scales are anchored by 0 (*never*) and 3 (*very often*).

Reliability: Alpha coefficients ranged from .20 to .83 across subscales.

Author: Torkelson, E., and Muhonen, T.

Article: Coping strategies and health symptoms among women and men in a downsizing organization.

Journal: *Psychological Reports*, June 2003, *92*, Part 1, 899–907.

Related Research: Muhonen, T., & Torkelson, E. (2001). A Swedish version of the COPE Inventory. *Lund (Sweden) Psychological Reports, 1*. Carver, C. S. (1997). You want to measure coping but your protocol is too long: Consider the brief COPE. *International Journal of Behavioral Medicine, 4*, 92–100.

10463

Test Name: COPING STRATEGIES INVENTORY

Purpose: To measure coping strategies.

Number of Items: 18

Format: Includes two subscales: Problem Solving and Social Support. Responses are made on a 5-point scale ranging from 1 (*not at all*) to 5 (*very much*).

Reliability: Alpha coefficients ranged from .67 to .89.

Validity: Correlations with other variables ranged from –.17 to .39 ($N = 86$).

Author: Su, J., et al.

Article: Intergenerational family conflict and coping among American college students.

Journal: *Journal of Counseling Psychology*, October 2005, *52*, 482–489.

Related Research: Tobin, D. L., et al. (1989). The hierarchical factor structure of the Coping Strategies Inventory. *Cognitive Therapy and Research, 13*, 343–361.

10464

Test Name: COPING STRATEGIES SCALE

Purpose: To measure coping strategies.

Number of Items: 28

Format: Includes four factors: problem solving, working harder, seeking advice, and avoidance. Responses are made on a 5-point scale ranging from 1 (*never*) to 5 (*always*). Sample items are presented.

Reliability: Alpha coefficients ranged from .68 to .76.

Validity: Correlations with other variables ranged from –.21 to .35 ($N = 600$).

Author: Ito, J. K., and Brotheridge, C. M.

Article: Resources, coping strategies, and emotional exhaustion: A conservation of resources perspective.

Journal: *Journal of Vocational Behavior*, December 2003, *63*, 490–509.

10465

Test Name: COPING STRATEGIES SCALE

Purpose: To measure coping as active-behavioral, active-cognitive, avoidant-behavioral, and avoidant-cognitive.

Number of Items: 59

Format: Frequency rating scales range from 1 (*never*) to 4 (*frequently*).

Reliability: Total alpha was .95. Subscale alphas ranged from .82 to .92.

Author: Litt, M. D., et al.

Article: Coping skills and treatment outcomes in cognitive–behavioral and interactional group therapy for alcoholism.

Journal: *Journal of Consulting and Clinical Psychology*, February 2003, *71*, 118–128.

Related Research: Prochaska, J. O., et al. (1988). Measuring processes of change: Applications to the cessation of smoking. *Journal of Consulting and Clinical Psychology, 56*, 520–528.

10466

Test Name: COPING STRATEGY QUESTIONNAIRE—SWEDISH VERSION

Purpose: To assess different strategies for coping with pain.

Number of Items: 15

Format: Consists of five strategies: reinterpreting pain sensation, coping self-statements, improving pain sensations, diverting attention, and catastrophizing. Responses are made on a 7-point scale ranging from 0 (*never*) to 6 (*always*).

Reliability: Alpha coefficients ranged from .66 to .86.

Author: Hellstrom, B., and Anderberg, U. M.

Article: Pain perception across the menstrual cycle phases in women with chronic pain.

Journal: *Perceptual and Motor Skills*, February 2003, *96*, 201–211.

Related Research: Rosenstiel, A. K., & Keefe, F. J. (1983). The use of coping strategies in chronic low back patients: Relationship to patient characteristic and current adjustment. *Pain, 17*, 33–44.

10467

Test Name: COPING SUBSCALES

Purpose: To measure coping as finding comfort in religion, active planning, humor, seeking emotional support, acceptance, and denial–disengagement.

Number of Items: 28

Format: Item response categories ranged from 1 (*don't do this at all*) to 4 (*usually do this a lot*). All items are presented.

Reliability: Alpha coefficients ranged from .64 to .88.

Author: Wade, S. L., et al.

Article: The relationship of caregiver coping to family outcomes during the initial year following pediatric traumatic injury.

Journal: *Journal of Consulting and Clinical Psychology*, June 2001, *69*, 406–415.

Related Research: Carver, C. S., et al. (1989). Assessing coping strategies: A theoretically based approach. *Journal of Personality and Social Psychology, 56*, 267–283.

10468

Test Name: COSTELLO–COMREY ANXIETY SCALE

Purpose: To measure predisposition to anxious affective states.

Number of Items: 9

Format: Scales range from 1 (*never*) to 4 (*always*).

Reliability: Coefficient alpha was .70.

Validity: Correlations with other variables ranged from −.24 to .45.

Author: Kuther, T. L., and Timoshin, A.

Article: A comparison of social cognitive and psychosocial predictors of alcohol use by college students.

Journal: *Journal of College Student Development*, March/April 2003, *44*, 143–154.

Related Research: Costello, C. G., & Comrey, A. L. (1967). Scales for measuring depression and anxiety. *The Journal of Psychology, 66*, 303–313.

10469

Test Name: COURTAULD EMOTIONAL CONTROL SCALE

Purpose: To assess the degree that women with breast cancer smother or bottle-up feelings of anger, madness, and fear.

Number of Items: 21

Format: Sample items are presented.

Reliability: Coefficient alpha was .95 for the total scale and ranged from .90 to .93 across subscales.

Author: Giese-Davis, J., et al.

Article: Change in emotion-regulation strategy for women with metastatic breast cancer following supportive–expressive group therapy.

Journal: *Journal of Consulting and Clinical Psychology*, August 2002, *70*, 916–925.

Related Research: Watson, M., & Greer, S. (1993). Development of a questionnaire measure of emotional control. *Journal of Psychosomatic Research, 27*, 299–305.

10470

Test Name: DAILY HASSLES MICROSYSTEM SCALE

Purpose: To measure the frequency and severity of daily hassles.

Number of Items: 28

Format: Scales range from 1 (*not at all a hassle*) to 4 (*a very big hassle*).

Reliability: Alpha coefficients were .77 (frequency) and .81 (severity).

Author: Vinokurov, A., et al.

Article: Acculturative hassles and immigrant adolescents: A life-domain assessment for Soviet Jewish refugees.

Journal: *The Journal of Social Psychology*, August 2002, *142*, 425–445.

Related Research: Seidman, E., et al. (1995). Development and validation of Adolescent Perceived Microsystem Scales: Social support, daily hassles, and involvement. *American Journal of Community Psychology, 23,* 355–388.

10471

Test Name: DAILY HASSLES QUESTIONNAIRE

Purpose: To identify typical day-to-day concerns of school-age children and adolescents.

Number of Items: 21

Format: Includes five domains: school, family, peer relations, physical appearance, and sports/athletics. Responses are made on a 4-point rating scale ranging from 0 (*not at all a hassle*) to 3 (*a very big hassle*). Sample items are presented.

Reliability: Alpha coefficients ranged from .69 to .91.

Author: Du Bois, D. L., et al.

Article: Race and gender influences on adjustment in early adolescence: Investigation of an integrative model.

Journal: *Child Development,* September/October 2002, *73,* 1573–1592.

Related Research: Rowlison, R., & Felner, R. (1988). Major life events, hassles, and adaptation in adolescence: Confounding in the conceptualization and measurement of life stress revisited. *Journal of Personality and Social Psychology, 55,* 432–444.

10472

Test Name: DEALING WITH ILLNESS SCALE

Purpose: To assess use of different coping strategies.

Number of Items: 76

Format: Responses are made on a 5-point scale ranging from 0 (*never*) to 5 (*always*). Examples are presented.

Reliability: Alpha coefficients ranged from .63 to .88.

Validity: Correlations with other variables ranged from −.12 to .60.

Author: Lightfoot, M., and Healy, C.

Article: Career development, coping, and emotional distress in youth living with HIV.

Journal: *Journal of Counseling Psychology,* October 2001, *48,* 484–489.

Related Research: Namir, S., et al. (1987). Coping with AIDS: Psychological and health implications. *Journal of Applied Social Psychology, 17,* 309–328.

10473

Test Name: DEATH ANXIETY INVENTORY—REVISED SPANISH VERSION

Purpose: To measure death anxiety.

Number of Items: 17

Format: Scales range from 1 (*totally disagree*) to 5 (*totally agree*). All items are presented.

Reliability: Coefficient alpha was .92.

Author: Tomás-Sábado, J., et al.

Article: The Death Anxiety Inventory: A revision.

Journal: *Psychological Reports,* December 2005, *97,* 793–796.

Related Research: Templar, D. I. (1970). The construction and validation of a death anxiety scale. *The Journal of General Psychology, 82,* 165–177.

10474

Test Name: DEATH ANXIETY INVENTORY—SPANISH FORM

Purpose: To measure internally and externally generated death anxiety.

Number of Items: 20

Format: Response scales range from 1 (*totally disagree*) to 5 (*totally agree*). All items are presented in English.

Reliability: Coefficient alpha was .90. Test–retest reliability (4 weeks) was .94.

Author: Tomás-Sábado, J., and Gómez-Benito, J.

Article: Death anxiety and death depression in Spanish nurses.

Journal: *Psychological Reports,* August 2005, *97,* 21–24.

Related Research: Tomás-Sábado, J., & Gómez-Benito, J. (2005). Construction and validation of the Death Anxiety Inventory. *European Journal of Psychological Assessment, 21,* 109–115.

10475

Test Name: DEATH ANXIETY SCALE

Purpose: To measure death anxiety.

Number of Items: 15

Format: Scales range from 1 (*strongly disagree*) to 7 (*strongly agree*). A sample item is presented.

Reliability: Various reliability coefficients ranged from .76 to .83.

Validity: Correlations with other variables ranged from −.34 to .16.

Author: Cohen, A. B., et al.

Article: Intrinsic and extrinsic religiosity, belief in the afterlife, death anxiety, and life satisfaction in young Catholics and Protestants.

Journal: *Journal of Research in Personality,* June 2005, *39,* 307–324.

Related Research: Templer, D. I. (1970). The construction and validation of a death anxiety scale.

The Journal of General Psychology, 82, 165–177.

10476

Test Name: DEATH DEPRESSION SCALE

Purpose: To quantify people's depressive reactions in relation to the idea of death.

Number of Items: 17

Format: Responses are true–false or Likert format. All items are presented.

Reliability: Coefficient alpha was .83. Test–retest (4 weeks) correlation coefficient was .87.

Validity: Correlations with other variables ranged from .23 to .78.

Author: Tomás-Sábado, J., and Gómez-Benito, J.

Article: The Spanish form of the Death Depression Scale.

Journal: *Perceptual of Motor Skills*, February 2003, *96*, 49–53.

Related Research: Templer, D. I., et al. (1990). The measurement of death depression. *Journal of Clinical Psychology, 46*, 834–841.

10477

Test Name: DENTAL APPEARANCE QUESTIONNAIRE

Purpose: To measure concern for dental appearance.

Number of Items: 23

Format: A Likert-type format is used. All items and response categories are presented.

Reliability: Cronbach's alpha was .84.

Author: Frazer, M., and Lindsay, S.

Article: Development of a questionnaire to measure concern for dental appearance.

Journal: *Psychological Reports*, October 2001, *89*, 425–430.

Related Research: Nuttall, N. (1996). Initial development of a questionnaire to measure dental indifference. *Community Dentistry and Oral Epidemiology, 24*, 112–116.

10478

Test Name: DENTAL FEAR SURVEY FOR CHILDREN

Purpose: To measure dental fear.

Number of Items: 15

Format: Scales range from 1 (*not afraid at all*) to 5 (*very afraid*).

Reliability: Coefficient alpha was .93.

Validity: Correlations with other variables ranged from .41 to .68.

Author: Ten Berge, M., et al.

Article: The Dental Subscale of the Children's Fear Survey Schedule: Predictive value and clinical usefulness.

Journal: *Journal of Psychopathology and Behavioral Assessment*, June 2002, *24*, 115–118.

Related Research: Klingberg, G., et al. (1995). Child dental fear: Cause related factors and clinical effects. *European Journal of Oral Sciences, 103*, 405–412.

10479

Test Name: DEPRESSION AND LOW WELL-BEING SUBSCALES

Purpose: To assess emotional distress.

Number of Items: 6

Format: Includes two subscales: Depression and Low Well-Being. Responses are made on 5-point scales ranging from 1 (*false*) to 5 (*true*). Examples are presented.

Reliability: Coefficient alpha was .80.

Author: Wentzel, K. R., et al.

Article: Friendships in middle school: Influences on motivation and school adjustment.

Journal: *Journal of Educational Psychology*, June 2004, *96*, 195–203.

Related Research: Weinberger, D. A., et al. (1987). *Construct validation of the Weinberger Adjustment Inventory*. Unpublished manuscript, Stanford University, Standford, CA.

10480

Test Name: DEPRESSION AND SOMATIC COMPLAINTS SCALE—JAPANESE VERSION

Purpose: To measure depression and somatic complaints.

Number of Items: 20

Format: Scales range from 1 (*not at all*) to 4 (*very much*). All items are presented in English.

Reliability: Alpha coefficients exceeded .83.

Validity: Correlations with other variables ranged from .10 to .52.

Author: Jou, Y. H., and Fukada, H.

Article: Stress, health, and reciprocity and sufficiency of social support: The care of university students in Japan.

Journal: *The Journal of Social Psychology*, June 2002, *142*, 353–370.

10481

Test Name: DEPRESSION ANXIETY STRESS SCALE—SPANISH VERSION

Purpose: To measure the negative emotional states of depression, anxiety, and stress.

Number of Items: 21

Format: All items are presented in Spanish.

Reliability: Alpha coefficients ranged from .86 to .93.

Validity: Correlations with other variables ranged from .60 to .86.

Author: Daza, P., et al.

Article: The Depression Anxiety Stress Scale—21: Spanish translation and validation with a Hispanic sample.

Journal: *Journal of Psychopathology and Behavioral Assessment*, September 2002, *24*, 195–205.

10482

Test Name: DEPRESSION–ANXIETY STRESS SCALES

Purpose: To measure depression and anxiety symptoms: anhedonia, skeletal–subjective, and easily upset–irritable.

Number of Items: 42 or 21

Format: Scales range from 0 (*did not apply to me at all*) to 3 (*applied to me very much or most of the time*). Sample items are presented.

Reliability: Alpha coefficients ranged from .89 to .96 across subscales on the 42-item version and from .81 to .92 on the 21-item version.

Author: Clara, I. P., et al.

Article: Confirmatory factor analysis of the depression–anxiety stress scales in depressed and anxious patients.

Journal: *Journal of Psychopathology and Behavioral Assessment*, March 2001, *23*, 61–67.

Related Research: Lovibond, P. F., & Lovibond, S. H. (1995). The structure of negative emotional states: Comparison of the Depression Anxiety Stress Scales (DASS) with the Beck Depression and Anxiety Inventories. *Behavior Research and Therapy, 33,* 335–343.

10483

Test Name: DEPRESSION SCALE

Purpose: To measure depression.

Number of Items: 4

Format: Scales range from 1 (*not at all true*) to 7 (*very true*). A sample item is presented.

Reliability: Coefficient alpha was .73.

Author: Chu, A. H. C., and Choi, J. N.

Article: Rethinking procrastination: Positive effects of "active" procrastination behavior on attitude and performance.

Journal: *The Journal of Social Psychology*, June 2005, *145*, 245–264.

Related Research: Sheikh, J. L., & Yesavage, J. A. (1982). *Geriatric Depression Scale (GDS)* [Department of Psychiatry and Behavioral Sciences, Stanford University]. Avaiable at *http://www.stanford.edu/~yesavage /GDS.english.long.html*

10484

Test Name: DEPRESSION SCALE

Purpose: To measure depression.

Number of Items: 7

Format: Scales range from 0 (*did not apply to me at all*) to 3 (*applied to me very much or most of the time*). Sample items are presented.

Reliability: Coefficient alpha was .89.

Validity: Correlations with other variables ranged from –.15 to .38.

Author: MacGeorge, E. L., et al.

Article: Stress, social support, and health among college students after September 11, 2001.

Journal: *Journal of College Student Development*, November/December 2004, 45, 655–670.

Related Research: Lovibond, P. F., & Lovibond, S. H. (1995). The structure of negative emotional states: Comparison of the Depression Anxiety Stress Scale

(DASS) with Beck Depression and Anxiety Inventories. *Behavior Research and Therapy, 35,* 335–343.

10485

Test Name: DEPRESSION SCALE

Purpose: To measure the frequency of symptoms of depression.

Number of Items: 20

Format: Scales range from 1 (*rarely or none of the time [less than 1 day]*) to 4 (*most or all of the time [5–7 days]*).

Reliability: Coefficient alpha was .91.

Validity: Correlations with other variables ranged from –.25 to .44.

Author: Major, V. S., et al.

Article: Work time, work interference with family, and psychological distress.

Journal: *Journal of Applied Psychology*, June 2002, 87, 427–436.

Related Research: Frone, M. R., et al. (1991). Relationship of work and family stressors to psychological distress: The independent moderating influence of social support, mastery, active coping and self-focused attention. *Journal of Social Behavior and Personality, 6,* 227–250.

10486

Test Name: DEPRESSION SELF-RATING SCALE

Purpose: To assess a child's current mood state.

Number of Items: 18

Format: Three-point scales range from *most of the time* to *never*. Samples items are presented.

Validity: Correlations with other variables ranged from –.34 to .81.

Author: Danielson, C. K., and Phelps, C. R.

Article: The assessment of children's social skills through self-report: A potential screening instrument for classroom use.

Journal: *Measurement and Evaluation in Counseling and Development*, January 2003, *35*, 218–229.

Related Research: Birleson, P., et al. (1987). Clinical evaluation of a self-rating scale for depressive disorder in childhood (Depression Rating Scale). *Journal of Child Psychology & Psychiatry & Allied Disciplines*, *28*, 43–60.

10487

Test Name: DEPRESSIVE MOOD LIST

Purpose: To assess the extent to which adolescents experience negative moods.

Number of Items: 6

Format: Responses are made on a 6-point scale ranging from 1 (*never*) to 6 (*always*).

Reliability: Internal consistency was .75.

Validity: Correlations with other variables ranged form –.47 to .28.

Author: Engels, R. C. M. E., et al.

Article: Parental attachment and adolescents' emotional adjustment: The associations with social skills and relational competence.

Journal: *Journal of Counseling Psychology*, October 2001, *48*, 428–439.

Related Research: Kandal, D., & Davies, M. (1982). Epidemiology of depressive mood in adolescents. *Archives of General Psychology*, *39*, 1205–1212.

10488

Test Name: DEPRESSIVE PERSONALITY DISORDER INVENTORY

Purpose: To assess depressive personality.

Number of Items: 41

Format: A Likert-type questionnaire is used. Sample items are presented.

Reliability: Alpha coefficients ranged from .94 to .96.

Validity: Correlations with other variables ranged from –.16 to .77.

Author: Huprich, S. K.

Article: Convergent and discriminant validity of three measures of depressive personality disorder.

Journal: *Journal of Personality Assessment*, June 2004, *82*, 321–328.

Related Research: Huprich, S. K., et al. (2002). Further psychometric evaluation of the Depressive Personality Disorder Inventory. *Journal of Personality Disorders*, *16*, 255–269.

10489

Test Name: DIAGNOSTIC INTERVIEW FOR DEPRESSIVE PERSONALITY DISORDER

Purpose: To provide a semistructured interview.

Number of Items: 63

Format: A 3-point scale is used.

Reliability: Coefficient alpha was .90.

Validity: Correlations with other variables ranged from –.14 to .55.

Author: Huprich, S. K.

Article: Convergent and discriminant validity of three measures of depressive personality disorder.

Journal: *Journal of Personality Assessment*, June 2004, *82*, 321–328.

Related Research: Gunderson, J. G., et al. (1994). The diagnostic interview for depressive

personality. *American Journal of Psychiatry*, *151*, 1300–1304.

10490

Test Name: DIFFICULTIES IN EMOTION REGULATION SCALES

Purpose: To assess the difficulties in emotion regulation in adults.

Number of Items: 36

Format: Scales range from 1 (*almost never, 0–10%*) to 5 (*almost always, 91–100%*). All items are presented.

Reliability: Coefficient alpha was .93. Subscale alphas exceeded .80.

Validity: Correlations with other variables ranged from –.69 to .20.

Author: Gratz, K. L., and Roemer, L.

Article: Multidimensional assessment of emotional regulation and dysregulation: Development, factor structure and initial validation of the Difficulties in Emotional Regulation Scale.

Journal: *Journal of Psychopathology and Behavioral Assessment*, March 2004, *26*, 41–54.

10491

Test Name: DISABILITY SEVERITY SCALE

Purpose: To assess disability severity of ALS patients.

Number of Items: 3

Format: Scales range from 1 (*no*) to 3 (*yes*). All items are presented.

Reliability: Coefficient alpha was .86.

Validity: Correlations with other variables ranged from –.24 to .01.

Author: Westaby, J. D., et al.

Article: Intentions to work during terminal illness: An exploratory study of antecedent conditions.

Journal: *Journal of Applied Psychology*, November 2005, *90*, 1297–1305.

10492

Test Name: DISGUST SCALE

Purpose: To measure disgust sensitivity.

Number of Items: 32

Format: Subjects respond to items on a true–false scale and a 3-point disgust scale anchored by 0 (*not disgusting at all*) and 2 (*very disgusting*). A sample item is presented.

Reliability: Alpha was .86. Spearman–Brown formula reliability was .79.

Validity: Correlations with other variables ranged from –.46 to .08.

Author: Sherman, N. C., et al.

Article: Disgust sensitivity and attitudes toward organ donation among African-American college students.

Journal: *Psychological Reports*, August 2001, *89*, 11–23.

Related Research: Haidt, J., et al. (1994). Individual differences in sensitivity to disgust: A scale sampling seven domains of disgust elicitors. *Personality and Individual Differences, 16*, 701–713.

10493

Test Name: DISPOSITIONAL COPING QUESTIONNAIRE— JAPANESE VERSION

Purpose: To assess coping with stress.

Number of Items: 32

Format: Scales range from 1 (*I usually do not do this at all*) to 5 (*I always do this*).

Reliability: Alpha coefficients exceeded .85. Nine-week test–retest reliabilities ranged from .67 to .81.

Author: Sasaki, M., and Yamasaki, K.

Article: Dispositional and situational coping and mental health status of university students.

Journal: *Psychological Reports*, December 2005, *97*, 797–809.

Related Research: Sasaki, M., & Yamasaki, K. (2002). [Development of a dispositional version of the General Coping Questionnaire (GCQ) and examination of its reliability and validity]. [*Japanese Journal of Public Health*], *49*, 399–408. [In Japanese with English abstract].

10494

Test Name: DISSOCIATIVE EXPERIENCES SCALE

Purpose: To measure dissociative experiences in daily life.

Number of Items: 28

Format: Eleven-point scales are used.

Validity: Correlations with other variables ranged from .28 to .54.

Author: Suszek, H.

Article: Self-pluralism and dissociation.

Journal: *Psychological Reports*, February 2005, *96*, 181–182.

Related Research: Ross, C. A., et al. (1995). A factor analysis of the Dissociative Experiences Scale (DES) in dissociative identity disorder. *Dissociation, 8*, 229–235.

10495

Test Name: DREAM SALIENCE SCALE

Purpose: To measure dream salience.

Number of Items: 4

Format: Includes vividness, bizarreness, emotionality, and color.

Reliability: Alpha coefficients ranged from .91 to .95

Author: Ebbean, M., et al.

Article: Effects of pryridoxine on dreaming: A preliminary study.

Journal: *Perceptual and Motor Skills*, February 2002, *94*, 135–140.

Related Research: Belicki, K. (1986). Recalling dreams: An examination of daily variation and individual differences. In J. Gackenbach (Ed.), *Sleep and dreams: A sourcebook* (pp. 187–206). New York: Garland.

10496

Test Name: DUAL-EMPLOYED COPING SCALE

Purpose: To measure coping behaviors of dual-employed couples.

Number of Items: 58

Format: Examples are presented.

Reliability: Overall internal reliabilities were .86 and .77.

Validity: Correlations with other variables ranged from –.11 to .25.

Author: Perrone, K. M., & Worthington, Jr., E. L.

Article: Factors influencing ratings of marital quality by individuals within dual-career marriages: A conceptual model.

Journal: *Journal of Counseling Psychology*, January 2001, *48*, 3–6.

Related Research: Skinner, D. A., & McCubbin, H. I. (1991). The Dual-Employed Coping Scales. In H. I. McCubbin & M. A. Thompson (Eds.), *Family assessment inventories for research and practice* (pp. 265–278). Madison: University of Wisconsin.

10497

Test Name: DYADIC COPING INVENTORY

Purpose: To assess dyadic coping and communication under conditions of stress.

Number of Items: 55

Format: Frequency scales range from 0 (*never*) to 5 (*always*).

Reliability: Coefficient alpha was .92. Subscale alphas ranged from .80 to .91.

Author: Bodenmann, G., et al.

Article: Differences in individual and dyadic coping among low and high depressed, partially remitted and nondepressed persons.

Journal: *Journal of Psychopathology and Behavioral Assessment*, June 2004, *26*, 75–85.

Related Research: Bodenmann, G. (2000). Stress and coping bei paaren [stress and coping couples]. Goettingen: Hogrefe.

10498

Test Name: DYSFUNCTIONAL ATTITUDES QUESTIONNAIRE

Purpose: To assess maladaptive beliefs related to depression.

Number of Items: 40

Format: Responses are made on a 7-point scale ranging from 1(*totally agree*) to 7 (*totally disagree*).

Reliability: Internal reliability estimates ranged from .82 to .97. Test–retest (6 weeks) reliability was 73.

Validity: Correlations with other variables ranged from .49 to .54.

Author: Dozois, D. J. A.

Article: The psychometric characteristics of the Hamilton Depression Inventory.

Journal: *Journal of Personality Assessment*, February 2003, *80*, 31–40.

Related Research: Weissman, A. N., & Beck, A. T. (1978, November). *Development and validation of the Dysfunctional Attitude Scale: A preliminary investigation*. Paper presented at the annual meeting of the American Educational Research Association, Toronto, Ontario, Canada.

10499

Test Name: EATING DISORDER INVENTORY

Purpose: To measure bulimia and anorexia symptoms.

Number of Items: 14

Format: Item responses are anchored by 1 (*strongly disagree*) and 5 (*strongly agree*). All items are presented.

Reliability: Cronbach's alpha was .90.

Validity: Correlations with other variables ranged from –.02 to .38.

Author: Ross, L. T., and Gill, J. L.

Article: Eating disorders: Relations with inconsistent discipline, anxiety, and drinking among college women.

Journal: *Psychological Reports*, August 2002, *91*, 289–298.

10500

Test Name: EATING DISORDERS INVENTORY

Purpose: To assess eating disorder symptomatology.

Number of Items: 23

Format: Item response scales are anchored by 1 (*never*) and 6 (*always*).

Reliability: Coefficient alpha was .70.

Author: Bravata, E. A., et al.

Article: Correlations among symptoms of depression and problematic eating patterns in intercollegiate athletes.

Journal: *Psychological Reports*, December 2003, *93*, Part 2, 1243–1246.

Related Research: Garner, D. M., et al. (1983). Development and validation of a multidimensional eating disorder inventory for anorexia nervosa and bulimia. *International Journal of Eating Disorders, 8*, 14–34.

10501

Test Name: EATING DISORDERS INVENTORY

Purpose: To measure drive for thinness, bulimia, body dissatisfaction, perfectionism, and maturity fears.

Number of Items: 64

Format: Six-point scales are anchored by *always* and *never*.

Reliability: Cronbach's alpha ranged from .65 to .82 across subscales and subgroups.

Author: Moeller, A. T., and Bothma, M. E.

Article: Body dissatisfaction and irrational beliefs.

Journal: *Psychological Reports*, April 2001, *88*, 423–430.

Related Research: Garner, D. M., et al. (1983). Development and validation of a multidimensional eating disorders inventory for anorexia nervosa and bulimia. *International Journal of Eating Disorders, 2*, 15–34.

10502

Test Name: EDINBURGH POSTNATAL DEPRESSION SCALE

Purpose: To assess maternal depression.

Number of Items: 10

Format: Responses are made on a 4-point scale ranging from 0 (*not at all*) to 3 (*yes, most of the time*). A sample item is presented.

Reliability: Coefficient alpha was .67.

Author: Asbury, K., et al.

Article: Nonshared environmental influences on individual differences in early behavioral development: A monozygotic twin differences study.

Journal: *Child Development,* May/June 2003, *74,* 933–943.

Related Research: Cox, J. L., et al. (1987). Development of the Edinburgh Postnatal Depression Scale. *British Journal of Psychiatry, 150,* 782–786.

10503

Test Name: EGO-RESILIENCY SCALE

Purpose: To measure the quality of resiliency by what individuals do about their own fluctuating life experiences.

Number of Items: 14

Format: Scales range from 1 (*does not apply*) to 4 (*applies very strongly*).

Reliability: Alpha coefficients ranged from .76 to .83.

Author: Greeff, A. P., and Ritman, I. N.

Article: Individual characteristics associated with resilience in single-parent families.

Journal: *Psychological Reports,* February 2005, *96,* 36–42.

Related Research: Block, J., & Kremen, A. M. (1996). IQ and ego-resiliency: Conceptual and empirical connections and separateness. *Journal of Personality and Social Psychology, 70,* 349–361.

10504

Test Name: EMOTIONAL AND GENERAL HEALTH SCALE

Purpose: To assess emotional and general health satisfaction.

Number of Items: 7

Format: Emotional health items use a yes–no format. Other items have scales that range from 1 (*definitely false*) to 5 (*definitely true*).

Reliability: Alpha coefficients ranged from .76 to .81.

Author: Munson, L. J., et al.

Article: Labeling sexual harassment in the military: An extension and replication.

Journal: *Journal of Applied Psychology,* April 2001, *86,* 293–303.

Related Research: Ware, J. E., & Sherbourne, C. D. (1992). The MOS 36-Item Short-Form Health Survey (SF-36): I. Conceptual framework and item selection. *Medical Care, 30,* 473–483.

10505

Test Name: EMOTIONAL DISSONANCE SCALES

Purpose: To assess emotional dissonance.

Number of Items: 5

Format: Includes two scales: three items with responses ranging on a 5-point scale from 1 (*strongly disagree*) to 5 (*strongly agree*) and two items with a 5-point scale ranging from 1 (*never*) to 5 (*always*). Examples are presented.

Reliability: Internal consistency reliabilities were .73 and .86.

Author: Glomb, T. M., and Tews, M. J.

Article: Emotional labor: A conceptualization and scale development.

Journal: *Journal of Vocational Behavior,* February 2004, *64,* 1–23.

Related Research: Morris, J. A., & Feldman, D. C. (1997). Managing emotions in the workplace. *Journal of Managerial Issues, 9,* 257–274. Brotheridge, C. M., & Lee, R. T (1998). *On the dimensionality of emotional labor: Development and validation of an emotional labor scale.* Paper presented at the first conference on Emotions in Organizational Life, San Diego, CA.

10506

Test Name: EMOTIONAL DISTRESS AND RISK-TAKING SCALES

Purpose: To measure emotional distress and risk-taking.

Number of Items: 7

Format: Four and 5-point response scales are used. Sample items are presented.

Reliability: Alpha coefficients ranged from .78 to .84.

Author: Colder, G. R., et al.

Article: A finite mixture model of growth trajectories of adolescent alcohol use: Predictors and consequences.

Journal: *Journal of Consulting and Clinical Psychology,* August 2002, *70,* 976–985.

Related Research: Simon, T. R., et al. (1998). Prospective psychosocial, interpersonal, and behavior predictors of handgun carrying among adolescents. *American Journal of Public Health, 88,* 960–963.

10507

Test Name: EMOTIONAL EATING SCALE

Purpose: To assess eating in response to negative emotions: anger–frustration, depression, and anxiety.

Number of Items: 25

Format: Scales range from 1 (*no desire to eat*) to 5 (*an overwhelming urge to eat*). A sample item is presented.

Reliability: Alpha coefficients ranged from .83 to .89 across subscales.

Validity: Correlations with other variables ranged from .27 to .68.

Author: Jackson, B., et al.

Article: Motivations to eat: Scale development and validation.

Journal: *Journal of Research in Personality*, August 2003, *37*, 297–318.

Related Research: Arnow, B., et al. (1995). The Emotional Eating Scale: The development of a measure to assess coping with negative affect by eating. *International Journal of Eating Disorders, 18*, 79–90.

10508

Test Name: EMOTIONAL EXHAUSTION SCALE

Purpose: To measure emotional exhaustion.

Number of Items: 9

Format: Scales range from 1 (*strongly disagree*) to 7 (*strongly agree*).

Reliability: Coefficient alpha was .92.

Validity: Correlations with other variables range from –.46 to .57.

Author: Cropanzano, R., and Rupp, D. E.

Article: The relationship of emotional exhaustion to work attitudes, job performance, and organizational citizenship behaviors.

Journal: *Journal of Applied Psychology*, February 2003, *88*, 160–169.

Related Research: Maslach, C. A., & Jackson, S. E. (1981). The measurement of experienced burnout. *Journal of Occupational Behavior, 2*, 99–113.

10509

Test Name: EMOTIONAL EXHAUSTION SCALE

Purpose: To measure emotional exhaustion.

Number of Items: 5

Format: Responses are made on a 5-point scale ranging from 1 (*never*) to 5 (*almost every day*). An example is given.

Reliability: Internal consistency reliability was .85.

Author: Glomb, T. M., and Tews, M. J.

Article: Emotional labor: A conceptualization and scale development.

Journal: *Journal of Vocational Behavior*, February 2004, *64*, 1–23.

Related Research: Wharton, A. S. (1993). The affective consequences of service work. *Work and Occupations, 20*, 205–232.

10510

Test Name: EMOTIONAL EXPERIENCES SCALE

Purpose: To assess the experience of seven emotions.

Number of Items: 7

Format: All items are presented.

Validity: Correlations with other variables ranged from –.32 to .37.

Author: Ashley, A., and Holtgraves, T.

Article: Repressors and memory: Effects of self-deception, impression management and mood.

Journal: *Journal of Research in Personality*, August 2003, *37*, 284–296.

Related Research: Storm, C., & Storm, T. (1987). A taxonomic study of the vocabulary of emotions. *Journal of Personality and Social Psychology, 4*, 805–816.

10511

Test Name: EMOTIONAL INTENSITY SCALE—REDUCED

Purpose: To measure intensity of emotions

Number of Items: 17

Format: Nine items are related to positive emotions and 8 to negative emotions. Five-point response

scales are used. All items are presented.

Reliability: Alpha coefficients ranged from .79 to .89.

Author: Geuens, M., and DePelsmacker, P.

Article: Validity and reliability of scores on the reduced emotional identity scale.

Journal: *Educational and Psychological Measurement*, April 2002, *62*, 299–315.

Related Research: Bachorowski, J. A., & Braaten, E. B. (1994). Emotional intensity: Measurement and theoretical implications. *Personality and Individual Differences, 17*, 191–199

10512

Test Name: EMOTIONAL OUTCOME MEASURE

Purpose: To measure emotional outcome.

Number of Items: 15

Format: Includes four scales: Career Satisfaction, Intent to Stay in the Profession, Met Expectations, and Work–Nonwork Conflict. Responses are made on a 5-point Likert-type scale ranging from 1 (*strongly disagree*) to 5 (*strongly agree*).

Reliability: Alpha coefficients ranged from .84 to .88.

Validity: Correlations with other variables ranged from –.53 to .52.

Author: Wallace, J. E.

Article: The benefits of mentoring for female lawyers.

Journal: *Journal of Vocational Behavior*, June 2001, *58*, 366–391.

Related Research: Greenshuas, J. H., et al. (1990). Effects of race on organizational experience, job performance evaluations, and career outcomes. *Academy of Management Journal, 33*, 64–86.

Price, J. L. (1990). *Wilford Hall Medical Center Retention Survey*. Lackland Airforce Base, TX. Kopelman, R. E., et al. (1983). A model of work, family and interrole conflict: A construct validation study. *Organizational Behavior and Human Performance, 32*, 198–215.

10513

Test Name: EMOTIONAL PAIN AND ACCEPTANCE SUBSCALES

Purpose: To measure emotional pain and acceptance associated with alcohol use.

Number of Items: 8

Format: Four-point Likert scales are used. All items are presented.

Reliability: Alpha coefficients ranged from .79 to .82.

Author: Ozegovic, J. J., et al.

Article: Trends and predictors of alcohol use among undergraduate female students.

Journal: *Journal of College Student Development*, September/October 2001, *42*, 447–455.

Related Research: Thombs, D. L., & Beck, K. H. (1995, November). *The social context of adolescent and college student drinking: An overview of recent findings*. Paper presented at the meeting of the Addiction Research Foundation on the Social and Health Effects of Different Drinking Patterns, Toronto, Ontario, Canada.

10514

Test Name: EMOTIONAL REACTIONS SCALE

Purpose: To assess positive and negative emotions.

Format: Scales range from 1 (*definitely not*) to 9 (*definitely*). Sample items are presented.

Reliability: Alpha coefficients ranged from .82 to .90.

Validity: Correlations with other variables ranged from –.60 to .50.

Author: Takaku, S.

Article: The effects of apology and perspective taking on interpersonal forgiveness: A dissonance–attribution model of interpersonal forgiveness.

Journal: *The Journal of Social Psychology*, August 2001, *141*, 494–508.

10515

Test Name: EMOTIONAL WELL-BEING SCALES

Purpose: To assess emotional well-being.

Number of Items: 24

Format: Includes three scales: Positive Affect, Negative Affect, and Test Anxiety. Examples are given.

Reliability: Alpha coefficients ranged from .65 to .92.

Validity: Correlations with other variables ranged from –.49 to .72.

Author: Linnenbrink, E. A.

Article: The dilemma of performance approach goals: The use of multiple goal contexts to promote students' motivation and learning.

Journal: *Journal of Educational Psychology*, May 2005, *97*, 197–213.

Related Research: Watson, D., & Tellegen, A. (1985). Toward a consensual structure of mood. *Psychological Bulletin, 98*, 219–235.

10516

Test Name: ENJOYMENT/BOREDOM SCALE

Purpose: To measure enjoyment and boredom in sport.

Number of Items: 8

Format: Items reflect enjoyment and boredom. Responses are made on a 100-point scale ranging from 0 (*strongly disagree*) to 100 (*strongly agree*). Examples are presented.

Reliability: Alphas were .80 and .68.

Author: Cervello, E. M., & Santos-Rosa, F. J.

Article: Motivation in sport: An achievement goal perspective in young Spanish recreational athletes.

Journal: *Perceptual and Motor Skills*, April 2001, *92*, 527–534.

Related Research: Duda, J. L., & Nicholls, J. G. (1992). Dimensions of achievement motivation in schoolwork and sport. *Journal of Educational Psychology, 84*, 290–299.

10517

Test Name: ESCAPIST AND CONTROL COPING SCALES

Purpose: To measure escapist and control strategies of coping.

Number of Items: 17

Format: Item responses are anchored by 1 (*hardly ever do this*) and 5 (*almost always do this*). Sample items are presented.

Reliability: Alpha coefficients were .86 (control coping) and .71 (escapist coping).

Author: Burke, R. J.

Article: Evidence for concurrent validity of responses by survivors of hospital restructuring.

Journal: *Psychological Reports*, June 2001, *88*, Part 2, 1259–1262.

Related Research: Latack, J. C. (1986). Coping with job stress: Measures and future directions of scale development. *Journal of Applied Psychology, 71*, 377–385.

10518

Test Name: ETIOLGY ATTRIBUTION SCALE

Purpose: To measure etiologic factor attributed to psychological problems.

Number of Items: 7

Format: Scales range from 1 (*most important*) to 6 (*least important*). All items are described.

Reliability: Test–retest reliabilities ranged from .53 to 74.

Validity: Correlations with other variables ranged from −.33 to .49.

Author: Worthington, R. L., and Dillon, F. R.

Article: The Theoretical Orientation Profile Scale—Revised: A validation study.

Journal: *Measurement and Evaluation in Counseling and Development*, July 2003, *36*, 95–105.

Related Research: Worthington, R. L. (1995). Etiology attributions, causal dimensions, responsibility attributions, treatment strategy recommendations and theoretical orientations. *Dissertation Abstracts International*, Vol. 56 (6), 3471B. (UMI No. 9532414)

10519

Test Name: EXCESSIVE REASSURANCE SEEKING

Purpose: To measure a tendency to repeatedly and persistently seek reassurance, even if reassurance has already been provided.

Number of Items: 4

Format: Responses are made on a 7-point scale ranging from 1 (*not at all*) to 7 (*very much*). An example is given.

Reliability: Alpha coefficients were .88 and .89.

Validity: Correlations with other variables ranged from −.39 to .46 (*n* = 425).

Author: Wei, M., et al.

Article: Adult attachment, depressive symptoms, and validation from self versus others.

Journal: *Journal of Counseling Psychology*, July 2005, *52*, 368–377.

Related Research: Joiner, T. E., & Metalsky, G. I. (2001). Excessive reassurance-seeking: Delineating a risk factor involved in the development of depressive symptoms. *Psychological Science*, *12*, 371–378.

10520

Test Name: EXERCISE-INDUCED FEELING INVENTORY

Purpose: To assess the feeling states associated with the stimulus properties of the exercise environment.

Number of Items: 12

Format: Responses are made on a 5-point scale ranging from 0 (*do not feel*) to 4 (*feel very strongly*).

Reliability: Alpha coefficients ranged from .70 to .85.

Author: Matsouka, O., et al.

Article: Mood alterations following an indoor and outdoor exercise program in healthy elderly women.

Journal: *Perceptual and Motor Skills*, June 2005, *100*, Part 1, 707–715.

Related Research: Gauvin, L., & Rejeski, J. W. (1993). The Exercise-Induced Feeling Inventory: Development and initial validation. *Journal of Sport and Exercise Psychology*, *15*, 403–423.

10521

Test Name: EXISTENTIAL INSECURITY SCALE

Purpose: To measure ontological insecurity.

Number of Items: 6

Reliability: Coefficient alpha was .62.

Validity: Correlations with other variables ranged from −.25 to .34.

Author: Lester, D., and Abdel-Khalek, A.

Article: Reliability of a scale to measure existential insecurity.

Journal: *Perceptual and Motor Skills*, June 2003, *96*, Part 2, 1152.

Related Research: Lester, D. (1992). Ontological insecurity and fear of death. *Psychological Reports*, *71*, 1178.

10522

Test Name: EXPERIENCES IN CLOSE RELATIONSHIPS SCALE

Purpose: To measure avoidance and anxiety.

Number of Items: 36

Format: Includes two subscales: Avoidance and Anxiety. Responses are made on a 7-point Likert-type scale ranging from 1 (*disagree strongly*) to 7 (*agree strongly*).

Reliability: Alpha coefficients were .91 and .94. Test–retest (3 weeks) reliability was .70.

Author: Mallinckrodt, B., and Weng, C.-C.

Article: Qualitative methods for verifying semantic equivalence of translated research instruments: A Chinese version of the Experiences in Close Relationships Scale.

Journal: *Journal of Counseling Psychology*, July 2004, *51*, 368–379.

Related Research: Brennan, K. A., et al. (1998). Self-report measurement of adult attachments: An integrative overview. In J. A. Simpson & W. S. Rholes (Eds.), *Attachment theory and close relationships* (pp. 46–76). New York: Guilford Press.

10523

Test Name: EXTENDED LIFE ORIENTATION TEST

Purpose: To measure optimism and pessimism.

Number of Items: 20

Format: Includes two scales: Optimism and Pessimism. Responses are made on a 5-point Likert-type scale ranging from 1 (*strongly disagree*) to 5 (*strongly agree*). Examples are given.

Reliability: Reliability coefficients ranged from .67 to .93.

Validity: Correlations with other variables ranged from −.44 to .56.

Author: Hardin, E. E., and Leong, F. T. L.

Article: Optimism and pessimism as mediators of the relations between self-discrepancies and distress among Asian and European Americans.

Journal: *Journal of Counseling Psychology*, January 2005, *52*, 25–35.

Related Research: Chang, E. C., et al. (1997). Optimism and pessimism as partially independent constructs: Relationship to positive and negative affectivity and psychological well-being. *Personality and Individual Differences*, *23*, 433–440.

10524

Test Name: EXTERNALIZING PROBLEMS SCALE

Purpose: To measure externalizing problems.

Number of Items: 24

Format: Responses are made on a 5-point scale ranging from 1 (*never*) to 5 (*almost every day*). Examples are given.

Reliability: Alpha coefficients ranged from .77 to .90.

Author: Galambos, N. L., et al.

Article: Parents do matter: Trajectories of change in

externalizing and internalizing problems in early adolescence.

Journal: *Child Development*, March/April 2003, *74*, 578–594.

Related Research: Brown, B. B., et al. (1986). Perceptions of peer pressure, peer conformity dispositions, and self-reported behavior among adolescents. *Developmental Psychology*, *22*, 521–530. Kaplan, H. B. (1978). Deviant behavior and self-enhancement in adolescence. *Journal of Youth and Adolescence*, *7*, 253–277.

10525

Test Name: FEAR AND CONCERN ABOUT AIDS SCALE

Purpose: To measure fear and concern about AIDS.

Number of Items: 9

Format: Response categories are anchored by 1 (*disagree strongly*) and 5 (*agree strongly*). All items are presented.

Reliability: Alpha was .64.

Validity: Correlations with other variables ranged from .05 to .26.

Author: Thompson, K. L., et al.

Article: Predictors for sexual behaviors related to AIDS transmission.

Journal: *Psychological Reports*, February 2001, *88*, 51–67.

Related Research: Some items were adapted with permission from other scales by Gray, L. A. (1993). Unpublished manuscript [Untitled], Oregon State University Counselor Education Program.

10526

Test Name: FEAR AND KNOWLEDGE OF ALZHEIMER'S DISEASE

Purpose: To measure fear and knowledge of Alzheimer's disease.

Number of Items: 40

Time Required: 10 minutes

Format: Five-point Likert scales are used.

Validity: Correlations with other variables ranged from −.27 to .27.

Author: Laforce, R., Jr., and McLean, S.

Article: Knowledge and fear of developing Alzheimer's disease in a sample of healthy adults.

Journal: *Psychological Reports*, February 2005, *96*, 204–206.

10527

Test Name: FEAR AROUSAL SCALE

Purpose: To assess fear, worry, and discomfort.

Number of Items: 4

Format: Subjects rank written scenarios on scales ranging from 1 (*not at all*) to 9 (*very much*).

Reliability: Coefficient alpha was .94.

Author: Ruiter, R. A. C., et al.

Article: Strengthening the persuasive impact of fear appeals: The role of action framing.

Journal: *The Journal of Social Psychology*, June 2003, *143*, 397–400.

Related Research: Mewborn, C. R., & Rogers, R. W. (1979). Effects of threatening and reassuring components of fear appeals on physiological and verbal measures of emotion and attitudes. *Journal of Experimental Social Psychology*, *15*, 242–253.

10528

Test Name: FEAR OF COMMITMENT SCALE

Purpose: To measure the generalized fear of making a career decision.

Number of Items: 40

Format: Responses are made on a 6-point Likert scale ranging from 1 (*strongly disagree*) to 6 (*strongly agree*). Examples are given.

Reliability: Internal consistencies were .91 and .93.

Validity: Correlations with other variables ranged from −.54 to .48.

Author: Wolfe, J. B., and Betz, N. E.

Article: The relationship of attachment variables to career decision-making self-efficacy and fear of commitment.

Journal: *The Career Development Quarterly*, June 2004, *52*, 363–369.

Related Research: Serling, D. A., & Betz, N. E. (1990). Development and evaluation of a measure of fear of commitment. *Journal of Counseling Psychology, 37*, 91–97.

10529

Test Name: FEAR OF FAILURE SCALE

Purpose: To measure fear of failure.

Number of Items: 27

Format: Scales range from 1 (*disagree*) to 5 (*agree*). Sample items are presented.

Reliability: Coefficient alpha was .83.

Author: Gable, S. L., et al.

Article: Evidence for bivariate systems: An empirical test of appetition and aversion across domains.

Journal: *Journal of Research in Personality*, October 2003, *37*, 349–372.

Related Research: Herman, W. (1990). Fear of failure as a distinctive personality trait measure of test anxiety. *Journal of Research and Development in Education, 23*, 180–185.

10530

Test Name: FEAR OF INTIMACY SCALE

Purpose: To measure fear of intimacy.

Number of Items: 35

Format: Responses are made on a 5-point scale ranging from 1 (*not at all characteristic of me*) to 5 (*extremely characteristic of me*).

Reliability: Alpha coefficients were .92 and .93. Test–retest (1 month) reliability was .89.

Author: Mallinckrodt, B., and Weng, C.-C.

Article: Quantitative methods for verifying semantic equivalence of translated research instruments: A Chinese version of the experiences in close relationships scale.

Journal: *Journal of Counseling Psychology*, July 2004, *51*, 368–379.

Related Research: Descutner, C. J., & Thelen, M. H. (1991). Development and validation of a fear-of-intimacy scale. *Psychological Assessment, 3*, 218–225.

10531

Test Name: FEAR OF NEGATIVE EVALUATION SCALE

Purpose: To assess the degree to which people experience apprehension at the prospect of being evaluated negatively.

Number of Items: 12

Format: Responses are made on a 5-point scale ranging from 1 (*not at all characteristic of me*) to 5 (*extremely characteristic*). An example is presented.

Reliability: Internal consistency was .90. Test–retest (4 weeks) reliability was .75.

Validity: Correlations with the Perfectionism Inventory Scales ranged from .16 to .83.

Author: Hill, R. W., et al.

Article: A new measure of perfectionism: The Perfectionism Inventory.

Journal: *Journal of Personality Assessment*, February 2004, *82*, 80–91.

Related Research: Leary, M. R. (1983). A brief version of the Fear of Negative Evaluation Scale. *Personality and Social Psychology Bulletin, 9*, 371–375.

10532

Test Name: FEAR OF NEGATIVE EVALUATION SCALE

Purpose: To assess expectations of being evaluated negatively.

Number of Items: 30

Format: A true–false format is used.

Reliability: Alpha coefficients ranged from .94 to .96. Test–retest (1 month) reliabilities ranged from .78 to .94.

Validity: Correlations with other variables ranged from .27 to .55.

Author: Hopko, D. R.

Article: Confirmatory factor analysis of the Math Anxiety Rating Scale—Revised.

Journal: *Educational and Psychological Measurement*, April 2003, *63*, 336–351.

Related Research: Watson, D., & Friend, R. (1969). Measurement of social–evaluative anxiety. *Journal of Consulting and Clinical Psychology, 33*, 448–457.

10533

Test Name: FEAR OF NEGATIVE EVALUATION SCALE—REVISED

Purpose: To measure apprehension over others' evaluations, distress over such evaluations, and expectations of negative evaluations.

Number of Items: 30

Format: Scales range from 0 (*not at all true of me*) to 4 (*very true of me*). Sample items are presented.

Reliability: Reliability coefficients ranged from .92 to .94.

Validity: Correlations with other variables ranged from −.50 to .32.

Author: Boatwright, K. J., and Egidio, R. K.

Article: Psychological predictors of college women's leadership aspirations.

Journal: *Journal of College Student Development*, September/October 2003, *44*, 653–669.

Related Research: Watson, D., & Friend, R. (1969). Measurement of social–evaluative anxiety. *Journal of Consulting and Clinical Psychology, 33,* 448–457.

10534

Test Name: FEAR QUESTIONNAIRE

Purpose: To assess degree of fear and avoidance of specific fears.

Number of Items: 17

Format: Nine-point scales are used.

Reliability: Coefficient alpha was .83.

Author: Weertman, A., et al.

Article: Influences of beliefs and personality disorders on treatment outcome in anxiety patients.

Journal: *Journal of Consulting and Clinical Psychology*, October 2005, *73*, 936–944.

Related Research: Marks, I. M., & Mathews, A. M. (1979). Brief standard self-rating scale for phobic patients. *Behavior Research and Therapy, 17,* 263–267.

10535

Test Name: FEAR SURVEY FOR CHILDREN II—IRANIAN VERSION

Purpose: To measure the intensity and prevalence of fears (from death, danger, unknown factors, failure, animals, and stress).

Number of Items: 53

Format: Scales range from 1 (*I do not fear*) to 3 (*I fear a lot*). A sample item is presented.

Reliability: Coefficient alpha was .68.

Author: Mazidi, M.

Article: Intensity and prevalence of current fears among Iranian university students.

Journal: *Psychological Reports*, February 2005, *96*, 190–196.

Related Research: King, N. J., & Gullone, E. (1993). The fears of youth in the 1990s: Contemporary normative data. *The Journal of Genetic Psychology, 154,* 137–153.

10536

Test Name: FLIGHT ANXIETY MODALITY SCALE

Purpose: To assess fear of flying.

Number of Items: 18

Format: Responses are made on a 5-point scale ranging from 0 (*no reaction*) to 4 (*very intense reaction*).

Reliability: Coefficient alpha was .95.

Validity: Correlations with other variables ranged from −.16 to .44.

Author: Bricker, J. B.

Article: Development and evaluation of the Air Travel Stress Scale.

Journal: *Journal of Counseling Psychology*, October 2005, *52*, 615–628.

Related Research: Van Gerwen, L. J., et al. (1999). Construction and psychometric characteristics of two self-report questionnaires for the assessment of fear of flying. *Psychological Assessment, 11,* 146–158.

10537

Test Name: FLIGHT ANXIETY SITUATIONS QUESTIONNAIRE

Purpose: To measure anxiety experienced in different flight-related situations.

Number of Items: 32

Format: Five-point Likert scales are used.

Reliability: Alpha coefficients ranged from .88 to .87. Test–retest reliabilities ranged from .90 to .92.

Author: Maltby, N., et al.

Article: Virtual reality exposure therapy for the treatment of fear of flying: A controlled investigation.

Journal: *Journal of Consulting and Clinical Psychology*, October 2002, *70*, 1112–1118.

Related Research: Van Gerwen, L. J., et al. (1999). Construction and psychometric characteristics of two self-report questionnaires for the assessment of fear of flying. *Psychological Assessment, 11,* 146–148.

10538

Test Name: FOCUSED EMOTIONS SCALES

Purpose: To assess inward- and outward-focused emotions.

Number of Items: 5

Format: Scales range from 1 (*strongly disagree*) to 5 (*strongly agree*). Sample items are presented.

Reliability: Alpha coefficients ranged from .64 to .76.

Author: Barclay, L. J., et al.

Article: Exploring the role of emotions in injustice perceptions and retaliation.

Journal: *Journal of Applied Psychology*, July 2005, *90*, 629–643.

Related Research: Weiss, H. M., et al. (1999). Effects of justice conditions on discrete emotions.

Journal of Applied Psychology, 84, 786–794.

10539

Test Name: FOOD NEOPHOBIA SCALE

Purpose: To measure food neophobia.

Number of Items: 10

Format: Responses are made on a 7-point rating scale.

Reliability: Alpha coefficients were .71 and .88. Test–retest reliabilities ranged from .80 to .90.

Author: Shariff, Z. M., and Yasin, Z. M.

Article: Correlates of Children's Eating Attitude Test scores among primary school children.

Journal: *Perceptual and Motor Skills,* April 2005, *100,* 463–472.

Related Research: Pliner, P., & Hobden, K. (1992). Development of a scale to measure the trait neophobia in humans. *Appetite, 19,* 105–120.

10540

Test Name: FOUR-DIMENSIONAL MOOD SCALE

Purpose: To measure four dimensions of dispositional mood.

Number of Items: 20

Format: Includes four areas: positive energy, tiredness, negative activation, and relaxation. Responses are made on a 5-point scale ranging from 1 (*slightly or not at all*) to 5 (*definitely*).

Reliability: Alpha coefficients were .83 and .85.

Validity: Correlations with other variables ranged from −.53 to .75.

Author: Huelsman, T. J., et al.

Article: Measurement of dispositional affect: Construct validity and convergence with a circumplex model of affect.

Journal: *Educational and Psychological Measurement,* August 2003, *63,* 655–673.

Related Research: Huelsman, T. J., et al. (1998). Scales to measure four dimensions of dispositional mood: Positive energy, tiredness, negative activation, and relaxation. *Educational and Psychological Measurement, 58,* 804–819.

10541

Test Name: FREQUENCY OF SELF-REINFORCEMENT QUESTIONNAIRE

Purpose: To measure participants' ability to encourage, support, and value their sense of self-worth.

Number of Items: 30

Format: A true–false format is used. An example is given.

Reliability: Alpha coefficients were .79 and .87.

Author: Wei, M., et al.

Article: Adult attachment, depressive symptoms, and validation from self versus others.

Journal: *Journal of Counseling Psychology,* July 2005, *52,* 368–377.

Related Research: Heiby, E. M. (1983). Assessment of frequency of self-reinforcement. *Journal of Personality and Social Psychology, 44,* 1304–1307.

10542

Test Name: FUNCTIONAL INDEPENDENCE MEASURE— MODIFIED

Purpose: To assess self-care, sphincter control, mobility, and locomotion.

Number of Items: 13

Format: Items are rated on a 7-point scale.

Reliability: Median interrater reliability was .95. Median test–retest reliability was .95.

Validity: Correlations with other variables ranged from −.21 to .35 (*N* = 102).

Author: Waldrop, D., et al.

Article: Self-efficacy, optimism, health competence, and recovery from orthopedic surgery.

Journal: *Journal of Counseling Psychology,* April 2001, *48,* 233–238.

Related Research: Ottenbacher, K. J., et al. (1996). The reliability of the Functional Independence Measure: A quantitative review. *Archives of Physical Medicine and Rehabilitation, 77,* 1226–1232.

10543

Test Name: GAY-RELATED STRESSFUL LIFE EVENTS MEASURE

Purpose: To measure stressful events related to homosexuality.

Number of Items: 12

Format: A checklist format is used. All items are presented.

Validity: Correlations with other variables ranged from −.09 to .30.

Author: Rosario, M., et al.

Article: Gay-related stress and emotional distress among gay, lesbian, and bisexual youths: A longitudinal examination.

Journal: *Journal of Consulting and Clinical Psychology,* August 2002, *70,* 967–975.

Related Research: Rosario, M., et al. (1996). Gay-related stress and its correlates among gay and bisexual adolescents of predominately Black and Hispanic background. *Journal of Community Psychology, 24,* 136–159.

10544

Test Name: GENERAL FUNCTIONING SCALE—ARABIC VERSION

Purpose: To assess general family health and pathology.

Number of Items: 12

Format: Four-point scales are used.

Reliability: Coefficient alpha was .63.

Author: Al-Krenawi, A., et al.

Article: Mental health aspects of Arab-Israeli adolescents from polygamous versus monogamous families.

Journal: *The Journal of Social Psychology*, August 2002, *142*, 446–460.

Related Research: Epstein, N. B., et al. (1983). The McMaster Family Assessment Device. *Journal of Marital and Family Therapy, 9,* 171–180.

10545

Test Name: GENERAL HEALTH QUESTIONNAIRE

Purpose: To measure general health.

Number of Items: 12

Format: Four-point scales are used.

Reliability: Alpha was .75.

Validity: Correlations with other variables ranged from −.39 to .70.

Author: Katerndahl, D. A., et al.

Article: Psychometric assessment of measures of psychological symptoms, functional status, life events and context for low income Hispanic patients in a primary care setting.

Journal: *Psychological Reports*, December 2002, *91*, Part 2, 1121–1128.

Related Research: Goldberg, D. P., & Williams, P. (1988). *Users guide to the General Health Questionnaire.* London, England: NFER.

10546

Test Name: GENERAL HEALTH QUESTIONNAIRE (GHQ-12)—ARABIC VERSION

Purpose: To measure general health.

Number of Items: 12

Reliability: Cronbach's alpha was .86.

Validity: The best balance was achieved with sensitivity at .88 and specificity at .84.

Author: Daradkeh, T. K., et al.

Article: Reliability, validity, and factor structure of the Arabic version of the 12-item General Health Questionnaire.

Journal: *Psychological Reports*, August 2001, *89*, 85–94.

Related Research: Goldberg, D. P., et al. (1997). The validity of two versions of the GHQ in the WHO study of mental illness in general health care. *Psychological Medicine, 27,* 191–197.

10547

Test Name: GENERAL HEALTH QUESTIONNAIRE—SHORT VERSION JAPANESE

Purpose: To assess general mental health.

Number of Items: 28

Format: A 4-point Likert format is used.

Reliability: Coefficient alpha was .92.

Author: Yukawa, S.

Article: Sex differences in relationships among anger, depression, and coping strategies of Japanese students.

Journal: *Psychological Reports*, December 2005, *97*, 769–776.

Related Research: Nakagawa, Y., & Daibo, I. (1985). [*Manual for the Japanese Version of the General Health Questionnaire GHQ*]. Tokyo, Japan: Nihon Bunka Kagaku sya.

10548

Test Name: GENERAL MENTAL HEALTH SCALE

Purpose: To measure feelings of distress and well-being among adults.

Number of Items: 5

Format: Rating scales are anchored by 1 (*none of the time*) and 6 (*all of the time*). Sample items are presented.

Reliability: Coefficient alpha was .81.

Validity: Correlations with other variables ranged from −.18 to .50.

Author: Razzino, B., et al.

Article: Central American adolescent acculturation and parental distress: Relationship to ratings of adolescent behavior problems.

Journal: *Psychological Reports*, June 2003, *92*, Part 2, 1255–1267.

Related Research: Ware, J., & Sherbourne, C. (1992). The MOS 36-Item Short-Form Health Survey (SF-36): I. Conceptual framework and item selection. *Medical Care, 30,* 473–483.

10549

Test Name: GENERAL SELF SCALE

Purpose: To measure satisfaction one has with oneself.

Number of Items: 8

Format: Response scales range from 1 (*false*) to 5 (*true*). A sample item is presented.

Reliability: Internal consistency reliabilities ranged from .81 to .84.

Validity: Correlations with other variables ranged from −.47 to .23.

Author: Annesi, J. J.

Article: Correlations of depression and total mood disturbance with physical activity and self-concept in preadolescents enrolled in an after-school exercise program.

Journal: *Psychological Reports*, June 2005, *96*, Part 2, 891–898.

Related Research: Marsh, H. W. (1990). *Self-description Questionnaire—I: Manual.* Sydney, Australia: University of Western Sydney.

10550

Test Name: GENERAL WELL-BEING SCHEDULE

Purpose: To measure subjective feelings of psychological well-being.

Number of Items: 18

Format: Six- and 10-point scales are used. All items are presented.

Reliability: Internal consistency measures ranged from .70 and .93.

Validity: Correlations with other variables ranged from −.74 to .43.

Author: Leonardson, G. R., et al.

Article: Validity and reliability of the General Well-Being Schedule with Northern Plains American Indians diagnosed with Type 2 Diabetes Mellitus.

Journal: *Psychological Reports*, August 2003, *93*, 49–58.

Related Research: Poston, W. S., et al. (1998). Evaluation of the factor structure of psychometric characteristics of the General Well-Being Schedule (GWB) with Mexican American women. *Women & Health*, 27(3), 51–64.

10551

Test Name: GENERALIZED CONTENTMENT SCALE

Purpose: To measure nonpsychotic depression.

Number of Items: 25

Format: Five-point scales are used. A sample item is presented.

Reliability: Coefficient alpha was .90.

Validity: Correlations with other variables ranged from −.30 to .65.

Author: Shahar, G.

Article: Maternal personality and distress as predictors of child neglect.

Journal: *Journal of Research in Personality*, December 2001, *35*, 537–545.

Related Research: Hudson, W. W. (1982). *The Clinical Measurement Package: A field manual.* Homewood, IL: Dorsey.

10552

Test Name: GENERALIZED EXPECTANCY FOR SUCCESS SCALE—REVISED

Purpose: To measure an individual's expectancy to attain desired goals.

Number of Items: 25

Format: Responses are made on a 5-point scale ranging from 1 (*highly improbable*) to 5 (*highly probable*).

Reliability: Coefficient alpha was .94. Test–retest (6 weeks) reliability was .69. Split-half reliability was .92.

Validity: Correlations with other variables ranged from −.52 to .66.

Author: Steed, L. G.

Article: A psychometric comparison of four measures of hope and optimism.

Journal: *Educational and Psychological Measurement*, June 2002, *62*, 466–482.

Related Research: Fibel, B., & Hale, W. D. (1978). The Generalized Expectancy for Success Scale—A new measure. *Journal of Consulting and Clinical Psychology, 46*, 924–931.

10553

Test Name: GENERIC QUESTIONNAIRE OF EVALUATION OF QUALITY OF LIFE

Purpose: To evaluate a person's self-perception of health and quality of life.

Number of Items: 36

Format: Includes seven subscales: Functional Capacity, Physical Aspects, Pain, General State of Health, Vitality, Emotional Aspects, and Mental Health.

Reliability: Coefficient alpha was .71. Split-half reliability was .74. Guttman split-half was .69.

Author: Rosa, D. A., et al.

Article: Mood changes after maximal exercise testing in subjects with symptoms of exercise dependence.

Journal: *Perceptual and Motor Skills*, August 2004, *99*, 341–353.

Related Research: Ware, J. E., & Sherbourne, C. D. (1992). The MOS 36-Item Short-Form Health Survey (SF-36): I. Conceptual frame work and item selection. *Medical Care, 30*, 473–483.

10554

Test Name: GERIATRIC DEPRESSION SCALE

Purpose: To provide an indicator of depression in older adults.

Number of Items: 4-, 10-, 15-, 30-item versions.

Format: A yes–no format is used.

Reliability: Mean reliability coefficients for the four versions ranged from .74 to .88.

Author: Kieffer, K. M., and Reese, R. J.

Article: A reliability generalization study of the Geriatric Depression Scale.

Journal: *Educational and Psychological Measurement*, December 2002, *62*(6), 969–994.

Related Research: Brink, T. L., et al. (1982). Screening test for geriatric depression. *Clinical Gerontologist*, 1, 37–43.

10555

Test Name: GERIATRIC DEPRESSION SCALE—SHORT FORM

Purpose: To assess depressive symptoms.

Number of Items: 15

Reliability: Coefficient alpha was .94.

Validity: Correlation with the Beck Depression Inventory was .86.

Author: Cameron, E. M., and Ferraro, F. R.

Article: Body satisfaction in college women after brief exposure to magazine images.

Journal: *Perceptual and Motor Skills*, June 2004, *98*, Part 1, 1093–1099.

Related Research: Ferraro, F. R., & Chelminski, I. (1996). Preliminary normative data on the Geriatric Depression Scale—Short Form (GDS–SF) in a young adult sample. *Journal of Clinical Psychology*, *52*, 443–447.

10556

Test Name: GOAL DISRUPTION/BEHAVIORAL INTERFERENCE SCALE

Purpose: To measure experiences and reactions to the 9/11 attacks.

Number of Items: 7

Format: Scales range from 1 (*strongly disagree*) to 7 (*strongly agree*). All items are presented.

Reliability: Alpha coefficients ranged from .81 to .88 across subscales.

Validity: Correlations with other variables ranged from –.03 to .18.

Author: MacGeorge, E. L., et al.

Article: Stress, social support, and health among college students after September 11, 2001.

Journal: *Journal of College Student Development*, November/December 2004, *45*, 655–670.

10557

Test Name: GOLDFARB FEAR OF FAT SCALE

Purpose: To assess subjects' concern with weight gain.

Number of Items: 10

Format: Responses are made on a 4-point scale ranging from 1 (*very untrue*) to 4 (*very true*). An example is given.

Reliability: Coefficient alpha was .85.

Author: Cameron, E. M., and Ferraro, F. R.

Article: Body satisfaction in college women after brief exposure to magazine images.

Journal: *Perceptual and Motor Skills*, June 2004, *98*, Part 1, 1093–1099.

Related Research: Goldfarb, L. A., et al. (1985). The Goldfarb Fear of Fat Scale. *Journal of Personality Assessment*, *49*, 329–332.

10558

Test Name: GRIEF PROCESSING AND GRIEF AVOIDANCE SCALES

Purpose: To measure the frequency of grief processing and grief avoidance with family and friends.

Number of Items: 20

Format: Scales range from 1 (*almost never*) to 5 (*almost constantly*). Sample items are presented.

Reliability: Alpha coefficients ranged from .62 to .97.

Validity: Correlations between processing and avoidance ranged from –.04 to –.02.

Author: Bonanno, G. A., et al.

Article: Grief processing and deliberate grief avoidance: A prospective comparison of bereaved spouses and parents in the United States and the People's Republic of China.

Journal: *Journal of Consulting and Clinical Psychology*, February 2005, *73*, 86–98.

10559

Test Name: GROSSMAN–COLE DEPRESSION INVENTORY

Purpose: To measure depression.

Number of Items: 19

Format: Response scales range from 1 (*not at all*) to 5 (*all of the day*). All items are presented.

Reliability: Coefficient alpha was .95.

Validity: Correlation with Beck Depression Inventory was .73.

Author: Cole, J. C., et al.

Article: Multimethod validation of the Beck Depression Inventory—II and Grossman–Cole Depression Inventory with an inpatient sample.

Journal: *Psychological Reports*, December 2003, *93*, Part 2, 1115–1129.

10560

Test Name: GROUP PERSONALITY PROJECTIVE TEST—ARABIC VERSION

Purpose: To distinguish between normal and neuropsychiatrically maladjusted individuals.

Number of Items: 90

Format: Subjects respond to drawing by selecting among

alternatives presented as multiple choice answers.

Reliability: Coefficient alpha was .86.

Author: Al-Musawi, N. M.

Article: Validation of the Arabic Version of the Group Personality Projective Test among university students in Bahrain.

Journal: *Psychological Reports,* April 2003, *92,* 389–392.

Related Research: Cassel, R. N., & Kahn, T. C. (1961). The Group Personality Projective Test. *Psychological Reports, 8,* 23–41.

10561

Test Name: HAMILTON ANXIETY RATING SCALE

Purpose: To assess state anxiety by structured interview.

Number of Items: 14

Reliability: Interrater reliability was .81.

Validity: Correlations with other variables ranged from .32 to .72.

Author: Wetherell, J. L., and Gatz, M.

Article: The Beck Anxiety Inventory in older adults with generalized anxiety disorder.

Journal: *Journal of Psychopathology and Behavioral Assessment,* March 2005, *27,* 17–24.

Related Research: Hamilton, M. (1959). The assessment of state anxiety by rating. *British Journal of Medical Psychiatry, 32,* 50–55.

10562

Test Name: HAMILTON DEPRESSION RATING SCALE

Purpose: To measure by structured interview.

Number of items: 17

Reliability: Interrater reliability was .88.

Validity: Correlations with other variables ranged from .39 to .51.

Author: Wetherell, J. L., and Gatz, M.

Article: The Beck Anxiety Inventory in older adults with generalized anxiety disorder.

Journal: *Journal of Psychopathology and Behavioral Assessment,* March 2005, *27,* 17–24.

Related research: Hamilton, M. (1960). A rating scale for depression. *Journal of Neurology, Neurosurgery, and Psychiatry, 23,* 56–62.

10563

Test Name: HAMILTON RATING SCALE FOR DEPRESSION—MODIFIED

Purpose: To assess severity of depression symptoms.

Number of Items: 17

Format: Scales range from 0 (*absent*) to 4 (*severe*).

Reliability: Coefficient alpha was .79.

Validity: Correlations with other variables ranged from −.36 to .60.

Author: Meyer, B.

Article: Coping with severe mental illness: Relations of the brief COPE with symptoms, functioning, and well-being.

Journal: *Journal of Psychopathology and Behavioral Assessment,* December 2001, *23,* 265–277.

Related Research: Miller, I. W., et al. (1985). The modified Hamilton Rating Scale for Depression: Reliability and validity. *Psychiatry Research, 14,* 131–142.

10564

Test Name: HAPPINESS SCALE

Purpose: To measure overall life happiness.

Number of Items: 3

Format: Responses are made on a 5-point scale. All items are presented.

Reliability: Coefficient alpha was .72.

Validity: Correlations with other variables ranged from .37 to .70.

Author: Mueller, D. J., and Kim, K.

Article: The Tenacious Goal Pursuit and Flexible Goal Adjustment Scales: Examination of their validity.

Journal: *Educational and Psychological Measurement,* February 2004, *64,* 120–142.

10565

Test Name: HASSLES AND UPLIFTS SCALE—SHORT FORM

Purpose: To measure daily hassles and uplifts.

Number of Items: 20

Format: Scales are anchored by 1 (*somewhat severe*) and 3 (*extremely severe*).

Reliability: Alpha coefficients were .84 (hassles) and .90 (uplifts).

Validity: Correlations with other variables ranged from −.40 to .43.

Author: Katerndahl, D. A., et al.

Article: Psychometric assessment of measures of psychological symptoms, functional status, life events and context for low income Hispanic patients in a primary care setting.

Journal: *Psychological Reports,* December 2002, *91,* Part 2, 1121–1128.

Related Research: Kanner, A., et al. (1981). Comparison of two modes of stress measurement: Daily hassles and uplifts versus life events. *Journal of Behavioral Medicine, 4,* 1–39.

10566

Test Name: HASSLES SCALE

Purpose: To assess interpersonal hassles and achievement hassles.

Number of Items: 53

Format: Includes two subscales: Interpersonal Hassles (social commitments) and Achievement Hassles (workload). Responses are either 0 (*have not experienced the hassle*) or 1 (*have experienced the hassle*).

Reliability: Alpha coefficients ranged from .70 to .90.

Validity: Correlations with other variables ranged from −.08 to .50.

Author: Sherry, S. B., et al.

Article: Perfectionism dimensions, perfectionistic attitudes, dependent attitudes, and depression in psychiatric patients and university students.

Journal: *Journal of Counseling Psychology*, July 2003, *50*, 373–386.

Related Research: DeLongis, A., et al. (1988). The impact of daily stress on health and mood: Psychological and social resources as mediators. *Journal of Personality and Social Psychology*, *54*, 486–495.

10567

Test Name: HASSLES SCALE

Purpose: To measure the number and severity of hassles experienced in a specified period of time.

Number of Items: 117

Format: Respondents rate each hassle they experience on a 3-point scale ranging from 1 (*somewhat*) to 3 (*severe*).

Reliability: Test–retest reliabilities were .79 (frequency) and .48 (intensity).

Author: Ziegler, D. J., and Leslie, Y. E.

Article: A test of the ABC Model underlying rational emotive behavior therapy.

Journal: *Psychological Reports*, February 2003, *92*, 235–240.

Related Research: Kanner, A. D., et al. (1981). Comparison of two modes of stress measurement: Daily hassles and uplifts versus major life events. *Journal of Behavioral Medicine*, *4*, 1–39.

10568

Test Name: HEALTH PERCEPTIONS QUESTIONNAIRE—REVISED

Purpose: To measure self-perceptions of health among older Spanish speakers.

Number of Items: 24

Format: A yes–no format is used. All items are presented in English.

Reliability: Coefficient alpha was .91. Test–retest correlation (2 months) was .59.

Author: Beaman, P. E., et al.

Article: Validation of the Health Perceptions Questionnaire for an older Mexican population.

Journal: *Psychological Reports*, June 2003, *92*, Part 1, 723–734.

Related Research: McDowell, I., & Newell, C. (1996). *Measuring health: A guide to rating scales and questionnaires* (2nd ed.). Oxford, England: Oxford University Press.

10569

Test Name: HEALTH SCALE

Purpose: To measure physical well-being.

Number of Items: 14

Format: Scales range from 1 (*strongly agree*) to 7 (*strongly disagree*).

Reliability: Coefficient alpha was .84.

Author: LeBlanc, M. M., and Kelloway, E. K.

Article: Predictors and outcomes of workplace violence and aggression.

Journal: *Journal of Applied Psychology*, June 2002, *87*, 444–453.

Related Research: Schat, A. C., & Kelloway, E. K. (2000). The effect of perceived control on the outcomes of workplace aggression and violence. *Journal of Occupational Health Psychology*, *4*, 386–402.

10570

Test Name: HEALTH SURVEY SF-36—SPANISH VERSION

Purpose: To measure eight components relevant to health status and well-being.

Number of Items: 36

Reliability: Alpha coefficients ranged from .66 to .91.

Validity: Correlations with other variables ranged from −.36 to .42.

Author: Extremera, N., and Fernández-Berrocal, P.

Article: Relation of perceived emotional intelligence and health-related quality of life of middle-aged women.

Journal: *Psychological Reports*, August 2002, *91*, 47–59.

Related Research: Ware, J. E., & Sherbourne, C. D. (1992). The MOS 36-Item Short-Form Health Survey (SF-36): I. Conceptual framework and item selection. *Medical Care*, *30*, 473–483.

10571

Test Name: HEALTH SYMPTOMS SCALE

Purpose: To rate frequency of health symptoms.

Number of Items: 20

Format: Responses are made on a 4-point scale ranging from 1 (*rarely/none*) to 4 (*most/all*).

Reliability: Coefficient alpha was .90.

Validity: Correlations with other variables ranged from −.30 to .66.

Author: Chemers, M. M., et al.

Article: Academic self-efficacy and first-year college student performance and adjustment.

Journal: *Journal of Educational Psychology*, March 2001, *93*, 55–64.

10572

Test Name: HELPLESSNESS, HOPELESSNESS AND HAPLESSNESS INVENTORY

Purpose: To measure helplessness, hopelessness, and haplessness.

Number of Items: 12

Format: A Likert format is used. All items are presented.

Reliability: Cronbach alpha coefficients ranged from .63 to .87 across subscales.

Validity: Correlations with other variables ranged from −.31 to .47.

Author: Lester, D.

Article: An inventory to measure helplessness, hopelessness, and haplessness.

Journal: *Psychological Reports*, December 2001, *89*, 495–498.

Related Research: Beck, A. T., et al. (1974). The measurement of pessimism. *Journal of Consulting and Clinical Psychology, 42*, 861–865.

10573

Test Name: HELPLESSNESS SCALE

Purpose: To measure externally located helplessness and internally located helplessness.

Number of Items: 12

Format: All items are presented.

Reliability: Coefficient alpha was .87.

Validity: Correlations with other variables ranged from .30 to .65.

Author: Ozmet, J. M., and Lester, D.

Article: Helplessness, locus of control, and psychological health.

Journal: *The Journal of Social Psychology*, February 2001, *141*, 137–138.

Related Research: Abrahamson, L. Y., et al. (1978). Learned helplessness in humans. *Journal of Abnormal Psychology, 87*, 49–74.

10574

Test Name: HELPLESSNESS SCALE

Purpose: To assess the degree of helplessness.

Number of Items: 20

Format: Responses are made on a 5-point scale ranging from 1 (*absolutely true*) to 5 (*not true at all*). Examples are given.

Reliability: Coefficient alpha was .96.

Author: Ziegler, A., et al.

Article: Predictors of learned helplessness among average and mildly gifted girls and boys attending initial high school physics instruction in Germany.

Journal: *Gifted Child Quarterly*, Winter 2005, *49*, 7–18.

Related Research: Breitkopf, L. (1985). Die Hilflosigkeitsskala [The Helplessness Scale]. *Diagnostica, 1*, 324–332.

10575

Test Name: HELPLESSNESS SCALE IN DAILY LIFE

Purpose: To assess one's daily life helplessness.

Number of Items: 26

Format: Includes five factors: lack of self-esteem, self-distrust, lack of self-responsibility, negativity and passivity, and lack of will power. Responses are made on a 5-point scale ranging from 1 (*not at all*) to 5 (*very much so*).

Reliability: Alpha coefficients ranged from .69 to .82.

Author: Yasunaga, M., and Inomata, K.

Article: Factors associated with helplessness among Japanese collegiate swimmers.

Journal: *Perceptual and Motor Skills*, October 2004, *99*, 581–590.

Related Research: Aoyagi, H., & Kyoya, H. (1986). [The reconstruction of the helplessness scale and its reliability and validity]. *[The Bulletin of the Tachikawa Junior College]*, *19*, 25–29.

10576

Test Name: HIMH TRICHOTILLOMANIA SEVERITY AND IMPAIRMENT SCALES

Purpose: To assess severity and severity of impairment resulting from hair pulling.

Number of Items: 6

Format: Four-, 5- and 10-point scales are used. All items are described.

Reliability: Alpha coefficients ranged from .63 to .61.

Validity: Correlations with other variables ranged from .25 to .77.

Author: Diefenbach, G. J., et al.

Article: Assessment of Trichotillomania: A psychometric evaluation of hair-pulling scales.

Journal: *Journal of Psychopathology and Behavioral Assessment*, September 2005, *27*, 169–178.

Related Research: Goodman, W. K., et al. (1989). The Yale–Brown Obsessive–Compulsive Scale: I. Development, use and reliability. *Archives of General Psychiatry, 46*, 1006–1011.

10577

Test Name: HONG KONG ACUTE LOW BACK PAIN SCREENING QUESTIONNAIRE—CHINESE VERSION

Purpose: To assess low back pain.

Number of Items: 24

Format: Eleven-point Likert scales are used.

Reliability: Coefficient alpha was .88.

Validity: Correlations with other variables ranged from −.62 to .74.

Author: Chan, S. F., et al.

Article: Pilot assessment of pain of orthopaedic patients in Hong Kong.

Journal: *Psychological Reports,* April 2005, *96,* 527–532.

10578

Test Name: HOPE SCALE

Purpose: To measure the trait-like construct of hopefulness.

Number of Items: 12

Format: Includes two subscales: Agency and Pathways. Responses are made on a 4-point scale ranging from 1 (*definitely false*) to 4 (*definitely true*).

Reliability: Test–retest (3-, 8-, and 10-week intervals) ranged from .73 to .85. Internal consistency ranged from .73 to .79.

Validity: Correlations with other variables ranged from −.49 to .50.

Author: Huprich, S. K., and Frisch, M. B.

Article: The Depressive Personality Disorder Inventory and its relationship to quality of life, hopefulness, and optimism.

Journal: *Journal of Personality Assessment,* August 2004, *83,* 22–28.

Related Research: Snyder, C. R., et al. (1991). The will and the ways:

Development and validation of an individual-differences measure of hope. *Journal of Personality and Social Psychology, 60,* 570–585.

10579

Test Name: HOPELESSNESS SCALE

Purpose: To assess the degree to which individual's cognitive schemas are characterized by pessimistic expectations.

Number of Items: 20

Format: A true–false format is used.

Reliability: Alpha coefficients were .78 and .93.

Validity: Correlations with other variables were .60 and .74.

Author: Wei, M., et al.

Article: Perceived coping as a mediator between attachment and psychological distress: A structural equation modeling approach.

Journal: *Journal of Counseling Psychology,* October 2003, *50,* 438–447.

Related Research: Beck, A. T., et al. (1974). The measurement of pessimism: The Hopelessness Scale. *Journal of Consulting and Clinical Psychology, 42,* 861–865.

10580

Test Name: HOPELESSNESS SCALE FOR CHILDREN

Purpose: To measure attitude toward the future.

Number of Items: 17

Format: A true–false format is used.

Reliability: Internal consistency coefficients ranged from .70 to .97.

Author: Vera, E. M., et al.

Article: Conflict resolution styles, self-efficacy, self-control, and future orientation of urban adolescents.

Journal: *Professional School Counseling,* October 2004, *8*(1), 73–80.

Related Research: Kazdin, A. E., et al. (1986). The Hopelessness Scale for Children: Psychometric characteristics and concurrent validity. *Journal of Consulting and Clinical Psychology, 54,* 241–245.

10581

Test Name: HOPKINS SYMPTOM CHECKLIST

Purpose: To measure depressive symptoms.

Number of Items: 5

Format: Item anchors range from 1 (*not at all*) to 5 (*extremely*).

Reliability: Alpha coefficients ranged from .74 to .82.

Author: Brook, J. S., et al.

Article: Cigarette smoking and depressive symptoms: A longitudinal study of adolescents and young adults.

Journal: *Psychological Reports,* August 2004, *95,* 159–166.

Related Research: Lipman, R. S., et al. (1979). The Hopkins Symptom Checklist (HSCL). *Journal of Affective Disorders, 1,* 9–24.

10582

Test Name: HOPKINS SYMPTOM CHECKLIST

Purpose: To assess psychological symptoms.

Number of Items: 30

Format: Includes three subscales: Depression, Anxiety, and Somatization. Responses are made on a 5-point scale ranging from 1 (*not at all*) to 5 (*extremely*).

Reliability: Internal consistency reliability coefficients ranged from .77 to .88. Test–retest (1 week)

reliabilities estimates ranged from .75 to .82.

Author: Corning, A. F.

Article: Self-esteem as a moderator between perceived discrimination and psychological distress among women.

Journal: *Journal of Counseling Psychology*, January 2002, *49*, 117–126.

Related Research: Derogatis, L. R., et al. (1974). The Hopkins Symptom Checklist. In P. Pichot (Ed.), *Psychological Measurements in Psychopharmacology* (pp.79–110). Basil, Switzerland: Karger.

10583

Test Name: HOPKINS SYMPTOM CHECKLIST

Purpose: To assess a variety of psychological symptoms.

Number of Items: 58

Format: Responses are made on a 4-point scale ranging from 1 (*not at all*) to 4 (*extremely*). Examples are given.

Reliability: Alpha coefficients ranged from .84 to .95.

Validity: Correlations with other variables ranged from −.49 to .96.

Author: Lopez, F. G., et al.

Article: Adult attachment orientation and college student distress: Test of a mediational model.

Journal: *Journal of Counseling Psychology*, October 2002, *49*, 460–467.

Related Research: Derogatis, L. R., et al. (1974). The Hopkins Symptoms Checklist (HSCL): A self-report symptom inventory. *Behavioral Science, 19*, 1–15.

10584

Test Name: HOPKINS SYMPTOM CHECKLIST

Purpose: To measure psychological distress.

Number of Items: 21

Format: Responses are made on a 4-point scale ranging from 1 (*not at all*) to 4 (*extremely*).

Reliability: Corrected split-half reliability was .91. Coefficient alpha was .90.

Validity: Correlations with other variables ranged from −.41 to .39.

Author: Vogel, D. L., and Wester, S. R.

Article: To seek help or not to seek help: The risks of self-disclosure.

Journal: *Journal of Counseling Psychology*, July 2003, *50*, 351–361.

Related Research: Green, D. E., et al. (1988). Development and evaluation of a 21-item version of the Hopkins Symptom Checklist with New Zealand and United States respondents. *Australian Journal of Psychology, 40*, 61–70.

10585

Test Name: HOPKINS SYMPTOM CHECKLIST—CAMBODIAN VERSION

Purpose: To assess psychopathology.

Number of Items: 44

Format: Four-point scales range from *not at all* to *extremely*.

Validity: Correlations with other variables ranged from .01 to .76.

Author: Hinton, D., et al.

Article: The psychophysiology of orthostatic panic in Cambodian refugees attending a psychiatric clinic.

Journal: *Journal of Psychopathology and Behavioral Assessment*, March 2004, *26*, 1–13.

Related Research: Rickels, K., et al. (1976). The Hopkins Symptom Checklist: Assessing emotional

distress in obstetric-gynecological practice. *Primary Care, 3*, 751–764. Mollica, R., et al. (1987). Indochinese versions of the Hopkins Symptom Checklist: A screening instrument for the psychiatric care of refugees. *American Journal of Psychiatry, 144*, 497–500.

10586

Test Name: HOSPITAL ANXIETY AND DEPRESSION SCALE

Purpose: To measure depression and anxiety.

Number of Items: 14

Format: Includes two subscales: Anxiety and Depression. Responses are made on a 4-point scale ranging from 0 to 3. Examples are given.

Reliability: Alpha coefficients were .61 and .73.

Validity: Correlations with other variables ranged from −.53 to .29.

Author: Cassidy, C., et al.

Article: Perceived discrimination and psychological distress: The role of personal and ethnic self-esteem.

Journal: *Journal of Counseling Psychology*, July 2004, *51*, 329–339.

Related Research: Zigmond, A. S., & Snaith, R. P. (1983). The Hospital Anxiety and Depression Scale. *Acta Psyciatrica Scandinavica, 67*, 361–370.

10587

Test Name: HOSPITAL ANXIETY AND DEPRESSION SCALE— JAPANESE VERSION

Purpose: To measure anxiety and depression.

Number of Items: 14

Format: Four-point response scales.

Reliability: Alpha coefficients ranged from .71 to .76.

Validity: Correlations with other variables ranged from −.43 to −.07.

Author: Kitamura, T., et al.

Article: Ryff's Psychological Well-Being Inventory: Factorial structure and life history correlates among Japanese university students.

Journal: *Psychological Reports*, February 2004, *94*, 83–103.

Related Research: Zigmond, A. S., & Snaith, R. P. (1983). The Hospital Anxiety and Depression Scale. *Acta Psychiatrica Scandinavica, 67*, 361–370.

10588

Test Name: HOSTILE ATTRIBUTION SCALE

Purpose: To measure hostility attributions in frustrating situations.

Number of Items: 10

Format: The multiple-choice format of items is described. A sample item is presented.

Reliability: Coefficient alpha was .60. Test–retest reliability was .80.

Validity: Correlations with other variables ranged from −.19 to .30.

Author: Homant, R. J., & Kennedy, D. B.

Article: Hostile attribution in perceived justification of workplace aggression.

Journal: *Psychological Reports*, February 2003, *92*, 185–194.

10589

Test Name: HOW I DEAL WITH THINGS SCALE

Purpose: To measure coping strategies.

Number of Items: 30

Format: Rating scales range from 1 (*rarely*) to 5 (*usually*).

Reliability: Alpha coefficients ranged from .76 to .80 across subscales.

Validity: Correlations with other variables ranged from −.04 to .38.

Author: Merrill, L. L., et al.

Article: Child sexual abuse and number of sexual partners in young women: The role of abuse severity, coping style, and sexual functioning.

Journal: *Journal of Consulting and Clinical Psychology*, December 2003, *71*, 987–996.

Related Research: Merrill, L. L., et al. (2001). Predicting the impact of child sexual abuse on women: The role of abuse severity, parental support, and coping strategies. *Journal of Consulting and Clinical Psychology, 69*, 992–1006.

10590

Test Name: HUMOR STYLES QUESTIONNAIRE

Purpose: To measure the use of humor to enhance the self, enhance relationships with others, enhance the self at the expense of others, and enhance relationships at the expense of self.

Number of Items: 32

Format: Scales range from 1 (*totally disagree*) to 7 (*totally agree*). All items are presented.

Reliability: Alpha coefficients ranged from .77 to .81 across subscales.

Validity: Correlations between subscales ranged from −.01 to .33. Correlations with other humor measures ranged from −.41 to .65.

Author: Martin, R. A., et al.

Article: Individual differences in uses of humor and their relation to psychological well-being: Development of the Humor Styles Questionnaire.

Journal: *Journal of Research in Personality*, February 2003, *37*, 48–75.

10591

Test Name: HUNTER OPINIONS AND PERSONAL EXPECTATIONS SCALE

Purpose: To measure global personal hopefulness.

Number of Items: 20.

Format: Includes equal numbers of hope and despair items. Responses are made on a 5-point scale ranging from 0 (*not at all*) to 4 (*extremely well*).

Reliability: Alpha coefficients ranged from .90 to .92.

Validity: Correlations with other variables ranged from −.63 to .67.

Author: Steed, L. G.

Article: A psychometric comparison of form measures of hope and optimism.

Journal: *Educational and Psychological Measurement*, June 2002, *62*, 466–482

Related Research: Nunn, K. P., et al. (1996). The construction and characteristics of an instrument to measure personal hopefulness. *Psychological Medicine, 26*, 531–545.

10592

Test Name: HURRICANE STORM QUESTIONNAIRE

Purpose: To measure fear of storms in children.

Number of Items: 9

Format: Scales range from 1 (*no fear*) to 3 (*a lot of fear*).

Validity: Correlations with a general fear scale ranged from .45 to .78.

Author: Muris, P.

Article: The Koala Fear Questionnaire: Its relationship with fear of storms and hurricanes in 4–14 year old Antillean Children.

Journal: *Journal of Psychopathology and Behavioral Assessment*, September 2002, *24*, 145–150.

10593

Test Name: IDEAL BODY STEREOTYPE SCALE—REVISED

Purpose: To assess internalization of the thin-ideal stereotype.

Number of Items: 10

Format: Responses are made on a 5-point scale ranging from 1 (*strongly disagree*) to 5 (*strongly agree*). An example is given.

Reliability: Coefficient alpha was .89.

Validity: Correlations with other variables ranged from –.17 to .66.

Author: Tylka, T. L., and Subich, L. M.

Article: Examining a multidimensional model of eating disorder symptomatology among college women.

Journal: *Journal of Counseling Psychology*, July 2004, *51*, 314–328.

Related Research: Stice, E., et al. (1996). The dual pathway model differentiates bulimics, subclinical bulimics, and controls: Testing the continuity hypothesis. *Behavior Therapy, 27*, 531–549.

10594

Test Name: ILLNESS COGNITION QUESTIONNAIRE

Purpose: To assess the constructs of helplessness, acceptance, and perceived benefits in patients with chronic diseases.

Number of Items: 18

Format: Response scales range from 1 (*not at all*) to 4 (*completely*). All items are presented.

Reliability: Alpha coefficients ranged from .84 to .91.

Validity: Correlations with other variables ranged from –.54 to .64.

Author: Evers, A. W. M., et al.

Article: Beyond unfavorable thinking: The Illness Cognition Questionnaire for chronic diseases.

Journal: *Journal of Consulting and Clinical Psychology*, December 2001, *69*, 1026–1036.

10595

Test Name: IMAGINARY AUDIENCE SCALE

Purpose: To measure children's and adolescents' concerns about being evaluated by an imaginary audience.

Number of Items: 12

Format: Includes two subscales: Transient Self and Abiding Self. All items are presented.

Reliability: Alpha Coefficients ranged from .56 to .87.

Validity: Correlations with other variables ranged from –.46 to .65.

Author: Kelly, K. M., et al.

Article: Using the Imaginary Audience Scale as a measure of social anxiety in young adults.

Journal: *Educational and Psychological Measurement*, October 2002, *62*, 896–914.

Related Research: Elkind, D., & Bowen, R. (1979). Imaginary audience behavior in children and adolescents. *Developmental Psychology, 15*, 38–44.

10596

Test Name: IMPACT OF EVENTS SCALE

Purpose: To measure two symptoms of trauma: intrusion and avoidance.

Number of Items: 15

Format: Four-point scales are used.

Reliability: Alpha coefficients ranged from .78 to .86.

Validity: Correlations with other variables ranged from –.45 to .87.

Author: Gearon, J. S., et al.

Article: Preliminary reliability and validity of the clinician-administered PTSD scale for schizophrenia.

Journal: *Journal of Consulting and Clinical Psychology*, February 2004, *72*, 121–125.

Related Research: Horowitz, M. J., et al. (1979). Impact of event scale: A measure of subjective stress. *Psychosomatic Medicine, 41*, 209–218.

10597

Test Name: IMPAIRED CONTROL OVER MENTAL ACTIVITIES SCALE—PERSIAN VERSION

Purpose: To measure obsessive thinking.

Number of Items: 17

Format: Scales range from 0 (*not at all*) to 4 (*very much*).

Reliability: Coefficient alpha was .90.

Validity: Correlations with other variables ranged from –.25 to .47.

Author: Ghorbani, N., et al.

Article: Private self-consciousness factors: Relationships with need for cognition, locus of control, and obsessive thinking in Iran and the United States.

Journal: *The Journal of Social Psychology*, August 2004, *144*, 359–372.

Related Research: Sanavio, E. (1988). Obsessions and compulsions: The Padua Inventory. *Behavior Research and Therapy, 26*, 169–177.

10598

Test Name: INDEX OF MOOD DISTURBANCE

Purpose: To measure emotional distress.

Number of Items: 10

Format: Scales range from 1 (*not at all*) to 5 (*extremely*). All items are presented.

Reliability: Coefficient alpha was .87.

Author: Wimberly, S. R., et al.

Article: Perceived partner reactions to diagnosis and treatment of breast cancer: Impact on psychosocial and psychosexual adjustment.

Journal: *Journal of Consulting and Clinical Psychology*, April 2005, *73*, 300–311.

Related Research: Trunzo, J. J., & Pinto, B. M. (2003). Social support as a mediator of optimism and distress in breast cancer survivors. *Journal of Consulting and Clinical Psychology*, *71*, 805–811.

10599

Test Name: INDIVIDUAL COPING QUESTIONNAIRE

Purpose: To assess a variety of coping strategies.

Number of Items: 23

Format: Scales range from 1 (*never*) to 5 (*always*).

Reliability: Total alpha was .72. Subscale alphas ranged from .70 to .86.

Author: Bodenmann, G., et al.

Article: Differences in individual and dyadic coping among low and high depressed, partially remitted and nondepressed persons.

Journal: *Journal of Psychopathology and Behavioral Assessment*, June 2004, *26*, 75–85.

Related Research: Carver, C. S., et al. (1984). Assessing coping strategies: A theoretically based approach. *Journal of Personality and Social Psychology*, *56*, 267–283.

10600

Test Name: INHIBITION SCALE

Purpose: To measure inhibition in children by teacher observation.

Number of Items: 13

Format: Three-point scales are anchored by 0 (*no inhibition*) and 2 (*strong inhibition*). A sample item is presented.

Reliability: Alpha coefficients ranged from .84 to .89.

Validity: Correlations with other variables ranged from −.58 to .42.

Author: Koomen, H. M. Y., and Hoeksma, J. B.

Article: Regulation of emotional security by children after entry to special and regular kindergarten classes.

Journal: *Psychological Reports*, December 2003, *93*, Part 2, 1319–1334.

Related Research: Koomen, H. M. Y., et al. (1999). Scales for teachers' assessment of inhibition and security seeking in kindergarten children. *Psychological Reports*, *84*, 767–772.

10601

Test Name: INJURY/SENSITIVITY INDEX

Purpose: To measure the fear of illness and injury.

Number of Items: 11

Format: Scales range from 1 (*agree very little*) to 5 (*agree very much*). All items are presented.

Reliability: Coefficient alpha was .80. Subscale alphas ranged from .84 to .89.

Validity: Correlations with other variables ranged from .20 to .50.

Author: Carleton, R. N., et al.

Article: Fear of physical harm: Factor structure and psychometric properties of the Injury/Illness Sensitivity Index.

Journal: *Journal of Psychopathology and Behavioral Assessment*, December 2005, *27*, 235–242.

Related Research: Taylor, S. (1993). The structure of fundamental fears. *Journal of Behavior Therapy and Experimental Psychiatry*, *24*, 289–299.

10602

Test Name: INTERNALIZING PROBLEMS SCALE

Purpose: To measure depressive and anxious affect.

Number of Items: 11

Format: Responses are made on a 6-point scale ranging from 1 (*does not describe me at all*) to 6 (*describes me very well*). Sample items are given.

Reliability: Alpha coefficients ranged from .79 to .86.

Author: Galambos, N. L., et al.

Article: Parents do matter: Trajectories of change in externalizing and internalizing problems in early adolescence.

Journal: *Child Development*, March/April 2003, *74*, 578–594.

Related Research: Petersen, A. C., et al. (1984). A Self-Image Questionnaire for Young Adolescents (SIQYA): Reliability and validity studies. *Journal of Youth and Adolescence*, *13*, 93–111.

10603

Test Name: INVENTORY FOR DEPRESSIVE SYMPTOMATOLOGY

Purpose: To assess the severity of depressive symptoms by self report and clinician report.

Number of Items: 28

Reliability: Internal consistency reliabilities ranged from .85 to .93.

Validity: Correlations with other variables ranged from .61 to .78.

Author: Vittengl, J. R., and Clark, L. A.

Article: Validity of sudden gains in acute phase treatment of depression.

Journal: *Journal of Consulting and Clinical Psychology*, February 2005, *73*, 173–182.

Related Research: Rush, A. J., et al. (1996). The Inventory for Depressive Symptomatology (IDS): Preliminary findings. *Psychiatry Research, 18*, 65–87.

10604

Test Name: INVENTORY OF COMPLICATED GRIEF

Purpose: To measure grief reactions following the death of a child.

Number of Items: 19

Format: Scales range from 1 (*never*) to 5 (*always*). Sample items are presented.

Reliability: Coefficient alpha was .90. Test–retest reliability was .81.

Author: Meij, L. W., et al.

Article: Couples at risk following death of their child: Predictors of grief versus depression.

Journal: *Journal of Consulting and Clinical Psychology*, August 2005, *73*, 617–623.

Related Research: Prigerson, H. G., et al. (1995). Inventory of Complicated Grief: A scale to measure maladaptive symptoms of loss. *Psychiatry Research, 59*, 65–79.

10605

Test Name: INVENTORY OF INTERPERSONAL PROBLEMS— SHORT FORM

Purpose: To rate the severity of interpersonal problems.

Number of Items: 32

Format: Scales range from 0 (*not at all*) to 4 (*extremely*).

Validity: Correlations of mean item scores with the full scale ranged from .94 to .96.

Author: Lutz, W., et al.

Article: Predicting change for individual psychotherapy clients on the basis of their nearest neighbor.

Journal: *Journal of Consulting and Clinical Psychology*, October 2005, *73*, 904–913.

Related Research: Horowitz, L. M., et al. (1988). Inventory of Interpersonal Problems: Psychometric properties and clinical applications. *Journal of Consulting and Clinical Psychology, 56*, 885–892.

10606

Test Name: INVENTORY OF TRAUMATIC GRIEF

Purpose: To assess symptoms of traumatic grief.

Number of Items: 29

Format: Five-point scales are anchored by 1 (*never*) and 5 (*always*).

Reliability: Coefficient alpha was .94.

Validity: Correlations with other variables ranged from −.48 to −.40.

Author: Boelen, P. A., and van den Bout, J.

Article: Positive thinking in bereavement: Is it related to depression, anxiety, or grief symptomatology?

Journal: *Psychological Reports*, December 2002, *91*, Part 1, 857–863.

Related Research: Prigerson, H. G., & Jacobs, S. C. (2001). Traumatic grief as a distinct disorder: A rationale, consensus criteria, and a preliminary empirical test. In M. S. Stroebe et al. (Eds.), *Handbook of bereavement research: Consequences, coping, and care* (pp. 613–647). Washington, DC: American Psychological Association.

10607

Test Name: INVENTORY TO DIAGNOSE DEPRESSION— LIFETIME VERSION

Purpose: To assess depressive symptoms.

Number of Items: 22

Format: Item responses are anchored by 1 (*absence of depressive symptomatology*) and 5 (*extreme presence of depressive symptomatology*).

Reliability: Coefficient alpha was .92.

Author: Bates, G. W., and Lavery, B. J.

Article: Social problem-solving and vulnerability to depression in a clinical sample.

Journal: *Psychological Reports*, June 2003, *92*, Part 2, 1277–1283.

Related Research: Zimmerman, M., & Coryell, W. (1987). The Inventory to Diagnose Depression, Lifetime Version. *Acta Psychiatrica Scandinavica, 75*, 495–499.

10608

Test Name: IRRATIONAL BELIEFS INVENTORY

Purpose: To measure worrying, rigidity, demand for approval, problem avoidance, and emotional irresponsibility.

Number of Items: 50

Format: Item responses range from 1 (*strongly disagree*) to 5 (*strongly agree*).

Reliability: Alpha coefficients ranged from .71 to .84 across subscales.

Validity: Correlations between subscales ranged from .03 to .45.

Author: DuPlessis, M., et al.

Article: The Irrational Beliefs Inventory: Cross-cultural comparisons between South African and previously published Dutch and American samples.

Journal: *Psychological Reports,* December 2004, *95,* Part 1, 841–849.

Related Research: Koopmans, P. C., et al. (1994). The Irrational Beliefs Inventory (IBI): Development and psychometric evaluation. *European Journal of Psychological Assessment, 10,* 15–27.

10609

Test Name: IRRATIONAL BELIEFS INVENTORY

Purpose: To measure childlike fantasy, special privilege, unlovability, unrealistic isolation, catastrophisizing, and task exaggeration.

Number of Items: 24

Format: Scoring and administration procedures are fully described. All items are presented.

Reliability: Alpha coefficients ranged from .56 to 67.

Author: Smith, J. C., et al.

Article: Factor structure of the Smith Irrational Beliefs Inventory: Results of an analysis on six independent samples.

Journal: *Psychological Reports,* October 2004, *95,* 696–704.

Related Research: Smith, J. C. (2002). *Stress management: A comprehensive handbook of techniques and strategies.* New York: Springer Publishing Company.

10610

Test Name: IRRATIONAL HEALTH BELIEFS SCALE—HIV VERSION

Purpose: To assess the tendency to make illogical assumptions about one's health.

Number of Items: 7

Format: Vignettes are followed by 5-point scales ranging from 1 (*not at all like I would think*) to 5 (*almost exactly how I would think*).

Reliability: Coefficient alpha was .81.

Author: Benotsch, E. G., et al.

Article: HIV–AIDS patients' evaluation of health information on the internet: The digital divide and vulnerability to fraudulent claims.

Journal: *Journal of Consulting and Clinical Psychology,* December 2004, *72,* 1004–1011.

Related Research: Christensen, A. J., et al. (1999). Assessment of irrational health beliefs: Relation to health practices and medical regimen adherence. *Health Psychology, 18,* 169–176.

10611

Test Name: JUNIOR HIGH LIFE EXPERIENCES SURVEY— ADAPTED

Purpose: To measure stressful life events.

Number of Items: 25

Format: Items are scored either 1 or 0. Sample items are presented.

Validity: Correlations with other variables ranged from .10 to .52 ($n = 451$).

Author: Kim, K. J., et al.

Article: Reciprocal influences between stressful life events and adolescent internalizing and externalizing problems.

Journal: *Child Development,* January/February 2003, *74,* 127–143.

Related Research: Ge, X., et al. (1994). Trajectories of stressful life events and depressive symptoms during adolescence. *Developmental Psychology, 30,* 467–483.

10612

Test Name: KJP DREAM INVENTORY

Purpose: To measure six dream dimensions: Recurring Pleasantness, Repetitive Traumatic Dreams, Openness/Death, Discontentedness, Dissociative Avoidance, and Uninhibitedness.

Number of Items: 17

Format: A Likert format is used.

Reliability: Test–retest reliability was .89 (2 weeks).

Validity: Correlations with other variables ranged from .16 to .56.

Author: Kroth, J., et al.

Article: Dream reports and marital satisfaction.

Journal: *Psychological Reports,* June 2005, *96,* Part 1, 647–650.

Related Research: Kroth, J., et al. (1999). Analysis of factor structure in a dream inventory. *Perceptual and Motor Skills, 89,* 657–658.

10613

Test Name: KOALA FEAR QUESTIONNAIRE

Purpose: To measure fear-provoking stimuli in children.

Number of Items: 31

Format: Children rate intensity of fear by choosing a visual scale of Koala bears that expresses degrees of fear: 1 (*no fear*) to 3 (*a lot of fear*).

Reliability: Alpha coefficients ranged from .89 to .92.

Author: Muris, P.

Article: The Koala Fear Questionnaire: Its relationship with fear of storms and hurricanes in 4- to 14-year-old Antillean Children.

Journal: *Journal of Psychopathology and Behavioral Assessment*, September 2002, *24*, 145–150.

Related Research: Muris, P., et al. (2000). *The Koala Fear Questionnaire: A standardized self-report scale for assessing fears in young children.* Maastricht: Masstricht University.

10614

Test Name: KUWAIT UNIVERSITY ANXIETY SCALE

Purpose: To measure anxiety.

Number of Items: 20

Format: Items are anchored by 1 (*rarely*) and 4 (*always*). All items are presented.

Reliability: Alpha coefficients were .73 (Kuwait) and .95 (United States).

Validity: Factor loadings in Kuwait and the United States differed slightly.

Author: Abdel-Khalek, A., and Lester, D.

Article: The Kuwait University Anxiety Scale: A cross-cultural evaluation in Kuwait and United States.

Journal: *Psychological Reports*, December 2003, *93*, Part 2, 1109–1114.

10615

Test Name: LAROCQUE OBESITY QUESTIONNAIRE

Purpose: To assess uncontrolled eating, stress responses, depression, and perfectionism.

Number of Items: 31

Reliability: Alpha coefficients ranged from .69 to .84.

Validity: Correlations with other variables ranged from −.54 to .84.

Author: Stotland, S. C., and Larocque, M.

Article: Covergent validity of the Larocque Obesity Questionnaire and self-reported behavior during obesity treatment.

Journal: *Psychological Reports*, December 2004, *95*, Part 1, 1031–1042.

Related Research: Stotland, S., & Larocque, M. (2003). Web-based psychological assessment in obesity treatment: Association with treatment continuation vs. dropout. *American Journal of Bariatric Medicine, 18*, 11–14.

10616

Test Name: LAUFER COMBAT SCALE

Purpose: To assess combat experiences.

Number of Items: 33

Format: Item anchors range from 0 (*never*) to 2 (*three or more times*).

Reliability: Coefficient alpha was .73.

Author: Erickson, D. J., et al.

Article: Posttraumatic stress disorder and depression symptomatology in a sample of Gulf War veterans: A prospective analysis.

Journal: *Journal of Consulting and Clinical Psychology*, February 2001, *69*, 41–49.

Related Research: Gallops, M., et al. (1981). Part III Appendix 1: The Combat Scale revised. In A. Egendorf et al. (Eds.), *Legacies of Vietnam: Comparative adjustment of veterans and their peers* (pp. 125–129). New York: Center for Policy Research.

10617

Test Name: LEVENSON SELF-REPORT PSYCHOPATHY

Purpose: To assess primary and secondary psychopathy.

Number of Items: 26

Reliability: Alpha coefficients ranged from .62 to .85.

Validity: Correlations with other variables ranged from −.67 to .55.

Author: Ross, S. R., et al.

Article: Psychopathy and the five-factor model in a noninstitutionalized sample: A domain and facet level analysis.

Journal: *Journal of Psychopathology and Behavioral Assessment*, December 2004, *26*, 213–223.

Related Research: Levenson, M. R., et al. (1995). Assessing psychopathic attributes in a noninstitutionalized population. *Journal of Personality and Social Psychology, 68*, 151–158.

10618

Test Name: LIFE ATTITUDES SCHEDULE—SHORT FORM

Purpose: To measure suicide proneness.

Number of Items: 24

Reliability: Total alpha coefficients ranged from .80 to .84.

Validity: Correlations with other variables ranged from −.05 to .26.

Author: Klibert, J. J., et al.

Article: Adaptive and maladaptive aspects of self-oriented versus socially prescribed perfectionism.

Journal: *Journal of College Student Development*, March/April 2005, *46*, 141–156.

Related Research: Rohde, P., et al. (1996). The Life Attitudes Schedule Short Form: An abbreviated measure of life enhancing and life-threatening behaviors in adolescents. *Suicide and Life Threatening Behavior, 26*, 272–281.

10619

Test Name: LIFE CHANGE MEASURE

Purpose: To assess life change following sexual assault as changes in self, changes in relationships, changes in spirituality, changes in beliefs, and changes in concern for others.

Number of Items: 17

Format: Five-point scales range from 1 (*much worse now*) to 5 (*much better now*). All items are described.

Reliability: K-R 20 coefficients ranged from .62 to .91 across subscales.

Validity: Correlations with other variables ranged from −.55 to .64.

Author: Frazier, P., et al.

Article: Positive and negative life changes following sexual assault.

Journal: *Journal of Consulting and Clinical Psychology*, December 2001, *69*, 1048–1055.

Related Research: Frazier, P., & Burnett, J. (1994). Immediate coping strategies among rape victims. *Journal of Counseling and Development, 72*, 633–639.

10620

Test Name: LIFE EXPERIENCES SURVEY

Purpose: To assess stressful life events.

Number of Items: 50

Format: Responses are made on a 6-point scale ranging from −3 (*extremely negative*) to 3 (*extremely positive*).

Reliability: Coefficient alpha was .72.

Validity: Correlations with other variables ranged from −.18 to .18.

Author: Bricker, J. B.

Article: Development and evaluation of the Air Travel Stress Scale.

Journal: *Journal of Counseling Psychology*, October 2005, *52*, 615–628.

Related Research: Sarason, I. G., et al. (1978). Assessing the impact of life changes: Development of the Life Experiences Survey. *Journal of Consulting and Clinical Psychology, 46*, 932–946.

10621

Test Name: LIFE EXPERIENCES SURVEY

Purpose: To assess positive and negative life experiences.

Number of Items: 70

Format: Responses are made on a 7-point scale ranging from −3 (*extremely negative*) to 3 (*extremely positive*). Examples are provided.

Reliability: Test–retest (5–6 weeks) reliabilities ranged from .19 to .88.

Author: Lopez, F. G. et al.

Article: Adult attachment orientation and college student distress: Test of a mediational model.

Journal: *Journal of Counseling Psychology*, October 2002, *49*, 460–467.

Related Research: Sarason, I. G., et al. (1978). Assessing the impact of life changes: Development of the Life Experiences Survey. *Journal of Consulting and Clinical Psychology, 46*, 932–946.

10622

Test Name: LIFE ORIENTATION TEST

Purpose: To measure optimism.

Number of Items: 8 (plus 4 filler) items.

Format: Half are positively worked and half are negatively worked.

Responses are made on a 5-point scale ranging from 0 (*strongly disagree*) to 4 (*strongly agree*). An example is given.

Reliability: Alpha coefficients were .79 (*N* = 207) and .84 (*N* = 205). Test–retest (4 weeks) reliability was .79.

Validity: Correlation with other variables ranged from −.44 to .44.

Author: Morris, J. E., and Long, B. C.

Article: Female clerical workers' occupational stress: The role of person and social resources, negative affectivity, and stress appraisals.

Journal: *Journal of Counseling Psychology*, October 2002, *49*, 395–410.

Related Research: Scheier, M. F., & Carver, C. S. (1985). Optimism, coping, and health: Assessment and implications of generalized outcome expectancies. *Health Psychology, 4*, 219–247.

10623

Test Name: LIFE ORIENTATION TEST

Purpose: To measure optimism.

Number of Items: 6

Format: Responses are made on a 5-point Likert scale ranging from 0 (*strongly disagree*) to 4 (*strongly agree*). A sample item is presented.

Reliability: Alpha coefficients ranged from .46 to .78. Test–retest reliabilities ranged from .68 (over 4 months) to .79 (over 2 of months).

Validity: Correlations with other variables ranged from −.12 to .37 (*N* = 102).

Author: Waldrop, D., et al.

Article: Self-efficacy, optimism, health competence, and recovery from orthopedic surgery.

Journal: *Journal of Counseling Psychology*, April 2001, *48*, 233–238.

Related Research: Scheier, M. F., et al. (1994). Distinguishing optimism form neuroticism (and trait anxiety, self-mastery, and self-esteem): A reevaluation of the Life Orientation Test. *Journal of Personality and Social Psychology*, *67*, 1063–1078.

10624

Test Name: LIFE ORIENTATION TEST

Purpose: To measure dispositional optimism.

Number of Items: 8

Format: Item responses range from 0 (*strongly disagree*) to 4 (*strongly agree*).

Reliability: Alpha coefficients range from .76 to .78. Test–retest reliability was .79 (4 weeks).

Validity: Correlations with other variables ranged from .19 to .54.

Author: Yarcheski, T. J., et al.

Article: Depression, optimism, and positive health practices in young adolescents.

Journal: *Psychological Reports*, December 2004, *95*, Part 1, 932–934.

Related Research: Scheier, M. F., & Carver, C. S. (1985). Optimism, coping, and health: Assessment and implications of generalized outcome expectancies. *Health Psychology, 4*, 219–247.

10625

Test Name: LIFE ORIENTATION TEST—R

Purpose: To measure individual differences in optimism.

Number of Items: 10

Format: Responses are made on a 5-point Likert scale ranging from

0 (*strongly disagree*) to 4 (*strongly agree*).

Reliability: Internal consistencies were .68 and .78. Test–retest (4, 12, 24, and 28 months) reliabilities ranged from .56 to .79.

Validity: Correlations with other variables ranged from −.66 to .50.

Author: Huprich, S. K., and Frisch, M. B.

Article: The Depressive Personality Disorder Inventory and its relationship to quality of life, hopefulness, and optimism.

Journal: *Journal of Personality Assessment*, August 2004, *83*, 22–28.

Related Research: Scheier, M. F., et al. (1994). Distinguishing optimism from neuroticism (and trait anxiety, self-mastery, and self-esteem): A reevaluation of the Life Orientation Test. *Journal of Personality and Social Psychology*, *67*, 1063–1078.

10626

Test Name: LIFE ORIENTATION TEST—REVISED JAPANESE VERSION

Purpose: To measure optimism and pessimism.

Number of Items: 8

Format: Item anchors are 0 (*strongly disagree*) and 4 (*strongly agree*). All items are presented in English.

Reliability: Alpha coefficients ranged from .69 to .81.

Validity: Correlations with other variables ranged from −.35 to .38.

Author: Nakano, K.

Article: Psychometric properties of the life Orientation Test—Revised in samples of Japanese students.

Journal: *Psychological Reports*, June 2004, *94*, Part 1, 849–855.

Related Research: Scheier, M. F., et al. (1994). Distinguishing

optimism from neuroticism (and trait anxiety, self-mastery, and self-esteem): A reevaluation of the Life Orientation Test. *Journal of Personality and Social Psychology*, *67*, 1063–1078.

10627

Test Name: LIFE REGARD INDEX—REVISED

Purpose: To measure a person's belief that he or she is filling a positively valued life goal.

Number of Items: 28

Format: A 5-point Likert format is used.

Reliability: Test–retest reliabilities (8 weeks) ranged from .81 to .87. Alphas ranged from .83 to .92.

Validity: Correlations with other variables ranged from −.54 to .64.

Author: Harris, A. H. S., and Standard, S.

Article: Psychometric properties of the Life Regard Index—Revised: A validation study of a measure of personal meaning.

Journal: *Psychological Reports*, December 2001, *89*, 759–773.

Related Research: Debats, D. L. (1998). Measurement of personal meaning: The psychometric properties of the Life Regard Index (LRI). In P. T. P. Wong & P. S. Fry (Eds.), *Handbook of personal meaning theory: Theory, research and application* (pp. 237–260). Mahwah, NJ: Erlbaum.

10628

Test Name: LIFE SATISFACTION INDEX—Z

Purpose: To measure satisfaction with life.

Number of Items: 13

Format: Two-point agreement–disagreement scales are used.

Reliability: Coefficient alpha was .84.

Validity: Correlations with other variables ranged from .64 to .79.

Author: O'Rourke, N., and Cappeliez, P.

Article: Marital satisfaction and marital aggrandizement among older adults: Analysis of gender invariance.

Journal: *Measurement and Evaluation in Counseling and Development*, July 2001, *34*, 66–79.

Related Research: Wood, V., et al. (1969). An analysis of a short self-report measure of life satisfaction: Correlations with rater judgments. *Journal of Gerontology, 24*, 465–469.

10629

Test Name: LIFE SATISFACTION SCALE

Purpose: To assess satisfaction with various aspects of life.

Number of Items: 7

Format: Responses are made on a 5-point scale ranging from 1 (*very dissatisfied*) to 5 (*very satisfied*).

Reliability: Coefficient alpha was .76.

Validity: Correlations with other variables ranged from −.22 to .57 ($n = 211$).

Author: Livingstone, H. A., and Day, A. L.

Article: Comparing the construct and criterion-related validity of ability-based and mixed-model measures of emotional intelligence.

Journal: *Educational and Psychological Measurement*, October 2005, *65*, 851–873.

Related Research: Tupperman, L., & Curtis, J. (1995). A Life Satisfaction Scale for use with national adult samples from the USA, Canada, and Mexico. *Social Indicator Research, 35*, 255–270.

10630

Test Name: LIFE SATISFACTION SCALE

Purpose: To measure life satisfaction.

Number of Items: 5

Format: Responses are made on a 7-point Likert scale. An example is given.

Reliability: Coefficient alpha was .90.

Validity: Correlations with other variables ranged from −.41 to .66.

Author: Zickar, M. J., et al.

Article: Job attitudes of workers with two jobs.

Journal: *Journal of Vocational Behavior*, February 2004, *64*, 222–235.

Related Research: Diener, E., et al (1985). The Satisfaction With Life Scale. *Journal of Personality Assessment, 49*, 71–75.

10631

Test Name: LOEBER YOUTH QUESTIONNAIRE

Purpose: To measure affect and control.

Number of Items: 58

Format: Item response scales are anchored by 1 (*almost never*) and 3 (*almost always*) on discreet categories. Sample items are presented.

Reliability: Test–retest reliabilities ranged from .59 to .82.

Validity: Convergent validity indices ranged from .24 to .57.

Author: Moser, R. P., and Jacob, T.

Article: Parental and sibling effects in adolescent outcomes.

Journal: *Psychological Reports*, October 2002, *91*, 463–479.

Related Research: Loeber, R., et al. (1998). *Antisocial behavior and mental health problems:*

Exploratory factors in childhood and adolescence. Mahwah, NJ: Erlbaum.

10632

Test Name: LONELINESS AND SOCIAL SATISFACTION QUESTIONNAIRE—REVISED

Purpose: To determine frequency of a child's feeling lonely and to measure social satisfaction.

Number of Items: 11

Format: Includes loneliness and social satisfaction items. Responses are made on a 3-point scale ranging from 1 (*no, never, or rarely*) to 3 (*a lot of the time*). Sample items are presented.

Reliability: Alphas ranged from .77 to .89.

Author: Kochenderfer-Ladd, B., and Wardrop, J. L.

Article: Chronicity and instability of children's peer victimization experiences as predictors of loneliness and social satisfaction trajectories.

Journal: *Child Development*, January/February 2001, *72*, 134–151.

Related Research: Cassidy, J., & Asher, S. R. (1992). Loneliness and peer relations in young children. *Child Development, 63*, 350–365.

10633

Test Name: LONELINESS EXPERIENCE QUESTIONNAIRE

Purpose: To measure emotional distress, social alienation and inadequacy, youth and discovery, interpersonal isolation, and self-alienation.

Number of Items: 30

Time Required: 10 minutes.

Format: Sample items are presented.

Reliability: Alpha coefficients ranged from .63 to .84. K-R 20 reliability for the total scale was .84.

Author: Rokach, A.

Article: Loneliness in cancer and multiple sclerosis patients.

Journal: *Psychological Reports*, April 2004, *94*, 637–648.

Related Research: Rokach, A., & Brock, H. (1997). Loneliness: A multidimensional experience. *Psychology: A Journal of Human Behavior, 34*, 1–9.

10634

Test Name: LOSS OF FACE QUESTIONNAIRE

Purpose: To measure the importance of the threat of loss of one's integrity.

Number of Items: 21

Format: Scales range from 1 (*strongly disagree*) to 5 (*strongly agree*). Sample items are presented.

Reliability: Alpha coefficients ranged from .83 to .89.

Author: Hall, G. C. N., et al.

Article: Ethnicity, culture, and sexual aggression: Risk and protective factors.

Journal: *Journal of Consulting and Clinical Psychology*, October 2005, *73*, 830–840.

Related Research: Zane, N., & Mak, W. (2003). Major approaches to the measurement of acculturation among ethnic minority populations: A content analysis and an alternative empirical strategy. In K. M. Chun et al. (Eds.), *Acculturation: Advances in theory, measurement, and applied research* (pp. 39–60). Washington, DC: American Psychological Association.

10635

Test Name: MANIC-DEPRESSIVENESS SCALE

Purpose: To measure manic and depressive tendencies.

Number of Items: 18

Format: A true–false format is used.

Reliability: Alpha coefficients ranged from .40 to .63. Total alpha was .65.

Author: Lester, D.

Article: The Manic-Depressiveness Scale.

Journal: *Psychological Reports*, December 2005, *97*, 690.

Related Research: Thalbourne, M. A., et al. (1994). An attempt to construct short scales measuring manic-depressive-like experience and behavior. *British Journal of Clinical Psychology, 33*, 205–207.

10636

Test Name: MANIFEST ANXIETY SCALE

Purpose: To measure anxiety.

Number of Items: 20

Format: A true–false format is used.

Validity: Correlations with other variables ranged from –.46 to .41.

Author: Ashley, A., and Holtgraves, T.

Article: Repressors and memory: Effects of self-deception, impression management, and mood.

Journal: *Journal of Research in Personality*, August 2003, *37*, 284–296.

Related Research: Hicks, R. A., et al. (1980). A undimensional short form of the TMAS. *Bulletin of the Psychometric Society, 16*, 447–448.

10637

Test Name: MASCULINE BODY IDEAL STRESS SCALE

Purpose: To measure stress associated with not having an ideal masculine body.

Number of Items: 8

Format: Scales range from 1 (*not distressing at all*) to 4 (*very distressing*). A sample item is presented.

Reliability: Coefficient alpha was .89.

Validity: Correlations with other variables ranged from –.30 to .47.

Author: Kimmel, S. B., and Mahalik, J. R.

Article: Body image concerns of gay men: The roles of minority stress and conformity to masculine norms.

Journal: *Journal of Consulting and Clinical Psychology*, December 2005, *73*, 1185–1190.

Related Research: Kimmel, S. B., & Mahalik, J. R. (2004). Measuring masculine body ideal distress: Development of a measure. *International Journal of Men's Health, 3*, 1–10.

10638

Test Name: MASSACHUSETTS GENERAL HOSPITAL HAIRPULLING SCALE

Purpose: To measure the frequency, intensity, and control of hair pulling and the distress associated with it.

Number of Items: 11

Format: Five-point scales are used.

Reliability: Internal consistency reliability was .89. Test–retest reliability was .95.

Validity: Correlations with other variables ranged from .10 to .55.

Author: Diefenbach, G. J., et al.

Article: Assessment of Trichotillomania: A psychometric evaluation of hair-pulling scales.

Journal: *Journal of Psychopathology and Behavioral Assessment*, September 2005, *27*, 169–178.

Related Research: Keuthen, N. J., et al. (1995). The Massachusetts

General Hospital (MGH) Hairpulling Scale: 1. Development and factor analysis. *Psychotherapy and Psychosomatics, 64,* 141–145.

10639

Test Name: MEANING IN LIFE QUESTIONNAIRE—PRESENCE SUBSCALE

Purpose: To measure the presence of meaning in life.

Number of Items: 5

Format: Responses are made on a 7-point scale ranging from 1 (*absolutely untrue*) to 7 (*absolutely true*). Examples are given.

Reliability: Alpha coefficients ranged from .82 to .86. Test–retest (1 month) stability was .70.

Validity: Correlations with other variables ranged from .27 to .86.

Author: Steger, M. F., and Frazier, P.

Article: Meaning in life: One link in the chain from religiousness to well-being.

Journal: *Journal of Counseling Psychology,* October 2005, *52,* 574–582.

10640

Test Name: MEASURE OF MENTAL ANTICIPATORY PROCESSES

Purpose: To assess adaptive and maladaptive forms of recurrent thought that arises in anticipatory coping processes.

Number of Items: 15

Format: Scales range from 1 (*never true for me*) to 5 (*always true for me*). All items are presented.

Reliability: Alpha coefficients ranged from .70 to .90.

Validity: Correlations with other variables ranged from –.40 to .60.

Author: Feldman, G., and Hayes, A.

Article: Preparing for problems: A measure of mental anticipatory processes.

Journal: *Journal of Research in Personality,* October 2005, *39,* 487–516.

10641

Test Name: MEDICAL OUTCOMES STUDY—SHORT FORM

Purpose: To measure functional limitations.

Number of Items: 36

Format: Three- and 5-point rating scales are used.

Reliability: Internal consistency coefficients ranged from .76 to .92.

Validity: Correlations with other variables ranged from –.49 to .43.

Author: Katerndahl, D. A., et al.

Article: Psychometric assessment of measures of psychological symptoms, functional status, life events, and context for low income Hispanic patients in a primary care setting.

Journal: *Psychological Reports,* December 2002, *91,* Part 2, 1121–1128.

Related Research: Hemingway, H., et al. (1997). Is the SF-36 a valid measure of change in population health? *British Medical Journal, 315,* 1273–1279.

10642

Test Name: MENTAL HEALTH INDEX

Purpose: To assess symptoms of anxiety and depression.

Number of Items: 15

Format: Six-point scales range from 1 (*not at this time*) to 6 (*all of the time*).

Reliability: Alpha coefficients ranged from .85 to .91.

Author: Harned, M. S.

Article: Does it matter what you call it? The relationship between labeling unwanted sexual experiences and distress.

Journal: *Journal of Consulting and Clinical Psychology,* December 2004, *72,* 1090–1099.

Related Research: Ware, J. E. (1984). The General Health Rating Index. In N. K. Wenger et al. (Eds.), *Assessment of Quality of Life in Clinical Trials of Cardiovascular Disease* (pp. 184–188). New York: Le Jacq Publishing.

10643

Test Name: MENTAL HEALTH INDEX

Purpose: To measure emotional distress.

Number of Items: 5

Format: Six-point scales range from 1 (*all of the time*) to 6 (*none of the time*). All items are presented.

Reliability: Alpha coefficients ranged from .72 to .74.

Author: Orlando, M., et al.

Article: The temporal relationship between emotional distress and cigarette smoking during adolescence and young adulthood.

Journal: *Journal of Consulting and Clinical Psychology,* December 2001, *69,* 959–970.

Related Research: Stewart, A. L., et al. (1988). The MOS Short-Form General Health Survey: Reliability and validity in a patient population. *Medical Care, 26,* 724–735.

10644

Test Name: MENTAL HEALTH INVENTORY

Purpose: To measure anxiety, depression, loss of emotional control, and well-being.

Number of Items: 18

Format: A Likert format is used.

Reliability: Alpha coefficients ranged from .80 to .91.

Author: Manne, S. L., et al.

Article: Couple-focused group intervention for women with early stage breast cancer.

Journal: *Journal of Consulting and Clinical Psychology*, August 2005, *73*, 634–646.

Related Research: Ware, J. E., et al. (1984). Health status and the use of outpatient mental health services. *American Psychologist*, *39*, 1090–1100.

10645

Test Name: MICHIGAN ALCOHOLISM SCREENING TEST (MAST)

Purpose: To assess alcohol-related problems.

Number of Items: 22

Format: A yes–no format is used.

Reliability: Alpha coefficients ranged from .76 to .78.

Author: Merrill, L. L., et al.

Article: Childhood abuse and premilitary sexual assault in male Navy recruits.

Journal: *Journal of Consulting and Clinical Psychology*, April 2001, *69*, 252–261.

Related Research: Selzer, M. L. (1971). The Michigan Alcoholism Screening Test: The quest for a new diagnostic instrument. *Journal of Psychiatry*, *127*, 1653–1658.

10646

Test Name: MISSISSIPPI SCALE—REVISED

Purpose: To measure PTSD symptoms: reexperiencing, avoidance-numbing, and hyperarousal.

Number of Items: 15

Format: Five-point Likert scales are used.

Reliability: Alpha coefficients ranged from .89 to .92.

Author: Erickson, D. J., et al.

Article: Posttraumatic stress disorder and depression symptomatology in a sample of Gulf War veterans: A prospective analysis.

Journal: *Journal of Consulting and Clinical Psychology*, February 2001, *69*, 41–49.

Related Research: Keane, T. M., et al. (1988). Mississippi Scale for Combat-Related Postraumatic Stress Disorder: Three studies in reliability and validity. *Journal of Consulting and Clinical Psychology*, *56*, 85–90.

10647

Test Name: MODIFIED COMPETITIVE STATE ANXIETY INVENTORY—2

Purpose: To measure competitive anxiety in sport.

Number of Items: 27

Format: Includes three subscales: Cognitive Anxiety, Somatic Anxiety, and Self-Confidence. Responses are made on a 4-point scale ranging from 1 (*not at all*) to 4 (*very much*).

Reliability: Coefficient alpha ranged from .75 to .83.

Validity: Correlations with other variables ranged from −.27 to .51.

Author: Kais, K., and Raudsepp, L.

Article: Cognitive and somatic anxiety and self-confidence in athletic performance of beach volleyball.

Journal: *Perceptual and Motor Skills*, April 2004, *98*, 439–449.

Related Research: Martens, R., et al. (1990). *Competitive anxiety in sport*. Champaign, IL: Human Kinetics.

10648

Test Name: MODIFIED SCALE FOR SUICIDE IDEATION

Purpose: To evaluate the extent of suicidal thoughts, their characteristics, and respondents' attitudes toward them.

Number of Items: 18.

Format: The score on each item ranges from 0 to 3.

Reliability: Coefficient alpha was .94.

Author: Zhang, J., and Norvilitis, J. M.

Article: Measuring Chinese psychological well-being with western developed instruments.

Journal: *Journal of Personality Assessment*, December 2002, *79*, 492–511.

Related Research: Miller, I. W., et al. (1986). The modified Scale for Suicidal Ideation: Reliability and validity. *Journal of Consulting and Clinical Psychology*, *54*, 724–725.

10649

Test Name: MOOD AND ANXIETY SYMPTOM QUESTIONNAIRE

Purpose: To measure affective symptoms.

Format: Scales range from 1 (*not at all*) to 5 (*extremely*).

Reliability: Alpha coefficients ranged from .86 to .93 across subscales.

Validity: Correlations between two subscales and other variables ranged from −.25 to .50.

Author: Bonn-Miller, M. O., et al.

Article: Marijuana use among daily tobacco smokers: Relationship to anxiety-related factors.

Journal: *Journal of Psychopathology and Behavioral Assessment*, December 2005, *27*, 279–289.

Related Research: Watson, D., et al. (1995). Testing a tripartite model: I. Evaluating the convergent and discriminate validity of anxiety and depression symptom scales. *Journal of Abnormal Psychology, 104*, 3–14.

10650

Test Name: MOOD IMPROVEMENT SCALE FOR RUNNERS

Purpose: To measure mood improvement after running.

Number of Items: 6

Format: All items are presented.

Reliability: Alpha was .73.

Validity: Correlations with other variables ranged from .13 to .57.

Author: O'Halloran, P. D., et al.

Article: Measure of beliefs about improvements in mood associated with running.

Journal: *Psychological Reports*, June 2002, *90*, Part 1, 834–840.

10651

Test Name: MOOD MODULES OF THYE PRIMARY CARE EVALUATION OF MENTAL DISORDERS (PRIME-MD)

Purpose: To classify and screen psychiatric inpatients on the basis of self-reported symptoms into depressed or not depressed groups.

Number of Items: 17

Format: A yes–no format is used.

Reliability: K-R 20 reliability was .80.

Validity: Correlation with the Patient Health Questionnaire was .87.

Author: Kumar, G., et al.

Article: Screening for major depressive disorders in adolescent psychiatric inpatients with the mood modules from the Primary Care Evaluation of Mental Disorders and the Patient Health Questionnaire.

Journal: *Psychological Reports*, October 2001, *89*, 274–278.

Related Research: Spitzer, R. L., et al. (1995). *PRIME-MD instruction manual updated for the DSM–IV.* New York: Biometrics Research Department, New York State Psychiatric Institute.

10652

Test Name: MOOD SCALES

Purpose: To measure positive and negative mood.

Number of Items: 6

Format: Response scales range from 0 (*not at all*) to 4 (*extremely*). All items are presented.

Reliability: Alpha coefficients ranged from .60 to .83.

Validity: Correlations with other variables ranged from .16 to .27.

Author: Kranzler, H. R., et al.

Article: Targeted Naltrexone treatment moderates the relations between mood and drinking behaviors among problem drinkers.

Journal: *Journal of Consulting and Clinical Psychology*, April 2004, *72*, 317–327.

10653

Test Name: MOOD SURVEY

Purpose: To assess the mood level and the frequency and intensity of mood changes.

Number of Items: 15

Format: Includes two subscales: Mood Level and Reactivity.

Reliability: Alpha coefficients were .90 (Mood) and .80 (Reactivity).

Author: Suslow, T., et al.

Article: Detection of facial expressions of emotions in depression.

Journal: *Perceptual and Motor Skills*, June 2001, *92*, Part 1, 857–868.

Related Research: Underwood, B., & Froming, W. J. (1980). The Mood Survey: A personality measure of happy and sad moods. *Journal of Personality Assessment, 44*, 404–414.

10654

Test Name: MULTIDIMENSIONAL ANXIETY SCALE FOR CHILDREN

Purpose: To assess physical symptoms, harm avoidance, social anxiety, and separation/panic by child self-report.

Number of Items: 39

Format: Scales range from 0 (*never true about me*) to 3 (*often true about me*).

Reliability: Alpha coefficients ranged from .88 to .91.

Author: Kemper, T. S., et al.

Article: Mother–child agreement on reports of internalizing symptoms among children referred for evaluation of ADHD.

Journal: *Journal of Psychopathology and Behavioral Assessment*, December 2003, *25*, 239–250.

Related Research: March, J. et al. (1997). The Multidimensional Anxiety Scale for Children (MASC): Factor structure, reliability, and validity. *Journal of the American Academy of Child and Adolescent Psychiatry, 36*, 554–565.

10655

Test Name: MULTIDIMENSIONAL BLOOD/INJURY PHOBIA INVENTORY

Purpose: To characterize the range of fears and reactions associated with blood–injury phobia.

Number of Items: 40

Format: All items are presented.

Reliability: Coefficient alpha was .91.

Validity: Correlations between subscales ranged from .41 to .69.

Author: Wenzel, A., and Holt, C. S.

Article: Validation of the Multidimensional Blood/Injury Phobia Inventory: Evidence for a unitary construct.

Journal: *Journal of Psychopathology and Behavioral Assessment*, September 2003, *25*, 203–211.

10656

Test Name: MULTIDIMENSIONAL CHILD AND ADOLESCENT DEPRESSION SCALE

Purpose: To measure depression.

Number of Items: 40

Format: Three-point response scales range from *none* to *a lot*. All items are presented.

Reliability: Alpha coefficients ranged from .65 to .92 across subscales.

Validity: Correlations with other variables ranged from .30 to .85.

Author: Abdel-Khalek, A. M.

Article: The Multidimensional Child and Adolescent Depression Scale: Psychometric properties.

Journal: *Psychological Reports*, October 2003, *93*, 544–560.

10657

Test Name: MULTIDIMENSIONAL FATIGUE INVENTORY—20

Purpose: To measure five dimensions of fatigue among persons with chronic disease.

Number of Items: 20

Time Required: 10 minutes

Format: 5-point response scales.

Reliability: Alpha coefficients ranged from .60 to .82 across subscales.

Validity: Correlations with the Rhoten Fatigue Scale ranged from .42 to .72.

Author: Schneider, R. A.

Article: Preliminary data on the Multidimensional Fatigue Inventory—20 from female caregivers of male hemodialysis patients.

Journal: *Psychological Reports*, June 2001, *88*, Part 1, 699–700.

Related Research: Smets, E. M., et al. (1996). Application of the Multidimensional Fatigue Inventory (MFI–20) in cancer patients receiving radiotherapy. *British Journal of Cancer, 73*, 241–245.

10658

Test Name: MULTIDIMENSIONAL PERSONALITY INDEX

Purpose: To measure negative affectivity.

Number of Items: 11

Format: A true–false format is used. An example is given.

Reliability: Coefficient alpha was .83.

Validity: Correlations with other variables ranged from –.19 to .23.

Author: Stoeva, A. Z., et al.

Article: Negative affectivity, role stress, and work–family conflict.

Journal: *Journal of Vocational Behavior*, February 2002, *60*, 1–16.

Related Research: Watson, D., & Clark, L. A. (1984). Negative affectivity: The disposition to experience aversive emotional states. *Psychological Bulletin, 96*, 235–254.

10659

Test Name: MULTIDIMENSIONAL SENSE OF HUMOR SCALE

Purpose: To measure sense of humor as coping with humor, humor appreciation, and attitudes toward humor.

Number of Items: 24

Format: Five-point scales are anchored by 1 (*strongly disagree*) and 5 (*strongly agree*).

Reliability: Internal consistencies ranged from .92 to .94.

Validity: Correlations with a worry scale ranged from –.22 to .07.

Author: Kelly, W. E.

Article: Correlations of sense of humor and sleep disturbance ascribed to worry.

Journal: *Psychological Reports*, December 2002, *91*, Part 2, 1202–1204.

Related Research: Thorson, J. A., & Powell, F. C. (1993). Development and validation of a multidimensional sense of humor scale. *Journal of Clinical Psychology, 49*, 13–23.

10660

Test Name: NEGATIVE ADDICTION SCALE—ADAPTED

Purpose: To focus on the negative psychological aspects of exercise dependence.

Number of Items: 14

Format: Items are scored either 0 (*absence*) or 1 (*presence*).

Reliability: Coefficient alpha was .79. Split-half reliability was .76. Guttman split-half was .76.

Author: Rosa, D. A., et al.

Article: Mood changes after maximal exercise testing in subjects with symptoms of exercise dependence.

Journal: *Perceptual and Motor Skills*, August 2004, *99*, 341–353.

Related Research: Hailey, B. J., & Bailey, L. A. (1982). Negative addiction in runners: A quantitative approach. *Journal of Sport Behavior, 5*, 150–154.

10661

Test Name: NEGATIVE AFFECT IN PE SCALE

Purpose: To assess typical negative affect experienced by students in physical education.

Number of Items: 4

Format: Items are adjectives. Responses are made on a 7-point scale ranging from 1 (*never*) to 7 (*always*). Examples are given.

Reliability: Coefficient alpha was .80.

Validity: Correlations with other variables ranged from −.32 to .43.

Author: Ntoumanis, N.

Article: A prospective study of participation in optional school physical education using a self-determination theory framework.

Journal: *Journal of Educational Psychology*, August 2005, *97*, 444–453.

Related Research: Ebbeck, V., & Weiss, M. R. (1998). Determinants of children's self-esteem: An examination of perceived competence and affect in sport. *Pediatric Exercise Science, 10*, 285–298.

10662

Test Name: NEGATIVE AFFECTIVITY SCALE

Purpose: To measure negative affectivity.

Number of Items: 10

Format: Responses are made on a 5-point scale ranging from 1 (*very slightly or not at all*) to 5 (*extremely*). Examples are given.

Reliability: Alpha coefficients were .87 and .88.

Validity: Correlations with other variables ranged from −.35 to .69 (*n* = 164).

Author: Bruck, C. S., and Allen, T. D.

Article: The relationship between the Big Five personality traits, negative affectivity, type A behavior, and work–family conflict.

Journal: *Journal of Vocational Behavior*, December 2003, *63*, 457–472.

Related Research: Watson, D., et al (1988). Development and validation of brief measures of positive and negative affect: The PANAS scales. *Journal of Personality and Social Psychology, 54*, 1063–1070.

10663

Test Name: NEGATIVE AFFECTIVITY SCALE

Purpose: To measure negative affectivity.

Number of Items: 11

Format: Five-point rating scales range from 1 (*strongly disagree*) to 5 (*strongly agree*).

Reliability: Coefficient alpha was .87.

Author: Lindfors, P.

Article: Positive health in a group of Swedish white-collar workers.

Journal: *Psychological Reports*, December 2002, *91*, Part 1, 839–845.

Related Research: Agho, A. O., et al. (1992). Discriminant validity of measures of job satisfaction, positive affectivity and negative affectivity. *Journal of Occupational and Organizational Psychology, 65*, 185–196.

10664

Test Name: NEGATIVE AFFECTIVITY SCALE

Purpose: To measure negative affectivity.

Number of Items: 12

Format: Five-point scales range from 1 (*never true of me*) to 5 (*always true of me*).

Reliability: Coefficient alpha was .82. Test–retest reliability (10 months) was .69.

Validity: Correlations with other variables ranged from .32 to .34.

Author: Stice, E., and Shaw, H.

Article: Prospective relations of body image, eating, and affective disturbances to smoking onset in adolescent girls: How Virginia slims.

Journal: *Journal of Consulting and Clinical Psychology*, February 2003, *71*, 129–135.

Related Research: Buss, A. H., & Plomin, R. (1984). *Temperament: Early developing personality traits*. Hillsdale, NJ: Erlbaum.

10665

Test Name: NEGATIVE AND POSITIVE AFFECT SCALE

Purpose: To measure positive and negative affect.

Number of Items: 12

Format: Scales range from 1 (*not*) to 5 (*very strongly*).

Reliability: Alpha coefficients were .77 (negative affect) and .91 (positive affect).

Validity: Correlations with other variables ranged from −.70 to .36.

Author: Deelstra, J. T., et al.

Article: Receiving instrumental support at work: When help is not welcome.

Journal: *Journal of Applied Psychology*, April 2003, *88*, 324–331.

Related Research: Warr, P. (1990). The measurement of well-being and other aspects of mental health. *Journal of Occupational Psychology, 63,* 193–210.

10666

Test Name: NEGATIVE EMOTION SCALE

Purpose: To measure negative emotions.

Number of Items: 8

Format: Responses are made on a 5-point scale ranging from 5 (*very*) to 1 (*not at all*). All items are presented, including anger, resentment, guilt, frustration, anxiety, distraction, worry, and helplessness.

Reliability: Reliabilities ranged from .88 to .92. Test–retest reliability was .64 (N = .70).

Validity: Correlations with other variables ranged from –.11 to 58.

Author: Fugate, M., et al.

Article: Coping with an organizational merger over four stages.

Journal: *Personnel Psychology,* Winter 2002, *55,* 905–928.

Related Research: Weiss, H. M., & Cropanzano, R. (1996). Affective events theory: A theoretical discussion of the structure, causes and consequences of affective experiences at work. In Staw, B. M., & Cummings, L. L. (Eds.), *Research in organizational behavior* (18th ed., pp. 1–74). Greenwich, CT: JAI Press.

10667

Test Name: NEGATIVE EMOTIONALITY SCALE

Purpose: To measure negative emotionality.

Number of Items: 30

Reliability: Internal consistency reliability was .83.

Validity: The correlation with a negative affect scale was .68.

Author: Lilienfeld, S. O., and Hess, T. H.

Article: Psychopathic personality traits and somatization: Sex differences and the mediating role of negative emotionality.

Journal: *Journal of Psychopathology and Behavioral Assessment,* March 2001, *23,* 11–24.

Related Research: Waller, N. G., et al. (1996). Exploring nonlinear models in personality assessment: Development and preliminary validation of a negative emotionality scale. *Journal of Personality, 64,* 545–576.

10668

Test Name: NEGATIVE EMOTIONS SCALE

Purpose: To measure negative emotions.

Number of Items: 14

Format: Seven-point scales range from *not at all* to *very much.*

Reliability: Coefficient alpha was .72.

Validity: Correlations with other variables ranged from –.07 to .33.

Author: Brown, S. P., et al.

Article: Good cope, bad cope: Adaptive and maladaptive coping strategies following a critical negative work event.

Journal: *Journal of Applied Psychology,* July 2005, *90,* 792–798.

10669

Test Name: NEGATIVE LIFE EVENTS SCALE

Purpose: To measure the occurrence of negative events.

Number of Items: 25

Format: A yes–no format is used.

Validity: Correlations with other variables ranged from .03 to .30.

Author: Westman, M., et al.

Article: Crossover of marital dissatisfaction during military downsizing among Russian Army officers and their spouses.

Journal: *Journal of Applied Psychology,* October 2004, *89,* 769–779.

Related Research: Holmes, T. H., & Rahe, R. H. (1967). The Social Readjustment Rating Scale. *Journal of Psychosomatic Research, 11,* 213–218.

10670

Test Name: NEGATIVE MASCULINITY SUBSCALE

Purpose: To assess unmitigated agency.

Number of Items: 8

Format: Responses are made on a 5-point bipolar scale ranging from 1 (*not at all*) to 5 (*very much*).

Reliability: Internal consistency reliabilities ranged from .71 to .85.

Validity: Correlations with other variables ranged from –.42 to .45.

Author: Bruch, M. A.

Article: The relevance of mitigated and unmitigated agency and commission for depression vulnerabilities and dysphoria.

Journal: *Journal of Counseling Psychology,* October 2002, *49,* 449–459.

Related Research: Spence, V. T., et al. (1979). Negative and positive components of psychological masculinity and femininity and their relationships to self-reports of neurotic and acting out behaviors. *Journal of Personality and Social Psychology, 37,* 1673–1682.

10671

Test Name: NEGATIVE MOOD RATING SCALE

Purpose: To measure the perceived ability to reduce negative mood.

Number of Items: 30

Reliability: Alpha coefficients ranged from .76 to .92 across subscales.

Validity: Correlations with other variables ranged from −.34 to .36.

Author: McCarthy, C. J., et al.

Article: Continued attachment to parents: Its relationship to affect regulation and perceived stress among college students.

Journal: *Measurement and Evaluation in Counseling and Development*, January 2001, *33*, 198–213.

Related Research: Kirsch, I., et al. (1990). Mood regulation expectancies as determinants of dysphoria in college students. *Journal of Counseling Psychology*, *37*, 306–312.

10672

Test Name: NEUROTICISM SCALE

Purpose: To measure neuroticism.

Number of Items: 8

Format: Scales range from 1 (*disagree strongly*) to 5 (*agree strongly*). Sample items are presented.

Reliability: Coefficient alpha was .81.

Author: Zautra, A. J., et al.

Article: Positive affect as a source of resilience for women in chronic pain.

Journal: *Journal of Consulting and Clinical Psychology*, April 2005, *73*, 212–220.

Related Research: John, O. P., et al. (1991). *The "Big Five" Inventory—Versions 4a and 54*. Berkeley: Institute for Personality and Social Research, University of California.

10673

Test Name: NUMBING SCALE

Purpose: To measure the frequency of experiences associated with the numbing response.

Number of Items: 35

Format: Self-report items are rated on 7-point Likert scales ranging from 1 (*never*) to 7 (*always*).

Reliability: Alpha was .93. Test–retest reliability was .80.

Validity: Correlations with other variables ranged from .71 to .76

Author: Ramirez, S. M., et al.

Article: Relationship of numbing to alexithymia, apathy, and depression.

Journal: *Psychological Reports*, February 2001, *88*, 189–200.

Related Research: Glover, H., et al. (1997). Numbing scale scores in female psychiatric inpatients diagnosed with self-injurious behavior, dissociative identity disorder, and major depression. *Psychiatric Research*, *70*, 115–123.

10674

Test Name: OBJECTIFIED BODY CONSCIOUSNESS SCALE

Purpose: To measure body awareness as body surveillance, body control, and body shame.

Number of Items: 24

Format: Seven-point Likert scales are used. Sample items are presented.

Reliability: Internal consistency reliabilities ranged from .67 to .89. Test–retest reliabilities ranged from .73 to .79.

Validity: Correlations with other variables ranged from −.51 to −.39.

Author: Befort, C., et al.

Article: Body image, self-esteem, and weight-related criticism from romantic partners.

Journal: *Journal of College Student Development*, September/October 2001, *42*, 407–419.

Related Research: McKinley, N. M., & Hyde, J. S. (1996). The Objectified Body Consciousness Scale: Development and validation. *Psychology of Women Quarterly*, *20*, 181–215.

10675

Test Name: OBSESSIVE BELIEFS QUESTIONNAIRE

Purpose: To assess obsessive beliefs associated with obsessive–compulsive disorder.

Number of Items: 86

Format: Scales range from 1 (*disagree very much*) to 7 (*agree very much*). All items are presented.

Reliability: Alpha coefficients range from .86 to .95.

Author: Woods, C. M., et al.

Article: Dimensionality of the Obsessive Beliefs Questionnaire (OBQ).

Journal: *Journal of Psychopathology and Behavioral Assessment*, June 2004, *26*, 113–126.

Related Research: Obsessive–compulsive cognitions working group. (2001). Development and initial validation of the Obsessive Beliefs Questionnaire and the Interpretations of Intrusions Inventory. *Behavior Research and Therapy*, *39*, 987–1006.

10676

Test Name: OBSESSIVE–COMPULSIVE INVENTORY

Purpose: To describe the presence and severity of obsessive–compulsive disorder symptoms.

Number of Items: 42

Format: Includes seven subscales: Washing, Checking, Doubting, Ordering, Obsessing, Hoarding, and Mental Neutralizing. Responses are made on a 5-point scale ranging from 0 (*not at all*) to 4 (*extremely*).

Reliability: Alpha coefficients ranged from .86 to .95.

Validity: Correlations with other variables ranged from .03 to .60.

Author: Hill, R. W., et al.

Article: A new measure of perfectionism: The Perfectionism Inventory.

Journal: *Journal of Personality Assessment*, February 2004, *82*, 80–91.

Related Research: Foa, E. B., et al. (1998). The validation of a new obsessive–compulsive disorder scale: The Obsessive–Compulsive Inventory. *Psychological Assessment, 10*, 206–214.

10677

Test Name: OBSESSIVE–COMPULSIVE INVENTORY—REVISED

Purpose: To assess how people rate the degree to which they are bothered by obsessive–compulsive disorder symptoms.

Number of Items: 18

Format: Scales range from 0 (*not at all*) to 4 (*extremely*).

Reliability: Subscale alpha coefficients range from .70 to .86.

Author: Woods, C. M., et al.

Article: Dimensionality of the Obsessive Beliefs Questionnaire (OBQ).

Journal: *Journal of Psychopathology and Behavioral Assessment*, June, 2004, *26*, 113–126.

Related Research: Foa, E. B., et al. (1998). The validation of a new obsessive–compulsive disorder scale: The Obsessive–Compulsive Inventory. *Psychological Assessment, 10*, 206–214.

10678

Test Name: OPERATION FAMILY STUDY QUESTIONNAIRE—PARENTS' LIFE SATISFACTION

Purpose: To measure parents' life satisfaction.

Number of Items: 3

Format: Each item is presented.

Reliability: Alpha coefficients ranged from .74 to .81.

Validity: Correlations with other variables ranged from –.25 to .05.

Author: Keltikangas-Järvinen, L., and Heinonen, K.

Article: Childhood roots of adulthood hostility: Family factors as predictors of cognitive and affective hostility.

Journal: *Child Development*, November/December 2003, *74*, 1751–1768.

Related Research: Makkonen, T., et al. (1981). *Operation family (child report, no. A 34)*. Helsinki, Finland: Mannerheim League of Child Welfare.

10679

Test Name: OPTIMISM AND PESSIMISM SCALE

Purpose: To measure optimism and pessimism

Number of Items: 56

Format: Includes separate scores for optimism and pessimism.

Validity: Correlations with other variables ranged from –.76 to .74 (*N* = 93).

Author: Terrill, D. R., et al.

Article: Construct validity of the Life Orientation Test.

Journal: *Journal of Personality Assessment*, December 2002, *79*, 550–563.

Related Research: Dember, W. N., et al. (1989). The measurement of optimism and pessimism. *Current Psychology: Research and Reviews, 8*, 102–119.

10680

Test Name: OPTIMISM SCALE

Purpose: To measure dispositional optimism.

Number of Items: 4

Format: Five-point scales are anchored by 0 (*strongly disagree*) and 4 (*strongly agree*).

Reliability: Coefficient alpha was .78.

Validity: Correlations with other variables ranged from –.56 to –.45.

Author: Boelen, P. A., and van den Bout, J.

Article: Positive thinking in bereavement: Is it related to depression, anxiety, or grief symptomatology?

Journal: *Psychological Reports*, December 2002, *91*, Part 1, 857–863.

Related Research: Scheier, M. F., & Carver, C. S. (1985). Optimism, coping, and health: Assessment and implications of generalized outcome expectancies. *Health Psychology, 4*, 219–247.

10681

Test Name: OXFORD HAPPINESS INVENTORY—PORTUGUESE VERSION

Purpose: To measure subjective well-being.

Number of Items: 29

Format: Item responses are anchored by 1 (*not at all*) and 7 (*extremely*). Sample items are presented in English.

Reliability: Alpha was .90.

Validity: Correlations with other variables ranged from −.54 to .65.

Author: Neto, F.

Article: Personality predictors of happiness.

Journal: *Psychological Reports*, June 2001, *88*, Part 1, 817–824.

Related Research: Argyle, M., & Crossland, J. (1987). Dimensions of positive emotions. *British Journal of Social Psychology, 26*, 127–137.

10682

Test Name: OXFORD–LIVERPOOL INVENTORY OF FEELINGS AND EXPERIENCES

Purpose: To measure unusual experiences, cognitive disorganization, introvertive anhedonia, and impulsive nonconformity. A lie scale is included.

Number of Items: 159

Format: A yes–no format is used.

Validity: Correlations with a transliminality scale ranged from .01 to .78.

Author: Thalbourne, M. A.

Article: Transliminality and the Oxford–Liverpool Inventory of Feelings and Experiences.

Journal: *Psychological Reports*, June 2005, *96*, Part 1, 579–585.

Related Research: Mason, O., et al. (1995). New scales for the assessment of schizotypy. *Personality and Individual Differences, 18*, 7–13.

10683

Test Name: PADUA INVENTORY—JAPANESE VERSION

Purpose: To measure disturbance associated with obsessive–compulsive symptoms.

Number of Items: 60

Format: Scales range from 0 (*not at all*) to 4 (*very much*).

Reliability: Alpha coefficients ranged from .81 to .92 across subscales.

Validity: Correlations with a perfectionism scale ranged from .14 to .56.

Author: Suzuki, T.

Article: Relationship between two aspects of perfectionism and obsessive–compulsive symptoms.

Journal: *Psychological Reports*, April 2005, *96*, 299–305.

Related Research: Sanavio, E. (1988). Obsessions and compulsions: The Padua Inventory. *Behavior Research and Therapy, 26*, 169–177.

10684

Test Name: PAIN CATASTROPHIZING SCALE

Purpose: To measure catastrophizing related to pain.

Number of Items: 13

Format: Includes three subscales: Rumination, Magnification, and Helplessness. Responses are made on a 4-point scale ranging from 1 (*not at all*) to 4 (*all the time*). Examples are given.

Validity: Correlations with other variables ranged from .07 to .63.

Author: Roelofs, J., et al.

Article: An examination of word relevance in a modified Stroop task in patients with chronic low back pain.

Journal: *Perceptual and Motor Skills*, June 2005, *100*, Part 2, 955–963.

Related Research: Sullivan, M. J., et al. (1995). The Pain Catastrophizing Scale: Development and validation. *Psychological Assessment, 7*, 624–632.

10685

Test Name: PAIN HELPLESSNESS INDEX

Purpose: To measure perceived helplessness about pain.

Number of Items: 15

Format: Sample items are presented.

Reliability: Coefficient alpha was .76.

Validity: Correlations with other variables ranged from −.34 to .66.

Author: Burns, J. W., et al.

Article: Do changes in cognitive factors influence outcome following multidisciplinary treatment for chronic pain? A cross-lagged panel analysis.

Journal: *Journal of Consulting and Clinical Psychology*, February 2003, *71*, 81–91.

Related Research: Burns, J. W., et al. (1998). Cognitive and physical capacity process variables predict long-term outcome following treatment of chronic pain. *Journal of Consulting and Clinical Psychology, 66*, 634–639.

10686

Test Name: PAIN VIGILANCE AND AWARENESS QUESTIONNAIRE

Purpose: To measure pain vigilance.

Number of Items: 16

Format: Includes two subscales: Attention to Pain and Attention to Changes in Pain. Responses are made on a 6-point scale ranging from 0 (*never*) to 5 (*always*). Examples are presented.

Validity: Correlations with other variables ranged from .08 to .58.

Author: Roelofs, J., et al.

Article: An examination of word relevance in a modified Stroop task in patients with chronic low back pain.

Journal: *Perceptual and Motor Skills*, June 2005, *100*, Part 2, 955–963.

Related Research: McCracken, L. M. (1997). Attention to pain in persons with chronic pain: A behavioral approach. *Behavior Therapy, 28*, 271–284.

10687

Test Name: PANIC DISORDER SEVERITY SCALE

Purpose: To assess panic disorder severity.

Number of Items: 7

Format: Clinician ratings range from 0 (*none*) to 4 (*extreme*).

Reliability: Coefficient alpha was .67.

Author: Hicks, T. V., et al.

Article: Physical, mental, and social catastrophic cognitions as prognostic factors in cognitive–behavioral and pharmacological treatments for panic disorder.

Journal: *Journal of Consulting and Clinical Psychology*, June 2005, *73*, 506–514.

Related Research: Shear, M. K., et al. (1997). Multicenter Collaborative Panic Disorder Severity Scale. *American Journal of Psychiatry, 154*, 1571–1575.

10688

Test Name: PARENTS WITH HIV/AIDS DISTRESS QUESTIONNAIRE

Purpose: To measure the severity of HIV-associated symptoms.

Number of Items: 23

Format: Rating scales range from 1 (*not at all*) to 6 (*extremely*).

Reliability: Coefficient alpha was .86.

Validity: Correlations with other variables ranged from −.09 to .53.

Author: Rotheram-Borus, M. J., et al.

Article: Impact of parent death and an intervention on the adjustment of adolescents whose parents have HIV/AIDS.

Journal: *Journal of Consulting and Clinical Psychology*, October 2001, *69*, 763–773.

Related Research: Rotheram-Borus, M. J., & Stein, J. A. (1999). Problem behaviors among adolescents whose parents are living with AIDS. *American Journal of Orthopsychiatry, 69*, 228–239.

10689

Test Name: PEDIATRIC SYMPTOM CHECKLIST

Purpose: To measure parents' impressions of their children's psychosocial functioning.

Number of Items: 35

Format: Items are scored *never*, *sometimes*, and *often*. Sample items are presented.

Reliability: Test–retest reliability (4 weeks) was .86.

Author: Kelly, M. L., and Fals-Stewart, W.

Article: Couples- versus individual-based therapy for alcohol and drug abuse: Effects on children's psychosocial functioning.

Journal: *Journal of Consulting and Clinical Psychology*, April 2002, *70*, 417–427.

Related Research: Jellinek, M. S., et al. (1999). Use of the Pediatric Symptom Checklist to screen for psychosocial problems in pediatric care: A national study. *Archives of Pediatric & Adolescent Medicine, 153*, 254–260.

10690

Test Name: PEER LIFE ORIENTATION TEST

Purpose: To measure optimism about peer relationships.

Number of Items: 12

Format: Responses are made on a 4-point scale ranging from *really agree* to *really disagree*.

Reliability: Coefficient alpha was .70.

Author: Barton, B. K., and Cohen, R.

Article: Classroom gender composition and children's peer relations.

Journal: *Child Study Journal*, 2004, *34*, 29–45.

Related Research: Deptula, D. P. (1998). *Expecting the best: Optimism as a predictor of children's social behaviors and peer relationships*. Unpublished master's thesis, University of Memphis, Memphis, TN.

10691

Test Name: PENN STATE WORRY QUESTIONNAIRE

Purpose: To assess worry.

Number of Items: 16

Format: Scales range from 1 (*not at all typical of me*) to 5 (*very typical of me*).

Reliability: Coefficient alpha was .93.

Validity: Correlations with other variables ranged from .00 to .29.

Author: Feldman, G., and Hayes, A.

Article: Preparing for problems: A measure of mental anticipatory processes.

Journal: *Journal of Research in Personality*, October 2005, *39*, 487–516.

Related Research: Meyer, T. J., et al. (1990). Development and validation of the Penn State Worry Questionnaire. *Behavior Research and Therapy, 28*, 487–496.

10692

Test Name: PENN STATE WORRY QUESTIONNAIRE

Purpose: To assess worry as a component of anxiety.

Number of Items: 6

Format: Scales range from 0 (*not at all typical*) to 4 (*very typical*).

Reliability: Coefficient alpha was .92.

Author: Wenzel, A., et al.

Article: Thought suppression in spider-fearful and nonfearful individuals.

Journal: *The Journal of General Psychology*. April 2003, *130*, 191–205.

Related Research: Meyer, T. J., et al. (1990). Development and validation of the Penn State Worry Questionnaire. *Behavior Research and Therapy, 28*, 487–495.

10693

Test Name: PENN STATE WORRY QUESTIONNAIRE

Purpose: To measure trait pathological worry by interview.

Number of Items: 14

Reliability: Coefficient alpha was .95.

Validity: Correlations with other variables ranged from –.02 to .40.

Author: Wetherell, J. L., and Gatz, M.

Article: The Beck Anxiety Inventory in older adults with generalized anxiety disorder.

Journal: *Journal of Psychopathology and Behavioral Assessment*, March 2005, 27, 17–24.

Related Research: Meyer, T. J., et al. (1990). Development and validation of the Penn State Worry Questionnaire. *Behavior Research and Therapy, 28*, 487–495.

10694

Test Name: PENN STATE WORRY QUESTIONNAIRE FOR CHILDREN

Purpose: To measure the severity of worrying.

Number of Items: 14

Format: Sample items are presented.

Reliability: Alpha was .88.

Validity: Correlations with other variables ranged from –.05 to .37.

Author: Muris, P.

Article: Parental rearing behaviors and worry of normal adolescents.

Journal: *Psychological Reports*, October 2002, *91*, 428–430.

Related Research: Chorpita, B. F., et al. (1997). Assessment of worry in children and adolescents: An adaptation of the Penn State Worry Questionnaire. *Behavior Research and Therapy, 35*, 569–581.

10695

Test Name: PENNEBAKER INVENTORY OF LIMBIC LANGUIDNESS

Purpose: To measure physical symptoms.

Number of Items: 54

Format: Responses are made on a 5-point scale ranging from 1 (*have never or almost never experienced the symptom in the past year*) to 5 (*more than once every week in the past year*).

Reliability: Alpha coefficients were .91 and .95.

Validity: Correlations with other variables ranged from –.12 to .39 ($N = 97$).

Author: Smith, N. G., and Ingram, K. M.

Article: Workplace heterosexism and adjustment among lesbian, gay,

and bisexual individuals: The role of unsupportive social interactions.

Journal: *Journal of Counseling Psychology*, January 2004, *51*, 57–67.

Related Research: Pennebaker, J. W. (1982). *The Psychology of physical symptoms*. New York: Springer-Verlag.

10696

Test Name: PERCEIVED COPING DIFFICULTIES SCALE

Purpose: To measure the perception of an ability to cope with extant stressors.

Number of Items: 4

Format: Responses are made on a 5-point scale ranging from 0 (*never*) to 4 (*very often*).

Reliability: Alpha coefficients ranged from .70 to .80.

Validity: Correlations with other variables ranged from –.12 to .29.

Author: Sherry, S. B., et al.

Article: Perfectionism dimensions, perfectionistic attitudes, dependent attitudes, and depression in psychiatric patients and university students.

Journal: *Journal of Counseling Psychology*, July 2003, *50*, 373–386.

Related Research: Hewitt, P. L., et al. (1992). The Perceived Stress Scale: Factor structure and relation to depression in a psychiatric sample. *Journal of Psychopathology and Behavioral Assessment, 14*, 247–257.

10697

Test Name: PERCEIVED STRESS SCALE

Purpose: To measure self-appraised life stress in the past month.

Number of Items: 14.

Format: Responses are made on a 5-point scale ranging from 0 (*never*) to 4 (*very often*). An example is given.

Reliability: Test–retest (6 weeks) reliability was .55.

Validity: Correlations with other variables ranged from –.59 to .60 (*N* = 150).

Author: Chang, E. C., et al.

Article: How adaptive and maladaptive perfectionism relate to positive and negative psychological functioning: Testing a stress-mediation model in Black and White female college students.

Journal: *Journal of Counseling Psychology*, January 2004, *51*, 93–102.

Related Research: Cohen, S., et al. (1983). A global measure of perceived stress. *Journal of Health and Social Behavior, 24*, 385–396.

10698

Test Name: PERCEIVED STRESS SCALE

Purpose: To measure level of stress experienced in the last month.

Number of Items: 4

Format: Scales range from 1 (*not at all true*) to 7 (*very true*). A sample item is presented.

Reliability: Coefficient alpha was .77.

Author: Chu, A. H. C., and Choi, J. N.

Article: Rethinking procrastination: Positive effects of "active" procrastination behavior on attitude and performance.

Journal: *The Journal of Social Psychology*, June 2005, *145*, 245–264.

Related Research: MacArthur, J. D., & MacArthur, C. T. (2001). *Perceived Stress Scale*. Department of Psychology, University of California, San Francisco. Available

at http://www.macses.ucsf.edu/ research/psychosocial/notebook/ PSS10.html

10699

Test Name: PERCEIVED STRESS SCALE

Purpose: To assess perceptions of stress over the past 3 months.

Number of Items: 10

Format: Scales range from 0 (*never*) to 4 (*very often*).

Reliability: Coefficient alpha was .85.

Validity: Correlations with other variables ranged from –.32 to .43.

Author: Winterowd, C., et al.

Article: The relationship of spiritual beliefs and involvement with the experience of anger and stress in college students.

Journal: *Journal of College Student Development*, September/October 2005, *46*, 515–529.

Related Research: Cohen, S., & Williamson, G. M. (1988). Perceived stress in a probability sample of the United States. In S. Spacapan & S. Oskamp (Eds.), *The social psychology of health* (pp. 31–67). Newbury Park, CA: Sage.

10700

Test Name: PERCEIVED STRESS SCALE—JAPANESE VERSION

Purpose: To assess global stress.

Number of Items: 14

Format: Five-point response categories are anchored by *never* and *very often*. A sample item is presented.

Reliability: Cronbach's alpha was .87.

Validity: Correlations with perfectionism ranged from .38 to .41.

Author: Sumi, K., et al.

Article: Neurotic perfectionism, perceived stress, and self-esteem among Japanese Men: A prospective study.

Journal: *Psychological Reports*, February 2001, *88*, 19–22.

Related Research: Cohen, S., et al. (1983). A global measure of perceived stress. *Journal of Health and Social Behavior, 24*, 385–396.

10701

Test Name: PERCEPTUAL ABERRATION SCALE

Purpose: To measure distortion in the perception of one's own body and external objects.

Number of Items: 35

Format: Sample items are presented.

Reliability: Coefficient alpha was .89.

Validity: Correlation with other variables ranged from –.30 to .40.

Author: Ross, S. R., et al.

Article: Positive and negative symptoms of schizotypy and the five-factor model: A domain and facet level analysis.

Journal: *Journal of Personality Assessment*, August 2002, *79*, 53–72.

Related Research: Chapman, L. J., et al. (1978). Body image aberration in schizophrenia. *Journal of Abnormal Psychology, 87*, 399–407.

10702

Test Name: PERSONAL ATTRIBUTES QUESTIONNAIRE

Purpose: To measure agency and commission.

Number of Items: 16

Format: Includes two subscales: Agency and Commission.

Reliability: Alpha coefficients ranged from .79 to .85. Test–retest (2.5 months) was .60.

Validity: Correlations with other variables ranged from −.42 to .45.

Author: Bruch, M. A.

Article: The relevance of mitigated and unmitigated agency and commission for depression vulnerabilities and dysphoria.

Journal: *Journal of Counseling Psychology*, October 2002, *49*, 449–459.

Related Research: Helgeson, V. S. (1994). Relation of agency and commission to well-being: Evidence and potential explanations. *Psychological Bulletin, 116*, 412–428.

10703

Test Name: PERSONAL CONTROL SCALE

Purpose: To assess the lack of mastery over daily events.

Number of Items: 4

Format: Scales range from 1 (*strongly disagree*) to 5 (*strongly agree*). All items are presented.

Reliability: Coefficient alpha was .80.

Author: Umberson, D., et al.

Article: Relationship dynamics, emotion state, and domestic violence: A stress and masculinities perspective.

Journal: *Journal of Marriage and Family*, February 2003, *65*, 233–247.

Related Research: Pearlin, L. I., & Schooler, C. (1978). The structure of coping. *Journal of Health and Social Behavior, 19*, 2–21.

10704

Test Name: PERSONAL COPING SCALE

Purpose: To measure personal organization and appropriate attitude.

Number of Items: 8

Format: Item responses are anchored by 1 (*not typical of me*) and 5 (*very typical of me*). Sample items are presented.

Reliability: Cronbach's alpha was .72.

Validity: Correlations with other variables ranged from −.30 to .23.

Author: Cohen, A., & Schwartz, H.

Article: An empirical examination among Canadian teachers of determinants of the need for employees' assistance programs.

Journal: *Psychological Reports*, June 2002, *90*, Part 2, 1221–1238.

Related Research: Kirchmeyer, C. (1993). Nonwork to work spillover: A more balanced view of the experiences and coping of professional women and men. *Sex Roles, 28*, 531–552.

10705

Test Name: PERSONAL DISTURBANCE SCALE

Purpose: To measure anxiety and depression.

Number of Items: 9

Format: Four-point scales are used.

Reliability: Alpha coefficients ranged from .76 to .86 across subscales. All items are presented.

Author: Bedford, A., et al.

Article: Personal Disturbance Scale: Factor structure confirmed in a large nonclinical sample.

Journal: *Psychological Reports*, February 2005, *96*, 107–188.

Related Research: Bedford, A., & Deary, I. J. (1997). The Personal Disturbance Scale (DSSI/SAD): Development, use and structure. *Personality and Individual Differences, 22*, 493–510.

10706

Test Name: PERSONAL FEAR OF INVALIDITY SCALE—ADAPTED CHINESE VERSION

Purpose: To measure one's reluctance to commit oneself to a given, potentially invalid hypothesis.

Number of Items: 14

Format: Responses are made on a 6-point scale ranging from 1 (*strongly disagree*) to 6 (*strongly agree*).

Reliability: Coefficient alpha was .72 ($n = 239$).

Validity: Correlations with other variables ranged from −.67 to .24 ($n = 239$).

Author: Moneta, G. B., and Yip, P. P. Y.

Article: Construct validity of the scores of the Chinese version of the Need for Closure Scale.

Journal: *Educational and Psychological Measurement*, June 2004, *64*, 531–548.

Related Research: Neuberg, S. L., et al. (1997). What the Need for Closure Scale measures and what it does not: Toward differentiating among related epistemic motives. *Journal of Personality and Social Psychology, 72*, 1396–1412.

10707

Test Name: PERSONAL FEELINGS QUESTIONNAIRE— SHAME SCALE

Purpose: To measure shame proneness.

Number of Items: 10

Format: Responses are made on a 5-point scale ranging from 0 (*never*) to 4 (*continuously or almost continuously*).

Reliability: Alpha coefficients were .73 and .78. Test–retest (2 weeks) reliability was .91.

Validity: Correlations with other variables ranged from –.48 to .58 (*N* = 299).

Author: Wei, M., et al.

Article: Adult attachment, shame, depression, and loneliness: The mediation role of basic psychological needs satisfaction.

Journal: *Journal of Counseling Psychology*, October 2005, *52*, 591–601.

Related Research: Harder, D. W., & Zalma, A. (1990). Two promising shame and guilt scales: A construct validity comparison. *Journal of Personality Assessment, 55*, 729–745.

10708

Test Name: PERSONAL MATURITY SCALE

Purpose: To assess a child's behavioral and emotional adjustment.

Number of Items: 14

Format: Scales range from 0 (*my child is not at all like that*) to 10 (*my child is exactly like that*).

Reliability: Coefficient alpha was .76.

Author: Jayakody, R., and Kalil, A.

Article: Social fathering in low-income, African American families with preschool children.

Journal: *Journal of Marriage and Family*, May 2002, *64*, 504–516.

Related Research: Zill, N., et al. (1991). *Welfare mothers as potential employees: A statistical profile based on national survey data.* Washington, DC: Child Trends.

10709

Test Name: PERSONAL PROBLEMS INVENTORY— MODIFIED

Purpose: To assess self-reported problem levels.

Number of Items: 20

Format: Responses are made on a 6-point rating scale ranging from 1 (*not at all a problem*) to 6 (*a very significant problem*). Examples are presented.

Reliability: Alpha coefficients were .83 and .85.

Validity: Correlations with other variables ranged from –.54 to .88.

Author: Lopez, F. G., et al.

Article: Adult attachment orientation and college student distress: Test of a mediational model.

Journal: *Journal of Counseling Psychology*, October 2002, *49*, 460–467.

Related Research: Cash, T. F., et al. (1975). When counselors are heard but not seen: Initial impact of physical attractiveness. *Journal of Counseling Psychology, 22*, 273–279.

10710

Test Name: PERSONAL REPORT OF COMMUNICATION APPREHENSION—24

Purpose: To measure apprehension or anxiety while speaking in public situations.

Number of Items: 24

Format: Includes four areas: dyads, groups, meetings, and public speaking. Responses are made on 5-point scales.

Validity: Correlations with other variables ranged from –.58 to .44.

Author: Diaz, R. J., et al.

Article: Cognition, anxiety, and prediction of performance in 1st year law students.

Journal: *Journal of Educational Psychology*, June 2001, *93*, 420–429.

Related Research: McCroskey, J. C. (1993). *Introduction to*

rhetorical communication (6th ed.). New Brunswick, NJ: Prentice Hall.

10711

Test Name: PERSONAL VIEWS SURVEY

Purpose: To measure hardiness as commitment, control, and challenge.

Number of Items: 45

Format: Sample items are presented.

Reliability: Alpha reliabilities ranged from .69 to .77 across subscales.

Validity: Correlations with the Millon Clinical Multiaxial Inventory, MMPI scales and five-factor scores are presented.

Author: Maddi, S. R., et al.

Article: The personality construct of hardiness: II. Relationships with comprehensive tests of personality and psychopathology.

Journal: *Journal of Research in Personality*, February 2002, *36*, 72–85.

Related Research: Maddi, S. R. (1997). Personal Views Survey II: A measure of dispositional hardiness. In C. P. Zalaquett & R. J. Woods (Eds.), *Evaluating stress: A book of resources*. Lanham, MD: Scarecrow Press.

10712

Test Name: PERSONAL VIEWS SURVEY

Purpose: To measure hardiness as challenge, control, and commitment.

Number of Items: 50

Format: Rating scales are anchored by 0 (*not true at all*) and 3 (*completely true*). Sample items are presented.

Reliability: Alpha coefficients ranged from .68 to .82.

Validity: Correlations with other variables ranged from .05 to .37. Correlations between subscales ranged from .55 to .86.

Author: Turnipseed, D. L.

Article: Hardy personality: A potential link with organizational citizenship behavior.

Journal: *Psychological Reports*, October 2003, *93*, 529–543.

Related Research: Kobasa, S. C. (1979). Stressful life events, personality, and health: An inquiry into hardiness. *Journal of Personality and Social Psychology*, *37*, 1–11.

10713

Test Name: PERSONAL WELL-BEING

Purpose: To measure health and mood.

Number of Items: 55

Format: Five-point scales anchored by *very often* and *rarely or never* are used with health items. Five-point scales anchored by *very slightly* and *extremely* are used with mood items.

Reliability: Alpha was .93 (health) and .90 (mood).

Validity: Correlations with other variables ranged from .00 to .45.

Author: Goldman, B. M., et al.

Article: Goal-directedness and personal identity as correlates of life outcomes.

Journal: *Psychological Reports*, August 2002, *91*, 153–166.

Related Research: Heath, D. H. (1991). *Fulfilling lives: Paths to maturity and success.* San Francisco: Jossey-Bass. Watson, D., et al. (1988). Development and validation of a brief measure of positive and negative affect: The PANAS Scales. *Journal of Personality and Social Psychology*, *54*, 1063–1070.

10714

Test Name: PHYSICAL ACTIVITY AFFECT SCALE

Purpose: To measure psychological response to exercise.

Number of Items: 12

Format: Includes four subscales: Positive Affect, Negative Affect, Fatigue, and Tranquility. Responses are made on a 5-point scale ranging from 0 (*do not feel*) to 4 (*feel very strongly*).

Reliability: Alpha coefficients ranged from .84 to .94.

Author: Butki, B. D., et al.

Article: Effects of a carbohydrate-restricted diet on affective responses to acute exercise among physically active participants.

Journal: *Perceptual and Motor Skills*, April 2003, *96*, 607–615.

Related Research: Lox, C. L., et al. (2000). Revisiting the measurement of exercise-induced feeling states: The Physical Activity Affect Scale (PAAS). *Measures in Physical Education and Exercise Science*, *4*, 79–95.

10715

Test Name: PHYSICAL ANHEDONIA SCALE

Purpose: To measure lack of pleasure derived from various physical domains such as eating, touching, and feeling.

Number of Items: 61

Format: Sample items are presented.

Reliability: Coefficient alpha was .83.

Validity: Correlation with other variables ranged from –.64 to .33.

Author: Ross, S. R., et al.

Article: Positive and negative symptoms of schizotypy and the five-factor model: A domain and facet level analysis.

Journal: *Journal of Personality Assessment*, August 2002, *79*, 53–72.

Related Research: Chapman, L. J., et al. (1976). Scales for physical and social anhedonia. *Journal of Abnormal Psychology*, *85*, 374–407.

10716

Test Name: PHYSICAL COMPLAINTS SCALE

Purpose: To measure well-being.

Number of Items: 10

Format: Nine-point scales are used.

Reliability: Coefficient alpha was .79.

Author: Kim, Y., et al.

Article: Self-concept, aspirations, and well-being in South Korea and the United States.

Journal: *The Journal of Social Psychology*, June 2003, *143*, 277–290.

Related Research: Emmons, R. A. (1991). Personal strivings, daily life events, and psychological and physical well-being. *Journal of Personality*, *59*, 453–472.

10717

Test Name: PHYSICAL HEALTH SCALE

Purpose: To assess physical health.

Number of Items: 20

Format: Symptoms are rated from 1 (*never*) to 5 (*15+ days*).

Reliability: Coefficient alpha was .69.

Author: Pritchard, M. E., and McIntosh, D. N.

Article: What predicts adjustment among law students? A longitudinal panel study.

Journal: *The Journal of Social Psychology*, December 2003, *143*, 727–745.

Related Research: McIntosh, D. N., et al. (1994). Stress and health in first-year law students. *Journal of Applied Social Psychology, 24,* 1474–1499.

10718

Test Name: PHYSICAL SYMPTOMS INVENTORY

Purpose: To assess physical health.

Number of Items: 18

Format: Responses are made on a 3-point scale ranging from 1 (*no*) to 3 (*yes, and I saw a doctor*). An example is given.

Reliability: Coefficient alpha was .80 (*n* = 195).

Validity: Correlations with other variables ranged from –.18 to .45 (*n* = 195).

Author: Lubbers, R., et al.

Article: Young workers' job self-efficacy and affect: Pathways to health and performance.

Journal: *Journal of Vocational Behavior,* October 2005, *67,* 199–214.

Related Research: Spector, P. E., & Jex, S. M. (1998). Development of four self-report measures of job stressors and strain: Interpersonal Conflict at Work Scale, Organizational Constraints Scale, Quantitative Workload Inventory, and Physical Symptoms Inventory. *Journal of Occupational Health Psychology, 3,* 356–367.

10719

Test Name: PHYSICAL SYMPTOMS SCALE

Purpose: To measure physical health symptoms.

Number of Items: 11

Format: Scales range from 1 (*not at all*) to 5 (*almost daily*). All items are presented.

Reliability: Coefficient alpha was .81.

Validity: Correlations with other variables ranged from –.26 to .57.

Author: Jokisaari, M.

Article: Regret appraisals, age, and subjective well-being.

Journal: *Journal of Research in Personality,* December 2003, *37,* 487–503.

Related Research: Nurmi, J.-E., & Salmela-Aro, K. (1996). *Physical Symptoms Scale.* Helsinki: Department of Psychology, University of Helsinki.

10720

Test Name: PITTSBURGH SLEEP QUALITY INDEX

Purpose: To measure sleep quality and sleep disturbance during the previous 1-month period.

Number of Items: 18

Format: Includes 4 open-ended questions and 14 questions rated on a 4-point scale ranging from 0 (*no difficulty*) to 3 (*severe difficulty*). Examples are given.

Reliability: Coefficient alpha was .83. Test–retest correlation was .85.

Validity: Correlations with other variables ranged from –.01 to .30.

Author: Howell, A. J., et al.

Article: Sleep quality, sleep propensity and academic performance.

Journal: *Perceptual and Motor Skills,* October 2004, *99,* 525–535.

Related Research: Buysse, D. J., et al. (1989). The Pittsburgh Sleep Quality Index: A new instrument for psychiatric practice and research. *Psychiatry Research, 28,* 193–213.

10721

Test Name: POSITIVE AFFECTIVE DELIVERY SCALE

Purpose: To rate employee positive affect delivery.

Number of Items: 6

Format: Scales range from 1 (*strongly disagree*) to 5 (*strongly agree*). A sample item is presented.

Reliability: Coefficient alpha was .89.

Validity: Correlations with other variables ranged from –.10 to .21.

Author: Gosserand, R. H., and Diefendorff, J. M.

Article: Emotional display rules and emotional labor: The moderating role of commitment.

Journal: *Journal of Applied Psychology,* November 2005, *90,* 1256–1264.

10722

Test Name: POSITIVE AND NEGATIVE AFFECT SCALE

Purpose: To assess trait negative affect and trait positive affect.

Number of Items: 10

Format: Responses are made on a 5-point scale.

Reliability: Coefficient alphas were .85 and .90.

Validity: Correlations with other variables ranged from –.68 to .74.

Author: Steed, L. G.

Article: A psychometric comparison of four measures of hope and optimism.

Journal: *Educational and Psychological Measurement,* June 2002, *62,* 466–482.

Related Research: Watson, D., et al. (1988). Development and validation of brief measures of positive and negative affect: The PANAS scales. *Journal of Personality of Social Psychology, 54,* 1063–1070.

10723

Test Name: POSITIVE AND NEGATIVE AFFECT SCHEDULE

Purpose: To assess both positive and negative affect.

Number of Items: 20

Format: Each adjective is rated on a 5-point rating scale ranging from 1 (*slightly or not at all*) to 5 (*definitely*).

Reliability: Alpha coefficients were .88 and .89.

Validity: Correlations with other variables ranged from –.48 to .79.

Author: Huelsman, T. J., et al.

Article: Measurement of dispositional affect: Construct validity and convergence with a circumflex model of affect.

Journal: *Educational and Psychological Measurement,* August 2003, *63,* 655–673.

Related Research: Watson, D., et al. (1988). Development and validation of brief measures of positive and negative affect: The PANAS scales. *Journal of Personality and Social Psychology, 54,* 1063–1070.

10724

Test Name: POSITIVE AND NEGATIVE AFFECT SCHEDULE—GERMAN SHORT FORM

Purpose: To assess emotional balance.

Number of Items: 20

Format: Responses are made on a 5-point scale.

Reliability: Coefficient alpha was .70.

Validity: Correlation with other variables ranged from .01 to .43.

Author: Wiese, B. S., et al.

Article: Subjective career success and emotional well-being: Longitudinal predictive power of selection, optimization, and compensation.

Journal: *Journal of Vocational Behavior,* June 2002, *60,* 321–335.

Related Research: Watson, D., et al. (1988). Development and

validation of brief measures of positive and negative affect: The PANAS scales. *Journal of Personality and Social Psychology, 54,* 1063–1070.

10725

Test Name: POSITIVE AND NEGATIVE EMOTIONS SCALES

Purpose: To measure positive and negative emotions.

Number of Items: 13

Format: Scales range from 1 (*not at all*) to 5 (*a great deal*). Sample items are presented.

Reliability: Alpha coefficients exceeded .83.

Author: Umberson, D., et al.

Article: Relationship dynamics, emotion state, and domestic violence: A stress and masculinities perspective.

Journal: *Journal of Marriage and Family,* February 2003, *65,* 233–247.

Related Research: Bradburn, N. M. (1969). *The structure of psychological well-being.* Chicago: Aldine.

10726

Test Name: POSITIVE AND NEGATIVE SUICIDE IDEATION INVENTORY

Purpose: To assess the frequency of negative risk and protective factors that are related to suicidal behavior.

Number of Items: 14

Format: Includes two subscales: Positive and Negative. Responses are made on a 5-point scale ranging from 1 (*not the time*) to 5 (*most of the time*).

Reliability: Alpha coefficients ranged from .80 to .96.

Validity: Correlations with other variables ranged from –.34 to .52 (*N* = 195).

Author: Osman, A., et al.

Article: The Positive and Negative Suicide Ideation (PANSI) Inventory: Psychometric evaluation with adolescent psychiatric inpatient samples.

Journal: *Journal of Personality Assessment,* December 2002, *79,* 512–530.

Related Research: Osman, A., et al. (1998). The Positive and Negative Suicide Ideation Inventory: Development and validation. *Psychological Reports, 82,* 783–793.

10727

Test Name: POSITIVE COPING SCALE

Purpose: To identify the likelihood of responding in the manner described.

Number of Items: 2

Format: Responses are made on a 7-point scale ranging from 1 (*not at all*) to 7 (*very much*).

Reliability: Alpha coefficients ranged from .84 to .88.

Author: Deffenbacher, J. L., et al.

Article: Characteristics of two groups of angry drivers.

Journal: *Journal of Counseling Psychology,* April 2003, *50,* 123–132.

Related Research: Novaco, R. W. (1975). *Anger Control.* Lexington, MA: Heath.

10728

Test Name: POSITIVE LIFE CHANGE SCALE

Purpose: To measure the extent to which life domains changed as a result of assault.

Number of Items: 17

Format: Response categories range from 1 (*much worse now*) to

5 (*much better now*). Sample items are presented.

Reliability: Coefficient alpha was .91.

Validity: Correlations with other variables ranged from –.06 to .47.

Author: Frazier, P., et al.

Article: Correlates of levels and patterns of positive life changes following sexual assault.

Journal: *Journal of Consulting and Clinical Psychology,* February 2004, *72,* 19–30.

Related Research: Frazier, P., et al. (2001). Positive and negative changes following sexual assault. *Journal of Consulting and Clinical Psychology, 69,* 1048–1055.

10729

Test Name: POSITIVE PSYCHOLOGY PROTECTIVE PROFILE

Purpose: To measure positive outlook, negative symptoms, and problem-solving.

Number of Items: 29

Format: Scales are anchored by 4 (*very much like me*) and 1 (*not at all like me*). All items are presented.

Reliability: Alpha coefficients ranged from .67 to .89.

Validity: Correlations with other variables ranged from –.55 to .46.

Author: Morse, L. W., et al.

Article: A validity study of the Positive Protective Profile.

Journal: *Psychological Reports,* October 2003, *93,* 441–447.

10730

Test Name: POSTTRAUMATIC GROWTH INVENTORY

Purpose: To measure the positive changes that follow trauma.

Number of Items: 21

Format: Scales range from 0 (*I did not experience this change as a result of my crisis*) to 5 (*I experienced this change to a very great degree as a result of my crisis*). All items are presented.

Reliability: Alpha coefficients ranged from .67 to .91 across subscales. Total alpha was .96.

Validity: Subscale correlations ranged from .41 to .82.

Author: Sheikh, A. I., and Marotta, S. A.

Article: A cross-validation study of the Posttraumatic Growth Inventory.

Journal: *Measurement and Evaluation in Counseling and Development,* July 2005, *38,* 66–77.

Related Research: Tedeschi, R. G., & Calhoun, L. G. (1996). The Posttraumatic Growth Inventory: Measuring the positive legacy of trauma. *Journal of Traumatic Stress, 9,* 455–472.

10731

Test Name: POSTTRAUMATIC STRESS DISORDER CHECKLIST (PCL)

Purpose: To measure posttraumatic stress.

Number of Items: 17

Format: Item responses are anchored by 1 (*not at all*) and 5 (*extremely*).

Reliability: Alpha was .97.

Validity: Correlations with other variables ranged from .77 to .93.

Author: Farley, M., and Patsalides, B. M.

Article: Physical symptoms, posttraumatic stress disorder, and healthcare utilization of women with abuse and without childhood physical and sexual abuse.

Journal: *Psychological Reports,* December 2001, *89,* 595–606.

Related Research: Weathers, F. W., et al. (1993). *The PTSD Checklist (PCL): Reliability, validity, and diagnostic utility.* Paper presented at the 9th Annual Meeting of the International Society for Traumatic Stress Studies, San Antonio, TX.

10732

Test Name: POSTTRAUMATIC STRESS DISORDER INVENTORY

Purpose: To assess symptoms of PTSD.

Number of Items: 17

Format: A yes–no format is used.

Reliability: Coefficient alpha was .87.

Author: Dekel, R., et al.

Article: World assumptions and combat-related posttraumatic stress disorder.

Journal: *The Journal of Social Psychology,* August 2004, *144,* 407–420.

Related Research: Solomon, Z. (1988). Convergent validity of posttraumatic stress disorder (PTSD) diagnosis: Self-report and clinical assessment. *Israel Journal of Psychiatry and Related Sciences, 25,* 46–55.

10733

Test Name: PROACTIVE COPING INVENTORY

Purpose: To measure coping in stressful situations: task-oriented coping, emotion-oriented coping, and avoidance-oriented coping.

Number of Items: 9

Format: Scales range from 1 (*not at all true*) to 7 (*very true*). Sample items are presented.

Reliability: Alpha coefficients ranged from .67 to .82 across subscales.

Author: Chu, A. H. C., and Choi, J. N.

Article: Rethinking procrastination: Positive effects of "active" procrastination behavior on attitudes and performance.

Journal: *The Journal of Social Psychology*, June 2005, *145*, 245–264.

Related Research: Greenglass, E., et al. (1999). The Proactive Coping Inventory (PCI): A multidimensional research instrument. Available at http://userpage.fuberlin.de/~health/greenpci.html

10734

Test Name: PROBLEM-FOCUSED STYLE OF COPING QUESTIONNAIRE

Purpose: To assess problem-focused activities associated with progress toward resolving problems.

Number of Items: 18

Format: Includes three subscales: Reflective Style, Suppressive Style, and Reactive Style. Responses are made on a 5-point scale ranging from 1 (*almost never*) to 5 (*almost all of the time*).

Reliability: Alpha coefficients ranged from .73 to .77. Test–retest (3 weeks) reliability coefficients ranged from .65 to .71.

Author: Wei, M., et al.

Article: Perceived coping as a mediator between attachment and psychological distress: A structural equation modeling approach.

Journal: *Journal of Counseling Psychology*, October 2003, *50*, 438–447.

Related Research: Heppner, P. P., et al. (1995). Progress in resolving problems: A problem-focused style of coping. *Journal of Counseling Psychology, 42*, 279–293.

10735

Test Name: PROBLEM-SOLVING AND SOCIAL SUPPORT SCALES

Purpose: To provide two measures of coping strategies.

Number of Items: 18

Format: Responses are made on 5-point scales ranging from 1 (*not at all*) to 5 (*very much*). Examples are given.

Reliability: Alpha coefficients ranged from .71 to .94. Test–retest (2 weeks) reliabilities ranged from .67 to .83.

Validity: Correlations with other variables ranged from –.08 to .40 ($n = 117$).

Author: Lee, R. M., et al.

Article: Coping with intergenerational family conflict among Asian American college students.

Journal: *Journal of Counseling Psychology*, July 2005, *52*, 389–399.

Related Research: Tobin, D. L., et al. (1984). *User's manual for the Coping Strategies Inventory.* Unpublished manuscript, Ohio State University.

10736

Test Name: PROCESS OF CHANGE SCALE

Purpose: To measure process of change: experiential and behavioral.

Number of Items: 40

Format: Five-point scales range from 1 (*never*) to 5 (*repeatedly*).

Reliability: Alpha coefficients ranged from .82 to .84.

Author: Stotts, A. L., et al.

Article: Motivational interviewing with cocaine-dependent patients: A pilot study.

Journal: *Journal of Consulting and Clinical Psychology*, October 2001, *69*, 858–862.

Related Research: DiClementi, C. C., & Prochaska, J. O. (1982). Self-change and therapy change of smoking behavior: A comparison of processes of change in cessation and maintenance. *Addictive Behaviors, 7*, 133–142.

10737

Test Name: PRODUCTION AND APPRECIATION OF HUMOR SCALE

Purpose: To measure humor production and appreciation.

Number of Items: 14

Format: Scales range from 1 (*rarely*) to 7 (*very often*). Sample items are presented.

Reliability: Alpha coefficients were .59 (production) and .76 (appreciation).

Author: Nevo, O., et al.

Article: Singaporean humor: A cross-cultural, cross-gender comparison.

Journal: *The Journal of General Psychology*, April 2001, *128*, 143–156.

Related Research: Ziv, A. (1981). *The psychology of humor.* Tel Aviv: Yahdav (in Hebrew).

10738

Test Name: PROFILE OF MOOD STATES DEPRESSION SCALE— SHORT FORM

Purpose: To assess depressive mood.

Number of Items: 8

Format: Items are rated on scales ranging from 0 (*not at all*) to 4 (*quite a bit*). Sample items are presented.

Reliability: Coefficient alpha was .90.

Validity: Correlations with other variables ranged from –.32 to .52.

Author: Hobfoll, S. E., et al.

Article: The impact of perceived child physical and sexual abuse history on Native American women's psychological well-being and AIDS risk.

Journal: *Journal of Consulting and Clinical Psychology*, February 2002, *70*, 252–257.

Related Research: Malouff, J. M., et al. (1985). Evaluation of a short form of the POMS–Depression Scale. *Journal of Clinical Psychology, 41*, 389–391.

10739

Test Name: PSYCHIATRIC INSTITUTE TRICHOTILLOMANIA SCALE

Purpose: To assess hair-pulling symptoms by clinician ratings.

Number of Items: 6

Format: Eight-point scales are used.

Reliability: Internal consistency reliability was .59. Interrater agreement ranged from .60 to 1.00.

Validity: Correlations with other variables ranged from .53 to .75.

Author: Diefenbach, G. J., et al.

Article: Assessment of trichotillomania: A psychometric evaluation of hair-pulling scales.

Journal: *Journal of Psychopathology and Behavioral Assessment*, September 2005, *27*, 169–178.

Related Research: Stanley, M.A., et al. (1999). Clinician-rated measures of hairpulling: A preliminary psychometric evaluation. *Journal of Psychopathology and Behavioral Assessment, 21*, 157–170.

10740

Test Name: PSYCHOLOGICAL AND PHYSICAL WELL-BEING SCALES

Purpose: To measure psychomatic symptoms, physical health, and medication use.

Number of Items: 41

Format: Varied 4-point scales, 2-point scales, and frequency scales are used. All are described.

Reliability: Alpha coefficients ranged from .29 to .92 across subscales.

Author: Burke, R. J.

Article: Work experiences and psychological well-being of former hospital-based nurses now employed elsewhere.

Journal: *Psychological Reports*, December 2002, *91*, Part 2, 1059–1064.

Related Research: Derogatis, L. R., et al. (1979). The Hopkins Symptom Checklist (HSCL): A self-report symptom inventory. *Behavioral Science, 19*, 1–15.

10741

Test Name: PSYCHOLOGICAL CONTROL SCALE—YOUTH SELF-REPORT

Purpose: To measure constraint of verbal expression, love withdrawal, invalidation of feelings, and personal attack.

Format: Subjects rank each parent on scales anchored by 1 (*not at all like him [her]*) and 3 (*a lot like him [her]*).

Reliability: Alpha coefficients ranged from .81 to .90.

Validity: Correlations with a peer and parent attachment scale ranged from –.51 to –.35.

Author: Leonardi, A., and Kiosseoglou, G.

Article: Parental psychological control and attachment in late adolescents and young adults.

Journal: *Psychological Reports*, June 2002, *90*, Part 1, 1015–1030.

Related Research: Barker, B. K. (1996). Parental psychological control: Revisiting a neglected

construct. *Child Development, 67*, 3276–3319.

10742

Test Name: PSYCHOLOGICAL DISTRESS SCALES

Purpose: To indicate psychological distress.

Number of Items: 9

Format: Includes two scales: Depressive Cognitions and Suicidal Ideation. Examples are presented.

Reliability: Alpha coefficients were .66 (depression) and .71 (suicidal ideation).

Validity: Correlation with other variables ranged from –.27 to .33.

Author: Goodyear, R. K., et al.

Article: Pregnant Latina teenagers: Psychosocial and developmental determinants of how they select and perceive the men who father their children.

Journal: *Journal of Counseling Psychology*, April 2002, *49*, 187–201.

Related Research: Newcomb, M. D., et al. (1999). Drug problems and psychological distress among a community sample of adults: Predictors, consequences, or confound? *Journal of Community Psychology, 27*, 405–429

10743

Test Name: PSYCHOLOGICAL TRAUMA AND PSYCHOLOGICAL RESOURCES SCALE

Purpose: To identify adolescents and adults who have experienced traumatic events such as physical and sexual abuse and neglect.

Number of Items: 92

Format: Response scales are anchored by 1 (*never*) and 4 (*often*). Sample items are presented.

Reliability: Alpha coefficients ranged from .75 to .96 across subscales.

Author: Stader, S. R., et al.

Article: Comparison of scores for abused and nonabused young adults on the Psychological Trauma and Resources Scale.

Journal: *Psychological Reports*, April 2004, *94*, 687–693.

Related Research: Holmes, G. R., et al. (1997). An interim report on the development of the Psychological Trauma and Resources Scales. *Psychological Reports*, *80*, 819–831.

10744

Test Name: PSYCHOLOGICAL WELL-BEING INVENTORY— JAPANESE VERSION

Purpose: To measure self-acceptance, positive relations, autonomy, environmental mastery, purpose in life, and personal growth.

Number of Items: 84

Format: Response scales are anchored by 1 (*yes*) and 2 (*no*). All items are presented in Japanese.

Reliability: Alpha coefficients ranged from .45 to .83.

Validity: Correlations with other variables ranged from −.43 to .14.

Author: Kitamura, T., et al.

Article: Ryff's Psychological Well-Being Inventory: Factorial structure and life history correlates among Japanese university students.

Journal: *Psychological Reports*, February 2004, *94*, 83–103.

Related Research: Ryff, C. D. (1989). Happiness is everything, or is it? Explorations on the meaning of psychological well-being. *Journal of Personality and Social Psychology*, *57*, 1069–1081.

10745

Test Name: PSYCHOLOGICAL WELL-BEING SCALE

Purpose: To measure psychological well-being.

Number of Items: 84

Format: Includes six subscales. Responses are made on a 6-point subscale ranging from 1 (*strongly disagree*) to 6 (*strongly agree*).

Reliability: Internal consistencies ranged from .86 to .96. Test–retest (6 weeks) reliabilities ranged from .81 to .88.

Author: Lease, S. H., et al.

Article: Affirming faith experiences and psychological health for Caucasian lesbian, gay, and bisexual individuals.

Journal: *Journal of Counseling Psychology*, July 2005, *52*, 378–388.

Related Research: Ryff, C. (1989). Happiness is everything, or is it? Explorations on the meaning of psychological well-being. *Journal of Personality and Social Psychology*, *57*, 1069–1081.

10746

Test Name: PSYCHOLOGICAL WELL-BEING SCALE

Purpose: To assess psychological well-being.

Number of Items: 5

Format: Scales range from 1 (*none of the time*) to 5 (*all of the time*). A sample item is presented.

Reliability: Alpha coefficients ranged from .83 to .85.

Author: Munson, L. J., et al.

Article: Labeling sexual harassment in the military: An extension and replication.

Journal: *Journal of Applied Psychology*, April 2001, *86*, 293–303.

Related Research: Viet, C. T., & Ware, J. E. (1983). The structure of psychological distress and well-being in general populations.

Journal of Consulting and Clinical Psychology, *51*, 730–742.

10747

Test Name: PSYCHOLOGICAL WELL-BEING SCALE

Purpose: To measure positive relations with others, self-acceptance, autonomy, environmental mastery, purpose in life, and personal growth.

Number of Items: 18

Format: Scales range from 1 (*strongly disagree*) to 5 (*strongly agree*).

Reliability: Alpha coefficients ranged from .71 to .80 following rescaling of scores by the POMP method.

Validity: Correlations with other variables ranged from −.14 to .43.

Author: Sheldon, K. M.

Article: Positive value change during college: Normative trends and individual differences.

Journal: *Journal of Research in Personality*, April 2005, *39*, 209–223.

Related Research: Ryff, C. D., & Keyes, C. L. M. (1995). The structure of psychological well-being revisited. *Journal of Personality and Social Psychology*, *69*, 719–727.

10748

Test Name: PSYCHOLOGICAL WELL-BEING SCALE—SWEDISH VERSION

Purpose: To assess personal growth, self-acceptance, environmental mastery, and positive relations with others.

Number of Items: 18

Format: Response scales range from 1 (*completely disagree*) to 6 (*completely agree*).

Reliability: Alpha coefficients ranged from .33 to .56 across subscales.

Validity: Correlations with other variables ranged from −.61 to −.29.

Author: Lindfors, P.

Article: Positive health in a group of Swedish white-collar workers.

Journal: *Psychological Reports*, December 2002, *91*, Part 1, 839–845.

Related Research: Ryff, C. D., & Keyes, C. L. (1995). The structure of psychological well-being revisited. *Journal of Personality and Social Psychology, 69,* 719–727.

10749

Test Name: PSYCHOPATHIC PERSONALITY INVENTORY

Purpose: To assess psychopathic personality traits.

Number of Items: 187

Format: Includes eight dimensions: Machiavellian Egocentricity, Social Potency, Fearlessness, Cold-Heartedness, Impulsive Nonconformity, Alienation (or blame externalization), and Carefree Nonplayfulness. Responses are made on a 4-point scale ranging from 1 (*false*) to 4 (*true*). Includes three validity scales.

Reliability: Alpha coefficients ranged from .53 to .94. Test–retest reliabilities ranged from .44 to .92.

Validity: Correlations with other variables ranged from −.67 to .81.

Author: Chapman, A. L., et al.

Article: Psychometric analysis of the Psychopathic Personality Inventory (PPI) with female inmates.

Journal: *Journal of Personality Assessment,* April 2003, *80,* 164–172.

Related Research: Lilienfeld, S. O., & Andrews, B. P. (1996). Development and preliminary validation of a self-report measure

of psychopathic personality traits in noncriminal populations. *Journal of Personality Assessment, 66,* 488–524.

10750

Test Name: PSYCHOSEXUAL WELL-BEING SCALE

Purpose: To measure psychosexual well-being in women.

Number of Items: 3

Format: All items are presented.

Reliability: Coefficient alpha was .87. Correlation between items ranged from .63 to .78.

Author: Wimberly, S. R., et al.

Article: Perceived partner reactions to diagnosis and treatment of breast cancer: Impact on psychosocial and psychosexual adjustment.

Journal: *Journal of Consulting and Clinical Psychology,* April 2005, *73,* 300–311.

Related Research: Carver, C. S., et al. (1988). Concerns about aspects of body image and adjustment to early stage breast cancer. *Psychosomatic Medicine, 60,* 168–174.

10751

Test Name: PSYCHOSIS RATING SCALE

Purpose: To assess delusionality, psychosis, and bizarre delusionality.

Number of Items: 3

Format: Scales range from 1 (*definitely not*) to 9 (*definitely*). All items are presented.

Reliability: Coefficient alpha was .92.

Author: O'Connor, S., and Vandenberg, B.

Article: Psychosis or faith? Clinicians' assessment of religious beliefs.

Journal: *Journal of Consulting and Clinical Psychology,* August 2005, *73,* 610–616.

Related Research: Sanderson, S., et al. (1999). Authentic religious experience or insanity? *Journal of Clinical Psychology, 55,* 607–616.

10752

Test Name: PSYCHOSOMATIC SYMPTOM SCORE II

Purpose: To assess somatic complaints common to secondary manifestations of anxiety.

Number of Items: 10

Format: Sample items are presented.

Reliability: Coefficient alpha was .75.

Validity: Correlations with other variables ranged from −.36 to .58.

Author: Szymanski, D. M., et al.

Article: Psychosocial correlates of internalized homophobia in lesbians.

Journal: *Measurement and Evaluation in Counseling and Development,* April 2001, *34,* 27–38.

Related Research: Rosenberg, M. (1965). *Society and the adolescent self-image.* Princeton, NJ: Princeton University Press.

10753

Test Name: PSYCHOSOMATIC SYMPTOMS SCALE

Purpose: To rate psychosomatic symptoms.

Number of Items: 21

Format: Response categories are anchored by 1 (*never*) and 5 (*very frequently*). Sample items are presented.

Reliability: Alpha coefficients ranged from .80 to .89.

Validity: Correlations with other variables ranged from −.13 to .01.

Author: Al-Mashaan, O. S.

Article: Associations among job satisfaction, optimism, pessimism, and psychosomatic symptoms for employees in the government sector in Kuwait.

Journal: *Psychological Reports*, August 2003, *93*, 17–25.

Related Research: Al-Otaibi, A. G. (1997). [The effect of job stress in psychosomatic disorders and absenteeism among government employees in Kuwait]. [*Journal of the Social Sciences* (Kuwait University)], *25*, 177–201. [in Arabic]

10754

Test Name: PTSD CHECKLIST

Purpose: To assess PTSD symptoms.

Number of Items: 17

Format: Five-point scales range from 1 (*not at all*) to 5 (*extremely*).

Reliability: Alpha coefficients ranged from .91 to .92.

Author: Harned, M. S.

Article: Does it matter what you call it? The relationship between labeling unwanted sexual experiences and distress.

Journal: *Journal of Consulting and Clinical Psychology*, December 2004, *72*, 1090–1099.

Related Research: Weathers, F. W., et al. (1993, April). *The PTSD Checklist: Reliability, validity, and diagnostic utility.* Paper presented at the annual meeting of the International Society for Traumatic Stress Studies, San Antonio, TX.

10755

Test Name: PTSD SYMPTOM SCALE—SELF-REPORT

Purpose: To measure symptoms of PTSD in three symptom clusters: intrusion, avoidance, and arousal.

Number of Items: 17

Format: Item responses are on a 4-point Likert scale.

Reliability: Alpha coefficients ranged from .78 to .82.

Validity: Correlations with other variables ranged from .16 to .32.

Author: Nortje, C., et al.

Article: Judgment of risk in traumatized and nontraumatized emergency medical service personnel.

Journal: *Psychological Reports*, December 2004, *95*, Part 2, 1119–1128.

Related Research: Foa, E. B., et al. (1993). Reliability and validity of a brief instrument for assessing posttraumatic stress disorder. *Journal of Traumatic Stress, 6,* 459–473.

10756

Test Name: PTSD SYMPTOMS QUESTIONNAIRE FOR WOMEN

Purpose: To measure women's reactions to victimization such as recurrent distressing recollections, avoidance, and hypervigilance.

Number of Items: 17

Format: Respondents report the age at every occurrence of a symptom.

Reliability: Alpha coefficients ranged from .63 to .75.

Author: Yoshihama, M., and Horrocks, J.

Article: Posttraumatic stress symptoms and victimization among Japanese American women.

Journal: *Journal of Consulting and Clinical Psychology*, February 2002, *70*, 205–215.

Related Research: Kilpatrick, D. G., et al. (1989). *National Women's Study PTSD Module.* Unpublished instrument, National Crime Victim's Research and Treatment Center, Charleston, SC.

10757

Test Name: PURPOSE IN LIFE SCALE

Purpose: To measure a range of directedness and intentionality in life.

Number of Items: 9

Reliability: Coefficient alpha was .84.

Validity: Correlations with other variables ranged from −.76 to .53.

Author: Heisel, M. J., and Flett, G. L.

Article: Purpose in life, satisfaction with life, and suicide ideation in a clinical sample.

Journal: *Journal of Psychopathology and Behavioral Assessment*, June 2004, *26*, 127–135.

Related Research: Ryff, C. D. (1989). Happiness is everything, or is it? Explorations on the meaning of psychological well-being. *Journal of Personality and Social Psychology, 57,* 1069–1081.

10758

Test Name: QUALITY OF LIFE INDEX—SWEDISH VERSION

Purpose: To measure satisfaction with and importance of areas of life.

Number of Items: 16

Format: Importance scales range from 0 (*not at all important*) to 7 (*extremely important*). Satisfaction scales range from −3 (*very dissatisfied*) to +3 (*very satisfied*).

Reliability: Alpha coefficients exceeded .79.

Author: Paunovic, N., and Öst, L.-G.

Article: Clinical validation of the Swedish version of the Quality of Life Inventory in crime victims with posttraumatic stress disorder and a nonclinical sample.

Journal: *Journal of Psychopathology and Behavioral Assessment*, March 2004, *26*, 15–21.

Related Research: Frisch, M. B., et al. (1992). Clinical validation of the Quality of Life Inventory: A measure of life satisfaction for use in treatment planning and outcome assessment. *Psychological Assessment, 4*, 92–101.

10759

Test Name: QUALITY OF LIFE QUESTIONNAIRE FOR ADOLESCENTS

Purpose: To measure quality of life of adolescents with chronic pain.

Number of Items: 44

Format: Most item responses are anchored by 4-point scales. Some items use visual analogue scales.

Reliability: Alpha coefficients ranged from .66 to .87.

Validity: Correlations with other variables ranged from –.71 to .05.

Author: Merlin, Y. P. B. M., et al.

Article: Shortening a Quality of Life Questionnaire for adolescents with chronic pain and its psychometric qualities.

Journal: *Psychological Reports,* June 2002, *90,* Part 1, 753–759.

Related Research: Langeveld, J. H., et al. (1996). A quality of life instrument for adolescents with chronic headache. *Cephalalgia, 16,* 183–196.

10760

Test Name: QUALITY OF LIFE SCALE

Purpose: To assess subjective well-being.

Number of Items: 47

Format: Five-point scales are used.

Reliability: Coefficient alpha was .93.

Author: Lim, H.-J., et al.

Article: Exercise, pain, perceived family support, and quality of life in Korean patients with ankylosing spondylitis.

Journal: *Psychological Reports,* February 2005, *96,* 3–8.

Related Research: Ro, Y. J. (1988). *Analytical study on quality of life of middle-age adults in Seoul.* Unpublished doctoral dissertation, Yonsei University, Seoul.

10761

Test Name: QUALITY OF LIFE SCALE

Purpose: To measure perceived quality of life.

Number of Items: 7

Format: Response scales range from 1 (*totally satisfying*) to 7 (*completely unsatisfying*).

Reliability: Coefficient alpha was .87.

Author: Livneh, H., and Martz, E.

Article: Psychosocial adaptation to spinal cord injury: A dimensional perspective.

Journal: *Psychological Reports,* October 2005, *97,* 577–586.

Related Research: Chibnall, J. T., & Tait, R. C. (1990). The Quality of Life Scale: A preliminary study with chronic pain subjects. *Psychology and Health, 4,* 283–292.

10762

Test Name: QUESTIONNAIRE OF EXPERIENCES OF DISSOCIATION

Purpose: To provide a self-report measure of dissociation.

Number of Items: 26

Reliability: Coefficient alpha was. 78. Test–retest reliability was .82.

Validity: Correlation with the Scale of Dissociative Activities was .73 and with the Curious Experiences Survey was .68.

Author: Mayer, J. L., and Farmer, R. F.

Article: The development and psychometric evaluation of a new measure of dissociative activities.

Journal: *Journal of Personality Assessment,* April 2003, *80,* 185–196.

Related Research: Riley, K. C. (1988). Measurement of dissociation. *Journal of Nervous and Mental Disease, 176,* 449–450.

10763

Test Name: QUESTIONNAIRE ON ATTITUDES TOWARD FLYING

Purpose: To measure fear of flying.

Number of Items: 36

Format: Ten-point rating scales are used.

Reliability: Test–retest reliability was .92. Split-half reliability was .99.

Author: Rothbaum, B. O., et al.

Article: Twelve-month follow-up of virtual reality and standard exposure therapies for the fear of flying.

Journal: *Journal of Consulting and Clinical Psychology,* April 2002, *70,* 428–432.

Related Research: Howard, W. A., et al. (1983). The nature and treatment of fear of flying: A controlled investigation. *Behavior Therapy, 14,* 557–567.

10764

Test Name: R–COPE (REVISED COPE SCALE)

Purpose: To measure coping in several dimensions: self-blame, self-focused rumination, expressing emotion, understanding emotion, maintaining optimism, goal replacement, other-blame, and mental disengagement.

Number of Items: 8

Format: All items are presented.

Reliability: Alpha coefficients ranged from .70 to .90 across subscales.

Validity: Correlations between subscales ranged from –.20 to .52.

Author: Zuckerman, M., and Gagne, M.

Article: The COPE revised: Proposing a 5-factor model of coping strategies.

Journal: *Journal of Research in Personality*, June 2003, *37*, 169–204.

Related Research: Carver, C. S., et al. (1989). Assessing coping strategies: A theoretically based approach. *Journal of Personality and Social Psychology, 56,* 267–283.

10765

Test Name: REACTIONS TO IMPAIRMENT AND DISABILITY INVENTORY

Purpose: To measure psychosocial adaptation to disability and chronic illness.

Number of Items: 60

Format: Response scales range from 1 (*never, for reaction has never been experienced*) to 4 (*often, for reaction has been frequently experienced*).

Reliability: Alpha coefficients ranged from .66 to .84.

Author: Livneh, H., and Martz, E.

Article: Psychosocial adaptation to spinal cord injury: A dimensional perspective.

Journal: *Psychological Reports,* October 2005, *97,* 577–586.

Related Research: Livneh, H., & Antonak, R. F. (1997). *Psychosocial adaptation to chronic illness and disability.* Gaithersburg, MD: Aspen.

10766

Test Name: REASONS FOR LIVING INVENTORY FOR ADOLESCENTS

Purpose: To assess reasons adolescents give for not killing themselves.

Number of Items: 30

Format: Responses are made on a 6-point scale ranging from 1 (*not at all important*) to 6 (*extremely important*).

Reliability: Coefficient alpha was .91

Validity: Correlations with other variables ranged from –.34 to .39.

Author: Osman, A., et al.

Article: The Positive and Negative Suicide Ideation (PANSI) Inventory: Psychometric evaluation with adolescent psychiatric inpatient samples.

Journal: *Journal of Personality Assessment,* December 2002, *79,* 512–530.

Related Research: Osman, A., et al. (1998). The Reasons for Living Inventory for Adolescents (RFL-A): Development and psychometric properties. *Journal of Clinical Psychology, 54,* 1063–1078.

10767

Test Name: RECENT LIFE EVENTS STRESS CHECKLIST

Purpose: To determine the occurrence and degree of stressfulness.

Number of Items: 15

Format: Responses are made on a 4-point scale ranging from 0 (*event not experienced or not stressful*) to 3 (*event experienced as very stressful*).

Reliability: Coefficient alpha was .74.

Author: Mulatu, M. S.

Article: Psychometric properties of scores on the preliminary Amharic version of the State–Trait Anxiety Inventory in Ethiopia.

Journal: *Educational and Psychological Measurement,* February 2002, *62,* 130–146.

Related Research: Mulatu, M. S. (1995). Prevalence and risk factors of psychopathology in Ethiopian children. *Journal of American*

Academy of Child and Adolescent Psychiatry, 34, 100–109.

10768

Test Name: RELIGIOUS COPING SCALE

Purpose: To assess religious coping thoughts and behaviors.

Number of Items: 10

Format: Five-point scales range from 1 (*not at all*) to 5 (*very much*). Sample items are presented.

Reliability: Coefficient alpha averaged .91 over four time points.

Author: Frazier, P., et al.

Article: Correlates of levels and patterns of positive life changes following sexual assault.

Journal: *Journal of Consulting and Clinical Psychology,* February 2004, *72,* 19–30.

Related Research: Pargament, K. I., et al. (1990). God help me: I. Religious coping efforts as predictors of the outcomes to significant negative life events. *American Journal of Community Psychology, 18,* 793–824.

10769

Test Name: RELIGIOUS PROBLEM-SOLVING SCALES— SHORT FORM

Purpose: To measure styles of religious coping.

Number of Items: 18

Format: Scales range from 1 (*never*) to 5 (*always*).

Reliability: Alpha coefficients ranged from .88 to .92 across subscales.

Validity: Correlations with other variables ranged from –.73 to .71.

Author: Constantine, M. G., et al.

Article: Religious participation, spirituality, and coping among African American college students.

Journal: *Journal of College Student Development*, September/October 2002, *43*, 605–613.

Related Research: Pargament, K. I., et al. (1988). Religion and the problem-solving process: Three styles of coping. *Journal for the Scientific Study of Religion, 27*, 90–104.

10770

Test Name: RESPONSES TO DEPRESSION QUESTIONNAIRE—REVISED

Purpose: To assess the extent to which individuals ruminate and the extent to which they distract themselves when they feel depressed.

Number of Items: 21

Format: Responses are made on a 4-point scale ranging from 1 (*almost never*) to 4 (*almost always*).

Reliability: Alpha coefficients ranged from .89 to .92.

Validity: Correlations with other variables ranged from .05 to .59.

Author: Rose, A. J.

Article: Corumination in the friendships of girls and boys.

Journal: *Child Development*, November/December 2002, *73*, 1830–1843.

Related Research: Nolen-Hoeksema, S., & Morrow, J. (1991). A prospective study of depression and distress following a natural disaster: The 1989 Loma Prieta Earthquake. *Journal of Personality and Social Psychology, 61*, 105–121.

10771

Test Name: RESTRAINT AND REPRESSIVE DEFENSIVENESS SCALE

Purpose: To measure repressive defensiveness.

Number of Items: 11

Format: All items are presented.

Reliability: Coefficient alpha was .69 for repressive defensiveness and .53 for restraint.

Author: Giese-Davis, J., et al.

Article: Change in emotion-regulation strategy for women with metastatic breast cancer following supportive-expressive group therapy.

Journal: *Journal of Consulting and Clinical Psychology*, August 2002, *70*, 916–925.

Related Research: Weinberger, D. A. (1997). Distress and self-restraint as measures of adjustment across the life span: Confirmatory factor analysis in clinical and nonclinical samples. *Psychological Assessment, 9*, 132–135.

10772

Test Name: RESULTANT SELF-ESTEEM SCALE

Purpose: To measure self-esteem, mood, and negative mood.

Number of Items: 36

Format: Eleven-point scales range from *not at all* to *extremely*.

Reliability: Alpha coefficients ranged from .78 to .87 across subscales.

Author: Rhodewalt, F., and Eddings, S. K.

Article: Narcissus reflects: Memory distortion in response to ego-relevant feedback among high- and low-narcissistic men.

Journal: *Journal of Research in Personality*, April 2002, *36*, 97–116.

Related Research: McFarland, C., & Ross, M. (1982). Impact of causal attributions on affective reactions to success and failure. *Journal of Personality and Social Psychology, 43*, 937–946.

10773

Test Name: REVISED PERSONAL LIFESTYLE QUESTIONNAIRE

Purpose: To measure positive health practices.

Number of Items: 24

Format: Item responses range from 1 (*never*) to 4 (*almost always*).

Reliability: Coefficient alpha was .85.

Validity: Correlations with other variables ranged from –.47 to .54.

Author: Yarcheski, T. J., et al.

Article: Depression, optimism, and positive health practices in young adolescents.

Journal: *Psychological Reports*, December 2004, *95*, Part 1, 932–934.

Related Research: Mahon, N. E., et al. (2003). The Revised Personal Lifestyle Questionnaire for early adolescents. *Western Journal of Nursing Research, 25*, 533–547.

10774

Test Name: REVISED TRANSLIMINALITY SCALE

Purpose: To measure the tendency for psychological material to cross thresholds in and out of consciousness.

Number of Items: 17

Format: A true–false format is used.

Reliability: Test–retest reliability was .66 (10 months). Coefficient alpha was .81.

Validity: Correlations with other variables ranged from .01 to .78.

Author: Thalbourne, M. A.

Article: Transliminality and the Oxford–Liverpool Inventory of Feelings and Experiences.

Journal: *Psychological Reports*, June 2005, *96*, Part 1, 579–585.

10775

Test Name: REVISED WAYS OF COPING CHECKLIST

Purpose: To assess coping with a current life stressor.

Number of Items: 42

Format: Includes five scales. Responses are made on a 4-point scale ranging from 0 (*not used*) to 3 (*used a great deal*).

Validity: Correlations with other variables ranged from −.55 to .45.

Author: DiTommaso, E., et al.

Article: Measurement and validity characteristics of the short version of the Social and Emotional Loneliness Scale for Adults.

Journal: *Educational and Psychological Measurement*, February 2004, *64*, 99–119.

Related Research: Vitaliano, P. P., et al. (1985). The Ways of Coping Checklist: Revision and psychometric properties. *Multivariate Behavioral Research*, *20*, 3–26.

10776

Test Name: RUMINATION SCALE

Purpose: To assess the extent to which individuals focus on themselves when depressed.

Number of Items: 22

Format: Scales range from 1 (*almost never*) to 4 (*almost always*).

Reliability: Alpha coefficients ranged from .83 to .94.

Validity: Correlations with other variables ranged from −.06 to .36.

Author: Feldman, G., and Hayes, A.

Article: Preparing for problems: A measure of mental anticipatory processes.

Journal: *Journal of Research in Personality*, October 2005, *39*, 487–516.

Related Research: Nolen-Hoeksema, S., & Morrow, J. (1991). A prospective study of depression and posttraumatic stress symptoms after a natural disaster: The 1989 Loma Prieta earthquake. *Journal of Personality and Social Psychology*, *61*, 115–121.

10777

Test Name: SARS FEAR SCALE

Purpose: To measure fear of SARS: fear of infection, insecurity, and instability.

Number of Items: 9

Format: Scales range from 0 (*definitely false*) to 3 (*definitely true*). All items are presented.

Reliability: Alpha coefficients ranged from .66 to .80 across subscales.

Validity: Correlations with other variables ranged from −.28 to .66.

Author: Ho, M. Y. S., et al.

Article: Fear of severe acute respiratory syndrome (SARS) among health care workers.

Journal: *Journal of Consulting and Clinical Psychology*, April 2005, *73*, 344–349.

10778

Test Name: SATISFACTION AND DISSATISFACTION WITH BODY PARTS SCALE

Purpose: To measure satisfaction with one's body.

Number of Items: 9

Format: Rating scales range from 1 (*extremely dissatisfied*) to 5 (*extremely satisfied*).

Reliability: Coefficient alpha was .94. Test–retest reliability was .90.

Validity: Correlations with other variables ranged from .32 to .59.

Author: Stice, E., and Shaw, H.

Article: Prospective relations of body image, eating, and affective disturbances to smoking onset in adolescent girls: How Virginia slims.

Journal: *Journal of Consulting and Clinical Psychology*, February 2003, *71*, 129–135.

Related Research: Berscheid, E., et al. (1973). The happy American body: A survey report. *Psychology Today*, *7*, 119–131.

10779

Test Name: SATISFACTION WITH LIFE SCALE

Purpose: To assess life satisfaction.

Number of Items: 5

Format: Responses are made on a 7-point Likert-type scale ranging from 1 (*strongly disagree*) to 7 (*strongly agree*). A sample item is given.

Reliability: Test–retest (8 weeks) reliability was .82.

Validity: Correlations with other variables ranged from −.57 to .58 ($N = 150$).

Author: Chang, E. C., et al.

Article: How adaptive and maladaptive perfectionism relate to positive and negative psychological functioning: Testing a stress-mediation model in Black and White female college students.

Journal: *Journal of Counseling Psychology*, January 2004, *51*, 93–102.

Related Research: Diemer, E., et al. (1985). The Satisfaction With Life Scale. *Journal of Personality Assessment*, *49*, 71–75.

10780

Test Name: SATISFACTION WITH LIFE SCALE—MODIFIED

Purpose: To measure satisfaction with dual-career lifestyle and global personal-life satisfaction.

Number of Items: 10

Format: Responses are made on a 7-point scale ranging from 1 (*strongly disagree*) to 7 (*strongly agree*). All items are presented.

Reliability: Alpha coefficients were .87 and .88. Test–retest (2 months) reliability was .87 for the original 5-item Satisfaction With Life Scale.

Validity: Correlation of dual-career lifestyle satisfaction items with other variables ranged from –.35 to .57.

Author: Perrone, K. M., & Worthington, E. L, Jr.

Article: Factors influencing ratings of marital quality by individuals within dual-career marriages: A conceptual model.

Journal: *Journal of Counseling Psychology*, January 2001, *48*, 3–9.

Related Research: Diener, E., et al. (1985). The Satisfaction With Life Scale. *Journal of Personality Assessment, 49*, 71–75.

10781

Test Name: SATISFACTION WITH LIFE SCALE—TURKISH VERSION

Purpose: To measure satisfaction with life.

Number of Items: 5

Format: Seven-point scales are anchored by 1 (*strongly disagree*) and 7 (*strongly agree*).

Reliability: Coefficient alpha was .88.

Validity: Correlations with other variables ranged from –.19 to .46.

Author: Öner-Özkan, B.

Article: Revised form of the Belief in Good Luck Scale in a Turkish sample.

Journal: *Psychological Reports*, October 2003, *93*, 585–594.

Related Research: Diener, E., et al. (1985). The Satisfaction With Life

Scale. *Journal of Personality Assessment, 49*, 71–75.

10782

Test Name: SCALE FOR COPING ADAPTIVENESS

Purpose: To measure coping styles as individuated style, alignment style, compartmentalized style, and conflicted style.

Number of Items: 26

Format: Scales range from 1 (*strongly disagree*) to 8 (*strongly agree*). All items are presented.

Reliability: Coefficient alpha was .83.

Author: Stroink, M. L.

Article: A conflicting standards dilemma and gender: A mediating model of its affective implications and coping styles.

Journal: *The Journal of Social Psychology*, June 2004, *144*, 273–292.

Related Research: Higgins, E. T. (1987). Self-discrepancy: A theory relating self and affect. *Psychological Review, 94*, 319–340.

10783

Test Name: SCALE FOR SUICIDE IDEATION—ADAPTED

Purpose: To evaluate the extent of suicidal thoughts, their characteristics, and respondents' attitudes toward them.

Number of Items: 19

Format: Each item consists of three alternative statements graded in intensity from 0 to 2.

Reliability: Internal consistency was .89.

Validity: Concurrent validity was .41.

Author: Zhang, J., and Norvilitis, J. M.

Article: Measuring Chinese psychological well-being with Western developed instruments.

Journal: *Journal of Personality Assessment*, December 2002, *79*, 492–511.

Related Research: Beck, A. T., et al. (1979). Assessment of suicidal intention: The Scale for Suicide Ideation. *Journal of Consulting and Clinical Psychology, 47*, 343–352.

10784

Test Name: SCALE OF DISSOCIATIVE ACTIVITIES

Purpose: To assess the degree to which individuals experience mild to severe forms of dissociative activity.

Number of Items: 35

Format: Responses are made on a 5-point scale ranging from 1 (*never*) to 5 (*very frequently*). All items are presented.

Reliability: Coefficient alpha was .95. Test–retest reliability was .77.

Validity: Correlations with the Curious Experiences Survey was .82 and with the Questionnaire of Experiences of Dissociation was .73.

Author: Mayer, J. L., and Farmer, R. F.

Article: The development and psychometric evaluation of a new measure of dissociative activities.

Journal: *Journal of Personality Assessment*, April 2003, *80*, 185–196.

10785

Test Name: SCALES OF PSYCHOLOGICAL WELL-BEING

Purpose: To measure psychological well-being as autonomy, environmental mastery, personal growth, positive relations with others, purpose in life, and self-acceptance.

Number of Items: 84

Format: Scales range from 1 (*strongly disagree*) to 5 (*strongly agree*).

Reliability: Alpha coefficients ranged from .83 to .91 across subscales.

Author: September, A., et al.

Article: The relation between well-being, imposter feelings, and gender role orientation among Canadian University students.

Journal: *The Journal of Social Psychology*, April 2001, *141*, 218–232.

Related Research: Ryff, C. D., & Singer, B. (1996). Psychological well-being: Meaning, measurement, and implications for psychotherapy research. *Psychotherapy and Psychosomatics, 65*, 14–23.

10786

Test Name: SCHEMA QUESTIONNAIRE

Purpose: To measure 13 maladaptive schemas.

Number of Items: 160

Format: Scales range from 1 (*completely untrue of me*) to 6 (*describes me perfectly*).

Reliability: The average alpha coefficient was .90. Test–retest reliability was .76.

Validity: Correlations with other variables ranged from .35 to .50.

Author: Schmidt, N. B., and Joiner, T. E., Jr.

Article: Global maladaptive schemas, negative life events, and psychological distress.

Journal: *Journal of Psychopathology and Behavioral Assessment*, March 2004, *26*, 65–72.

Related Research: Schmidt, N. B., et al. (1995). The Schema Questionnaire: Investigation of

psychometric properties and hierarchical structure of a measure of maladaptive schemas. *Cognitive Therapy and Research, 19*, 295–231.

10787

Test Name: SCHIZOPHRENIA SYMPTOMS SCALE

Purpose: To assess schizophrenia symptomology.

Number of Items: 7

Format: Scales range from 1 (*not present*) to 7 (*extremely severe*).

Reliability: Coefficient alpha was .77.

Validity: Correlations with other variables ranged from −.55 to .19.

Author: Meyer, B.

Article: Coping with severe mental illness: Relations of the brief COPE with symptoms, functioning, and well-being.

Journal: *Journal of Psychopathology and Behavioral Assessment*, December 2001, *23*, 265–277.

Related Research: Eisele, R., et al. (1991). Rationale for BPRS use in routine clinical practice: Quantitative assessment of psychopathology consistent with clinical sense. *European Psychiatry, 6*, 261–268.

10788

Test Name: SCHIZOTYPAL PERSONALITY QUESTIONNAIRE—BRIEF

Purpose: To index schizotypal traits.

Number of Items: 22

Format: Includes three subscales: Cognitive–Perceptual, Interpersonal, and Disorganized.

Reliability: Coefficient alpha was .72.

Validity: Correlations with other variables ranged from −.07 to .48.

Author: Hergovich, A.

Article: Paranormal belief, schizotypy, and body mass index.

Journal: *Perceptual and Motor Skills*, June 2005, *100*, Part 1, 883–891.

Related Research: Raine, A., & Benishay, D. (1995). The SPQ–B: A brief screening instrument for schizotypal personality disorder. *Journal of Personality Disorders, 9*, 346–355.

10789

Test Name: SCHWARTZ OUTCOME SCALE

Purpose: To measure a broad domain of psychological health.

Number of Items: 10

Format: Responses are made on a 7-point scale ranging from 0 (*never*) to 6 (*all of the time or nearly all of the time*). All items are presented.

Reliability: Test–retest correlation coefficients for the items ranged from .53 to .86.

Author: Young, J. L., et al.

Article: Four studies extending the utility of the Schwartz Outcome Scale (SOS-10).

Journal: *Journal of Personality Assessment*, April 2003, *80*, 130–138.

Related Research: Blais, M. A., et al. (1999). Development and initial validation of a brief mental health outcome measure. *Journal of Personality Assessment, 73*, 359–373.

10790

Test Name: SECURITY SEEKING SCALE

Purpose: To measure security seeking in children by teacher observation.

Number of Items: 13

Format: Rating scales are anchored by 0 (*no security seeking*) and 2 (*high security seeking*). A sample item is presented.

Reliability: Alpha coefficients ranged from .86 to .91.

Validity: Correlations with other variables ranged from −.50 to −.26.

Author: Koomen, H. M. Y., and Hoeksma, J. B.

Article: Regulation of emotional security by children after entry to special and regular kindergarten classes.

Journal: *Psychological Reports*, December 2003, *93*, Part 2, 1319–1334.

10791

Test Name: SELF-IMAGE SCALE

Purpose: To assess body image of women with cancer. The scale measures self-acceptance and partner acceptance.

Number of Items: 11

Format: Scales range from 1 (*strongly agree*) to 5 (*strongly disagree*). Sample items are presented.

Reliability: Alpha coefficients ranged from .82 to .92.

Author: Scott, J. L., et al.

Article: United we stand? The effects of a couple-coping intervention on adjustment to early stage breast or gynecological cancer.

Journal: *Journal of Consulting and Clinical Psychology*, December 2004, *72*, 1122–1135.

Related Research: Halford, W. K., et al. (2001). Helping each other through the night: Couples and coping with cancer. In K. R.

Schmaling & T. G. Sher (Eds.), *The Psychology of Couples and Illness* (pp. 135–170). Washington, DC: American Psychological Association.

10792

Test Name: SELF-INVENTORY QUESTIONNAIRE: PTSD

Purpose: To measure the frequency of psychological health problems.

Number of Items: 47

Format: Four-point scales are anchored by *not at all* and *very much*.

Reliability: Total alpha was .96. Subscale alphas ranged from .79 to .86.

Author: Berghout, C., et al.

Article: Should subjects be forewarned of the possible psychological consequences of filling out a PTSD Questionnaire?

Journal: *Psychological Reports*, April 2002, *90*, 461–465.

Related Research: Hovens, J. E. (1994). *Research into the psychodiagnostics of posttraumatic stress disorder*. Delft, the Netherlands: Eburon.

10793

Test Name: SELF-PERCEPTION PROFILE FOR ADULTS

Purpose: To assess three domains of well-being.

Number of Items: 12

Format: Includes three well-being domains: view of oneself as a good worker, perception of how well one provided financially for the household, and general self-competence.

Reliability: Coefficient alpha was .63.

Author: Kossek, E. E., et al.

Article: Sustaining work force inclusion and well-being of mothers on public assistance: Individual deficit and social ecology perspectives.

Journal: *Journal of Vocational Behavior*, February 2003, *62*, 155–175.

Related Research: Harter, S. (1985). Process underlying the construction, maintenance, and enhancement of the self-concept in children. In J. Suls & A. Greenwald (Eds.), *Psychological perspectives on the self* (Vol. 3, pp. 137–181). Hillsdale, NJ: Erlbaum.

10794

Test Name: SELF-PREOCCUPATION SCALE

Purpose: To measure the tendency to focus more on the self than on external objects.

Number of Items: 19

Format: Items are rated on scales anchored by 1 (*does not apply to me at all*) and 5 (*applies to me very well*).

Reliability: Cronbach's alpha was .89.

Validity: Correlations with other variables ranged from −.32 to .12.

Author: Sakamoto, S., and Tomoda, A.

Article: Association of self-preoccupation and self-reported duration and severity of depressive episodes.

Journal: *Psychological Reports*, June 2002, *90*, Part 1, 861–868.

Related Research: Sakamoto, S., et al. (1998). The Preoccupation Scale: Its development and relationship with depression scales. *Journal of Clinical Psychology*, *54*, 645–654.

10795

Test Name: SELF-RATING DEPRESSION SCALE

Purpose: To measure depressive symptoms.

Number of Items: 20

Format: Includes three categories of depressive symptoms: pervasive affect, physiological features, and psychological concomitants. Responses are made on a 4-point scale ranging from 1 (*some or a little of the time*) to 4 (*most or all of the time*).

Reliability: Alpha coefficients were .84 and .85.

Validity: Correlations with other variables ranged from −.63 to .75 (*N* = 299).

Author: Wei, M., et al.

Article: Adult attachment, shame, depression, and loneliness: The mediation role of basic psychological needs satisfaction.

Journal: *Journal of Counseling Psychology*, October 2005, *52*, 591–601.

Related Research: Zung, W. W. (1965). A self-rating depression scale. *Archives of General Psychiatry, 12*, 63–70.

10796

Test Name: SELF-RATING DEPRESSION SCALE— JAPANESE VERSION

Purpose: To measure depression.

Number of Items: 20

Format: Scales range from 1 (*a little of the time*) to 4 (*most of the time*).

Reliability: Coefficient alpha was .80.

Author: Yukawa, S.

Article: Sex differences in relationships among anger, depression, and coping strategies of Japanese students.

Journal: *Psychological Reports*, December 2005, *97*, 769–776.

Related Research: Fukuda, K., & Kobayashi, S. (1983). [*Manual for the Japanese version of the Self-Rating Depression Scale (SDS)*]. Tokyo, Japan: Sankyou Bou.

10797

Test Name: SELF-REPORT COPING SCALE

Purpose: To measure child coping strategies.

Number of Items: 34

Format: A Likert format is used with responses ranging from 1 (*never*) to 5 (*always*).

Reliability: Alpha coefficients ranged from .63 to .86.

Author: Holmbeck, G. N., et al.

Article: A multimethod, multi-informant, and multidimensional perspective on psychosocial adjustment in preadolescents with Spina Bifida.

Journal: *Journal of Consulting and Clinical Psychology*, August 2003, *71*, 702–796.

Related Research: Causey, D. L., & Dubow, E. F. (1992). Development of a self-report coping measure for elementary school children. *Journal of Clinical Child Psychology, 50*, 332–345.

10798

Test Name: SELF-REPORT PSYCHOPATHY SCALE

Purpose: To assess psychopathic traits.

Number of Items: 26

Format: Includes a primary and a secondary scale. Responses are made on 4-point Likert-type scales ranging from 1 (*disagree strongly*) to 4 (*agree strongly*).

Reliability: Internal consistencies ranged from .66 to .88.

Validity: Correlations with other variables ranged from −.30 to .37.

Author: Campbell, J. S., and Elison, J.

Article: Shame coping styles and psychopathic personality traits.

Journal: *Journal of Personality Assessment*, February 2005, *84*, 96–104.

Related Research: Levenson, M., et al. (1995). Assessing psychopathic attributes in a noninstitutionalized population. *Journal of Personality and Social Psychology, 68*, 151–158.

10799

Test Name: SELF-REPORTING QUESTIONNAIRE

Purpose: To assess global psychiatric symptoms.

Number of Items: 24

Format: Responses are made on a 3-point scale ranging from 0 (*no*) to 2 (*yes*).

Reliability: Coefficient alpha was .84.

Author: Mulatu, M. S.

Article: Psychometric properties of scores on the preliminary Amharic version of the State–Trait Anxiety Inventory in Ethiopia.

Journal: *Educational and Psychological Measurement*, February 2002, *62*, 130–146.

Related Research: Harding, T. M., et al. (1983). The WHO collaborative study on strategies for extending mental health care: II. The development of reserved methods. *American Journal of Psychiatry, 140*, 1474–1480.

10800

Test Name: SEMANTIC DIFFERENTIAL MEASURE OF EMOTIONAL STATES— VALENCE SUBSCALE

Purpose: To assess dream valence.

Number of Items: 6

Format: Employs bipolar adjectives on 9-point scales. All items are presented.

Reliability: Internal consistencies were .89 and .90.

Validity: Correlations with other variables ranged from −.22 to .01 ($N = 94$).

Author: Hill, C. E., et al.

Article: Working with dreams using the Hill cognitive–experiential model: A comparison of computer-assisted, therapist empathy, and therapist empathy + input conditions.

Journal: *Journal of Counseling Psychology*, April 2003, *50*, 211–220.

Related Research: Mehrabian, A., & Russell, J. A. (1974). *An approach to environmental psychology.* Cambridge, MA: MIT Press.

10801

Test Name: SENSITIVITY TO DISGUST SCALE

Purpose: To measure disgust related to contact with bodies of water.

Number of Items: 7

Format: Six-point scales are used. All items are described.

Reliability: Coefficient alpha was .90.

Author: Bixler, R. D., and Powell, G.

Article: Sensitivity to disgust and perceptions of natural bodies of water and watercraft activities.

Journal: *Psychological Reports*, August 2003, *93*, 73–74.

Related Research: Bixler, R. D., & Floyd, M. F. (1999). Hands on or off? Disgust sensitivity and preference for environmental education activities. *Journal of Environmental Education, 30*, 4–11.

10802

Test Name: SEPARATION–INDIVIDUATION INVENTORY—CHINESE VERSION

Purpose: To measure disturbances in the separation–individuation process.

Format: Ten-point Likert format.

Reliability: Coefficient alpha was .88.

Validity: Correlations with other variables ranged from .47 to .50.

Author: Tam, W.-C. C., et al.

Article: Chinese version of the Separation–Individuation Inventory.

Journal: *Psychological Reports*, August 2003, *93*, 291–299.

Related Research: Christenson, R. M., & Wilson, W. P. (1985). The Separation–Individuation Inventory: Association with borderline phenomena. *Journal of Nervous and Mental Disease, 180*, 529–533.

10803

Test Name: SEPARATION–INDIVIDUATION TEST OF ADOLESCENCE— ADAPTED

Purpose: To measure separation–individuation.

Format: Includes three subscales: Separation Anxiety, Engulfment Anxiety, and Rejection Expectancy. Examples are given.

Reliability: Alpha coefficients ranged from .71 to .83.

Validity: Correlations with other variables ranged from −.55 to .57.

Author: Mattanah, J. F., et al.

Article: Parental attachment, separation–individuation, and college student adjustment: A structural equation analysis of mediational effects.

Journal: *Journal of Counseling Psychology*, April 2004, *51*, 213–225.

Related Research: Levine, J. B., et al. (1986). The separation–individuation test of adolescence. *Journal of Personality Assessment, 50*, 123–137.

10804

Test Name: SERIOUSNESS OF ILLNESS RATING SCALE

Purpose: To assess the seriousness of medical conditions (symptoms).

Number of Items: 37

Format: Scales range from 0 (*no problems*) to 4 (*serious problems*).

Validity: Correlations with other variables ranged from −.31 to .74.

Author: Pettit, J. W., et al.

Article: Are happy people healthier? The specific role of positive affect in predicting self-reported health symptoms.

Journal: *Journal of Research in Personality*, December 2001, *35*, 521–536.

Related Research: Wyler, A. R., et al. (1970). The Seriousness of Illness Rating Scale: Reproducibility. *Journal of Psychosomatic Research, 14*, 59–64.

10805

Test Name: SEXUAL PREOCCUPATION SCALE

Purpose: To assess preoccupation with sexual thoughts and fantasies.

Number of Items: 10

Format: Scales range from −2 (*disagree*) to +2 (*agree*). Sample items are presented.

Reliability: Coefficient alpha was .91. Test–retest reliability was .76.

Validity: Correlations with other variables ranged from −.16 to .56.

Author: Koukounas, E., and Letch, N. M.

Article: Psychological correlates of perception of sexual intent in women.

Journal: *The Journal of Social Psychology*, August 2001, *141*, 443–456.

Related Research: Snell, W. E., & Papini, D. R. (1989). The Sexuality

Scale: An instrument to measure sexual-esteem, sexual-depression, and sexual-preoccupation. *Journal of Sex Research, 26,* 256–263.

10806

Test Name: SHEEHAN DISABILITY SCALE

Purpose: To measure global impairment caused by a presenting problem.

Number of Items: 3

Format: Scales range from 0 (*not at all*) to 10 (*severe*). All items are described. (A fourth item is scored on a 5-point scale).

Validity: Correlations with other variables ranged from .18 to .49.

Author: Smits, J. A. J., et al.

Article: Mechanism of change in cognitive–behavioral treatment of panic disorder: Evidence for the fear of fear mediational hypothesis.

Journal: *Journal of Consulting and Clinical Psychology,* August 2004, *72,* 645–652.

Related Research: Ballenger, J. C., et al. (1988). Alprazolam in panic disorder and agoraphobia: Results from a multicenter trial: I. Efficacy in short-term treatment. *Archives of General Psychiatry, 45,* 413–422.

10807

Test Name: SHEEHAN PATIENT-RELATED ANXIETY SCALE

Purpose: To assess the intensity of anxiety symptoms.

Number of Items: 35

Format: Rating scales range from 0 (*not at all distressing*) to 4 (*extremely distressing*).

Validity: Correlations with other variables ranged from .36 to .58.

Author: Smits, J. A. J., et al.

Article: Mechanism of change in cognitive–behavioral treatment of

panic disorder: Evidence for the fear of fear mediational hypothesis.

Journal: *Journal of Consulting and Clinical Psychology,* August 2004, *72,* 645–652.

Related Research: Sheehan, D. (1983). *The anxiety disease.* New York: Scribner.

10808

Test Name: SHORT AFFECT INTENSITY SCALE

Purpose: To measure positive emotions, negative emotions, and reversed positive emotions.

Number of Items: 20

Format: Six-point response categories range from 1 (*I never feel like that*) to 6 (*I always feel like that*). All items are presented.

Reliability: Alpha coefficients ranged from .60 to .94 across scales and samples.

Validity: Correlations with other variables ranged from −.41 to .38.

Author: Geuens, M., and DePelsmacker, P.

Article: Developing a short Affect Intensity Scale.

Journal: *Psychological Reports,* October 2002, *91,* 657–670.

Related Research: Larsen, R. J., & Diener, E. (1987). Affect intensity as an individual difference characteristic: A review. *Journal of Research in Personality, 21,* 1–39.

10809

Test Name: SHORT MOOD AND FEELINGS QUESTIONNAIRE

Purpose: To assess depressed mood.

Number of Items: 13

Format: Responses are made on a 3-point scale ranging from 0 (*not at all*) to 2 (*almost all the time*).

Reliability: Coefficient alpha was .90.

Validity: Correlations with other variables ranged from −.66 to .60.

Author: Newman, D. L.

Article: Ego development and ethnic identity formation in rural American Indian adolescents.

Journal: *Child Development,* May/June 2005, *76,* 734–746.

Related Research: Angold, A., et al. (1995). Development of a short questionnaire for use in epidemiological studies of depression in children and adolescents. *International Journal of Methods in Psychiatric Research, 5,* 237–249.

10810

Test Name: SITUATIONAL HUMOR RESPONSE QUESTIONNAIRE

Purpose: To measure the extent to which subjects laugh or smile in a variety of situations.

Number of Items: 21

Format: A Likert format is used.

Reliability: Cronbach's alpha was .79.

Validity: Correlation with empathic concern was .23.

Author: Hampes, W. P.

Article: Relation between humor and empathic concern.

Journal: *Psychological Reports,* February 2001, *88,* 241–244.

Related Research: Martin, R. A., & Lefcourt, H. M. (1994). Situational Humor Response Questionnaire: Quantitative measure of a sense of humor. *Journal of Personality and Social Psychology, 47,* 145–155.

10811

Test Name: SLEEP DISTURBANCE ASCRIBED TO WORRY SCALE

Purpose: To measure individual differences in the attribution of sleep disturbance to worry.

Number of Items: 5

Format: Eleven-point scales are anchored by *never* and *very often*.

Reliability: Internal consistency coefficients ranged from .85 to .89.

Validity: Correlations with measures of humor ranged from −.22 to .07.

Author: Kelly, W. E.

Article: Correlations of sense of humor and sleep disturbance ascribed to worry.

Journal: *Psychological Reports*, December 2002, *91*, Part 2, 1202–1204.

Related Research: Kelly, W. E. (2002). Worry and sleep length revisited: Worry, sleep length, and sleep disturbance ascribed to worry. *Journal of Genetic Psychology, 163*, 296–304.

10812

Test Name: SMITH STRESS SYMPTOMS INVENTORY

Purpose: To measure stress symptoms and stress-related behaviors.

Number of Items: 54

Format: Includes six symptom scales: Worry, Attention Deficit, Autonomic Arousal/Anxiety, Striated Muscle Tension, Depression, and Anger. Responses are made on a 4-point scale ranging from 1 (*does not fit me at all*) to 4 (*fits me very well*).

Reliability: Alpha coefficients ranged from .76 to .89.

Author: Piiparinen, R., and Smith, J. C.

Article: Stress symptoms one year after 9/11/01: A follow-up.

Journal: *Perceptual and Motor Skills*, October 2004, *99*, 577–580.

Related Research: Smith, J. C. (2002). *The Smith Stress Symptoms Inventory (SSSI)*. Unpublished manuscript, Roosevelt University Stress Institute, Chicago, IL.

10813

Test Name: SOCIAL ANXIETY SCALE

Purpose: To measure social anxiety.

Number of Items: 24

Format: Item responses are anchored by 0 (*never or none*) and 3 (*severe or usually*).

Reliability: Alpha coefficients ranged from .81 to .92.

Author: Soykan, C., et al.

Article: Liebowitz Social Anxiety Scale: The Turkish version.

Journal: *Psychological Reports*, December 2003, *93*, Part 2, 1059–1069.

Related Research: Libowitz, M. R. (1987). Social phobia. *Modern Problems of Pharmacopsychiatry, 22*, 141–173.

10814

Test Name: SOCIAL ANXIETY SCALE FOR ADOLESCENTS

Purpose: To assess adolescents' subjective experience of social anxiety.

Number of Items: 18

Format: Includes three subscales: Fear of Negative Evaluation, Social Avoidance and Distress—New, and Social Avoidance and Distress—General. Examples are given.

Reliability: Alpha coefficients ranged from .70 to .89.

Author: Storch, E. A., et al.

Article: The relationship of peer victimization to social anxiety and loneliness in adolescence.

Journal: *Child Study Journal*, 2003, *33*, 1–18.

Related Research: LaGreca, A. M., & Lopez, N. (1998). Social anxiety among adolescents: Linkages with peer relations and friendships. *Journal of Abnormal Child Psychology, 26*, 83–94.

10815

Test Name: SOCIAL BEHAVIORS QUESTIONNAIRE

Purpose: To assess the frequency of lifetime suicide ideation, suicide attempts, threats of suicide, and self-reported suicide likelihood.

Number of Items: 4

Reliability: Coefficient alpha was .88.

Validity: Correlations with the Positive and Negative Suicide Ideation Inventory ranged from −.37 to .50.

Author: Osman, A., et al.

Article: The Positive and Negative Suicide Ideation (PANSI) Inventory: Psychometric evaluation with adolescent psychiatric inpatient samples.

Journal: *Journal of Personality Assessment*, December 2002, *79*, 512–530.

Related Research: Osman, A., et al. (2001). The Suicidal Behaviors Questionnaire—Revised (SBQ–R): Validation with clinical and nonclinical samples. *Assessment, 4*, 443–454.

10816

Test Name: SOCIAL PHOBIA AND ANXIETY INVENTORY

Purpose: To measure social phobia and agoraphobia.

Number of Items: 45

Format: Scales range from 1 (*never*) to 7 (*always*).

Reliability: Test–retest reliabilities ranged from .77 to .86 across subscales.

Validity: Correlations with other variables ranged from .39 to .78.

Author: Garcia-López, L. J., et al.

Article: Psychometric properties of the Social Phobia and Anxiety Inventory, the Social Anxiety Scale for Adolescents, the Fear of Negative Evaluation Scale, and the Social Avoidance and Distress Scale in an adolescent Spanish-speaking sample.

Journal: *Journal of Psychopathology and Behavioral Assessment*, March 2001, *23*, 51–59.

Related Research: Turner, S. M., et al. (1989). An empirically derived inventory to measure social fears and anxiety: The Social Phobia and Anxiety Inventory. *Psychological Assessment: A Journal of Consulting and Clinical Psychology*, *1*, 35–40.

10817

Test Name: SOCIAL PHYSIQUE ANXIETY SCALE

Purpose: To measure anxiety individuals have about their perceptions that others are evaluating their bodies.

Number of Items: 12

Format: Item responses range from 1 (*not at all true*) to 5 (*extremely true*). Some items are presented.

Reliability: Coefficient alpha was .90.

Validity: Correlations with other variables ranged from −.82 to .33.

Author: Lanning, B. A., et al.

Article: Relations of sex, age, perceived fitness, and aerobic activity with social physique anxiety in adults sixty years and older.

Journal: *Psychological Reports*, December 2004, *95*, Part 1, 761–766.

Related Research: Hart, E. A., et al. (1989). The measurement of

social physique anxiety. *Journal of Sport and Exercise Psychology*, *11*, 94–104.

10818

Test Name: SOCIAL READJUSTMENT RATING SCALE

Purpose: To measure stressful life events.

Number of Items: 43

Time Required: 10 minutes

Format: A yes–no format is used.

Author: Meehan, D.-C.-M., and Negy, C.

Article: Undergraduate students' adaptation to college: Does being married make a difference?

Journal: *Journal of College Student Development*, September/October 2003, *44*, 670–690.

Related Research: Holmes, T. H., & Rahe, R. H. (1967). The Social Readjustment Rating Scale. *Journal of Psychosomatic Research*, *11*, 213–218.

10819

Test Name: SOCIAL STRESS INVENTORY

Purpose: To measure stressful recent life events, chronic stress, and lifetime traumatic events.

Number of Items: 110

Format: All items are presented with response formats.

Validity: Correlations with depression ranged from .24 to .38.

Author: Taylor, J., and Turner, R. J.

Article: Perceived discrimination, social stress, and depression in the transition to adulthood: Racial contrasts.

Journal: *Social Psychology Quarterly*, September 2002, *65*, 213–225.

Related Research: Turner, R. J., et al. (1995). The epidemiology of social stress. *American Sociological Review*, *60*, 104–125.

10820

Test Name: SOCIOCULTURAL ATTITUDES TOWARDS APPEARANCE QUESTIONNAIRE— INTERNALIZATION SUBSCALE

Purpose: To assess internalization of the thin-ideal stereotype.

Number of Items: 8

Format: Responses are rated on a 5-point scale ranging from 1 (*completely disagree*) to 5 (*completely agree*). An example is given.

Reliability: Coefficient alpha was .88.

Validity: Correlations with other variables ranged from −.16 to .67.

Author: Tylka, T. L., and Subich, L. M.

Article: Examining a multidimensional model of eating disorder symptomatology among college women.

Journal: *Journal of Counseling Psychology*, July 2004, *51*, 314–328.

Related Research: Heinberg, L. J., et al. (1995). Development and validation of the Sociocultural Attitudes Towards Appearance Questionnaire. *International Journal of Eating Disorders*, *17*, 81–89.

10821

Test Name: SOMATIC COMPLAINTS INVENTORY

Purpose: To measure frequency of somatic complaints as a second indicator of well-being.

Number of Items: 10

Format: Responses are made on a scale of *often*, *sometimes*, and *rarely*. An example is given.

Reliability: Coefficient alpha was .89.

Validity: Correlations with other variables ranged from −.19 to .28.

Author: Meir, E. I., and Melamed, S.

Article: Occupational specialty congruence: New data and future directions.

Journal: *Journal of Vocational Behavior*, August 2005, *67*, 21–34.

Related Research: Caplan, R. D., et al. (1975). *Job demands and worker health: Main effects and occupational differences* (HEW Pub. No. NIOSH 75–160). Washington, DC: National Institute for Occupational Safety and Health.

10822

Test Name: SOMATIC COMPLAINTS SCALE

Purpose: To assess psychological distress arising from perceptions of bodily dysfunctions.

Number of Items: 12

Format: Scales range from 1 (*never*) to 5 (*very often*).

Reliability: Coefficient alpha was .87.

Validity: Correlations with other variables ranged from –.22 to .44.

Author: Major, V. S., et al.

Article: Work time, work interference with family, and psychological distress.

Journal: *Journal of Applied Psychology*, June 2002, *87*, 427–436.

Related Research: Derogates, L. R. (1977). *S. L.-90 administration, scoring, and procedures: Manual-I for the revised version and other instruments of the psychopathology rating scale series.* Baltimore: Johns Hopkins University School of Medicine.

10823

Test Name: SOURCES OF DEPRESSION SCALES

Purpose: To measure (a) perceptions of depression as beyond personal control, (b) how much

patients blame depression on personal inadequacy, and (c) how much patients think that depression does not reflect actual realities.

Number of Items: 29

Format: Seven-point DAS scales are used. All items are presented.

Reliability: Alpha coefficients ranged from .71 to .93.

Author: Teasdale, J. D., et al.

Article: How does cognitive therapy prevent relapse in residual depression? Evidence from a controlled trial.

Journal: *Journal of Consulting and Clinical Psychology*, June 2001, *69*, 347–357.

Related Research: Imber, S. D., et al. (1990). Mode-specific effects among three treatments for depression. *Journal of Consulting and Clinical Psychology*, *58*, 352–359.

10824

Test Name: SOUTH OAKS GAMBLING SCREEN—REVISED

Purpose: To screen individuals with pathological and problem gambling in the general population and clinical settings.

Number of Items: 16

Format: A yes–no format is used. Examples are presented.

Reliability: Coefficient alpha was .97.

Validity: Correlations with other variables ranged from –.53 to .40.

Author: Lightsey, O. R., Jr., and Hulsey, C. D.

Article: Impulsivity, coping, stress, and problem gambling among university students.

Journal: *Journal of Counseling Psychology*, April 2002, *49*, 202–211.

Related Research: Lesieur, H. R., & Blume, S. B. (1993). Revising the South Oaks Gambling Screen in

different settings. *Journal of Gambling Studies*, *9*, 213–223

10825

Test Name: SPATIAL ANXIETY SCALE

Purpose: To measure intensity of anxiety.

Number of Items: 8

Format: Responses are made on a 5-point scale ranging from 1 (*not at all*) to 5 (*very much*). An example is given.

Reliability: Coefficient alpha was .80.

Author: Devlin, A. S.

Article: Sailing experience and sex as correlates of spatial ability.

Journal: *Perceptual and Motor Skills*, June 2004, *98*, Part 2, 1409–1421.

Related Research: Lawton, C. A. (1994). Gender differences in way-finding strategies: Relationship to spatial ability and spatial anxiety. *Sex Roles*, *20*, 765–779.

10826

Test Name: SPIDER PHOBIA QUESTIONNAIRE

Purpose: To measure fear of spiders.

Number of Items: 43

Format: Scales range from 0 (*almost never*) to 3 (*almost always*).

Reliability: Coefficient alpha was .91.

Author: Wenzel, A., et al.

Article: Thought suppression in spider-fearful and nonfearful individuals.

Journal: *The Journal of General Psychology*, April 2003, *130*, 191–205.

Related Research: Watts, F. N., & Sharrock, R. (1984). Questionnaire dimensions of spider phobia.

Behavior Research and Therapy,
22, 575–580.

10827

Test Name: SPIRITUAL
WELL-BEING SCALE

Purpose: To measure religious and
existential well-being.

Number of Items: 20

Format: Seven-point scales range
from 1 (*strongly agree*) to 7
(*strongly disagree*).

Reliability: Alpha coefficients
ranged from .78 to .94.

Validity: Correlations with other
variables ranged from –.66 to .82.

Author: Pollard, L. J., and Bates,
L. W.

Article: Religion and perceived
stress among undergraduates
during fall 2001 final examinations.

Journal: *Psychological Reports,*
December 2004, *95,* Part 1,
999–1007.

Related Research: Ellison, C. W.
(1983). Spiritual well-being:
Conceptualization and
measurement. *Journal of
Psychology and Theology, 11,*
330–340.

10828

Test Name: SPORT ANXIETY
QUESTIONNAIRE

Purpose: To measure sport anxiety.

Number of Items: 6

Format: Item anchors ranged from
1 (*not at all true*) to 5 (*always
true*). A sample item is presented.

Reliability: Coefficient alpha was .82.

Author: Storch, E. A.

Article: Reliability and factor
structure of the Sport Anxiety
Questionnaire in fifth- and sixth-
grade children.

Journal: *Psychological Reports,*
August 2003, *93,* 160.

Related Research: Storch, E. A.,
et al. (2002). Generalization of
social anxiety to sport: An
investigation of Hispanic
elementary-aged children. *Child
Study Journal, 32,* 81–88.

10829

Test Name: SPORT ANXIETY
SCALE

Purpose: To measure sport anxiety.

Number of Items: 21

Format: Includes three subscales:
Somatic Anxiety, Worry, and
Concentration Disruption.
Responses are made on a 4-point
scale ranging from 1 (*not at all*) to 4
(*very much so*).

Reliability: Alpha coefficients
ranged from .74 to .88.

Validity: Correlations with other
variables ranged from –.85 to .82.

Author: Cresswell, S., and Hodge, K.

Article: Coping skills: Role of trait
sport confidence and trait anxiety.

Journal: *Perceptual and Motor
Skills,* April 2004, *98,* 433–438.

Related Research: Smith, R. E.,
et al. (1990). Measurement and
correlates of sport-specific cognitive
and somatic trait anxiety: The
Sport Anxiety Scale. *Anxiety
Research, 2,* 263–280.

10830

Test Name: STAGES OF CHANGE
SCALE

Purpose: To measure a client's
readiness to change.

Number of Items: 32

Format: Includes four stages.
Responses are made on a 5-point
Likert scale.

Reliability: Alpha coefficients
ranged from .97 to .84.

Author: Whipple, J. L., et al.

Article: Improving the effects of
psychotherapy: The use of early

identification of treatment failure
and problem-solving strategies in
routine practice.

Journal: *Journal of Counseling
Psychology,* January 2003, *50,*
59–68.

Related Research: McConnaughy,
E. A., et al. (1983). Stages of change
in psychotherapy: Measurement
and sample profile. *Psychotherapy:
Theory, Research & Practice, 20,*
368–375.

10831

Test Name: STATE OF MIND
AND CONSCIOUSNESS
QUESTIONNAIRE

Purpose: To measure proneness to
altered states of consciousness.

Number of Items: 60

Format: Responses are made on a
5-point scale ranging from 1 (*never*)
to 5 (*very often*). Examples are
given.

Reliability: Coefficient alpha was .96.

Validity: Correlation with altered
states of consciousness was .26.

Author: Suszek, H., and Kopera, M.

Article: Altered states of
consciousness, dissociation, and
dream recall.

Journal: *Perceptual and Motor
Skills,* February 2005, *100,*
176–178.

Related Research: Kokoszka, A.
(1992). Occurrence of altered states
of consciousness among students:
Profoundly and superficially
altered states in wakefulness.
*Imagination, Cognition and
Personality, 12,* 231–247.

10832

Test Name: STATE–TRAIT
ANXIETY INVENTORY—SHORT
VERSION

Purpose: To measure state anxiety.

Number of Items: 6

Format: Scales range from 1 (*not at all*) to 4 (*very much so*).

Reliability: Alpha coefficients ranged from .67 to .86.

Author: Gohm, C. L., et al.

Article: Personality in extreme situations: Thinking (or not) under acute stress.

Journal: *Journal of Research in Personality*, September 2001, *35*, 388–399.

Related Research: Marteau, T. M., & Bekker, H. (1992). The development of a six-item short form of the state scale of the Speilberger State–Trait Anxiety Inventory (STAI). *British Journal of Clinical Psychology, 31,* 301–306.

10833

Test Name: STRAIN-FREE NEGATIVE AFFECTIVITY SCALE—REVISED

Purpose: To measure negative affectivity.

Number of Items: 20

Format: Responses are made on a 5-point scale ranging from 1 (*strongly disagree*) to 5 (*strongly agree*). An example is given.

Reliability: Coefficient alpha was .90.

Validity: Correlations with other variables ranged from –.25 to .61.

Author: Crossley, C. D., and Stanton, J. M.

Article: Negative affect and job search: Further examination of the reverse causation hypothesis.

Journal: *Journal of Vocational Behavior*, June 2005, *66*, 549–560.

Related Research: Fortunato, V. J., & Goldblatt, A. M. (2002). Construct validation of revised Strain-Free Negative Affectivity Scale. *Educational and Psychological Measurement, 62,* 45–63.

10834

Test Name: STRAINS SCALES

Purpose: To measure five types of strain.

Number of Items: 40

Format: Includes five types of strain: psychological distress-type strain, somatic strain, emotional strain, attitudinal strain, and behavioral strain. Responses are made on a 7-point scale ranging from 1 (*strongly disagree*) to 7 (*strongly agree*).

Reliability: Alpha coefficients ranged from .75 to .91.

Validity: Correlations with other variables ranged from –.41 to .69 (*n* = 309).

Author: Fortunato, V. J.

Article: A comparison of the construct validity of three measures of negative affectivity.

Journal: *Educational and Psychological Measurement*, April 2004, *64*, 271–289.

Related Research: Quinn, R. P., & Shepard, L. J. (1974). *Quality of employment survey.* Ann Arbor, MI: Institute for Social Research. Goldberg, D. (1978). *Manual of the General Health Questionnaire.* Windsor, England: National Foundation for Educational Research. Peters, L. H., et al. (1980). The behavioral and affective consequences of performance-relevant situational variables. *Organizational Behavior and Human Performance, 25,* 79–96. Cammann, C., et al. (1979). *The Michigan Organizational Assessment Questionnaire.* Unpublished manuscript, University of Michigan, Ann Arbor. Meyer, J. P., & Allen, N. J. (1997). *Commitment in the workplace: Theory, research, and application.* Thousand Oaks, CA: Sage. Wayne, S. J., et al. (1997). Perceived organizational support and leader–member exchange: A social exchange perspective. *Academy of Management Journal, 40,* 82–111. Smith, C. A., et al. (1983). Organizational citizenship behavior: Its nature and antecedents. *Journal of Applied Psychology, 68,* 653–663.

10835

Test Name: STRATEGIC APPROACH TO COPING SCALE—ITALIAN VERSION

Purpose: To measure coping as assertive action, cautious action, social joining, seeking social support, antisocial action, aggressive action, instinctive action, avoidance, and indirect action.

Number of Items: 52

Format: Item response scales range from 1 (*not at all*) to 5 (*very much*).

Reliability: Coefficient alpha was .80. Subscale reliabilities ranged from .64 to .72.

Author: Comunian, A. L.

Article: Hobfoll's Strategic Approach to Coping: Reliability and validity of the Italian adaptation.

Journal: *Psychological Reports*, December 2003, *93*, Part 2, 1130–1132.

Related Research: Hobfoll, S. E., et al. (1993). *Preliminary test manual: Strategic Approach to Coping Scale (SACS).* Unpublished test manual, Kent State University, OH.

10836

Test Name: STRESS AND COPING QUESTIONNAIRE FOR CHILDREN

Purpose: To assess children's emotional responses and coping strategies when confronted with school-related and asthma-related stressors.

Number of Items: 28

Format: Item responses are anchored by 1 (*almost never*) and

4 (*almost always*). All items are presented.

Reliability: Cronbach's alpha ranged from .60 to .78 across factors (subscales).

Author: Röder, I., et al.

Article: The Stress and Coping Questionnaire for Children (school version and asthma version): Construction, factor structure, and psychometric properties.

Journal: *Psychological Reports,* August 2002, *91,* 29–36.

Related Research: Röder, I. (2000). *Stress in children with asthma: Coping and social support in the school context* [Dissertation]. Leiden, the Netherlands: Print Partners Ipskanp.

10837

Test Name: STRESS APPRAISAL MEASURE—REVISED

Purpose: To assess stress appraisal.

Number of Items: 19

Format: Includes four factors: challenge, threat, centrality, and resources. All items are presented.

Reliability: Alpha coefficients ranged from .68 to .85.

Author: Roesch, S. C., and Rowley, A. A.

Article: Evaluating and developing a multidimensional, dispositional measure of appraisal.

Journal: *Journal of Personality Assessment,* October 2005, *85,* 188–196.

Related Research: Peacock, E. J., & Wong, P. T. (1990). The Stress Appraisal Measure (SAM): A multidimensional approach to cognitive appraisal. *Stress Medicine, 6,* 227–236.

10838

Test Name: STRESS PREDISPOSITION SCALE

Purpose: To measure Type A and Type B stress predisposition.

Number of Items: 10

Format: Bipolar statement format.

Reliability: Alpha was .69.

Validity: Correlations with variables ranged from −.13 to .15.

Author: Sightler, K. W., and Wilson, M. G.

Article: Correlates of the impostor phenomenon among undergraduate entrepreneurs.

Journal: *Psychological Reports,* June 2001, *88,* Part 1, 679–689.

Related Research: Kindler, H. S. (1998). Personal Stress Assessment Inventory—Predisposition. In D. Marcie & J. Seltzer (Eds.), *Occupational behavior: Experiences and cases* (pp. 90–91). Cincinnati, OH: Southwestern College.

10839

Test Name: STRESS SCALE

Purpose: To measure stress.

Number of Items: 7

Format: Responses are made on a 5-point scale ranging from *never* to *very often.* All items are presented.

Reliability: Coefficient alpha was .87.

Validity: Correlations with other variables ranged from −.38 to .63.

Author: Behson, S. J.

Article: The relative contribution of formal and informal organizational work–family support.

Journal: *Journal of Vocational Behavior,* June 2005, *66,* 487–500.

Related Research: Kandel, D. B., et al. (1985). The stressfulness of daily social roles for women: Marital, occupational and household roles. *Journal of Health and Social Behavior, 26,* 64–78.

10840

Test Name: STRESS SCALE

Purpose: To assess stress.

Number of Items: 11

Format: Includes two areas: challenge-related stress and hindrance-related stress. Responses are made on a 5-point scale ranging from 1 (*produces no stress*) to 5 (*produces a great deal of stress*). Examples are given.

Reliability: Alpha coefficients were .90 (challenge-related stress) and .68 (hindrance-related stress).

Validity: Correlations with other variables ranged from −.30 to .47 ($n = 392$).

Author: Boswell, W. R., et al.

Article: Relations between stress and work outcomes: The role of felt challenge, job control, and psychological strain.

Journal: *Journal of Vocational Behavior,* February 2004, *64,* 165–181.

Related Research: Cavanaugh, M. A., et al. (2000). An empirical examination of self-reported work stress among U.S. managers. *Journal of Applied Psychology, 85,* 65–74.

10841

Test Name: STRESS SCALE

Purpose: To assess stress.

Number of Items: 2

Format: Responses are made on a 5-point scale. Both items are presented.

Reliability: Coefficient alpha was .64.

Validity: Correlations with other variables ranged from −.44 to .50.

Author: Greenhaus, J. H., et al.

Article: The relation between work–family balance and quality of life.

Journal: *Journal of Vocational Behavior*, December 2003, *63*, 510–531.

Related Research: Patchen, M. (1970). *Participation, achievement, and involvement on the job*. Englewood Cliffs, NJ: Prentice-Hall.

10842

Test Name: STRESS SCALES— JAPANESE VERSION

Purpose: To measure academic, interpersonal, health, life–environmental, and part-time work stressors.

Number of Items: 30

Format: Scales range from 1 (*not at all*) to 4 (*very much*). All items are presented in English.

Reliability: Coefficient alpha was .84.

Validity: Correlations with other variables ranged from .14 to .52.

Author: Jou, Y. H., and Fukada, H.

Article: Stress, health, and reciprocity and sufficiency of social support: The care of university students in Japan.

Journal: *The Journal of Social Psychology*, June 2002, *142*, 353–370.

10843

Test Name: STUDENT WORRY QUESTIONNAIRE

Purpose: To measure worrisome thinking, financial-related concerns, significant others' well-being, social adequacy concerns, academic concerns, and general anxiety symptoms.

Number of Items: 30

Format: Responses are anchored by 0 (*almost never characteristic of me*) and 4 (*almost always characteristic of me*). All items are presented.

Reliability: Alpha coefficients ranged from .80 to .94 across subscales.

Validity: Correlations between scales ranged from .21 to .51. Correlations with other variables ranged from .25 to .68.

Author: Osman, A. et al.

Article: Development and psychometric properties of the Student Worry Questionnaire.

Journal: *Psychological Reports*, February 2001, *88*, 277–290.

10844

Test Name: SUBJECTIVE HAPPINESS SCALE

Purpose: To measure perceived happiness.

Number of Items: 4

Format: A 7-point Likert format is used.

Reliability: Alpha coefficients ranged from .79 to .94.

Validity: Correlations with other variables ranged from .32 to .66.

Author: Mattei, D., and Schaefer, C. E.

Article: An investigation of the validity of the Subjective Happiness Scale.

Journal: *Psychological Reports*, February 2004, *94*, 288–290.

Related Research: Lyubomersky, S., & Lepper, H. (1999). A measure of subjective happiness: Preliminary reliability and construct validation. *Social Indicators Research, 46*, 137–155.

10845

Test Name: SUBJECTIVE HEALTH QUESTIONNAIRE

Purpose: To measure health complaints.

Number of Items: 13

Format: Responses are 0 (*no*) and 1 (*yes*). Examples are given.

Reliability: Alpha coefficients ranged from .69 to .79.

Author: Geurts, S. A. E., et al.

Article: Does work–home interference mediate the relationship between workload and well-being?

Journal: *Journal of Vocational Behavior*, December 2003, *63*, 532–559.

Related Research: Dirken, J. M. (1969). *Arbeid en stress* [*Work and stress*]. Groningen: Wolters Noordhuff.

10846

Test Name: SUICIDE OPINION QUESTIONNAIRE—ADAPTED

Purpose: To measure suicidal ideation.

Number of Items: 13

Reliability: Coefficient alpha was .78.

Validity: Correlation with the Suicide Ideation Questionnaire was .60.

Author: Lester, D.

Article: Derivation of a proxy measure of suicidal ideation from the Suicide Opinion Questionnaire.

Journal: *Perceptual and Motor Skills*, December 2004, *99*, Part 1, 1046.

Related Research: Domino, G., et al. (1980). Students' attitudes toward suicide. *Social Psychiatry, 15*, 127–130.

10847

Test Name: SUICIDE OPINION QUESTIONNAIRE—REVISED

Purpose: To provide a proxy measure of death anxiety when only the Suicide Opinion Questionnaire has been administered to a sample.

Number of Items: 10

Reliability: Coefficient alpha was .65.

Validity: Correlation with death anxiety scores was .43.

Author: Lester, D.

Article: Derivation of a proxy measure of death anxiety from the Suicide Opinion Questionnaire.

Journal: *Perceptual and Motor Skills*, August 2003, *97*, 120.

Related Research: Domino, G., et al. (1980). Students' attitudes toward suicide. *Social Psychiatry*, *15*, 127–130.

10848

Test Name: SUICIDE RESILIENCE INVENTORY—25

Purpose: To assess factors that defend against suicidal thoughts and behaviors in three dimensions: Internal, Protective Emotional Stability, and External Protective.

Number of Items: 25

Format: Item anchors are 1 (*strongly disagree*) and 6 (*strongly agree*).

Reliability: Alpha coefficients ranged from .86 to .96.

Validity: Cohen *d* statistics ranged from .72 to .95 across known-groups comparisons.

Author: Osman, A., et al.

Article: Suicide Resilience Inventory—25: Development and preliminary psychometric properties.

Journal: *Psychological Reports*, June 2004, *94*, Part 2, 1349–1360.

10849

Test Name: SURVEY OF CHILDREN'S STRESS SYMPTOMS

Purpose: To measure stress in children by report of the mother.

Number of Items: 27

Format: Scales range from 1 (*never occurs*) to 4 (*occurs a lot of the time*).

Reliability: Coefficient alpha was .92.

Author: Ceballo, R., et al.

Article: Inner-city children's exposure to community violence: How much do parents know?

Journal: *Journal of Marriage and Family*, November 2001, *63*, 527–540.

Related Research: Pynoos, R., et al. (1998). *The Survey of Children's Stress Symptoms.* Unpublished text, University of California at Los Angeles.

10850

Test Name: SURVEY OF RECENT LIFE EXPERIENCES

Purpose: To measure stress.

Number of Items: 51

Time Required: Five to 10 minutes.

Format: Four-point scales are anchored by 1 (*not at all part of my life*) and 4 (*very much part of my life*).

Validity: Correlation with a stress scale was .57.

Author: Bass, M. A., and Enochs, W. K.

Article: Comparison of two exercise programs on general well-being of college students.

Journal: *Psychological Reports*, December 2002, *91*, Part 2, 1195–1201.

Related Research: Kohn, P. M., & Macdonald, J. E. (1991). The Survey of Recent Life Experiences: A decontaminated hassles scale for adults. *Journal of Behavioral Medicine*, *15*, 221–236.

10851

Test Name: SURVEY OF RECENT LIFE EXPERIENCES

Purpose: To assess recent hassles.

Number of Items: 41

Format: Responses are made on a 5-point scale ranging from 1 (*not at all part of my life*) to 5 (*very much part of my life*).

Reliability: Coefficient alpha was .90.

Validity: Correlations with other variables ranged from –.20 to .37.

Author: Bricker, J. B.

Article: Development and evaluation of the Air Travel Stress Scale.

Journal: *Journal of Counseling Psychology*, October 2005, *52*, 615–628.

Related Research: Kohn, P. M., & Macdonald, J. E. (1992). The Survey of Recent Life Experiences: A decontaminated hassles scale for adults. *Journal of Behavioral Medicine*, *15*, 221–236.

10852

Test Name: SURVEY OF TRAUMATIC CHILDHOOD EVENTS

Number of Items: 30

Format: Five-point scales are anchored by A (*none*) and D (*6 to 10*). Sample items are presented.

Reliability: Alpha coefficients ranged from .72 to .92.

Validity: Correlations with other variables ranged from .19 to .31.

Author: Thalbourne, M. A., and Houran, J.

Article: Childhood trauma as a possible antecedent of transliminality.

Journal: *Psychological Reports*, December 2003, *93*, Part 1, 687–694.

Related Research: Council, J. R., & Edwards, P. W. (1987). *Survey of Traumatic Childhood Events.* Unpublished measure, North Dakota State University, Fargo.

10853

Test Name: SYMPTOM CHECKLIST—REVISED

Purpose: To measure psychological symptomatology.

Number of Items: 35

Format: Four-point scales are anchored by 0 (*not at all*) and 4 (*extremely*).

Reliability: Alpha coefficients ranged from .81 to .90 across subscales.

Validity: Correlations with other variables ranged from −.66 to .70.

Author: Katerndahl, D. A., et al.

Article: Psychometric assessment of measures of psychological symptoms, functional status, life events, and context for low income Hispanic patients in a primary care setting.

Journal: *Psychological Reports*, December 2002, *91*, Part 2, 1121–1128.

Related Research: Winokur, A., et al. (1994). Symptoms of emotional distress in a family planning service. *British Journal of Psychiatry, 144*, 395–399.

10854

Test Name: SYMPTOM INTERPRETATION QUESTIONNAIRE

Purpose: To measure attribution of symptoms.

Number of Items: 13

Format: Four-point scales are used.

Reliability: Alpha coefficients ranged from .74 to .84.

Author: Ayalon, L., and Young, M. A.

Article: Racial group differences in help-seeking behaviors.

Journal: *The Journal of Social Psychology*, August 2005, *145*, 391–403.

Related Research: Robbins, J. M., & Kirmayer, L. J. (1991). Attributions of common somatic symptoms. *Psychological Medicine, 21*, 1029–1045.

10855

Test Name: SYMPTOMS OF STRESS INVENTORY

Purpose: To measure somatic, behavioral, and psychological symptomology of stress among firefighters and paramedics.

Format: Each symptom is rated on a 4-point scale ranging from 0 (*never*) to 4 (*frequently*).

Reliability: Alpha was .96. Test–retest reliabilities (6 weeks) were .47 to .86 over subscales.

Validity: Correlation with the Sources of Occupational Stress Scale was .60.

Author: Beaton, R., et al.

Article: Outcomes of a leadership intervention for a metropolitan fire department.

Journal: *Psychological Reports*, June 2001, *88*, Part 2, 1049–1066.

Related Research: Beaton, R., et al. (1991). Self-reported symptoms of stress with temporomandibular disorders: Comparisons to healthy men and women. *Journal of Prosthetic Dentistry, 65*, 289–293.

10856

Test Name: TAMPA SCALE FOR KINESIOPHOBIA

Purpose: To measure fear of pain.

Number of Items: 17

Format: Includes two subscales: Somatic Focus and Activity Avoidance. Responses are made on a 4-point Likert-type scale ranging from 1 (*strongly agree*) to 4 (*strongly disagree*). Examples are given.

Validity: Correlations with other variables ranged from .35 to .65.

Author: Roelofs, J., et al.

Article: An examination of word relevance in a modified Stroop task in patients with chronic low back pain.

Journal: *Perceptual and Motor Skills*, June 2005, *100*, Part 2, 955–963.

Related Research: Miller, R. P., et al. (1991). *The Tampa Scale.* Unpublished report.

10857

Test Name: TAYLOR MANIFEST ANXIETY SCALE

Purpose: To measure neuroticism

Number of Items: 50

Format: A true–false format is used.

Validity: Correlations with other variables from −.52 to .72 (*N* = 93).

Author: Terrill, D. R., et al.

Article: Construct validity of the Life Orientation Test.

Journal: *Journal of Personality Assessment*, December 2002, *79*, 550–563.

Related Research: Taylor, J. A. (1953). A personality scale of manifest anxiety. *The Journal of Abnormal and Social Psychology, 48*, 285–290.

10858

Test Name: TAYLOR MANIFEST ANXIETY SCALE— UNIDIMENSIONAL SHORT FORM

Purpose: To measure anxiety in a global context.

Number of Items: 20

Reliability: Test–retest reliability was .88.

Validity: Correlation with other variables ranged from .26 to .52.

Author: Nguyen, T. T., et al.

Article: Nightmare frequency, nightmare distress, and anxiety.

Journal: *Perceptual and Motor Skills*, August 2002, *95*, 219–225.

Related Research: Hicks, R. A., et al. (1980). A unidimensional short form of the TMAS. *Bulletin of the Psychonomic Society, 16*, 447–448.

10859

Test Name: TEMPLAR DEATH ANXIETY SCALE—SPANISH VERSION

Purpose: To measure fear of death.

Number of Items: 15

Format: A true–false format is used. All items are presented in Spanish and in English.

Reliability: Coefficient alpha was .73. Test–retest correlation was .87 (3 weeks).

Author: Tomás-Sábado, J., and Gómez-Benito, J.

Article: Psychometric properties of the Spanish form of Templar's Death Anxiety Scale.

Journal: *Psychological Reports*, December 2002, *91*, Part 2, 1116–1120.

Related Research: Templar, D. I. (1969). Death Anxiety Scale. *Proceedings of the Annual Convention of the American Psychological Association, 4*, 737–738.

10860

Test Name: THINGS I WORRY ABOUT SCALE

Purpose: To measure the extent to which people worry about things.

Number of Items: 20

Format: Item responses are anchored by 1 (*not true for me*) and 5 (*very true for me*). All items are presented.

Reliability: Alpha coefficients ranged from .60 to .85 across subscales.

Author: Kroll, J., et al.

Article: Moral conflict as a component of ordinary worry.

Journal: *Psychological Reports*, June 2002, *90*, Part 1, 997–1006.

Related Research: Tallis, F., et al. (1992). A questionnaire for the measurement of nonpathological worry. *Personality and Individual Differences, 13*, 161–168.

10861

Test Name: THOUGHTS ABOUT PSYCHOTHERAPY SURVEY

Purpose: To measure treatment fears.

Number of Items: 19

Format: Includes three subscales: Therapist Responsiveness, Image Concerns, and Coercion Concerns. Responses are made on a 5-point scale ranging from 1 (*no concern*) to 5 (*very concerned*). Examples are given.

Reliability: Internal consistency coefficients ranged from .81 to .92.

Validity: Correlations with other variables ranged from −.19 to .38 ($N = 354$).

Author: Vogel, D. L., et al.

Article: The role of outcome expectations and attitudes on decisions to seek professional help.

Journal: *Journal of Counseling Psychology*, October 2005, *52*, 459–470.

Related Research: Kushner, M. G., & Sher, K. J. (1989). Fears of psychological treatment and its relation to mental health service avoidance. *Professional Psychology: Research and Practice, 20*, 251–257.

10862

Test Name: THOUGHTS RATING FORM

Purpose: To measure extent of catastrophic cognitions associated with panic disorder.

Number of Items: 17

Format: Scales range from 0 (*none*) to 8 (*extremely*). All items are presented.

Reliability: Alpha coefficients ranged from .83 to .88. Test–retest reliabilities ranged from .68 to .81.

Author: Hicks, T. V., et al.

Article: Physical, mental, and social catastrophic cognitions as prognostic factors in cognitive–behavioral and pharmacological treatments for panic disorder.

Journal: *Journal of Consulting and Clinical Psychology*, June 2005, *73*, 506–514.

Related Research: Barlow, D. H., et al. (2000). Cognitive–behavioral therapy, imipramine, or their combination for panic disorder: A randomized controlled trial. *Journal of the American Medical Association, 283*, 2529–2536.

10863

Test Name: TRAIT ANXIETY SCALE

Purpose: To measure trait anxiety expressed through somatic symptoms.

Number of Items: 4

Format: Scales range from 1 (*none or a little of the time*) to 4 (*most or all of the time*). A sample item is presented.

Reliability: Coefficient alpha was .77.

Author: Woods, C. M., et al.

Article: Dimensionality of the Obsessive Beliefs Questionnaire (OBQ).

Journal: *Journal of Psychopathology and Behavioral Assessment*, June 2004, *26*, 113–126.

Related Research: Zung, W. W. K. (1971). A rating instrument for anxiety disorders. *Psychosomatics, 12*, 371–379

10864

Test Name: TRAIT META-MOOD SCALE

Purpose: To evaluate mood regulations skills.

Number of Items: 48

Format: Scales range from 1 (*strongly disagree*) to 5 (*strongly agree*). Sample items are presented.

Reliability: Coefficient alpha was .82.

Validity: Correlations with other variables ranged from −.37 to −.05.

Author: Williams, F. M., et al.

Article: Mood regulation skill and the symptoms of endogenous and hopelessness depression in Spanish high school students.

Journal: *Journal of Psychopathology and Behavioral Assessment*, December 2004, *26*, 233–240.

Related Research: Salovey, P., et al. (1995). Emotional attention, clarity, and repair: Exploring emotional intelligence using the Trait Meta-Mood Scale. In J. W. Pennebaker (Ed.), *Emotion, disclosure, and health* (pp. 125–151). Washington, DC: American Psychological Association.

10865

Test Name: TRAIT META-MOOD SCALE—SPANISH VERSION

Purpose: To measure three aspects of intrapersonal emotional intelligence: attention, clarity, and repair.

Number of Items: 48

Format: Item responses are anchored by 1 (*strongly disagree*) and 5 (*strongly agree*). Sample items are presented.

Reliability: Alphas ranged from .76 to .87 (Spanish version).

Validity: Correlations with other variables ranged from −.36 to .42.

Author: Extremera, N., and Fernández-Berrocal, P.

Article: Relation of perceived emotional intelligence and health-related quality of life of middle-aged women.

Journal: *Psychological Reports*, August 2002, *91*, 47–59.

Related Research: Salovey, P., et al. (1995). Emotional attention, clarity, and repair: Exploring emotional intelligence using the Trait Meta-Mood Scale. In J. W. Pennebaker (Ed.), *Emotion, disclosure, and health* (pp. 125–151). Washington, DC: American Psychological Association.

10866

Test Name: TRANSLIMINALITY SCALE

Purpose: To measure the tendency for psychological material to move into or out of consciousness.

Number of Items: 17

Format: A true–false format is used. Sample items are presented.

Reliability: K-R 20 reliability was .85.

Validity: Correlations with other variables ranged from .23 to .37.

Author: Thalbourne, M. A., and Houran, J.

Article: Childhood trauma as a possible antecedent of transliminality.

Journal: *Psychological Reports*, December 2003, *93*, Part 1, 687–694.

Related Research: Lange, R., et al. (2000). The Revised Transliminality Scale: Reliability and validity data from a Rasch top-down purification procedure. *Consciousness and Cognition, 9*, 591–617.

10867

Test Name: TRAUMA STAGES OF RECOVERY TEST

Purpose: To assess stages of recovery in terms of emotional awareness and control, symptom mastery, coping, memory, and relationships.

Number of Items: 44

Format: Scales range from 1 (*strongly disagree*) to 5 (*strongly agree*). All items are presented.

Reliability: Alpha coefficients ranged from .59 to .86 across subscales.

Validity: Correlations with other variables ranged from −.60 to .68.

Author: Hansen, C. E.

Article: Psychometric properties of the Trauma Stages of Recovery.

Journal: *Psychological Reports*, August 2005, *97*, 217–235.

10868

Test Name: TRAUMA SYMPTOM CHECKLIST

Purpose: To measure symptoms of emotional distress.

Number of Items: 40

Format: Response scales range from 0 (*never*) to 3 (*very often*).

Validity: Correlations with other variables ranged from −.07 to .38.

Author: Wolfe, D. A., et al.

Article: Dating violence prevention with at-risk youth: A controlled outcome evaluation.

Journal: *Journal of Consulting and Clinical Psychology*, April 2003, *71*, 279–291.

Related Research: Elliot, D. M., & Briere, J. (1992). Sexual abuse trauma among professional women: Validating the trauma symptom checklist—40 (TSC-40). *Child Abuse and Neglect, 16,* 391–398.

10869

Test Name: TRI-AXIAL COPING SCALE—JAPANESE VERSION

Purpose: To measure tendencies to adapt particular coping strategies.

Number of Items: 24

Format: Sample items are presented.

Reliability: Alpha coefficients ranged from .66 to .87.

Author: Yukawa, S.

Article: Sex differences in relationships among anger, depression, and coping strategies of Japanese students.

Journal: *Psychological Reports,* December 2005, *97,* 769–776.

Related Research: Kaminura, E., et al. (1995). [A validation three-dimensional model of coping response and the development of the Tri-Axial Coping Scale (TAC-24)]. [*Bulletin of Counseling and School Psychology*], *33,* 41–47.

10870

Test Name: TYPE A BEHAVIOR ASSESSMENT SCALE—REVISED

Purpose: To measure impatience and hostile speech style, achievement striving and job commitment, and time urgency.

Number of Items: 25

Format: Four-point response scales are anchored by 1 (*no*) and 4 (*yes*). Sample items are presented.

Reliability: Alpha coefficients ranged from .73 to .84.

Validity: Correlations with other variables ranged from .04 to .48.

Author: Oashi, O.

Article: Relation of type A behavior and multidimensionally measured narcissistic personality of Japanese university students.

Journal: *Psychological Reports,* February 2004, *94,* 51–54.

Related Research: Okazaki, N., et al. (1995, October). [*Reconstruction of the Type A Behavior Assessment Scale.*] Paper presented at the 59th meeting of the Japanese Psychological Association, Okinawa, Japan. [in Japanese]

10871

Test Name: UCLASOCIAL SUPPORT INVENTORY— MODIFIED

Purpose: To assess support related to the participant's stress or worry about his or her HIV disease in the past 30 days.

Number of Items: 16

Format: Responses are made on a 5-point scale ranging from 1 (*never*) to 5 (*very often*).

Reliability: Coefficient alpha was .85.

Author: Simoni, J. M.

Article: Spirituality and psychological adaptation among women with HIV/AIDS: Implications for counseling.

Journal: *Journal of Counseling Psychology,* April 2002, *49,* 139–147.

Related Research: Schwarzer, R., et al. (1994). The multidimensional nature of received social support in gay men at risk of HIV infection and AIDS. *American Journal of Community Psychology, 22,* 319–339.

10872

Test Name: UNIVERSITY OF RHODE ISLAND CHANGE ASSESSMENT SCALE

Purpose: To measure precontemplation, contemplation, action, and maintenance as stages of change in psychotherapy.

Number of Items: 32

Format: Five-point Likert Scales are used. Sample items are presented.

Reliability: Alpha coefficients ranged from .81 to .87 across subscales.

Author: Scott, K. L., and Wolfe, D. A.

Article: Readiness to change as a predictor of outcome in batterer treatment.

Journal: *Journal of Consulting and Clinical Psychology,* October 2003, *71,* 879–889.

Related Research: McConnaughy, E. A., et al. (1989). Stages of change in psychotherapy: A follow-up report. *Psychotherapy: Theory, Research & Practice, 26,* 494–503.

10873

Test Name: UNIVERSITY OF WALES MOOD ADJECTIVE CHECKLIST

Purpose: To evaluate mood.

Number of Items: 29

Format: Includes three scales: Energetic Arousal, Tense Arousal, and Hedonic Tone. Responses are made on a 4-point scale ranging from 1 (*definitely*) to 4 (*definitely not*).

Reliability: Alpha coefficients exceeded .74.

Author: Reilley, S., et al.

Article: Workload, error detection, and experienced stress in a simulated pharmacy verification task.

Journal: *Perceptual and Motor Skills,* August 2002, *95,* 27–46.

Related Research: Matthews, G., et al. (1990). Refining the measurement of mood: The UWIST

Mood Adjective Checklist. *British Journal of Psychology, 81*, 17–42.

10874

Test Name: UNMITIGATED COMMISSION SCALE

Purpose: To measure unmitigated commission.

Number of Items: 9

Format: Responses are made on a 5-point scale ranging from 1 (*strongly disagree*) to 5 (*strongly agree*). Sample items are presented.

Reliability: Internal consistency reliabilities ranged from .70 to .80.

Validity: Correlations with other variables ranged from –.26 to .58.

Author: Bruch, M. A.

Article: The relevance of mitigated and unmitigated agency and commission for depression vulnerabilities and dysphoria.

Journal: *Journal of Counseling Psychology*, October 2002, *49*, 449–459.

Related Research: Fritz, H. L., & Helgeson, V. S. (1998). Distinctions of unmitigated communion from communion: Self-neglect and overinvolvement with others. *Journal of Personality and Social Psychology, 75*, 121–140.

10875

Test Name: VITALITY SCALE

Purpose: To measure well-being.

Number of Items: 7

Format: Nine-point scales are used.

Reliability: Coefficient alpha was .86.

Author: Kim, Y., et al.

Article: Self-concept, aspirations, and well-being in South Korea and the United States.

Journal: *The Journal of Social Psychology*, June 2003, *143*, 277–290.

Related Research: Ryan, R. M., & Frederick, C. (1997). On energy,

personality, and health: Subjective vitality as a dynamic reflection of well-being. *Journal of Personality, 65*, 529–565.

10876

Test Name: WAYS OF COPING SCALE—ADAPTED

Purpose: To assess coping responses to stressful life events.

Number of Items: 27

Format: Includes five factors: community involvement, constructive cognitions, avoidance, realistic acceptance, and spiritually based coping. Responses are made on a 4-point scale ranging from 1 (*never*) to 4 (*a great deal*). Examples are presented.

Reliability: Alpha coefficients ranged from .69 to .82.

Validity: Correlations with other variables ranged from –.21 to .60 (*N* = 230).

Author: Simoni, J. M.

Article: Spirituality and psychological adaptation among women with HIV/AIDS: Implications for counseling.

Journal: *Journal of Counseling Psychology*, April 2002, *49*, 139–147.

Related Research: Reed, G. M., et al. (1994). Realistic acceptance as a predictor of decreased survival time in gay men with AIDS. *Health Psychology, 13*, 299–307.

10877

Test Name: WAYS OF COPING SCALE—TURKISH VERSION

Purpose: To measure cognitive and behavioral strategies used to manage stress: approach coping, avoidant coping, fatalism, and social support seeking.

Number of Items: 66

Format: Response scales are anchored by 0 (*does not apply*) and 3 (*does apply a great deal*).

Reliability: Alpha coefficients ranged from .64 to .91.

Author: Ogul, M., and Gençöz, T.

Article: Roles of perceived control and coping strategies on depressive and anxiety symptoms of Turkish adolescents.

Journal: *Psychological Reports*, December 2003, *93*, Part 1, 659–672.

Related Research: Folkman, S., & Lazarus, R. S. (1980). An analysis of coping in a middle-aged community sample. *Journal of Health and Social Behavior, 21*, 219–239.

10878

Test Name: WAYS OF RELIGIOUS COPING SCALE

Purpose: To measure religious coping as religious cognitions and behaviors used to deal with stress.

Number of Items: 40

Format: Self-report format.

Reliability: Coefficient alpha was .95.

Validity: Correlations with other variables ranged from –.29 to .08.

Author: Daugherty, T. K., and McLarty, L. M.

Article: Religious coping, drinking motivation, and sex.

Journal: *Psychological Reports*, April 2003, *92*, 643–647.

Related Research: Boudreaux, E., et al. (1995). The Ways of Religious Coping Scale: Reliability, validity, and scale development. *Psychological Assessment, 2*, 233–244.

10879

Test Name: WEINBERGER ADJUSTMENT INVENTORY: DEPRESSION AND LOW WELL-BEING SUBSCALES

Purpose: To assess emotional distress.

Number of Items: 6

Format: Includes two subscales: Depression and Low Well-Being. Responses are made on 5-point scales ranging from 1 (*false*) to 5 (*true*). Examples are given.

Reliability: Coefficient alpha was .80.

Author: Wentzel, K. R., et al.

Article: Friendships in middle school: Influences on motivation and school adjustment.

Journal: *Journal of Educational Psychology*, June 2004, *96*, 195–203.

Related Research: Weinberger, D. A., et al. (1987). *Construct validation of the Weinberger Adjustment Inventory*. Unpublished manuscript, Stanford University, Stanford, CA.

10880

Test Name: WELL-BEING AND FUNCTIONAL STATUS BATTERY

Purpose: To assess well-being and functional status.

Number of Items: 149

Format: Includes 11 areas: psychosocial distress and well-being, physical functioning, role functioning, social family and sexual function, cognitive functioning, health perceptions, health distress, energy fatigue, sleep disturbance, pain, and physical or psychophysiologic symptoms. Responses are made on 5-point and on 6-point scales. Many items are presented.

Reliability: Alpha coefficients ranged from .74 to .80+.

Author: Marshall, G. N., et al.

Article: The tripartite model of anxiety and depression: Symptom structure in depressive and hypertensive patient groups.

Journal: *Journal of Personality Assessment*, April 2003, *80*, 139–153.

Related Research: Hays, R. D., & Stewart, A. L. (1990). The structure of self-reported health in chronic disease patients. *Psychological Assessment, 2*, 22–30.

10881

Test Name: WELL-BEING SCALE

Purpose: To assess psychological well-being.

Number of Items: 18

Reliability: Coefficient alpha was .81.

Validity: Correlations with other variables ranged from –.37 to .20.

Author: Feldman, G., and Hayes, A.

Article: Preparing for problems: A measure of mental anticipatory processes.

Journal: *Journal of Research in Personality*, October 2005, *39*, 487–516.

Related Research: Ryff, C. D., & Keyes, C. L. M. (1995). The structure of psychological well-being revisited. *Journal of Personality and Social Psychology, 69*, 719–727.

10882

Test Name: WELL-BEING SCALES

Purpose: To measure personal growth, purpose in life, and self-acceptance.

Number of Items: 27

Format: Rating scales range from 1 (*strongly disagree*) to 6 (*strongly agree*).

Validity: Correlations with other variables ranged from –.76 to .36.

Author: Cordova, M. J., et al.

Article: Social constraints, cognitive processing, and adjustment to breast cancer.

Journal: *Journal of Consulting and Clinical Psychology*, August 2001, *69*, 706–711.

Related Research: Ryff, C. D. (1989). Happiness is everything, or is it? Explorations on the meaning of psychological well-being. *Journal of Personality and Social Psychology, 57*, 1069–1089.

10883

Test Name: WELLNESS EVALUATION OF LIFESTYLE— TEENAGE VERSION

Purpose: To measure adolescents' wellness for six life tasks.

Number of Items: 105

Format: Scales range from 1 (*strongly agree*) to 4 (*strongly disagree*).

Reliability: Alpha coefficients ranged from .51 to .88.

Author: Rayle, A. D. and Meyers, J. E.

Article: Counseling adolescents toward wellness: The roles of ethnic identity, acculturation, and mattering.

Journal: *Professional School Counseling*, October 2004, *8*, 81–90.

Related Research: Meyers, J. E., & Sweeney, T. J. (2001). *The Wellness Evaluation of Lifestyle—Teenagers*. Greensboro, NC: Authors.

10884

Test Name: WENDER UTAH RATING SCALE

Purpose: To measure attention-deficit/hyperactivity disorder.

Format: Responses are made on 4- and 5-point scales.

Reliability: Coefficient alpha was .87

Validity: Correlation with the Barrett Impulsiveness Scale II-A was .43.

Author: Fossati, A., et al.

Article: Psychometric properties of an adolescent version of the Barrett Impulsiveness Scale—11 for a sample of Italian high school students.

Journal: *Perceptual and Motor Skills*, October 2002, *95*, 621–635.

Related Research: Ward, M. F., et al. (1993). The Wender Utah Rating Scale: An aid in the retrospective diagnosis of childhood attention deficit hyperactivity disorder. *American Journal of Psychiatry, 150*, 885–890.

10885

Test Name: WHITE BEAR SUPPRESSION INDEX

Purpose: To assess mood regulation through thought suppression.

Number of Items: 15

Reliability: Alpha coefficients ranged from .87 to .88. Test–retest reliabilities ranged from .69 to .92 (1 week–3 months).

Validity: Correlations with other variables ranged from −.33 to.58.

Author: McCarthy, C. J., et al.

Article: Continued attachment to parents: Its relationship to affect regulation and perceived stress among college students.

Journal: *Measurement and Evaluation in Counseling and Development*, January 2001, *33*, 198–213.

Related Research: Wagner, K., & Zanakos, S. (1994). Chronic thought suppression. *Journal of Personality, 62*, 615–640.

10886

Test Name: WHITE BEAR SUPPRESSION INVENTORY— SPANISH VERSION

Purpose: To measure the habitual tendency to suppress thoughts.

Number of Items: 15

Format: Item anchors are 1 (*strongly disagree*) and 5 (*strongly agree*). Sample items are presented in English.

Reliability: Coefficient alpha was .88. Test–retest reliability was .72 (4 weeks).

Validity: Correlations with other variables ranged from −.28 to .53.

Author: Fernández-Berrocal, P., et al.

Article: Validity and reliability of the Spanish version of the White Bear Suppression Inventory.

Journal: *Psychological Reports*, June 2004, *94*, Part 1, 782–784.

Related Research: Wenzlaff, R. M., & Wegner, D. M. (2000). Thought suppression. *Annual Review of Psychology, 51*, 59–91.

10887

Test Name: WILL TO LIVE SCALE

Purpose: To measure the will to live.

Number of Items: 3

Format: Scales range from 1 (*no*) to 3 (*yes*). All items are presented.

Reliability: Coefficient alpha was .82.

Validity: Correlations with other variables ranged from −.24 to .36.

Author: Westaby, J. D., et al.

Article: Intentions to work during terminal illness: An exploratory study of antecedent conditions.

Journal: *Journal of Applied Psychology*, November 2005, *90*, 1297–1305.

10888

Test Name: WOMEN'S HEALTH QUESTIONNAIRE

Purpose: To measure emotional and physical well-being among midlife women.

Number of Items: 35

Format: Includes nine subscales: Depressed Mood, Somatic Symptoms, Memory and Concentration Concerns, Vasomotor Symptoms, Anxiety, Sexual Behavior, Sleep Problems, Menstrual Symptoms, and Attractiveness. Responses are made on a 4-point scale ranging from *yes, definitely* to *no, not at all*.

Reliability: Test–retest (1 week) reliability was .86. Kuder–Richardson internal consistency reliability was .64.

Validity: Correlations with Kupperman's Index was .62 and .78.

Author: Kurpius, S. E. R., et al.

Article: Mood, marriage, and menopause.

Journal: *Journal of Counseling Psychology*, January 2001, *48*, 77–84.

Related Research: Hunter, M., et al. (1986). Relationships between psychological symptoms, somatic complaints, and menopausal status. *Maturitas, 8*, 217–218.

10889

Test Name: ZUNG SELF-RATING ANXIETY SCALE—SPANISH VERSION

Purpose: To assess anxiety.

Number of Items: 12

Format: Four-point scales range from 1 (*none or a little of the time*) to 4 (*most or all of the time*). All items are presented in English.

Reliability: Coefficient alpha was .81.

Validity: Correlations with other variables ranged from −.23 to .69.

Author: Kliewer, W., et al.

Article: Exposure to violence against a family member and internalizing symptoms in Columbian adolescents: The protective effects of family support.

Journal: *Journal of Consulting and Clinical Psychology*, December 2001, *69*, 971–982.

Related Research: Zung, W. W. K. (1971). A rating instrument for anxiety disorders. *Psychosomatics*, *12*, 164–167.

10890

Test Name: ZUNG SELF-RATING DEPRESSION SCALE

Purpose: To measure the psychological, affective, and somatic aspects of depression.

Number of Items: 20

Format: Items are rated on a 0 to 4 scale indicating frequency of experiencing symptoms over the past few days.

Reliability: Alpha coefficients ranged from .79 to .88. Split-half reliability was .94.

Validity: Correlations with other variables ranged from .70 to .76.

Author: Dozois, D. J. A.

Article: The psychometric characteristics of the Hamilton Depression Inventory.

Journal: *Journal of Personality Assessment*, February 2003, *80*, 31–40.

Related Research: Zung, W. W. K. (1965). A self-rating depression scale. *Archives of General Psychiatry*, *12*, 63–70.

10891

Test Name: ZUNG SELF-RATING DEPRESSION SCALE—SPANISH VERSION

Purpose: To measure depression in two dimensions: Melancholia and Helplessness.

Number of Items: 19

Format: Response scales range from 1 (*none or little of the time*) to 4 (*most or all of the time*). All items are presented in English.

Reliability: Coefficient alpha was .73 on both subscales.

Validity: Correlations with other variables ranged from −.26 to .69.

Author: Kliewer, W., et al.

Article: Exposure to violence against a family member and internalizing symptoms in Columbian adolescents: The protective effects of family support.

Journal: *Journal of Consulting and Clinical Psychology*, December 2001, *69*, 971–982.

Related Research: Zung, W. W. K. (1965). A self-rating depression scale. *Archives of General Psychiatry*, *12*, 63–70.

CHAPTER 4
Adjustment—Social

10892

Test Name: ACCULTURATION ATTITUDES SCALE

Purpose: To measure assimilation, integration, and separation in Israel.

Number of Items: 18

Format: Scales range from 1) *totally disagree*) to 6 (*totally agree*). All items are presented.

Reliability: Alpha coefficients ranged from .56 to .77.

Validity: Correlations with other variables ranged from −.39 to .33.

Author: Kurman, J., et al.

Article: Acculturation attitudes, perceived attitudes of the majority, and adjustment of Israeli-Arab and Jewish-Ethiopian students to an Israeli university.

Journal: *The Journal of Social Psychology*, October 2005, *145*, 593–612.

10893

Test Name: ACCULTURATION RATING SCALE FOR MEXICAN AMERICANS—II

Purpose: To assess association and identity with the Mexican and Anglo cultures.

Number of Items: 30

Format: Includes two subscales: Anglo Orientation and Mexican Orientation. Responses are made on a 5-point scale ranging from 1 (*not at all*) to 5 (*extremely often or almost always*).

Reliability: Internal consistency coefficients ranged from .77 to .91. Test–retest (2 weeks) reliability estimates were .94 and .96.

Validity: Correlations with other variables ranged from −.47 to .23.

Author: Flores, L. Y., and O'Brien, K. M.

Article: The career development of Mexican American adolescent women: A test of social cognitive career theory.

Journal: *Journal of Counseling Psychology*, January 2002, *49*, 14–27.

Related Research: Cuéllar, I., et al. (1995). Acculturation Rating Scale for Mexican Americans—II: A revision of the original ARSMA Scale. *Hispanic Journal of Behavioral Sciences, 17*, 275–304.

10894

Test Name: ACCULTURATION RATING SCALE FOR MEXICAN AMERICANS—II

Purpose: To measure Mexican American acculturation.

Number of Items: 30

Format: Includes two scales: Mexican Orientation and Anglo Orientation. Responses are made on a 5-point scale ranging from 1 (*not at all*) to 5 (*extremely often or almost always*).

Reliability: Internal consistency estimates ranged from .68 to .88. Test–retest (1 week) reliability estimates were .94 and .96.

Validity: Correlations with other variables ranged from −.07 to .53.

Author: Robitschek, C.

Article: Validity of Personal Growth Initiative Scale scores with a Mexican American college student population.

Journal: *Journal of Counseling Psychology*, October 2003, *50*, 496–502.

Related Research: Cuéllar, I., et al. (1995). Acculturation Rating Scale for Mexican Americans—II: A revision of the original ARSMA Scale. *Hispanic Journal of Behavioral Sciences, 17*, 275–304.

10895

Test Name: ACCULTURATION RATING SCALE FOR MEXICAN AMERICANS—II (SCALES 1 AND 2)

Purpose: To assess the behavioral domain of participants' acculturation and White attitudinal marginalization.

Number of Items: 48

Format: Includes five subscales: Mexican Orientation, Anglo Orientation, Anglo Marginality, Mexican Marginality, and Mexican American Marginality. Responses are made on 5-point scales ranging from 1 (*not at all*) to 5 (*extremely often or almost always*).

Reliability: Test–retest reliability was .96. Alpha coefficients were .76 and .88.

Validity: Correlations with other variables ranged from −.10 to .17.

Author: Castillo, L. G., et al.

Article: Acculturation, White marginalization, and family support as predictors of perceived distress in Mexican American female college students.

Journal: *Journal of Counseling Psychology*, April 2004, *51*, 151–157.

Related Research: Cuéllar, I., et al. (1995). Acculturation Rating Scale for Mexican Americans—II: A revision of the original ARSMA Scale. *Hispanic Journal of Behavioral Sciences, 17*, 275–304.

10896

Test Name: ACCULTURATION SCALE FOR MEXICAN AMERICANS

Purpose: To measure parent and adolescent acculturation of Mexican Americans.

Number of Items: 9

Format: Rating scales ranged from 1 (*only Spanish, no English*) to 5 (*only English, no Spanish*). Sample items are presented.

Reliability: Alpha coefficients were .70 (parents) and .68 (adolescents).

Validity: Correlations with other variables ranged from –.37 to .55.

Author: Razzino, B., et al.

Article: Central American adolescent acculturation and parental distress: Relationship to ratings of adolescent behavior problems.

Journal: *Psychological Reports*, June 2003, *92*, Part 2, 1255–1267.

Related Research: Burnam, A., et al. (1987). Measurement of acculturation in a community population of Mexican Americans. *Hispanic Journal of Behavioral Sciences, 9*, 105–130.

10897

Test Name: ACCULTURATIVE HASSLES INVENTORY

Purpose: To measure hassles experienced by Soviet Jewish refugee adolescents.

Number of Items: 39

Format: Scales range from 1 (*not at all a hassle*) to 4 (*a very big hassle*). All items are presented.

Reliability: Alpha coefficients ranged from .64 to .83.

Validity: Correlations with other variables ranged from .25 to .47.

Author: Vinokurov, A., et al.

Article: Acculturative hassles and immigrant adolescents: A life-domain assessment for Soviet Jewish refugees.

Journal: *The Journal of Social Psychology*, August 2002, *142*, 425–445.

10898

Test Name: ACCULTURATIVE STRESS SCALE

Purpose: To measure stress resulting from the experience of being in a new culture.

Number of Items: 6

Format: Scales ranged from 1 (*very stressed*) to 7 (*not at all stressed*). Sample items are presented.

Reliability: Alpha coefficients ranged from .78 to .88.

Author: Greenland, K., and Brown, R.

Article: Acculturation and contact in Japanese students studying in the United Kingdom.

Journal: *The Journal of Social Psychology*, August 2005, *145*, 373–389.

Related Research: Ward, C., et al. (1998). The U-curve on trial: A longitudinal study of psychological and sociocultural adjustment during cross-cultural transition. *International Journal of Intercultural Relations, 22*, 277–279.

10899

Test Name: ADOLESCENT INTERPERSONAL COMPETENCE QUESTIONNAIRE

Purpose: To measure four domains of competence related to adolescent dating relationships.

Number of Items: 32

Format: Response categories range from 1 (*poor at this time*) to 5 (*extremely good at this time*). Sample items are presented.

Reliability: Alpha coefficients ranged from .84 to .90.

Validity: Correlations with other variables ranged from –.23 to .30.

Author: Wolfe, D. A., et al.

Article: Dating violence prevention with at-risk youth: A controlled outcome evaluation.

Journal: *Journal of Consulting and Clinical Psychology*, April 2003, *71*, 279–291.

Related Research: Buhrmeister, D. (1990). Intimacy of friendship, interpersonal competence, and adjustment during preadolescence and adolescence. *Child Development, 61*, 1101–1111.

10900

Test Name: ADOLESCENTS RELATIONAL SELF-VIEWS SCALES

Purpose: To assess adolescents' relational self-views.

Number of Items: 19

Format: Includes three areas: social self-worth, social self-competence, and perceived control. Responses are made on 4-point scales ranging from 1 (*not at all*) to 4 (*very much*). Examples are given.

Reliability: Internal consistencies ranged from .46 to .82.

Validity: Correlations with other variables ranged from −.46 to .53.

Author: Caldwell, M. S., et al.

Article: Reciprocal influences among relational self-views, social disengagement, and peer stress during early adolescence.

Journal: *Child Development,* July/August 2004, 75, 1140–1154.

Related Research: Rudolph, K. D., & Clark, A. G. (2001). Conceptions of relationships in children with depressive and aggressive symptoms. Social–cognitive distortion of reality? *Journal of Abnormal Child Psychology, 25,* 447–475. Rudolph, K. D., et al. (2001). Negotiating the transition to middle school: The role of self-regulatory processes. *Child Development, 72,* 929–946.

10901

Test Name: ADULT ATTACHMENT SCALE

Purpose: To measure attachment styles.

Number of Items: 18

Format: Includes three subscales: Depend, Close, and Anxiety. Responses are made on a 5-point scale ranging from 1 (*not at all characteristic of me*) to 5 (*very characteristic of me*).

Reliability: Internal consistency reliability estimates ranged from .69 to .75. Test–retest (2 months) reliabilities ranged from .52 to .71.

Validity: Correlations with other variables ranged from −.41 to .34.

Author: Tokar, D. M., et al.

Article: Psychological separation, attachment security, vocational self-concept crystallization, and career indecision: A structural equation analysis.

Journal: *Journal of Counseling Psychology,* January 2003, *50,* 3–19.

Related Research: Collins, N. L., & Read, S. J. (1990). Adult attachment, working models, and relationship quality in dating couples. *Journal of Personality and Social Psychology, 58,* 644–663.

10902

Test Name: ADVERSARIAL HETEROSEXUAL BELIEFS SCALE

Purpose: To measure various aspects of adversarial relationships between the sexes.

Number of Items: 15

Format: Scales range from 1 (*strongly disagree*) to 7 (*strongly agree*).

Reliability: Alpha coefficients ranged from .83 to .84.

Author: Hall, G. C. N., et al.

Article: Ethnicity, culture, and sexual aggression: Risk and protective factors.

Journal: *Journal of Consulting and Clinical Psychology,* October 2005, *73,* 830–840.

Related Research: Lonsway, K. A., & Fitzgerald, L. F. (1995). Attitudinal antecedents of rape myth acceptance: A theoretical and empirical reexamination. *Journal of Personality and Social Psychology, 68,* 704–711.

10903

Test Name: AFRICAN AMERICAN IDENTITY SCALE

Purpose: To measure the strength of identity among African Americans.

Number of Items: 4

Format: Scales range from 1 (*definitely disagree*) to 5 (*definitely agree*).

Reliability: Coefficient alpha was .86.

Author: Heaven, P. C. L., and Greene, R. L.

Article: African Americans' stereotypes of Whites: Relationships with social dominance orientation, right-wing authoritarianism, and group identity.

Journal: *The Journal of Social Psychology,* February 2001, *141,* 141–143.

Related Research: Hinkle, S., et al. (1989). Intragroup identification and intergroup differentiation: A multicomponent approach. *British Journal of Social Psychology, 28,* 305–317.

10904

Test Name: AFRICAN SELF-CONSCIOUSNESS SCALE

Purpose: To assess a Black person's degree of pro-Black Afrocentric versus anti-Black Eurocentric values.

Number of Items: 42

Format: Scales range from 1 (*strongly disagree*) to 8 (*strongly agree*). Sample items are presented.

Reliability: Alpha coefficients ranged from .76 to .80.

Validity: Correlations with other variables ranged from −.36 to .36.

Author: Kelly, S.

Article: Underlying components of scores assessing African-Americans' racial perspective.

Journal: *Measurement and Evaluation in Counseling and Development,* April 2004, *37,* 28–40.

Related Research: Baldwin, J. A., & Bell, Y. (1985). The African

Self-Consciousness Scale: An Afrocentric personality questionnaire. *The Western Journal of Black Studies, 9,* 61–68.

10905

Test Name: AFRICULTURAL COPING SYSTEMS INVENTORY

Purpose: To measure culture-specific coping strategies of African Americans in everyday stressful situations.

Number of Items: 30

Format: Includes four subscales: Cognitive/Emotional Debriefing, Spiritual-Centered Coping, Collective-Centered Coping, and Ritual-Centered Coping. Responses are made on a 4-point scale ranging from 0 (*did not use*) to 3 (*used a great deal*). All items are presented.

Reliability: Alpha coefficients ranged from .60 to .83.

Author: Utsey, S. O., et al.

Article: Testing the structural invariance of the Africultural Coping Systems Inventory across three samples of African descent populations.

Journal: *Educational and Psychological Measurement,* February 2004, *64,* 185–195.

Related Research: Utsey, S. O., et al. (2000). Development and initial validation of the Africultural Coping Systems Inventory. *Journal of Black Psychology, 26,* 194–215.

10906

Test Name: AGGRESSION FROM COWORKERS AND THE PUBLIC SCALES

Purpose: To measure the frequency of aggression from coworkers and the public.

Number of Items: 3

Format: Scales range from 0 (*never*) to 4 (*four or more times*). A sample item is presented.

Reliability: Alpha coefficients were .91 (public) and .82 (coworker).

Validity: Correlations with other variables ranged from −.39 to .64.

Author: LeBlanc, M. M., and Kelloway, E. K.

Article: Predictors and outcomes of workplace violence and aggression.

Journal: *Journal of Applied Psychology,* June 2002, *87,* 444–453.

10907

Test Name: AGGRESSIVE CULTURE EXPOSURE SCALE

Purpose: To assess the extent to which persons have experienced aggression in their neighborhoods and at home.

Number of Items: 6

Format: Scales range from 1 (*absolutely not true*) to 5 (*absolutely true*). All items are presented.

Reliability: Reliability was .95.

Validity: Correlations with other variables ranged from −.09 to .54.

Author: Douglas, S. C., and Martinko, M. J.

Article: Exploring the role of individual differences in the prediction of workplace aggression.

Journal: *Journal of Applied Psychology,* August 2001, *86,* 547–559.

10908

Test Name: ANXIOUS SOLITUDE SCALE

Purpose: To assess anxious solitude.

Number of Items: 8

Format: Responses are made on a 3-point scale ranging from 0 (*not true*) to 2 (*often true*). All items are presented.

Reliability: Alpha coefficients were .73 and .74.

Validity: Correlations with other variables ranged from −.37 to .59.

Author: Gazelle, H., and Rudolph, K. D.

Article: Moving toward and away from the world: Social approach and avoidance trajectories in anxious solitary youth.

Journal: *Child Development,* May/June 2004, *75,* 829–849.

Related Research: Achenbach, T. (1991). *Manual for the Teacher's Report Form and 1991 Profile.* Burlington: University of Vermont, Department of Psychiatry. Ladd, G. W., & Profilet, S. M. (1996). The Child Behavior Scale: A teacher-report measure of young children's aggressive, withdrawn, and prosocial behaviors. *Developmental Psychology, 32,* 1008–1024.

10909

Test Name: ASHER LONELINESS SCALE

Purpose: To assess adolescents' feelings of loneliness.

Number of Items: 16

Format: Responses are made on a 5-point scale. Sample items are presented.

Reliability: Coefficient alpha was .92.

Validity: Correlations with other variables ranged from −.61 to .58.

Author: Storch, E. A., et al.

Article: The relationship of peer victimization to social anxiety and loneliness in adolescence.

Journal: *Child Study Journal,* 2003, *33,* 1–18.

Related Research: Asher, S. R., & Wheeler, V. A. (1985). Children's loneliness: A comparison of rejected and neglected peer status. *Journal*

of Consulting and Clinical Psychology, 53, 500–505.

10910

Test Name: ASHER LONELINESS SCALE

Purpose: To assess children's experience of loneliness.

Number of Items: 24

Format: Responses are made on a 5-point scale ranging from 1 (*not true at all*) to 5 (*always true*).

Reliability: Coefficient alpha for 16 items was .88.

Author: Storch, E. A., et al.

Article: The relationship of communication beliefs and abilities to peer victimization in elementary school children.

Journal: *Child Study Journal,* 2002, *32,* 231–240.

Related Research: Asher, S. R., et al. (1984). Loneliness in children. *Child Development, 55,* 1457–1464.

10911

Test Name: ASIAN ACCULTURATION SCALE

Purpose: To assess the degree of acculturation of Asian immigrants to North America in terms of interpersonal matters, exposure to English mass media, and English–Canadian interactions.

Number of Items: 11

Format: Scales range from 1 (*strongly disagree*) to 7 (*strongly agree*). All items are presented.

Reliability: Alpha coefficients ranged from .87 to .92.

Validity: Goodness of fit indexes were .90 or higher for a three-factor model.

Author: Kim, C., et al.

Article: The Chinese in Canada: A study in ethnic change with emphasis on gender roles.

Journal: *The Journal of Social Psychology,* February 2004, *144,* 5–29.

10912

Test Name: ASIAN AMERICAN RACISM-RELATED STRESS INVENTORY

Purpose: To measure racism-related stress for Asian Americans.

Number of Items: 29

Format: Includes three subscales: Socio-Historical Racism, General Racism, and Perpetual Foreigner Racism. Responses are made on a 5-point scale ranging from 1 (*This event never happened to me or someone I know*) to 5 (*This event happened and I was extremely upset*). All items are presented.

Reliability: Alpha coefficients ranged from .75 to .95.

Validity: Correlations with other variables ranged from –.09 to .58.

Author: Liang, C. T. H., et al.

Article: The Asian American Racism-Related Stress Inventory: Development, factor analysis, reliability, and validity.

Journal: *Journal of Counseling Psychology,* January 2004, *51,* 103–114.

10913

Test Name: ATTACHMENT ANXIETY AND AVOIDANCE IN CLOSE RELATIONSHIPS SCALE—HEBREW

Purpose: To measure attachment anxiety and avoidance in close relationships.

Number of Items: 10

Format: Includes five items tapping avoidant attachment and five items tapping anxious attachment. Responses are made on 7-point scales ranging from 1 (*not at all*) to 7 (*very much*). Examples are given.

Reliability: Alpha coefficients were .75 and .79.

Validity: Correlations with other variables ranged from –.14 to .48.

Author: Berant, E., et al.

Article: Rorschach correlates of self-reported attachment dimensions: Dynamic manifestations of hyperactivating and deactivating strategies.

Journal: *Journal of Personality Assessment,* February 2005, *84,* 70–81.

Related Research: Mikulincer, M., et al. (1990). Attachment styles and fear of personal death: A case study of affect regulation. *Journal of Personality and Social Psychology, 58,* 273–280.

10914

Test Name: ATTACHMENT SCALE

Purpose: To measure healthy attachment.

Number of Items: 18

Format: Includes three factors: close, depend, and anxiety. Responses are made on a 5-point scale ranging from 1 (*not at all characteristic of me*) to 5 (*very characteristic of me*). Examples are presented.

Reliability: Alpha coefficients ranged from .59 to .77.

Validity: Correlations with other variables ranged from –.24 to .23.

Author: Goodyear, R. K., et al.

Article: Pregnant Latina teenagers: Psychosocial and developmental determinants of how they select and perceive the men who father their children.

Journal: *Journal of Counseling Psychology,* April 2002, *49,* 187–201.

Related Research: Collins, N. L., & Read, S. J. (1990). Adult attachment, working models, and relationship quality in dating couples. *Journal of Personality and Social Psychology, 58,* 644–663.

10915

Test Name: ATTACHMENT STYLE QUESTIONNAIRE

Purpose: To provide a self-evaluation of attachment style.

Number of Items: 40

Format: Includes five scales: Confidence, Discomfort with Closeness, Relationships as Secondary, Need for Approval, and Preoccupation with Relationships. Responses are made on a 6-point scale ranging from 1 (*totally disagree*) to 6 (*totally agree*).

Reliability: Alpha coefficients ranged from .61 to .73.

Validity: Correlations with the Parental Attitude Research Instrument subscales ranged from −.37 to .32.

Author: Trombini, E., et al.

Article: Maternal attitudes and attachment styles in mothers of obese children.

Journal: *Perceptual and Motor Skills,* October 2003, *97,* 613–620.

Related Research: Feeney, J. A., et al. (1994). Assessing adult attachment. In M. B. Sperling & W. H. Berman (Eds.), *Attachment in adults: Clinical and developmental perspectives* (pp. 128–152). New York: Guilford Press.

10916

Test Name: BALANCED INVENTORY OF DESIRABLE RESPONDING

Purpose: To assess social desirability and response bias.

Number of Items: 40

Format: Includes two constructs: self-deceptive positivity and impression management. Responses are made on a 7-point scale ranging from 1 (*not true*) to 7 (*very true*).

Reliability: Alpha coefficients ranged from .62 to .86.

Validity: Correlations with other variables ranged from −.35 to .19.

Author: Inman, A. G., et al.

Article: Development and preliminary validation of the Cultural Values Conflict Scale for South Asian women.

Journal: *Journal of Counseling Psychology,* January 2001, *48,* 17–27.

Related Research: Paulhus, D. L. (1991). Measurement and control of response bias. In J. P. Robinson et al. (Eds.), *Measures of personality and social psychological attitudes* (Vol. 1, pp. 17–57). San Diego, CA: Academic Press.

10917

Test Name: BELIEFS ABOUT WORKING IN GROUPS QUESTIONNAIRE

Purpose: To measure the quality of social interactions and the quality of learning in student work groups.

Number of Items: 15

Format: Item responses are anchored by 1 (*totally disagree*) and 5 (*totally agree*). All items are presented.

Reliability: Test–retest reliabilities ranged from .45 to .55 over a 6-week interval. Internal consistency ranged from .70 to .72.

Author: Boekaerts, M.

Article: Assessment of attitudes about new learners' roles: Factor analysis of the Beliefs about Working in Groups Scale.

Journal: *Psychological Reports,* June 2002, *90,* Part 1, 986–996.

Related Research: Boekaerts, M. (1997). Self-regulated learning: A new concept embraced by researchers, policy makers, educators, teachers, and students. *Learning and Instruction, 7,* 161–186.

10918

Test Name: BELONGINGNESS SCALE

Purpose: To assess the sense of belonging with a partner.

Number of Items: 11

Reliability: Alpha coefficients exceeded .86.

Validity: Correlations with chance of marrying ranged from −.48 to .01.

Author: Umaña-Taylor, A. J., and Fine, M.

Article: Predicting commitment to wed among Hispanic and Anglo partners.

Journal: *Journal of Marriage and Family,* February 2003, *65,* 117–139.

Related Research: Barker, H. B., & Kelley. H. H. (1979). Conflict in the development of close relationships. In R. L. Burgess & T. L. Houston (Eds.), *Social Exchange in Developing Relationships* (pp. 135–168). New York: Academic Press.

10919

Test Name: BEST FRIEND EXPERIENCES QUESTIONNAIRE

Purpose: To measure the intimacy and negativity of best friend relationships.

Number of Items: 17

Format: Five-point scales are used. Sample items are presented.

Reliability: Alpha coefficients were .80 (intimacy) and .72 (negativity).

Author: Updegraph, K. A., et al.

Article: Parents' involvement in adolescents' peer relationships: A comparison of mothers' and fathers' roles.

Journal: *Journal of Marriage and Family*, August 2001, *63*, 655–668.

Related Research: Blyth, D. A., et al. (1982). Early adolescents' significant others: Grade and gender differences in perceived relationships with familial and nonfamilial adults and young people. *Journal of Youth and Adolescence*, *11*, 425–450.

10920

Test Name: BLACK RACIAL IDENTITY ATTITUDE SCALE— LONG FORM

Purpose: To measure black racial identity.

Number of Items: 50

Format: Scales range from 1 (*strongly disagree*) to 5 (*strongly agree*).

Reliability: Alpha coefficients ranged from .51 to .80 across subscales.

Author: Sanchez, D., and Carter, R. T.

Article: Exploring the relationship between racial identity and religious orientation among African American college students.

Journal: *Journal of College Student Development*, May/June 2005, *46*, 280–295.

Related Research: Parham, T. A., & Helms, J. E. (1985). Attitudes of racial identity and self-esteem of Black students: An exploratory investigation. *Journal of College Student Personnel, 26,* 143–147.

10921

Test Name: BLAME ATTRIBUTION SCALE

Purpose: To assess victimization in terms of cognitions entertained by a victim.

Number of Items: 4

Format: Scales range from 1 (*never*) to 5 (*always*). All items are presented.

Reliability: Coefficient alpha was .77.

Validity: Correlations with other variables ranged from –.40 to .45.

Author: Aquino, K., et al.

Article: How employees respond to personal offense: The effects of blame attribution, victim status, and offender status on revenge and reconciliation in the workplace.

Journal: *Journal of Applied Psychology*, February 2001, *86*, 52–59.

Related Research: Wade, S. H. (1989). *The development of a scale to measure forgiveness.* Unpublished doctoral dissertation, Fuller Theological Seminary, Pasadena, CA.

10922

Test Name: BRIEF SOCIAL DESIRABILITY SCALE

Purpose: To measure social desirability.

Number of Items: 10

Format: A true–false format is used.

Reliability: Coefficient alpha was .88.

Validity: The correlation with the full 33-item scale was .96.

Author: Amodei, N., et al.

Article: Interview versus self-answer methods of assessing health and emotional functioning in primary care patients.

Journal: *Psychological Reports*, June 2003, *92*, Part 1, 937–948.

Related Research: Fischer, D. G., & Fick, C. (1993). Measuring social desirability: Short forms of the Marlowe–Crowne Social Desirability Scales. *Educational and Psychological Measurement*, *53*, 417–424.

10923

Test Name: CENTRALITY AND REGARD SCALES

Purpose: To measure racial identity.

Number of Items: 14

Format: Scales range from 1 (*strongly disagree*) to 7 (*strongly agree*). Sample items are presented.

Reliability: Alpha coefficients ranged from .67 to .88.

Validity: Correlations with self-esteem ranged from –.01 to .37.

Author: Johnston, T. M., et al.

Article: The Multidimensional Inventory of Black Identity: Its use with Euro-American, Latino, and Native American undergraduates.

Journal: *Measurement and Evaluation in Counseling and Development*, July 2005, *38*, 92–103.

10924

Test Name: CHILDREN'S SELF-REPORT SOCIAL SKILLS SCALE

Purpose: To assess children's social skills: adherence to rules, perceived popularity, and finesse in applying interaction skills.

Number of Items: 21

Format: Scales range from 1 (*never*) to 5 (*always*). All items are presented.

Reliability: Coefficient alpha for the total scale was .96. Alpha coefficients ranged from .84 to .90 across subscales.

Validity: Subscale correlations with other variables ranged from −.34 to .30.

Author: Danielson, C. K., and Phelps, C. R.

Article: The assessment of children's social skills through self-report: A potential screening instrument for classroom use.

Journal: *Measurement and Evaluation in Counseling and Development*, January 2003, *35*, 218–229.

10925

Test Name: CLASSROOM COHESION SCALE

Purpose: To measure cohesion in a group.

Number of Items: 10

Format: Response scales range from 1 (*strongly disagree*) to 5 (*strongly agree*).

Reliability: Coefficient alpha was .95.

Validity: Correlations with other variables ranged from −.50 to .79.

Author: Myers, S. A., and Goodboy, A. K.

Article: A study of grouphate in a course on small group communication.

Journal: *Psychological Reports*, October 2005, *97*, 381–386.

Related Research: Rosenfeld, L. B., & Gilbert, J. R. (1989). The measurement of cohesion and its relationship to dimensions of self-disclosure in classroom settings. *Small Group Behavior, 20*, 291–301.

10926

Test Name: CLASSROOM PEER NOMINATIONS SCALES

Purpose: To measure within class peer prosocial leadership, aggression, and social withdrawal.

Number of Items: 18

Format: Includes three scales: Prosocial Leadership, Aggression, and Social Withdrawal. All items are presented in abbreviated format.

Reliability: Internal consistency reliabilities ranged from .87 to .94.

Author: Chang, L.

Article: Variable effects of children's aggression, social withdrawal, and prosocial leadership as functions of teacher beliefs and behaviors.

Journal: *Child Development*, March/April 2003, *74*, 535–548.

Related Research: Schwartz, D., et al. (1998). Peer group victimization as a predictor of children's behavior problems at home and in school. *Development and Psychopathology, 10*, 87–99.

10927

Test Name: COLLECTIVE SELF-ESTEEM SCALE—MODIFIED, SHORTENED

Purpose: To measure how individuals evaluate the ethnic group with which they identify.

Number of Items: 8

Format: Responses are made on a 7-point scale ranging from 1 (*strongly disagree*) to 7 (*strongly agree*). Examples are given.

Reliability: Coefficient alpha was .81.

Validity: Correlations with other variables ranged from −.46 to .67.

Author: Cassidy, C., et al.

Article: Perceived discrimination and psychological distress: The role of personal and ethnic self-esteem.

Journal: *Journal of Counseling Psychology*, July 2004, *51*, 329–339.

Related Research: Luhtanen, R., & Crocker, J. (1992). A collective self-esteem scale: Self-evaluation of one's social identity. *Personality and Social Psychology Bulletin, 18*, 302–318.

10928

Test Name: COLLECTIVISM SCALE

Purpose: To assess preferences for working alone or in a group.

Number of Items: 3

Format: All items are presented.

Reliability: Coefficient alpha was .68.

Validity: Correlations with other variables ranged from −.07 to .15.

Author: Colquitt, J. A.

Article: Does the justice of the one interact with the justice of the many? Reactions to procedural justice in teams.

Journal: *Journal of Applied Psychology*, August 2004, *89*, 633–646.

Related Research: Wagner, J. A., III. (1995). Studies of individualism–collectivism: Effects on cooperation in groups. *Academy of Management Journal, 38*, 152–172.

10929

Test Name: COLLEGIATE PSYCHOLOGICAL SENSE OF COMMUNITY SCALE

Purpose: To measure community well-being.

Number of Items: 14

Format: Responses are made on a 5-point Likert Scale ranging from 1 (*strongly disagree*) to 5 (*strongly agree*).

Reliability: Coefficient alpha was .86.

Validity: Correlations with other variables ranged from −.36 to .70 ($N = 88$).

Author: Lee, R. M.

Article: Do ethnic identity and other-group orientation protect against discrimination for Asian Americans?

Journal: *Journal of Counseling Psychology*, April 2003, *50*, 133–141.

Related Research: Lounsbury, J. W., & Deneui, D. (1996). Collegiate psychological sense of community in relation to size of college/university and extroversion. *Journal of Community Psychology*, *24*, 381–394.

10930

Test Name: COMFORT FROM COMPANION ANIMALS SCALE

Purpose: To measure the perceived emotional comfort provided by pets.

Number of Items: 11

Format: Item responses are anchored on 4-point agreement scales.

Reliability: Cronbach's alpha was .85.

Author: Castelli, P., et al.

Article: Companion cats and the social support systems of men with AIDS.

Journal: *Psychological Reports*, August 2001, *89*, 177–187.

Related Research: Zasloff, R. L. (1996). Measuring attachment to companion animals: A dog is not a cat is not a bird. *Applied Animal Behavior Science*, *47*, 43–48.

10931

Test Name: COMMITMENT SCALE

Purpose: To measure the desire for a committed relationship.

Number of Items: 15

Format: Item responses are anchored by 1 (*strongly disagree*) and 5 (*strongly agree*). Sample items are presented.

Reliability: K-R reliability was .96.

Author: Mathes, E. W., et al.

Article: An evolutionary perspective on the interaction of age and sex differences in short-term sexual strategies.

Journal: *Psychological Reports*, June 2002, *90*, Part 1, 949–956.

Related Research: Sternberg, R. J. (1988). *The triangle of love*. New York: Basic Books.

10932

Test Name: COMMUNITY FUNCTIONING HASSLES SCALES

Purpose: To assess the ability to function in the community, to function with friends and others, and to function financially.

Number of Items: 21

Format: Scales range from 1 (*not at all a hassle*) to 4 (*a great deal of a hassle*).

Reliability: Alpha coefficients ranged from .62 to .82 across subscales.

Author: Oyserman, D., et al.

Article: Positive parenting among African American mothers with a serious mental illness.

Journal: *Journal of Marriage and Family*, February 2002, *64*, 65–77.

Related Research: Lazarus, R., & Folkman, S. (1984). *Stress, appraisal, and coping*. New York: Springer-Verlag.

10933

Test Name: COMPANIONATE LOVE SCALE

Purpose: To measure the expectation of a lasting love.

Number of Items: 8

Format: Scales range from 1 (*not at all true*) to 9 (*definitely true*). Sample items are presented.

Reliability: Coefficient alpha was .90.

Author: Kito, M.

Article: Self-disclosure in romantic relationships and friendships among American and Japanese college students.

Journal: *The Journal of Social Psychology*, April 2005, *145*, 127–140.

Related Research: Hatfield, E. (1988). Passionate and companionate love. In R. J. Sternberg & M. L. Barnes (Eds.), *The psychology of love* (pp. 191–217). New Haven, CT: Yale University Press.

10934

Test Name: COMPREHENSION OF CONSENT/COERCION MEASURE

Purpose: To measure the ability to recognize consent and coercion in sexual situations.

Number of Items: 10

Format: Two vignettes are followed by five items with scales ranging from 1 (*strongly agree*) to 5 (*strongly disagree*).

Reliability: Internal consistency reliabilities ranged from .75 to .84. Test–retest reliability was .60 (5 weeks).

Author: Davis, T. L., and Liddell, D. L.

Article: Getting inside the house: The effectiveness of a rape prevention program for college fraternity men.

Journal: *Journal of College Student Development*, January/February 2002, *43*, 35–50.

Related Research: Gibson, D. B., & Humphrey, C. F. (1993). *Educating in regards to sexual violence: An interactional dramatic acquaintance rape intervention.* Unpublished manuscript, University of Minnesota, Sexual Violence Program, Minneapolis.

10935

Test Name: CONCERN FOR APPROPRIATENESS SCALE

Purpose: To assess participants' tendencies to be aware of norms for socially appropriate behavior and to attempt to meet those norms.

Number of Items: 13

Format: Responses are made on a 5-point scale ranging from 1 (*strongly disagree*) to 5 (*strongly agree*). An example is presented.

Reliability: Internal consistency was .83.

Author: Mohr, J. J., et al.

Article: Counselors' attitudes regarding bisexuality as predictors of counselors' clinical responses: An analogue study of a female bisexual client.

Journal: *Journal of Counseling Psychology*, April 2001, *48*, 212–222

Related Research: Lennox, R. D., & Wolfe, R. N. (1984). Revision of the Self-Monitoring Scale. *Journal of Personality and Social Psychology*, *46*, 1349–1364.

10936

Test Name: CONFLICT MANAGEMENT STRATEGIES SCALE

Purpose: To assess the propensity to handle conflict by problem

solving, contention, avoidance, and yielding.

Number of Items: 16

Format: Scales range from 1 (*definitely disagree*) to 7 (*definitely agree*). Sample items are presented.

Reliability: Alpha coefficients ranged from .60 to .76 across subscales.

Validity: Correlations with other variables ranged from –.24 to .38.

Author: Bizman, A., and Yinon, Y.

Article: Intergroup conflict management strategies as related to perceptions of dual identity and separate groups.

Journal: *The Journal of Social Psychology*, April 2004, *144*, 115–126.

10937

Test Name: CONNECTEDNESS SCALE

Purpose: To measure the degree to which individuals value and need relational ties to others.

Number of Items: 50

Format: Five-point Likert scales are used. Sample items are presented.

Reliability: Alpha coefficients ranged from .94 to .95.

Validity: Correlations with other variables ranged from –.09 to .32.

Author: Boatwright, K. J., and Egidio, R. K.

Article: Psychological predictors of college women's leadership aspirations.

Journal: *Journal of College Student Development*, September/October 2003, *44*, 653–669.

Related Research: Welch, N. C. (1997). The development and validation of a scale measuring the construct of connectedness. Doctoral dissertation, University of Texas at Austin. *Dissertation Abstracts International*, *59*, 0085.

10938

Test Name: CONSENSUS SCALE

Purpose: To assess participants' feelings about group decision-making processes.

Number of Items: 21

Format: Response scales range from 1 (*strongly disagree*) to 2 (*strongly agree*).

Reliability: Coefficient alpha was .92.

Validity: Correlations with other variables ranged from –.45 to .72.

Author: Myers, S. A., and Goodboy, A. K.

Article: A study of grouphate in a course on small group communication.

Journal: *Psychological Reports*, October 2005, *97*, 381–386.

Related Research: DeStephen, R. S., & Hirokawa, R. Y. (1988). Small group consensus: Stability of group support of the decision, task process, and group relationships. *Small Group Behavior*, *19*, 227–239.

10939

Test Name: CONTACT SCALES

Purpose: To measure contact, intergroup anxiety, and in-group bias.

Number of Items: 23

Format: Various formats are used. All items are described. Sample items are presented.

Reliability: Alpha coefficients ranged from .38 to .76.

Author: Greenland, K., and Brown, R.

Article: Acculturation and contact in Japanese students studying in the United Kingdom.

Journal: *The Journal of Social Psychology*, August 2005, *145*, 373–389.

Related Research: Islam, M. R., & Hewstone, M. (1993). Dimensions of contact as predictors of intergroup anxiety, perceived out-group variability, and out-group attitude: An integrative account. *Personality and Social Psychology Bulletin, 19,* 700–710.

10940

Test Name: CONTACT WITH DELINQUENT FRIENDS SCALE

Purpose: To measure contact with delinquent friends.

Number of Items: 12

Format: Item responses range from *none* to *above three-fourths*. All items are presented.

Reliability: Coefficient alpha was .85.

Validity: Correlations with other variables ranged from .03 to .30.

Author: Lee, E., and Kim, M.

Article: Exposure to media violence and bullying at school: Mediating influences of anger and contact with delinquent friends.

Journal: *Psychological Reports,* October 2004, *95,* 659–672.

Related Research: Kim, B. H. (1999). [*A study on school violence and its causes*]. Unpublished master's thesis, Catholic University of Daegu, Korea. [in Korean]

10941

Test Name: COOPERATION SCALE

Purpose: To measure group member cooperation.

Number of Items: 6

Format: Responses are made on a 7-point scale ranging from 1 (*strongly disagree*) to 7 (*strongly agree*). Examples are given.

Reliability: Coefficient alpha was .83.

Validity: Correlations with other variables ranged from .34 to .55.

Author: Erez, A., et al.

Article: Effects of rotated leadership and peer evaluations on the functioning and effectiveness of self-managed teams: A quasi-experiment.

Journal: *Personnel Psychology,* Winter 2002, *55,* 929–948.

10942

Test Name: CO-RUMINATION QUESTIONNAIRE

Purpose: To assess the extent to which participants typically coruminate with close, same-sex friends.

Number of Items: 27.

Format: Includes nine content areas. Responses are made on a 5-point scale ranging from 1 (*not at all true*) to 5 (*really true*). Examples are presented.

Reliability: Coefficient alpha was .96.

Validity: Correlations with other variables ranged from .10 to .61.

Author: Rose, A. J.

Article: Co-rumination in the friendships of girls and boys.

Journal: *Child Development,* November/December 2002, *73,* 1830–1843.

10943

Test Name: COWORKER REACTION SCALE

Purpose: To assess coworker treatment of gay and lesbian workers.

Number of Items: 10

Format: Scales range from 1 (*strongly disagree*) to 5 (*strongly agree*). A sample item is presented.

Reliability: Coefficient alpha was .89.

Validity: Correlations with other variables ranged from –.45 to .85.

Author: Griffith, K. H., and Hebl, M. R.

Article: The disclosure dilemma for gay men and lesbians: "Coming out" at work.

Journal: *Journal of Applied Psychology,* December 2002, *87,* 1191–1199.

10944

Test Name: CROSS-CULTURAL ADJUSTMENT SCALE— ADAPTED

Purpose: To measure nonwork/general and work adjustments.

Number of Items: 10

Format: Includes two scales: Nonwork/General and Work Adjustments. Responses are made on a 7-point scale ranging from 1 (*very unadjusted*) to 7 (*very adjusted*). Sample items are given.

Reliability: Reliability coefficients were .81 and .88.

Validity: Correlations with other variables ranged from –.48 to .37 ($n = 133$).

Author: Takeuchi, R., et al.

Article: Antecedents and consequences of psychological workplace strain during expatriation: A cross-sectional and longitudinal investigation.

Journal: *Personnel Psychology,* Winter 2005, *58,* 925–948.

Related Research: Black, J. S., & Stephens, G. K. (1989). The influence of the spouse on American expatriate adjustment and intent to stay in Pacific Rim overseas assignments. *Journal of Management, 15,* 529–544.

10945

Test Name: CROSS RACIAL IDENTITY SCALE

Purpose: To assess racial identity.

Number of Items: 40

Format: Includes six subscales: Pre-Encounter Assimilation, Pre-Encounter Miseducation, Pre-Encounter Self-Hatred, Immersion-Emersion Anti-White, Internalization Afrocentricity, and Internalization Multiculturalist Inclusive. Responses are made on a 7-point Likert-scale ranging from 1 (*strongly disagree*) to 7 (*strongly agree*).

Reliability: Internal consistency correlations ranged from .74 to .89.

Validity: Correlations with other variables ranged from −.22 to .35 ($N = 153$).

Author: Cokley, K. O.

Article: Testing Cross's Revised Identity Model: An examination of the relationship between racial identity and internalized racialism.

Journal: *Journal of Counseling Psychology*, October 2002, *49*, 476–483.

Related Research: Vandiver, B. J., et al. (2000). *The Cross Racial Identity Scale.* Unpublished scale created by a team of researchers from Penn State University and Southern Illinois University at Carbondale.

10946

Test Name: CROSS RACIAL IDENTITY SCALE

Purpose: To provide a measure of six Black racial identities.

Number of Items: 50

Format: Includes six subscales: Pre-Encounter Assimilation, Pre-Encounter Miseducation, Pre-Encounter Self-Hatred, Immersion-Emerson Anti-White, Internalization Black Nationalist, and Internalization Multiculturalist Inclusive. Responses are made on a 7-point scale ranging from 1 (*strongly disagree*) to 7 (*strongly agree*).

Reliability: Reliability estimates ranged from .59 to .91.

Author: Vandiver, B. J., et al.

Article: Validating the Cross Racial Identity Scale.

Journal: *Journal of Counseling Psychology*, January 2002, *49*, 71–85.

Related Research: Vandiver, B. J., et al. (2000). *The Cross Racial Identity Scale.* Unpublished scale.

10947

Test Name: CULTURAL ADJUSTMENT DIFFICULTIES CHECKLIST

Purpose: To assess the acculturation-induced stresses of Asians in the United States.

Number of Items: 59

Format: Includes two subscales: Acculturative Distress and Intercultural Competence Concerns.

Reliability: Alpha coefficients ranged from .88 to .93 ($N = 80$).

Validity: Correlations with other variables ranged from −.01 to .52.

Author: Inman, A. G., et al.

Article: Development and preliminary validation of the Cultural Values Conflict Scale for South Asian women.

Journal: *Journal of Counseling Psychology*, January 2001, *48*, 17–27.

Related Research: Sodowsky, G. R., & Lai, E. W. M. (1997). Asian immigrant variables and structured models of cross-cultural distress. In A. Booth, A. C. Crouter, & N. Landale (Eds.), *Immigration and the family: Research and policy on U.S. immigrants* (pp. 211–234). Hillsdale, NJ: Erlbaum.

10948

Test Name: CULTURAL MISTRUST INVENTORY

Purpose: To assess African Americans' mistrust toward European Americans and European American–related organizations.

Number of Items: 48

Format: Includes four subscales: Politics and Law, Education and Training, Business and Work, and Interpersonal Relations. Responses are made on a 9-point Likert-type scale ranging from 1 (*not in the least agree*) to 9 (*entirely agree*).

Reliability: Alpha coefficients for three of the subscales ranged from .78 to .52. Interpersonal relations was reported as low.

Author: Liang, C. T. H., et al.

Article: The Asian American Racism-Related Stress Inventory: Development, factor analysis, reliability, and validity.

Journal: *Journal of Counseling Psychology*, January 2004, *51*, 103–114.

Related Research: Terrell, F., & Terrell, S. (1981). An inventory to measure cultural mistrust among Blacks. *The Western Journal of Black Studies, 5*, 180–184.

10949

Test Name: CULTURAL NOVELTY SCALE

Purpose: To assess the difference between one's home culture and the culture of the location one has been assigned by an employer.

Number of Items: 8

Format: Scales range from 1 (*very similar*) to 5 (*very different*).

Reliability: Coefficient alpha was .76.

Validity: Correlations with other variables ranged from −.32 to .16.

Author: Shaffer, M. A., and Harrison, D. A.

Article: Forgotten partners of international assignments: Development and test of a model of spouse adjustment.

Journal: *Journal of Applied Psychology*, April 2001, *86*, 238–254.

10950

Test Name: CULTURAL VALUES CONFLICT SCALE

Purpose: To assess the degree to which South Asian women living in the United States experience cultural value conflicts.

Number of Items: 24

Format: Includes two subscales: Intimate Relations and Sex Role Expectations. All items are presented.

Reliability: Alpha coefficients ranged from .84 to .87 ($N = 319$).

Validity: Correlations with other variables ranged from −.35 to .52.

Author: Inman, A. G., et al.

Article: Development and preliminary validation of the Cultural Values Conflict Scale for South Asian women.

Journal: *Journal of Counseling Psychology*, January 2001, *48*, 17–27.

10951

Test Name: CULTURE SHOCK ADAPTATION INVENTORY

Purpose: To assess the degree to which culture shock symptoms are lacking for international students in the United States.

Number of Items: 37

Format: Includes four aspects of adaptation to another culture: emotional well-being, physical well-being, perceived control of the environment, and perceived compatibility with others. Responses are made on a 4-point scale ranging from 1 (*strongly agree*) to 4 (*strongly disagree*).

Reliability: Coefficient alpha was .80. Spearman–Brown reliability was .92.

Author: Swagler, M. A., and Ellis, M. V.

Article: Crossing the distance: Adjustment of Taiwanese graduate students in the United States.

Journal: *Journal of Counseling Psychology*, October 2003, *50*, 420–437.

Related Research: Juffer, K. A. (1983). *The initial development and validation of an instrument to assess the degree of culture shock adaptation.* Unpublished doctoral dissertation, University of Iowa.

10952

Test Name: DEPRESSIVE INTERPERSONAL RELATIONSHIPS INVENTORY

Purpose: To measure reassurance-seeking, general dependency, and doubt in the sincerity of others.

Number of Items: 16

Format: Seven-point scales are used. Sample items are presented.

Reliability: Alpha coefficients ranged from .74 to .89 across subscales.

Author: Joiner, T. E., Jr., et al.

Article: The relative specificity of excessive reassurance-seeking to depression symptoms and diagnosis among clinical samples of adults and youth.

Journal: *Journal of Psychopathology and Behavioral Assessment*, March 2001, *23*, 35–41

Related Research: Joiner, T. E., Jr., et al. (1992). When depression breeds contempt: Reassurance-seeking, self-esteem, and rejection of depressed college students by their roommates. *Journal of Abnormal Psychology, 101,* 165–173.

10953

Test Name: DEVIANT PEERS ASSOCIATION SCALE

Purpose: To measure associating with deviant peers.

Number of Items: 6

Format: Item response scales range from 1 (*none of my friends*) to 5 (*four or more of my friends*).

Reliability: Coefficient alpha was .95.

Author: Higgins, G. E., and Makin, D. A.

Article: Self-control, deviant peers, and software piracy.

Journal: *Psychological Reports*, December 2004, *95*, Part 1, 921–931.

Related Research: Krohn, M. D., et al. (1985). Social learning theory and adolescent cigarette smoking: A longitudinal study. *Social Problems, 32*, 455–473.

10954

Test Name: DUKE SOCIAL SUPPORT AND STRESS SCALE

Purpose: To measure family and nonfamily support and stress.

Number of Items: 22

Format: Scales range from 0 (*none*) to 3 (*a lot*).

Reliability: Alpha coefficients were .72 (support) and .58 (stress).

Validity: Correlations with other variables ranged from −.23 to .43.

Author: Katerndahl, D. A., et al.

Article: Psychometric assessment of measures of psychological symptoms, functional status, life events, and context for low income Hispanic patients in a primary care setting.

Journal: *Psychological Reports,* December 2002, *91*, Part 2, 1121–1128.

10955

Test Name: DYADIC TRUST SCALE

Purpose: To measure trust in a benevolent partner and trust in an honest partner.

Number of Items: 8

Reliability: Alpha coefficients exceeded .69.

Validity: Correlations with chance of marrying ranged from –.65 to –.01.

Author: Umaña-Taylor, A. J., and Fine, M.

Article: Predicting commitment to wed among Hispanic and Anglo partners.

Journal: *Journal of Marriage and Family,* February 2003, *65*, 117–139.

Related Research: Larzalere, R. E., & Huston, T. L. (1980). The Dyadic Trust Scale: Toward understanding interpersonal trust in close relationships. *Journal of Marriage and the Family, 42,* 595–604.

10956

Test Name: EMBARRASSABILITY SCALE

Purpose: To measure a person's propensity for embarrassment in various situations.

Number of Items: 26

Reliability: Coefficient alpha was .88.

Validity: Correlation with the Imaginary Audience Scale ranged from .53 to .65.

Author: Kelly, K. M., et al.

Article: Using the Imaginary Audience Scale as a measure of social anxiety in young adults.

Journal: *Educational and Psychological Measurement,* October 2002, *62*, 896–914.

Related Research: Modigliani, A. (1966). *Embarrassment and social influence.* Unpublished doctoral dissertation, University of Michigan, Ann Arbor.

10957

Test Name: EMOTIONAL EMPATHY SCALE

Purpose: To measure the extent to which individuals are reactive to the emotional experience of others.

Number of Items: 33

Format: Responses are made on an 8-point scale ranging from +4 (*very strongly agree*) to –4 (*very strongly disagree*). An example is presented.

Reliability: Coefficient alpha was .82.

Validity: Correlations with other variables ranged from –.34 to .48.

Author: Lopez, F. G.

Article: Adult attachment orientation, self–other boundary regulation, and splitting tendencies in a college sample.

Journal: *Journal of Counseling Psychology,* October 2001, *48*, 440–446.

Related Research: Mehrabian, A., & Epstein, N. (1972). A measure of emotional empathy. *Journal of Personality, 40,* 525–543.

10958

Test Name: EMOTIONAL SOCIAL SUPPORT SCALE

Purpose: To measure social support from coworkers.

Number of Items: 18

Format: Scales range from 1 (*never or rarely*) to 5 (*very often*). Sample items are presented.

Reliability: Alpha coefficients ranged from .78 to .93 across subscales.

Validity: Correlations with other variables ranged from –.29 to .30.

Author: Zellars, K. L., and Perrewé, P. L.

Article: Affective personality and the content of emotional social support: Coping in organizations.

Journal: *Journal of Applied Psychology,* June 2001, *86*, 459–467.

Related Research: Fenlason, K. J., & Beehr, T. A. (1994). Social support and occupational stress: Effects of talking to others. *Journal of Organizational Behavior, 15,* 157–175.

10959

Test Name: ETHNIC BELONGING SUBSCALE

Purpose: To assess cultural pride.

Number of Items: 4

Format: Responses are made on a 5-point scale ranging from 1 (*strongly disagree*) to 5 (*strongly agree*). Examples are presented.

Reliability: Coefficient alpha was .82.

Validity: Correlations with other variables ranged from –.42 to .26.

Author: Goodyear, R. K., et al.

Article: Pregnant Latina teenagers: Psychosocial and developmental determinants of how they select and perceive the men who father their children.

Journal: *Journal of Counseling Psychology,* April 2002, *49*, 187–201.

Related Research: Phinney, J. S. (1992). The Multigroup Ethnic Identity Measure: A new scale for use with diverse groups. *Journal of Adolescent Research, 7,* 156–176.

10960

Test Name: ETHNIC DISPARITY PERCEPTION INVENTORY

Purpose: To measure ethnic disparity as physical disparity, cultural disparity, linguistic disparity, ethnic involvement, and involvement in host culture.

Number of Items: 44

Format: Seven-point scales are anchored by 1 (*strongly disagree*) and 7 (*strongly agree*). Sample items are presented.

Reliability: Alpha coefficients ranged from .72 to .89 across subscales.

Validity: Correlations between subscales ranged from –.27 to .60.

Author: Bahk, C.-M., et al.

Article: Relations of perceived ethnic disparity to involvement in ethnic and host cultures.

Journal: *Psychological Reports,* August 2003, *93,* 251–262.

10961

Test Name: ETHNIC IDENTIFICATION SCALE

Purpose: To measure the strength of ethnic identification.

Number of Items: 10

Format: Scales range from 1 (*strongly disagree*) to 6 (*strongly agree*).

Reliability: Alpha coefficients exceeded .70.

Validity: Correlations with other variables ranged from –.67 to .76.

Author: Korf, L., and Malan, J.

Article: Threat to ethnic identity: The experience of White Afrikaans-speaking participants in postapartheid South Africa.

Journal: *The Journal of Social Psychology,* April 2002, *142,* 149–169.

Related Research: Brown, R. J., et al. (1986). Explaining intergroup differentiation in an industrial organization. *Journal of Occupational Psychology, 59,* 273–286.

10962

Test Name: ETHNIC IDENTITY ACHIEVEMENT SUBSCALE

Purpose: To measure ethnic identity.

Number of Items: 7

Format: Responses are made on a 6-point scale ranging from 1 (*strongly disagree*) to 6 (*strongly agree*). Examples are given.

Reliability: Coefficient alpha was .76.

Validity: Correlations with other variables ranged from –.17 to .18.

Author: Linnehan, F., et al.

Article: African-American students' early trust beliefs in work-based mentors.

Journal: *Journal of Vocational Behavior,* June 2005, *66,* 501–515.

Related Research: Phinney, J. S. (1992). The Multigroup Ethnic Identity Measure: A new scale for use with diverse groups. *Journal of Adolescent Research, 7,* 156–176.

10963

Test Name: ETHNIC IDENTITY SCALE

Purpose: To measure ethnic pride and belonging and ethnic differentiation.

Number of Items: 20

Format: Five-point scales range from 0 (*strongly disagree*) to 4 (*strongly agree*). All items are presented.

Reliability: Coefficient alpha was .85 for the total scale. Subscale alphas were .86 (pride) and .82 (differentiation).

Validity: Correlations with rational attitudes ranged from –.33 to .39.

Author: Valk, A., and Karu, K.

Article: Ethnic attitudes in relation to ethnic pride and ethnic differentiation.

Journal: *The Journal of Social Psychology,* October 2001, *141,* 583–601.

10964

Test Name: ETHNIC SOCIETY IMMERSION SCALE

Purpose: To measure participation in ethnic activities.

Number of Items: 17

Format: A true–false format is used.

Reliability: Alpha coefficients ranged from .67 to .83.

Author: Hall, G. C. N., et al.

Article: Ethnicity, culture, and sexual aggression: Risk and protective factors.

Journal: *Journal of Consulting and Clinical Psychology,* October 2005, *73,* 830–840.

Related Research: Stephenson, M. (2000). Development and validation of the Stephenson Multigroup Identification Scale (SMIS). *Psychological Assessment, 12,* 77–88.

10965

Test Name: EXCLUDED BY PEERS SUBSCALE—ADAPTED

Purpose: To measure exclusion by peers.

Number of Items: 4

Format: Responses are made on a 3-point scale ranging from 0 (*doesn't apply*) to 2 (*certainly applies*). All items are presented.

Reliability: Coefficient alpha was .94.

Validity: Correlations with other variables ranged from −.49 to .33.

Author: Buhs, E. S.

Article: Peer rejection, negative peer treatment, and school adjustment: Self-concept and classroom engagement as mediating processes.

Journal: *Journal of School Psychology*, November 2005, *43*, 407–424.

Related Research: Ladd, G. W., & Profilet, S. M. (1996). The Child Behavior Scale: A teacher-report measure of young children's aggressive, withdrawn, and prosocial behaviors. *Developmental Psychology, 32*, 1008–1024.

10966

Test Name: EXPATRIATE ADJUSTMENT SCALE

Purpose: To measure expatriate adjustment.

Number of Items: 14

Format: Scales range from 1 (*extremely unadjusted*) to 7 (*extremely adjusted*).

Reliability: Coefficient alpha was .88.

Validity: Correlations with other variables ranged from −.29 to .52.

Author: Shaffer, M. A., and Harrison, D. A.

Article: Forgotten partners of international assignments: Development and test of a model of spouse adjustment.

Journal: *Journal of Applied Psychology*, April 2001, *86*, 238–254.

Related Research: Black, J. S. (1988). Work role transitions: A study of expatriate managers in

Japan. *Journal of International Business Studies, 19*, 277–294.

10967

Test Name: EXPATRIATE CROSS-CULTURAL ADJUSTMENT SCALE

Purpose: To measure cross-cultural adjustment as general adjustment and work adjustment.

Number of Items: 7

Format: Scales range from 1 (*strongly disagree*) to 7 (*strongly agree*).

Reliability: Coefficient alpha was .81.

Validity: Correlations with other variables ranged from −.55 to .55.

Author: Takeuchi, R., et al.

Article: An examination of crossover and spillover effects on spousal and expatriate cross-cultural adjustment on expatriate outcomes.

Journal: *Journal of Applied Psychology*, August 2002, *87*, 655–666.

Related Research: Black, J. S., & Stephens, G. K. (1989). The influence of the spouse on American expatriate adjustment and intent to stay in Pacific Rim overseas assignments. *Journal of Management, 15*, 529–544.

10968

Test Name: EXPECTATIONS OF OTHERS SCALE

Purpose: To measure the perception of the participants that significant others in their lives felt they should engage in a program of leisure-time physical activity.

Number of Items: 10

Format: Responses are made on a 7-point scale ranging from −3 to +3. An example is given.

Reliability: Coefficient alpha was .79.

Validity: Correlations with other variables ranged from −.04 to .37.

Author: Kerner, M. S., and Kurrant, A. B.

Article: Psychosocial correlates to high school girls' leisure-time physical activity: A test of the theory of planned behavior.

Journal: *Perceptual and Motor Skills*, December 2003, *97*, Part 2, 1175–1183.

10969

Test Name: EXPERIENCE OF THREAT SCALE

Purpose: To measure threat perceived by Afrikaners in South Africa.

Number of Items: 15

Format: Scales range from 1 (*absence of threat*) to 6 (*highest possible threat*). All items are presented.

Reliability: Coefficient alpha was .77. Subscale alphas ranged from .74 to .82.

Validity: Correlations with other variables ranged from −.74 to .36.

Author: Korf, L., and Malan, J.

Article: Threat to ethnic identity: The experience of White Afrikaans-speaking participants in postapartheid South Africa.

Journal: *The Journal of Social Psychology*, April 2002, *142*, 149–169.

10970

Test Name: EXPERIENCE SUPPORT SCALE

Purpose: To measure emotional, instrumental, and tangible social support.

Number of Items: 21

Format: Scales range from 1 (*don't receive at all*) to 5 (*receive a great deal*). Sample items are presented.

Reliability: Alpha coefficients ranged from .83 to .87 across subscales.

Validity: Correlations with other variables ranged from –.17 to .04.

Author: MacGeorge, E. L., et al.

Article: Stress, social support, and health among college students after September 11, 2001.

Journal: *Journal of College Student Development*, November/December 2004, *45*, 655–670.

Related Research: Xu, Y., & Burleson, B. R. (2001). Effects of gender, culture, and support type on perceptions of spousal social support: An assessment of the "support gap" hypothesis in early marriage. *Human Communication Research*, *27*, 535–566.

10971

Test Name: EXPERIENCES IN CLOSE RELATIONSHIPS SCALE

Purpose: To measure adult attachment.

Number of Items: 36

Format: Includes two subscales: Anxiety and Avoidance. Responses are made on a 7-point Likert-type scale ranging from 1 (*disagree strongly*) to 7 (*agree strongly*).

Reliability: Alpha coefficients ranged from .91 to .94.

Validity: Correlations with other variables ranged from –.46 to .54 (*N* = 299).

Author: Wei, M., et al.

Article: Adult attachment, shame, depression, and loneliness: The mediation role of basic psychological needs satisfaction.

Journal: *Journal of Counseling Psychology*, October 2005, *52*, 591–601.

Related Research: Brennan, K. A., et al. (1998). Self-report measurement of adult attachment: An integrative overview. In J. A. Simpson & W. S. Rholes (Eds.), *Attachment theory and close relationships* (pp. 46–76). New York: Guilford Press.

10972

Test Name: FEAR OF INTIMACY SCALE

Purpose: To measure anxiety about close dating relationships.

Number of Items: 30

Format: Scales range from 1 (*not at all characteristic of me*) to 5 (*extremely characteristic of me*). Sample items are presented.

Reliability: Coefficient alpha was .89.

Validity: Correlations with other variables ranged from –.16 to .15.

Author: Rochlen, A. B., et al.

Article: The Online and Face-to-Face Counseling Attitudes Scales: A validation study.

Journal: *Measurement and Evaluation in Counseling and Development*, July 2004, *37*, 95–111.

Related Research: Descutner, C. J., & Thelen, M. H. (1991). Development and validation of a fear-of-intimacy scale. *Psychological Assessment*, *3*, 218–225.

10973

Test Name: FORGIVENESS LIKELIHOOD SCALE

Purpose: To assess participants' likelihood to forgive others across various situations.

Number of Items: 10

Format: Responses are made on a 5-point scale ranging from 1 (*not at all likely*) to 5 (*extremely likely*). An example is given.

Reliability: Test–retest reliability was .81. Coefficient alpha was .85.

Validity: Correlations with other variables ranged from –.02 to .56 (*n* = 147).

Author: Ross, S. R., et al.

Article: A personological examination of self- and other-forgiveness in the five factor model.

Journal: *Journal of Personality Assessment*, April 2004, *82*, 207–214.

Related Research: Rye, M. S., et al. (2001). Evaluation of the psychometric properties of two forgiveness scales. *Current Psychology*, *20*, 260–277.

10974

Test Name: FORGIVENESS SCALE

Purpose: To measure forgiveness.

Number of Items: 15

Format: Responses are made on a 5-point Likert-type scale ranging from 1 (*strongly disagree*) to 5 (*strongly agree*). A sample item is given.

Reliability: Test–retest reliability was .80. Coefficient alpha was .87 (*n* = 147).

Validity: Correlations with other variables ranged from .10 to .52 (*n* = 147).

Author: Ross, S. R., et al.

Article: A personological examination of self- and other-forgiveness in the five factor model.

Journal: *Journal of Personality Assessment*, April 2004, *82*, 207–214.

Related Research: Rye, M. S., et al. (2001). Evaluation of the psychometric properties of two forgiveness scales. *Current Psychology*, *20*, 260–277.

10975

Test Name: FRIENDSHIP CLOSENESS INVENTORY

Purpose: To measure the way people engage in friendships, the way people express friendship, and the way they interact with friends.

Number of Items: 49

Format: Item responses are made on 7-point scales anchored by 1 (*not at all*) and 7 (*very frequently*). All items are presented.

Reliability: Alpha was .91. Subscale alphas ranged from .87 to .93.

Author: Polimeni, A. M., et al.

Article: Friendship Closeness Inventory: Development and psychometric evaluation.

Journal: *Psychological Reports*, August 2002, *91*, 142–152.

Related Research: Berscheid, E., et al. (1989). The Relationship Closeness Inventory: Assessing the closeness of interpersonal relationships. *Journal of Personality and Social Psychology, 57*, 792–807.

10976

Test Name: FRIENDSHIP QUALITY QUESTIONNAIRE

Purpose: To measure friendship relationship quality.

Number of Items: 18

Format: Includes six subscales: Conflict Resolution, Companionship and Recreation, Conflict and Betrayal, Intimate Exchange, Help and Guidance, and Validation and Caring. Responses are made on a 5-point scale ranging from *not at all true* to *really true*.

Reliability: Alpha coefficients ranged from .73 to .90.

Author: Barton, B. K., and Cohen, R.

Article: Classroom gender composition and children's peer relations.

Journal: *Child Study Journal*, 2004, *34*, 29–45.

Related Research: Parker, J. G., & Asher, S. R. (1993). Friendship and friendship quality in middle childhood: Links with peer group acceptance and feelings of loneliness and social dissatisfaction. *Developmental Psychology, 29*, 611–621.

10977

Test Name: FRIENDSHIP QUALITY QUESTIONNAIRE

Purpose: To characterize a friendship or one's friend.

Number of Items: 40

Format: Responses are made on a 5-point scale ranging from 0 (*not at all true*) to 4 (*really true*). Responses are partitioned according to six subscales: Disclosure, Help, Conflict, Conflict Resolution, Companionship, and Validation.

Reliability: Alpha coefficients ranged from .85 to .90.

Author: Simpkins, S. D., & Parke, R. D.

Article: The relations between parental friendships and children's friendships: Self-report and observational analysis.

Journal: *Child Development*, March/April 2001, *72*, 569–582.

Related Research: Parker, J. G., & Asher, S. R. (1993). Friendship and friendship quality in middle childhood: Links with peer group acceptance and feelings of loneliness and social dissatisfaction. *Developmental Psychology, 29*, 611–621.

10978

Test Name: FRIENDSHIP QUALITY QUESTIONNAIRE— REVISED

Purpose: To assess friendship quality and closeness with a friend.

Number of Items: 19

Format: Includes two factors: friendship quality and closeness. Responses are made on a 5-point scale ranging from 0 (*not at all true*) to 4 (*really true*). An example is given.

Reliability: Coefficient alpha was .92.

Validity: Correlations with other variables ranged from .03 to .58.

Author: Rose, A. J.

Article: Co-rumination in the friendships of girls and boys.

Journal: *Child Development*, November/December 2002, *73*, 1830–1843.

Related Research: Parker, J. G., and Asher, S. R. (1993). Friendship and friendship quality in middle childhood: Links with peer group acceptance and feeling of loneliness and social dissatisfaction. *Developmental Psychology, 29*, 611–621.

10979

Test Name: GENERAL MATTERING SCALE

Purpose: To measure general mattering—the sense of belonging in relation to others.

Number of Items: 5

Format: Scales range from 1 (*not at all*) to 4 (*very much*).

Reliability: Alpha coefficients ranged from .73 to .86.

Author: Rayle, A. D., and Meyers, J. E.

Article: Counseling adolescents toward wellness: The roles of ethnic identity, acculturation and mattering.

Journal: *Professional School Counseling*, October 2004, *8*(1), 81–90.

Related Research: Marcus, F. M. (1991). *Mattering: Its measurement and theoretical significance*. Unpublished manuscript.

10980

Test Name: GROUP CONFLICT SCALE

Purpose: To assess a group member's perception of conflict with other group members.

Number of Items: 7

Reliability: Coefficient alpha was .79.

Validity: Correlations with other variables ranged from −.40 to .01.

Author: Colquitt, J. A.

Article: Does the justice of the one interact with the justice of the many: Reactions to procedural justice in teams.

Journal: *Journal of Applied Psychology*, August 2004, *89*, 633–646.

Related Research: Saavedra, R., et al. (1993). Complex interdependence in task-performing groups. *Journal of Applied Psychology, 78*, 61–72.

10981

Test Name: GROUPHATE SCALE

Purpose: To measure general feelings about working in groups.

Number of Items: 6

Format: Response scales are anchored by 1 (*strongly disagree*) and 5 (*strongly agree*).

Reliability: Coefficient alpha was .86.

Validity: Correlations with other variables ranged from −.58 to .03.

Author: Myers, S. A., and Goodboy, A. K.

Article: A study of grouphate in a course on small group communication.

Journal: *Psychological Reports*, October 2005, *97*, 381–386.

Related Research: Keyton, J. H., et al. (1996). *Grouphate: Implications for teaching group*

communication. Paper presented at the meeting of the National Communication Association, San Diego, CA.

10982

Test Name: HEARTLAND FORGIVENESS SCALE

Purpose: To measure forgiveness of self and others and situational forgiveness as separate constructs.

Number of Items: 18

Format: Includes three subscales: Self-Forgiveness, Other-Forgiveness, and Situational Forgiveness. Responses are true–false. Sample items are given.

Reliability: Alpha coefficients ranged from .76 to .87. Test–retest reliability was .82.

Validity: Correlations with other variables ranged from −.04 to .62 (*n* = 147).

Author: Ross, S. R., et al.

Article: A personological examination of self-and other-forgiveness in the five factor model.

Journal: *Journal of Personality Assessment*, April 2004, *82*, 207–214.

Related Research: Edwards, L. M., et al. (2002). A positive relationship between religious faith and forgiveness: Faith in the absence of data? *Pastoral Psychology, 50*, 147–152.

10983

Test Name: HOLYOAKE CODEPENDENCY INDEX

Purpose: To measure an individual's endorsement of codependent beliefs: self-sacrifice, external focus, and reactivity.

Number of Items: 13

Format: Five-point scales are anchored by *strongly agree* and *strongly disagree*.

Reliability: Internal consistency reliabilities ranged from .72 to .73. Test–retest correlations ranged from .76 to .88.

Author: Dear, G. E.

Article: Test–retest reliability of the Holyoake Codependency Index with Australian students.

Journal: *Psychological Reports*, April 2004, *94*, 482–484.

Related Research: Dear, G. E. (2002). The Holyoake Codependency Index: Further evidence of factorial validity. *Drug and Alcohol Review, 21*, 59–64.

10984

Test Name: HUMAN–ANIMAL RELATIONSHIP QUESTIONNAIRE

Purpose: To measure human–animal relationships as friendship and power.

Number of Items: 21

Format: Item anchors range from 1 (*disagree quite a lot*) and 5 (*agree*). All items are presented.

Reliability: Coefficient alpha was .73.

Validity: Various criterion validity tests are presented.

Author: Porcher, J., and Cousson-Gélie, F.

Article: Affective components of the human–animal relationship in animal husbandry: Development and validation of a questionnaire.

Journal: *Psychological Reports*, August 2004, *95*, 275–290.

10985

Test Name: HUMANISTIC TREATMENT SCALE

Purpose: To assess the treatment of a specified target immigrant from a specified background.

Number of Items: 7

Format: Scales range from 1 (*strongly disagree*) to 7 (*strongly agree*). The scale follows a descriptive vignette describing the target. All items are presented.

Reliability: Alpha coefficients were .87 (U.S. sample) and .64 (Mexican sample).

Validity: Multiple correlation coefficients ranged from .07 to .45.

Author: Lee, Y.-T., and Ottati, V.

Article: Attitudes toward U.S. immigration policy: The roles of in-group–out-group bias, economic concern, and obedience to the law.

Journal: *The Journal of Social Psychology*, October 2002, *142*, 617–634.

10986

Test Name: IMMATURE LOVE SCALE

Purpose: To measure immature love.

Number of Items: 4

Format: A true–false format is used. All items are presented.

Reliability: Coefficient alpha was .55.

Validity: Correlations with other variables ranged from –.46 to .21.

Author: Le, T. N., and Levenson, M. R.

Article: Wisdom as self-transcendence: What's love (& individualism) got to do with it?

Journal: *Journal of Research in Personality*, August 2005, *39*, 443–457.

10987

Test Name: IN-GROUP IDENTIFICATION SCALE

Purpose: To measure in-group identification.

Number of Items: 3

Format: Three-point scales are used. All items and scales are presented.

Reliability: Coefficient alpha was .81.

Validity: Correlations with other variables ranged from –.28 to .37.

Author: Florack, A., et al.

Article: Perceived intergroup threat and attitudes of host community members toward immigrant acculturation.

Journal: *The Journal of Social Psychology*, October 2003, *143*, 633–648.

10988

Test Name: INTERACTION ANXIOUSNESS SCALE

Purpose: To measure the tendency to experience subjective social anxiety.

Number of Items: 15

Format: Scales range from 1 (*The statement is not at all characteristic of me*) to 5 (*The statement is extremely characteristic of me*). Sample items are presented.

Reliability: Coefficient alpha was .87.

Validity: Correlations with stigmatization ranged from .20 to .58.

Author: Harvey, R. D.

Article: Individual differences in the phenomenological impact of social stigma.

Journal: *The Journal of Social Psychology*, April 2001, *141*, 174–189.

Related Research: Leary, M. R. (1983). Social anxiousness: The construct and its measurement. *Journal of Personality Assessment*, *44*, 66–75.

10989

Test Name: INTERNALIZED HOMOPHOBIA SCALE

Purpose: To measure the degree to which gay men are uneasy about their homosexuality and seek to hide homosexual feelings.

Number of Items: 9

Format: Scales range from 1 (*never*) to 4 (*often*). A sample item is presented.

Reliability: Coefficient alpha was .86.

Validity: Correlations with other variables ranged from –.30 to .09.

Author: Kimmel, S. B., and Mahalik, J. R.

Article: Body image concerns of gay men: The roles of minority stress and conformity to masculine norms.

Journal: *Journal of Consulting and Clinical Psychology*, December 2005, *73*, 1185–1190.

Related Research: Martin, J., & Dean, L. (1987). *Summary of measures: Mental health effects of AIDS on at-risk homosexual men.* Unpublished manuscript, Division of Sociomedical Science, Columbia University at New York, School of Public Health, NY.

10990

Test Name: INTERPERSONAL COGNITIVE DISTORTIONS SCALE

Purpose: To assess cognitive distortions in interpersonal relationships.

Number of Items: 19

Format: Item anchors range from 1 (*not appropriate*) to 3 (*appropriate*). All items are presented.

Reliability: Alpha coefficients ranged from .63 to .72 for the total scale. Subscale alphas ranged from .39 to .73.

Validity: Correlations with other variables ranged from .17 to .94.

Author: Hamamce, Z., and Büyüköztürk, S.

Article: The Interpersonal and Cognitive Distortions Scale: Development and psychometric characteristics.

Journal: *Psychological Reports,* August 2004, *95,* 291–303.

10991

Test Name: INTERPERSONAL COMPETENCE SCALE

Purpose: To assess adolescent interpersonal competence.

Number of Items: 18

Format: Responses are made on a 7-point scale.

Reliability: Alpha coefficients were .80 and .84.

Validity: Correlations with other variables ranged from .17 to .44.

Author: Mahoney, J. L., et al.

Article: Promoting interpersonal competence and educational success through extracurricular activity participation.

Journal: *Journal of Educational Psychology,* June 2003, *95,* 409–418.

Related Research: Cairns, R. B., et al. (1995). A brief method for assessing social development: Structure, reliability, stability, and developmental validity of the Interpersonal Competence Scale. *Behavior Research and Therapy, 33,* 725–736.

10992

Test Name: INTERPERSONAL COMPETENCE SCALE

Purpose: To measure social skills: conflict management, comfort with disclosure, and emotional supportiveness.

Number of Items: 24

Format: Five-point response scales are used.

Reliability: Alpha coefficients ranged from .81 to .90.

Author: Scott, K. L., and Wolfe, D. A.

Article: Readiness to change as a predictor of outcome in batterer treatment.

Journal: *Journal of Consulting and Clinical Psychology,* October 2003, *71,* 879–889.

Related Research: Buhrmeister, D., et al. (1988). Five domains of interpersonal competence in peer relationships. *Journal of Personality and Social Psychology, 55,* 991–1008.

10993

Test Name: INTERPERSONAL DEPENDENCY INVENTORY

Purpose: To measure emotional reliance on others, lack of social self-confidence, and assertion of autonomy.

Number of Items: 48

Format: Scales range from 1 (*not at all like me*) to 4 (*very much like me*).

Reliability: Alpha coefficients ranged from .72 to .83 across subscales.

Validity: Correlations with other variables ranged from –.18 to .52.

Author: Beck, J. G., and Davila, J.

Article: Development of an interview for anxiety-relevant interpersonal styles: Preliminary support for convergent and discriminant validity.

Journal: *Journal of Psychopathology and Behavioral Assessment,* March 2003, *25,* 1–9.

Related Research: Hirschfield, R. M. A., et al. (1977). A measure of interpersonal dependency. *Journal of Personality Assessment, 41,* 610–618.

10994

Test Name: INTERPERSONAL EVALUATION INDEX

Purpose: To measure liking and willingness to interact with a target person.

Number of Items: 10

Format: Rating scales range from 0 (*not very much*) to 2 (*very much*). Sample items are presented.

Reliability: Coefficient alpha was .83. The intraclass agreement coefficient was .72.

Validity: Correlations with other variables ranged from .06 to .24.

Author: Perez, M., et al.

Article: The interpersonal consequences of inflated self-esteem in an inpatient psychiatric youth sample.

Journal: *Journal of Consulting and Clinical Psychology,* August 2001, *69,* 712–716.

Related Research: Joiner, T. E., Jr., et al. (1992). When depression breeds contempt: Reassurance-seeking, self-esteem, and rejection of depressed college students by their roommates. *Journal of Abnormal Psychology, 101,* 165–173.

10995

Test Name: INTERPERSONAL INTERACTION SCALES

Purpose: To measure frequency, duration, and routines of interactions.

Number of Items: 7

Format: Includes three scales: Frequency, Duration, and Routines of Interactions. Responses are made on a 5-point Likert scale ranging from 1 (*strongly disagree*) to 5 (*strongly agree*). All items are presented.

Reliability: Alpha coefficients ranged from .72 to .82.

Validity: Correlations with other variables ranged from −.14 to .28.

Author: Diefendorff, J. M., et al.

Article: The dimensionality and antecedents of emotional labor strategies.

Journal: *Journal of Vocational Behavior*, April 2005, *66*, 339–357.

Related Research: Withey, M., et al. (1983). Measures of Perrow's work unit technology: An empirical assessment and a new scale. *Academy of Management Journal, 26*, 45–63.

10996

Test Name: INTERPERSONAL JUDGMENT SCALE

Purpose: To measure discrimination.

Number of Items: 4

Format: Seven-point rating scales are used. All items are described.

Reliability: Alpha coefficients ranged from .77 to .78.

Author: Singh, R., et al.

Article: Intergroup perception as a compromise between in-group bias and fair-mindedness.

Journal: *The Journal of Social Psychology*, August 2004, *144*, 373–387.

Related Research: Singh, R., et al. (1998). In-group bias and fair-mindedness as strategies of self-presentation in intergroup perceptions. *Personality and Social Psychology Bulletin, 24*, 147–162.

10997

Test Name: INTERPERSONAL MISTRUST–TRUST MEASURE

Purpose: To measure trusting stance one takes with others.

Number of Items: 18

Format: Scales range from 1 (*strongly disagree*) to 7 (*strongly agree*).

Reliability: Coefficient alpha was .76.

Author: Spector, M. D., and Jones, G. E.

Article: Trust in the workplace: Factors affecting trust formation between team members.

Journal: *The Journal of Social Psychology*, June 2004, *144*, 311–321.

Related Research: McLennan, J., & Omodei, M. M. (2000). Conceptualizing and measuring global personal mistrust–trust. *The Journal of Social Psychology, 140*, 279–294.

10998

Test Name: INTERPERSONAL POWER INVENTORY

Purpose: To assess 11 individual power bases.

Number of Items: 44

Format: Responses are made on a 7-point scale ranging from 1 (*much more likely to comply*) to 7 (*much less likely to comply*).

Reliability: Alpha coefficients ranged from .63 to .90.

Author: Erchul, W. P., et al.

Article: School psychologist and teacher perceptions of social power in consultation.

Journal: *Journal of School Psychology*, November/December 2001, *39*, 483–497.

Related Research: Raven, B. H., et al. (1998). Conceptualizing and measuring a power/interaction model of interpersonal influence. *Journal of Applied Social Psychology, 28*, 307–332.

10999

Test Name: INTERPERSONAL REACTIVITY INDEX

Purpose: To measure interpersonal reactivity.

Number of Items: 28

Format: Includes four subscales: Fantasy, Empathic Concern, Perspective Taking, and Personal Distress. Responses are made on a 5-point scale ranging from 0 (*does not describe me well*) to 4 (*describes me very well*). A few examples are given.

Reliability: Alpha coefficients ranged from .71 to .77.

Author: Burkard, A. W., and Knox, S.

Article: Effect of therapist color-blindness on empathy and attributions in cross-cultural counseling.

Journal: *Journal of Counseling Psychology*, October 2004, *51*, 387–397.

Related Research: Davis, M. H. (1983). Measuring individual differences in empathy: Evidence for a multidimensional approach. *Journal of Personality and Social Psychology, 44*, 113–126.

11000

Test Name: INTERPERSONAL REACTIVITY INDEX— PERSPECTIVE-TAKING SCALE

Purpose: To identify those more likely to help others.

Number of Items: 7

Format: Responses are made on a 5-point Likert-type scale. An example is given.

Reliability: Coefficient alpha was .72.

Validity: Correlation with empathy was .14 and with helping the correlation was .28.

Author: Oswald, P. A.

Article: Does the Interpersonal Reactivity Index Perspective-Taking Scale predict who will volunteer time to counsel adults entering college?

Journal: *Perceptual and Motor Skills*, December 2003, *97*, Part 2, 1184–1186.

Related Research: Davis, M.
(1980). A multidisciplinary
approach to individual differences
in empathy. *JSAS: Catalog of
Selected Documents in Psychology,
10*, 85.

11001

Test Name: INTERPERSONAL
REACTIVITY SCALE

Purpose: To measure empathic
perspective taking, empathic
fantasy, empathic concern, and
personal distress.

Number of Items: 28

Format: Scales range from 1 (*doesn't
describe me well*) to 5 (*describes me
very well*). Sample items are
presented.

Reliability: Alpha coefficients
ranged from .68 to .79 across
subscales.

Author: Schutte, N. S., et al.

Article: Emotional intelligence and
interpersonal relations.

Journal: *The Journal of Social
Psychology*, August 2001, *141*,
523–536.

Related Research: Davis, M. H.
(1980). A multidimensional
approach to individual differences
in empathy. *JSAS Catalog of
Selected Documents in Psychology,
10*, 85.

11002

Test Name: INTERPERSONAL
RELATIONSHIP INVENTORY—
JAPANESE VERSION

Purpose: To measure interpersonal
relationships.

Number of Items: 39

Format: Includes three subscales:
Social Support, Reciprocity, and
Conflict. Responses are made on
a 5-point scale ranging from
1 (*strongly disagree*) to 5 (*strongly
agree*).

Reliability: Alpha coefficients
ranged from .93 to .96. Test–retest
(3 weeks) reliability ranged from .69
to .74.

Validity: Correlations with other
variables ranged from –.37 to .42.

Author: Sumi, K.

Article: Reliability and construct
validity of the Japanese version of
the Interpersonal Relationship
Inventory.

Journal: *Perceptual and Motor
Skills*, August 2003, *97*, 135–140.

Related Research: Tilden, V. P.,
et al. (1990). The IPR Inventory:
Development and psychometric
characteristics. *Nursing Research,
39*, 337–343. Makabe, R. (1998).
[The Interpersonal Relationship
Inventory: Translation process
from English into Japanese].
[*Japanese Journal of Nursing
Research*], *31*, 423–432. [in
Japanese]

11003

Test Name: INTERPERSONAL
SOLIDARITY SCALE

Purpose: To measure personal
closeness.

Number of Items: 20

Format: Seven-point scales are
anchored by 1 (*strongly disagree*)
and 7 (*strongly agree*).

Reliability: Coefficient alpha was .95.

Author: Myers, S. A., and Johnson,
A. D.

Article: Scores on liking and
solidarity in interpersonal
relationships.

Journal: *Psychological Reports*,
December 2002, *91*, Part 1,
855–856.

Related Research: Wheeless, L. R.
(1978). A follow-up study of the
relationships among trust,
disclosure, and interpersonal
solidarity. *Human Communication
Research, 4*, 143–157.

11004

Test Name: INTERPERSONAL
SUPPORT EVALUATION LIST

Purpose: To assess four social
support areas.

Number of Items: 40

Format: Includes four areas:
tangible assistance, appraisal,
self-esteem, and belonging.
Responses are made on a 4-point
scale ranging from 0 (*definitely
false*) to 3 (*definitely true*).

Reliability: Alpha coefficients
ranged from .84 to .93. Test–retest
reliability coefficients were .83
(4 months) and .74 (6 months).

Validity: Correlations with other
variables ranged from –.48 to .28.

Author: Liao, H.-Y., et al.

Article: A test of Cramer's (1999)
help-seeking model and
acculturation effects with Asian and
Asian American college students.

Journal: *Journal of Counseling
Psychology*, July 2005, *52*, 400–411.

Related Research: Cohen, S., et al.
(1985). Measuring the functional
components of social support. In
I. G. Sarason & B. R. Sarason
(Eds.), *Social support: Theory,
research, and applications*
(pp. 73–94). The Hague, the
Netherlands: Martinus Nijhoff.

11005

Test Name: INTERPERSONAL
SUPPORT EVALUATION LIST—
SHORT FORM

Purpose: To measure social
support.

Number of Items: 15

Format: Response categories range
from 1 (*completely false*) to
4 (*completely true*).

Reliability: Coefficient alpha was .81.

Author: Jacobsen, P. B., et al.

Article: Predictors of posttraumatic
stress disorder symptomatology

following bone marrow transplantation for cancer.

Journal: *Journal of Consulting and Clinical Psychology*, February 2002, *70*, 235–240.

Related Research: Pierce, R. S., et al. (1996). Financial stress, social support, and alcohol involvement: A longitudinal test of the buffering hypothesis in a general population survey. *Health Psychology, 15*, 38–47.

11006

Test Name: INTERPERSONAL TRUST SCALE

Purpose: To measure interpersonal trust in various situations.

Number of Items: 25

Format: Responses are made on a 5-point Likert-type scale ranging from 1 (*strongly agree*) to 5 (*strongly disagree*).

Validity: Correlations with other variables ranged from –.07 to –.26.

Author: DiTommaso, E., et al.

Article: Measurement and validity characteristics of the Short Version of the Social and Emotional Loneliness Scale for Adults.

Journal: *Educational and Psychological Measurement*, February 2004, *64*, 99–119.

Related Research: Rotter, J. (1967). A new scale for the measurement of interpersonal trust. *Journal of Personality, 35*, 651–665.

11007

Test Name: INVENTORY OF INTERPERSONAL PROBLEMS

Purpose: To assess distress arising from interpersonal sources.

Number of Items: 127

Format: Scales range from 0 (*not at all*) to 4 (*extremely*).

Reliability: Alpha coefficients ranged from .82 to .94. Test–retest reliabilities ranged from .80 to .90.

Author: Missirlian, T. M., et al.

Article: Emotional arousal, client perceptual processing, and the working alliance in experimental psychotherapy for depression.

Journal: *Journal of Consulting and Clinical Psychology*, October 2005, *73*, 861–871.

Related Research: Horowitz, L. M., et al. (1988). Inventory of Interpersonal Problems: Psychosomatic properties and clinical applications. *Journal of Consulting and Clinical Psychology, 56*, 885–892.

11008

Test Name: INVENTORY OF INTERPERSONAL PROBLEMS

Purpose: To assess interpersonal functioning such as vindictiveness, avoidant and intrusive behavior.

Number of Items: 64

Format: Subjects rate the degree to which a problem applies to themselves on 5-point scales.

Reliability: Alpha coefficients ranged from .72 to .85.

Author: Taft, C. T., et al.

Article: Personality, interpersonal, and motivational predictors of the working alliance in group–cognitive behavioral therapy for partner violent men.

Journal: *Journal of Consulting and Clinical Psychology*, April 2004, *72*, 349–354.

Related Research: Alden, L. E., et al. (1990). Construction of circumplex scales for the inventory of personal problems. *Journal of Personality Assessment, 55*, 521–536.

11009

Test Name: INVENTORY OF INTERPERSONAL PROBLEMS— SHORT VERSION

Purpose: To rate the severity of interpersonal difficulties.

Number of Items: 32

Format: Item responses range from 0 (*not at all*) to 4 (*extremely*).

Validity: Correlations between the mean item score and a longer version ranged from .94 to .96.

Author: Stiles, W. B., et al.

Article: Early sudden gains in psychotherapy under routine clinic conditions: Practice-based evidence.

Journal: *Journal of Consulting and Clinical Psychology*, February 2003, *71*, 14–21.

Related Research: Barkham, M., et al. (1996). The development of the IIP-32: A short version of the Inventory of Interpersonal Problems. *British Journal of Clinical Psychology, 35*, 21–35.

11010

Test Name: IOWA–NETHERLANDS COMPARISON ORIENTATION MEASURE

Purpose: To measure social comparison orientation.

Number of Items: 9

Format: Responses are made on a 5-point scale ranging from 1 (*strongly disagree*) to 5 (*strongly agree*). Sample items are presented.

Reliability: Coefficient alpha was .80.

Validity: Correlations with other variables ranged from –.09 to .43.

Author: Buunk, B. P., et al.

Article: Engaging in upward and downward comparisons as a determinant of relative deprivation at work: A longitudinal study.

Journal: *Journal of Vocational Behavior*, April 2003, *62*, 370–388.

Related Research: Gibbons, F. X., & Buunk, B. P. (1999). Individual differences in social comparison: Development and validation of a measure of social comparison orientation. *Journal of Personality and Social Psychology, 76*, 129–142.

11011

Test Name: ISRAELI IDENTITY SCALE

Purpose: To assess the degree to which Israeli's perceive themselves as belonging to a religious, secular, or a combination of these sectors of Israeli society.

Number of Items: 5

Format: Scales range from 1 (*definitely disagree*) to 7 (*definitely agree*). All items are presented.

Reliability: Alpha coefficients exceeded .83.

Validity: Correlations with other variables ranged from –.58 to .38.

Author: Bizman, A., and Yinon, Y.

Article: Intergroup conflict management strategies as related to perceptions of dual identity and separate groups.

Journal: *The Journal of Social Psychology*, April 2004, *144*, 115–126.

11012

Test Name: JOB-SEEKING SOCIAL SUPPORT SCALE

Purpose: To measure job-seeking social support.

Number of Items: 5

Format: Five-point scales range from 1 (*not at all*) to 5 (*a very great deal*).

Reliability: Coefficient alpha was .92.

Validity: Correlations with other variables ranged from –.02 to .29.

Author: Adams, G., and Rau, B.

Article: Job-seeking among retirees seeking bridge employment.

Journal: *Personnel Psychology*, Autumn 2004, *57*, 719–744.

Related Research: Vinokur, A., & Caplan, R. D. (1987). Attitudes and social support: Determinants of job-seeking behavior and well-being among the unemployed. *Journal of Applied Social Psychology, 17*, 1007–1024.

11013

Test Name: JOB SOCIALIZATION OUTCOMES SCALE

Purpose: To measure job socialization.

Number of Items: 34

Format: Sample items are presented.

Reliability: Alpha coefficients ranged from .84 to .93.

Validity: Correlations with other variables ranged from –.40 to .44.

Author: Wesson, M. J., and Gogus, C. I.

Article: Shaking hands with a computer: An examination of two methods of organizational newcomer orientation.

Journal: *Journal of Applied Psychology*, September 2005, *90*, 1018–1026.

11014

Test Name: KAPLAN SOCIAL SUPPORT SCALE

Purpose: To measure general social support.

Number of Items: 9

Format: Responses are made on a 5-point scale. An example is given.

Reliability: Alpha coefficients were .86 ($N = 205$) and .88 ($N = 207$). Test–retest (6 months) reliabilities were .62 and .71. Other internal consistencies ranged from .81 to .83.

Validity: Correlations with other variables ranged from –.38 to .44.

Author: Morris, J. E., and Long, B. C.

Article: Female clerical workers' occupational stress: The role of person and social resources, negative affectivity, and stress appraisals.

Journal: *Journal of Counseling Psychology*, October 2002, *49*, 395–410.

Related Research: Turner, J. R., et al. (1983). Social support: Conceptualization, measurement, and implications for mental health. *Research in Community and Mental Health, 3*, 67–111.

11015

Test Name: KOREAN SELF-IDENTITY ACCULTURATION SCALE

Purpose: To measure acculturation in a Korean immigrant population.

Number of Items: 18

Format: Multiple 5-point scales are used. All are described.

Reliability: Alpha coefficients ranged from .51 to .85 across subscales.

Author: Oh, Y., et al.

Article: Acculturation, stress, and depressive symptoms among Korean immigrants in the United States.

Journal: *The Journal of Social Psychology*, August 2002, *142*, 511–526.

Related Research: Suinn, R., et al. (1987). The Suinn-Lew Asian Self-identity Acculturation Scales: An initial report. *Educational and Psychological Measurement, 47*, 401–407.

11016

Test Name: LANGUAGE, IDENTITY, AND BEHAVIOR ACCULTURATION SCALE

Purpose: To measure global level of acculturation to both American and Russian cultures.

Number of Items: 51

Format: Includes three dimensions: Language, Identity, and Behavior. Responses are made on a 4-point scale ranging from *not at all* to *very well, like a native.* Examples are given.

Reliability: Alpha coefficients ranged from .88 to .95.

Author: Jeltova, I., et al.

Article: Risky sexual behaviors in immigrant adolescent girls from the former Soviet Union: Role of natal and host culture.

Journal: *Journal of School Psychology,* January/February 2005, *43,* 3–22.

Related Research: Birman, D., & Trickett, E. J. (2001). Cultural transitions in first-generation immigrants. *Journal of Cross-Cultural Psychology, 32,* 456–477.

11017

Test Name: LANGUAGE IDENTITY AND BEHAVIORAL ACCULTURATION INDEX

Purpose: To assess acculturation of adolescents and their mothers.

Number of Items: 50

Format: A Likert format is used. Sample items are presented.

Reliability: Alpha coefficients ranged from .72 to .94 across subscales.

Author: Jones, C. J., and Trickett, E. J.

Article: Immigrant adolescents behaving as culture brokers: A

study of families from the Former Soviet Union.

Journal: *The Journal of Social Psychology,* August 2005, *145,* 405–427.

Related Research: Birman, D., & Trickett, E. J. (2001). The process of acculturation in first generation immigrants: A study of Soviet Jewish refugee adolescents and parents. *Journal of Cross-Cultural Psychology, 32,* 456–477.

11018

Test Name: LIKING FOR PEOPLE SCALE

Purpose: To measure interpersonal orientation and liking for people.

Number of Items: 15

Format: Responses are made on a 5-point Likert-type scale ranging from 1 (*strongly disagree*) to 5 (*strongly agree*).

Validity: Correlations with other variables ranged from −.21 to −.34.

Author: DiTommaso, E., et al.

Article: Measurement and validity characteristics of the short version of the Social and Emotional Loneliness Scale for Adults.

Journal: *Educational and Psychological Measurement,* February 2004, *64,* 99–119.

Related Research: Filsinger, E. E. (1981). A measure of interpersonal orientation: The Liking People Scale. *Journal of Personality Assessment, 45,* 295–300.

11019

Test Name: LIKING SCALE

Purpose: To measure general feelings of liking.

Number of Items: 13

Format: Seven-point rating scales ranged from 1 (*strongly disagree*) to 7 (*strongly agree*).

Reliability: Coefficient alpha was .92.

Validity: Correlation with a solidarity measure was .73.

Author: Myers, S. A., and Johnson, A. D.

Article: Scores on liking and solidarity in interpersonal relationships.

Journal: *Psychological Reports,* December 2002, *91,* Part 1, 855–856.

Related Research: Rubin, Z. (1970). Measurement of romantic love. *Journal of Personality and Social Psychology, 16,* 265–273.

11020

Test Name: LIST OF SOCIAL SITUATION PROBLEMS— SPANISH VERSION

Purpose: To identify social situations that children and adolescents find difficult.

Number of Items: 60

Format: A yes–no format is used. All items are presented in English.

Reliability: Internal reliability coefficients ranged from .58 to .86 across subscales.

Validity: Correlations with other variables ranged from .00 to .60.

Author: Inglés, C. J., et al.

Article: The List of Social Situation Problems: Reliability and validity in an adolescent Spanish-speaking sample.

Journal: *Journal of Psychopathology and Behavioral Assessment,* March 2003, *25,* 65–74.

Related Research: Spence, S. H. (1980). *Social skill training with children and adolescents: A counselor's manual.* Windsor, England: NFER-NELSON.

11021

Test Name: LONELINESS AND SOCIAL SATISFACTION QUESTIONNAIRE—REVISED

Purpose: To measure loneliness.

Number of Items: 4

Format: Responses are made on a 5-point scale. An example is given.

Reliability: Coefficient alpha was .84.

Validity: Correlations with other variables ranged from −.55 to .28.

Author: Ladd, G. W., and Troop-Gordon, W.

Article: The role of chronic peer difficulties in the development of children's psychological adjustment problems.

Journal: *Child Development*, September/October 2003, *74*, 1344–1367.

Related Research: Cassidy, J., & Asher, S. R. (1992). Loneliness and peer relations in young children. *Child Development, 63*, 350–365.

11022

Test Name: LONELINESS QUESTIONNAIRE

Purpose: To assess loneliness.

Number of Items: 24

Format: Responses are made on a 5-point scale ranging from *always true* to *not true at all*. A sample item is presented.

Reliability: Coefficient alpha was .90.

Validity: Correlations with other variables ranged from −.68 to .40.

Author: Browning, C., et al.

Article: Peer social competence and the stability of victimization.

Journal: *Child Study Journal*, 2003, *33*, 73–90.

Related Research: Asher, S. R., et al. (1984). Loneliness in childhood. *Child Development, 55,* 1456–1464.

11023

Test Name: LOVING AND LIKING SCALES

Purpose: To measure emotional involvement and dependence of a spouse and respect and admiration for a spouse.

Number of Items: 26

Format: Eight-point scales are used. Sample items are presented.

Reliability: Alpha coefficients ranged from .77 to .87.

Author: Tallman, I., and Hsiao, Y.-L.

Article: Resources, cooperation, and problem solving in early marriage.

Journal: *Social Psychology Quarterly*, June 2004, 67, 172–188.

Related Research: Rubin, Z., (1973). *Liking and loving: An invitation to social psychology.* New York: Holt.

11024

Test Name: MALE PARTNERS' HARM RISK SCALE

Purpose: To assess women's perception of their partner's risk of personal harm.

Number of Items: 4

Format: Responses are made on a 5-point scale ranging from 1 (*strongly disagree*) to 5 (*strongly agree*). A sample item is presented.

Reliability: Coefficient alpha was .71.

Validity: Correlation with other variables ranged from −.32 to .23.

Author: Goodyear, R. K., et al.

Article: Pregnant Latina teenagers: Psychosocial and developmental determinants of how they select and perceive the men who father their children.

Journal: *Journal of Counseling Psychology*, April 2002, *49*, 187–201.

11025

Test Name: MALE PARTNERS' NEGATIVE RELATIONSHIP WITH WOMEN SCALE

Purpose: To assess male partners' negative relationships with women.

Number of Items: 13

Format: Includes two scales: Young Woman's Perception of Her Partner's Willingness to Engage in Coercive Sexual Activity and Changes in Batterers' Behaviors. Sample items are presented.

Reliability: Alpha coefficients were .64 and .94.

Author: Goodyear, R. K., et al.

Article: Pregnant Latina teenagers: Psychosocial and developmental determinants of how they select and perceive the men who father their children.

Journal: *Journal of Counseling Psychology*, April 2002, *49*, 187–201.

Related Research: Kirby, D. (1984). *Sexuality education: A handbook for evaluating programs.* Santa Cruz, CA: Network. Tolman, R. M. (1999). The validation of the Psychological Maltreatment of Women Inventory. *Violence and Victims, 14*, 25–37.

11026

Test Name: MANAGING AFFECT AND DIFFERENCES SCALE

Purpose: To rate conflict management tactics with one's romantic partner.

Number of Items: 109

Format: Includes nine subscales: Love and Affection, Emotional Expressivity, Validation, Focusing, Communication Over Time, Editing, Feedback, Stop Actions, and Leveling.

Reliability: Alpha coefficients ranged from .68 to .85.

Author: Creasey, G., & Hesson-McInnis, M.

Article: Affective responses, cognitive appraisals, and conflict tactics in late adolescent romantic relationships: Association with attachment orientations.

Journal: *Journal of Counseling Psychology*, January 2001, *48*, 85–96.

Related Research: Arellano, C. & Markman, H. (1995). The Managing Affect and Differences Scale (MADS): A self-report measure assessing conflict management in couples. *Journal of Family Psychology*, *9*, 319–334.

11027

Test Name: MANIA SCALE

Purpose: To assess dependent and possessive love.

Number of Items: 7

Format: Response scales range from 1 (*strongly disagree*) to 5 (*strongly agree*). All items are presented.

Reliability: Coefficient alpha was .73.

Validity: Correlations with other variables ranged from –.57 to .16.

Author: Loving, T. J., et al.

Article: Stress hormone changes and marital conflict: Spouses' relative power makes a difference.

Journal: *Journal of Marriage and Family*, August 2004, *66*, 595–612.

Related Research: Hendrick, S. S., et al. (1988). Romantic relationships: Love, satisfaction, and staying

together. *Journal of Personality and Social Psychology*, *54*, 980–988.

11028

Test Name: MARLOWE–CROWNE SOCIAL DESIRABILITY SCALE

Purpose: To assess one's need to gain social approval.

Number of Items: 33

Format: A true–false format is used

Reliability: Internal consistency was .88. Test–retest (1 month) reliability was .89.

Validity: Correlations with other variables ranged from –.04 to –.18 (*n* = 368).

Author: Hill, R. W., et al.

Article: A new measure of perfectionism: The Perfectionism Inventory.

Journal: *Journal of Personality Assessment*, February 2004, *82*, 80–91.

Related Research: Crowne, D., & Marlowe, D. (1960). A new scale of social desirability independent of psychopathology. *Journal of Consulting Psychology*, *24*, 349–354.

11029

Test Name: MARLOWE–CROWNE SOCIAL DESIRABILITY SCALE—20

Purpose: To assess socially desirable responding.

Number of Items: 20

Format: A yes–no format is used.

Validity: Correlations with other variables ranged from .02 to .12.

Author: Jackson, B., et al.

Article: Motivations to eat: Scale development and validation.

Journal: *Journal of Research in Personality*, August 2003, *37*, 297–318.

Related Research: Strahan, R., & Gerbasi, K. C. (1972). Short, homogeneous versions of the Marlowe–Crowne Social Desirability Scale. *Journal of Clinical Psychology*, *28*, 191–193.

11030

Test Name: MARLOWE–CROWN SOCIAL DESIRABILITY SCALE— SHORT FORM

Purpose: To assess social desirability response bias.

Number of Items: 13

Format: A true–false format is used.

Reliability: Coefficient alpha was .72.

Author: Abbey, A., and McAuslan, P.

Article: A longitudinal examination of male college students' perpetration of sexual assault.

Journal: *Journal of Consulting and Clinical Psychology*, October 2004, *72*, 747–756.

Related Research: Ballard, R. (1992). Short form of the Marlowe–Crowne Social Desirability Scale. *Psychological Reports*, *71*, 1155–1160.

11031

Test Name: MATTERING TO OTHERS QUESTIONNAIRE

Purpose: To evaluate positive perceived mattering for early to late adolescence.

Number of Items: 11

Format: Includes three versions of 11 items each for mother, father, and friends. Responses are made on a 5-point scale ranging from 1 (*not much*) to 5 (*a lot*). A sample item is given.

Reliability: Alpha coefficients ranged from .93 to .96.

Author: Marshall, S. K.

Article: Relative contributions of perceived mattering to parents and friends in predicting adolescents' psychological well-being.

Journal: *Perceptual and Motor Skills*, October 2004, *99*, 591–601.

Related Research: Marshall, S. K. (2001). Do I matter? Construct validation of adolescents' perceived mattering to parents and friends. *Journal of Adolescence, 24*, 473–490.

11032

Test Name: MAUGER FORGIVENESS SCALE

Purpose: To measure self-forgiveness and forgiveness of others.

Number of Items: 30

Format: Includes two subscales: Forgiveness of Self and Forgiveness of Others. Responses are true–false.

Reliability: Alpha coefficients ranged from .68 to .82. Test–retest reliability was .67 and .94.

Validity: Correlations with other variables ranged from −.05 to .62 ($n = 147$).

Author: Ross, S. R., et al.

Article: A personological examination of self- and other-forgiveness in the five factor model.

Journal: *Journal of Personality Assessment*, April 2004, *82*, 207–214.

Related Research: Mauger, P. A., et al. (1992). The measurement of forgiveness: Preliminary research. *Journal of Psychology and Christianity, 11*, 170–180.

11033

Test Name: MEANINGLESSNESS SCALE

Purpose: To measure meaninglessness in the South African context.

Number of Items: 3

Format: Item responses range from 1 (*strongly disagree*) to 4 (*strongly agree*). All items are presented.

Reliability: Coefficient alpha was .66.

Author: Morojele, N. K., and Brook, J. S.

Article: Sociodemographic, sociocultural, and individual predictors of reported feelings of meaninglessness among South African adolescents.

Journal: *Psychological Reports*, December 2004, *95*, Part 2, 1271–1278.

Related Research: Neal, A., & Groat, H. T. (1974). Social class correlates of stability and change in levels of alienation. *Sociological Quarterly, 15*, 548–558.

11034

Test Name: MEXICAN AMERICAN ENCULTURATION/ACCULTURATION SCALE

Purpose: To assess family support and closeness, family obligations, and family as referent.

Number of Items: 17

Format: Scales range from 1 (*strongly disagree*) to 5 (*strongly agree*). Sample items are presented.

Reliability: Alpha coefficients ranged from .79 to .92.

Author: McHale, S. M., et al.

Article: Siblings' differential treatment in Mexican American families.

Journal: *Journal of Marriage and Family*, December 2005, *67*, 1259–1274.

Related Research: Gonzales, N., et al. (2000). *Mexican American Enculturation/Acculturation Scale.* Unpublished scale, Arizona State University, Tempe.

11035

Test Name: MILLER SOCIAL INTIMACY SCALE

Purpose: To measure the level of social intimacy and the current relationship with a closest friend.

Number of Items: 25

Format: Responses are made on a 5-point scale ranging from 1 (*very rarely*) to 5 (*almost always*).

Validity: Correlations with other variables ranged from −.06 to −.35.

Author: DiTommaso, E., et al.

Article: Measurement and validity characteristics of the short version of the Social and Emotional Loneliness Scale for Adults.

Journal: *Educational and Psychological Measurement*, February 2004, *64*, 99–119.

Related Research: Miller, R. S., & Lefcourt, H. M. (1982). The assessment of social intimacy. *Journal of Personality Assessment, 46*, 514–518.

11036

Test Name: MIVILLE–GUZMAN UNIVERSALITY–DIVERSITY SCALE

Purpose: To measure the awareness and acceptance of similarities and differences among people.

Number of Items: 45

Format: Scales range from 1 (*strongly disagree*) to 6 (*strongly agree*).

Reliability: Coefficient alpha was .91.

Validity: Correlations with other variables ranged from −.17 to .40.

Author: Constantine, M. G., and Arorash, T. J.

Article: Universal–diverse orientation and general expectations about counseling: Their relation to college students' multicultural counseling expectations.

Journal: *Journal of College Student Development*, November/December 2001, *42*, 535–544.

Related Research: Miville, M. L., et al. (1999). Appreciating similarities and valuing differences: The Miville–Guzman Universality–Diversity Scale. *Journal of Counseling Psychology*, *46*, 291–307.

11037

Test Name: MODERN RACISM SCALE

Purpose: To assess racial antagonism.

Number of Items: 7

Format: Scales range from 1 (*strongly disagree*) to 5 (*strongly agree*). All items are presented.

Reliability: Coefficient alpha was .82.

Validity: Correlations with other variables ranged from –.30 to .11.

Author: Hogan, D. E., and Mallott, M.

Article: Changing racial prejudice through diversity education.

Journal: *Journal of College Student Development*, March/April 2005, *46*, 115–125.

Related Research: McConahay, J. B. (1986). Modern racism, ambivalence, and the Modern Racism Scale. In J. F. Dovidio & S. L. Gaertner (Eds.), *Prejudice, discrimination, and racism* (pp. 91–126). New York: Academic Press.

11038

Test Name: MULTICULTURAL COMPETENCE SCALE

Purpose: To assess competence in dealing with diverse populations.

Number of Items: 21

Format: Scales range from 1 (*inappropriate*) to 4 (*very appropriate*). All items are presented.

Reliability: Subscale alphas ranged from .72 to .97.

Validity: Correlations between subscales ranged from .29 to .50.

Author: Garnst, G., et al.

Article: Cultural competency revisited: The California Brief Multicultural Competence Scale.

Journal: *Measurement and Education in Counseling and Development*, July 2004, *37*, 163–183.

11039

Test Name: MULTICULTURAL PERSONALITY INVENTORY

Purpose: To measure cultural empathy, open-mindedness, emotional stability, orientation to action, adventurousness–curiosity, flexibility, and extraversion.

Number of Items: 78

Time Required: 15 minutes.

Format: Scales range from 1 (*not at all applicable*) to 5 (*totally applicable*). Sample items are presented.

Reliability: Alpha coefficients ranged from .74 to .91.

Author: Van der Zee, K. I., and Van Oudenhoven, J. P.

Article: The Multicultural Personality Questionnaire: Reliability and validity of self and other ratings of multicultural effectiveness.

Journal: *Journal of Research in Personality*, September 2001, *35*, 278–288.

Related Research: Van dee Zee, K. I., & Van Oudenhoven, J. P. (2000). The Multicultural Personality Questionnaire: A multidimensional instrument of multicultural effectiveness. *European Journal of Personality*, *14*, 291–309.

11040

Test Name: MULTICULTURAL PERSPECTIVE INDEX

Purpose: To measure multicultural perspective.

Number of Items: 42

Format: Items are anchored by 1 (*not like me at all*) and 5 (*very much like me*). All items are presented.

Reliability: Coefficient alpha was .80.

Validity: Correlations with other variables ranged from .06 to .29.

Author: Mower, R. R., and McCarver, D. M.

Article: A preliminary investigation of Multicultural Perspective and Life Satisfaction.

Journal: *Psychological Reports*, February 2002, *90*, 251–256.

11041

Test Name: MULTIDIMENSIONAL INVENTORY OF BLACK IDENTITY

Purpose: To assess African Americans' racial identity.

Number of Items: 56

Format: Scales range from 1 (*strongly disagree*) to 7 (*strongly agree*). All items are presented.

Reliability: Subscale reliability coefficients ranged from .60 to .79.

Validity: Correlations with other variables ranged from –.31 to .50.

Author: Cokley, K. O., and Helm, K.

Article: Testing the construct validity of scores on the Multidimensional Inventory of Black Identity.

Journal: *Measurement and Evaluation in Counseling and Development*, July 2001, *34*, 80–95.

Related Research: Sellers, R. M., et al. (1997). Multidimensional Inventory of Black Identity: A preliminary investigation of reliability and construct validity. *Journal of Personality and Social Psychology, 73*, 805–815.

11042

Test Name: MULTIDIMENSIONAL INVENTORY OF BLACK IDENTITY—THREE SUBSCALES

Purpose: To measure three aspects of racial identity.

Number of Items: 9

Format: Includes three aspects of racial identity: centrality, public regard, and private regard. Responses are made on a 7-point Likert Scale ranging from 1 (*strongly disagree*) to 7 (*strongly agree*). Sample items are presented.

Reliability: Alpha coefficients were .65 and .67.

Validity: Correlations with other variables ranged from −.03 to .15.

Author: Chavous, T. M., et al.

Article: Racial identity and academic attainment among African American adolescents.

Journal: *Child Development*, July/August 2003, *74*, 1076–1090.

Related Research: Hawkins, J. D., et al. (1992). Risk and protective factors for alcohol and other drug problems in adolescence and early adulthood: Implications for substance abuse prevention. *Psychological Bulletin, 112*, 64–105.

11043

Test Name: MULTIDIMENSIONAL SCALE OF PERCEIVED SOCIAL SUPPORT

Purpose: To measure perceived social support.

Number of Items: 12

Format: Includes three subscales: Support From Friends, Support From Family, and Support From Significant Others. Responses are made on a 7-point scale ranging from 1 (*very strongly disagree*) to 7 (*very strongly agree*).

Reliability: Alpha coefficients ranged from .92 to .94.

Author: Clara, I. P., et al.

Article: Confirmatory factor analysis of the Multidimensional Scale of Perceived Social Support in clinically distressed and student samples.

Journal: *Journal of Personality Assessment*, December 2003, *81*, 265–270.

Related Research: Zimet, G. D., et al. (1988). The Multidimensional Scale of Perceived Social Support. *Journal of Personality Assessment, 52*, 30–41.

11044

Test Name: MULTIGENERATIONAL INTERCONNECTEDNESS SCALES

Purpose: To measure separation–individuation.

Number of Items: 31

Format: Seven-point Likert scales are used. Sample items are presented.

Reliability: Alpha coefficients ranged from .83 to .87.

Author: Kalsner, L., and Pistole, M. C.

Article: College adjustment in a multiethnic sample: Attachment, separation–individuation, and ethnic identity.

Journal: *Journal of College Student Development*, January/February 2003, *44*, 92–109.

Related Research: Gavazzi, S. M., et al. (1999). Measurement of financial, functional, and psychological connections in families: The conceptual development and empirical use of the Multigenerational Interconnectedness Scale. *Psychological Reports, 84*, 1361–1371.

11045

Test Name: MULTIGROUP ETHNIC IDENTITY MEASURE

Purpose: To assess ethnic identity.

Number of Items: 1 open-ended question + 12 items

Format: Responses to the 12 items are made on a 5-point scale ranging from 1 (*strongly disagree*) to 5 (*strongly agree*). All items are presented.

Reliability: Coefficient alpha was .72.

Validity: Correlations with other variables ranged from .14 to .74.

Author: Kim, S. S., and Gelfand, M. J.

Article: The influence of ethnic identity on perceptions of organizational recruitment.

Journal: *Journal of Vocational Behavior*, December 2003, *63*, 396–416.

Related Research: Phinney, J. S. (1992). The Multigroup Ethnic Identity Measure: A new scale for use with diverse groups. *Journal of Adolescent Research, 7*, 156–176.

11046

Test Name: MULTIGROUP ETHNIC IDENTITY MEASURE

Purpose: To measure ethnic identity.

Number of Items: 20

Format: Includes three dimensions: Ethnic Identity Achievement, Affirmation and Belonging, and Ethnic Behaviors. Also included is a 6-item measure of other-group orientation. Responses are made on a 4-point scale ranging from 1 (*strongly disagree*) to 4 (*strongly agree*).

Reliability: Alpha coefficients ranged from .72 to .88.

Author: Lee, R. M., and Yoo, H. C.

Article: Structure and measurement of ethnic identity for Asian American college students.

Journal: *Journal of Counseling Psychology*, April 2004, *51*, 263–269.

Related Research: Phinney, J. S. (1992). The Multigroup Ethnic Identity Measure: A new scale for use with diverse groups. *Journal of Adolescent Research*, 7, 156–176.

11047

Test Name: MULTIGROUP ETHNIC IDENTITY MEASURE

Purpose: To assess ethnic identity formation.

Number of Items: 14

Format: Includes three subscales: Affirmation/Belonging, Ethnic Identity Achievement, and Ethnic Behaviors. Responses are made on a 4-point Likert scale ranging from 1 (*strongly disagree*) to 4 (*strongly agree*).

Reliability: Alpha coefficients were .63 and .83.

Validity: Correlations with other variables ranged from −.25 to .43.

Author: Newman, D. L.

Article: Ego development and ethnic identity formation in rural American Indian adolescents.

Journal: *Child Development*, May/June 2005, *76*, 734–746.

Related Research: Phinney, J. S. (1992). The Multigroup Ethnic Identity Measure: A new scale for use with diverse groups. *Journal of Adolescent Research*, 7, 156–176.

11048

Test Name: MULTIGROUP ETHNIC IDENTITY MEASURE

Purpose: To measure ethnic identity development.

Number of Items: 22

Format: Includes two subscales: Ethnic Identity and Other-Group Orientation. Responses are made on a Likert-type scale ranging from 1 (*strongly disagree*) to 4 (*strongly agree*).

Reliability: Alpha coefficients were .59 and .89.

Author: Ponterotto, J. G., et al.

Article: The Multigroup Ethnic Identity Measure (MEIM): Psychometric review and further validity testing.

Journal: *Educational and Psychological Measurement*, June 2003, *63*, 502–515.

Related Research: Phinney, J. S. (1992). The Multigroup Ethnic Identity Measure: A new scale for use with diverse groups. *Journal of Adolescent Research*, 7, 156–176.

11049

Test Name: MULTIGROUP ETHNIC IDENTITY MEASURE

Purpose: To measure ethnic belonging, identity achievement, and ethnic behaviors.

Number of Items: 23

Format: Scales range from 1 (*strongly disagree*) to 4 (*strongly agree*).

Reliability: Alpha coefficients ranged from .54 to .90 across samples.

Author: Rayle, A. D., and Meyers, J. E.

Article: Counseling adolescents toward wellness: The roles of ethnic identity, acculturation, and mattering.

Journal: *Professional School Counseling*, October 2004, *8*, 81–90.

Related Research: Phinney, J. S. (1992). The Multigroup Ethnic Identity Measure: A new scale for use with diverse groups. *Journal of Adolescent Research*, 7, 156–176.

11050

Test Name: MULTIGROUP ETHNIC IDENTITY MEASURE

Purpose: To measure ethnic identity.

Number of Items: 12

Format: Four-point Likert scales were used.

Reliability: Coefficient alpha was .87.

Validity: Correlations with other variables ranged from −.25 to .27.

Author: Smith, T. B., and Stratton, J.

Article: Ethnic identity and racial attitudes in a minority group of mixed racial origin.

Journal: *Psychological Reports*, February 2003, *92*, 284–290.

Related Research: Phinney, J. S. (1992). The Multigroup Ethnic Identity Measure: A new scale for use with diverse groups. *Journal of Adolescent Research*, 7, 156–176.

11051

Test Name: MULTIGROUP ETHNIC IDENTITY MEASURE

Purpose: To measure global ethnic identity.

Number of Items: 12

Format: Includes two subscales: Affirmation and Belonging and Ethnic Identity Achievement. Responses are made on a 4-point

Likert-type scale ranging from 1 (*strongly disagree*) to 4 (*strongly agree*).

Reliability: Alpha coefficients were .84 (affirmation and belonging) and .78 (ethnic identity and achievement).

Validity: Correlations with other variables ranged from –.16 to .33.

Author: Yip, T., and Fuligni, A. J.

Article: Daily variation in ethnic identity, ethnic behavior, and psychological well-being among American adolescents of Chinese descent.

Journal: *Child Development*, September/October 2002, *73*, 1557–1572.

Related Research: Phinney, J. S. (1992). The Multigroup Ethnic Identity Measure: A new scale for use with diverse groups. *Journal of Adolescent Research*, 7, 156–176.

11052

Test Name: NADANOLITIZATION—RACIST DIMENSION

Purpose: To measure the internalization of negative and positive racial stereotypes of Blacks.

Number of Items: 49

Format: Includes three factors: mental/genetic deficiencies, sexual prowess, and natural ability. Responses are made on a 7-point Likert scale ranging from 1 (*strongly disagree*) to 7 (*strongly agree*).

Reliability: Internal consistency coefficients ranged from .67 to .88.

Author: Cokley, K. O.

Article: Racial(ized) identity, ethnic identity, and Afrocentric values: Conceptual and methodological challenges in understanding African American identity.

Journal: *Journal of Counseling Psychology*, October 2005, *52*, 517–526.

Related Research: Cokley, K. O. (2002). Testing Cross's revised racial identity model: An examination of the relationship between racial identity and internalized racialism. *Journal of Counseling Psychology, 49*, 476–483.

11053

Test Name: NEED FOR SOCIAL APPROVAL SUBSCALE

Purpose: To measure dependence of happiness and personal worth on approval from others.

Number of Items: 11

Format: Seven-point scales range from *totally agree* to *totally disagree*.

Reliability: Coefficient alpha was .82.

Author: Teasdale, J. D., et al.

Article: How does cognitive therapy prevent relapse in residual depression? Evidence from a controlled trial.

Journal: *Journal of Consulting and Clinical Psychology*, June 2001, *69*, 347–357.

Related Research: Weissman, A., & Beck, A. T. (1978, November). *The Dysfunctional Attitudes Scale.* Paper presented at the annual meeting of the Association for the Advancement of Behavior Therapy, Chicago, IL.

11054

Test Name: NETWORK BUILDING SCALE

Purpose: To assess to what extent individuals develop and use networks.

Number of Items: 6

Format: Scales range from 1 (*very strongly disagree*) to 7 (*very strongly agree*). A sample item is presented.

Reliability: Coefficient alpha was .94.

Validity: Correlations with other variables ranged from .22 to .46.

Author: Thompson, J. A.

Article: Proactive personality and job performance: A social capital perspective.

Journal: *Journal of Applied Psychology*, September 2005, *90*, 1011–1017.

11055

Test Name: NETWORK OF RELATIONSHIPS INVENTORY

Purpose: To measure perceptions of experiences in close relationships.

Number of Items: 18

Format: Includes six different aspects of support: companionship, reliable alliance, enhancement of worth, instrumental help, affection, and intimacy. Responses are made on 5-point Likert scales. Examples are presented.

Reliability: Alpha coefficients exceeded .89.

Author: Furman, W., et al.

Article: Adolescents' working models and styles for relationships with parents, friends, and romantic partners.

Journal: *Child Development*, January/February 2002, *73*, 241–255.

Related Research: Furman, W., & Buhrmester, D. (1985). Children's perceptions of the personal relationships in their social networks. *Developmental Psychology, 21*, 1016–1024.

11056

Test Name: NETWORK OF RELATIONSHIPS INVENTORY

Purpose: To enable children to rate persons in their social network relative to social support or conflict.

Number of Items: 33

Format: Includes 11 scales.

Reliability: Alpha coefficients ranged from .86 to .94.

Author: Meehan, B. T., et al.

Article: Teacher–student relationships as compensatory resources for aggressive children.

Journal: *Child Development*, July/August 2003, *74*, 1145–1157.

Related Research: Furman, W., & Buhrmester, D. (1985). Children's perceptions of the personal relationships in their social networks. *Developmental Psychology, 21*, 1016–1024.

11057

Test Name: NEWCOMER SOCIALIZATION QUESTIONNAIRE

Purpose: To measure knowledge of expected role behaviors.

Number of Items: 43

Format: Includes three dimensions: Organizational Socialization, Group Socialization, and Task Socialization. Responses are made on a 7-point scale ranging from *strongly disagree* to *strongly agree*. All items are presented.

Reliability: Alpha coefficients ranged from .88 to .92. Test–retest reliabilities ranged from .71 to .79.

Validity: Correlations with other variables ranged from −.10 to .80.

Author: Haueter, J. A., et al.

Article: Measurement of newcomer socialization: Construct validation of a multidimensional scale.

Journal: *Journal of Vocational Behavior*, August 2003, *63*, 20–39.

11058

Test Name: NORBECK SOCIAL SUPPORT QUESTIONNAIRE— ADAPTED

Purpose: To assess multiple dimensions of social support.

Number of Items: 13

Format: Responses are made on a 5-point scale ranging from 0 (*not at all*) to 4 (*a great deal*).

Reliability: Alpha coefficients ranged from .72 to .98.

Author: Huth-Bocks, A.-C., et al.

Article: The impact of maternal characteristics and contextual variables on infant–mother attachment.

Journal: *Child Development*, March/April 2004, *75*, 480–496.

Related Research: Norbeck, J., et al. (1981). The development of an instrument to measure social support. *Nursing Research, 30*, 264–269.

11059

Test Name: NOVELTY SCALES

Purpose: To measure perceived national culture novelty and role novelty.

Number of Items: 12

Format: Includes two scales: Cultural Novelty and Role Novelty. Responses are made on a 5-point scale ranging from 1 (*not at all*) to 5 (*fluently*).

Reliability: Alpha coefficients were .70 to .81.

Validity: Correlations with other variables ranged from −.40 to .15 ($N = 213$).

Author: Kraimer, M. L., et al.

Article: Sources of support and expatriate performance: The mediating role of expatriate adjustment.

Journal: *Personnel Psychology*, Spring 2001, *54*, 71–99.

Related Research: Torbiorn, I. (1982). *Living abroad*. New York: Wiley. Shaffer, M. A., et al. (1999). Dimensions, determinants, and differences in the expatriate adjustment process. *Journal of International Business Studies, 30*, 557–581.

11060

Test Name: OBSERVED FRIENDSHIP QUALITY SCALE

Purpose: To rate observed friendship quality.

Number of Items: 27 codes.

Format: Each child is rated on a 5-point scale ranging from 1 (*not at all characteristic*) to 5 (*highly characteristic*) for 17 individual codes and 10 dyadic codes. All 27 codes are described.

Reliability: Alpha coefficients ranged from .45 to .91.

Author: Simpkins, S. D., & Parke, R. D.

Article: The relations between parental friendships and children's friendships: Self-report and observational analysis.

Journal: *Child Development*, March/April 2001, *72*, 569–582.

Related Research: Flyr, M. L., et al. (1995). *Observed Friendship Quality Scale*. Unpublished coding system, University of California, Riverside.

11061

Test Name: OPERATING PRINCIPLES SCALE

Purpose: To determine how collaboratively group members operate.

Number of Items: 10

Format: Responses are made on a 5-point scale ranging from

5 (*strongly agree*) to 1 (*strongly disagree*). Sample items are presented.

Reliability: Coefficient alpha was .87.

Validity: Correlations with other variables ranged from –.25 to .69.

Author: Mebane, D. J., and Galassi, J. P.

Article: Variables affecting collaborative research and learning in a professional development school partnership.

Journal: *The Journal of Educational Research*, May/June 2003, *96*, 259–268.

11062

Test Name: ORGANIZATIONAL TRUST INVENTORY—MODIFIED

Purpose: To assess individual trust in dyadic bargaining situations.

Number of Items: 12

Format: Scales range from 1 (*strongly disagree*) to 7 (*strongly agree*). All items are presented.

Reliability: Coefficient alpha was .70.

Author: Naquin, C. E., and Paulson, G. D.

Article: Online bargaining and interpersonal trust.

Journal: *Journal of Applied Psychology*, February 2003, *88*, 113–120.

Related Research: Cummings, L. L., & Bromiley, P. (1966). The Organizational Trust Inventory (OTI): Development and validation. In R. M. Kramer & T. R. Tyler (Eds.), *Trust in organizations: Frontiers in theory and research* (pp. 302–330). Thousand Oaks, CA: Sage.

11063

Test Name: OVER- AND UNDERINVOLVED SCALES

Purpose: To assess involvement with others.

Number of Items: 21

Format: Sample items are presented. Five-point response scales are used.

Reliability: Alpha coefficients ranged from .56 to .90.

Validity: Correlations with other variables ranged from –.47 to .47.

Author: Hardy, G. E., et al.

Article: Client interpersonal and cognitive styles as predictors of response to time-limited cognitive therapy for depression.

Journal: *Journal of Consulting and Clinical Psychology*, October 2001, *69*, 841–845.

Related Research: Weissman, A. N., & Beck, A. T. (1978, August/September). *Development and validation of the Dysfunctional Attitude Scale: A preliminary investigation.* Paper presented at the annual convention of the American Psychological Association, Toronto, Ontario, Canada.

11064

Test Name: PARENT'S EXPERIENCES OF RACIAL SOCIALIZATION SCALE—ADAPTED

Purpose: To measure parent's racial socialization practices.

Number of Items: 40

Format: Responses are made on a 3-point scale ranging from 1 (*never*) to 3 (*lots of times*).

Reliability: Internal reliability coefficients ranged from .76 to .86.

Author: Caughy, M. O., et al.

Article: The influence of racial socialization practices on the cognitive and behavioral competence of African American preschoolers.

Journal: *Child Development*, September/October 2002, *73*, 1611–1625

Related Research: Stevenson, H. (1999). *Parents' experience of racial socialization.* Unpublished measure, University of Pennsylvania, Graduate School of Education, Philadelphia.

11065

Test Name: PASSIONATE LOVE SCALE

Purpose: To measure passionate love.

Number of Items: 15

Format: Scales range from 0 (*not at all true*) to 9 (*definitely true*). A sample item is presented.

Reliability: Coefficient alpha was .93.

Author: Kito, M.

Article: Self-disclosure in romantic relationships and friendships among American and Japanese college students.

Journal: *The Journal of Social Psychology*, April 2005, *145*, 127–140.

Related Research: Hatfield, E., & Sprecher, S. (1986). Measuring passionate love in intimate relations. *Journal of Adolescence*, *9*, 383–410.

11066

Test Name: PASSIONATE LOVE SCALE

Purpose: To assess passionate love.

Number of Items: 30

Format: Scales range from 1 (*not at all true*) to 9 (*definitely true*). Sample items are presented.

Reliability: Coefficient alpha was .94.

Author: Myers, J. E., and Shurts, M.

Article: Measuring positive emotionality: A review of instruments assessing love.

Journal: *Measurement and Evaluation in Counseling and Development*, January 2002, *34*, 238–254.

Related Research: Hatfield, E., & Sprecher, S. (1986). Measuring passionate love in intimate relationships. *Journal of Adolescence, 9*, 383–410.

11067

Test Name: PEER BELIEF INVENTORY—ADAPTED

Purpose: To assess children's perceptions of their peers in general.

Number of Items: 15

Format: Responses are made on a 5-point scale. Examples are given.

Reliability: Coefficient alpha was .84.

Author: Ladd, G. W., and Troop-Gordon, W.

Article: The role of chronic peer difficulties in the development of children's psychological adjustment problems.

Journal: *Child Development*, September/October 2003, *74*, 1344–1367.

Related Research: Rabiner, D. L., et al. (1993). Children's beliefs about familiar and unfamiliar peers in relation to their sociometric status. *Developmental Psychology, 29*, 236–243.

11068

Test Name: PEER EXCLUSION SCALE

Purpose: To assess peer exclusion.

Number of Items: 5

Format: Responses are made on a 3-point scale ranging from 0 (*not true*) to 2 (*often true*). All items are presented.

Reliability: Alpha coefficients were .90 and .93.

Validity: Correlations with other variables ranged from –.44 to .59.

Author: Gazelle, H., and Rudolph, K. D.

Article: Moving toward and away from the world: Social approach and avoidance trajectories in anxious solitary youth.

Journal: *Child Development*, May/June 2004, *75*, 829–849.

Related Research: Ladd, G. W., & Profilet, S. M. (1996). The Child Behavior Scale: A teacher-report measure of young children's aggressive, withdrawn, and prosocial behaviors. *Developmental Psychology, 32*, 1008–1024.

11069

Test Name: PEER FRIENDSHIP AND SUPPORT SCALE

Purpose: To assess peer support in time of need.

Number of Items: 4

Format: Scales range from 0 (*not at all or never true of me*) to 4 (*definitely or always true of me*).

Reliability: Coefficient alpha was .83.

Validity: Correlations with other variables ranged from .06 to .10.

Author: Fenzel, L. M.

Article: Multivariate analysis of predictors of heavy episodic drinking and drinking-related problems among college students.

Journal: *Journal of College Student Development*, March/April 2005, *46*, 126–140.

11070

Test Name: PEER NOMINATIONS SCALE

Purpose: To measure antisocial disruption and prosocial leadership.

Number of Items: 15

Format: Includes two types of items: antisocial—disruption and prosocial—leadership. Examples are given.

Reliability: Alpha coefficients ranged from .82 to .95.

Validity: Correlations with other variables ranged from –.16 to .25.

Author: Chang, L., et al.

Article: Mediating teacher liking and moderating authoritative teachering on Chinese adolescents' perceptions of antisocial and prosocial behaviors.

Journal: *Journal of Educational Psychology*, June 2004, *96*, 369–380.

Related Research: Schwartz, D., et al. (2001). Correlates of victimization in Chinese children's peer groups. *Developmental Psychology, 37*, 520–532.

11071

Test Name: PENN INTERACTIVE PEER PLAY SCALE

Purpose: To assess peer-play interaction across classroom and home settings.

Number of Items: 32.

Format: Includes a teacher version and a parent version. Comprises three underlying dimensions of children's peer-play behaviors: Play Interaction, Play Disruption, and Play Disconnection.

Reliability: Internal consistency reliability coefficients ranged from .74 to .92.

Author: Fantuzzo, J., and McWayne, C.

Article: The relationship between peer-play interactions in the family context and dimensions of school readiness for low-income preschool children.

Journal: *Journal of Educational Psychology*, March 2002, *94*, 79–87.

Related Research: Fantuzzo, J., & Hampton, V. (2000). Penn Interactive Peer Play Scale: A parent and teacher rating system for young children. In K. Gitlin-Weine et al. (Eds.), *Play diagnosis and assessment* (pp. 599–620). New York: Wiley.

11072

Test Name: PERCEIVED COMPETENCE SCALE FOR CHILDREN

Purpose: To assess students' cognitive and social competence.

Number of Items: 8.

Format: Includes two factors: cognitive competence and social competence. All items are included.

Reliability: Alpha coefficients were .77 and .84.

Validity: Correlations with other variables ranged from −.44 to .53 (*N* = 131).

Author: Tanaka, A., et al.

Article: Achievement motives, cognitive and social competence, and achievement goals in the classroom.

Journal: *Perceptual and Motor Skills*, October 2002, *95*, 445–458.

Related Research: Harter, S. (1982). The Perceived Competence Scale for Children. *Child Development*, *53*, 87–97.

11073

Test Name: PERCEIVED DISCRIMINATION SCALE

Purpose: To measure perceived personal ethnic discrimination.

Number of Items: 3

Format: Responses are made on a 4-point scale ranging from 1 (*strongly disagree*) to 4 (*strongly agree*). All items are presented.

Reliability: Internal reliability estimates ranged from .63 to .81.

Validity: Correlations with other variables ranged from −.36 to .28 (*N* = 84).

Author: Lee, R. M.

Article: Resilience against discrimination: Ethnic identity and other-group orientation as protective factors for Korean Americans.

Journal: *Journal of Counseling Psychology*, January 2005, *52*, 36–44.

Related Research: Finch, B. K., et al. (2000). Perceived discrimination and depression among Mexican-origin adults in California. *Journal of Health and Social Behavior*, *41*, 295–313.

11074

Test Name: PERCEIVED RACISM SCALE

Purpose: To measure emotional reactions to racism.

Number of Items: 32

Format: Includes eight emotions: angry, hurt, frustrated, sad, powerless, hopeless, ashamed, and strengthened. Responses are made on a 5-point scale ranging from 1 (*not at all*) to 5 (*extremely*).

Reliability: Alpha coefficients ranged from .75 to .96. Test–retest reliability coefficients ranged from .71 to .80.

Validity: Correlations with other variables ranged from −.04 to .41.

Author: Liang, C. T. H., et al.

Article: The Asian American Racism-Related Stress Inventory: Development, factor analysis, reliability, and validity.

Journal: *Journal of Counseling Psychology*, January 2004, *51*, 103–114.

Related Research: McNeilly, M. D., et al. (1996). The Perceived Racism Scale: A multidimensional assessment of the experience of White racism among African-Americans. *Ethnicity and Disease*, *6*, 154–166.

11075

Test Name: PERCEIVED SOCIAL SUPPORT—FRIENDS AND FAMILY SUBSCALES

Purpose: To assess friends and family social support.

Number of Items: 40

Format: Includes two subscales: Friend Social Support and Family Social Support. Responses to each item are *yes*, *no*, or *don't know*. Examples are given.

Reliability: Alpha coefficients were .88 and .90.

Validity: Correlations with other variables ranged from −.05 to −.41.

Author: Tylka, T. L., and Subich, L. M.

Article: Examining a multidimensional model of eating disorder symptomatology among college women.

Journal: *Journal of Counseling Psychology*, July 2004, *51*, 314–328.

Related Research: Procidano, M. E., & Heller, K. (1983). Measures of perceived social support from friends and family: Three validation studies. *American Journal of Community Psychology*, *11*, 1–24.

11076

Test Name: PERCEPTIONS OF FAIR INTERPERSONAL TREATMENT SCALE—MODIFIED

Purpose: To measure fair interpersonal treatment.

Number of Items: 18

Format: Responses are made on a 7-point scale ranging from *strongly disagree* to *strongly agree*.

Reliability: Alpha coefficients were .90 and .92.

Validity: Correlations with other variables ranged from −.36 to .60.

Author: Behson, S. J.

Article: Which dominates? The relative importance of work–family organizational support and general organizational context on employee outcomes.

Journal: *Journal of Vocational Behavior*, August 2002, *61*, 53–72.

Related Research: Donovan, M. A., et al. (1998). The Perceptions of Fair Interpersonal Treatment Scale: Development and validations of a measure of interpersonal treatment in the workplace. *Journal of Applied Psychology*, *83*, 683–692.

11077

Test Name: PERCEPTIONS OF PEER SUPPORT SCALE— ADAPTED

Purpose: To measure victimization.

Number of Items: 4

Format: One item each estimates verbal, physical, general, and indirect forms of victimization. Responses are made on a 5-point scale ranging from 1 (*almost never*) to 5 (*almost always*). All items are presented.

Reliability: Coefficient alpha was .78.

Validity: Correlations with other variables ranged from −.35 to .33.

Author: Buhs, E. S.

Article: Peer rejection, negative peer treatment, and school adjustment: Self-concept and classroom engagement as mediating processes.

Journal: *Journal of School Psychology*, November 2005, *43*, 407–424.

Related Research: Kochenderfer, B. J., & Ladd, G. W. (1996). Peer victimization: Cause or consequence of school maladjustment? *Child Development*, *67*, 1305–1317.

11078

Test Name: PERSONAL RESOURCE QUESTIONNAIRE (PRQ85)

Purpose: To measure social support.

Number of Items: 25

Format: Response scales are anchored by *strongly agree* and *strongly disagree*. Sample items are presented.

Reliability: Alpha coefficients ranged from .89 to .92.

Author: Yarcheski, T. J., et al.

Article: Social support, self-esteem, and positive health practices of early adolescents.

Journal: *Psychological Reports*, February 2003, *92*, 99–103.

Related Research: Weinert, C. (1987). A social support measure: PRQ85. *Nursing Research*, *36*, 273–277.

11079

Test Name: POWERLESSNESS SCALE

Purpose: To measure powerlessness.

Number of Items: 10

Format: Scales range from 1 (*strongly disagree*) to 5 (*strongly agree*). Sample items are presented.

Reliability: Coefficient alpha was .88.

Validity: Correlations with stigmatization ranged from .20 to .44.

Author: Harvey, R. D.

Article: Individual differences in the phenomenological impact of social stigma.

Journal: *The Journal of Social Psychology*, April 2001, *141*, 174–189.

Related Research: Neal, A., & Goat, H. T. (1974). Social class correlates of stability and change in levels of alienation. *Sociological Quarterly*, *15*, 548–558.

11080

Test Name: PRESCHOOL BEHAVIOR Q-SORT—MODIFIED

Purpose: To rate classroom social competence.

Number of Items: 72

Format: Includes two factors: positive engagement and conflict management.

Reliability: Alpha coefficients were .88 and .92.

Author: Smith, M., and Walden, T.

Article: An exploration of African American preschool-aged children's behavioral regulations in emotionally arousing situations.

Journal: *Child Study Journal*, 2001, *31*, 13–45.

Related Research: Baumrind, D. (1968). *Preschool Behavior Q-Sort: Manual*. Unpublished manuscript, University of California, Berkeley.

11081

Test Name: PRESCHOOL SOCIOAFFECTIVE PROFILE— SHORT FORM

Purpose: To assess children's emotional competence with peers.

Number of Items: 30

Format: Taps three areas of children's emotional competence: positive emotional behaviors with peers; angry, aggressive, and oppositional behaviors; and anxious, isolated, and withdrawn behaviors. Responses are made on a 6-point scale ranging from 1 (*never*) to 6 (*always*).

Reliability: Alpha coefficients ranged from .85 to .95. Test–retest (2 weeks) reliabilities ranged from .78 to .86.

Author: Lindsey, E. W., and Colwell, M. J.

Article: Preschoolers' emotional competence: Links to pretend and physical play.

Journal: *Child Study Journal,* 2003, *33,* 39–52.

Related Research: La Freniere, P. J., et al. (1992). Development and validation of the Preschool Socioaffective Profile. *Psychological Assessment, 4,* 442–450.

11082

Test Name: PROPENSITY TO TRUST MEASURE

Purpose: To measure the propensity to trust.

Number of Items: 8

Format: Responses are made on a 7-point Likert scale ranging from 1 (*strongly disagree*) to 7 (*strongly agree*). A sample item is given.

Reliability: Coefficient alpha was .66.

Validity: Correlations with other variables ranged from −.25 to .24.

Author: Alge, B. J., et al.

Article: Remote control: Predictors of electronic monitoring intensity and secrecy.

Journal: *Personnel Psychology,* Summer 2004, *57,* 377–410.

Summer Related Research: Mayer, R. C., & Davis, J. H. (1999). The effect of the performance appraisal system on trust for management: A field quasi-experiment. *Journal of Applied Psychology, 84,* 123–136.

11083

Test Name: PROSOCIAL GOAL SCALE

Purpose: To assess efforts to be prosocial.

Number of Items: 7

Format: Responses are made on a 5-point scale ranging from 1 (*never*) to 5 (*always*). A sample item is given.

Reliability: Alpha coefficients were .79 and .86.

Validity: Correlations with other variables ranged from .08 to .43.

Author: Wentzel, K. R., et al.

Article: Friendships in middle school: Influences on motivation and school adjustment.

Journal: *Journal of Educational Psychology,* June 2004, *96,* 195–203.

Related Research: Wentzel, K. R. (1993). Social and academic goals at school: Motivation and achievement in early adolescence. *Journal of Early Adolescence, 13,* 4–20.

11084

Test Name: PSYCHOLOGICAL SEPARATION–INDIVIDUATION

Purpose: To measure two dimensions of psychological separation–individuation: general independence and conflictual independence.

Number of Items: 138

Format: Includes four subscales: Functional Independence, Emotional Independence, Attitudinal Independence, and Conflictual Independence. Responses are made on a 5-point scale ranging from 1 (*not at all true of me*) to 5 (*very true of me*).

Reliability: Alpha coefficients ranged from .84 to .96. Test–retest (2–3 weeks) reliabilities ranged from .74 to .96.

Validity: Correlations with other variables ranged from −.47 to .34.

Author: Choi, K.-H.

Article: Psychological separation–individuation and adjustment to college among Korean American students: The roles of collectivism and individualism.

Journal: *Journal of Counseling Psychology,* October 2002, *49,* 468–475.

Related Research: Hoffman, J. (1984). Psychological separation of late adolescents from their parents. *Journal of Counseling Psychology, 34,* 157–163.

11085

Test Name: PSYCHOSOCIAL COSTS OF RACISM TO WHITES SCALE

Purpose: To measure the psychosocial costs of racism to Whites.

Number of Items: 16

Format: Includes three factors: White empathetic reactions toward racism, White guilt, and White fear of others.

Reliability: Alpha coefficients ranged from .69 to .85. Test–retest (2 weeks) reliability ranged from .69 to .95.

Validity: Correlations with other variables ranged from −.70 to .67 (*N* = 366).

Author: Spanierman, L. B., and Heppner, M. J.

Article: Psychological Costs of Racism to Whites Scale (PCRW): Construction and initial validation.

Journal: *Journal of Counseling Psychology,* April 2004, *51,* 249–262.

11086

Test Name: QUESTIONNAIRE ABOUT INTERPERSONAL DIFFICULTIES FOR ADOLESCENTS

Purpose: To assess the situations that present difficulties for adolescents.

Number of Items: 36

Format: Scales range from 0 (*no difficulty*) to 4 (*maximum difficulty*). Sample items are presented.

Reliability: Coefficient alpha was .90. Test–retest reliability was .78 (2 weeks).

Validity: Correlations with other variables ranged from .00 to .57.

Author: Inglés, C. J., et al.

Article: The List of Social Situation Problems: Reliability and validity in an adolescent Spanish-speaking sample.

Journal: *Journal of Psychopathology and Behavioral Assessment*, March 2003, *25*, 65–74.

11087

Test Name: RACIAL CENTRALITY SCALE

Purpose: To measure how central race is to one's identity.

Number of Items: 8

Format: Scales range from 1 (*strongly disagree*) to 7 (*strongly agree*).

Reliability: Coefficient alpha was .77.

Validity: Correlations with other variables ranged from –.08 to .31.

Author: Cokley, K. O.

Article: Gender differences among African American students in the impact of racial identity on academic psychosocial development.

Journal: *Journal of College Student Development*, September/October 2001, *42*, 480–487.

Related Research: Sellers, R. M., et al. (1997). Multidimensional Inventory of Black Identity: A

preliminary investigation of reliability and construct validity. *Journal of Personality and Social Psychology*, *73*, 805–815.

11088

Test Name: RACIAL TENSIONS SUBSCALE

Purpose: To measure perceived minority group discrimination on campus.

Number of Items: 6

Format: Responses are made on a 6-point Likert scale ranging from 1 (*strongly disagree*) to 6 (*strongly agree*). Examples are given.

Reliability: Coefficient alpha was .79.

Validity: Correlations with other variables ranged from –.36 to .04 ($N = .88$).

Author: Lee, R. M.

Article: Do ethnic identity and other-group orientation protect against discrimination for Asian Americans?

Journal: *Journal of Counseling Psychology*, April 2003, *50*, 133–141.

Related Research: Ancis, J. R., et al. (2000). Student perceptions of the campus cultural climate by race. *Journal of counseling and Development*, *78*, 180–185.

11089

Test Name: RATING OF SELF AND OTHERS

Purpose: To measure to what extent people rate themselves and others positively and negatively.

Number of Items: 20

Format: Items were anchored by 1 (*not at all true of me [most other people]*) and 9 (*very true of me [most other people]*).

Reliability: Alpha was .83. Test–retest reliability (1 week) was .85.

Author: Lee, D. Y., et al.

Article: Self and other ratings of Canadian and Korean groups of mental health professionals and their clients.

Journal: *Psychological Reports*, April 2002, *90*, 667–676.

Related Research: Brown, J. D. (1986). Evaluations of self and others: Self-enhancement biases in social judgments. *Social Cognition*, *4*, 353–376.

11090

Test Name: REACTIONS TO HOMOSEXUALITY

Purpose: To assess reactions to homosexuality.

Number of Items: 26

Format: Includes four dimensions: Public Identification As Gay, Perception of Stigma Associated With Being Gay, Social Comfort With Gay Men, and Moral and Religious Acceptability With Being Gay. Responses are made on a 7-point Likert-type scale ranging from 1 (*strongly disagree*) to 7 (*strongly agree*).

Reliability: Alpha coefficients ranged from .62 to .85.

Author: Currie, M., et al.

Article: The Short Internalized Homonegativity Scale: Examination of the factorial structure of a new measure of internalized homophobia.

Journal: *Educational and Psychological Measurement*, December 2004, *64*, 1053–1067.

Related Research: Ross, M. W., & Rosser, S. B. R. (1996). Measurement and correlates of internalized homophobia: A factor analytic study. *Journal of Clinical Psychology*, *52*, 15–21.

11091

Test Name: RECIPROCAL ATTACHMENT QUESTIONNAIRE

Purpose: To measure adult attachment.

Number of Items: 43

Format: Includes five dimensions—Proximity Seeking, Separation Protest, Feared Loss, Availability, and Use—and 4 patterns—angry withdrawal, compulsive caregiving, compulsive self-reliance, and compulsive care seeking. Responses are made on a 5-point scale ranging from 1 (*strongly agree*) to 5 (*strongly disagree*).

Validity: Correlations with other variables ranged from −.27 to .49.

Author: DiTommaso, E., et al.

Article: Measurement and validity characteristics of the short version of the Social and Emotional Loneliness Scale for Adults.

Journal: *Educational and Psychological Measurement*, February 2004, *64*, 99–119.

Related Research: West, L. M., & Sheldon-Keller, A.-E. (1994). *Patterns of relating: An adult attachment perspective*. New York: Guilford Press.

11092

Test Name: RELATIONAL–INTERDEPENDENT SELF-CONSTRUAL SCALE

Purpose: To assess one's feelings of being close to and connected to other people.

Number of Items: 11

Format: Responses are made on a 7-point scale.

Validity: Correlations with the Relationship Profile Test ranged from −.21 to .33.

Author: Bornstein, R. F., et al.

Article: Construct validity of the Relationship Profile Test: A self-report measure of dependency–detachment.

Journal: *Journal of Personality Assessment*, February 2003, *80*, 64–74.

Related Research: Cross, S. E., et al. (2000). The relational–interdependent self-construal and relationships. *Journal of Personality and Social Psychology, 78*, 791–808.

11093

Test Name: RELATIONAL SATISFACTION SCALE

Purpose: To measure relationship satisfaction.

Number of Items: 12

Format: Response scales range from 1 (*strongly disagree*) to 5 (*strongly agree*).

Reliability: Coefficient alpha was .87.

Validity: Correlations ranged from −.58 to .72.

Author: Myers, S. A., and Goodboy, A. K.

Article: A study of grouphate in a course on small group communication.

Journal: *Psychological Reports*, October 2005, *97*, 381–386.

Related Research: Anderson, C. M., et al. (2001). Small Group Relational Satisfaction Scale: Development, reliability and validity. *Communication Studies, 52*, 220–233.

11094

Test Name: RELATIONSHIP ASSESSMENT SCALE

Purpose: To measure relationship satisfaction.

Number of Items: 7

Format: Five-point response scales are used. Sample items are presented.

Reliability: Alpha coefficients ranged from .65 to .87.

Author: Sprecher, S.

Article: Equity and social exchange in dating couples: Associations with satisfaction, commitment, and stability.

Journal: *Journal of Marriage and Family*, August 2001, *63*, 599–613.

Related Research: Hendrick, S. S. (1988). A generic measure of relationship satisfaction. *Journal of Marriage and the Family, 50*, 93–98.

11095

Test Name: RELATIONSHIP COMMITMENT SCALE

Purpose: To measure commitment to a relationship.

Number of Items: 5

Format: Seven-point response scales are used. Sample items are presented.

Reliability: Alpha coefficients ranged from .52 to .97.

Author: Sprecher, S.

Article: Equity and social exchange in dating couples: Associations with satisfaction, commitment, and stability.

Journal: *Journal of Marriage and Family*, August 2001, *63*, 599–613.

Related Research: Lund, M. (1985). The development of investment and commitment scales for predicting continuity of personal relationships. *Journal of Personal and Social Relationships, 2*, 3–23.

11096

Test Name: RELATIONSHIP PROFILE TEST

Purpose: To measure dependency–detachment.

Number of Items: 30

Format: Includes three subscales: Destructive Dependence, Dysfunctional Detachment, and Healthy Dependency. Responses are made on a 7-point scale ranging from 1 (*not at all true of me*) to 7 (*very true of me*). Sample items are presented.

Reliability: Alpha coefficients ranged from .68 to .83. Test–retest (23 weeks) correlations ranged from .23 to .80. Test–retest (85 weeks) correlations ranged from .45 to .67.

Validity: Correlations with other variables ranged from –.48 to .71.

Author: Bornstein, R. F., et al.

Article: Constant validity of the Relationship Profile Test: A self-report measure of dependency–detachment.

Journal: *Journal of Personality Assessment*, February 2003, *80*, 64–74.

Related Research: Bornstein, R. F., & Languirand, M. A. (2003). *Healthy dependency.* New York: Newmarket.

11097

Test Name: RELATIONSHIP QUESTIONNAIRE

Purpose: To measure adult relational orientation.

Number of Items: 4

Format: Includes four descriptive paragraphs: secure, dismissive, preoccupied, and fearful attachment styles. Responses are made on a 5-point scale ranging from 1 (*not at all like me*) to 5 (*very much like me*). Examples are given.

Validity: Correlations with other variables ranged from –.30 to .48.

Author: Wolfe, J. B., and Betz, N. E.

Article: The relationship of attachment variables to career

decision-making self-efficacy and fear of commitment.

Journal: *The Career Development Quarterly*, June 2004, *52*, 363–369.

Related Research: Bartholomew, K., & Horowitz, L. M. (1991). Attachment styles among young adults: A test of a four-category model. *Journal of Personality and Social Psychology, 61*, 226–244.

11098

Test Name: RELATIONSHIP SCALES QUESTIONNAIRE

Purpose: To assess adult attachment prototypes.

Number of Items: 30

Format: Includes four adult attachment prototypes: secure, fearful, preoccupied, and dismissing. Responses are made on a 5-point scale ranging from 1 (*not at all like me*) to 5 (*very like me*).

Validity: Correlations with other variables ranged from –.43 to .42.

Author: DiTommaso, E., et al.

Article: Measurement and validity characteristics of the short version of the Social and Emotional Loneliness Scale for Adults.

Journal: *Educational and Psychological Measurement*, February 2004, *64*, 99–119.

Related Research: Griffin, D. W., & Bartholomew, K. (1994). The metaphysics of measurement: The case of adult attachment. In K. Bartholomew & D. P. Pearlman (Eds.), *Advances in personal relationships: Vol. 5. Adult attachment relationships* (pp. 17–52). London: Jessica Kingsley.

11099

Test Name: RELATIONSHIPS WITH OTHER PEOPLE SCALE

Purpose: To assess social support.

Number of Items: 11

Format: Scales range from 1 (*none of the time*) to 6 (*all of the time*). A sample item is presented.

Reliability: Coefficient alpha was .90.

Author: Mulsow, M., et al.

Article: Multilevel factors influencing maternal stress during the first three years.

Journal: *Journal of Marriage and Family*, November 2002, *64*, 944–956.

Related Research: Marshall, N. L., & Barnett, R. C. (1993). Work–family strains and gains among two-earner couples. *Journal of Community Psychology, 21*, 64–78.

11100

Test Name: RELATIVE DEPRIVATION SCALE

Purpose: To assess relative deprivation.

Number of Items: 8

Format: Responses are made on a 5-point scale ranging from 1 (*never*) to 5 (*often*). All items are presented.

Reliability: Coefficient alpha was .78.

Validity: Correlations with other variables ranged from –.09 to .36.

Author: Buunk, B. P., et al.

Article: Engaging in upward and downward comparisons as a determinant of relative deprivation at work: A longitudinal study.

Journal: *Journal of Vocational Behavior*, April 2003, *62*, 370–388.

Related Research: Buunk, B. P., & Janssen, P. P. M. (1992). Relative deprivation and mental health among men in midlife. *Journal of Vocational Behavior, 40*, 338–350.

11101

Test Name: RESTRICTIVE EMOTIONALITY SCALE

Purpose: To assess a male participant's difficulty in expressing his feelings as well as his denying others their right to emotional expression.

Number of Items: 10

Format: Responses are made on a 6-point scale ranging from 1 (*strongly disagree*) to 6 (*strongly agree*). An example is presented.

Reliability: Alpha coefficients were .84 and .85. Test–retest (4 weeks) reliability was .76.

Validity: Correlations with other variables ranged from –.38 to .51.

Author: Bruch, M. A.

Article: Shyness and toughness: Unique and moderated relations with men's emotional impression.

Journal: *Journal of Counseling Psychology,* January 2002, *49,* 28–34.

Related Research: O'Neil, J. M., et al. (1995). Fifteen years of research on men's gender role conflict: New paradigms for empirical research. In R. Levent & W. Pollack (Eds.), *Foundations for a new psychology of men* (pp. 164–206). New York: Basic Books.

11102

Test Name: REVISED AESTHETIC EXPERIENCE SCALE

Purpose: To measure cognitive synergies and elaboration, emotional closeness, experimental emotional distancing, paratelic mode, and expressive perception.

Number of Items: 28

Format: Item responses are anchored by 1 (*never*) and 5 (*very often*). All items are presented.

Reliability: Alpha coefficients ranged from .63 to .75 across subscales.

Validity: Correlations with other variables ranged from .27 to .50.

Author: Stamatopoulou, D.

Article: Integrating the philosophy and psychology of aesthetic experience: Development of the Aesthetic Experience Scale.

Journal: *Psychological Reports,* October 2004, *95,* 673–695.

11103

Test Name: REVISED CLASS PLAY—CHINESE VERSION

Purpose: To provide peer assessments of social functioning.

Number of Items: 30

Format: Includes three variables: sociability–cooperation, aggression–disruption, and shyness–sensitivity. Examples are given.

Reliability: Internal reliabilities ranged from .73 to .97. Test–retest (2 weeks) reliabilities ranged from .84 to .97 ($N = 132$).

Validity: Correlations with other variables ranged from –.76 to .75.

Author: Chen, X., et al.

Article: Social functioning and adjustment in Chinese children: The imprint of historical time.

Journal: *Child Development,* January/February 2005, *76,* 182–195.

Related Research: Masten, A., et al. (1985). A revised class play method of peer assessment. *Developmental Psychology, 21,* 523–533.

11104

Test Name: REVISED SOCIAL ANHEDONIA SCALE

Purpose: To measure lack of interest or pleasure in interpersonal relationships.

Number of Items: 40

Format: Sample items are presented.

Reliability: Coefficient alpha was .79.

Validity: Correlation with other variables ranged from –.59 to .44.

Author: Ross, S. R., et al.

Article: Positive and negative symptoms of schizotypy and the five-factor model: A domain and facet level analysis.

Journal: *Journal of Personality Assessment,* August 2002, *79,* 53–72.

Related Research: Mishlove, M., & Chapman, L. J. (1985). Social anhedonia in the prediction of psychosis proneness. *Journal of Abnormal Psychology, 94,* 384–396.

11105

Test Name: REVISED TEASING QUESTIONNAIRE

Purpose: To measure memories for teasing during childhood.

Number of Items: 35

Format: Responses are made on 5-point scales ranging from 0 (*I was never teased about this*) to 4 (*I was always teased about this*) and 0 (*I did not feel upset about this at all*) to 4 (*I felt extremely upset about this*).

Reliability: Alpha coefficients were .85 and .88.

Validity: Correlations with other variables ranged from –.29 to .41.

Author: Storch, E. A., et al.

Article: Psychosocial adjustment in early adulthood: The role of childhood teasing and father support.

Journal: *Child Study Journal,* 2003, *33,* 153–163.

Related Research: Roth, D., et al. (2002). The relationship between memories for childhood teasing and anxiety and depression in adulthood. *Journal of Anxiety Disorders, 16*, 149–164.

11106

Test Name: ROMANTIC ACTS SCALE

Purpose: To measure the importance of romantic acts (trust and support, kindness and offerings, and sexual relationships).

Number of Items: 18

Format: Scales range from 1 (*not important at all*) to 7 (*extremely important*).

Reliability: Alpha coefficients ranged from .79 to .91.

Validity: Correlations with other variables ranged from .15 to .21.

Author: Neto, F.

Article: The Satisfaction With Love Life Scale.

Journal: *Measurement and Evaluation in Counseling and Development*, April 2005, *38*, 2–13.

11107

Test Name: ROMANTIC LOVE AND LIKING FOR PARTNER SCALES

Purpose: To measure romantic love.

Number of Items: 26

Format: Scales range from 1 (*not at all true*) to 5 (*definitely true*). Sample items are presented.

Reliability: Alpha coefficients ranged from .83 to .89 across subscales and husband and wife respondents.

Validity: Correlations with other variables ranged from –.24 to .57.

Author: Kurdek, L. A.

Article: Predicting the timing of separation and marital satisfaction: An eight-year prospective longitudinal study.

Journal: *Journal of Marriage and Family*, February 2002, *64*, 163–179.

Related Research: Rubin, Z. (1970). Measurement of romantic love. *Journal of Personality and Social Psychology, 16*, 265–273.

11108

Test Name: RUBIN LOVE SCALE

Purpose: To measure romantic love.

Number of Items: 11

Format: Responses are made on a 7-point Likert-type scale ranging from 1 (*strongly disagree*) to 7 (*strongly agree*).

Reliability: Internal consistency ranged from .68 to .86.

Validity: Correlations with other variables ranged from –.03 to .56.

Author: Perrone, K. M., & Worthington, E. L, Jr.

Article: Factors influencing ratings of marital quality by individuals within dual-career marriages: A conceptual model.

Journal: *Journal of Counseling Psychology*, January 2001, *48*, 3–9.

Related Research: Rubin, Z. (1970). Measurement of romantic love. *Journal of Personality and Social Psychology, 16*, 265–273.

11109

Test Name: SATISFACTION WITH LOVE LIFE SCALE

Purpose: To measure satisfaction with love life.

Number of Items: 5

Format: Seven-point agreement scales are used. All items are presented.

Reliability: Coefficient alpha was .91.

Validity: Correlations with other variables ranged from –.25 to .77.

Author: Neto, F.

Article: The Satisfaction With Love Life Scale.

Journal: *Measurement and Evaluation in Counseling and Development*, April 2005, *38*, 2–13.

11110

Test Name: SCALE OF ACCULTURATION STRATEGIES—CROATIAN AND POLISH VERSIONS

Purpose: To measure relationships with a host group and maintenance of original culture.

Number of Items: 26

Format: Scales range from 1 (*completely disagree*) to 5 (*completely agree*). Sample items are presented in English.

Reliability: Alpha coefficients exceeded .74.

Validity: Correlations with other variables ranged from –.30 to .51.

Author: Kosic, A.

Article: Acculturation attitudes, need for cognitive closure, and adaptation of immigrants.

Journal: *The Journal of Social Psychology*, April 2002, *142*, 179–201.

11111

Test Name: SCALE OF ETHNOCULTURAL EMPATHY

Purpose: To measure ethnocultural empathy.

Number of Items: 31

Format: Includes four subscales: Empathic Feeling and Expression, Empathic Perspective Taking, Acceptance of Cultural Differences, and Empathic Awareness.

Reliability: Alpha coefficients ranged from .61 to .90.

Validity: Correlations with other variables ranged from −.46 to .67.

Author: Spanierman, L. B., and Heppner, M. J.

Article: Psychological Costs of Racism to Whites Scale (PCRW): Construction and initial validation.

Journal: *Journal of Counseling Psychology*, April 2004, *51*, 249–262.

Related Research: Wand, Y., et al. (2003). The Scale of Ethnocultral Empathy: Development, validation, and reliability. *Journal of Counseling Psychology, 50,* 221–234.

11112

Test Name: SCALE OF FEELINGS AND BEHAVIOR OF LOVE—REVISED

Purpose: To measure the feelings and behavior of people who say they are in love.

Number of Items: 120

Format: Scales range from 1 (*never*) to 5 (*always*).

Reliability: Alpha coefficients ranged from .78 to .97 across subscales. Total alpha was .95.

Author: Myers, J. E., and Shurts, M.

Article: Measuring positive emotionality: A review of instruments assessing love.

Journal: *Measurement and Evaluation in Counseling and Development*, January 2002, *34*, 238–254.

Related Research: Swenson, C. H. et al. (1992). Scale of Feelings and Behavior

of Love: Revised. In L. Vandecreek et al. (Eds.), *Innovations in clinical practice: A source book*. (Vol. 11 pp. 303–314). Sarasota, FL: Professional Resource Press.

11113

Test Name: SCALE OF INTERPERSONAL BEHAVIOR

Purpose: To measure discomfort and tension an individual perceives in four situations.

Number of Items: 50

Format: Scales range from 1 (*not at all*) to 5 (*extremely*). Sample items are presented in English.

Reliability: Alpha coefficients ranged from .78 to .83.

Author: Nota, L., and Soresi, S.

Article: An assertiveness training program for indecisive students attending an Italian university.

Journal: *The Career Development Quarterly*, June 2003, *51*, 322–334.

Related Research: Arrindell, W. A., et al. (1984). *Se Schaal voor Interpersoonlijk Gedrag (SIG): Handluding deel I* [The Scale for Interpersonal Behavior (SIB)]. Lisse, the Netherlands: Swets and Zeitlinger.

11114

Test Name: SELF-CONSTRUAL SCALE

Purpose: To assess the degree to which individuals see themselves as connected to or separate from others.

Number of Items: 24

Format: Sample items are presented.

Reliability: Alpha coefficients ranged from .54 to .74.

Validity: Correlations with other variables ranged from −.53 to .18.

Author: Dinnel, D. L., et al.

Article: A cross-cultural comparison of social phobia symptoms.

Journal: *Journal of Psychopathology and Behavioral Assessment*, June 2001, *24*, 75–84.

Related Research: Singelis, T. M. (1994). The measurement of independent and interdependent self-construals. *Personality and Social Psychology Bulletin, 20,* 580–591.

11115

Test Name: SELF–OTHER DIFFERENTIATION SCALE

Purpose: To assess the degree to which people experience a separate sense of self in their relationships with others.

Number of Items: 11

Format: Responses are either 0 (*true*) or 1 (*false*). An example is given.

Reliability: Alpha coefficients were .76 and .78.

Validity: Correlations with other variables ranged from −.50 to .09.

Author: Lopez, F. G.

Article: Adult attachment orientation, self–other boundary regulation, and splitting tendencies in a college sample.

Journal: *Journal of Counseling Psychology*, October 2001, *48*, 440–446.

Related Research: Olver, R. R., et al. (1990). Self–other differentiation and the mother–child relationship: The effects of sex and birth order. *Journal of Genetic Psychology, 150,* 311–321.

11116

Test Name: SELF PERCEPTION PROFILE

Purpose: To measure social competence.

Number of Items: 12.

Format: Includes two subscales: Social and Global. Examples are presented.

Reliability: Alpha coefficients for each subscale were .75.

Validity: Correlations with other variables ranged from –.62 to .44 ($N = 53$).

Author: Lockwood, R. L., et al.

Article: The impact of sibling warmth and conflict on children's social competence with peers.

Journal: *Child Study Journal,* 2001, *31,* 47–69

Related Research: Harter, S. (1982). The Perceived Competence Scale for Children. *Child Development, 53,* 87–97.

11117

Test Name: SELF-PERCEPTION PROFILE FOR CHILDREN—2 SUBSCALES

Purpose: To measure children's perceived social and self-acceptance.

Number of Items: 12

Format: Includes measures of perceived social acceptance and perceptions of self-acceptance. Examples are given.

Reliability: Alpha coefficients were .74 and .75.

Author: Ladd, G. W., and Troop-Gordon, W.

Article: The role of chronic peer difficulties in the development of children's psychological adjustment problems.

Journal: *Child Development,* September/October 2003, *74,* 1344–1367.

Related Research: Harter, S. (1985). *The self-perception profile for children.* Unpublished manual, University of Denver, Denver, CO.

11118

Test Name: SENSE OF COHERENCE SCALE

Purpose: To measure sense of coherence in interactions in terms of comprehensibility, manageability, and meaningfulness.

Number of Items: 29

Format: Sample items are presented with their appropriate 7-point response scales.

Reliability: Alpha coefficients ranged from .86 to .96.

Validity: Correlations with other variables ranged from –.37 to –.29.

Author: Lustig, D. C., and Strauser, D. R.

Article: The relationship between sense of coherence and career thoughts.

Journal: *The Career Development Quarterly,* September 2002, *51,* 2–11.

Related Research: Antonovsky, A. (1993). The structure and properties of the Sense of Coherence Scale. *Social Science and Medicine, 36,* 725–733.

11119

Test Name: SENSE OF COMMUNITY SCALE

Purpose: To measure sense of community.

Number of Items: 10

Format: All items are presented. A Likert format is used.

Reliability: Coefficient alpha was .87.

Validity: Correlations with other variables ranged from –.23 to .57.

Author: Clark, S. C.

Article: Work cultures and work/family balance.

Journal: *Journal of Vocational Behavior,* June 2001, *58,* 348–365.

Related Research: Clark, S. C., & Farmer, P. M. K. (1998, October). *Living in two different worlds: Measuring cultural and value differences between work and home, and their effect on border-crossing.* Paper presented at the annual meeting of the Institute of Behavioral and Applied Management, Orlando, FL.

11120

Test Name: SEPARATENESS SCALE

Purpose: To measure feelings of being separate from others.

Number of Items: 9

Format: Includes two factors: independence/individuality and self–other boundary. Responses are made on a 5-point scale.

Validity: Correlations with the Relationship Profile Test ranged from –.09 to .27.

Author: Bornstein, R. F., et al.

Article: Construct validity of the Relationship Profile Test: A self-report measure of dependency–detachment.

Journal: *Journal of Personality Assessment,* February 2003, *80,* 64–74.

Related Research: Wang, C. L., & Mowen, J. C. (1997). The separateness–connectedness self-schema. *Psychology and Marketing, 14,* 185–207.

11121

Test Name: SERVICE ORIENTATION SCALE

Purpose: To assess the degree to which an employee tries to get along and be helpful to others.

Number of Items: 5

Format: Scales range from 1 (*strongly disagree*) to 7 (*strongly agree*). All items are presented.

Reliability: Coefficient alpha was .77.

Validity: Correlations with other variables ranged from .18 to .53.

Author: Bettencourt, L. A., et al.

Article: A comparison of attitude, personality, and knowledge predictors of service-oriented organizational citizenship behaviors.

Journal: *Journal of Applied Psychology*, February 2001, *86*, 29–41.

Related Research: Cran, D. J. (1994). Towards validation of the service orientation construct. *The Services Industries Journal*, *14*, 34–44.

11122

Test Name: SEXUAL HARASSMENT COPING STRATEGIES SCALE

Purpose: To measure coping with sexual harassment as avoidance–denial, social coping, confrontation, and advocacy-seeking.

Number of Items: 26

Format: A yes–no format is used. All items are presented.

Reliability: Alpha coefficients ranged from .57 to .81.

Validity: Correlations with other variables ranged from −.10 to .55.

Author: Malamut, A. B., and Offermann, L. R.

Article: Coping with sexual harassment: Personal, environmental, and cognitive determinants.

Journal: *Journal of Applied Psychology*, December 2001, *86*, 1152–1166.

11123

Test Name: SEXUAL MINORITY DISCRIMINATION SCALE

Purpose: To assess the prevalence of treatment discrimination faced by lesbians and gay men in an organization.

Number of Items: 9

Format: Scales range from 1 (*strongly disagree*) to 7 (*strongly agree*). All items are presented. Scoring methods are described.

Reliability: Coefficient alpha was .97 (calculated on the basis of averaged item intercorrelations in the between-group matrix).

Validity: Correlations with other variables ranged from −.78 to .24.

Author: Button, S. B.

Article: Organizational efforts to affirm sexual diversity: A cross-level examination.

Journal: *Journal of Applied Psychology*, February 2001, *86*, 17–28.

11124

Test Name: SHORT ACCULTURATION SCALE

Purpose: To assess the extent to which one used English versus Spanish and interacted with Latinos versus Americans.

Number of Items: 12

Format: Includes three subscales: Language, Media, and Ethnic Social Relations. Responses are made on a 5-point scale ranging from 1 (*mostly Spanish/Mexican*) to 5 (*mostly English/American*).

Reliability: Alpha coefficients ranged from .78 to .92.

Validity: Correlations with other variables ranged from −.27 to .19.

Author: Caldera, Y. M., et al.

Article: Intrapersonal, familial, and cultural factors in the commitment to a career choice of Mexican

American and non-Hispanic White college woman.

Journal: *Journal of Counseling Psychology*, July 2003, *50*, 309–323.

Related Research: Marin, G., et al. (1987). Development of a short acculturation scale for Hispanics. *Hispanic Journal of Behavioral Sciences*, *9*, 183–205.

11125

Test Name: SILENCING THE SELF SCALE

Purpose: To identify behaviors and beliefs about oneself in relationships with others.

Number of Items: 31

Format: Includes four subscales: Externalized Self-Perception, Care as Self-Sacrifice, Silencing the Self, and Divided Self. Responses are made on a 5-point scale ranging from 1 (*strongly disagree*) to 5 (*strongly agree*). Examples are given.

Reliability: Alpha coefficients ranged from .86 to .94. Test–retest reliabilities ranged from .88 to .93.

Validity: Correlations with other variables ranged from .27 to .53.

Author: Piran, N., and Cormier, H. C.

Article: The social construction of women and disordered eating patterns.

Journal: *Journal of Counseling Psychology*, October 2005, *52*, 549–558.

Related Research: Jack, D., & Dill, D. (1992). The Silencing the Self Scale. *Psychology of Women Quarterly*, *16*, 97–106.

11126

Test Name: SITUATIONAL, ATTITUDINAL, FAMILIAL, AND ENVIRONMENTAL ACCULTURATION STRESS SCALE—SHORT FORM

Purpose: To measure acculturative stress.

Number of Items: 24

Format: Responses are made on a 5-point scale ranging from 1 (*not stressful*) to 5 (*extremely stressful*). A sample item is presented.

Reliability: Alpha coefficients were .89 and .93.

Validity: Correlations with other variables ranged from −.16 to .17.

Author: Kim, B. S. K., and Omizo, M. M.

Article: Asian and European American cultural values, collective self-esteem, acculturative stress, cognitive flexibility, and general self-efficacy among Asian American college students.

Journal: *Journal of Counseling Psychology*, July 2005, *52*, 412–419.

Related Research: Padilla, A. M., et al. (1985). Acculturation and personality as predictors of stress in Japanese and Japanese-Americans. *The Journal of Social Psychology*, *125*, 295–305. Mena, F. J., et al. (1987). Acculturative stress and specific coping strategies among immigrant and later generation college students. *Hispanic Journal of Behavioral Sciences*, *9*, 207–225.

11127

Test Name: SOCIAL AND EMOTIONAL LONELINESS SCALE FOR ADULTS—S

Purpose: To provide a multidimensional loneliness measure.

Number of Items: 15

Format: Includes three factors: romantic, family, and social. Responses are made on a 7-point Likert-type scale ranging from 1 (*strongly disagree*) to 7 (*strongly agree*). All items are presented.

Reliability: Alpha coefficients ranged from .85 to .90 (*n* = 1,526).

Validity: Correlations with other variables ranged from −.62 to .48.

Author: DiTommaso, E., et al.

Article: Measurement and validity characteristics of the short version of the Social and Emotional Loneliness Scale for Adults.

Journal: *Educational and Psychological Measurement*, February 2004, *64*, 99–119.

Related Research: DiTommaso, E. (1997). *Assessing an attachment model of loneliness: The relationship between attachment style, chronic loneliness, and coping.* Unpublished dissertation, University of New Brunswick, Fredericton, New Brunswick, Canada.

11128

Test Name: SOCIAL ANXIETY AND SOCIAL AVOIDANCE SCALE

Purpose: To assess social adjustment.

Number of Items: 12

Format: Responses are anchored by 1 (*not at all true about me*) and 5 (*always true about me*). A sample item is presented.

Reliability: Alpha coefficients ranged from .74 to .91.

Author: Johnson, H. D., et al.

Article: Peer conflict avoidance: Associations with loneliness, social anxiety, and social avoidance.

Journal: *Psychological Reports*, February 2001, *88*, 227–235.

Related Research: Franke, S., & Hymel, S. (1984). Social anxiety and avoidance in children: The development of a self-report measure. Paper presented at the Biennial University of Waterloo Conference on Child Development, Waterloo, Ontario.

11129

Test Name: SOCIAL ANXIETY SCALE

Purpose: To evaluate fear and avoidance of 11 social interactions.

Number of Items: 24

Format: Scales range from 0 (*no anxiety/avoidance*) to 100 (*severe anxiety/avoidance*).

Reliability: Coefficient alpha was .94.

Author: Moscovitch, D. A., et al.

Article: Mediation of changes in anxiety and depression during treatment of social phobia.

Journal: *Journal of Consulting and Clinical Psychology*, October 2005, *73*, 945–952.

Related Research: Liebowitz, M. R. (1987). Social phobia. *Modern Problems of Pharmacopsychiatry*, *22*, 141–173.

11130

Test Name: SOCIAL ANXIETY SCALE FOR ADOLESCENTS

Purpose: To measure fear of negative evaluation and social avoidance and distress.

Number of Items: 22

Format: Scales range from 1 (*not at all*) to 5 (*all the time*).

Validity: Total scale correlations with other variables ranged from .56 to .92.

Author: Garcia-López, L. J., et al.

Article: Psychometric properties of the Social Phobia and Anxiety Inventory, the Social Anxiety Scale for Adolescents, the Fear of Negative Evaluation Scale, and the Social Avoidance and Distress Scale in an adolescent Spanish-speaking sample.

Journal: *Journal of Psychopathology and Behavioral Assessment*, March 2001, *23*, 51–59.

Related Research: LeGreca, A. M., & Stone, W. L. (1993). The Social Anxiety Scale for Children—Revised: Factor structure and concurrent validity. *Journal of Clinical Child Psychology, 22,* 17–27.

11131

Test Name: SOCIAL ANXIETY SCALE FOR CHILDREN—REVISED

Purpose: To measure subjective experiences of social anxiety and its behavioral consequences.

Number of Items: 22

Format: Scales range from 1 (*not at all*) to 5 (*all the time*). Sample items are presented.

Reliability: Alpha coefficients ranged from .69 to .86.

Validity: Correlations with other variables ranged from –.09 to .75.

Author: Higa, C. K., et al.

Article: Psychometric properties and clinical utility of the School Refusal Assessment Scale in a multiethnic sample.

Journal: *Journal of Psychopathology and Behavioral Assessment,* December 2002, *24,* 247–258.

Related Research: LaGreca, A. M., & Stone, W. L. (1993). The Social Anxiety Scale for Children—Revised: Factor structure and concurrent validity. *Journal Clinical Child Psychology, 22,* 17–27.

11132

Test Name: SOCIAL ANXIETY SUBSCALE

Purpose: To measure social reticence and social performance difficulties.

Number of Items: 6

Format: Includes new situations, being observed, embarrassing events, and large groups. Responses are made on a 3-point scale ranging from 1 (*a little like me*) to 2 (*somewhat like me*) to 3 (*a lot like me*). An example is given.

Reliability: Coefficient alpha was .70. Test–retest reliability was .73.

Author: Anderson, S. L., and Betz, N. E.

Article: Sources of social self-efficacy expectation: Their measurement and relation to career development.

Journal: *Journal of Vocational Behavior,* February 2001, *58,* 98–117.

Related Research: Scheier, M. F., & Carver, C. S. (1985). The Self-Consciousness Scale: A revised version for use with general populations. *Journal of Applied Social Psychology, 15,* 687–699.

11133

Test Name: SOCIAL AVOIDANCE AND DISTRESS SCALE

Purpose: To measure social anxiety.

Number of Items: 28

Format: Responses are made on a 5-point Likert-type response scale. An example is given.

Reliability: Reliability coefficients were .91 to .94.

Validity: Correlations with other variables ranged from –.44 to .54.

Author: Hardin, E. E., and Leong, F. T. L.

Article: Optimism and pessimism as mediators of the relations between self-discrepancies and distress among Asian and European Americans.

Journal: *Journal of Counseling Psychology,* January 2005, *52,* 25–35.

Related Research: Watson, D., & Friend, R. (1969). Measurements of social-evaluative anxiety. *Journal of Consulting and Clinical Psychology, 33,* 448–457.

11134

Test Name: SOCIAL COGNITION AND OBJECT RELATIONS SCALE

Purpose: To measure interpersonal functioning, personality functioning, and object relations.

Number of Items: 8

Format: The eight subscales involve: Complexity, Affect, Relationships, Morals, Causality, Aggression, Self-Esteem, and Identity. Responses are made on a 7-point scale.

Reliability: Interater reliability ranged from .70 to .95.

Author: Callahan, K. L., et al.

Article: Psychological assessment of adult survivors of childhood sexual abuse within a naturalistic clinical sample.

Journal: *Journal of Personality Assessment,* April 2003, *80,* 173–184.

Related Research: Westen, D. (1995). *Social Cognition and Object Relations Scale: Q-sort for projective stories (SCORES-Q).* Unpublished manuscript, Department of Psychiatry, The Cambridge Hospital and Harvard Medical School, Cambridge, MA.

11135

Test Name: SOCIAL COHESION MEASURE

Purpose: To measure social cohesion.

Number of Items: 4

Format: Encompasses team unity, interpersonal trust, team spirit, and cooperative communication.

Responses are made on a 6-point scale ranging from 1 (*strongly disagree*) to 6 (*strongly agree*). All items are given.

Reliability: Coefficient alpha was .82.

Validity: Correlations with other variables ranged from –.01 to .61.

Author: Hirschfeld, R. R., et al.

Article: Teams' female representation and perceived potency as inputs to team outcomes in a predominantly male field setting.

Journal: *Personnel Psychology*, Winter 2005, *58*, 893–924.

Related Research: Seers, A. (1989). Team-member exchange quality: A new construct for role-making research. *Organizational Behavior and Human Decision Processes, 43*, 118–135.

11136

Test Name: SOCIAL CONNECTEDNESS SCALE—CAMPUS VERSION

Purpose: To measure social adjustment–distress among various Asian ethnic groups.

Number of Items: 14

Format: Responses are made on a 6-point scale ranging from 1 (*strongly disagree*) to 6 (*strongly agree*).

Reliability: Internal reliability estimates ranged from .90 to .93.

Validity: Correlations with other variables ranged from –.66 to .52.

Author: Lee, R. M.

Article: Resilience against discrimination: Ethnic identity and other-group orientation as protective factors for Korean Americans.

Journal: *Journal of Counseling Psychology*, January 2005, *52*, 36–44.

Related Research: Lee, R. M., et al. (2001). Social connectedness, dysfunctional interpersonal behaviors, and psychological distress: Testing a mediator model. *Journal of Counseling Psychology, 48*, 310–318.

11137

Test Name: SOCIAL CONNECTEDNESS SCALE—REVISED

Purpose: To assess social connectedness.

Number of Items: 20

Format: Responses are made on a 6-point Likert scale ranging from 1 (*strongly disagree*) to 6 (*strongly agree*). All items are presented.

Reliability: Coefficient alpha was .94.

Author: Lee, R. M., et al.

Article: Social connectedness, dysfunctional interpersonal behaviors, and psychological distress: Testing a mediator model.

Journal: *Journal of Counseling Psychology*, July 2001, *48*, 310–318.

Related Research: Lee, R. M., & Robbins, S. B. (1995). Measuring belongingness: The Social Connectedness and the Social Assurances scales. *Journal of Counseling Psychology, 42*, 232–241.

11138

Test Name: SOCIAL CONSTRAINTS SCALE

Purpose: To measure the responses that inhibit the expression of cancer-related thoughts.

Number of Items: 15

Format: Rating scales range from 1 (*never*) to 4 (*often*).

Validity: Correlations with other variables ranged from –.57 to .62.

Author: Cordova, M. J., et al.

Article: Social constraints, cognitive processing, and adjustment to breast cancer.

Journal: *Journal of Consulting and Clinical Psychology*, August 2001, *69*, 706–711.

Related Research: Lepore, S. J., & Ituarte, P. H. G. (1999). Optimism about cancer enhances mood by reducing negative social relations. *Cancer Research, Therapy and Control, 8*, 165–174.

11139

Test Name: SOCIAL CONSTRAINTS SCALE—SPOUSE

Purpose: To assess a cancer patient's perceptions of their spouse's responses that they perceived to block cancer-related thoughts and feelings.

Number of Items: 15

Format: Scales range from 1 (*never*) to 4 (*often*). Sample items are presented.

Reliability: Coefficient alpha was .86.

Validity: Correlations with other variables ranged from .03 to .48.

Author: Quartana, P. J., et al.

Article: Gender, neuroticism, and emotional expressivity: Effects on spousal constraints among individuals with cancer.

Journal: *Journal of Consulting and Clinical Psychology*, August 2005, *73*, 769–776.

11140

Test Name: SOCIAL DISTANCE SCALE

Purpose: To measure the willingness to associate with a target person or group.

Number of Items: 5

Format: Item anchors range from 0 (*definitely willing*) to 3 (*definitely unwilling*). All items are presented.

Reliability: Coefficient alpha was .72.

Author: Walkup, J., et al.

Article: How is stigmatization affected by the "layering" of stigmatized conditions such as serious mental illness and HIV?

Journal: *Psychological Reports*, December 2004, *95*, Part 1, 771–779.

Related Research: Link, B. G., et al. (1987). The social rejection of former mental patients: Understanding why labels matter. *American Journal of Sociology, 92,* 1461–1499.

11141

Test Name: SOCIAL DOMINANCE ORIENTATION SCALE

Purpose: To assess social dominance orientation.

Number of Items: 16

Format: Responses are made on a 7-point scale ranging from 1 (*very negative*) to 7 (*very positive*). Examples are given.

Reliability: Coefficient alpha was .90.

Validity: Correlations with other variables ranged from −.25 to .18.

Author: Aquino, K., et al.

Article: How social dominance orientation and job status influence perceptions of African-American affirmative action beneficiaries.

Journal: *Personnel Psychology*, Autumn 2005, *58*, 703–744.

Related Research: Sidanius, J., & Pratto, F. (1999). *Social dominance: An intergroup theory of social hierarchy and oppression.* New York: Cambridge University Press.

11142

Test Name: SOCIAL DOMINANCE ORIENTATION SCALE

Purpose: To measure group dominance and anti-egalitarianism.

Number of Items: 5

Format: Scales range from 1 (*strongly disagree*) to 5 (*strongly agree*). All items are presented.

Reliability: Reliability coefficients exceeded .77.

Validity: Correlations with other variables ranged from −.25 to .16.

Author: Peña, Y., and Sidanius, J.

Article: U.S. patriotism and ideologies of group dominance: A tale of asymmetry.

Journal: *The Journal of Social Psychology*, December 2002, *142*, 782–790.

Related Research: Pratto, F., et al. (1994). Social dominance orientation: A personality variable predicting social and political attitudes. *Journal of Personality and Social Psychology, 67,* 741–763.

11143

Test Name: SOCIAL DOMINANCE ORIENTATION SCALE

Purpose: To measure social dominance orientation.

Number of Items: 14

Format: Responses are made on a 7-point scale ranging from 1 (*very negative*) to 7 (*very positive*). Examples are given.

Reliability: Alpha coefficients ranged from .70 to .93.

Validity: Correlations with other variables ranged from −.41 to .30 ($n = 312$).

Author: Worthington, R. L., et al.

Article: Development, reliability, and validity of the Lesbian, Gay,

and Bisexual Knowledge and Attitudes Scale for Heterosexuals (LGB-KASH).

Journal: *Journal of Counseling Psychology*, January 2005, *52*, 104–118.

Related Research: Sidanius, J., & Pratto, F. (1999). *Social dominance: An intergroup theory of social hierarchy and oppression.* New York: Cambridge University Press.

11144

Test Name: SOCIAL ENGAGEMENT/ DISENGAGEMENT SCALES

Purpose: To measure social engagement/disengagement behaviors.

Number of Items: 18

Format: Includes three areas: social helplessness, social withdrawal, and prosocial behavior. Responses are made on 5-point scales. Examples are given.

Reliability: Internal consistencies ranged from .65 to .94.

Validity: Correlations with other variables ranged from −.25 to .36.

Author: Caldwell, M. S., et al.

Article: Reciprocal influences among relational self-views, social disengagement, and peer stress during early adolescence.

Journal: *Child Development*, July/August 2004, *75*, 1140–1154.

Related Research: Nolen-Hochsema, S., et al. (1992). Predictors and consequences of childhood depressive symptoms: A 5-year longitudinal study. *Journal of Abnormal Psychology, 101,* 405–422. Cassidy, J., & Asher, S. R. (1992). Loneliness and peer relations in young children. *Child Development, 63,* 350–365.

11145

Test Name: SOCIAL EXPERIENCE QUESTIONNAIRE

Purpose: To identify experience with peers.

Number of Items: 15

Format: Includes two dimensions: Overt Victimization and Relational Victimization. Responses are made on a 5-point scale. Examples are presented.

Reliability: Alpha coefficients were .85 (girls) and .86 (boys).

Validity: Correlations with other variables ranged from −.43 to .47

Author: Luther, S. S., and Becker, B. E.

Article: Privileged but pressured? A study of affluent youth.

Journal: *Child Development*, September/October 2002, *73*, 1593–1610.

Related Research: Crick, N. R., & Grotpeter, J. K. (1996). Children's treatment by peers: Victims of relational and overt aggression. *Development and Psychopathology*, *8*, 367–380.

11146

Test Name: SOCIAL HELPLESSNESS SCALE

Purpose: To assess helpless behavior in the context of peer interactions.

Number of Items: 12

Format: Responses are made on a 5-point scale ranging from 1 (*not true*) to 5 (*very true*). Sample items are given.

Reliability: Alpha coefficients were .92 and .94.

Validity: Correlations with other variables ranged from −.61 to .59.

Author: Gazelle, H., and Rudolph, K. D.

Article: Moving toward and away from the world: Social approach and avoidance trajectories in anxious solitary youth.

Journal: *Child Development*, May/June 2004, *75*, 829–849.

Related Research: Nolen-Hocksema, S., et al. (1992). Predictors and consequences of childhood depressive symptoms: A 5-year longitudinal study. *Journal of Abnormal Psychology, 101*, 405–422.

11147

Test Name: SOCIAL HOPELESSNESS QUESTIONNAIRE

Purpose: To measure hopelessness regarding social or interpersonal cognitions and expectations of future relationships.

Number of Items: 20

Format: Likert scales are used.

Reliability: Coefficient alpha was .92.

Validity: Correlations with other variables ranged from −.68 to .81.

Author: Heisel, M. J., and Flett, G. L.

Article: Purpose in life, satisfaction with life, and suicide ideation in a clinical sample.

Journal: *Journal of Psychopathology and Behavioral Assessment*, June 2004, *26*, 127–135.

11148

Test Name: SOCIAL INTERACTION ANXIETY AND PHOBIA SCALES.

Purpose: To measure anxiety in social situations.

Number of Items: 40

Format: Scales range from 0 (*not at all characteristic or true of me*) to 4 (*extremely characteristic or true of me*). A sample item is presented.

Reliability: Reliability coefficients exceeded .87.

Validity: Correlations with other variables ranged from −.53 to .79.

Author: Dinnel, D. L., et al.

Article: A cross-cultural comparison of social phobia symptoms.

Journal: *Journal of Psychopathology and Behavioral Assessment*, June 2002, *24*, 75–84.

Related Research: Mattick, R. P., & Clarke, J. C. (1998). Development and validation of measures of social phobia scrutiny fear and social interaction anxiety. *Behavior Research and Therapy, 36*, 455–470.

11149

Test Name: SOCIAL INTERACTION QUESTIONNAIRES

Purpose: To measure social interaction in the work group, department, and organization.

Number of Items: 17 items for each of three questionnaires.

Format: Includes three questionnaires for social interaction in the work group, department, and organization. Responses are made on a 7-point Likert-type scale ranging from 1 (*strongly disagree*) to 7 (*strongly agree*).

Reliability: Alpha coefficients ranged from .94 to .95 (*N* ranged from 150–154).

Validity: Correlations with other variables ranged from −.16 to .66 (*N* ranged 150–154).

Author: Heffner, T. S., and Rentsch, J. R.

Article: Organizational commitment and social interaction: A multiple constituencies approach.

Journal: *Journal of Vocational Behavior*, December 2001, *59*, 471–490.

11150

Test Name: SOCIAL INTERACTION SCALE

Purpose: To assess social interactions about work in a work unit.

Number of Items: 3

Format: Scales range from 1 (*never*) to 5 (*quite frequently*). A sample item is presented.

Reliability: Coefficient alpha was .91.

Validity: Correlations with other variables at the work unit level ranged from .00 to .27.

Author: González-Romá, V., et al.

Article: An examination of the antecedents and moderator influences of climate strength.

Journal: *Journal of Applied Psychology*, June 2002, *87*, 465–473.

11151

Test Name: SOCIAL INTERACTION SCALE

Purpose: To measure social interaction among employees as friends outside of work.

Number of Items: 9

Format: Scales range from 1 (*not at all*) to 5 (*very much*) or from 1 (*not true*) to 5 (*true*). Sample items are presented.

Reliability: Coefficient alpha was .85.

Validity: Correlations with other variables ranged from –.24 to .20.

Author: Klein, K. J., et al.

Article: Is everyone in agreement? An exploration of within-group agreement in employee perceptions of the work environment.

Journal: *Journal of Applied Psychology*, February 2001, *86*, 3–16.

11152

Test Name: SOCIAL INTERACTION SELF-STATEMENT TEST—PUBLIC SPEAKING

Purpose: To measure thoughts in social interactions.

Number of Items: 30

Format: Includes two similar positive and negative thought subscales. Responses are made on a 5-point scale ranging from 0 (*never*) to 4 (*very often*). Example is given.

Validity: Correlations with other variables ranged from –.38 to .65.

Author: Diaz, R. J., et al.

Article: Cognition, anxiety, and prediction of performance in 1st-year law students.

Journal: *Journal of Educational Psychology*, June 2001, *93*, 420–429.

Related Research: Glass, C. R. et al. (1982). Cognitive assessment of social anxiety: Development and validations of a self-statement questionnaire. *Cognitive Therapy and Research, 6,* 37–55.

11153

Test Name: SOCIAL PHYSIQUE ANXIETY SCALE

Purpose: To measure social physique anxiety.

Number of Items: 12

Format: Scales range from 1 (*not at all*) to 5 (*extremely.*)

Reliability: Alpha coefficients ranged from .89 to .90.

Author: Bowden, R. G., et al.

Article: Changes in social physique anxiety during a 16-week physical activity course.

Journal: *Psychological Reports,* June 2005, *96,* Part 1, 690–692.

Related Research: Hart, E. A., et al. (1989). The measurement of social physique anxiety. *Journal of Sport and Exercise Psychology, 11,* 94–104.

11154

Test Name: SOCIAL PHYSIQUE ANXIETY SCALE—REVISED

Purpose: To measure social physique anxiety.

Number of Items: 7

Format: Responses are made on a 5-point Likert-type scale ranging from 1 (*strongly agree*) to 5 (*strongly disagree*).

Reliability: Coefficient alpha was .90. Test–retest (8 weeks) reliability was .82.

Author: Jordan, E. H., et al.

Article: An examination of Euro-American and African-American differences in social physique anxiety among college women.

Journal: *Perceptual and Motor Skills,* February 2005, *100,* 96–98.

Related Research: Motl, R. W., et al. (2000). The Social Physique Anxiety Scale: An example of the potential consequence of negatively worded items in factorial validity studies. *Journal of Applied Measurement, 1,* 327–345.

11155

Test Name: SOCIAL PROVISIONS SCALE

Purpose: To measure perceived social support.

Number of Items: 24

Format: Includes six subscales: Attachment, Social Integration, Reassurance of Worth, Reliable Alliance, Guidance, and Opportunity for Nurturance.

Responses are made on a 4-point Likert-type scale ranging from 1 (*strongly disagree*) to 4 (*strongly agree*).

Reliability: Internal consistencies ranged from .65 to .83.

Validity: Correlations with other variables ranged from −.68 to .56.

Author: Mallinckrodt, B., and Wei, M.

Article: Attachment, social competencies, social support, and psychological distress.

Journal: *Journal of Counseling Psychology*, July 2005, *52*, 358–367.

Related Research: Cutrona, C. E., & Russell, D. W. (1990). Type of social support and specific stress: Toward a theory of optimal matching. In B. R. Sarason et al. (Eds.), *Social support: An interactive view* (pp. 319–366). New York: Wiley.

11156

Test Name: SOCIAL RESPONSIBILITY SCALE

Purpose: To measure social responsibility toward respect for a specific target group.

Number of Items: 10

Format: Scales range from 1 (*highly disagree*) to 5 (*highly agree*). All items are presented.

Reliability: Coefficient alpha was .88.

Author: Johnson, L. M., et al.

Article: General versus specific victim blaming.

Journal: *The Journal of Social Psychology*, April 2002, *142*, 249–263.

Related Research: Mulford, C. L., et al. (1996). Victim-blaming and society-blaming scales for social problems. *Journal of Applied Social Psychology*, *26*, 1324–1336.

11157

Test Name: SOCIAL–SEXUAL EFFECTIVENESS SCALE

Purpose: To assess a person's confidence in sexual situations and his or her ability to interpret sexual signals accurately.

Number of Items: 14

Format: Scales range from 1 (*never true*) to 7 (*always true*). A sample item is presented.

Reliability: Coefficient alpha was .85.

Validity: Correlations with other variables ranged from −.15 to .27.

Author: Koukounas, E., and Letch, N. M.

Article: Psychological correlates of perception of sexual intent in women.

Journal: *The Journal of Social Psychology*, August 2001, *141*, 443–456.

Related Research: Quackenbush, R. L. (1989). Assessing men's social–sexual effectiveness: A self-report instrument. *Psychological Reports*, *64*, 969–970.

11158

Test Name: SOCIAL SKILL SCALE

Purpose: To assess how one is perceived by others.

Number of Items: 7

Format: Scales range from 1 (*strongly disagree*) to 5 (*strongly agree*). All items are presented.

Reliability: Alpha coefficients ranged from .77 to .81.

Validity: Correlations with other variables ranged from −.13 to .27.

Author: Witt, L. A., and Ferris, G. R.

Article: Social skill as moderator of the conscientiousness–performance

relationship: Convergent results across four studies.

Journal: *Journal of Applied Psychology*, October 2003, *88*, 809–820.

11159

Test Name: SOCIAL SUPPORT FOR ADOLESCENTS SCALE

Purpose: To measure adolescents' perceived support from friends, family, and school personnel.

Number of Items: 21

Format: Includes three factors: family support, formal support, and informal support. Responses are made on a 3-point scale ranging from 1 (*not at all helpful*) to 3 (*a great deal helpful*).

Reliability: Alpha coefficients were .80 and .82.

Validity: Correlations with other variables ranged from −.13 to .50.

Author: Wettersten, K. B., et al.

Article: Predicting educational and vocational attitudes among rural high school students.

Journal: *Journal of Counseling Psychology*, October 2005, *52*, 658–663.

Related Research: Cauce, A., et al. (1982). Social support in high-risk adolescents: Structural components and adaptive impact. *American Journal of Community Psychology*, *10*, 417–428.

11160

Test Name: SOCIAL SUPPORT LIST—ENGLISH VERSION

Purpose: To measure support satisfaction and support interactions.

Number of Items: 34

Format: Items are rated on two 4-point scales anchored by 1 (*I miss it*) and 4 (*It happens too often*).

Reliability: Alpha coefficients ranged from .77 to .94 across subscales and the total scale.

Author: Bridges, K. R., et al.

Article: An English language version of the Social Support List: Preliminary reliability.

Journal: *Psychological Reports*, June 2002, *90*, Part 1, 1055–1058.

Related Research: van Soderen, E. (1990). Hiet meten van sociale steun [The assessment of social support]. Unpublished doctoral dissertation, University of Groningen, Groningen, the Netherlands.

11161

Test Name: SOCIAL SUPPORT NETWORK RESOURCES

Purpose: To measure the extent and depth of support from personal networks.

Number of Items: 6

Format: Various 5-point scales are used. All are described.

Reliability: Alpha coefficients ranged from .68 to .84 across three subscales.

Validity: Correlations with other variables ranged from −.32 to .41.

Author: Shaffer, M. A., and Harrison, D. A.

Article: Forgotten partners of international assignments: Development and test of a model of spouse adjustment.

Journal: *Journal of Applied Psychology*, April 2001, *86*, 238–254.

Related Research: Vaux, A., & Harrison, D. A. (1985). Support network characteristics associated with support satisfaction and perceived support. *American*

Journal of Community Psychology, 13, 245–268.

11162

Test Name: SOCIAL SUPPORT QUESTIONNAIRE—6

Purpose: To measure social support.

Number of Items: 6

Format: Response scales range from 1 (*seldom*) to 3 (*always*). Sample items are presented.

Reliability: Coefficient alpha was .94.

Validity: Correlations with other variables ranged from −.37 to .34.

Author: Hobfoll, S. E., et al.

Article: The impact of perceived child physical and sexual abuse history on Native American women's psychological well-being and AIDS risk.

Journal: *Journal of Consulting and Clinical Psychology*, February 2002, *70*, 252–257.

Related Research: Sarason, I. G., et al. (1987). A brief measure of social support: Practical and theoretical implications. *Journal of Social and Personal Relationships, 4*, 497–511.

11163

Test Name: SOCIAL SUPPORT QUESTIONNAIRE—FRENCH SHORT FORM

Purpose: To measure availability and satisfaction.

Number of Items: 6

Format: All items are presented in English.

Reliability: Alpha coefficients ranged from .82 to .89. Test–retest reliabilities (2 weeks) ranged from .84 to .89.

Validity: Correlations with other variables ranged from −.18 to .14.

Author: Rascle, N., and Bruchon-Schweitzer, M.

Article: Short-form of Sarason's Social Support Questionnaire: French adaptation and validation.

Journal: *Psychological Reports*, August 2005, *97*, 195–202.

11164

Test Name: SOCIAL SUPPORT SCALE

Purpose: To measure social support from friends, negative social support, instrumental support, and cultural support.

Number of Items: 20

Format: Various rating scales are used. All items and scales are presented.

Reliability: Alpha coefficients ranged from .62 to .86.

Author: Duran, B., et al.

Article: Obstacles for rural American Indians seeking alcohol, drug, or mental health treatment.

Journal: *Journal of Consulting and Clinical Psychology*, October 2005, *73*, 819–829.

Related Research: National Center for Posttraumatic Stress Disorder & National Center for American Indian and Alaska Native Mental Health Research. (1996). *Matsunaga Vietnam Veterans Project*. White River Junction, VT: National Center for Posttraumatic Stress Disorder.

11165

Test Name: SOCIAL SUPPORT SCALE

Purpose: To measure social support.

Number of Items: 24

Format: Responses are made on a 5-point Likert scale ranging from 5 (*very much*) to 1 (*I don't have any such person*).

Reliability: Reliabilities ranged from .63 to .93.

Validity: Correlations with other variables ranged from −.29 to .46.

Author: Fugate, M., et al.

Article: Coping with an organizational merger over four stages.

Journal: *Personnel Psychology,* Winter 2002, *55,* 905–928.

Related Research: Caplan, R., et al. (1975). *Job demands and work health.* (NIOSH Pub. No. 75–160). Washington, DC: U.S. Department of Health, Education, and Welfare.

11166

Test Name: SOCIAL SUPPORT SCALE

Purpose: To measure emotional and instrumental help received by clients from their own social network.

Number of Items: 3

Format: Responses are made on a 5-point Likert scale ranging from 1 (*strongly disagree*) to 5 (*strongly agree*). All items are presented.

Reliability: Reliability was .74.

Author: Kossek, E. E., et al.

Article: Sustaining work force inclusion and well-being of mothers on public assistance: Individual deficit and social ecology perspectives.

Journal: *Journal of Vocational Behavior,* February 2003, *62,* 155–175.

Related Research: Wilcox, B. L. (1981). Social support, life stress, and psychological adjustment: A test of the buffering hypothesis.

American Journal of Community Psychology, 9, 371–386.

11167

Test Name: SOCIAL SUPPORT SCALE

Purpose: To assess support from family, neighbors, and friends.

Number of Items: 11

Format: Various formats are used. All items are presented.

Reliability: Alpha coefficients ranged from .78 to .84 across two subscales.

Validity: Correlations with other variables ranged from −.29 to .19.

Author: Kotchick, B. A., et al.

Article: Predictors of parenting among African American single mothers: Personal and contextual factors.

Journal: *Journal of Marriage and Family,* May 2005, *67,* 448–460.

11168

Test Name: SOCIAL SUPPORT SCALE

Purpose: To assess how coworkers pay attention to one's feelings and emotions.

Number of Items: 4

Format: Scales range from 1 (*not at all*) to 5 (*a great deal*).

Reliability: Alpha coefficients exceeded .85.

Author: Totterdell, P., et al.

Article: Affect networks: A structured analysis of the relationship between work ties and job-related affect.

Journal: *Journal of Applied Psychology,* October 2004, *89,* 854–867.

Related Research: Peeters, M. C. W., et al. (1995). Social

interactions, stressful events and negative affect at work: A micro-analytic approach. *European Journal of Social Psychology, 25,* 391–401.

11169

Test Name: SOCIAL SUPPORT SCALE FOR CHILDREN AND ADOLESCENTS

Purpose: To assess the extent to which students perceive their parents, teachers, and friends as supportive.

Number of Items: 18

Format: Includes three subscales: Teacher, Parent, and Close Friend. An example is given.

Reliability: Alpha coefficients ranged from .68 to .90.

Validity: Correlations with other variables ranged from −.28 to .30.

Author: Kenny, M. E., and Bledsoe, M.

Article: Contributions of the relational context to career adaptability among urban adolescents.

Journal: *Journal of Vocational Behavior,* April 2005, *66,* 257–272.

Related Research: Harter, S. (1985). *Manual for the Social Support Scale for Children and Adolescents.* Unpublished manuscript, University of Denver, Denver, CO.

11170

Test Name: SOCIAL SUPPORT SCALE FOR OLDER CHILDREN AND ADOLESCENTS—ADAPTED

Purpose: To assess students' perceived support for math/science schoolwork.

Number of Items: 10

Format: Includes two subscales: Approval Support and Instrumental

Support. Sample items are presented.

Reliability: Alpha coefficients ranged from .77 to .84.

Validity: Correlations with other variables ranged from −.12 to .51.

Author: Bouchey, H. A., and Harter, S.

Article: Reflected appraisals, academic self-perceptions, and math/science performance during early adolescence.

Journal: *Journal of Educational Psychology*, November 2005, *97*, 673–686.

Related Research: Harter, S., & Robinson, N. (1988). *The Social Support Scale for Older Children and Adolescents (Revised): Approval, emotional, and instrumental support*. Unpublished manuscript, University of Denver, Denver, CO.

11171

Test Name: SOCIAL SUPPORT SCALES—JAPANESE VERSION

Purpose: To measure social support.

Number of Items: 18

Format: Scales range from 1 (*not at all*) to 4 (*very much*). All items are presented in English.

Reliability: Alpha coefficients ranged from .85 to .89 across subscales.

Validity: Correlations with other variables ranged from .08 to .28.

Author: Jou, Y. H., and Fukada, H.

Article: Stress, health, and reciprocity and sufficiency of social support: The care of university students in Japan.

Journal: *The Journal of Social Psychology*, June 2002, *142*, 353–370.

11172

Test Name: SOCIALIZATION SCALE

Purpose: To measure dimensions of socialization.

Number of Items: 34

Format: Includes six dimensions: Organizational Goals and Values, Language, Politics, History, People, and Performance Proficiency. Responses are made on a 7-point scale ranging from *strongly disagree* to *strongly agree*.

Reliability: Alpha coefficients ranged from .80 to .92.

Validity: Correlations with other variables ranged from −.14 to .77.

Author: Haueter, J. A., et al.

Article: Measurement of newcomer socialization: Construct validation of a multidimensional scale.

Journal: *Journal of Vocational Behavior*, August 2003, *63*, 20–39.

Related Research: Chao, G. T., et al. (1994). Organizational socialization: Its content and consequences. *Journal of Applied Psychology*, *79*, 730–743.

11173

Test Name: SOCIOCULTURAL ADAPTATION SCALE

Purpose: To measure an individual's ability to function in everyday situations in a foreign culture.

Number of Items: 29

Format: Includes two factors: behavioral and cognitive. Responses are made on a 5-point scale ranging from 1 (*no difficulty*) to 5 (*extreme difficulty*). Sample items are presented.

Reliability: Alpha coefficients were .88 and .89.

Validity: Correlations with other variables ranged from −.41 to .47 (*N* = 125).

Author: Swagler, M. A., and Jome, L. M.

Article: The effects of personality and acculturation on the adjustment of North American sojourners in Taiwan.

Journal: *Journal of Counseling Psychology*, October 2005, *52*, 527–536.

Related Research: Ward, C., & Kennedy, A. (1999). The measurement of sociocultural adaptation. *International Journal of Intercultural Relations*, *23*, 659–677.

11174

Test Name: SPLITTING INDEX— MODIFIED

Purpose: To measure the disposition to use splitting as an ego defense.

Number of Items: 16

Format: Includes two subscales: Self-Splitting and Other-Splitting. Responses are made on a 5-point scale ranging from 1 (*strongly disagree*) to 5 (*strongly agree*). Sample items are presented.

Reliability: Alpha coefficients ranged from .84 to .90.

Validity: Correlations with other variables ranged from −.40 to .58.

Author: Lopez, F. G.

Article: Adult attachment orientation, self–other boundary regulation, and splitting tendencies in a college sample.

Journal: *Journal of Counseling Psychology*, October 2001, *48*, 440–446.

Related Research: Gould, J. R., et al. (1996). The Splitting Index: Construction of a scale measuring the defense mechanism of splitting.

Journal of Personality Assessment,
66, 414–430.

11175

Test Name: SPORT ANXIETY
SCALE

Purpose: To assess social anxiety
and avoidance within sports.

Number of Items: 7

Format: Responses are made on
a 5-point scale ranging from
1 (*never true about me*) to
5 (*always true about me*).

Reliability: Coefficient alpha was .75.

Validity: Correlations with other
variables ranged from .17 to .68.

Author: Storch, E. A., et al.

Article: Overt and relational
victimization and psychosocial
adjustment in minority
preadolescents.

Journal: *Child Study Journal,*
2002, *32,* 81–88.

11176

Test Name: STEPHENSON
MULTIGROUP
ACCULTURATION SCALE

Purpose: To measure behavioral
and attitudinal aspects of
acculturation.

Number of Items: 32

Format: Scales range from 1 (*true*)
to 4 (*false*).

Reliability: Alpha coefficients
ranged from .75 to .94.

Author: Rayle, A. D., and Meyers,
J. E.

Article: Counseling adolescents
toward wellness: The roles of ethnic
identity, acculturation, and
mattering.

Journal: *Professional School
Counseling,* October 2004, *8*(1),
81–90.

Related Research: Stephenson, M.
(2000). Development and validation
of the Stephenson Multigroup
Acculturation Scale (SMAS).
Psychological Assessment, 12,
77–88.

11177

Test Name: STERNBERG
TRIANGULAR LOVE SCALE

Purpose: To measure intimacy,
commitment, and passion.

Number of Items: 45

Format: Nine-point scales range
from *extremely* to *not at all.*

Reliability: Alpha coefficients were
around .90.

Author: Myers, J. E., and Shurts, M.

Article: Measuring positive
emotionality: A review of
instruments assessing love.

Journal: *Measurement and
Evaluation in Counseling and
Development,* January 2002, *34,*
238–254.

Related Research: Sternberg, R. J.
(1986). A triangular theory of love.
Psychological Review, 93, 119–135.
Acker, M., & Davis, M. H. (1992).
Intimacy, passion and commitment
in adult romantic relationships: A
test of the triangular theory of love.
*Journal of Social and Personal
Relationship, 9,* 21–50.

11178

Test Name: STORYTELLING
INTERVIEW

Purpose: To assess children's
understanding of situations in
which one could feel two emotions
of opposite valence.

Number of Items: 6

Format: Responses are scored on a
3-point scale ranging from 0 (*no
emotions explained*) to 2 (*two
opposite-valenced emotions for
each story*).

Reliability: Coefficient alpha was .74.

Author: Dunn, J., et al.

Article: Old friends, new friends:
Predictors of children's perspective
on their friends at school.

Journal: *Child Development,*
March/April 2002, *73,* 621–635.

Related Research: Gordis, F. W.,
et al. (1982, April). *Young children's
understanding of simultaneous
conflicting emotions.* Paper
presented at the biennial meeting of
the Society of Research in Child
Development, Kansas City, MO.

11179

Test Name: STRENGTHS AND
DIFFICULTIES
QUESTIONNAIRE

Purpose: To assess prosocial
behavior.

Number of Items: 25

Reliability: Coefficient alpha was
.87 (prosocial subscale).

Validity: Correlations of prosocial
behavior subscale with other
variables ranged from −.50 to .57.

Author: Dunn, J., et al.

Article: Old friends, new friends:
Predictors of children's perspective
on their friends at school.

Journal: *Child Development,*
March/April 2002, *73,* 621–635.

Related Research: Goodman, R.
(1997). The Strengths and
Difficulties Questionnaire: A
research note. *Journal of Child
Psychology of Psychiatry, 38,*
581–586.

11180

Test Name: STRESS FROM
ACCULTURATION SCALE

Purpose: To assess stress arising
from acculturation in a Korean
immigrant population.

Number of Items: 30

Format: Scales range from 1 (*strongly disagree*) to 5 (*strongly agree*). Sample items are presented.

Reliability: Coefficient alpha was .95.

Author: Oh, Y., et al.

Article: Acculturation, stress, and depressive symptoms among Korean immigrants in the United States.

Journal: *The Journal of Social Psychology,* August 2002, *142,* 511–526.

Related Research: Sandhu, D. S., & Asrabadi, B. R. (1994). Development of an acculturation stress scale for international students: Preliminary findings. *Psychological Reports, 75,* 435–448.

11181

Test Name: STUDENT SOCIAL SUPPORT SCALE—REVISED

Purpose: To measure social support students received from various people in their lives.

Number of Items: 15

Format: Includes three subscales: Parental Support, Teachers Support, and Close Friend Support. Responses are made on a 5-point Likert-type scale ranging from *strongly agree* to *strongly disagree*. An example is given.

Reliability: Coefficient alpha was .87.

Author: Powell, C. L. and Arriola, K. R. J.

Article: Relationship between psychosocial factors and academic achievement among African American students.

Journal: *The Journal of Educational Research,* January/February 2003, *96,* 175–181.

Related Research: Malecki, C. K., & Elliott, S. N. (1999). Adolescents'

ratings of perceived social support and its importance. Validation of the student support scale. *Psychology in the Schools, 36,* 473–483.

11182

Test Name: SUINN–LEW ASIAN SELF-IDENTITY ACCULTURATION SCALE

Purpose: To assess acculturation level.

Number of Items: 21

Reliability: Alpha coefficients ranged from .88 to .91.

Validity: Correlation with the Social Phobia and Anxiety Inventory was −.28.

Author: Okazaki, S.

Article: Self–other agreement on affective distress scales in Asian Americans and White Americans.

Journal: *Journal of Counseling Psychology,* October 2002, *49,* 428–437.

Related Research: Suinn, R. M., et al. (1987). The Suinn–Lew Asian Self-Identity Acculturation Scale: An initial report. *Educational & Psychological Measurement, 47,* 401–407.

11183

Test Name: TAIJIN KYOFUSHO SCALE

Purpose: To measure an allocentric component of social anxiety in which a patient is concerned that his or her shortcomings may harm others.

Number of Items: 31

Format: Scales range from 1 (*totally false*) to 7 (*exactly true*). A sample item is presented.

Reliability: Alpha coefficients exceeded .80.

Validity: Correlations with other variables ranged from −.44 to .79.

Author: Dinnel, D. L., et al.

Article: A cross-cultural comparison of social phobia symptoms.

Journal: *Journal of Psychopathology and Behavioral Assessment,* June 2002, *24,* 75–84.

Related Research: Kleinknecht, R. A., et al. (1997). Cultural factors in social anxiety: A comparison of social phobia symptoms and *Taijin Kyofusho. Journal of Anxiety Disorders, 11,* 157–177.

11184

Test Name: TEACHER CHECKLIST OF PEER RELATIONS

Purpose: To measure a child's peer relations.

Number of Items: 17

Format: Includes three areas: peer acceptance, social skills, and aggressiveness. Examples are presented.

Reliability: Internal consistency coefficients ranged from .69 to .95.

Author: Lindsey, E. W.

Article: Preschool children's friendships and peer acceptance: Links to social competence.

Journal: *Child Study Journal,* 2002, *32,* 145–155.

Related Research: Coie, J. D., & Dodge, K. A. (1988). Multiple sources of data on social behavior and social status in the school: A cross-age comparison. *Child Development, 59,* 815–829.

11185

Test Name: TEACHER–CHILD RATING SCALE—SOCIAL COMPETENCE

Purpose: To enable teachers to rate their children on social competence.

Number of Items: 20

Format: Responses are made on a 5-point scale ranging from 1 (*not at all*) to 5 (*very well*). Examples are given.

Reliability: Internal reliabilities ranged from .92 to .96. Test–retest reliability was .86.

Validity: Correlations with other variables ranged from −.45 to .65.

Author: Chen, X., et al.

Article: Social functioning and adjustment in Chinese children: The imprint of historical time.

Journal: *Child Development*, January/February 2005, *76*, 182–195.

Related Research: Hightower, A. D., et al. (1986). The Teacher–Child Rating Scale: A brief objective measure of elementary children's school problem behaviors and competencies. *School Psychology Review, 15*, 393–409.

11186

Test Name: TEAM PERCEIVED POTENCY MEASURE

Purpose: To assess team perceived potency.

Number of Items: 8

Format: Responses are made on a 6-point scale ranging from 1 (*strongly disagree*) to 6 (*strongly agree*). Examples are given.

Reliability: Coefficient alpha was .85.

Validity: Correlations with other variables ranged from .07 to .33 (*n* = 92).

Author: Hirschfeld, R. R., et al.

Article: Teams' female representation and perceived potency as inputs to team outcomes

in a predominantly male field setting.

Journal: *Personnel Psychology,* Winter 2005, *58*, 893–924.

Related Research: Guzzo, R. A., et al. (1993). Potency in groups: Articulating a construct. *British Journal of Social Psychology, 32*, 87–106.

11187

Test Name: TEAM SOCIAL COHESION QUESTIONNAIRE

Purpose: To measure team social cohesion.

Number of Items: 17

Format: Responses are made on a 4-point scale ranging from 1 (*strongly disagree*) to 4 (*strongly agree*).

Reliability: Coefficient alpha was .70.

Author: Tziner, A., et al.

Article: Relation between social cohesion and team performance in soccer teams.

Journal: *Perceptual and Motor Skills*, February 2003, *96*, 145–148.

Related Research: Elron, E. (1997). Top management teams within multinational corporations: Effects of cultural heterogeneity. *Leadership Quarterly, 8*, 393–412.

11188

Test Name: TEAMWORK AND CONTINUOUS IMPROVEMENT SCALES

Purpose: To measure teamwork and continuous improvement.

Number of Items: 16

Format: Includes four factors: teamwork, active involvement, allegiance to quality, and personal accountability. All items are presented.

Reliability: Alpha coefficients ranged from .66 to .90.

Validity: Correlations with other variables ranged from −.21 to .52.

Author: Coyle-Shapiro, J. A.-M., and Morrow, P. C.

Article: The role of individual differences in employee adoption of TQM orientation.

Journal: *Journal of Vocational Behavior*, April 2003, *62*, 320–340.

11189

Test Name: TENDENCY TO FORGIVE SCALE

Purpose: To assess the tendency to forgive in reaction to interpersonal offenses.

Number of Items: 4

Format: Scales range from 1 (*strongly disagree*) to 7 (*strongly agree*). Sample items are presented.

Validity: Correlations with other variables ranged from −.59 to .30.

Author: Brown, R. P.

Article: Vengeance is mine: Narcissism, vengeance, and the tendency to forgive.

Journal: *Journal of Research in Personality*, December 2004, *38*, 576–584.

Related Research: Brown, R. P. (2005). Letting bygones be bygones: Further validation for the Tendency to Forgive Scale. *Personality and Individual Differences, 38*, 627–638.

11190

Test Name: TEST OF NEGATIVE SOCIAL EXCHANGE

Purpose: To assess the frequency of unpleasant social interactions.

Number of Items: 18

Format: Scales range from 1 (*not at all*) to 5 (*about every day*). Sample items are presented.

Reliability: Alpha coefficients ranged from .92 to .95.

Validity: Correlations with other variables ranged from −.70 to .52.

Author: Schumacher, J. A., and Leonard, K. E.

Article: Husbands' and wives' marital adjustment, verbal aggression, and physical aggression as longitudinal predictors of physical aggression in early marriage.

Journal: *Journal of Consulting and Clinical Psychology*, February 2005, *73*, 28–37.

Related Research: Ruehlman, L. S., & Karaly, P. (1991). With a little flack from my friends: Development and preliminary validation of the Test of Negative Social Exchange (TENSE). *Psychological Assessment, 3,* 97–104.

11191

Test Name: TEXAS SOCIAL BEHAVIOR INVENTORY

Purpose: To measure feelings of self-worth or social skill.

Number of Items: 16

Format: Items are anchored by 0 (*not at all*) and 4 (*very much characteristic of me*).

Reliability: Alternate form reliability was .89.

Author: Cox, R. L., et al.

Article: Anger expression: Parental and cognitive factors.

Journal: *Psychological Reports*, August 2003, *93*, 59–65.

Related Research: Helmreich, R. H., & Stapp, J. (1974). Short forms of the Texas Social Behavior Inventory (TB-SI): An objective measure of self-esteem. *Bulletin of the Psychometric Society, 4,* 473–475.

11192

Test Name: TRANSGRESSION NARRATIVE TEST OF FORGIVINGNESS

Purpose: To measure forgiveness as a cross-situational disposition.

Number of Items: 5

Format: Responses are made on a 5-point scale ranging from 1 (*definitely not forgive*) to 5 (*definitely forgive*). An example is given.

Reliability: Test–retest reliability was .95. Alpha coefficients were .73 and .74.

Validity: Correlations with other variables ranged from −.05 to .56 ($n = 147$).

Author: Ross, S. R., et al.

Article: A personological examination of self- and other-forgiveness in the five factor model.

Journal: *Journal of Personality Assessment*, April 2004, *82*, 207–214.

Related Research: Berry, J. W., et al. (2001). Dispositional forgiveness: Development and construct validity of the Transgression Narrative Test of Forgivingness (TNTF). *Personality and Social Psychology Bulletin, 27,* 1277–1290.

11193

Test Name: TRUST IN COLLEAGUES SCALE

Purpose: To measure trust in colleagues.

Number of Items: 6

Format: Responses are made on a 7-point Likert scale.

Reliability: Alpha coefficients ranged from .80 to .86.

Validity: Correlations with other variables ranged from −.17 to .52.

Author: Coyle-Shapiro, J. A.-M., and Morrow, P. C.

Article: The role of individual differences in employee adoption of TQM orientation.

Journal: *Journal of Vocational Behavior*, April 2003, *62*, 320–340.

Related Research: Cook, J., & Wall, T. (1980). New work attitude measures of trust, organizational commitment and personal need non-fulfillment. *Journal of Occupational Psychology, 53,* 39–52.

11194

Test Name: TRUST IN MANAGEMENT SCALE

Purpose: To measure trust in management.

Number of Items: 7

Format: Scales range from 1 (*strongly disagree*) to 5 (*strongly agree*). Sample items are presented.

Reliability: Alpha coefficients ranged from .94 to .96 across two samples.

Validity: Correlations with other variables ranged from −.53 to .75.

Author: Kernan, M. C., and Hanges, P. J.

Article: Survivor reactions to reorganization: Antecedents and consequences of procedural, interpersonal, and informational justice.

Journal: *Journal of Applied Psychology*, October 2002, *87*, 916–928.

Related Research: Cook, J., & Wall, T. (1980). New work attitude measures of trust, organizational commitment and personal need non-fulfillment. *Journal of Occupational Psychology, 53,* 39–52.

11195

Test Name: TURKISH INTERPERSONAL RELATIONS INVENTORY

Purpose: To assess sociability, benevolence, tenderheartedness, tolerance, and insistence.

Number of Items: 25

Format: Includes five subscales: Sociability, Benevolence, Tenderheartedness, Tolerance, and Insistence. Responses are made on a 0 to 3 scale.

Reliability: Reliability coefficients ranged from .51 to .66.

Author: Dane, S., and Sekertekin, M. A.

Article: Differences in handedness and scores of aggressiveness and interpersonal relations of soccer players.

Journal: *Perceptual and Motor Skills*, June 2005, *100*, Part 1, 743–746.

Related Research: Özkan, N. (1993). *[Interpersonal Relations Inventory and its reliability]*. Unpublished master's thesis, Ankara University. [in Turkish]

11196

Test Name: UCLA LONELINESS SCALE—ADAPTED

Purpose: To measure feelings of solitude, disconnection, and lack of closeness.

Number of Items: 8

Format: Responses are made on a 4-point scale ranging from 1 (*never*) to 4 (*often*). All items are presented.

Reliability: Alpha coefficients ranged from .62 to .92.

Author: Joiner, Jr., T. E., et al.

Article: The core of loneliness: Lack of pleasurable engagement—more so than painful disconnection—predicts social impairment, depression onset, and recovery from depressive disorders among adolescents.

Journal: *Journal of Personality Assessment*, December 2002, *79*, 472–491.

Related Research: Roberts, R. E., et al. (1993). A brief measure of loneliness suitable for use with adolescents. *Psychological Reports*, 72, 1379–1391.

11197

Test Name: UCLA LONELINESS SCALE—REVISED

Purpose: To measure the experience of loneliness.

Number of Items: 20

Format: Responses are made on a 4-point scale ranging from 1 (*never*) to 4 (*often*).

Reliability: Alpha coefficients were .91 and .94.

Validity: Correlations with other variables ranged from –.18 to .35.

Author: Storch, E. A., et al.

Article: Psychosocial adjustment in early adulthood: The role of childhood teasing and father support.

Journal: *Child Study Journal*, 2003, *33*, 153–163.

Related Research: Russell, D., et al. (1980). The revised UCLA Loneliness Scale: Concurrent and discriminant validity evidence. *Journal of Personality and Social Psychology*, 39, 472–480.

11198

Test Name: UCLA SOCIAL ATTAINMENT SCALE

Purpose: To assess peer relationships, leaderships, and sexual relationships and other social activities by interviewer rating.

Number of Items: 10

Format: Scales range from 1 (*very low functioning*) to 5 (*very high functioning*).

Reliability: Coefficient alpha was .66.

Validity: Correlations with other variables ranged from –.16 to .33.

Author: Meyer, B.

Article: Coping with severe mental illness: Relations of the brief COPE with symptoms, functioning, and well-being.

Journal: *Journal of Psychopathology and Behavioral Assessment*, December 2001, *23*, 265–277.

Related Research: Goldstein, M. J. (1978). Further data concerning the relation between premorbid adjustment and paranoid symptomatology. *Schizophrenia Bulletin*, 4, 236–243.

11199

Test Name: UNSUPPORTIVE SOCIAL INTERACTIONS INVENTORY—ADAPTED

Purpose: To measure heterosexism-specific unsupportive social interactions.

Number of Items: 12

Format: Two of the 4 subscales were used: Minimizing and Blaming. Responses are made on a 4-point scale ranging from 0 (*none*) to 4 (*a lot*). Examples are given.

Reliability: Alpha coefficients were .76 and .90.

Validity: Correlations with other variables ranged from –.15 to .73 ($N = 97$).

Author: Smith, N. G., and Ingram, K. M.

Article: Workplace heterosexism and adjustment among lesbian, gay, and bisexual individuals: The role of unsupportive social interactions.

Journal: *Journal of Counseling Psychology*, January 2004, *51*, 57–67.

Related Research: Ingram, K. M., et al. (2001). Unsupportive responses from others concerning a stressful life event: Development of the unsupportive social interactions inventory. *Journal of Social and Clinical Psychology, 20,* 173–207.

11200

Test Name: WEIGHT-RELATED CRITICISM SCALE

Purpose: To measure weight-related criticism from romantic partners.

Number of Items: 4

Format: Scales range from 1 (*never*) to 6 (*all the time*). All items are presented.

Reliability: Internal consistency was .71.

Author: Befort, C., et al.

Article: Body image, self-esteem, and weight-related criticism from romantic partners.

Journal: *Journal of College Student Development*, September/October 2001, *42*, 407–419.

Related Research: Levine, M. P., et al. (1994). The relation of sociocultural factors to eating attitudes and behaviors among middle school girls. *Journal of Early Adolescence, 14,* 471–490.

11201

Test Name: WHITE RACIAL IDENTITY ATTITUDE SCALE

Purpose: To measure racial identity.

Number of Items: 50

Reliability: Alpha coefficients ranged from .45 to .67 across subscales.

Validity: Correlations with other variables ranged from −.27 to .51.

Author: Milville, M. L., et al.

Article: Integrating identities: The relationships of racial, gender, and ego identities among White college students.

Journal: *Journal of College Student Development*, March/April 2005, *46*, 157–175.

Related Research: Helms, J. E., & Carter, R. T. (1990). The development of the White Racial Identity Inventory. In J. E. Helms (Ed.), *Black and White racial identity: Theory, research, and practice* (pp. 67–80). New York: Greenwood Press.

11202

Test Name: WILLINGNESS TO DISCRIMINATE SCALE

Purpose: To measure the willingness to discriminate against a target group.

Number of Items: 6

Format: Scales range from 1 (*highly disagree*) to 6 (*highly agree*). All items are presented.

Reliability: Coefficient alpha was .77.

Author: Johnson, L. M., et al.

Article: General versus specific victim blaming.

Journal: *The Journal of Social Psychology*, April 2002, *142*, 249–263.

Related Research: Mulford, C. L., et al. (1996). Victim-blaming and society-blaming scales for social problems. *Journal of Applied Social Psychology, 26,* 1324–1336.

11203

Test Name: WORK INTERDEPENDENCE SCALE

Purpose: To assess the degree to which employees coordinate and depend on each other to complete their work.

Number of Items: 6

Format: Scales range from 1 (*not at all*) to 5 (*very much*). A sample item is presented.

Reliability: Coefficient alpha was .80.

Validity: Correlations with other variables ranged from −.43 to .46.

Author: Klein, K. J., et al.

Article: Is everyone in agreement? An exploration of within-group agreement in employee perceptions of the work environment.

Journal: *Journal of Applied Psychology*, February 2001, *86*, 3–16.

11204

Test Name: WORTMAN SOCIAL SUPPORT SCALE

Purpose: To measure social support: emotional support, material support, affirmation–validation, and social integration.

Number of Items: 23

Format: Five-point scales are used.

Reliability: Alpha coefficients ranged from .78 to .89. Total alpha was .77.

Validity: Correlations with other variables ranged from −.54 to .80.

Author: Johnson, J. G., et al.

Article: Hopelessness as a mediator of the association between social support and depressive symptoms: Findings of a study of men with HIV.

Journal: *Journal of Consulting and Clinical Psychology*, December 2001, *69*, 1056–1060.

Related Research: O'Brien, K. O., et al. (1993). Social relationships of men at risk for AIDS. *Social Science and Medicine, 36,* 1161–1167.

11205

Test Name: VANCOUVER INDEX OF ACCULTURATION

Purpose: To measure acculturation.

Number of Items: 20

Format: Includes two dimensions of acculturation: Mainstream Culture and Heritage Culture. Responses are made on a 9-point Likert-type scale ranging from 1 (*strongly disagree*) to 9 (*strongly agree*). Examples are given.

Reliability: Internal consistency coefficients ranged from .80 to .92.

Validity: Correlations with other variables ranged from –.41 to .23 ($N = 125$).

Author: Swagler, M. A., and Jome, L. M.

Article: The effects of personality and acculturation on the adjustment of North American sojourners in Taiwan.

Journal: *Journal of Counseling Psychology*, October 2005, 52, 527–536.

Related Research: Ryder, A. G., et al. (2000). Is acculturation unidimensional or bidimensional? A head-to-head comparison in the prediction of personality, self-identity, and adjustment. *Journal of Personality and Social Psychology, 79,* 49–65.

CHAPTER 5
Adjustment—Vocational

11206

Test Name: ABRIDGED JOB IN GENERAL SCALE

Purpose: To measure global satisfaction with one's job.

Number of Items: 8

Format: Scoring procedure employed 0 (*no*), 1 (*?*), and 3 (*yes*).

Reliability: Alpha coefficients were .85 and .87.

Validity: Correlations with other variables ranged from −.67 to .66.

Author: Russell, S. S., et al.

Article: Shorter can also be better: The Abridged Job in General Scale.

Journal: *Educational and Psychological Measurement*, October 2004, *64*, 878–893.

Related Research: Ironson, G. H., et al. (1989). Construction of a Job in General scale: A comparison of global, composite, and specific measures. *Journal of Applied Psychology, 74*, 193–200.

11207

Test Name: ACTIVE COPING SCALE

Purpose: To measure coping with job stress.

Number of Items: 9

Format: Responses are anchored by 1 (*not used at all*) and 4 (*used a great deal*). A sample item is presented in English.

Reliability: Coefficient alpha was .88.

Validity: Correlations with other variables ranged from −.22 to .35.

Author: Shimazu, A., et al.

Article: Job control and social support as coping resources in job satisfaction.

Journal: *Psychological Reports*, April 2004, *94*, 449–456.

Related Research: Kosugi, S. (2000). [Mental health activities in the workplace by a general checkup using the Job Stress Scale]. [*Job Stress Research*], 7, 141–150. [in Japanese]

11208

Test Name: ADJUSTMENT TO TELECOMMUTING SCALE

Purpose: To measure adjustment to telecommuting.

Number of Items: 5

Format: Responses are made on a 7-point scale ranging from 1 (*strongly disagree*) to 7 (*strongly agree*). A sample item is presented.

Reliability: Coefficient alpha was .77.

Validity: Correlations with other variables ranged from −.05 to .57.

Author: Raghuram, S., et al.

Article: Technology enabled work: The role of self-efficacy in determining telecommuter adjustment and structuring behavior.

Journal: *Journal of Vocational Behavior*, October 2003, *63*, 180–198.

Related Research: Saks, A. M. (1995). Longitudinal field investigation of the moderating and mediating effects of self-efficacy on the relationship between training and newcomer adjustment. *Journal of Applied Psychology, 80*, 211–225.

11209

Test Name: AFFECT BEFORE WORK SCALE

Purpose: To measure affective well-being at work.

Number of Items: 10

Format: Responses are made on a 6-point scale ranging from 1 (*not at all*) to 6 (*very much*). Examples are given.

Reliability: Coefficient alpha was .89.

Validity: Correlations with other variables ranged from −.36 to .52.

Author: Daniels, K., and Harris, C.

Article: A daily diary study of coping in the context of the job demands–control–support model.

Journal: *Journal of Vocational Behavior*, April 2005, *66*, 219–237.

Related Research: Daniels, K. (2000). Measures of five aspects of affective well-being at work. *Human Relations, 53*, 275–294.

11210

Test Name: BALANCE MEASURE

Purpose: To assess the balance between challenges and skills.

Number of Items: 5

Format: Sample items are presented.

Reliability: Alpha coefficients were .76 and .79.

Validity: Correlations with other variables ranged from −.04 to .34.

Author: Bakker, A. B.

Article: Flow among music teachers and their students: The crossover of peak experiences.

Journal: *Journal of Vocational Behavior*, February 2005, *66*, 26–44.

Related Research: French, J. R. P., et al. (1982). *The mechanisms of job stress and strain*. New York: Wiley.

11211

Test Name: BARRIER-COPING EFFICACY SCALE

Purpose: To assess participants' indication of their confidence in their ability to cope with a variety of barriers or problems that engineering students could potentially experience.

Number of Items: 7

Format: Responses are made on a 10-point scale ranging from 0 (*no confidence*) to 9 (*complete confidence*). Examples are given.

Reliability: Coefficient alpha was .89.

Validity: Correlations with other variables ranged from −.24 to .52 ($N = 287$).

Author: Lent, R. W., et al.

Article: Relation of contextual supports and barriers to choice behavior in engineering majors: Test of alternative social cognitive models.

Journal: *Journal of Counseling Psychology*, October 2003, *50*, 458–465.

Related Research: Lent, R. W., et al. (2001). The role of contextual supports and barriers in the choice of math/science education options: A test of social cognitive hypotheses. *Journal of Counseling Psychology*, *48*, 474–483.

11212

Test Name: BRIEF JOB STRESS QUESTIONNAIRE

Purpose: To measure job demands, job control and social support.

Number of Items: 9

Format: Four-point scales are anchored by 1 (*agree*) and 4 (*disagree*).

Reliability: Alpha coefficients ranged from .65 to .82.

Validity: Correlations with other variables ranged from −.21 to .56.

Author: Shimazu, A., et al.

Article: Job control and social support as coping resources in job satisfaction.

Journal: *Psychological Reports*, April 2004, *94*, 449–456.

Related Research: Shimomitsu, T., et al. (1998). [Development of a novel brief job stress questionnaire]. In S. Kato (Ed.), [*Report of the research grant for the prevention of work-related diseases from the ministry of labor*] (pp. 107–115). Tokyo: Ministry of Labor. [in Japanese]

11213

Test Name: BURNOUT INVENTORY FOR ATHLETES

Purpose: To provide a unidimensional measure of burnout.

Format: Responses are made on a 5-point scale ranging from 1 (*never*) to 5 (*always*).

Reliability: Test–retest reliability coefficients were .56 and .58. Internal consistency coefficient was .91.

Validity: Correlations with other variables ranged from −.37 to .22.

Author: Wiggins, M. S., et al.

Article: Anxiety and burnout in female collegiate ice hockey and soccer athletes.

Journal: *Perceptual and Motor Skills*, October 2005, *101*, 519–524.

Related Research: Van Yperen, N. W. (1997). Inequity and vulnerability to dropout symptoms: An exploratory causal analysis among highly skilled young soccer players. *The Sport Psychologist*, *11*, 318–325.

11214

Test Name: CAREER SATISFACTION SCALE

Purpose: To measure career satisfaction.

Number of Items: 5

Format: Responses are made on a 7-point scale ranging from 1 (*strongly disagree*) to 7 (*strongly agree*). An example is given.

Reliability: Reliability coefficients were .73 and .84.

Validity: Correlations with other variables ranged from −.18 to .55.

Author: Erdogan, B., and Bauer, T. N.

Article: Enhancing career benefits of employee proactive personality: The role of fit with jobs and organizations.

Journal: *Personnel Psychology*, Winter 2005, *58*, 859–891.

Related Research: Greenhaus, J. H., et al. (1990). Effects of race on organizational experiences, job performance evaluations, and career outcomes. *Academy of Management Journal*, *33*, 64–86.

11215

Test Name: COACHING ISOMORPHISM QUESTIONNAIRE

Purpose: To measure mimetic, normative, and coercive pressures exerted on athletic coaches.

Number of Items: 18

Format: Response categories are anchored by 1 (*not at all*) and 7 (*very much so*).

Reliability: Alpha coefficients ranged from .63 to .71.

Validity: Cohen's Kappa was .84.

Author: Cunningham, G. B., et al.

Article: Initial reliability of the Coaching Isomorphism Questionnaire for NCAA coaches.

Journal: *Psychological Reports*, April 2001, *88*, 332–334.

Related Research: DiMaggio, P. J., & Powell, W. W. (1983). The iron cage revisited: Institutional isomorphism and collective rationality in organizational fields. *American Sociological Review, 48*, 147–160.

11216

Test Name: CONSEQUENCE OF COMMITMENT SCALE

Purpose: To measure turnover intention.

Number of Items: 3

Format: Responses are made on a 5-point scale ranging from *strongly disagree* to *strongly agree*. A sample item is presented.

Reliability: Alpha coefficients were .79 and .82.

Author: Cheng, Y., and Stockdale, M. S.

Article: The validity of the three-component model of organizational commitment in a Chinese context.

Journal: *Journal of Vocational Behavior*, June 2003, *62*, 465–489.

Related Research: Colarelli, S. M. (1984). Methods of communication and mediating processes in realistic job previews. *Journal of Applied Psychology, 69*, 633–642.

11217

Test Name: CONTROLLABILITY SCALE

Purpose: To assess if work events are controllable by a worker.

Number of Items: 5

Format: Scales range from 1 (*not at all*) to 6 (*completely*). A sample item is presented.

Reliability: Coefficient alpha was .75.

Validity: Correlations with other variables ranged from −.09 to .31.

Author: Schaubroeck, J., et al.

Article: Individual differences in utilizing control to cope with job demands: Effects on susceptibility to infectious disease.

Journal: *Journal of Applied Psychology*, April 2001, *86*, 265–278.

Related Research: Furnham, A., et al. (1992). The development of an occupational attributional style questionnaire. *Journal of Organizational Behavior, 13*, 27–39.

11218

Test Name: CYNICISM SCALE

Purpose: To measure cynicism in organization: pessimism, dispositional attribution, and situational attribution.

Number of Items: 12

Format: Item anchors are 1 (*strongly disagree*) and 5 (*strongly agree*). All items are presented.

Reliability: Alpha coefficients ranged from .60 to .86.

Author: Wanous, J. P., et al.

Article: Cynicism about organizational change: An attribution process perspective.

Journal: *Psychological Reports*, June 2004, *94*, Part 2, 1421–1434.

Related Research: Wanous, J. P., et al. (2000). Cynicism about organizational change: Measurement, antecedents, and correlates. *Group and Organization Management, 25*, 132–153.

11219

Test Name: EMOTION MANAGEMENT BEHAVIOR SCALE

Purpose: To assess how emotions are managed at work.

Number of Items: 6

Format: Scales range from 1 (*strongly disagree*) to 7 (*strongly agree*). All items are presented.

Reliability: Coefficient alpha was .85.

Validity: Correlations with other variables ranged from −.24 to .40.

Author: Diefendorff, J. M., and Richard, E. M.

Article: Antecedents and consequences of emotional display rule perceptions.

Journal: *Journal of Applied Psychology*, April 2003, *88*, 284–294.

11220

Test Name: EMOTIONAL DEMANDS SCALE

Purpose: To assess whether employees deal with emotionally charged situations and whether they are confronted with events that touch them personally.

Format: Responses are made on a 5-point scale ranging from 1 (*never*) to 5 (*always*). An example is given.

Reliability: Alpha coefficients were .81 and .83 (*n* = 191).

Validity: Correlations with other variables ranged from −.16 to .56 (*n* = 191).

Author: Demerouti, E., et al.

Article: Spillover and crossover of exhaustion and life satisfaction among dual-earner parents.

Journal: *Journal of Vocational Behavior*, October 2005, *67*, 266–289.

Related Research: Van Veldhoven, M., et al. (2002). Specific relationships between psychological job conditions and job-related stress: A three-level analytic approach. *Work & Stress, 16*, 207–228.

11221

Test Name: EMOTIONAL DISPLAY MEASURE

Purpose: To measure the expression of positive and negative emotions while at work.

Number of Items: 8

Format: Five-point scales assess the frequency and duration of expressions. Sample items and response scales are presented.

Reliability: Alpha coefficients ranged from .87 to .96.

Author: Diefendorff, J. M., and Richard, E. M.

Article: Antecedents and consequences of emotional display rule perceptions.

Journal: *Journal of Applied Psychology*, April 2003, *88*, 284–294.

Related Research: Schaubroeck, J., & Jones, J. R. (2000). Antecedents of workplace emotional labor dimensions and moderators of their effects on physical symptoms. *Journal of Organizational Behavior, 21*, 163–183.

11222

Test Name: EMPLOYEE ATTITUDE SURVEY

Purpose: To measure job satisfaction as satisfaction with

empowerment, fulfillment, pay, work group, and security.

Number of Items: 24

Format: Scales range from 1 (*very dissatisfied or strongly disagree or very poor*) to 5 (*very satisfied or strongly agree or very good*). All items are presented.

Reliability: Alpha coefficients ranged from .53 to .93.

Validity: Correlations between subscales ranged from .03 to .83.

Author: Schneider, B., et al.

Article: Which comes first: Employee attitudes or organizational financial and market performance?

Journal: *Journal of Applied Psychology*, October 2003, *88*, 836–851.

11223

Test Name: EMPLOYEE-FOCUSED EMOTIONAL LABOR SCALE

Purpose: To measure modifying and faking expressions as well as measuring the extent to which the employee modifies feelings to meet display rules.

Number of Items: 6

Format: Includes two factors: surface acting and deep acting. All items are presented.

Reliability: Alpha coefficients were .74 and .83.

Validity: Correlations with other variables ranged from −.18 to .49.

Author: Brotheridge, C. M., and Grandey, A. A.

Article: Emotional labor and burnout: Comparing two perspectives of "people work."

Journal: *Journal of Vocational Behavior*, February 2002, *60*, 17–39.

Related Research: Brotheridge, C. M., & Lee, R. T. (1998). *On the*

dimensionality of emotional labour: Development and validation of the Emotional Labour Scale. Paper presented at the First Conference on Emotions in Organizational Life, San Diego.

11224

Test Name: EMPLOYEE PERFORMANCE SCALE

Purpose: To measure empathy and excellence in job performance.

Number of Items: 6

Format: Scales range from 1 (*completely agree*) to 7 (*completely disagree*). All items are presented.

Reliability: Coefficient alpha was .88.

Validity: Correlations with other variables ranged from .07 to .67.

Author: Salanova, M., et al.

Article: Linking organizational resources and work engagement to employee performance and customer loyalty: The mediation of service climate.

Journal: *Journal of Applied Psychology*, November 2005, *90*, 1217–1227.

11225

Test Name: EMPLOYEE SATISFACTION INVENTORY

Purpose: To measure job satisfaction as satisfaction with the job itself, promotion, supervision, working conditions, the organization as a whole, and pay.

Number of Items: 24

Format: Five-point scales range from 1 (*strongly disagree*) to 5 (*strongly agree*). Sample items are presented.

Reliability: Coefficient alpha was .74.

Validity: Correlations with an autonomy scale ranged from −.05 to .27.

Author: Koustelios, A., et al.

Article: Autonomy and job satisfaction for a sample of Greek teachers.

Journal: *Psychological Reports*, December 2004, *95*, Part 1, 883–886.

Related Research: Koustelios, A., et al. (1997). The Employee Satisfaction Inventory (ESI): Development of a scale to measure satisfaction of Greek employees. *Educational and Psychological Measurement*, *57*, 469–476.

11226

Test Name: EMPLOYEE SATISFACTION INVENTORY— GREEK VERSION

Purpose: To measure satisfaction with work, pay, promotion, supervision, and the organization as a whole.

Number of Items: 21

Format: Item responses are anchored by 1 (*strongly agree*) and 5 (*strongly disagree*). Sample items are presented in English.

Reliability: Alpha coefficients ranged from .62 to .81 across subscales.

Validity: Correlations with other variables ranged from –.56 to .50.

Author: Koustelios, A.

Article: Organizational factors as predictors of teachers' burnout.

Journal: *Psychological Reports*, June 2001, *88*, Part 1, 627–634.

Related Research: Koustelios, A., & Bagiatis, K. (1997). The Employee Satisfaction Inventory (ESI): Development of a scale to measure satisfaction of Greek employees. *Educational and Psychological Measurement*, *57*, 469–476.

11227

Test Name: EMPLOYEES' PERCEPTIONS OF GLOBAL FIT SCALE

Purpose: To measure employees' perceptions of global fit.

Number of Items: 8

Format: Includes two subscales: Person–Job Fit and Person–Organization Fit. Responses are made on a 5-point scale ranging from 1 (*to a very little extent*) to 5 (*to a very large extent*). Examples are given.

Reliability: Coefficient alpha was .92.

Author: Lyons, H. Z., et al.

Article: A multicultural test of the theory of work adjustment: Investigating the role of heterosexism and fit perceptions in the job satisfaction of lesbian, gay, and bisexual employees.

Journal: *Journal of Counseling Psychology*, October 2005, *52*, 537–548.

Related Research: Saks, A. M., & Ashforth, B. E. (1997). A longitudinal investigation of the relationships between job information sources, applicant perceptions of fit, and work outcomes. *Personnel Psychology*, *50*, 395–427.

11228

Test Name: EQUITY SENSITIVITY SCALE

Purpose: To assess the degree to which a member of an organization is concerned about equity; that is, what one gets from the organization and what one contributes to it.

Format: Respondents assign 0 to 10 points to each of two paired statements. Sample items are presented.

Reliability: Coefficient alpha was .75.

Validity: Correlations with other variables ranged from –.13 to .17.

Author: Colquitt, J. A.

Article: Does the justice of the one interact with the justice of the many? Reactions to procedural justice in teams.

Journal: *Journal of Applied Psychology*, August 2004, *89*, 633–646.

Related Research: King, W. C., & Miles, E. W. (1994). The measure of equity sensitivity. *Journal of Occupational and Organizational Psychology*, *67*, 133–142.

11229

Test Name: ERROR ORIENTATION SCALE

Purpose: To measure error strain and learning from errors at work.

Number of Items: 9

Format: Sample items are presented.

Reliability: Alpha coefficients ranged from .81 to .82.

Author: Keith, N., and Frese, M.

Article: Self-regulation in error management training: Emotion control and metacognition as mediators of performance effects.

Journal: *Journal of Applied Psychology*, July 2005, *90*, 677–691.

Related Research: Rybowiak, V., et al. (1999). Error Orientation Questionnaire [EOQ]: Reliability, validity, and different language equivalence. *Journal of Organizational Behavior*, *20*, 527–547.

11230

Test Name: EXCESSIVE JOB DEMANDS SCALE

Purpose: To assess excessive job demands.

Number of Items: 5

Format: Scales range from 1 (*strongly disagree*) to 5 (*strongly agree*).

Reliability: Coefficient alpha was .76.

Validity: Correlations with other variables ranged from −.41 to .41.

Author: Griffin, M. A.

Article: Dispositions and work reactions: A multilevel approach.

Journal: *Journal of Applied Psychology*, December 2001, *86*, 1142–1151.

Related Research: Hart, P. M., et al. (2000). Development of the School Organizational Health Questionnaire: A measure for assessing teacher morale and school organizational climate. *British Journal of Educational Psychology*, *70*, 211–228.

11231

Test Name: FACET-FREE JOB SATISFACTION SCALE

Purpose: To assess one's satisfaction with one's current or most recent job.

Number of Items: 5

Format: Responses are made on a 1 to 5 scale.

Reliability: Internal consistency coefficients ranged from .77 to .84.

Author: Schaefer, B. M., et al.

Article: The work lives of child molesters: A phenomenological perspective.

Journal: *Journal of Counseling Psychology*, April 2004, *51*, 226–239.

Related Research: Quinn, R. P., & Staines, G. L. (1979). *The 1977 Quality of Employment Survey.* Ann Arbor: Institute for Social Research, University of Michigan.

11232

Test Name: FEAR OF LOSING ONE'S JOB

Purpose: To measure workers' fear of losing their jobs/job security.

Number of Items: 2

Format: Responses are made on a 6-point scale ranging from *strongly agree* to *strongly disagree*. Both items are presented.

Reliability: Coefficient alpha was .71.

Validity: Correlations with other variables ranged from −.15 to .39.

Author: Goulet, L. R., and Singh, P.

Article: Career commitment: A reexamination and an extension.

Journal: *Journal of Vocational Behavior*, August 2002, *61*, 73–91.

11233

Test Name: GAINS AND LOSSES IN RETIREMENT SCALE— ADAPTED

Purpose: To measure retirement negativity.

Number of Items: 4

Format: All items are presented.

Reliability: Coefficient alpha was .78.

Validity: Correlations with other variables ranged from −.06 to .24.

Author: Adams, G., and Rau, B.

Article: Job seeking among retirees seeking bridge employment.

Journal: *Personnel Psychology*, Autumn 2004, *57*, 719–744.

Related Research: Anson, O., et al. (1989). Family, gender, and attitudes toward retirement. *Sex Roles*, *20*, 355–368.

11234

Test Name: GENDER COMFORT IN ATHLETIC TRAINING QUESTIONNAIRE

Purpose: To assess the comfort of athletic trainers in providing care to athletes of the same- and opposite-sex.

Number of Items: 8

Format: Responses are made on a 5-point scale ranging from 1 (*strongly disagree*) to 5 (*strongly agree*). All items are presented.

Reliability: Coefficient alpha was .72.

Author: Drummond, J. L., et al.

Article: Self-reported comfort in athletic training to same- and opposite-sex athletes.

Journal: *Perceptual and Motor Skills*, August 2004, *99*, 337–340.

Related Research: Paluska, S., & D'Amico, F. (2000). The comfort of family practice residents with health care of patients of opposite gender. *Family Medicine*, *32*, 612–617.

11235

Test Name: GENERAL JOB SATISFACTION SCALE

Purpose: To measure job satisfaction.

Number of Items: 5

Format: Scales range from 1 (*strongly disagree*) to 7 (*strongly agree*).

Reliability: Coefficient alpha was .77.

Validity: Correlations with other variables ranged from −.19 to .12.

Author: Noor, N. M.

Article: Work-family conflict, locus of control, and women's well being: Tests of alternative pathways.

Journal: *The Journal of Social Psychology*, October 2002, *142*, 645–662.

Related Research: Hackman, J. R., & Oldham, G. R. (1975). Development of the Job Diagnostic

Inventory. *Journal of Applied Psychology, 60,* 159–170.

11236

Test Name: GROUP DEVELOPMENT QUESTIONNAIRE

Purpose: To assess the developmental level of work groups.

Number of Items: 60

Format: Includes four subscales: Dependency and Inclusion, Counterdependency and Fight, Trust and Structure, and Work. Responses are made on a 5-point scale ranging from 1 (*never true of this group*) to 5 (*always true of this group*).

Reliability: Test–retest reliability ranged from .69 to .89. Alpha coefficients ranged from .66 to .88.

Author: Wheelan, S. A., and Kesselring, J.

Article: Link between faculty group development and elementary student performance on standardized tests.

Journal: *The Journal of Educational Research,* July/August 2005, *98,* 323–330.

Related Research: Wheelan, S., & Hochberger, J. (1996). Validation studies of the Group Development Questionnaire. *Small Group Research, 27,* 143–170.

11237

Test Name: HEALTH PROFESSIONS STRESS INVENTORY

Purpose: To measure stress in the health professions.

Number of Items: 30

Format: Item responses are anchored by 0 (*never*) and 4 (*very often*). All items are presented.

Reliability: Alpha coefficients ranged from .61 to .80 across subscales.

Validity: Correlations with other variables ranged from −.25 to .53.

Author: Akhtar, S., and Lee, J. S. Y.

Article: Confirmatory factor analysis and job burnout correlates of the Health Professions Stress Inventory.

Journal: *Psychological Reports,* February 2002, *90,* 243–250.

Related Research: Wolfgang, A. P. (1988). The Health Professions Stress Inventory. *Psychological Reports, 62,* 220–222.

11238

Test Name: HOURLY EMPLOYEES' SATISFACTION SCALE

Purpose: To measure hourly employees' satisfaction.

Number of Items: 4

Format: Responses are made on a 7-point scale ranging from 1 (*strongly disagree*) to 7 (*strongly agree*). Examples are presented.

Reliability: Coefficient alpha was .86.

Validity: Correlations with other variables ranged from −.18 to .61.

Author: Koys, D. J.

Article: The effects of employer satisfaction, organizational citizenship behavior, and turnover on organizational effectiveness: A unit-level, longitudinal study.

Journal: *Personnel Psychology,* Spring 2001, *54,* 101–114.

Related Research: Foodservice Research Forum. (1997). *Industry of choice.* Chicago: The Educational Foundation, National Restaurant Association.

11239

Test Name: INDEX OF OVERALL JOB SATISFACTION

Purpose: To measure job satisfaction.

Number of Items: 5

Format: Responses are made on a 7-point scale ranging from 1 (*strongly disagree*) to 7 (*strongly agree*). Sample items are presented.

Validity: Correlations with other variables ranged from −.46 to .68 (*n* = 311).

Author: Hochwarter, W. A., et al.

Article: Perceived organizational support as a mediator of the relationship between politics perceptions and work outcomes.

Journal: *Journal of Vocational Behavior,* December 2003, *63,* 438–456.

Related Research: Brayfield, A., & Rothe, H. (1951). An index of job satisfaction. *Journal of Applied Psychology, 35,* 307–311.

11240

Test Name: INDIVIDUAL JOB IMPACT SCALE

Purpose: To assess the personal-level impact of a change in job responsibilities.

Number of Items: 6

Format: Scales range from 1 (*strongly disagree*) to 5 (*strongly agree*). All items are presented.

Reliability: Coefficient alpha was .81.

Validity: Correlations with other variables ranged from −.13 to .08.

Author: Caldwell, S. D., et al.

Article: Toward an understanding of the relationships among organizational change, individual differences, and changes in person–environment fit: A cross-level study.

Journal: *Journal of Applied Psychology*, October 2004, *89*, 868–882.

11241

Test Name: INFLUENCE OVER DECISION-MAKING SCALE

Purpose: To assess how a person can influence organizational matters.

Number of Items: 4

Format: Scales range from 1 (*not at all*) to 5 (*a great deal*). A sample item is presented.

Reliability: Coefficient alpha was .90.

Validity: Correlations with other variables ranged from −.02 to .50.

Author: Totterdell, P., et al.

Article: Affect networks: A structured analysis of the relationship between work ties and job-related affect.

Journal: *Journal of Applied Psychology*, October 2004, *89*, 854–867.

Related Research: Parker, S. K. (1998). Enhancing role breadth self-efficacy: The role of job enrichment and other organizational interventions. *Journal of Applied Psychology, 83*, 835–852.

11242

Test Name: INFORMATION TECHNOLOGY IMPACT ON HUMAN RESOURCES' PROFESSIONAL ROLE SCALE

Purpose: To measure the impact of informational technology on human resources' professional role.

Number of Items: 26

Format: Includes five dimensions: Information Responsiveness, Information Autonomy, External Professional Link, Time on Transformational Activities, and Time on Information Technology Support Activities.

Reliability: Alpha coefficients ranged from .88 to .94.

Validity: Correlations with other variables ranged from −.05 to .23.

Author: Gardner, S. D., et al.

Article: Virtual HR: The impact of information technology on the human resource professional.

Journal: *Journal of Vocational Behavior*, October 2003, *63*, 159–179.

11243

Test Name: INTENT TO QUIT SCALE

Purpose: To measure employee's intent to quit.

Number of Items: 3

Format: Responses are made on a 7-point Likert scale. All items are presented.

Reliability: Coefficient alpha was .85.

Validity: Correlations with other variables ranged from −.68 to .17.

Author: Lauver, K. L., and Kristof-Brown, A.

Article: Distinguishing between employees' perceptions of person–job and person–organization fit.

Journal: *Journal of Vocational Behavior*, December 2001, *59*, 454–470.

Related Research: O'Reilly, C. A. III., et al. (1991). People and organizational culture: A profile comparison approach to assessing person–organization fit. *Academy of Management Journal, 34*, 487–516.

11244

Test Name: INTENT TO REMAIN WITH ORGANIZATION SCALE

Purpose: To measure turnover intention.

Number of Items: 3

Format: Likert scales are used. All items are described.

Reliability: Coefficient alpha was .76.

Validity: Correlations with other variables ranged from .14 to .60.

Author: Simons, T., and Roberson, Q.

Article: Why managers should care about fairness: The effects of aggregate justice perceptions on organizational outcomes.

Journal: *Journal of Applied Psychology*, June 2003, *88*, 432–443.

Related Research: Robinson, S. L. (1996). Trust and breach of the psychological contract. *Administrative Science Quarterly, 41*, 574–599.

11245

Test Name: INTENT TO TURNOVER SCALE

Purpose: To measure intent to turnover.

Number of Items: 3

Format: Responses are made on a 5-point scale ranging from 1 (*strongly disagree*) to 5 (*strongly agree*). An example is presented.

Reliability: Coefficient alpha was .91.

Validity: Correlations with other variables ranged from −.68 to .35.

Author: Allen, T. D.

Article: Family-supportive work environment: The role of organizational perceptions.

Journal: *Journal of Vocational Behavior*, June 2001, *58*, 414–435.

11246

Test Name: INTENTION TO QUIT INDEX

Purpose: To measure intention to quit.

Number of Items: 3

Format: Scales range from 1 (*terrible*) to 7 (*excellent*). All items are presented.

Reliability: Coefficient alpha was .92.

Author: Griffeth, R. W., et al.

Article: The development of a multidimensional measure of job market cognitions: The Employment Opportunity Index [EOI].

Journal: *Journal of Applied Psychology*, March 2005, *90*, 335–349.

Related Research: Bluedorn, A. (1982). A unified model of turnover from organizations. *Human Relations, 35,* 135–153.

11247

Test Name: INTENTION TO QUIT SCALE

Purpose: To measure one's intention to quit.

Number of Items: 4

Reliability: Coefficient alpha was .71.

Validity: Correlations with other variables ranged from −.17 to .21.

Author: Baruch, Y., et al.

Article: Generalist and specialist graduate business degrees: Tangible and intangible value.

Journal: *Journal of Vocational Behavior*, August 2005, *67*, 51–68.

Related Research: Kirschenbaum, A., & Weisberg, J. (1994). Job search, intentions, and turnover: The mismatched trilogy. *Journal of Vocational Behavior, 44,* 17–31.

11248

Test Name: INTENTION TO QUIT SCALE

Purpose: To measure intention to quit.

Number of Items: 2

Format: Responses are made on a 7-point scale ranging from 1 (*strongly disagree*) to 7 (*strongly agree*). Both items are presented.

Reliability: Alpha coefficients were .66 and .71.

Validity: Correlations with other variables ranged from −.59 to .09.

Author: Conway, N., and Briner, R. B.

Article: Full-time versus part-time employees: Understanding the links between work status, the psychological contract, and attitudes.

Journal: *Journal of Vocational Behavior*, October 2002, *61*, 279–301.

Related Research: Cook, J. D., et al. (1981). *The experience of work: A compendium of 249 measures and their use.* New York: Academic Press.

11249

Test Name: INTENTION TO TURNOVER SCALE

Purpose: To measure turnover intentions.

Number of Items: 3

Format: Scales range from 1 (*strongly disagree*) to 7 (*strongly agree*).

Reliability: Coefficient alpha was .70.

Validity: Correlations with other variables ranged from −.49 to .20.

Author: LeBlanc, M. M., and Kelloway, E. K.

Article: Predictors and outcomes of workplace violence and aggression.

Journal: *Journal of Applied Psychology*, June 2002, *87*, 444–453.

Related Research: Cammann, C., et al. (1979). *The Michigan Occupational Assessment Questionnaire.* Unpublished

manuscript, University of Michigan, Ann Arbor.

11250

Test Name: INTENTIONS TO QUIT SCALE

Purpose: To measure intentions to quit.

Number of Items: 3

Format: An example is given.

Reliability: Coefficient alpha was .87.

Validity: Correlations with other variables ranged from −.64 to .18.

Author: Jokisaari, M., and Nurmi, J.-E.

Article: Company matters: Goal-related social capital in the transition to working life.

Journal: *Journal of Vocational Behavior*, December 2005, *67*, 413–428.

Related Research: Colarelli, S. M. (1984). Methods of communication and mediating processes in realistic job previews. *Journal of Applied Psychology, 69,* 633–642.

11251

Test Name: INTENTIONS TO QUIT SCALE

Purpose: To measure one's intentions to quit the organization.

Number of Items: 6

Format: Scoring procedure employed 0 (*no*), 1 (*?*), and 3 (*yes*). An example is given.

Validity: Correlations with other variables ranged from −.20 to −.68.

Author: Russell, S. S., et al.

Article: Shorter can also be better: The Abridged Job in General Scale.

Journal: *Educational and Psychological Measurement*, October 2004, *64*, 878–893.

Related Research: Parra, L. F. (1995). *Development of an Intention to Quit Scale.* Unpublished manuscript, Bowling Green State University, Bowling Green, OH.

11252

Test Name: INTERPERSONAL CONFLICT AT WORK SCALE

Purpose: To measure how often one experienced arguments, yelling, and rudeness with coworkers.

Number of Items: 4

Format: Responses are made on a 5-point Likert scale ranging from 1 (*less than once per month or never*) to 5 (*several times per day*).

Reliability: Alpha coefficients were .74 and .76.

Validity: Correlations with other variables ranged from −.35 to .40 (*N* = 292).

Author: Fox, S., et al.

Article: Counterproductive work behavior (CWB) in response to job stressors and organizational justice: Some mediator and moderator tests for autonomy and emotions.

Journal: *Journal of Vocational Behavior,* December 2001, *59,* 291–309.

Related Research: Spector, P. E., & Jex, S. M. (1998). Development of four self-report measures of job stressors and strain: Interpersonal Conflict at Work Scale, Organizational Constraints Scale, Quantitative Workload Inventory, and Physical Symptoms Inventory. *Journal of Occupational Health Psychology, 3,* 356–367.

11253

Test Name: INTERPERSONAL CONFLICT AT WORK SCALE

Purpose: To measure both coworker and supervisor sources of conflict.

Number of Items: 8

Format: Responses are made on a 5-point scale ranging from 1 (*never*) to 5 (*very often*). An example is given.

Reliability: Alpha coefficients were .64 and .79 (*n* = 195).

Validity: Correlations with other variables ranged from −.40 to .09 (*n* = 195).

Author: Lubbers, R., et al.

Article: Young workers' job self-efficacy and affect: Pathways to health and performance.

Journal: *Journal of Vocational Behavior,* October 2005, *67,* 199–214.

Related Research: Frone, M. R. (2000). Interpersonal conflict at work and psychological outcomes: Testing a model among young workers. *Journal of Occupational Health Psychology, 5,* 246–255.

11254

Test Name: JOB AFFECT SCALE—MODIFIED

Purpose: To measure energy, fatigue, nervousness, and relaxation.

Number of Items: 20

Format: Includes four areas: energy, fatigue, nervousness, and relaxation. Responses are made on a 5-point scale ranging from 1 (*slightly or not at all*) to 5 (*definitely*).

Reliability: Alpha coefficients were .72 and .81.

Validity: Correlations with other variables ranged from −.53 to .82.

Author: Huelsman, T. J., et al.

Article: Measurement of dispositional affect: Construct validity and convergence with a circumplex model of affect.

Journal: *Educational and Psychological Measurement,* August 2003, *63,* 655–673.

Related Research: Burke, M. J., et al. (1989). Measuring affect at work: Confirmatory analyses of competing structures with conceptual linkage to cortical regulatory systems. *Journal of Personality and Social Psychology, 57,* 1091–1102.

11255

Test Name: JOB ANXIETY AND DEPRESSION SCALE

Purpose: To measure job-related anxiety and depression.

Number of Items: 6

Format: Scales range from 1 (*never*) to 5 (*all of the time*). Sample items are presented.

Reliability: Alpha coefficients ranged from .76 to .87.

Validity: Correlations with other variables ranged from −.55 to .26.

Author: Parker, S. K.

Article: Longitudinal effects of lean production on employee outcomes and the mediating role of work characteristics.

Journal: *Journal of Applied Psychology,* August 2003, *88,* 620–634.

Related Research: Warr, P. (1990). The measurement of well-being and other aspects of mental health. *Journal of Occupational Psychology, 63,* 193–210.

11256

Test Name: JOB DESCRIPTION FORM

Purpose: To measure job satisfaction.

Number of Items: 7

Format: Scales range from 1 (*completely dissatisfied*) to 7 (*completely satisfied*).

Reliability: Coefficient alpha was .78.

Author: Maier, G. W., and Brunstein, J. C.

Article: The role of personal work goals in newcomers' job satisfaction and organizational commitment: A longitudinal analysis.

Journal: *Journal of Applied Psychology*, October 2001, *86*, 1034–1042.

Related Research: Neuberger, O., & Allerbeck, M. (1978). *Messung und analyse von arbeitszufriedenheit* [Measurement and analysis of job satisfaction]. Bern, Switzerland: Huber.

11257

Test Name: JOB DIAGNOSTIC SURVEY

Purpose: To measure job satisfaction.

Number of Items: 14

Format: Responses are made on a 7-point scale. Sample items are presented.

Reliability: Alpha coefficients were .76 and .88.

Validity: Correlations with other variables ranged from −.12 to .59.

Author: Goulet, L. R., and Singh, P.

Article: Career Commitment: A reexamination and an extension.

Journal: *Journal of Vocational Behavior*, August 2002, *61*, 73–91.

Related Research: Hackman, J. R., & Oldham, G. R. (1974). Development of the Job Diagnostic Survey. *Journal of Applied Psychology, 65*, 159–170.

11258

Test Name: JOB DIAGNOSTIC SURVEY

Purpose: To measure overall job satisfaction.

Number of Items: 5

Format: Examples are given.

Reliability: Coefficient alpha was .83.

Validity: Correlations with other variables ranged from −.14 to .54.

Author: Haueter, J. A., et al.

Article: Measurement of newcomer socialization: Construct validation of a multidimensional scale.

Journal: *Journal of Vocational Behavior*, August 2003, *63*, 20–39.

Related Research: Hackman, J. R., & Oldham, G. R. (1975). Development of the Job Diagnostic Survey. *Journal of Applied Psychology, 60*, 159–170.

11259

Test Name: JOB-FOCUSED EMOTIONAL SCALE

Purpose: To measure job-focused emotional labor.

Number of Items: 7

Format: Includes variety, intensity, duration, and frequency. Responses are made on a 5-point scale ranging from 1 (*never*) to 5 (*always*). All items are presented.

Reliability: Alpha coefficients were .74 and .76.

Validity: Correlations with other variables ranged from −.12 to .49.

Author: Brotheridge, C. M., and Grandey, A. A.

Article: Emotional labor and burnout: Comparing two perspectives of "people work."

Journal: *Journal of Vocational Behavior*, February 2002, *60*, 17–39.

Related Research: Brotheridge, C. M., & Lee, R. T. (1998). *On the dimensionality of emotional labour: Development and validation of the Emotional Labour Scale*. Paper presented at the First Conference on Emotions in Organizational Life, San Diego.

11260

Test Name: JOB IN GENERAL SCALE

Purpose: To provide a global measurement of job satisfaction.

Format: Adjective scales are anchored by *yes*, *no* and *?*.

Reliability: Alpha coefficients ranged from .91 to .95.

Validity: Correlations with other variables ranged from −.05 to .80.

Author: Harris, J. I., et al.

Article: The comparative contributions of congruence and social support in career outcomes.

Journal: *The Career Development Quarterly*, June 2001, *49*, 314–323.

Related Research: Ironson, G. H., et al. (1989). Construction of a Job in General scale: A comparison of global, composite, and specific measures. *Journal of Applied Psychology, 74*, 193–200.

11261

Test Name: JOB-INDUCED TENSION SCALE

Purpose: To measure stress symptoms.

Number of Items: 7

Format: Responses are made on a 7-point scale ranging from *strongly disagree* to *strongly agree*. Sample items are presented.

Reliability: Coefficient alpha was .85.

Validity: Correlations with other variables ranged from −.03 to −.15.

Author: Haueter, J. A., et al.

Article: Measurement of newcomer socialization: Construct validation of a multidimensional scale.

Journal: *Journal of Vocational Behavior*, August 2003, *63*, 20–39.

Related Research: House, R. J., & Rizzo, J. R. (1972). Role conflict and ambiguity as critical variables in a model of organizational behavior. *Organizational Behavior and Human Performance, 7,* 467–505.

11262

Test Name: JOB-INDUCED TENSION SCALE

Purpose: To measure job-induced tension.

Number of Items: 6

Format: Responses are made on a 5-point scale ranging from 1 (*strongly disagree*) to 5 (*strongly agree*). Sample items are presented.

Validity: Correlations with other variables ranged from –.39 to .31 (*n* = 311).

Author: Hochwarter, W. A., et al.

Article: Perceived organizational support as a mediator of the relationship between politics perceptions and work outcomes.

Journal: *Journal of Vocational Behavior*, December 2003, *63*, 438–456.

Related Research: House, R., & Rizzo, J. (1972). Toward the measurement of organizational practices: Scale development and validation. *Journal of Applied Psychology, 56,* 338–396.

11263

Test Name: JOB-RELATED AFFECT SCALE

Purpose: To assess how an individual feels at work: calm, anxious, gloomy, and enthusiastic.

Number of Items: 12

Format: Frequency scales range from 1 (*never*) to 5 (*all of the time*). Sample items are presented.

Reliability: Alpha coefficients ranged from .77 to .88 across subscales.

Validity: Correlations with other variables ranged from –.18 to .32.

Author: Totterdell, P., et al.

Article: Affect networks: A structured analysis of the relationship between work ties and job-related affect.

Journal: *Journal of Applied Psychology*, October 2004, *89*, 854–867.

Related Research: Sevastos, P., et al. (1992). Evidence on the reliability and construct validity of Warr's (1990) well-being and mental health measures. *Journal of Occupational and Organizational Psychology, 65,* 33–49.

11264

Test Name: JOB-RELATED AFFECTIVE WELL-BEING SCALE

Purpose: To measure job-experienced emotions.

Number of Items: 30

Format: Includes positive and negative emotions. Responses are made on a 5-point scale ranging from 1 (*almost never*) to 5 (*extremely often or always*).

Reliability: Coefficient alpha was .95.

Author: Fox, S., et al.

Article: Counterproductive work behavior (CWB) in response to job stressors and organizational justice: Some mediator and moderator tests for autonomy and emotions.

Journal: *Journal of Vocational Behavior*, December 2001, *59*, 291–309.

Related Research: Van Katwyk, P. T., et al. (2000). Using the Job-Related Affective Well-Being Scale (JAWS) to investigate affective responses to work stressors. *Journal of Occupational Health Psychology, 5,* 219–230.

11265

Test Name: JOB-RELATED EXHAUSTION SCALE

Purpose: To measure emotional exhaustion on the job.

Number of Items: 6

Format: Scales range from 0 (*never felt this way*) to 6 (*felt this way every day*). Sample items are presented.

Reliability: Alpha coefficients ranged from .85 to .89.

Author: Grandey, A. A., et al.

Article: Must "service with a smile" be stressful? The moderating role of personal control for American and French employees.

Journal: *Journal of Applied Psychology*, September 2005, *90*, 893–904.

Related Research: Wharton, A. S. (1993). The affective consequences of service work: Managing emotions on the job. *Work and Occupations, 20,* 205–232.

11266

Test Name: JOB-ROLE QUALITY SCALE

Purpose: To assess job characteristics as being rewarding or a concern.

Number of Items: 28

Format: Scales range from 1 (*not at all*) to 4 (*considerably*). Sample items are presented.

Reliability: Alpha coefficients were .77 (rewards) and .81 (concerns).

Author: Gareis, K. C., et al.

Article: Individual and crossover effects of work schedule fit: A within-couple analysis.

Journal: *Journal of Marriage and Family*, November 2003, *65*, 1041–1054.

Related Research: Barnett, R. C., & Brennan, R. T. (1997). Change in job conditions, change in psychological distress, and gender: A longitudinal study of dual-earner couples. *Journal of Organizational Behavior, 18*, 253–274.

11267

Test Name: JOB SATISFACTION BLANK

Purpose: To measure general job satisfaction.

Number of Items: 4

Reliability: Split-half reliability was .93 (*n* = 310).

Validity: Correlations with other variables ranged from −.03 to −.13.

Author: Jepsen, D. A., and Sheu, H.-B.

Article: General job satisfaction from a developmental perspective: Exploring choice-job matches at two career stages.

Journal: *The Career Development Quarterly*, December 2003, *52*, 162–179.

Related Research: Hoppock, R. (1935). *Job satisfaction*. New York: Harper.

11268

Test Name: JOB SATISFACTION INDEX

Purpose: To measure job satisfaction.

Number of Items: 5

Format: Five-point scales are used. A sample item is presented.

Reliability: Alpha coefficients ranged from .85 to .88.

Validity: Correlations with other variables ranged from −.61 to .67.

Author: Ambrose, M. L., and Cropanzano, R.

Article: A longitudinal analysis of organizational fairness: An examination of reactions to tenure and promotion decisions.

Journal: *Journal of Applied Psychology*, April 2003, *88*, 266–275.

Related Research: Brayfield, A. H., & Rothe, H. F. (1951). An index of job satisfaction. *Journal of Applied Psychology, 35*, 307–311.

11269

Test Name: JOB SATISFACTION INVENTORY

Purpose: To measure level of job satisfaction.

Number of Items: 10

Format: Responses are made on a 20-point scale. An example is given.

Reliability: Split-half reliability coefficient was .91.

Validity: Correlations with other variables ranged from −.23 to .70.

Author: Meir, E. I., and Melamed, S.

Article: Occupational specialty congruence: New data and future directions.

Journal: *Journal of Vocational Behavior*, August 2005, *67*, 21–34.

Related Research: Meir, E. I., & Yaari, Y. (1988). The relationship between congruent specialty choice within occupations and satisfaction. *Journal of Vocational Behavior, 33*, 99–117.

11270

Test Name: JOB SATISFACTION MEASURE

Purpose: To measure job satisfaction.

Number of Items: 3

Format: Each item is accompanied by a different response format, e.g. 1 = *yes*, 0 = *no*. All items are presented.

Reliability: Coefficient alpha was .83.

Validity: Correlations with other variables ranged from −.40 to .25.

Author: Boudreau, J. W., et al.

Article: Personality and cognitive ability as predictors of job search among employed managers.

Journal: *Personnel Psychology*, Spring 2001 *54*, 25–50.

Related Research: Judge, T. A., et al. (1994). Job and life attitudes of male executives. *Journal of Applied Psychology, 79*, 767–782.

11271

Test Name: JOB SATISFACTION SCALE

Purpose: To measure job satisfaction.

Number of Items: 4

Format: Scales range from 1 (*never*) to 7 (*always*). A sample item is presented.

Reliability: The scale reliability was .83.

Validity: Correlations with other variables ranged from −.52 to .36.

Author: Allen, D. G., and Griffeth, R. W.

Article: Test of a mediated performance–turnover relationship highlighting the moderating roles of visibility and reward contingency.

Journal: *Journal of Applied Psychology*, October 2001, *86*, 1014–1021.

Related Research: Hoppock, R. (1935). *Job satisfaction*. New York: Harper.

11272

Test Name: JOB SATISFACTION SCALE

Purpose: To measure job satisfaction.

Number of Items: 5

Format: Responses are made on a 4-point response format ranging from *very unsatisfied* to *very satisfied*. All items are presented.

Reliability: Coefficient alpha was .80.

Validity: Correlations with other variables ranged from −.38 to .58.

Author: Behson, S. J.

Article: The relative contribution of formal and informal organizational work–family support.

Journal: *Journal of Vocational Behavior,* June 2005, *66,* 487–500.

Related Research: Iverson, R. D., et al. (1998). Affectivity, organizational stressors, and absenteeism: A causal model of burnout and its consequences. *Journal of Vocational Behavior, 52,* 1–23.

11273

Test Name: JOB SATISFACTION SCALE

Purpose: To measure job satisfaction.

Number of Items: 8

Format: Scales range from 1 (*extremely dissatisfied*) to 7 (*extremely satisfied*). All items are presented.

Reliability: Coefficient alpha was .82.

Validity: Correlations with other variables ranged from .13 to .70.

Author: Bettencourt, L. A., et al.

Article: A comparison of attitude, personality, and knowledge predictors of service-oriented organizational citizenship behaviors.

Journal: *Journal of Applied Psychology,* February 2001, *86,* 29–41.

11274

Test Name: JOB SATISFACTION SCALE

Purpose: To measure job satisfaction.

Number of Items: 6

Format: Item responses are anchored by 1 (*very dissatisfied*) and 5 (*very satisfied*). All items are presented.

Reliability: Reliabilities ranged from .73 to .77.

Validity: Correlations with other variables ranged from −.17 to .36.

Author: Cohen, A., and Schwartz, H.

Article: An empirical examination among Canadian teachers of determinants of the need for employees' assistance programs.

Journal: *Psychological Reports,* June 2002, *90,* Part 2, 1221–1238.

Related Research: Schriesheim, C., & Tsui, A. S. (1980). *Development and validation of a short satisfaction instrument for use in survey feedback interventions.* Paper presented at the meeting of the Western Academy of Management, Phoenix, AZ.

11275

Test Name: JOB SATISFACTION SCALE

Purpose: To measure job satisfaction.

Number of Items: 2

Format: Responses are made on a 5-point scale ranging from 1 (*I am not satisfied at all*) to 5 (*I am extremely satisfied and couldn't be more satisfied*).

Reliability: Coefficient alpha was .83.

Validity: Correlations with other variables ranged from −.06 to .57.

Author: Conway, N., and Briner, R. B.

Article: Full-time versus part-time employees: Understanding the links between work status, the psychological contract, and attitudes.

Journal: *Journal of Vocational Behavior,* October 2002, *61,* 279–301.

Related Research: Warr, P. B. (1987). *Work, unemployment, and mental health.* Oxford, England: Oxford University Press.

11276

Test Name: JOB SATISFACTION SCALE

Purpose: To evaluate job satisfaction.

Number of Items: 3

Format: An example is given.

Reliability: Coefficient alpha was .79.

Validity: Correlations with other variables ranged from −.64 to .11.

Author: Jokisaari, M., and Nurmi, J.-E.

Article: Company matters: Goal-related social capital in the transition to working life.

Journal: *Journal of Vocational Behavior,* December 2005, *67,* 413–428.

Related Research: Cammann, C., et al. (1983). Assessing the attitudes and perceptions of organizational members. In S. E. Seashore et al. (Eds.), *Assessing organizational change: A guide to methods, measures, and practices* (pp. 71–138). New York: Wiley.

11277

Test Name: JOB SATISFACTION SCALE

Purpose: To assess job satisfaction with momentary time instructions (e.g., right now and at this moment).

Number of Items: 5

Format: Scales range from 1 (*strongly disagree*) to 5 (*strongly agree*). Sample items are presented.

Reliability: Coefficient alpha was .95.

Validity: Correlations with other variables ranged from −.46 to .49.

Author: Judge, T. A., and Ilies, R.

Article: Affect and job satisfaction: A study of their relationship at work and at home.

Journal: *Journal of Applied Psychology*, August 2004, *89*, 661–673.

Related Research: Brayfield, A. H., & Rothe, H. F. (1951). An index of job satisfaction. *Journal of Applied Psychology*, *35*, 307–311.

11278

Test Name: JOB SATISFACTION SCALE

Purpose: To measure job satisfaction.

Number of Items: 5

Format: Responses are made on a 7-point Likert scale. Examples are presented.

Reliability: Coefficient alpha was .84.

Validity: Correlations with other variables ranged from −.68 to .47.

Author: Lauver, K. L. and Kristof-Brown, A.

Article: Distinguishing between employees' perceptions of person–job and person–organization fit.

Journal: *Journal of Vocational Behavior*, December 2001, *59*, 454–470.

11279

Test Name: JOB SATISFACTION SCALE

Purpose: To measure job satisfaction.

Number of Items: 4

Format: Responses are made on a 5-point scale ranging from 1 (*does not apply at all*) to 5 (*applies very strongly*). Examples are presented.

Reliability: Coefficient alpha was .67.

Validity: Correlations with other variables ranged form −.35 to .27 (*n* = 391).

Author: Pinquart, M., et al.

Article: Self-efficacy and successful school-to-work transition: A longitudinal study.

Journal: *Journal of Vocational Behavior*, December 2003, *63*, 329–346.

Related Research: Erwins, C. J. (2001). The relationship of women's role strain to social support, role satisfaction, and self-efficacy. *Family Relations*, *50*, 230–238.

11280

Test Name: JOB SATISFACTION SCALE

Purpose: To measure job satisfaction.

Number of Items: 10

Format: Four-point scales are anchored by 1 (*disagree*) and 4 (*agree*).

Reliability: Coefficient alpha was .86.

Validity: Correlations with other variables ranged from −.04 to .56.

Author: Shimazu, A., et al.

Article: Job control and social support as coping resources in job satisfaction.

Journal: *Psychological Reports*, April 2004, *94*, 449–456.

Related Research: McLean, A. A. (1979). *Work stress*. Boston: Addison-Wesley.

11281

Test Name: JOB SATISFACTION SCALE

Purpose: To measure job satisfaction.

Number of Items: 4

Format: Scales range from 1 (*strongly disagree*) to 5 (*strongly agree*). Sample items are presented.

Reliability: Coefficient alpha was .89.

Validity: Correlations with other variables ranged from .23 to .67.

Author: Tan, H. H., and Aryee, S.

Article: Antecedents and outcomes of union loyalty: A constructive replication and an extension.

Journal: *Journal of Applied Psychology*, August 2002, *87*, 715–722.

Related Research: Fricko, M. A., & Beehr, T. A. (1992). A longitudinal investigation of interest congruence and gender concentration as predictors of job satisfaction. *Personnel Psychology*, *45*, 99–117.

11282

Test Name: JOB SATISFACTION SCALE—ADAPTED

Purpose: To assess job satisfaction.

Number of Items: 5

Reliability: Coefficient alpha was .70.

Validity: Correlations with other variables ranged from −.22 to .59.

Author: Kolodinsky, R. W., et al.

Article: Nonlinearity in the relationship between political skill and work outcomes: Convergent evidence from three studies.

Journal: *Journal of Vocational Behavior*, October 2004, *65*, 294–308.

Related Research: Brayfield, A., & Rothe, H. (1951). An index of job satisfaction. *Journal of Applied Psychology*, *35*, 307–311.

11283

Test Name: JOB SATISFACTION SCALE (ARABIC)

Purpose: To measure intrinsic and extrinsic satisfaction with the job and the organization.

Number of Items: 22

Format: Six-point scales are anchored by 1 (*very much dissatisfaction*) and 6 (*very much satisfaction*).

Reliability: Alpha coefficients ranged from .94 to .95.

Validity: Correlations with other variables ranged from –.35 to .33.

Author: Al-Mashaan, O. S.

Article: Associations among job satisfaction, optimism, pessimism, and psychosomatic symptoms for employees in the government sector in Kuwait.

Journal: *Psychological Reports*, August 2003, *93*, 17–25.

Related Research: Al-Mashaan, O. S. (1998). Job satisfaction. In R. A. Amed & U. P. Gielen (Eds.), *Psychology in the Arab Countries* (pp. 363–383). Cairo, Egypt: Menoufia University Press.

11284

Test Name: JOB SATISFACTION SCALE—MODIFIED

Purpose: To measure "facet-free job satisfaction."

Number of Items: 5

Format: Responses are made on a 5-point scale ranging from 1 (*not at all what I wanted*) to 5 (*just what I wanted*).

Reliability: Alpha coefficients ranged from .89 to .93.

Author: Schirmer, L. L., and Lopez, F. G.

Article: Probing the social support and work strain relationship among adult workers: Contributions of adult attachment orientations.

Journal: *Journal of Vocational Behavior*, August 2001, *59*, 17–33.

Related Research: Pond, S. B., & Geyer, P. D. (1987). Employee age as a moderator of the relations between perceived work alternatives and job satisfaction. *Journal of Applied Psychology, 72*, 552–557. Lent, E. B. (1992). The predictive ability of congruence and career self-efficacy in adult workers: A study of job satisfaction (Doctoral dissertation, Michigan State University, 1992). *Dissertation Abstracts International, 53* (6-B), 3195.

11285

Test Name: JOB SATISFACTION SCALES

Purpose: To measure job satisfaction.

Number of Items: 11

Format: Includes three scales: Satisfaction With Job Autonomy, Satisfaction With Personal Fulfillment From Job, and Satisfaction With Financial Characteristics of Job. Responses are made on a 5-point scale ranging from 1 (*very dissatisfied*) to 5 (*very satisfied*). All items are presented.

Reliability: Alpha coefficients ranged from .73 to .88.

Author: Wolniak, G. C., and Pascarella, E. T.

Article: The effects of college major and job field congruence on job satisfaction.

Journal: *Journal of Vocational Behavior*, October 2005, *67*, 233–251.

Related Research: Chartrand, J., & Walsh, W. B. (1999). What should we expect from congruence? *Journal of Vocational Behavior, 55*, 136–146.

11286

Test Name: JOB SATISFACTION SURVEY

Purpose: To measure composite job satisfaction.

Number of Items: 36

Format: Includes nine facets: pay, promotion, supervision, fringe benefits, contingent rewards, operating conditions, coworkers, nature of work, and communication. Responses are made on a 6-point scale. ranging from 1 (*disagree very much*) to 6 (*agree very much*). A sample item is provided.

Reliability: Alpha coefficients ranged from .45 to .91.

Validity: Correlations with other variables ranged from –.43 to .68.

Author: Bruck, C. S., et al.

Article: The relation between work–family conflict and job satisfaction: A finer-grained analysis.

Journal: *Journal of Vocational Behavior*, June 2002, *60*, 336–353.

Related Research: Spector, P. E. (1985). Measurement of human service staff satisfaction: Development of the Job Satisfaction Survey. *American Journal of Community Psychology, 13*, 693–713.

11287

Test Name: JOB STRESS SCALE

Purpose: To assess job stress.

Number of Items: 4

Format: Scales range from 1 (*strongly disagree*) to 5 (*strongly agree*). All items are presented.

Reliability: Coefficient alpha was .87.

Validity: Correlations with other variables ranged from –.21 to .63.

Author: Bolino, M. C., and Turnley, W. H.

Article: The personal costs of citizenship behavior: The relationship between individual initiative and role overload, job stress, and work–family conflict.

Journal: *Journal of Applied Psychology*, July 2005, *90*, 740–748.

Related Research: Motowidlo, S. J., et al. (1986). Occupational stress: Its causes and consequences for job performance. *Journal of Applied Psychology, 71*, 618–629.

11288

Test Name: JOB STRESS SCALE

Purpose: To measure job stress.

Number of Items: 8

Format: Responses are made on a 5-point scale ranging from *very stressful* to *not stressful*. An example is given.

Reliability: Coefficient alpha was .71.

Validity: Correlation with other variables ranged from –.18 to .44.

Author: Stoeva, A. Z., et al.

Article: Negative affectivity, role stress, and work–family conflict.

Journal: *Journal of Vocational Behavior*, February 2002, *60*, 1–16.

Related Research: Arsenault, A., et al. (1991). Stress and mental strain in hospital work: Exploring the relationship beyond personality. *Journal of Organizational Behavior, 12*, 483–493.

11289

Test Name: JOB STRESSOR SCALES

Purpose: To measure job stressors.

Number of Items: 30

Format: Includes five scales: Interpersonal Conflict at Work, Work Demands, Job Ambiguity, Role Ambiguity, and Role Conflict.

Reliability: Alpha coefficients ranged from .84 to .92.

Validity: Correlations with other variables ranged from –.41 to .69 (*n* = 309).

Author: Fortunato, V. J.

Article: A comparison of the construct validity of three measures of negative affectivity.

Journal: *Educational and Psychological Measurement*, April 2004, *64*, 271–289.

Related Research: Spector, P. E., & Jex, S. M. (1998). Development of four self-report measures of job stressors and strain: Interpersonal Conflict at Work Scale, Organizational Constraints Scale, Quantitative Workload Inventory, and Physical Symptoms Inventory. *Journal of Occupational Health Psychology, 3*, 356–367. Karasek, R. A., Jr. (1979). Job demands, job decision latitude, and mental strain: Implications for job redesign. *Administrative Science Quarterly, 24*, 285–308. Breaugh, J. A., & Colihan, J. P. (1994). Measuring facets of job ambiguity: Construct validity evidence. *Journal of Applied Psychology, 79*, 191–202. Rizzo, J. R., et al. (1970). Role conflict and ambiguity in complex organizations. *Administrative Science Quarterly, 15*, 150–163.

11290

Test Name: JOB TENSION SCALE

Purpose: To measure job tension.

Number of Items: 7

Reliability: Coefficient alpha was .80.

Validity: Correlations with other variables ranged from –.22 to .53.

Author: Kolodinsky, R. W., et al.

Article: Nonlinearity in the relationship between political skill and work outcomes: Convergent evidence from three studies.

Journal: *Journal of Vocational Behavior*, October 2004, *65*, 294–308.

Related Research: House, R. J., & Rizzo, J. (1972). Toward the measurement of organizational practices: Scale development and validation. *Journal of Applied Psychology, 56*, 338–396.

11291

Test Name: JOB WITHDRAWAL SCALE

Purpose: To measure turnover intentions.

Number of Items: 3

Format: Responses are made on a 5-point multiple-choice format.

Reliability: Alpha coefficients were .74 and .77.

Validity: Correlations with other variables ranged from –.59 to .53.

Author: Wasti, S. A.

Article: Commitment profiles: Combinations of organizational commitment forms and job outcomes.

Journal: *Journal of Vocational Behavior*, October 2005, *67*, 290–308.

Related Research: Hanisch, K. A., & Hulin, C. L. (1991). General attitudes and organizational withdrawal: An evaluation of a causal model. *Journal of Vocational Behavior, 39*, 110–128.

11292

Test Name: LOYALTY AND INTENTION TO QUIT SCALES

Purpose: To assess loyalty and intention to quit.

Number of Items: 5

Format: Includes two parts: Loyalty and Intention to Quit. Responses are made on a 5-point Likert scale ranging from 1 (*strongly disagree*) to 5 (*strongly agree*). Examples are presented.

Reliability: Alpha coefficients were .65 (loyalty) and .93 (intention to quit).

Validity: Correlations with other variables ranged from −.27 to .54 (*n* = 392).

Author: Boswell, W. R., et al.

Article: Relations between stress and work outcomes: The role of felt challenge, job control, and psychological strain.

Journal: *Journal of Vocational Behavior*, February 2004, *64*, 165–181.

Related Research: Boroff, K. E., & Lewin, D. (1997). Loyalty, voice, and intent to exit a union firm: A conceptual and empirical analysis. *Industrial and Labor Relations Review*, *51*, 50–63.

11293

Test Name: MANIPULATION OF DEPENDENCE ON TEAM MEMBERS MEASURE

Purpose: To measure manipulation of dependence on team members.

Number of Items: 3

Format: Responses are made on 7-point scales ranging from 1 (*strongly disagree*) to 7 (*strongly agree*). A sample item is presented.

Reliability: Coefficient alpha was .71.

Author: Alge, B. J., et al.

Article: Remote control: Predictors of electronic monitoring intensity and secrecy.

Journal: *Personnel Psychology*, Summer 2004, *57*, 377–410.

Related Research: Emerson, R. M. (1962). Power–dependence relations. *American Sociological Review*, *27*, 31–41.

11294

Test Name: MASLACH BURNOUT INVENTORY—CHINESE VERSION

Purpose: To assess emotional exhaustion, depersonalization, and personal accomplishment.

Number of Items: 22

Format: Seven-point scales are anchored by 0 (*feeling has never been experienced*) and 6 (*feeling is experienced daily*).

Reliability: Internal consistency coefficients ranged from .80 to .88.

Author: Yuen, M., et al.

Article: Confirmatory factor analysis and reliability of the Chinese Version of the Maslach Burnout Inventory among guidance teachers in Hong Kong.

Journal: *Psychological Reports*, December 2002, *91*, Part 2, 1081–1086.

Related Research: Mo, K. W. (1991). Teacher burnout: Relations with stress, personality, and social support. *Education Journal*, *19*, 3–11.

11295

Test Name: MEANING OF WORK SCALE

Purpose: To measure the meaning of work in terms of intrinsic and extrinsic rewards and work centrality.

Number of Items: 46

Format: Response scales are anchored by 5 (*strongly agree*) and 1 (*strongly disagree*). All items are presented in English.

Reliability: Alpha coefficients ranged from .69 to .86. Total alpha was .82.

Validity: Correlation with job involvement was .65.

Author: Hasan, H.

Article: Meaning of work among a sample of Kuwaiti workers.

Journal: *Psychological Reports*, February 2004, *94*, 195–207.

11296

Test Name: MICHIGAN ORGANIZATIONAL ASSESSMENT QUESTIONNAIRE

Purpose: To assess global satisfaction.

Number of Items: 3

Format: Responses are made on a 7-point scale ranging from 1 (*strongly disagree*) to 7 (*strongly agree*).

Reliability: Alpha coefficients were .77 and .82.

Validity: Correlations with other variables ranged from −.36 to .54.

Author: Bruck, C. S., et al.

Article: The relation between work–family conflict and job satisfaction: A finer-grained analysis.

Journal: *Journal of Vocational Behavior*, June 2002, *60*, 336–353.

Related Research: Cammann, C., et al. (1979). *The Michigan Organizational Assessment Questionnaire*. Unpublished manuscript, University of Michigan, Ann Arbor.

11297

Test Name: MILITARY JOB SATISFACTION SCALE

Purpose: To measure military job satisfaction: job fulfillment, supervision, job opportunities, and recognition.

Number of Items: 14

Format: Items are anchored by 4 (*very satisfied*) and 1 (*very dissatisfied*). All items are presented.

Reliability: Alpha coefficients ranged from .74 to .86 across subscales.

Validity: Correlations with other variables ranged from −.04 to .27.

Author: Schumm, W. R., et al.

Article: Dimensionality of military job satisfaction items: An exploratory factor analysis of data from the Spring 1996 Sample of Military Personnel.

Journal: *Psychological Reports,* June 2003, *92,* Part 1, 809–819.

11298

Test Name: MULTIDIMENSIONAL RESEARCH BURNOUT SCALE

Purpose: To measure burnout in an academic setting.

Number of Items: 8

Format: Item responses range from 1 (*strongly disagree*) to 5 (*strongly agree*). All items are presented.

Reliability: Alpha coefficients ranged from .74 to .80.

Author: Singh, S. N., et al.

Article: Research burnout: A refined multidimensional scale.

Journal: *Psychological Reports,* December 2004, *95,* Part 2, 1253–1263.

Related Research: Singh, S. N., & Bush, R. F. (1997). Research burnout in tenured marketing professors: An empirical investigation. *Journal of Marketing Education, 20,* 4–15.

11299

Test Name: NEGATIVE SPILLOVER SCALE

Purpose: To measure negative nonwork-to-work spillover.

Number of Items: 8

Format: Five-point scales are used. Sample items are presented.

Reliability: Cronbach's alpha was .81.

Validity: Correlations with other variables ranged from −.37 to .39.

Author: Cohen, A., and Schwartz, H.

Article: An empirical examination among Canadian teachers of determinants of the need for employees' assistance programs.

Journal: *Psychological Reports,* June 2002, *90,* Part 2, 1221–1238.

Related Research: Kirchmeyer, C. (1993). Nonwork-to-work spillover: A more balanced view of the experiences and coping of professional women and men. *Sex Roles, 28,* 531–552.

11300

Test Name: OCCUPATIONAL POSITIVE AND NEGATIVE AFFECT SCALE

Purpose: To measure positive and negative work affect.

Number of Items: 14

Format: Scales range from 1 (*not at all*) to 7 (*all the time*).

Reliability: Alpha coefficients ranged from .86 to .92.

Author: Griffin, M. A.

Article: Dispositions and work reactions: A multilevel approach.

Journal: *Journal of Applied Psychology,* December 2001, *86,* 1142–1151.

Related Research: Hart, P. M., et al. (1996). *QPASS: Manual for the Queensland Public Agency Staff Survey.* Brisbane, Queensland, Australia: Public Sector Management Commission.

11301

Test Name: OCCUPATIONAL STRAIN SCALE

Purpose: To measure occupational strain symptoms.

Number of Items: 4

Format: Scales range from 1 (*very seldom*) to 5 (*very often*).

Reliability: Coefficient alpha was .75.

Validity: Correlations with other variables ranged from −.24 to .01.

Author: Elovainio, M., et al.

Article: Organizational justice evaluations, job control, and occupational strain.

Journal: *Journal of Applied Psychology,* June 2001, *86,* 418–424.

Related Research: Elo, A.-L., et al. (1992). *OSQ Occupational Stress Questionnaire: User's instructions.* Helsinki, Finland: Finnish Institute of Occupational Health.

11302

Test Name: OLDENBERG BURNOUT INVENTORY

Purpose: To measure job burnout.

Number of Items: 15

Format: Scales range from 1 (*totally disagree*) to 4 (*totally agree*). Sample items are presented.

Reliability: Alpha coefficients ranged from .82 to .83 across two subscales.

Validity: Correlations with other variables ranged from .06 to .53.

Author: Demerouti, E., et al.

Article: The job demands–resources model of burnout.

Journal: *Journal of Applied Psychology,* June 2001, *86,* 499–512.

11303

Test Name: ONTARIO SOCCER OFFICIALS SURVEY—REVISED FOR BASKETBALL

Purpose: To measure the sources and magnitude of perceived psychological stress of certified high school basketball officials.

Number of Items: 16

Format: Includes four factors: fear of physical harm, fear of failure, lack of respect, and time pressure. Examples are given.

Reliability: Alpha coefficients ranged from .68 to .86.

Author: Stewart, M. J., et al.

Article: Perceived psychological stress among high school basketball officials.

Journal: *Perceptual and Motor Skills*, October 2004, *99*, 463–469.

Related Research: Taylor, A. H. (1990). Perceived stress, psychological burnout and paths to turnover intentions among sport officials. *Applied Sport Psychology*, *2*, 84–97.

11304

Test Name: OPPORTUNITY SATISFACTION SCALE

Purpose: To measure satisfaction with career and developmental opportunities.

Number of Items: 6

Format: Responses are made on a 5-point scale ranging from 1 (*strongly dissatisfied*) to 5 (*strongly satisfied*). All items are presented.

Reliability: Coefficient alpha was .89.

Validity: Correlations with other variables ranged from .18 to .45.

Author: Prince, J. B.

Article: Career opportunity and organizational attachment in a blue-collar unionized environment.

Journal: *Journal of Vocational Behavior*, August 2003, *63*, 136–150.

11305

Test Name: ORGANIZATIONAL CONSTRAINTS SCALE

Purpose: To measure work constraints.

Number of Items: 11

Reliability: Alpha coefficients were .84 and .85.

Validity: Correlations with other variables ranged from −.42 to .47 ($N = 292$.)

Author: Fox, S., et al.

Article: Counterproductive work behavior (CWB) in response to job stressors and organizational justice: Some mediator and moderator tests for autonomy and emotions.

Journal: *Journal of Vocational Behavior*, December 2001, *59*, 291–309.

Related Research: Spector, P. E., & Jex, S. M. (1998). Development of four self-report measures of job stressors and strain: Interpersonal Conflict at Work Scale, Organizational Constraints Scale, Quantitative Workload Inventory, Physical Symptoms Inventory. *Journal of Occupational Health Psychology*, *3*, 356–367.

11306

Test Name: ORGANIZATIONAL SATISFACTION SCALE

Purpose: To measure organizational satisfaction.

Number of Items: 5

Format: Scales range from 1 (*strongly disagree*) to 7 (*strongly agree*). A sample item is presented.

Reliability: Coefficient alpha was .81.

Validity: Correlations with other variables ranged from .10 to .59.

Author: Liao, H., and Rupp, D. E.

Article: The impact of justice climate and justice orientation on

work outcomes: A cross-level multifoci framework.

Journal: *Journal of Applied Psychology*, March 2005, *90*(2), 242–256.

Related Research: King, D. C. (1960). A multiplant factor analysis of employees' attitudes toward their company. *Journal of Applied Psychology*, *44*, 285–300.

11307

Test Name: ORGANIZATIONAL WITHDRAWAL COGNITIONS

Purpose: To measure organizational withdrawal cognitions.

Number of Items: 3

Format: Responses are made on a 4-point scale ranging from 1 (*strongly disagree*) to 4 (*strongly agree*). A sample item is presented.

Reliability: Reliability estimates were .75 and .82.

Validity: Correlations with other variables ranged from −.35 to .67.

Author: Blau, G., et al.

Article: Correlates of professional versus organizational withdrawal cognitions.

Journal: *Journal of Vocational Behavior*, August 2003, *63*, 72–85.

Related Research: Blau, G. (1989). Testing the generalizability of a career commitment measure and its impact on employee turnover. *Journal of Vocational Behavior*, *35*, 88–103.

11308

Test Name: OUTCOME FAVORABILITY SCALE

Purpose: To assess response to a layoff.

Number of Items: 8

Format: Scales range from 1 (*strongly disagree*) to 5 (*strongly agree*). Sample items are presented.

Reliability: Internal reliability was .80.

Validity: Correlations with other variables ranged from −.40 to .39.

Author: Barclay, L. J., et al.

Article: Exploring the role of emotions in injustice perceptions and retaliation.

Journal: *Journal of Applied Psychology*, July 2005, *90*, 629–643.

Related Research: Brockner, J., et al. (1990). When it is especially important to explain why: Factors affecting the relationship between manager's explanations of a layoff and survivor's reactions to the layoff. *Journal of Experimental Social Psychology, 26*, 389–407.

11309

Test Name: OVERALL JOB SATISFACTION INDEX

Purpose: To measure job satisfaction.

Number of Items: 18

Format: Scales range from 1 (*strongly disagree*) to 5 (*strongly agree*).

Reliability: Coefficient alpha was .92.

Validity: Correlations with other variables ranged from −.04 to .63.

Author: Schleicher, D. J., et al.

Article: Reexamining the job satisfaction–performance relationship: The complexity of attitudes.

Journal: *Journal of Applied Psychology*, February 2004, *89*, 165–177.

Related Research: Brayfield, A. H., & Rothe, H. F. (1951). An index of job satisfaction. *Journal of Applied Psychology, 35*, 307–311.

11310

Test Name: OVERALL JOB SATISFACTION SCALE

Purpose: To measure job satisfaction.

Number of Items: 3

Format: Responses are made on a 5-point scale ranging from 1 (*strongly disagree*) to 5 (*strongly agree*). A sample item is given.

Reliability: Coefficient alpha was .88.

Validity: Correlations with other variables ranged from −.68 to .70.

Author: Allen, T. D.

Article: Family-supportive work environment: The role of organizational perceptions.

Journal: *Journal of Vocational Behavior*, June 2001, *58*, 414–435.

Related Research: Cammann, C., et al. (1979). *The Michigan Organizational Assessment Questionnaire*. Unpublished manuscript. Ann Arbor: University of Michigan.

11311

Test Name: OVERT INTENTION TO STAY SCALE

Purpose: To measure the intention to stay in a job.

Number of Items: 4

Format: Scales range from 1 (*strongly disagree*) to 5 (*strongly agree*).

Reliability: Alpha coefficients ranged from .75 to .82.

Validity: Correlations with other variables ranged from −.18 to .51.

Author: Barrick, M. R., and Zimmerman, R. D.

Article: Reducing voluntary, avoidable turnover through selection.

Journal: *Journal of Applied Psychology*, January 2005, *90*, 159–166.

Related Research: Chatman, J. J. (1991). Matching people and organizations: Selection and socialization in public accounting firms. *Administrative Science Quarterly, 36*, 459–484.

11312

Test Name: PERCEIVED COWORKER SUPPORT SCALE

Purpose: To measure employees' perceived coworker support.

Number of Items: 4

Format: Responses are made on a 5-point scale ranging from 1 (*not at all*) to 5 (*completely*).

Reliability: Coefficient alpha was .86.

Validity: Correlations with other variables ranged from −.16 to .37.

Author: Liao, H., et al.

Article: Sticking out like a sore thumb: Employee dissimilarity and deviance at work.

Journal: *Personnel Psychology*, Winter 2004, *57*, 969–1000.

Related Research: Haynes, C. E., et al. (1999). Measures of perceived work characteristics for health services research: Test of a measurement model and normative data. *British Journal of Health Psychology, 4*, 257–275.

11313

Test Name: POSITIVE AND NEGATIVE AFFECT SCHEDULE—EXPANDED FORM

Purpose: To measure affect at work as fear, hostility, quiet, sadness, joviality, attentiveness, self-assurance, shyness, fatigue, serenity, and surprise.

Number of Items: 60

Format: Scales range from 1 (*very slightly or not at all*) to 5 (*extremely*).

Reliability: Alpha coefficients ranged from .77 to .92 over seven of the subscales.

Author: Lee, K., and Allen, N. J.

Article: Organizational citizenship behavior and workplace deviance: The role of affect and cognitions.

Journal: *Journal of Applied Psychology*, February 2002, *87*, 131–142.

Related Research: Watson, D., & Clark, L. A. (1994). *Manual for the Positive and Negative Affect Schedule (Expanded Form)*. Unpublished manuscript, University of Iowa, Iowa City.

11314

Test Name: POSITIVE AND NEGATIVE JOB AFFECT SCALE

Purpose: To measure positive and negative mood states associated with a job.

Number of Items: 12

Format: Item responses are anchored by 0 (*very little*) and 4 (*very much*). All items are presented.

Reliability: Alphas were .76 (positive mood) and .73 (negative mood).

Validity: Correlations with other variables ranged from −.38 to .52.

Author: LaMastro, V.

Article: Influence of perceived institutional and faculty support on college students' attitudes and behavioral intentions.

Journal: *Psychological Reports*, April 2001, *88*, 567–580.

Related Research: Brief, A., et al. (1988). Should negative affectivity remain an unmeasured variable in the study of job stress. *Journal of Applied Psychology, 73*, 193–198.

11315

Test Name: POSITIVE ASPECTS OF PEACEKEEPING SCALE

Purpose: To measure the fulfilling and uplifting experiences of military personnel in Somalia.

Number of Items: 7

Format: A 5-point Likert scale is used.

Reliability: Internal consistency reliability was .83.

Author: Gray, M. J., et al.

Article: A longitudinal analysis of PTSD symptom course: Delayed-onset PTSD in Somalia peacekeepers.

Journal: *Journal of Consulting and Clinical Psychology*, October 2004, *72*, 909–913.

Related Research: Litz, B. T., et al. (1997). Warriors as peacekeepers: Features of the Somalia experience and PTSD. *Journal of Consulting and Clinical Psychology, 65,* 1001–1010.

11316

Test Name: PROBLEMS WITH REORGANIZATION SCALE

Purpose: To assess problems with reorganization.

Number of Items: 4

Format: Responses are made on a 4-point scale ranging from 1 (*never*) to 4 (*always*). A sample item is presented.

Reliability: Coefficient alpha was .76.

Validity: Correlations with other variables ranged from −.31 to .38 (*n* = 214).

Author: Bakker, A. B., et al.

Article: Job demands and job resources as predictors of absence duration and frequency.

Journal: *Journal of Vocational Behavior*, April 2003, *62*, 341–356.

Related Research: Van Veldhoven, M., & Mejman, T. (1994). *Het meten van psychosociale arbeidsbelasting met een uragenlijst: de Vrogenlijst Belevng en Beoordeling van de Arbad (VVBA)*. [Measurement of psychosocial job demands with a questionnaire: The questionnaire experience and evaluation of work (VBBA)]. Amsterdam: NIA.

11317

Test Name: PROCEDURAL JUSTICE SCALE

Purpose: To assess reaction to a layoff.

Number of Items: 3

Format: Scales range from 1 (*strongly disagree*) to 5 (*strongly agree*). Sample items are presented.

Reliability: Coefficient alpha was .74.

Validity: Correlations with other variables ranged from −.49 to .39.

Author: Barclay, L. J., et al.

Article: Exploring the role of emotions in injustice perceptions and retaliation.

Journal: *Journal of Applied Psychology*, July 2005, *90*, 629–643.

Related Research: Brockner, J., et al. (1994). Interactive effects of procedural justice and outcome negativity on victims and survivors of job loss. *Academy of Management Journal, 37,* 397–409.

11318

Test Name: PROFESSIONAL WITHDRAWAL COGNITIONS SCALE

Purpose: To measure professional withdrawal cognitions.

Number of Items: 3

Format: Responses are made on a 4-point scale ranging from

1 (*strongly disagree*) to 4 (*strongly agree*). A sample item is presented.

Reliability: Coefficient alpha was .87.

Validity: Correlations with other variables ranged from −.46 to .67.

Author: Blau, G., et al.

Article: Correlates of professional versus organizational withdrawal cognitions.

Journal: *Journal of Vocational Behavior*, August 2003, *63*, 72–85.

Related Research: Blau, G. (1989). Testing the generalizability of a career commitment measure and its impact on employee turnover. *Journal of Vocational Behavior, 35*, 88–103.

11319

Test Name: PROXIMAL JOB ADJUSTMENT OUTCOME SCALES

Purpose: To assess task mastery, role clarity, work group integration, and politics.

Number of Items: 18

Format: Scales range from 1 (*strongly disagree*) to 5 (*strongly agree*). Sample items are presented.

Reliability: Alpha coefficients ranged from .67 to .91.

Author: Kammeyer-Mueller, J. D., and Wanberg, C. R.

Article: Unwrapping the organizational entry process: Disentangling multiple antecedents and their pathways to adjustment.

Journal: *Journal of Applied Psychology*, October 2003, *88*, 779–794.

Related Research: Morrison, E. W. (1993). Longitudinal study of the effects of information seeking on newcomer socialization. *Journal of Applied Psychology, 78*, 173–183. Chao, G. T., et al. (1994). Organizational socialization: Its

content and consequences. *Journal of Applied Psychology, 79*, 730–743. Rizzo, J. R., et al. (1970). Role conflict and ambiguity in complex organizations. *Administrative Science Quarterly, 15*, 150–163.

11320

Test Name: PSYCHOLOGICAL EMPOWERMENT SCALE

Purpose: To measure psychological empowerment.

Number of Items: 12

Format: Response scales range from 1 (*strongly disagree*) to 7 (*strongly agree*). All items are presented.

Reliability: Coefficient alpha was .89.

Author: Hancer, M., et al.

Article: An examination of dimensions of Psychological Empowerment Scale for service employees.

Journal: *Psychological Reports*, October 2005, *97*, 667–672.

Related Research: Spreitzer, G. M., et al. (1997). A dimensional analysis of the relationship between psychological empowerment and effectiveness, satisfaction, and strain. *Journal of Management, 23*, 679–704.

11321

Test Name: QUALITY OF EMPLOYMENT QUESTIONNAIRE

Purpose: To assess job satisfaction and work self-esteem.

Number of Items: 9

Format: Includes two scales: Job Satisfaction and Work Self-Esteem. Responses are made on a 5-point Likert scale.

Validity: Correlations with other variables ranged from −.14 to .43.

Author: Waters, L.

Article: Protégé–mentor agreement about the provision of psychosocial support: The mentoring relationship, personality, and workload.

Journal: *Journal of Vocational Behavior*, December 2004, *65*, 519–532.

Related Research: Quinn, R., & Sheppard, L. (1974). *The 1972–73 Quality of Employment Survey: Descriptive statistics, with comparison data from the 1969–70 Survey of Working Conditions*. Ann Arbor: Institute for Social Research, University of Michigan.

11322

Test Name: QUALITY OF THE EMPLOYMENT RELATIONSHIP SCALE

Purpose: To measure met expectations and perceived future continuity.

Number of Items: 8

Format: Scales range from 1 (*not at all*) to 5 (*to a great extent*).

Reliability: Alpha coefficients were .88 (met expectations) and .89 (continuity).

Author: Dabos, G. E., and Rousseau, D. M.

Article: Mutuality and reciprocity in psychological contracts of employees and employers.

Journal: *Journal of Applied Psychology*, February 2004, *89*, 52–72.

Related Research: Wade-Benzoni, K. A., & Rousseau, D. M. (1998, July). Building relationships around tasks: Psychological contracts in faculty–doctoral student collaborations (Working paper No. 1998-13). Pittsburgh, PA: The Heinz School of Public Policy and Management, Carnegie Mellon University.

11323

Test Name: RECIPROCAL TASK INTERDEPENDENCE SCALE

Purpose: To assess reciprocal task interdependence.

Number of Items: 5

Format: Responses are made on a 5-point Likert scale ranging from *strongly disagree* to *strongly agree*. An example is presented.

Reliability: Coefficient alpha was .76.

Validity: Correlations with other variables ranged from –.27 to .16.

Author: Parker, L., and Allen, T. D.

Article: Work/family benefits: Variables related to employees' fairness perception.

Journal: *Journal of Vocational Behavior*, June 2001, *58*, 453–468.

Related Research: Pearce, J. L., & Gregersen, H. B. (1991). Task interdependence and extrarole behavior: A test of the mediating effects of felt responsibility. *Journal of Applied Psychology, 76,* 838–844.

11324

Test Name: RELATIVE DEPRIVATION SCALE

Purpose: To assess relative deprivation.

Number of Items: 3

Format: Responses are made on a 5-point Likert scale ranging from 1 (*strongly disagree*) to 5 (*strongly agree*). All items are presented.

Reliability: Coefficient alpha was .79.

Validity: Correlations with other variables ranged from –.69 to .79.

Author: Feldman, D. C., and Turnley, W. H.

Article: Contingent employment in academic careers: Relative deprivation among adjunct faculty.

Journal: *Journal of Vocational Behavior*, April 2004, *64*, 284–307.

Related Research: Olson, J., et al. (1995). The preconditions and consequences of relative deprivation: Two field studies. *Journal of Applied Psychology, 25,* 944–964.

11325

Test Name: RESPONSIBILITY FOR THE WORK OF OTHERS SCALE

Purpose: To measure job demands.

Number of Items: 3

Format: Scales range from 1 (*almost none*) to 5 (*almost total*). A sample item is presented.

Reliability: Coefficient alpha was .73.

Validity: Correlations with other variables ranged from –.24 to .44.

Author: Schaubroeck, J., et al.

Article: Individual differences in utilizing control to cope with job demands: Effects on susceptibility to infectious disease.

Journal: *Journal of Applied Psychology*, April 2001, *86*, 265–278.

Related Research: Caplan, R. D., et al. (1975). *Job demands and worker health* (NIOSH Publication No. 75-160). Washington, DC: Department of Health Education and Welfare.

11326

Test Name: RETENTION SCALE

Purpose: To assess the probability that the employee will remain with the organization.

Number of Items: 5

Format: Responses are made on a 5-point Likert scale ranging from 1 (*strongly disagree*) to 5 (*strongly agree*).

Reliability: Coefficient alpha was .89.

Validity: Correlations with other variables ranged from –.27 to .11.

Author: Andrews, M. C., et al.

Article: The interactive effects of organizational politics and exchange ideology on manager ratings of retention.

Journal: *Journal of Vocational Behavior*, April 2003, *62*, 357–369.

11327

Test Name: ROLE AMBIGUITY AND OCCUPATIONAL STRAIN SCALES

Purpose: To measure role ambiguity and psychic strain.

Number of Items: 16

Format: Scales range from 1 (*very seldom*) to 5 (*very often*). Sample items are presented.

Reliability: Alpha coefficients were .89 (role ambiguity) and .79 (psychic strain).

Author: Elovainio, M., and Kivimäki, M.

Article: The effects of personal need for structure and occupational identity in the role stress process.

Journal: *The Journal of Social Psychology*, June 2001, *141*, 365–378.

Related Research: Elo, A.-L., et al. (1992). *Occupational Stress Questionnaire: User's Instructions* (Rev. No.19). Helsinki, Finland: Finnish Institute of Occupational Health.

11328

Test Name: ROLE OVERLOAD SCALE

Purpose: To measure work role overload.

Number of Items: 3

Format: Scales range from 1 (*strongly disagree*) to 5 (*strongly agree*). All items are presented.

Reliability: Coefficient alpha was .84.

Validity: Correlations with other variables ranged from –.17 to .65.

Author: Bolino, M. C., and Turnley, W. H.

Article: The personal costs of citizenship behavior: The relationship between individual initiative and role overload, job stress, and work–family conflict.

Journal: *Journal of Applied Psychology*, July 2005, *90*, 740–748.

11329

Test Name: ROLE OVERLOAD SCALE

Purpose: To measure role overload.

Number of Items: 3

Format: Scales range from 1 (*rarely or never*) to 5 (*constantly*).

Reliability: Alpha coefficients ranged from .80 to .85.

Validity: Correlations with other variables ranged from –.10 to .34.

Author: Parker, S. K.

Article: Longitudinal effects of lean production on employee outcomes and the mediating role of work characteristics.

Journal: *Journal of Applied Psychology*, August 2003, *88*, 620–634.

Related Research: Caplan, R. D., et al. (1975). *Job demands and worker health: Main effects and occupational differences.* Washington, DC: U.S. Department of Health, Education, and Welfare.

11330

Test Name: SATISFACTION IN SPORT QUESTIONNAIRE— SPANISH VERSION

Purpose: To assess satisfaction in sport.

Number of Items: 11

Format: Includes three subscales: Normative Success, Social Approval, and Mastery Experiences. Responses are made on a 100-point rating scale ranging from 0 (*strongly disagree*) to 100 (*strongly agree*). Examples are presented.

Reliability: Alpha coefficients ranged from .68 to .87.

Author: Cervellô, E. M., & Santos-Rosa, F. J.

Article: Motivation in sport: An achievement goal perspective in young Spanish recreational athletes.

Journal: *Perceptual and Motor Skills*, April 2001, *92*, 527–534.

Related Research: Cervello, E. M., et al. (1999). Relaciones entre la orientacion de metas disposicional y la satisfaccion con la practica deportiva. *Revista de Psicologia del Deporte*, *8*(1), 7–19. Treasure, D. C., & Roberts, G. C. (1994). Cognitive and affective concomitants of task and ego goal orientations during the middle school years. *Journal of Sport and Exercise Psychology*, *16*, 15–28.

11331

Test Name: SATISFACTION SCALE

Purpose: To measure satisfaction.

Number of Items: 6

Format: Responses are made of a 5-point scale ranging from (*strongly disagree*) to 5 (*strongly agree*). All items are presented.

Reliability: Coefficient alpha was .87 (*N* = 989).

Validity: Correlations with other variables ranged from .03 to .52 (*N* = 989).

Author: Allen, D. G., et al.

Article: Recruitment communication media: Impact on prehire outcomes.

Journal: *Personnel Psychology*, Spring 2004, *57*, 143–171.

Related Research: Downs, C. W., & Hazen, M. (1977). A factor analytic study of communication satisfaction. *Journal of Business Communication*, *14*, 63–73.

11332

Test Name: SCALE OF EMPLOYEE AUTONOMY

Purpose: To measure employees' sense of control.

Number of Items: 4

Format: All items are presented. Likert format is used.

Reliability: Coefficient alpha was .76.

Validity: Correlations with other variables ranged from –.25 to .40.

Author: Clark, S. C.

Article: Employees' sense of community, sense of control, and work/family conflict in Native American organizations.

Journal: *Journal of Vocational Behavior*, August 2002, *61*, 92–108.

Related Research: Clark, S. C. (2001). Work cultures and work/family balance. *Journal of Vocational Behavior*, *58*, 348–365.

11333

Test Name: SCHOOL COUNSELOR ACTIVITY RATING SCALE

Purpose: To assess how school counselors actually spend their time and how they would prefer to spend their time in job-related activities.

Number of Items: 40

Format: Scales range from 1 (*never do this* or *would prefer never to do*

this) to 5 (*routinely do this* or *would prefer to routinely do this*). Sample items are presented.

Reliability: Alpha coefficients ranged form .43 to .93 across subscales.

Validity: Correlations with other variables ranged form .19 to .21.

Author: Scarborough, J. L.

Article: The School Counselor Activity Rating Scale: An instrument for gathering process data.

Journal: *Professional School Counseling*, February 2005, *8*, 274–283.

11334

Test Name: SCHOOL PRINCIPAL BURNOUT SCALE—FARSI VERSION

Purpose: To measure exhaustion, aloofness, and deprecation among school principals.

Number of Items: 22

Format: All items are presented in English.

Reliability: Total alpha was .86. Alpha coefficients ranged from .82 to .87 across subscales.

Validity: Correlations with other variables ranged from .18 to .78.

Author: Rashidzadeh, M. A.

Article: Burnout among Iranian school principals.

Journal: *Psychological Reports*, February 2002, *90*, 61–64.

Related Research: Friedman, I. A. (1995). School principal burnout: The concept and its components. *Journal of Organizational Behavior, 16*, 191–198.

11335

Test Name: SHARED VISION SCALE

Purpose: To measure the extent to which employees feel united by their joint work.

Number of Items: 3

Format: All items are presented.

Reliability: Coefficient alpha was .65.

Validity: Correlations with other variables ranged from −.36 to .50.

Author: Wong, A., et al.

Article: Organizational partnerships in China: Self-interest, goal interdependence, and opportunism.

Journal: *Journal of Applied Psychology*, July 2005, *90*, 782–791.

11336

Test Name: SOCIAL SUPPORT RECEIVED FROM COWORKERS SCALES

Purpose: To assess social support received from coworkers.

Number of Items: 12

Format: Includes three scales: Receipt of Nonjob Social Support, Positive Job-Related Social Support, and Negative Job-Related Social Support. Responses are made on a 7-point agreement scale.

Reliability: Alpha coefficients ranged from .83 to .91.

Validity: Correlations with other variables ranged from −.26 to .55.

Author: Bowling, N. A., et al.

Article: Giving and receiving social support at work: The roles of personality and reciprocity.

Journal: *Journal of Vocational Behavior*, December 2005, *67*, 476–489.

Related Research: Fenlason, K. J., & Beehr, T. A. (1994). Social support and occupational stress: Effects of talking to others. *Journal of Organizational Behavior, 15*, 157–175.

11337

Test Name: SOCIALIZING INFLUENCES SCALE

Purpose: To identify agents of socialization in the workplace as organizational influence, leader influence, or coworker influence.

Number of Items: 7

Format: A multiple choice format is used. All items are presented.

Reliability: Alpha coefficients were .94 (organization), .92 (coworker) and .93 (leader).

Validity: Correlations with other variables ranged from −.18 to .23.

Author: Kammeyer-Mueller, J. D., and Wanberg, C. R.

Article: Unwrapping the organizational entry process: Disentangling multiple antecedents and their pathways to adjustment.

Journal: *Journal of Applied Psychology*, October 2003, *88*, 779–794.

11338

Test Name: STRESS IN GENERAL SCALE

Purpose: To measure general job stress.

Number of Items: 15

Format: Includes two factors: pressure and threat. Responses are made on a 3-point scale: *no, ?,* and *yes.*

Reliability: Alpha coefficients ranged from .79 to .90.

Validity: Correlations with other variables ranged from −.57 to .70.

Author: Stanton, J. M., et al.

Article: A general measure of work stress: The Stress in General Scale.

Journal: *Educational and Psychological Measurement*, October 2001, *61*, 866–888.

11339

Test Name: STRESS IN GENERAL SCALE

Purpose: To assess job stress.

Number of Items: 9

Format: Responses are made on a *yes–?–no* format scale.

Reliability: Alpha coefficients were .75 and .82.

Validity: Correlations with other variables ranged from –.24 to .39.

Author: Wasti, S. A.

Article: Commitment profiles: Combinations of organizational commitment forms and job outcomes.

Journal: *Journal of Vocational Behavior*, October 2005, *67*, 290–308.

Related Research: Smith, P. C., et al. (1992). *Development and validation of the Stress in General (SIG) Scale.* Paper presented at Society for Industrial and Organizational Psychology, Montreal, Quebec, Canada.

11340

Test Name: STRESSFUL OCCUPATIONAL EVENTS SCALE

Purpose: To measure stress coping in law enforcement.

Number of Items: 29

Format: Checklist format, followed by 3-point stress scales anchored by *not very* and *very*.

Reliability: K-R 20 reliabilities ranged from .83 to .65 across two subscales.

Author: Patterson, G. T.

Article: Development of a law enforcement stress and coping questionnaire.

Journal: *Psychological Reports*, April 2002, *90*, Part 1, 789–799.

Related Research: Spielberger, C. D., et al. (1981). *The Police Stress Survey: Sources of stress in law enforcement.* Tampa, FL: Human Resources Institute.

11341

Test Name: STUDENT AFFAIRS WORK LIFE SCALE

Purpose: To measure seven work perceptions of student affairs mid-level leaders, the level of morale and satisfaction, and intent to leave.

Number of Items: 68

Format: Scales ranged from 1 (*strongly disagree*) to 5 (*strongly agree*). All items are presented.

Reliability: Alpha coefficients ranged from .66 to .94 across subscales.

Validity: Correlations between the variables in the final structural equation ranged from –41 to .71.

Author: Rosser, V. J., and Javinar, J. M.

Article: Midland student affairs leaders' intentions to leave: Examining the quality of their professional and institutional work life.

Journal: *Journal of College Student Development*, November/December 2003, *44*, 813–830.

11342

Test Name: SUBORDINATES' RESISTANCE SCALE

Purpose: To measure subordinates' dysfunctional and constructive resistance.

Number of Items: 14

Format: Scales range from 0 (*I cannot remember ever using this tactic*) to 4 (*I use this tactic very often*). Sample items are presented.

Reliability: Alpha coefficients were .89 (dysfunctional) and .79 (constructive).

Validity: Correlations with other variables ranged from –.26 to .23.

Author: Tepper, B. J., et al.

Article: Personality moderators of the relationship between abusive supervision and subordinates' resistance.

Journal: *Journal of Applied Psychology*, October 2001, *86*, 974–983.

Related Research: Tepper, B. J., et al. (1998, August). *The multidimensionality and multifunctionality of subordinates' resistance to downward influence attempts.* Paper presented at the annual meeting of the Academy of Management, San Diego, CA.

11343

Test Name: SUCCESSFUL LIFE MANAGEMENT IN THE OCCUPATIONAL DOMAIN SCALES

Purpose: To assess successful life management in the occupational domain.

Number of Items: 13

Format: Includes two scales: Subjective Success in the Work Domain and Job-Satisfaction. Responses are made on 7-point scales. Examples are given.

Reliability: Alpha coefficients were .79 and .89.

Validity: Correlations with other variables ranged from –.08 to .25.

Author: Wiese, B. S., et al.

Article: Subjective career success and emotional well-being: Longitudinal predictive power of selection, optimization, and compensation.

Journal: *Journal of Vocational Behavior*, June 2002, *60*, 321–335.

11344

Test Name: SURVIVOR RESPONSES ON DOWNSIZING AND RESTRUCTURING

Purpose: To measure hopefulness, obliging, cynical, and fearful responses to organizational change.

Number of Items: 20

Format: Item responses are anchored by 1 (*not at all*) and 4 (*to a great extent*).

Reliability: Internal consistency reliabilities ranged from .56 to .86 across subscales.

Author: Burke, R. J.

Article: Evidence for concurrent validity of responses by survivors of hospital restructuring.

Journal: *Psychological Reports*, June 2001, *88*, Part 2, 1259–1262.

Related Research: Sprietzer, G. M., & Mishra, A. K. (2000). An empirical examination of a stress-based framework of survivor responses to downsizing. In R. J. Burke & C. L. Cooper (Eds.), *The organization in crisis* (pp. 77–118). London: Blackwell Publishers.

11345

Test Name: TASK SATISFACTION SCALE

Purpose: To assess how much employees like doing a task.

Number of Items: 3

Format: Scales range from 1 (*strongly disagree*) to 5 (*strongly agree*). A sample item is presented.

Reliability: Coefficient alpha was .89.

Validity: Correlations with other variables ranged from −.17 to .35.

Author: Douthitt, E. A., and Aiello, J. R.

Article: The role of participation and control in the effects of computer monitoring on fairness perceptions, task satisfaction and performance.

Journal: *Journal of Applied Psychology*, October 2001, *86*, 867–874.

11346

Test Name: TASK SATISFACTION SCALE

Purpose: To measure task satisfaction.

Number of Items: 4

Format: Responses are made on a 7-point scale ranging from 1 (*strongly disagree*) to 7 (*strongly agree*). A sample item is presented.

Reliability: Coefficient alpha was .93.

Author: Towler, A. J.

Article: Effects of charismatic influence training on attitudes, behavior, and performance.

Journal: *Personnel Psychology*, Summer 2003, *56*, 363–381.

Related Research: Kirkpatrick, S. A., & Locke, E. A. (1996). Direct and indirect effects of three core charismatic leadership components on performance and attitudes. *Journal of Applied Psychology, 81*, 36–51.

11347

Test Name: TEACHER SATISFACTION SCALE

Purpose: To measure teachers' job satisfaction.

Number of Items: 25

Format: Scales range from 1 (*never*) to 5 (*always*).

Reliability: Alpha coefficients ranged from .72 to .93 across subscales. Total alpha was .94.

Validity: Correlations with other variables ranged from −.21 to .65.

Author: Bogler, R.

Article: Satisfaction of Jewish and Arab teachers in Israel.

Journal: *The Journal of Social Psychology*, February 2005, *145*, 19–33.

Related Research: Tarabeh, H. (1995). *Principals' and teachers' job satisfaction as a function of the gap between principals' perception and teachers' perception of the principal's role.* Unpublished master's thesis, University of Haifa, Israel.

11348

Test Name: TURNOVER INTENTIONS SCALE

Purpose: To measure intentions to quit the organization.

Number of Items: 3

Format: Scales range from 1 (*definitely not*) to 5 (*definitely yes*).

Reliability: Scale reliability was .95.

Validity: Correlations with other variables ranged from −.52 to .45.

Author: Allen, D. G., and Griffeth, R. W.

Article: Test of a mediated performance–turnover relationship highlighting the moderating roles of visibility and reward contingency.

Journal: *Journal of Applied Psychology*, October 2001, *86*, 1014–1021.

Related Research: Griffeth, R. W., & Hom, P. W. (1995). The employee turnover process. *Research in Personnel and Human Resource Management, 13*, 245–293.

11349

Test Name: TURNOVER INTENTIONS SCALE

Purpose: To measure turnover intentions.

Number of Items: 3

Format: Scales range from 1 (*strongly disagree*) to 7 (*strongly agree*). A sample item is presented.

Reliability: Alpha coefficients ranged from .79 to .89.

Validity: Correlations with other variables ranged from −.80 to .13.

Author: Ambrose, M. L., and Cropanzano, R.

Article: A longitudinal analysis of organizational fairness: An examination of reactions to tenure and promotion decisions.

Journal: *Journal of Applied Psychology*, April 2003, *88*, 266–275.

Related Research: Cropanzano, R., et al. (1993). Dispositional affectivity as a predictor of work attitudes and performance. *Journal of Organizational Behavior, 14*, 595–606.

11350

Test Name: UNION LOYALTY AND SOCIALIZATION SCALES

Purpose: To assess union loyalty and individual union socialization.

Number of Items: 14

Format: Loyalty scales range from 1 (*strongly disagree*) to 5 (*strongly agree*). Sample items are presented. Socialization scales were 5-point accuracy scales.

Reliability: Alphas were .92 (for loyalty) and .93 (socialization).

Validity: Correlations with other variables ranged from .27 to .83.

Author: Tan, H. H., and Aryee, S.

Article: Antecedents and outcomes of union loyalty: A constructive replication and an extension.

Journal: *Journal of Applied Psychology*, August 2002, *87*, 715–722.

Related Research: Gordon, M. E., et al. (1980). Commitment to the

union: Development of a measure and an examination of its correlates. *Journal of Applied Psychology, 65*, 479–499.

11351

Test Name: UNION PARTICIPATION SCALES

Purpose: To measure union loyalty, prounion behavior, and perceived union instrumentality.

Number of Items: 25

Reliability: Alpha coefficients ranged from .81 to .93.

Validity: Correlations with other variables ranged from .11 to .77.

Author: Fuller, J. B., Jr., and Hester, K.

Article: A closer look at the relation between justice perceptions and union participation.

Journal: *Journal of Applied Psychology*, December 2001, *86*, 1096–1105.

Related Research: Parks, J., et al. (1995). Operationalizing the outcomes of union commitment: The dimensionality of participation. *Journal of Organizational Behavior, 16*, 533–555.

11352

Test Name: UNION TURNOVER INTENTIONS SCALE

Purpose: To measure turnover intentions with respect to union membership.

Number of Items: 3

Format: Scales range from 1 (*very unlikely or strongly disagree*) to 5 (*very likely or strongly agree*). All items are presented.

Reliability: Coefficient alpha was .94.

Validity: Correlations with other variables ranged from −.32 to −.03.

Author: Aryee, S., and Chay, Y. W.

Article: Workplace justice, citizenship behavior, and turnover intentions in a union context: Examining the mediating role of perceived union support and union instrumentality.

Journal: *Journal of Applied Psychology*, February 2001, *86*, 154–160.

11353

Test Name: VOCATIONAL ADAPTATION SCALE

Purpose: To assess satisfaction about key sources of vocational adjustment.

Number of Items: 28

Format: Five-point scales anchored by *very satisfied* and *rarely dissatisfied*. Sample items are presented.

Reliability: Alpha was .95.

Validity: Correlations with other variables ranged from .13 to .26.

Author: Goldman, B. M., et al.

Article: Goal-directedness and personal identity as correlates of life outcomes.

Journal: *Psychological Reports*, August 2002, *91*, 153–166.

Related Research: Heath, D. H. (1991). *Fulfilling lives: Paths to maturity and success*. San Francisco: Jossey-Bass.

11354

Test Name: WORK ADDICTION RISK TEST

Purpose: To measure workaholism.

Number of Items: 25

Format: Includes five dimensions: Compulsive Tendencies, Control, Impaired Communication/Self-Absorption, Inability to Delegate, and Self-Worth. Responses are made on a 4-point scale ranging from 1 (*never true*) to 4 (*always true*). All items are presented.

Reliability: Test–retest (2 weeks) correlation coefficient was .83. Alpha coefficients were .85 and .88. Spearman–Brown split-half reliability coefficient was .85 ($N = 442$).

Validity: Correlations with "Type A" behaviors and with state trait anxiety ranged from .20 to .50.

Author: Flowers, C. P., and Robinson, B. E.

Article: A structural and discriminant analysis of the Work Addiction Risk Test.

Journal: *Educational and Psychological Measurement*, June 2002, *62*, 517–526.

Related Research: Robinson, B. E. (1999). The Work Addiction Risk Test: Development of a tentative measure of workaholism. *Perceptual and Motor Skills, 88*, 199–210.

11355

Test Name: WORK AND NONWORK EMPLOYEE DEVELOPMENT SCALES

Purpose: To assess the dimensions of employee development.

Number of Items: 37

Reliability: Alpha coefficients were .93 (work support) and .89 (nonwork support).

Validity: Correlations with other variables ranged from .29 to .50.

Author: Maurer, T. J., et al.

Article: A model of involvement in work-related learning and development activity: The effects of individual, situational, motivational, and age variables.

Journal: *Journal of Applied Psychology*, August 2003, *88*, 707–724.

Related Research: Maurer, T., et al. (2002). Predictors of attitudes toward a 360-degree feedback system and involvement in post-feedback management development activity. *Journal of Occupational and Organizational Psychology, 75*, 87–107.

11356

Test Name: WORK EMOTIONS/ AFFECTIVE WELL-BEING SCALE

Purpose: To measure affect at work as positive emotions and negative emotions.

Number of Items: 19

Format: Scales range from 1 (*never*) to 5 (*every day*). All items are presented.

Reliability: Alpha coefficients were .96 (positive emotions) and .90 (negative emotions).

Author: Simpson, P. A., and Stroh, L. K.

Article: Gender differences: Emotional expression and feelings of personal inauthenticity.

Journal: *Journal of Applied Psychology*, August 2004, *89*, 715–721.

Related Research: Van Katwyk, P. T., et al. (2000). Using the Job-Related Affective Well-Being Scale (JAWS) to investigate affective responses to work stressors. *Journal of Occupational Health Psychology, 5*, 219–230.

11357

Test Name: WORK ENGAGEMENT SCALE

Purpose: To measure the vigor of, the dedication to, and the degree of absorption in work.

Number of Items: 17

Format: Scales range from 0 (*never*) to 6 (*always*). All items are presented.

Reliability: Alpha coefficients ranged from .70 to .77.

Validity: Correlations with other variables ranged from .07 to .43.

Author: Salanova, M., et al.

Article: Linking organizational resources and work engagement to employee performance and customer loyalty: The mediation of service climate.

Journal: *Journal of Applied Psychology*, November 2005, *90*, 1217–1227.

11358

Test Name: WORK–NONWORK CONFLICT SCALE

Purpose: To measure work–nonwork conflict.

Number of Items: 6

Format: Sample items are present.

Reliability: Cronbach's alpha was .80.

Validity: Correlations with other variables ranged from −.33 to .39.

Author: Cohen, A., and Schwartz, H.

Article: An empirical examination among Canadian teachers of determinants of the need for employees' assistance programs.

Journal: *Psychological Reports*, June 2002, *90*, Part 2, 1221–1238.

Related Research: Shamir, B. (1983). Some antecedents of work–nonwork conflict. *Journal of Vocational Behavior, 23*, 98–111.

11359

Test Name: WORK OUTCOMES SCALE

Purpose: To measure job satisfaction, intention to quit, absenteeism, and job insecurity feelings.

Number of Items: 13

Format: Four-point scales are used. Sample items are presented.

Reliability: Alpha coefficients ranged from .82 to .87 across subscales.

Author: Burke, R. J.

Article: Work experiences and psychological well-being of former hospital-based nurses now employed elsewhere.

Journal: *Psychological Reports,* December 2002, *91,* Part 2, 1059–1064.

Related Research: Quinn, R. P., & Shepard, L. J. (1974). *The 1972–73 quality of employment survey.* Ann Arbor: Institute for Social Research, University of Michigan.

11360

Test Name: WORK OVERLOAD SCALE

Purpose: To measure work overload.

Number of Items: 5

Format: Scales range from 1 (*strongly disagree*) to 5 (*strongly agree*). Sample items are presented.

Reliability: Coefficient alpha was .82.

Validity: Correlations with other variables ranged from –.19 to .32.

Author: Aryee, S., et al.

Article: Rhythms of life: Antecedents and outcomes of work–family balance in employed parents.

Journal: *Journal of Applied Psychology,* January 2005, *90,* 132–146.

11361

Test Name: WORK OVERLOAD SCALE

Purpose: To measure the extent to which a person believes work interferes with his/her personal life.

Number of Items: 3

Format: Scales range from 1 (*strongly disagree*) to 5 (*strongly agree*). All items are presented.

Reliability: Coefficient alpha was .80.

Validity: Correlations with other variables ranged from –.34 to .70.

Author: Brett, J. M., and Stroh, L. K.

Article: Working 61 plus hours a week: Why do managers do it?

Journal: *Journal of Applied Psychology,* February 2003, *88,* 67–78.

11362

Test Name: WORK OVERLOAD SCALE

Purpose: To measure the degree of overload experienced on the job.

Number of Items: 7

Format: Scales range from 1 (*very little*) to 5 (*very great*). Sample items are presented.

Reliability: Coefficient alpha was .88.

Validity: Correlations with other variables ranged from –.40 to .50.

Author: Major, V. S., et al.

Article: Work time, work interference with family, and psychological distress.

Journal: *Journal of Applied Psychology,* June 2002, *87,* 427–436.

11363

Test Name: WORK PRESSURE SCALE

Purpose: To measure quantitative, demanding aspects of the job.

Number of Items: 3

Format: Responses are made on a 5-point scale ranging from 1 (*never*) to 5 (*always*). An example is given.

Reliability: Alpha coefficients ranged from .83 to .85.

Author: Demerouti, E., et al.

Article: The loss spiral of work pressure, work–home interference, and exhaustion: Reciprocal relations in a three-wave study.

Journal: *Journal of Vocational Behavior,* February 2004, *64,* 131–149.

Related Research: De Jonge, J., et al. (2000). The demanding control model: Specific demands, specific control, and well-defined groups. *International Journal of Stress Management,* 7, 269–287.

11364

Test Name: WORK-RELATED FLOW SCALE

Purpose: To measure work-related flow.

Number of Items: 13

Format: Includes three areas: absorption, work enjoyment, and intrinsic work motivation. Responses are made on a 7-point scale ranging from 0 (*never*) to 6 (*always*). Examples are given.

Reliability: Alpha coefficients ranged from .63 to .96. Test–retest correlations ranged from .71 to .77.

Author: Bakker, A. B.

Article: Flow among music teachers and their students: The crossover of peak experiences.

Journal: *Journal of Vocational Behavior,* February 2005, *66,* 26–44.

Related Research: Bakker, A. B. (2001). *Vragenlijst voor het meten van werkgerelateerde flow: De Wolf* [Questionnaire for the assessment of work-related flow: The WOLF].

Utrecht, the Netherlands: Department of Social and Organizational Psychology, Utrecht University.

11365

Test Name: WORK-RELATED RESEARCH MEASURE

Purpose: To assess the extent to which one perceives stress-related research.

Number of Items: 6

Format: Responses are made on a 5-point scale ranging from 1 (*rarely or never*) to 5 (*constantly or always*). An example is given.

Reliability: Alpha coefficients were .77 and .85.

Author: Fernet, C., et al.

Article: Adjusting to job demands: The role of work self-determination and job control in predicting burnout.

Journal: *Journal of Vocational Behavior*, August 2004, *65*, 39–56.

Related Research: Singh, S. N., et al. (1998). Research-related burnout among faculty in higher education. *Psychological Reports*, *83*, 463–473.

11366

Test Name: WORK ROLE SALIENCE SCALE

Purpose: To assess the relative importance of work.

Number of Items: 27

Format: Responses are made on a 5-point scale ranging from 1 (*strongly disagree*) to 5 (*strongly agree*). Sample items are presented.

Reliability: Alpha coefficients ranged from .72 to .98.

Author: Kenny, M. E., et al.

Article: The role of perceived barriers and relational support in

the educational and vocational lives of urban high school students.

Journal: *Journal of Counseling Psychology*, April 2003, *50*, 142–153.

Related Research: Greenhaus, J. H. (1971). An investigation of the role of career salience in vocational behavior. *Journal of Vocational Behavior*, *1*, 209–216.

11367

Test Name: WORK SATISFACTION SCALE

Purpose: To measure overall work satisfaction.

Number of Items: 22

Format: Scales range from 1 (*strongly dissatisfied*) to 5 (*strongly satisfied*). Sample items are presented.

Reliability: Coefficient alpha was .89.

Validity: Correlations with other variables ranged from .05 to .60 aggregated at the work-unit level.

Author: González-Romá, V., et al.

Article: An examination of the antecedents and moderator influences of climate strength.

Journal: *Journal of Applied Psychology*, June 2002, *87*, 465–473.

11368

Test Name: WORK SOCIAL SUPPORT SCALE

Purpose: To rate expressive and instrumental support received from coworkers.

Number of Items: 6

Format: Scales range from 1 (*they are not at all that way*) to 7 (*they are very much that way*). Sample items are presented.

Reliability: Coefficient alpha was .93.

Validity: Correlations with other variables ranged from .00 to .34.

Author: Wise, D., and Stake, J. E.

Article: The moderating roles of personal and social resources on the relationship between dual expectation (for instrumentality and expressiveness) and well-being.

Journal: *The Journal of Social Psychology*, February 2002, *142*, 109–119.

Related Research: House, J. S. (1981). *Work stress and social support*. Reading, MA: Addison-Wesley.

11369

Test Name: WORK STATUS CONGRUENCE SCALE

Purpose: To assess the extent to which conditions of work (hours, shift, for example) are congruent with an employees' preferences.

Number of Items: 7

Format: Scales ranged from 1 (*strongly agree*) to 5 (*strongly disagree*). All items are presented.

Reliability: Coefficient alpha was .82.

Validity: Correlations with other variables ranged from −.21 to .42.

Author: Holtom, B. C., et al.

Article: The relationship between work status congruence and work-related attitudes and behavior.

Journal: *Journal of Applied Psychology*, October 2002, *87*, 903–915.

11370

Test Name: WORK STRESS INVENTORY

Purpose: To assess respondent's experience with organizational stress and with job risk.

Number of Items: 40

Format: Responses are made on 5-point rating scales. Examples are presented.

Reliability: Alpha coefficients ranged from .84 to .90.

Validity: Correlations with other variables ranged from −.46 to .65.

Author: Schirmer, L. L., and Lopez, F. G.

Article: Probing the social support and work strain relationship among adult workers: Contributions of adult attachment orientations.

Journal: *Journal of Vocational Behavior*, August 2001, *59*, 17–33.

Related Research: Barone, D. F., et al. (1988). The Work Stress Inventory: Organizational stress and job risk. *Educational and Psychological Measurement, 48*, 141–154.

11371

Test Name: WORK STRESSORS SCALE

Purpose: To measure work overload and role clarity.

Number of Items: 6

Format: Scales range from 1 (*strongly disagree*) to 5 (*strongly agree*).

Reliability: Alpha coefficients were .65 (overload) and .66 (clarity).

Validity: Correlations with other variables ranged from −.19 to .66.

Author: Jex, S. M., et al.

Article: The impact of self-efficacy on stressor–strain relations: Coping style as an explanatory mechanism.

Journal: *Journal of Applied Psychology*, June 2001, *86*, 401–409.

Related Research: Cammann, C., et al. (1983). Michigan Organizational Assessment Questionnaire. In S. E. Seashore et al. (Eds.), *Assessing*

organizational change: A guide to methods, measures, and practices (pp. 71–138). New York: Wiley.

11372

Test Name: WORK WELL-BEING SCALE

Purpose: To measure well-being at work.

Number of Items: 7

Format: Scales range from 1 (*I don't at all feel this way about myself at work*) to 7 (*I feel very much this way about myself at work*). Sample items are presented.

Reliability: Coefficient alpha was .83.

Author: Wise, D., and Stake, J. E.

Article: The moderating roles of personal and social resources on the relationship between dual expectations (for instrumentality and expressiveness) and well being.

Journal: *The Journal of Social Psychology*, February 2002, *142*, 109–119.

Related Research: Monge, R. H. (1973). Development trends in factors of adolescent self-concept. *Developmental Psychology, 8*, 382–393.

11373

Test Name: WORK WITHDRAWAL BEHAVIOR SCALE

Purpose: To measure work withdrawal behavior.

Number of Items: 18

Format: Responses are made on a 5-point Likert scale. An example is provided.

Reliability: Coefficient alpha was .85.

Validity: Correlations with other variables ranged from −.26 to .54.

Author: Boswell, W. R., et al.

Article: Relations between stress and work outcomes: The role of felt challenge, job control, and psychological strain.

Journal: *Journal of Vocational Behavior*, February 2004, *64*, 165–181.

Related Research: Hanisch, K. A., & Hulin, C. L. (1990). Job attitudes and organizational withdrawal: An examination of retirement and other involuntary withdrawal behaviors. *Journal of Vocational Behavior, 37*, 60–78.

11374

Test Name: WORK WITHDRAWAL BEHAVIOR SCALE

Purpose: To assess the frequency of work withdrawal behavior.

Number of Items: 12

Format: Frequency scales range from 1 (*never*) to 5 (*once a week or more*). Sample items are described.

Reliability: Coefficient alpha was .69.

Validity: Correlations with other variables ranged from −.27 to .19.

Author: Glomb, T. M., and Welsh, E. T.

Article: Can opposites attract? Personality heterogeneity in supervisor–subordinate dyads as a predictor of subordinate outcomes.

Journal: *Journal of Applied Psychology*, July 2005, *90*, 749–757.

11375

Test Name: WORKAHOLISM TYPE MEASURES

Purpose: To measure work involvement, being driven to work, and work enjoyment.

Number of Items: 25

Format: Sample items are presented.

Reliability: Alpha coefficients ranged from .45 to .85.

Validity: Correlations between scales ranged from .02 to .22.

Author: Burke, R. J., et al.

Article: Psychometric properties of Spence and Robbins' Measures of Workaholism Components.

Journal: *Psychological Reports*, December 2002, *9*, Part 2, 1098–1104.

Related Research: Spence, J. T., & Robbins, A. S. (1992). Workaholism: Definition, measurement, and preliminary results. *Journal of Personality Assessment, 58*, 160–178.

11376

Test Name: WORKER EMOTIONAL EXHAUSTION SCALE

Purpose: To measure worker emotional exhaustion.

Number of Items: 4

Format: Scales range from 1 (*once a month or less*) to 5 (*several times a day*). All items are presented.

Reliability: Coefficient alpha was .78.

Validity: Correlations with other variables ranged from –.33 to .16.

Author: Wilk, S. L., and Moynihan, L. M.

Article: Display rule "regulators": The relationship between supervisors and worker emotional exhaustion.

Journal: *Journal of Applied Psychology*, September 2005, *90*, 917–927.

Related Research: Maslach, C., & Jackson, S. E. (1981). The measurement of experienced burnout. *Journal of Occupational Behavior, 2*, 99–113.

11377

Test Name: WORKPLACE HETEROSEXIST EXPERIENCES QUESTIONNAIRE

Purpose: To measure participants' experiences with heterosexism.

Number of Items: 22

Format: Responses are made on a 5-point scale ranging from 0 (*never*) to 4 (*most of the time*). Sample items are presented.

Reliability: Alpha coefficients ranged from .88 to .93.

Author: Lyons, H. Z., et al.

Article: A multicultural test of the theory of work adjustment: Investigating the role of heterosexism and fit perceptions in the job satisfaction of lesbian, gay, and bisexual employees.

Journal: *Journal of Counseling Psychology*, October 2005, *52*, 537–548.

Related Research: Waldo, C. R. (1999). Working in a majority context: A structural model of heterosexism as minority stress in the workplace. *Journal of Counseling Psychology, 46*, 218–232.

CHAPTER 6
Aptitude

11378

Test Name: AUDITORY MOVING WINDOWS PARADIGM

Purpose: To assess online syntactic processing.

Number of Items: 208

Format: Includes an equal number of semantically plausible and semantically implausible sentences.

Validity: Correlations with other variables ranged from −.45 to .41.

Author: Titone, D., et al.

Article: Memory and encoding of spoken discourse following right hemispheric damage: Evidence from the auditory moving window (AMW) technique.

Journal: *Brain and Language*, April 2001, 77, 10–24.

Related Research: Ferreira, F., et al. (1996). Effects of lexical frequency and syntactic complexity in spoken language comprehension: Evidence from the auditory moving window technique. *Journal of Experimental Psychology: Learning, Memory, and Cognition, 22, 324–335.*

11379

Test Name: CANADIAN FORCES APTITUDE TEST

Purpose: To measure general cognitive ability.

Number of Items: 60

Format: Includes three subscales: Verbal Skills, Spatial Ability, and Problem-Solving Ability.

Validity: Correlations with other variables ranged from −.22 to .15 ($n = 211$).

Author: Livingstone, H. A., and Day, A. L.

Article: Comparing the construct and criterion-related validity of ability-based and mixed-model measures of emotional intelligence.

Journal: *Educational and Psychological Measurement*, October 2005, 65, 851–873.

Related Research: Albert, J. (1998). *Cognitive measures: Comparison of the Canadian Forces Aptitude Test (CFAT), Raven's Progressive Matrices, and the Wonderlic Personnel Test* (Technical Note 98-5). Ottawa, Canada: Director, Human Resources Research and Evaluation.

11380

Test Name: EMOTIONAL INTELLIGENCE INVENTORY

Purpose: To measure empathy, utilization of feelings, handling relationships, and self-control.

Number of Items: 41

Format: Item responses are anchored by 1 (*never like me*) and 5 (*always like me*). All items are presented.

Reliability: Total alpha was .81. Subscale alphas ranged from .67 to .75. Test–retest reliabilities ranged from .64 to .70 across subscales.

Author: Tapia, M.

Article: Measuring emotional intelligence.

Journal: *Psychological Reports*, April 2001, 88, 353–364.

Related Research: Tapia, M., & Burry-Stock, J. (1988). *Emotional Intelligence Inventory.* Tuscaloosa: The University of Alabama.

11381

Test Name: EMOTIONAL INTELLIGENCE SCALE

Purpose: To measure attention to feelings, emotions, and moods.

Number of Items: 35

Format: Scales range from 1 (*strongly disagree*) to 5 (*strongly agree*).

Reliability: Reliability coefficients ranged from .78 to .90.

Validity: Correlations with other variables ranged from −.31 to .45.

Author: Constantine, M. G., and Gainor, K. A.

Article: Emotional intelligence and empathy: Their relation to multicultural counseling knowledge and awareness.

Journal: *Professional School Counseling*, December 2001, 5, 131–137.

Related Research: Schutte, N. S., et al. (1998). Development and validation of a measure of emotional intelligence. *Personality and Individual Differences, 25, 167–177.*

11382

Test Name: EMOTIONAL INTELLIGENCE SCALE

Purpose: To measure emotional intelligence as maturity, compassion, morality, sociability, and stable disposition.

Number of Items: 65

Format: All items are presented.

Validity: Correlations with other variables ranged from −.65 to −.01.

Author: Fukunishi, I., et al.

Article: Association of emotional intelligence with alexithymic characteristics.

Journal: *Psychological Reports*, December 2001, *89*, 651–658.

Related Research: Uchiyama, K., et al. (2001). [EQS Manual]. Tokyo: Jitsumu-Kyolku Syuppan. [in Japanese]

11383

Test Name: EMOTIONAL INTELLIGENCE SCALE

Purpose: To measure self-emotions appraisal, others-emotions appraisal, use of emotions, and regulation of emotions.

Number of Items: 16

Format: Scales range from 1 (*totally disagree*) to 7 (*totally agree*). All items are presented.

Reliability: Alpha coefficients ranged from .79 to .93 across subscales.

Validity: Correlations with other variables ranged from −.45 to .48.

Author: Law, K. S., et al.

Article: The construction and criterion validity of emotional intelligence and its potential utility for management studies.

Journal: *The Journal of Applied Psychology*, June 2004, *89*, 483–496.

Related Research: Wong, C. S., & Law, K. S. (2002). The effects of leader and follower emotional intelligence on performance and attitude: An exploratory study. *The Leadership Quarterly, 13*, 243–274.

11384

Test Name: EMOTIONAL INTELLIGENCE SCALE

Purpose: To measure the ability to know one's feelings and emotions and to understand the feelings and emotions of others.

Number of Items: 25

Format: Five-point scales range from *strongly disagree* to *strongly agree*. All items are presented.

Reliability: Alphas ranged from .66 to .80 across subscales.

Validity: Correlations between subscales ranged from .25 to .48.

Author: Wu, S. M.

Article: Development and application of a brief measure of emotional intelligence for vocational high school teachers.

Journal: *Psychological Reports*, December 2004, *95*, Part 2, 1207–1218.

11385

Test Name: SCHUTTE SELF-REPORT INVENTORY OF EMOTIONAL INTELLIGENCE

Purpose: To assess emotional intelligence.

Number of Items: 33

Format: Responses are made on a 5-point Likert scale ranging from 1 (*strongly disagree*) to 5 (*strongly agree*). Examples are given.

Reliability: Alpha coefficients ranged from .58 to .89.

Validity: Correlations with other variables ranged from −.47 to .53.

Author: Chapman, B. P., and Hayslip, B., Jr.

Article: Incremental validity of a measure of emotional intelligence.

Journal: *Journal of Personality Assessment*, October 2005, *85*, 154–169.

Related Research: Schutte, N. S., et al. (1998). Development and validation of a measure of emotional intelligence. *Personality and Individual Differences, 25*, 167–177.

CHAPTER 7
Attitude

11386

Test Name: ACCEPTANCE OF VERBAL PRESSURE SCALE

Purpose: To assess the extent to which it is acceptable for a man to verbally pressure a woman to have sex.

Number of Items: 13

Format: Seven-point scales range from *not at all acceptable* to *very acceptable.*

Reliability: Coefficient alpha was .97.

Validity: Correlations with other variables ranged from –.13 to .32.

Author: Abbey, A., and McAuslan, P.

Article: A longitudinal examination of male college students' perpetration of sexual assault.

Journal: *Journal of Consulting and Clinical Psychology,* October 2004, *72,* 747–756.

Related Research: Cook, S. L. (1995). Acceptance and expectation of sexual aggression in college students. *Psychology of Women Quarterly, 19,* 181–194.

11387

Test Name: ADOLESCENT, PARENT, AND TEACHER SCALES

Purpose: To measure adolescents' and parents' beliefs and attitudes about mathematics and science as well as teachers' ratings of children's mathematics performance and ability.

Number of Items: 14

Format: Five-point and 7-point scales are used. Sample items are presented.

Reliability: Alpha coefficients ranged from .60 to .88.

Author: Bleeker, M. M., and Jacobs, J. E.

Article: Achievement in math and science: Do mothers' beliefs matter 12 years later?

Journal: *Journal of Educational Psychology,* March 2004, *96,* 97–100.

Related Research: Jacobs, J. E., & Eccles, J. S. (1992). The impact of mothers' gender-role stereotypic beliefs on mothers' and children's ability perceptions. *Journal of Personality and Social Psychology, 63,* 932–944.

11388

Test Name: ADULT ATTACHMENT SCALE

Purpose: To assess beliefs and attitudes about adult relationships analogous to those thought to be important in early attachment relationships.

Number of Items: 18

Format: Includes three subscales: Close, Depend, and Anxiety.

Reliability: Alpha coefficients ranged from .74 to .85. Test–retest (6 months) reliabilities ranged from .64 to .71.

Author: Wei, M., et al.

Article: Perceived coping as a mediator between attachment and psychological distress: A structural equation modeling approach.

Journal: *Journal of Counseling Psychology,* October 2003, *50,* 438–447.

Related Research: Collins, N. L., & Read, S. J. (1990). Adult attachments, working models, and relationship quality in dating couples. *Journal of Personality and Social Psychology, 58,* 644–663.

11389

Test Name: AFFECTIVE LEARNING SCALE

Purpose: To measure six dimensions of affective learning attitudes and behavior.

Number of Items: 24

Format: Seven-point good–bad scales are used. A sample item is presented.

Reliability: Alpha coefficients ranged from .88 to .95.

Author: Clark, R. K., et al.

Article: Experimentally assessing the student impacts of out-of-class communication: Office visits and the student experience.

Journal: *Journal of College Student Development,* November/December 2002, *43,* 824–837.

Related Research: Christophel, D. M. (1990). The relationship among teacher immediacy behaviors, student motivation, and learning. *Communication Education, 39,* 323–340.

11390

Test Name: AFFECTIVE ORGANIZATIONAL ATTITUDES SCALE

Purpose: To assess employees' overall attitude toward the organization.

Number of Items: 4

Format: Three items employ a 5-point rating scale ranging from 1 (*strongly disagree*) to 5 (*strongly agree*), and one item employs a 5-point rating scale ranging from *yes, definitely,* to *not at all.* All items are presented.

Reliability: Coefficient alpha was .76.

Validity: Correlations with other variables ranged from –.07 to .46.

Author: Wegner, S. H., et al.

Article: Employees that think and act like owners: Effects of ownership beliefs and behaviors on organizational effectiveness.

Journal: *Personnel Psychology,* Winter 2003, *56,* 847–871.

11391

Test Name: AIDS HEALTH BELIEF SCALE

Purpose: To measure AIDS health beliefs.

Number of Items: 15

Format: Item responses range from 1 (*strongly agree*) to 4 (*strongly disagree*).

Reliability: Coefficient alpha was .78.

Author: Mashegoane, S., et al.

Article: The prediction of condom use intention among South African university students.

Journal: *Psychological Reports,* October 2004, *95,* 407–417.

Related Research: Zagumny, M. J., & Brady, D. B. (1998). Development of the AIDS Health Belief Scale (AHBS). *AIDS Education and Prevention, 10,* 173–179.

11392

Test Name: AIDS HEALTH BELIEF SCALE

Purpose: To measure perceived susceptibility to HIV/AIDS, perceived severity of HIV/AIDS, perceived benefits of preventive behavior, and barriers to preventive behavior.

Number of Items: 16

Format: Item responses are anchored by 1 (*strongly disagree*) and 6 (*strongly agree*).

Reliability: Coefficient alpha was .67.

Author: Peltzer, K., and Oladimeji, Y.

Article: Some factors in condom use amongst first-year Nigerian University students and Black and White South Africans.

Journal: *Psychological Reports,* April 2004, *94,* 583–586.

Related Research: Zagumny, M. J., & Brady, D. B. (1998). Development of the AIDS Health Belief Scale (AHBS). *AIDS Education and Prevention, 10,* 173–179.

11393

Test Name: ALTRUISM TEST

Purpose: To measure attitudes toward helping others.

Number of Items: 21

Format: Responses are made on a 5-point Likert scale ranging from *strongly agree* to *strongly disagree.* An example is presented.

Reliability: Coefficient alpha was .76.

Author: Powell, C. L., and Arriola, K. R. J.

Article: Relationship between psychosocial factors and academic achievement among African American students.

Journal: *The Journal of Educational Research,* January/February 2003, *96,* 175–181.

Related Research: Kool, V. K., et al. (1992). Nonviolence test: Nonviolence and moral reasoning. *The Journal of Social Psychology, 133,* 745–746.

11394

Test Name: ANOMALOUS EXPERIENCES SCALE

Purpose: To measure paranormal beliefs.

Number of Items: 70

Format: A true–false format is used. Sample items are presented.

Reliability: K-R 20 reliability coefficients ranged from .64 to .85 across subscales.

Author: Houran, J., and Lange, R.

Article: Redefining delusion based on studies of subjective paranormal ideation.

Journal: *Psychological Reports,* April 2004, *94,* 501–513.

Related Research: Kumar, V. K., et al. (1994). *The Anomalous Experiences Inventory.* Unpublished manuscript, West Chester University, West Chester, PA.

11395

Test Name: ASSESSMENT OF ATTITUDES FOR CAREER DECISION-MAKING

Purpose: To measure attributional style toward making career decisions. Controllability, causality, and stability.

Number of Items: 9

Format: Five-point scales are used.

Reliability: Coefficient alpha was .78. Subscale alphas ranged from .64 to .89.

Author: Maples, M. R., and Luzzo, D. A.

Article: Evaluating DISCOVERS's effectiveness in enhancing college students' social cognitive career development.

Journal: *The Career Development Quarterly*, March 2005, *53*, 263–273.

Related Research: Luzzo, D. A., & Jenkins-Smith, A. (1998). Development and initial validation of the assessment of attributions for career decision-making. *Journal of Vocational Behavior, 52*, 224–245.

11396

Test Name: ASSESSMENT OF ATTRIBUTIONS FOR CAREER DECISION MAKING

Purpose: To measure attributional style toward making career decisions.

Number of Items: 9

Format: Includes three factors: causality, stability, and controllability. Responses are made on a 5-point scale.

Reliability: Internal consistency reliabilities ranged from .64 to .89. Test–retest (6 weeks) reliabilities ranged from .64 to .89.

Author: Maples, M. R., and Luzzo, D. A.

Article: Evaluating DISCOVER's effectiveness in enhancing college students' social cognitive career development.

Journal: *The Career Development Quarterly*, March 2005, *53*, 274–285.

Related Research: Luzzo, D. A., & Jenkins-Smith, A. (1998). Development and initial validation of the Assessment of Attributions

for Career Decision Making. *Journal of Vocational Behavior, 52*, 224–245.

11397

Test Name: ATTITUDE CHECKLIST

Purpose: To measure levels of participant's satisfaction, enjoyment, perceived autonomy, motivation, and sense of fairness associated with their experiences in the research project.

Number of Items: 12

Format: Responses are made on a 5-point rating scale ranging from 1 (*strongly disagree*) to 5 (*strongly agree*).

Validity: Correlations with other variables ranged from −.03 to .76.

Author: Flowerday, T., et al.

Article: The role of choice and interest in reader engagement.

Journal: *The Journal of Experimental Education*, Winter 2004, *72*, 93–114.

Related Research: Kohn, A. (1993, September). Choices for children: Why and how to let students decide. *Phi Delta Kappan, 75*, 8–16, 18–21.

11398

Test Name: ATTITUDE TOWARD CHRISTIANITY SHORT-FORM

Purpose: To measure attitudes toward Christianity.

Number of Items: 7

Format: Scales range from 1 (*disagree strongly*) to 5 (*agree strongly*). Sample items are presented.

Reliability: Alpha coefficients ranged from .91 to .93. Test–retest reliability was .92 (1 week).

Author: Lewis, C. A., et al.

Article: Temporal stability of the Francis Scale of Attitude toward

Christianity Short-Form: Test-retest data over one week.

Journal: *Psychological Reports*, April 2005, *96*, 266–268.

Related Research: Francis, L. J. (1993). Reliability and validity of a short scale of attitude towards Christianity among adults. *Psychological Reports, 72*, 615–618.

11399

Test Name: ATTITUDE TOWARD ECONOMICS INVENTORY— ADAPTED

Purpose: To measure high school students' attitudes toward economics.

Number of Items: 14

Format: Responses are made on a 5-point Likert-type scale ranging from 1 (*strongly agree*) to 5 (*strongly disagree*). Examples are given.

Reliability: Alpha coefficients were .87 to .88.

Validity: Correlations with other variables ranged from −.17 to .38.

Author: Mergendoller, J. R., et al.

Article: Comparing problem-based learning and traditional instruction in high school economics.

Journal: *The Journal of Educational Research*, July/August 2000, *93*, 374–382.

Related Research: Hodgin, R. F. (1984). *Attitude assessment for research in economics education* (ERIC Document Reproduction Service No. ED 248 779).

11400

Test Name: ATTITUDE TOWARD FAMILY OBLIGATION SCALE

Purpose: To assess adolescents' attitude toward assisting and spending time with the family.

Number of Items: 12

Format: Responses are made on a 5-point scale ranging from 1 (*almost never*) to 5 (*almost always*).

Reliability: Coefficients alpha was .86.

Author: Fuligni, A. J., et al.

Article: The impact of family obligation on the daily activities and psychological well-being of Chinese American adolescents.

Journal: *Child Development*, January/February 2002, *73*, 302–314.

Related Research: Fuligni, A. J., et al. (1999). Attitudes toward family obligations among American adolescents from Asian, Latin American, and European backgrounds. *Child Development*, *70*, 1030–1044.

11401

Test Name: ATTITUDE TOWARD MATERNAL EMPLOYMENT QUESTIONNAIRE

Purpose: To measure mother's attitudes and beliefs related to maternal employment and maternal role when infant was 1 month old.

Number of Items: 11

Format: Includes two areas: beneficial beliefs and harmful beliefs.

Reliability: Coefficient alpha was .88.

Author: Huston, A. C., and Aronson, S. R.

Article: Mothers' time with infant and time in employment as predictors of mother–child relationships and children's early development.

Journal: *Child Development*, March/April 2005, *76*, 467–482.

Related Research: Greenberger, E., et al. (1988). Beliefs about the benefits of maternal employment for children. *Psychology of Women Quarterly, 12*, 35–59.

11402

Test Name: ATTITUDE TOWARD MORAL BEHAVIOR SCALE

Purpose: To assess attitude toward moral behavior.

Number of Items: 5

Format: Semantic differential consisting of five pairs of adjectives. All items are presented. Responses are made on a 7-point scale.

Reliability: Coefficient alpha was .92.

Validity: Correlations with other variables ranged from .45 to .65.

Author: Tsorbatzoudis, H., and Emmanouilidou, M.

Article: Predicting moral behavior in physical education classes: An application of the theory of planned behavior.

Journal: *Perceptual and Motor Skills*, June 2005, *100*, Part 2, 1055–1065.

11403

Test Name: ATTITUDE TOWARD PREVENTION SCALE

Purpose: To measure attitudes toward HIV prevention.

Number of Items: 15

Format: A sample item is presented.

Reliability: Coefficient alpha was .72.

Author: St. Lawrence, J. S., et al.

Article: Reducing STD and HIV risk behavior of substance-dependent adolescents: A randomized controlled trial.

Journal: *Journal of Consulting and Clinical Psychology*, August 2002, *70*, 1010–1021.

Related Research: Torabi, M. R., & Yarber, W. (1992). Alternate forms of HIV prevention attitude scale for teenagers. *AIDS Education and Prevention, 4*, 172–182.

11404

Test Name: ATTITUDE TOWARD RELIGION SCALE

Purpose: To measure attitude toward religion.

Number of Items: 4

Format: Item responses are anchored by *strongly disagree* and *strongly agree*. All items are presented.

Reliability: Alpha was .89.

Validity: Correlations with other variables ranged from −.21 to .41.

Author: Lin, Y.

Article: Age, sex, education, religion, and perceptions of tattoos.

Journal: *Psychological Reports*, April 2002, *90*, 654–658.

11405

Test Name: ATTITUDE TOWARD THE ADVERTISEMENT SCALE

Purpose: To measure attitude toward advertisements as pleasantness, clarity, and interest.

Number of Items: 9

Format: Seven-point semantic differential format. All items are presented.

Reliability: Alpha coefficients ranged from .74 to .82 across subscales.

Author: Chebat, J.-C., et al.

Article: Drama advertisements: Moderating effects of self-relevance on the relations among empathy, information processing, and attitudes.

Journal: *Psychological Reports*, June 2003, *92*, Part 1, 997–1014.

Related Research: Chebat, J.-C., & Gélinas-Chebat, C. (1991). What makes open vs. closed conclusion advertisements more persuasive? The moderating role of prior knowledge and involvement. *Journal of Business Research, 53*, 93–102.

11406

Test Name: ATTITUDES REGARDING BISEXUALITY SCALE

Purpose: To measure attitudes toward bisexuality.

Number of Items: 18

Format: Includes two constructs: Stability and Tolerance. Responses are made on a 5-point scale ranging from 1 (*strongly disagree*) to 5 (*strongly agree*). Examples are presented.

Reliability: Internal consistencies were .77 and .89. Test–retest (3 weeks) reliabilities were .84 and .91.

Validity: Correlations with other variables ranged from .26 to .57.

Author: Dillon, F. R., and Worthington, R. L.

Article: The Lesbian, Gay, and Bisexual Affirmative Counseling Self-Efficacy Inventory (LGB-CSI): Development, validation, and training implications.

Journal: *Journal of Counseling Psychology*, April 2003, *50*, 235–251.

Related Research: Mohr, J. J., & Rochlen, A. B. (1999). Measuring attitudes regarding bisexuality in lesbian, gay male, and heterosexual populations. *Journal of Counseling Psychology, 46*, 353–369.

11407

Test Name: ATTITUDES REGARDING BISEXUALITY SCALE

Purpose: To measure attitudes toward bisexuality.

Number of Items: 24

Format: Responses are made on a 5-point rating scale ranging from 1 (*strongly disagree*) to 5 (*strongly agree*). Examples are given.

Reliability: Internal consistency estimates ranged from .83 to .94.

Test–retest (3 weeks) estimates ranged from .71 to .92.

Validity: Correlations with other variables ranged from −.49 to .74 ($n = 45$).

Author: Worthington, R. L., et al.

Article: Development, reliability, and validity of the Lesbian, Gay, and Bisexual Knowledge and Attitudes Scale for Heterosexuals (LGB-KASH).

Journal: *Journal of Counseling Psychology*, January 2005, *52*, 104–118.

Related Research: Mohr, J. J., & Rochlen, A. B. (1999). Measuring attitudes regarding bisexuality in lesbian, gay male, and heterosexual populations. *Journal of Counseling Psychology, 45*, 353–369.

11408

Test Name: ATTITUDES TO CHRISTIANITY INVENTORY

Purpose: To assess attitudes toward prayer, God, Jesus, the Bible, Christian practice, and social justice.

Number of Items: 30

Format: Scales range from 1 (*strongly disagree*) to 5 (*strongly agree*). Sample items are presented.

Reliability: Alpha coefficients ranged from .75 to .94 across subscales.

Validity: Correlations with religious behaviors ranged from .15 to .69.

Author: Dorman, J. P.

Article: Associations between religious behavior and attitude to Christianity among Australian Catholic adolescents: Scale validation.

Journal: *The Journal of Social Psychology*, October 2001, *141*, 629–639.

11409

Test Name: ATTITUDES TOWARD AGING SCALE

Purpose: To measure attitude toward aging.

Number of Items: 21

Format: Employs bipolar adjective pairs with a 7-point format scale. An example is presented.

Reliability: Coefficient alpha was .89.

Author: Griffith, J. D., and Hart, C. L.

Article: A summary of U.S. skydiving fatalities: 1993–1999.

Journal: *Perceptual and Motor Skills*, June 2002, *94*, Part 2, 1089–1090.

Related Research: Netz, Y., & Ben-Sira, D. (1993). Attitudes of young people, adults, and older adults from the three-generation families toward the concepts 'Ideal Person,' 'Youth,' 'Adult,' and 'Old Person.' *Educational Gerontology, 19*, 607–621.

11410

Test Name: ATTITUDES TOWARD BODY ART

Purpose: To measure attitudes toward individuals with body art.

Number of Items: 30

Format: A 7-point semantic differential format is used. All items are presented.

Reliability: Alpha coefficients ranged from .86 to .87.

Validity: Correlations with a religiosity scale ranged from −.14 to −.01.

Author: Koch, J. R., et al.

Article: Religious belief and practice in attitudes toward individuals with body piercing.

Journal: *Psychological Reports*, October 2004, *95*, 583–586.

Related Research: Stuppy, D. J., et al. (1998). Attitudes of health care providers and students towards tattooed people. *Journal of Advanced Nursing, 27,* 1165–1170.

11411

Test Name: ATTITUDES TOWARD CAREER COUNSELING SCALE

Purpose: To assess attitudes toward career counseling.

Number of Items: 16

Format: Includes two factors: value and stigma.

Reliability: Internal consistency estimates ranged from .80 to .90. Test–retest (3 weeks) reliability was .80.

Author: Whitaker, L. A., et al.

Article: Influencing client expectations about career counseling using a videotaped intervention.

Journal: *The Career Development Quarterly,* June 2004, *52,* 309–322.

Related Research: Rochlen, A.-B., et al. (1999). Development of the Attitudes Toward Career Counseling Scale. *Journal of Counseling Psychology, 46,* 196–206.

11412

Test Name: ATTITUDES TOWARD CHILDREN WITH DISABILITIES QUESTIONNAIRE

Purpose: To measure personal and professional attitudes toward children with disabilities.

Number of Items: 24

Format: Seven-point scales are anchored by –3 (*strongly disagree*) and +3 (*strongly agree*).

Reliability: Total alpha was .56. Subscale alphas ranged from .66 to .73.

Validity: Correlations with other variables ranged from –.45 to .13.

Author: Gaje, G. D., et al.

Article: Anxiety, attitudes, and sex roles of male college students in a "buddy program" for persons with disabilities.

Journal: *Psychological Reports,* June 2002, *90,* Part 2, 1211–1220.

Related Research: Daugherty, T., et al. (1994). *Measuring attitudes toward children with disabilities and their parents.* Presented at the annual meeting of the American Psychological Association, Los Angeles, CA.

11413

Test Name: ATTITUDES TOWARD CONDOM USE SCALE

Purpose: To measure attitudes toward condoms.

Number of Items: 10

Format: Scales range from 1 (*strongly disagree*) to 6 (*strongly agree*). A sample item is presented.

Reliability: Coefficient alpha was .74.

Author: Carey, M. P., et al.

Article: Reducing HIV-risk behavior among adults receiving outpatient psychiatric treatment: Results from a randomized controlled trial.

Journal: *Journal of Consulting and Clinical Psychology,* April 2004, *72,* 252–268.

Related Research: Sacco, W. P., et al. (1991). Attitudes about condom use as an AIDS-relevant behavior: Their factor structure and relation to condom use. *Psychological Assessment, 3,* 265–272.

11414

Test Name: ATTITUDES TOWARD CREDIT CARD Q-SORT SCALE

Purpose: To measure knowledge/beliefs, behavior, and affect associated with credit cards.

Number of Items: 10

Format: All items are presented.

Reliability: Alpha coefficients ranged from .66 to .79.

Author: Pinto, M. B., et al.

Article: Relationship of credit attitude and debt to self-esteem and locus of control in college-age consumers.

Journal: *Psychological Reports,* June 2004, *94,* Part 2, 1405–1418.

Related Research: Pinto, M. B, et al. (2000). Materialism and credit card use by college students. *Psychological Reports, 86,* 643–652.

11415

Test Name: ATTITUDES TOWARD EDUCATIONAL PRACTICES SCALE

Purpose: To assess teachers' attitudes and beliefs toward traditional and reform-recommended educational practices.

Number of Items: 55

Format: Includes 13 subscales.

Reliability: Alpha coefficients ranged from .50 to .91.

Author: Seitsinger, A. M.

Article: Service-learning and standards-based instruction in middle schools.

Journal: *The Journal of Educational Research,* September/October 2005, *99,* 19–30.

Related Research: National Center on Public Education and Social Policy (1998). *Scale reliability of self-study staff survey across years (1994–1998).* Kingston, RI: Author.

11416

Test Name: ATTITUDES TOWARD FEMINISM AND THE WOMEN'S MOVEMENT SCALE

Purpose: To measure feminist attitudes.

Number of Items: 10

Format: Responses are made on a 5-point scale ranging from 1 (*strongly disagree*) to 5 (*strongly agree*).

Reliability: Alpha coefficients ranged from .68 to .89. Test–retest (2 weeks) reliability was .81.

Validity: Correlations with other variables ranged from −.13 to .31.

Author: Flores, L. Y., and O'Brien, K. M.

Article: The career development of Mexican American adolescent women: A test of social cognitive career theory.

Journal: *Journal of Counseling Psychology*, January 2002, *49*, 14–27.

Related Research: Fassinger, R. E. (1994). Development and testing of the Attitude Toward Feminism and the Women's Movement (FWM) Scale. *Psychology of Women Quarterly*, *18*, 389–402.

11417

Test Name: ATTITUDES TOWARD GAY, LESBIAN, BISEXUAL, AND TRANSGENDER PERSONS

Purpose: To assess attitudes toward GLBT persons.

Number of Items: 3

Format: Scales range from 1 (*strongly disagree*) to 4 (*strongly agree*). All items are presented.

Reliability: Coefficient alpha was .85.

Author: Brown, R. D., et al.

Article: Assessing the campus climate for gay, lesbian, bisexual, and transgender (GLBT) students using a multiple perspectives approach.

Journal: *Journal of College Student Development*, January/February 2004, *45*, 8–26.

Related Research: Malaney, G. D., et al. (1997). Assessing campus climate for gays, lesbians, and bisexuals at two institutions. *Journal of College Student Development*, *38*, 365–375.

11418

Test Name: ATTITUDES TOWARD HOMELESS CHILDREN SCALE

Purpose: To measure children's overall evaluation of homeless children.

Number of Items: 8

Format: Responses are made on a 4- and 5-point response scales. Examples are presented.

Reliability: Coefficient alpha was .83.

Validity: Correlations with other variables ranged from .20 to .43.

Author: Karafantis, D. M., and Levy, S. R.

Article: The role of children's lay theories about the malleability of human attributes in beliefs about and volunteering for disadvantaged groups.

Journal: *Child Development*, January/February 2004, *75*, 236–250.

11419

Test Name: ATTITUDES TOWARD HOMOSEXUALS IN THE MILITARY

Purpose: To measure trust, threat, acceptance, and comfort of homosexuals in the military.

Number of Items: 14

Format: Item responses are anchored by 1 (*strongly agree*) and 4 (*strongly disagree*). All items are presented.

Reliability: Total alpha was .87. Subscale alphas ranged from .63 to .78.

Validity: Correlations with the Attitudes Toward Lesbians and Gay Men ranged from .59 to .75.

Author: Estrada, A. X.

Article: A preliminary scale for assessing attitudes toward homosexuals in the military.

Journal: *Psychological Reports*, April 2002, *90*, 583–592.

11420

Test Name: ATTITUDES TOWARD IMMIGRANT ACCULTURATION SCALE

Purpose: To measure attitudes toward integration, assimilation, segregation, and exclusion.

Number of Items: 14

Format: Scales range from 1 (*completely disagree*) to 7 (*completely agree*). Sample items are presented.

Reliability: Alpha coefficients ranged from .62 to .70.

Validity: Correlations with other variables ranged from −.57 to .59.

Author: Florack, A., et al.

Article: Perceived intergroup threat and attitudes of host community members toward immigrant acculturation.

Journal: *The Journal of Social Psychology*, October 2003, *143*, 633–648.

11421

Test Name: ATTITUDES TOWARD LAW SCHOOL SCALES

Purpose: To measure attitudes toward law school.

Number of Items: 26

Format: Scales range from −2 (*strongly disagree*) to 2 (*agree strongly*). Sample items are presented.

Reliability: Alpha coefficients ranged from .78 to .89 across baseline and follow-up measurements.

Author: Pritchard, M. E., and McIntosh, D. N.

Article: What predicts adjustment among law students? A longitudinal panel study.

Journal: *The Journal of Social Psychology*, December 2003, *143*, 727–745.

Related Research: Homer, S., & Schwartz, L. (1990). Admitted but not accepted: Outsiders take an inside look at law school. *Berkeley Women's Law Journal, 5*, 1–74.

11422

Test Name: ATTITUDES TOWARD LEARNING AND DEVELOPMENT

Purpose: To measure how interested and how favorable employees are about career development.

Number of Items: 8

Format: Sample items are presented.

Reliability: Coefficient alpha was .91.

Validity: Correlations with other variables ranged from –.28 to .58.

Author: Maurer, T. J., et al.

Article: A model of involvement in work-related learning and development activity: The effects of individual, situational, motivational, and age variables.

Journal: *Journal of Applied Psychology*, August 2003, *88*, 707–724.

11423

Test Name: ATTITUDES TOWARD LEARNING ENGLISH SCALE

Purpose: To measure attitudes toward learning English among Arab students.

Number of Items: 30

Format: Likert response categories were anchored by 1 (*like*) and 3 (*dislike*).

Reliability: Test–retest reliability was .79.

Validity: Correlations between subscales ranged from .47 to .80. Correlations with other variables ranged from –.02 to .16.

Author: Lori, A. A., and Al-Ansari, S. H.

Article: Relations of some sociocultural variables and attitudes and motivations of young Arab students learning English as a second language.

Journal: *Psychological Reports*, February 2001, *88*, 91–101.

Related Research: Gardner, R. C., & Lambert, W. E. (1972). *Attitudes and motivation in second language learning.* Rowley, MA: Newbury House.

11424

Test Name: ATTITUDES TOWARD LESBIAN AND GAY MEN SCALE—SHORT FORM

Purpose: To assess attitudes toward lesbian women and gay men along a cognitive continuum of condemnation to tolerance.

Number of Items: 10

Format: Responses are made on a 5-point scale ranging from 1 (*strongly disagree*) to 5 (*strongly agree*). Examples are given.

Reliability: Alpha coefficients ranged from .85 to .92.

Validity: Correlations with other variables ranged from .23 to .59.

Author: Dillon, F. R., and Worthington, R. L.

Article: The Lesbian, Gay, and Bisexual Affirmative Counseling Self-Efficacy Inventory (LGB-CSI):

Development, validation, and training implications.

Journal: *Journal of Counseling Psychology*, April 2003, *50*, 235–251.

Related Research: Herek, G. M. (1988). Heterosexuals' attitudes toward lesbians and gay men: Correlates and gender differences. *Journal of Sex Research, 25*, 451–477.

11425

Test Name: ATTITUDES TOWARD LESBIANS AND GAY MEN SCALE

Purpose: To assess attitudes toward lesbian women and gay men.

Number of Items: 20

Format: Includes two parts: lesbian and gay male. Responses are made on a 9-point scale ranging from 1 (*strongly disagree*) to 9 (*strongly agree*). Examples are given.

Reliability: Alpha coefficients ranged from .85 to .92.

Validity: Correlations with other variables ranged from –.89 to .57 (*n* = 45).

Author: Worthington, R. L., et al.

Article: Development, reliability, and validity of the Lesbian, Gay, and Bisexual Knowledge and Attitudes Scale for Heterosexuals (LGB-KASH).

Journal: *Journal of Counseling Psychology*, January 2005, *52*, 104–118.

Related Research: Herek, G. M. (1984). Attitudes towards lesbians and gay men: A factor analytic study. *Journal of Homosexuality, 10*, 39–51.

11426

Test Name: ATTITUDES TOWARD LESBIANS AND GAY MEN SCALE—DUTCH VERSION

Purpose: To measure attitudes towards lesbians and gay men.

Number of Items: 10

Format: Response scales are anchored by 1 (*strongly agree*) and 5 (*strongly disagree*). All items are presented in English.

Reliability: Alpha coefficients ranged from .88 to .94.

Validity: Correlations with other variables ranged from .30 to .76.

Author: van de Meerendonk, B., et al.

Article: Application of Herek's Attitudes Toward Lesbians and Gay Men Scale in the Netherlands.

Journal: *Psychological Reports*, August 2003, *93*, 265–275.

Related Research: Herek, G. M. (1984). Attitudes toward lesbians and gay men: A factor analytic study. *Journal of Homosexuality*, *10*, 39–51.

11427

Test Name: ATTITUDES TOWARD MARRIAGE SCALE

Purpose: To measure attitudes toward marriage.

Number of Items: 14

Format: Scales range from 1 (*not at all difficult*) to 5 (*very difficult*). A sample item is presented.

Reliability: Alpha coefficients exceeded .84.

Validity: Correlations with chance of marrying ranged from −.52 to .21.

Author: Umaña-Taylor, A. J., and Fine, M.

Article: Predicting commitment to wed among Hispanic and Anglo partners.

Journal: *Journal of Marriage and Family*, February 2003, *65*, 117–139.

Related Research: Kinnaird, K. L., & Gerrard, M. (1986). Premarital sexual behavior and attitudes toward marriage and divorce among young women as a function of their mother's marital status. *Journal of Marriage and the Family*, *48*, 757–765.

11428

Test Name: ATTITUDES TOWARD MEN SCALE

Purpose: To assess attitudes toward men regarding marriage and parenthood, sexuality, work, and physical and personality attributes.

Number of Items: 32

Format: Scales range from 1 (*disagree strongly*) to 4 (*agree strongly*).

Reliability: Alpha coefficients ranged from .77 to .89.

Author: Maltby, J., and Day, L.

Article: Applying a social identity paradigm to examine the relationship between men's self-esteem and their attitudes toward men and women.

Journal: *The Journal of Social Psychology*, February 2003, *143*, 111–126.

Related Research: Iazzo, A. N. (1983). The construction and validation of Attitudes Toward Men Scale. *The Psychological Record*, *33*, 371–378.

11429

Test Name: ATTITUDES TOWARD MULTIPLE ROLE PLANNING

Purpose: To assess knowledge–certainty, commitment to multiple roles, independence, and involvement.

Number of Items: 40

Format: Includes four subscales: Knowledge/Certainty, Commitment to Multiple Roles, Independence, and Involvement. Responses are made on a 5-point Likert scale. Sample items are presented.

Reliability: Alpha items ranged from .72 to .84.

Validity: Correlations with other variables ranged from −.35 to .28.

Author: Peake, A., and Harris, K. L.

Article: Young adults' attitude toward multiple role planning: The influence of gender, career traditionality, and marriage plans.

Journal: *Journal of Vocational Behavior*, June 2002, *60*, 405–421.

Related Research: Weitzman, L. M., & Fitzgerald, L. F. (1996). The development and initial validation of scales to assess attitudes toward multiple role planning. *Journal of Career Assessment*, *4*, 269–284.

11430

Test Name: ATTITUDES TOWARD OBESE PEOPLE SCALE

Purpose: To measure attitudes toward obese people in four dimensions: Stigmatization, Social, Self-Confidence, and Diet and Exercise.

Number of Items: 44

Format: A 5-point Likert format was used. All items are presented.

Reliability: Alpha coefficients ranged from .78 to .89 across subscales. Total alpha was .92.

Author: Glenn, C. V., and Chow, P.

Article: Measurement of attitudes toward obese people among a Canadian sample of men and women.

Journal: *Psychological Reports*, October 2002, *91*, 627–640.

Related Research: Yuker, H. E., et al. (1995). Methods for measuring attitudes and behavior about obese people. In Allison, D. B. (Ed.), *Handbook of assessment methods for eating behavior and weight related problems: Measures, theory, and research* (pp. 81–105). London: Sage.

11431

Test Name: ATTITUDES TOWARD ONLINE AND TRADITIONAL COURSES

Purpose: To measure attitudes toward online and traditional courses.

Number of Items: 9

Format: Five-point scales range from 1 (*strongly disagree*) to 5 (*strongly agree*). All items are presented.

Reliability: Test–retest reliability coefficients ranged from .51 to .79.

Author: Jenkins, S. J., and Downs, E.

Article: Demographic, attitude, and personality differences reported by students enrolled in online versus traditional courses.

Journal: *Psychological Reports,* August 2003, *93*, 213–221.

Related Research: Sankaran, S. R., et al. (2000). Effect of student attitude to course format on learning performance: An empirical study in Web vs. lecture instruction. *Journal of Instructional Psychology, 27*, 67–73.

11432

Test Name: ATTITUDES TOWARD PHYSICAL EDUCATION SCALE

Purpose: To measure attitudes toward physical education.

Number of Items: 24

Format: Responses are made on a 5-point Likert-type scale ranging from 1 (*strongly disagree*) to 5 (*strongly agree*).

Reliability: Coefficient alpha was .93.

Author: Koca, C., and Demirhan, G.

Article: An examination of high school students' attitudes toward physical education with regard to sex and sport participation.

Journal: *Perceptual and Motor Skills,* June 2004, *98*, Part 1, 754–758.

Related Research: Demirhan, G., & Altay, F. (2001). [Attitudes scale of high school first graders towards physical education and sport: II]. *Spor Bilimleri Dergisi, 12*(2), 9–20.

11433

Test Name: ATTITUDES TOWARD RAPE VICTIMS SCALE

Purpose: To assess attitudes about rape victims.

Number of Items: 25

Format: Responses are made on a 7-point scale. An example is given.

Reliability: Alpha coefficients were .83 and .85.

Author: Jimenez, J. A., and Abreu, J. M.

Article: Race and sex effects on attitudinal perceptions of acquaintance rape.

Journal: *Journal of Counseling Psychology,* April 2003, *50*, 252–256.

Related Research: Ward, C. (1988). The Attitudes Toward Rape Victims Scale: Construction, validation, and cross-cultural applicability. *Psychology of Women Quarterly, 12*, 127–146.

11434

Test Name: ATTITUDES TOWARD RESEARCH SCALE— ADAPTED

Purpose: To assess students' interest in doing research.

Number of Items: 4

Format: Likert-style items are used.

Reliability: Alpha coefficients ranged from .88 to .91.

Validity: Correlations with other variables ranged from .01 to .46.

Author: Schlosser, L. Z., and Gelso, C. J.

Article: Measuring the working alliance in advisor–advisee relationships in graduate school.

Journal: *Journal of Counseling Psychology,* April 2001, *48*, 157–167.

Related Research: Royalty, G. M., et al. (1986). The environment and the student in counseling psychology: Does the research training environment influence graduate students' attitudes towards research? *The Counseling Psychologist, 14*, 9–30.

11435

Test Name: ATTITUDES TOWARD SCIENCE SCALE

Purpose: To measure attitudes towards science.

Number of Items: 22

Format: Item responses are anchored by 1 (*strongly disagree*) and 5 (*strongly agree*). All items are presented.

Reliability: Cronbach's alpha was .98.

Author: Cherian, L.

Article: Attitudes towards science of South African Northern Sotho-speaking pupils.

Journal: *Psychological Reports,* August 2002, *91*, 127–130.

Related Research: Simpson, R. D., et al. (1985). Attitude toward science and achievement motivation profiles of male and female science students in grades six to ten. *Science Education, 69*, 511–526.

11436

Test Name: ATTITUDES TOWARD SEEKING PROFESSIONAL HELP SCALE— SHORT FORM

Purpose: To assess general attitudes toward seeking professional psychological help.

Number of Items: 10

Format: Scales range from 0 (*strongly disagree*) to 3 (*strongly agree*). Sample items are presented.

Reliability: Coefficient alpha was .75.

Validity: Correlations with other variables ranged from −.43 to .65.

Author: Rochlen, A. B., et al.

Article: The Online and Face-to-Face Counseling Attitudes Scales: A validation study.

Journal: *Measurement and Evaluation in Counseling and Development*, July 2004, *37*, 95–111.

Related Research: Fischer, E. H., & Farina, A. (1995). Attitudes toward seeking professional psychological help: A shortened form and considerations for research. *Journal of College Student Development, 36*, 368–373.

11437

Test Name: ATTITUDES TOWARD SEEKING PROFESSIONAL PSYCHOLOGICAL HELP SCALE

Purpose: To measure attitudes toward counseling.

Number of Items: 29

Format: Responses are made on a 4-point Likert-type scale ranging from 0 (*disagree*) to 3 (*agree*).

Reliability: Internal consistencies ranged from .83 to .90. Test–retest (5 days) reliability was .86, for 2 weeks it was .89, for 4 weeks it was .82, for 6 weeks it was .73, and for 2 months it was .84.

Validity: Correlations with other variables ranged from −.33 to .61.

Author: Vogel, D. L., and Wester, S. R.

Article: To seek help or not to seek help: The risks of self-disclosure.

Journal: *Journal of Counseling Psychology*, July 2003, *50*, 351–361.

Related Research: Fischer, E. H., & Turner, J. L. (1970). Development and research utility of an attitude scale. *Journal of Consulting and Clinical Psychology, 35*, 79–90.

11438

Test Name: ATTITUDES TOWARD SEEKING PROFESSIONAL PSYCHOLOGICAL HELP SCALE—REVISED

Purpose: To measure overall attitude toward seeking professional help for psychological problems.

Number of Items: 29

Format: Responses are made on a 5-point scale ranging from 1 (*strongly disagree*) to 5 (*strongly agree*).

Reliability: Alpha coefficients ranged from .80 to .89.

Validity: Correlations with other variables ranged from −.42 to .43.

Author: Liao, H.-Y., et al.

Article: A test of Cramer's (1999) help-seeking model and acculturation effects with Asian and Asian American college students.

Journal: *Journal of Counseling Psychology*, July 2005, *52*, 400–411.

Related Research: Fischer, E. H., & Turner, J. L. (1970). Orientations to seeking professional help: Development and research utility of an attitude scale. *Journal of Consulting and Clinical Psychology, 35*, 79–90.

11439

Test Name: ATTITUDES TOWARD SEEKING PROFESSIONAL PSYCHOLOGICAL HELP SCALE—SHORTENED

Purpose: To measure attitudes toward seeking professional help.

Number of Items: 10

Format: Responses are made on a 4-point Likert-type scale ranging from 1 (*disagree*) to 4 (*agree*). An example is given.

Reliability: Test–retest (1 month) reliability was .80. Internal consistency reliabilities were .82 and .84.

Validity: Correlations with other variables ranged from −.31 to .56 ($N = 354$).

Author: Vogel, D. L., et al.

Article: The role of outcome expectations and attitudes on decisions to seek professional help.

Journal: *Journal of Counseling Psychology*, October 2005, *52*, 459–470.

Related Research: Fischer, E. H., & Farina, A. (1995). Attitudes Toward Seeking Professional Psychological Help: A shortened form and considerations for research. *Journal of College Student Development, 36*, 368–373.

11440

Test Name: ATTITUDES TOWARD STATISTICS SCALE

Purpose: To measure attitudes toward statistics.

Number of Items: 29

Format: Includes two subscales: Attitude Toward the Field of Statistics and Attitude Toward the Course of Statistics. Responses are made on a 5-point Likert-type scale. Examples are given.

Reliability: Alpha coefficients ranged from .88 to .94.

Validity: Correlations with other variables ranged from .22 to .92.

Author: Cashin, S. E., and Elmore, P. B.

Article: The Survey of Attitudes Toward Statistics Scale: A construct validity study.

Journal: *Educational and Psychological Measurement*, June 2005, *65*, 509–524.

Related Research: Wise, S. L. (1985). The development and validation of a scale measuring attitudes toward statistics. *Educational and Psychological Measurement, 45*, 401–405.

11441

Test Name: ATTITUDES TOWARD TV VIOLENCE SCALE

Purpose: To survey attitudes toward TV violence.

Number of Items: 11

Format: Responses are made on a 5-point Likert-type scale ranging from 1 (*strongly disagree*) to 5 (*strongly agree*). All items are presented.

Reliability: Alpha coefficients were .87 and .88.

Author: Nussbaum, E. M., and Kardash, C. A. M.

Article: The effects of goal instructions and text on the generation of counterarguments during writing.

Journal: *Journal of Educational Psychology*, May 2005, *97*, 157–169.

Related Research: Nussbaum, E. M., et al. (2003, April). *Writing arguments and counterarguments: Do goals and need for cognition overcome the "my-side" bias?* Paper presented at the annual meeting of the American

Educational Research Association, Chicago, IL.

11442

Test Name: ATTITUDES TOWARD USING FEEDBACK SCALE

Purpose: To measure attitudes toward using feedback.

Number of Items: 3

Format: Responses are made on a 7-point scale ranging from *strongly agree* to *strongly disagree*. An example is given.

Reliability: Coefficient alpha was .75.

Validity: Correlations with other variables ranged from –.16 to .31.

Author: Atwater, L. E., and Brett, J. F.

Article: Antecedents and consequences of reactions to developmental 360° feedback.

Journal: *Journal of Vocational Behavior*, June 2005, *66*, 532–548.

11443

Test Name: ATTITUDES TOWARD WIFE ABUSE SCALE

Purpose: To measure attitudes toward male violence against an intimate female partner.

Number of Items: 8

Format: Scales range from 1 (*strongly disagree*) to 7 (*strongly agree*).

Reliability: Coefficient alpha was .63.

Author: Ali, A., and Toner, B. B.

Article: Self-esteem as a predictor of attitudes toward wife abuse among Muslim women and men in Canada.

Journal: *The Journal of Social Psychology*, February 2001, *141*, 23–30.

Related Research: Briere, J. (1987). Predicting self-reported likelihood of battering: Attitudes and childhood experiences. *Journal of Research on Personality, 21*, 61–69.

11444

Test Name: ATTITUDES TOWARD WOMEN SCALE

Purpose: To measure an individual's beliefs about the rights, roles, and privileges of women.

Number of Items: 15

Format: Four-point scales range from *agree strongly* to *disagree strongly*.

Reliability: Various reliability coefficients ranged from .81 to .87.

Validity: The correlation with a 55-item version of the scale was .91.

Author: Davis, T. L., and Liddell, D. L.

Article: Getting inside the house: The effectiveness of a rape prevention program for college fraternity men.

Journal: *Journal of College Student Development*, January/February 2002, *43*, 35–50.

Related Research: Spence, J. T., & Helmreich, R. L. (1972). The Attitudes Toward Women Scale: An objective instrument to measure the rights and roles of women in contemporary society. *Catalog of Selected Documents in Psychology, 153*, 66–67.

11445

Test Name: ATTITUDES TOWARD WOMEN SCALE FOR ADOLESCENTS

Purpose: To measure sex role attitudes.

Number of Items: 12

Format: Responses are made on a 4-point scale ranging from *strongly agree* to *strongly disagree*.

Reliability: Alpha coefficients ranged from .66 to .69.

Author: Jeltova, I., et al.

Article: Risky sexual behaviors in immigrant adolescent girls from the former Soviet Union: Role of natal and host culture.

Journal: *Journal of School Psychology*, January/February 2005, *43*, 3–22.

Related Research: Galambos, N. L., et al. (1985). The Attitudes Toward Women Scale for Adolescents (AWS–A): A study of reliability and validity. *Sex Roles*, *13*, 343–356.

11446

Test Name: ATTITUDES TOWARD WOMEN'S ROLES SCALE

Purpose: To assess gender role attitudes.

Number of Items: 15

Format: Responses are made on a 4-point scale. Examples are given.

Reliability: Alpha coefficients ranged from .71 to .82.

Author: McHale, S. M., et al.

Article: Developmental and individual differences in girls' sex-typed activities in middle childhood and adolescence.

Journal: *Child Development*, September/October 2004, *75*, 1575–1593.

Related Research: Spence, J., & Helmreich, R. L. (1972). The Attitudes Toward Women Scale: An objective instrument to measure attitudes toward the rights and roles of women in contemporary society. *JSAS Catalog of Selected Documents in Psychology*, *2*, 153.

11447

Test Name: ATTITUDES TOWARD WORKING SINGLE PARENTS SCALE

Purpose: To measure attitudes toward working single parents.

Number of Items: 12

Format: Includes two subscales: Effect on Work and Effect on Children. Responses are made on a 5-point Likert scale ranging from 1 (*strongly disagree*) to 5 (*strongly agree*). All items are presented.

Reliability: Alpha coefficients were .69 and .81.

Validity: Correlations with other variables ranged from −.24 to .94.

Author: Noble, C. L., et al.

Article: Attitudes toward working single parents: Initial development of a measure.

Journal: *Educational and Psychological Measurement*, December 2004, *64*, 1030–1052.

11448

Test Name: ATTITUDES TOWARD AIDS VICTIMS SCALE

Purpose: To assess attitudes toward AIDS victims.

Number of Items: 20

Format: Response categories are anchored by 1 (*disagree strongly*) and 5 (*agree strongly*).

Reliability: Alpha was .91. Split-half reliability was .87.

Validity: Correlations with other variables ranged from −.01 to .28.

Author: Thompson, K. L., et al.

Article: Psychological predictors of sexual behaviors related to AIDS transmission.

Journal: *Psychological Reports*, February 2001, *88*, 51–67.

Related Research: Larsen, K. W., et al. (1988). AIDS victims and heterosexual attitudes. *Proceedings of the Oregon Academy of Sciences*, *24*, 99–107.

11449

Test Name: ATTITUDES TOWARD BLACKS SCALE

Purpose: To measure old-fashioned racist attitudes.

Number of Items: 20

Format: Seven-point scales are used.

Reliability: Coefficient alpha was .89.

Validity: Correlations with other variables ranged from −.15 to .73.

Author: Ziegert, J. C., and Hanges, P. J.

Article: Employment discrimination: The role of implicit attitudes, motivation, and a climate for racial bias.

Journal: *Journal of Applied Psychology*, May 2005, *90*, 553–562.

Related Research: Brigham, J. C. (1993). College students' racial attitudes. *Journal of Applied and Social Psychology*, *23*, 1933–1967.

11450

Test Name: ATTITUDES TOWARD BODY ART

Purpose: To measure attitudes toward individuals with body art.

Number of Items: 30

Format: A 7-point semantic differential format is used. All items are presented.

Reliability: Alpha coefficients ranged from .86 to .87.

Validity: Correlations with a religiosity scale ranged from −.14 to −.01.

Author: Koch, J. R., et al.

Article: Religious belief and practice in attitudes toward individuals with body piercing.

Journal: *Psychological Reports*, October 2004, *95*, 583–586.

Related Research: Stuppy, D. J., et al. (1998). Attitudes of health care providers and students towards tattooed people. *Journal of Advanced Nursing, 27*, 1165–1170.

11451

Test Name: ATTITUDES TOWARD LESBIAN/GAY/BISEXUAL RELATIONSHIPS

Purpose: To assess acceptance, comfort and support of lesbian, gay, and bisexual people and issues.

Number of Items: 4

Format: All items are presented. Four-point scales are used.

Reliability: Alpha coefficients ranged from .72 to .80.

Validity: Correlations with other variables ranged from .36 to .46.

Author: Laing, C. T. H., and Alimo, C.

Article: The impact of white heterosexual students' interactions on attitude toward lesbian, gay, and bisexual people: A longitudinal study.

Journal: *Journal of College Student Development*, May/June 2005, *46*, 237–250.

11452

Test Name: ATTITUDES TOWARDS VIOLENCE SCALE

Purpose: To measure the acceptance of violence.

Number of Items: 20

Format: Scales range from 1 (*strongly disagree*) to 7 (*strongly agree*).

Reliability: Alpha coefficients ranged from .89 to .91.

Author: Hall, G. C. N., et al.

Article: Ethnicity, culture, and sexual aggression: Risk and protective factors.

Journal: *Journal of Consulting and Clinical Psychology*, October 2005, *73*, 830–840.

Related Research: Lonsway, K. A., & Fitzgerald, L. F. (1995). Attitudinal antecedents of rape myth acceptance: A theoretical and empirical reexamination. *Journal of Personality and Social Psychology, 68*, 704–711.

11453

Test Name: ATTITUDINAL AND PERCEPTUAL MEASURES

Purpose: To assess attitudinal and perceptual measures

Number of Items: 17

Format: Includes five scales: Job Satisfaction, Organizational Commitment, Comparing Commitment to Employees, Risk, and Desire for Promotion. Responses are made on 5-point scales. Examples are presented.

Reliability: Alpha coefficients ranged from .76 to .92.

Validity: Correlations with other variables ranged from –.89 to .88.

Author: Ostroff, C., and Clark, M. A.

Article: Maintaining an internal market: Antecedents of willingness to change jobs.

Journal: *Journal of Vocational Behavior*, December 2002, *59*, 425–453.

Related Research: Cammann, C., et al. (1979). *The Michigan Organizational Assessment Questionnaire.* Unpublished manuscript, University of Michigan, Ann Arbor. Mowday, R. T. et al. (1979). The measurement of

organizational commitment. *Journal of Vocational Behavior, 14*, 224–247. Bretz, R. D., et al. (1994). Job search behavior of employed manager. *Personnel Psychology, 47*, 275–315.

11454

Test Name: ATTITUDINAL PROFESSIONAL COMMITMENT SCALE

Purpose: To measure attitudinal professional commitment.

Number of Items: 5

Format: A sample item is presented.

Reliability: An estimate of reliability was .83.

Validity: Correlations with other variables ranged from –.46 to .27 (*n* = 226).

Author: Blau, G., et al.

Article: Correlates of professional versus organizational withdrawal cognitions.

Journal: *Journal of Vocational Behavior*, August 2003, *63*, 72–85.

Related Research: Blau, G. (1985). The measurement and prediction of career commitment. *Journal of Occupational Psychology, 58*, 277–288.

11455

Test Name: BASIC BELIEFS INVENTORY

Purpose: To measure basic beliefs.

Number of Items: 102

Format: Includes eight scales: Self-Esteem, Relationships, Benign World, Meaningful World, Personal Directedness, Predictable/Controllable World, Optimism, and Validity.

Reliability: Consistency coefficients are in the mid .80s.

Validity: Correlations with other variables ranged from –.25 to.36.

Author: Mumford, M. D., et al.

Article: Alternative approaches for measuring values: Direct and indirect assessments in performance prediction.

Journal: *Journal of Vocational Behavior*, October 2002, *61*, 348–373.

Related Research: Caitlin, G., & Epstein, S. (1992). Unforgettable experiences: The relation of life events to basic beliefs about the self and world. *Social Cognition, 10*, 189–209.

11456

Test Name: BEHAVIORAL INTERVENTION RATING SCALE—REVISED

Purpose: To assess parents' and teachers' subjective beliefs of treatment efficacy.

Number of Items: 24

Format: Includes three factors: acceptability, effectiveness, and time to effect. Responses are made on a 6-point Likert scale.

Reliability: Alpha coefficients ranged from .87 to .97.

Author: Sheridan, S. M., et al.

Article: The effects of conjoint behavioral consultation results of a 4-year investigation.

Journal: *Journal of School Psychology*, September/October 2001, *39*, 361–385.

Related Research: Von Brock, M. B., & Elliott, S. N. (1987). Influence of treatment effectiveness information on the acceptability of classroom interventions. *Journal of School Psychology, 25*, 131–144.

11457

Test Name: BELIEF IN AFTERLIFE SCALE

Purpose: To assess strength of belief in an afterlife.

Number of Items: 10

Format: Scales range from 1 (*strongly disagree*) to 7 (*strongly agree*). A sample item is presented.

Reliability: Coefficient alpha was .87. The split-half correlation was .78.

Validity: Correlations with other variables ranged from –.35 to .42.

Author: Cohen, A. B., et al.

Article: Intrinsic and extrinsic religiosity, belief in the afterlife, death anxiety, and life satisfaction in young Catholics and Protestants.

Journal: *Journal of Research in Personality*, June 2005, *39*, 307–324.

Related Research: Osarchuk, M., & Tatz, S. J. (1973). Effect of induced fear of death on belief in an afterlife. *Journal of Personality and Social Psychology, 27*, 256–260.

11458

Test Name: BELIEF IN GOOD LUCK SCALE—EXTENDED TURKISH VERSION

Purpose: To measure belief in general luck, personal luck, and trust in luck.

Number of Items: 16

Format: Response scales are anchored by 1 (*strongly disagree*) and 5 (*strongly agree*). All items are presented in English.

Reliability: Coefficient alpha was .71.

Validity: Correlations with other variables ranged from –.23 to .71.

Author: Öner-Özkan, B.

Article: Revised form of the Belief in Good Luck Scale in a Turkish sample.

Journal: *Psychological Reports*, October 2003, *93*, 585–594.

Related Research: Darke, P. R., & Freedman, J. L. (1997). The Belief in Good Luck Scale. *Journal of Research in Personality, 31*, 486–511.

11459

Test Name: BELIEF IN SPORTS SUPERSTITIONS

Purpose: To measure beliefs in sports-related superstitions.

Number of Items: 9

Format: Item anchors are 1 (*strongly disagree*) and 4 (*strongly agree*). All items are presented.

Reliability: Coefficient alpha was .83.

Validity: Correlations with other variables ranged from .31 to .34.

Author: McClearn, D. G.

Article: Interest in sports and belief in sports superstitions.

Journal: *Psychological Reports*, June 2004, *94*, Part 1, 1043–1047.

11460

Test Name: BELIEFS ABOUT HUMAN NATURE SCALE

Purpose: To measure entity beliefs and incremental beliefs about human nature.

Number of Items: 4

Format: Sample items are presented.

Reliability: Alpha coefficients ranged from .71 to .93.

Author: Heslin, P. A., et al.

Article: The effect of implicit person theory on performance appraisals.

Journal: *Journal of Applied Psychology*, September 2005, *90*, 842–856.

Related Research: Levy, S. R., & Dweck, C. S. (1997). *Implicit theory measures: Reliability and validity data for adults and children.*

Unpublished manuscript, Columbia University, NY.

11461

Test Name: BELIEFS ABOUT ORGANIZATIONAL CITIZENSHIP BEHAVIOR SCALE

Purpose: To measure participant beliefs about organizational citizenship behavior.

Number of Items: 4

Format: Responses are made on a 5-point Likert ranging from 1 (*strongly disagree*) to 5 (*strongly agree*). All items are presented.

Reliability: Alpha coefficients were .77 and .80.

Validity: Correlations with other variables ranged from .28 to .42.

Author: Haworth, C. L., and Levy, P. E.

Article: The importance of instrumentality beliefs in the prediction of organizational citizenship behaviors.

Journal: *Journal of Vocational Behavior*, August 2001, *59*, 64–75.

11462

Test Name: BELIEFS ABOUT THE CAUSES OF SUCCESS

Purpose: To assess whether athletes believe that ability, deception, and high effort lead to success.

Number of Items: 14

Format: Includes three factors: deception, hard work, and high ability. Responses are made on a 5-point rating scale ranging from 1 (*strongly disagree*) to 5 (*strongly agree*). All items are presented.

Reliability: Alpha coefficients ranged from .69 to .76.

Validity: Correlations with other variables ranged from −.21 to .40.

Author: Laparidis, K., et al.

Article: Motivational climate, beliefs about the bases of success, and sportsmanship behaviors of professional basketball athletes.

Journal: *Perceptual and Motor Skills*, June 2003, *96*, Part 2, 1141–1151.

Related Research: Duda, J. L., & Nicholls, J. (1992). Dimensions of achievement motivation in schoolwork and sport. *Journal of Educational Psychology, 84*, 290–299.

11463

Test Name: BELIEFS ABOUT THE CONSEQUENCES OF MATERNAL EMPLOYMENT FOR CHILDREN

Purpose: To measure attitudes about maternal employment.

Number of Items: 11

Format: Scales range from 1 (*disagree very strongly*) to 6 (*agree very strongly*). A sample item is presented.

Reliability: Coefficient alpha was .88.

Author: Booth, C., et al.

Article: Child-care usage and mother–infant "quality time."

Journal: *Journal of Marriage and Family*, February 2002, *64*, 16–26.

Related Research: Greenberger, E., et al. (1988). Beliefs about the consequences of maternal employment for children. *Psychology of Women Quarterly, 12*, 35–59.

11464

Test Name: BELIEFS AND ATTITUDES ABOUT SLEEP SCALE—FRENCH VERSION

Purpose: To assess sleep-related thoughts and beliefs about perceived causes, consequences,

control, and predictability of insomnia.

Number of Items: 30

Format: Visual analogy scales range from 0 (*strongly disagree*) to 100 (*strongly agree*).

Reliability: Coefficient alpha was .90.

Author: Bastien, C. H., et al.

Article: Cognitive–behavioral therapy for insomnia: Comparison of individual therapy, group therapy, and telephone consultations.

Journal: *Journal of Consulting and Clinical Psychology*, August 2004, *72*, 653–659.

Related Research: Blais, F. C., et al. (1997). Evaluation de l'insomnie: Validation de trios questionnaires [Evaluation of insomnia: Validation of three questionnaires]. *L' Encephale, XIII*, 447–453.

11465

Test Name: BLACK RACIAL IDENTITY ATTITUDE SCALE

Purpose: To measure preencounter, immersion, and internalization racial identity attitudes.

Number of Items: 50

Format: Scales range from 1 (*strongly disagree*) to 5 (*strongly agree*). Sample items are presented.

Reliability: Alpha coefficients ranged from .53 to .77 across subscales.

Validity: Correlations with other variables ranged from −.36 to −.48.

Author: Kelly, S.

Article: Underlying components of scores assessing African Americans' racial perspective.

Journal: *Measurement and Evaluation in Counseling and Development*, April 2004, *37*, 28–40.

Related Research: Parham, T. A., & Helms, J. E. (1985). The relationship of racial identity attitudes to self-actualization of Black students and affective states. *Journal of Counseling Psychology, 32,* 431–440.

11466

Test Name: BLACK RACIAL IDENTITY ATTITUDE SCALE

Purpose: To measure racial identity ego statuses.

Number of Items: 39

Format: Includes four subscales: Pre-Encounter, Encounter, Immediate-Immersion, and Internalization. Responses are made on a 5-point Likert scale ranging from 1 (*strongly disagree*) to 5 (*strongly agree*).

Reliability: Internal consistencies ranged from .23 to .79.

Author: Nghe, L. T., and Mahalik, J. R.

Article: Examining racial identity statuses as predictors of psychological defenses in African American college students.

Journal: *Journal of Counseling Psychology,* January 2001, *48,* 10–16.

Related Research: Helms, J. E., & Parham, T. A. (1996). The development of the Racial Identity Attitude Scale. In R. L. Jones (Ed.), *Handbook of tests and measurements for Black populations* (Vol. 2, pp. 167–174). Hampton, VA: Cobb & Henry.

11467

Test Name: BODY ATTITUDES QUESTIONNAIRE

Purpose: To reflect women's principal body-related concerns.

Number of Items: 44

Format: Includes six subscales: Feelings of General Fatness, Feelings of Self-Loathing Related to the Body, Subjective Assessment of Individual's Physical Strength and Fitness, the Personal Relevance of Body Weight and Shape, Overall Sense of Attractiveness Primarily in Relation to the Opposite Sex, and Feelings That the Lower Body is Fat. Responses are made on a 5-point Likert-type scale ranging from 1 (*strongly disagree*) to 5 (*strongly agree*). Examples are given. All items are presented in Portuguese.

Reliability: Internal consistency was .87. Test–retest coefficients ranged from .64 to .91.

Validity: Correlations with other variables ranged from −.46 to .75.

Author: Scagliusi, F. B., et al.

Article: Psychometric testing and applications of the Body Attitudes Questionnaire translated into Portuguese.

Journal: *Perceptual and Motor Skills,* August 2005, *101,* 25–41.

Related Research: Ben-Tovim, D. I., & Walker, M. K. (1991). The development of the Ben-Tovim Walker Body Attitudes Questionnaire (BAQ), a new measure of women's attitudes towards their own bodies. *Psychological Medicine, 21,* 775–784.

11468

Test Name: BODY ELIMINATION ATTITUDE SCALE

Purpose: To measure disgust with body elimination.

Number of Items: 26

Format: Likert format. All items are presented.

Reliability: Correlations with other variables ranged from −.42 to .28.

Author: Corgiat, C. A., and Templer, D. I.

Article: Relation of attitude toward body elimination to parenting style and attitude toward the body.

Journal: *Psychological Reports,* April 2003, *92,* 621–626.

Related Research: Templer, D. I., et al. (1984). Assessment of body elimination attitude. *Journal of Clinical Psychology, 40,* 754–759.

11469

Test Name: BODY–SELF RELATIONS QUESTIONNAIRE

Purpose: To measure body-image attitudes: appearance evaluation, appearance orientation, fitness evaluation, fitness orientation, health evaluation, health orientation, and illness orientation.

Number of Items: 54

Format: Five-point agreement scales are used.

Reliability: Alpha coefficients ranged from .69 to .90 across subscales.

Author: Kuff, E., et al.

Article: Body-image attitudes and psychological functioning in Euro-American and Asian-American college women.

Journal: *Psychological Reports,* June 2001, *88,* Part 1, 917–928.

Related Research: Brown, T. A., et al. (1990). Attitudinal body-image assessment: Factor analysis of the Body–Self Relations Questionnaire. *Journal of Personality Assessment, 55,* 135–144.

11470

Test Name: CAREER MATURITY ATTITUDE INVENTORY REVISED

Purpose: To measure the maturity of attitudes that are important to realistic decision making.

Number of Items: 25

Reliability: Internal consistency was .74.

Validity: Correlations with other variables ranged from −.43 to .39.

Author: Kornspan, A. S., and Etzel, E. F.

Article: The relationship of demographic and psychological variables to career maturity of junior college student–athletes.

Journal: *Journal of College Student Development*, March/April 2001, *42*, 122–132.

Related Research: Crites, J. O., & Savickas, M. L. (1996). Revision of the Career Maturity Inventory. *Journal of Career Assessment, 4,* 131–138.

11471

Test Name: CAREERISM SCALE

Purpose: To measure careerist attitudes toward work.

Number of Items: 4

Format: Responses are made on a 5-point scale ranging from 1 (*strongly disagree*) to 5 (*strongly agree*). A sample item is given.

Reliability: Coefficient alpha was .74.

Validity: Correlations with other variables ranged from −.52 to .61.

Author: Feldman, D. C., and Turnley, W. H.

Article: Contingent employment in academic careers: Relative deprivation among adjunct faculty.

Journal: *Journal of Vocational Behavior*, April 2004, *64*, 284–307.

Related Research: Feldman, D. C., & Weitz, B. A. (1991). From the invisible hand to the gladhand: Understanding a careerist orientation to work. *Human Resource Management, 30,* 237–257.

11472

Test Name: CHEATING JUSTIFICATION SCALE— REVISED

Purpose: To measure justification for cheating.

Number of Items: 8

Format: Five-point Likert scales are used. Sample items are presented.

Reliability: Coefficient alpha was .93 on the original scale.

Author: Lester, M. C., and Diekoff, G. M.

Article: A comparison of traditional and Internet cheaters.

Journal: *Journal of College Student Development*, November/December 2002, *43*, 906–911.

Related Research: Haines, V. J., et al. (1996). College cheating: Immaturity, lack of commitment, and the neutralizing attitude. *Research in Higher Education, 25,* 342–354.

11473

Test Name: CHILDREN'S ATTITUDES TOWARD WOMEN'S ROLES SCALE

Purpose: To assess girls' gender role attitudes.

Number of Items: 19

Format: Responses are made on a 4-point scale. Examples are given.

Reliability: Alpha coefficients ranged from .67 to .88.

Author: McHale, S. M., et al.

Article: Developmental and individual differences in girls' sex-typed activities in middle childhood and adolescence.

Journal: *Child Development*, September/October 2004, *75*, 1575–1593.

Related Research: Antill, J., et al. (1994). *Measures of children's sex-typing in middle childhood II.* Unpublished manuscript, Macquarie University, Sydney, Australia.

11474

Test Name: CHILDREN'S EATING ATTITUDE TEST

Purpose: To measure dieting behaviors, food preoccupations, bulimia, and concerns about being overweight.

Number of Items: 26

Format: Responses are made on a 6-point scale ranging from *always* to *never.*

Reliability: Alpha coefficients were .76 and .81. Test–retest reliability was .81.

Author: Shariff, Z. M., and Yasin, Z. M.

Article: Correlates of children's Eating Attitude Test scores among primary school children.

Journal: *Perceptual and Motor Skills*, April 2005, *100*, 463–472.

Related Research: Maloney, M. J., et al. (1988). Reliability testing of a children's version of the Eating Attitude Test. *Journal of the American Academy of Child and Adolescent Psychiatry, 5,* 541–543.

11475

Test Name: COLLEGE DEGREE OUTCOME EXPECTATION MEASURE

Purpose: To assess beliefs about the consequences of obtaining a college degree.

Number of Items: 3

Format: Responses are made on a 4-point scale ranging from 1 (*not al all useful*) to 4 (*extremely useful*). All items are presented.

Reliability: Alpha coefficients were .77 and .84.

Validity: Correlations with other variables ranged from −.11 to .32.

Author: Kahn, J. H., and Nauta, M. M.

Article: Social–cognitive prediction of first year college persistence: The importance of proximal assessment.

Journal: *Research in Higher Education*, December 2001, *42*, 633–652.

Related Research: Bean, J. P. (1985). Interaction effects based on class level in an explanatory model of college student dropout syndrome. *American Educational Research Journal, 22*, 35–64.

11476

Test Name: COLOR-BLIND RACIAL ATTITUDES SCALE

Purpose: To measure color-blind racial attitudes.

Number of Items: 20

Format: Includes three subscales: Racial Privilege, Institutional Discrimination, and Blatant Racial Issues. Responses are made on a 6-point Likert-type scale ranging from 1 (*strongly disagree*) to 6 (*strongly agree*).

Reliability: Alpha coefficients ranged from .64 to .91. Temporal stability over 2 weeks was .68.

Validity: Correlations with other variables ranged from −.43 to .19 ($N = 354$).

Author: Spanierman, L. B., and Heppner, M. J.

Article: Psychological Costs of Racism to Whites Scale (PCRW): Construction and initial validation.

Journal: *Journal of Counseling Psychology*, April 2004, *51*, 249–262.

Related Research: Neville, H. A., et al. (2000). Construction and initial validation of the Color-Blind Racial Attitudes scale (CoBRAS).

Journal of Counseling Psychology, 47, 59–70.

11477

Test Name: COMMUNICATION ATTITUDES TEST

Purpose: To assess self-perceived speech beliefs.

Number of Items: 35

Format: A true–false format is used. Examples are presented.

Reliability: Test–retest reliabilities were .83 (1 week) and .76 (12 weeks). Coefficient alpha was .74.

Author: Storch, E. A., et al.

Article: The relationship of communication beliefs and abilities to peer victimization in elementary school children.

Journal: *Child Study Journal*, 2002, *32*, 231–240.

Related Research: Brutten, G. J. (1984). *The Communication Attitude Test*. Unpublished manuscript, Southern Illinois University, Carbondale.

11478

Test Name: COMPETITION–COOPERATION ATTITUDE SCALE

Purpose: To measure attitude toward competition and cooperation.

Number of Items: 28

Format: Responses are made on a 5-point Likert type scale ranging from *strongly disagree* to *strongly agree*. Examples are presented.

Reliability: Split-half reliability was .82. Coefficient alpha was .91.

Validity: Correlations with other variables ranged from −.33 to .66.

Author: Houston, J. M., et al.

Article: A factorial analysis of scales measuring competitiveness.

Journal: *Educational and Psychological Measurement*, April 2002, *62*, 284–298.

Related Research: Martin, H. J., & Larsey, K. S. (1976). Measurement of competitive–cooperative attitudes. *Psychological Reports, 39*, 303–306.

11479

Test Name: COMPETITIVE INDEX

Purpose: To assess both positive and negative attitudes toward competition.

Number of Items: 20.

Format: A true–false format is used. Examples are presented.

Reliability: Coefficient alpha was .90.

Validity: Correlations with other variables ranged from .01 to .75.

Author: Houston, J. M., et al.

Article: A factorial analysis of scales measuring competitiveness.

Journal: *Educational and Psychological Measurement*, April 2002, *62*, 284–298.

Related Research: Smither, R. D., & Houston, J. M. (1992). The nature of competitiveness: The development and validation of the Competitiveness Index. *Educational and Psychological Measurement, 52*, 407–418.

11480

Test Name: COMPUTER ATTITUDES/ATTRIBUTES SCALES

Purpose: To measure perceived computer attitudes and computer attributes.

Number of Items: 17

Format: All items are presented.

Reliability: Alpha coefficients ranged from .91 to .85.

Validity: Correlations with other variables ranged from .21 to .46.

Author: Van Braak, J. P., and Goeman, K.

Article: Differences between general computer attitudes and perceived computer attributes: Development and validation of a scale.

Journal: *Psychological Reports,* April 2003, *92,* 655–660.

11481

Test Name: CONDOM ATTITUDE SCALE FOR ADOLESCENTS

Purpose: To measure attitude toward condom use.

Number of Items: 23

Format: Five-point scales range from 1 (*strongly disagree*) to 5 (*strongly agree*). Sample items are presented.

Reliability: Coefficient alpha was .84.

Author: St. Lawrence, J. S., et al.

Article: Reducing STD and HIV risk behavior of substance-dependent adolescents: A randomized controlled trial.

Journal: *Journal of Consulting and Clinical Psychology,* August 2002, *70,* 1010–1021.

Related Research: St. Lawrence, J. S., et al. (1994). Factor structure and validation of an adolescent version of the Condom Attitude Scale: An instrument for measuring adolescents' attitudes toward condoms. *Psychological Assessment, 6,* 352–359.

11482

Test Name: CONSERVATISM–LIBERALISM SCALE

Purpose: To measure conservative attitudes.

Number of Items: 26

Format: A multiple-choice format is used.

Reliability: Coefficient alpha was .66.

Author: Crowson, H. M., et al.

Article: Is political conservatism synonymous with authoritarianism?

Journal: *The Journal of Social Psychology,* October 2005, *145,* 571–592.

Related Research: McClosky, H., & Bann, C. A. (1979). On the reappraisal of the Classical Conservatism Scale. *Political Methodology, 6,* 149–172.

11483

Test Name: CREDIBILITY SCALE

Purpose: To assess how much participants believe an intervention is credible and potentially efficacious.

Number of Items: 5

Format: Response options ranged from 0 to 9. Sample items are presented.

Reliability: Coefficient alpha was .93.

Author: Lumley, M. A., and Provenzano, K. M.

Article: Stress management through written emotional disclosure improves academic performance among college students with physical symptoms.

Journal: *Journal of Educational Psychology,* September 2003, *95,* 641–649.

Related Research: Borkovec, T. D., & Nau, S. D. (1972). Credibility of analogue therapy rationale. *Journal of Behavior Therapy and Experimental Psychiatry, 3,* 257–260.

11484

Test Name: CRITICAL THINKING BELIEF APPRAISAL SCALE

Purpose: To assess teachers' beliefs about classroom use of critical-thinking activities.

Number of Items: 36

Format: Includes six high critical-thinking prompts and six low critical-thinking prompts.

Reliability: Alpha coefficients ranged from .79 to .96.

Validity: Correlations with other variables ranged from .02 to .31.

Author: Torf, B., and Warburton, E. C.

Article: Assessment of teachers' beliefs about classroom use of critical-thinking activities.

Journal: *Educational and Psychological Measurement,* February 2005, *65,* 155–179.

11485

Test Name: CUSTOMER SERVICE ATTITUDE QUESTIONNAIRE

Purpose: To measure employees' perceptions of customer service standards, support, orientation to customers, and customer satisfaction.

Number of Items: 16

Format: Scales range from 1 (*strongly disagree*) to 5 (*strongly agree*). All items are presented.

Reliability: Alpha coefficients ranged from .68 to .96.

Validity: Correlations between subscales ranged from .08 to .64.

Author: Susskind, A. M., et al.

Article: Customer service providers' attitudes relating to customer service and customer satisfaction in the customer–server exchange.

Journal: *Journal of Applied Psychology,* February 2003, *88,* 179–187.

11486

Test Name: CYNICAL ATTITUDE TOWARD COLLEGE SCALE

Purpose: To measure undergraduate student cynicism.

Number of Items: 18.

Format: Includes four factors: policy, academic, social, and institutional. Responses are made on a 5-point scale ranging from 1 (*strongly disagree*) to 5 (*strongly agree*). All items are presented.

Reliability: Alpha coefficients ranged from .67 to .84.

Validity: Discriminant validity coefficients ranged from −.44 to .72

Author: Brockway, J. H., et al.

Article: Development and validation of a scale from measuring cynical attitude toward college.

Journal: *Journal of Educational Psychology*, March 2002, *94*, 210–224.

11487

Test Name: DAILY SUBJECTIVE SLEEP EXPERIENCE QUESTIONNAIRE

Purpose: To measure subjective aspects of the sleep experience.

Number of Items: 12

Format: Eleven-point scales are used that are unique to each item. All items are presented.

Reliability: Coefficient alpha was .91.

Author: Rose, D. A., and Kahan, T. L.

Article: Melatonin and sleep qualities in healthy adults: Pharmacological and expectancy effects.

Journal: *The Journal of General Psychology*, December 2001, *128*, 401–421.

Related Research: Parrott, A. C., & Hirdmarch, I. (1978). Factor analysis of a sleep evaluation questionnaire. *Psychological Medicine, 8*, 325–329.

11488

Test Name: DATE RAPE MYTH ACCEPTANCE SCALE

Purpose: To assess attitudes toward sexual violence.

Number of Items: 19

Reliability: Internal consistency estimates were .85 and .86.

Validity: Correlations with other variables ranged from .21 to .57 (*N* = 114).

Author: Hill, M. S., and Fischer, A. R.

Article: Does entitlement mediate the link between masculinity and rape-related variables?

Journal: *Journal of Counseling Psychology*, January 2001, *48*, 39–50.

Related Research: Truman, D. M., et al. (1996). Dimensions of masculinity: Relations to date rape supportive attitudes and sexual aggression in dating situations. *Journal of Counseling and Development, 74*, 555–562.

11489

Test Name: DECISIONAL BALANCE SCALE

Purpose: To measure the perceived pros and cons of condom use.

Number of Items: 5

Format: Scales range from 1 (*not at all important*) to 5 (*extremely important*). Sample items are presented.

Reliability: Coefficient alpha was .76 (pros) and .70 (cons).

Author: Carey, M. P., et al.

Article: Reducing HIV-risk behavior among adults receiving outpatient psychiatric treatment: Results from a randomized controlled trial.

Journal: *Journal of Consulting and Clinical Psychology*, April 2004, *72*, 252–268.

Related Research: Galavotti, C., et al. (1995). Validation of measures of condom and other contraceptive use among women at high risk for HIV infection and unintended pregnancy. *Health Psychology, 14*, 570–578.

11490

Test Name: DRUG ATTITUDES SCALE

Purpose: To assess students' attitudes toward substance use.

Number of Items: 14

Format: Responses are made on a 4-point scale ranging from 1 (*strongly disagree*) to 4 (*strongly agree*). An example is given.

Reliability: Coefficient alpha was .85.

Author: Brand, S., et al.

Article: Middle school improvement and reform: Development and validation of a school-level assessment of climate, cultural pluralism, and school safety.

Journal: *Journal of Educational Psychology*, September 2003, *95*, 570–588.

Related Research: Blau, G. M., et al. (1988). Predisposition to drug use in rural adolescents: Preliminary relationships and methodological considerations. *Journal of Drug Education, 18*, 13–22.

11491

Test Name: DYSFUNCTIONAL ATTITUDE SCALE—FORM A

Purpose: To assess perfectionistic and dependent attitudes.

Number of Items: 26

Format: Includes two factors: perfectionistic attitudes and dependent attitudes. Responses are made on a 7-point scale ranging from 1 (*disagree*) to 7 (*agree*).

Reliability: Test–retest (18 months) correlations were .68 and .76. Alpha coefficients ranged from .70 to .95.

Validity: Correlations with other variables ranged from .14 to .84.

Author: Sherry, S. B., et al.

Article: Perfectionism dimensions, perfectionistic attitudes, dependent attitudes, and depression in psychiatric patients and university students.

Journal: *Journal of Counseling Psychology*, July 2003, *50*, 373–386.

Related Research: Weissman, A. N. (1979). The Dysfunctional Attitude Scale: A validation study. *Dissertation Abstracts International, 40*, 1389B–1390B. (UMI No. 70-19, 533)

11492

Test Name: DYSFUNCTIONAL BELIEFS AND ATTITUDES ABOUT SLEEP SCALE

Purpose: To measure dysfunctional beliefs and attitudes about sleep.

Number of Items: 28

Format: Six-point scales range from 0 (*strongly disagree*) to 5 (*strongly agree*).

Reliability: Coefficient alpha was .72. For poor sleepers alpha was .81. For good sleepers alpha was .80.

Author: Strom, L., et al.

Article: Internet based treatment for insomnia: A controlled evaluation.

Journal: *Journal of Consulting and Clinical Psychology*, February 2004, *72*, 113–120.

Related Research: Morin, C. M. (1993). *Insomnia: Psychological assessment and management.* New York: Guilford Press.

11493

Test Name: EATING ATTITUDES TEST

Purpose: To measure the broad range of disordered eating behaviors and attitudes.

Number of Items: 26

Format: Responses are made on a 6-point scale ranging from 1 (*always*) to 6 (*never*). Examples are given.

Reliability: Alpha coefficients ranged from .79 to .94.

Validity: Correlations with other variables ranged from .21 to .59.

Author: Moradi, B., et al.

Article: Roles of sexual objectification experiences and internalization of standards of beauty in eating disorder symptomatology: A test and extension of objectification theory.

Journal: *Journal of Counseling Psychology*, July 2005, *52*, 420–428.

Related Research: Garner, D. M., et al. (1982). The Eating Attitudes Test: Psychometric features and clinical correlates. *Psychological Medicine, 12*, 871–878.

11494

Test Name: EATING ATTITUDES TEST

Purpose: To measure eating attitudes: dieting, food preoccupation, social pressure to eat, and vomiting/laxatives.

Number of Items: 40

Format: Items are anchored by 1 (*never true*) and 5 (*always true*).

Reliability: Theta coefficients ranged from .48 to .86.

Validity: Correlations with other variables ranged from −.43 to .24.

Author: Tomotake, M., et al.

Article: Temperament, character, and eating attitudes in Japanese college women.

Journal: *Psychological Reports*, June 2003, *92*, Part 2, 1162–1168.

Related Research: Garner, D. M., & Garfinkel, P. E. (1979). The Eating Attitude Test: An index of the symptoms of anorexia nervosa. *Psychological Medicine, 9*, 273–279.

11495

Test Name: EATING ATTITUDES TEST—FRENCH VERSION

Purpose: To assess eating disorder symptoms.

Number of Items: 26

Format: Includes three subscales: Dieting, Bulimia and Food Preoccupation, and Oral Control. Responses are made on a 6-point scale ranging from 1 (*never*) to 6 (*always*).

Reliability: Alpha coefficients ranged from .61 to .77.

Validity: Correlations with other variables ranged from .38 to .42.

Author: Ferrand, C., and Brunet, E.

Article: Perfectionism and risk for disordered eating among young French male cyclists of high performance.

Journal: *Perceptual and Motor Skills*, December 2004, *99*, Part 1, 959–967.

Related Research: Leichner, P., et al. (1994). Validation d'une échelle d'attitudes alimentaires auprès d'une population québécoise francophone. *Revue Canadienne de Psychiatrie, 39*, 49–54.

11496

Test Name: EDUCATIONAL BELIEFS SCALES

Purpose: To measure educational beliefs.

Number of Items: 19

Format: Includes four scales: School Attachment, School Relevance, School Efficacy, and

School Importance. Four-point and 5-point scales are employed. Examples are given.

Reliability: Alpha coefficients ranged from .64 to .85.

Validity: Correlations with other variables ranged from −.06 to .14.

Author: Chavous, T. M., et al.

Article: Racial identity and academic attainment among African American adolescents.

Journal: *Child Development*, July/August 2003, *74*, 1076–1090.

Related Research: Hawkins, J. D., et al. (1992). Risk and protective factors for alcohol and other drug problems in adolescence and early adulthood: Implications for substance abuse prevention. *Psychological Bulletin, 112*, 64–105. Roeser, R. W., et al. (1994, February). *A portrait of academic alienation in adolescence: Motivation, mental health, and family experience.* Paper presented at the biennial meeting of the Society for Research on Adolescence, San Diego, CA. Midgley, C., et al. (1993). *Manuals for the Patterns of Adaptive Learning Survey (PALS).* Ann Arbor: University of Michigan.

11497

Test Name: EMAIL COMFORT SCALE

Purpose: To measure the degree of liking for sending and receiving email.

Number of Items: 4

Format: Scales range from 1 (*strongly disagree*) to 6 (*strongly agree*). Sample items are presented.

Reliability: Coefficient alpha .77.

Validity: Correlations with other variables ranged from −.16 to .22.

Author: Rochlen, A. B., et al.

Article: The Online and Face-to-Face Counseling Attitudes Scales: A validation study.

Journal: *Measurement and Evaluation in Counseling and Development*, July 2004, *37*, 95–111.

11498

Test Name: ENTITLEMENT ATTITUDES SCALE

Purpose: To assess men's level of general entitlement.

Number of Items: 27

Format: Responses are made on a 7-point Likert-type scale ranging from 1 (*strongly disagree*) to 7 (*strongly agree*). An example is presented.

Reliability: Alpha coefficients were .76 and .85.

Validity: Correlations with other variables ranged from .09 to .58 ($N = 114$).

Author: Hill, M. S., & Fischer, A. R.

Article: Does entitlement mediate the link between masculinity and rape-related variables?

Journal: *Journal of Counseling Psychology*, January 2001, *48*, 39–50.

Related Research: Nadkarni, L., & Malone, J. A. (1989, April). *The development of a self-report inventory to measure personal entitlement.* Paper presented at the meeting of the Eastern Psychological Association, Boston.

11499

Test Name: ENTITY AND INCREMENTAL BELIEFS ABOUT SPORT ABILITY SUBSCALES

Purpose: To measure entity and incremental beliefs about sport ability.

Number of Items: 7

Format: Responses are made on a 5-point rating scale ranging from 1 (*don't agree at all*) to 5 (*agree completely*). Examples are presented.

Reliability: Alpha coefficients were .79 and .84.

Validity: Correlations with other variables ranged from −.34 to .36.

Author: Cury, F., et al.

Article: Perceptions of competence, implicit theory of ability, perceptions of motivational climate, and achievement goals: A test of the trichotomous conceptualization of endorsement of achievement motivational in the physical educational setting.

Journal: *Perceptual and Motor Skills*, August 2002, *95*, 233–244.

Related Research: Sarrazin, P., et al. (1996). Goal orientations and conceptions of the nature of sport ability in children: A social cognitive approach. *British Journal of Social Psychology, 35*, 399–414.

11500

Test Name: EPISTEMOLOGICAL BELIEFS INVENTORY

Purpose: To measure epistemological beliefs.

Number of Items: 32

Format: Includes innate ability, simple knowledge, certain knowledge, omniscient authority, and quick learning. Responses are made on a 6-point Likert-type scale ranging from 1 (*strongly disagree*) to 6 (*strongly agree*).

Reliability: Alpha coefficients ranged from .54 to .78.

Author: Ravindran, B., et al.

Article: Predicting preservice teachers' cognitive engagement with goals and epistemological beliefs.

Journal: *The Journal of Educational Research*, March/April 2005, *98*, 222–232.

Related Research: Bendixen, L. D., et al. (1998). Epistemic beliefs and moral reasoning. *The Journal of Psychology, 132*, 187–200.

11501

Test Name: FACE-TO-FACE COUNSELING ATTITUDE SCALE

Purpose: To measure the discomfort and value of face-to-face counseling.

Number of Items: 10

Format: All items are presented.

Reliability: Alpha coefficients ranged from .69 to .90.

Validity: Correlations with other variables ranged from −.51 to .64.

Author: Rochlen, A. B., et al.

Article: The Online and Face-to-Face Counseling Attitudes Scales: A validation study.

Journal: *Measurement and Evaluation in Counseling and Development*, July 2004, *37*, 95–111.

11502

Test Name: FACULTY BELIEFS ABOUT GRADES INVENTORY

Purpose: To measure faculty orientations toward norm-referenced or criterion-referenced grading and beliefs about the sorting and selecting function of grades.

Number of Items: 24

Format: Includes two scales: Frame of Reference and Gatekeeping. Responses are a 7-point Likert-type scale ranging from *strongly agree* to *strongly disagree*.

Reliability: Alpha coefficients ranged from .21 to .83.

Author: Barnes, L. L. B., et al.

Article: Effects of academic discipline and teaching goals in

predicting grading beliefs among undergraduate teaching faculty.

Journal: *Research in Higher Education*, August 2001, *42*, 455–467.

Related Research: Barnes, L. L. B. (1997). Development of the Faculty Beliefs About Grades Inventory. *Educational and Psychological Measurement, 57*, 459–468.

11503

Test Name: FENNEMA–SHERMAN MATHEMATICS ATTITUDE SCALES—ADAPTED

Purpose: To measure mathematics attitudes.

Number of Items: 23

Format: Includes five separate scales. Responses are made on 5-point Likert scales ranging from 1 (*strongly disagree*) to 5 (*strongly agree*). Examples are presented.

Reliability: Alpha coefficients ranged from .72 to .88. Split-half reliability estimates ranged from .86 to .93. Six-month stability coefficients ranged from .46 to .69 ($n = 278$).

Author: Turner, S. L., et al.

Article: Family factors associated with sixth-grade adolescents' math and science career interests.

Journal: *The Career Development Quarterly*, September 2004, *53*, 41–52.

Related Research: Fennema, E., & Sherman, J. A. (1976). Fennema–Sherman Mathematics Attitude Scales: Instruments designed to measure attitudes toward the learning of mathematics by females and males. *JSAS Catalog of Selected Documents in Psychology, 6* (31, Manuscript No. 1225).

11504

Test Name: FENNEMA–SHERMAN MATHEMATICS SCALES—MODIFIED

Purpose: To measure attitudes toward mathematics.

Number of Items: 36

Format: Includes three subtests: Confidence in Using Mathematics, Perceived Usefulness of Mathematics, and Mathematics Anxiety. Responses are made on a 5-point Likert-type scale.

Reliability: Reliabilities ranged from .88 to .93.

Author: McCoy, L. P.

Article: Effect of demographic and personal variables on achievement in eighth-grade algebra.

Journal: *The Journal of Educational Research*, January/February 2005, *98*, 131–135.

Related Research: Fennema, E., & Sherman, J. (1976). Fennema–Sherman Mathematics Attitude Scales: Instruments designed to measure attitude toward the learning of mathematics by females and males. *JSAS Catalog of Selected Documents in Psychology, 6*(31, Manuscript No. 1225).

11505

Test Name: FOCAL ORGANIZATION ATTITUDE SCALE

Purpose: To measure attitude toward the focal organization.

Number of Items: 5

Format: Responses are made of a 5-point scale ranging from 1 (*strongly disagree*) to 5 (*strongly agree*). All items are presented.

Reliability: Coefficient alpha was .86 ($N = 989$).

Validity: Correlations with other variables ranged from .06 to .48 ($N = 989$).

Author: Allen, D. G., et al.

Article: Recruitment communication media: Impact on prehire outcomes.

Journal: *Personnel Psychology*, Spring 2004, 57, 143–171.

Related Research: Fishbein, M., & Ajzen, I. (1975). *Belief, attitude, intention, and behavior: An introduction to theory and research.* Reading, MA: Addison-Wesley.

11506

Test Name: FRABONI SCALE OF AGEISM

Purpose: To assess the cognitive and affective components of ageism.

Number of Items: 29

Format: Scales range from 1 (*strongly disagree*) to 4 (*strongly agree*). All items are presented.

Reliability: Alpha coefficients ranged from .65 to .79 across subscales.

Validity: Correlations between subscales ranged from .65 to .73.

Author: Rupp, D. E., et al.

Article: The multidimensional nature of ageism: Construct validity and group differences.

Journal: *The Journal of Social Psychology*, June 2005, 145, 335–362.

Related Research: Fraboni, M., et al. (1990). The Fraboni Scale of Ageism (FSA): An attempt at a more precise measure of ageism. *Canadian Journal on Aging, 9,* 56–66.

11507

Test Name: FRANCIS SCALE OF ATTITUDE TOWARD ALCOHOL

Purpose: To measure attitude toward alcohol.

Number of Items: 16

Format: Scales range from 1 (*agree strongly*) to 5 (*disagree strongly*). All items are presented.

Reliability: Coefficient alpha was .89.

Author: Fearn, M., et al.

Article: Internal consistency reliability of the Francis Scale of Attitude toward Alcohol among adolescents in northern Ireland.

Journal: *Psychological Reports,* August, 2005, 97, 321–324.

Related Research: Francis, L. J. (1992). Attitudes toward alcohol, church attendance and denominational identity. *Drug and Alcohol Dependence, 31,* 45–50.

11508

Test Name: FRANCIS SCALE OF ATTITUDE TOWARD CHRISTIANITY

Purpose: To measure attitude toward Christianity as affective responses to God, Jesus, Bible, prayer, and church.

Number of Items: 24

Format: Response scales are anchored by 1 (*disagree strongly*) and 5 (*agree strongly*).

Reliability: Coefficient alpha was .92.

Validity: Correlations with other variables ranged from .27 to .31.

Author: Robbins, M., et al.

Article: Reliability of the Francis Scale of Attitude toward Christianity among 8-year-olds.

Journal: *Psychological Reports,* February 2003, 92, 104.

Related Research: Francis, L. J., & Stubbs, M. T. (1987). Measuring attitudes toward Christianity: From childhood into adulthood.

Personality and Individual Differences, 8, 741–743.

11509

Test Name: FREE-WILL–DETERMINISM SCALE

Purpose: To assess beliefs in the role of causality and human life.

Number of Items: 9

Format: Item response scales are anchored by 1 (*determinant*) and 7 (*strong libertarian*).

Reliability: Alpha coefficients ranged from .62 to .83.

Author: Haynes, S. D., and Rojas, D.

Article: Free will, determinism, and punishment.

Journal: *Psychological Reports,* December 2003, 93, Part 2, 1013–1021.

Related Research: Viney, W., et al. (1984). Validity of a scale designed to measure beliefs in free will and determinism. *Psychological Reports, 54,* 867–872.

11510

Test Name: GAMBLING BELIEF QUESTIONNAIRE

Purpose: To measure illusion of control, erroneous beliefs of winning, gamblers fallacy, superstition, impaired control, the "near" miss, memory bias, biased evaluation, positive state, relief, and money as a solution to problems.

Number of Items: 65

Format: Rating scales are anchored by 0 (*not at all*) and 4 (*very much*). Sample items are presented.

Reliability: Coefficient alpha was .97.

Author: Joukhador, J., et al.

Article: Differences in cognitive distortions between problem and social gamblers.

Journal: *Psychological Reports*, June 2003, *92*, Part 2, 1203–1214.

Related Research: Toneatto, T. (1999). Cognitive psychopathology of problem gambling. *Substance Use and Misuse, 34*, 1593–1604.

11511

Test Name: GENDER BASED ATTITUDES TOWARD MARITAL ROLES

Purpose: To measure attitudes about marital roles.

Number of Items: 6

Format: Scales range from 1 (*strongly agree*) to 4 (*strongly disagree*).

Reliability: Coefficient alpha was .87.

Author: Klute, M. M., et al.

Article: Occupational self-direction, values, and egalitarian relationships: A study of dual-earner couples.

Journal: *Journal of Marriage and Family*, February 2004, *64*, 139–151.

Related Research: Hoffman, L. W., & Kloska, D. D. (1995). Parents' gender-based attitudes toward marital roles and childrearing: Development and validation of new measures. *Sex Roles, 32*, 273–295.

11512

Test Name: GENDER LIBERALISM SCALE

Purpose: To measure attitudes towards women.

Number of Items: 15

Format: Four-point scales range from *strongly agree* to *strongly disagree*. Sample items are presented.

Reliability: Alpha coefficients were .84 (wives) and .79 (husbands).

Validity: Correlations with other variables ranged from −.22 to .35.

Author: Marks, S. R., et al.

Article: Role balance among White married couples.

Journal: *Journal of Marriage and Family*, November 2001, *63*, 1083–1098.

Related Research: Atkinson, J., & Huston, T. L. (1984). Sex role orientation and division of labor early in marriage. *Journal of Personality and Social Psychology, 46*, 330–345.

11513

Test Name: GENDER ROLE ATTITUDES SCALE

Purpose: To assess gender role attitudes at home, at work, and in society.

Number of Items: 12

Format: Scales range from 1 (*strongly agree*) to 7 (*strongly disagree*).

Reliability: Alpha coefficients ranged from .82 to .83.

Validity: Correlations with other variables ranged from −.43 to .59.

Author: Kulik, L.

Article: The impact of family status on gender identity and on sex-role typing of household tasks in Israel.

Journal: *The Journal of Social Psychology*, June 2005, *145*, 299–316.

Related Research: Kulik, L. (2000). Intrafamiliar congruence in gender role ideology: Husband–wife versus parents–offspring. *Journal of Comparative Family Studies, 31*, 91–106.

11514

Test Name: GROUP ATTITUDE SCALE

Purpose: To assess perceptions of group cohesiveness.

Number of Items: 20

Format: Responses are made on a 5-point scale ranging from 5 (*strongly agree*) to 1 (*strongly disagree*). Sample items are presented.

Reliability: Coefficient alpha was .92.

Validity: Correlations with other variables ranged from −.24 to .69.

Author: Mebane, D. J., and Galassi, J. P.

Article: Variables affecting collaborative research and learning in a professional development school partnership.

Journal: *The Journal of Educational Research*, May/June 2003, *96*, 259–268.

Related Research: Evans, N. J., & Jarvis, P. A. (1986). The Group Attitude Scale: A measure of attraction to group. *Small Group Behavior, 17*, 203–216.

11515

Test Name: HANSON SEX ATTITUDE QUESTIONNAIRE— SEXUAL ENTITLEMENT SUBSCALE

Purpose: To assess men's level of sexual entitlement.

Number of Items: 9

Format: Responses are made on a 5-point Likert-type scale ranging from 1 (*completely disagree*) to 5 (*completely agree*). An example is presented.

Reliability: Alpha coefficients were .70 and .81.

Validity: Correlations with other variables ranged from .26 to .59 (*N* = 114).

Author: Hill, M. S., and Fischer, A. R.

Article: Does entitlement mediate the link between masculinity and rape-related variables?

Journal: *Journal of Counseling Psychology*, January 2001, *48*, 39–50.

Related Research: Hanson, R. K., et al. (1994). The attitudes of incest offenders: Sexual entitlement and acceptance of sex with children. *Criminal Justice and Behavior, 21*, 187–202.

11516

Test Name: HEALTH-RELATED ATTITUDES AND BEHAVIOR SCALES

Purpose: To measure attitudes, intentions, perceived behavioral control, and health-related behaviors.

Number of Items: 16

Format: Seven-point rating scales and a 6-point frequency scale are used. Sample items are presented.

Reliability: Alpha coefficients ranged from .72 to .92.

Author: Theodorakis, Y., et al.

Article: Relations between family structure and students' health-related attitudes and behaviors.

Journal: *Psychological Reports*, December 2004, *95*, Part 1, 851–858.

Related Research: Theodorakis, Y., et al. (2003). Greek students' attitudes toward physical activity and health-related behavior. *Psychological Reports, 92*, 275–283.

11517

Test Name: HEALTH TEAM STEREOTYPE SCALE

Purpose: To measure stereotypic attitudes of occupational and physical therapy students toward their own profession and toward each other.

Number of Items: 67

Format: Items are pairs of bipolar adjectives. Responses are made on a 7-point scale.

Reliability: Internal consistency was .93.

Author: Katz, J. S., et al.

Article: Physical and occupational therapy undergraduates' stereotypes of one another.

Journal: *Perceptual and Motor Skill*, June 2001, *92*, Part 1, 843–851.

Related Research: Osgood, C. E., et al. (1957). *The measurement of meaning.* Urbana: University of Illinois Press.

11518

Test Name: HOMOSEXUAL ATTITUDES INVENTORY

Purpose: To measure negative attitudes and discomfort with homosexuality.

Number of Items: 33

Format: Four-point scales range from 1 (*disagree strongly*) to 4 (*agree strongly*). Sample items are presented.

Reliability: Alpha coefficients ranged from .83 to .91.

Validity: Correlations with other variables ranged from –.07 to .33.

Author: Rosario, M., et al.

Article: Gay-related stress and emotional distress among gay, lesbian, and bisexual youths: A longitudinal examination.

Journal: *Journal of Consulting and Clinical Psychology*, August 2002, *70*, 967–975.

Related Research: Nungesser, L. (1983). *Homosexual acts, actions, and identities.* New York: Praeger.

11519

Test Name: HOSTILE GENDER ROLE BELIEFS

Purpose: To measure three of Burt's rape supportive attitudes and hostility toward women.

Format: Seven-point scales range from *strongly disagree* to *strongly agree*.

Reliability: Coefficient alpha was .90.

Validity: Correlations with other variables ranged from –.13 to .27.

Author: Abbey, A., and McAuslan, P.

Article: A longitudinal examination of male college students' perpetration of sexual assault.

Journal: *Journal of Consulting and Clinical Psychology*, October 2004, *72*, 747–756.

Related Research: Lonsway, K. A., & Fitzgerald, L. F. (1995). Attitudinal antecedents of rape myth acceptance: A theoretical and empirical reexamination. *Journal of Personality and Social Psychology, 68*, 704–711.

11520

Test Name: HYPERFEMININITY SCALE

Purpose: To assess strength of traditional beliefs and the ways in which women can manipulate men.

Number of Items: 26

Reliability: Alpha coefficients ranged from .76 to .79.

Validity: Correlations with other variables ranged from –.15 to .54.

Author: Bartolucci, A. D., and Zeichner, A.

Article: Sex, hypermasculinity, and hyperfemininity in perception of social cues in neutral interactions.

Journal: *Psychological Reports*, February 2003, *92*, 75–83.

Related Research: Murnen, S. K., & Byrne, D. (1991). Hyperfemininity: Measurement and initial validation of the construct.

Journal of Sex Research, 28, 479–489.

11521

Test Name: HYPERMASCULINITY INDEX

Purpose: To assess extreme machismo attitudes in men: callused sexual beliefs, violence as manly, and danger as exciting.

Number of Items: 30

Reliability: Alpha coefficients ranged from .89 to .93.

Validity: Correlations with other variables ranged from −.36 to .41.

Author: Bartolucci, A. D., and Zeichner, A.

Article: Sex, hypermasculinity, and hyperfemininity in perception of social cues in neutral interactions.

Journal: *Psychological Reports,* February 2003, *92,* 75–83.

Related Research: Mosher, D. L., & Sirkin, M. (1994). Measuring a macho personality constellation. *Journal of Research in Personality, 18,* 150–163.

11522

Test Name: IDEAS AND ATTITUDES TOWARD ACADEMIC-CAREER FUTURE INSTRUMENT

Purpose: To measure career indecision.

Number of Items: 54

Format: Includes four areas: level of decision related to one's academic-career future, locus of control associated with professional problem-solving, ability to gather information useful to making a choice, and importance attributed to making an academic-career choice. Responses are made on a 7-point scale. Examples are presented.

Reliability: Alpha coefficients ranged from .77 to .91.

Author: Nota, L., and Soresi, S.

Article: An assertiveness training program for indecisive students attending an Italian university.

Journal: *The Career Development Quarterly,* June 2003, *51,* 322–334.

Related Research: Nota, L. (1997). La dimensione "decisione–indecisione" [The "decision–indecision" dimension]. *Psicologia e Scuola, 87,* 83–95.

11523

Test Name: IDENTIFICATION WITH SCHOOL QUESTIONNAIRE

Purpose: To assess attitudinal aspects of school engagement.

Number of Items: 21

Format: Responses are made on a 4-point Likert scale ranging from 1 (*strongly agree*) to 4 (*strongly disagree*). Examples are given.

Reliability: Alpha coefficients were .78 and .84.

Validity: Correlations with other variables ranged from −.20 to .44 ($N = 181$).

Author: Kenny, M. E., et al.

Article: The role of perceived barriers and relational support in the educational and vocational lives of urban high school students.

Journal: *Journal of Counseling Psychology,* April 2003, *50,* 142–155.

Related Research: Voelkl, K. (1996). Measuring students' identification with school. *Educational and Psychological Measurement, 56,* 760–770.

11524

Test Name: ILLEGAL IMMIGRATION SCALE

Purpose: To measure attitudes toward illegal aliens.

Number of Items: 20

Format: All items are presented.

Reliability: Alpha coefficients ranged from .79 to .93 across national samples.

Author: van der Veer, K., et al.

Article: Structure of attitudes toward illegal immigration: Development of cross national cumulative scales.

Journal: *Psychological Reports,* June 2004, *94,* Part 1, 897–906.

Related Research: Ommundsen, R., & Larsen, K. S. (1997). Attitudes toward illegal immigration in Scandinavia and United States. *Psychological Reports, 84,* 1331–1338.

11525

Test Name: IMPLICIT ASSOCIATION TEST

Purpose: To measure implicit racial attitudes.

Number of Items: 40

Format: Subject sorts words into racial categories. Scoring methods are described.

Reliability: Coefficient alpha was .70.

Validity: Correlations with other variables ranged from −.29 to .12.

Author: Ziegert, J. C., and Hanges, P. J.

Article: Employment discrimination: The role of implicit attitudes, motivation, and a climate for racial bias.

Journal: *Journal of Applied Psychology,* May 2005, *90,* 553–562.

11526

Test Name: IMPORTANCE OF CLOTHING QUESTIONNAIRE— CHINESE VERSION

Purpose: To measure experimentation, self-enhancement, and conformity.

Number of Items: 20

Format: Items are anchored by 1 (*strongly disagree*) and 5 (*strongly agree*). All items are presented.

Reliability: Alpha coefficients ranged from .76 to .89 across subscales.

Author: Fung, M. S. C., and Yuen, M.

Article: Clothing interest among Chinese adolescent girls in Hong Kong in relation to socioeconomic status.

Journal: *Psychological Reports*, April 2002, *90*, 387–390.

Related Research: Littrel, M. A., et al. (1990). Clothing interests, body satisfaction, and eating behavior of adolescent females: Related or independent dimensions? *Adolescence, 25*, 77–95.

11527

Test Name: IMPORTANCE OF WORK REWARDS SCALE

Purpose: To assess the importance of work-related rewards such as promotion, pay, and recognition.

Number of Items: 6

Format: Scales range from 1 (*very unimportant*) to 6 (*very important*).

Reliability: Coefficient alpha was .73.

Validity: Correlations with other variables ranged from −.03 to .14.

Author: Boswell, W. R., et al.

Article: The outcomes and correlates of job search objectives: Searching to leave or searching for leverage?

Journal: *Journal of Applied Psychology*, December 2004, *89*, 1083–1091.

Related Research: Wollack, S., et al. (1971). Development of the Survey of Work Values. *Journal of Applied Psychology, 55*, 331–338.

11528

Test Name: INDEX OF ATTITUDES TOWARD HOMOSEXUALS

Purpose: To measure prejudice toward homosexuals.

Number of Items: 25

Format: Item responses are anchored by 1 (*strongly agree*) and 5 (*strongly disagree*).

Reliability: Alpha was .91. Guttman split-half reliability was .89.

Author: Hayes, R. A., et al.

Article: Stigma directed toward chronic illness is resistant to change through education and exposure.

Journal: *Psychological Reports*, June 2002, *90*, Part 2, 1161–1173.

Related Research: Hudson, W. W., & Ricketts, W. A. (1980). A strategy for measuring homophobia. *Journal of Homosexuality, 5*, 357–371.

11529

Test Name: INDEX OF DEVIANCE-PRONE ATTITUDES AND BEHAVIOR

Purpose: To measure deviance-prone attitudes and behavior.

Number of Items: 15

Format: Three sets of 5-point scales are used. Sample items are presented.

Reliability: Coefficient alpha was .73.

Author: Brody, G. H., et al.

Article: Neighborhood disadvantage moderates associations of parenting and older sibling problem attitudes and behavior with conduct disorders in African American children.

Journal: *Journal of Consulting and Clinical Psychology*, April 2003, *71*, 211–222.

Related Research: Blanton, H., et al. (1997). Role of family and peers in the development of prototypes associated with substance use. *Journal of Family Psychology, 11*, 271–288.

11530

Test Name: INDEX OF HOMOPHOBIA

Purpose: To measure homophobia.

Number of Items: 25

Format: Five-point rating scales are anchored by 1 (*strongly agree*) and 5 (*strongly disagree*). Sample items are presented.

Reliability: Alpha coefficient was .94.

Validity: The correlation with a gay and lesbian attitude scale was .71.

Author: Span, S. A., and Vidal, L. A.

Article: Cross-cultural differences in female university students' attitudes toward homosexuals: A preliminary study.

Journal: *Psychological Reports*, April 2003, *92*, 565–572.

Related Research: Hudson, W. W., & Ricketts, W. A. (1980). A strategy for the measurement of homophobia. *Journal of Homosexuality, 54*, 357–372.

11531

Test Name: INTERNALIZED HOMONEGATIVITY INVENTORY

Purpose: To measure internalized homonegativity.

Number of Items: 23

Format: Includes three subscales: Personal Homonegativity, Gay Affirmation, and Morality of

Homosexuality. Examples are presented.

Reliability: Alpha coefficients were .70 and .91.

Author: Currie, M. R., et al.

Article: The Short Internalized Homonegativity Scale: Examination of the factorial structure of a new measure of internalized homophobia.

Journal: *Educational and Psychological Measurement*, December 2004, *64*, 1053–1067.

Related Research: Mayfield, W. (2001). The development of an internalized homonegativity inventory for gay men. *Journal of Homosexuality, 41*(2), 53–76.

11532

Test Name: INTERNALIZED HOMOPHOBIA SCALE

Purpose: To measure internalized homophobia.

Number of Items: 9

Format: Responses are made on a 5-point Likert scale ranging from 1 (*strongly agree*) to 5 (*strongly disagree*). Sample items are presented.

Reliability: Alpha coefficients ranged from .81 to .87. Test–retest (6 months) reliability was .56.

Validity: Correlation with psychological distress was .12. Correlation with self-esteem was –.60.

Author: Rostosky, S. S., and Riggle, E. D. B.

Article: "Out" at work: The relation of actor and partner workplace policy and internalized homophobia to disclosure status.

Journal: *Journal of Counseling Psychology*, October 2002, *49*, 411–419.

Related Research: Wright, E., et al. (1999). Empowering gay, lesbian,

and bisexual youth: Findings from the Indiana Youth Assess Project (Final Evolution Report). Indianapolis: Indiana University.

11533

Test Name: INVENTORY OF BELIEFS ABOUT WIFE BEATING

Purpose: To measure attitudes about the appropriateness of violence by husbands towards wives.

Number of Items: 31

Format: Scales range from 1 (*strongly agree*) to 7 (*strongly disagree*).

Reliability: Alpha coefficients ranged from .73 to .86 across subscales.

Validity: Correlations with other variables ranged from –.29 to .27.

Author: Berkel, L. A., et al.

Article: Gender role attitudes, religion, and spirituality as predictors of domestic violence attitudes in White college students.

Journal: *Journal of College Student Development*, March/April 2004, *45*, 119–133.

Related Research: Saunders, T. A., et al. (1987). The Inventory of Beliefs about Wife Beating: The construction and initial validation of beliefs and attitudes. *Violence and Victims, 2*, 39–57.

11534

Test Name: IRRATIONAL BELIEFS INVENTORY

Purpose: To measure child-like fantasy, special privilege, unlovability, unrealistic isolation, catastrophizing, and task exaggerations.

Number of Items: 24

Format: Scoring and administration procedures are fully described. All items are presented.

Reliability: Alpha coefficients ranged from .56 to .67.

Author: Smith, J. C., et al.

Article: Factor structure of the Smith Irrational Beliefs Inventory: Results of an analysis on six independent samples.

Journal: *Psychological Reports*, December 2004, *95*, 696–704.

Related Research: Smith, J. C. (2002). *Stress management: A comprehensive handbook of techniques and strategies*. New York: Springer Publishing Company.

11535

Test Name: JOB ATTITUDES SCALE

Purpose: To measure job satisfaction and anxiety.

Number of Items: 4

Format: Scales range from 1 (*strongly disagree*) to 7 (*strongly agree*). Sample items are presented.

Reliability: Coefficient alpha was .95.

Validity: Correlations with other variables ranged from –.45 to .85.

Author: Griffith, K. H., and Hebl, M. R.

Article: The disclosure dilemma for gay men and lesbians: "Coming out" at work.

Journal: *Journal of Applied Psychology*, December 2002, *87*, 1191–1199.

Related Research: Ironson, G. H., et al. (1989). Construction of a job in general scale: A comparison of global, composite, and specific measures. *Journal of Applied Psychology, 74*, 193–200.

11536

Test Name: JOINING THE FOCAL ORGANIZATION ATTITUDE SCALE

Purpose: To measure attitude toward joining the focal organization.

Number of Items: 3

Format: Responses are made of a 5-point scale ranging from (*strongly disagree*) to 5 (*strongly agree*). All items are presented.

Reliability: Coefficient alpha was .83 (*N* = 989).

Validity: Correlations with other variables ranged from .01 to .51 (*N* = 989).

Author: Allen, D. G., et al.

Article: Recruitment communication media: Impact on prehire outcomes.

Journal: *Personnel Psychology*, Spring 2004, *57*, 143–171.

Related Research: Fishbein, M., & Ajzen, I. (1975). *Belief, attitude, intention, and behavior: An introduction to theory and research.* Reading, MA: Addison-Wesley.

11537

Test Name: LEADERSHIP ATTITUDES AND BELIEFS SCALE

Purpose: To evaluate the thinking of college students about leadership and organization in terms of hierarchical and systematic thinking.

Number of Items: 28

Format: Five-point scales range from *strongly agree* to *strongly disagree*.

Reliability: Alpha coefficients ranged from .84 to .88.

Validity: Correlations with other variables ranged from −.35 to .18.

Author: Wielkiewicz, R. M.

Article: Validity of the Leadership Attitudes and Beliefs Scale: Relationships with personality,

communal orientation, and social desirability.

Journal: *Journal of College Student Development*, January/February 2002, *43*, 108–118.

11538

Test Name: LEARNING BEHAVIOR, GENERAL ATTITUDE, AND GENERAL INFORMATION SCALES

Purpose: To measure learning behaviors, general attitudes toward learning, and general information about education requirements.

Number of Items: 32

Format: Attitude and information, scales range from *strongly agree* to *strongly disagree*.

Reliability: Test–retest reliability ranged from .98 to .99.

Author: Schlossberg, S. M., et al.

Article: The effects of a counselor-led guidance intervention on students' behaviors and attitudes.

Journal: *Professional School Counseling*, February 2001, *4*(3), 156–164.

Related Research: Myrick, R. D., et al. (1986). Changing student attitudes through classroom guidance. *The School Counselor, 33*, 244–254.

11539

Test Name: LEARNING ORIENTATION/GRADE-ORIENTATION SCALE II (LOGO–II)

Purpose: To assess learning-oriented attitudes and grade-oriented attitudes and behavior.

Number of Items: 32

Format: Attitude response scales are anchored by 1 (*strongly disagree*) and 5 (*strongly agree*). Behavior scales are anchored by 1 (*never*) and 5 (*always*).

Reliability: Alpha coefficients ranged from .79 to .81.

Validity: Correlations with academic performance ranged from −.18 to .14.

Author: Page, S., and Alexitch, L. R.

Article: Learning- and grade-orientation, sex, and prediction of self-reported academic performance.

Journal: *Psychological Reports*, February 2003, *92*, 320–324.

Related Research: Eison, J., et al. (1986). Educational and personal characteristics of four different types of learning and grade oriented students. *Contemporary Educational Psychology, 11*, 54–67.

11540

Test Name: LEISURE-TIME PHYSICAL ACTIVITY ATTITUDE SCALE

Purpose: To measure attitude toward leisure-time physical activity.

Number of Items: 32

Format: Responses are made on a 7-point scale ranging from −3 (*strongly disagree*) to 3 (*strongly agree*). An example is given.

Reliability: Coefficient alpha was .92.

Validity: Correlations with other variables ranged from .06 to .66.

Author: Kerner, M. S., and Kurrant, A. B.

Article: Psychosocial correlates to high school girls' leisure-time physical activity: A test of the theory of planned behavior.

Journal: *Perceptual and Motor Skills*, December 2003, *97*, Part 2, 1175–1183.

Related Research: Kerner, M. S., & Kalinski, M. I. (2002). Scale construction for measuring adolescent boys' and girls' attitude, beliefs, perception of control, and intention to engage in leisure-time physical activity. *Perceptual and Motor Skills, 95,* 109–117.

11541

Test Name: LESBIAN, GAY, AND BISEXUAL KNOWLEDGE AND ATTITUDES SCALE FOR HETEROSEXUALS

Purpose: To measure heterosexuals' attitudes toward lesbians, gays, and bisexuals.

Number of Items: 28

Format: Includes four subscales: LGB Knowledge, Religious Conflict, LGB Civil Rights, and Internalized Affirmativeness. Responses are made on a 7-point scale ranging from 1 (*very uncharacteristic of me*) to 7 (*very characteristic of me or my views*). All items are presented.

Reliability: Alpha coefficients ranged from .54 to .94.

Validity: Correlations with other variables ranged from −.89 to .74.

Author: Worthington, R. L., et al.

Article: Development, reliability, and validity of the Lesbian, Gay, and Bisexual Knowledge and Attitudes Scale for Heterosexuals (LGB-KASH).

Journal: *Journal of Counseling Psychology,* January 2005, *52,* 104–118.

11542

Test Name: LIFE ATTITUDE PROFILE

Purpose: To measure existential meaning and purpose in life.

Number of Items: 44

Format: Scales range from 1 (*strongly disagree*) to 7 (*strongly agree*). Sample items are presented.

Reliability: Alpha coefficients ranged from .55 to .83.

Author: Sinha, S. P., et al.

Article: Social support and self-control as variables in attitude toward life and perceived control among older people in India.

Journal: *The Journal of Social Psychology,* August 2002, *142,* 527–540.

Related Research: Recker, G. T., & Peacock, E. J. (1981). The Life Attitude Profile (LAP): A multidimensional instrument for assessing attitude toward life. *Canadian Journal of Behavioral Science, 13,* 264–273.

11543

Test Name: LOVE AND LIKING SCALES

Purpose: To measure current attitudes about the relationship partner.

Number of Items: 26

Format: Includes two scales: Romantic Love and General Liking. Responses are made on a 9-point scale ranging from 1 (*not at all true; disagree completely*) to 9 (*definitely true; agree completely*).

Reliability: Alpha coefficients were .96 and .98.

Validity: Correlations with other variables ranged from −.43 to .62.

Author: Berry, J. W., and Worthington, Jr., E. L.

Article: Forgiveness, relationship quality, stress while imagining relationship events, and physical and mental health.

Journal: *Journal of Counseling Psychology,* October 2001, *48,* 447–455.

Related Research: Rubin, Z. (1970). Measurement of romantic love. *Journal of Personality and Social Psychology, 16,* 265–273. Tzeng, O. C. S. (1993).

Measurement of love and intimate relations: Theories, scales, and applications for love development, maintenance, and dissolution. Westport, CT: Praeger Publishers.

11544

Test Name: LOVE ATTITUDES SCALE

Purpose: To measure eros, ludus, storge, pragma, mania, and agape.

Number of Items: 24

Reliability: Alpha coefficients ranged from .65 to .81.

Validity: Correlations with other variables ranged from −.10 to .45.

Author: Neto, F.

Article: The Satisfaction with Love Life Scale.

Journal: *Measurement and Evaluation in Counseling and Development,* April 2005, *38,* 2–13.

Related Research: Hendrick, S., et al. (1998). The Love Attitudes Scale: Short Form. *Journal of Social and Personal Relationships, 15,* 147–159.

11545

Test Name: MAGICAL IDEATION SCALE

Purpose: To measure idiosyncratic beliefs about cause and effect relations.

Number of Items: 30

Format: Examples are presented.

Reliability: Coefficient alpha was .83.

Validity: Correlations with other variables ranged from −.29 to .39.

Author: Ross, S. R., et al.

Article: Positive and negative symptoms of schizotypy and the Five-Factor Model: A domain and facet level analysis.

Journal: *Journal of Personality Assessment*, August 2002, *79*, 53–72.

Related Research: Eckblad, M., & Chapman, L. J. (1983). Magical ideation as a measure of schizotypy. *Journal of Consulting and Clinical Psychology, 51*, 215–225.

11546

Test Name: MATERIALISM SCALE

Purpose: To measure three dimensions of materialism: success, centrality, and happiness.

Number of Items: 18

Format: Seven-point agreement scales are used.

Reliability: Alpha was .74.

Author: Jusoh, W. J. W., et al.

Article: Self-ratings of materialism and status consumption in a Malaysian sample: Effects of answering during an assumed recession versus economic growth.

Journal: *Psychological Reports*, June 2001, *88*, Part 2, 1142–1144.

Related Research: Richins, M. L., & Dawson, S. (1992). A consumer values orientation for materialism and its measurement: Scale development and validation. *Journal of Consumer Research, 19*, 303–316.

11547

Test Name: MATHEMATICS ATTITUDE AND ANXIETY SCALES

Purpose: To measure attitudes toward success in mathematics and math anxiety.

Number of Items: 24

Format: Five-point agreement scales are used. Sample items are presented.

Reliability: Alphas were .87 (attitudes) and .94 (anxiety).

Author: Alkhateeb, H. M.

Article: A preliminary study of achievement, attitudes toward success in mathematics, and mathematics anxiety with technology-based instruction in brief calculus.

Journal: *Psychological Reports*, February 2002, *90*, 47–57.

Related Research: Fennema, E., & Sherman, J. A. (1976). Fennema–Sherman Mathematics Attitude Scales: Instruments designed to measure attitudes toward the learning of mathematics by females and males. *JSAS Catalog of Selected Documents in Psychology, 6* (31, Ms. No. 1225)

11548

Test Name: MATHEMATICS ATTITUDE SCALE

Purpose: To measure mathematics attitude.

Number of Items: 20

Format: Responses are made on a 5-point scale ranging from 1 (*strongly agree*) to 5 (*strongly disagree*). Examples are presented.

Reliability: Coefficient alpha was .97.

Author: Alkhateeb, H. M.

Article: Attitudes of undergraduate majors in elementary education toward mathematics through a hands-on manipulative approach.

Journal: *Perceptual and Motor Skills*, February 2002, *94*, 55–58.

Related Research: Aiken, L. R. (1972). Research on attitudes toward mathematics. *The Arithmetic Teacher, 19*, 229–234.

11549

Test Name: MATHEMATICS ATTITUDES SCALE—ARABIC SHORT FORM

Purpose: To measure attitudes towards the study of mathematics.

Number of Items: 51

Format: Five-point scales are anchored by 1 (*strongly disagree*) and 5 (*strongly agree*).

Reliability: Alpha coefficients ranged from .72 to .89 across subscales. Total alpha was .89.

Author: Alkhateeb, H. M.

Article: Internal consistency reliability and construct validity of an Arabic translation of the shortened form of the Fennema–Sherman Mathematics Attitudes Scales.

Journal: *Psychological Reports*, April 2004, *94*, 565–571.

Related Research: Fennema, E., & Sherman, J. A. (1976). Fennema–Sherman Mathematics Attitudes Scale: Instruments designed to measure attitudes toward the learning of mathematics by males and females. *JSAS Catalog of Selected Documents in Psychology, 6* (31, Manuscript No. 1225).

11550

Test Name: MATHEMATICS TEACHING EFFICACY BELIEFS INSTRUMENT—ARABIC VERSION

Purpose: To measure beliefs about mathematics teaching efficacy.

Number of Items: 21

Format: Item anchors are 1 (*strongly disagree*) and 5 (*strongly agree*). All items are presented in English.

Reliability: Alpha coefficients ranged from .75 to .84 across subscales.

Author: Alkhateeb, H. M.

Article: Internal consistency reliability and validity of the Arabic translation of the Mathematics Teaching Efficacy Beliefs Instrument.

Journal: *Psychological Reports*, June 2004, *94*, Part 1, 833–838.

Related Research: Enochs, L. G., et al. (2000). Establishing factorial validity of the Mathematics Teaching Efficacy Beliefs Instrument. *School Science and Mathematics, 100*, 194–202.

11551

Test Name: MEAN WORLD INDEX

Purpose: To assess if a person believes that people are trustworthy and altruistic.

Number of Items: 3

Format: Item responses are anchored by 1 (*strongly disagree*) and 5 (*strongly agree*).

Reliability: Coefficient alpha was .75.

Author: Martin, M. M., et al.

Article: Verbal aggression and viewing the world as a mean place.

Journal: *Psychological Reports*, February 2003, *92*, 151–152.

Related Research: Gerbner, G., et al. (1977). TV violence profile No. 8: The highlights. *Journal of Communication, 27*, 171–180.

11552

Test Name: MEANINGLESSNESS SCALE

Purpose: To measure meaninglessness in the South African context.

Number of Items: 3

Format: Item responses range from 1 (*strongly disagree*) to 4 (*strongly agree*). All items are presented.

Reliability: Coefficient alpha was .66.

Author: Morojele, N. K., and Brook, J. S.

Article: Sociodemographic, sociocultural, and individual predictors of reported feelings of meaninglessness among South African adolescents.

Journal: *Psychological Reports*, December 2004, *95*, Part 2, 1271–1278.

Related Research: Neal, A., & Groat, H. T. (1974). Social class correlates of stability and change in levels of alienation. *Sociological Quarterly, 15*, 548–558.

11553

Test Name: MILLENNIAL APOCALYPTIC EVENTS QUESTIONNAIRE

Purpose: To assess endorsement of apocalyptic views.

Number of Items: 4

Format: Multiple-choice format. All items are presented with scoring rules.

Reliability: Cronbach's alpha was .87.

Author: Morris, N., and Johnson, M. P.

Article: Apocalyptic thinking, autonomy, and sociotropy.

Journal: *Psychological Reports*, June 2002, *90*, Part 2, 1069–1074.

Related Research: Thompson, D. (1997). *The end of time: Faith and fear in the shadow of the millennium.* London: Minerva Press.

11554

Test Name: MIND-READING BELIEFS SCALE

Purpose: To assess mind-reading beliefs.

Number of Items: 8

Format: Scales range from 0 (*strongly disagree*) to 4 (*strongly agree*). All items are presented.

Reliability: Alpha coefficients ranged from .64 to .82 across samples.

Validity: Correlations with NEO-FFI scales ranged from −.09 to .23.

Author: Realo, A., et al.

Article: Mind-reading ability: Beliefs and performance.

Journal: *Journal of Research in Personality*, October 2003, *37*, 420–445.

11555

Test Name: MODERN RACISM SCALE

Purpose: To measure subtle contemporary anti-Black attitudes.

Number of Items: 8

Format: Scales range from 1 (*disagree strongly*) to 5 (*agree strongly*). All items are presented.

Reliability: Coefficient alpha was .81.

Validity: Correlations with other variables ranged from .15 to .23.

Author: Chang, M. J.

Article: Is it more than about getting along? The broader educational relevance of reducing students' racial biases.

Journal: *Journal of College Student Development*, March/April 2001, *42*, 93–105.

Related Research: McConahay, J. B., et al. (1981). Has racism declined in America? *Journal of Conflict Resolution, 25*, 563–579.

11556

Test Name: MODERN RACISM SCALE

Purpose: To measure modern racism.

Number of Items: 7

Format: Seven-point scales are used. A sample item is presented.

Reliability: Coefficient alpha was .81.

Validity: Correlations with other variables ranged from −.22 to .73.

Author: Ziegert, J. C., and Hanges, P. J.

Article: Employment discrimination: The role of implicit attitudes, motivation, and a climate for racial bias.

Journal: *Journal of Applied Psychology*, May 2005, *90*, 553–562.

Related Research: McConahay, J. B. (1986). Modern racism, ambivalence, and the Modern Racism Scale. In J. F. Dovidio & S. L. Gaertner (Eds.), *Prejudice, discrimination, and racism* (pp. 91–125). Orlando, FL: Academic Press.

11557

Test Name: MODERNITY SCALE

Purpose: To measure progressive attitudes about childrearing.

Number of Items: 8

Format: Responses are made on a 5-point scale.

Reliability: Coefficient alpha was .60.

Validity: Correlations with other variables ranged from −.09 to .26.

Author: Huston, A. C., and Aronson, S. R.

Article: Mothers' time with infant and time in employment as predictors of mother–child relationships and children's early development.

Journal: *Child Development*, March/April 2005, *76*, 467–482.

Related Research: Schaeffer, E. S., & Edgerton, M. (1985). Parent and child correlates of parental modernity. In I. E. Siegel (Ed.), *Parental belief systems: The psychological consequences for children* (pp. 297–318). Hillsdale, NJ: Erlbaum.

11558

Test Name: MONEY ATTITUDE SCALE

Purpose: To measure attitude about money.

Number of Items: 29

Format: Seven-point scales are anchored by *never* and *always*.

Reliability: Alpha coefficients ranged from .73 to .86 across subscales.

Author: Yang, B., and Lester, D.

Article: Internal consistency of the Yamauchi/Templar Money Attitude Scale.

Journal: *Psychological Reports*, December 2002, *91*, Part 1, 994.

Related Research: Yamauchi, K. T., & Templar, D. C. (1982). The development of a Money Attitude Scale. *Journal of Personality Assessment, 46*, 522–528.

11559

Test Name: MULTIDIMENSIONAL BODY–SELF RELATIONS QUESTIONNAIRE

Purpose: To provide an attitudinal assessment of body-image and weight-related variables.

Number of Items: 69

Format: Includes 10 subscales: Appearance Evaluation, Appearance Orientation, Fitness Evaluation, Fitness Orientation, Health Evaluation, Health Orientation, Illness Orientation, Overweight Preoccupation, Body-Areas Satisfaction, and Self-Classified Weight.

Reliability: Alpha coefficients ranged from .66 to .91.

Author: Radell, S. A., et al.

Article: Effects of teaching with minors on body image and locus of control in women college ballet dancers.

Journal: *Perceptual and Motor Skills*, December 2002, *95*, Part 2, 1239–1247.

Related Research: Cash, T. F., et al. (1989). Gender and body images: Stereotypes and realities. *Sex Roles, 21*, 361–373.

11560

Test Name: MULTIDIMENSIONAL SPORTSMANSHIP ORIENTATIONS SCALE

Purpose: To assess respect for one's involvement in sport, the opponent, social conventions, the rules, and negative approach towards sport participation.

Number of Items: 18

Format: Responses are made on a 5-point scale ranging from 1 (*strongly disagree*) to 5 (*strongly agree*). All items are presented.

Reliability: Alpha coefficients ranged from .62 to .82.

Validity: Correlations with other variables ranged from −.25 to .41.

Author: Leperidis, K., et al.

Article: Motivational climate, beliefs about the bases of success, and sportsmanship behaviors of professional basketball athletes.

Journal: *Perceptual and Motor Skills*, June 2003, *96*, Part 2, 1141–1151.

Related Research: Vellerand, R. J., et al. (1996). Toward a multidimensional definition of sportsmanship. *Journal of Applied Sport Psychology, 8*, 89–101.

11561

Test Name: MY CLASS ACTIVITIES

Purpose: To assess students' attitudes toward their class activities.

Number of Items: 31

Format: Includes four dimensions: Interest, Challenge, Choice, and Enjoyment. Responses are made on a 5-point scale ranging from *never* to *always*. All items are presented.

Reliability: Alpha coefficients ranged from .63 to .92.

Author: Gentry, M., et al.

Article: Gifted students' perceptions of their class activities: Differences among rural, urban, and suburban student attitudes.

Journal: *Gifted Child Quarterly,* Spring 2001, *45,* 115–129.

Related Research: Gentry, M., et al. (1999, April). *Assessing middle school students' perceptions of classroom activities: Rationale and instrumentation.* Paper presented at the annual meeting of the American Educational Research Association, Montreal, Canada.

11562

Test Name: NEGATIVE ATTITUDE TOWARD ATHEISTS SCALE

Purpose: To measure attitudes towards atheists.

Number of Items: 5

Format: Seven-point scales range from 1 (*strongly disagree*) to 7 (*strongly agree*). All items are presented.

Reliability: Coefficient alpha was .84.

Author: Bloesch, E., et al.

Article: A brief, reliable measure of negative attitudes toward atheists.

Journal: *Psychological Reports,* December 2004, *95,* Part 1, 1161–1162.

Related Research: Morrison, T. G., et al. (1999). The psychometric properties of the Homonegativity Scale. *Journal of Homosexuality, 37,* 111–126.

11563

Test Name: NEW ENVIRONMENTAL PARADIGM SCALE

Purpose: To measure the new environmental paradigm sentiment (balance of nature and belief in human dominance).

Number of Items: 8

Format: All items are presented.

Reliability: Alpha coefficients ranged from .60 to .74.

Author: Chang-Ho, C. J.

Article: Factor structure of the New Environmental Paradigm Scale: Evidence from an urban sample in Southern California.

Journal: *Psychological Reports,* February 2004, *94,* 125–130.

Related research: Dunlap, R. E., & Van Liere, K. (1978). The New Environmental Paradigm: A proposed measuring instrument and preliminary results. *Journal of Environmental Education, 9,* 10–19.

11564

Test Name: NORMATIVE BELIEFS ABOUT AGGRESSION SCALE

Purpose: To measure normative beliefs about aggression.

Number of Items: 20

Format: Responses are made on a 4-point scale ranging from *perfectly OK* to *really wrong.*

Reliability: Coefficient alpha was .87.

Author: Guerra, N. G., et al.

Article: Community violence exposure, social cognition, and aggression among urban elementary school children.

Journal: *Child Development,* September/October 2003, *74,* 1561–1576.

Related Research: Huesmann, L. R., & Guerra, N. G. (1997). Children's normative beliefs about aggression and aggressive behavior. *Journal of Personality and Social Psychology, 72,* 408–419.

11565

Test Name: NUNGESSER HOMOSEXUAL ATTITUDES INVENTORY

Purpose: To assess internalized homophobia.

Number of Items: 34

Format: Includes three subscales: Self, Other, and Disclosure. Examples are presented.

Reliability: Alpha coefficients ranged from .68 to .94.

Author: Currie, M. R., et al.

Article: The Short Internalized Homonegativity Scale: Examination of the factorial structure of a new measure of internalized homophobia.

Journal: *Educational and Psychological Measurement,* December 2004, *64,* 1053–1067.

Related Research: Nungesser, G. (1983). *Homosexual acts, actors, and identities.* New York: Praeger Publishers.

11566

Test Name: NUNGESSER HOMOSEXUALITY ATTITUDES INVENTORY—ADAPTED

Purpose: To assess personalized homonegativity.

Number of Items: 15

Format: Responses are made on a 4-point scale ranging from 1 (*strongly disagree*) to 4 (*strongly agree*). Examples are given.

Reliability: Coefficient alpha was .83.

Author: Lease, S. H., et al.

Article: Affirming faith experiences and psychological health for Caucasian lesbian, gay, and bisexual individuals.

Journal: *Journal of Counseling Psychology*, July 2005, *52*, 378–388.

Related Research: Shidlo, A. (1994). Internalized homophobia: Conceptual and empirical issues in measurement. In B. Greene & G. M. Herek (Eds.), *Lesbian and gay psychology: Theory, research, and clinical application* (pp. 176–205). Thousand Oaks, CA: Sage.

11567

Test Name: OKLAHOMA RACIAL ATTITUDES SCALE

Purpose: To measure racial attitudes.

Number of Items: 35

Format: Includes six subscales. Responses are made on a 5-point Likert-type scale ranging from 1 (*strongly disagree*) to 5 (*strongly agree*).

Reliability: Alpha coefficients ranged from .60 to .84.

Author: Spanierman, L. B., and Heppner, M. J.

Article: Psychological Costs of Racism to Whites Scale (PCRW): Construction and initial validation.

Journal: *Journal of Counseling Psychology*, April 2004, *51*, 249–262.

Related Research: LaFleur, N. K., et al. (2002). *Manual: Oklahoma Racial Attitudes Scale.* Unpublished manual.

11568

Test Name: OKLAHOMA RACIAL ATTITUDES SCALE— PRELIMINARY FORM

Purpose: To measure racial attitudes and behaviors associated with White racial consciousness.

Number of Items: 50

Format: Scales range from 1 (*strongly disagree*) to 5 (*strongly agree*).

Reliability: Alpha coefficients ranged from .50 to .82 across subscales.

Validity: Correlations with multicultural competence ranged from −.61 to .58.

Author: Mueller, J. A., and Pope, R. L.

Article: The relationship between multicultural competence and White racial consciousness among student affairs practitioners.

Journal: *Journal of College Student Development*, March/April 2001, *42*, 133–144.

Related Research: Choney, S. K., & Behrens, J. T. (1996). Development of the Oklahoma Racial Attitudes Scale— Preliminary Form (ORAS–P). In G. R. Sodowsky & J. Impara (Eds.), *Multicultural assessment in counseling and clinical psychology* (pp. 225–240). Lincoln, NE: Buros Institute of Mental Measurements.

11569

Test Name: ONLINE COUNSELING ATTITUDES SCALE

Purpose: To measure attitudes toward online counseling in terms of its discomfort and value.

Number of Items: 10

Format: All items are presented.

Reliability: Alpha coefficients ranged from .77 to .89.

Validity: Correlations with other variables ranged from −.49 to .69.

Author: Rochlen, A. B., et al.

Article: The Online and Face-to-Face Counseling Attitudes Scales: A validation study.

Journal: *Measurement and Evaluation in Counseling and Development*, July 2004, *37*, 95–111.

11570

Test Name: ORGAN DONATION ATTITUDE SCALE—REVISED

Purpose: To measure attitudes toward organ donation including donation across racial groups.

Number of Items: 22

Format: Six-point response scales are anchored by 1 (*strongly agree*) and 6 (*strongly disagree*). Sample items are presented.

Reliability: Alpha was .87.

Author: Sherman, N. C., et al.

Article: Disgust sensitivity and attitudes toward organ donation among African-American college students.

Journal: *Psychological Reports*, August 2001, *89*, 11–23.

Related Research: Parisi, N. B., & Katz, I. (1986). Attitudes toward posthumous organ donation and commitment to donate. *Health Psychology*, *5*, 565–580.

11571

Test Name: OWNERSHIP BELIEFS SCALE

Purpose: To assess ownership beliefs.

Number of Items: 4

Format: Responses are made on a 5-point scale ranging from 1 (*strongly disagree*) to 5 (*strongly agree*). All items are presented.

Reliability: Coefficient alpha was .72.

Validity: Correlations with other variables ranged from .15 to .79.

Author: Wagner, S. H., et al.

Article: Employees that think and act like owners: Effect of ownership beliefs and behaviors on organizational effectiveness.

Journal: *Personnel Psychology,* Winter 2003, *56,* 847–871.

11572

Test Name: PARANORMAL BELIEFS SCALE

Purpose: To assess paranormal beliefs.

Number of Items: 30

Format: Scales range from 1 (*do not agree at all*) to 5 (*agree completely*). A sample item is presented.

Reliability: Coefficient alpha was .95.

Author: Patry, A. L., and Pelletier, L. G.

Article: Extraterrestrial beliefs and experiences: An application of the theory of reasoned action.

Journal: *The Journal of Social Psychology,* April 2001, *141,* 199–217.

Related Research: Tobacyk, J., & Milford, G. (1983). Belief in paranormal phenomena: Assessment instrument development and implications for personality functioning. *Journal of Personality and Social Psychology, 44,* 1029–1037.

11573

Test Name: PARENT CHILD-REARING ATTITUDE QUESTIONNAIRE—FRENCH VERSION

Purpose: To assess three dimensions of the emotional climate created by parental practices toward their child.

Number of Items: 43

Format: Includes three dimensions: Pleasure, Stimulation, and

Discipline. Responses are made on a 9-point scale ranging from *very strong agreement* to *very strong disagreement.* Examples are given.

Reliability: Alpha coefficients ranged from .58 to .72. Stability over 1 year ranged from .55 to .68.

Author: Vitaro, F., et al.

Article: Kindergarten disruptive behaviors, protective factors, and educational achievement by early adulthood.

Journal: *Journal of Educational Psychology,* November 2005, *97,* 617–629.

Related Research: Falender, C. A., & Mehrabian, A. (1980). The emotional climate for children as inferred from parental attitudes: A preliminary validation of three scales. *Educational and Psychological Measurement, 40,* 1033–1042.

11574

Test Name: PARENTAL ATTITUDE RESEARCH INSTRUMENT

Purpose: To measure early childhood parental attitude.

Number of Items: 35

Format: Includes six subscales which form two higher order constructs of Egalitarian parenting and Authoritarian parenting.

Reliability: Internal consistency reliabilities were .79 and .83.

Validity: Correlations with other variables ranged from −.29 to .18.

Author: Belsky, J., et al.

Article: Intergenerational transmission of warm–sensitive–stimulating parenting: A prospective study of mothers and fathers of 3-year-olds.

Journal: *Child Development,* March/April 2005, *76,* 384–396.

Related Research: Schaefer, R., & Bell, R. Q. (1958). Development of

a parental attitude research instrument. *Child Development, 29,* 339–361.

11575

Test Name: PARENTAL ATTITUDE RESEARCH INSTRUMENT

Purpose: To measure opinions and attitudes of mothers towards their educational task and family life.

Number of Items: 115

Format: Includes 23 scales. The names of all scales are listed.

Reliability: Alpha coefficients ranged from .54 to .84.

Validity: Correlations with the Attachment Style Questionnaire ranged from −.37 to .32.

Author: Trombini, E., et al.

Article: Maternal attitudes and attachment styles in mothers of obese children.

Journal: *Perceptual and Motor Skills,* October 2003, *97,* 613–620.

Related Research: Schaefer, E. S., & Bell, R. Q. (1958). Development of a parental attitude research instrument. *Child Development, 29,* 339–361.

11576

Test Name: PEER APPROVAL OF FORCED SEX SCALE

Purpose: To assess the extent to which friends approve of strategies to obtain sex with a woman.

Number of Items: 6

Format: Five-point scales range from *not at all* to *very much.*

Reliability: Coefficient alpha was .80.

Validity: Correlations with other variables ranged from −.21 to .35.

Author: Abbey, A., and McAuslan, P.

Article: A longitudinal examination of male college students' perpetration of sexual assault.

Journal: *Journal of Consulting and Clinical Psychology*, October 2004, 72, 747–756.

Related Research: Boeringer, S. B., et al. (1991). Social contexts and social learning in sexual coercion and aggression: Assessing the contribution of fraternity membership. *Family Relations, 40,* 58–64.

11577

Test Name: PEER CONTROL AND AUTONOMY SUPPORT SCALE

Purpose: To assess students' perceptions of their peers' attitudes toward career decision.

Number of Items: 22

Format: Includes four subscales: Competence Feedback, Controlling Behaviors, Involvement, and Informational Feedback. Responses are made on a 7-point scale ranging from 1 (*does not correspond at all*) to 7 (*corresponds completely*).

Reliability: Alpha coefficients ranged from .64 to .69.

Author: Guay, F., et al.

Article: Predicting career indecision: A self-determination theory perspective.

Journal: *Journal of Counseling Psychology*, April 2003, 50, 165–177.

Related Research: Pelletier, L. G. (1992). *Construction et validation de l' Echelle des Perceptions du Style Interpersonal* [Construction and validation of the perceptions of the Interpersonal Style Scale]. Unpublished manuscript, University of Ottawa, Canada.

11578

Test Name: PEOPLE OF COLOR RACIAL IDENTITY ATTITUDE SCALE

Purpose: To measure social identity in terms of conformity, dissonance, immersion–emersion, and internalization.

Number of Items: 50

Format: Scales range from 1 (*strongly agree*) to 5 (*strongly disagree*). All items are presented.

Reliability: Alpha coefficients ranged from .61 to .87 across samples.

Author: Bryant, A., Jr., and Baker, S. B.

Article: The feasibility of constructing profiles of Native Americans from the People of Color Racial Identity Attitudes Scale: A brief report.

Journal: *Measurement and Evaluation in Counseling and Development*, April 2003, 36, 2–8.

Related Research: Helms, J. E. (1995). *The People of Color (POC) Racial Identity Attitude Scale.* Unpublished manuscript, University of Maryland, College Park.

11579

Test Name: PERCEIVED ATTITUDES AND ATTRIBUTES SCALE

Purpose: To assess the perceived attitudes toward and attributes of a potential employer.

Number of Items: 14

Format: Attitude scales range from 1 (*strongly disagree*) to 5 (*strongly agree*). Attribute scales range from 1 (*not very likely*) to 2 (*extremely likely*).

Reliability: Alpha coefficients were .86 (attitudes) and .79 (attributes).

Author: Collins, C. J., and Stevens, C. K.

Article: The relationship between early recruitment-related activities and the application decisions of new labor-market entrants: A brand equity approach to recruitment.

Journal: *Journal of Applied Psychology*, December 2002, 87, 1121–1133.

Related Research: Harris, M. M., & Fink, L. S. (1987). A field study of applicant reactions to employment opportunities: Does the recruiter make a difference? *Personnel Psychology, 40,* 765–786.

11580

Test Name: PERSONAL DEVELOPMENT COMPETITIVE ATTITUDE SCALE

Purpose: To identify an attitude that values the enjoyment and process of the task over the outcome of winning.

Number of Items: 15

Format: Responses are made on a 5-point Likert-type scale. Examples are presented.

Reliability: Internal consistency reliabilities were .90 to .94.

Validity: Correlations with other variables ranged from .08 to .66.

Author: Houston, J. M., et al.

Article: A factorial analysis of scales measuring competitiveness.

Journal: *Educational and Psychological Measurement*, April 2002, 62, 284–298.

Related Research: Ryckman, R. M., et al. (1996). Construction of a personal development competitive attitude scale. *Journal of Personality Assessment, 66,* 374–385.

11581

Test Name: PERSONALITY BELIEF QUESTIONNAIRE

Purpose: To assess beliefs associated with personality disorders.

Number of Items: 126

Format: Response scales range from 0 (*I don't believe in it at all*) to 4 (*I*

believe in it totally). A sample item is presented.

Reliability: Reliability coefficients ranged from .77 to .93.

Author: Kuyden, W., et al.

Article: Response to cognitive therapy in depression: The role of maladaptive beliefs and personality disorders.

Journal: *Journal of Consulting and Clinical Psychology,* June 2001, *69,* 560–566.

Related Research: Beck, A. T., & Beck, J. S. (1991). *The Personality Belief Questionnaire.* Unpublished assessment instrument, The Beck Institute for Cognitive Therapy and Research, Bala Cynwyd, PA.

11582

Test Name: PHILOSOPHIES OF HUMAN NATURE SCALE

Purpose: To assess beliefs that people are conventionally good, cynicism, and locus of control.

Number of Items: 23

Format: All items are presented.

Reliability: Alpha coefficients ranged from .51 to .69.

Author: Callen, K. S., and Owenby, S. F.

Article: Associations of demographic information and philosophies of human nature.

Journal: *Psychological Reports,* October 2005, *97,* 363–377.

Related Research: Wrightsman, L. S. (1964). Measurement of philosophies of human nature. *Psychological Reports, 14,* 743–751.

11583

Test Name: PHYSICAL ACTIVITY ENJOYMENT SCALE

Purpose: To measure the degree to which participants perceived the

running activity as an enjoyable experience.

Number of Items: 18

Format: Bipolar statements each containing a 7-point scoring scale.

Reliability: Internal consistency ranged from .89 to .93.

Validity: Correlations with other variables ranged from –.20 to .46.

Author: Ryska, T. A.

Article: Enjoyment of evaluative physical activity among young participants: The role of self-handicapping and intrinsic motivation.

Journal: *Child Study Journal,* 2003, *33,* 213–234.

Related Research: Kendzierski, D., & De Carlo, K. J. (1991). Physical Activity Enjoyment Scale: Two validation studies. *Journal of Sport & Exercise Psychology, 13,* 50–64.

11584

Test Name: PHYSICAL ACTIVITY QUESTIONNAIRE

Purpose: To identify attitude toward and perceptions of physical activity.

Number of Items: 8

Format: Includes attitude towards physical activity, perception of parents' participation in physical activities, and perceived barriers to exercise. Sample items are presented.

Reliability: Alpha coefficients ranged from .73 to .92.

Author: Papacharisis, V., and Goudas, M.

Article: Perceptions about exercise and intrinsic motivation of students attending a health-related physical education program.

Journal: *Perceptual and Motor Skills,* December 2003, *97,* Part 1, 689–696.

Related Research: Theodorakis, Y. (1994). Planned behavior, attitude strength, self-identify, and the perception of exercise behavior. *The Sport Psychologist, 8,* 149–165.

11585

Test Name: PHYSICAL EDUCATOR'S ATTITUDE TOWARD TEACHING INDIVIDUALS WITH DISABILITIES—III

Purpose: To measure physical educator's attitude toward teaching individuals with disabilities.

Number of Items: 12

Format: Includes three dimensions: Outcomes of Teaching Students With Disabilities in Regular Classes, Effects on Students' Learning, and Need for Academic Preparation to Teach Students With Disabilities. Responses are made on a 5-point Likert-type scale ranging from 1 (*strongly agree*) to 5 (*strongly disagree*). All items are presented.

Reliability: Alpha coefficients ranged from .71 to .88.

Author: Goyakla Apache, R. R., and Rizzo, T.

Article: Evaluating effectiveness of an infusion learning model on attitudes of physical education majors.

Journal: *Perceptual and Motor Skills,* August 2005, *101,* 177–186.

Related Research: Rizzo, T. L. (1993). *Physical Educator's Attitude Toward Teaching Individuals With Disabilities—III.* Unpublished survey [available from the author], Department of Kinesiology, California State University, San Bernadino, CA.

11586

Test Name: POLITICAL ORIENTATION SCALES

Purpose: To measure political orientation.

Number of Items: 22

Format: Includes six scales: Equality of Income and Possession, Social Justice and Equality, Abortion and Euthanasia, Acceptability of Alternative Forms of Cohabitation, Ethnocentrism, and Sexism. Responses are made on a 5-point Likert scale. Examples are given.

Reliability: Alpha coefficients ranged from .69 to .90.

Author: ter Bogt, T., et al.

Article: Socialization and development of the work ethic among adolescents and young adults.

Journal: *Journal of Vocational Behavior*, June 2005, *66*, 420–437.

Related Research: Middendorp, C. P. (1979). *Progressiveness and conservatism: The fundamental dimensions of ideological controversy and their relationship to social class.* The Hague/Paris/New York: Mouton.

11587

Test Name: PROACTIVE ATTITUDE SCALE

Purpose: To measure how much responsibility individuals take for their own lives and the belief that they could affect their own life changes.

Number of Items: 15

Format: Four-point rating scales are anchored by 1 (*not at all true of me*) and 4 (*exactly true of me*). Sample items are presented.

Reliability: Coefficient alpha was .65.

Validity: Correlations with other variables ranged from –.55 to .59.

Author: Sachs, J.

Article: Psychometric properties of the Proactive Attitude Scale in students at the University of Hong Kong.

Journal: *Psychological Reports*, December 2003, *93*, Part 1, 805–815.

11588

Test Name: PROENVIRONMENTAL ATTITUDES SCALE

Purpose: To measure proenvironmental attitudes including approach to information about environmental problems, rejection of driving, survival in pollution, antipollution purchasing behavior, and support for population control.

Number of Items: 27

Format: Scales range from 1 (*strongly disagree*) to 5 (*strongly agree*). Sample items are presented.

Validity: Correlations with other variables ranged from –.20 to .31.

Author: Iwata, O.

Article: Relationships between proenvironmental attitudes and concepts of nature.

Journal: *The Journal of Social Psychology*, February 2001, *141*, 75–83.

Related Research: Iwata, O. (1995). Relationships of pro-environmental attitudes with materialism and its associated attitudes toward money. *Psychologia, 38*, 252–257.

11589

Test Name: PROTÉGÉ TRUST BELIEFS SCALE

Purpose: To measure protégé trust beliefs.

Number of Items: 15

Format: Includes four factors: benevolence, honesty, competence, and predictability. Responses are made on a 6-point scale ranging from 1 (*strongly disagree*) to 6 (*strongly agree*). Sample items are given.

Reliability: Alpha coefficients ranged from .82 to .91.

Validity: Correlations with other variables ranged from –.21 to .44.

Author: Linnehan, F., et al.

Article: African-American students' early trust beliefs in work-based mentors.

Journal: *Journal of Vocational Behavior*, June 2005, *66*, 501–515.

Related Research: Gefen, D., et al. (2001). What drives eGovernment Adoption? An antecedent model of intended use of online public services. In *Americas Conference on Information Systems* (*AMCIS*) (pp. 569–576), August 9–11, Dallas, TX.

11590

Test Name: PRO-UNION ATTITUDE SCALE

Purpose: To measure pro-union attitudes.

Number of Items: 8

Format: Scales range from 1 (*strongly disagree*) to 5 (*strongly agree*). Sample items are presented.

Reliability: Coefficient alpha was .88.

Validity: Correlations with other variables ranged from .38 to .67.

Author: Tan, H. H., and Aryee, S.

Article: Antecedents and outcomes of union loyalty: A constructive replication and an extension.

Journal: *Journal of Applied Psychology*, August 2002, *87*, 715–722.

Related Research: Desphande, S., & Fiorito, J. (1989). Specific and general beliefs in union voting models. *Academy of Management Journal, 32*, 883–897.

11591

Test Name: PSYCHOSEXUAL SCALES

Purpose: To measure intentions towards sexual intercourse: coital intentions, attitudes towards negative sexual outcomes, social norms towards premarital sex, and self-efficacy or refusal skills.

Number of Items: 13

Format: Five-point scales are anchored by 1 (*strongly disagree*) and 5 (*strongly agree*) or 1 (*very unlikely*) and 5 (*very likely*).

Reliability: Alpha coefficients ranged from .69 to .78.

Validity: Correlations between subscales ranged from .09 to .44.

Author: Nagy, S., et al.

Article: Scales measuring psychosocial antecedents of coital initiation among adolescents in a rural southern state.

Journal: *Psychological Reports*, June 2003, *92*, Part 1, 981–990.

11592

Test Name: QUICK DISCRIMINATION INDEX

Purpose: To assess attitudes toward women and racial minorities.

Number of Items: 23

Format: Five-point scales are anchored by 1 (*strongly disagree*) and 5 (*strongly agree*). All items are presented.

Reliability: Alpha coefficients ranged from .69 to .83.

Author: Green, R. G., et al.

Article: Some normative data on mental health professionals' attitudes about racial minorities and women.

Journal: *Psychological Reports*, April 2004, *94*, 485–494.

Related Research: Ponterotto, J., et al. (1995). Development and initial evaluation of the Quick Discrimination Index (QDI). *Educational and Psychological Measurement, 55*, 1016–1031.

11593

Test Name: QUICK DISCRIMINATION INDEX

Purpose: To measure racial and gender attitudes.

Number of Items: 30

Format: Includes three subscales: General, Affective, and Attitudes Toward Women's Equity.

Reliability: Alpha coefficients ranged from .71 to .88.

Author: Spanierman, L. B., and Heppner, M. J.

Article: Psychological Costs of Racism to Whites Scale (PCRW): Construction and initial validation.

Journal: *Journal of Counseling Psychology*, April 2004, *51*, 249–262.

Related Research: Ponterotto, J. G., et al. (1995). Development and initial validation of the Quick Discrimination Index (QDI). *Educational and Psychological Measurement, 55*, 1026–1031.

11594

Test Name: RAPE MYTH ACCEPTANCE SCALE

Purpose: To measure beliefs that deny and justify male sexual aggression.

Number of Items: 19

Format: Scales range from 1 (*strongly disagree*) to 7 (*strongly agree*).

Reliability: Alpha coefficients ranged from .93 to .94.

Author: Hall, G. C. N., et al.

Article: Ethnicity, culture, and sexual aggression: Risk and protective factors.

Journal: *Journal of Consulting and Clinical Psychology*, October 2005, *73*, 830–840.

Related Research: Lonsway, K. A., & Fitzgerald, L. F. (1995).

Attitudinal antecedents of rape myth acceptance: A theoretical and empirical reexamination. *Journal of Personality and Social Psychology, 68*, 704–711.

11595

Test Name: RAPE MYTH ACCEPTANCE SCALE

Purpose: To measure men's endorsement of myths about rape.

Number of Items: 45

Format: Responses are made on a 7-point scale.

Reliability: Alpha coefficients were .93 and .95.

Validity: Correlations with other variables ranged from .03 to .41 ($n = 254$).

Author: Locke, B. D., and Mahalik, J. R.

Article: Examining masculinity norms, problem drinking, and athletic involvement as predictors of sexual aggression in college men.

Journal: *Journal of Counseling Psychology*, July 2005, *52*, 279–283.

Related Research: Payne, D. L., et al. (1999). Rape myth acceptance: Exploration of its structure and its measurement using the Illinois Rape Myth Acceptance Scale. *Journal of Research in Personality, 33*, 27–68.

11596

Test Name: RELATIONSHIP SATISFACTION QUESTIONNAIRE

Purpose: To measure five attitudes: satisfying–dissatisfying, fulfilling–disappointing, rewarding–punishing, positive–negative, and good–bad.

Number of Items: 35

Format: A semantic differential is used.

Reliability: Coefficient alpha was .95.

Author: Punyanunt-Carter, N. M.

Article: Reported affectionate communication and satisfaction in marital and dating relationships.

Journal: *Psychological Reports*, December 2004, *95*, Part 2, 1154–1160.

Related Research: Beatty, M. J., & Dobus, J. A. (1992). Relationship between sons' perceptions of fathers' messages and satisfaction in adult son–father relationships. *Southern Communication Journal*, *57*, 277–284.

11597

Test Name: RESEARCH ATTITUDES MEASURE

Purpose: To assess students' confidence in their ability to perform research-related activities.

Number of Items: 23

Format: Includes six subscales: Discipline and Intrinsic Motivation, Analytic Skills, Preliminary Conceptualization, Writing Skills, Application of Ethics and Procedures, and Contribution and Utilization of Resources. Responses are made on a 5-point scale ranging from 0 (*no confidence*) to 4 (*absolute confidence*).

Reliability: Coefficient alpha was .92.

Validity: Correlations with other variables ranged from .11 to .46.

Author: Schlosser, L. Z., and Gelso, C. J.

Article: Measuring the working alliance in advisor–advisee relationships in graduate school.

Journal: *Journal of Counseling Psychology*, April 2001, *48*, 157–167.

Related Research: O'Brien, K. M., et al. (1998, August). *Research self-efficacy: Improvements in*

instrumentation. Poster presented at the 1998 convention of the American Psychological Association, San Francisco, CA.

11598

Test Name: RIOT SURVEY

Purpose: To assess student perceptions and beliefs about a campus riot.

Number of Items: 12

Format: Various formats are used. All items are presented.

Reliability: Alpha coefficients ranged from .55 to .83 across subscales.

Author: Kaplowitz, S. A., and Campo, S.

Article: Drinking, alcohol policy, and attitudes toward a campus riot.

Journal: *Journal of College Student Development*, September/October 2004, *45*, 501–516.

Related Research: Perkins, H. W. (2002). Surveying the damage: A review of research on consequences of alcohol misuse among college populations. *Journal of Studies on Alcohol*, *14*, 91–100.

11599

Test Name: RUBIN LOVE SCALE

Purpose: To assess the attitude of love.

Number of Items: 13

Format: Scales range from 1 (*not true at all; disagree completely*) to 9 (*definitely true; agree completely*).

Reliability: Alpha coefficients exceeded .83.

Author: Myers, J. E., and Shurts, M.

Article: Measuring positive emotionality: A review of instruments assessing love.

Journal: *Measurement and Evaluation in Counseling and Development*, January 2002, *34*, 238–254.

Related Research: Rubin, Z. (1970). Measurement of romantic love. *Journal of Personality and Social Psychology*, *16*, 265–273.

11600

Test Name: SCALES OF SELF- AND COLLECTIVE EFFICACY BELIEFS WITH TEACHERS' JOB SATISFACTION

Purpose: To assess teachers' self- and collective efficacy beliefs with teachers' job satisfaction.

Number of Items: 52

Format: Includes measures of perceived self-efficacy, perceived collective efficacy, perceptions of the behavior of various constituents in the school community, and job satisfaction. Responses are made on a 7-point scale ranging from 1 (*strongly disagree*) to 7 (*strongly agree*). All items are presented.

Reliability: Alpha coefficients ranged from .74 to .91.

Author: Capara, G. V., et al.

Article: Efficacy beliefs as determinants of teachers' job satisfaction.

Journal: *Journal of Educational Psychology*, December 2003, *95*, 821–832.

Related Research: Capara, G. V., et al. (2003). Teachers', school staff's and parents' efficacy beliefs as determinants of attitudes toward school. *European Journal of Psychology of Education*, *18*, 15–31.

11601

Test Name: SCHOOL ATTITUDE ASSESSMENT SURVEY

Purpose: To measure attitudes that predict academic achievement in adolescents: academic self-perceptions, attitudes toward school, peer attitudes, and self-regulation.

Number of Items: 20

Format: All items are presented.

Reliability: Alpha coefficients ranged from .87 to .90.

Validity: Correlations with grade point average ranged from .26 to .53 across subscales.

Author: McCoach, P. B.

Article: A validation study of the School Attitude Assessment Survey.

Journal: *Measurement and Evaluation in Counseling and Development*, April 2002, *35*, 66–77.

11602

Test Name: SCHOOL ATTITUDE ASSESSMENT SURVEY—REVISED

Purpose: To assess school attitude.

Number of Items: 43

Format: Includes five factors: academic self-perceptions, attitudes toward school, attitudes toward teachers and classes, motivation and self-regulation, and goal valuation. Responses are made on a 7-point Likert scale ranging from *strongly disagree* to *strongly agree*.

Reliability: Alpha coefficients ranged from .89 to .95.

Author: McCoach, D. B., and Siegle, D.

Article: Factors that differentiate underachieving gifted students from high-achieving gifted students.

Journal: *Gifted Child Quarterly*, Spring 2003, *47*, 144–154.

Related Research: McCoach, D. B. (2000). *The School Attitude Assessment Survey—Revised (SAAS–R)*. Unpublished instrument.

11603

Test Name: SCHOOL ATTITUDE ASSESSMENT SURVEY—REVISED

Purpose: To measure secondary school students' academic self-perceptions, attitude toward school, attitudes toward teachers, goal valuation, and motivation/self-regulation.

Number of Items: 35

Format: Includes five factors: academic self-perceptions, attitudes toward teachers, attitudes toward school, goal valuation, and motivation/self-regulation.

Reliability: Internal consistency reliability coefficients ranged from .86 to .91.

Author: McCoach, D. B., and Siegle, D.

Article: The School Attitude Assessment Survey—Revised: A new instrument to identify academically able students who underachieve.

Journal: *Educational and Psychological Measurement*, June 2003, *63*, 414–429.

Related Research: McCoach, D. B. (2002). A validation study of the School Attitude Assessment Survey. *Measurement and Evaluation in Counseling and Development, 35*, 66–77.

11604

Test Name: SCIENCE ACTIVITY QUESTIONNAIRE—ADAPTED

Purpose: To measure science attitudes, goal orientations, and cognitive engagement.

Number of Items: 39

Format: Includes three subscales: Science Attitudes, Goal Orientations, and Cognitive Engagement.

Reliability: Alpha coefficients ranged from .36 to .87.

Author: Stefanou, C., and Parkes, J.

Article: Effects of classroom assessment on student motivation in fifth-grade science.

Journal: *The Journal of Educational Research*, January/February 2003, *96*, 152–162.

Related Research: Meece, J. L., et al. (1988). Students' goal orientations and cognitive engagement in classroom activities. *Journal of Educational Psychology, 80*, 514–523.

11605

Test Name: SCIENCE ATTITUDES SCALE

Purpose: To measure teacher attitudes toward teaching science to children.

Number of Items: 22

Format: Scales range from 1 (*strongly disagree*) to 5 (*strongly agree*). All items are presented.

Reliability: Coefficient alpha for the total scale was .92. Subscale alphas ranged from .68 to .84.

Author: Cho, H.-S., et al.

Article: Early childhood teachers' attitudes toward science teaching: A scale validation study.

Journal: *Educational Research Quarterly*, December 2003, *27*, 39–42.

Related Research: Thompson C., and Shrigley, R. L. (1986). What research says: Revising the Science Attitudes Scale. *School Science and Mathematics, 86*, 331–343.

11606

Test Name: SEX ROLE ATTITUDES SCALE—REVISED

Purpose: To assess attitudes concerning traditional sex roles.

Number of Items: 12

Format: A sample item is given.

Reliability: Coefficient alpha was .76.

Validity: Correlations with other variables ranged from −.22 to .39.

Author: Noble, C. L., et al.

Article: Attitudes toward working single parents: Initial development of a measure.

Journal: *Educational and Psychological Measurement*, December 2004, *64*, 1030–1052.

Related Research: Vanyperen, N. W., & Buunk, B. P. (1991). Sex-role attitudes, social comparison, and satisfaction with relationships. *Social Psychology Quarterly, 54*, 169–180.

11607

Test Name: SEX ROLE EGALITARIANISM SCALE (FORM KK)

Purpose: To measure beliefs about appropriate sex roles.

Number of Items: 25

Format: Scales range from 1 (*strongly agree*) to 5 (*strongly disagree*).

Reliability: Coefficient alpha was .91.

Validity: Correlations with other variables ranged from −.40 to .27.

Author: Berkel, L. A., et al.

Article: Gender role attitudes, religion, and spirituality as predictors of domestic violence attitudes in White college students.

Journal: *Journal of College Student Development*, March/April 2004, *45*, 119–133.

Related Research: King, L. A., & King, D. W. (1990). Abbreviated measures of sex role egalitarian attitudes. *Sex Roles, 23*, 659–673.

11608

Test Name: SEXUAL HARASSMENT ATTITUDE SCALE FOR WORKERS

Purpose: To assess attitudes toward sexual harassment.

Number of Items: 18

Format: Sample items are presented. A Likert format is used.

Reliability: Coefficient alpha was .86.

Author: McCabe, M. P., and Hardman, L.

Article: Attitudes and perceptions of workers to sexual harassment.

Journal: *The Journal of Social Psychology*, December 2005, *145*, 719–740.

Related Research: Mazer, D. B., & Percival, E. F. (1989). Ideology or experience? The relationships among perceptions, attitudes, and experiences of sexual harassment in university students. *Sex Roles, 20*, 135–147.

11609

Test Name: SHEEP–GOAT SCALE

Purpose: To measure belief in and experience of extrasensory perception and autokinetics.

Number of Items: 18

Format: Six-point Likert format. Sample items are presented.

Validity: Correlations with other variables ranged from .16 to .63.

Author: Roe, C. A., and Morgan, C. L.

Article: Narcissism and belief in the paranormal.

Journal: *Psychological Reports*, April 2002, *90*, 405–411.

Related Research: Thalbourne, M. A., & Delin, P. S. (1993). A new instrument for measuring the sheep–goat variable: Its psychometric properties and factor structure. *Journal for the Society for Psychical Research, 59*, 172–186.

11610

Test Name: SOCIOCULTURAL ATTITUDES TOWARDS APPEARANCE QUESTIONNAIRE— INTERNALIZATION SUBSCALE

Purpose: To assess levels of agreement with societal standards of appearance.

Number of Items: 8

Format: Responses are made on a 5-point scale ranging from 1 (*completely disagree*) to 5 (*completely agree*).

Reliability: Alpha coefficients were .88 and .92.

Validity: Correlations with other variables ranged from .46 to .70.

Author: Tylka, T. L., and Subich, L. M.

Article: Revisiting the latent structure of eating disorders: Taxometric analyses with nonbehavioral indicators.

Journal: *Journal of Counseling Psychology*, July 2003, *50*, 276–286.

Related Research: Heinberg, L. J., et al. (1995). Development and validation of the Sociocultural Attitudes Towards Appearance Questionnaire. *International Journal of Eating Disorders, 17*, 81–89.

11611

Test Name: SOFTWARE PIRACY SCALE

Purpose: To measure attitude toward software piracy.

Number of Items: 11

Format: Item responses range from 1 (*strongly disagree*) to 5 (*strongly agree*).

Reliability: Coefficient alpha was .89.

Validity: Correlations with other variables ranged from −.37 to .36.

Author: Higgins, G. E., and Makin, D. A.

Article: Self-control, deviant peers, and software piracy.

Journal: *Psychological Reports,* December 2004, *95* Part 1, 921–931.

Related Research: Rahim, M. M., et al. (2001). Factors affecting softlifting intention of computing students: An empirical study. *Journal of Educational Computing Research, 24,* 385–405.

11612

Test Name: STATISTICS ATTITUDE SURVEY

Purpose: To measure attitudes toward statistics.

Number of Items: 33

Format: Responses are made on a 5-point Likert-type scale. Examples are given.

Reliability: Alpha coefficients were .93 and .94.

Validity: Correlations with other variables ranged from .48 to .87.

Author: Cashin, S. E., and Elmore, P. B.

Article: The Survey of Attitudes Toward Statistics Scale: A construct validity study.

Journal: *Educational and Psychological Measurement,* June 2005, *65,* 509–524.

Related Research: Roberts, D. M., & Bilderback, E. W. (1980). Reliability and validity of a statistics attitude survey. *Educational and Psychological Measurement, 40,* 235–238.

11613

Test Name: STEREOTYPE SCALE

Purpose: To measure the internalization of negative, anti-Black myths.

Number of Items: 52

Format: Scales range from 1 (*strongly agree*) to 5 (*strongly disagree*). Sample items are presented.

Reliability: Alpha coefficients ranged from .93 to .94.

Validity: Correlations with other variables ranged from −.23 to .55.

Author: Kelly, S.

Article: Underlying components of scores assessing African Americans' racial perspective.

Journal: *Measurement and Evaluation in Counseling and Development,* April 2004, *37,* 28–40.

Related Research: Kelly, S., and Floyd, F. J. (2001). The effects of negative racial stereotypes and Afrocentricity on Black couple relationships. *Journal of Family Psychology, 15,* 110–123.

11614

Test Name: STEREOTYPE THREAT QUESTIONNAIRE

Purpose: To measure stereotype threat.

Number of Items: 5

Format: Responses are made on a 7-point Likert-type scale ranging from 1 (*strongly disagree*) to 7 (*strongly agree*). An example is given.

Reliability: Coefficient alpha was .77.

Validity: Correlations with other variables ranged from −.07 to .32 (*n* = 166).

Author: Roberson, L., et al.

Article: Stereotype threat and feedback seeking in the workplace.

Journal: *Journal of Vocational Behavior,* February 2003, *62,* 176–188.

Related Research: Steele, C. M., & Aronson, J. (1995). Stereotype threat and the intellectual test performance of African Americans. *Journal of Personality and Social Psychology, 69,* 797–811.

11615

Test Name: STRUCTURAL ASSURANCE BELIEFS SCALE

Purpose: To measure structural assurance beliefs.

Number of Items: 6

Format: Responses are made on a 6-point scale ranging from 1 (*strongly disagree*) to 6 (*strongly agree*).

Reliability: Coefficient alpha was .79.

Validity: Correlations with other variables ranged from −.15 to .06.

Author: Linnehan, F., et al.

Article: African-American students' early trust beliefs in work-based mentors.

Journal: *Journal of Vocational Behavior,* June 2005, *66,* 501–515.

Related Research: McKnight, D. H., et al. (1998). Initial trust formation in new organizational relationships. *Academy of Management Review, 22,* 473–490.

11616

Test Name: STUDENT ANTI-INTELLECTUALISM SCALE

Purpose: To measure anti-intellectual attitudes.

Number of Items: 25

Format: Item anchors are −3 (*disagree*) and +3 (*agree*). Sample items are presented.

Reliability: Coefficient alpha was .91.

Validity: Correlations with other variables ranged from −.17 to −.54.

Author: Hook, R. J.

Article: Students' anti-intellectual attitudes and adjustment to college.

Journal: *Psychological Reports*, June 2004, *94*, Part 1, 909–914.

Related Research: Eigenberger, M. E., & Sealander, K. A. (2001). A scale for measuring students' anti-intellectualism. *Psychological Reports*, *89*, 387–402.

11617

Test Name: STUDENT'S ATTITUDE TOWARD WORK SCALE

Purpose: To measure student's attitude toward work.

Number of Items: 8

Format: Responses are made on a 7-point scale ranging from 1 (*strongly disagree*) to 7 (*strongly agree*). Sample items are presented.

Reliability: Alpha coefficients were .68 and .73.

Validity: Correlations with other variables ranged from −.03 to .65.

Author: Linnehan, F.

Article: A longitudinal study of work-based, adult–youth mentoring.

Journal: *Journal of Vocational Behavior*, August 2003, *63*, 40–54.

Related Research: Stern, D., et al. (1990). Quality of students' work experience and orientation toward work. *Youth & Society*, *22*, 263–282.

11618

Test Name: STUDENT'S BELIEF IN THE RELEVANCE OF SCHOOL SCALE

Purpose: To measure student's belief in the relevance of school.

Number of Items: 10

Format: Responses are made on a 7-point scale ranging from 1 (*strongly disagree*) to 7 (*strongly agree*). Sample items are presented.

Reliability: Alpha coefficients were .70 and .79.

Validity: Correlations with other variables ranged from .00 to .60.

Author: Linnehan, F.

Article: A longitudinal study of work-based, adult–youth mentoring.

Journal: *Journal of Vocational Behavior*, August 2003, *63*, 40–54.

Related Research: Roy, K., & Rosenbaum, J. (1996, August). *Students' perceptions of school relevance: A test of Stinchcombe's hypothesis.* Paper presented at the annual meeting of the American Sociological Association, New York.

11619

Test Name: STUDENTS' IRRATIONAL BELIEFS SCALE

Purpose: To measure perfectionism, negativism, blame proneness, escapism, anxious over concern, and absolute demands.

Number of Items: 33

Format: Item anchors are 1 (*not at all*) and 5 (*always applicable to me*).

Reliability: Alpha coefficients ranged from .52 to .71 across subscales.

Author: Hassan, N., and Ismail, H. N.

Article: Factor analysis of responses to the Irrational Beliefs Scale in a sample of Iraqi university students.

Journal: *Psychological Reports*, June 2004, *94*, Part 1, 775–781.

Related Research: Watson, C. G., et al. (1990). A factor analysis of Ellis' Irrational Beliefs. *Journal of Clinical Psychology*, *46*, 413–420.

11620

Test Name: STUDY HABITS AND ATTITUDES INVENTORY

Purpose: To assess college students' study habits and attitudes.

Number of Items: 31

Format: Multiple choice format. Involves attitudes toward learning, motivation, goal-setting, study behaviors and procrastination, and self-efficacy.

Reliability: Internal consistency coefficients were .75 and .77. Test–retest (1 week) reliability was .94.

Validity: Correlations with GPA were .46 and .64.

Author: Chapman, B. P., and Hayslip, B., Jr.

Article: Incremental validity of a measure of emotional intelligence.

Journal: *Journal of Personality Assessment*, October 2005, *85*, 154–169.

Related Research: Nixon, C. T., & Frost, A. G. (1990). The Study Habits and Attitudes Inventory and its implications for students' success. *Psychological Reports*, *66*, 1075–1085.

11621

Test Name: SUBSTANCE ABUSE ATTITUDE SURVEY

Purpose: To assess attitudes among clinicians toward aspects of alcohol and drug abuse.

Number of Items: 39

Format: Six-point scales range from *strongly disagree* to *strongly agree*.

Reliability: Test–retest reliabilities ranged from .65 to .86.

Author: Beckstead, J. W.

Article: Attitudes accentuate attributes in social judgment: The combined effects of substance use, depression, and technical incompetence on judgments of professional impairment.

Journal: *The Journal of Social Psychology*, April 2003, *143*, 185–201.

Related Research: Chappel, J. N., et al. (1985). The Substance Abuse Attitude Survey: An instrument for measuring attitudes. *Journal of Studies on Alcohol, 46*, 48–52.

11622

Test Name: SUPERNATURAL AND PARANORMAL BELIEFS SCALES

Purpose: To measure belief in the supernatural and in the paranormal.

Number of Items: 19

Format: Scales range from 1 (*I don't believe this*) to 5 (*I definitely believe this*). Sample items are presented.

Reliability: Alpha coefficients were .81 (supernatural) and .71 (paranormal).

Validity: The correlation between the scales was .01.

Author: Beck, R., and Miller, J. P.

Article: Erosion of belief and disbelief: Effects of religiosity and negative affect on beliefs in the paranormal and supernatural.

Journal: *The Journal of Social Psychology*, April 2001, *141*, 277–287.

11623

Test Name: SUPERSTITION QUESTIONNAIRE

Purpose: To measure personal superstitious beliefs.

Number of Items: 28

Format: Scales range from 1 (*strongly disagree*) to 7 (*strongly agree*). All items are presented.

Validity: Correlations with perceived personal superstition ranged from .32 to .66 across subscales.

Author: Rudski, J.

Article: What does a "superstitious" person believe? Impressions of participants.

Journal: *The Journal of General Psychology*, October 2003, *130*, 431–445.

Related Research: Grimmer, M. R., & White, K. D. (1992). Non-conventional beliefs among Australian science and non-science students. *The Journal of Psychology, 126*, 521–528.

11624

Test Name: SURVEY IN UFO'S AND ALIEN ABDUCTIONS

Purpose: To assess peoples' attitudes, beliefs, and experiences regarding UFO's and alien abductions.

Number of Items: 51

Format: Various formats are used. All are described. Sample items are presented.

Reliability: Alpha coefficients ranged from .79 to .94 across subscales.

Author: Patry, A. L., and Pelletier, L. G.

Article: Extraterrestrial beliefs and experiences: An application of the theory of reasoned action.

Journal: *The Journal of Social Psychology*, April 2001, *141*, 199–217.

Related Research: Bartholomew, R. E., et al. (1991). UFO abductees and contactees: Psychopathology or fantasy proneness. *Professional Psychology: Research and Practice, 22*, 215–222

11625

Test Name: SURVEY OF ATTITUDES TOWARD STATISTICS SCALE

Purpose: To measure attitudes toward statistics.

Number of Items: 28

Format: Includes four subscales: Affect, Cognitive Competence, Value, and Difficulty. Responses are made on a 7-point Likert-type scale. Examples are given.

Reliability: Alpha coefficients ranged from .74 to .94.

Validity: Correlations with other variables ranged from –.15 to .89.

Author: Cashin, S. E., and Elmore, P. B.

Article: The Survey of Attitudes Toward Statistics Scale: A construct validity study.

Journal: *Educational and Psychological Measurement*, June 2005, *65*, 509–524.

Related Research: Schau, C., et al. (1995). The development and validation of the Survey of Attitudes Toward Statistics. *Educational and Psychological Measurement, 55*, 868–875.

11626

Test Name: SURVEY OF ATTITUDES TOWARD STATISTICS—SPANISH VERSION

Purpose: To measure attitudes toward statistics as affect, cognitive competence, value, and difficulty.

Number of Items: 28

Format: Scales range from 1 (*strongly disagree*) to 7 (*strongly agree*). Sample items are presented in English.

Reliability: Alpha coefficients ranged from .65 to .84 across subscales.

Author: Carmona, J., et al.

Article: Mathematical background and attitude toward statistics in a sample of Spanish college students.

Journal: *Psychological Reports,* August 2005, 97, 56–62.

Related Research: Schau, C., et al. (1995). The development and validation of the Survey of Attitudes toward Statistics. *Educational and Psychological Measurement, 55,* 868–875.

11627

Test Name: SURVEY OF PERSONAL BELIEFS

Purpose: To measure catastrophizing, self-directed shoulds, other-directed shoulds, low frustration tolerance, and self-worth.

Number of Items: 50

Format: A 6-point Likert format was used.

Reliability: Alpha was .89. Test–retest reliabilities ranged from .74 to .87 across subscales.

Validity: Correlations with other variables ranged from −.47 to .11.

Author: Moeller, A. T., and Bothma, M. E.

Article: Body dissatisfaction and irrational beliefs.

Journal: *Psychological Reports,* April 2001, 88, 423–430.

Related Research: Kassinove, H. (1986). Self-reported affect and core irrational thinking: A preliminary analysis. *Journal of Rational-Emotive Therapy, 4,* 119–130.

11628

Test Name: TEACHER BELIEF SCALE

Purpose: To assess teachers' beliefs.

Number of Items: 48

Format: Includes four subscales: the Role of the Learner, Relationship Between Skills, Socioconstructivism, and the Role of the Teacher. Responses are made on a 5-point Likert scale ranging from 0 (*strongly disagree*) to 4 (*strongly agree*). Examples are presented.

Reliability: Alpha coefficients ranged from .60 to .90. Mean score stability after one year was .69

Author: Staub, F. C., and Stern, E.

Article: The nature of teachers' pedagogical content beliefs matters for students' achievement gains: Quasi-experimental evidence from elementary mathematics.

Journal: *Journal of Educational Psychology,* June 2002, 94, 344–355.

Related Research: Fennema, E., et al. (1990, March). *Teacher Belief Scale: Cognitively guided instruction project.* Madison: University of Wisconsin.

11629

Test Name: TEACHER WARMTH AND ATTITUDES SCALES

Purpose: To measure teacher warmth, averse attitudes toward aggression, and empathic attitudes toward social withdrawal.

Number of Items: 22

Format: Includes three scales: Teacher Warmth, Teachers' Averse Attitudes Toward Aggression, and Teachers' Empathic Attitudes Toward Social Withdrawal. Most items are presented in abbreviated format. Responses are made on a 5-point scale ranging from 0 (*never*) to 4 (*always*).

Reliability: Internal consistency reliabilities ranged from .63 to .87.

Author: Chang, L.

Article: Variable effects of children's aggression, social withdrawal, and prosocial

leadership as functions of teacher beliefs and behaviors.

Journal: *Child Development,* March/April 2003, 74, 535–548.

Related Research: Jiang, G. (2001). *Teacher behaviors and classroom management styles and students' social emotional development.* Unpublished doctoral dissertation, The Chinese University of Hong Kong.

11630

Test Name: TEACHERS' CULTURALLY RELEVANT BELIEFS MEASURE

Purpose: To measure teachers' culturally relevant beliefs.

Number of Items: 48

Format: Includes six dimensions: Knowledge; Student's Race, Ethnicity, and Culture; Social Relations in and Beyond the Classroom; Teaching as a Profession; Teaching Practice; and Students' Needs and Strengths. All items are presented.

Reliability: Alpha coefficients ranged from .72 to .85.

Validity: Correlations with other variables ranged from −.43 to .41.

Author: Love, A., and Kruger, A. C.

Article: Teacher beliefs and student achievement in urban schools serving African American students.

Journal: *The Journal of Educational Research,* November/December 2005, 99, 87–98.

Related Research: Ladson-Billings, G. (1994). *The dreamkeepers: Successful teachers of African American children.* San Francisco: Jossey-Bass.

11631

Test Name: TEST ATTITUDE SURVEY

Purpose: To measure test-taking attitude.

Number of Items: 45

Format: Includes three components: Motivation, Self-Doubts Regarding Test-Taking, and Dislike of Tests. Responses are made on a 5-point Likert scale ranging from 1 (*strongly agree*) to 5 (*strongly disagree*). Items are presented.

Reliability: Alpha coefficients ranged from .44 to .90.

Author: McCarthy, J. M., and Goffin, R. D.

Article: Is the Test Attitude Survey psychometrically sound?

Journal: *Educational and Psychological Measurement*, June 2003, *63*, 446–464.

Related Research: Arvey, R. D., et al. (1990). Motivational components of test-taking. *Personnel Psychology, 43*, 695–716.

11632

Test Name: THEORETICAL ORIENTATION TO READING PROFILE

Purpose: To identify teachers' beliefs about reading.

Number of Items: 28

Format: Includes three areas: phonics, skill-based, and whole language.

Reliability: Test–retest reliability was .81.

Validity: Correlations with the Approaches to Beginning Reading and Reading Instruction Questionnaire ranged from –.52 to .58.

Author: Evans, M. A., et al.

Article: Beginning reading: The views of parents and teachers of young children.

Journal: *Journal of Educational Psychology*, March 2004, *96*, 130–141.

Related Research: Deford, D. E. (1985). Validating the construct of theoretical orientation in reading instruction. *Reading Research Quarterly, 20*, 351–381.

11633

Test Name: THEORIES OF INTELLIGENCE MEASURE

Purpose: To assess the extent to which individuals agree with an entity viewpoint.

Number of Items: 3

Format: Responses are made on a 6-point Likert-type scale ranging from 1 (*very strongly disagree*) to 6 (*very strongly agree*). An example is given.

Reliability: Coefficient alpha was .91

Validity: Correlations with other variables ranged from –.18 to .25.

Author: Jagacinski, C. M., and Duda, J. L.

Article: A comparative analysis of contemporary achievement goal orientation measures.

Journal: *Education and Psychological Measurement*, December 2001, *61*, 1013–1039.

Related Research: Dweck, C. S., et al. (1995). Implicit theories and their role in judgments and reactions: A world from two perspectives. *Psychological Inquiry, 6*, 267–285.

11634

Test Name: VALUE AND ATTITUDINAL SIMILARITY SCALE

Purpose: To measure perceptions of similarities between mentor/protégé's values and attitudes concerning work and family balance.

Number of Items: 5

Format: Responses are made on a 5-point scale ranging from 1 (*strongly disagree*) to 5 (*strongly agree*). All items are presented.

Reliability: Reliability coefficient was .92.

Validity: Correlations with other variables ranged from –.22 to .57.

Author: Nielson, T. R., et al.

Article: The supportive mentor as a means of reducing work–family conflict.

Journal: *Journal of Vocational Behavior*, December 2001, *59*, 364–381.

11635

Test Name: VENGEANCE SCALE

Purpose: To measure a person's attitude toward revenge.

Number of Items: 20

Format: Seven-point Likert scales are used.

Reliability: Coefficient alpha was .95.

Validity: Correlations with other variables ranged from –.07 to .73.

Author: Douglas, S. C., and Martinko, M. J.

Article: Exploring the role of individual differences in the prediction of workplace aggression.

Journal: *Journal of Applied Psychology*, August 2001, *86*, 547–559.

Related Research: Stuckless, N., & Goranson, R. (1992). The Vengeance Scale: Development of a measure of attitudes toward revenge. *Journal of Social Behavior and Personality*, 7, 25–42.

11636

Test Name: WHITE RACIAL IDENTITY ATTITUDES SCALE—MODIFIED

Purpose: To measure White racial identity.

Number of Items: 50

Format: Scales range from 1 (*strongly disagree*) to 5 (*strongly agree*).

Reliability: Alpha coefficients ranged from .45 to .76 (original) and from .63 to .87 (modified).

Validity: Correlations between modified subscales ranged from −.42 to .27.

Author: Mercer, S. H., and Cunningham, M.

Article: Racial identity in White American college students: Issues of conceptualization and measurement.

Journal: *Journal of College Student Development*, March/April 2003, *44*, 217–230.

Related Research: Helms, J. E., & Carter, R. T. (1991). Relationships of White and Black racial identity attitudes and demographic similarity to counselor performance. *Journal of Counseling Psychology*, *38*, 446–457.

11637

Test Name: WOMANIST IDENTITY ATTITUDE SCALE

Purpose: To assess gender attitudes associated with the four components of the womanist identity development model.

Number of Items: 43

Format: Scales range from 1 (*strongly disagree*) to 5 (*strongly agree*).

Reliability: Alpha coefficients ranged from .30 to .74 across subscales.

Validity: Correlations with other variables ranged from −.33 to .16. Correlations between subscales ranged from −.26 to .36.

Author: Constantine, M. G., and Watt, S. K.

Article: Cultural congruity, womanist identity attitudes, and life satisfaction among African American college women attending historically Black and predominately White institutions.

Journal: *Journal of College Student Development*, March/April 2002, *43*, 184–194.

Related Research: Ossana, S. M., et al. (1992). Do "womanist" identity attitudes influence college women's self-esteem and perceptions of environmental bias? *Journal of Counseling and Development*, *70*, 402–408.

11638

Test Name: WORK ATTITUDES SCALES

Purpose: To assess job satisfaction, job-related well-being, and employee, intrinsic motivation.

Number of Items: 33

Format: Seven-point agreement scales and 6-point frequency scales are used.

Reliability: Alpha coefficients ranged from .74 to .91.

Author: Epitropaki, O., and Martin, R.

Article: From ideal to real: A longitudinal study of the role of implicit leadership theories on leader–member exchange and employee outcomes.

Journal: *Journal of Applied Psychology*, July 2005, *90*, 659–676.

Related Research: Warr, P. D., et al. (1979). Scales for the measurement of work attitudes and aspects of psychological well-being. *Journal of Occupational Psychology*, *52*, 129–148.

11639

Test Name: WRITING ORIENTATION SCALE

Purpose: To measure teachers' beliefs about writing instruction.

Number of Items: 13

Format: Includes three factors: explicit instruction, correct writing, and natural learning. Responses are made on a 6-point Likert-type scale ranging from 1 (*strongly disagree*) to 6 (*strongly agree*).

Reliability: Internal consistency coefficients ranged from .60 to .70.

Author: Graham, S., et al.

Article: Primary grade teachers' instructional adaptations for struggling writers: A national survey.

Journal: *Journal of Educational Psychology*, June 2003, *95*, 279–292.

Related Research: Graham, S., et al. (2002). Primary grade teachers' theoretical orientations concerning writing instruction: Construct validation and nationwide survey. *Contemporary Educational Psychology*, *27*, 147–166.

11640

Test Name: YOUTH ATTITUDES TOWARD FAMILY OBLIGATION SCALES

Purpose: To measure youth attitudes toward family obligations.

Number of Items: 24

Format: Includes three areas: assisting with household tasks and spending time with their families, respecting and following the wishes of family members, and supporting and being near their families in the future. Responses are made on 5-point scales. Examples are given.

Reliability: Alpha coefficients ranged from .68 to .89.

Author: Tseng, V.

Article: Family interdependence and academic adjustment in college: Youth from immigrant and U.S.-born families.

Journal: *Child Development*, May/June 2004, 75, 966–983.

Related Research: Fuligni, A. J., et al. Attitudes toward family obligations among American adolescents with Asian, Latin American, and European backgrounds. *Child Development*, 70, 1030–1044.

CHAPTER 8
Behavior

11641

Test Name: ABSORPTION SCALE

Purpose: To measure involvement, engagement, and responsiveness in stimuli that narrows or widens attention.

Number of Items: 34

Format: A true–false format and 4-point Likert response scales are used.

Reliability: Alpha coefficients exceeded .86.

Validity: Correlations with other variables ranged from –.57 to 52.

Author: Kremen, A. M., and Block, J.

Article: Absorption: Construct explication by Q-sort assessments of personality.

Journal: *Journal of Research in Personality*, June 2002, *36*, 252–259.

Related Research: Tellegen, A. (1992). *Note on the structures and meaning of the MPQ Absorption Scale.* Unpublished manuscript, University of Minnesota.

11642

Test Name: ABUSIVE SUPERVISION BEHAVIOR SCALE

Purpose: To measure abusive supervision in a military context.

Number of Items: 27

Format: Scales range from 0 (*never*) to 5 (*frequently, if not always*). Sample items are presented.

Reliability: Coefficient alpha was .93.

Validity: Correlations with other variables ranged from –.35 to .32.

Author: Zellars, K. L., et al.

Article: Abusive supervision and subordinates' organizational citizenship behavior.

Journal: *Journal of Applied Psychology*, December 2002, *87*, 1068–1076.

Related Research: Duffy, M. K., et al. (2002). Social undermining and social support in the workplace. *Academy of Management Journal, 45*, 331–351.

11643

Test Name: ABUSIVE SUPERVISION SCALE

Purpose: To assess the extent of use of abusive supervision.

Number of Items: 15

Format: Scales range from 1 (*I cannot remember him/her ever using this behavior with me*) to 5 (*He/She uses this behavior very often with me*). Sample items are presented.

Reliability: Coefficient alpha was .91.

Validity: Correlations with other variables ranged from –.20 to .23.

Author: Tepper, B. J., et al.

Article: Personality moderators of the relationship between abusive supervision and subordinates' resistance.

Journal: *Journal of Applied Psychology*, October 2001, *86*, 974–983.

Related Research: Tepper, B. J. (2000). Consequences of abusive supervision. *Academy of Management Journal, 43*, 178–190.

11644

Test Name: ACADEMIC PROCRASTINATION SCALE

Purpose: To measure degree of procrastination.

Number of Items: 6

Format: Scales range from 1 (*not at all true*) to 7 (*very true*).

Reliability: Coefficient alpha was .82.

Validity: Correlations with other variables ranged from –.40 to .25.

Author: Chu, A. H. C., and Choi, J. N.

Article: Rethinking procrastination: Positive effects of "active" procrastination behavior on attitudes and performance.

Journal: *The Journal of Social Psychology*, June 2005, *145*, 245–264.

Related Research: Ferrari, J. R., et al. (1995). *Procrastination and task avoidance: Theory, research, and treatment.* New York: Plenum Press.

11645

Test Name: ACQUIESCENCE SCALE

Purpose: To measure acquiescence.

Number of Items: 5

Format: Responses are made on a 5-point scale ranging from *never true* to *always true*. All items are presented.

Reliability: Alpha coefficients ranged from .64 to .81.

Author: Cook, W. L.

Article: Interpersonal influence in family systems: A social relations model analysis.

Journal: *Child Development*, July/August 2001, *72*, 1179–1197.

Related Research: Cook, W. L. (1993). Interdependence and the interpersonal sense of control: An analysis of family relationships. *Journal of Personality and Social Psychology, 64*, 587–601.

11646

Test Name: ACTION CONTROL SCALE—ADAPTED, DUTCH TRANSLATION

Purpose: To measure initiative versus hesitation dimension of action–state orientation.

Number of Items: 8

Format: Responses are either action or state orientation. A sample item is given.

Reliability: Coefficient alpha was .78.

Validity: Correlations with other variables ranged from −.58 to .37.

Author: van Hooft, E. A. J., et al.

Article: Bridging the gap between intentions and behavior: Implementation intentions, action control, and procrastination.

Journal: *Journal of Vocational Behavior*, April 2005, *66*, 238–256.

Related Research: Kuhl, J. (1994). Action versus state orientation: Psychometric properties of the Action Control Scale (ACS–90). In J. Kuhl & J. Beckmann (Eds.),

Volition and personality: Action versus state orientation. Seattle, WA: Hogrede & Huber.

11647

Test Name: ACTIVATION–DEACTIVATION ADJECTIVE CHECKLIST— SHORT FORM

Purpose: To measure arousal.

Number of Items: 20

Format: Subjects record feelings at the moment on scales ranging from 1 (*certainly, always false*) to 6 (*certainly, always true*).

Reliability: Alpha coefficients exceeded .86.

Author: Vancouver, J. B., and Tischner, E. C.

Article: The effect of feedback sign on task performance depends on self-concept discrepancies.

Journal: *Journal of Applied Psychology*, December 2004, *89*, 1092–1098.

Related Research: Thayer, R. E. (1967). Measurement of activation through self-report. *Psychological Reports, 20*, 663–778.

11648

Test Name: ACTIVE JOB SEARCH SCALE

Purpose: To assess the degree to which respondents engaged in active job search behaviors in the past 6 months.

Format: Responses are made on a 6-point Likert scale ranging from 0 (*never or no times*) to 5 (*very frequently or at least ten times*). Examples are presented.

Reliability: Coefficient alpha was .86.

Validity: Correlations with other variables ranged from −.28 to .21.

Author: Dunford, B., et al.

Article: Out-of-the-money: The impact of underwater stock options on executive job search.

Journal: *Personnel Psychology*, Spring 2005, *58*, 67–101.

Related Research: Blau, G. (1993). Further exploring the relationship between job search and voluntary individual turnover. *Personnel Psychology, 46*, 313–330.

11649

Test Name: ACTIVE PROCRASTINATION SCALE

Purpose: To distinguish active from passive procrastinators.

Number of Items: 12

Format: Scales range from 1 (*not at all true*) to 7 (*very true*). Sample items are presented.

Reliability: Coefficient alpha was .67.

Validity: Correlations with other variables ranged from −.31 to .34.

Author: Chu, A. H. C., and Choi, J. N.

Article: Rethinking procrastination: Positive effects of "active" procrastination behavior on attitudes and performance.

Journal: *The Journal of Social Psychology*, June 2005, *145*, 245–264.

11650

Test Name: ACTIVITIES OF DAILY LIFE SCALE

Purpose: To measure physical functioning such as washing, dressing, and eating.

Number of Items: 7

Format: Item responses range from 0 (*complete disability*) to 3 (*no difficulty*). All items are presented.

Reliability: Coefficient alpha was .95.

Author: Shmotkin, D., et al.

Article: Tracing long-term effects of early trauma: A broad-scope view of Holocaust survivors in late life.

Journal: *Journal of Consulting and Clinical Psychology*, April 2003, *71*, 223–234.

Related Research: Branch, L. G., et al. (1984). A prospective study of functional status among community elders. *American Journal of Public Health*, *74*, 266–268.

11651

Test Name: ADAPTIVE SOCIAL BEHAVIOR INVENTORY

Purpose: To assess social competence and disruptive behavior.

Number of Items: 30

Format: Includes three factors: express, comply, and disrupt. Responses are made on a 3-point scale ranging from 1 (*rarely*) to 3 (*almost always*).

Reliability: Alpha coefficients ranged from .62 to .82.

Author: Belsky, J., et al.

Article: Testing a core emotion-regulation prediction: Does early attentional persistence moderate the effect of infant negative emotionality on later development?

Journal: *Child Development*, January/February 2001, *72*, 123–133.

Related Research: Hogan, A., et al. (1992). The Adaptive Social Behavior Inventory (ASBI): A new assessment of social competence in high risk three-year-olds. *Journal of Psychoeducational Assessment*, *10*, 230–239.

11652

Test Name: ADOLESCENT ALCOHOL USE SCALE

Purpose: To measure adolescent alcohol use.

Number of Items: 9

Format: Various item response scales are used. All are described along with scoring procedures.

Reliability: Coefficient alpha was .88.

Author: Bray, J. H., et al.

Article: Individuation, peers, and adolescent alcohol use: A latent growth analysis.

Journal: *Journal of Consulting and Clinical Psychology*, June 2003, *71*, 533–564.

Related Research: Baer, P. E., et al. (1987). Stress, coping, family conflict, and adolescent alcohol use. *Journal of Behavioral Medicine*, *10*, 449–466.

11653

Test Name: ADOLESCENT ANGER RATING SCALE

Purpose: To measure adolescence instrumental and reactive anger.

Number of Items: 16

Format: Includes three subscales: Reactive, Instrumental, and Anger Control.

Reliability: Alpha coefficients ranged from .70 to .83. Test–retest (2 weeks) reliability coefficients ranged from .58 to .69.

Validity: Correlations with the Multidimensional Anger Inventory ranged from –.11 to .46.

Author: McKinnie Burney, D., and Kromrey, J.

Article: Initial development and score validation of the Adolescent Anger Rating Scale.

Journal: *Educational and Psychological Measurement*, June 2001, *61*, 446–460.

11654

Test Name: ADOLESCENT RISKY BEHAVIOR SCALE

Purpose: To assess risky behavior.

Number of Items: 24

Format: Scales range from 1 (*never*) to 4 (*more than 10 times*). Sample items are presented.

Reliability: Alpha coefficients ranged from .88 to .93.

Author: McHale, S. M., et al.

Article: Siblings' differential treatment in Mexican American families.

Journal: *Journal of Marriage and Family*, December 2005, *67*, 1259–1274.

Related Research: Eccles, J. S., & Barber, B. (1990). *Risky behavior measure*. Unpublished scale, University of Michigan, Ann Arbor.

11655

Test Name: ADOLESCENTS' BEHAVIORAL MISCONDUCT SCALE

Purpose: To measure adolescents' behavioral misconduct.

Number of Items: 16

Format: Includes three domains: Substance Use, Disobeying Parents, and Antisocial Behavior.

Reliability: Alpha coefficients ranged from .77 to .87.

Author: Marshall, S. K.

Article: Relative contributions of perceived mattering to parents and friends in predicting adolescents' psychological well-being.

Journal: *Perceptual and Motor Skills*, October 2004, *99*, 591–601.

Related Research: Maggs, J. L., et al. (1995). Risky business: The paradoxical meaning of problem behavior for young adolescents.

Journal of Early Adolescence, 15, 344–362.

11656

Test Name: ADULT BEHAVIOR CHECKLIST

Purpose: To measure ADHD in adults by self-report.

Number of Items: 18

Format: Scales range from 0 (*never or rarely*) to 3 (*very often*).

Reliability: Alpha coefficients exceeded .73.

Author: Wallace, J. G., et al.

Article: The cognitive failures questionnaire revisited: Dimensions and correlates.

Journal: *The Journal of General Psychology,* July 2002, *129,* 238–256.

Related Research: Barkley, R. A., & Murphy, K. R. (1996). *Attention-deficit hyperactivity disorder: A handbook for diagnosis and treatment* (2nd ed.). New York: Guilford Press.

11657

Test Name: AFRICULTURAL COPING SYSTEMS INVENTORY

Purpose: To measure culture-specific coping behaviors used by African Americans during stressful experiences.

Number of Items: 30

Format: Scales range from 0 (*does not apply or did not use*) to 3 (*used a great deal*). Sample items are presented.

Reliability: Alpha coefficients ranged from .71 to .80 across subscales.

Validity: Correlations with other variables ranged from −.73 to .71.

Author: Constantine, M. G., et al.

Article: Religious participation, spirituality, and coping among African American college students.

Journal: *Journal of College Student Development,* September/October 2002, *43,* 605–613.

Related Research: Utsey, S. O., et al. (2000). Development and initial validation of the Africultural Coping Systems Inventory. *Journal of Black Psychology, 26,* 194–215.

11658

Test Name: AGGRESSION QUESTIONNAIRE

Purpose: To measure aggressiveness.

Format: Includes four subscales: Physical Aggression, Verbal Aggression, Anger, and Hostility.

Reliability: Alpha coefficients ranged from .53 to .85. Test–retest coefficients ranged from .72 to .80.

Validity: Correlations with the Barrett Impulsiveness Scale—II-A ranged from .14 to .46.

Author: Fossati, A., et al.

Article: Psychometric properties of an adolescent version of the Barrett Impulsiveness Scale—II for a sample of Italian high school students.

Journal: *Perceptual and Motor Skills,* October 2002, *95,* 621–635.

Related Research: Buss, A. H., & Perry, M. (1992). The Aggression Questionnaire. *Journal of Personality and Social Psychology, 63,* 452–459.

11659

Test Name: AGGRESSION SCALE

Purpose: To assess aggressive attitude, verbal aggression, and physical aggression.

Number of Items: 18

Format: Four-point scales are anchored by 0 (*not true at all*) and 4 (*very true*). Sample items are presented.

Reliability: Alpha coefficients ranged from .65 to .77 across subscales.

Validity: Correlations with other variables ranged from −.22 to −.16.

Author: Storch, E. A., and Storch, J. B.

Article: Intrinsic religiosity and aggression in a sample of intercollegiate athletes.

Journal: *Psychological Reports,* December 2002, *91,* Part 2, 1041–1042.

11660

Test Name: AGGRESSIVE BEHAVIOR SUBSCALE

Purpose: To assess aggressive behavior.

Number of Items: 3

Format: Responses are made on a 5-point scale ranging from 1 (*very uncharacteristic*) to 5 (*very characteristic*). All items are presented.

Reliability: Alpha coefficients were .89 and .91.

Validity: Correlations with other variables ranged from −.62 to .53.

Author: Gazelle, H., and Rudolph, K. D.

Article: Moving toward and away from the world: Social approach and avoidance trajectories in anxious solitary youth.

Journal: *Child Development,* May/June 2004, *75,* 829–849.

Related Research: Cassidy, J., & Asher, S. R. (1992). Loneliness and peer relations in young children. *Child Development, 63,* 350–365.

11661

Test Name: ALCOHOL COMPOSITE USE INDEX

Purpose: To measure alcohol use.

Number of Items: 4

Format: Response categories are 0 (*no use/ no recent use*) and 1 (*use/ recent use*). All items are presented.

Reliability: The average alpha coefficient ranged from .70 to .79 across waves of data collection.

Author: Spoth, R., et al.

Article: Brief family intervention effects on adolescent substance initiation: School-level growth curve analysis 6 years following baseline.

Journal: *Journal of Consulting and Clinical Psychology*, June 2004, 72, 535–542.

Related Research: Spoth, R., et al. (1999). Alcohol initiation outcomes of universal family-focused preventive interventions: One and two year follow-ups of a controlled study. *Journal of Studies on Alcohol, 13*(Suppl.), 103–111.

11662

Test Name: ALCOHOL CONSUMPTION INDEX

Purpose: To measure alcohol consumption.

Number of Items: 8

Format: Six-point scales are used. A sample item is presented.

Reliability: Alpha coefficients ranged from .94 to .95 over two follow-up periods.

Author: Neighbors, C., et al.

Article: Targeting misperceptions of descriptive drinking norms: Efficacy of a computer-delivered personalized normative feedback intervention.

Journal: *Journal of Consulting and Clinical Psychology*, June 2004, 72, 434–447.

Related Research: Knee, C. R., & Neighbors, C. (2002). Self-determination, perception of peer pressure, and drinking among college students. *Journal of Applied Social Psychology, 32*, 522–543.

11663

Test Name: ALCOHOL USE SCALES

Purpose: To measure alcohol use, perceived parental norms regarding alcohol use, perceived peer norms regarding alcohol use, and perceived control over drinking.

Number of Items: 14

Format: Various 4-point scales are used. All scales and sample items are presented.

Reliability: Alpha coefficients ranged from .78 to .94.

Validity: Correlations with alcohol use ranged from –.35 to .87.

Author: Kuther, T. L., and Timoshin, A.

Article: A comparison of social cognitive and psychosocial predictors of alcohol use by college students.

Journal: *Journal of College Student Development*, March/April 2003, 44, 143–154.

11664

Test Name: AMSTERDAM CHILD BEHAVIOR CHECKLIST

Purpose: To obtain teacher ratings of behavior problems in elementary school children.

Number of Items: 21

Format: Responses are made on a 4-point scale ranging from *hardly applies* to *applies very well*.

Reliability: Alpha coefficients ranged from .75 to .91.

Author: van den Oord, E. J. C. G., and Rossem, R. V.

Article: Difference in first graders' school adjustment: The role of classroom characteristics and social structure of the group.

Journal: *Journal of School Psychology*, September/October 2002, 40, 371–394.

Related Research: De Jong, P. F. (1995). Validity of the Amsterdam Child Behavior Checklist: A short rating scale for children. *Psychological Reports*, 77, 1139–1144.

11665

Test Name: ANGER/FRUSTRATION SUBSCALE

Purpose: To enable parents and teachers to rate anger.

Number of Items: 24

Format: Responses are made on a 7-point scale ranging from 1 (*extremely untrue*) to 7 (*extremely true*). An example is given.

Reliability: Coefficient alpha was .61.

Author: Eisenberg, N., et al.

Article: The relations of regulation and negative emotionality in Indonesian children's social functioning.

Journal: *Child Development*, November/December 2001, 72, 1747–1763.

Related Research: Goldsmith, H. H., & Rothbart, M. K. (1991). Contemporary instruments for assessing early temperament by questionnaire and in the laboratory. In A. Angleitner & J. Strelan (Eds.), *Explorations in temperament* (pp. 249–272). New York: Plenum.

11666

Test Name: ANGER SCALE

Purpose: To assess anger.

Number of Items: 6

Format: Item anchors range from 1 (*rarely*) to 5 (*almost always*).

Reliability: Coefficient alpha was .83.

Validity: Correlations with other variables ranged from .03 to .20.

Author: Lee, E., and Kim, M.

Article: Exposure to media violence and bullying at school: Mediating influences of anger and contact with delinquent friends.

Journal: *Psychological Reports*, October 2004, *95*, 659–672.

Related Research: Watson, D., & Clark, L. A. (1993). Behavioral disinhibition versus constraint: A dispositional perspective. In D. M. Wegner & J. W. Pennebaker (Eds.), *Handbook of mental control* (pp. 506–526), New York: Prentice-Hall.

11667

Test Name: ANTISOCIAL BEHAVIOR CHECKLIST

Purpose: To assess parental antisocial behavior.

Number of Items: 46

Format: Item scores range from 0 (never) to 3 (often).

Reliability: Test–retest (4 weeks) was .91. Coefficient alpha was .80 (for mothers) and .91 (for fathers).

Author: Bingham, C. R., et al.

Article: Parental ratings of son's behavior problems in high-risk families: Convergent validity, internal structure, and interparent agreement.

Journal: *Journal of Personality Assessment*, June 2003, *80*, 237–251.

Related Research: Zucker, R. A., & Noll, R. B. (1980). *The Antisocial Behavior Checklist*. Unpublished manuscript, Michigan State University, East Lansing.

11668

Test Name: ANTISOCIAL BEHAVIOR SCALE

Purpose: To reflect a latent construct of antisocial behavior.

Number of Items: 16

Format: Includes three factors: stealing episodes, property damage, and confrontational acts. Examples are presented.

Reliability: Alpha coefficients ranged from .64 to .88.

Author: Goodyear, R. K., et al.

Article: Pregnant Latina teenagers: Psychosocial and developmental determinants of how they select and perceive the men who father their children.

Journal: *Journal of Counseling Psychology*, April 2002, *49*, 187–201.

Related Research: Stacy, A. W., & Newcomb, M. D. (1993). Adolescent drug use and adult drug problems in women: Direct, interactive, and mediational effects. *Experimental and Clinical Psychopharmacology*, *7*, 160–173.

11669

Test Name: ANXIETY AND CONDUCT PROBLEMS SCALES

Purpose: To measure children's anxious symptoms and conduct problems by the children's own reports.

Number of Items: 7

Format: A yes–no format is used.

Reliability: Alpha coefficients ranged from .65 to .76.

Author: Hill, N., and Bush, K. R.

Article: Relationships between parenting environment and children's mental health among African American and European American mothers and children.

Journal: *Journal of Marriage and Family*, November 2001, *63*, 954–966.

Related Research: Kusche, C. A., et al. (1988). *Seattle Personality Questionnaire for Young School-Age Children*. Unpublished manuscript, Department of Psychology, University of Washington, Seattle.

11670

Test Name: ARABIC SCALE OF TYPE A BEHAVIOR

Purpose: To measure Type A behavior.

Number of Items: 20

Format: Five-point scales are anchored by 1 (*no*) and 5 (*very much*).

Reliability: Coefficient alpha was .90. Subscale alphas ranged from .52 to .85.

Validity: Correlations with other variables ranged from −.62 to −.02.

Author: Hasan, H. J. T. M.

Article: Relations of the Arabic Type A Behavior Scale with measures of optimism and pessimism.

Journal: *Psychological Reports*, December 2002, *91*, Part 2, 1043–1051.

Related Research: Abdel-Khalek, A. M. (2000). [The problem of the relationship between personality and Type A behavior]. [*The Egyptian Journal of Psychology*], *10*, 9–24. [In Arabic].

11671

Test Name: ARTISTIC AND SCIENTIFIC ACTIVITIES SURVEY

Purpose: To identify the extent of involvement with various artistic and scientific activities during the past 3 years.

Format: Includes eight subscales.

Reliability: Reliability coefficients were .71 and .88.

Validity: Correlations with other variables ranged from −.11 to .52.

Author: Perrine, N. E., and Brodersen, R. M.

Article: Artistic and scientific creative behavior: Openness and the mediating role of interests.

Journal: *The Journal of Creative Behavior*, Fourth Quarter 2005, *39*, 217–236.

Related Research: Guastello, S. J., & Shissler, J. E. (1994). A two-factor taxonomy of creative behavior. *The Journal of Creative Behavior, 28*, 211–221.

11672

Test Name: ASIAN AMERICAN PERCEIVED RACIAL DISCRIMINATION SCALE

Purpose: To identify the extent to which one believes he or she has personally encountered racial discrimination.

Number of Items: 10

Format: Responses are made on a 5-point scale ranging from 1 (*almost never*) to 5 (*almost always*). An example is given.

Reliability: Internal reliability estimate was .84.

Validity: Correlations with other variables ranged from −.20 to .24 (*N* = 147).

Author: Yoo, H. C., and Lee, R. M.

Article: Ethnic identity and approach-type coping as moderators of the racial discrimination/well-being relation in Asian Americans.

Journal: *Journal of Counseling Psychology*, October 2005, *52*, 497–506.

11673

Test Name: ASSOCIATION WITH DELINQUENT PEERS SCALE

Purpose: To measure association with peers involved in delinquent behavior.

Number of Items: 15

Format: Scales range from 1 (*none*) to 5 (*almost all*). Sample items are presented.

Reliability: Alpha coefficients ranged from .56 to .92.

Validity: Correlations with other variables ranged from −.21 to .40.

Author: Roosa, M. W., et al.

Article: Family and child characteristics linking neighborhood context and child externalizing behavior.

Journal: *Journal of Marriage and Family*, May 2005, *67*, 515–529.

11674

Test Name: AUTONOMY-SUPPORTIVE MOTIVATING STYLE SCALE

Purpose: To measure a teacher's autonomy-supportive behavior.

Number of Items: 9

Format: Includes seven instructional behaviors and two impressions of the teacher's style. Items are presented.

Reliability: Coefficient alpha was .83.

Author: Reeve, J., et al.

Article: Testing models of the experience of self-determination in intrinsic motivation and the conundrum of choice.

Journal: *Journal of Educational Psychology*, June 2003, *95*, 375–392.

Related Research: Reeve, J., et al. (1999). Autonomy-supportive teachers: How they teach and motivate students. *Journal of Educational Psychology, 91*, 537–548.

11675

Test Name: BAECKE QUESTIONNAIRE OF HABITUAL ACTIVITY

Purpose: To assess exercise habits.

Number of Items: 16

Format: Includes three sections: Workplace, Sports, and Nonsports Leisure Activities. Responses are

made on a 5-point scale ranging from 1 (*never*) to 5 (*very often*). Examples are given.

Validity: Correlations with other variables ranged from .05 to .29.

Author: Tsorbatzoudis, H.

Article: Evaluation of a school-based intervention programme to promote physical activity: An application of the theory of planned behavior.

Journal: *Perceptual and Motor Skills*, December 2005, *101*, 787–802.

Related Research: Baecke, J., et al. (1982). A short questionnaire for the measurement of habitual activity in epidemiological studies. *American Journal of Clinical Nutrition, 36*, 936–942.

11676

Test Name: BALANCED INVENTORY OF DESIRABLE RESPONDING

Purpose: To provide estimates of desirable responding.

Number of Items: 40

Format: Includes two scales: Self-Deception Scale and Impression Management Scale.

Reliability: Alpha coefficients were .63 and .78.

Validity: Correlations with other variables ranged from −.25 to .23.

Author: Davis, M. H., et al.

Article: Measuring conflict-related behaviors: Reliability and validity evidence regarding the conflict dynamics profile.

Journal: *Educational and Psychological Measurement*, August 2004, *64*, 707–731.

Related Research: Paulhus, D. L. (1988). *Assessing self deception and impression management in self-reports: The Balanced Inventory of Desirable Responding.* Vancouver,

Canada: Department of Psychology, University of British Columbia.

11677

Test Name: BARRATT IMPULSIVENESS SCALE—II-A

Purpose: To measure impulsivity.

Number of Items: 30

Format: Responses are made on a 4-point scale ranging from 1 (*rarely/never*) to 4 (*almost always/always*). All items are presented.

Reliability: Coefficient alpha was .78.

Author: Fossati, A., et al.

Article: Psychometric properties of an adolescent version of the Barrett Impulsiveness Scale—II for a sample of Italian high school students.

Journal: *Perceptual and Motor Skills*, October 2002, *95*, 621–635.

Related Research: Patton, J. H., et al. (1995). Factor structure of the Barratt Impulsiveness Scale. *Journal of Clinical Psychology, 51,* 768–774.

11678

Test Name: BEHAVIOR PROBLEMS INDEX

Purpose: To measure aspects of problem behavior by the focal child.

Number of Items: 28

Format: Includes two subscales: Externalizing and Internalizing. Responses range from 0 (*not true*) to 2 (*often true*). Examples are presented.

Reliability: Reliability coefficients ranged from .80 to .92.

Author: Gennetian, L. A., and Miller, C.

Article: Children and welfare reform: A view from an experimental welfare program in Minnesota.

Journal: *Child Development*, March/April 2002, *73*, 601–620.

Related Research: Peterson, J. L., & Zill, N. (1986). Marital disruption, parent–child relationships, and behavioral problems in children. *Journal of Marriage and the Family, 48,* 295–307.

11679

Test Name: BEHAVIOR PROBLEMS INDEX

Purpose: To provide an inventory of behavior problems.

Number of Items: 26

Format: Responses are made on a 3-point scale ranging from 1 (*not true*) to 3 (*often true*). Sample items are presented.

Reliability: Coefficient alpha was .87.

Author: Yoshikawa, H., et al.

Article: Variation in teenage mothers' experiences of child care and other components of welfare reform: Selection processes and development consequences.

Journal: *Child Development*, January/February 2001, *72*, 299–317.

Related Research: Peterson, J. L., & Zill, N. (1986). Marital disruption, parent–child relationships, and behavioral problems in children. *Journal of Marriage and the Family, 48,* 295–307.

11680

Test Name: BEHAVIOR PROBLEMS INDEX— EXTERNALIZING AND INTERNALIZING SUBSCALES

Purpose: To measure externalizing behaviors and internalizing symptoms.

Number of Items: 23

Format: Includes two subscales: Externalizing Behaviors and Internalizing Symptoms.

Reliability: Alpha coefficients were .80 and .87.

Author: Yoshikawa, H., et al.

Article: Effects of earnings-supplement policies on adult economic and middle-childhood outcomes differ for the "hardest to employ."

Journal: *Child Development*, September/October 2003, *74*, 1500–1521.

Related Research: Peterson, J. L., & Zill, N. (1986). Marital disruption, parent–child relationships, and behavioral problems in children. *Journal of Marriage and the Family, 48,* 295–307.

11681

Test Name: BEHAVIORAL ACTIVATION SYSTEM SCALE

Purpose: To measure behavioral activation.

Number of Items: 13

Format: Includes three subscales: Reward Responsiveness, Drive, and Fun Seeking.

Reliability: Internal consistencies ranged from .66 to .84.

Validity: Correlations with other variables ranged from −.12 to .64.

Author: Meyer, T. D., and Hofmann, B. U.

Article: Assessing the dysregulation of the Behavioral Activation System: The Hypomanic Personality Scale and the BIS-BAS scales.

Journal: *Journal of Personality Assessment*, December 2005, *85*, 318–324.

Related Research: Gray, J. A. (1981). A critique of Eysenck's theory of personality. In H. J.

Eysenck (Ed.), *A model for personality* (pp. 246–276). Berlin: Springer-Verlag.

11682

Test Name: BEHAVIORAL INTENTION SCALE

Purpose: To assess intention to donate money to help fight AIDS or malaria.

Number of Items: 4

Format: Seven-point semantic differential. Sample items are presented.

Reliability: Coefficient alpha was .80.

Author: Chebat, J.-C., et al.

Article: Drama advertisements: Moderating effects of self-relevance on the relations among empathy, information processing, and attitudes.

Journal: *Psychological Reports*, June 2003, *92*, Part 1, 997–1014.

Related Research: Grossbart, S., et al. (1986). Verbal and visual references to competition in comparative advertising. *Journal of Advertising, 15*, 10–23.

11683

Test Name: BEHAVIORAL INTENTIONS SCALE

Purpose: To assess the extent to which people advocate forgiveness in response to misbehavior.

Number of Items: 4

Format: Scales range from 1 (*definitely not*) to 9 (*definitely*). All items are presented.

Reliability: Coefficient alpha was .90.

Validity: Correlations with other variables ranged from −.60 to .58.

Author: Takaku, S.

Article: The effects of apology and perspective taking on interpersonal

forgiveness: A dissonance-attribution model of interpersonal forgiveness.

Journal: *The Journal of Social Psychology*, August 2001, *141*, 494–508.

11684

Test Name: BEHAVIORAL OBSERVATION SCALES— ADAPTED

Purpose: To measure individual team member performance ratings.

Number of Items: 47

Format: Responses are made on a 7-point scale ranging from 1 (*almost never*) to 7 (*very frequently*).

Reliability: Alpha coefficients were .72 and .79.

Validity: Correlations with other variables ranged from −.07 to .08.

Author: Taggar, S., and Neubert, M.

Article: The impact of poor performers on team outcomes: An empirical examination of attribution theory.

Journal: *Personnel Psychology*, Winter 2004, *57*, 935–968.

Related Research: Taggar, S., et al. (1999). Leadership emergence in autonomous work teams: Antecedents and outcomes. *Personnel Psychology, 52*, 899–926.

11685

Test Name: BLAME FOR CHEATING SCALE

Purpose: To identify students' assignment of blame for cheating within the hypothetical classroom.

Number of Items: 4

Format: Includes two categories: fault or blame assigned to the student and fault or blame assigned to the teacher. Responses are made on 5-point scales.

Reliability: Assigned to the student: two items, $r = .72$. Assigned to the teacher: two items, $r = .87$.

Validity: Correlations with other variables ranged from −.70 to .69.

Author: Murdock, T. B.

Article: Effects of classroom context variables on high school students' judgments of the acceptability and likelihood of cheating.

Journal: *Journal of Educational Psychology*, December 2004, *96*, 765–777.

11686

Test Name: BOYHOOD GENDER CONFORMITY SCALE

Purpose: To measure gender atypicality.

Number of Items: 8

Format: Scales range from 0 (*never*) to 6 (*always*).

Reliability: Alpha coefficients ranged from .77 to .85.

Author: D'Augelli, A. R., et al.

Article: Parents' awareness of lesbian, gay, and bisexual youths' sexual orientation.

Journal: *Journal of Marriage and Family*, May 2005, *67*, 474–482.

Related Research: Hockenberry, S. L., & Billingham, R. E. (1987). Sexual orientation and boyhood gender conformity: Development of the Boyhood Gender Conformity Scale (BGCS). *Archives of Sexual Behavior, 16*, 475–492.

11687

Test Name: BULLYING AT SCHOOL SCALE

Purpose: To measure the amount of bullying at school.

Number of Items: 11

Format: Item anchors range from *one or two times* to *above 5 times*. All items are presented.

Reliability: Coefficient alpha was .68.

Validity: Correlations with other variables ranged from .16 to .30.

Author: Lee, E., and Kim, M.

Article: Exposure to media violence and bullying at school: Mediating influences of anger and contact with delinquent friends.

Journal: *Psychological Reports*, October 2004, *95*, 659–672.

Related Research: Lee, C. J., & Kwak, K. (2000). [*Prevalence and characteristics of bullying at school*]. Seoul, Korea. [in Korean]

11688

Test Name: BUSS–PERRY AGGRESSION QUESTIONNAIRE

Purpose: To measure physical aggression, verbal aggression, anger, and hostility.

Number of Items: 29

Format: Five-point scales range from *extremely uncharacteristic of me* to *extremely characteristic of me*.

Reliability: Alpha coefficients ranged from .72 to .85 across subscales.

Validity: Correlations with several behavior scales ranged from –.04 to .53.

Author: Wu, K. D., and Clark, L. A.

Article: Relations between personality traits and self-reports of daily behavior.

Journal: *Journal of Research in Personality*, August 2003, *37*, 231–256.

Related Research: Buss, A. H., & Perry, M. (1992). The Aggression Questionnaire. *Journal of Personality and Social Psychology*, *63*, 452–459.

11689

Test Name: BUSS–PERRY AGGRESSION QUESTIONNAIRE—ADAPTED

Purpose: To assess aggressiveness

Number of Items: 29

Format: Includes four scales: Physical Aggression, Verbal Aggression, Hostility, and Anger. Responses are made on a 5-point scale ranging from 1 (*completely false*) to 5 (*completely true*).

Reliability: Test–retest correlation ranged from .57 to .81

Author: Reynes, E., and Lorant, J.

Article: Effect of traditional judo training on aggressiveness among young boys.

Journal: *Perceptual and Motor Skills*, February 2002, *94*, 21–25.

Related Research: Buss, A. H., & Perry, M. (1992). The Aggression Questionnaire. *Journal of Personality and Social Psychology*, *63*, 452–459.

11690

Test Name: CAGE QUESTIONNAIRE

Purpose: To provide an alcohol screening instrument.

Number of Items: 4

Format: Responses are either 1 (*yes*) or 0 (*no*). All items are presented.

Reliability: Alpha coefficients ranged from .52 to .90 ($n = 22$). Test–retest (7 days) reliability coefficients were .80 and .95. Test–retest (24–48 hours) reliability coefficient was .67.

Author: Shields, A. L., and Caruso, J. C.

Article: A reliability induction and reliability generalization study of the CAGE Questionnaire.

Journal: *Educational and Psychological Measurement*, April 2004, *64*, 254–270.

Related Research: Ewing, J. A. (1984). Detecting alcoholism: The CAGE Questionnaire. *Journal of the American Medical Association*, *252*, 1905–1907.

11691

Test Name: CALMNESS DUE TO PREPARATION

Purpose: To assess calmness due to preparation.

Number of Items: 2

Format: Both are presented. Responses are made on a 7-point scale ranging from 1 (*strongly disagree*) to 7 (*strongly agree*).

Reliability: Alpha coefficients were .84 and .87.

Validity: Correlations with other variables ranged from –.31 to .28.

Author: McGregor, H. A., and Elliot, A. J.

Article: Achievement goals as predictors of achievement-relevant processes prior to task engagement.

Journal: *Journal of Educational Psychology*, June 2002, *94*, 381–395.

11692

Test Name: CAREER-RELATED HELP-SEEKING SCALE

Purpose: To measure career help-seeking behavior.

Number of Items: 4

Format: Scales range from 1 (*strongly disagree*) to 5 (*strongly agree*). All items are presented.

Reliability: Coefficient alpha was .82.

Author: Perrone, K. M., et al.

Article: Gender and ethnic differences in career goal attainment.

Journal: *The Career Development Quarterly*, December 2001, *50*, 168–178.

Related Research: Feij, J. A., et al. (1995). The development of career enhancing strategies and content innovation: A longitudinal study of new workers. *Journal of Vocational Behavior, 46,* 231–256.

11693

Test Name: CHEATING SCALE

Purpose: To measure academic dishonesty on examinations and written assignments.

Number of Items: 9

Format: A yes–no format is used. All items are presented with a scoring procedure.

Reliability: Coefficient alpha was .79.

Validity: Correlations with other variables ranged from –.52 to .38.

Author: Bichler, G., and Tibbetts, S. G.

Article: Conditional covariation of binge drinking with predictors of college students' cheating.

Journal: *Psychological Reports,* December 2003, *93,* Part 1, 735–749.

11694

Test Name: CHEATING SCALE

Purpose: To assess the frequency of four types of academic cheating.

Number of Items: 4

Format: Responses are made on a 5-point response scale ranging from *never* to *very often.* All items are presented.

Reliability: Coefficient alpha was .75.

Validity: Correlations with other variables ranged from –.43 to .30.

Author: Finn, K. V., and Frone, M. R.

Article: Academic performance and cheating: Moderating role of school identification and self-efficacy.

Journal: *The Journal of Educational Research,* January/February 2004, *97,* 115–122.

11695

Test Name: CHILD ADAPTIVE BEHAVIOR INVENTORY— SHORT FORM

Purpose: To capture subtle behavioral problems in children related to emotional and cognitive functioning.

Number of Items: 21

Format: Includes three subscales: Poor Emotional Control, Social Isolation, and Intellectual Engagement.

Reliability: Alpha coefficients ranged from .82 to .89.

Author: Kertes, D. A., and Gunnar, M. R.

Article: Evening activities as a potential confound in research on the adrenocortical system in children.

Journal: *Child Development,* January/February 2004, *75,* 193–204.

Related Research: Groterant, H. D., & McRoy, R. G. (1997). The Minnesota/Texas Adoption Research Project: Implications of openness in adoption for development and relationships. *Applied Developmental Science, 1,* 168–186. Groterant, H. D., & van Dolmen, M. (2000). *Child Adaptive Behavior Inventory— Short Form* (Report for the International Adoption Project). Minneapolis: University of Minnesota.

11696

Test Name: CHILD AGGRESSIVE BEHAVIOR SCALE.

Purpose: To assess the frequency of child aggressive behavior by teacher ratings.

Number of Items: 12

Format: Scales range from 1 (*never*) to 5 (*almost always*). Sample items are described.

Reliability: Alpha coefficients were .96 (girls) and .97 (boys).

Author: Sim, T. N., and Ong, L. P.

Article: Parent physical punishment and child aggression in a Singapore Chinese preschool sample.

Journal: *Journal of Marriage and Family,* February 2005, *67,* 85–99.

Related Research: Dodge, K. A., & Coie, J. D. (1987). Social information processing factors in reactive and proactive aggression in children's peer groups. *Journal of Personality and Social Psychology, 53,* 1146–1158.

11697

Test Name: CHILD BEHAVIOR CHECKLIST

Purpose: To measure internality and externality.

Number of Items: 102

Format: Checklist format. Item descriptions are presented.

Reliability: Internal consistency coefficients ranged from .59 to .89. Test–retest reliabilities (7 days) ranged from .45 to .83.

Author: Crofoot, T. L., et al.

Article: Mental health screening results for Native American and Euro-American youth in Oregon juvenile justice settings.

Journal: *Psychological Reports,* June 2003, *92,* Part 2, 1053–1060.

Related Research: Achenbach, T. M. (1991). *Manual for youth self-report and 1991 profile.* Burlington: Department of Psychiatry, University of Vermont.

11698

Test Name: CHILD BEHAVIOR CHECKLIST

Purpose: To measure parents' perceptions of social, emotional, and behavioral symptoms in their adolescents.

Number of Items: 122

Format: Rating scales are anchored by 1 (*not true*) and 3 (*very true or often true*). Items are described.

Reliability: Alpha coefficients ranged from .87 (internalizing symptoms) and .82 (externalizing symptoms).

Validity: Correlations with other variables ranged from –.05 to .50.

Author: Razzino, B., et al.

Article: Central American adolescent acculturation and parental distress: Relationship to ratings of adolescent behavior problems.

Journal: *Psychological Reports*, June 2003, 92, Part 2, 1255–1267.

Related Research: Achenbach, T. M. (1991). *Manual for the Child Behavior Checklist/4-18 and 1991 Profile*. Burlington: Department of Psychiatry, University of Vermont.

11699

Test Name: CHILD BEHAVIOR INVENTORY

Purpose: To measure descriptive behaviors by children and adolescents.

Number of Items: 36

Format: Frequency scales range from 1 (*never*) to 7 (*always*). Problem scales range from 1 (*no*) to 2 (*yes*). All items are presented.

Reliability: Coefficient alpha was .98. Test–retest reliability was .86 (3 weeks).

Author: Weis, R., et al.

Article: Factor structure and discriminative validity of the Eyberg Childhood Behavior Inventory with young children.

Journal: *Journal of Psychopathology and Behavioral Assessment*, December 2005, 27, 269–278.

Related Research: Eyberg, S. M., & Ross, A. W. (1978). Assessment of child behavior problems: The validation of a new inventory. *Journal of Clinical Child Psychology*, 7, 113–116.

11700

Test Name: CHILD BEHAVIOR QUESTIONNAIRE

Purpose: To assess child behaviors and emotions by parent report.

Number of Items: 194

Format: Scales range from 1 (*extremely untrue*) to 7 (*extremely true*).

Reliability: Alpha coefficients ranged from .56 to .82.

Author: Hayden, E. P., et al.

Article: Parent reports and laboratory assessments of child temperament: A comparison of their associations with risk for depression and externalizing disorders.

Journal: *Journal of Psychopathology and Behavioral Assessment*, June 2005, 27, 89–100.

Related Research: Rothbart, M. K., et al. (2001). Investigations of temperament at three to seven years: The Child Behavior Questionnaire (CBQ). *Child Development*, 72, 1394–1408.

11701

Test Name: CHILD BEHAVIOR QUESTIONNAIRE—3 SUBSCALES

Purpose: To enable caregiving parents and teachers to rate children's temperamental emotionality.

Number of Items: 39 (parents) and 29 (teachers).

Format: Includes three subscales: Anger/Frustration, Sadness, and Fear. Responses are made on a 7-point scale ranging from 1 (*extremely untrue*) to 7 (*extremely true*).

Reliability: Alpha coefficients ranged from .73 to .91.

Author: Eisenberg, N., et al.

Article: The relations of regulation and emotionality to children's externalizing and internalizing problem behavior.

Journal: *Child Development*, July/August 2001, 72, 1112–1134.

Related Research: Rothbart, M. K., & Bates, J. E. (1998). Temperament. In N. Eisenberg (Ed.) & W. Damon (Series Ed.), *Handbook of child psychology: Vol. 3. Social, emotional, and personality development* (pp. 105–176). New York: Wiley.

11702

Test Name: CHILD BEHAVIOR QUESTIONNAIRE—4 SUBSCALES

Purpose: To enable teachers and parents to rate attentional and behavioral regulations.

Number of Items: 46 (parents) and 44 (teachers).

Format: Includes attentional and behavioral regulation subscales. Responses are made on a 7-point scale ranging from 1 (*extremely untrue*) to 7 (*extremely true*).

Reliability: Alpha coefficients ranged from .74 to .88.

Author: Eisenberg, N., et al.

Article: The relations of regulation and emotionality to children's externalizing and internalizing problem behavior.

Journal: *Child Development*, July/August 2001, 72, 1112–1134.

Related Research: Ahadi, S. A., & Rothbart, M. K. (1994). Temperament, development, and the Big Five. In C. F. Halverson Jr. et al. (Eds.), *The developing structure of temperament and personality from infancy to adulthood* (pp. 189–207). Hillsdale, NJ: Erlbaum.

11703

Test Name: CHILD BEHAVIOR RATING SCALE

Purpose: To assess child behaviors.

Number of Items: 84

Format: Contains both desirable and undesirable child behaviors. Responses are made in a 7-point scale ranging from 1 (*never*) to 7 (*always*).

Reliability: Reliability for the aggression scale was .90 (mothers) and .94 (fathers).

Author: Bingham, C. R., et al.

Article: Parental ratings of son's behavior problems in high-risk families: Convergent validity, internal structure, and interparent agreement.

Journal: *Journal of Personality Assessment*, June 2003, *80*, 237–251.

Related Research: Maguin, E., et al. (1994). The path to alcohol problems through conduct problems: A family-based approach to very early intervention with risk. *Journal of Research on Adolescence, 4*, 249–269.

11704

Test Name: CHILD ROUTINES INVENTORY

Purpose: To measure commonly occurring routines in school-age children in terms of their frequency and importance.

Number of Items: 28

Format: Frequency scales range from 0 (*almost never*) to 4 (*nearly always*).

Reliability: Alpha coefficients ranged from .79 to .83 across subscales. Total alpha was .90. Test–retest reliabilities ranged from .75 to .86.

Validity: Correlations with other variables ranged from −.35 to .54.

Author: Sytsma, S. E., et al.

Article: Development and initial validation of the Child Routines Inventory.

Journal: *Journal of Psychopathology and Behavioral Assessment*, December 2001, *23*, 241–251.

11705

Test Name: CHILDHOOD SEXUAL ABUSE SCALE

Purpose: To measure a history of childhood sexual abuse in family of origin.

Number of Items: 8

Format: A yes–no format is used. Sample items are presented.

Reliability: Alpha coefficients ranged from .89 to .91.

Author: Hall, G. C. N., et al.

Article: Ethnicity, culture, and sexual aggression: Risk and protective factors.

Journal: *Journal of Consulting and Clinical Psychology*, October 2005, *73*, 830–840.

Related Research: Malamuth, N. M., et al. (1995). Using the confluence model of sexual aggression to predict men's conflict with women: A 10-year follow-up study. *Journal of Personality and Social Psychology, 69*, 353–369.

11706

Test Name: CHILDHOOD TRAUMA QUESTIONNAIRE

Purpose: To measure childhood sexual and physical–emotional abuse.

Number of Items: 10

Format: Item responses range from 1 (*never true*) to 5 (*very often true*). Sample items are presented.

Reliability: Alpha coefficients ranged from .83 to .93 across subscales. Test–retest reliabilities ranged from .83 to .86.

Validity: Correlations with other variables ranged from −.18 to .33.

Author: Hobfoll, S. E., et al.

Article: The impact of perceived child physical and sexual abuse history on Native American women's psychological well-being and AIDS risk.

Journal: *Journal of Consulting and Clinical Psychology*, February 2002, *70*, 252–257.

Related Research: Bernstein, D. P., et al. (1994). Internal reliability and validity of a new retrospective measure of child abuse and neglect. *American Journal of Psychiatry, 151*, 1132–1136.

11707

Test Name: CHILDHOOD TRAUMA QUESTIONNAIRE

Purpose: To measure the extent of physical, psychological, and sexual abuse and emotional and physical neglect by retrospective self-reports of adolescents.

Number of Items: 35

Format: Scales range from 1 (*never true*) to 5 (*very often true*).

Reliability: Alpha coefficients ranged from .71 to .93 across subscales.

Author: Wolfe, D. A., et al.

Article: Dating violence prevention with at-risk youth: A controlled outcome evaluation.

Journal: *Journal of Consulting and Clinical Psychology*, April 2003, *71*, 279–291.

Related Research: Bernstein, D. P., et al. (1997). Validity of the

Childhood Trauma Questionnaire in an adolescent psychiatric population. *Journal of the American Academy of Child and Adolescent Psychiatry, 36,* 340–348.

11708

Test Name: CHILDREN'S BEHAVIOR SCALE FOR BEHAVIOR RELATED TO OTITIS MEDIA WITH EFFUSION

Purpose: To measure effusion-specific behavior in young children by parental report.

Number of Items: 30 (for 12–24-month-old children). 33 (for 24–48-month-old children).

Format: All items are presented. Scales range from 1 (*do not agree at all*) to 5 (*totally agree*).

Reliability: Alpha coefficients ranged from .52 to .83 across subscales.

Validity: Correlations between factors ranged from .03 to .42.

Author: Timmerman, A., et al.

Article: First psychometric evaluation of a disease-specific questionnaire for children's behavior related to otitis media with effusion.

Journal: *Psychological Reports,* December 2005, *97,* 819–831.

11709

Test Name: CHILDREN'S HOSTILITY INVENTORY

Purpose: To measure children's exhibited and internally experienced hostility.

Number of Items: 26

Format: A true–false format is used.

Reliability: Coefficient alpha was .66.

Validity: Correlations with other variables ranged from −.07 to .41.

Author: Gordis, E. B., et al.

Article: Parents' hostility in dyadic marital and triadic family settings and children's behavior problems.

Journal: *Journal of Consulting and Clinical Psychology,* August 2001, *69,* 727–734.

Related Research: Kazdin, A. E., et al. (1987). Children's Hostility Inventory: Measurement of aggression and hostility in psychiatric inpatient children. *Journal of Clinical Child Psychology, 16,* 320–328.

11710

Test Name: CHILDREN'S MEMORY MODEL-BASED EXPECTANCY QUESTIONNAIRE

Purpose: To distinguish between heavier and lighter drinking children and adults.

Number of Items: 41

Format: Four-point Likert-type scales are used. A sample item is presented.

Reliability: Alpha coefficients ranged from .69 to .95 across samples.

Author: Cruz, I. Y., and Dunn, M. E.

Article: Lowering risk for early alcohol use by challenging alcohol expectancies in elementary school children.

Journal: *Journal of Consulting and Clinical Psychology,* June 2003, *71,* 493–503.

Related Research: Dunn, M. E., et al. (2000). Changes in activation of alcohol expectancies in memory as related to changes in alcohol use after participation in an expectancy challenge program. *Experimental and Clinical Psychopharmacology, 8,* 566–575.

11711

Test Name: CHILDREN'S OVERT REACTIVITY TO

INTERPERSONAL CONFLICT MEASURE

Purpose: To enable parents to report on overt signs of children's emotional and behavioral activity.

Number of Items: 12

Format: Includes three scales: Overt Distress, Behavioral Dysregulation, and Behavioral Involvement.

Reliability: Alpha coefficients ranged from .64 to .78.

Author: Davies, P. T., et al.

Article: Assessing children's emotional security in the interpersonal relationship: The security in the Interparental Subsystem Scales.

Journal: *Child Development,* March/April 2002, *73,* 544–562.

Related Research: Garcia-O'Hearn, H., et al. (1997). Mothers' and fathers' reports of children's reaction to naturalistic marital conflict. *Journal of the American Academy of Child Psychiatry, 36,* 1366–1373.

11712

Test Name: CHRONIC SELF-DESTRUCTIVENESS SCALE

Purpose: To assess chronic self-destructive attitudes and behavior.

Number of Items: 52

Format: Rating scales range from 1 (*I strongly agree*) to 5 (*I strongly disagree*).

Reliability: Test–retest reliabilities ranged from .90 to .98 (1 month). Alpha coefficients ranged from .73 to .97.

Validity: Correlations with other variables ranged from −.28 to .41.

Author: Kelly, D. B., et al.

Article: Chronic self-destructiveness, hopelessness, and risk-taking in college students.

Journal: *Psychological Reports,* June 2005, *9,* Part 1, 620–624.

Related Research: Kelley, K., et al. (1985). Chronic self-destructiveness: Conceptualization, measurement, and initial validation of the construct. *Motivation and Emotion, 9,* 135–151.

11713

Test Name: CITIZENSHIP BEHAVIORS SCALE

Purpose: To assess organizational citizenship behavior.

Number of Items: 12

Reliability: Coefficient alpha was .88.

Validity: Correlations with other variables ranged from .01 to .29.

Author: Cable, D. M., and DeRue, D. S.

Article: The convergent and discriminant validity of subjective fit perceptions.

Journal: *Journal of Applied Psychology,* October 2002, *87,* 875–884.

Related Research: Van Dyne, L., & LePine, J. A. (1998). Helping and voice extra-role behaviors: Evidence of construct and predictive validity. *Academy of Management Journal, 41,* 108–119.

11714

Test Name: CLASSROOM BEHAVIOR INVENTORY— RESEARCH VERSION

Purpose: To enable teachers to rate the child's social and cognitive skills.

Number of Items: 42

Format: Includes three factors: cognitive/attention, sociability, and problem behaviors.

Reliability: Alpha coefficients ranged from .65 to .84.

Validity: Correlations with other variables ranged from –.42 to .55.

Author: Peisner-Feinberg, E. S., et al.

Article: The relation of preschool child-care quality to children's cognitive and social development trajectories through second grade.

Journal: *Child Development,* September/October 2001, *72,* 1534–1553.

Related Research: Schaefer, E. S., et al. (1978). *Classroom Behavior Inventory.* Unpublished manuscript, University of North Carolina at Chapel Hill.

11715

Test Name: CLIENT PROBLEM PROFILE

Purpose: To measure drug use, family problems, HIV/AIDS risk, and criminal involvement.

Number of Items: 14

Format: All items are presented.

Reliability: Coefficient alpha was .56.

Validity: Correlations with other variables ranged from –.12 to .49.

Author: Joe, G. W., et al.

Article: Development and validation of a client problem profile and index for drug treatment.

Journal: *Psychological Reports,* August 2004, *95,* 215–234.

11716

Test Name: COALITION SUBSCALE—REVISED

Purpose: To measure use of coalitions as a means of influence.

Number of Items: 2

Format: Responses are made on a 5-point scale ranging from 1 (*never do it*) to 5 (*nearly always do it*). Both items are presented.

Reliability: Coefficient alpha was .83 (*N* = 221).

Validity: Correlation with other variables ranged from .10 to .43 (*N* = 221).

Author: Andrews, M. C., and Kacmar, K. M.

Article: Impression management by association: Construction and validation of a scale.

Journal: *Journal of Vocational Behavior,* February 2001, *58,* 142–161.

Related Research: Schriescheim, C. A., & Hinkin, T. R. (1990). Influence tactics used by subordinates: A theoretical analysis and refinement of the Kipnis, Schmidt, and Wilkinson subscale. *Journal of Applied Psychology, 75,* 246–257.

11717

Test Name: COERCIVE SEXUALITY SCALE

Purpose: To assess men's self-reported sexually coercive behaviors.

Number of Items: 19

Format: Responses are made on a 4-point scale ranging from 1 (*never*) to 4 (*often*). An example is given.

Reliability: Internal consistency estimates were .84 and .96.

Author: Hill, M. S., & Fischer, A. R.

Article: Does entitlement mediate the link between masculinity and rape-related variables?

Journal: *Journal of Counseling Psychology,* January 2001, *48,* 39–50.

Related Research: Rapaport, K., & Burkhart, B. R. (1984). Personality and attitudinal characteristics of sexually coercive college males. *Journal of Abnormal Psychology, 93,* 216–221.

11718

Test Name: COMPASS OF SHAME SCALE

Purpose: To measure withdrawal, attack self, avoidance, and attack other.

Number of Items: 30

Format: Subjects use 5-point scales to respond to scenarios. Two sample items are presented.

Reliability: Alpha coefficients ranged from .57 to .87. Test–retest reliabilities ranged from .75 to .85.

Validity: Correlations with other variables ranged from −.55 to .65.

Author: Yelsma, P., et al.

Article: Shame-focused coping styles and their associations with self-esteem.

Journal: *Psychological Reports,* June 2002, *90,* Part 2, 1179–1189.

Related Research: Elison, J. (2000). *The Compass of Shame Scale: An assessment of shame-focused coping* [Master's thesis]. Ann Arbor, MI: Proquest.

11719

Test Name: COMPLEX PARTIAL EPILEPTIC-LIKE SIGNS SCALE

Purpose: To assess frequency of signs of complex partial epilepsy.

Number of Items: 16

Format: A yes–no format is used.

Reliability: Internal consistency was about .70. Stability coefficients ranged from .70 to .90.

Validity: Correlations with other variables ranged from −.16 to .41.

Author: MacDonald, D. A., and Holland, D.

Article: Spirituality and complex partial epileptic-like signs.

Journal: *Psychological Reports,* December 2002, *91,* Part 1, 785–792.

Related Research: Persinger, M. A., & Makerec, K. (1993). Complex partial epileptic signs as a continuum from normals to epileptics: Normative data and clinical populations. *Journal of Clinical Psychology, 49,* 33–45.

11720

Test Name: COMPULSIVE BUYING SCALE

Purpose: To measure compulsive buying.

Number of Items: 11

Format: All items are presented.

Reliability: Alpha was .86.

Validity: Correlations with other variables ranged from −.14 to .13.

Author: Roberts, J. A., and Tanner, J. F., Jr.

Article: Compulsive buying and sexual attitudes, intentions and activity: An extension of Roberts and Tanner.

Journal: *Psychological Reports,* June 2002, *90,* Part 2, 1259–1260.

11721

Test Name: COMPUTER PLAYFULNESS SCALE

Purpose: To assess the playfulness with which individuals interact with computers.

Number of Items: 7

Reliability: Coefficient alpha was .88.

Validity: Correlations with other variables ranged from −.34 to .61.

Author: Potosky, D., and Bobko, P.

Article: Selection testing via the internet: Practical considerations and exploratory empirical findings.

Journal: *Personnel Psychology,* Winter 2004, *57,* 1003–1034.

Related Research: Webster, J., & Martocchio, J. J. (June, 1992). Microcomputer playfulness: Development of a measure with workplace implications. *MIS Quarterly,* 201–226.

11722

Test Name: COMPUTER USE SCALE

Purpose: To measure students' computer use.

Number of Items: 3

Format: Response categories range from 1 (*never*) to 4 (*a lot*).

Reliability: Coefficient alpha was .74.

Validity: Correlations with other variables ranged from −.17 to .21.

Author: Higgins, G. E., and Makin, D. A.

Article: Self-control, deviant peers, and software piracy.

Journal: *Psychological Reports,* December 2004, *95,* Part 1, 921–931.

Related Research: Igbaria, M., & Chakrabarti, A. (1990). Computer technology and attitudes towards microcomputer use. *Behaviour and Information Technology, 9,* 229–241.

11723

Test Name: CONDUCT PROBLEMS SCALE

Purpose: To measure the frequency of students' participation in relatively common problem behaviors.

Number of Items: 27

Format: Responses are made on a 5-point scale ranging from 0 (*zero times*) to 4 (*five or more times*).

Reliability: Coefficient alpha was .79.

Validity: Correlations with other variables ranged from −.21 to .39.

Author: Pearce, M. J., et al.

Article: The protective effects of religiousness and parent involvement on the development of conduct problems among youth exposed to violence.

Journal: *Child Development*, November/December 2003, *74*, 1682–1696.

11724

Test Name: CONFLICT IN ADOLESCENT DATING RELATIONSHIPS INVENTORY

Purpose: To measure the abusive strategies among teens by their dating partners and by themselves.

Number of Items: 70

Format: Scales range from *never* to *often*. Sample items are presented.

Reliability: Coefficient alpha was .83. Subscale alphas ranged from .66 to .83. Test–retest reliability was .68 (2 weeks).

Validity: Correlations with other variables ranged from –.19 to .38.

Author: Wolfe, D. A., et al.

Article: Dating violence prevention with at-risk youth: A controlled outcome evaluation.

Journal: *Journal of Consulting and Clinical Psychology*, April 2003, *71*, 279–291.

Related Research: Wolfe, D. A., et al. (2001). Development and validation of the conflict in adolescent dating relationships inventory. *Psychological Assessment, 13,* 277–293.

11725

Test Name: CONFLICT RESPONSE QUESTIONNAIRE

Purpose: To assess direct aggression and indirect aggression.

Number of Items: 28

Format: Response categories range from 1 (*never or almost never*) to 5

(*often or very often*). Sample items are presented.

Reliability: Alpha coefficients ranged from .91 to .92.

Author: Gregoski, M., et al.

Article: Measuring direct and indirect aggression: Is there a response bias?

Journal: *Psychological Reports*, October 2005, *97*, 563–566.

Related Research: Green, L., et al. (1996). How do friendship, indirect, and direct aggression relate? *Aggressive Behavior, 22,* 81–86.

11726

Test Name: CONFLICT TACTICS SCALE

Purpose: To index strategies couples use during conflict.

Number of Items: 18

Format: Responses are made on a 7-point scale ranging from 0 (*never*) to 6 (*more than 20 times*).

Reliability: Alpha coefficients ranged from .35 to .79.

Author: Cummings, E. M., et al.

Article: Children's responses to everyday marital conflict tactics in the home.

Journal: *Child Development*, November/December 2003, *74*, 1918–1929.

Related Research: Straus, M. A. (1979). Measuring intrafamily conflict and violence: The Conflict Tactics (CT) Scales. *Journal of Marriage and the Family, 41,* 75–88.

11727

Test Name: CONFLICT TACTICS SCALE—REVISED

Purpose: To provide an overall current measure of partner aggression.

Number of Items: 15

Format: Includes psychological and physical aggression.

Reliability: Alpha coefficients ranged from .62 to .82.

Author: Linares, L. O., et al.

Article: A mediational model for the impact of exposure to community violence on early child behavior problems.

Journal: *Child Development*, March/April 2001, *72*, 639–652.

Related Research: Straus, M. A. (1990). The Conflict Tactics Scale and its critics: An evaluation and new data on validity and reliability. In M. A. Straus & R. J. Gelles (Eds.), *Physical violence in American families* (pp. 49–74). New Brunswick, NJ: Transaction.

11728

Test Name: CONSCIENTIOUS AND ALTRUISTIC ORGANIZATIONAL CITIZENSHIP BEHAVIORS SCALES

Purpose: To measure conscientious and altruistic organizational citizenship behavior.

Number of Items: 10

Format: Includes two dimensions of organizational citizenship behavior: Conscientious and Altruistic. Sample items are presented.

Reliability: Alpha coefficients ranged from .73 to .83.

Validity: Correlations with other variables ranged from .18 to .38.

Author: Haworth, C. L., and Levy, P. E.

Article: The importance of instrumentality beliefs in the prediction of organizational citizenship behaviors.

Journal: *Journal of Vocational Behavior*, August 2001, *59*, 64–75.

Related Research: Podsakoff, P. M., et al. (1990). Transformational leader behaviors and their effects on followers' trust in leader, satisfaction, and organizational citizenship behaviors. *Leadership Quarterly, 1*, 107–142.

11729

Test Name: CONSEQUENCES OF INTOXICATION QUESTIONNAIRE

Purpose: To measure the number of times a person has experienced seven consequences of being intoxicated in the past month.

Number of Items: 7

Format: Responses range from 0 to 99 times. All items are presented.

Reliability: Coefficient alpha was .79. Test–retest reliability was .79.

Author: Fromme, K., and Corbin, W.

Article: Prevention of heavy drinking and associated negative consequences among mandated and voluntary college students.

Journal: *Journal of Consulting and Clinical Psychology*, December 2004, *72*, 1038–1049.

Related Research: D'Amico, E. J., & Fromme, K. (2000). Implementation of the risk skills training program: A brief intervention targeting adolescent participation in risk behaviors. *Cognitive and Behavioral Practice, 7*, 101–117.

11730

Test Name: CONTACT WITH DELINQUENT FRIENDS SCALE

Purpose: To measure contact with delinquent friends.

Number of Items: 12

Format: Item responses range from *none* to *above three-fourths*. All items are presented.

Reliability: Coefficient alpha was .85.

Validity: Correlations with other variables ranged from .03 to .30.

Author: Lee, E., and Kim, M.

Article: Exposure to media violence and bullying at school: Mediating influences of anger and contact with delinquent friends.

Journal: *Psychological Reports*, October 2004, *95*, 659–672.

Related Research: Kim, B. H. (1999). [A study on the school violence and its causes]. Unpublished master's thesis, Catholic University of Daegu, Korea. [in Korean]

11731

Test Name: CONTEXTUAL PERFORMANCE BEHAVIORS SCALE

Purpose: To rate coworker conceptual performance behaviors.

Number of Items: 16

Format: Responses are made on a 5-point scale ranging from 1 (*not at all likely*) to 5 (*extremely likely*). Includes the dimensions of Persisting With Extra Effort, Volunteering to Carry Out Extra Activities, Helping/Cooperating With Others, Following Rules/Procedures, and Endorsing Organizational Objectives.

Reliability: Coefficient alpha was .93.

Validity: Correlations with other variables ranged from −.42 to .28.

Author: Lauver, K. L., and Kristof-Brown, A.

Article: Distinguishing between employees' perceptions of person–job and person–organization fit.

Journal: *Journal of Vocational Behavior*, December 2001, *59*, 454–470.

Related Research: Motowidlo, S. J., & Van Scotter, J. R. (1994). Evidence that task performance should be distinguished from contextual performance. *Journal of Applied Psychology, 79*, 475–480.

11732

Test Name: COOK–MEDLEY HOSTILITY SCALE

Purpose: To measure hostility.

Number of Items: 50

Format: A true–false format is used.

Reliability: Test–retest reliability was .84.

Validity: Correlations with other variables ranged from −.23 to −.15.

Author: Davidson, K. W., et al.

Article: The relation between defense use and adaptive behavior.

Journal: *Journal of Research in Personality*, April 2004, *38*, 85–104.

Related Research: Barefoot, J. C., et al. (1989). The Cook–Medley Hostility Scale: Item content and the ability to predict survival. *Psychosomatic Medicine, 5*, 146–157.

11733

Test Name: COPING BEHAVIOR VIA VENTING SCALE

Purpose: To assess children's coping behavior when faced with emotionally difficult situations with peers.

Number of Items: 4

Format: Includes instrumental aggression, emotional intervention, emotional outbursts, and emotional aggression. Responses are made on a 7-point scale ranging from 1 (*never*) to 7 (*usually*).

Reliability: Coefficient alpha was .67.

Author: Denham, S. A., et al.

Article: Preschool emotional competence: Pathway to social competence?

Journal: *Child Development,* January/February 2003, *74,* 238–256.

Related Research: Eisenberg, N., et al. (1994). The relation of emotionality and regulation to preschoolers' anger-related reactions. *Child Development, 65,* 1352–1366.

11734

Test Name: CORE ALCOHOL AND DRUG SURVEY

Purpose: To assess negative consequences of substance abuse in college students.

Number of Items: 11

Format: Frequency scales range from 1 (*never*) to 6 (*10 or more times*). All items are presented.

Reliability: Alpha coefficients ranged from .77 to .79 across two subscales.

Validity: Correlations with other variables ranged from .23 to .77.

Author: Martens, M. P., et al.

Article: Measuring negative consequences of college student substance use: A psychometric evaluation of the Core Alcohol and Drug Survey.

Journal: *Measurement and Evaluation in Counseling and Development,* October 2005, *38,* 164–176.

Related Research: Presley, C. A., et al. (1998). *Core Alcohol and Drug Survey: Users manual* (6th ed.). Carbondale: Southern Illinois University at Carbondale.

11735

Test Name: COUNTERPRODUCTIVE WORK BEHAVIOR CHECKLIST

Purpose: To assess counterproductive work behavior.

Number of Items: 64

Format: Includes organizational and personnel counterproductive work behavior. Responses are made on a 5-point scale from 1 (*never*) to 5 (*everyday*). Examples are presented.

Reliability: Alpha coefficients were .88 and .96.

Validity: Correlations with other variables ranged from −.26 to .45.

Author: Fox, S., et al.

Article: Counterproductive work behavior (CWB) in response to job stressors and organizational justice: Some mediator and moderator tests for autonomy and emotions.

Journal: *Journal of Vocational Behavior,* December 2001, *59,* 291–309.

Related Research: Fox, S., & Spector, P. E. (1999). A model of work frustration–aggression. *Journal of Organizational Behavior, 20,* 915–931.

11736

Test Name: COWORKERS' ORGANIZATIONAL CITIZENSHIP BEHAVIOR SCALE

Purpose: To assess the extent to which helping, initiative, industry, and boosterism are embraced by employees.

Number of Items: 20

Format: Scales range from 1 (*strongly disagree*) to 5 (*strongly agree*). Sample items are presented.

Reliability: Coefficient alpha was .91.

Validity: Correlations with other variables ranged from −.26 to .39.

Author: Tepper, B. J., et al.

Article: Moderators of the relationships between coworkers' organizational citizenship behavior and fellow employees' attitudes.

Journal: *The Journal of Applied Psychology,* June 2004, *89,* 455–465.

Related Research: Moorman, R. H., & Blakely, G. L. (1995). Individualism–collectivism as an individual difference predictor of organizational citizenship behavior. *Journal of Organizational Behavior, 16,* 127–142.

11737

Test Name: CULTURE BROKER SCALE

Purpose: To measure behaviors that children use to aid their parents with culture and language.

Number of Items: 7

Format: Scales range from 0 (*never*) to 4 (*all the time*).

Reliability: Coefficient alpha was .86.

Validity: Correlations ranged from −.27 to .30.

Author: Jones, C. J., and Trickett, E. J.

Article: Immigrant adolescents behaving as culture brokers: A study of families from the Former Soviet Union.

Journal: *The Journal of Social Psychology,* August 2005, *145,* 405–427.

Related Research: Buchman, R. M. (1994). *Intergenerational and gender differences in acculturation: Implications for adolescent–family adjustment.* Unpublished master's thesis, University of Maryland, College Park.

11738

Test Name: DAILY BEHAVIOR QUESTIONNAIRE

Purpose: To measure exhibitionism, aggression, failure to plan, and carefree–spontaneous behavior.

Number of Items: 55

Format: A yes–no format is used. All items are presented.

Reliability: Alpha coefficients ranged from .52 to .89 across subscales.

Validity: Correlations with personality scales ranged from −.10 to .55.

Author: Wu, K. D., and Clark, L. A.

Article: Relations between personality traits and self-reports of daily behavior.

Journal: *Journal of Research in Personality*, August 2003, *37*, 231–256.

11739

Test Name: DAILY DRINKING QUESTIONNAIRE

Purpose: To assess typical and the heaviest weekly alcohol use.

Number of Items: 3

Format: Scoring procedures are presented.

Reliability: Alpha coefficients ranged from .84 to .87.

Author: Fromme, K., and Corbin, W.

Article: Prevention of heavy drinking and associated negative consequences among mandated and voluntary college students.

Journal: *Journal of Consulting and Clinical Psychology*, December 2004, *72*, 1038–1049.

Related Research: Collins, R. L., et al. (1985). Social determinants of alcohol consumption: The effects of social interaction and model status on the self-administration of alcohol. *Journal of Consulting and Clinical Psychology*, *53*, 189–200.

11740

Test Name: DEFENSE STYLE QUESTIONNAIRE

Purpose: To measure maladaptive action, image-distorting, self-sacrificing, and adaptive defenses.

Number of Items: 88

Format: Item anchors are 1 (*strongly disagree*) and 9 (*strongly agree*).

Reliability: Subscale alpha coefficients ranged from .50 to .88.

Validity: Correlations with other variables ranged from −.08 to .35.

Author: Randolph, D. E., et al.

Article: Social desirability, defense styles, and the Children's Role Inventory Scale.

Journal: *Psychological Reports*, June 2003, *92*, Part 1, 842–846.

Related Research: Bond, M. (1986). Defense Style Questionnaire. In G. E. Vaillant (Ed.), *Empirical studies of ego mechanisms of defense* (pp. 146–152). Washington, DC: American Psychiatric Press.

11741

Test Name: DEFENSE STYLE QUESTIONNAIRE—40

Purpose: To enable persons to rate their defense style.

Number of Items: 40

Format: Includes three subscales: Mature, Neurotic, and Immature.

Reliability: Internal consistency reliability estimates ranged from .58 to .80. Test–retest (4 weeks) reliabilities ranged from .75 to .85.

Validity: Correlations with other variables ranged from −.48 to .60.

Author: Nghe, L. T., & Mahalik, J. R.

Article: Examining racial identity statuses as predictors of

psychological defenses in African American college students.

Journal: *Journal of Counseling Psychology*, January 2001, *48*, 10–16.

Related Research: Andrews, G., et al. (1993). The Defense Style Questionnaire. *Journal of Nervous and Mental Disease*, *181*, 246–254.

11742

Test Name: DELIBERATE SELF-HARM INVENTORY

Purpose: To measure self-harm.

Number of Items: 17 self-harm items.

Format: Self-harm items are followed by a yes–no response and five related questions. All items are presented.

Reliability: Coefficient alpha was .83.

Validity: Correlations with other variables ranged from −.21 to .49.

Author: Gratz, K. L.

Article: Measurement of deliberate self-harm: Preliminary data on the deliberate self-harm inventory.

Journal: *Journal of Psychopathology and Behavioral Assessment*, December 2001, *23*, 253–263.

11743

Test Name: DELINQUENCY SCALE

Purpose: To measure nonconforming and antisocial behavior.

Number of Items: 45

Format: Frequency scales range from *0* to *9+* times. Sample items are presented.

Reliability: Alpha coefficients ranged from .56 to .64.

Author: Hall, G. C. N., et al.

Article: Ethnicity, culture, and sexual aggression: Risk and protective factors.

Journal: *Journal of Consulting and Clinical Psychology*, October 2005, *73*, 830–840.

Related Research: Malamuth, N. M., et al. (1995). Using the confluence model of sexual aggression to predict men's conflict with women: A 10-year follow-up study. *Journal of Personality and Social Psychology, 69*, 353–369.

11744

Test Name: DELINQUENT ACTIVITY SCALE

Purpose: To measure delinquent activity.

Number of Items: 16

Format: Six-point scales range from 1 (*never*) to 6 (*10 or more times*).

Reliability: Coefficient alpha was .75. Test–retest reliability was .70.

Author: Windle, M., and Windle, R. C.

Article: Depressive symptoms and cigarette smoking among middle adolescents: Prospective associations and intrapersonal and interpersonal influences.

Journal: *Journal of Consulting and Clinical Psychology*, April 2001, *69*, 215–226.

Related Research: Elliott, D. S., et al. (1989). *Multiple problem youth: Delinquency, substance use, and mental health*. New York: Springer-Verlag.

11745

Test Name: DEVIANCE BEHAVIOR SCALE

Purpose: To measure extent of deviant behavior.

Number of Items: 8

Format: Subjects report the number of times in the last year they engaged in eight behaviors. Sample items are presented.

Reliability: Coefficient alpha was .76.

Author: Orlando, M., et al.

Article: The temporal relationship between emotional distress and cigarette smoking during adolescence and young adulthood.

Journal: *Journal of Consulting and Clinical Psychology*, December 2001, *69*, 959–970.

Related Research: Jessor, R., et al. (1972). On becoming a drinker: Social–psychological aspects of an adolescent transition. *Annals of the New York Academy of Sciences, 197*, 199–213.

11746

Test Name: DEVIANT BEHAVIOR SCALE

Purpose: To measure deviance.

Number of Items: 16

Format: Responses are made on a 5-point scale ranging from 1 (*never*) to 5 (*six or more times*).

Reliability: Alpha coefficients ranged from .89 to .92.

Author: McQueen, A., et al.

Article: Acculturation, substance use, and deviant behavior: Examining separation and family conflict as mediators.

Journal: *Child Development*, November/December 2003, *74*, 1737–1750.

Related Research: Jessor, R. (1987). Problem-behavior theory, psychosocial development, and adolescent problem drinking. *British Journal of Addiction, 82*, 331–342.

11747

Test Name: DEVIANT PEER AFFILIATION SCALE

Purpose: To measure the extent of deviant peer affiliations by adult retrospective reports.

Number of Items: 6

Format: Scales range from *none* to *all of them*. Sample items are described.

Reliability: Coefficient alpha was .80.

Author: Roche, K. M., et al.

Article: Establishing independence in low-income urban areas: The relationship to adolescent aggressive behavior.

Journal: *Journal of Marriage and Family*, August 2003, *65*, 668–680.

Related Research: Patterson, G. R., et al. (1992). *A social learning approach: 4. Antisocial boys*. Eugene, OR: Castalia.

11748

Test Name: DEVIANT PEERS SCALE

Purpose: To assess the extent to which the adolescent's friends engaged in misconduct or problem behavior.

Number of Items: 4

Format: Responses are made on a 4-point scale ranging from 1 (*disagree strongly*) to 4 (*agree strongly*). Examples are given.

Reliability: Alpha coefficients ranged from .69 to .78.

Author: Galambos, N. L., et al.

Article: Parents do matter: Trajectories of change in externalizing and internalizing problems in early adolescence.

Journal: *Child Development*, March/April 2003, *74*, 578–594.

Related Research: Galambos, N. L., & Maggs, J. L. (1991). Out-of-school care of young adolescents and self-reported behavior. *Developmental Psychology, 27*, 644–655.

11749

Test Name: DEVIANT PEERS SCALES

Purpose: To measure how many respondents' friends engage in delinquent acts.

Number of Items: 15

Format: Response scales range from 1 (*none*) to 5 (*all*).

Reliability: Coefficient alpha was .80.

Author: Simons, R. L., et al.

Article: Quality of parenting as a mediator of the effect of childhood deviance on adolescent friendship choices and delinquency: A growth curve analysis.

Journal: *Journal of Marriage and Family*, February 2001, *63*, 63–79.

Related Research: Elliott, D. S., et al. (1989). *Multiple problem youth: Delinquency, substance use, and mental health problems*. New York: Springer-Verlag.

11750

Test Name: DISCIPLINED–UNDISCIPLINED BEHAVIOR INVENTORY— REVISED

Purpose: To measure disciplined and undisciplined behaviors in physical education classes.

Number of Items: 16

Format: Includes two factors: disciplined behavior and undisciplined behavior. Responses are made on a Likert-type scale ranging from 0 (*total disagreement*) to 100 (*total agreement*). Examples are given.

Reliability: Alpha coefficients were .77 and .78.

Validity: Correlations with other variables ranged from −.39 to .41.

Author: Cervelló E. M., et al.

Article: Goal orientations, motivational climate, equality, and discipline of Spanish physical education students.

Journal: *Perceptual and Motor Skills*, August 2004, *99*, 271–283.

Related Research: Cervelló, E. M., et al. (2002). Una aproximación social cognitiva al estudio de la coeducación y los comportamientos de disciplina en las clases de educación física [A social cognitive approximation of the study of coeducation and the behaviors of discipline in physical education classes]. *Revista Internacional de Ciencias Sociales y Humanidades*, *11*, 43–64.

11751

Test Name: DISRUPTIVE BEHAVIORS DISORDER SCALE

Purpose: To measure the presence and severity of symptoms of ADHD disorders, operational defiant disorders, and conduct disorders.

Number of Items: 45

Format: Four-point scales range from 0 (*not at all present*) to 3 (*very much present*). Sample items are presented.

Reliability: Reliabilities ranged from .72 to .95.

Author: Owens, J. S., and Hoza, B.

Article: The role of inattention and hyperactivity/impulsivity in the positive illusory bias.

Journal: *Journal of Consulting and Clinical Psychology*, August 2003, *71*, 680–691.

Related Research: Pelham, W. E., Jr. (2002). *Attention deficit hyperactivity disorder: Diagnosis, nature, etiology, and treatment.* Unpublished manuscript.

11752

Test Name: DRINKING PROBLEMS INVENTORY

Purpose: To measure problems experienced because of "too much alcohol."

Number of Items: 8

Format: A yes–no format is used.

Reliability: Coefficient alpha was .75.

Author: Holahan, C. J., et al.

Article: Unipolar depression, life context vulnerabilities, and drinking to cope.

Journal: *Journal of Consulting and Clinical Psychology*, April 2004, *72*, 269–275.

Related Research: Finney, J. W., & Moos, R. H. (1995). Entering treatment for alcohol abuse: A stress and coping model. *Addiction*, *90*, 1223–1240.

11753

Test Name: DRIVER BEHAVIOR QUESTIONNAIRE

Purpose: To measure driver behavior in four dimensions: Error, Ordinary Violation, Aggressive Violation, and Lapse.

Number of Items: 28

Format: Five-point response categories ranged from *never* to *nearly all the time*. All items are presented.

Reliability: Alpha coefficients ranged from .51 to .82 across subscales. Total alpha was .84.

Author: Bianchi, A., and Summala, H.

Article: Moral judgment and drivers' behavior among Brazilian students.

Journal: *Psychological Reports*, December 2002, *91*, Part 1, 759–766.

Related Research: Lawton, R. J., et al. (1997). The role of affect in predicting social behaviors: The case of road traffic violations. *Journal of Applied Social Psychology*, *27*, 1258–1276.

11754

Test Name: DRIVER'S ANGRY THOUGHTS QUESTIONNAIRE

Purpose: To rate how often drivers have angry thoughts while behind the wheel.

Number of Items: 65

Format: Scales range from 1 (*not at all*) to 5 (*all the time*). Sample items are presented.

Reliability: Subscale alpha coefficients ranged from .83 to .93.

Validity: Correlations with other variables ranged from −.43 to .81.

Author: Deffenbacher, J. L., et al.

Article: Evaluation of two new scales assessing driving anger: The Driving Anger Expression Inventory and the Driver's Angry Thoughts Questionnaire.

Journal: *Journal of Psychopathology and Behavioral Assessment*, June 2004, *26*, 87–99.

11755

Test Name: DRIVING ANGER EXPRESSION INVENTORY

Purpose: To measure verbal aggression, personal physical aggression, use of vehicle to express anger, and adaptive constructive expression.

Number of Items: 49

Reliability: Cronbach alpha coefficients ranged from .84 to .89 across subscales.

Validity: Correlations with other variables ranged from −.40 to .61.

Author: Deffenbacher, J. L., et al.

Article: Further evidence of reliability and validity for the Driving Anger Expression Index.

Journal: *Psychological Reports*, December 2001, *89*, 535–540.

Related Research: Deffenbacher, J. L., et al. (2003) Anger, aggression, risky behavior, and crash-related outcomes in three groups of drivers. *Behavior Research and Therapy, 41*, 333–349.

11756

Test Name: DRIVING ANGER SCALE

Purpose: To assess anger when driving.

Number of Items: 14

Format: Responses are made on a 5-point scale ranging from 1 (*not at all*) to 5 (*very much*).

Reliability: Coefficient alpha was .87.

Validity: Correlations with other variables ranged from −.14 to .50.

Author: Bricker, J. B.

Article: Development and evaluation of the Air Travel Stress Scale.

Journal: *Journal of Counseling Psychology*, October 2005, *52*, 615–628.

Related Research: Deffenbacher, J. L., et al. (1994). Development of a driving anger scale. *Psychological Reports, 74*, 83–91.

11757

Test Name: DRIVING SURVEY

Purpose: To assess the frequency of aggressive and risky behavior on the road and crash-related outcomes.

Number of Items: 38

Format: Employs 0 to 5+ scales.

Reliability: Alpha coefficients ranged from .41 to .89.

Author: Deffenbacher, J. L., et al.

Article: Characteristics of two groups of angry drivers.

Journal: *Journal of Counseling Psychology*, April 2003, *50*, 123–132.

Related Research: Deffenbacher, J. L., et al, (2000). Characteristics and treatment of high anger drivers. *Journal of Counseling Psychology, 47*, 5–17.

11758

Test Name: DRIVING SURVEY

Purpose: To measure the frequency of aggressive behavior, accidents and moving violations over the past three months.

Number of Items: 28

Format: Scales range from 0 to 5+.

Reliability: Alpha coefficients ranged from .41 to .89.

Validity: Correlations with other variables ranged from −.40 to .64.

Author: Deffenbacher, J. L., et al.

Article: Evaluation of two new scales assessing driving anger: The Driving Anger Expression Inventory and the Driver's Angry Thoughts Questionnaire.

Journal: *Journal of Psychopathology and Behavioral Assessment*, June 2004, *26*, 87–99.

11759

Test Name: DRUG USE SCALES

Purpose: To assess the willingness and the intention to use drugs.

Number of Items: 9

Format: Five-point response scales range from 1 (*not at all or do not intend*) to 5 (*very willing or do intend*). Sample items are presented.

Reliability: Alpha coefficients were .77 (willingness) and .79 (intention).

Author: Brody, G. H., et al.

Article: Neighborhood disadvantage moderates associations of parenting and older sibling problem attitudes and behavior with conduct disorders in African American children.

Journal: *Journal of Consulting and Clinical Psychology*, April 2003, *71*, 211–222.

Related Research: Gibbons, F. X., et al. (1995). Prototype perceptions predict (lack of) pregnancy prevention. *Personality and Social Psychology Bulletin, 21*, 85–93.

11760

Test Name: DURATION OF EMOTIONAL DISPLAYS SCALE

Purpose: To measure assessed duration of emotional displays.

Number of Items: 3

Format: Responses are made on a 5-point scale ranging from 1 (*strongly disagree*) to 5 (*strongly agree*). An example is given.

Reliability: Internal consistency reliability was .78.

Author: Glomb, T. M., and Tews, M. J.

Article: Emotional labor: A conceptualization and scale development.

Journal: *Journal of Vocational Behavior*, February 2004, *64*, 1–23.

Related Research: Morris, J. A., & Feldman, D. C. (1997). Managing emotions in the workplace. *Journal of Managerial Issues, 9*, 257–274.

11761

Test Name: DUTCH EATING BEHAVIOR QUESTIONNAIRE

Purpose: To measure eating behavior.

Number of Items: 33

Format: Scales range from 1 (*never*) to 5 (*very often*).

Reliability: Alpha coefficients ranged from .71 to .94 across subscales.

Validity: Correlations with other variables ranged from .03 to .68.

Author: Jackson, B., et al.

Article: Motivations to eat: Scale development and validation.

Journal: *Journal of Research in Personality*, August 2003, *37*, 297–318.

Related Research: van Strien, T., et al. (1986). The Dutch Eating Behavior Questionnaire (DEBQ) for assessment of restrained, emotional and, external eating. *International Journal of Eating Disorders, 5*, 295–315.

11762

Test Name: DUTCH RESTRAINED EATING SCALE

Purpose: To measure frequency of dieting behaviors.

Format: Scales range from 1 (*never*) to 5 (*always*).

Reliability: Coefficient alpha was .95. Test–retest reliabilities ranged from .62 to .82.

Validity: Correlations with other variables ranged from –.15 to .41.

Author: Stice, E., et al.

Article: Psychological and behavioral risk factors for obesity onset in adolescent girls: A prospective study.

Journal: *Journal of Consulting and Clinical Psychology*, April 2005, *73*, 195–202.

Related Research: van Strien, T., et al. (1986). Predictive validity of the Dutch Restrained Eating Scale. *International Journal of Eating Disorders, 5*, 747–755.

11763

Test Name: EARLY SCHOOL BEHAVIOR SCALE

Purpose: To measure the frequency of child behaviors that indicates a child's mental health.

Number of Items: 18

Format: Mothers rate their child's behavior on scales that range from 0 (*never*) to 4 (*almost always*).

Reliability: Coefficient alpha was .77.

Author: Hill, N., and Bush, K. R.

Article: Relationships between parenting environment and children's mental health among African American and European American mothers and children.

Journal: *Journal of Marriage and Family*, November 2001, *63*, 954–966.

Related Research: Caldwell, C. B., & Pianta, R. G. (1991). A measure of young children's problem and competence behaviors: The Early School Behavior Scale. *Journal of Psychoeducational Assessment, 9*, 32–44.

11764

Test Name: EATING DISORDER EXAMINATION— QUESTIONNAIRE

Purpose: To assess behavioral eating disorder symptoms.

Format: Scales range from 0 (*never*) to 4 (*very often*).

Reliability: Alpha coefficients ranged from .67 to .71.

Validity: Correlations with other variables ranged from –.26 to .35.

Author: Harned, M. S., and Fitzgerald, L. F.

Article: Understanding a link between sexual harassment and eating disorder symptoms: A mediational analysis.

Journal: *Journal of Consulting and Clinical Psychology*, October 2002, *70*, 1170–1181.

Related Research: Beglin, S. J., & Fairburn, C. G. (1992). Evaluation of a new instrument for the detection of eating disorders in community samples. *Psychiatric Research, 44*, 191–201.

11765

Test Name: EFFECTANCE SCALE

Purpose: To measure effectance.

Number of Items: 6

Format: Responses are made on a 5-point scale ranging from *never true* to *always true*. All items are presented.

Reliability: Reliability coefficients ranged from .73 to .85.

Author: Cook, W. L.

Article: Interpersonal influence in family systems: A social relations model analysis.

Journal: *Child Development,* July/August 2001, *72,* 1179–1197.

Related Research: Cook, W. L. (1993). Interdependence and the interpersonal sense of control: An analysis of family relationships. *Journal of Personality and Social Psychology, 64,* 587–601.

11766

Test Name: EMOTION REGULATION SCALE

Purpose: To measure emotion suppression and emotion-faking.

Number of Items: 7

Format: Scales range from 1 (*never/not at all*) to 5 (*always/ constantly*). Sample items are presented.

Reliability: Alpha coefficients ranged from .83 to .89.

Author: Grandey, A. A., et al.

Article: Must "service with a smile" be stressful? The moderating role of personal control for American and French employees.

Journal: *Journal of Applied Psychology,* September 2005, *90,* 893–904.

Related Research: Brotheridge, C., & Lee, R. T. (2003). Development and validation of the Emotional Labour Scale. *Journal of Occupational and Organizational Psychology, 76,* 365–379.

11767

Test Name: EMOTIONAL INTENSITY SCALE

Purpose: To enable parents and teachers to rate children's emotionality.

Number of Items: 12

Format: Items are rated on a 7-point scale ranging from 1 (*never*) to 7 (*always*). Examples are presented.

Reliability: Coefficient alpha was .43.

Author: Eisenberg, N., et al.

Article: The relations of regulation and negative emotionality in Indonesian children's social functioning.

Journal: *Child Development,* November/December 2001, *72,* 1747–1763.

Related Research: Larsen, R. J., & Diener, E. (1987). Affect intensity as an individual difference characteristic: A review. *Journal of Research in Personality, 21,* 1–39.

11768

Test Name: EMOTIONAL LABOR STRATEGY SCALE

Purpose: To measure emotional labor strategies.

Number of Items: 14

Format: Includes three scales: Surface Acting, Deep Acting, and Expression of Naturally Felt Emotions. All responses are made on a 5-point scale ranging from 1 (*strongly disagree*) to 5 (*strongly agree*). All items are given.

Reliability: Alpha coefficients ranged from .75 to .92.

Validity: Correlations with other variables ranged from −.31 to .40.

Author: Diefendorff, J. M., et al.

Article: The dimensionality and antecedents of emotional labor strategies.

Journal: *Journal of Vocational Behavior,* April 2005, *66,* 339–357.

Related Research: Grandley, A. (2003). When the show must go on: Surface and deep acting as determinants of emotional exhaustion and peer-rated service delivery. *Academy of Management Journal, 46,* 86–96.

11769

Test Name: EMPLOYEES' ORGANIZATIONAL CITIZENSHIP BEHAVIOR SCALE

Purpose: To measure employees' organizational citizenship behavior.

Number of Items: 5

Format: Includes conscientiousness, altruism, civic virtue, sportsmanship, and courtesy. Responses are made on a 7-point scale ranging from 1 (*strongly disagree*) to 7 (*strongly agree*). All items are presented.

Reliability: Alpha coefficients were .85 and .86.

Validity: Correlations with other variables ranged from −.21 to .61

Author: Koys, D. J.

Article: The effects of employer satisfaction, organizational citizenship behavior, and turnover on organizational effectiveness: A unit-level, longitudinal study.

Journal: *Personnel Psychology,* Spring 2001, *54,* 101–114.

11770

Test Name: ENTREPRENEURIAL EXPERIENCE SCALE

Purpose: To assess level of entrepreneurial experience.

Number of Items: 3

Format: A 5-point Likert format is used.

Reliability: Coefficient alpha was .60.

Validity: Correlations with other variables ranged from –.15 to .32.

Author: Zhao, H., et al.

Article: The mediating role of self-efficacy in the development of entrepreneurial intentions.

Journal: *Journal of Applied Psychology*, November 2005, *90*, 1265–1272.

11771

Test Name: EPWORTH SLEEPINESS SCALE

Purpose: To assess general amount of daytime sleepiness.

Number of Items: 8

Format: Responses are scored on a 4-point scale ranging from 0 (*would never doze*) to 3 (*high chance of dozing*).

Reliability: Coefficient alpha was .73. Test–retest correlation was .82.

Validity: Correlations with other variables ranged from –.03 to .30.

Author: Howell, A. J., et al.

Article: Sleep quality, sleep propensity and academic performance.

Journal: *Perceptual and Motor Skills*, October 2004, *99*, 525–535.

Related Research: Johns, M. W. (1991). A new method for measuring daytime sleepiness: The Epworth Sleepiness Scale. *Sleep, 14*, 540–545.

11772

Test Name: EXHIBITIONISM SCALE

Purpose: To measure exhibitionism.

Number of Items: 7

Reliability: Coefficient alpha was .63.

Validity: Correlations with other scales ranged from –.03 to .57.

Correlations with several behaviors ranged from –.02 to .46.

Author: Wu, K. D., and Clark, L. A.

Article: Relations between personality traits and self-reports of daily behavior.

Journal: *Journal of Research in Personality*, August 2003, *37*, 231–256.

Related Research: Raskin, R., & Hall, C. (1979). The Narcissistic Personality Inventory. *Psychological Reports, 45*, 590.

11773

Test Name: EXPECTED INVOLVEMENT SCALE

Purpose: To measure expected involvement in risk-taking behavior.

Number of Items: 30

Format: Rating scales range from 1 (*not at all likely*) to 7 (*extremely likely*). Sample items are presented.

Reliability: Cronbach's alpha was .89.

Validity: Correlations with a self-destructiveness scale ranged from –.28 to .41.

Author: Kelly, D. B., et al.

Article: Chronic self-destructiveness, hopelessness, and risk-taking in college students.

Journal: *Psychological Reports*, June 2005, *96*, Part 1, 620–624.

Related Research: Fromme, K., et al. (1997). Outcome expectancies and risk-taking behavior. *Cognitive Therapy and Research, 21*, 421–442.

11774

Test Name: EXPERIENCES OF DISCRIMINATION SCALE

Purpose: To measure racial discrimination.

Number of Items: 13

Format: Scales range from 1 (*never*) to 4 (*several times*). All items are presented.

Reliability: Coefficient alpha was .92.

Validity: Correlations with other variables ranged from –.15 to .27.

Author: Murry, V. M., et al.

Article: Racial discrimination as a moderator of the links among stress, maternal psychological functioning, and family relationships.

Journal: *Journal of Marriage and Family*, November 2001, *63*, 915–926.

11775

Test Name: FRAMINGHAM SELF-RATING QUESTIONNAIRE

Purpose: To evaluate parents' Type A behavior.

Number of Items: 9

Format: Includes two factors: hard-driving competitiveness and job involvement. Examples are presented.

Reliability: Alpha coefficients ranged from .60 to .76.

Validity: Correlations with other variables ranged from –.25 to .21.

Author: Keltikangas-Järvinen, L., and Heinonen, K.

Article: Childhood roots of adulthood hostility: Family factors as predictors of cognitive and affective hostility.

Journal: *Child Development*, November/December 2003, *74*, 1751–1768.

Related Research: Haynes, S. G., et al. (1978). The relationship of psychosocial factors to coronary heart disease in the Framingham study: I. Methods and risk factors. *American Journal of Epidemiology, 107*, 362–383.

11776

Test Name: FREE-RIDING SCALE

Purpose: To measure the magnitude of free-riding.

Number of Items: 4

Format: Five-point scales are anchored by 1 (*none/not at all*) and 5 (*to a great extent*). A sample item is presented.

Reliability: Alpha was .69.

Author: Miles, J. A., and Klein, H. J.

Article: Perception in consequences of free riding.

Journal: *Psychological Reports*, February 2002, *90*, 215–225.

Related Research: Mulvey, P. W., & Klein, H. J. (1998). The impact of perceived loafing and collective efficacy on group processes and group performance. *Organizational Behavior and Human Decision Processes*, 74, 62–87.

11777

Test Name: FREQUENCY AND ACCEPTABILITY OF PARTNER BEHAVIOR INVENTORY

Purpose: To measure the frequency and acceptability of positive and negative partner behavior.

Number of Items: 20

Format: Sample items are presented.

Reliability: Alpha coefficients ranged from .65 to .85.

Validity: Correlations between self- and partner reports ranged from .43 to .58.

Author: Doss, B. D., et al.

Article: Improving relationships: Mechanisms of change in couple therapy.

Journal: *Journal of Consulting and Clinical Psychology*, August 2005, *73*, 624–633.

11778

Test Name: FRONTAL SYSTEMS BEHAVIOR SCALE

Purpose: To measure frontal system dysfunction.

Number of Items: 46

Format: Responses are made on a 5-point scale ranging from 1 (*almost never*) to 5 (*almost always*). Examples are given.

Validity: Correlations with other variables ranged from −.23 to .16.

Author: Spinella, M., et al.

Article: Gambling and delaying rewards as a function of frontal system dysfunction: A study in neuroeconomics.

Journal: *Perceptual and Motor Skills*, December 2004, *99*, Part 1, 993–994.

Related Research: Grace, J., et al. (1999). Assessing frontal behavior syndromes with the Frontal Lobe Personality Scale. *Assessment, 6*, 269–284.

11779

Test Name: FUNCTIONAL ASSESSMENT OF SELF-MUTILATION

Purpose: To measure the frequency, methods, and functions of self-mutilation.

Number of Items: 11 behaviors, 22 reasons

Format: Scales range from 0 (*never*) to 3 (*often*). All items are presented.

Reliability: Internal consistency coefficients ranged from .65 to .66.

Author: Nock, M. K., and Prinstein, M. J.

Article: A functional approach to the assessment of self-mutilative behavior.

Journal: *Journal of Consulting and Clinical Psychology*, October 2004, *72*, 885–890.

Related Research: Lloyd, E. E., et al. (1997, April). *Self-mutilation in a community sample of adolescents: Descriptive characteristics and provisional prevalence rates.* Paper presented at the annual meeting of the Society for Behavioral Medicine, New Orleans, LA.

11780

Test Name: GANG MEMBERSHIP INVENTORY—MODIFIED

Purpose: To assess adolescent gang-related behaviors.

Number of Items: 6

Format: Items consist of descriptions of gang-related behaviors. Responses are made on a 6-point scale ranging from 0 (*never*) to 5 (*more than once a day*). Includes two factors: gang involvement and gang delinquency.

Reliability: Alpha coefficients were .74 and .83.

Author: Walker-Barnes, C. J., & Mason, C. A.

Article: Ethnic differences in the effect of parenting on gang involvement and gang delinquency: A longitudinal, hierarchical linear modeling perspective.

Journal: *Child Development*, November/December 2001, *72*, 1814–1831.

Related Research: Pilen, M. B., & Hoewing-Roberson, R. C. (1992). Determining youth gang membership: Development of a self-report instrument (ERIC Document Reproduction Service No. ED 352 412). Bloomington, IL: Chestnut Health Systems.

11781

Test Name: GENERAL COUNTERPRODUCTIVE BEHAVIOR SCALE

Purpose: To assess counterproductive behavior such as fraud, deception, sabotage, and lateness.

Number of Items: 50

Format: Scales range from 0 (*never*) to 4 (*often*).

Reliability: Coefficient alpha was .88.

Validity: Correlations with other variables ranged from −.63 to .37.

Author: Marcus, B., and Shuler, H.

Article: Antecedents of counterproductive behavior at work: A general perspective.

Journal: *Journal of Applied Psychology*, August 2004, *89*, 647–660.

Related Research: Marcus, B., et al. (2002). Measuring counterproductivity: Development and initial validation of a German self-report questionnaire. *International Journal of Selection and Assessment, 10*, 18–35.

11782

Test Name: GRONINGEN MEMORY FAILURES QUESTIONNAIRE

Purpose: To identify everyday memory problems.

Number of Items: 28

Format: Responses are on a 5-point scale ranging from 1 (*almost never*) to 5 (*almost always*).

Reliability: Test–retest (5 weeks) reliability coefficients were .84 and .88.

Author: Schmidt, I. W., et al.

Article: Relations between subjective evaluations of memory and objective memory performance.

Journal: *Perceptual and Motor Skills*, December 2001, *93*, 761–776.

Related Research: Schmidt, I. W., et al. (1999). Evaluation of an

intervention directed at enhancing memory by modifying memory beliefs and expectations in older adults. *Educational Gerontology, 25*, 365–385.

11783

Test Name: HELP-SEEKING BEHAVIOR SCALE

Purpose: To assess help-seeking behavior.

Number of Items: 16

Format: Includes three scales: Help-Seeking, Expedient Help-Seeking, and Avoidant Help-Seeking. Examples are given.

Reliability: Alpha coefficients ranged from .64 to .79.

Author: Linnenbrink, E. A.

Article: The dilemma of performance approach goals: The use of multiple goal contexts to promote students' motivation and learning.

Journal: *Journal of Educational Psychology*, May 2005, *97*, 197–213.

Related Research: Ryan, A. M., et al. (2005). Differential profiles of students identified by their teacher as having avoidant, appropriate, or dependent help-seeking tendencies in the classroom. *Journal of Educational Psychology, 97*, 275–285.

11784

Test Name: HISTORICAL, CLINICAL, RISK MANAGEMENT—20

Purpose: To assess the risk of the occurrence of violence based on individual's history, clinical information, and risk management information.

Number of Items: 20

Format: Three-point scales range from 0 (*available information contraindicates presence of this*

item) and 2 (*available information indicates presence of this item*).

Validity: Correlations with other variables ranged from .15 to .62.

Author: McNiel, D. E., et al.

Article: Utility of decision support tools for assessing acute risk of violence.

Journal: *Journal of Consulting and Clinical Psychology*, October 2003, *71*, 945–953.

Related Research: Webster, C. D., et al. (1997). *HCR–20: Assessing the Risk for Violence (Version 2)*. Buruby, British Columbia, Canada: Mental Health, Law and Policy Institute, Simon Fraser University.

11785

Test Name: HISTORICAL ORGANIZATIONAL CITIZENSHIP SCALE

Purpose: To assess an employee's past organizational citizenship behavior.

Number of Items: 15

Format: Scales range from 1 (*strongly disagree*) to 7 (*strongly agree*). Sample items are presented.

Reliability: Coefficient alpha was .72.

Validity: Correlations with other variables ranged from .01 to .46.

Author: Williams, S., et al.

Article: Justice and organizational citizenship behavior intentions: Fair rewards versus fair treatment.

Journal: *The Journal of Social Psychology*, February 2002, *142*, 33–44.

Related Research: Williams, S., & Wong, T. S. (1999). Mood and organizational citizenship behavior: The effects of positive affect on employee organizational citizenship behavior intentions. *Journal of Psychology: Interdisciplinary and Applied, 133*, 656–668.

11786

Test Name: HORROCKS PROSOCIAL PLAY BEHAVIOR INVENTORY

Purpose: To assess five moral behaviors.

Number of Items: 10

Format: Responses are made on a 4-point scale ranging from 1 (*not at all*) to 4 (*very much*). An example is given.

Reliability: Coefficient alpha was .87.

Validity: Correlations with other variables ranged from .37 to .62.

Author: Tsorbatzoudis, H., and Emmanouilidou, M.

Article: Predicting moral behavior in physical education classes: An application of the theory of planned behavior.

Journal: *Perceptual and Motor Skills*, June 2005, *100*, Part 2, 1055–1065.

11787

Test Name: IDENTITY MANAGEMENT STRATEGIES SCALES

Purpose: To measure identity management strategies.

Number of Items: 15

Format: Scales range from 1 (*strongly disagree*) to 5 (*strongly agree*). All items are presented.

Validity: Correlations with other variables ranged from −.67 to .36.

Author: Niens, U., and Cairns, E.

Article: Identity management strategies in Northern Ireland.

Journal: *The Journal of Social Psychology*, June 2002, *142*, 371–380.

11788

Test Name: ILLINOIS BULLY SCALE

Purpose: To assess frequency of teasing, name calling, social exclusion, and rumor spreading.

Number of Items: 9

Format: Responses are made on a scale ranging from *never* to 7 *or more times*.

Reliability: Coefficient alpha was .87.

Author: Espelage, D. L., et al.

Article: Examination of peer-group contextual effects on aggression during early adolescence.

Journal: *Child Development*, January/February 2003, *74*, 205–220.

Related Research: Espelage, D., & Holt, M. K. (2001). Bullying and victimization during early adolescence: Peer influences and psychosocial correlates. *Journal of Emotional Abuse, 2,* 123–142.

11789

Test Name: ILLINOIS FIGHT SCALE

Purpose: To evaluate the frequency of physical fighting.

Number of Items: 5

Format: Responses are made on a scale ranging from *never* to 7 *or more times*.

Reliability: Coefficient alpha was .83.

Author: Espelage, D. L., et al.

Article: Examination of peer-group contextual effects on aggression during early adolescence.

Journal: *Child Development*, January/February 2003, *74*, 205–220.

Related Research: Espelage, D., & Holt, M. K. (2001). Bullying and victimization during early adolescence: Peer influences and psychosocial correlates. *Journal of Emotional Abuse, 2,* 123–142.

11790

Test Name: IMPACT OF EVENT SCALE

Purpose: To assess intrusion and avoidance in response to a critical incident or trauma.

Number of Items: 15

Format: Scales range from 0 (*not at all*) to 5 (*often*).

Reliability: Alpha coefficients ranged from .66 to .72.

Author: Witteveen, A. B., et al.

Article: Utility of the Impact of Event Scale in screening for posttraumatic stress disorder.

Journal: *Psychological Reports*, August 2005, *97*, 297–308.

Related Research: Horowitz, M. J., et al. (1979). Impact of Event Scale: A measure of subjective stress. *Psychosomatic Medicine, 41,* 209–218.

11791

Test Name: IMPLEMENTATION INTENTIONS MEASURE

Purpose: To measure implementation intentions.

Number of Items: 5

Format: Responses are made on a 5-point Likert scale ranging from 1 (*strongly disagree*) to 5 (*strongly agree*). All items are presented.

Reliability: Coefficient alpha was .75.

Validity: Correlations with other variables ranged from −.21 to .56.

Author: van Hooft, E. A. J., et al.

Article: Bridging the gap between intentions and behavior: Implementation intentions, action control, and procrastination.

Journal: *Journal of Vocational Behavior*, April 2005, *66*, 238–256.

11792

Test Name: IMPLICIT LEADERSHIP SCALE

Purpose: To measure six dimensions of implicit leadership.

Number of Items: 21

Format: Nine-point scales range from *not at all characteristic* to *extremely characteristic*.

Reliability: Alpha coefficients ranged from .73 to .90 across subscales.

Author: Epitropaki, O., and Martin, R.

Article: From ideal to real: A longitudinal study of the role of implicit leadership theories on leader–member exchange and employee outcomes.

Journal: *Journal of Applied Psychology*, July 2005, *90*, 659–676.

Related Research: Offermann, L. R., et al. (1994). Implicit leadership theories: Content, structure, and generalizability. *Leadership Quarterly, 5*, 43–58.

11793

Test Name: IMPRESSION MANAGEMENT BY ASSOCIATION SCALE

Purpose: To measure the use of association tactics.

Number of Items: 12

Format: Responses are made on a 5-point scale ranging from 1 (*never do it*) to 5 (*nearly always do it*).

Reliability: Coefficient alpha was .86 ($N = 221$).

Validity: Correlations with other variables ranged from .17 to .82.

Author: Andrews, M. C., and Kacmar, K. M.

Article: Impression management by association: Construction and validation of a scale.

Journal: *Journal of Vocational Behavior*, February 2001, *58*, 142–161.

11794

Test Name: IMPRESSION MANAGEMENT SCALE

Purpose: To measure impression management.

Number of Items: 10

Format: Responses are made on a 5-point scale ranging from 1 (*never do it*) to 5 (*nearly always do it*). Examples are presented.

Reliability: Coefficient alpha was .24 ($N = 221$).

Validity: Coefficient with other variables ranged from –.02 to .29 ($N = 221$).

Author: Andrews, M. C., and Kacmar, K. M.

Article: Impression management by association: Construction and validation of a scale.

Journal: *Journal of Vocational Behavior*, February 2001, *58*, 142–161.

Related Research: Wayne, S. J., & Ferris, G. R. (1990). Influence tactics, affect, and exchange quality in supervisor–subordinate interactions: A laboratory experiment and field study. *Journal of Applied Psychology, 75*, 487–499.

11795

Test Name: IMPRESSION MANAGEMENT SCALE

Purpose: To measure types of impression management.

Format: Scales range from 1 (*never behave in this way*) to 5 (*often behave in this way*). Sample items are presented.

Reliability: Alpha coefficients ranged from .70 to .88 across subscales.

Validity: Correlations with other variables ranged from –.29 to .65.

Author: Lewis, M. A., and Neighbors, C.

Article: Self-determination and the use of self-presentation strategies.

Journal: *The Journal of Social Psychology*, August 2005, *145*, 469–489.

Related Research: Bolino, M. C., & Turnley, W. H. (1999). Measuring impression management in organizations: A scale development based on the Jones and Pittman typology. *Organizational Research Methods, 2*, 187–206.

11796

Test Name: INDEX OF SPOUSE ABUSE

Purpose: To assess the severity of abuse inflicted on a woman by her partner.

Number of Items: 30

Format: Five-point scales range from *never* to *very frequently*.

Reliability: Internal consistency reliability was .90 or above.

Author: Kaslow, N. J., et al.

Article: Risk and protective factors for suicidal behavior in abused African American women.

Journal: *Journal of Consulting and Clinical Psychology*, April 2002, *70*, 311–319.

Related Research: Hudson, W. W., & McIntosh, S. R. (1981). The assessment of spouse abuse: Two quantifiable dimensions. *Journal of Marriage and the Family, 43*, 873–888.

11797

Test Name: INDIRECT AGGRESSION SCALE

Purpose: To enable teachers to rate girls' indirect aggressive behavior.

Number of Items: 5

Format: Responses are made on a 5-point scale ranging from 1 (*never true*) to 5 (*usually true*). Examples are given.

Reliability: Coefficient alpha was .91.

Author: Gazelle, H., et al.

Article: Anxious solitude across contexts: Girls' interactions with familiar and unfamiliar peers.

Journal: *Child Development*, January/February 2005, *76*, 227–246.

Related Research: Crick, N. R. (1996). The role of overt aggression, relational aggression, and prosocial behavior in the prediction of children's future social adjustment. *Child Development*, *67*, 2317–2327.

11798

Test Name: INFANT BEHAVIOR QUESTIONNAIRE— SHORTENED

Purpose: To measure infant behavior.

Number of Items: 43

Format: Includes three scales: Smiling and Laughter, Duration of Orienting, and Distress (to Novelty, to Limitation).

Reliability: Alpha coefficients ranged from .52 to .92.

Author: Watamura, S. E., et al.

Article: Morning-to-afternoon increases in cortisol concentrations for infants and toddlers at child care: Age differences and behavioral correlates.

Journal: *Child Development*, July/August 2003, *74*, 1006–1020.

Related Research: Rothbart, M. K. (1981). Measurement of temperament in infancy. *Child Development*, *52*, 569–578.

11799

Test Name: INFLUENCE BEHAVIOR QUESTIONNAIRE

Purpose: To measure influence tactics used by leaders including legitimating, rational persuasion, personal appeals, pressure, exchanges, ingratiating, consultative, inspirational, and coalition.

Number of Items: 50

Reliability: Alpha coefficients ranged from .67 to .89.

Validity: Correlations with other variables ranged from −.16 to .33.

Author: Barbuto, J. E., Jr., et al.

Article: A field examination of two measures of work motivation as predictors of leaders' influence tactics.

Journal: *The Journal of Social Psychology*, October 2002, *142*, 601–616.

Related Research: Yukl, G. A. (1998). *Leadership in organizations*. Englewood Cliffs, NJ: Prentice Hall.

11800

Test Name: INFLUENCE TACTICS SCALE

Purpose: To measure ingratiation and self-promotion.

Number of Items: 14

Format: Scales range from 1 (*strongly disagree*) to 7 (*strongly agree*). All items are presented.

Reliability: Alpha coefficients were .85 (ingratiation) and .77 (self-promotion).

Validity: Correlations with other variables ranged from −.22 to .40.

Author: Higgins, C. A., and Judge, T. A.

Article: The effect of applicant influence tactics on recruiter perceptions of fit and hiring recommendations: A field study.

Journal: *Journal of Applied Psychology*, August 2004, *89*, 622–632.

Related Research: Stevens, C. K., & Kristof, A. L. (1995). Making the right impression: A field study of applicant impression management during job interviews. *Journal of Applied Psychology*, *80*, 587–606.

11801

Test Name: INFLUENCE TACTICS SCALES

Purpose: To assess ingratiation, rational persuasion, upward appeals, exchange, legitimizing, pressure, personal appeals, consultation, and inspirational appeals.

Number of Items: 45

Reliability: Alpha coefficients ranged from .70 to .89 across subscales.

Validity: Correlations with other variables ranged from −.09 to .59.

Author: Moss, J. A., and Barbuto, J. E., Jr.

Article: Machiavellianism's association with sources of motivation and downward influence strategies.

Journal: *Psychological Reports*, June 2004, *94*, Part 1, 933–943.

Related Research: Kipnis, D., et al. (1980). Intraorganizational influence tactics: Explorations of getting one's way. *Journal of Applied Psychology*, *65*, 440–452.

11802

Test Name: INFORMATION TECHNOLOGY INDEX

Purpose: To measure the extent to which human resources professionals use information technology.

Format: Responses are made on a 5-point scale ranging from 1 (*very low*) to 5 (*very high*).

Reliability: Coefficient alpha was .87.

Validity: Correlations with other variables ranged from –.07 to .26.

Author: Gardner, S. D., et al.

Article: Virtual HR: The impact of information technology on the human resource professional.

Journal: *Journal of Vocational Behavior*, October 2003, *63*, 159–179.

Related Research: Greengard, S. (1999). How to fill technology's promise. *Workforce*, 10–18.

11803

Test Name: IN-ROLE PERFORMANCE SCALE

Purpose: To measure in-role performance.

Number of Items: 5

Format: Responses are made on a 5-point scale ranging from 1 (*very uncharacteristic*) to 5 (*very characteristic*). A sample item is given.

Reliability: Coefficient alpha was .78.

Validity: Correlations with other variables ranged from –.33 to .71.

Author: Feldman, D. C., and Turnley, W. H.

Article: Contingent employment in academic careers: Relative deprivation among adjunct faculty.

Journal: *Journal of Vocational Behavior*, April 2004, *64*, 284–307.

Related Research: Williams, L. J., & Anderson, S. E. (1991). Job satisfaction and organizational commitment as predictors of organizational citizenship and in-role behaviors. *Journal of Management*, 17, 601–617.

11804

Test Name: INSOMNIA SEVERITY INDEX—FRENCH VERSION

Purpose: To assess insomnia severity.

Number of Items: 7

Format: Scales range from 0 (*not at all*) to 4 (*extremely*).

Reliability: Coefficient alpha was .88.

Author: Bastien, C. H., et al.

Article: Cognitive–behavioral therapy for insomnia: Comparison of individual therapy, group therapy, and telephone consultations.

Journal: *Journal of Consulting and Clinical Psychology*, August 2004, *72*, 653–659.

Related Research: Blais, F. C., et al. (1997). Evaluation de l'insomnie: Validation de trios questionnaires. [Evaluation of insomnia: Validation of three questionnaires]. *L' Encephale*, *XIII*, 447–453.

11805

Test Name: INSTRUMENTAL ACTIVITIES OF DAILY LIFE SCALE

Purpose: To measure activities such as shopping and housekeeping.

Number of Items: 7

Format: Scales range from 0 (*complete disability*) to 3 (*no difficulty*). All items are presented.

Reliability: Coefficient alpha was .88.

Author: Shmotkin, D., et al.

Article: Tracing long-term effects of early trauma: A broad-scope view of Holocaust survivors in late life.

Journal: *Journal of Consulting and Clinical Psychology*, April 2003, *71*, 223–234.

Related Research: Lawton, M. P., & Brody, E. M. (1969). Assessment of older people: Self-maintaining in instrumental activities of daily living. *The Gerontologist*, *9*, 179–186.

11806

Test Name: INTENDED SOCIALIZATION BEHAVIOR SCALE

Purpose: To measure intended behavior used by supervisors to socialize an employee into an organization.

Number of Items: 40 (16-item short version)

Format: Seven-point scales are anchored by 1 (*not at all*) and 7 (*to a very large extent*). All items are presented.

Reliability: Alpha coefficients were .94 (supervisor) and .97 (subordinates). Reliabilities of a 16-item version were .91 and .81.

Validity: Correlations between supervisor and subordinate responses ranged from –.09 to .44.

Author: La Preze, M. W.

Article: Supervisors' behavior during new employees' socialization: Scale development.

Journal: *Psychological Reports*, October 2003, *93*, 379–392.

11807

Test Name: INTENTION TO ENGAGE IN PHYSICAL ACTIVITY SCALE

Purpose: To measure intention to engage in leisure-time physical activity.

Number of Items: 24

Format: Responses are made on a 7-point scale ranging from –3 (*very unlikely*) to 3 (*very likely*).

Reliability: Coefficient alpha was .94.

Validity: Correlations with other variables ranged from .19 to .66.

Author: Kerner, M. S., and Kurrant, A. B.

Article: Psychosocial correlates to high school girls' leisure-time physical activity: A test of the theory of planned behavior.

Journal: *Perceptual and Motor Skills*, December 2003, *97*, Part 2, 1175–1183.

11808

Test Name: INTENTIONS FOR SAFER SEX SCALE

Purpose: To assess behavioral intentions for safer sex.

Number of Items: 6

Format: Subjects respond to scenarios by answering six questions on a scale ranging from 1 (*definitely will not do*) to 5 (*definitely will do*). A sample item is presented.

Reliability: Coefficient alpha was .89.

Author: Carey, M. P., et al.

Article: Reducing HIV-risk behavior among adults receiving outpatient psychiatric treatment: Results from a randomized controlled trial.

Journal: *Journal of Consulting and Clinical Psychology*, April 2004, *72*, 252–268.

Related Research: Carey, M. P., et al. (1997). Enhancing motivation to reduce the risk of HIV infection for economically disadvantaged urban women. *Journal of Consulting and Clinical Psychology*, *65*, 531–541.

11809

Test Name: INTENTIONS TO PERFORM BEHAVIOR ASSOCIATED WITH JOINING THE FOCAL ORGANIZATION SCALE

Purpose: To measure intentions to perform behavior associated with joining the focal organization.

Number of Items: 9

Format: Responses are made on a 5-point scale ranging from 1 (*very unlikely*) to 5 (*very likely*). All items are presented.

Reliability: Coefficient alpha was .96 (*N* = 989).

Validity: Correlations with other variables ranged from .02 to .51 (*N* = 989).

Author: Allen, D. G., et al.

Article: Recruitment communication media: Impact on prehire outcomes.

Journal: *Personnel Psychology*, Spring 2004, *57*, 143–171.

11810

Test Name: INTENTIONS TO SEEK COUNSELING INVENTORY

Purpose: To measure intentions to seek counseling.

Number of Items: 17

Format: Responses are made on a 6-point scale ranging from 1 (*very unlikely*) to 6 (*very likely*).

Reliability: Internal consistency ranged from .84 to .95.

Validity: Correlations with other variables ranged from −.26 to .61.

Author: Vogel, D. L., and Wester, S. R.

Article: To seek help or not to seek help: The risks of self-disclosure.

Journal: *Journal of Counseling Psychology*, July 2003, *50*, 351–361.

Related Research: Cash, T. F., et al. (1975). When counselors are heard but not seen: Initial impact of physical attractiveness. *Journal of Counseling Psychology*, *22*, 273–279.

11811

Test Name: INTERACTION BEHAVIOR QUESTIONNAIRE— SHORT FORM

Purpose: To measure positive interaction.

Number of Items: 15

Format: A true–false format is used. Examples are given.

Reliability: Alpha coefficients ranged from .81 to .91.

Validity: Correlations with other variables ranged from −.64 to .56.

Author: Brody, G. H., et al.

Article: Protective longitudinal paths linking child competence to behavioral problems among African American siblings.

Journal: *Child Development*, March/April 2004, *75*, 455–467.

Related Research: Prinz, R. J., et al. (1979). Multivariate assessment of conflict in distressed and nondistressed mother adolescent dyads. *Journal of Applied Behavior Analysis, 12*, 691–700.

11812

Test Name: INTERPERSONAL DEVIANCE SCALE—ADAPTED

Purpose: To assess interpersonal deviance.

Number of Items: 6

Format: Responses are made on a 5-point scale ranging from 1 (*never*) to 5 (*once a week or more*). All items are given.

Reliability: Coefficient alpha was .83.

Validity: Correlations with other variables ranged from −.40 to .52.

Author: Liao, H., et al.

Article: Sticking out like a sore thumb: Employee dissimilarity and deviance at work.

Journal: *Personnel Psychology,* Winter 2004, *57,* 969–1000.

Related Research: Bennett, R. J., & Robinson, S. L. (2000). The development of a measure of workplace deviance. *Journal of Applied Psychology, 85,* 349–360.

11813

Test Name: INTRINSIC/EXTRINSIC— REVISED SCALE

Purpose: To measure religious behaviors that meet personal intrinsic and extrinsic needs.

Number of Items: 14

Format: Item responses range from *strongly disagree* to *strongly agree.* Sample items are presented.

Reliability: Alpha coefficients ranged from .57 to .83.

Validity: Correlations with other variables ranged from −.44 to .82.

Author: Pollard, L. J., and Bates, L. W.

Article: Religion and perceived stress among undergraduates during fall 2001 final examinations.

Journal: *Psychological Reports,* December 2004, *95,* Part 1, 999–1007.

Related Research: Gorsuch, R. L., & McPherson, S. E. (1989). Intrinsic/Extrinsic Measurement: I/E–Revised and single-item scales. *Journal for the Scientific Study of Religion, 28,* 348–354.

11814

Test Name: INVENTORY OF CHILDHOOD MEMORIES AND IMAGININGS

Purpose: To single out individuals with fantasy-prone characteristics.

Number of Items: 48

Format: Each item that applies to the respondent is checked. Examples are given.

Reliability: Kuder–Richardson reliability coefficient was .89.

Validity: Correlations with other variables ranged from .30 to .81.

Author: Dunn, L. W., et al.

Article: The relationship between scores on the ICMIC and selected talent domains: An investigation with gifted adolescents.

Journal: *Gifted Child Quarterly,* Spring 2004, *48,* 133–142.

Related Research: Myers, S. A. (1983). The Winston–Barber Inventory of Childhood Memories and Imaginings: Children's Form and norms for 1,337 children and adolescents. *Journal of Mental Imagery, 7,* 83–94.

11815

Test Name: INVENTORY OF CHILDREN'S ACTIVITIES— REVISED

Purpose: To identify children's commonly engaged activities.

Number of Items: 30

Format: Includes two sections: extent of engagement and competence. Responses are made on 5-point scales.

Reliability: Alpha coefficients ranged from .60 to .81. Test–retest (1 week) reliabilities ranged from .58 to .84.

Validity: Correlations with other variables ranged from .63 to .95.

Author: Tracey, T. J. G.

Article: Development of interests and competency beliefs: A 1-year longitudinal study of fifth-to-eighth-grade students using the ICA–R and structural equation modeling.

Journal: *Journal of Counseling Psychology,* April 2002, *49,* 148–163.

Related Research: Tracey, T. J. G., & Ward, C. C. (1998). The structure of children's interests and competence perceptions. *Journal of Counseling Psychology, 45,* 290–303.

11816

Test Name: JENKINS ACHIEVEMENT STRIVING ACTIVITY SCALE

Purpose: To assess presence of achievement-related behaviors and attitudes.

Number of Items: 7

Format: Responses are made on a 5-point scale ranging from 1 (*much less*) to 5 (*much more than others*).

Reliability: Coefficient alpha was .79.

Validity: Correlations with other variables ranged from −.10 to .22.

Author: Kwallek, N., et al.

Article: Effect of color schemes and environmental sensitivity on job satisfaction and perceived performance.

Journal: *Perceptual and Motor Skills,* October 2005, *101,* 473–486.

Related Research: Helmreich, R. L., et al. (1988). Making it without losing it: Type A, achievement motivation, and scientific attainment revisited. *Personality and Social Psychology Bulletin, 14,* 495–504.

11817

Test Name: JENKINS ACTIVITY SURVEY—SPANISH VERSION

Purpose: To measure Type A behavior.

Number of Items: 31

Format: Scales range from *not at all* to *in complete agreement.*

Reliability: Alpha coefficients ranged from .75 to .88.

Author: Moriana, J. A., and Herruzo, J.

Article: Type A behavior pattern as a predictor of psychiatric sick-leaves of Spanish teachers.

Journal: *Psychological Reports*, February 2005, *96*, 77–82.

Related Research: Burmúdez, J., et al. (1990). Type A behavior pattern and attentional performance. *Personality and Individual Differences*, *11*, 13–18.

11818

Test Name: JOB SEARCH BEHAVIOR INDEX

Purpose: To assess job search behavior.

Number of Items: 11

Format: Responses are made on a 5-point scale ranging from 1 (*no time at all*) to 5 (*very much time*).

Reliability: Coefficient alpha was .90.

Validity: Correlations with other variables ranged from –.42 to .54.

Author: Van Hooft, E. A. J., et al.

Article: Predictors and outcomes of job search behavior: The moderating effects of gender and family situation.

Journal: *Journal of Vocational Behavior*, October 2005, *67*, 133–152.

Related Research: Van Hooft, E. A. J., et al. (2004). Job search and the theory of planned behavior: Minority–majority group differences in the Netherlands. *Journal of Vocational Behavior*, *65*, 366–390.

11819

Test Name: JOB SEARCH BEHAVIOR SCALE—DUTCH VERSION

Purpose: To assess job search behavior.

Number of Items: 11

Format: Responses are made on a 5-point scale ranging from 1 (*no time at all*) to 5 (*very much time*). All items are presented.

Reliability: Alpha coefficients were .86 and .89.

Validity: Correlations with other variables ranged from –.22 to .47.

Author: van Hooft, E. A. J., et al.

Article: Job search and the theory of planned behavior: Minority–majority group differences in the Netherlands.

Journal: *Journal of Vocational Behavior*, December 2004, *65*, 366–390.

Related Research: Blau, G. (1994). Testing a two-dimensional measure of job-search behavior. *Organizational Behavior and Human Decision Processes*, *59*, 288–312.

11820

Test Name: JOB SEARCH BEHAVIOR SCALES

Purpose: To measure general, preparatory, and active job search behavior.

Number of Items: 18

Format: Scales range from 1 (*never [0 times] or strongly disagree*) to 5 (*frequently [6–9 times] or strongly agree*). Sample items are presented.

Reliability: Alpha coefficients ranged from .72 to .94 across subscales.

Validity: Correlations with other variables ranged from –.15 to .89.

Author: Saks, A. M., and Ashforth, B. E.

Article: Is job search related to employment quality? It all depends on the fit.

Journal: *Journal of Applied Psychology*, August 2002, *87*, 646–654.

Related Research: Blau, G. (1994). Testing a two-dimensional measure of job-search behavior. *Organizational Behavior and Human Decision Processes*, *59*, 288–312.

11821

Test Name: JOB SEARCH BEHAVIORAL INDEX— ADAPTED

Purpose: To measure job search behavior.

Number of Items: 10

Format: Responses are 1 (*yes*) to 0 (*no*). Examples are given.

Reliability: Coefficient alpha was .81.

Validity: Correlations with other variables ranged from –.30 to .54 (*n* = 392).

Author: Boswell, W. R., et al.

Article: Relations between stress and work outcomes: The role of felt challenge, job control, and psychological strain.

Journal: *Journal of Vocational Behavior*, February 2004, *64*, 165–181.

Related Research: Kopelman, R. E., et al. (1992). Rationale and construct validity evidence for the Job Search Behavior Index: Because intentions (and New Year's resolutions) often come to naught. *Journal of Vocational Behavior*, *40*, 269–287.

11822

Test Name: JOB SEARCH INTENSITY AND CLARITY SCALES

Purpose: To assess the frequency of job search behavior and the clarity of the search.

Number of Items: 14

Format: Intensity scales range from 1 (*never*) to 5 (*very often*). Clarity responses are "agree" and "disagree." All items are presented.

Reliability: Alpha coefficients were .82 (intensity) and .85 (clarity).

Validity: Correlations with other variables ranged from –.14 to .37.

Author: Wanberg, C. R., et al.

Article: Predictive validity of a multidisciplinary model of reemployment success.

Journal: *Journal of Applied Psychology,* December 2002, *87,* 1100–1120.

11823

Test Name: JOB SEARCH INTERACTION SCALE—DUTCH VERSION

Purpose: To assess job search intention.

Number of Items: 11

Format: Responses are made on a 5-point scale ranging from 1 (*no time at all*) to 5 (*very much time*).

Reliability: Coefficient alpha was .92.

Validity: Correlations with other variables ranged from –.24 to .54.

Author: van Hooft, E. A. J., et al.

Article: Job search and the theory of planned behavior: Minority–majority group differences in the Netherlands.

Journal: *Journal of Vocational Behavior,* December 2004, *65,* 366–390.

Related Research: Ajzen, I. (1990). The theory of planned behavior. *Organizational Behavior and Human Decision Processes, 50,* 179–211.

11824

Test Name: JOB-SEEKING SCALE

Purpose: To measure job seeking.

Number of Items: 12

Format: Includes two dimensions: Traditional Job Seeking and Assertive Job Seeking. Sample items are presented.

Reliability: Coefficient alpha was .94.

Author: Adams, G., and Rau, B.

Article: Job seeking among retirees seeking bridge employment.

Journal: *Personnel Psychology,* Autumn 2004, *57,* 719–744.

Related Research: Blau, G. (1994). Testing a two-dimensional measure of job search behavior. *Organizational Behavior and Human Decision Processes, 59,* 288–312.

11825

Test Name: KINDERGARTEN BEHAVIOR RATING SCALE

Purpose: To identify pupils at risk for later academic difficulties.

Number of Items: 7

Format: Ratings are made on a 9-point scale.

Reliability: Coefficient alpha was .92. Test–retest correlations ranged between .92 and .97.

Validity: Correlations with academic achievement in Grades 1 and 2 ranged between .27 and .66.

Author: Cadieux, A.

Article: A 3-year longitudinal study of self-concept and classroom behavior of grade 1 retained pupils.

Journal: *Perceptual and Motor Skills,* April 2003, *96,* 371–378.

Related Research: Cadieux, A., & Boudreault, P. (2002). Psychometric properties of a Kindergarten Behavior Rating Scale to predict later academic achievement. *Psychological Reports, 91,* 687–698.

11826

Test Name: LEADER BEHAVIOR SCALE

Purpose: To assess preparation, supportive coaching, active coaching, sense making, event novelty, event description, perceptions of leader effectiveness

and satisfaction with external team leadership.

Number of Items: 26

Format: Scales range from 1 (*not at all*) to 5 (*to a very large extent*). Sample items are presented.

Reliability: Alpha coefficients ranged from .65 to .91 across subscales.

Validity: Correlations between subscales ranged from –.35 to .55.

Author: Morgeson, F. P.

Article: The external leadership of self-managing teams: Intervening in the context of novel and disruptive events.

Journal: *Journal of Applied Psychology,* May 2005, *90,* 497–508.

11827

Test Name: LEADER INFORMING BEHAVIOR SCALE

Purpose: To assess leader-informing behavior in a work unit.

Number of Items: 3

Format: Scales range from 1 (*strongly in disagreement*) to 5 (*strongly in agreement*). All items are presented.

Reliability: Coefficient alpha was .89.

Validity: Correlations with other variables ranged from .00 to .56 aggregated at the work-unit level.

Author: González-Romá, V., et al.

Article: An examination of the antecedents and moderator influences of climate strength.

Journal: *Journal of Applied Psychology,* June 2002, *87,* 465–473.

11828

Test Name: LEADERSHIP BEHAVIOR SCALES

Purpose: To measure contingent reward behaviors, noncontingent reward behaviors, contingent punishment behaviors, noncontingent punishment behaviors, leader likeability, and leader member exchange.

Number of Items: 31

Format: Scales range from 1 (*not at all, never true*) to 5 (*to a very great extent, almost always true*), from 1 (*not at all, never true*) to 5 (*to a very great extent, almost always true*), and from 1 (*not at all*) to 4 (*fully*). Sample items are presented.

Reliability: Alpha coefficients ranged from .55 to .93 across subscales.

Author: Dionne, S. D., et al.

Article: Neutralizing substitutes for leadership theory: Leadership effects and common-source bias.

Journal: *Journal of Applied Psychology*, June 2002, *87*, 454–464.

Related Research: Podsakoff, P. M., et al. (1982). Effects of leader contingent and noncontingent reward and punishment behaviors on subordinate performance and satisfaction. *Academy of Management Journal, 25*, 810–821.

11829

Test Name: LEADERSHIP EMPOWERMENT BEHAVIOR SCALE

Purpose: To assess the meaningfulness of work, fostering participation in decision making, expression of confidence, and providing autonomy.

Number of Items: 10

Format: Sample items are presented.

Reliability: Coefficient alpha was .88.

Validity: Correlations with other variables ranged from –.01 to .22.

Author: Ahearne, M., et al.

Article: To empower or not to empower your sales force? An empirical examination of the influence of leadership empowerment behavior on customer satisfaction and performance.

Journal: *Journal of Applied Psychology*, September 2005, *90*, 945–955.

11830

Test Name: LEADERSHIP PROTOTYPICALITY SCALES

Purpose: To measure productivity effectiveness, group-orientedness, charisma, and self-sacrificing leadership behavior.

Number of Items: 13

Format: Various Likert-type formats are used. All are presented along with sample items.

Reliability: Alpha coefficients ranged from .92 to .95 across subscales.

Author: van Knippenberg, B., and van Knippenberg, D.

Article: Leader self-sacrifice and leadership effectiveness: The moderating role of leader prototypicality.

Journal: *Journal of Applied Psychology*, January 2005, *90*, 25–37.

Related Research: Platow, M. J., & van Knippenberg, D. (2001). A social identity analysis of leadership endorsement: The effects of leader ingroup prototypicality and distributive intergroup fairness. *Personality and Social Psychology Bulletin, 27*, 1508–1519.

11831

Test Name: LIKELIHOOD TO SEXUALLY HARASS SCALE

Purpose: To measure male likelihood to harass.

Number of Items: 10

Format: Items are scenarios that males rate on a scale that ranges from 1 (*not at all likely*) to 5 (*very likely to engage in sexually harassing behavior*).

Reliability: Coefficient alpha was .91.

Author: Robb, L. A., and Doverspike, D.

Article: Self-reported proclivity to harass as a moderator of the effectiveness of sexual harassment–presentation training.

Journal: *Psychological Reports*, February 2001, *88*, 85–88.

Related Research: Pryor, J. B. (1988). The Likelihood to Sexually Harass Scale. In C. M. Davis et al. (Eds.), *Sexually-related measures: A compendium* (pp. 295–298). Beverly Hills, CA: Sage.

11832

Test Name: LOW SELF-CONTROL SCALE

Purpose: To measure low self-control.

Number of Items: 24

Format: Four-point response categories range from 1 (*strongly disagree*) to 4 (*strongly agree*).

Reliability: Coefficient alpha was .83.

Validity: Correlations with other variables ranged from –.25 to .31.

Author: Higgins, G. E., and Makin, D. A.

Article: Self-control, deviant peers, and software piracy.

Journal: *Psychological Reports*, December 2004, *95*, Part 1, 921–931.

Related Research: Grasmick, H. G., et al. (1993). Testing the core empirical implications of Gottfredson and Hirschi's general theory of crime. *Journal of Research in Crime and Delinquency, 30*, 5–29.

11833

Test Name: MACHIAVELLIAN BEHAVIOR SCALE

Purpose: To measure Machiavellian behavior.

Number of Items: 7

Format: Four-point approval scales are anchored by *strongly approve* and *strongly disapprove*. All items (scenarios) are presented.

Reliability: Coefficient alpha was .70.

Validity: Correlations with other variables ranged from .37 to .79.

Author: Aziz, A., et al.

Article: Relations of Machiavellian behavior with sales performance of stockbrokers.

Journal: *Psychological Reports*, April 2002, *90*, 451–460.

Related Research: Aziz, A., & Meeks, J. (1990). *A new scale for measuring Machiavellianism.* Unpublished paper, School of Business and Economics, College of Charleston, Charleston, SC.

11834

Test Name: MARIJUANA COPING STRATEGIES SCALE

Purpose: To assess change processes for modifying marijuana use.

Number of Items: 48

Format: Scales ranged from 0 (*never*) to 3 (*frequently*).

Reliability: Coefficient alpha was .94.

Author: Litt, M. D., et al.

Article: Coping and self-efficacy in marijuana treatment: Results from the Marijuana Treatment Project.

Journal: *Journal of Consulting and Clinical Psychology*, December 2005, *73*, 1015–1025.

Related Research: Prochaska, J. O., et al. (1988). Measuring processes of change: Applications to the cessation of smoking. *Journal of Consulting and Clinical Psychology, 56,* 520–528.

11835

Test Name: MEASURE OF INGRATIATORY BEHAVIORS IN ORGANIZATIONAL SETTINGS

Purpose: To measure ingratiation.

Number of Items: 24

Format: Includes four dimensions: Other-Enhancement, Favor Rendering, Opinion Conformity, and Self-Promotion. Examples are given.

Reliability: Alpha coefficients ranged from .71 to .82.

Validity: Correlations with other variables ranged from –.36 to .34.

Author: Kacmar, K. M., et al.

Article: Situational and dispositional factors as antecedents of ingratiatory behaviors in organizational settings.

Journal: *Journal of Vocational Behavior*, October 2004, *65,* 309–331.

Related Research: Kumar, K., & Beyerlein, M. (1991). Construction and validation of an instrument for measuring ingratiatory behaviors in organizational settings. *Journal of Applied Psychology, 76,* 619–627.

11836

Test Name: METACOGNITIVE ACTIVITY SCALE

Purpose: To assess the degree to which trainees engaged in metacognitive monitoring and control activities during web-page training.

Number of Items: 15

Format: Responses are made on a 5-point scale ranging from 1 (*almost never*) to 5 (*almost always*). All items are presented.

Reliability: Coefficient alpha was .92.

Validity: Correlations with other variables ranged from –.35 to .52.

Author: Schmidt, A. M., and Ford, J. K.

Article: Learning within a learner control training environment: The interactive effects of goal orientation and metacognitive instruction on learning outcomes.

Journal: *Personnel Psychology,* Summer 2003, *56*, 405–429.

Related Research: Ford, J. K., et al. (1998). Relationships of goal orientation, metacognitive activity, and practice strategies with learning outcomes and transfer. *Journal of Applied Psychology, 83,* 218–233.

11837

Test Name: MISREPRESENTATION OF INFORMATION SCALE

Purpose: To assess the degree to which subjects misrepresent information.

Number of Items: 4

Format: Seven-point scales are anchored by 1 (*always*) and 2 (*never*). All items are presented.

Reliability: Cronbach's alpha was .88.

Author: Yurtsever, G.

Article: Tolerance of ambiguity, information, and negotiation.

Journal: *Psychological Reports,* August 2001, *89*, 57–64.

Related Research: Lewicki, R. J. (1983). Lying and deception: A behavioral model. In M. H. Bazerman & R. J. Lewicki (Eds.), *Negotiating in organizations* (pp. 64–112). Beverly Hills, CA: Sage.

11838

Test Name: MONITORING THE FUTURE STUDY SURVEY

Purpose: To determine frequency of use of substances.

Format: Responses are made on a 7-point scale ranging from *never* to *40+ times*.

Reliability: Alpha coefficients were .66 (girls) and .83 (boys).

Validity: Correlations with other variables ranged from −.49 to .78.

Author: Luther, S. S., and Becker, B. E.

Article: Privileged but pressured? A study of affluent youth.

Journal: *Child Development,* September/October 2002, 73, 1593–1610.

Related Research: Johnston, L. D., et al. (1984). *Drugs and American high school students* (DHHS No. ADM 85-1374). Washington, DC: U.S. Government Printing Office.

11839

Test Name: MORAL DISENGAGEMENT SCALE

Purpose: To assess a child's proneness to moral disengagement.

Number of Items: 28

Format: Scales range from 1 (*not sure*) to 2 (*agree*). All items are presented.

Reliability: Coefficient alpha was .82.

Validity: Correlations with other variables ranged from −.16 to .32.

Author: Pelton, J., et al.

Article: The Moral Disengagement Scale: Extension with an American minority sample.

Journal: *Journal of Psychopathology and Behavioral Assessment,* March 2004, 26, 31–39.

Related Research: Bandura, A. (1995). *Multifaceted Scale of the Mechanisms of Moral Disengagement.* (Available from A. Bandura, Stanford University, Stanford, CA)

11840

Test Name: MOTHER-RATED EMOTION REGULATION MEASURE

Purpose: To enable mothers to rate their child's skills at emotion regulation.

Number of Items: 17

Format: Includes two scales: Soothability and Emotionality. Responses are made on a 7-point scale. Examples are presented.

Reliability: Coefficient alpha was .87.

Validity: Correlations with other variables ranged from −.19 to .56.

Author: Lindsey, E. W., and Colwell, M. J.

Article: Preschoolers' emotional competence: Links to pretend and physical play.

Journal: *Child Study Journal,* 2003, 33, 39–52.

Related Research: Finegan, J., et al. (1989). Factor structure of the Preschool Characteristics Questionnaire. *Infant Behavior and Development,* 12, 221–227.

11841

Test Name: MOTIVATIONAL STYLE PROFILE—ADAPTED

Purpose: To assess paratelic and negativistic dominance.

Number of Items: 20

Format: Includes four subscales. Responses are made on a 6-point scale ranging from *never* to *always*.

Reliability: Alpha coefficients ranged from .70 to .83. Temporal stability coefficients ranged from .71 to .86.

Author: Thatcher, J., et al.

Article: Motivation, stress, and cortisol responses in sky diving.

Journal: *Perceptual and Motor Skills,* December 2003, 97, Part 1, 995–1002.

Related Research: Apter, M. J., et al. (1998). The development of the Motivational Style Profile. *Personality and Individual Differences,* 24, 7–18.

11842

Test Name: NATIONAL YOUTH SURVEY—ADAPTED

Purpose: To enable adolescents to report their delinquent behaviors.

Number of Items: 20

Format: Includes major and minor delinquent activities. Responses are made on a 5-point scale ranging from 0 (*never*) to 4 (*six or more times*).

Reliability: Alpha coefficients ranged from .69 to .77.

Validity: Correlations with other variables ranged from −.05 to .52 ($n = 451$).

Author: Kim, K. J., et al.

Article: Reciprocal influences between stressful life events and adolescent internalizing and externalizing problems.

Journal: *Child Development,* January/February 2003, 74, 127–143.

Related Research: Elliott, D. S., et al. (1989). *Multiple problem youth: Delinquency, substance use, and mental health problems.* New York: Springer-Verlag.

11843

Test Name: OPPORTUNISTIC BEHAVIOR SCALE

Purpose: To measure the extent to which a copartner would be willing to pursue his or her goals with guile.

Number of Items: 6

Reliability: Coefficient alpha was .73.

Validity: Correlations with other variables ranged from −.43 to .47.

Author: Wong, A., et al.

Article: Organizational partnerships in China: Self-interest, goal interdependence, and opportunism.

Journal: *Journal of Applied Psychology*, July 2005, *90*, 782–791.

Related Research: Parkhe, A. (1993). Strategic alliance structuring: A game theoretic and transaction cost examination of interfirm cooperation. *Academy of Management Journal, 36*, 794–829.

11844

Test Name: ORGANIZATIONAL ATTRIBUTIONAL STYLE QUESTIONNAIRE

Purpose: To measure the extent which a person exhibits a hostile attributional style.

Number of Items: 32

Format: Various 7-point scales are used as responses to scenarios. Sample items are presented.

Reliability: Internal reliability was .89.

Validity: Correlations with other variables ranged from −.12 to .64.

Author: Douglas, S. C., and Martinko, M. J.

Article: Exploring the role of individual differences in the prediction of workplace aggression.

Journal: *Journal of Applied Psychology*, August 2001, *86*, 547–559.

Related Research: Kent, R., & Martinko, M. J. (1995). The development and evaluation of a scale to measure organizational attributional style. In M. J. Martinko (Ed.), *Attribution theory: An organizational perspective* (pp. 53–75). Delray Beach, FL: St. Lucie Press.

11845

Test Name: ORGANIZATIONAL CITIZENSHIP BEHAVIOR

Purpose: To measure loyalty, obedience, social participation, advocacy participation, and functional participation.

Number of Items: 34

Reliability: Alpha coefficients ranged from .54 to .68.

Validity: Correlations with other variables ranged from .55 to .86. Correlations between subscales ranged from .03 to .48.

Author: Turnipseed, D. L.

Article: Hardy personality: A potential link with organizational citizenship behavior.

Journal: *Psychological Reports*, October 2003, *93*, 529–543.

Related Research: Van Dyne, L., et al. (1994). Organization citizenship behavior: Construct redefinition, measurement, and validation. *Academy of Management Journal, 37*, 765–802.

11846

Test Name: ORGANIZATIONAL CITIZENSHIP BEHAVIOR— ADAPTED

Purpose: To measure the dimensions of boosterism and conscientiousness.

Number of Items: 6

Format: Includes measures of conscientiousness and boosterism.

Reliability: Alpha coefficients were .79 and .80.

Validity: Correlations with other variables ranged from .23 to .67 (*n* = 186).

Author: Chen, Z. X., et al.

Article: Test of a mediation model of perceived organizational support.

Journal: *Journal of Vocational Behavior*, June 2005, *66*, 457–470.

Related Research: Farh, J. L., et al. (1997). Impetus for extraordinary action: A cultural analysis of justice and organizational citizenship behavior in Chinese society. *Administrative Science Quarterly, 42*, 421–444.

11847

Test Name: ORGANIZATIONAL CITIZENSHIP BEHAVIOR INTENTIONS SCALE

Purpose: To measure intention to be altruistic and conscientious in one's organizational behavior.

Number of Items: 11

Format: Scales range from 1 (*most unlikely*) to 7 (*most likely*). Sample items are presented.

Reliability: Coefficient alpha was .65.

Validity: Correlations with other variables ranged from −.06 to .46.

Author: Williams, S., et al.

Article: Justice and organizational citizenship behavior intentions: Fair rewards versus fair treatment.

Journal: *The Journal of Social Psychology*, February 2002, *142*, 33–44.

11848

Test Name: ORGANIZATIONAL CITIZENSHIP BEHAVIOR MEASURE

Purpose: To measure organizational citizenship behavior.

Number of Items: 10

Format: Includes two measures: Helping and Conscientiousness. Responses are made on a 5-point scale ranging from 1 (*to a very small extent*) to 5 (*to a great extent*). All items are presented.

Reliability: Alpha coefficients ranged from .80 to .95.

Validity: Correlations with other variables ranged from .24 to .60.

Author: Ehrhart, M. G.

Article: Leadership and procedural justice climate as antecedents of unit-level organizational citizenship behavior.

Journal: *Personnel Psychology,* Spring 2004, *57,* 61–94.

Related Research: Podsakoff, P. M., et al. (1990). Transformational leader behaviors and their effects on followers' trust in leader, satisfaction, and organizational citizenship behaviors. *Leadership Quarterly, 1,* 107–142.

11849

Test Name: ORGANIZATIONAL CITIZENSHIP BEHAVIOR SCALE

Purpose: To measure organizational citizenship behavior: loyalty, service delivery, and participation.

Number of Items: 16

Format: Scales range from 1 (*not at all characteristic of me*) to 7 (*extremely characteristic of me*). All items are presented.

Reliability: Alpha coefficients ranged from .80 to .87 across subscales.

Validity: Correlations with other variables ranged from .11 to .53.

Author: Bettencourt, L. A., et al.

Article: A comparison of attitude, personality, and knowledge predictors of service-oriented organizational citizenship behaviors.

Journal: *Journal of Applied Psychology,* February 2001, *86,* 29–41.

11850

Test Name: ORGANIZATIONAL CITIZENSHIP BEHAVIOR SCALE

Purpose: To measure altruism and conscientiousness.

Number of Items: 6

Format: Includes two dimensions: Altruism and Conscientiousness. Sample items are presented.

Reliability: Alpha coefficients were .78 and .87.

Validity: Correlations with other variables ranged from −.17 to .68 ($n = 253$).

Author: Chen, Z. X., and Francesco, A. M.

Article: The relationship between the three components of commitment and employee performance in China.

Journal: *Journal of Vocational Behavior,* June 2003, *62,* 490–510.

Related Research: Chen, Z. X., et al. (2002). Loyalty to supervisor versus organizational commitment: Relationship with the performance of Chinese employees. *Journal of Occupational and Organizational Psychology, 75,* 339–356.

11851

Test Name: ORGANIZATIONAL CITIZENSHIP BEHAVIOR SCALE

Purpose: To measure organizational citizenship behaviors.

Number of Items: 4

Format: Responses are made on a 7-point scale ranging from 1 (*strongly disagree*) to 7 (*strongly agree*).

Reliability: Alpha coefficients were .79 to .80.

Validity: Correlations with other variables ranged from −.32 to .49.

Author: Conway, N., and Briner, R. B.

Article: Full-time versus part-time employees: Understanding the links between work status, the psychological contract, and attitudes.

Journal: *Journal of Vocational Behavior,* October 2002, *61,* 279–301.

11852

Test Name: ORGANIZATIONAL CITIZENSHIP BEHAVIOR SCALE

Purpose: To measure organizational citizenship behavior as loyalty and civic virtue.

Number of Items: 7

Format: Scales range from *not at all* to *a very great extent.*

Reliability: Alpha coefficients ranged from .79 to .81.

Validity: Correlations with other variables ranged from −.02 to .35.

Author: Coyle-Shapiro, J. A.-M., and Conway, N.

Article: Exchange relationships: Examining psychological contracts and perceived organizational support.

Journal: *Journal of Applied Psychology,* July 2005, *90,* 774–781.

11853

Test Name: ORGANIZATIONAL CITIZENSHIP BEHAVIOR SCALE

Purpose: To assess organizational citizenship behaviors oriented to the organization as a whole.

Number of Items: 5

Format: Responses are made on a 5-point scale ranging from 1 (*very uncharacteristic*) to 5 (*very characteristic*). A sample item is presented.

Reliability: Coefficient alpha was .81.

Validity: Correlations with other variables ranged from −.34 to .71.

Author: Feldman, D. C., and Turnley, W. H.

Article: Contingent employment in academic careers: Relative deprivation among adjunct faculty.

Journal: *Journal of Vocational Behavior*, April 2004, *64*, 284–307.

Related Research: Williams, L. J., & Anderson, S. E. (1991). Job satisfaction and organizational commitment as predictors of organizational citizenship and in-role behaviors. *Journal of Management, 17*, 601–617.

11854

Test Name: ORGANIZATIONAL CITIZENSHIP BEHAVIOR SCALE

Purpose: To assess altruism, sportsmanship, civic virtue, and courtesy.

Number of Items: 21

Format: Frequency scales range from 1 (*never*) to 5 (*always*).

Reliability: Coefficient alpha was .78.

Validity: Correlations with other variables ranged from –.19 to .19.

Author: Glomb, T. M., and Welsh, E. T.

Article: Can opposites attract? Personality heterogeneity in supervisor–subordinate dyads as a predictor of subordinate outcomes.

Journal: *Journal of Applied Psychology*, July 2005, *90*, 749–757.

11855

Test Name: ORGANIZATIONAL CITIZENSHIP BEHAVIOR SCALE

Purpose: To measure altruism, conscientiousness, civic virtue, courtesy, and sportsmanship.

Number of Items: 23

Format: A 5-point Likert format is used. All items are presented.

Reliability: Alphas ranged from .72 to .91 across subscales. Test–retest reliability was .83.

Author: Lam, S. S.

Article: Test–retest reliability and factor structures of organizational

citizenship behavior for Hong Kong workers.

Journal: *Psychological Reports*, February 2001, *88*, 262–264.

Related Research: Podsakoff, P. M., et al. (1990). Transformational leader behaviors and their effects on followers' trust in leader, satisfaction, and organizational citizenship behaviors. *Leadership Quarterly, 1*, 107–142.

11856

Test Name: ORGANIZATIONAL CITIZENSHIP BEHAVIOR SCALE

Purpose: To measure individual and organizational components of organizational citizenship behavior.

Number of Items: 16

Format: Scales range from 1 (*never*) to 7 (*always*). All items are presented.

Reliability: Alpha coefficients were .81 (individual) and .88 (organizational).

Validity: Correlations with other variables ranged from –.47 to .30.

Author: Lee, K., and Allen, N. J.

Article: Organizational citizenship behavior and workplace deviance: The role of affect and cognitions.

Journal: *Journal of Applied Psychology*, February 2002, *87*, 131–142.

11857

Test Name: ORGANIZATIONAL CITIZENSHIP BEHAVIOR SCALE

Purpose: To measure aspects of organizational citizenship.

Number of Items: 20

Format: Scales range from 1 (*strongly disagree*) to 5 (*strongly agree*).

Reliability: Alpha coefficients ranged from .73 to .85.

Validity: Correlations with other variables ranged from –.29 to .40.

Author: Tepper, B. J., et al.

Article: Justice, citizenship, and role definition effects.

Journal: *Journal of Applied Psychology*, August 2001, *86*, 789–796.

Related Research: Moorman, R. H., & Blakely, G. L. (1995). Individualism–collectivism as an individual difference predictor of organizational citizenship behavior. *Journal of Organizational Behavior, 16*, 127–142.

11858

Test Name: ORGANIZATIONAL CITIZENSHIP BEHAVIORS SCALE

Purpose: To measure organizational citizenship behaviors.

Number of Items: 24

Format: Includes five dimensions: Altruism, Courtesy, Sportsmanship, Civic Virtue, and Conscientiousness.

Reliability: Reliabilities ranged from .67 to .86.

Validity: Correlations with other variables ranged from .06 to .35.

Author: Norris-Watts, C., and Levy, P. E.

Article: The mediating role of affective commitment in the relation of the feedback environment to work outcomes.

Journal: *Journal of Vocational Behavior*, December 2004, *65*, 351–365.

Related Research: Podsakoff, P. M., et al. (1990). Transformational leader behaviors and their effects on followers' trust in leader, satisfaction, and organizational citizenship behaviors. *Leadership Quarterly, 1*, 107–142.

11859

Test Name: ORGANIZATIONAL CITIZENSHIP BEHAVIORS SCALES

Purpose: To measure organizational citizenship behaviors.

Number of Items: 10

Format: Includes two scales: Altruism Towards Colleagues and Loyal Boosterism. Examples are given.

Reliability: Alpha coefficients were .77 and .82.

Validity: Correlations with other variables ranged from –.29 to .47.

Author: Wasti, S. A.

Article: Commitment profiles: Combinations of organizational commitment forms and job outcomes.

Journal: *Journal of Vocational Behavior*, October 2005, *67*, 290–308.

Related Research: Moorman, R. H., & Blakely, G. L. (1995). Individualism–collectivism as an individual difference predictor of organizational citizenship behavior. *Journal of Organizational Behavior, 16*, 127–142.

11860

Test Name: ORGANIZATIONAL CITIZENSHIP SCALE

Purpose: To measure organizational citizenship.

Number of Items: 8

Format: Scales range from 1 (*not at all characteristic of me*) to 5 (*very characteristic of me*). Sample items are presented.

Reliability: Alpha coefficients ranged from .87 to .88 across subscales.

Validity: Correlations with other variables ranged from –.32 to .59.

Author: Aryee, S., and Chay, Y. W.

Article: Workplace justice, citizenship behavior, and turnover intentions in a union context: Examining the mediating role of perceived union support and union instrumentality.

Journal: *Journal of Applied Psychology*, February 2001, *86*, 154–160.

Related Research: Skarlicki, D. P., & Latham, G. P. (1996). Increasing citizenship behavior in a labor union: A test of organizational justice theory. *Journal of Applied Psychology, 50*, 617–633.

11861

Test Name: ORGANIZATIONAL MISBEHAVIOR SCALES

Purpose: To assess intentions, attitudes, and norms in organizational misbehavior.

Number of Items: 22

Format: Seven-point scales are used. All items are described.

Validity: Correlations among intention, attitude, and norms ranged from .23 to .40.

Author: Vardi, Y., and Weitz, E.

Article: Using the theory of reasoned action to predict organizational misbehavior.

Journal: *Psychological Reports*, December 2002, *91*, Part 2, 1027–1040.

Related Research: Vardi, Y., & Wiener, Y. (1996). Misbehavior in organizations: A motivational framework. *Organization Science, 7*, 151–165.

11862

Test Name: ORIENTATION TOWARD CONTROL VERSUS AUTONOMY SCALE

Purpose: To assess teachers' styles of managing behavioral problems in the classroom.

Number of Items: 32

Format: Includes four subscales: Highly Directive, Moderately Directive, Moderately Autonomy-Oriented, and Highly Autonomy-Oriented. Responses are made on a 7-point scale.

Reliability: Alpha coefficients ranged from .62 to .76.

Author: Vitaro, F., et al.

Article: Kindergarten disruptive behaviors, protective factors, and educational achievement by early adulthood.

Journal: *Journal of Educational Psychology*, November 2005, *97*, 617–629.

Related Research: Deci, E. L., et al. (1981). An instrument to assess adults' orientations toward control versus autonomy with children: Reflections on intrinsic motivation and perceived competence. *Journal of Educational Psychology, 73*, 642–650.

11863

Test Name: OVERT–COVERT AGGRESSION INVENTORY

Purpose: To measure obvious and direct aggression and latent indirect aggression.

Number of Items: 10

Format: All items are presented.

Reliability: Alpha coefficients ranged from .73 to .74. Test–retest reliability ranged from .84 to .88. Item-total correlations ranged from .42 to .56.

Validity: Correlations with other variables ranged from –.23 to .73.

Author: Miyazaki, T., et al.

Article: Development of the Overt–Covert Aggression Inventory.

Journal: *Psychological Reports*, August 2003, *93*, 24–36.

11864

Test Name: OWNERSHIP BEHAVIORS SCALE

Purpose: To assess ownership behaviors.

Number of Items: 4

Format: Responses are made on a 5-point scale ranging from *all the time* to *never.* All items are presented.

Reliability: Coefficient alpha was .83.

Validity: Correlations with other variables ranged from .21 to .79.

Author: Wagner, S. H., et al.

Article: Employees that think and act like owners: Effect of ownership beliefs and behaviors on organizational effectiveness.

Journal: *Personnel Psychology,* Winter 2003, *56,* 847–871.

11865

Test Name: PARTICIPATION IN CLASS QUESTIONNAIRE

Purpose: To measure class participation by observer (teacher) report.

Number of Items: 4

Format: Scales range from 1 (*never*) to 5 (*always*). All items are presented.

Reliability: Alpha coefficients ranged from .65 to .77.

Validity: Correlations with other variables ranged from –.51 to .37.

Author: Oyserman, D., et al.

Article: Possible selves as roadmaps.

Journal: *Journal of Research in Personality,* April 2004, *38,* 130–147.

Related Research: Finn, J., et al. (1995). Disruptive and inattentive–withdrawn behavior and achievement among fourth graders. *Elementary School Journal, 95,* 421–434.

11866

Test Name: PARTICIPATION IN SCHOLARLY ACTIVITIES SCALE

Purpose: To determine activities in which doctoral students are or were involved while a student.

Number of Items: 11

Format: Respondents check items representing activities in which they are or have been involved while a student. All items are presented.

Reliability: Coefficient alpha was .77.

Validity: Correlations with other variables ranged from –.10 to .31 (N = 50).

Author: Weidman, J. C., and Stein, E. L.

Article: Socialization of doctoral students to academic norms.

Journal: *Research in Higher Education,* December 2003, *44,* 641–656.

11867

Test Name: PAST YEAR LEISURE PHYSICAL ACTIVITY SCALE

Purpose: To assess exercise level.

Number of Items: 24

Format: Each activity endorsed is rated on a scale of times per year, months per year, days per week, and minutes per day.

Reliability: Test–retest reliability (1 year) ranged from .55 to .66.

Validity: Correlations with other variables ranged from –.07 to .13.

Author: Stice, E., et al.

Article: Psychological and behavioral risk factors for obesity onset in adolescent girls: A prospective study.

Journal: *Journal of Consulting and Clinical Psychology,* April 2005, *73,* 195–202.

Related Research: Aaron, D. J., et al. (1993). The epidemiology of leisure physical activity in an adolescent population. *Medicine and Science in Sports and Exercise, 25,* 847–853.

11868

Test Name: PATTERNS OF DECISION MAKING QUESTIONNAIRE

Purpose: To assess behavioral control.

Number of Items: 28

Format: Responses are made on a 5-point scale ranging from 1 (*My parents tell me exactly what to do, without discussing it with me*) to 5 (*I decide alone*).

Reliability: Coefficient alpha was .87.

Author: Walker-Barnes, C. J., & Mason, C. A.

Article: Ethnic differences in the effect of parenting on gang involvement and gang delinquency: A longitudinal, hierarchical linear modeling perspective.

Journal: *Child Development,* November/December 2001, *72,* 1814–1831.

Related Research: Steinberg, L. (1987). Single parents, stepparents, and the susceptibility of adolescents to antisocial peer pressure. *Child Development, 58,* 269–275.

11869

Test Name: PEER EVALUATION INVENTORY—TWO SUBSCALES

Purpose: To assess children's likeability and aggressive disturbance.

Format: Two subscales: Likeability and Aggressive-Disturbance.

Reliability: Alpha coefficients were .89 and .93.

Validity: Correlations with other variables ranged from –.31 to .29.

Author: Charlebois, P., et al.

Article: Examining dosage effects on prevention outcomes: Results from a multi-model longitudinal preventive intervention for young disruptive boys.

Journal: *Journal of School Psychology*, May/June 2004, *42*, 201–220.

Related Research: Pekarik, E. G., et al. (1974). The Pupil Evaluation Inventory: A sociometric technique for assessing children's social behaviors. *Journal of Abnormal Child Psychology, 4*, 83–97.

11870

Test Name: PEER VICTIMIZATION SCALE

Purpose: To assess peer victimization.

Number of Items: 4

Format: Responses are coded 1 (*no/never*), 2 (*sometimes*), or 3 (*a lot*).

Reliability: Alpha coefficients were .74+.

Author: Ladd, G. W., & Burgess, K. B.

Article: Do relational risks and protective factors moderate the linkages between childhood aggression and early psychological and school adjustment?

Journal: *Child Development*, September/October 2001, *72*, 1579–1601.

Related Research: Kochenderfer, B. J., & Ladd, G. W. (1996). Peer victimization: Cause or consequence of school maladjustment? *Child Development, 67*, 1305–1317.

11871

Test Name: PEER VICTIMIZATION SCALE

Purpose: To assess the degree to which students perceived

themselves to be targets of persistent victimization.

Number of Items: 4

Format: Responses are either *somewhat true for me* or *really true for me*.

Reliability: Coefficient alpha was .76.

Author: Nishina, A., and Juvonen, J.

Article: Daily reports of witnessing and experiencing peer harassment in middle school.

Journal: *Child Development*, March/April 2005, *76*, 435–450.

Related Research: Neary, A., & Joseph, S. (1994). Peer victimization and its relationship to self-concept and depression among schoolgirls. *Personality and Individual Differences, 16*, 183–186.

11872

Test Name: PERCEIVED DISCRIMINATION SCALE

Purpose: To measure perceived discrimination.

Number of Items: 6

Format: Includes two areas: perceived frequency of being treated unfairly or negatively because of one's ethnic background at school and outside school; feeling unaccepted in society because of one's ethnicity. Responses are made on a 7-point scale ranging from 1 (*almost never*) to 7 (*very often*). Examples are given.

Reliability: Coefficient alpha was .82.

Validity: Correlations with other variables ranged from −.33 to .29.

Author: Cassidy, C., et al.

Article: Perceived discrimination and psychological distress: The role of personal and ethnic self-esteem.

Journal: *Journal of Counseling Psychology*, July 2004, *51*, 329–339.

Related Research: Verkuyten, M. (1998). Perceived discrimination and self-esteem among ethnic minority adolescents. *The Journal of Social Psychology, 138*, 479–493.

Phinney, J., et al. (1998). Psychological variables as predictors of perceived ethnic discrimination among minority and immigrant adolescents. *Journal of Applied Social Psychology, 28*, 937–953.

11873

Test Name: PERCEIVED PARTNER CRITICISM AND AVOIDANCE SCALE

Purpose: To assess partner behavior.

Number of Items: 38

Format: Item responses range from 1 (*never*) to 4 (*often*). Sample items are presented.

Reliability: Alpha coefficients ranged from .79 to .93.

Author: Manne, S., et al.

Article: Perceived partner critical and avoidant behavior as predictors of anxious and depressive symptoms among mothers of children undergoing hemopaietic stem cell transplantation.

Journal: *Journal of Consulting and Clinical Psychology*, December 2003, *71*, 1076–1083.

Related Research: Manne, S., et al. (1999). Spouse support, coping, and mood among individuals with cancer. *Annals of Behavioral Medicine, 21*, 111–121.

11874

Test Name: PERSONAL LIFESTYLE QUESTIONNAIRE

Purpose: To measure health-related practices: exercise, nutrition, relaxation, substance abuse, safety and health promotion.

Number of Items: 24

Format: Item responses are anchored by 1 (*never*) and 4 (*always*).

Reliability: Alpha coefficients ranged from .58 to .84.

Validity: Correlations between subscales ranged from .26 to .53.

Author: Mahon, N. E., et al.

Article: Mental health variables and positive health practices in early adolescents.

Journal: *Psychological Reports*, June 2001, *88*, Part 2, 1023–1030.

Related Research: Brown, N., et al. (1983). The relationship among health beliefs, health values, and health promotion activities. *Western Journal of Nursing Research, 5*, 155–163.

11875

Test Name: PHYSICAL PERFORMANCE SCALE

Purpose: To assess and rate the difficulty of performing activities that require motion and vigor, such as climbing stairs.

Number of Items: 7

Format: Response scales range from 0 (*complete disability*) to 3 (*no difficulty*). All items are presented.

Reliability: Coefficient alpha was .91.

Author: Shmotkin, D., et al.

Article: Tracing long-term effects of early trauma: A broad-scope view of Holocaust survivors in late life.

Journal: *Journal of Consulting and Clinical Psychology*, April 2003, *71*, 223–234.

Related Research: Rosow, I., & Breslaw, N. (1966). A Guttman health scale for the aged. *Journal of Gerontology, 21*, 556–559.

11876

Test Name: PHYSIOLOGICAL AROUSAL CHECKLIST

Purpose: To assess physiological arousal.

Number of Items: 7

Format: Five-point rating scales ranged from 0 (*not at all*) to 4 (*greatly*). All items are presented.

Reliability: Coefficient alpha was .77.

Author: Duggan, S., et al.

Article: Young adults' immediate and delayed reactions to simulated marital conflicts: Implications for intergenerational patterns of violence in intimate relationships.

Journal: *Journal of Consulting and Clinical Psychology*, February 2001, *69*, 13–24.

Related Research: Shields, S. A., & Stern, R. M. (1979). Emotion: The perception of bodily change. In P. Pliner et al. (Eds.), *Perception of emotion in self and others* (pp. 85–106). New York: Plenum Press.

11877

Test Name: PLANNED BEHAVIOR QUESTIONNAIRE

Purpose: To measure behavioral intentions.

Number of Items: 3

Format: Responses are made on 7-point scales. All items are presented.

Reliability: Coefficient alpha was .90.

Validity: Correlations with other variables ranged from −.08 to .54.

Author: Hagger, M. S., et al.

Article: The processes by which perceived autonomy support in physical education promotes leisure-time physical activity intentions and behavior: A trans-contextual model.

Journal: *Journal of Educational Psychology*, December 2003, *95*, 784–795.

Related Research: Courneya, K. S., & McAuley, E. (1994). Factors affecting the intention–physical activity relationship: Intention versus expectation and scale correspondence. *Research Quarterly for Exercise and Sports, 65*, 280–285.

11878

Test Name: PLEASANT EVENTS SCHEDULE

Purpose: To measure the frequency of relaxation, social skills, and pleasant activities.

Number of Items: 52

Format: Multiple formats are used. All are presented.

Reliability: Reliability coefficients ranged from .75 to .90 across subscales.

Author: Kaufman, N. K., et al.

Article: Potential mediators of cognitive–behavioral therapy for adolescents with comorbid major depression and conduct disorder.

Journal: *Journal of Consulting and Clinical Psychology*, February 2005, *73*, 38–46.

Related Research: MacPhillamy, D. J., & Lewinsohn, P. M. (1982). The Pleasant Events Schedule: Studies on reliability, validity, and scale intercorrelation. *Journal of Consulting and Clinical Psychology, 50*, 363–380.

11879

Test Name: POSITIVE BEHAVIOR SCALE

Purpose: To measure positive aspects of the child's behavior.

Number of Items: 25

Format: Includes three subscales: Compliance, Social Competence, and Autonomy. Responses are made on an 11-point scale ranging from 0 (*not at all like my child*) to

10 (*completely like my child*). Examples are presented.

Reliability: Reliability coefficients ranged from .79 to .95.

Author: Gennetian, L. A., and Miller, C.

Article: Children and welfare reform: A view from an experimental welfare program in Minnesota.

Journal: *Child Development*, March/April 2002, *73*, 601–620.

Related Research: Polit, D. F. (1996). *Parenting and child outcome measures in the New Chance 42-month survey.* New York: Manpower Demonstration Research Corporation.

11880

Test Name: PRE-SCHOOL ACTIVITIES INVENTORY

Purpose: To assess gender role behavior.

Number of Items: 24

Format: Includes three categories: toys, activities, and characteristics. Responses are made on a 5-point scale ranging from 1 (*never*) to 5 (*very often*). Examples are given.

Reliability: Test–retest (1 year) reliabilities were .62 and .66. Split-half reliabilities were .66 and .80. Alpha coefficients ranged from .65 to .91.

Author: Iervolino, A. C., et al.

Article: Genetic and environmental influences on sex-typed behavior during the preschool years.

Journal: *Child Development*, July/August 2005, *76*, 826–840.

Related Research: Golombok, S., & Rust, J. (1993). The Pre-School Activities Inventory: A standardized assessment of gender role in children. *Psychological Assessment, 5*, 131–136.

11881

Test Name: PROACTIVE BEHAVIORS SCALE

Purpose: To measure proactive behaviors.

Number of Items: 22

Format: Includes four proactive behaviors: voice, innovation, political knowledge, and career initiative. Examples are given.

Reliability: Alpha coefficients ranged from .74 to .88.

Validity: Correlations with other variables ranged from −.05 to .34 ($N = 180$).

Author: Seibert, S. E., et al.

Article: What do proactive people do? A longitudinal model linking proactive personality and career success.

Journal: *Personnel Psychology*, Winter 2001, *54*, 845–874.

Related Research: VanDyne, L., & LePine, J. A. (1998). Helping and voice extra-role behaviors: Evidence of construct and predictive validity. *Academy of Management Journal, 41*, 108–119. Welbourne, T. M., et al. (1998). The role-based performance scale: Validity analysis and theory-based measure. *Academy of Management Journal, 41*, 540–555. Chao, G. T., et al. (1994). Organizational socialization: Its content and consequences. *Journal of Applied Psychology, 79*, 730–743. Tharenou, P., & Terry, D. J. (1998). Reliability and validity of scores on scales to measure managerial aspirations. *Educational and Psychological Measurement, 58*, 475–492.

11882

Test Name: PROACTIVE BEHAVIORS SCALE—KOREAN VERSION

Purpose: To assess subordinates' proactive behavior by supervisor report.

Number of Items: 25

Format: Scales range from 1 (*strongly disagree*) to 7 (*strongly agree*). Sample items are presented in English.

Reliability: Reported reliability coefficients ranged from .83 to .90 across subscales.

Validity: Correlations with other variables ranged from −.26 to .26.

Author: Kim, T.-Y., et al.

Article: Socialization tactics, employee proactivity, and person–organization fit.

Journal: *Journal of Applied Psychology*, March 2005, *90*, 232–241.

Related Research: Ashford, S. J., & Black, S. J. (1996). Proactivity during organizational entry: The role of desire for control. *Journal of Applied Psychology, 81*, 199–214.

11883

Test Name: PROBLEM BEHAVIOR INVENTORY FOR ADOLESCENTS

Purpose: To assess alcohol and drug use, smoking, sexual activity, major and minor delinquency, direct and indirect aggression, and gambling.

Number of Items: 40

Format: Various response scales are used. All are described. Sample items are presented.

Reliability: Alpha coefficients ranged from .60 to .91.

Validity: Correlations among problem behaviors ranged from .08 to .60.

Author: Willoughby, T., et al.

Article: Where is the syndrome? Examining co-occurrence among multiple problem behaviors in adolescence.

Journal: *Journal of Consulting and Clinical Psychology*, December 2004, *72*, 1022–1037.

11884

Test Name: PROBLEM BEHAVIOR SCALE

Purpose: To assess the problem behavior of a focal child.

Number of Items: 28

Format: Scales range from 0 (*not true*) to 2 (*often true*).

Reliability: Coefficient alpha was .92.

Author: Morris, P. A., and Gennetian, L. A.

Article: Identifying the effects of income on children's development using experimental data.

Journal: *Journal of Marriage and Family*, August 2003, *65*, 716–729.

Related Research: Peterson, J. L., & Zill, N. (1986). Marital disruption, parent–child relationships, and behavior problems in children. *Journal of Marriage and the Family*, *48*, 295–307.

11885

Test Name: PROBLEM BEHAVIOR SCALE FOR CHILDREN—SELF-RATING FORM

Purpose: To measure problem behavior.

Number of Items: 14

Format: Includes internal problem behavior and external problem behavior. Responses are either "true" or "not true."

Reliability: Test–retest reliability coefficients were .78 and .82. K-R 20 coefficients ranged from .57 to .78. Split-half (unequal length Spearman–Brown) coefficients ranged from .63 to .80.

Author: Aunola, K., and Nurmi, J.-E.

Article: The role of parenting styles in children's problem behavior.

Journal: *Child Development*, November/December 2005, *76*, 1144–1159.

Related Research: Aunola, K., & Nurmi, J.-E. (1999). *Problem Behavior Scale for Children (Self-Rating Form)*. Unpublished test material, University of Jyvaskyla, Jyvaskyla, Finland.

11886

Test Name: PROCRASTINATION SCALE

Purpose: To measure procrastination.

Number of Items: 3

Format: Responses are made on a 7-point scale ranging from 1 (*strongly disagree*) to 7 (*strongly agree*). An example is given.

Reliability: Alpha coefficients were .83 and .92.

Validity: Correlations with other variables ranged from –.28 to .37.

Author: McGregor, H. A., and Elliot, A. J.

Article: Achievement goals as predictors of achievement-relevant processes prior to task engagement.

Journal: *Journal of Educational Psychology*, June 2002, *94*, 381–395.

11887

Test Name: PROCRASTINATION SCALE—SHORT FORM

Purpose: To measure procrastination tendencies.

Number of Items: 16

Format: Scales range from 1 (*That is never me*) to 4 (*That's me for sure*).

Reliability: Alpha coefficients ranged from .86 to .89.

Validity: Correlations with other variables ranged from –.28 to .05.

Author: Klibert, J. J., et al.

Article: Adaptive and maladaptive aspects of self-oriented versus socially prescribed perfectionism.

Journal: *Journal of College Student Development*, March/April 2005, *46*, 141–156.

Related Research: Tuckman, B. W. (1991). The development and concurrent validity of the Procrastination Scale. *Educational and Psychological Measurement*, *51*, 437–480.

11888

Test Name: PROSOCIAL BEHAVIOR SCALE

Purpose: To rate prosocial behavior.

Number of Items: 24

Format: Responses are made on a 5-point scale. Examples are presented.

Reliability: Alpha coefficients were .94 and .95.

Validity: Correlations with other variables ranged from –.26 to .66.

Author: Bandura, A., et al.

Article: Role of affective self-regulatory efficacy in diverse spheres of psychosocial functioning.

Journal: *Child Development*, May/June 2003, *74*, 769–782.

Related Research: Caprara, G. V., & Pastorelli, C. (1993). Early emotional instability, prosocial behaviour, and aggression: Some methodological aspects. *European Journal of Personality*, *7*, 19–36.

11889

Test Name: PROSOCIAL BEHAVIOR SCALE

Purpose: To assess prosocial behavior.

Number of Items: 3

Format: Responses are made on a 5-point scale ranging from 1 (*very uncharacteristic*) to 5 (*very characteristic*). All items are presented.

Reliability: Coefficient alphas were .83 and .87.

Validity: Correlations with other variables ranged from −.16 to −.62.

Author: Gazelle, H., and Rudolph, K. D.

Article: Moving toward and away from the world: Social approach and avoidance trajectories in anxious solitary youth.

Journal: *Child Development*, May/June 2004, *75*, 829–849.

Related Research: Cassidy, J., & Asher, S. R. (1992). Loneliness and peer relations in young children. *Child Development*, *63*, 350–365.

11890

Test Name: PSYCHOLOGICAL CONTRACT INVENTORY

Purpose: To measure the three psychological contract forms: balanced, relational, transactional.

Number of Items: 11

Format: Six-point scales are used. All items are presented.

Reliability: Alpha coefficients ranged from .63 to .87 across subscales.

Author: Hui, C., et al.

Article: Psychological contract and organizational citizenship behavior in China: Investigating generalizability and instrumentality.

Journal: *Journal of Applied Psychology*, April 2004, *89*, 311–321.

Related Research: Rousseau, D. M. (2000). *Psychological Contract Inventory: Technical report* (Tech Rep. No. 2). Pittsburgh, PA: Carnegie Mellon University.

11891

Test Name: PSYCHOLOGICAL CONTRACT SCALES

Purpose: To assess the system of beliefs an individual and an employer hold regarding their exchange agreement.

Number of Items: 23

Format: Scales range from 1 (*not at all*) to 5 (*to a great extent*). All items are presented.

Reliability: Alpha coefficients ranged from .78 to .92 across subscales.

Author: Dabos, G. E., and Rousseau, D. M.

Article: Mutuality and reciprocity in psychological contracts of employees and employers.

Journal: *Journal of Applied Psychology*, February 2004, *89*, 52–72.

Related Research: Rousseau, D. M. (2000). *Psychological Contract Inventory: Technical report* (Tech. Rep. No. 2000-02). Pittsburgh, PA: Carnegie Mellon University.

11892

Test Name: PSYCHOLOGICAL MALTREATMENT OF WOMEN INVENTORY—ADAPTED VERSION

Purpose: To measure psychological aspects of domestic violence among lesbians, gays, and bisexuals.

Number of Items: 14

Format: Scales range from 1 (*never*) to 5 (*very frequently*).

Reliability: Alpha coefficients ranged from .87 to .91.

Author: Balsam, K. F., et al.

Article: Victimization over the life span: A comparison of lesbian, gay, bisexual, and heterosexual siblings.

Journal: *Journal of Consulting and Clinical Psychology*, June 2005, *73*, 477–487.

Related Research: Tolman, R. (1989). The development of a measure of psychological maltreatment of women by their male partners. *Violence and Victims*, *4*, 159–177.

11893

Test Name: PUNISHMENT INVENTORY

Purpose: To assess a student's recollections of punishment during their childhood.

Number of Items: 20

Format: Includes four factors: Living With Rules, Physical Punishment, Consequences of Misbehavior, and Verbal Punishment.

Reliability: Coefficient alpha was .83.

Validity: Correlations with other variables ranged from −.60 to .17.

Author: Cohen, J. H., and Amidon, E. J.

Article: Reward and punishment histories: A way of predicting teaching style?

Journal: *Journal of Educational Research*, May/June 2004, *97*, 269–277.

Related Research: Kaplan, C. (1992). Teachers' punishment histories and their selection of disciplinary strategies. *Contemporary Educational Psychology*, *17*, 258–265.

11894

Test Name: QUESTIONNAIRE FOR PLANNED BEHAVIOR MODEL

Purpose: To measure planned behavior for explaining intention toward healthy eating behavior: attitude toward healthy eating, subjective norms, perceived behavioral control, role identity, attitude strength, behavioral intention.

Format: Various 7-point scales are used. All are illustrated with sample items.

Reliability: Subscale alpha reliabilities ranged from .71 to .89.

Validity: Correlations with a health behavior questionnaire ranged from .10 to .74.

Author: Bebetsos, E., et al.

Article: Physically active students' intentions and self-efficacy towards healthy eating.

Journal: *Psychological Reports*, October 2002, *91*, 485–495.

Related Research: Theodorakis, Y. (1992). Prediction of athletic participation: A test of a planned behavior theory. *Perceptual and Motor Skills*, 74, 371–379.

11895

Test Name: QUESTIONNAIRE OF LEVEL OF HABITUAL PHYSICAL ACTIVITY

Purpose: To measure level of habitual physical activity.

Number of Items: 21

Format: Includes three dimensions: Work, Sports, and Leisure. Each item is scored from 1 to 5.

Reliability: Coefficient alpha was .61. Split-half reliability was .72. Guttman split-half was .66.

Author: Rosa, D. A., et al.

Article: Mood changes after maximal exercise testing in subjects with symptoms of exercise dependence.

Journal: *Perceptual and Motor Skills*, August 2004, *99*, 341–353.

Related Research: Baecke, J. A. H., et al. (1982). A short questionnaire for the measurement of habitual physical activity in epidemiological studies. *American Journal of Clinical Nutrition, 36*, 936–942.

11896

Test Name: REACTIVE AND PROACTIVE AGGRESSION QUESTIONNAIRE

Purpose: To assess reactive and proactive aggression.

Number of Items: 23

Format: Includes two scales: Proactive Aggression and Reactive Aggression. Responses are made on a 3-point scale ranging from 0 (*never*) to 2 (*often*).

Reliability: Alpha coefficients were .74 and .78.

Validity: Correlations with other variables ranged from −.29 to .43.

Author: Miller, J. D., and Lynam, D. R.

Article: Psychopathy and the five-factor model of personality: A replication and extension.

Journal: *Journal of Personality Assessment*, October 2003, *81*, 168–178.

11897

Test Name: REACTIVE–PROACTIVE AGGRESSION SCALE

Purpose: To enable teachers to rate the child's reactive and proactive behavior.

Number of Items: 6

Format: Items reflect both reactive (angry) and proactive (bullying) behavior. Responses are made on a 5-point scale.

Reliability: Coefficient alpha was .91.

Author: Allen, J. P., et al.

Article: A secure base in adolescence: Markers of attachment security in the mother–adolescent relationship.

Journal: *Child Development*, January/February 2003, *74*, 292–307.

Related Research: Dodge, K. A., & Coie, J. D. (1987). Social information-processing factors in reactive and proactive aggression in children's peer groups. *Journal of Personality and Social Psychology, 53*, 1146–1158.

11898

Test Name: REBELLIOUSNESS SCALE

Purpose: To measure rebelliousness.

Number of Items: 4

Format: Four-point rating scales are used. All items are presented.

Reliability: Coefficient alpha was .67.

Author: Orlando, M., et al.

Article: The temporal relationship between emotional distress and cigarette smoking during adolescence and young adulthood.

Journal: *Journal of Consulting and Clinical Psychology*, December 2001, *69*, 959–970.

Related Research: Smith, G. M., & Fogg, C. P. (1979). Psychological antecedents of teenage drug use. *Research in Community and Mental Health, 1*, 87–102.

11899

Test Name: REGULATION PROCESS SCALES

Purpose: To measure goal choice activities and goal striving activities.

Number of Items: 15

Format: Scales range from 1 (*never*) to 5 (*constantly*). All items are presented.

Reliability: Alpha coefficients ranged from .73 to .81.

Validity: Correlations with other variables ranged from −.03 to .45.

Author: Chen, G., et al.

Article: A multilevel examination of the relationships among training outcomes, mediating regulatory processes, and adaptive performance.

Journal: *Journal of Applied Psychology*, September 2005, *90*, 827–841.

11900

Test Name: REINVESTMENT SCALE

Purpose: To assess reinvestment actions and skill breakdown under pressure.

Number of Items: 20

Format: Responses are either true–false or yes–no. Examples are presented.

Reliability: Coefficient alpha was .80. Test–retest reliability was .74.

Author: Chell, B. J., et al.

Article: Manipulated stress and dispositional reinvestment in a wall-volley task: An investigation into controlled processing.

Journal: *Perceptual and Motor Skills*, October 2003, *97*, 435–448.

Related Research: Masters, R. S. W., et al. (1993). "Reinvestment": A dimension of personality implicated in skill breakdown under pressure. *Personality and Individual Differences*, *14*, 655–666.

11901

Test Name: RELATIONAL AGGRESSION SCALE

Purpose: To assess relational aggression among children by teachers.

Number of Items: 5

Format: Response scales are anchored by 1 (*never or almost never true of this child*) and 5 (*always or almost always true of this child*). All items are presented.

Reliability: Coefficient alpha was .88.

Author: Isobe, M., et al.

Article: Behavioral orientations and peer-contact patterns of relationally aggressive girls.

Journal: *Psychological Reports*, February 2004, *94*, 327–334.

Related Research: Crick, N. R., et al. (1997). Relational and overt aggression in preschool. *Developmental Psychology*, *33*, 579–588.

11902

Test Name: RELIGIOUS BEHAVIOR SCALE

Purpose: To measure religious behavior.

Number of Items: 6

Format: Item responses are anchored by 0 (*never*) and 4 (*daily*). All items are presented.

Reliability: Coefficient alpha was .88.

Validity: Correlations with other variables ranged from −.25 to .55.

Author: Buchko, K. J., and Witzig, T. F., Jr.

Article: Relationship between God-image and religious behaviors.

Journal: *Psychological Reports*, December 2003, *93*, Part 2, 1141–1148.

11903

Test Name: RESTRICTIVE AFFECTIONATE BEHAVIOR BETWEEN MEN SCALE

Purpose: To assess a male participant's concerns and limitations in expressing his feelings and affection to other men.

Number of Items: 8

Format: Responses are made on a 6-point scale ranging from 1 (*strongly disagree*) to 6 (*strongly agree*). An example is presented.

Reliability: Alpha coefficients were .83 and .84. Test–retest (4 weeks) reliability was .86.

Validity: Correlations with other variables ranged from −.19 to .51.

Author: Bruch, M. A.

Article: Shyness and toughness: Unique and moderated relations with men's emotional inexpression.

Journal: *Journal of Counseling Psychology*, January 2002, *49*, 28–34.

Related Research: O'Neil, J. M., et al. (1986). Gender Role Conflict Scale: College men's fear of femininity. *Sex Roles*, *14*, 335–350.

11904

Test Name: RETROSPECTIVE BEHAVIORAL SELF-CONTROL SCALE

Purpose: To assess noncriminal and nonoccupational behavioral manifestations of low self-control.

Number of Items: 67

Format: Frequency scales range from *never* to *often*.

Reliability: Coefficient alpha was .94.

Validity: Correlations with other variables ranged from −.63 to .26.

Author: Marcus, B., and Shuler, H.

Article: Antecedents of counterproductive behavior at work: A general perspective.

Journal: *Journal of Applied Psychology*, August 2004, *89*, 647–660.

Related Research: Marcus, B. (2003). An empirical examination of the construct validity of two alternative self-control measures. *Educational and Psychological Measurement, 63*, 674–706.

11905

Test Name: RETROSPECTIVE BEHAVIORAL SELF-CONTROL SCALE—REVISED

Purpose: To measure self-control.

Number of Items: 23

Format: Includes six subscales: Impulsivity, Simple Tasks, Risk Seeking, Physical Activities, Self-Centeredness, and Volatile Temper. Responses are made on a 5-point scale. All items are presented.

Reliability: Coefficient alpha was .75.

Validity: Correlations with other variables ranged from .42 to .67.

Author: Marcus, B.

Article: An empirical examination of the construct validity of two alternative self-control measures.

Journal: *Educational and Psychological Measurement*, August 2003, *63*, 674–706.

Related Research: Grasmick, H. G., et al. (1993). Testing the core empirical implications of Gottfredson and Hirschi's general theory of crime. *Journal of Research in Crime and Delinquency, 30*, 5–29.

11906

Test Name: REVENGE AND RECONCILIATION SCALES

Purpose: To measure revenge and forgiveness.

Number of Items: 10

Format: All items are presented.

Reliability: Alpha coefficients were .83 (revenge) and .83 (reconciliation).

Validity: Correlations with other variables ranged from –.40 to .24.

Author: Aquino, K., et al.

Article: How employees respond to personal offense: The effects of blame attribution, victim status, and offender status on revenge and reconciliation in the workplace.

Journal: *Journal of Applied Psychology*, February 2001, *86*, 52–59.

Related Research: Wade, S. H. (1989). *The development of a scale to measure forgiveness.* Unpublished doctoral dissertation, Fuller Theological Seminary, Pasadena, CA.

11907

Test Name: REVISED BEHAVIOR PROBLEM CHECKLIST

Purpose: To measure the severity of child conduct problems by parental report.

Number of Items: 21

Format: Scales range from 0 (*no problem*) to 3 (*severe problem*). Sample items are described.

Reliability: Alpha coefficients were .90 (fathers) and .93 (mothers).

Author: Simons, R. L., et al.

Article: Quality of parenting as a mediator of the effect of childhood deviance on adolescent friendship choices and delinquency: A growth curve analysis.

Journal: *Journal of Marriage and Family*, February 2001, *63*, 63–79.

Related Research: Quay, H. C., & Peterson, D. R. (1983). *Interim manual for the Revised Behavior Problem Checklist.* Miami, FL: University of Miami.

11908

Test Name: REVISED CLASS PLAY MEASURE

Purpose: To assess peer social behavior.

Number of Items: 30

Format: Includes three variables: sociability–leadership, aggression–disruption, and shyness–sensitivity. Examples are presented.

Reliability: Internal consistency ranged from .80 to .93.

Author: Chen, X., et al.

Article: The peer group as a context: Mediating and moderating effects on relations between academic achievement and social functioning in Chinese children.

Journal: *Child Development*, May/June 2003, *74*, 710–727.

Related Research: Master, A., et al. (1985). A Revised Class Play method of peer assessment. *Developmental Psychology, 21*, 523–533.

11909

Test Name: REVISED NONVERBAL IMMEDIACY MEASURE

Purpose: To measure nonverbal immediacy behavior of teachers by student report.

Number of Items: 10

Format: Scales range from 1 (*never*) to 4 (*very often*). A sample item is presented.

Reliability: Alpha coefficients ranged from .77 to .78.

Author: Clark, R. K., et al.

Article: Experimentally assessing the student impacts of out-of-class communication: Office visits and the student experience.

Journal: *Journal of College Student Development*, November/December 2002, *43*, 824–837.

Related Research: McCroskey, J. C., et al. (1995). A cross-cultural and multi-behavioral analysis of the relationship between nonverbal immediacy and teacher evaluation. *Communication Education, 44,* 281–291.

11910

Test Name: REVISED PERSONAL LIFESTYLE QUESTIONNAIRE

Purpose: To measure positive health practices.

Number of Items: 24

Format: Item responses range from 1 (*never*) to 4 (*almost always*).

Reliability: Coefficient alpha was .85.

Validity: Correlations with other variables ranged from −.47 to .54.

Author: Yarcheski, T. J., et al.

Article: Depression, optimism, and positive health practices in young adolescents.

Journal: *Psychological Reports,* December 2004, *95*, Part 1, 932–934.

Related Research: Mahon, N. E., et al. (2003). The Revised Personal Lifestyle Questionnaire for early adolescents. *Western Journal of Nursing Research, 25,* 533–547.

11911

Test Name: REWARD INVENTORY

Purpose: To assess a person's recollections of his or her experiences with rewarding practices while growing up.

Number of Items: 20

Format: Includes four factors: individuality, physical affection, positive reinforcement, and social independence. Responses are made on a 5-point scale ranging from 1 [*never (not even once)*] to 5 [*very often (so common I couldn't even begin to guess how often I experienced this)*].

Reliability: Coefficient alpha was .94.

Validity: Correlations with other variables ranged from −.60 to .23.

Author: Cohen, J. H., and Amidon, E. J.

Article: Reward and punishment histories: A way of predicting teaching style?

Journal: *The Journal of Educational Research,* May/June 2004, *97*, 269–277.

Related Research: Cohen, J. (1999). Beginning preservice teachers' perceptions of their reward and punishment histories and teaching style (Doctoral dissertation, Temple University, 1999). *Dissertation Abstracts International, 60,* 7.

11912

Test Name: RISK ASSESSMENT BEHAVIOR

Purpose: To assess preadolescents' participation in health compromising or risky behavior.

Number of Items: 3

Format: A yes–no format is used. All items are presented.

Reliability: Coefficient alpha was .62.

Validity: Correlations with other variables ranged from −.42 to .29.

Author: Markey, C. N., et al.

Article: Personality, puberty, and preadolescent girls' risky behaviors: Examining the predictive value of the five-factor model of personality.

Journal: *Journal of Research in Personality,* October 2003, *37*, 405–419.

Related Research: Markey, C. N., et al. (2001). Personality and family determinants of preadolescents' participation in health-compromising and health-promoting behaviors. *Adolescent and Family Health, 2,* 83–90.

11913

Test Name: RISK-TAKING SCALE

Purpose: To determine one's risk-taking tendency.

Number of Items: 6

Format: Responses are made on a 3-point scale ranging from 1 (*not at all true*) to 3 (*very true*).

Reliability: Coefficient alpha was .59.

Author: Cleveland, M. J., et al.

Article: The impact of parenting on risk cognitions and risk behavior: A study of mediation and moderation in a panel of African American adolescents.

Journal: *Child Development,* July/August 2005, *76*, 900–916.

Related Research: Eysenck, S. B., & Eysenck, H. J. (1977). The place of impulsiveness in a dimensional system of personality description. *British Journal of Social and Clinical Psychology, 16,* 57–68.

11914

Test Name: RISKY BEHAVIOR SCALE

Purpose: To identify youth involvement in behaviors.

Number of Items: 18

Format: Responses are made on a 4-point scale ranging from 1 (*never*) to 4 (*more than 10 times*).

Reliability: Alpha coefficients ranged from .82 to .89.

Author: Crouter, A. C., et al.

Article: How do parents learn about adolescents' experiences? Implications for parental knowledge and adolescent risky behavior.

Journal: *Child Development,* July/August 2005, *76,* 869–882.

Related Research: Eccles, J., & Barber, B. (1990). *The Risky Behavior Scale.* Unpublished measure, University of Michigan.

11915

Test Name: RISKY BEHAVIOR SCALE

Purpose: To assess sexual activities during the past year.

Number of Items: 11

Format: A yes–no format is used. All items are presented.

Reliability: Alpha was .92.

Validity: Correlations with other variables ranged from −.17 to .23.

Author: Thompson, K. L., et al.

Article: Psychological predictors of sexual behaviors related to AIDS transmission.

Journal: *Psychological Reports,* February 2001, *88,* 51–67.

Related Research: Gray, L. A. (1993). Survey on HIV/AIDS: Oregon State University Students. Unpublished manuscript, University Counselor Education Program, Oregon State University.

11916

Test Name: ROSE'S WRITER'S BLOCK QUESTIONNAIRE— CHINESE VERSION

Purpose: To measure writer's block.

Number of Items: 14

Format: Includes three subscales: Blocking, Premature Editing, and Complexity. Responses are made on a 5-point scale ranging from *almost always* to *almost never.* All items are presented.

Reliability: Alpha coefficients ranged from .76 to .84.

Author: Lee, S.-Y., and Krashen, S.

Article: Writer's block in a Chinese sample.

Journal: *Perceptual and Motor Skills,* October 2003, *97,* 537–542.

Related Research: Rose, M. (1984). *Writer's block: The cognitive dimension.* Carbondale: Southern Illinois University Press.

11917

Test Name: RUTGERS ALCOHOL PROBLEMS INDEX

Purpose: To assess alcohol-related problems.

Number of Items: 25

Format: Item responses range from 0 (*never*) to 4 (*more than 10 times*).

Reliability: Alpha coefficients ranged from .82 to .89 over three follow-up periods.

Author: Neighbors, C., et al.

Article: Targeting misperceptions of descriptive drinking norms: Efficacy of a computer-delivered personalized normative feedback intervention.

Journal: *Journal of Consulting and Clinical Psychology,* June 2004, *72,* 434–447.

Related Research: White, H. R., & Labouvie, E. U. (1989). Towards the assessment of adolescent problem drinking. *Journal of Studies on Alcohol, 50,* 30–37.

11918

Test Name: SCHEDULE OF RACIST EVENTS

Purpose: To assess the frequency of racist events experienced by African Americans during the past year, during one's lifetime, and its stressfulness.

Number of Items: 18

Format: Responses are made on 6-point scales.

Reliability: Reliability coefficients ranged from .94 to .95. Split-half coefficients ranged from .91 to .93. Alpha coefficients ranged from .84 to .89.

Validity: Correlations with other variables ranged from −.09 to .55.

Author: Liang, C. T. H., et al.

Article: The Asian American Racism-Related Stress Inventory: Development, factor analysis, reliability, and validity.

Journal: *Journal of Counseling Psychology,* January 2004, *51,* 103–114.

Related Research: Landrine, H., & Klonoff, E. A. (1996). The Schedule of Racist Events: A measure of racial discrimination and a study of its negative physical and mental health consequences. *Journal of Black Psychology, 22,* 144–168.

11919

Test Name: SCHEDULE OF SEXIST EVENTS

Purpose: To assess the perceived frequency and appraisal of sexist events.

Number of Items: 20

Format: Responses are made on 6-point scales.

Reliability: Internal consistency reliability estimates ranged from .90 to .93.

Validity: Correlations with other variables ranged from −.08 to .39.

Author: Moradi, B., and Subich, L. M.

Article: Examining the moderating role of self-esteem in the link between experiences of perceived sexist events and psychological distress.

Journal: *Journal of Counseling Psychology,* January 2004, *51,* 50–56.

Related Research: Klonoff, E. A., & Landrine, H. (1995). The Schedule of Sexist Events: A measure of lifetime and recent sexist discrimination in women's lives. *Psychology of Women Quarterly, 19*, 439–472.

11920

Test Name: SCHOLARLY ACTIVITY SCALE

Purpose: To measure students' level of scholarly activity.

Number of Items: 9

Format: Responses are either 1 (*some experience, no matter how much*) or 0 (*no experience*).

Reliability: K-R 20 values were .68 and .70.

Validity: Correlations with other variables ranged from .14 to .31 ($N = 149$).

Author: Kahn, J. H.

Article: Predicting the scholarly activity of counseling psychology students: A refinement and extension.

Journal: *Journal of Counseling Psychology*, July 2001, *48*, 344–354.

Related Research: Kahn, J. H., & Scott, N. A. (1997). Predictors of research productivity and science-related career goals among counseling psychology graduate students. *The Counseling Psychologist, 25*, 38–67.

11921

Test Name: SCHOLASTIC BEHAVIORS DEVOTED TO MATH/SCIENCE COURSEWORK SCALE

Purpose: To assess the extent to which students engaged in a range of behaviors devoted to specific coursework in math/science.

Number of Items: 7

Format: Examples are given.

Reliability: Coefficient alpha was .79.

Validity: Correlations with other variables ranged from .05 to .47.

Author: Bouchey, H. A., and Harter, S.

Article: Reflected appraisals, academic self-perceptions, and math/science performance during early adolescence.

Journal: *Journal of Educational Psychology*, November 2005, *97*, 673–686.

11922

Test Name: SCHOOL ENGAGEMENT SCALE

Purpose: To measure high school students' self-reported time spent on English and math courses.

Number of Items: 8

Format: Responses are made on a 5-point Likert-type scale.

Reliability: Alpha coefficients were .77 and .80.

Validity: Correlations with other variables ranged from −.10 to .34.

Author: Wettersten, K. B., et al.

Article: Predicting educational and vocational attitudes among rural high school students.

Journal: *Journal of Counseling Psychology*, October 2005, *52*, 658–663.

Related Research: Dornbusch, S., & Steinberg, L. (1990). *Measures of school engagement.* Unpublished manuscript, Temple University, Philadelphia, PA.

11923

Test Name: SCHOOL REFUSAL ASSESSMENT SCALE—REVISED

Purpose: To identify the primary function of a child's school refusal behavior.

Number of Items: 24

Format: Scales range from 0 (*never*) to 6 (*always*). All items are presented.

Reliability: Item reliability coefficients ranged from .21 to .86.

Author: Keorney, C. A.

Article: Identifying the function of school refusal behavior: A revision of the school refusal assessment scale

Journal: *Journal of Psychopathology and Behavioral Assessment*, December 2002, *24*, 235–245.

Related Research: Higa, C. K., et al. (2004). Psychometric properties and clinical utility of the School Refusal Assessment Scale in a multiethnic sample. *Journal of Psychopathology and Behavioral Assessment, 24*, 247–258.

11924

Test Name: SELECTIVE OPTIMIZATION WITH COMPENSATION QUESTIONNAIRE

Purpose: To assess selective optimization with compensation behaviors.

Number of Items: 12

Format: Includes four components: Elective selection, loss-based selection, optimization, and compensation. Responses are made on a 4-point scale ranging from 1 (*a little*) to 4 (*exactly*). All items are presented.

Reliability: Alpha coefficients ranged from .25 to .81. Test–retest reliability ranged from .70 to .80.

Validity: Correlations with other variables ranged from −.20 to .52.

Author: Bajor, J. K., and Baltes, B. B.

Article: The relationship between selection optimization with compensation, conscientiousness, motivation, and performance.

Journal: *Journal of Vocational Behavior*, December 2003, *63*, 347–367.

Related Research: Baltes, B. B., et al. (1999). *The measurement of selection, optimization, and compensation (SOC) by self-report: Technical report 1999.* Berlin, Germany: Max Planck Institute for Human Development.

11925

Test Name: SELF-CONTROL SCALE

Purpose: To assess one's sense of autonomy and control over future events.

Number of Items: 15

Reliability: Coefficient alpha was .66.

Validity: Correlations with other variables ranged from −.28 to .12.

Author: Klibert, J. J., et al.

Article: Adaptive and maladaptive aspects of self-oriented versus socially prescribed perfectionism.

Journal: *Journal of College Student Development*, March/April 2005, *46*, 141–156.

Related Research: Bartone, P., et al. (1989). The impact of a military air disaster on the health of assistance workers. *Journal of Nervous and Mental Disease, 117*, 317–328.

11926

Test Name: SELF-CONTROL SCALE

Purpose: To measure self-control.

Number of Items: 7

Format: Response scales are anchored by 1 (*strongly agree*) and 5 (*strongly disagree*).

Reliability: Coefficient alpha was .55.

Validity: Correlations with other variables ranged from −.52 to .38.

Author: Bichler, G., and Tibbetts, S. G.

Article: Conditional covariation of binge drinking with predictors of college students' cheating.

Journal: *Psychological Reports*, December 2003, *93*, Part 1, 735–749.

Related Research: Grasmick, H., et al. (1993). Testing the core implications of Gottfredson and Hirschi's general theory of crime. *Journal of Research in Crime and Delinquency, 30*, 5–29.

11927

Test Name: SELF-CONTROL SCALE

Purpose: To measure self-control in six dimensions: Self-Centered, Physical Activity, Impulsivity, Simple Tasks, Temper, and Risk Seeking.

Number of Items: 24

Format: Item response categories are anchored by 1 (*never*) and 7 (*very often*). All items are presented.

Reliability: Alpha coefficients ranged from .76 to .87 across subscales.

Author: Mansfield, P. M., et al.

Article: Self-control and credit-card use among college students.

Journal: *Psychological Reports*, June 2003, *92*, Part 2, 1067–1078.

Related Research: Grasmick, H. G., et al. (1993). Testing the core empirical implications of Gottfredson and Hirschi's general theory of crime. *Journal of Research in Crime and Delinquency, 30*, 5–29.

11928

Test Name: SELF-CONTROL SCALE

Purpose: To measure self-control.

Number of Items: 12

Format: Item responses are anchored by 1 (*never*) and 5 (*very often*).

Reliability: Alpha was .82.

Author: Tibbetts, S. G., and Whittimore, J. N.

Article: The interactive effects of low self-control and commitment to school on substance abuse among college students.

Journal: *Psychological Reports*, February 2002, *90*, 327–337.

Related Research: Grasmick, H. G., et al. (1993). Testing the core empirical implications of Gottfredson and Hirschi's general theory of crime. *Journal of Research in Crime and Delinquency, 30*, 5–29.

11929

Test Name: SELF-CONTROL SCHEDULE

Purpose: To assess strategies of self-control.

Number of Items: 36

Format: Scales range from 1 (*very characteristic*) to 6 (*not at all characteristic*). Sample items are presented.

Reliability: Alpha coefficients ranged from .76 to .86 across subscales.

Author: Sinha, S. P., et al.

Article: Social support and self-control as variables in attitude toward life and perceived control among older people in India.

Journal: *The Journal of Social Psychology*, August 2002, *142*, 527–540.

Related Research: Rosenbaum, M. (1980). A schedule for assessing self-control behavior: Preliminary findings. *Behavior Therapy, 11*, 109–121.

11930

Test Name: SELF-DISCIPLINE QUIZ

Purpose: To measure facets of self-discipline.

Number of Items: 20

Format: Item responses are anchored by *strongly agree* and *strongly disagree*. Sample items are presented.

Reliability: Test–retest reliability (28 days) was .90.

Validity: Correlations with other variables ranged from .09 to .44.

Author: Du Brin, A. J.

Article: Career-related correlates of self-discipline.

Journal: *Psychological Reports*, August 2001, *89*, 107–110.

11931

Test Name: SELF-MONITORING SCALE

Purpose: To measure the degree to which individuals observe and control their behavior in diverse social situations.

Format: Includes three factors: extraversion, other-directedness, and acting.

Reliability: Alpha coefficients ranged from .66 to .71

Validity: Correlations with other variables ranged from –.56 to .38.

Author: Kelly, K. M., et al.

Article: Using the Imaginary Audience Scale as a measure of social anxiety in young adults.

Journal: *Educational and Psychological Measurement*, October 2002, *62*, 896–914.

Related Research: Snyder, M. (1974). Self-monitoring of expressive behavior. *Journal of Personality and Social Psychology*, *30*, 526–537.

11932

Test Name: SELF-OBSERVATION AUTO-VERBALIZATIONS INVENTORY—GERMAN VERSION

Purpose: To measure self-talk used for introspection purposes.

Number of Items: 27

Format: Scales range from 1 (*never*) to 6 (*very often*). Sample items are presented in English.

Reliability: Coefficient alpha was .89.

Validity: Correlations with other variables ranged from –.48 to .50.

Author: Schneider, J. F., et al.

Article: Does self-consciousness mediate the relation between self-talk and self-knowledge?

Journal: *Psychological Reports*, April 2005, *96*, 387–396.

Related Research: Morin, A. (1993). Self-talk and self-awareness: On the nature of the relation. *The Journal of Mind and Behavior, 14*, 223–234.

11933

Test Name: SELF-PRESENTATION TACTICS SCALE

Purpose: To assess self-presentation tactics.

Number of Items: 63

Format: Scales range from 1 (*very infrequently*) to 9 (*very frequently*). Sample items are presented.

Reliability: Alpha coefficients ranged from .56 to .84 across subscales.

Author: Lewis, M. A., and Neighbors, C.

Article: Self-determination and the use of self-presentation strategies.

Journal: *The Journal of Social Psychology*, August 2005, *145*, 469–489.

Related Research: Lee, S., et al. (1999). Development of a self-presentation tactics scale. *Personality and Individual Differences, 26*, 701–722.

11934

Test Name: SELF-RATING INVENTORY FOR PTSD

Purpose: To rate intrusion, avoidance, and hyperarousal.

Number of Items: 22

Format: Scales range from 1 (*not at all*) to 4 (*extremely*).

Reliability: Alpha coefficients ranged from .85 to .87 across subscales.

Author: Witteveen, A. B., et al.

Article: Utility of the Impact of Event Scale in screening for posttraumatic stress disorder.

Journal: *Psychological Reports*, August 2005, *97*, 297–308.

Related Research: Hovens, J. E., et al. (1994). The development of the Self-Rating Inventory for Posttraumatic Stress Disorder. *Acta Psychiatrica Scandinavica, 90*, 172–183.

11935

Test Name: SELF-REGULATION BEHAVIORS FOR ONLINE LEARNING SCALE

Purpose: To measure self-regulation behaviors for online learning.

Number of Items: 4

Format: Responses are made on a 5-point scale ranging from 1 (*not well at all*) to 5 (*very well*). All items are presented.

Reliability: Coefficient alpha was .79.

Author: Williams, P. E., and Hellman, C. M.

Article: Differences in self-regulation for online learning between first- and second-generation college students.

Journal: *Research in Higher Education*, February 2004, *45*, 71–82.

Related Research: Bandura, A. (1989). *The Multidimensional Self-Efficacy Scales*. Unpublished test, Stanford University.

11936

Test Name: SELF-REGULATION OF WITHHOLDING NEGATIVE EMOTIONS QUESTIONNAIRE

Purpose: To measure individual differences in the self-regulation of withholding negative emotions.

Number of Items: 28

Format: Includes four self-regulatory styles: external, introjected, identified, and integrated. Responses are made on a 7-point scale ranging from 1 (*strongly disagree*) to 7 (*strongly agree*). All items are presented.

Reliability: Alpha coefficients ranged from .67 to .78.

Author: Kim, Y., et al.

Article: The development of the self-regulation of withholding negative emotions questionnaire.

Journal: *Educational and Psychological Measurement*, April 2002, *62*, 316–336.

Related Research: Ryan, R. M., & Connell, J. P. (1989). Perceived locus of causality and internalization: Examining reasons for acting in two domains. *Journal of Personality and Social Psychology*, *57*, 749–761.

11937

Test Name: SELF-REGULATION QUESTIONNAIRE

Purpose: To assess self-regulation for people with mental retardation.

Number of Items: 53

Format: Responses are made on a 5-point scale.

Reliability: Coefficient alpha was .97.

Author: Kojima, M., and Ikeda, Y.

Article: Relationships between self-regulation and personality scores of persons with Down syndrome.

Journal: *Perceptual and Motor Skills*, December 2001, *93*, 705–708.

Related Research: Kojima, M., & Ikeda, Y. (2000). [Self-regulation in persons with Down syndrome]. [*The Japanese Journal of Special Education*], *37*, 37–48. [In Japanese]

11938

Test Name: SELF-REGULATION SCALE

Purpose: To assess self-regulation.

Number of Items: 33

Format: Includes self-cuing, self-reinforcement, self-punishment, and related cognitive strategies. Responses are made on a 5-point Likert-type scale.

Reliability: Coefficient alpha was .89.

Validity: Correlations with other variables ranged from −.21 to .42.

Author: Edwards, W. R., and Schleicher, D. J.

Article: On selecting psychology graduate students: Validity evidence for a test of tacit knowledge.

Journal: *Journal of Educational Psychology*, September 2004, *96*, 592–602.

Related Research: Manz, C. (1992). *Mastering self-leadership: Empowering yourself for personal excellence*. Englewood Cliffs, NJ: Prentice Hall.

11939

Test Name: SELF-REGULATION SCALE

Purpose: To provide children a self-report of self-regulation.

Number of Items: 16

Format: Responses are made on a 4-point scale. Examples are presented.

Reliability: Coefficient alpha was .81.

Author: Eisenberg, N., et al.

Article: The relations of regulation and negative emotionality in Indonesian children's social functioning.

Journal: *Child Development*, November/December 2001, *72*, 1747–1763.

Related Research: Rohrbeck, C. A., et al. (1991). Child Self-Control Rating Scale: Validation of a child self-report measure. *Journal of Clinical Child Psychology*, *20*, 179–183.

11940

Test Name: SELF-REGULATION TEST FOR CHILDREN

Purpose: To measure self-regulation.

Format: A computerized behavioral task.

Reliability: Test–retest (4 weeks) was .92

Validity: Correlations with other variables ranged from −.30 to .40.

Author: Howse, R. B., et al.

Article: Motivation and self-regulation as predictors of achievement in economically disadvantaged young children.

Journal: *Journal of Experimental Education*, Winter 2003, *71*, 151–174.

Related Research: Kuhl, J., & Kraska, K. (1993). Self-regulation: Psychometric properties of a computer-aided instrument. *German Journal of Psychology*, *17*, 11–24.

11941

Test Name: SELF-REINFORCEMENT QUESTIONNAIRE

Purpose: To measure self-control skills.

Number of Items: 30

Format: A sample item is presented.

Validity: Multiple correlation coefficients with other variables ranged from .25 to .40.

Author: Heiby, E. M., and Mearig, A.

Article: Self-control skills and negative emotional state: A focus of hostility.

Journal: *Psychological Reports*, April 2002, *90*, 627–633.

Related Research: Heiby, E. M. (1982). A Self-Reinforcement Questionnaire. *Behavior Research and Therapy, 20*, 397–401.

11942

Test Name: SELF-REPORT ALTRUISM SCALE

Purpose: To assess participants' self-reported prosocial behavior

Number of Items: 23

Format: Responses are made on a 5-point scale ranging from *never* to *very often*. An example is presented.

Reliability: Coefficient alpha was .88.

Author: Eisenberg, N., et al.

Article: Brazilian adolescents' prosocial moral judgment and behavior: Relations to sympathy, perspective taking, gender-role orientation, and demographic characteristics.

Journal: *Child Development*, March/April 2001, *72*, 518–534.

Related Research: Rushton, J. P., et al. (1981). The altruistic personality and the Self-Report Altruism Scale. *Personality and Individual Differences, 2*, 293–302.

11943

Test Name: SELF-REPORT DELINQUENCY CHECKLIST—REVISED

Purpose: To identify the occurrence of delinquent acts at home, at school, and in the community.

Number of Items: 31

Format: Responses are made on a 4-point scale.

Reliability: Alpha coefficients were .92 (girls) and .94 (boys).

Validity: Correlations with other variables ranged from −.49 to .78.

Author: Luther, S. S., and Becker, B. E.

Article: Privileged but pressured? A study of affluent youth.

Journal: *Child Development*, September/October 2002, *73*, 1593–1610.

Related Research: Elliot, D. C., et al. (1987). The identification and prediction of career offenders utilizing self-reported and official data. In J. Buchard & S. Burchard (Eds.), *Prevention of delinquent behavior*. Newbury Park, CA: Sage.

11944

Test Name: SELF-REPORT OF ANTISOCIAL BEHAVIOR QUESTIONNAIRE

Purpose: To measure antisocial behavior.

Number of Items: 18

Format: Responses are made on a 4-point scale ranging from 0 (*never*) to 3 (*frequently*). Examples are given.

Reliability: Coefficient alpha was .87.

Author: Kiesner, J., and Pastore, M.

Article: Differences in the relations between antisocial behavior and peer acceptance across contexts and across adolescence.

Journal: *Child Development*, November/December 2005, *76*, 1278–1293.

Related Research: Kiesner, J. (2002). Depressive symptoms in early adolescence: Their relations with classroom problem behavior and peer status. *Journal of Research on Adolescence, 12*, 463–478.

11945

Test Name: SELF-REPORT PERFORMANCE MEASURE

Purpose: To measure self-report performance.

Number of Items: 10

Format: Responses are made on a continuum ranging from 1 (*0% of the time*) to 8 (*100% of the time*). A sample item is presented.

Validity: Correlations with other variables ranged from −.17 to .29 ($n = 311$).

Author: Hochwarter, W. A., et al.

Article: Perceived organizational support as a mediator of the relationship between politics perceptions and work outcomes.

Journal: *Journal of Vocational Behavior*, December 2003, *63*, 438–456.

Related Research: Wright, P., et al. (1995). P=f(MxA): Cognitive ability as a moderator of the relationship between personality and performance. *Journal of Management, 21*, 1129–1140.

11946

Test Name: SELF-VERBALIZATION SCALE—GERMAN VERSION

Purpose: To measure cognitive, mnemonic, and attentional uses of self-directed speech.

Number of Items: 22

Format: Scales range from 1 (*completely false*) to 6 (*completely true*).

Reliability: Coefficient alpha was .91.

Validity: Correlations with other variables ranged from –.21 to .32.

Author: Schneider, J. F., et al.

Article: Does self-consciousness mediate the relation between self-talk and self-knowledge?

Journal: *Psychological Reports*, April 2005, *96*, 387–396.

Related Research: Duncan, R. M., & Cheyne, J. A. (1999). Incidence and functions of self-reported private speech in young adults: A self-verbalization questionnaire. *Canadian Journal of Behavioral Science, 31*, 133–136.

11947

Test Name: SERVANT–LEADERSHIP MEASURE

Purpose: To measure seven major categories of servant–leadership behavior.

Number of Items: 14

Format: Includes two dimensions: Ethical Behavior and Prioritization of Subordinates' Concerns. Responses are made on a 5-point scale ranging from 1 (*to a very small extent*) to 5 (*to a great extent*). All items are presented.

Reliability: Coefficient alpha was .98.

Validity: Correlations with other variables ranged from .24 to .72.

Author: Ehrhart, M. G.

Article: Leadership and procedural justice climate as antecedents of

unit-level organizational citizenship behavior.

Journal: *Personnel Psychology*, Spring 2004, *57*, 61–94.

Related Research: Ehrhart, M. G. (1998). *Servant–leadership: An overview and directions for future research*. Working paper, University of Maryland.

11948

Test Name: SEVERITY OF VIOLENCE AGAINST WOMEN SCALES

Purpose: To measure domestic violence experienced by mothers.

Number of Items: 46

Format: Includes nine dimensions ranging from Threats of Mild Violence to Severe Physical and Sexual Violence.

Reliability: Alpha coefficients ranged from .89 to .98.

Author: Huth-Bocks, A.-C., et al.

Article: The impact of maternal characteristics and contextual variables on infant–mother attachment.

Journal: *Child Development*, March/April 2004, *75*, 480–496.

Related Research: Marshall, L. L. (1992). Development of the Severity of Violence Against Women Scales. *Journal of Family Violence, 7*, 103–121.

11949

Test Name: SEXUAL ABUSE SUBSCALE

Purpose: To assess severity of child sexual abuse.

Number of Items: 6

Format: Responses are made on a 5-point scale ranging from 0 (*never*) to 4 (*always*). An example is given.

Reliability: Alpha coefficients ranged from .72 to .86.

Validity: Correlations with other variables ranged from .03 to .73.

Author: Hund, A. R., and Espelage, D. L.

Article: Childhood sexual abuse, disordered eating, alexithymia, and general distress: A mediation model.

Journal: *Journal of Counseling Psychology*, October 2005, *52*, 559–573.

Related Research: Sanders, B., & Becker-Lausen, E. (1995). The measurement of psychological maltreatment: Early data on the Child Abuse and Trauma Scale. *Child Abuse and Neglect, 19*, 315–323.

11950

Test Name: SEXUAL BEHAVIOR ASSESSMENT

Purpose: To measure sexual experience and behavior.

Number of Items: 26

Format: A yes–no format is used.

Reliability: Alpha coefficients ranged from .79 to .87.

Author: Hall, G. C. N., et al.

Article: Ethnicity, culture, and sexual aggression: Risk and protective factors.

Journal: *Journal of Consulting and Clinical Psychology*, October 2005, *73*, 830–840.

Related Research: Bentler, P. M. (1968). Heterosexual Behavior Assessment I: Males. *Behavior Research and Therapy, 6*, 21–25.

11951

Test Name: SEXUAL EXCITATION SCALE

Purpose: To measure one's level of sexual excitation elicited by social interactions, visual stimuli, fantasy, and nonsexual stimuli.

Number of Items: 20

Format: Responses are made on a 4-point Likert scale.

Reliability: Coefficient alpha was .90.

Validity: Correlations with the Sexual Sensation Seeking Scale were .55 (men) and .59 (women).

Author: Gaither, G. A., and Sellbom, M.

Article: The Sexual Sensation Seeking Scale: Reliability and validity within a heterosexual college student sample.

Journal: *Journal of Personality Assessment*, October 2003, *81*, 157–167.

Related Research: Janssen, E., et al. (2002). The Sexual Inhibition (SIS) and Sexual Excitation (SES) Scales: I. Measuring sexual inhibition and excitation proneness in men. *The Journal of Sex Research*, *39*, 114–126.

11952

Test Name: SEXUAL EXPERIENCES QUESTIONNAIRE

Purpose: To measure frequency of offensive sex-related behaviors: gender harassment, unwanted sexual attention, and sexual coercion.

Number of Items: 18

Format: Items are anchored by 1 (*never*) and 5 (*often*).

Reliability: Coefficient alpha was .82.

Author: Kakuyama, T., et al.

Article: Organizational tolerance as a correlate of sexual harassment of Japanese working women.

Journal: *Psychological Reports*, June 2003, *92*, Part 2, 1268–1270.

Related Research: Gefland, M. J., et al. (1995). The structure of sexual harassment: A confirmatory analysis across cultures and settings. *Journal of Vocational Behavior*, *47*, 164–177.

11953

Test Name: SEXUAL EXPERIENCES QUESTIONNAIRE

Purpose: To measure sexual harassment.

Number of Items: 23

Format: Scales range from 0 (*never*) to 4 (*very often*).

Reliability: Coefficient alpha was .93.

Author: Sims, C. S., et al.

Article: The effects of sexual harassment on turnover in the military: Time-dependent modeling.

Journal: *Journal of Applied Psychology*, November 2005, *90*, 1141–1152.

Related Research: Fitzgerald, L. F., et al. (1999). Measuring sexual harassment in the military: The Sexual Experiences Questionnaire (SEQ–DoD). *Military Psychology*, *11*, 243–263.

11954

Test Name: SEXUAL EXPERIENCES QUESTIONNAIRE

Purpose: To measure sexual harassment.

Number of Items: 25

Format: Responses are made on a 3-point scale ranging from 1 (*never*) to 3 (*more than once*).

Reliability: Alpha coefficients ranged from .75 to .92.

Author: Smith, N. G., and Ingram, K. M.

Article: Workplace heterosexism and adjustment among lesbian, gay, and bisexual individuals: The role of unsupportive social interactions.

Journal: *Journal of Counseling Psychology*, January 2004, *51*, 57–67.

Related Research: Fitzgerald, L. F., et al. (1998). The incidence and dimensions of sexual harassment in academia and the workplace. *Journal of Vocational Behavior*, *32*, 152–175.

11955

Test Name: SEXUAL EXPERIENCES QUESTIONNAIRE—REVISED ABBREVIATED VERSION

Purpose: To measure gender harassment, sexual coercion, and unwanted sexual attention in the workplace.

Number of Items: 14

Format: Scales range from 0 (*never*) to 4 (*most of the time*). Sample items are presented.

Reliability: Alpha coefficients ranged from .57 to .87.

Validity: Correlations with other variables ranged from –.24 to .82.

Author: Lim, S., and Cortina, L. M.

Article: Interpersonal mistreatment in the workplace: The interface and impact of general incivility and sexual harassment.

Journal: *Journal of Applied Psychology*, May 2005, *90*, 483–496.

Related Research: Fitzgerald, L. F., et al. (1995). Measuring sexual harassment: Theoretical and psychometric advances. *Basic and Applied Social Psychology*, *17*, 425–427.

11956

Test Name: SEXUAL EXPERIENCES

QUESTIONNAIRE—SHORT FORM

Purpose: To measure unwanted sex-related experiences.

Number of Items: 12

Format: Five-point scales range from 0 (*never*) to 4 (*many times*).

Reliability: Alpha coefficients ranged from .85 to .95.

Validity: Correlations with other variables ranged from –.25 to .45.

Author: Harned, M. S., and Fitzgerald, L. F.

Article: Understanding a link between sexual harassment and eating disorder symptoms: A mediational analysis.

Journal: *Journal of Consulting and Clinical Psychology*, October 2002, *70*, 1170–1181.

Related Research: Fitzgerald, L. F., et al. (1999). Measuring sexual harassment in the military: The Sexual Experiences Questionnaire (SEQ-DOD). *Military Psychology*, *11*, 243–263.

11957

Test Name: SEXUAL EXPERIENCES SURVEY

Purpose: To measure unwanted sexual experiences with dating partners.

Number of Items: 10

Format: Scales range from 0 (*never*) to 4 (*very frequently*).

Reliability: Alpha coefficients ranged from .71 to .82.

Author: Harned, M. S.

Article: Does it matter what you call it? The relationship between labeling unwanted sexual experiences and distress.

Journal: *Journal of Consulting and Clinical Psychology,*, December 2004, *72*, 1090–1099.

Related Research: Koss, M. P., & Gidyzc, C. A. (1985). The Sexual Experiences Survey: Reliability and validity. *Journal of Consulting and Clinical Psychology*, *53*, 422–423.

11958

Test Name: SEXUAL EXPERIENCES SURVEY

Purpose: To measure men's sexually aggressive behavior toward women.

Number of Items: 11

Format: Responses are made on a 5-point scale ranging from *never* to *often*. An example is given.

Reliability: Alpha coefficients were .69 and .89. Test–retest (1 week) reliability was .93.

Validity: Correlations with other variables ranged from –.01 to .37 (*N* = 254).

Author: Locke, B. D., and Mahalik, J. R.

Article: Examining masculinity norms, problem drinking, and athletic involvement as predictors of sexual aggression in college men.

Journal: *Journal of Counseling Psychology*, July 2005, *52*, 279–283.

Related Research: Koss, M. P., & Gaines, J. A. (1993). The prediction of sexual aggression by alcohol use, athletic participation, and fraternity affiliation. *Journal of Interpersonal Violence*, *8*, 94–108.

11959

Test Name: SEXUAL INHIBITION SCALE—1

Purpose: To measure one's level of sexual inhibition as a result of a lack of focus on the sexual situation, partner concerns, and performance concerns or distraction.

Number of Items: 14

Format: Responses are made on a 4-point Likert scale.

Reliability: Coefficient alpha was .70.

Validity: Correlations with the Sexual Sensation Seeking Scale were .13 (men) and .15 (women).

Author: Gaither, G. A., and Sellbom, M.

Article: The Sexual Sensation Seeking Scale: Reliability and validity within a heterosexual college student sample.

Journal: *Journal of Personality Assessment*, October 2003, *81*, 157–167.

Related Research: Janssen, E., et al. (2002). The Sexual Inhibition (SIS) and Sexual Excitation (SES) Scales: I. Measuring sexual inhibition and excitation proneness in men. *The Journal of Sex Research*, *39*, 114–126.

11960

Test Name: SEXUAL INHIBITION SCALE—2

Purpose: To measure one's level of sexual inhibition as a result of the risk of being caught engaging in sexual behavior, the negative consequences of sexual behaviors (e.g., sexually transmitted diseases, unwanted pregnancy), pain, and values related to sexuality.

Number of Items: 11

Format: Responses are made on a 4-point Likert scale.

Reliability: Coefficient alpha was .69.

Validity: Correlations with the Sexual Sensation Seeking Scale were –.20 (women) and –.32 (men).

Author: Gaither, G. A., and Sellbom, M.

Article: The Sexual Sensation Seeking Scale: Reliability and validity within a heterosexual college student sample.

Journal: *Journal of Personality Assessment*, October 2003, *81*, 157–167.

Related Research: Janssen, E., et al. (2002). The Sexual Inhibition (SIS) and Sexual Excitation (SES) Scales: I. Measuring sexual inhibition and excitation proneness in men. *The Journal of Sex Research, 39*, 114–126.

11961

Test Name: SEXUAL OBJECTIFICATION SUBSCALE

Purpose: To measure daily sexist events.

Number of Items: 25

Format: Responses are made on a 5-point scale ranging from 1 (*never*) to 5 (*about 2 or more times per week last semester*). Examples are given.

Reliability: Coefficient alpha was .87.

Validity: Correlations with other variables ranged from .16 to .27.

Author: Moradi, B., et al.

Article: Roles of sexual objectification experiences and internalization of standards of beauty in eating disorder symptomatology: A test and extension of objectification theory.

Journal: *Journal of Counseling Psychology*, July 2005, *52*, 420–428.

Related Research: Swim, J. K., et al. (1998). Experiencing everyday prejudice and discrimination. In J. K. Swim & C. Stangor (Eds.), *Prejudice: The target's perspective* (pp. 37–60). San Diego, CA: Academic Press.

11962

Test Name: SEXUAL ORIENTATION DISCLOSURE BEHAVIOR AT WORK SCALE

Purpose: To measure the extent to which individuals engage in

avoidant behaviors concerning sexual orientation.

Number of Items: 12

Format: Scales range from 1 (*strongly disagree*) to 7 (*strongly agree*). A sample item is presented.

Reliability: Coefficient alpha was .91.

Validity: Correlations with other variables ranged from −.28 to .58.

Author: Griffith, K. H., and Hebl, M. R.

Article: The disclosure dilemma for gay men and lesbians: "Coming out" at work.

Journal: *Journal of Applied Psychology*, December 2002, *87*, 1191–1199.

Related Research: Croteau, J. M. (1996). Research on the work experience of lesbian, gay, and bisexual people: An integrative review of methodology and findings. *Journal of Vocational Behavior, 48*, 195–209.

11963

Test Name: SHAME QUESTIONNAIRE

Purpose: To measure the experience of shame and the protective and adaptive behaviors following shame.

Number of Items: 27

Format: Scales range from 1 (*totally disagree*) to 7 (*totally agree*). All items are presented.

Reliability: Alpha coefficients ranged from .72 to .88.

Validity: Correlations with other variables ranged from −.36 to .69.

Author: Bagozzi, R. P., et al.

Article: Culture moderates the self-regulation of shame and its effects on performance: The case of salespersons in the Netherlands and the Philippines.

Journal: *Journal of Applied Psychology*, April 2003, *88*, 219–233.

11964

Test Name: SHORT MICHIGAN ALCOHOL SCREENING TEST— MODIFIED

Purpose: To measure problem drinking of a respondent's parents.

Number of Items: 10

Format: A yes–no format is used.

Reliability: Coefficient alpha was .88.

Author: Wolfe, D. A., et al.

Article: Dating violence prevention with at-risk youth: A controlled outcome evaluation.

Journal: *Journal of Consulting and Clinical Psychology*, April 2003, *71*, 279–291.

Related Research: Wolfe, D. A., et al. Comparative pathways to dating violence for adolescent girls and boys: Stability and change over one year. Manuscript submitted for publication.

11965

Test Name: SITUATIONAL HUMOR RESPONSE SCALE

Purpose: To assess sense of humor by the frequency of smiling, laughing, or other display of amusement.

Number of Items: 18

Format: Five-point scales range from 1 (*wouldn't have found it particularly amusing*) to 5 (*I would have laughed heartily*). A sample item is presented.

Reliability: Coefficient alpha was .73.

Author: Nevo, O., et al.

Article: Singaporean humor: A cross-cultural, cross-gender comparison.

Journal: *The Journal of General Psychology*, April 2001, *128*, 143–156.

Related Research: Martin, R. A., & Lefcourt, H. M. (1983). Sense of humor as a moderator of the relation between stressors and mood. *Journal of Personality and Social Psychology, 45*, 1313–1324.

11966

Test Name: SKILL UTILIZATION SCALE

Purpose: To assess skill utilization.

Number of Items: 4

Format: Scales for three items range from 1 (*not at all*) to 5 (*a great deal*). One item used a 5-point satisfaction scale.

Reliability: Alpha coefficients ranged from .72 to .77.

Validity: Correlations with other variables ranged from −.30 to .47.

Author: Parker, S. K.

Article: Longitudinal effects of lean production on employee outcomes and the mediating role of work characteristics.

Journal: *Journal of Applied Psychology*, August 2003, *88*, 620–634.

Related Research: Jackson, P. R., & Mullarkey, S. (2000). Lean production teams and health in garment manufacture. *Journal of Occupational Health Psychology, 5*, 231–245.

11967

Test Name: SLEEP SURVEY

Purpose: To assess sleep-related behaviors.

Number of Items: 15

Format: All items are presented. Most use a yes–no format. Others use a 17-point hours scale.

Reliability: Alpha coefficients ranged from .53 to .80 across subscales.

Validity: Correlations with other variables ranged from −.29 to .06.

Author: Peters, B. R., et al.

Article: Individual differences in the Considerations of Future Consequences Scale correlate with sleep habits, sleep quality, and GPA in university students.

Journal: *Psychological Reports*, June 2005, *96*, Part 1, 817–824.

11968

Test Name: SMOKING BEHAVIOR QUESTIONNAIRE

Purpose: To measure the reasons people smoke and the behavior associated with smoking in four dimensions: Dependence, Need for Social Integration, Regulation of Negative Effects, and Hedonism.

Number of Items: 28

Format: All items are presented.

Reliability: Alpha coefficients ranged from .55 to .84 across subscales.

Validity: Multiple correlations between sets of prediction variables and smoking behavior ranged from .10 to .50.

Author: Gilliard, J., and Bruchon-Schweitzer, M.

Article: Development and validation of a multidimensional smoking behaviour questionnaire.

Journal: *Psychological Reports*, December 2001, *89*, 499–509.

11969

Test Name: SOCIAL BEHAVIOR RATING SCALE

Purpose: To enable teachers to rate the child's social behavior.

Number of Items: 44

Format: Responses are made on a 5-point scale ranging from 1 (*almost never true for the child*) to 5 (*almost always true for the child*). Examples are given.

Reliability: Alpha coefficients ranged from .88 to .94.

Author: Schwartz, D., et al.

Article: Victimization of the peer group and children's academic functioning.

Journal: *Journal of Educational Psychology*, August 2005, *97*, 425–435.

Related Research: Schwartz, D., et al. (2002). Victimization in South Korean children's peer groups. *Journal of Abnormal Child Psychology, 30*, 113–125.

11970

Test Name: SOCIAL EXPERIENCE QUESTIONNAIRE

Purpose: To measure relational and overt victimization and lack of prosocial treatment.

Number of Items: 14

Format: Scales range from 1 (*never*) to 5 (*all the time*). All items are presented.

Reliability: Subscale alphas ranged from .77 to .80.

Author: Casey-Cannon, S., et al.

Article: Middle-school girls' reports of peer victimization: Concerns, consequences, and implications.

Journal: *Professional School Counseling*, December 2001, *5*, 139–147.

Related Research: Crick, N. R., & Grotpeter, J. K. (1996). Children's treatment by peers: Victims of relational and overt aggression. *Development and Psychopathology, 8*, 367–380.

11971

Test Name: SOCIAL EXPERIENCE QUESTIONNAIRE—REVISED

Purpose: To measure children's victimization.

Number of Items: 15

Format: Includes two subscales: Overt Victimization and Relational Victimization. Examples are given.

Reliability: Alpha coefficients were .87 and .88.

Author: Rudolph, K. D., et al.

Article: Need for approval and children's well-being.

Journal: *Child Development*, March/April 2005, *76*, 309–323.

Related Research: Crick, N. R., & Grotpeter, J. K. (1996). Children's treatment by peers: Victims of relational and overt aggression. *Development and Psychopathology*, *8*, 367–380.

11972

Test Name: SOCIAL EXPERIENCE QUESTIONNAIRE—SELF REPORT

Purpose: To assess peer victimization.

Number of Items: 10

Format: Includes two subscales: Relational Victimization and Overt Victimization. Responses are made on a 5-point scale ranging from 1 (*never*) to 5 (*all the time*). Examples are presented.

Validity: Correlations with other variables ranged from –.23 to .40.

Author: Storch, E. A., et al.

Article: Overt and relational victimization and psychosocial adjustment in minority preadolescents.

Journal: *Child Study Journal*, 2002, *32*, 73–80.

Related Research: Crick, N. R., & Grotpeter, J. K. (1996). Children's treatment by peers: Victims of relational and overt aggression. *Development and Psychopathology*, *8*, 367–380.

11973

Test Name: SOCIAL EXPERIENCE QUESTIONNAIRE—SELF-REPORT—MODIFIED

Purpose: To assess self-reports of victimization.

Number of Items: 22

Format: Includes three subscales: Relational Victimization, Overt Victimization, and Prosocial Behaviors. Examples are given.

Reliability: Alpha coefficients ranged from .84 to .86.

Author: Storch, E. A., et al.

Article: The relationship of peer victimization to social anxiety and loneliness in adolescence.

Journal: *Child Study Journal*, 2003, *33*, 1–18.

Related Research: Crick, N. R., & Grotpeter, J. K. (1996). Children's treatment by peers: Victims of relational and overt aggression. *Developmental Psychopathology*, *8*, 367–380.

11974

Test Name: SOCIAL/PHYSICAL PLEASURE SCALE

Purpose: To assess pleasure derived from alcohol consumption.

Number of Items: 9

Format: A true–false format is used.

Reliability: Coefficient alpha was .81.

Author: Greenbaum, P. E., et al.

Article: Variation in the drinking trajectories of freshmen college students.

Journal: *Journal of Consulting and Clinical Psychology*, April 2005, *73*, 229–238.

Related Research: Brown, S. A., et al. (1980). Expectations of reinforcement from alcohol: Their domain and relation to drinking patterns. *Journal of Consulting and Clinical Psychology*, *48*, 419–426.

11975

Test Name: SOCIOSEXUAL ORIENTATION INVENTORY

Purpose: To measure individuals' willingness to engage in uncommitted sexual relationships.

Number of Items: 8

Format: Two items are presented.

Reliability: Coefficient alpha was .82.

Validity: Correlations with the Sexual Sensation Seeking Scale were .51 (women) and .54 (men).

Author: Gaither, G. A., and Sellbom, M.

Article: The Sexual Sensation Seeking Scale: Reliability and validity within a heterosexual college student sample.

Journal: *Journal of Personality Assessment*, October 2003, *81*, 157–167.

Related Research: Kalichman, S. C., & Rompa, D. (1995). Sexual Sensation Seeking and Sexual Compulsivity Scales: Reliability, validity, and predicting HIV-risk behavior. *Journal of Personality Assessment*, *65*, 586–601.

11976

Test Name: STRENGTHS AND DIFFICULTIES QUESTIONNAIRE

Purpose: To provide a measure of behavior difficulties.

Number of Items: 25

Format: Includes five scales: Conduct Problems, Hyperactivity,

Emotional Symptoms, Peer Problems, and Prosocial Behavior.

Validity: Correlation with the Child Behavior Checklist was greater than .80.

Author: Woods, S., and Wolke, D.

Article: Direct and relational bullying among primary school children and academic achievement.

Journal: *Journal of School Psychology*, March/April 2004, *42*, 135–155.

Related Research: Goodman, R. (1997). The Strengths and Difficulties Questionnaire: A research note. *Journal of Child Psychology and Psychiatry*, *38*, 581–586.

11977

Test Name: STRENGTHS AND DIFFICULTIES QUESTIONNAIRE—ADAPTED

Purpose: To assess behavioral outcomes.

Number of Items: 19

Format: Includes four subscales: Anxiety, Prosocial Behavior, Hyperactivity, and Conduct Problems.

Reliability: Test–retest (1 year) reliabilities ranged from .42 to .55. Alpha coefficients ranged from .51 to .73.

Author: Asbury, K., et al.

Article: Nonshared environmental influences on individual differences in early behavioral development: A monozygotic twin differences study.

Journal: *Child Development*, May/June 2003, *74*, 933–943.

Related Research: Goodman, R. (1997). The Strengths and Difficulties Questionnaire: A research note. *Journal of Child Psychology and Psychiatry*, *38*, 581–586.

11978

Test Name: STRENGTHS AND DIFFICULTIES QUESTIONNAIRE—PROSOCIAL SCALE

Purpose: To provide a general assessment of prosocial behavior.

Number of Items: 5

Format: All items are presented.

Reliability: Alpha coefficients ranged from .68 to .85.

Validity: Correlations with other variables ranged from –.56 to .09.

Author: Hay, D. F., and Pawlby, S.

Article: Prosocial development in relation to children's and mothers' psychological problems.

Journal: *Child Development*, September/October 2003, *74*, 1314–1327.

Related Research: Goodman, R., et al. (1998). The Strengths and Difficulties Questionnaire: A pilot study on the validity of the self-report version. *European Child and Adolescent Psychiatry*, *7*, 125–130.

11979

Test Name: STUDENT–FACULTY AND STUDENT–PEER INTERACTIONS SURVEY

Purpose: To indicate a student's interactions with faculty and peers.

Number of Items: 8

Format: A yes–no format is used. All items are presented.

Reliability: Alpha coefficients were .64 and .81.

Validity: Correlations with other variables ranged from –.32 to .46. ($N = 50$).

Author: Weidman, J. C., and Stein, E. L.

Article: Socialization of doctoral students to academic norms.

Journal: *Research in Higher Education*, December 2003, *44*, 641–656.

Related Research: Trow, M. (ed.) (1975). *Teachers and students: Aspects of American higher education.* New York: McGraw-Hill.

11980

Test Name: STUDENT LEADERSHIP PRACTICE INVENTORY

Purpose: To identify the behaviors and the frequency of behaviors.

Number of Items: 30

Format: Scales range from 1 (*rarely*) to 5 (*very frequently*).

Reliability: Alpha coefficients ranged from .56 to .90 across types of student leaders and across leadership practices.

Author: Posner, B. Z.

Article: A leadership development instrument for students: Updated.

Journal: *Journal of College Student Development*, July/August 2004, *45*, 443–456.

Related Research: Kouzes, J. M., & Posner, B. Z. (1987). *Student Leadership Practices Inventory.* San Francisco: Jossey-Bass.

11981

Test Name: STUDY HABITS INVENTORY

Purpose: To assess typical study behaviors of college students.

Number of Items: 63

Format: A true–false format is used.

Reliability: Alpha coefficients ranged from .84 to .86.

Validity: Correlations with other variables ranged from –.51 to .22.

Author: Onwuegbuzie, A. J.

Article: Modeling statistics achievement among graduate students.

Journal: *Educational and Psychological Measurement,* December 2003, *63,* 1020–1038.

Related Research: Jones, C. H., & Slate, J. R. (1992). *Technical manual for the Study Habits Inventory.* Unpublished manuscript, Arkansas State University, Jonesboro.

11982

Test Name: SUBSTANCE USE SCALE

Purpose: To identify frequency of substance use.

Number of Items: 4

Format: Responses are made on a 6-point scale ranging 1 (*never*) to 6 (*usually use every day*) for three items and on a 4-point scale ranging from 1 (*none*) to 4 (*happened more than twice*) for one item.

Reliability: Coefficient alpha was .82.

Author: Davies, P. T., and Forman, E. M.

Article: Children's pattern of preserving emotional security in the interparental subsystem.

Journal: *Child Development,* November/December 2002, *73,* 1880–1903.

Related Research: Wills, T. A., & Cleary, S. D. (1996). How are social support effects mediated? A test with parental support and adolescent substance use. *Journal of Personality and Social Psychology, 71,* 937–952.

11983

Test Name: SUBSTANCE USE SCALE

Purpose: To measure cigarette, alcohol, and marijuana use.

Number of Items: 3

Format: Item responses range from 0 (*never used*) to 5 (*usually use everyday*).

Reliability: Alpha coefficients ranged from .62 to .82.

Validity: Subscale correlations ranged from .33 to .54.

Author: Wills, T. A., and Stoolmiller, M.

Article: The role of self-control in early escalation of substance use: A time-varying analysis.

Journal: *Journal of Consulting and Clinical Psychology,* August 2002, *70,* 986–997.

Related Research: Needle, R., et al. (1989). A comparison of the empirical utility of three composite measures of adolescent drug involvement. *Addictive Behaviors, 14,* 429–441.

11984

Test Name: SURFACE ACTING SCALE

Purpose: To measure surface acting.

Number of Items: 5

Format: Responses are made on a 5-point scale ranging from 1 (*never*) to 5 (*always*). Examples are presented.

Reliability: Internal consistency reliability was .87.

Author: Glomb, T. M., and Tews, M. J.

Article: Emotional labor: A conceptualization and scale development.

Journal: *Journal of Vocational Behavior,* February 2004, *64,* 1–23.

Related Research: Brotheridge, C. M., & Lee, R. T. (1998). *On the dimensionality of emotional labor: Development and validation of an emotional labor scale.* Paper presented at the first conference on Emotions in Organizational Life, San Diego, CA.

11985

Test Name: SYMLOG ADJECTIVE RATING FORM

Purpose: To assess team member roles.

Number of Items: 36

Format: Includes two dimensions: Task Role and Social Role. Responses are made on a 5-point scale ranging from *never* to *always*.

Reliability: Alpha coefficients were .65 and .87.

Validity: Correlations with other variables ranged from –.16 to .25 ($n = 220$).

Author: Stewart, G. L., et al.

Article: An exploration of member roles as a multilevel linking mechanism for individual traits and team outcomes.

Journal: *Personnel Psychology,* Summer 2005, *58,* 343–365.

Related Research: Bales, R. F., & Cohen, S. P. (1979). *SYMLOG: A system for the multiple level observation of groups.* New York: Free Press.

11986

Test Name: TEACHER ASSESSMENT OF SOCIAL BEHAVIOR—ADAPTED

Purpose: To assess social behavior.

Number of Items: 9

Format: Includes three subscales: Prosocial Behavior, Overt Aggression, and Social Withdrawal. Responses are made on a 5-point scale ranging from 1 (*very uncharacteristic*) to 5 (*very characteristic*). Examples are given.

Reliability: Alpha coefficients ranged from .72 to .77.

Validity: Correlations with other variables ranged from −.35 to .32.

Author: Rudolph, K. D., et al.

Article: Need for approval and children's well-being.

Journal: *Child Development*, March/April 2005, *76*, 309–323.

Related Research: Cassidy, J., & Asher, S. R. (1992). Loneliness and peer relations in young children. *Child Development, 63*, 350–365.

11987

Test Name: TEACHER BEHAVIORS INVENTORY— ABBREVIATED

Purpose: To identify teacher behaviors.

Number of Items: 16

Format: Includes the following dimensions: Clarity, Enthusiasm, Interaction, Organization, Pacing, and Disclosure. Responses are made on a 5-point scale ranging from 1 (*almost never*) to 5 (*almost always*). All items are presented.

Reliability: Reliability coefficients ranged from .72 to .98.

Author: Renaud, R. D., and Murray, H. G.

Article: Factorial validity of student ratings of instruction.

Journal: *Research in Higher Education*, December 2005, *46*, 929–953.

Related Research: Murray, H. G. (1983). Low-inference classroom teaching behaviors and student ratings of college teaching effectiveness. *Journal of Educational Psychology, 75*, 138–149.

11988

Test Name: TEACHER BEHAVIORS INVENTORY— ABBREVIATED VERSION

Purpose: To identify low-inference classroom teaching behaviors.

Number of Items: 16

Format: Includes eight dimensions: Clarity, Enthusiasm, Interaction, Organization, Pacing, Disclosure, Speech, and Rapport. Responses are made on a 5-point frequency-of-occurrence scale ranging from 1 (*almost never*) to 5 (*almost always*). All items are presented.

Reliability: Interrater reliabilities ranged from .57 to .98.

Author: Renaud, R. D., and Murray, H. G.

Article: Factorial validity of student ratings of instruction.

Journal: *Research in Higher Education*, December 2005, *46*, 929–953.

Related Research: Murray, H. G. (1983). Low-inference classroom teaching behaviors and student ratings of college teaching effectiveness. *Journal of Educational Psychology, 75*, 138–149.

11989

Test Name: TEACHER–CHILD RATING SCALE

Purpose: To provide teachers' ratings of children's classroom behavior.

Number of Items: 38

Format: Includes seven subscales: Conduct Problems, Learning Problems, Shy/Anxious Problems, Frustration Tolerance, Work Habits, Assertive Social Skills, and Peer Sociability.

Reliability: Internal consistency reliabilities on a composite of three subscales (Conduct Problems, Learning Problems, and Shy/Anxious Problems) exceeded .90.

Author: Hamre, B. K., and Pianta, R. C.

Article: Early teacher–child relationships and the trajectory of

children's school outcomes through eighth grade.

Journal: *Child Development*, March/April 2001, *72*, 625–638.

Related Research: Hightower, A. D., et al. (1986). The Teacher–Child Rating Scale: A brief objective measure of elementary children's school problem behaviors and competencies. *School Psychology Review, 15*, 393–409.

11990

Test Name: TEACHER–CHILD RATING SCALE

Purpose: To enable teachers to assess student behaviors.

Number of Items: 36

Format: Includes two domains: Problems and Competence.

Reliability: Alpha coefficients ranged from .92 to .95.

Validity: Correlations with other variables ranged from −.75 to .75.

Author: Luther, S. S., and Becker, B. E.

Article: Privileged but pressured? A study of affluent youth.

Journal: *Child Development*, September/October 2002, *73*, 1593–1610.

Related Research: Hightower, A. D., et al. (1986). The Teacher–Child Rating Scale: A brief objective measure of elementary school children's school problem behaviors and competencies. *School Psychology Review, 15*, 393–409.

11991

Test Name: TEACHER INTERACTION AND INSTRUCTION BEHAVIOR QUESTIONNAIRE

Purpose: To measure three dimensions of teaching: Providing

Guidance, Providing Encouragement, and Providing Order.

Format: Sample items are presented.

Reliability: Alpha coefficients ranged from .92 and .94.

Validity: Correlations between scales ranged from −.31 to .70.

Author: van Velzen, J. H., and Tillema, H. H.

Article: Students' use of self-reflective thinking: When teaching becomes coaching.

Journal: *Psychological Reports*, December 2004, *95*, Part 1, 1229–1238.

Related Research: Crèton, H. A., & Wubbels, T. (1984). [*Disciplinary problems of beginning teachers*] [Thesis]. Utrecht, the Netherlands: W. C. C.

11992

Test Name: TEACHER OBSERVATION OF CLASSROOM ADAPTATION—REVISED

Purpose: To enable teachers to rate frequency of children's behavior.

Number of Items: 16

Format: Includes three scales: Aggression, Poor Peer Relations, and Poor Academic Focus.

Reliability: Alpha coefficients were greater than .85.

Author: Barth, J. M., et al.

Article: Classroom environment influences on aggression, peer relations, and academic focus.

Journal: *Journal of School Psychology*, March/April 2004, *42*, 115–133.

Related Research: Werthamer-Larsson, L., et al. (1991). Effect of first-grade classroom environment on shy behavior, aggressive behavior, and concentration problems. *American Journal of Community Psychology, 19*, 585–602.

11993

Test Name: TEACHER OBSERVATION OF CLASSROOM ADAPTATION—REVISED

Purpose: To enable teachers to rate child attention and behavior.

Number of Items: 19

Format: Includes three scales: Attention, Aggressive Behavior, and Social and Emotional Competence. Responses are made on a 6-point scale.

Reliability: Internal consistency reliabilities ranged from .92 to .95.

Author: Blair, C., et al.

Article: Cortisol reactivity is positively related to executive function in preschool children attending Head Start.

Journal: *Child Development*, May/June 2005, *76*, 554–557.

Related Research: Werthamer-Larsson, L., et al. (1991). Effect of first-grade classroom environment on shy behavior, aggressive behavior, and concentration problems. *American Journal of Community Psychology, 19*, 585–602.

11994

Test Name: TEACHER RATING FORM

Purpose: To identify low-inference classroom teaching behaviors.

Number of Items: 9

Format: Includes nine dimensions: Clarity, Enthusiasm, Interaction, Organization, Pacing, Disclosure, Speech, Rapport, and Overall Teaching Effectiveness. Responses are made on a 5-point scale ranging from 1 (*poor*) to 5 (*excellent*).

Reliability: Interrater reliabilities ranged from .64 to .97.

Author: Renaud, R. D., and Murray, H. G.

Article: Factorial validity of student ratings of instruction.

Journal: *Research in Higher Education*, December 2005, *46*, 929–953.

Related Research: Murray, H. G. (1983). Low-inference classroom teaching behaviors and student ratings of college teaching effectiveness. *Journal of Educational Psychology, 75*, 138–149.

11995

Test Name: TEACHER RATING SCALE OF SCHOOL ADJUSTMENT

Purpose: To identify children's classroom participation.

Number of Items: 9

Format: Includes two subscales: Cooperative and Autonomous Participation. Responses are made on 3-point scales ranging from 0 (*doesn't apply*) to 2 (*certainly applies*). All items are presented.

Reliability: Alpha coefficients are .76 and .93.

Validity: Correlations with other variables ranged from −.31 to .45.

Author: Buhs, E. S.

Article: Peer rejection, negative peer treatment, and school adjustment: Self-concept and classroom engagement as mediating processes.

Journal: *Journal of School Psychology*, November 2005, *43*, 407–424.

Related Research: Birch, S. H., & Ladd, G. W. (1997). The teacher–child relationship and children's early school adjustment. *Journal of School Psychology, 35*, 61–79.

11996

Test Name: TEACHER REPORT FORM

Purpose: To assess teacher reports of children's externalizing behavior.

Number of Items: 28

Format: Responses are made on a 3-point scale.

Reliability: Alpha coefficients were .86 and .95.

Author: Troop-Gordon, W., and Ladd, G. W.

Article: Trajectories of peer victimization and perceptions of the self and schoolmates: Precursors to internalizing and externalizing problems.

Journal: *Child Development*, September/October 2005, *76*, 1072–1091.

Related Research: Achenbach, T. M. (1991). *Integrative guide for the 1991 CBCL/4–18, YSR, and TRF profiles.* Burlington: Department of Psychiatry, University of Vermont.

11997

Test Name: TEACHER REPORT FORM—WITHDRAWN AND DEPRESSION/ANXIOUS SUBSCALES

Purpose: To assess teacher reports of children's internalizing behavior.

Number of Items: 19

Format: Responses are made on a 3-point scale.

Reliability: Alpha coefficients were .88 and .95.

Author: Troop-Gordon, W., and Ladd, G. W.

Article: Trajectories of peer victimization and perceptions of the self and schoolmates: Precursors to internalizing and externalizing problems.

Journal: *Child Development*, September/October 2005, *76*, 1072–1091.

Related Research: Achenbach, T. M. (1991). *Integrative guide for the 1991 CBCL/4–18, YSR, and TRF profiles.* Burlington:

Department of Psychiatry, University of Vermont.

11998

Test Name: TEACHER REPORT OF PROBLEM BEHAVIOR QUESTIONNAIRE—ADAPTED

Purpose: To measure problem behavior in the classroom during the past week.

Number of Items: 6

Format: Responses are made on a 6-point scale ranging from *no, not at all* to *yes*. Examples are given.

Reliability: Coefficient alpha was .92.

Author: Kiesner, J., and Pastore, M.

Article: Differences in the relations between antisocial behavior and peer acceptance across contexts and across adolescence.

Journal: *Child Development*, November/December 2005, *76*, 1278–1293.

Related Research: Kiesner, J. (2002). Depressive symptoms in early adolescence: Their relations with classroom problem behavior and peer status. *Journal of Research on Adolescence, 12,* 463–478.

11999

Test Name: TEACHER–STUDENT RATING SCALE

Purpose: To measure classroom behavior problems.

Number of Items: 18

Format: Responses are made on a 5-point scale ranging from 1 (*not a problem*) to 5 (*a very serious problem*).

Reliability: Coefficient alpha was .93.

Validity: Correlations with other variables ranged from −.40 to .26.

Author: Brand, S., et al.

Article: Middle school improvement and reform: Development and validation of a school-level assessment of climate, cultural pluralism, and school safety.

Journal: *Journal of Educational Psychology*, September 2003, *95*, 570–588.

Related Research: Hightower, A. D., et al. (1986). The Teacher–Child Rating Scale: A brief objective measure of elementary school children's school problem behaviors and competencies. *School Psychology Review, 15,* 393–409.

12000

Test Name: TEACHERS' REACTION TO SCHOOL VIOLENCE SCALE

Purpose: To measure teachers' reactions to school violence.

Number of Items: 35

Format: Includes six components: Intrusion, Perceived Safety With Students, Avoidance of Students/Situations, Trust of Students, Environmental Safety, and Feelings of Relief. All items are presented.

Reliability: Alpha coefficients ranged from .60 to .95.

Validity: Correlation with the Impact of Events Scale was .87.

Author: Ting, L., et al.

Article: The Teachers' Reactions to School Violence Scale: Psychometric properties and scale development.

Journal: *Educational and Psychological Measurement*, December 2002, *62*, 1006–1019.

12001

Test Name: TEASING QUESTIONNAIRE—REVISED (DUTCH VERSION)

Purpose: To assess recollections of childhood teasing.

Format: Sample items are presented.

Reliability: Coefficient alpha was .89.

Validity: Correlations with other variables ranged from .31 to .49.

Author: Muris, P., and Littel, M.

Article: Domains of childhood teasing and psychopathological symptoms in Dutch adolescents.

Journal: *Psychological Reports*, June 2005, *96*, Part 1, 707–708.

Related Research: Storch, E. A., et al. (2004). The measurement and impact of childhood teasing in a sample of young adults. *Journal of Anxiety Disorders, 18*, 681–694.

12002

Test Name: TELECOMMUTERS' STRUCTURING BEHAVIOR SCALE

Purpose: To measure telecommuters' structuring behavior.

Number of Items: 5

Format: Responses are made on a 7-point scale ranging from 1 (*strongly disagree*) to 7 (*strongly agree*). A sample item is presented.

Reliability: Coefficient alpha was .82.

Validity: Correlations with other variables ranged from −.06 to .34.

Author: Raghuram, S., et al.

Article: Technology enabled work: The role of self-efficacy in determining telecommuter adjustment and structuring behavior.

Journal: *Journal of Vocational Behavior*, October 2003, *63*, 180–198.

12003

Test Name: TENDENCY TO CONFORM SCALE

Purpose: To measure the tendency to conform.

Number of Items: 7

Format: Seven-point semantic differential scales are used. All items are presented.

Reliability: Internal consistency was .74.

Validity: Correlations with a psychological reactance scale ranged from −.32 to −.31.

Author: Goldsmith, R. E., et al.

Article: Tendency to conform: A new measure and its relationship to psychological reactance.

Journal: *Psychological Reports*, June 2005, *96*, Part 1, 591–594.

12004

Test Name: THERAPEUTIC REACTANCE SCALE

Purpose: To measure psychological reactance.

Number of Items: 28

Format: Response scales ranged from 1 (*strongly agree*) to 7 (*strongly disagree*).

Reliability: Coefficient alpha was .80.

Validity: Correlations with a conformity scale ranged from −.32 to −.31.

Author: Goldsmith, R. E., et al.

Article: Tendency to conform: A new measure and its relationship to psychological reactance.

Journal: *Psychological Reports*, June 2005, *96*, Part 1, 591–594.

Related Research: Dowd, E. T., et al. (1991). The Therapeutic Reactance Scale: A measure of psychological reactance. *Journal of Counseling and Development, 69*, 541–545.

12005

Test Name: TIME MANAGEMENT BEHAVIOR SCALE

Purpose: To measure time management as setting goals and priorities, mechanics–planning–scheduling, control, and preference for disorganization.

Number of Items: 34

Format: Scales range from 1 (*seldom true*) to 5 (*very often true*).

Reliability: Alpha coefficients ranged from .65 to .85 across subscales.

Author: Baltes, B. B., and Heydens-Gahir, H. A.

Article: Reduction of work–family conflict through the use of selection, organization, and compensation behaviors.

Journal: *The Journal of Applied Psychology*, December 2003, *88*, 1005–1018.

Related Research: Macan, T. H., et al. (1990). College students' time management: Correlations with academic performance. *Journal of Educational Psychology, 82*, 760–768.

12006

Test Name: TIME MANAGEMENT BEHAVIOR SCALE

Purpose: To measure college students' time management.

Number of Items: 46

Format: Includes four subscales; Setting Goals and Priorities; Mechanics, Planning, and Scheduling; Perceived Control of Time; and Preference for (Dis)Organization. Responses are made on a 5-point Likert-type scale.

Reliability: Coefficient alpha was .91.

Validity: Correlations with other variables ranged from −.28 to .59.

Author: Edwards, W. R., and Schleicher, D. J.

Article: On selecting psychology graduate students: Validity evidence for a test of tacit knowledge.

Journal: *Journal of Educational Psychology*, September 2004, *96*, 592–602.

Related Research: Macan, T. H., et al. (1990). College students' time management: Correlations with academic performance and stress. *Journal of Educational Psychology, 82*, 760–768.

12007

Test Name: TODDLER BEHAVIOR ASSESSMENT QUESTIONNAIRE

Purpose: To measure toddler behavior.

Number of Items: 111

Format: Scales range from 1 (*never*) to 7 (*always*).

Reliability: Two subscales' alpha coefficients were .89 and .92.

Author: Hayden, E. P., et al.

Article: Parent reports and laboratory assessments of child temperament: A comparison of their associations with risk for depression and externalizing disorders.

Journal: *Journal of Psychopathology and Behavioral Assessment*, June 2005, *27*, 89–100.

Related Research: Goldsmith, H. H. (1996). Studying temperament via construction of the Toddler Behavior Assessment Questionnaire. *Child Development, 67*, 218–235.

12008

Test Name: TODDLER BEHAVIOR ASSESSMENT QUESTIONNAIRE—MODIFIED

Purpose: To assess toddler behavior.

Number of Items: 35

Format: Includes four scales: Pleasure, Attention Focusing, Social Fear, and Anger Proneness.

Reliability: Alpha coefficients ranged from .75 to .90.

Author: Watamura, S. E., et al.

Article: Morning-to-afternoon increases in cortisol concentrations for infants and toddlers at child care: Age differences and behavioral correlates.

Journal: *Child Development*, July/August 2003, *74*, 1006–1020.

Related Research: Goldsmith, H. H. (1996). Studying temperament via construction of the Toddler Behavior Assessment Questionnaire. *Child Development, 67*, 218–235.

12009

Test Name: TRANSFORMATIONAL LEADERSHIP SCALE

Purpose: To measure charisma, consideration, and intellectual stimulation.

Number of Items: 27

Format: Five-point response scales are anchored by 1 (*not at all*) and 5 (*frequently if not always*).

Reliability: Alpha coefficients ranged from .83 to .96.

Validity: Correlations with other variables ranged from .64 to .80.

Author: Harvey, S., et al.

Article: Instructors transformational leadership: University student attitudes and ratings.

Journal: *Psychological Reports*, April 2003, *92*, 395–402.

12010

Test Name: TRANSFORMATIONAL LEADERSHIP SCALE

Purpose: To assess individualized consideration, intellectual stimulation, inspirational motivation, and idealized influence.

Number of Items: 16

Format: Frequency scales range from 1 to 5.

Reliability: Coefficient alpha was .93.

Validity: Correlations with other variables ranged from .13 to .73.

Author: Kark, R., et al.

Article: The two faces of transformational leadership: Empowerment and dependency.

Journal: *Journal of Applied Psychology*, April 2003, *88*, 246–255.

Related Research: Avolio, B. J., et al. (1999). Reexamining the components of transformational and transactional leadership using the Multifactor Leadership Questionnaire. *Journal of Occupational and Organizational Psychology, 72*, 441–462.

12011

Test Name: TUCKMAN PROCRASTINATION SCALE

Purpose: To measure the tendency to procrastinate.

Number of Items: 16

Format: Response scales range from 1 (*That's me for sure*) to 4 (*That's not me for sure*). Sample items are presented.

Reliability: Alpha coefficients ranged from .90 to .92.

Validity: Correlation with self-regulation was –.54.

Author: Tuckman, B. W.

Article: Relations of academic procrastination, rationalizations, and performance in a web course with deadlines.

Journal: *Psychological Reports*, June 2005, *96*, Part 2, 1015–1021.

12012

Test Name: TURKISH AGGRESSIVENESS INVENTORY

Purpose: To assess destructiveness, assertiveness, and passive aggressiveness.

Number of Items: 30

Format: Includes three subscales: Destructiveness, Assertiveness, and Passive Aggressiveness. Responses are made on a 0 to 5 scale.

Reliability: Internal consistency reliabilities ranged from .81 to .93.

Author: Dane, S., and Sekertekin, M. A.

Article: Differences in handedness and scores of aggressiveness and interpersonal relations of soccer players.

Journal: *Perceptual and Motor Skills*, June 2005, *100*, Part 1, 743–746.

Related Research: Kiper, I. (1984). *[Relations among aggressiveness subscales and economic social and academic factors]*. Unpublished master's thesis, Ankara University. [in Turkish]

12013

Test Name: UNION CITIZENSHIP BEHAVIOR SCALE

Purpose: To measure union citizenship behavior at the organizational and individual member levels.

Number of Items: 8

Format: Scales range from 1 (*not at all*) to 5 (*at every available opportunity*).

Reliability: Alpha coefficients ranged from .78 to .87.

Validity: Correlations with other variables ranged from −.21 to .46.

Author: Redman, T., and Snape, E.

Article: Exchange ideology and member–union relationships: An evaluation of moderation effects.

Journal: *Journal of Applied Psychology*, July 2005, *90*, 765–773.

12014

Test Name: UNION CITIZENSHIP BEHAVIOR SCALE

Purpose: To assess individually and organizationally directed union citizenship behavior.

Number of Items: 10

Format: Scales range from 1 (*almost never*) to 5 (*almost always*). Sample items are presented.

Reliability: Coefficient alpha was .93 (individual) and .92 (organization).

Validity: Correlations with other variables ranged from .23 to .48.

Author: Tan, H. H., and Aryee, S.

Article: Antecedents and outcomes of union loyalty: A constructive replication and an extension.

Journal: *Journal of Applied Psychology*, August 2002, *87*, 715–722.

Related Research: Skarlicki, D. P., & Latham, G. P. (1997). Leadership training in organizational justice to increase citizenship behavior within a labor union: A replication. *Personnel Psychology, 50*, 617–633.

12015

Test Name: UNIVERSITY OF RHODE ISLAND CHANGE ASSESSMENT SCALE— GAMBLING

Purpose: To measure stages of change related to gambling: precontemplation, contemplation, action, and maintenance.

Number of Items: 32

Format: Scales range from 1 (*strongly disagree*) to 5 (*strongly agree*). All items are presented.

Reliability: Alpha coefficients range from .80 to .88 across subscales.

Validity: Correlations between subscales ranged from −.56 to .54. Correlations with readiness ranged from −.57 to .76.

Author: Petry, N. M.

Article: Stages of change in treatment-seeking pathological gamblers.

Journal: *Journal of Consulting and Clinical Psychology*, April 2005, *73*, 312–322.

Related Research: DiClemente, C. C., & Hughes, S. O. (1990). Stages of change profiles in outpatient alcoholism treatment. *Journal of Substance Abuse, 2*, 217–235.

12016

Test Name: UNIVERSITY STUDENT LAWBREAKING SCALE

Purpose: To measure the rate of lawbreaking among college students.

Number of Items: 34

Format: Scales range from 0 (*never*) to 4 (*more than 15 times*).

Reliability: Alpha coefficients ranged from .34 to .84 across subscales.

Author: Low, J. M., et al.

Article: Predictors of university student lawbreaking behaviors.

Journal: *Journal of College Student Development*, September/October 2004, *4*, 535–548.

Related Research: Elliott, D. S., et al. (1983). The prevalence and incidence of delinquent behavior: 1976–1980. Boulder, CO: Behavioral Research Institute.

12017

Test Name: VERBAL ABUSE SCALE

Purpose: To assess childhood psychological abuse using retrospective reports by youth.

Number of Items: 14

Format: Scales range from 1 (*never*) to 3 (*often*).

Reliability: Coefficient alpha was .90.

Author: D'Augelli, A. R., et al.

Article: Parents' awareness of lesbian, gay, and bisexual youths' sexual orientation.

Journal: *Journal of Marriage and Family*, May 2005, *67*, 474–482.

Related Research: Briere, J., & Runtz, M. (1990). Differential adult symptomatology associated with three types of child abuse histories. *Child Abuse & Neglect, 14,* 357–364.

12018

Test Name: VOLUNTEERISM QUESTIONNAIRE

Purpose: To measure planned behavior and functional variables associated with volunteer activity.

Number of Items: 42

Format: Various 7-point scales are used. All items are presented.

Reliability: Alpha coefficients ranged from .72 to .97.

Validity: Correlations between subscales ranged from .02 to .81.

Author: Greenslade, J. H., and White, K. M.

Article: The prediction of above-average participation in volunteerism: A test of the theory of planned behavior and the Volunteers' Function Inventory in older Australian adults.

Journal: *The Journal of Social Psychology,* April 2005, *145,* 155–172.

12019

Test Name: WORK BEHAVIOR SCALE

Purpose: To measure work behaviors in the school psychology service.

Number of Items: 20

Format: Includes four factors: individual level treatment, individual level prevention, systemic level treatment, and systemic level prevention. Responses are made on a 6-point scale ranging from 1 (*never*) to 6 (*very often*). All items are presented.

Reliability: G coefficients said to be analogous to alpha coefficients ranged from .79 to .87.

Author: Idsoe, T.

Article: Work behavior in the school psychology service: Conceptual framework and construct validity approached by two different methodologies.

Journal: *Journal of School Psychology,* September/October 2003, *41,* 313–335.

Related Research: Anthun, R. (1999). Quality and improvement potential in school psychology services. *School Psychology International, 20,* 163–175.

12020

Test Name: WORK WITHDRAWAL SCALE

Purpose: To assess how often employees engage in withdrawal behaviors.

Format: Scales range from 1 (*never*) to 5 (*once a week or more*).

Reliability: Coefficient alpha was .76.

Validity: Correlations with other variables ranged from –.27 to .10.

Author: Kammeyer-Mueller, J. D., and Wanberg, C. R.

Article: Unwrapping the organizational entry process: Disentangling multiple antecedents and their pathways to adjustment.

Journal: *Journal of Applied Psychology,* October 2003, *88,* 779–794.

Related Research: Roznowski, M., & Hanisch, K. A. (1990). Building systematic heterogeneity into work attitudes and behavior measures. *Journal of Vocational Behavior, 36,* 361–375.

12021

Test Name: WORK WITHDRAWAL SCALE

Purpose: To measure frequency of withdrawal behaviors.

Number of Items: 12

Format: Responses are made on an 8-point ranging from *never* to *more than once a week.* An example is given.

Reliability: Alpha coefficients were .74 and .75.

Validity: Correlations with other variables ranged from –.44 to .53.

Author: Wasti, S. A.

Article: Commitment profiles: Combinations of organizational commitment forms and job outcomes.

Journal: *Journal of Vocational Behavior,* October 2005, *67,* 290–308.

Related Research: Hanisch, K. A., & Hulin, C. L. (1991). General attitudes and organizational withdrawal: An evaluation of a causal model. *Journal of Vocational Behavior, 39,* 110–128.

12022

Test Name: WORKPLACE DEVIANT BEHAVIOR SCALE

Purpose: To measure deviant behavior in the workplace.

Number of Items: 23

Format: Scales range from 1 (*never*) to 7 (*always*).

Reliability: Coefficient alpha was .82.

Author: Lee, K., and Allen, N. J.

Article: Organizational citizenship behavior and workplace deviance: The role of affect and cognitions.

Journal: *Journal of Applied Psychology*, February 2002, *87*, 131–142.

Related Research: Bennett, R. J., & Robinson, S. L. (2000). Development of a measure of workplace deviance. *Journal of Applied Psychology, 85,* 349–360.

12023

Test Name: YOUTH PROBLEM BEHAVIORS SCALE

Purpose: To measure the extent of cigarette smoking, alcohol use, theft, aggression, and criminal behavior.

Number of Items: 27

Format: Seven-point rating scales are used. Sample items are presented.

Reliability: Coefficient alpha was .61.

Validity: Correlations with other variables ranged from –.32 to .62.

Author: Rotheram-Borus, M. J., et al.

Article: Impact of parent death and an intervention on the adjustment of adolescents whose parents have HIV/AIDS.

Journal: *Journal of Consulting and Clinical Psychology,* October 2001, *69,* 763–773.

CHAPTER 9

Communication

12024

Test Name: AFFECTIONATE COMMUNICATION INDEX

Purpose: To assess the amount of verbal and nonverbal affectionate communication and support.

Number of Items: 19

Format: Seven-point Likert scales range from 1 (*Partners* always *engage in this type of affectionate behavior*) to 7 (*Partners* never *engage in this type of affectionate behavior*)

Reliability: Alpha coefficients ranged from .82 to .88.

Author: Punyanunt-Carter, N. M.

Article: Reported affectionate communication and satisfaction in marital and dating relationships.

Journal: *Psychological Reports*, December 2004, *95*, Part 2, 1154–1160.

Related Research: Floyd, K., & Morman, M. T. (1998). The measurement of affectionate communication. *Communications Quarterly, 46*, 144–162.

12025

Test Name: AFFECTIVE TONE AND ACTIVATION OR POTENCY SCALES

Purpose: To measure the aspects of experience including affective tone and activation or potency.

Number of Items: 7

Format: Responses are made on 7-point semantic differential scales. All items are presented.

Reliability: Alpha coefficients ranged from .63 to .71.

Author: Peterson, S. E., and Miller, J. A.

Article: Comparing the quality of students' experiences during cooperative learning and large-group instruction.

Journal: *The Journal of Educational Research*, January/February 2004, *97*, 123–133.

Related Research: Csikszentmihalyi, M., & Larson, R. (1987). Validity and reliability of the experience-sampling method. *Journal of Nervous and Mental Disease, 175*, 526–536.

12026

Test Name: CEO SCALES

Purpose: To measure the perceived autonomy, communication, and apparent objective gap experienced by CEOs working for Chinese-based international joint ventures.

Number of Items: 11

Format: Five-point Likert scales are used. Sample items are presented.

Reliability: Alpha coefficients ranged from .69 to .85.

Validity: Correlations with other variables ranged from −.56 to .36.

Author: Gang, Y., et al.

Article: Role conflict and ambiguity of CEOs in international joint ventures: A transaction cost perspective.

Journal: *Journal of Applied Psychology*, August 2001, *86*, 764–773.

12027

Test Name: COMMITMENT TO THE EXCHANGE RELATIONSHIP SCALE

Purpose: To assess reviewers' and givers' commitment to an exchange relationship.

Number of Items: 4

Format: Scales range from 1 (*not at all*) to 7 (*to a great extent*). All items are presented.

Reliability: Alpha coefficients were .83 (givers) and .93 (receivers).

Author: Flynn, F. J., and Brockner, J.

Article: It's different to give than to receive: Predictions of givers' and receivers' reactions to favor exchange.

Journal: *Journal of Applied Psychology*, December 2003, *88*, 1034–1045.

Related Research: Brockner, J., et al. (2000). Culture and procedural fairness: When the effects of what you do depend upon how you do it. *Administrative Science Quarterly, 45*, 138–159.

12028

Test Name: COMMUNICATION ABOUT SEXUAL ISSUES SCALE

Purpose: To assess parent–child communication about sexual issues by adult children's self-reports. Issues addressed include: relationships, sexual facts, protection, and values.

Number of Items: 19

Format: Scales range from 1 (*never*) to 5 (*more than 10 times*). Sample items are presented.

Reliability: Total alpha was .93. Subscale alphas ranged from .82 to .93.

Author: Raffaelli, M., and Green, S.

Article: Parent–adolescent communication about sex: Retrospective reports by Latino college students.

Journal: *Journal of Marriage and Family*, May 2003, *65*, 474–481.

Related Research: Raffaelli, M., et al. (1999). Do mothers and teens disagree about sexual communication? A methodological reappraisal. *Journal of Youth and Adolescence*, *23*, 395–402.

12029

Test Name: COMMUNICATION PATTERNS QUESTIONNAIRE

Purpose: To assess problematic interaction and communication in close relationships.

Number of Items: 7

Reliability: Alpha coefficients ranged from .67 to .84.

Validity: Correlations with other variables ranged from –.37 to .12.

Author: Atkins, D. C., et al.

Article: Prediction of response to treatment in a randomized clinical trial of marital therapy.

Journal: *Journal of Consulting and Clinical Psychology*, October 2005, *73*, 893–903.

Related Research: Heavey, C. L., et al. (1996). The Communication Patterns Questionnaire: The reliability and validity of a

constructive communication subscale. *Journal of Marriage and Family*, *58*, 796–800.

12030

Test Name: COMPLEMENTARY RELATIONSHIP ORIENTATION SCALE

Purpose: To measure the importance a person places on the difference in age or status and the person's tendency to adapt communicative behavior according to the difference.

Number of Items: 10

Format: Responses are made on a 5-point Likert-type scale ranging from 1 (*not at all characteristic of me*) to 5 (*very much characteristic of me*). All items are presented.

Reliability: Alpha coefficients were .77 and .79.

Validity: Correlations with other variables ranged from .06 to .24.

Author: Sakuragi, T.

Article: Association of culture with shyness among Japanese and American university students.

Journal: *Perceptual and Motor Skills*, June 2004, *98*, Part 1, 803–813.

Related Research: Sakuragi, T. (1994). Family independence/dependence and symmetrical/complementary relationship orientation as cultural values: Their measurement and relation to communicative predispositions (Doctoral dissertation, University of Minnesota). *Dissertation Abstracts International*, *55*, 3352.

12031

Test Name: CONFLICT BEHAVIOR QUESTIONNAIRE

Purpose: To assess conflictual communication patterns.

Number of Items: 20

Format: A true–false format is used.

Reliability: Alpha coefficients ranged from .86 to .92.

Author: Hock, E., et al.

Article: Separation anxiety in parents of adolescents: Theoretical significance and scale development.

Journal: *Child Development*, January/February 2001, *72*, 284–298.

Related Research: Prinz, R., et al. (1979). Multivariate assessment of conflict in distressed and nondistressed mother–adolescent dyads. *Journal of Applied Behavioral Analysis*, *12*, 691–700.

12032

Test Name: COUNSELING APPROPRIATENESS CHECK LIST—REVISED

Purpose: To enable participants to indicate appropriate problems they would discuss with counselors.

Number of Items: 66

Format: Responses are made on a 5-point Likert-type scale ranging from 1 (*most appropriate*) to 5 (*definitely inappropriate*).

Reliability: Test–retest reliability coefficients ranged form .63 to .95.

Author: Rose, E. M., et al.

Article: Spiritual issues in counseling: Clients' beliefs and preferences.

Journal: *Journal of Counseling Psychology*, January 2001, *48*, 61–71.

Related Research: Warman, R. (1961). The counseling role of college and university counseling centers. *Journal of Counseling Psychology*, *8*, 231–238.

12033

Test Name: COUPLE'S COMMUNICATIVE EVALUATION SCALE

Purpose: To measure intimate communication.

Number of Items: 400

Format: A 5-point Likert format is used. Sample items are presented.

Reliability: Alpha coefficients ranged from .94 to .99 across subscales.

Validity: Correlations with other variables ranged from −.86 to .74.

Author: West, C. E.

Article: Clinical utility and validation of the Couple's Communicative Evaluation Scale.

Journal: *Psychological Reports*, October 2005, *97*, 599–622.

12034

Test Name: DISCLOSURE EXPECTATIONS SCALE

Purpose: To measure anticipated risk and anticipated utility of self-disclosing emotional material to a counselor.

Number of Items: 8

Format: Includes two factors: anticipated risk and anticipated utility. Responses are made on a 5-point scale ranging from 1 (*not at all*) to 5 (*very*). All items are presented.

Reliability: Alpha coefficients were .74 (anticipated risk) and .83 (anticipated utility).

Validity: Correlations with other variables ranged from −.30 to .39.

Author: Vogel, D. L., and Wester, S. R.

Article: To seek help or not to seek help: The risks of self-disclosure.

Journal: *Journal of Counseling Psychology*, July 2003, *50*, 351–361.

12035

Test Name: DISCLOSURE OF EMOTION SCALE

Purpose: To measure to what extent individuals disclose their feelings and emotions to others.

Number of Items: 5

Format: Four-point response categories are used. Sample items are presented.

Reliability: Alpha coefficients ranged from .75 to .81.

Author: Stroebe, M., et al.

Article: Does disclosure of emotions facilitate recovery from bereavement? Evidence from two prospective studies.

Journal: *Journal of Consulting and Clinical Psychology*, February 2002, *70*, 169–178.

Related Research: Schut, H. (1992). *Omgaan met dedood van de partner: Effecten op gezoudheid en effecten van rouwbegeleiding* [Coping with conjugal bereavement: Effects on psychological functioning and effects of grief counseling]. Amsterdam: Thesis Publishers. [In Dutch]

12036

Test Name: DISCLOSURE-TO-THERAPIST ASSESSMENT PROTOCOL

Purpose: To assess client perceptions of the nature of self-disclosure in psychotherapy.

Number of Items: 20

Format: Includes 10 open-ended interview items and 10 items answered on a 7-point scale ranging from 1 (*very little*) to 7 (*to a great extent*). Examples are given.

Reliability: Coefficient alpha for the items answered on the 7-point scale was .66.

Author: Farber, B. A., et al.

Article: Clients' perceptions of the process and consequences of self-disclosure in psychotherapy.

Journal: *Journal of Counseling Psychology*, July 2004, *51*, 340–346.

Related Research: Farber B. A., et al. (2001, November). *Self-disclosure in psychotherapy: The client's perspective.* Paper presented at the North American Society for Psychotherapy Research Conference, Puerto Vallerta, Mexico.

12037

Test Name: DISCLOSURE TO THERAPIST INVENTORY— REVISED

Purpose: To measure the extent to which topics are discussed with therapists by patients.

Number of Items: 80

Format: Item responses are anchored by 1 (*not at all*) and 5 (*discussed thoroughly*). Sample items are presented.

Reliability: Alpha was .96. Split-half reliability was .92.

Author: Roe, D., and Farber, B. A.

Article: Differences in self-disclosure in psychotherapy between American and Israeli patients.

Journal: *Psychological Reports*, June 2001, *88*, Part 1, 611–624.

Related Research: Hall, D. A. (1993). *Factors impacting disclosure in therapy: Alliance as facilitatory and shame as inhibitor.* Unpublished doctoral thesis, Teachers College, Columbia University, New York.

12038

Test Name: DISTRESS DISCLOSURE INDEX

Purpose: To measure the degree to which a person is comfortable talking to others about personally distressing information.

Number of Items: 12

Format: Responses are made on a 5-point Likert-type scale ranging from 1 (*strongly disagree*) to 5 (*strongly agree*). An example is given.

Reliability: Internal consistency coefficients ranged from .92 to .95. Test–retest (2 months) correlation was .80. Test–retest (3 months) correlation was .81.

Validity: Correlations with other variables ranged from –.54 to .41 ($N = 354$).

Author: Vogel, D. L., et al.

Article: The role of outcome expectations and attitudes on decisions to seek professional help.

Journal: *Journal of Counseling Psychology*, October 2005, *52*, 459–470.

Related Research: Kahn, J. H., & Hessling, R. M. (2001). Measuring the tendency to conceal versus disclose psychological distress. *Journal of Social and Clinical Psychology*, *20*, 41–65.

12039

Test Name: EMOTIONAL SELF-DISCLOSURE SCALE

Purpose: To measure emotional disclosures.

Number of Items: 40

Format: Includes eight subscales: Depression, Happiness, Jealousy, Anxiety, Anger, Calmness, Apathy, and Fear. Items are scored from 0 (*not at all*) to 4 (*totally willing*).

Reliability: Alpha coefficients ranged from .83 to .96. Test–retest (12 weeks) reliabilities ranged from .35 to .76.

Author: Vogel, D. L., and Wester, S. R.

Article: To seek help or not to seek help: The risks of self-disclosure.

Journal: *Journal of Counseling Psychology*, July 2003, *50*, 351–361.

Related Research: Snell, W. E., Jr., et al. (1988). Development of the Emotional Self-Disclosure Scale. *Sex Roles*, *18*, 59–74.

12040

Test Name: FEEDBACK DISCOUNTING SCALE

Purpose: To assess discounting of performance feedback.

Number of Items: 4

Format: Responses are made on a 6-point scale ranging from 1 (*not at all*) to 6 (*completely*). A sample item is given.

Reliability: Reliability coefficient was .77.

Validity: Correlations with other variables ranged from –.19 to .32 ($n = 166$).

Author: Roberson, L., et al.

Article: Stereotype threat and feedback seeking in the workplace.

Journal: *Journal of Vocational Behavior*, February 2003, *62*, 176–188.

Related Research: Crocker, J., et al. (1991). Social stigma: The affective consequences of attributional ambiguity. *Journal of Personality and Social Psychology*, *60*, 218–228.

12041

Test Name: FEEDBACK SATISFACTION SCALE

Purpose: To assess feedback satisfaction.

Number of Items: 4

Format: Responses are made on a 5-point Likert scale ranging from 1 (*strongly disagree*) to 5 (*strongly agree*). Examples are given.

Reliability: Reliability coefficient was .80 ($N = 146$).

Validity: Correlations with other variables ranged from –.08 to .43.

Author: Bono, J. E., and Colbert, A. E.

Article: Understanding responses to multisource feedback: The role of core self-evaluations.

Journal: *Personnel Psychology*, Spring 2005, *58*, 171–203.

Related Research: Facteau, C. L., et al. (1998). Reactions of leaders to 360-degree feedback from subordinates and peers. *Leadership Quarterly*, *9*, 427–448.

12042

Test Name: FEEDBACK SEEKING STRATEGIES SCALES

Purpose: To measure feedback seeking strategies.

Number of Items: 11

Format: Includes two scales: Direct Inquiry Feedback Seeking and Feedback Monitoring. All items are included.

Reliability: Reliability coefficients ranged from .75 to .81.

Validity: Correlations with other variables ranged from –.19 to .22 ($n = 166$).

Author: Roberson, L., et al.

Article: Stereotype threat and feedback seeking in the workplace.

Journal: *Journal of Vocational Behavior*, February 2003, *62*, 176–188.

Related Research: Ashford, S. J., & Tsui, A. S. (1991). Self-regulation for managerial effectiveness: The role of active feedback seeking. *Academy of Management Journal*, *34*, 251–280.

12043

Test Name: FEEDBACK VALANCE SCALE

Purpose: To measure supervisor feedback.

Number of Items: 7

Format: Scales range from 1 (*strongly disagree*) to 7 (*strongly agree*). All items are presented.

Reliability: Coefficient alpha was .79.

Validity: Correlations with other variables ranged from −.38 to .28.

Author: George, J. M., and Zhou, J.

Article: When openness to experience and conscientiousness are related to creative behavior: An interactional approach.

Journal: *Journal of Applied Psychology*, June 2001, *86*, 513–524.

12044

Test Name: GERMAN INNER SPEECH QUESTIONNAIRE

Purpose: To measure overt and covert talking to oneself about oneself.

Number of Items: 9

Reliability: Coefficient alpha was .86.

Validity: Correlations with other variables ranged from .01 to .51.

Author: Schneider, J. F.

Article: Relations among self-talk, self-consciousness, and self-knowledge.

Journal: *Psychological Reports*, December 2002, *91*, Part 1, 807–812.

Related Research: Siegrist, M. (1995). Inner speech as a cognitive process mediating self-consciousness and inhibiting self-deception. *Psychological Reports*, *76*, 259–265.

12045

Test Name: IMPRESSION-MANAGEMENT SCALE

Purpose: To measure the extent of engagement in impression-management activities.

Number of Items: 23

Format: Scales range from 1 (*very inaccurate*) to 5 (*very accurate*).

Reliability: Alpha coefficients ranged from .72 to .83 across subscales.

Author: Turnley, W. H., and Bolino, M. C.

Article: Achieving desired images while avoiding undesired images: Exploring the role of self-monitoring in impression management.

Journal: *Journal of Applied Psychology*, April 2001, *86*, 351–360.

Related Research: Bolino, M. C., & Turnley, W. H. (1999). Measuring impression management in organizations: A scale based on the Jones and Pittman Taxonomy. *Organizational Research Methods*, *2*, 187–206.

12046

Test Name: INACCURATE COMMUNICATION FROM COWORKERS SCALE

Purpose: To measure inaccurate communication.

Number of Items: 5

Format: Scales range from 1 (*strongly disagree*) to 5 (*strongly agree*).

Reliability: Coefficient alpha was .82.

Author: George, J. M., and Zhou, J.

Article: When openness to experience and conscientiousness are related to creative behavior: An interactional approach.

Journal: *Journal of Applied Psychology*, June 2001, *86*, 513–524.

Related Research: O'Reilly, C. A., & Roberts, K. H. (1976). Relationships among components of credibility and communication behaviors in work units. *Journal of Applied Psychology*, *61*, 99–102.

12047

Test Name: INDIRECT SEXUAL COMMUNICATION SCALE

Purpose: To assess the frequency of indirect sexual communication from parents to children by adult children's self-reports.

Number of Items: 3

Format: Scales range from 1 (*never*) to 5 (*more than 10 times*). A sample item is presented.

Reliability: Alpha coefficients were .66 (mothers) and .74 (fathers).

Author: Raffaelli, M., and Green, S.

Article: Parent–adolescent communication about sex: Retrospective reports by Latino college students.

Journal: *Journal of Marriage and Family*, May 2003, *65*, 474–481.

Related Research: Raffaelli, M., & Ontai, L. L. (2001). "She's 16 years old and there's boys calling over to the house": An exploratory study of sexual socialization in Latino families. *Culture, Health, and Sexuality*, *3*, 295–310.

12048

Test Name: INEFFECTIVE ARGUING INVENTORY

Purpose: To identify a pattern of conflict.

Number of Items: 8

Format: Examples are given.

Reliability: Alpha coefficients ranged from .57 to .71.

Validity: Correlations with other variables ranged from −.64 to .35.

Author: Brody, G. H., et al.

Article: Protective longitudinal paths linking child competence to behavioral problems among African American siblings.

Journal: *Child Development,* March/April 2004, *75,* 455–467.

Related Research: Kurdek, L. A. (1994). Conflict resolution styles in gay, lesbian, heterosexual nonparent, and heterosexual parent couples. *Journal of Marriage and the Family, 56,* 705–722.

12049

Test Name: INSPIRATION/MODELING SUBSCALE

Purpose: To assess the degree to which students received inspiration and influence from others when making academic and career decisions.

Number of Items: 7

Format: Responses are made on a 5-point Likert-type scale ranging from 1 (*strongly disagree*) to 5 (*strongly agree*). Examples are given.

Reliability: Alpha coefficients ranged from .87 to .91.

Author: Karunanayake, D., and Nauta, M. M.

Article: The relationship between race and students' career role models and perceived role model influence.

Journal: *The Career Development Quarterly,* March 2004, *52,* 225–234.

Related Research: Nauta, M. M., & Kokaly, M. L. (2001). Assessing role model influences on students' academic and vocational decisions. *Journal of Career Assessments, 9,* 81–99.

12050

Test Name: INSTRUCTIONAL ACTIVITIES FEEDBACK FORM

Purpose: To enable students to provide feedback to their instructors.

Number of Items: 38

Format: Responses are made on a 5-point scale ranging from A (*almost never*) to E (*almost always*). All items are given.

Validity: Correlations with other variables ranged from .07 to .56.

Author: Hampton, S. E., and Reiser, R. A.

Article: Effects of a theory-based feedback and consultation process on instruction and learning in college classrooms.

Journal: *Research in Higher Education,* August 2004, *45,* 497–527.

Related Research: Hampton, S. E., & Reiser, R. A. (2000). *Instructional activities feedback form.* Unpublished manuscript, Florida State University.

12051

Test Name: INTERCULTURAL WILLINGNESS TO COMMUNICATE SCALE

Purpose: To measure willingness to communicate with someone from another culture.

Number of Items: 12

Format: Anchors for items ranged from 0 to 100 percent. Sample items are presented.

Reliability: Coefficient alpha was .91.

Author: Lin, Y., and Rancer, A. S.

Article: Sex differences in intercultural communication apprehension, ethnocentrism, and intercultural willingness to communicate.

Journal: *Psychological Reports,* February 2003, *92,* 195–200.

Related Research: Kassing, J. W. (1997). Development of the Intercultural Willingness to Communicate Scale. *Communication Research Reports, 14,* 399–407.

12052

Test Name: INTERPERSONAL COMMUNICATION SATISFACTION INVENTORY

Purpose: To assess satisfaction in interpersonal communication.

Number of Items: 19

Format: Likert response scales range from 1 (*strongly agree*) to 7 (*strongly disagree*).

Reliability: Coefficient alpha was .90.

Author: Punyanunt-Carter, N. M.

Article: Reported affectionate communication and satisfaction in marital and dating relationships.

Journal: *Psychological Reports,* December 2004, *95,* Part 2, 1154–1160.

Related Research: Hecht, M. L. (1978). The conceptualization and measurement of interpersonal communication. *Human Communication Research, 4,* 253–264.

12053

Test Name: INTERPERSONAL COMMUNICATION WITH CUSTOMERS SCALE

Purpose: To measure the expression and regulation of emotions in dealing with customers: giving information, listening, persuading, negotiating, and calming.

Number of Items: 6

Format: Scales range from 1 (*not important at all*) to 7 (*very important*).

Reliability: Coefficient alpha was .78.

Author: Wilk, S. L., and Moynihan, L. M.

Article: Display rule "regulators": The relationship between supervisors and worker emotional exhaustion.

Journal: *Journal of Applied Psychology*, September 2005, *90*, 917–927.

Related Research: Morris, J. A., & Feldman, D. C. (1996). The dimensions, antecedents, and consequences of emotional labor. *Academy of Management Review, 21*, 986–1010.

12054

Test Name: JOB INTERVIEW PREPARATION AND RESPONSE STRATEGIES SCALE

Purpose: To measure the extent to which subjects use job interview strategies.

Number of Items: 26

Format: Scales range from 1 (*not at all*) to 5 (*to a very great extent*). Sample items are presented.

Reliability: Alpha coefficients ranged from .75 to .92 across subscales.

Validity: Correlations with other variables ranged from –.15 to .54.

Author: Maurer, T. J., et al.

Article: Interviewee coaching, preparation strategies, and response strategies in relation to performance in situational employment interviews: An extension of Maurer, Solamon and Troxtel (1988).

Journal: *Journal of Applied Psychology*, August 2001, *86*, 709–717.

12055

Test Name: JUSTICE ANTECEDENTS SCALE

Purpose: To measure employee input, communication, support, and individual treatment prior to reorganization.

Number of Items: 17

Format: Scales range from 1 (*strongly disagree*) to 7 (*strongly agree*). Sample items are presented.

Reliability: Alpha coefficients ranged from .58 to .96.

Author: Kernan, M. C., and Hanges, P. J.

Article: Survivor reactions to reorganization: Antecedents and consequences of procedural, interpersonal, and informational justice.

Journal: *Journal of Applied Psychology*, October 2002, *87*, 916–928.

Related Research: Colquitt, J. A. (2001). On the dimensionality of organizational justice: A construct validation measure. *Journal of Applied Psychology, 86*, 386–400.

12056

Test Name: LEADER–MEMBER EXCHANGE QUALITY

Purpose: To measure the leader's contribution to an exchange relationship and the overall quality of the relationship as seen from the member's perspective.

Number of Items: 7

Format: Items are anchored by 1 (*very ineffective*) and 5 (*very effective*) and 1 (*not at all*) and 5 (*a great deal*). Sample items are presented.

Reliability: Cronbach's alpha was .90.

Validity: Correlations with other variables ranged from –.31 to .40.

Author: van Breukelen, W., et al.

Article: Effects of LMX and differential treatment on work unit commitment.

Journal: *Psychological Reports*, August 2002, *91*, 220–230.

Related Research: Graen, G. B., & Uhl-Bien, M. (1995). Relationship-based approach to leadership: Development of Leader–Member Exchange (LMX) theory of leadership over 25 years: Applying a multi-level multi-domain perspective. *Leadership Quarterly, 6*, 219–247.

12057

Test Name: LEADER–MEMBER EXCHANGE SCALE

Purpose: To measure perceptions of the quality of the supervisor–subordinate relationship.

Number of Items: 7

Format: A sample item is given.

Reliability: Internal reliability estimate was .89.

Validity: Correlations with other variables ranged from –.25 to .25.

Author: Kacmar, K. M., et al.

Article: Situational and dispositional factors as antecedents of ingratiatory behaviors in organizational settings.

Journal: *Journal of Vocational Behavior*, October 2004, *65*, 309–331.

Related Research: Scandura, T. A., et al. (1986). When managers decide not to decide autocratically: An investigation of leader–member exchange and decision influence. *Journal of Applied Psychology, 71*, 579–584.

12058

Test Name: LEADER–MEMBER EXCHANGES SCALE

Purpose: To measure leader–member exchanges.

Number of Items: 11

Format: Includes four dimensions: Affect, Loyalty, Contribution, and Professional Respect. Examples are given.

Reliability: Reliabilities ranged from .59 to .90.

Author: Vandenberghe, C., et al.

Article: Affective commitment to the organization, supervisor, and work group: Antecedents and outcomes.

Journal: *Journal of Vocational Behavior*, February 2004, *64*, 47–71.

Related Research: Liden, R. C., & Maslyn, J. M. (1998). Multidimensionality of leader–member exchange: An empirical assessment through scale development. *Journal of Management*, *24*, 43–72.

12059

Test Name: LMX-MDM SCALE

Purpose: To measure leader–member exchange.

Number of Items: 12

Format: A sample item is presented.

Reliability: Coefficient alpha was .94 (*N* = 267).

Validity: Correlations with other variables ranged from –.05 to .62 (*N* = 267).

Author: Erdogan, B., et al.

Article: Work value congruence and intrinsic career success: The compensatory roles of leader–member exchange and perceived organizational support.

Journal: *Personnel Psychology*, Summer 2004, *57*, 305–332.

Related Research: Liden, R. C., & Maslyn, J. M. (1998). Multidimensionality of leader–member exchange: An empirical assessment through scale development. *Journal of Management*, *24*, 43–72.

12060

Test Name: MENTORING AND COMMUNICATIONS SUPPORT SCALE

Purpose: To measure workplace social support.

Number of Items: 15

Format: Includes four factors: collegial task support, career mentoring, coaching mentoring, and collegial social support. Responses are made on a 5-point scale ranging from 1 (*strongly disagree*) to 5 (*strongly agree*).

Reliability: Alpha coefficients ranged from .75 to .89.

Validity: Correlations with other variables ranged from –.12 to .29.

Author: Harris, J. I., et al.

Article: The comparative contributions of congruence and social support in career outcomes.

Journal: *The Career Development Quarterly*, June 2001, *49*, 314–323.

Related Research: Hill, S. E. K., et al. (1989). Mentoring and other communication support in the academic setting. *Groups and Organization Studies*, *14*, 355–368.

12061

Test Name: MOTHER–DAUGHTER COMMUNICATION SCALE

Purpose: To measure the warmth and openness of mother–daughter communication.

Number of Items: 24

Format: Response scales range from 1 (*strongly disagree*) to 5 (*strongly agree*). Sample items are presented.

Reliability: Coefficient alpha was .92.

Author: Milan, S., et al.

Article: Prevalence, cause, and predictors of emotional distress in pregnant and parenting adolescents.

Journal: *Journal of Consulting and Clinical Psychology*, April 2004, *72*, 328–340.

Related Research: Fox, G., & Inazu, J. (1980). Patterns and outcomes of mother–daughter communication about sexuality. *Journal of Social Issues*, *36*, 7–29.

12062

Test Name: NEGATIVE EXPRESSION SCALE

Purpose: To measure family communication by mothers' reports.

Number of Items: 13

Format: Four-point scales range from 0 (*never happens*) to 3 (*happens all the time*).

Reliability: Alpha coefficients ranged from .83 to .87.

Author: Hill, N., and Bush, K. R.

Article: Relationships between parenting environment and children's mental health among African American and European American mothers and children.

Journal: *Journal of Marriage and Family*, November 2001, *63*, 954–966.

Related Research: Greenberg, M., et al. (1995). *Family Expressiveness Questionnaire* (Technical report: Fast Track). Durham, NC: Duke University.

12063

Test Name: OPENER SCALE

Purpose: To assess the ability of participants to elicit self-disclosure from others.

Number of Items: 10

Format: Responses are made on a 5-point scale ranging from 1 (*strongly disagree*) to 5 (*strongly agree*). An example is given.

Reliability: Alpha coefficients were .79 and .88. Test–retest reliability (6 weeks) was .69.

Validity: Correlations with other variables ranged from –.38 to .53.

Author: Bruch, M. A.

Article: Shyness and toughness: Unique and moderated relations with men's emotional inexpression.

Journal: *Journal of Counseling Psychology*, January 2002, *49*, 28–34.

Related Research: Miller, L. C., et al. (1983). Openers: Individuals who elicit intimate self-disclosure. *Journal of Personality and Social Psychology*, *44*, 1234–1244.

12064

Test Name: PARTICIPATION IN DECISION-MAKING SCALE

Purpose: To measure participation in decision making.

Number of Items: 4

Format: Responses are made on a 5-point scale. A sample item is given.

Reliability: Coefficient alpha was .87.

Validity: Correlations with other variables ranged from −.23 to .35 ($N = 600$).

Author: Ito, J. K., and Brotheridge, C. M.

Article: Resources, coping strategies, and emotional exhaustion: A conservation of resources perspective.

Journal: *Journal of Vocational Behavior*, December 2003, *63*, 490–509.

Related Research: Ito, J. K., & Peterson, R. B. (1986). Effects of task difficulty and interunit interdependence on information processing systems. *Academy of Management Journal*, *29*, 139–149.

12065

Test Name: PARTICIPATIVE DECISION-MAKING SCALE

Purpose: To assess the level of involvement that job holders have in decision making.

Number of Items: 7

Format: Scales range from 1 (*never*) to 7 (*always*). Sample items are presented.

Reliability: Coefficient alpha was .96.

Validity: Correlations with other variables ranged from .31 to .71.

Author: Pierce, J. L., et al.

Article: Work environment structure and psychological ownership: The mediating effects of control.

Journal: *The Journal of Social Psychology*, October 2004, *144*, 507–534.

12066

Test Name: PERCEIVED POSITIVE INFORMATIONAL FEEDBACK SCALE

Purpose: To measure the amount of positive and informational feedback a student experiences in academic contexts.

Number of Items: 5

Format: Responses are made on a 6-point scale ranging from 1 (*not at all true*) to 6 (*completely true*). An example is given.

Reliability: Internal reliability ranged from .81 to .85.

Author: Levesque, C., et al.

Article: Autonomy and competence in German and American university students: A comparative study based on self-determination theory.

Journal: *Journal of Educational Psychology*, March 2004, *96*, 68–84.

Related Research: Deci, E. L., et al. (1989). Self-determination in a work organization. *Journal of Applied Psychology*, *74*, 580–590.

12067

Test Name: PERSONAL REPORT OF COMMUNICATION APPREHENSION

Purpose: To measure apprehension in oral communication.

Number of Items: 24

Format: Item anchors are 1 (*strongly agree*) and 5 (*strongly disagree*).

Reliability: Coefficient alpha was .96.

Validity: Correlations with other variables ranged from −.53 to .42.

Author: Simmons, D., et al.

Article: Correlations among applicants' communication apprehension, argumentativeness, and verbal aggressiveness in selection interviews.

Journal: *Psychological Reports*, June 2003, *92*, Part 1, 804–808.

12068

Test Name: PERSONAL REPORT OF INTERCULTURAL COMMUNICATION APPREHENSION SCALE

Purpose: To measure apprehension about intercultural communication.

Number of Items: 14

Format: Rating scales range from *strongly disagree* to *strongly agree*. A sample item is presented.

Reliability: Coefficient alpha was .92.

Author: Lin, Y., and Rancer, A. S.

Article: Sex differences in intercultural communication apprehension, ethnocentrism, and intercultural willingness to communicate.

Journal: *Psychological Reports*, February 2003, *92*, 195–200.

Related Research: Neuliep, J. W., & McCroskey, J. C. (1997). The development of intercultural and interethnic communication apprehension scales. *Communication Research Reports*, *14*, 145–156.

12069

Test Name: QUALITY OF LEADER–MEMBER EXCHANGE QUESTIONNAIRE—MANDARIN VERSION

Purpose: To measure perceived exchange relationships with supervisors.

Number of Items: 8

Format: Seven-point Likert scales are used. Sample items are presented in English.

Reliability: Coefficient alpha was .92.

Validity: Correlations with other variables ranged from .07 to .38.

Author: Chi, S.-C., and Lo, H.-H.

Article: Taiwanese employees' justice perceptions of co-workers' punitive events.

Journal: *The Journal of Social Psychology*, February 2003, *143*, 27–42.

Related Research: Bauer, T. N., & Green, S. G. (1996). Development of leader–member exchange: A longitudinal test. *Academy of Management Journal, 39*, 1538–1567.

12070

Test Name: REACTIONS TO FEEDBACK SCALE

Purpose: To measure reactions to feedback.

Number of Items: 24

Format: Includes three factors: positive emotions, negative emotions, and motivation. Responses are made on a 5-point scale ranging from *not at all* to *very much*.

Reliability: Alpha coefficients ranged from .77 to .91.

Validity: Correlations with other variables ranged from −.56 to .36.

Author: Atwater, L. E., and Brett, J. F.

Article: Antecedents and consequences of reactions to developmental 360° feedback.

Journal: *Journal of Vocational Behavior*, June 2005, *66*, 532–548.

12071

Test Name: REASSURANCE-SEEKING SCALE—TURKISH VERSION

Purpose: To assess reassurance-seeking.

Number of Items: 4

Format: Scales range from 1 (*no, not at all*) to 7 (*yes, very much*). All items are presented in Turkish.

Reliability: Coefficient alpha was .86.

Validity: Correlations with other variables ranged from −.26 to .36.

Author: Gençöz, T., and Gençöz, F.

Article: Psychometric properties of the Reassurance-Seeking Scale in a Turkish sample.

Journal: *Psychological Reports*, February 2005, *96*, 47–50.

Related Research: Coyne, J. C. (1976). Toward an interactional description of depression. *Psychiatry, 39*, 28–40.

12072

Test Name: SCALE FOR INNER SPEECH—GERMAN VERSION

Purpose: To measure overt and covert self-talk.

Number of Items: 9

Format: Scales range from 1 (*completely false*) to 6 (*completely true*).

Reliability: Coefficient alpha was .85.

Validity: Correlations with other variables ranged from −.26 to .56.

Author: Schneider, J. F., et al.

Article: Does self-consciousness mediate the relation between self-talk and self-knowledge?

Journal: *Psychological Reports*, April 2005, *96*, 387–396.

Related Research: Siegrist, M. (1995). Inner speech as a cognitive process mediating self-consciousness and inhibiting self-deception. *Psychological Reports, 76*, 259–265.

12073

Test Name: SELF-CONCEALMENT SCALE

Purpose: To assess the desire to actively conceal personal information from others.

Number of Items: 10

Format: Responses are made on a 5-point Likert-type scale ranging from 1 (*strongly disagree*) to 5 (*strongly agree*).

Reliability: Internal consistencies ranged from .83 to .88. Test–retest reliabilities ranged from .74 to .81.

Validity: Correlations with other variables ranged from −.47 to .31 (N = 354).

Author: Vogel, D. L., et al.

Article: The role of outcome expectations and attitudes on decisions to seek professional help.

Journal: *Journal of Counseling Psychology*, October 2005, *52*, 459–470.

Related Research: Larson, D. G., & Chastain, R. L. (1990). Self-concealment: Conceptualization, measurement, and health implications. *Journal of Social and Clinical Psychology, 9*, 439–455.

12074

Test Name: SELF-DISCLOSURE SCALE

Purpose: To assess the extent to which one typically self-discloses with same-sex friendships.

Number of Items: 5

Format: Responses are made on a 5-point scale ranging from 1 (*not at all true*) to 5 (*really true*). An example is presented.

Reliability: Coefficient alpha was .85.

Validity: Correlations with other variables ranged from .14 to .61.

Author: Rose, A. J.

Article: Co-rumination in the friendships of girls and boys.

Journal: *Child Development*, November/December 2002, *73*, 1830–1843.

Related Research: Parke, J. G., & Asher, S. R. (1993). Friendship and friendship quality in middle childhood: Links with peer group acceptance and feelings of loneliness and social dissatisfaction. *Developmental Psychology, 29*, 611–621.

12075

Test Name: SELF-PERCEPTION OF SAFE COMMUNICATION SCALE

Purpose: To assess the likelihood of various kinds of communication with potential sex partners.

Number of Items: 12

Format: Response categories are anchored by 1 (*unlikely*) and 4 (*likely*). All items are prevented.

Reliability: Coefficient alpha was .86.

Validity: Correlations with other variables ranged from −.17 to .26.

Author: Thompson, K. L., et al.

Article: Psychological predictors of sexual behaviors related to AIDS transmission.

Journal: *Psychological Reports*, February 2001, *88*, 51–67.

Related Research: Gray, L. A. (1993). Unpublished manuscript, Oregon State University Counselor Education Program.

12076

Test Name: SELF-VERBALIZATION QUESTIONNAIRE— GERMAN VERSION

Purpose: To measure cognitive, mnemonic, and attentional uses of overtly vocalized self-directed speech.

Number of Items: 27

Reliability: Coefficient alpha was .91.

Validity: Correlations with other variables ranged from .17 to .42.

Author: Schneider, J. F.

Article: Relations among self-talk, self-consciousness, and self-knowledge.

Journal: *Psychological Reports*, December 2002, *91*, Part 1, 807–812.

Related Research: Duncan, R. M., & Cheyne, T. A. (1999). Incidence and functions of self-reported private speech in young adults: A Self-Verbalization Questionnaire. *Canadian Journal of Behavioral Science, 31*, 133–136.

12077

Test Name: SELLING TECHNIQUES SCALE

Purpose: To measure responsiveness to objection-addressing and closing strategies in the selling process.

Number of Items: 30

Format: Seven-point scales are anchored by *very responsive* and *very nonresponsive*. All items are presented.

Validity: Correlations with buyers' ratings ranged from −.19 to .15.

Author: Claxton, R., et al.

Article: Industrial buyers' perception of effective selling.

Journal: *Psychological Reports*, December 2001, *89*, 476–482.

Related Research: Dubinsky, A. J., & Staples, W. A. (1981). Are industrial sales people buyer oriented? *Journal of Purchasing and Materials Management, 17*, 12–19.

12078

Test Name: STUDENT ENGAGEMENT QUESTIONNAIRE

Purpose: To obtain feedback on the students' perceptions of the development of generic capabilities and of the teaching and learning environment.

Number of Items: 39

Format: Includes 10 teaching and learning environment domain scales and 8 capability scales. Responses are made on a 5-point Likert scale ranging from *strongly disagree* to *strongly agree*. All items are presented.

Reliability: Alpha coefficients ranged from .53 to .88.

Author: Leung, D. Y. P., and Kember, D.

Article: Comparability of data gathered from evaluation questionnaires on paper and through the internet.

Journal: *Research in Higher Education*, August 2005, *46*, 571–591.

Related Research: Kember, D., & Leung, D. Y. P. (2005). The influence of active learning experiences on the development of graduate capabilities. *Studies in Higher Education, 30*, 157–172.

12079

Test Name: TEAM COLLECTIVISM SCALE

Purpose: To measure collectivism.

Number of Items: 6

Format: Responses are made on a 5-point scale ranging from 1 (*strongly disagree*) to 5 (*strongly agree*). All items are presented.

Reliability: Coefficient alpha was .82.

Author: Colquitt, J. A., et al.

Article: Justice in teams: Antecedents and consequences of procedural justice climate.

Journal: *Personnel Psychology,* Spring 2002, *55,* 83–109.

Related Research: Wagner, J. A., III. (1995). Studies of individualism–collectivism: Effects on cooperation in groups. *Academy of Management Journal, 38,* 152–172.

12080

Test Name: TEAM EMPOWERMENT SCALE

Purpose: To measure team empowerment.

Number of Items: 26

Format: Includes the following dimensions: Potency, Meaningfulness, Autonomy, and Impact. Responses are made on a 7-point Likert scale ranging from 1 (*strongly disagree*) to 7 (*strongly agree*).

Reliability: Alpha coefficients were .96 and .98.

Validity: Correlations with other variables ranged from .33 to .64.

Author: Kirkman, B. L., et al.

Article: Assessing the incremental validity of team consensus ratings over aggregation of individual-level data in predicting team effectiveness.

Journal: *Personnel Psychology,* Autumn 2001, *54,* 645–667.

Related Research: Kirkman, B. L., & Rosen, B. (1999). Beyond self-management: The antecedents and consequences of team empowerment. *Academy of Management Journal, 42,* 59–75.

12081

Test Name: THE SELF-DISCLOSURE INDEX

Purpose: To measure the willingness to disclose personal information.

Number of Items: 40

Format: Scales range from 0 (*discuss not at all*) to 4 (*discuss fully and completely*). Sample items are presented.

Reliability: Alpha coefficients ranged from .83 to .91.

Author: Kito, M.

Article: Self-disclosure in romantic relationships and friendships among American and Japanese college students.

Journal: *The Journal of Social Psychology,* April 2005, *145,* 127–140.

Related Research: Miller, L. C., et al. (1983). Openers: Individuals who elicit intimate self-disclosure. *Journal of Personality and Social Psychology, 44,* 1234–1244.

12082

Test Name: VERBAL AGGRESSIVENESS SCALE

Purpose: To measure verbal aggressiveness as a communication behavior that involves attacking the self-concept of another person.

Number of Items: 20

Format: Response scales are anchored by 1 (*strongly disagree*) and 5 (*strongly agree*).

Reliability: Coefficient alpha was .86.

Author: Martin, M. M., et al.

Article: Verbal aggression and viewing the world as a mean place.

Journal: *Psychological Reports,* February 2003, *92,* 151–152.

Related Research: Infante, D. A., & Wigley, C. J. (1986). Verbal aggressiveness: An interpersonal model and measure. *Communication Monographs, 53,* 61–69.

12083

Test Name: WILLINGNESS TO SELF-DISCLOSE SYMPTOMS SCALE

Purpose: To measure willingness to disclose symptoms and fears to a physician.

Number of Items: 13

Format: A Likert format is used.

Reliability: Coefficient alpha was .94.

Author: Aruguete, M. S., and Roberts, C. A.

Article: Participants' ratings of male physicians who vary in race and communication style.

Journal: *Psychological Reports,* December 2002, *91,* Part 1, 793–806.

Related Research: Young, J. W. (1980). The effects of perceived physician competence in patients' symptom disclosure to male and female physicians. *Journal of Behavioral Medicine, 3,* 279–290.

CHAPTER 10

Concept Meaning

12084

Test Name: CONCEPTIONS OF MATHEMATICS QUESTIONNAIRE

Purpose: To measure fragmented and cohesive conceptions of mathematics.

Number of Items: 19

Format: Likert scales are anchored by 1 (*strongly disagree*) and 5 (*strongly agree*). All items are presented.

Reliability: Alpha coefficients were .80 (fragmented) and .90 (cohesive).

Author: Mji, A., and Klass, E. N.

Article: Psychometric characteristics of the Conceptions of Mathematics Questionnaire.

Journal: *Psychological Reports*, June 2001, *88*, Part 1, 825–831.

Related Research: Crawford, K., et al. (1998). University mathematics students' conceptions of mathematics. *Studies in Higher Education, 23*, 87–94.

12085

Test Name: CONCEPTIONS OF MATHEMATICS SCALE

Purpose: To measure fragmented and cohesive conceptions of mathematics.

Number of Items: 18

Format: Agreement scales are anchored by 1 (*strongly disagree*) and 5 (*strongly agree*). All items are presented.

Reliability: Alpha coefficients were .87 (cohesive conceptions) and .80 (fragmented conceptions).

Author: Alkhateeb, H. M.

Article: University students' conceptions of first-year mathematics.

Journal: *Psychological Reports*, August 2001, *89*, 41–47.

Related Research: Crawford, K., et al. (1998). University mathematics students' conceptions of mathematics. *Studies in Higher Education, 23*, 131–152.

12086

Test Name: CONDOM MEANING SCALE

Purpose: To measure the connotative meaning of the term condom.

Number of Items: 15

Format: A 7-point semantic differential format is used. All adjective pairs are presented.

Reliability: Coefficient alpha was .93.

Author: McDermott, R. J., and Noland, V. J.

Article: Condom use history as a determinant of university students' Condom Evaluative Index.

Journal: *Psychological Reports*, June 2004, *94*, Part 1, 889–893.

Related Research: Sarvela, P., et al. (1992). Connotative meanings assigned to contraceptive options.

Journal of American College Health, 46, 221–225.

12087

Test Name: FORGIVENESS CONCEPT SURVEY

Purpose: To assess knowledge of forgiveness.

Number of Items: 10

Format: Scales range from 1 (*strongly agree*) to 5 (*strongly disagree*).

Reliability: Mean alpha coefficient was .70.

Validity: Correlations with other variables ranged from −.11 to .10.

Author: Rye, M. S., et al.

Article: Can group interventions facilitate forgiveness of an ex-spouse? A randomized clinical trial.

Journal: *Journal of Consulting and Clinical Psychology*, October 2005, *73*, 880–892.

12088

Test Name: SYMBOLISM MEASURE

Purpose: To measure symbolism.

Number of Items: 3

Format: Responses are made on a 5-point scale ranging from 1 (*strongly disagree*) to 5 (*strongly agree*). All items are presented.

Reliability: Coefficient alpha was .64 ($N = 989$).

Validity: Correlations with other variables ranged from .01 to .48 ($N = 989$).

Author: Allen, D. G., et al.

Article: Recruitment communication media: Impact on prehire outcomes.

Journal: *Personnel Psychology,* Spring 2004, *57,* 143–171.

Related Research: Trevino, L. K., et al. (1987). Media symbolism, media richness, and media choice in organizations. *Communication Research, 14,* 553–574.

CHAPTER 11

Creativity

12089

Test Name: CHINESE CREATIVE WRITING SCALE

Purpose: To assess creativity of writing.

Number of Items: 13

Format: Includes three factors: fluency, flexibility, and originality. All items are presented.

Reliability: Alpha coefficients ranged from .06 to .79. Interrater reliability ranged from .90 to .98.

Author: Cheung, W. M., et al.

Article: Development and validation of the Chinese Creative Writing Scale for primary school students in Hong Kong.

Journal: *The Journal of Creative Behavior,* Fourth Quarter, 2001, *35*(4), 249–259.

Related Research: Carlson, R. K. (1965). An originality story scale. *The Elementary School Journal,* *65,* 366–374.

12090

Test Name: CREATIVE BEHAVIOR INVENTORY— REVISED

Purpose: To measure creative behavior.

Number of Items: 28

Format: Includes accomplishments in visual, literary and performing arts, and crafts. Responses are made on a 4-point scale ranging from *never did this* to *did this more than five times.* An example is given.

Reliability: Alpha coefficients were .89 and .90.

Validity: Correlations with other variables ranged from –.27 to .54.

Author: Dollinger, S. J., et al.

Article: Creativity and intuition revisited.

Journal: *The Journal of Creative Behavior,* Fourth Quarter 2004, *38*(4), 58–78.

Related Research: Dollinger, S. J. (2003). Need for uniqueness, need for cognition, and creativity. *The Journal of Creative Behavior, 37* (2), 99–116.

12091

Test Name: CREATIVE BEHAVIOR SCALE

Purpose: To measure employee creativity in meeting organizational goals.

Number of Items: 13

Format: Scales range from 1 (*not at all characteristic*) to 5 (*very characteristic*). All items are presented.

Reliability: Coefficient alpha was .96.

Validity: Correlations with other variables ranged from –.26 to .26.

Author: George, J. M., and Zhou, J.

Article: When openness to experience and conscientiousness are related to creative behavior: An interactional approach.

Journal: *Journal of Applied Psychology,* June 2001, *86,* 513–524.

12092

Test Name: CREATIVE CONFIDENCE SCALE

Purpose: To assess creative confidence.

Number of Items: 12

Format: All items are presented.

Reliability: Reliability estimates were .89 and .90.

Validity: Correlations with other variables ranged from .15 to .70.

Author: Phelan, S., and Young, A. M.

Article: Understanding creativity in the workplace: An examination of individual styles and training in relation to creative confidence and creative self-leadership.

Journal: *The Journal of Creative Behavior,* Fourth Quarter 2003, *37*(4), 266–281.

Related Research: Harrison, A., et al. (1997). Testing the self-efficacy–performance linkage of social-cognitive theory. *The Journal of Social Psychology, 137,* 79–87. Stevens, C., & Gist, M. (1997). Effects of self-efficacy and goal-orientation training on negotiation skill maintenance. *Personnel Psychology, 50,* 955–978.

12093

Test Name: CREATIVE PERFORMANCE RATING SCALE

Purpose: To assess employee creativity by supervisor report.

Number of Items: 13

Format: Scales range from 1 (*not at all characteristic*) to 5 (*very characteristic*). Sample items are presented.

Reliability: Coefficient alpha was .98.

Validity: Correlations with other variables ranged from −.13 to .23.

Author: George, J. M., and Zhou, J.

Article: Understanding when bad moods foster creativity and good ones don't: The role of context and clarity of feelings.

Journal: *Journal of Applied Psychology*, August 2002, 87, 687–697.

Related Research: George, J. M., & Zhou, J. (2001). When openness to experience and conscientiousness are related to creative behavior: An interactional approach. *Journal of Applied Psychology, 86*, 513–524.

12094

Test Name: CREATIVE SELF-LEADERSHIP SCALE

Purpose: To assess creative self-leadership.

Number of Items: 11

Format: All items are presented.

Reliability: Reliability estimates were .88 and .90.

Validity: Correlations with other variables ranged from .00 to .70.

Author: Phelan, S., and Young, A. M.

Article: Understanding creativity in the workplace: An examination of individual styles and training in relation to creative confidence and creative self-leadership.

Journal: *The Journal of Creative Behavior*, Fourth Quarter 2003, 37(4), 266–281.

Related Research: Neck, S., & Manz, C. (1995). Thought–self–leadership as a framework for

enhancing the performance of performance appraisers. *The Journal of Applied Behavioral Science, 31*, 278–302.

12095

Test Name: CREATIVE STYLES QUESTIONNAIRE—REVISED

Purpose: To assess styles of creativity.

Number of Items: 76.

Format: Includes seven creativity styles: belief in unconscious processes, use of techniques, use of other people, final product orientation, environmental control and behavioral self-regulation, superstition, and use of the senses. Included is the Self-Perceived Creative Capacity containing two items. Responses are made on a 5-point scale ranging from 1 (*strongly agree*) to 5 (*strongly disagree*).

Reliability: Alpha coefficients ranged from .40 to .77.

Validity: Correlations with other variables ranged from −.26 to .40.

Author: Lack, S. A., et al.

Article: Fantasy proneness, creative capacity, and styles of creativity.

Journal: *Perceptual and Motor Skills*, February 2003, 96, 19–24.

Related Research: Kumar, V. K., & Holman, E. R. (1997). Creative Styles Questionnaire—Revised. Unpublished psychological test, West Chester University, West Chester, PA.

12096

Test Name: CREATIVITY FOSTERING ACTIVITIES QUESTIONNAIRE

Purpose: To rate the degree of usefulness of activities for fostering elementary school students creativity.

Number of Items: 33

Format: Responses are made on a 5-point scale ranging from 1 (*not very useful*) to 5 (*very useful*).

Reliability: Coefficient alpha was .94.

Author: Tan, A.-G.

Article: Singaporean teachers' perception of activities useful for fostering creativity.

Journal: *The Journal of Creative Behavior*, Second Quarter 2001, 35(2), 131–148.

Related Research: Tan, A.-G. (1998). An exploratory study of Singaporean primary pupils' desirable activities for English lessons. *Education Journal, 26*, 59–76.

12097

Test Name: FINKE CREATIVE INVENTION TASK

Purpose: To measure creativity.

Format: Includes originality of preinventive forms, originality of the inventions, and composite creativity. Judges rated on a 5-point scale ranging from 1 (*not at all original*) to 5 (*highly original*).

Reliability: Interrater reliabilities ranged from .73 to .84.

Validity: Correlations with other variables ranged from .07 to .51.

Author: Sligh, A. C., et al.

Article: Relation of creativity to fluid and crystallized intelligence.

Journal: *The Journal of Creative Behavior*, Second Quarter 2005, 39(2), 123–136.

Related Research: Finke, R. A. (1990). *Creative imagery: Discoveries as inventions in visualization.* Hillsdale, NJ: Laurence Erlbaum.

12098

Test Name: HOW DO YOU THINK? FORM E

Purpose: To assess creativity.

Number of Items: 100

Format: Includes areas of energy level, originality, interests, activities, self-confidence, sense of humor, flexibility, risk taking, and playfulness. Responses are made on a 5-point Likert-type scale.

Reliability: Coefficient alpha was .90.

Validity: Correlations with other variables ranged from .06 to .71.

Author: Clapham, M. M.

Article: The convergent validity of the Torrance Tests of Creative Thinking and creative interest inventories.

Journal: *Educational and Psychological Measurement*, October 2004, *64*, 828–841.

Related Research: Davis, G. A. (1975). In frumious pursuit of the creative person. *The Journal of Creative Behavior, 9*, 75–87.

12099

Test Name: OBSTACLES TO PERSONAL CREATIVITY INVENTORY

Purpose: To identify obstacles to personal creativity.

Number of Items: 66

Format: Includes four factors: inhibition/shyness, lack of time/opportunity, social repression, and lack of motivation. Responses are made on a 5-point scale ranging from 1 (*totally disagree*) to 5 (*totally agree*). Examples are given.

Reliability: Alpha coefficients ranged from .85 to .91.

Author: Alencar, E. M. L. S., et al.

Article: Obstacles to personal creativity between Brazilian and Mexican university students: A comparative study.

Journal: *The Journal of Creative Behavior*, Third Quarter 2003, *37*(3), 179–192.

Related Research: Alencar, E. M. L. S. (1999). Barreiras à criatividade pessoal: Desenvolvimento de um instrumento de medida [Obstacles to personal creativity: The development of a measurement instrument]. *Psicologia Escolar e Educacional, 3*, 123–132.

12100

Test Name: ORIGINALITY SUBSCALE

Purpose: To measure idea generation and preference for change.

Number of Items: 11

Format: Five-point response scales.

Reliability: Coefficient alpha was .87.

Author: Im, S., et al.

Article: Exploring the dimensionality of the Originality Subscale of the Kirton Adaptation–Innovation Inventory.

Journal: *Psychological Reports*, December 2003, *93*, Part 1, 883–894.

Related Research: Kirton, M. J. (1976). Adaptors and innovators: A description and measure. *Journal of Applied Psychology, 61*, 622–629.

12101

Test Name: TEST OF CREATIVE THINKING—DRAWING PRODUCTION

Purpose: To provide a culturally fair measure of creative potential.

Format: Includes five figural fragments in a large square frame and a small square open on its fourth side outside the frame. Respondents are to complete the drawing.

Reliability: Coefficient alpha was .86.

Validity: Correlations with other variables ranged from .01 to .39.

Author: Dollinger, S. J.

Article: Need for uniqueness, need for cognition, and creativity.

Journal: *The Journal of Creative Behavior*, Second Quarter 2003, *37*(2), 99–116.

Related Research: Urban, K. K. (1991). On the development of creativity in children. *Creativity Research Journal, 4*, 177–191.

12102

Test Name: UNUSUAL USES OF CHOPSTICKS

Purpose: To measure verbal creativity.

Number of Items: 1

Time Required: 10 minutes

Format: Responses are scored for fluency, flexibility, and originality. The question is given.

Validity: Correlations with other variables ranged from −.23 to .71.

Author: Yeh, Y.-C.

Article: Seventh graders' academic achievement, creativity, and ability to construct a cross-domain concept map—A brain function perspective.

Journal: *The Journal of Creative Behavior*, Second Quarter 2004, *38*(2), 125–144.

Related Research: Wu, J. J. (1998). *A newly developed creativity test.* Unpublished project report supported by the Ministry of Education, Taipei, Taiwan.

12103

Test Name: WALLACH–KOGAN CREATIVITY TEST—MODIFIED

Purpose: To measure creativity.

Format: Includes three subtests: Alternate Uses, Similarities, and Pattern Meanings.

Reliability: Alpha coefficients ranged from .77 to .93.

Validity: Correlations with the Real-World Divergent Thinking Test ranged from .33 to .63.

Author: Han, K.-S.

Article: Domain-specificity of creativity in young children: How quantitative and qualitative data support it.

Journal: *The Journal of Creative Behavior*, Second Quarter 2003, 37(2), 117–142.

Related Research: Wallach, M. A., & Kogan, N. (1965). *Modes of thinking in young children*. New York: Holt, Rinehart & Winston.

12104

Test Name: WEB PAGE CREATING SKILL SCALE

Purpose: To provide self-evaluation of one's web page creating ability.

Number of Items: 3

Format: Responses are made on a 5-point scale ranging from 1 (*strongly disagree*) to 5 (*strongly agree*). An example is presented.

Reliability: Coefficient alpha was .91.

Validity: Correlations with other variables ranged from −.09 to .56.

Author: Schmidt, A. M., and Ford, J. K.

Article: Learning within a learner control training environment: The interactive effects of goal orientation and metacognitive instruction on learning outcomes.

Journal: *Personnel Psychology*, Summer 2003, 56, 405–429.

12105

Test Name: WORD ASSOCIATION MEASURE

Purpose: To obtain unconventional word associations.

Number of Items: 10

Format: Two responses per stimulus word are requested. All items are given.

Reliability: Alpha coefficients were .60 and .66.

Validity: Correlations with other variables ranged from −.02 to .31.

Author: Dollinger, S. J.

Article: Need for uniqueness, need for cognition, and creativity.

Journal: *The Journal of Creative Behavior*, Second Quarter 2003, 37(2), 99–116.

Related Research: Merten, T. (1995). Factors influencing word-association responses: A reanalysis. *Creativity Research Journal, 8*, 249–263.

CHAPTER 12

Development

12106

Test Name: ADULT SELF-TRANSCENDENCE INVENTORY

Purpose: To assess the development of wisdom.

Number of Items: 10

Format: Scales range from 1 (*disagree strongly*) to 4 (*agree strongly*). All items are presented.

Reliability: Coefficient alpha was .73.

Validity: Correlations with other variables ranged from –.46 to .19.

Author: Le, T. N., and Levenson, M. R.

Article: Wisdom as self-transcendence: What's love (& individualism) got to do with it?

Journal: *Journal of Research in Personality*, August 2005, *39*, 443–457.

12107

Test Name: CONCEPTS OF DEVELOPMENT QUESTIONNAIRE—CATEGORICAL THINKING SUBSCALE

Purpose: To provide single explanations of behavior based on either environmental or temperamental factors alone.

Number of Items: 10

Format: Responses are made on a 4-point scale ranging from 1 (*strongly disagree*) to 4 (*strongly agree*). Sample items are presented.

Reliability: Internal consistency was .54 and .65.

Author: Guzell, J., and Vernon-Feagons, L.

Article: Parental perceived control over caregiving and its relationship to parent–infant interaction.

Journal: *Child Development*, January/February 2004, *75*, 134–146.

Related Research: Sameroff, A. J., & Feil, A. A. (1985). Parental concepts of development. In J. Sigel (Ed.), *Parental belief systems* (pp. 83–108). Hillsdale, NJ: Erlbaum.

12108

Test Name: DEAF IDENTITY DEVELOPMENT SCALE—REVISED

Purpose: To measure four deaf identity constructs.

Number of Items: 47

Format: Includes four scales: Hearing, Marginal, Immersion, and Bicultural. In addition to the scale's 60 items there are 15 items pertaining to demographic information. Responses to the 60 items are made on a 5-point scale ranging from 1 (*strongly agree*) to 5 (*strongly disagree*).

Reliability: Alpha coefficients ranged from .78 to .87.

Author: Fischer, L. C., and McWhirter, J. J.

Article: The Deaf Identity Development Scale: A revision and validation.

Journal: *Journal of Counseling Psychology*, July 2001, *48*, 355–358.

Related Research: Glickman, N. S. (1993). *Deaf identity development: Construction and validation of a theoretical model.* Unpublished doctoral dissertation, University of Massachusetts, Amherst.

12109

Test Name: DISTRIBUTIVE JUSTICE SCALE

Purpose: To measure stage of moral reasoning and sense of justice.

Number of Items: 15

Format: Children match captions to drawings indicating which caption is most fair. Scoring rules are described.

Reliability: Internal consistency reliabilities ranged from .35 to .79.

Author: Vandiver, T.

Article: Children's social competence, academic competence, and aggressiveness as related to ability to make judgments of fairness.

Journal: *Psychological Reports*, August 2001, *89*, 111–121.

Related Research: Enright, R. D., et al. (1980). Children's distributive justice reasoning: A standardized and objective scale. *Developmental Psychology, 16*, 193–202.

12110

Test Name: INTERPERSONAL COMPETENCE SCALE

Purpose: To assess social development.

Number of Items: 36

Format: Includes two scales: One for teachers to complete for participants and a self-report version. Responses are made on a 7-point Likert format.

Reliability: Test–retest (3 weeks) reliabilities ranged from .80 to .92 for the teacher version. Test–retest (1 year) ranged from .40 to .50. Reliabilities for the self-report version parallel the teacher version.

Author: Farmer, T. W., et al.

Article: Deviant or diverse peer groups? The peer affiliation of aggressive elementary students.

Journal: *Journal of Educational Psychology*, September 2002, *94*, 611–620.

Related Research: Cairns, R. B., et al. (1995). A brief method for assessing social development: Structure, reliability, stability, and developmental validity of the Interpersonal Competence Scale. *Behavior Research and Therapy*, *33*, 725–736.

12111

Test Name: LOYOLA GENERATIVITY SCALE— KOREAN VERSION

Purpose: To assess individual differences in generative concern such as being remembered and passing knowledge to the next generation.

Number of Items: 18

Format: Seven-point scales are anchored by 1 (*never applies to me*) and 7 (*applies to me very often*). Sample items are presented in English.

Reliability: Coefficient alpha was .86.

Author: Kim, G., and Youn, G.

Article: Role of education in generativity differences of employed and unemployed women in Korea.

Journal: *Psychological Reports*, December 2002, *91*, Part 2, 1205–1212.

Related Research: McAdams, D. P., & de St. Aubin, E. (1992). A theory of generativity and its assessment through self-report, behavioral acts, and narrative themes in autobiography. *Journal of Personality and Social Psychology*, *62*, 1003–1015.

12112

Test Name: MEASURE OF SEXUAL IDENTITY EXPLORATION AND COMMITMENT

Purpose: To measure sexual identity development.

Number of Items: 26

Format: Includes four subscales: Exploration, Commitment, Sexual Orientation Uncertainty, and Synthesis. Responses are made on a 6-point rating scale ranging from 1 (*very uncharacteristic of me*) to 6 (*very characteristic of me*). Examples are given.

Reliability: Alpha coefficients ranged from .74 to .89.

Validity: Correlations with other variables ranged from –.23 to .40 ($n = 312$).

Author: Worthington, R. L., et al.

Article: Development, reliability, and validity of the Lesbian, Gay, and Bisexual Knowledge and Attitudes Scale for Heterosexuals (LGB-KASH).

Journal: *Journal of Counseling Psychology*, January 2005, *52*, 104–118.

Related Research: Worthington, R. L., et al. (2002). *The Measure of Sexual Identity Exploration and Commitment (MoSIEC): Development, reliability, and validity*. Unpublished manuscript.

12113

Test Name: PERVASIVE DEVELOPMENTAL DISORDERS RATING SCALE

Purpose: To measure arousal, affect, and cognition.

Number of Items: 51

Format: Five-point Likert scales are used. Sample items are presented.

Reliability: Alpha coefficients ranged from .77 to .89. Test–retest reliabilities ranged from .86 to .92.

Validity: Specificity, sensitivity, and classification indicies ranged from 77 to 91 percent.

Author: Williams, T. O., Jr., and Eaves, R. C.

Article: Pervasive Developmental Disorders Rating Scale: Development and construct validity.

Journal: *Psychological Reports*, August 2005, *97*, 245–257.

12114

Test Name: PUBERTAL DEVELOPMENT SCALE

Purpose: To assess adolescent pubertal development by parental report.

Number of Items: 11 (6 for boys, 5 for girls).

Format: Response scales range from 1 (*not started*) to 5 (*already passed or finished*). Sample items are presented.

Reliability: Interitem reliabilities were .75 (boys) and .80 (girls).

Validity: Correlations with other variables ranged from –.08 to .26.

Author: McBride, C. K., et al.

Article: Individual and familial influences on the onset of sexual intercourse among urban African American adolescents

Journal: *Journal of Consulting and Clinical Psychology*, February 2003, *71*, 159–167.

Related Research: Peterson, A. C., et al. (1988). A self-report measure of pubertal status: Reliability, validity, and initial norms. *Journal of Youth and Adolescence, 17,* 117–133.

12115

Test Name: SENTENCE COMPLETION TEST—JAPANESE VERSION

Purpose: To measure ego development.

Number of Items: 12

Format: Respondents complete 12 sentences. Scoring methods are briefly described.

Validity: Correlations with other variables ranged from .10 to .33.

Author: Takenouchi, A., et al.

Article: Relationship of sports experience and ego development of adolescent Japanese athletes.

Journal: *Psychological Reports,* August 2004, *95*, 13–26.

Related Research: Sasaki, M. (1981). [Measuring ego development of female adolescents by sentence completions]. *[Japanese Journal of Educational Psychology]*, *29*, 147–151. [in Japanese]

12116

Test Name: STAGES OF CHANGE SCALE FOR PRESCRIPTION DRUGS

Purpose: To measure change as a process through five dimensions: Precontemplation, Contemplation,

Preparation, Action, and Maintenance.

Number of Items: 15

Format: Response scales are anchored by 1 (*strongly disagree*) and 5 (*strongly agree*). All items are presented.

Reliability: Alpha coefficients ranged from .60 to .87.

Validity: Correlation with a single item measure of the same construct was .91.

Author: Cook, C. L., and Perri, M., III.

Article: Single-item vs. multiple-item measures of stage of change in compliance with prescribed medications.

Journal: *Psychological Reports,* February 2004, *94*, 115–124.

12117

Test Name: STAGES OF CHANGE SCALE

Purpose: To measure a client's readiness to change.

Number of Items: 32

Format: Includes four stages. Responses are made on a 5-point Likert scale.

Reliability: Alpha coefficients ranged from .79 to .84.

Author: Whipple, J. L., et al.

Article: Improving the effects of psychotherapy: The use of early identification of treatment failure and problem-solving strategies in routine practice.

Journal: *Journal of Counseling Psychology,* January 2003, *50*, 59–68.

Related Research: McConnaughy, E. A., et al. (1983). Stages of change in psychotherapy: Measurement and sample profiles. *Psychotherapy: Theory, Research & Practice, 20*, 368–375.

12118

Test Name: STRESS-RELATED GROWTH SCALE—REVISED

Purpose: To assess stress-related growth.

Number of Items: 29

Format: Includes three factors: mature thinking, affective growth, and religious growth. All items are presented.

Reliability: Alpha coefficients ranged from .78 to .90.

Validity: Correlations with other variables ranged from –.22 to .32.

Author: Roesch, S. C., et al.

Article: On the dimensionality of the Stress-Related Growth Scale: One, three, or seven factors?

Journal: *Journal of Personality Assessment,* June 2004, *82*, 281–290.

Related Research: Park, C. L., et al. (1996). Assessment and prediction of stress-related growth. *Journal of Personality, 64*, 71–105.

12119

Test Name: STUDENT GROWTH SCALES

Purpose: To rate improvement in cognitive, communication, self-confidence, and interpersonal skills.

Number of Items: 11

Format: Scales range from 1 (*very little*) to 5 (*very much*). All items are presented.

Validity: Correlations between subscales ranged from .42 to .61.

Author: Huang, Y.-R., and Chang, S.-M.

Article: Academic and cocurricular involvement: Their relationship and the best combinations for student growth.

Journal: *Journal of College Student Development*, July/August 2004, *45*, 391–406.

Related Research: Chang, S. M. (1999). *Dah Shyue jiaw yuh duey shyue sheng chong jyi* [The impacts of colleges on students]. Taipei, Taiwan: Teacher Chang Culture Press.

12120

Test Name: UNIVERSITY OF RHODE ISLAND CHANGE ASSESSMENT

Purpose: To measure readiness for change as precontemplation, contemplation, action, and maintenance.

Number of Items: 32

Format: Scales range from 1 (*strongly disagree*) to 5 (*strongly agree*). All items are presented.

Reliability: Alpha coefficients ranged from .69 to .82. Split-half reliabilities ranged from .66 to .84.

Author: Cohen, P. J., et al.

Article: Examining readiness for change: A preliminary evaluation of the University of Rhode Island Change Assessment with incarcerated adolescents.

Journal: *Measurement and Evaluation in Counseling and Development*, April 2005, *38*, 45–62.

Related Research: McConnaughy, E. I., et al. (1983). Stages of change in psychotherapy: Measurement and sample profiles. *Psychotherapy: Theory, Research & Practice, 20*, 368–375.

12121

Test Name: WASHINGTON UNIVERSITY SENTENCE COMPLETION TEST

Purpose: To assess ego development.

Number of Items: 36

Format: Responses are made on an ego-level rating scale ranging from E2 to E8.

Reliability: Alpha coefficients were .83 and .86.

Author: Kurtz, J. E., and Tiegreen, S. B.

Article: Matters of conscience and conscientiousness: The place of ego development in the five-factor model.

Journal: *Journal of Personality Assessment*, December 2005, *85*, 312–317.

Related Research: Hy, L. X., & Loevinger, J. (1996). *Measuring ego development.* Mahwah, NJ: Erlbaum.

CHAPTER 13
Family

12122

Test Name: ACCEPTANCE–INVOLVEMENT SCALE—REVISED

Purpose: To enable adolescents to report the frequency with which parents engaged in specific behaviors indicative of warmth and engagement.

Number of Items: 6

Format: All items are presented.

Reliability: Coefficient alpha was .59.

Validity: Correlations with other variables ranged from −.13 to .38.

Author: Fletcher, A. C., et al.

Article: Parental influences on adolescent problem behavior: Revisiting Stattin and Kerr.

Journal: *Child Development*, May/June 2004, *75*, 781–796.

Related Research: Lamborn, S. D., et al. (1991). Patterns of competence and adjustment among adolescents from authoritative, indulgent, and neglectful families. *Child Development*, *62*, 1049–1065.

12123

Test Name: ADEQUACY OF FINANCIAL SUPPORT MEASURE.

Purpose: To measure the ability to pay for the basic needs of family life.

Number of Items: 8

Format: A checklist format is used.

Reliability: Coefficient alpha was .79.

Author: Oyserman, D., et al.

Article: Positive parenting among African American mothers with a serious mental illness.

Journal: *Journal of Marriage and Family*, February 2002, *64*, 65–77.

Related Research: Mowbray, C.T., et al. (1997). Analysis of post discharge change in a dual diagnosis population. *Health and Social Work*, *24*, 91–101.

12124

Test Name: ADOPTION DYNAMICS QUESTIONNAIRE

Purpose: To measure adolescents' sense of preoccupation with their adoptions.

Number of Items: 17

Format: Various 5-point scales are used. A sample item is presented.

Reliability: Coefficient alpha was .91.

Author: Kohler, J. K., et al.

Article: Adopted adolescents' preoccupation with adoption: The impact on adoptive family relationships.

Journal: *Journal of Marriage and Family*, February 2002, *64*, 93–104.

Related Research: Benson, P. L., et al. (1994). *The Adoption Dynamics Questionnaire*. Search Institute, Minneapolis, MN.

12125

Test Name: ADULT ATTACHMENT INVENTORY

Purpose: To measure attachment-related feelings and behavior.

Number of Items: 15

Format: Item responses are anchored by 1 (*not at all*) and 5 (*very much*). Sample items are presented.

Reliability: Alpha coefficients ranged from .83 to .89.

Author: Besharat, M. A.

Article: Relation of attachment style with marital conflict.

Journal: *Psychological Reports*, June 2003, *92*, Part 2, 1135–1140.

Related Research: Hazan, C., & Shaver, P. (1987). Romantic love conceptualized as an attachment process. *Journal of Personality and Social Psychology*, *52*, 511–524.

12126

Test Name: ADULT ATTACHMENT SCALE

Purpose: To measure parents' attachment style.

Number of Items: 18

Format: Includes three dimensions of attachment: Comfort With Closeness and Intimacy, Comfort With Dependency, and Anxiety About Rejection or Abandonment. Responses are made on a 5-point scale ranging from 1 (*not at all characteristic of me*) to 5 (*very characteristic of me*).

Reliability: Alpha coefficients ranged from .78 to .87.

Author: Hock, E., et al.

Article: Separation anxiety in parents of adolescents: Theoretical significance and scale development.

Journal: *Child Development*, January/February 2001, *72*, 284–298.

Related Research: Collins, N., & Reed, S. (1990). Adult attachment, working models, and relationship quality in dating couples. *Journal of Personality and Social Psychology, 58*, 644–663.

12127

Test Name: AFFECTIVE COMMITMENT SCALES

Purpose: To measure fathers' perceptions of their spouse's satisfaction with them as fathers, fathers' perception of spouse's perception of their worth as fathers, and reflected appraisal of fathers' competence.

Number of Items: 26

Format: Five-point agreement scales, 7-point semantic differential scales and 5-point frequency scales are used. Sample items are presented.

Reliability: Alpha coefficients ranged from .71 to .90 across subscales.

Validity: Correlations with other variables ranged from .29 to .54.

Author: Pasley, K., et al.

Article: Effects of commitment and psychological centrality on fathering.

Journal: *Journal of Marriage and Family*, February 2004, *64*, 130–138.

Related Research: Guidubaldi, J., & Cleminshaw, H. K. (1988). Development and validation of the Cleminshaw Guidubaldi Parent Satisfaction Scale. In M. J. Fine (Ed.), *The second handbook on parent education: Contemporary perspectives* (pp. 257–277). San Diego, CA: Academic Press. Secas,

V. (1971). Parental behaviors and dimensions of adolescent self-evaluation. *Sociometry, 34*, 466–482. Ahrons, C. R. (1983). Predictors of paternal involvement post divorce: Mothers' and fathers' perceptions. *Journal of Divorce, 6*, 55–69.

12128

Test Name: ASIAN AMERICAN FAMILY CONFLICT SCALE

Purpose: To measure intergenerational family conflict.

Number of Items: 10

Format: Includes two subscales: Likelihood and Seriousness. Responses are made on 5-point scales. An example is given.

Reliability: Alpha coefficients ranged from .81 to .91. Test–retest (3 weeks) reliabilities ranged from .80 to .85.

Validity: Correlations with other variables ranged from –.60 to .42 ($n = 117$).

Author: Lee, R. M., et al.

Article: Coping with intergenerational family conflict among Asian American college students.

Journal: *Journal of Counseling Psychology*, July 2005, *52*, 389–399.

Related Research: Lee, R. M., et al. (2000). Construction of the Asian American Family Conflicts Scale. *Journal of Counseling Psychology, 47*, 211–222.

12129

Test Name: ASPECTS OF MARRIED LIFE QUESTIONNAIRE

Purpose: To measure marital satisfaction.

Number of Items: 7

Format: Scales range from 1 (*very dissatisfied*) to 9 (*very satisfied*).

Reliability: Alpha coefficients were .86 (husbands) and .88 (wives).

Author: Helms-Erickson, H.

Article: Marital quality ten years after the transition to parenthood: Implications of the timing of parenthood and the division of housework.

Journal: *Journal of Marriage and Family*, November 2001, *63*, 1099–1110.

Related Research: Huston, T. L., et al. (1986). Changes in the marital relationship during the first year of marriage. In R. Gilmour & S. Duck (Eds.), *The emerging field of personal relationships*. (pp. 109–132). Hillsdale, N.J.: Erlbaum.

12130

Test Name: ATTACHMENT Q-SET—VERSON 3.0

Purpose: To describe infant attachment behavior in the home setting.

Number of Items: 90

Format: A rectangular forced nine-category distribution was used.

Reliability: Correlations of independent sorts exceeded .75.

Validity: Correlations with other variables ranged from –.15 to .48.

Author: Van Bakel, H. J. A., and Riksen-Walraven, J. M.

Article: Parenting and development of one-year-olds: Links with parental, contextual, and child characteristics.

Journal: *Child Development*, January/February 2002, *73*, 256–273.

Related Research: Waters, E. (1995). The Attachment Q-Set, Version 3.0. [Appendix A]. *Monographs of the Society for Research in Child Development, 60* (2–3, Serial No. 244).

12131

Test Name: AUTONOMY AND RELATEDNESS INVENTORY

Purpose: To measure marital functioning as acceptance, autonomy, control, hostile control, hostile detachment, and relatedness.

Number of Items: 24

Format: Five-point scales are used. Sample items are presented.

Reliability: Coefficient alpha was .92.

Validity: Correlations with perfectionism ranged from –.60 to –.01.

Author: Haring, M., et al.

Article: Perfectionism, coping, and quality of intimate relationships.

Journal: *Journal of Marriage and Family,* February 2003, *65,* 143–158.

Related Research: Schaefer, E. S., & Burnett, C. K. (1987). Stability and predictability of quality of women's marital relationships and demoralization. *Journal of Personality and Social Psychology, 53,* 1129–1136.

12132

Test Name: BEHAVIORAL CONTROL MEASURE

Purpose: To enable adolescents to report on their parents' knowledge of their activities and provision of behavioral control.

Number of Items: 7

Format: Responses are made on 3-point and 7-point scales. Examples are given.

Reliability: Coefficient alpha was .71.

Author: Coley, L., et al.

Article: Out-of-school care and problem behavior trajectories among low-income adolescents: Individual, family, and

neighborhood characteristics as added risks.

Journal: *Child Development,* May/June 2004, *75,* 948–965.

Related Research: Pittman, L.D., & Chase-Lansdale, P. L. (2001). African American adolescent girls in impoverished communities: Parenting style and adolescent outcomes. *Journal of Research on Adolescence, 11,* 199–224.

12133

Test Name: CAREER-RELATED PARENT SUPPORT SCALES

Purpose: To measure parent support for self-efficacy information for adolescent vocational and educational development. Subscales include Instrumental Assistance, Career-Related Modeling, Emotional Support, and Verbal Encouragement.

Number of Items: 27

Format: Scales range from 1 (*strongly disagree*) to 5 (*strongly agree*). A sample item is presented.

Reliability: Alpha coefficients ranged from .80 to .85 across subscales.

Author: Alliman-Brissett, A. E., et al.

Article: Parent support and African American adolescents' career self-efficacy.

Journal: *Professional School Counseling,* February 2004, *7*(3), 124–132.

Related Research: Turner, S. L., et al. (2003). Career-Related Parent Support Scale. *Measurement and Evaluation in Counseling and Development, 56,* 44–55.

12134

Test Name: CAREER SUPPORT SCALE—ADAPTED

Purpose: To assess the amount of perceived support and encouragement that participants received in their career pursuits from their parents.

Number of Items: 10

Format: Responses are made on a 5-point scale ranging from 1 (*almost never*) to 5 (*almost always*). Sample items are presented.

Reliability: Internal consistency was .76.

Validity: Correlations with other variables ranged from –.09 to .14.

Author: Flores, L. Y., and O'Brien, K. M.

Article: The career development of Mexican American adolescent women: A test of social cognitive career theory.

Journal: *Journal of Counseling Psychology,* January 2002, *49,* 14–27.

Related Research: Binen, L. M., et al. (1995). *Career Support Scale.* Unpublished manuscript, University of Missouri, Columbia.

12135

Test Name: CHILD ABUSE POTENTIAL INVENTORY

Purpose: To screen and assess the potential for child abuse among parents.

Number of Items: 37

Format: Scales range from 1 (*disagree*) to 0 (*agree*). Sample items are presented.

Validity: Correlations with other variables ranged from –.11 to .26.

Author: Medora, N. P., et al.

Article: Attitudes toward parenting strategies, potential for child abuse, and parental satisfaction of ethnically diverse low-income U.S. mothers.

Journal: *The Journal of Social Psychology*, June 2001, *141*, 335–348.

Related Research: Milner, J. S., & Wimberley, R. C. (1980). Prediction and explanation of child abuse. *Journal of Clinical Psychology, 36*, 875–884.

12136

Test Name: CHILD REPORT OF PARENTAL BEHAVIOR INVENTORY—SHORTENED VERSION

Purpose: To measure types of control and warmth.

Number of Items: 63

Format: Responses are made on a 5-point scale ranging from 1 (*not like his or her parents*) to 5 (*very much like his or her parents*). Includes three subscales: Lax Control, Psychological Control, and Parental Warmth.

Reliability: Alpha coefficients ranged from .72 to .92.

Author: Walker-Barnes, C. J., & Mason, C. A.

Article: Ethnic differences in the effect of parenting on gang involvement and gang delinquency: A longitudinal, hierarchical linear modeling perspective.

Journal: *Child Development*, November/December 2001, *72*, 1814–1831.

Related Research: Schaefer, E. S. (1965). Children's reports of parental behavior: An inventory. *Child Development, 36*, 413–424.

12137

Test Name: CHILD REPORT OF PARENTING BEHAVIOR INVENTORY

Purpose: To assess acceptance, psychological control, and lax behavioral control by mothers and fathers.

Number of Items: 30

Format: Response scales range from 1 (*not like her/him*) to 3 (*a lot like her/him*). Sample items are presented.

Reliability: Alpha coefficients ranged from .66 to .90.

Author: Krishnakumar, A., et al.

Article: Cross-ethnic equivalence of socialization measures in European American and African American youth.

Journal: *Journal of Marriage and Family*, August 2004, *66*, 809–820.

Related Research: Schaefer, E. (1965). Children's reports of parental behavior: An inventory. *Child Development, 71*, 1072–1085.

12138

Test Name: CHILD'S PERCEPTION QUESTIONNAIRE—MARITAL DISCORD SUBSCALE

Purpose: To measure adolescents' perceptions of interparental conflict.

Number of Items: 6

Reliability: Internal consistency was .90.

Validity: Correlations with other variables ranged from –.01 to .27.

Author: Epstein, M. K., et al.

Article: Interparental conflict, adolescent behavioral problems, and adolescent competence: Convergent and discriminant validity.

Journal: *Educational and Psychological Measurement*, June 2004, *64*, 475–495.

Related Research: Emery, R. E., & O'Leary, K. D. (1982). Children's perceptions of marital discord and behavior problems of boys and girls. *Journal of Abnormal Child Psychology, 10*, 11–24.

12139

Test Name: CHILD'S REPORT OF PARENTAL BEHAVIOR INVENTORY

Purpose: To measure paternal acceptance among adolescents.

Number of Items: 24

Format: Scales range from 1 (*not at all*) to 5 (*very much*). Sample items are presented.

Reliability: Alpha coefficients ranged from .69 to .79.

Author: Crouter, A. C., et al.

Article: Implications of overwork and overload for the quality of men's family relationships.

Journal: *Journal of Marriage and Family*, May 2001, *63*, 404–416.

Related Research: Schafer, E. S. (1965). Children's reports of parental behavior: An inventory. *Child Development, 36*, 417–424.

12140

Test Name: CHILD'S REPORT OF PARENTAL BEHAVIOR INVENTORY

Purpose: To assess mothers' and fathers' perceptions of their own support, behavioral control, and psychological control in relation to their adolescent.

Number of Items: 56

Format: Includes three measures: their own support, behavioral control, and psychological control. Responses are made on 5-point scales.

Reliability: Alpha coefficients ranged from .80 to .92.

Author: Galambos, N. L., et al.

Article: Parents do matter: Trajectories of change in externalizing and internalizing problems in early adolescence.

Journal: *Child Development*, March/April 2003, *74*, 578–594.

Related Research: Burger, G. K., & Armentrout, J. A. (1971). Comparative study of methods to estimate factor scores for reports of parental behaviors. *Proceedings of the 79th American Psychological Association Annual Convention, 6,* 149–150.

12141

Test Name: CHILD'S REPORT OF PARENTAL BEHAVIOR INVENTORY—SUBSCALE PARENT VERSION

Purpose: To identify feelings of warmth and acceptance in the parent–child relationship.

Number of Items: 24

Format: Responses are made on a 4-point scale ranging from 1 (*not like you*) to 4 (*a lot like you*). An example is given.

Reliability: Alpha coefficients were .92 and .93.

Author: Crouter, A. C., et al.

Article: How do parents learn about adolescents' experiences? Implications for parental knowledge and adolescent risky behavior.

Journal: *Child Development,* July/August 2005, *76,* 869–882.

Related Research: Schwarz, J. C., et al. (1985). Assessing child-rearing behaviors: A comparison of ratings made by mother, father, and sibling on the CRPBI. *Child Development, 55,* 462–479.

12142

Test Name: CHILDREN'S ATTRIBUTIONS AND PERCEPTIONS SCALE— SPANISH VERSION

Purpose: To assess perceptions and attributions relevant to sexually abused children.

Number of Items: 18

Format: Scales range from 1 (*never*) to 5 (*always*).

Reliability: Alpha coefficients ranged from .54 to .73.

Validity: Correlations between factors ranged from .00 to .47.

Author: Pereda, N., and Forns, M.

Article: Use of the Children's Attributions and Perceptions Scale in an underprivileged Spanish sample.

Journal: *Psychological Reports,* December 2005, *97,* 835–846.

12143

Test Name: CHILDREN'S COMPETENCY SCALE

Purpose: To measure children's abilities by parent report.

Number of Items: 14

Format: Item responses range from 1 (*very little*) to 5 (*clearly above average*). All items are presented.

Reliability: Reliability coefficients ranged from .78 to .88.

Validity: Correlations between scales averaged .60.

Author: Räty, H.

Article: A measure of parents' assessments of their children's abilities.

Journal: *Psychological Reports,* December 2004, *95,* Part 1, 957–963.

12144

Test Name: CHILDREN'S PERCEPTION OF INTERPARENTAL CONFLICT SCALE

Purpose: To identify children's exposure to destructive conflict.

Number of Items: 17

Format: Includes three subscales: Intensity, Resolution, and Content. Examples are presented.

Reliability: Alpha coefficients ranged from .84 to .87.

Author: Davies, P. T., and Forman, E. M.

Article: Children's pattern of pressuring emotional security in the interparental subsystem.

Journal: *Child Development,* November/December 2002, *73,* 1880–1903.

Related Research: Grych, J. H., et al. (1992). Assessing marital conflict from the child's perspective. *Child Development, 63,* 550–572.

12145

Test Name: CHILDREN'S PERCEPTION OF INTERPARENTAL CONFLICT SCALE

Purpose: To assess interpretation and response to interpersonal conflict.

Number of Items: 48

Format: Items are anchored by a response scale ranging from 0 (*false*) to 2 (*true*). Sample items are presented.

Reliability: Alpha was .95.

Validity: Correlations with other variables ranged from −.58 to .67.

Author: Johnson, H. D.

Article: Associations among family adaptability and cohesion, interparental conflict, and tactics used during young adults' conflicts with parents.

Journal: *Psychological Reports,* August 2002, *91,* 315–325.

Related Research: Grych, J. H., et al. (1992). Assessing marital conflict from the child's perspective: The Children's Perception of Interparental Conflict Scale. *Child Development, 63,* 558–572.

12146

Test Name: CHILDREN'S PERCEPTION OF

INTERPARENTAL CONFLICT SCALE—ADAPTED

Purpose: To provide children's reports of their exposure to destructive conflict histories.

Number of Items: 23

Format: Includes four subscales: Frequency, Intensity, Resolution, and Content. Responses are made on a scale of true, sort of true, or false. Examples are presented.

Reliability: Alpha coefficients ranged from .78 to .92.

Author: Davies, P. T., et al.

Article: Assessing children's emotional security in the interparental relationship: The Security in the Interpersonal Subsystem Scales.

Journal: *Child Development*, March/April 2002, *73*, 544–562.

Related Research: Grych, J. H., et al. (1992). Assessing marital conflict from the child's perspective. *Child Development*, *63*, 558–572.

12147

Test Name: CHILDREN'S PERCEPTIONS OF PARENTS SCALE

Purpose: To assess children's perceptions of their mothers and fathers.

Number of Items: 21

Format: For each item one of two descriptions is chosen which best describes parents and then indicates whether the statement is "sort of true" or "really true."

Reliability: Alpha coefficients ranged from .55 to .70.

Author: d'Ailly, H.

Article: Children's autonomy and perceived control in learning: A model of motivation and achievement in Taiwan.

Journal: *Journal of Educational Psychology*, March 2003, *95*, 84–96.

Related Research: Grolnick, W. S., et al. (1991). Inner resources for school achievements: Motivational mediators of children's perceptions of their parents. *Journal of Educational Psychology*, *83*, 508–517.

12148

Test Name: CHILDREN'S REPORT OF PARENTAL BEHAVIOR INVENTORY—108

Purpose: To measure control–autonomy, acceptance–rejection, and firm–lax control.

Number of Items: 108

Format: Sample items are presented without response categories.

Reliability: Reliabilities ranged from .87 to .99 across subscales.

Validity: Correlations with other variables ranged from –.37 to .42.

Author: Seibel, F. L., and Johnson, W. B.

Article: Parental control, trait anxiety, and satisfaction with life in college students.

Journal: *Psychological Reports*, April 2001, *88*, 473–480.

Related Research: Schudermann, S., & Shulderman, E. (1970). Replicability of factors in children's reports of parental behavior (CRPBI). *The Journal of Psychology*, *76*, 239–249.

12149

Test Name: CHILDREN'S ROLE INVENTORY

Purpose: To measure roles of children in dysfunctional families: hero role, mascot role, scapegoat role, and lost child role.

Number of Items: 56

Format: Item anchors are 1 (*strongly disagree*) and 5 (*strongly agree*).

Reliability: Subscale alpha coefficients ranged from .78 to .87.

Validity: Correlations with other variables ranged from –.08 to .35.

Author: Randolph, D. E., et al.

Article: Social desirability, defense styles, and the Children's Role Inventory Scale.

Journal: *Psychological Reports*, June 2003, *92*, Part 1, 842–846.

Related Research: Potter, A. E., & Williams, D. E. (1994). Factor and factorial replication of the Childrens' Role Inventory. *Educational and Psychological Measurement*, *54*, 417–427.

12150

Test Name: CLOSENESS AND INDEPENDENCE INVENTORY

Purpose: To measure spouses' desired level of closeness in a relationship.

Number of Items: 6

Format: Nine-point rating scales are used. Sample items are presented.

Reliability: Alpha coefficients ranged from .75 to .76.

Validity: Correlations with other variables ranged from –.32 to .08.

Author: Atkins, D. C., et al.

Article: Prediction of response to treatment in a randomized clinical trial of marital therapy.

Journal: *Journal of Consulting and Clinical Psychology*, October 2005, *73*, 893–903.

12151

Test Name: CLOSENESS TO PARENTS MEASURE

Purpose: To assess adolescents' relationships with their parents.

Number of Items: 8

Format: Includes relationships with father and relationships with mother. Responses are made on a 5-point scale. All items are presented.

Reliability: Alpha coefficients were .88 and .89.

Validity: Correlations with other variables ranged from −.30 to .15.

Author: Crosnoe, R., and Elder, G. H., Jr.

Article: Adolescent twins and emotional distress: The interrelated influence of nonshared environment and social structure.

Journal: *Child Development*, November/December 2002, 73, 1761–1774.

12152

Test Name: COMPUTER-PRESENTED PARENTING DILEMMAS

Purpose: To assess monitoring of peer interaction, reactions to child noncompliance, and reactions to child distress.

Number of Items: 9

Format: Each dilemma includes multiple responses rated on a 7-point scale ranging from 7 (*very, very likely*) to 1 (*very, very unlikely*).

Reliability: Coefficient alpha was .60.

Validity: Correlations with other variables ranged from −.10 to 30 (*N* = 110).

Author: Hubbs-Tait, L., et al.

Article: Relation of maternal cognitive stimulation, emotional support, and intrusive behavior during Head Start to children's kindergarten cognitive abilities.

Journal: *Child Development*, January/February 2002, 73, 110–131.

Related Research: Holden, G. W., & Ritchie, K. L. (1991). Linking extreme marital discord, child rearing, and child behavior problems: Evidence from battered women. *Child Development, 62,* 311–317.

12153

Test Name: CONCERN ABOUT FUTURE CAREER–MARRIAGE CONFLICT SCALE

Purpose: To assess degree of concern about future career–marriage conflict.

Number of Items: 4

Format: Responses are made on a 4-point scale ranging from 1 (*a great deal*) to 4 (*not at all*).

Reliability: Coefficient alpha was .92.

Validity: Correlations with other variables ranged from −.07 to .10 (*n* = 324).

Author: Barnett, R. C., et al.

Article: Planning ahead: College seniors' concerns about career–marriage conflict.

Journal: *Journal of Vocational Behavior*, April 2003, 62, 305–319.

Related Research: Barnett, R. C. (1971). Personality correlates of vocational planning. *Genetic Psychology Monographs, 83,* 309–356.

12154

Test Name: CONFLICT BEHAVIOR QUESTIONNAIRE

Purpose: To assess communication style and level of conflict in parent–adolescent interaction.

Number of Items: 20

Format: A true–false format is used. Sample items are presented. Scoring procedures are described.

Reliability: Coefficient alpha was .90. Test–retest reliabilities ranged from .37 to .84 (6 to 8 weeks).

Author: Barkley, R. A., et al.

Article: The efficacy of problem-solving communication training alone, behavior management training alone, and their combination for parent–adolescent conflict in teenagers with ADHD and ODD.

Journal: *Journal of Consulting and Clinical Psychology*, December 2001, 69, 926–941.

Related Research: Prinz, R. J., et al. (1979). Multivariate assessment of conflict in distressed and nondistressed mother–adolescent dyads. *Journal of Applied Behavior Analysis, 12,* 691–700.

12155

Test Name: CONFLICT TACTICS SCALE—MODIFIED

Purpose: To assess severity of interadult violence in participants' homes.

Number of Items: 19

Format: Includes three subscales: Levels of Reasoning, Verbal Aggression, and Physical Violence With the Family Context.

Reliability: Alpha coefficients were .83 (very aggressive) and .90 (physical violence).

Author: Maughan, A., and Cicchetti, D.

Article: Impact of child maltreatment and interadult violence on children's emotion regulation abilities and socioemotional adjustment.

Journal: *Child Development*, September/October 2002, 73, 1525–1542.

Related Research: Straus, M. A. (1979). Measuring interfamilial conflict and violence: The Conflict

Tactics Scale (CTS). *Journal of Marriage and the Family, 41,* 75–88.

12156

Test Name: CONFLICTS AND PROBLEM-SOLVING SCALES

Purpose: To assess the level of interparental conflict in the home.

Number of Items: 43

Format: Includes three subscales: Verbal Aggression, Physical Aggression, and Resolution. Examples are presented.

Reliability: Alpha coefficients ranged from .80 to .89.

Author: Davies, P. T., and Forman, E. M.

Article: Children's pattern of pressuring emotional security in the interparental subsystem.

Journal: *Child Development,* November/December 2002, *73,* 1880–1903.

Related Research: Kerig, P. (1996). Assessing the links between interparental conflict and child adjustment: The Conflicts and Problem-Solving scales. *Journal of Family Psychology, 10,* 454–473.

12157

Test Name: CONFUSION, HUBBUB, AND ORDER SCALE

Purpose: To assess degree of home chaos.

Number of Items: 6

Format: Responses are made on a 5-point scale ranging from 1 (*definitely untrue*) to 5 (*definitely true*). Examples are given.

Reliability: Coefficient alpha was .63.

Author: Asbury, K., et al.

Article: Nonshared environmental influences on individual differences

in early behavioral development: A monozygotic twin differences study.

Journal: *Child Development,* May/June 2003, *74,* 933–943.

Related Research: Matheny, A. P., et al. (1995). Bringing order out of chaos: Psychometric characteristics of the Confusion, Hubbub and Order Scale. *Journal of Applied Developmental Psychology, 16,* 429–444.

12158

Test Name: CONTINUED ATTACHMENT SCALE

Purpose: To assess spontaneous thoughts about parents and curiosity and efforts to make contact with them.

Number of Items: 12

Reliability: Alpha coefficients ranged from .58 to .91.

Validity: Correlations with other variables ranged from –.22 to.62.

Author: McCarthy, C. J., et al.

Article: Continued attachment to parents: Its relationship to affect regulation and perceived stress among college students.

Journal: *Measurement and Evaluation in Counseling and Development,* January 2001, *33,* 198–213.

Related Research: Berman, W. H., et al. (1994). Measuring continued attachment to parents: The Continued Attachment Scale— Parent Version. *Psychological Reports, 75,* 171–182.

12159

Test Name: CRISIS IN FAMILY SYSTEMS—REVISED

Purpose: To measure family stressors in three dimensions: Balance, Difficulty, and Chronicity. Content domains include: Financial, Legal, Career,

Relationships, Safety, Medical Issues, Authority, and Prejudice.

Number of Items: 63

Format: Respondents rate the difficulty of an experience on four-point scales anchored by 1 (*not at all*) and 4 (*a lot*).

Validity: Correlations with depression ranged from –.27 to .58.

Author: Berry, C., et al.

Article: Validation of the Crisis in Family Systems—Revised, A contemporary measure of life stressors.

Journal: *Psychological Reports,* June 2001, *88,* Part 1, 713–724.

Related Research: Shalowitz, M. U., et al. (1998). A new measure of contemporary life stress: Development, validation, and reliability of the Crisis in Family Systems. *Health Services Research, 33,* 1381–1402.

12160

Test Name: DAILY DISCIPLINE INVENTORY

Purpose: To assess parenting strategies including verbal criticism, supportive parenting, and harsh parenting.

Number of Items: 38

Format: Open-ended responses of mothers are coded into 1 of 75 categories.

Reliability: Alpha coefficients ranged from .59 to .62.

Author: Bauchaine, T. P., et al.

Article: Mediators, moderators, and predictors of 1-year outcomes among children treated for early-onset conduct problems: A latent growth curve analysis.

Journal: *Journal of Consulting and Clinical Psychology,* June 2005, *73,* 371–388.

Related Research: Webster-Stratton, C., & Spitzer, A. (1991).

Development, reliability, and validity of the Daily Telephone Discipline Interview. *Behavioral Assessment, 13,* 221–239.

12161

Test Name: DECISION-MAKING QUESTIONNAIRE

Purpose: To rate parents' and children's perception of who makes the decisions in the family.

Number of Items: 15

Format: Items are rated on a four-point scale ranging from *a* (*parents tell the child what to do*) to *d* (*the child decides*).

Reliability: Alpha coefficients ranged from .74 to 81.

Validity: Correlations with other variables ranged from –.30 to .44.

Author: Holmbeck, G. N., et al.

Article: Observed and perceived parental overprotection in relation to psychosocial adjustment in preadolescents with a physical disability: The mediational role of behavioral autonomy.

Journal: *Journal of Consulting and Clinical Psychology,* February 2002, *70,* 96–110.

Related Research: Steinberg, L. (1987). The impact of puberty on family relations: Effects of pubertal status and pubertal timing. *Developmental Psychology, 23,* 451–460.

12162

Test Name: DIFFERENTIATION IN THE FAMILY SYSTEM SCALE

Purpose: To measure respect, empathy, tolerance for individuality, and acceptance within sex dyadic relationships.

Number of Items: 66

Format: Sample items are presented.

Reliability: Alpha coefficients exceeded .85.

Author: Sabatelli, R. M., and Bartle-Haring, S.

Article: Family-of-origin experiences and adjustment in married couples.

Journal: *Journal of Marriage and Family,* February 2003, *65,* 159–169.

Related Research: Anderson, S. A., & Sabatelli, R. M. (1992). The Differentiation in the Family System Scale (DIFS). *American Journal of Family Therapy, 20,* 77–89.

12163

Test Name: DIFFERENTIATION IN THE FAMILY SYSTEM SCALE

Purpose: To assess patterns of differentiation in the family.

Number of Items: 11

Format: Likert-type items.

Reliability: Alpha coefficients for four subscales ranged from .83 to .94.

Author: Hock, E., et al.

Article: Separation anxiety in parents of adolescents: Theoretical significance and scale development.

Journal: *Child Development,* January/February 2001, 72, 284–298.

Related Research: Anderson, S. A., & Sabatelli, R. M. (1992). The Differentiation in the Family System Scale (DIFS). *The American Journal of Family Therapy, 20,* 77–89.

12164

Test Name: DISCIPLINARY CONSISTENCY AND APPROPRIATENESS SCALES

Purpose: To measure disciplinary laxness and appropriateness.

Number of Items: 18

Reliability: Alpha coefficients ranged from .66 to .67.

Validity: Correlations with other variables ranged from –.29 to .43.

Author: Dorsey, S., and Forehand, R.

Article: The relation of social capital to child psychosocial adjustment difficulties: The role of positive parenting and neighborhood dangerousness.

Journal: *Journal of Psychopathology and Behavioral Assessment,* March 2003, 25, 11–23.

Related Research: Arnold, D. S., et al. (1993). The Parenting Scale: A measure of dysfunctional parenting in discipline situations. *Psychological Assessment, 5,* 137–144.

12165

Test Name: DOMESTIC TASK INVOLVEMENT SCALE

Purpose: To assess the degree that husbands or wives were responsible for household tasks.

Number of Items: 10

Format: Scales range from 1 (*myself entirely*) to 7 (*my spouse entirely*). All items are presented.

Reliability: Alpha coefficients ranged from .71 to .86 across subscales and husbands and wives.

Validity: Goodness of fit coefficients exceeded .84.

Author: Kim, C., et al.

Article: The Chinese in Canada: A study in ethnic change with emphasis on gender roles.

Journal: *The Journal of Social Psychology,* February 2004, *144,* 5–29.

12166

Test Name: DYSCONTROL EXPERIENCES QUESTIONNAIRE

Purpose: To assess childhood experiences of parental (or other) uncontrolled behavior by adult retrospective reports.

Number of Items: 30

Format: Scales range from 0 (*never*) to 3 (*often*).

Reliability: Alpha coefficients ranged from .89 to .93 across subscales.

Validity: Correlations with other variables ranged from −.38 to .54.

Author: Watt. M. C., and Stewart, S. H.

Article: Dyscontrol Experiences Questionnaire: Development, reliability, and validity.

Journal: *Journal of Psychopathology and Behavioral Assessment*, September 2003, *23*, 155–165.

12167

Test Name: EMOTIONAL INTIMACY SUBSCALE

Purpose: To measure emotional intimacy between spouses/partners.

Number of Items: 6

Format: Five-point scales are used. A sample item is presented.

Reliability: Alpha coefficients ranged from .80 to .83.

Author: Mulsow, M., et al.

Article: Multilevel factors influencing maternal stress during the first three years.

Journal: *Journal of Marriage and Family*, November 2002, *64*, 944–956.

Related Research: Schaefer, M. T., & Olson, D. H. (1981). Assessing intimacy: The PAIR Inventory.

Journal of Marital and Family Therapy, 7, 47–60.

12168

Test Name: EMOTIONAL SUPPORT SCALE

Purpose: To identify mothers' emotional attentiveness and responsiveness toward each of their children.

Number of Items: 8

Format: Includes two versions: mothers' version and children's version. Examples are given.

Reliability: Alpha coefficients ranged from .81 to .85.

Validity: Correlations with other variables ranged from −.37 to .44.

Author: Brody, G. H., et al.

Article: Protective longitudinal paths linking child competence to behavioral problems among African American siblings.

Journal: *Child Development,* March/April 2004, *75,* 455–467.

Related Research: Wills, T. A., et al. (1992). The role of life events, family support, and competence in adolescent substance use: A test of vulnerability and protective factors. *American Journal of Community Psychology, 20,* 349–374.

12169

Test Name: EXPRESSION OF AFFECTION INVENTORY— EMOTION AND INSTRUMENTAL SCALES

Purpose: To measure emotion and instrumental expressions of affection.

Number of Items: 22

Format: Responses are made on a 7-point Likert scale.

Reliability: Alpha coefficients ranged from .69 to .88.

Author: Feinberg, M., et al.

Article: Adolescent, parent, and observer perceptions of parenting: Genetic and environmental influences on shared and distinct perceptions.

Journal: *Child Development,* July/August 2001, *72,* 1266–1284.

Related Research: Hetherington, E. M., & Clingempeel, W. G. (1992). Coping with marital transitions: A family systems perspective. *Monographs of the Society for Research in Child Development, 57* (2–3, Serial No. 227).

12170

Test Name: FAMILY ADAPTATION, PARTNERSHIP, GROWTH, AFFECTION, AND RESOLVE

Purpose: To measure global family functioning.

Number of Items: 5

Time Required: 5 minutes

Format: Items are anchored by *almost always* and *hardly ever.*

Reliability: Internal consistency measures ranged from .80 and .86.

Validity: Concurrent validity measures ranged from .64 to .80.

Author: Leonardson, G. R., et al.

Article: Validity and reliability of the General Well-Being Schedule with Northern Plains American Indians diagnosed with Type 2 diabetes mellitus.

Journal: *Psychological Reports,* August 2003, *93,* 49–58.

12171

Test Name: FAMILY ALIENATION SCALE

Purpose: To measure isolation and detachment from spouse and children.

Number of Items: 3

Format: Scales range from 1 (*never*) to 5 (*very often*). All items are presented.

Reliability: Coefficient alpha was .83.

Validity: Correlations with other variables ranged from −.30 to .63.

Author: Brett, J. M., and Stroh, L. K.

Article: Working 61 plus hours a week: Why do managers do it?

Journal: *Journal of Applied Psychology*, February 2003, *88*, 67–78.

12172

Test Name: FAMILY AND CAREER SCALE

Purpose: To measure family versus career orientation

Number of Items: 16

Format: Responses are made on a 5-point scale ranging from 1 (*strongly disagree*) to 5. (*strongly agree*). All items are presented.

Reliability: Coefficient alpha was .89.

Author: Battle, A., and Wigfield, A.

Article: College women's value orientations toward family, career, and graduate school.

Journal: *Journal of Vocational Behavior*, February 2003, *62*, 56–75.

Related Research: Hallett, M., & Gilbert, L. (1997). Variables differentiating university women considering role-sharing and conventional dual-career marriages. *Journal of Vocational Behavior, 50*, 308–322.

12173

Test Name: FAMILY AND COMMUNITY SCALES

Purpose: To assess family and community as factors related to willingness to change jobs.

Number of Items: 12

Format: Includes two scales: Community Ties and Family Concerns. Responses are made on a 5-point scale ranging from 1 (*would be of very little or no concern*) to 5 (*would be a very major concern or problem*).

Reliability: Alpha coefficients were .75 and .78.

Validity: Correlations with other variables ranged from −.89 to .65.

Author: Ostroff, C., and Clark, M. A.

Article: Maintaining an internal market: Antecedents of willingness to change jobs.

Journal: *Journal of Vocational Behavior*, December 2002, *59*, 425–453.

Related Research: Landau, J. C., et al. (1992). Predictors of willingness to relocate for managerial and professional employees. *Journal of Organizational Behavior, 13*, 667–680.

12174

Test Name: FAMILY AND JOB INVOLVEMENT SCALES

Purpose: To measure family and job involvement.

Number of Items: 8

Format: Scales range from 1 (*strongly disagree*) to 5 (*strongly agree*). Sample items are presented.

Reliability: Alpha coefficients were .86 (family) and .85 (job).

Author: Aryee, S., et al.

Article: Rhythms of life: Antecedents and outcomes of work–family balance in employed parents.

Journal: *Journal of Applied Psychology*, January 2005, *90*, 132–146.

Related Research: Lodahl, T. M., & Kejner, M. (1965). Definition and measurement of job involvement. *Journal of Applied Psychology, 49*, 239–257.

12175

Test Name: FAMILY AND WORK SUPPORT SCALES

Purpose: To measure quality of relationships in the family and at work.

Number of Items: 18

Format: Scales range from 1 (*very little*) to 5 (*very much*). Sample items are presented.

Reliability: Alpha coefficients were .89 (work) and .92 (family).

Author: Aryee, S., et al.

Article: Rhythms of life: Antecedents and outcomes of work–family balance in employed parents.

Journal: *Journal of Applied Psychology*, January 2005, *90*, 132–146.

Related Research: Etzion, D. (1984). Moderation effect of social support on the stress–burnout relationship. *Journal of Applied Psychology, 69*, 615–622.

12176

Test Name: FAMILY ASSESSMENT DEVICE—ADAPTED

Purpose: To assess family functioning.

Number of Items: 19

Format: Includes three subscales: Problem Solving, Communication, and Roles. Responses are made on a 4-point Likert-type scale ranging from 1 (*strongly agree*) to 4 (*strongly disagree*).

Reliability: Estimates of internal consistency ranged from .60 to .82. Test–retest (1 week) reliability ranged from .66 to .75.

Validity: Correlations with other variables ranged from −.61 to .50.

Author: Whitaker, A. E., and Robitschek, C.

Article: Multidimensional family functioning: Predicting personal growth initiative.

Journal: *Journal of Counseling Psychology*, October 2001, *48*, 420–427.

Related Research: Epstein, N. B., et al. (1983). The McMaster Family Assessment Device. *Journal of Marital and Family Therapy, 9,* 171–180.

12177

Test Name: FAMILY ATTACHMENT AND CHANGEABILITY INDEX 8

Purpose: To measure adaptability to changing family circumstances.

Number of Items: 16

Format: Scales range from 1 (*never*) to 5 (*always*).

Reliability: Alpha coefficients exceeded .75. Guttman reliability for the total scale was .64.

Author: Greeff, A. P., and Ritman, I. N.

Article: Individual characteristics associated with resilience in single-parent families.

Journal: *Psychological Reports,* February 2005, *96,* 36–42.

Related Research: McCubbin, H. I., et al. (1996). *Family assessment: Resiliency, coping and adaptation inventories for research and practice.* Madison: University of Wisconsin.

12178

Test Name: FAMILY DECISION-MAKING SCALE

Purpose: To measure adolescents' perceptions of parental autonomy granting.

Number of Items: 7

Format: A yes–no format is used. All items are presented.

Reliability: Coefficient alpha was .65.

Validity: Correlations with other variables ranged from −.22 to .01.

Author: Crosnoe, R., and Elder, G. H., Jr.

Article: Adolescent twins and emotional distress: The interrelated influence of nonshared environment and social structure.

Journal: *Child Development,* November/December 2002, *73,* 1761–1774.

12179

Test Name: FAMILY ENVIRONMENT SCALE— CHINESE VERSION

Purpose: To assess three aspects of family environment relevant to talent development.

Number of Items: 12

Format: Includes three aspects: Parental Expectations, Independence, and Family Cohesion. Responses are made on a 5-point scale ranging from 1 (*strongly disagree*) to 5 (*strongly agree*).

Reliability: Alpha coefficients ranged from .79 to .84.

Author: Chan, D. W.

Article: Family environment and talent development of Chinese gifted students in Hong Kong.

Journal: *Gifted Child Quarterly,* Summer 2005, *49,* 211–221.

Related Research: Harrington, D. M., et al. (1987). Testing aspects of Carl Rogers's theory of creative environments: Child-rearing antecedents of creative potential in young adolescents. *Journal of Personality and Social Psychology, 52,* 851–856.

12180

Test Name: FAMILY EXPRESSIVITY QUESTIONNAIRE

Purpose: To measure general family emotional expressivity.

Number of Items: 40

Format: Includes four subscales: Positive and Negative Affect; and Dominant and Nondominant Power. Responses are made on a 4-point scale.

Reliability: Alpha coefficients were .77 and .91.

Author: Smith, M., and Walden, T.

Article: An exploration of African American preschool-aged children's behavioral regulation in emotionally arousing situations.

Journal: *Child Study Journal,* 2001, *31,* 13–43.

Related Research: Halberstadt, A. (1986). Family socialization of emotional expression and nonverbal communication styles and skills. *Journal of Personality and Social Psychology, 51,* 827–836.

12181

Test Name: FAMILY INTERDEPENDENCE SCALE

Purpose: To identify the relationship between a parent and a child.

Number of Items: 14

Format: Responses are made on a 5-point scale ranging from 1 (*strongly disagree*) to 5 (*strongly agree*). All items are presented.

Reliability: Alpha coefficients were .66 and .73.

Validity: Correlations with other variables ranged from −.03 to .24.

Author: Sakuragi, T.

Article: Association of culture with shyness among Japanese and American university students.

Journal: *Perceptual and Motor Skills*, June 2004, *98*, Part 1, 803–813.

Related Research: Sakuragi, T. (1994). Family independence/dependence and symmetrical/complementary relationship orientation as cultural values: Their measurement and relation to communicative predispositions. *Dissertation Abstracts International, 55*, 3352.

12182

Test Name: FAMILY INVOLVEMENT SCALE

Purpose: To assess the centrality of an individual's family in his/her life.

Number of Items: 4

Format: Scales range from 1 (*strongly agree*) to 5 (*strongly disagree*). All items are presented.

Reliability: Coefficient alpha was .63.

Validity: Correlations with other variables ranged from −.27 to .71.

Author: Brett, J. M., and Stroh, L. K.

Article: Working 61 plus hours a week: Why do managers do it?

Journal: *Journal of Applied Psychology*, February 2003, *88*, 67–78.

12183

Test Name: FAMILY INVOLVEMENT SCALE

Purpose: To measure family involvement.

Number of Items: 6

Format: Responses are made on a 7-point scale. Examples are given.

Reliability: Coefficient alpha was .82.

Validity: Correlations with other variables ranged from −.11 to .21.

Author: Goulet, L. R., and Singh, P.

Article: Career commitment: A reexamination and an extension.

Journal: *Journal of Vocational Behavior*, August 2002, *61*, 73–91.

Related Research: Misra, S., et al. (1990). Measurement of family involvement: A cross-national study of managers, *Journal of Cross-Cultural Psychology, 21*, 232–248.

12184

Test Name: FAMILY–JOB BALANCE SCALE

Purpose: To measure the consequences of meeting job and other obligations.

Number of Items: 5

Format: Scales range from 1 (*rarely*) to 5 (*very often*). All items are presented.

Reliability: Coefficient alpha was .79.

Validity: Correlations with other variables range from −.19 to .66.

Author: Brett, J. M., and Stroh, L. K.

Article: Working 61 plus hours a week: Why do managers do it?

Journal: *Journal of Applied Psychology*, February 2003, *88*, 67–78.

12185

Test Name: FAMILY MANAGEMENT SCALE

Purpose: To measure the objective demands of the couples' work and family roles.

Number of Items: 12

Format: Responses are made on a 4-point scale ranging from *very easy* to *very difficult*.

Reliability: Test–retest (2 weeks) reliability was .88. Coefficient alpha was .87.

Validity: Correlations with other variables ranged from −.32 to .34.

Author: Perrone, K. M., and Worthington, E. L., Jr.

Article: Factors influencing ratings of marital quality by individuals within dual-career marriages: A conceptual model.

Journal: *Journal of Counseling Psychology*, January 2001, *48*, 3–6.

Related Research: Bohen, H. H., & Viveros-Long, A. (Eds.) (1981). *Balancing jobs and family life.* Philadelphia: Temple University Press.

12186

Test Name: FAMILY OF INFLUENCE AND SUPPORT SCALE

Purpose: To assess how much family members influence and how much support family members are perceived to offer in a person's personal life.

Number of Items: 3

Format: Various 7-point response scales are used. All items and responses are presented.

Reliability: Alpha coefficients exceeded .73.

Validity: Correlations with chance of marrying ranged from −.45 to .30.

Author: Umaña-Taylor, A. J., and Fine, M. A.

Article: Predicting commitment to wed among Hispanic and Anglo partners.

Journal: *Journal of Marriage and Family*, February 2003, *65*, 117–129.

Related Research: Bryant, C. M., et al. (1996, November). *A test of the dyadic withdrawal hypothesis: Do African American, Anglo and Hispanic couples exhibit similar patterns of social regression?* Paper presented at the National Council on Family Relations, Kansas City, MO.

12187

Test Name: FAMILY ORIENTATION SCALE

Purpose: To assess students' feelings of family orientation.

Number of Items: 4

Format: Responses are made on a 5-point scale ranging from 1 (*not at all true*) to 5 (*very true*). All items are presented.

Reliability: Alpha coefficients were .72 and .73.

Author: Urdan, T.

Article: Predictors of academic self-handicapping and achievement: Examining achievement goals, classroom goal structures, and culture.

Journal: *Journal of Educational Psychology*, June 2004, 96, 251–264.

Related Research: Hui, C. H., & Yee, C. (1994). The Shortened Individualism–Collectivism Scale: Its relationship to demographic and work-related variables. *Journal of Research in Personality*, 28, 409–424.

12188

Test Name: FAMILY PROCESS INVENTORY

Purpose: To measure beliefs about one's family, family structure, deviant beliefs, and cohesion and communication.

Number of Items: 98

Format: Five-point scales are used. All items are presented.

Reliability: Alpha coefficients ranged from .71 to .97.

Author: Smith, E. P., et al.

Article: Latent models of family processes in African American families: Relationships to child competence, achievement, and problem behavior.

Journal: *Journal of Marriage and Family*, November 2001, 63, 967–980.

Related Research: Tolan, P. H., et al. (1977). Assessment of family relationship characteristics: A measure to explain risk for antisocial behavior and depression among urban youth. *Psychological Assessment*, 9, 212–223.

12189

Test Name: FAMILY RISK FACTOR CHECKLIST—PARENT

Purpose: To assess a child's exposure to multiple concurrent family risk factors.

Number of Items: 48

Format: Includes five domains: Life Events, SES, Parenting, Conflict and Mood, and Psychopathology.

Reliability: Test–retest intraclass correlation coefficients ranged from .61 to .89.

Author: Dwyer, S. B., et al.

Article: Teachers' knowledge of children's exposure to family risk factors: Accuracy and usefulness.

Journal: *Journal of School Psychology*, January/February 2005, 43, 23–38.

Related Research: Dwyer, S. B., et al. (2003). Population level assessment of the family risk factors related to the onset or persistence of children's mental health problems. *Journal of Child Psychology and Psychiatry*, 44, 699–711.

12190

Test Name: FAMILY ROUTINES INVENTORY

Purpose: To provide a report by parents of family routines and their predictability.

Number of Items: 28

Format: Frequency scales range from 0 (*almost never*) to 3 (*always*). Importance scales range from 0 (*not at all important*) to 2 (*very important*).

Reliability: Reliability coefficients ranged from .67 to .79.

Validity: Correlations with other variables ranged from .14 to .54.

Author: Sytsma, S. E., et al.

Article: Development and initial validation of the Child Routines Inventory.

Journal: *Journal of Psychopathology and Behavioral Assessment*, December 2001, 23, 241–251.

Related Research: Jensen, E. W., et al. (1983). The Family Routines Inventory: Development and validation. *Social Science and Medicine*, 17, 201–211.

12191

Test Name: FAMILY SATISFACTION SCALE

Purpose: To measure satisfaction with marriage and spouse.

Number of Items: 2

Format: Scales range from 1 (*very unhappy*) to 5 (*very happy*). All items are presented.

Reliability: Coefficient alpha was .82.

Validity: Correlations with other variables ranged from −.40 to .62.

Author: Brett, J. M., and Stroh, L. K.

Article: Working 61 plus hours a week: Why do managers do it?

Journal: *Journal of Applied Psychology*, February 2003, *88*, 67–78.

12192

Test Name: FAMILY SATISFACTION SCALE

Purpose: To measure overall support from and emotional satisfaction with one's family.

Number of Items: 20

Format: Responses are made on a 5-point scale ranging from 1 (*strongly disagree*) to 5 (*strongly agree*).

Reliability: Alpha coefficients were .88 and .95.

Validity: Correlations with other variables ranged from −.54 to .39 ($N = 86$).

Author: Su, J., et al.

Article: Intergenerational family conflict and coping among among American college students.

Journal: *Journal of Counseling Psychology*, October 2005, *52*, 482–489.

Related Research: Carver, M. D., & Jones, W. H. (1992). The Family Satisfaction Scale. *Social Behavior and Personality, 20*, 71–84.

12193

Test Name: FAMILY SATISFACTION SCALE

Purpose: To measure family satisfaction.

Number of Items: 5

Format: Responses are made on a 7-point Likert scale. An example is given.

Reliability: Coefficient alpha was .93.

Validity: Correlations with other variables ranged from −.37 to .66.

Author: Zickar, M. J., et al.

Article: Job attitudes of workers with two jobs.

Journal: *Journal of Vocational Behavior*, February 2004, *64*, 222–235.

Related Research: Rothausen, T. J. (1994). *Expanding the boundaries of job satisfaction: The effects of job facets, life satisfaction, and family situation.* Unpublished doctoral dissertation, University of Minnesota.

12194

Test Name: FAMILY SENSE OF COHERENCE SCALE

Purpose: To assess children's coping.

Number of Items: 21

Format: Includes three scales: Family Worries, Family Investment, and Family Disengagement. Examples are presented.

Reliability: Alpha coefficient ranged from .83 to .87. Test–retest (2 weeks) reliability coefficients were >.77.

Author: Davies, P. T., and Forman, E. M.

Article: Children's pattern of pressuring emotional security in the interparental subsystem.

Journal: *Child Development*, November/December 2002, *73*, 1880–1903.

Related Research: Forman, E. M. (1999). *Family instability and adolescent adjustment: Exploration of intrapsychic and parenting mediating mechanism.* Unpublished doctoral dissertation, University of Rochester.

12195

Test Name: FAMILY-SENSITIVE SUPERVISION SCALE

Purpose: To measure family-sensitive supervision.

Number of Items: 3

Format: All items are presented. A Likert format is used.

Reliability: Coefficient alpha was .85.

Validity: Correlations with other variables ranged from −.20 to .36.

Author: Clark, S. C.

Article: Employees' sense of community, sense of control, and work/family conflict in Native American organizations.

Journal: *Journal of Vocational Behavior*, August 2002, *61*, 92–108.

Related Research: Clark, S. C. (2001). Work cultures and work/family balance. *Journal of Vocational Behavior, 58*, 348–365.

12196

Test Name: FAMILY STRENGTHS SCALES

Purpose: To measure several dimensions of family strengths: Personal Worth, Affective and Normative Commitment, Conflict Resolution, Communication, Positive Interaction, and Time Together.

Number of Items: 20

Format: Seven-point response categories are used. All items are presented.

Reliability: Alpha coefficients ranged from .64 to .91 across subscales.

Author: Schumm, W. R., et al.

Article: Family strengths and the Kansas Marital Satisfaction Scale: A factor analytic study.

Journal: *Psychological Reports*, June 2001, *88*, Part 2, 965–973.

Related Research: Schumm, W. R. (1985). Beyond relationship characteristics of strong families:

Constructing a model of family strengths. *Family Perspective, 19,* 1–9.

12197

Test Name: FAMILY STRESS SCALE

Purpose: To measure family stress.

Number of Items: 5

Format: Responses are made on a 5-point scale ranging from *very stressful* to *not stressful.*

Reliability: Coefficient alpha was .77.

Validity: Correlations with other variables ranged from −.08 to .39.

Author: Stoeva, A. Z., et al.

Article: Negative affectivity, role stress, and work–family conflict.

Journal: *Journal of Vocational Behavior,* February 2002, *60,* 1–16.

12198

Test Name: FAMILY SUPPORT SCALE

Purpose: To measure family support when raising a small child.

Number of Items: 18

Format: Item anchors are 1 (*not at all adequate*) and 2 (*almost always adequate*).

Reliability: Reliability estimates ranged from .75 to .77.

Author: Saylor, C. F., et al.

Article: Age-related parenting stress differences in mothers of children with spina bifida.

Journal: *Psychological Reports,* December 2003, *93,* Part 2, 1223–1232.

Related Research: Dunst, C. J., et al. (1984). The Family Support Scale: Reliability and validity. *Journal of Individual, Family and Community Wellness, 1,* 45–52.

12199

Test Name: FAMILY SUPPORT SCALE

Purpose: To measure family support.

Number of Items: 14

Format: Response scales are anchored by 1 (*strongly agree*) and 4 (*strongly disagree*). Sample items are presented.

Reliability: Coefficient alpha was .87.

Validity: Correlations with other variables ranged from .30 to .75.

Author: Weinman, M. L., et al.

Article: Associations of family support, resiliency, and depression symptoms among indigent teens attending a family planning clinic.

Journal: *Psychological Reports,* December 2003, *93*(3) Part 1, 719–731.

Related Research: Gillmore, M. R., et al. (1992). Substance use and other factors associated with risky sexual behavior among pregnant adolescents. *Family Planning Perspectives, 24,* 255–268.

12200

Test Name: FAMILY-SUPPORTIVE ORGANIZATION PERCEPTIONS SCALE

Purpose: To assess family-supportive organization perceptions.

Number of Items: 14

Format: Responses are made on a 5-point scale ranging from 1 (*strongly disagree*) to 5 (*strongly agree*). All items are presented.

Validity: Correlations with other variables ranged from −.47 to .62.

Author: Allen, T. D.

Article: Family-supportive work environments: The role of organizational perceptions.

Journal: *Journal of Vocational Behavior,* June 2001, *58,* 414–435.

Related Research: Friedman, D. E. (1990). Work and family: The new strategic plan. *Human Resource Planning, 13,* 79–89. Friedman, D. E., & Galinsky, E. (1992). Work and family issues: A legitimate business concern. In S. Zedeck (Ed.), *Work, families, and organization* (pp. 168–207). San Francisco: Jossey-Bass.

12201

Test Name: FAMILY-SUPPORTIVE ORGANIZATION PERCEPTIONS SCALE

Purpose: To measure family-supportive organization perceptions.

Number of Items: 14

Format: Responses are made on a 7-point scale ranging from *strongly disagree* to *strongly agree.*

Reliability: Alpha coefficients were .89 and .91.

Validity: Correlations with other variables ranged from −.29 to .69.

Author: Behson, S. J.

Article: Which dominates? The relative importance of work–family organizational support and general organizational context on employee outcomes.

Journal: *Journal of Vocational Behavior,* August 2002, *61,* 53–72.

Related Research: Allen, T. D. (2001). Family-supportive work environments: The role of organizational perceptions. *Journal of Vocational Behavior, 58,* 414–415.

12202

Test Name: FAMILY UNPREDICTABILITY SCALE

Purpose: To measure unpredictability in nurturance, finances, discipline, and meals.

Number of Items: 22

Format: Sample items are presented.

Reliability: Alpha coefficients ranged from .73 to .84.

Author: Ross, L. T., and Hill, E. M.

Article: Comparing alcoholic and nonalcoholic parents on the Family Unpredictability Scale.

Journal: *Psychological Reports,* June 2004, *94,* Part 2, 1385–1391.

Related Research: Ross, L. T., & Hill, E. M. (2000). The Family Unpredictability Scale: Reliability and validity. *Journal of Marriage and the Family, 62,* 549–562.

12203

Test Name: FAMILY VIOLENCE SCALE

Purpose: To measure family violence by adult child report.

Number of Items: 17

Format: Scales range from 1 (*never*) to 4 (*very often*). Sample items are presented.

Reliability: Alpha coefficients ranged from .88 to .90.

Author: Hall, G. C. N., et al.

Article: Ethnicity, culture, and sexual aggression: Risk and protective factors.

Journal: *Journal of Consulting and Clinical Psychology,* October 2005, *73,* 830–840.

Related Research: Bardis, P. (1973). Violence: Theory and quantification. *Journal of Political and Military Sociology, 1,* 121–146.

12204

Test Name: FAMILY–WORK STRESS AND INVOLVEMENT SCALES

Purpose: To measure job and family stressors and job and family involvement.

Number of Items: 43

Format: Scales range from 1 (*disagree strongly or almost always*) to 5 (*agree strongly or almost never/never*). Four-point frequency scales are used on eight items.

Reliability: Alpha coefficients ranged from .80 to .90.

Author: Baltes, B. B., and Heydens-Gahir, H. A.

Article: Reduction of work–family conflict through the use of selection, organization, and compensation behaviors.

Journal: *Journal of Applied Psychology,* December 2003, *88,* 1005–1018.

Related Research: Frone, M. R., et al. (1992). Antecedents and outcomes of work–family conflict: Testing a model of the work–family interface. *Journal of Applied Psychology, 77,* 65–78.

12205

Test Name:
FATHER–DAUGHTER RELATIONSHIP RATING SCALE

Purpose: To measure daughters' perceived relationships to fathers.

Number of Items: 9

Format: Seven-point scales are anchored by *not at all* and *very much.* All items are presented.

Reliability: Alpha was .93.

Author: Brown, J., et al.

Article: The Father–Daughter Relationship Rating Scale.

Journal: *Psychological Reports,* February 2002, *90,* 212–214.

Related Research: Cabrera, N., et al. (2000). Fatherhood in the twenty-first century. *Child Development, 71,* 127–136.

12206

Test Name: FATHER INVOLVEMENT SCALE

Purpose: To assess actual and desired expressive involvement, instrumental involvement, and mentoring/advising involvement of subjects' fathers in their lives.

Number of Items: 20

Format: Scales range from 1 (*not at all involved or desired much less involvement*) to 5 (*very involved or desired much more involvement*).

Reliability: Alpha coefficients ranged from .90 to .93 across subscales.

Author: Schwartz, S. J., and Finley, G. E.

Article: Fathering in intact and divorced families: Ethnic differences in retrospective reports.

Journal: *Journal of Marriage and Family,* February 2005, *67,* 207–215.

Related Research: Finley, G. E., & Schwartz, S. J. (2004). The Father Involvement and Nurturant Fathering Scales: Retrospective measures for adolescent and adult children. *Educational and Psychological Measurement, 64,* 143–164.

12207

Test Name: FATHER SUPPORT SCALE

Purpose: To assess father support.

Number of Items: 5

Format: All items are presented.

Reliability: Alpha coefficients were .78 and .88.

Validity: Correlations with other variables ranged from −.35 to .02.

Author: Storch, E. A., et al.

Article: Psychosocial adjustment in early adulthood: The role of childhood teasing and father support.

Journal: *Child Study Journal,* 2003, *33,* 153–163.

Related Research: Flouri, E., & Buchanan, A. (2002). Life satisfaction in teenage boys: The moderating role of father involvement and bullying. *Aggressive Behavior, 28*, 126–133.

12208

Test Name: FATIGUE INDEX

Purpose: To measure the degree of fatigue at home.

Number of Items: 6

Format: Scales range from 1 (*strongly disagree*) to 5 (*strongly agree*). All items are presented.

Reliability: Coefficient alpha was .75.

Author: Yoon, J.

Article: The role of structure and motivation for workplace empowerment: The case of Korean employees.

Journal: *Social Psychology Quarterly*, June 2001, *64*, 195–206.

Related Research: Moen, P., & Forest, K. B. (1990). Working parents, workplace supports, and well-being: The Swedish experience. *Social Psychology Quarterly, 53*, 117–131.

12209

Test Name: FINANCIAL CONNECTEDNESS SUBSCALE

Purpose: To assess financial independence.

Number of Items: 8

Format: Responses are made on a 7-point Likert-type scale. Sample items are presented.

Reliability: Alpha coefficients were .86 and .88.

Author: Scott, D. J., and Church, A. T.

Article: Separation/attachment theory and career decidedness and

commitment: Effects of parental divorce.

Journal: *Journal of Vocational Behavior*, June 2001, *58*, 328–347.

Related Research: Gavazzi, S. M., & Sabatelli, R. M. (1988, November). *Multigenerational interconnectedness and family involvement: Assessing levels of individuation in adolescence and early childhood.* Paper presented at the National Council on Family Relations 50th Annual Conference, Philadelphia.

12210

Test Name: FORGIVENESS SCALE

Purpose: To measure level of forgiveness toward an ex-spouse.

Number of Items: 15

Format: Scales range from 1 (*strongly disagree*) to 5 (*strongly agree*).

Reliability: Coefficient alpha was .88.

Validity: Correlations with other variables ranged from −.39 to .32.

Author: Rye, M. S., et al.

Article: Can group interventions facilitate forgiveness of an ex-spouse? A randomized clinical trial.

Journal: *Journal of Consulting and Clinical Psychology*, October 2005, *73*, 880–892.

Related Research: Rye, M. S., et al. (2001). Evaluation of the psychometric properties of two forgiveness scales. *Current Psychology, 20*, 260–277.

12211

Test Name: GENERAL FAMILY FUNCTIONING SCALE

Purpose: To measure family functioning.

Number of Items: 12

Format: Scales range from 1 (*strongly agree*) to 4 (*strongly disagree*).

Reliability: Coefficient alpha was .86.

Author: Kazarian, S. S.

Article: Family functioning, cultural orientation, and psychological well-being among university students in Lebanon.

Journal: *The Journal of Social Psychology*, April 2005, *145*, 141–152.

Related Research: Epstein, N. B., et al. (1983). The McMaster Family Assessment Device. *Journal of Marital and Family Therapy, 9*, 171–180.

12212

Test Name: HOME DATA QUESTIONNAIRE—REVISED

Purpose: To measure children's reactions to interparental arguments over the past year.

Number of Items: 13

Format: Includes three scales: Overt Distress, Behavioral Avoidance, and Behavioral Involvement. Examples are presented.

Reliability: Alpha coefficients ranged from .35 to .79.

Validity: Correlations with other variables ranged from −.10 to .37.

Author: Davies, P. T., and Forman, E. M.

Article: Children's pattern of pressuring emotional security in the interparental subsystem.

Journal: *Child Development*, November/December 2002, *73*, 1880–1903.

Related Research: Garcia-O'Hearn, C., et al. (1997). Mothers' and fathers' reports of children's reaction to naturalistic marital conflict. *Journal of American*

Academy of Child and Adolescent Psychiatry, 36, 1366–1373.

12213

Test Name: HOME ENVIRONMENT RISK SCALE— PORTUGUESE VERSION

Purpose: To measure the home environment to identify children at risk of school failure.

Number of Items: Items per subscale ranged from 6 to 18.

Format: A multiple-choice format is used. Sample items are presented in English.

Reliability: Alpha coefficients ranged from .55 to .80.

Validity: Correlations with other variables ranged from .01 to .54.

Author: Marturano, E. M., et al.

Article: An evaluation scale of family environment for identification of children at risk of school failure.

Journal: *Psychological Reports,* April 2005, *96*, 307–321.

12214

Test Name: IMPACT OF EVENT SCALE—REVISED

Purpose: To assess mothers' post-traumatic reactions.

Number of Items: 22

Format: Includes three subscales: Intrusion, Avoidance, and Hyperarousal. Responses are made on a 6-point scale ranging from 0 (*never*) to 5 (*often*).

Reliability: Alpha coefficients were .96 and .93.

Author: Dybdahl, R.

Article: Children and mothers in war: An outcome study of a psychosocial intervention program.

Journal: *Child Development,* July/August 2001, *72*, 1214–1230.

Related Research: Weiss, D. (1996). Psychometric review of the Impact of Events Scale—Revised. In B. H. Stamm (Ed.), *Measurement of stress, trauma, and adaptation*. Lutherville, MD: Sidran.

12215

Test Name: INDEX OF SPOUSE ABUSE

Purpose: To assess the severity of physical and nonphysical abuse among spouses.

Number of Items: 30

Format: Response scales range from 1 (*never*) to 5 (*very frequently*). Sample items are presented.

Reliability: Alpha coefficients ranged from .86 to .88 across subscales and samples.

Author: Thompson, M. P., et al.

Article: The mediating roles of perceived social support and resources in the self-efficacy-suicide attempts relation among African American abused women.

Journal: *Journal of Consulting and Clinical Psychology,* August 2002, *70*, 942–949.

Related Research: Hudson, W., & McIntosh, S. R. (1981). The assessment of spouse abuse: Two quantifiable dimensions. *Journal of Marriage and the Family, 43*, 873–888.

12216

Test Name: INFORMAL WORK–FAMILY ORGANIZATIONAL SUPPORT SCALES

Purpose: To measure informal work–family organizational support.

Number of Items: 13

Format: Includes three scales: Job Autonomy, Manager Support, and

Career Impact. Responses are made on 4-point scales ranging from *strongly disagree* to *strongly agree*. All items are presented.

Reliability: Alpha coefficients ranged from .68 to .89.

Validity: Correlations with other variables ranged from −.38 to .58.

Author: Behson, S. J.

Article: The relative contribution of formal and informal organizational work–family support.

Journal: *Journal of Vocational Behavior,* June 2005, *66*, 487–500.

Related Research: Thompson, C. A., et al. (1999). When work–family benefits are not enough: The influence of work–family culture on benefit utilization, organizational attachment, and work–family conflict. *Journal of Vocational Behavior, 54*, 392–415.

12217

Test Name: INTERACTION BEHAVIOR QUESTIONNAIRE— SHORT FORM

Purpose: To assess level of support and involvement in the mother–child relationship.

Number of Items: 15

Format: A true–false format is used. Examples are presented.

Reliability: Correlation alpha was .85.

Validity: Correlation with other variables ranged from −.26 to .43 (*N* = 277).

Author: Brody, G. H., et al.

Article: Unique and protective contributions of parenting and classroom processes to the adjustment of African American children living in single-parent families.

Journal: *Child Development,* January/February 2002, *73*, 274–286.

Related Research: Prinz, R. J., et al. (1979). Multivariate assessment of conflict in distressed and nondistressed mother–adolescent dyads. *Journal of Applied Behavior Analysis, 12,* 691–700.

12218

Test Name: INTERACTION STRAIN SCALE

Purpose: To measure strain experienced by employed women as they cope with domestic and paid work.

Number of Items: 12

Format: Scales range from 1 (*true*) to 3 (*untrue*).

Reliability: Alpha coefficients ranged from .69 to .75.

Validity: Correlations with other variables ranged from –.20 to .24.

Author: Noor, N. M.

Article: Work–family conflict, locus of control, and women's well-being: Tests of alternative pathways.

Journal: *The Journal of Social Psychology,* October 2002, *142,* 645–662.

Related Research: Parry, G., & Warr, P. B. (1980). The measurement of mothers' work attitudes. *Journal of Occupational Psychology, 53,* 245–252.

12219

Test Name: INTERACTIVE BEHAVIOR QUESTIONNAIRE

Purpose: To assess level of support and involvement in the parent–child relationship.

Number of Items: 15

Format: A true–false format is used. Examples are given.

Reliability: Coefficient alpha was .84.

Author: Brody, G. H., et al.

Article: Longitudinal pathways to competence and psychological adjustment among African American children living in rural single-parent households.

Journal: *Child Development,* September/October 2002, *73,* 1505–1515.

Related Research: Prinz, R. J., et al. (1979). Multivariate assessment of conflict in distressed and nondistressed monther–adolescent dyads. *Journal of Applied Behavior Analysis, 12,* 691–700.

12220

Test Name: INTERACTIVE BEHAVIOR QUESTIONNAIRE— SHORT FORM

Purpose: To assess warmth and support in the mother–child relationship.

Number of Items: 14

Format: A true–false format is used.

Reliability: Coefficient alpha was .85.

Validity: The correlation with the long form was .96.

Author: Pelton, J., et al.

Article: The Moral Disengagement Scale: Extension with an American minority sample.

Journal: *Journal of Psychopathology and Behavioral Assessment,* March 2004, *26,* 31–39.

Related Research: Prinz, R. J., et al. (1979). Multivariate assessment of conflict in distressed and nondistressed mother–adolescent dyad. *Journal of Applied Behavioral Analysis, 12,* 691–700.

12221

Test Name: INTERGENERATIONAL AMBIVALENCE SCALE

Purpose: To assess the ambivalence felt between parents and their adult children.

Number of Items: 5

Format: Scales range from 1 (*strongly agree*) to 5 (*strongly disagree*). All items are presented.

Reliability: Coefficient alpha was .68.

Validity: Correlations with other variables ranged from –.25 to .52.

Author: Pillemer, K., and Suitor, J. J.

Article: Explaining mothers' ambivalence toward their adult children.

Journal: *Journal of Marriage and Family,* August 2002, *64,* 602–613.

12222

Test Name: INTIMATE RELATIONS SCALE

Purpose: To assess four interpersonal aspects of the marital relationship.

Number of Items: 25

Format: Includes Maintenance, Conflict, Love, and Ambivalence. Responses are made on a 9-point scale ranging from 1 (*very little or not at all*) to 9 (*very much or extremely*).

Reliability: Alpha coefficients range from .67 to .93.

Author: Volling, B. L., et al.

Article: Emotion regulation in context: The jealousy complex between young siblings and its relations with child and family characteristics.

Journal: *Child Development,* March/April 2002, *73,* 581–600.

Related Research: Braiker, H., & Kelley, H. H. (1979). Conflict in the development of close relationships (pp. 135–168). In R. Burgess & T. Huston (Eds.), *Social exchange in*

developing relationships. New York: Academic.

12223

Test Name: INVENTORY OF PARENT AND PEER ATTACHMENT

Purpose: To measure parent and peer attachment in adolescence.

Number of Items: 75

Format: Includes three subscales: Trust, Communication, and Alienation. Responses are made on a 5-point scale ranging from 1 (*almost never or never true*) to 5 (*almost always or always true*).

Validity: Correlations with other variables ranged from –.77 to .69.

Author: DiTommaso, E., et al.

Article: Measurement and validity characteristics of the short version of the Social and Emotional Loneliness Scale for Adults.

Journal: *Educational and Psychological Measurement,* February 2004, *64,* 99–119.

Related Research: Armsden, G. C., & Greenberg, M. T. (1987). The Inventory of Parent and Peer Attachment: Individual differences and their relationship to psychological well-being in adolescence. *Journal of Youth and Adolescence, 16,* 427–454.

12224

Test Name: INVENTORY OF PARENT AND PEER ATTACHMENT

Purpose: To measure the degree of trust, communication, and alienation in relationships with parents.

Number of Items: 50

Format: Responses are made on a 4-point Likert scale. Sample items are presented. Examples are given.

Reliability: Alpha coefficients ranged from .74 to .93.

Author: Luther, S. S., and Becker, B. E.

Article: Privileged but pressured? A study of affluent youth.

Journal: *Child Development,* September/October 2002, *73,* 1593–1610.

Related Research: Armsden, G. C., & Greenburg, M. T. (1987). The Inventory of Parent and Peer Attachment: Individual differences and their relationship to psychological well-being in adolescence. *Journal of Youth and Adolescence, 16,* 427–454.

12225

Test Name: INVENTORY OF PARENT AND PEER ATTACHMENT

Purpose: To assess adolescents' perceptions of the current degree of trust, communication, and alienation in their relationships with their mothers.

Number of Items: 25

Format: Responses are made on a 5-point scale ranging from *never* to *almost always.* Sample items are presented.

Reliability: Alpha coefficients ranged from .86 to .91.

Author: McElhaney, K. B., and Allen, J. P.

Article: Autonomy and adolescent social functioning: The moderating effect of risk.

Journal: *Child Development,* January/February 2001, *72,* 220–235.

Related Research: Armsden, G. C., & Greenberg, M. T. (1987). The inventory of parent and peer attachment: Individual differences and their relationship to psychological well-being in adolescents. *Journal of Youth and Adolescence, 16,* 427–454.

12226

Test Name: INVENTORY OF PARENT AND PEER ATTACHMENT

Purpose: To assess affective and cognitive dimensions of adolescents to peers and to parents.

Number of Items: 53

Format: Scales range from 1 (*almost never or never*) to 5 (*almost always or always*).

Reliability: Alpha coefficients ranged from .68 to .91 across subscales.

Validity: Correlations with other variables ranged from –.47 to .61.

Author: Schwartz, J. P., and Buboltz, W. C., Jr.

Article: The relationship between attachment to parents and psychological separation in college students.

Journal: *Journal of College Student Development,* September/October 2004, *45,* 566–577.

Related Research: Armsden, G. C., & Greenberg, M. T. (1987). The Inventory of Parent and Peer Attachment: Individual differences and their relationship to psychological well-being in adolescence. *Journal of Youth and Adolescence, 16,* 427–454.

12227

Test Name: INVENTORY OF PARENT AND PEER ATTACHMENT—MODIFIED

Purpose: To measure parental attachment.

Number of Items: 16

Format: Includes two subscales: Trust and Communication. Responses are made on a 4-point scale ranging from 1 (*never*) to 4 (*almost always*). Sample items are presented.

Reliability: Alpha coefficients were .76 and .79.

Validity: Correlations with other variables ranged from −.27 to .33.

Author: Engels, R. C. M. E., et al.

Article: Parental attachment and adolescents' emotional adjustment: The associations with social skills and relational competence.

Journal: *Journal of Counseling Psychology*, October 2001, *48*, 428–439.

Related Research: Armsden, G. C., & Greenberg, M. T. (1987). The Inventory of Parent and Peer Attachment: Individual differences and their relationship to psychological well-being in adolescence. *Journal of Youth and Adolescence*, *16*, 427–454.

12228

Test Name: INVENTORY OF PARENT AND PEER ATTACHMENT—REVISED, ADAPTED

Purpose: To measure security of attachment to each parent.

Number of Items: 50

Format: For each parent there are three subscales: Trust, Communication, and Alienation. Responses are made on a 5-point scale ranging from 1 (*almost never or never true*) to 5 (*almost always or always true*). Examples are given.

Reliability: Alpha coefficients ranged from .76 to .94. Test–retest (3 weeks) reliability was .93.

Validity: Correlations with other variables ranged from −.54 to .57.

Author: Mattanah, J. F., et al.

Article: Parental attachment, separation–individuation, and college student adjustment: A structural equation analysis of mediational effects.

Journal: *Journal of Counseling Psychology*, April 2004, *51*, 213–225.

Related Research: Armsden, G. C., & Greenberg, M.T. (1987). The Inventory of Parent and Peer Attachment: Individual differences and their relationship to psychological well-being in adolescence. *Journal of Youth and Adolescence*, *16*, 427–454.

12229

Test Name: INVENTORY OF PARENT AND PEER ATTACHMENT—SHORT VERSION

Purpose: To measure daughter–father and daughter–mother relationships.

Number of Items: 14

Format: Scales range from 1 (*never*) to 5 (*always*).

Reliability: Alpha coefficients ranged from .63 to .88 across subscales.

Author: Coley, R. L.

Article: Daughter–father relationships and psychosocial functioning in low-income African American families.

Journal: *Journal of Marriage and Family*, November 2003, *65*(4), 867–875.

Related Research: Armsden, G.C., & Greenberg, M. T. (1987). The Inventory of Parent and Peer Attachment: Relationships to well-being in adolescence. *Journal of Youth and Adolescence*, *16*, 427–454.

12230

Test Name: INVOLVEMENT IN CHILD CARE SCALE

Purpose: To measure mothers' and fathers' involvement in child care.

Number of Items: 36

Format: Scales range from 1 (*almost always my spouse*) to 5 (*almost always myself*).

Reliability: Coefficient alpha was .93.

Validity: Correlations with other variables ranged from −.32 to .43.

Author: Gaunt, R.

Article: The role of value priorities in paternal and maternal involvement in child care.

Journal: *Journal of Marriage and Family*, August 2005, *67*, 643–655.

12231

Test Name: ISSUES CHECKLIST

Purpose: To measure the diversity and the intensity of family conflict.

Number of Items: 44

Format: A yes–no format, frequency rating, and anger intensity scale are used for each item. Scoring procedures are described.

Reliability: Test–retest reliabilities ranged from .47 to .80.

Validity: Correlations with other variables ranged from −.52 to .55.

Author: Barkley, R. A., et al.

Article: The efficacy of problem-solving communication training alone, behavior management training alone, and their combination for parent–adolescent conflict in teenagers with ADHD and ODD.

Journal: *Journal of Consulting and Clinical Psychology*, December 2001, *69*, 926–941.

Related Research: Prinz, R. J., et al. (1979). Multivariate assessment of conflict in distressed and nondistressed mother–adolescent dyads. *Journal of Applied Behavior Analysis*, *12*, 691–700.

12232

Test Name: ISSUES CHECKLIST

Purpose: To measure the frequency of parental–adolescent conflict during the past two weeks and the intensity of discussions about those conflicts.

Number of Items: 18

Format: Intensity scales range from 1 (*calm*) to 5 (*angry*).

Reliability: Coefficient alpha was .87.

Author: Kaufman, N. K., et al.

Article: Potential mediators of cognitive–behavioral therapy for adolescents with comorbid major depression and conduct disorder.

Journal: *Journal of Consulting and Clinical Psychology*, February 2005, 73, 38–46.

Related Research: Robin, A. L., & Weiss, J. G. (1980). Criterion-related validity of behavioral and self-report measures of problem-solving communication skills in distressed and nondistressed parent–adolescent dyads. *Behavioral Assessment, 2*, 339–352.

12233

Test Name: ISSUES CHECKLISTS—BRIEF VERSION

Purpose: To assess family conflict.

Number of Items: 17

Format: Each item/issue is rated from 1 (*calm*) to 5 (*angry*) in terms of its discussion in the family.

Reliability: Interitem correlations ranged from .80 (child report) to .84 (parent report).

Validity: Correlations with other variables ranged from −.20 to .14.

Author: McBride, C. K., et al.

Article: Individual and familial influences on the onset of sexual intercourse among urban African American adolescents.

Journal: *Journal of Consulting and Clinical Psychology*, February 2003, 71, 159–167.

Related Research: Robin, A. L., & Foster, S. L. (1989). *Negotiating parent–adolescent conflict: A behavioral-family systems approach.* (pp. 295–328). New York: Guilford Press.

12234

Test Name: JOB–FAMILY ROLE STRAIN SCALE—MODIFIED

Purpose: To measure values and emotions about job and family roles.

Number of Items: 16

Format: Responses are made on a 5-point Likert scale ranging from *strongly agree* to *strongly disagree*.

Reliability: Test–retest (2 weeks) reliability was .72. Coefficient alpha was .80.

Validity: Correlation with other variables ranged from −.35 to .34.

Author: Perrone, K. M., & Worthington, E. L., Jr.

Article: Factors influencing ratings of marital quality by individuals without dual-career marriages: A conceptual model.

Journal: *Journal of Counseling Psychology*, January 2001, 48, 3–9.

Related Research: Bohen, H. H., & Viveros-Long, A. (Eds.) (1981). *Balancing jobs and family life.* Philadelphia: Temple University Press.

12235

Test Name: KANSAS MARITAL SATISFACTION AND FAMILY STRENGTHS SCALES

Purpose: To measure Satisfaction, Personal Worth, Affective Commitment, Normative Commitment, Conflict Resolution, Communication, Positive Interaction, and Time Together.

Number of Items: 22

Format: All items are presented.

Reliability: Alpha coefficients ranged from .53 to .91 across subscales.

Author: Akagi, C. G., et al.

Article: Dimensionality of the Kansas Family Strengths Scale and the Kansas Marital Satisfaction Scale as revised to capture changes in marital satisfaction.

Journal: *Psychological Reports*, December 2003, 93, Part 2, 1267–1274.

Related Research: Schumm, W. R., et al. (2001). Family strengths and the Kansas Marital Satisfaction Scale: A factor analytic study. *Psychological Reports, 88*, 965–973.

12236

Test Name: KANSAS MARITAL SATISFACTION SCALE

Purpose: To measure marital satisfaction.

Number of Items: 3

Format: Scales range from 1 (*not at all true*) to 9 (*extremely true*). A sample item is presented.

Reliability: Coefficient alpha was .97.

Author: Kurdek, L. A.

Article: Predicting the timing of separation and marital satisfaction: An eight-year prospective longitudinal study.

Journal: *Journal of Marriage and Family*, February 2002, 64, 163–179.

Related Research: Schumm, W. R., et al. (1986). Concurrent and discriminant validity of the Kansas Marital Satisfaction Scale. *Journal of Marriage and the Family, 48*, 381–387.

12237

Test Name: KANSAS MARITAL SATISFACTION SCALE—KOREAN VERSION

Purpose: To measure marital satisfaction.

Number of Items: 4

Format: Item responses range from 1 (*very dissatisfied*) to 7 (*very satisfied*).

Reliability: Alpha coefficients ranged from .93 to .95.

Validity: Correlations with other variables ranged from −.36 to .73.

Author: Chung, H.

Article: Application and revision of the Kansas Marital Satisfaction Scale for use with Korean couples.

Journal: *Psychological Reports*, December 2004, *95*, Part 1, 1015–1022.

Related Research: Schumm, W. R., et al. (1983). Characteristics of responses to the Kansas Marital Satisfaction Scale by a sample of 84 married mothers. *Psychological Reports, 53*, 567–572.

12238

Test Name: KINSHIP SUPPORT SCALE

Purpose: To assess adolescents' perceptions of adult family members as sources of social and emotional support.

Number of Items: 13

Format: Responses are made on a 4-point Likert scale ranging from 1 (*strongly disagree*) to 4 (*strongly agree*). Examples are given.

Reliability: Alpha coefficients were .72 and .86.

Validity: Correlations with other variables ranged from −.12 to .43.

Author: Kenny, M. E., et al.

Article: The role of perceived barriers and relational support in the educational and vocational lives of urban high school students.

Journal: *Journal of Counseling Psychology*, April 2003, *50*, 142–155.

Related Research: Taylor, R. D., et al. (1993). Influence of kinship social support on the parenting experiences and psychosocial adjustment of African American adolescents. *Developmental Psychology, 29*, 382–388.

12239

Test Name: LAXNESS SCALE

Purpose: To assess disciplinary consistency in parenting.

Number of Items: 10

Format: Sample items are presented.

Reliability: Coefficient alpha was .66.

Validity: Correlations with other variables ranged from −.24 to .44.

Author: Kotchick, B. A., et al.

Article: Predictors of parenting among African American single mothers: Personal and contextual factors.

Journal: *Journal of Marriage and Family*, May 2005, *67*, 448–460.

12240

Test Name: LIFE AND HOME SATISFACTION SCALES

Purpose: To measure satisfaction with life and with home and family.

Number of Items: 10

Format: Scales range from 1 (*very dissatisfied*) to 5 (*very satisfied*).

Reliability: Alpha coefficients were .90 (satisfaction with life) and .93 (satisfaction with home).

Validity: Correlations with other variables ranged from −.27 to .90.

Author: Sumer, H. C., and Knight, P. A.

Article: How do people with different attachment styles balance work and family? A personality perspective on work–family linkage.

Journal: *Journal of Applied Psychology*, August 2001, *86*, 653–663.

Related Research: Diener, E., et al. (1985). The Satisfaction with Life Scale. *Journal of Personality Assessment, 49*, 71–75.

12241

Test Name: LOVE-WITHDRAWAL SCALE

Purpose: To capture memories of parents' highly contingent style of expressing affection.

Number of Items: 20

Format: Includes two 10-item parallel forms; one assesses mothers, the other assesses fathers. Responses are made on 4-point scales ranging from 1 (*very unlike*) to 4 (*very like*). An example is given.

Reliability: Test–retest (2 weeks) reliabilities were .83 and .94. Alpha coefficients were .90 and .91.

Author: Scott, A. B., and Mallinckrodt, B.

Article: Parental emotional support, science self-efficacy, and choice of science major in undergraduate women.

Journal: *The Career Development Quarterly*, March 2005, *53*, 263–273.

Related Research: Swanson, L. B., & Mallinckrodt, B. (2001). Family environment, love withdrawal, childhood sexual abuse, and adult attachment. *Psychotherapy Research, 11*, 455–472.

12242

Test Name: LUM EMOTIONAL AVAILABILITY OF PARENT SCALE

Purpose: To measure parental emotional availability.

Number of Items: 15

Format: Scales range from 1 (*never*) to 6 (*always*). All items are presented.

Reliability: Test–retest reliabilities ranged from .85 to .92 (4 to 16 days). Alpha coefficients ranged from .93 to .97.

Validity: Correlations with other variables ranged from −.62 to .88.

Author: Lum, J. J., and Phares, V.

Article: Assessing the emotional availability of parents.

Journal: *Journal of Psychopathology and Behavioral Assessment*, September 2005, *27*, 211–226.

12243

Test Name: MARITAL ADJUSTMENT SCALE

Purpose: To measure marital satisfaction.

Number of Items: 16

Format: Six-point scales anchored by *always agree* and *always disagree*. A sample item is presented.

Reliability: Alpha was .93.

Validity: Correlations with other variables ranged from .00 to .34.

Author: Goldman, B. M., et al.

Article: Goal-directedness and personal identity as correlates of life outcomes.

Journal: *Psychological Reports*, August 2002, *91*, 153–166.

Related Research: Heath, D. H. (1991). *Fulfilling lives: Paths to maturity and success.* San Francisco: Jossey-Bass.

12244

Test Name: MARITAL AGGRANDIZEMENT SCALE

Purpose: To measure biased responding in married couples.

Number of Items: 18

Format: Seven-point Likert scales are used. Sample items are presented. Scoring procedures are described.

Reliability: Alpha coefficients ranged from .82 to .84.

Validity: The comparative fit index was .95 indicating that a single-factor model is tenable for men and women.

Author: O'Rourke, N., and Cappeliez, P.

Article: Marital satisfaction and marital aggrandizement among older adults: Analysis of gender invariance.

Journal: *Measurement and Evaluation in Counseling and Development*, July 2001, *34*, 66–79.

12245

Test Name: MARITAL COMPARISON LEVEL INDEX— CHINESE VERSION

Purpose: To measure the discrepancy between marital experience and expectations.

Number of Items: 43

Format: Seven-point scales are used. All items are presented in English.

Reliability: Coefficient alpha was .97.

Author: Chan, Y.-T., and Rudowicz, E.

Article: The Chinese version of the Marital Comparison Level Index revisited.

Journal: *Psychological Reports*, December 2002, *91*, Part 2, 1143–1147.

Related Research: Sabatelli, R. M. (1984). The Marital Comparison Level Index: A measure for assessing outcomes relative to expectations. *Journal of Marriage and the Family*, *46*, 651–662.

12246

Test Name: MARITAL COPING INVENTORY

Purpose: To measure marital coping as Conflict, Introspective Self-Blame, Avoidance, Self-Interest, and Positive Approach.

Number of Items: 64

Format: Five-point scales are used. Sample items are presented.

Reliability: Alpha coefficients ranged from .80 to .93 across subscales.

Author: Haring, M., et al.

Article: Perfectionism, coping, and quality of intimate relationships.

Journal: *Journal of Marriage and Family*, February 2003, *65*, 143–158.

Related Research: Bowman, M. L. (1990). Coping efforts and marital satisfaction: Measuring marital coping and its correlates. *Journal of Marriage and the Family*, *52*, 463–474.

12247

Test Name: MARITAL HAPPINESS AND CONFLICTS SCALE

Purpose: To measure marital happiness.

Number of Items: 15

Format: Scales range from 1 (*not very happy*) to 3 (*very happy*) or from *often* to *never*.

Reliability: Alphas were .87 (happiness) and .54 (conflict).

Author: Rogers, S. J.

Article: Dollars, dependency, and divorce: Four perspectives on the role of wives' income.

Journal: *Journal of Marriage and Family,* February 2004, *66,* 59–74.

Related Research: Johnson, D. R., et al. (1986). Dimensions of marital quality: Toward methodological and conceptual refinement. *Journal of Family Issues, 7,* 31–49.

12248

Test Name: MARITAL HAPPINESS SCALE

Purpose: To measure 10 types of marital satisfaction.

Number of Items: 10

Format: All items are described.

Reliability: Coefficient alpha was .90.

Validity: Correlations with perfectionism ranged from −.44 to .17.

Author: Haring, M., et al.

Article: Perfectionism, coping, and quality of intimate relationships.

Journal: *Journal of Marriage and Family,* February 2003, *65,* 143–158.

Related Research: Azrin, N., et al. (1973). Reciprocity counseling: A rapid learning-based procedure for marital counseling. *Behavior Research and Therapy, 11,* 365–382.

12249

Test Name: MARITAL LOVE AND CONFLICT SCALES

Purpose: To measure marital closeness and conflict.

Number of Items: 18

Format: Scales range from 1 (*not at all*) to 9 (*very much*). Sample items are presented.

Reliability: Alpha coefficients were .87 (husbands) and .91 (wives) for marital love and .76 (husbands) and .79 (wives) for marital conflict.

Author: Crouter, A. C., et al.

Article: Implications of overwork and overload for the quality of men's family relationships.

Journal: *Journal of Marriage and Family,* May 2001, *63,* 404–416.

Related Research: Braiker, H. B., & Kelley, H. H. (1979). Conflict in the development of close relationships. In R. L. Burgess & T. L. Huston (Eds.), *Social Exchange in Developing Relationships.* New York: Academic Press.

12250

Test Name: MARITAL PERSPECTIVE-TAKING SCALE

Purpose: To measure how well the respondent takes the point of view of the partner and how well the partner takes the respondent's perspective.

Number of Items: 8

Format: Scales range from 1 (*never*) to 5 (*often*).

Reliability: Alpha coefficients ranged from .74 to .80.

Author: Crouter, A. C., et al.

Article: Implications of overwork and overload for the quality of men's family relationships.

Journal: *Journal of Marriage and Family,* May 2001, *63,* 404–416.

Related Research: Stets, J. E. (1993). Control in dating relationships. *Journal of Marriage and Family, 55,* 673–685.

12251

Test Name: MARITAL PROBLEMS INVENTORY

Purpose: To measure the severity of marital problems.

Number of Items: 19

Format: Scales range from 1 (*not a problem*) to 11 (*major problem*).

Reliability: Alpha coefficients were .83 (husbands) and .85 (wives).

Author: Cohan, C. L., and Kleinbaum, S.

Article: Toward a greater understanding of the cohabitation effect: Premarital cohabitation and marital communication.

Journal: *Journal of Marriage and Family,* February 2002, *64,* 180–192.

Related Research: Geiss, S. L., & O'Leary, K. D. (1981). Therapist ratings of frequency and severity of marital problems: Implications for research. *Journal of Marital and Family Therapy, 7,* 515–520.

12252

Test Name: MARITAL PROBLEMS MEASURE

Purpose: To assess quality of marriage.

Number of Items: 19

Format: Includes marital problems and marital instability. Fourteen responses are in a yes–no format and five responses are made on a 4-point scale ranging from 1 (*never*) to 4 (*very often*).

Reliability: Alpha coefficients ranged from .73 to .86.

Author: Parke, R. D., et al.

Article: Economic stress, parenting, and child adjustment in Mexican American and European American families.

Journal: *Child Development,* November/December 2004, *75,* 1632–1656.

Related Research: Johnson, D. R., et al. (1986). Dimensions of marital quality: Towards methodological and conceptual refinement. *Journal of Family Issues, 7,* 31–49.

12253

Test Name: MARITAL QUALITY SCALE

Purpose: To assess marital quality.

Number of Items: 22

Format: Various scales are used. Sample items are presented.

Reliability: Coefficient alpha was .81 (husbands) and .82 (wives).

Validity: Correlations with other variables ranged from −.40 to .07. The correlation between husband and wife quality scores was .52.

Author: Booth, A., et al.

Article: Testosterone, marital quality, and role overload.

Journal: *Journal of Marriage and Family*, May 2005, *67*, 483–498.

12254

Test Name: MARITAL ROLE QUALITY

Purpose: To measure if specific features of a marriage are rewarding or a matter of concern.

Number of Items: 52

Format: Four-point scales are used.

Reliability: Alpha coefficients ranged from .89 to .93.

Author: Brennan, R. T., et al.

Article: When she earns more than he does: A longitudinal study of dual-earner couples.

Journal: *Journal of Marriage and Family*, February 2001, *63*, 168–182.

Related Research: Barnett, R. C., et al. (1993). Gender and the relationship between job experiences and psychological distress: A study of dual-earner couples. *Journal of Personality and Social Psychology, 64,* 794–806.

12255

Test Name: MARITAL ROLE QUALITY SCALE

Purpose: To measure the rewards and concerns of marital relationships.

Number of Items: 15

Format: Four-point reward/concern scales are used.

Reliability: Alpha coefficients exceeded .87.

Author: Gareis, K. C., et al.

Article: Individual and crossover effects of work schedule fit: A within-couple analysis.

Journal: *Journal of Marriage and Family*, November 2003, *65*, 1041–1054.

Related Research: Hyde, J. S., & Plant, G. A. (1996). *Factor structure of Barnett's Partner Rewards and Concerns Scale.* Madison: University of Wisconsin.

12256

Test Name: MARITAL SATISFACTION SCALE

Purpose: To measure marital satisfaction.

Number of Items: 7

Format: Response categories ranged from *always dissatisfied* to *always satisfied*. All items are presented.

Reliability: Coefficient alpha was .79 (.81 for men and .78 for women).

Validity: Correlations with other variables ranged from −.27 to .54.

Author: Stevens, D., et al.

Article: Working hard and hardly working: Domestic labor and marital satisfaction among dual-earner couples.

Journal: *Journal of Marriage and Family*, May 2001, *63*, 514–526.

Related Research: Spanier, G. H. (1976). Measuring dyadic

adjustment: New scales for assessing the quality of marriage. *Journal of Marriage and the Family, 38,* 15–28.

12257

Test Name: MARITAL SATISFACTION SUBSCALE

Purpose: To measure marital satisfaction.

Number of Items: 10

Format: Eight-point scales are used. Sample items are presented.

Reliability: Alpha coefficients ranged from .86 to .90.

Author: Kuijer, R. G., et al.

Article: Are equity concerns important in the intimate relationship when one partner has cancer?

Journal: *Social Psychology Quarterly*, September 2001, *64*, 267–282.

Related Research: Arrindell, W. A., et al. (1983). On the psychometric properties of the Maudsley Marital Questionnaire (MMQ): Evaluation of self-ratings in distressed and "normal" volunteer couples based on the Dutch version. *Personality and Individual Differences, 4,* 293–306.

12258

Test Name: MARITAL TRUST SCALE—JAPANESE VERSION

Purpose: To measure mothers' sense of trust from their partners and mothers' trust for their partners.

Number of Items: 8

Format: Scales range from 1 (*strongly disagree*) to 5 (*strongly agree*). Sample items are presented in English.

Reliability: Coefficient alpha was .83.

Author: Sakai, A.

Article: Parenting and marital trust in Japan.

Journal: *Psychological Reports,* April 2005, *96,* 515–526.

Related Research: Griffin, D. W., & Bartholomew, K. (1994). Models of the self and other: Fundamental dimensions underlying measures of adult attachment. *Journal of Personality and Social Psychology, 67,* 430–445.

12259

Test Name: MARITAL WELL-BEING SCALE

Purpose: To measure marital well-being.

Number of Items: 5

Format: All items are presented.

Reliability: Alpha coefficients exceeded .86.

Author: Goodwin, P. Y.

Article: African American and European American women's marital well-being.

Journal: *Journal of Marriage and Family,* August 2003, *65,* 550–560.

Related Research: Crohan, S. E., & Veroff, J. (1989). Dimensions of marital well-being among White and Black newlyweds. *Journal of Marriage and the Family, 51,* 373–383.

12260

Test Name: MARRIAGE TRUST SCALE

Purpose: To measure support and trust expected from marriage partner.

Number of Items: 18

Format: Scales range from 1 (*strongly disagree*) to 7 (*strongly agree*). A sample item is presented.

Reliability: The average coefficient alpha for husbands was .88 and for wives .89.

Validity: Correlations with other variables ranged from −.31 to .55.

Author: Kurdek, L. A.

Article: Predicting the timing of separation and marital satisfaction: An eight-year prospective longitudinal study.

Journal: *Journal of Marriage and Family,* February 2002, *64,* 163–179.

Related Research: Rempel, J. K., et al. (1985). Trust in close relationships. *Journal of Personality and Social Psychology, 49,* 95–112.

12261

Test Name: MATERNAL ACCEPTANCE–REJECTION QUESTIONNAIRE

Purpose: To measure adolescents' perceptions of two key components of the attachment relationship with the mother: acceptance and rejection.

Number of Items: 35

Format: Includes two scales: Warmth/Affection and Aggression/Hostility. Responses are made on a 4-point scale ranging from *almost never true* to *almost always true.*

Reliability: Coefficient alpha was .94.

Author: Cassidy, J., et al.

Article: Feedback seeking in children and adolescents: Associations with self-perceptions, attachment representations, and depression.

Journal: *Child Development,* March/April 2003, *74,* 612–628.

Related Research: Rohner, R. P. (1991). *Handbook for the study of parental acceptance and rejection.* Storrs: University of Connecticut, Center for the Study of Parental Acceptance and Rejection.

12262

Test Name: MATERNAL CHARACTERISTICS SCALE

Purpose: To rate mothers on observed patterns of maternal behavior and attitudes: Relatedness, Confidence, Impulse Control, and Verbal Accessibility.

Number of Items: 35

Format: Raters use a yes–no format. Sample items are presented.

Validity: Correlations with other variables ranged from −.67 to −.12.

Author: Shahar, G.

Article: Maternal personality and distress as predictors of child neglect.

Journal: *Journal of Research in Personality,* December 2001, *35,* 537–545.

Related Research: Polansky, N. A., et al. (1992). The Maternal Characteristics Scale: A cross validation. *Child Welfare, 71,* 271–280.

12263

Test Name: MATERNAL EFFICACY QUESTIONNAIRE

Purpose: To measure self-reported maternal self-efficacy.

Number of Items: 10

Format: Responses are made on a 4-point Likert scale.

Reliability: Alpha coefficients were .65 and .86.

Validity: Correlation with the Parenting Stress Index, Sense of Competence scale was .75.

Author: Huth-Bocks, A.-C., et al.

Article: The impact of maternal characteristics and contextual variables on infant–mother attachment.

Journal: *Child Development,* March/April 2004, *75,* 480–496.

Related Research: Teti, D. M., & Gelfand, D. M. (1991). Behavioral competence among mothers of infants in the first year: The mediational role of maternal self-efficacy. *Child Development, 62,* 918–929.

12264

Test Name: MATERNAL EMPATHY SCALE

Purpose: To assess maternal empathy.

Number of Items: 33

Format: Responses are made on a 4-point scale ranging from 1 (*strongly disagree*) to 4 (*strongly agree*).

Reliability: Coefficient alpha was .81

Author: Smith, M., and Walden, T.

Article: An exploration of African American preschool-aged children's behavioral regulation in emotionally arousing situations.

Journal: *Child Study Journal,* 2001, *31,* 13–43.

Related Research: Mehrabian, A., & Epstein, N. (1972). A measure of emotional empathy. *Journal of Personality, 40,* 525–543.

12265

Test Name: MATERNAL MONITORING SCALE

Purpose: To assess maternal monitoring of children's activities.

Number of Items: 17

Format: Scales range from 1 (*never*) to 4 (*always*). Sample items are presented.

Reliability: Coefficient alpha was .91.

Validity: Correlations with other variables ranged from –.25 to .43.

Author: Kotchick, B. A., et al.

Article: Predictors of parenting among African American single

mothers: Personal and contextual factors.

Journal: *Journal of Marriage and Family,* May 2005, *67,* 448–460.

12266

Test Name: MATERNAL NEGATIVITY TOWARD THE CHILD SCALE

Purpose: To measure maternal negativity toward the child.

Number of Items: 23

Format: Includes four scales: Frequency of Parent–Child Conflict, Parental Criticism and Nagging of the Child, Frequency of Different Types of Punitive Discipline Techniques, and Hostility. Responses are made on 4-, 5-, and 7-point scales.

Reliability: Alpha coefficients ranged from .57 to .86.

Author: Jenkins, J., et al.

Article: Mutual influence of marital conflict and children's behavior problems: Shared and nonshared family risks.

Journal: *Child Development,* January/February 2005, *76,* 24–39.

Related Research: Hetherington, E. M., & Chingempeel, W. G. (1992). Coping with marital transitions. *Monographs of the Society for Research in Child Development,* 57 (2–3, Serial No. 227).

12267

Test Name: MATERNAL PARENTING SCALES— JAPANESE VERSION

Purpose: To measure parenting stress and maladjusted parenting behavior.

Number of Items: 9

Format: Scales range from 1 (*strongly disagree*) to 5 (*strongly*

agree). All items are presented in English.

Reliability: Alpha coefficients ranged from .62 to .78.

Author: Sakai, A.

Article: Parenting and marital trust in Japan.

Journal: *Psychological Reports,* April 2005, *96,* 515–526.

Related Research: Sato, T., et al. (1994). Ikuji ni Karen suru sutoresa to sono yokuntsu jyuushoudo tono Karen [Rearing-related stress and depressive severity]. [*The Japanese Journal of Psychology*], *64,* 409–416.

12268

Test Name: MATERNAL REACTIONS TO CHILD'S DEVIANT BEHAVIOR SCALE

Purpose: To assess a mother's reaction to a child's behavior in specific circumstances.

Number of Items: 23

Format: Scales range from 1 (*strongly disagree*) to 7 (*strongly agree*). Sample items are presented.

Reliability: Alpha coefficients ranged from .61 to .83 across subscales.

Validity: Correlations with other variables ranged from –.11 to .25.

Author: Medora, N. P., et al.

Article: Attitudes toward parenting strategies, potential for child abuse, and parental satisfaction of ethnically diverse low-income U.S. mothers.

Journal: *The Journal of Social Psychology,* June 2001, *141,* 335–348.

Related Research: Rickard, K. M., et al. (1984). Parental expectations and childhood deviance in clinic-referred and non-clinic children. *Journal of Clinical Psychology, 13,* 179–186.

12269

Test Name: MATERNAL SEPARATION ANXIETY SCALE

Purpose: To assess a mother's sadness and guilt about separation from her infant and beliefs about the importance of maternal care.

Number of Items: 21

Format: Five-point scales range from 1 (*strongly disagree*) to 5 (*strongly agree*).

Reliability: Coefficient alpha was .93.

Author: Booth, C. L., et al.

Article: Child-care usage and mother–infant "quality time."

Journal: *Journal of Marriage and Family*, February 2002, *64*, 16–26.

Related Research: Hock E., et al. (1983). Mothers of infants: Attitudes toward employment and motherhood following birth of first child. *Journal of Marriage and Family, 46*, 425–431

12270

Test Name: MEASURE OF PARENTING STYLE

Purpose: To measure, by child self-report, mother and father dysfunctional behavior toward children in three dimensions: Overcontrol, Indifference, and Abuse.

Number of Items: 15

Format: Four-point scales range from 0 (*not true at all*) to 3 (*extremely true*).

Reliability: Alpha coefficients ranged from .76 to .93 across subscales.

Author: Ma, S. H., and Teasdale, J. D.

Article: Mindfulness-based cognitive therapy for depression: Replication and exploration of differential relapse prevention effects.

Journal: *Journal of Consulting and Clinical Psychology*, February 2004, *72*, 31–40.

Related Research: Parker, G., et al. (1997). The development of a refined measure of dysfunctional parenting and assessment of its relevance in patients with affective disorders. *Psychological Medicine, 27*, 1193–1203.

12271

Test Name: MEMORIES OF UPBRINGING SCALE

Purpose: To assess memories of parental rearing in four domains: Anxious Rearing, Overprotection, Emotional Warmth, and Rejection.

Number of Items: 40

Format: Sample items are presented.

Reliability: Alpha reliabilities ranged from .72 to .84 across subscales.

Validity: Correlations with a worry scale ranged from –.05 to .37.

Author: Muris, P.

Article: Parental rearing behaviors and worry of normal adolescents.

Journal: *Psychological Reports*, October 2002, *91*, 428–430.

Related Research: Castro, J., et al. (1993). Exploring the feasibility of assessing perceived parental rearing styles in Spanish children with the EMBU. *International Journal of Social Psychiatry, 39*, 47–57.

12272

Test Name: MONITORING AND CONTROL QUESTIONNAIRE

Purpose: To measure monitoring of children's activities.

Number of Items: 26

Format: Scales range from 1 (*never*) to 4 (*always*).

Reliability: Coefficient alpha was .91.

Validity: Correlations with other variables ranged from –.29 to .36.

Author: Dorsey, S., and Forehand, R.

Article: The relation of social capital to child psychosocial adjustment difficulties: The role of positive parenting and neighborhood dangerousness.

Journal: *Journal of Psychopathology and Behavioral Assessment*, March 2003, *25*, 11–23.

Related Research: Patterson, G. R., & Strouthamer-Loeber, M. (1984). The correlation of family management practices and delinquency. *Child Development, 55*, 1299–1307.

12273

Test Name: MONITORING AND CONTROL QUESTIONNAIRE

Purpose: To assess a mother's degree of monitoring a child's behavior.

Number of Items: 17

Format: Scales range from 1 (*never*) to 4 (*always*). Sample items are presented.

Reliability: Coefficient alpha was .86.

Author: Pelton, J., et al.

Article: The Moral Disengagement Scale: Extension with an American minority sample.

Journal: *Journal of Psychopathology and Behavioral Assessment*, March 2004, *26*, 31–39.

Related Research: Kotchick, B. A., et al. (1997). The impact of HIV infection on parenting in inner-city African American families. *Journal of Family Psychology, 11*, 447–461.

12274

Test Name: MOTHER–FATHER–PEER SCALE—ADAPTED

Purpose: To assess the adolescent's deidealization of mother.

Number of Items: 7

Format: Responses are made on a 5-point Likert scale. An example is given.

Reliability: Coefficient alpha was .82.

Author: Allen, J. P., et al.

Article: A secure base in adolescence: Markers of attachment security in the mother–adolescent relationship.

Journal: *Child Development*, January/February 2003, *74*, 292–307.

Related Research: Epstein, S. (1983). *Scoring and interpretation of the Mother–Father–Peer Scale.* Unpublished manuscript. Amherst, MA.

12275

Test Name: MOTHER, FATHER SUPPORT FOR SEXUAL ORIENTATION SCALES

Purpose: To assess mothers' and fathers' support for sexual orientation.

Number of Items: 18

Format: Includes two subscales: Mother and Father. Responses are made on a 7-point scale. Examples are given.

Reliability: Internal consistency estimates were .91 and .92.

Validity: Correlations with other variables ranged from −.45 to .30.

Author: Mohr, J. J., and Fassinger, R. E.

Article: Self-acceptance and self-disclosure of sexual orientation in lesbian, gay and bisexual adults: An attachment perspective.

Journal: *Journal of Counseling Psychology*, October 2003, *50*, 483–495.

Related Research: Mohr, J. J., & Fassinger, R. E. (1997, August). *Romantic attachments, parental attachment, and lesbian identity development.* Poster session presented at the 105th annual convention of the American Psychological Association, Chicago.

12276

Test Name: MOTHERS' PERCEIVED SOCIAL SUPPORT SCALE

Purpose: To measure mothers' perceived social support.

Number of Items: 3

Format: Responses are made on a 7-point semantic differential scale.

Reliability: Alpha coefficients were .88 and .75.

Author: Dybdahl, R.

Article: Children and mothers in war: An outcome study of a psychosocial intervention program.

Journal: *Child Development*, July/August 2001, *72*, 1214–1230.

Related Research: Flannery, R. B. (1990). Social support and psychological trauma: A methodological review. *Journal of Traumatic Stress, 3*, 593–611.

12277

Test Name: MULTIDIMENSIONAL WORK–FAMILY CONFLICT SCALE

Purpose: To assess work–family conflict.

Number of Items: 18

Format: Includes six subsections. Responses are made on a 5-point Likert scale ranging from 1 (*strongly disagree*) to 5 (*strongly agree*).

Reliability: Internal consistency reliabilities ranged from .70 to .88.

Validity: Correlations with other variables ranged from −.26 to .89 ($n = 164$).

Author: Bruck, C. S., and Allen, T. D.

Article: The relationship between the Big Five personality traits, negative affectivity, type A behavior, and work–family conflict.

Journal: *Journal of Vocational Behavior*, December 2003, *63*, 457–472.

Related Research: Carlson, D. S., et al. (2000). Construction and validation of a multidimensional measure of work–family conflict. *Journal of Vocational Behavior, 56*, 249–276.

12278

Test Name: MULTIGENERATIONAL INTERCONNECTEDNESS SCALE—ARABIC VERSION

Purpose: To assess emotional, financial, and functional connectedness between an adolescent and his or her family.

Number of Items: 31

Format: Seven-point rating scales indicate the frequency of an experience. All items are presented in English.

Reliability: Alpha coefficients ranged from .68 to .71.

Validity: No main or interactive effects on age or sex were found.

Author: Dwairy, M.

Article: Validation of a Multigenerational Interconnectedness Scale among Arab adolescents.

Journal: *Psychological Reports*, December 2003, *93*, Part 1, 697–704.

Related Research: Glavazzi, S. M., et al. (1999). Measurement of financial, functional, and psychological connectedness in families: Conceptual development and empirical use of a Multigenerational Interconnectedness Scale. *Psychological Reports, 84,* 1361–1371.

12279

Test Name: MY MEMORIES OF UPBRINGING QUESTIONNAIRE

Purpose: To measure aspects of parental behavior that could lead to anxiety.

Number of Items: 40

Format: Scales range from 1 (*no, never*) to 4 (*yes, most of the time*). All items are presented in English.

Reliability: Alpha coefficients ranged from .66 to .81.

Validity: Correlations with other variables ranged from −.08 to .33.

Author: Muris, P., et al.

Article: Assessment of anxious rearing behaviors with a modified version of "Egna Minnen Beträffande Uppfostran" questionnaire for children.

Journal: *Journal of Psychopathology and Behavioral Assessment,* December 2003, *25,* 229–237.

12280

Test Name: NETWORK OF RELATIONSHIP INVENTORY—REVISED

Purpose: To enable adolescents to rate the quality of their relationships with their parents.

Number of Items: 15

Format: Includes two dimensions: Perceptions of Positive Social Support and Perceptions of Negative Interactions. Responses

are made on a 5-point scale ranging from 1 (*little or none*) to 5 (*the most*).

Validity: Correlations with other variables ranged from −.33 to .52.

Author: Smetana, J. G., et al.

Article: African American late adolescents' relationships with parents: Developmental transitions and longitudinal patterns.

Journal: *Child Development,* May/June 2004, *75,* 932–947.

Related Research: Furman, W., & Buhrmester, D. (1992). Age and sex in perceptions of networks of personal relationships. *Child Development, 63,* 103–115.

12281

Test Name: NONJOB RESPONSIBILITIES SCALE

Purpose: To measure nonjob tasks.

Number of Items: 22

Format: Scales ranged from 1 (*not applicable*) to 5 (*mostly you*).

Reliability: Coefficient alpha was .79.

Validity: Correlations with other variables ranged from −.10 to .23.

Author: Major, V. S., et al.

Article: Work time, work interference with family, and psychological distress.

Journal: *Journal of Applied Psychology,* June 2002, *87,* 427–436.

Related Research: Broman, C. (1988). Household work and family life satisfaction of Blacks. *Journal of Marriage and Family, 50,* 743–748.

12282

Test Name: NURTURANT FATHERING SCALE

Purpose: To measure the characteristics of subject's relationship to his or her father.

Number of Items: 9

Format: Five-point rating scales are used. A sample item is presented.

Reliability: Coefficient alpha was .94.

Author: Schwartz, S. J., and Finley, G. E.

Article: Fathering in intact and divorced families: Ethnic differences in retrospective reports.

Journal: *Journal of Marriage and Family,* February 2005, *67,* 207–215.

Related Research: Finley, G. E., & Schwartz, S. J. (2004). The Father Involvement and Nurturant Fathering Scales: Retrospective measures for adolescent and adult children. *Educational and Psychological Measurement, 64,* 143–164.

12283

Test Name: NURTURANT/INVOLVED PARENTING SCALE

Purpose: To assess the quality of mother and father parenting by adolescent self-report.

Number of Items: 5

Format: Scales range from 1 (*strongly agree*) to 5 (*strongly disagree*). All items are presented.

Reliability: Coefficient alpha was .90.

Author: Wickrama, K. A. S., and Bryant, C. M.

Article: Community context of social resources and adolescent mental health.

Journal: *Journal of Marriage and Family,* November 2003, *65,* 850–866.

Related Research: Borowsky, I. W., et al. (2001). Adolescent suicide attempts: Risks and protectors. *Pediatrics, 107,* 485–493.

12284

Test Name: NURTURANT PARENTING SCALE

Purpose: To measure the frequency of actions of parents that are nurturing.

Number of Items: 18

Format: Scales range from 1 (*never*) to 5 (*always*). Sample items are presented.

Reliability: Alpha coefficients exceeded .70.

Validity: Correlations with other variables ranged from −.05 to .25.

Author: Murry, V. M., et al.

Article: Parental involvement promotes rural African American youths' self-pride and sexual self-concepts.

Journal: *Journal of Marriage and Family*, August 2005, *67*, 627–642.

12285

Test Name: O'LEARY–PORTER SCALE

Purpose: To assess child exposure to overt interparental hostility.

Number of Items: 9

Format: Responses are made on a 5-point scale ranging from 1 (*never*) to 5 (*very often*).

Reliability: Alpha coefficients were .75 and .80.

Author: Cummings, E. M., et al.

Article: Children's responses to everyday marital conflict tactics in the home.

Journal: *Child Development*, November/December 2003, *74*, 1918–1929.

Related Research: Porter, B., & O'Leary, K. D. (1980). Marital discord and child behavior problems. *Journal of Abnormal Child Psychology, 8,* 287–295.

12286

Test Name: O'LEARY–PORTER SCALE

Purpose: To measure frequency of adolescent exposure to overt and subtle forms of interparental discord.

Number of Items: 10

Format: Responses are made on a 5-point scale. An example is presented.

Reliability: Coefficient alpha was .87. Test–retest reliability was .96.

Author: Davies, P. T., and Windle, M.

Article: Interparental discord and adolescent adjustment trajectories: The potentiating and protective role of interpersonal attributes.

Journal: *Child Development*, July/August 2001, *72*, 1163–1178.

Related Research: Porter, B., & O'Leary, K. D. (1980). Marital discord and childhood behavior problems. *Journal of Abnormal Child Psychology, 8,* 287–295.

12287

Test Name: PARENT–ADOLESCENT CONFLICT SCALE

Purpose: To measure the frequency of parent–adolescent conflict.

Number of Items: 10

Reliability: Alpha coefficients ranged from .78 to .85.

Validity: Correlations with other variables ranged from −.28 to .43.

Author: Roosa, M. W., et al.

Article: Family and child characteristics linking neighborhood context and child externalizing behavior.

Journal: *Journal of Marriage and Family*, May 2005, *67*, 515–529.

Related Research: Rulz, S. Y., & Gonzales, N. A. (1998).

Multicultural, multidimensional assessment of parent–adolescent conflict. Poster presented at the Seventh Biennial Meeting of the Society for Research on Adolescence, San Diego, CA.

12288

Test Name: PARENT–ADOLESCENT CONFLICT SCALE

Purpose: To measure parent–adolescent conflict.

Number of Items: 11

Format: Scales range from 1 (*not at all*) to 6 (*several times a day*).

Reliability: Alpha coefficients ranged form .80 to .85.

Author: Crouter, A. C., et al.

Article: Implications of overwork and overload for the quality of men's family relationships.

Journal: *Journal of Marriage and Family*, May 2001, *63*, 404–416.

Related Research: Smetana, J. G. (1988). Concepts of self and social convention: Adolescents' and parents' reasoning about hypothetical and actual family conflicts. In M. R. Gunnor and W. H. Collins (Eds.), *Development During the Transition to Adolescence: Minnesota Symposia on Child Psychology, Vol. 21,* (pp. 79–122). Hillsdale, NJ: Erlbaum.

12289

Test Name: PARENT AND PEER ATTACHMENT INVENTORY—FRENCH VERSION

Purpose: To assess the degree of the adolescents' attachments to father and mother.

Number of Items: 14

Format: Includes three subscales: Trust, Communication, and Alienation. Responses are made on a 5-point scale ranging from 1 (*almost never or never*) to 5 (*almost always or always*). Examples are given.

Reliability: Internal consistency ranged from .75 to .91.

Author: Vignoli, E., et al.

Article: Career exploration in adolescents: The role of anxiety, attachment, and parenting style.

Journal: *Journal of Vocational Behavior*, October 2005, *67*, 153–168.

Related Research: Vignoli, E., & Mallet, P. (2004). Validation of a brief measure of adolescents' parent attachment based on Armsden and Greenberg's three-dimension model. *European Review of Applied Psychology*, *54*, 251–260.

12290

Test Name: PARENT ATTRIBUTION TEST

Purpose: To assess parents' attributions about the relative influence of self versus a child on caregiving outcomes.

Number of Items: 12

Format: Includes two subscales: Child Control Over Failure and Adult Control Over Failure. Responses are made on a 7-point scale ranging from *not at all important* to *very important*. Examples are given.

Reliability: Alpha coefficients ranged from .59 to .91.

Author: Guzell, J., and Vernon-Feagons, L.

Article: Parental perceived control over caregiving and its relationship to parent–infant interaction.

Journal: *Child Development*, January/February 2004, *75*, 134–146.

Related Research: Bugental, D. B., et al. (1998). Measuring parental

attributions: Conceptual and methodological issues. *Journal of Family Psychology*, *12*, 459–480.

12291

Test Name: PARENT–CHILD CLOSENESS SCALE

Purpose: To measure closeness between parents and adult children.

Number of Items: 4

Format: Scales range from 1 (*never*) to 5 (*very often*). A sample item is presented.

Reliability: Coefficient alpha was .66.

Validity: Correlations with other variables ranged from –.30 to .27.

Author: Pillemer, K., and Suitor, J. J.

Article: Explaining mothers' ambivalence toward their adult children.

Journal: *Journal of Marriage and Family*, August 2002, *64*, 602–613.

12292

Test Name: PARENT–CHILD DISCUSSION QUALITY SCALE

Purpose: To assess mother–child discussion quality.

Number of Items: 6

Format: Three topics are employed: school, religion, and prosocial behavior. Two 4-point scales are used.

Reliability: Coefficient alpha was .84.

Validity: Correlations with other variables ranged from –.26 to .36.

Author: Brody, G. H., et al.

Article: Longitudinal pathways to competence and psychological adjustment among African American children living in rural single-parent households.

Journal: *Child Development*, September/October 2002, *73*, 1505–1516.

Related Research: Brody, G. H., et al. (1998). Coparenting processes and child competence among rural African American families. In M. Lewis & C. Feiring (Eds.), *Families, risk, and competence.* (pp. 227–243). Mahwah, NJ: Erlbaum.

12293

Test Name: PARENT–CHILD DISCUSSION QUALITY SCALE

Purpose: To assess mother–child discussion quality.

Number of Items: 9

Format: Includes three areas: school, religion, and prosocial behavior. Responses are made on a 0 to 3 scale. Examples are given.

Reliability: Alpha coefficients exceeded .70.

Author: Brody, G. H., et al.

Article: Protective longitudinal paths linking child competence to behavioral problems among African American siblings.

Journal: *Child Development*, March/April 2004, *75*, 455–467.

Related Research: Brody, G. H., et al. (1998). Children's development of alcohol use norms: Contributions of parent and sibling norms, children's temperaments, and parent–child discussions. *Journal of Family Psychology*, *12*, 209–219.

12294

Test Name: PARENT–CHILD INTERPERSONAL STRESS SCALE

Purpose: To measure stress between parents and their adult children.

Number of Items: 3

Format: Scales range from 1 (*never*) to 5 (*very often*) and from 1 (*not at all tense and strained*) to 4 (*very tense and strained*). Sample items are presented.

Reliability: Coefficient alpha was .50.

Validity: Correlations with other variables ranged from −.16 to .52.

Author: Pillemer, K., and Suitor, J. J.

Article: Explaining mothers' ambivalence toward their adult children.

Journal: *Journal of Marriage and Family*, August 2002, *64*, 602–613.

12295

Test Name: PARENT–CHILD RELATIONSHIP SURVEY

Purpose: To assess warmth/support.

Number of Items: 36 (parents), 31 (children).

Format: Responses are made on a 5-point Likert scale.

Reliability: Alpha coefficients ranged from .85 to .92

Author: Feinberg, M., et al.

Article: Adolescent, parent, and observer perceptions of parenting: Genetic and environmental influences on shared and distinct perceptions.

Journal: *Child Development*, July/August 2001, *72*, 1266–1284.

Related Research: Hetherington, E. M., & Clingempeel, W. G. (1992). Coping with marital transitions: A family systems perspective. *Monographs of the Society for Research in Child Development, 57* (2–3, Serial No. 227).

12296

Test Name: PARENT DISCIPLINE BEHAVIOR INVENTORY— PARENT–CHILD DISAGREEMENT SCALE

Purpose: To measure parental conflict/negativity.

Number of Items: 42

Format: Responses are made on a 7-point Likert scale.

Reliability: Alpha coefficients ranged from .78 to .91.

Author: Feinberg, M., et al.

Article: Adolescent, parent, and observer perceptions of parenting: Genetic and environmental influences on shared and distinct perceptions.

Journal: *Child Development*, July/August 2001, *72*, 1266–1284.

Related Research: Hetherington, E. M., & Clingempeel, W. G. (1992). Coping with marital transitions: A family systems perspective. *Monographs of the Society for Research in Child Development, 57* (2–3, Serial No. 227).

12297

Test Name: PARENT DISCIPLINE BEHAVIOR INVENTORY— PUNITIVE SCALE

Purpose: To measure parental conflict/negativity.

Number of Items: 43

Format: Responses are made on a 7-point Likert scale.

Reliability: Alpha coefficients ranged from .89 to .91.

Author: Feinberg, M., et al.

Article: Adolescent, parent, and observer perceptions of parenting: Genetic and environmental influences on shared and distinct perceptions.

Journal: *Child Development*, July/August 2001, *72*, 1266–1284.

Related Research: Hetherington, E. M., & Clingempeel, W. G. (1992). Coping with marital transitions: A family systems perspective. *Monographs of the Society for Research in Child Development, 57* (2–3, Serial No. 227).

12298

Test Name: PARENT INVOLVEMENT SCALE

Purpose: To assess youth perceptions of the degree to which their parents or primary guardians were involved and interested in their lives.

Number of Items: 6

Format: Responses are made on a 4-point scale ranging from 1 (*never*) to 4 (*often*).

Reliability: Coefficient alpha was .80.

Validity: Correlations with other variables ranged from −.21 to .16.

Author: Pearce, M. J., et al.

Article: The protective effects of religiousness and parent involvement on the development of conduct problems among youth exposed to violence.

Journal: *Child Development*, November/December 2003, *74*, 1682–1696.

12299

Test Name: PARENT RELATIONSHIP QUALITY SCALE

Purpose: To assess perceptions of warmth, respect, and support from parents.

Number of Items: 6

Format: Scales range from 0 (*not at all or never true of me*) to 4 (*definitely or always true of me*).

Reliability: Coefficient alpha was .86.

Validity: Correlations with other variables ranged from −.19 to −.04.

Author: Fenzel, L. M.

Article: Multivariate analysis of predictors of heavy episodic drinking and drinking-related problems among college students.

Journal: *Journal of College Student Development*, March/April 2005, *46*, 126–140.

Related Research: Lamborn, S. D., et al. (1991). Patterns of competence and adjustment among adolescents from authoritative, authoritarian, indulgent, and neglectful families. *Child Development*, *62*, 1049–1065.

12300

Test Name: PARENT REPORTS OF INVOLVEMENT ACTIVITIES SCALE

Purpose: To assess how often parents get involved in their adolescents' activities at home and in school.

Number of Items: 24

Format: Includes two factors: parent involvement at home and in school. Responses are made on a 6-point scale ranging from 1 (*never*) to 6 (*once or more per week*). Examples are given.

Reliability: Alpha coefficients were .67 and .87.

Author: Deslandes, R., and Bertrand, R.

Article: Motivation of parent involvement in secondary-level schooling.

Journal: *The Journal of Educational Research*, January/February 2005, *98*, 164–175.

Related Research: Deslandes, R., & Cloutier, R. (2002). Adolescents' perception of parent–school involvement. *School Psychology International*, *23*, 220–232.

12301

Test Name: PARENT SUPPORT SCALE

Purpose: To measure parent support.

Number of Items: 10

Format: Includes two scales: Parent Involvement and Parent Supervision. Responses are made on 4-point scales.

Reliability: Coefficient alpha was .75.

Author: Brookmeyer, K. A., et al.

Article: Adolescents who witness community violence: Can parent support and prosocial cognitions protect them from committing violence?

Journal: *Child Development*, July/August 2005, *76*, 917–929.

Related Research: Henrich, C. C., et al. (2004). The association of violence exposure with academic achievement and feeling safe at school: Is it moderated by parent support? A prospective study. *Journal of Applied Developmental Psychology*, *25*, 327–348.

12302

Test Name: PARENT–YOUTH CONFLICT SCALE

Purpose: To measure the frequency of open disagreement with parents.

Number of Items: 10

Format: Scales range from 1 (*never*) to 6 (*almost every day*).

Reliability: Alpha coefficients ranged from .80 to .86.

Author: Krishnakumar, A., et al.

Article: Cross-ethnic equivalence of socialization measures in European American and African American youth.

Journal: *Journal of Marriage and Family*, August 2004, *66*, 809–820.

Related Research: Sweet, J., et al. (1992). *National survey of families and households 1988*. Madison: Center for Demography and Ecology, University of Wisconsin.

12303

Test Name: PARENTAL ACCEPTANCE SCALE

Purpose: To measure adolescent perceptions of parental acceptance.

Number of Items: 8

Format: Scales range from 1 (*almost never*) to 5 (*almost always*). A sample item is presented.

Reliability: Alpha coefficients ranged from .79 to .86.

Author: McHale, S. M., et al.

Article: Siblings' differential treatment in Mexican American families.

Journal: *Journal of Marriage and Family*, December 2005, *67*, 1259–1274.

Related Research: Schludermann, E., & Schludermann, S. (1970). Replicability of factors in children's reports of parent behavior (CRPBI). *Journal of Psychology*, *76*, 239–249.

12304

Test Name: PARENTAL AFFECTIVE INVOLVEMENT SCALE

Purpose: To measure parents' affective involvement in their child's vocational process through discussion during the last year in high school.

Number of Items: 10

Format: Responses are made on a 5-point scale ranging from 1 (*totally disagree*) to 5 (*totally agree*). An example is given.

Reliability: Coefficient alpha was .81.

Author: Ratelle, C. F., et al.

Article: Family correlates of trajectories of academic motivation during a school transition: A semiparametric group-based approach.

Journal: *Journal of Educational Psychology*, December 2004, *96*, 743–754.

Related Research: Barnes, H., & Olson, D. H. (1992). Parent–adolescent communication. In H. I. McCubbin, et al. (Eds.), *Family inventories* (2nd rev. ed., pp. 29–44). St. Paul, MN: Family Social Science.

12305

Test Name: PARENTAL ATTACHMENT QUESTIONNAIRE

Purpose: To assess attachment to a mother figure and a father figure.

Number of Items: 40

Format: Scales range from 1 (*not at all*) to 5 (*very much*). Sample items are presented.

Reliability: Alpha coefficients ranged from .93 to .96.

Validity: Correlations with other variables ranged from −.01 to .34.

Author: Hinderlie, H. H., and Kenny, M.

Article: Attachment, social support, and college adjustment among Black students at predominately White universities.

Journal: *Journal of College Student Development*, May/June 2002, *43*, 327–340.

Related Research: Kenny, M. E. (1987). The extent and function of parental attachment among first-year college students. *Journal of Youth and Adolescence, 16*, 17–27.

12306

Test Name: PARENTAL ATTACHMENT QUESTIONNAIRE

Purpose: To assess student perceptions of their parental relationship.

Number of Items: 70

Format: Includes three dimensions: Affect Quality of Relationship, Parental Fostering of Autonomy, and Parental Role in Providing Emotional Support.

Reliability: Internal consistency coefficients ranged from .84 to .93. Test–retest coefficients ranged from .85 to .94.

Author: Reese, R. J., et al.

Article: A reliability generalization study of select measures of adult attachment style.

Journal: *Educational and Psychological Measurement*, August 2002, *62*, 619–646.

Related Research: Kenny, M. E. (1987). The extent and function of parental attachment among first-year college students. *Journal of Youth and Adolescence, 16*, 17–27.

12307

Test Name: PARENTAL ATTACHMENT QUESTIONNAIRE

Purpose: To measure a young person's perceived level of secure attachment to his or her parents.

Number of Items: 55

Format: Includes three factors: affective quality of relationships, parents as facilitators of independence, and parents as source of support. Responses are made on a 5-point scale ranging from 1 (*not at all*) to 5 (*very much*). Sample items are given.

Reliability: Alpha coefficients ranged from .80 to .96. Test–retest (2 weeks) reliabilities ranged from .82 to .91.

Author: Scott, D. J., and Church, A. T.

Article: Separation/attachment theory and career decidedness and commitment: Effects of parental divorce

Journal: *Journal of Vocational Behavior*, June 2001, *58*, 328–347.

Related Research: Kenny, M. E. (1987). The extent and function of parental attachment among first-year college students. *Journal of Youth and Adolescence, 16*, 17–27.

12308

Test Name: PARENTAL ATTITUDE RESEARCH INSTRUMENT—AMSTERDAM VERSION

Purpose: To assess parental child-rearing attitudes: authoritarian control, promotion of autonomy, over protection, and self-complaints.

Number of Items: 15

Format: Four-point scales are anchored by 1 (*do not agree at all*) and 4 (*agree totally*). Sample items are presented in English.

Reliability: Alpha coefficients ranged from .57 to .83.

Author: ten Berge, M., et al.

Article: Childhood dental fear in relation to parental child-rearing attitudes.

Journal: *Psychological Reports*, February 2003, *92*, 43–50.

Related Research: Schaefer, E. S., & Bell, R. Q. (1958). Development of a parental attitude instrument. *Child Development, 29*, 339–361.

12309

Test Name: PARENTAL AUTHORITY QUESTIONNAIRE

Purpose: To assess parental authority or disciplinary practices from the child's point of view.

Number of Items: 30

Format: Includes three subscales: Authoritarian, Authoritative, and Permissive. Responses are made on a 5-point Likert scale ranging from 1 (*do not agree*) to 5 (*agree*).

Reliability: Test–retest (2 weeks) reliabilities ranged from .77 to .92.

Alpha coefficients ranged from .57 to .87.

Validity: Correlations with other variables ranged from −.46 to .40.

Author: Dwairy, M.

Article: Parenting styles and mental health of Arab gifted adolescents.

Journal: *Gifted Child Quarterly,* Fall 2004, *48,* 275–286.

Related Research: Buri, J. R. (1991). Parental Authority Questionnaire. *Journal of Personality and Social Assessment,* 57, 110–119.

12310

Test Name: PARENTAL AUTHORITY QUESTIONNAIRE—REVISED CHINESE VERSION

Purpose: To assess mothers' and fathers' authoritative child control methods by mother and father self-report.

Number of Items: 10

Format: Scales range from 1 (*strongly disagree*) to 5 (*strongly agree*). Sample items are presented in English.

Reliability: Alpha coefficients ranged from .74 to .80.

Author: Sim, T. N., and Ong, L. P.

Article: Parent physical punishment and child aggression in a Singapore Chinese preschool sample.

Journal: *Journal of Marriage and Family,* February 2005, *67,* 85–99.

Related Research: Buri, J. R. (1991). Parental Authority Questionnaire. *Journal of Personality Assessment,* 57, 110–119.

12311

Test Name: PARENTAL AUTONOMY SUPPORT SCALE

Purpose: To assess parents' support of their child's autonomy in making the decision to pursue a college education in science during the child's last year in high school.

Number of Items: 8

Format: Responses are made on a 5-point scale ranging from 1 (*totally disagree*) to 5 (*totally agree*). A sample item is given.

Reliability: Coefficient alpha was .87.

Author: Ratelle, C. F., et al.

Article: Family correlates of trajectories of academic motivation during a school transition: A semiparametric group-based approach.

Journal: *Journal of Educational Psychology,* December 2004, *96,* 743–754.

Related Research: Paulson, S. E., et al. (1994, October). *Constructs underlying students' perceptions of parents, teachers, and schools.* Paper presented at the annual meeting of the Midwestern Educational Research Association, Chicago. Robinson, C. C., et al. (1995, March). *Authoritative, authoritarian, and permissive parenting practices: Psychometric support for a new measure.* Paper presented at the biennial meeting of the Society for Research in Child Development, Indianapolis, IN.

12312

Test Name: PARENTAL BONDING INSTRUMENT

Purpose: To examine parental contributions to a parent–child bond.

Number of Items: 40

Format: Includes two dimensions: Care and Overprotection. Responses are made on a 4-point scale ranging from 1 (*not true*) to 4 (*true*). Sample items are presented.

Reliability: Alpha coefficients ranged from .71 to .89.

Validity: Correlations with other variables ranged from −.34 to .23.

Author: Overbeek, G., et al.

Article: Parental attachment and romantic relationships: Association with emotional disturbance during late adolescence.

Journal: *Journal of Counseling Psychology,* January 2003, *50,* 28–39.

Related Research: Parker, G., et al. (1979). A parental bonding instrument. *British Journal of Medical Psychology,* 52, 1–10.

12313

Test Name: PARENTAL BONDING INSTRUMENT

Purpose: To measure the constructs of care and overprotection.

Number of Items: 25

Format: There are two parallel forms. Responses are made on a 4-point Likert-type scale.

Reliability: Internal consistency coefficients ranged from .83 to .85. Test–retest coefficients ranged from .68 to .80.

Author: Reese, R. J., et al.

Article: A reliability generalization study of select measures of adult attachment style.

Journal: *Educational and Psychological Measurement,* August 2002, *62,* 619–646.

Related Research: Parker, G., et al. (1979). A parental bonding instrument. *British Journal of Medical Psychology,* 52, 1–10.

12314

Test Name: PARENTAL BONDING INSTRUMENT

Purpose: To measure adults' memories of their parents'

emotional responsiveness and intrusive control.

Number of Items: 50

Format: Includes two separate 25 item parallel forms, one for mother and one for father. There is a Care Scale and an Overprotection Scale for each form. Responses are made on a 4-point scale ranging from 1 (*very unlike*) to 4 (*very like*).

Reliability: Test–retest (3 weeks) reliabilities were .63 and .76. Split-half reliabilities were .79 and .88. Alpha coefficients were .87 and .95.

Author: Scott, A. B., and Mallinckrodt, B.

Article: Parental emotional support, science self-efficacy, and choice of science major in undergraduate women.

Journal: *The Career Development Quarterly*, March 2005, *53*, 263–273.

Related Research: Parker, G., et al. (1979). A parental bonding instrument. *British Journal of Medical Psychology, 52*, 1–10.

12315

Test Name: PARENTAL CARE QUESTIONNAIRE

Purpose: To measure separation anxiety.

Number of Items: 21

Reliability: Coefficient alpha was .93.

Validity: Correlations with other variables ranged from −.30 to .23.

Author: Huston, A. C., and Aronson, S. R.

Article: Mothers' time with infant and time in employment as predictors of mother–child relationships and children's early development.

Journal: *Child Development*, March/April 2005, *76*, 467–482.

Related Research: DeMeis, D. K., et al. (1986). The balance of employment and motherhood: Longitudinal study of mothers' feelings about separation from their first-born infants. *Developmental Psychology, 22*, 627–632.

12316

Test Name: PARENTAL CAREGIVING STYLES SCALE

Purpose: To assess perceptions of childhood relationships with parents.

Number of Items: 3

Format: Includes three care giving styles: warm/responsive, cold/rejecting, and ambivalent/inconsistent. Responses are made separately for the mother and father on a 7-point scale ranging from 1 (*not at all like my parent*) to 7 (*very much like my parent*).

Reliability: Alpha coefficients were .70 and .74.

Validity: Correlations with other variables ranged from −.29 to .30.

Author: Mohr, J. J., and Fassinger, R. E.

Article: Self-acceptance and self-disclosure of sexual orientation in lesbian, gay and bisexual adults: An attachment perspective.

Journal: *Journal of Counseling Psychology*, October 2003, *50*, 482–495.

Related Research: Collins, N. L., & Read, S. J. (1990). Adult attachments, working models, and relationship quality in dating couples. *Journal of Personality and Social Psychology, 58*, 644–663.

12317

Test Name: PARENTAL CONTROL AND AUTONOMY SUPPORT SCALE

Purpose: To assess students' perceptions of their parents' attitudes toward career decisions.

Number of Items: 29

Format: Includes five subscales: Incompetence Feedback, Autonomy Supportive Behaviors, Controlling Behaviors, Involvement, and Informational Feedback. Responses are made on a 7-point scale ranging from 1 (*does not correspond at all*) to 7 (*corresponds completely*).

Reliability: Alpha coefficients ranged from .76 to .91.

Author: Guay, F., et al.

Article: Predicting career indecision: A self-determination theory perspective.

Journal: *Journal of Counseling Psychology*, April 2003, *50*, 165–177.

Related Research: Pelletier, L. G. (1992). *Construction et validation de l' Echelle des Perceptions du Style Interpersonal.* [Construction and validation of the Perceptions of the Interpersonal Style Scale]. Unpublished manuscript, University of Ottawa, Ontario, Canada.

12318

Test Name: PARENTAL CONTROL SCALE

Purpose: To assess parental control of adolescent behaviors.

Number of Items: 6

Format: All items are presented.

Reliability: Coefficient alpha was .67.

Author: Fletcher, A. C., et al.

Article: Parental influences on adolescent problem behavior: Revisiting Stattin and Kerr.

Journal: *Child Development*, May/June 2004, *75*, 781–796.

Related Research: Dornbusch, S., et al. (1985). Single parents, extended households, and the control of adolescents. *Child Development, 56,* 326–341.

12319

Test Name: PARENTAL CONTROL SCALE

Purpose: To measure perceived parental control recalled by respondents from childhood.

Number of Items: 13

Format: Response scales are anchored by 4 (*almost always true*) and 1 (*almost never true*).

Reliability: Coefficient alpha was .89.

Author: Khaleque, A.

Article: Perceived parental control in childhood and sexual preferences of adult offspring.

Journal: *Psychological Reports,* June 2003, *92,* Part 1, 755–756.

Related Research: Rohner, R. P. (1990). *Handbook for the study of parental acceptance and rejection.* Storrs, CT: Rohner Research.

12320

Test Name: PARENTAL CONTROL SCALE

Purpose: To assess parental monitoring, consistency of discipline, and positive reinforcement.

Number of Items: 14

Format: Response categories range from 1 (*never*) to 4 (*always*). Samples items are presented.

Reliability: Coefficient alpha was .75.

Validity: Correlations with other variables ranged from –.15 to .16.

Author: Simons R. L., et al.

Article: Community differences in the association between parenting practices and child conduct problems.

Journal: *Journal of Marriage and Family,* May 2002, *64,* 331–345.

Related Research: Conger, R. D., et al. (1992). A family process model of economic hardship and influences on adjustment of early adolescent boys. *Child Development, 63,* 526–541.

12321

Test Name: PARENTAL DISCIPLINE HARSHNESS QUESTIONNAIRE

Purpose: To measure harshness of parental discipline.

Number of Items: 6

Format: Responses are rated on a 6-point scale ranging from *I rarely or never do this* to *I usually do this.* Additional responses are made on a 5-point scale ranging from *a lot more* to *a lot less.*

Reliability: Test–retest (1 year) reliability was .52.

Author: Asbury, K., et al.

Article: Nonshared environmental influences on individual differences in early behavioral development: A monozygotic twin differences study.

Journal: *Child Development,* May/June 2003, *74,* 933–943.

Related Research: Deater-Deckard, K., et al. (1998). Multiple risk factors in the development of externalizing behavior problems: Group and individual differences. *Development and Psychopathology, 10,* 469–493.

12322

Test Name: PARENTAL FEELINGS QUESTIONNAIRE— SHORTENED

Purpose: To assess negative parental feelings.

Number of Items: 7

Format: Responses are made on a 5-point scale ranging from *definitely true* to *definitely untrue.* Additional responses are made on a 5-point scale ranging from *a lot more* to *a lot less.*

Reliability: Test–retest (1 year) reliability was .50.

Author: Asbury, K., et al.

Article: Nonshared environmental influences on individual differences in early behavioral development: A monozygotic twin differences study.

Journal: *Child Development,* May/June 2003, *74,* 933–943.

Related Research: Deater-Deckard, K. (2000). Parenting and child behavioral adjustment in early childhood: A quantitative genetic approach to studying family processes. *Child Development, 71,* 468–484.

12323

Test Name: PARENTAL IDENTIFICATION QUESTIONNAIRE

Purpose: To assess parental identification.

Number of Items: 11

Format: Includes three types of items: to imitate mother/father's beliefs, to imitate mother/father's status, and to surpass mother/father. Responses are made on a 5-point scale ranging from 1 (*not like me at all*) to 5 (*very much like me*).

Reliability: Alpha coefficients ranged from .49 to .87.

Validity: Correlations with other variables ranged from –.27 to .64.

Author: Caldera, Y. M., et al.

Article: Intrapersonal, familial, and cultural factors in the commitment to a career choice of Mexican American and non-Hispanic White college women.

Journal: *Journal of Counseling Psychology,* July 2003, *50,* 309–323.

Related Research: Parsons, A. D., & Hubbs-Tait, L. (1996, March). *Career exploration of adolescent and young adult daughters: Comparison of socialization by mothers and fathers.* Poster presented at the biennial meeting of the Southwestern Society for Research in Human Development, Park City, UT.

12324

Test Name: PARENTAL INVOLVEMENT AND AUTONOMY SCALES

Purpose: To measure perceived connection and responsiveness in parent–child relationships and parental encouragement of autonomy and expression of individuality.

Number of Items: 18

Format: Four-point scales are used. Sample items are presented.

Reliability: Alpha coefficients ranged from .69 to .78.

Author: Sessa, F. M.

Article: The influence of perceived parenting on substance use during the transition to college: A comparison of male residential and commuter students.

Journal: *Journal of College Student Development,* January/February 2005, *46,* 62–74.

Related Research: Steinberg, L., et al. (1991). Authoritative parenting and adolescent adjustment across varied environmental niches. *Journal of Research on Adolescence, 1,* 19–36.

12325

Test Name: PARENTAL INVOLVEMENT AND MONITORING SCALE

Purpose: To measure parental involvement and monitoring.

Number of Items: 20

Format: Response scales range from 1 (*never*) to 5 (*always*). Sample items are presented. Parent and child formats are available.

Reliability: Alpha coefficients ranged from .73 to .75.

Author: Kimonis, E. R., et al.

Article: Callous-unemotional traits and delinquent peer affiliation.

Journal: *Journal of Consulting and Clinical Psychology,* December 2004, *72,* 956–966.

Related Research: Shelton, K. K., et al. (1996). The assessment of parenting practices in families of elementary school-aged children. *Journal of Clinical and Child Psychology, 25,* 317–327.

12326

Test Name: PARENTAL INVOLVEMENT SCALE

Purpose: To assess parental involvement.

Number of Items: 16

Format: Responses are made on a 3-point scale.

Reliability: Alpha coefficients ranged from .74 to .85.

Author: Luther, S. S., and Becker, B. E.

Article: Privileged but pressured? A study of affluent youth.

Journal: *Child Development,* September/October 2002, *73,* 1593–1610.

Related Research: Dornbusch, S. M. (1985). Single parents, extended households, and the control of adolescents. *Child Development, 56,* 326–341.

12327

Test Name: PARENTAL INVOLVEMENT SCALE

Purpose: To assess student perceptions of parental involvement in schooling.

Number of Items: 12

Format: Scales range from 1 (*never involved*) to 4 (*highly involved*).

Reliability: Coefficient alpha was .92.

Validity: Correlations with other variables ranged from –.42 to .36.

Author: Mji, A., and Mbinda, Z.

Article: Exploring high school science students' perceptions of parental involvement in their education.

Journal: *Psychological Reports,* August 2005, *97,* 325–336.

12328

Test Name: PARENTAL KNOWLEDGE MEASURE

Purpose: To provide an estimate of how much parents knew about their adolescents' daily experiences.

Number of Items: 9

Format: Responses are made on a 5-point scale ranging from 1 (*almost never*) to 5 (*almost always*). An example is given.

Reliability: Alpha coefficients were .83 and .85.

Author: Crouter, A. C., et al.

Article: How do parents learn about adolescents' experiences? Implications for parental knowledge and adolescent risky behavior.

Journal: *Child Development,* July/August 2005, *76,* 869–882.

Related Research: Stattin, H., & Kerr, M. (2000). Parental monitoring: A reinterpretation. *Child Development, 71,* 1072–1085.

12329

Test Name: PARENTAL KNOWLEDGE OF YOUTH ACTIVITIES SCALE

Purpose: To assess parent's knowledge of youth activities.

Number of Items: 5

Format: Scales range from 1 (*don't know*) to 3 (*know a lot*). Sample items are presented.

Reliability: Alpha coefficients ranged from .77 to .80.

Author: Krishnakumar, A., et al.

Article: Cross-ethnic equivalence of socialization measures in European American and African American youth.

Journal: *Journal of Marriage and Family*, August 2004, *66*, 809–820.

Related Research: Barker, B. K. (1996). Parental psychological control: Revisiting a neglected construct. *Child Development, 67*, 3296–3319.

12330

Test Name: PARENTAL MONITORING SCALE

Purpose: To measure the extent of parental monitoring by self-reports of adult children.

Number of Items: 6

Format: Scales range from 1 (*all the time*) to 5 (*never*). Sample items are described.

Reliability: Coefficient alpha was .69.

Author: Roche, K. M., et al.

Article: Establishing independence in low-income urban areas: The relationship to adolescent aggressive behavior.

Journal: *Journal of Marriage and Family*, August 2003, *65*, 668–680.

Related Research: Capaldi, D. M., & Patterson, G. R. (1989). *Psychometric properties of fourteen latent constructs from the Oregon Youth Study*. New York: Springer-Verlag.

12331

Test Name: PARENTAL MONITORING SCALE

Purpose: To measure perceptions of parental monitoring on the part of adolescents.

Number of Items: 10

Format: Three-point scales range from *not like* to *a lot alike*. Sample items are presented.

Reliability: Coefficient alpha was .67.

Author: Sessa, F. M.

Article: The influence of perceived parenting on substance use during the transition to college: A comparison of male residential and commuter students.

Journal: *Journal of College Student Development*, January/February 2005, *46*, 62–74.

Related Research: Schluderman, E., & Schluderman, S. (1970). Replicability of factors in children's report of parent behavior (CRPBI). *The Journal of Psychology, 76*, 239–249.

12332

Test Name: PARENTAL MONITORING SUBSCALE

Purpose: To assess efforts to obtain the types of information indicative of parental monitoring efforts.

Number of Items: 5

Format: Responses are made on a 3-point scale ranging from 1 (*don't try to know*) to 3 (*try a lot to know*). All items are presented.

Reliability: Coefficient alpha was .72.

Validity: Correlations with other variables ranged from –.11 to .45.

Author: Fletcher, A. C., et al.

Article: Parental influences on adolescent problem behavior: Revisiting Stattin and Kerr.

Journal: *Child Development*, May/June 2004, *75*, 781–796.

Related Research: Steinberg, L., et al. (1994). Parental monitoring and peer influences on adolescent substance use. *Pediatrics, 93*, 1060–1063.

12333

Test Name: PARENTAL NURTURANCE SCALE

Purpose: To assess listening to and sharing feelings and experiences with one's children.

Number of Items: 13

Format: Scales range from 1 (*not at all*) to 4 (*very much*).

Reliability: Coefficient alpha was .83.

Author: Oyserman, D., et al.

Article: Positive parenting among African American mothers with a serious mental illness.

Journal: *Journal of Marriage and Family*, February 2002, *64*, 65–77.

Related Research: Rickel, A., & Biasatti, L. (1982). Modification of the Black Child Rearing Practice Report. *Journal of Clinical Psychology, 38*, 129–134.

12334

Test Name: PARENTAL OVERLOAD SCALE

Purpose: To measure the extent of parental obligations.

Number of Items: 5

Format: Scales range from 1 (*never*) to 5 (*always*). Sample items are presented.

Reliability: Coefficient alpha was .83.

Validity: Correlations with other variables ranged from –.19 to .25.

Author: Aryee, S., et al.

Article: Rhythms of life: Antecedents and outcomes of work–family balance in employed parents.

Journal: *Journal of Applied Psychology*, January 2005, *90*, 132–146.

Related Research: Aryee, S., et al. (1999). Role stressors, interrole conflict, and well-being: The moderating influence of spousal support and coping behaviors among employed parents in Hong Kong. *Journal of Vocational Behavior, 54*, 259–278.

12335

Test Name: PARENTAL OVERPROTECTION SCALE

Purpose: To measure acceptance, rejection, control, enforcement, lax discipline, enforcement, and hostile control.

Number of Items: 49

Format: A three-point Likert scale is used. Sample items are presented.

Reliability: Alpha coefficients ranged from .61 to .69.

Validity: Correlations with other variables ranged from −.42 to .39.

Author: Holmbeck, G. N., et al.

Article: Observed and perceived parental overprotection in relation to psychosocial adjustment in preadolescents with a physical disability: The mediational role of behavioral autonomy.

Journal: *Journal of Consulting and Clinical Psychology*, February 2002, *70*, 96–110.

Related Research: Schwartz, J. C., et al. (1985). Assessing child rearing behaviors: A comparison of ratings made by mother, father, child, and sibling on the CRPBI. *Child Development, 56*, 462–479. Parker, G., et al. (1979). A parental bonding instrument. *British Journal of Medical Psychology, 52*, 1–10.

12336

Test Name: PARENTAL PERCEIVED ACADEMIC EFFICACY—SUBSCALE

Purpose: To measure parents' beliefs in their efficacy to promote their children's intellectual development.

Number of Items: 8

Format: Responses are made on 5-point scales.

Reliability: Coefficient alpha was .87.

Author: Bandura, A., et al.

Article: Self-efficacy beliefs as shapers of children's aspirations and career trajectories.

Journal: *Child Development*, January/February 2001, *72*, 187–206.

Related Research: Bandura, A. (1990). Reflections on nonability determinants of competence. In R. J. Sternberg & J. Kolligian, Jr. (Eds.), *Competence considered* (pp. 161–191). Cambridge, England: Cambridge University Press.

12337

Test Name: PARENTAL PRACTICES QUESTIONNAIRE

Purpose: To measure hostile parenting.

Number of Items: 58

Format: Includes two subscales: Hostile/Rejecting and Passive/Inconsistent.

Reliability: Alpha coefficients ranged from .72 to .89.

Author: Parke, R. D., et al.

Article: Economic stress, parenting, and child adjustment in Mexican American and European American families.

Journal: *Child Development*, November/December 2004, *75*, 1632–1656.

Related Research: Schaefer, E. S. (1965). Children's report of parental behavior: An inventory. *Child Development, 36*, 413–424.

12338

Test Name: PARENTAL RESPONSIBILITY SCALE

Purpose: To assess the amount of child care in which mothers and fathers take responsibility.

Number of Items: 14

Format: Scales range from 1 (*mother almost always*) to 5 (*father almost always*).

Reliability: Alpha coefficients were .77 (mothers) and .79 (fathers).

Author: McBride, B. A., et al.

Article: Child characteristics, parenting stress, and parental involvement: Fathers vs. mothers.

Journal: *Journal of Marriage and Family*, November 2002, *64*, 988–1101.

Related Research: McBride, B. A., & Mills, G. (1993). A comparison of mother and father involvement with their preschool age children. *Early Childhood Research Quarterly, 12*, 173–197.

12339

Test Name: PARENTAL SATISFACTION SCALE

Purpose: To measure the enjoyment of parenthood.

Number of Items: 4

Format: Scales range from 1 (*strongly agree*) and 4 (*strongly disagree*). All items are presented.

Reliability: Coefficient alpha was .85.

Validity: Correlations with other variables ranged from −.04 to .26.

Author: Medora, N. P., et al.

Article: Attitudes toward parenting strategies, potential for child abuse, and parental satisfaction of ethnically diverse low-income U.S. mothers.

Journal: *The Journal of Social Psychology*, June 2001, *141*, 335–348.

Related Research: Medora, N. P., et al. (1996). Parenting strategies of low-income African-American, Latino-American, Anglo-American, and Asian-American mothers. *Family Science Review, 9*, 107–122.

12340

Test Name: PARENTAL SOCIALIZATION QUESTIONNAIRE

Purpose: To measure parental socialization.

Number of Items: 18

Format: Responses are made on a 5-point scale ranging from 1 (*not at all characteristic of mother/father*) to 5 (*very characteristic of mother/father*).

Reliability: Alpha coefficients ranged from .90 to .98.

Validity: Correlations with other variables ranged from −.16 to .67.

Author: Caldera, Y. M., et al.

Article: Intrapersonal, familial, and cultural factors in the commitment to a career choice of Mexican American and non-Hispanic white college women.

Journal: *Journal of Counseling Psychology*, July 2003, *50*, 309–323.

Related Research: Parsons, A. D., & Hubbs-Tait, L. (1996, March). *Career exploration of adolescent and young adult daughters: Comparison of socialization by mothers and fathers.* Poster presented at the biennial meeting of the Southwestern Society for Research in Human Development, Park City, UT.

12341

Test Name: PARENTAL SUPPORT SCALE

Purpose: To measure the degree to which individuals perceive their parents as supportive of them.

Number of Items: 11

Format: Five-point Likert scales are used. Paternal and maternal support scores are averaged to form a total score.

Reliability: Alpha coefficients ranged from .87 to .90.

Author: Merrill, L. L., et al.

Article: Predicting the impact of child sexual abuse on women: The role of abuse severity, parental support, and coping strategies.

Journal: *Journal of Consulting and Clinical Psychology*, December 2001, *69*, 992–1006.

Related Research: Fromuth, M. (1986). The relationship of childhood sexual abuse with later psychological and sexual adjustment in a sample of college women. *Child Abuse and Neglect, 4*, 265–273.

12342

Test Name: PARENTING ALLIANCE MEASURE

Purpose: To measure the degree to which parents believe they have a sound parenting relationship with their child's other parent.

Number of Items: 20

Reliability: Coefficient alpha was .96.

Validity: Correlations with other variables ranged from −.40 to .69.

Author: Hughes, F. M., et al.

Article: Predicting spouses' perceptions of their parenting alliance.

Journal: *Journal of Marriage and Family*, May 2004, *66*, 506–514.

Related Research: Abidin, R. R., & Brunner, J. F. (1995). Development of a parenting alliance inventory. *Journal of Clinical Child Psychology, 24*, 31–40.

12343

Test Name: PARENTING DIMENSION INVENTORY— SHORT FORM

Purpose: To assess parenting practices.

Number of Items: 26

Format: Includes four areas: nurturance, responsiveness, nonrestrictiveness, and consistency.

Reliability: Alpha coefficients ranged from .54 to .79.

Author: Robinson, N. M., et al.

Article: Family factors associated with high academic competence in former Head Start children at third grade.

Journal: *Gifted Child Quarterly*, Fall 2002, *46*, 278–290.

Related Research: Slater, M. A., & Power, T. G. (1987). Multidimensional assessment of parenting in single-parent families. In J. P. Vincent (Ed.), *Advances in family intervention, assessment, and theory* (pp. 197–228). Greenwich, CT: JAI Press.

12344

Test Name: PARENTING SCALE

Purpose: To assess how parents would respond to various discipline scenarios. Laxness, Over-Reactivity, and Verbosity are measured dimensions.

Number of Items: 30

Format: Seven-point scales range from a *parenting mistake* to *an adaptive parenting response*.

Reliability: Alpha coefficients ranged from the .63 to .83 across subscales. Total alpha was .84. Two week test–retest reliabilities ranged from .79 to .84.

Validity: Correlations with an ADHD scale ranged from .10 to .30.

Author: Collett, B. R., et al.

Article: Assessment of discipline styles among parents of preschool through school-age children.

Journal: *Journal of Psychopathology and Behavioral Assessment*, September 2001, *23*, 163–170.

Related Research: Arnold, D. S., et al. (1993). The Parenting Scale: A measure of dysfunctional parenting in discipline situations. *Psychological Assessment, 5*, 137–144.

12345

Test Name: PARENTING SENSE OF COMPETENCE SCALE

Purpose: To measure parenting satisfaction and sense of competence.

Number of Items: 8.

Format: Scales range from 1 (*not at all*) to 5 (*very much*).

Reliability: Coefficient alpha was .83.

Author: Oyserman, D., et al.

Article: Positive parenting among African American mothers with a serious mental illness.

Journal: *Journal of Marriage and Family*, February 2002, *64*, 65–77.

Related Research: Gibaud-Wallston, J., & Wandersman, L. P. (1978). *Development and utility of the Parenting Sense of Competence Scale.* Paper presented at the American Psychological Association, Toronto, Canada.

12346

Test Name: PARENTING STYLE INDEX

Purpose: To measure Acceptance or Involvement, Strictness or Supervision, and Psychological Autonomy.

Number of Items: 46

Format: Four-point scales are anchored by 1 (*strongly disagree*) and 4 (*strongly agree*). Fourteen items are anchored by 1 (*didn't know*) and 7 (*knew a lot*). Sample items are presented.

Reliability: Reliabilities ranged from .72 to .76.

Author: Joshi, A., et al.

Article: Parenting styles and academic achievement in college students.

Journal: *Psychological Reports*, December 2003, *93*, Part 1, 823–828.

Related Research: Steinberg, L., et al. (1994). Over-time changes in adjustment and competence among adolescents from authoritative, authoritarian, indulgent, and neglectful families. *Child Development, 65*, 754–770.

12347

Test Name: PARENTING STYLES FRENCH SELF-REPORT QUESTIONNAIRE

Purpose: To assess four parenting styles.

Number of Items: 29

Format: Includes four scales: Authoritative, Authoritarian, Permissive, and Neglectful. Responses are made on a 4-point scale ranging from 1 (*definitely wrong*) to 4 (*definitely right*). Examples are given.

Reliability: Internal consistencies ranged from .57 to .81.

Author: Vignoli, E., et al.

Article: Career exploration in adolescents: The role of anxiety, attachment, and parenting style.

Journal: *Journal of Vocational Behavior*, October 2005, *67*, 153–168.

Related Research: Bourcet, C. (1994). *Evaluation de soi, climat familial et adaptation scolaire à l'adolescence* [Self-evaluation, family climate and school adjustment in adolescence]. Unpublished doctoral dissertation, University of Paris V, France.

12348

Test Name: PARENTS' ROLE CONSTRUCTION SCALE

Purpose: To measure the extent to which parents believed that it is their responsibility to help the school educate their adolescent.

Number of Items: 10

Format: Includes behaviors that are parent focused, school focused, and mainly partnership focused in accordance with the adolescents' education. Responses are made on a 6-point Likert-type scale ranging from 1 (*disagree very strongly*) to 6 (*agree very strongly*). Examples are given.

Reliability: Coefficient alpha was .72.

Author: Deslandes, R., and Bertrand, R.

Article: Motivation of parent involvement in secondary-level schooling.

Journal: *Journal of Educational Research*, January/February 2005, *98*, 164–175.

Related Research: Reed, R. P., et al. (2000, April). *Parents' motivations for involvement in children's education: Testing a theoretical model.* Paper presented at the annual meeting of the American Educational Research Association, New Orleans, LA.

12349

Test Name: PERCEIVED FAIRNESS OF WORK/FAMILY BENEFITS SCALE

Purpose: To assess perceived fairness of work/family benefits.

Number of Items: 10

Format: Responses are made on a 5-point Likert scale ranging from *strongly disagree* to *strongly agree*. All items are presented.

Reliability: Internal consistency was .80.

Validity: Correlations with other variables ranged from –.26 to .20.

Author: Parker, L., and Allen, T. D.

Article: Work/family benefits: Variables related to employees' fairness perceptions.

Journal: *Journal of Vocation Behavior*, June 2001, *58*, 453–468.

Related Research: Grover, S. L. (1991). Predicting the perceived fairness of parental leave policies. *Journal of Applied Psychology, 76*, 247–255. Halpert, J. A., et al. (1993). Pregnancy as a source of bias in performance appraisals. *Journal of Organizational Behavior, 14*, 649–663. Higgins, C. A., & Duxbury, L. E. (1992). Work–family conflict: A comparison of dual-career and traditional-career men. *Journal of Organizational Behavior, 13*, 389–411.

12350

Test Name: PERCEIVED FAMILY SUPPORT SCALE

Purpose: To measure perceived family support.

Number of Items: 10

Format: Scales range from 1 (*strongly disagree*) to 5 (*strongly agree*).

Reliability: Coefficient alpha was .86.

Author: Lim, H.-J., et al.

Article: Exercise, pain, perceived family support, and quality of life in Korean patients with ankylosing spondylitis.

Journal: *Psychological Reports*, February 2005, *96*, 3–8.

Related Research: Kang, H. S. (1985). *Experimental study of the effects of reinforcement education for rehabilitation on hemiplegia patients' self-care activities.* Unpublished doctoral dissertation, Yonsei University, Seoul, South Korea.

12351

Test Name: PERCEIVED SOCIAL SUPPORT SCALE

Purpose: To assess social support provided by the family.

Number of Items: 20

Format: Response scales ranged from *generally false* to *generally true*. Sample items are presented.

Reliability: Internal consistency was .95.

Author: Windle, M., and Windle, R. C.

Article: Depressive symptoms and cigarette smoking among middle adolescents: Prospective associations and intrapersonal and interpersonal influences.

Journal: *Journal of Consulting and Clinical Psychology*, April 2001, *69*, 215–226.

Related Research: Windle, M., & Miller-Tutzauer, C. (1992). Confirmatory factor analysis and concurrent validity of the Perceived Social Support—Family Measure among adolescents. *Journal of Marriage and the Family, 54*, 777–787.

12352

Test Name: PERCEIVED SOCIAL SUPPORT SCALE—FAMILY

Purpose: To measure support from family.

Number of Items: 20

Format: A checklist format is used. An example is given.

Reliability: Test–retest (1 month) reliability was .83. Alpha coefficients were .90 and .91.

Validity: Correlations with other variables ranged from –.24 to .02.

Author: Castillo, L. G., et al.

Article: Acculturation, White marginalization, and family support as predictors of perceived distress in Mexican American female college students.

Journal: *Journal of Counseling Psychology*, April 2004, *51*, 151–157.

Related Research: Procidano, M. E., & Heller, K. (1983). Measure of perceived social support from friends and family: Three validation studies. *American Journal of Community Psychology, 11*, 1–24.

12353

Test Name: PERCEPTION OF EMOTION WORK SCALE

Purpose: To measure emotion work in a marriage.

Number of Items: 7

Format: Scales range from 1 (*partner much more*) to 5 (*I much more*). All items are presented.

Reliability: Alpha coefficients were .79 (men) to .69 (women).

Validity: Correlations with other variables ranged from –.50 to .35.

Author: Stevens, D., et al.

Article: Working hard and hardly working: Domestic labor and marital satisfaction among dual-earner couples.

Journal: *Journal of Marriage and Family*, May 2001, *63*, 514–526.

12354

Test Name: PERCEPTIONS OF ADULT ATTACHMENT QUESTIONNAIRE

Purpose: To assess mothers' attachment experiences.

Number of Items: 60

Format: Includes eight scales: Rejection, Love, Role-Reversal, Anger, Derogation, Forgiveness, Vulnerability, and No Memory. Responses are made on a 5-point Likert scale ranging from 1 (*strongly disagree*) to 5 (*strongly agree*).

Reliability: Alpha coefficients ranged from .49 to .94. Test–retest reliabilities ranged from .64 to .86.

Author: Huth-Bocks, A.-C., et al.

Article: The impact of maternal characteristics and contextual variables on infant–mother attachment.

Journal: *Child Development*, March/April 2004, *75*, 480–496.

Related Research: Lichtenstein, J., & Cassidy, J. (1991, April). The Inventory of Adult Attachment (INVAA): Validation of a new measure of adult attachment. Paper presented at the biennial meeting of the Society for Research in Child Development, Seattle, WA.

12355

Test Name: PERCEPTIONS OF CONTROL AND SUPPORT AT WORK SCALES

Purpose: To assess control and support at work.

Number of Items: 11

Format: Scales range from 1 (*not at all*) to 5 (*very much* or *absolutely*).

Reliability: Alpha reliabilities ranged from .79 to .88.

Validity: Correlations with other variables ranged from −.07 to .43.

Author: Maier, G. W., and Brunstein, J. C.

Article: The role of personal work goals in newcomers' job satisfaction and organizational commitment: A longitudinal analysis.

Journal: *Journal of Applied Psychology*, October 2001, *86*, 1034–1042.

12356

Test Name: PERSONAL CHARACTERISTICS SCALES

Purpose: To identify adolescents' reports of their own expressivity and parents' reports of children's openness to supervision.

Number of Items: 18

Format: Responses are made on 5-point scales. Sample items are given.

Reliability: Alpha coefficients ranged from .78 to .92.

Author: Crouter, A. C., et al.

Article: How do parents learn about adolescents' experiences? Implications for parental knowledge and adolescent risky behavior.

Journal: *Child Development*, July/August 2005, *76*, 869–882.

Related Research: Antill, J. K., et al. (1993). Measures of children's sex typing in middle childhood. *Australian Journal of Psychology*, *45*, 25–33.

12357

Test Name: PERSPECTIVE TAKING SCALE

Purpose: To measure the extent to which husbands and wives perceive that they are able to role-take with their spouses.

Number of Items: 5

Format: Scales range from 1 (*never*) to 5 (*very often*). All items are presented.

Reliability: Omega reliabilities ranged from .70 to .76.

Author: Cast, A. D., and Bird, S. R.

Article: Participation in household and paid labor: Effects on perceptions of role-taking ability.

Journal: *Social Psychology Quarterly*, June 2005, *68*, 143–159.

Related Research: Stets, J. E. (1993). Control in dating relationships. *Journal of Marriage and the Family*, *55*, 673–685.

12358

Test Name: PLANNING INVENTORY

Purpose: To measure the extent of multiple role planning.

Number of Items: 10

Format: Respondents check each item they discussed with their partner and seriously considered using. All items are presented.

Validity: Correlations with other variables ranged from −.33 to .63.

Author: Peake, A., and Harris, K. L.

Article: Young adults' attitude toward multiple role planning: The influence of gender, career traditionality, and marriage plans.

Journal: *Journal of Vocational Behavior*, June 2002, *60*, 405–421.

Related Research: Weitzman, L. M. (1994). Multiple-role realism: A theoretical framework for the process of planning to combine career and family roles. *Applied and Preventive Psychology*, *3*, 15–25.

12359

Test Name: PORTRAIT VALUES QUESTIONNAIRE—MODIFIED

Purpose: To measure nine values plus two security values for adolescents and their parents.

Number of Items: 40

Format: Each item is a short verbal portrait describing a person's goals, aspirations, or wishes that point implicitly to the importance of a single broad value. Responses are made on 6-point scales.

Reliability: Alpha coefficients ranged from .57 to .65.

Author: Knafo, A., and Schwartz, S. H.

Article: Parenting and adolescents' accuracy in perceiving parental values.

Journal: *Child Development*, March/April 2003, *74*, 595–611.

Related Research: Schwartz, S. H., et al. (2001). Extending the cross-cultural validity of the theory of basic human values with a different method of measurement. *Journal of Cross-Cultural Psychology, 32*, 519–542.

12360

Test Name: POSITIVE FEELINGS QUESTIONNAIRE

Purpose: To measure marital satisfaction.

Number of Items: 17

Format: Scales range from 1 (*extremely negative*) to 7 (*extremely positive*).

Reliability: Coefficient alpha was .94. Test–retest reliability was .92 (3 weeks).

Validity: Correlations with other marital satisfaction measures ranged from .40 to .70.

Author: O'Rourke, N., and Cappeliez, P.

Article: Marital satisfaction and marital aggrandizement among older adults: Analysis of gender invariance.

Journal: *Measurement and Evaluation in Counseling and Development*, July 2001, *34*, 66–79.

Related Research: O'Leary, K. D., et al. (1983). Assessment of positive feelings toward spouse. *Journal of Consulting and Clinical Psychology, 51*, 949–951.

12361

Test Name: POSITIVE RELATIONAL INVOLVEMENT SCALE

Purpose: To assess positive aspects of father–son relationships.

Number of Items: 12

Format: Scales range from 1 (*strongly disagree*) to 7 (*strongly agree*).

Reliability: Coefficient alpha was .90.

Author: Floyd, K., et al.

Article: Human affection exchange: VI. Further tests of reproductive probability as a predictor of men's affection with their adult sons.

Journal: *The Journal of Social Psychology*, April 2004, *144*, 191–206.

Related Research: Floyd, K., & Morman, M. T. (2000) Affection received from fathers as a predictor of men's affection with their own sons: Test of the modeling and compensation hypotheses. *Communication Monographs, 67*, 347–361.

12362

Test Name: POWER–PARTNER SCALE

Purpose: To assess perceptions of influence in relationships with partners.

Number of Items: 5

Reliability: Coefficient alpha was .71.

Validity: Correlations with other variables ranged from −.65 to .46.

Author: Hughes, F. M., et al.

Article: Predicting spouses' perceptions of their parenting alliance.

Journal: *Journal of Marriage and Family*, May 2004, *66*, 506–514.

Related Research: Daiuto, A., & Baucom, D. (1995). *The Relationship Dimensions Profile*. Unpublished manuscript, University of North Carolina, Chapel Hill.

12363

Test Name: PROBLEM-SOLVING CHECKLIST

Purpose: To measure mother–adolescent disagreements.

Number of Items: 27

Format: Scales range from 0 (*never*) to 4 (*all the time*). Sample items are presented.

Reliability: Alpha coefficients ranged from .88 to .92.

Author: Jones, C. J., and Trickett, E. J.

Article: Immigrant adolescents behaving as culture brokers: A study of families from the former Soviet Union.

Journal: *The Journal of Social Psychology*, August 2005, *145*, 405–427.

Related Research: Reuter, M. A., & Conger, R. D. (1995). Antecedents of parent–adolescent disagreements. *Journal of Marriage and the Family, 57*, 435–448.

12364

Test Name: PROVISION OF SOCIAL RELATIONS SCALE

Purpose: To measure perceived support from family and friends.

Number of Items: 15

Format: Scales range from 1 (*not at all like me*) to 5 (*very much like me*). Sample items are presented.

Reliability: Coefficient alpha was .85.

Validity: Correlations with other variables ranged from −.30 to .23.

Author: Kuther, T. L., and Timoshin, A.

Article: A comparison of social cognitive and psychosocial predictors of alcohol use by college students.

Journal: *Journal of College Student Development*, March/April 2003, *44*, 143–154.

Related Research: Turner, R. J., et al. (1983). Social support: Conceptualization, measurement, and implications for mental health. *Research in Community & Mental Health*, 3, 67–111.

12365

Test Name: PSYCHOLOGICAL CONTROL SCALE

Purpose: To assess psychological control

Number of Items: 7

Format: Responses are made on a 3-point scale ranging from 1 (*not like the parent*) to 3 (*a lot like the parent*).

Reliability: Alpha coefficients were .72 to .76.

Author: Smetana, J. G., and Daddis, C.

Article: Domain-specific antecedents of parental psychological control and monitoring: The role of parenting beliefs and practices.

Journal: *Child Development*, March/April 2002, *73*, 563–580.

Related Research: Dornbusch, S. M., et al. (1985). Single-parents, extended households, and control of adolescents. *Child Development*, 56, 326–341.

12366

Test Name: PSYCHOLOGICAL CONTROL SCALE—YOUTH SELF-REPORT

Purpose: To assess parent psychological control.

Number of Items: 8

Format: Likert-type scale. An example is presented.

Reliability: Coefficient alpha was .88.

Author: Davies, P. T., and Forman, E. M.

Article: Children's pattern of pressuring emotional security in the interparental subsystem.

Journal: *Child Development*, November/December 2002, *73*, 1880–1903.

Related Research: Barber, B. K. (1996). Parental psychological control: Revisiting a neglected construct. *Child Development*, 67, 3296–3319.

12367

Test Name: PSYCHOLOGICAL PRESENCE OF CHILD TO FATHER SCALE

Purpose: To assess the cognitive presence of a child to his or her father.

Number of Items: 8

Format: Scales range from 1 (*never*) to 5 (*always*). Sample items are presented.

Reliability: Coefficient alpha was .79.

Validity: Correlations with other variables ranged from .18 to .51.

Author: Pasley, K., et al.

Article: Effects of commitment and psychological centrality on fathering.

Journal: *Journal of Marriage and Family*, February 2004, *64*, 130–138.

Related Research: Ryan, C. M. (1991). *The prediction of fathers' child support compliance from the quality of the former spouse*

relationship and psychological presence. Unpublished doctoral dissertation, University of Tennessee, Knoxville.

12368

Test Name: PSYCHOLOGICAL SEPARATION INVENTORY

Purpose: To measure aspects of maternal and paternal separation.

Number of Items: 138

Format: Includes four subscales: Functional Independence, Emotional Independence, Attitudinal Independence, and Conflictual Independence. Responses are made on a 5-point scale ranging from 1 (*not at all true of me*) to 5 (*very much true of me*).

Reliability: Alpha coefficients ranged from .84 to .92. Test–retest (2 weeks) coefficients ranged from .49 to .96.

Author: Tokar, D. M., et al.

Article: Psychological separation, attachment security, vocational self-concepts crystallization, and career indecision: A structural equation analysis.

Journal: *Journal of Counseling Psychology*, January 2003, *50*, 3–19.

Related Research: Hoffman, J. A. (1984). Psychological separation of late adolescents from their parents. *Journal of Counseling Psychology*, *31*, 170–178.

12369

Test Name: QUALITY MARRIAGE INDEX

Purpose: To measure marital satisfaction.

Number of Items: 7

Format: Six items use a 7-point Likert scale. A sample item is presented. One item uses a 10-point scale.

Reliability: Coefficient alpha was .97.

Author: Sacco, W. P., and Phares, V.

Article: Partner appraisal and marital satisfaction: The role of self-esteem and depression.

Journal: *Journal of Marriage and Family*, May 2001, *63*, 504–513.

Related Research: Norton, R. (1983). Measuring marital quality: A critical look at the dependent variable. *Journal of Marriage and the Family, 45*, 141–151.

12370

Test Name: QUALITY OF MARRIAGE INDEX

Purpose: To measure marital satisfaction.

Number of Items: 5

Format: Scales range from 1 (*strongly disagree*) to 5 (*strongly agree*). A sample item is presented.

Reliability: Coefficient alpha was .94.

Validity: Correlations with other variables ranged from –.46 to .63.

Author: Heller, D., and Watson, D.

Article: The dynamic spillover of satisfaction between work and marriage: The role of time and mood.

Journal: *Journal of Applied Psychology*, November 2005, *90*, 1273–1279.

12371

Test Name: RAISING CHILDREN CHECKLIST—HARSH CONTROL

Purpose: To measure mother's harsh control methods.

Number of Items: 8

Format: Responses are made on a 4-point scale ranging from 1 (*definitely no*) to 4 (*definitely yes*). Sample items are given.

Reliability: Coefficient alpha was .69.

Author: NICHD Study of Early Child Care.

Article: Are child developmental outcomes related to before- and after-school care arrangements?

Journal: *Child Development*, January/February 2004, *75*, 280–295.

Related Research: Shumow, L., et al. (1998). Harsh, firm, and permissive parenting in low-income families: Relations to children's academic achievement and behavioral adjustment. *Journal of Family Issues, 19*, 483–507.

12372

Test Name: RELATIONSHIPS QUESTIONNAIRE

Purpose: To measure quality of the marital relationship.

Number of Items: 14

Format: Includes two scales: Love and Conflict. Responses are made on a 9-point scale. Examples are given.

Reliability: Alpha coefficients ranged from .71 to .94.

Author: Crouter, A. C., et al.

Article: How do parents learn about adolescents' experiences? Implications for parental knowledge and adolescent risky behavior.

Journal: *Child Development*, July/August 2005, *76*, 869–882.

Related Research: Braiker, H. B., & Kelly, H. H. (1979). Conflict in the development of close relationships. In R. Burgess & T. Huston (Eds.), *Social exchange in developing relationships* (pp. 135–168). New York: Academic Press.

12373

Test Name: RETROSPECTIVE FAMILY UNPREDICTABILITY SCALE

Purpose: To measure inconsistent discipline and nurturance.

Number of Items: 14

Format: Items are anchored by 1 (*not at all*) and 5 (*extremely*). A sample item is presented.

Reliability: Cronbach alpha was .91.

Validity: Correlations with other variables ranged from –.02 to .44.

Author: Ross, L. T., and Gill, J. L.

Article: Eating disorders: Relation with inconsistent discipline, anxiety, and drinking among college women.

Journal: *Psychological Reports*, August 2002, *91*, 289–298.

Related Research: Ross, L. T. (1999, March). *The Retrospective Family Unpredictability Scale.* Poster presented at the meeting of the Southeastern Psychological Association, Savannah, GA.

12374

Test Name: ROLE BALANCE SCALE

Purpose: To assess to what extent respondents can balance the demands placed upon them in their daily lives.

Number of Items: 4

Format: Response scales range from 1 (*strongly disagree*) to 5 (*strongly agree*). All items are presented.

Reliability: Alpha coefficients were .64 (wives) and .56 (husbands).

Validity: Correlations with other variables ranged from –.44 to .42.

Author: Marks, S. R., et al.

Article: Role balance among White married couples.

Journal: *Journal of Marriage and Family*, November 2001, *63*, 1083–1098.

Related Research: Marks, S. R., & MacDermid, S. M. (1996). Multiple roles and the self: A theory of role balance. *Journal of Marriage and the Family, 58,* 417–432.

12375

Test Name: ROLE CONFLICT SCALES

Purpose: To measure role conflict.

Number of Items: 17

Format: Includes three scales: Work-to-Family Conflict, Family-to-Work Conflict, and Work-to-School Conflict. Responses are made on a 5-point scale ranging from 1 (*strongly disagree*) to 5 (*strongly agree*). Examples are presented.

Reliability: Alpha coefficients ranged from .77 to .85.

Validity: Correlations with other variables ranged from –.08 to .21.

Author: Rau, B. L., and Hyland, M. M.

Article: Role conflict and flexible work arrangements: The effects on applicant attraction.

Journal: *Personnel Psychology,* Spring 2002, *55,* 111–136.

Related Research: Eagle, B. W., et al. (1997). Interrole conflicts and the permeability of work and family domains: Are there gender differences? *Journal of Vocational Behavior, 50,* 168–184.

12376

Test Name: ROLE IDENTITY SCALE

Purpose: To identify the degree of agreement between how one should behave as a spouse and how one's partner expects one to behave.

Number of Items: 11

Format: All items are presented along with scoring procedures.

Reliability: Omega reliability was .88.

Author: Stets, J., and Burke, P. J.

Article: Identity verification, control, and aggression in marriage.

Journal: *Social Psychology Quarterly,* June 2005, *68,* 160–178.

Related Research: Swann, W. B., Jr., et al. (1994). Authenticity and positivity strivings in marriage and courtship. *Journal of Personality and Social Psychology, 66,* 857–869.

12377

Test Name: ROLE OVERLOAD SCALE

Purpose: To measure the feeling of being overwhelmed by multiple commitments.

Number of Items: 13

Format: Response scales range from 1 (*strongly agree*) to 5 (*strongly disagree*). A sample item is presented.

Reliability: Coefficient alpha was .92.

Author: Crouter, A. C., et al.

Article: Implications of overwork and overload for the quality of men's family relationships.

Journal: *Journal of Marriage and Family,* May 2001, *63,* 404–416.

Related Research: Reilly, M. D. (1982). Working wives and convenience consumption. *Journal of Consumer Research, 8,* 407–418.

12378

Test Name: ROLE PERFORMANCE SCALE

Purpose: To assess frequency of involvement by fathers in child related activities.

Number of Items: 11

Format: Scales range from 1 (*not at all*) to 5 (*very much*).

Reliability: Coefficient alpha was .77.

Validity: Correlations with other variables ranged from .28 to .54.

Author: Pasley, K., et al.

Article: Effects of commitment and psychological centrality on fathering.

Journal: *Journal of Marriage and Family,* February 2004, *64,* 130–138.

Related Research: Ahrons, C. R. (1983). Predictors of parental involvement post divorce: Mothers' and fathers' perceptions. *Journal of Divorce, 6,* 55–69.

12379

Test Name: SATISFACTION WITH CHILDHOOD SCALE

Purpose: To ascertain participants' perceptions of family functioning quality.

Number of Items: 3

Format: Responses are made on 7-point scales. All items are presented.

Reliability: Coefficient alpha was .65.

Validity: Correlations with other variables ranged from –.14 to .36.

Author: Goodyear, R. K., et al.

Article: Pregnant Latina teenagers: Psychosocial and developmental determinants of how they select and perceive the men who father their children.

Journal: *Journal of Counseling Psychology,* April 2002, *49,* 187–201.

12380

Test Name: SCHEDULE FLEXIBILITY SCALE

Purpose: To measure how difficult it would be to do nonwork activity between 9 A.M. and 5 P.M.

Number of Items: 21

Format: Scales range from 1 (*very difficult*) to 6 (*very easy*). A sample item is presented.

Reliability: Coefficient alpha was .96.

Validity: Correlations with other variables ranged from –.40 to .13.

Author: Major, V. S., et al.

Article: Work time, work interference with family, and psychological distress.

Journal: *Journal of Applied Psychology*, June 2002, *87*, 427–436.

Related Research: Berman, L. (1997). *When flextime "works" and when it "fails": An in-depth analysis of alternatives to the nine-to-five work week.* Unpublished doctoral dissertation, University of Maryland, College Park.

12381

Test Name: SECURITY IN THE INTERPARENTAL SUBSYSTEM SCALE

Purpose: To assess how children perceive emotional security in the naturalistic context of interparental conflict.

Number of Items: 37

Format: Includes seven factors: emotional reactivity, behavioral dysregulation, avoidance, involvement, constructive family representations, destructive family representations, and conflict spillover representations. Responses are made on a 4-point scale ranging from 1 (*not at all true of me*) to 4 (*very true of me*). All items are presented.

Reliability: Alpha coefficients ranged from .52 to .89. Test–retest reliabilities ranged from .59 to .87.

Author: Davies, P. T., et al.

Article: Assessing children's emotional security in the interpersonal relationship: The

Security of the Interpersonal Systems Scales.

Journal: *Child Development*, March/April 2002, *73*, 544–562.

Related Research: Davies, P. T., & Cummings, E. M. (1998). Exploring children's emotional security as a mediator of the link between marital relations and child adjustment. *Child Development, 69*, 124–139.

12382

Test Name: SECURITY SCALE

Purpose: To assess children's perceptions of security in parent–child relationships.

Number of Items: 15

Format: Includes two forms: Mother and Father. Items are scored on a 4-point scale. An example is given.

Reliability: Alpha coefficients were .74 (mother form) and .81 (father form).

Validity: Correlations with other variables ranged from .05 to .42.

Author: Verschueren, K., and Marcoen, A.

Article: Perceptions of self and relationships with parents in aggressive and nonaggressive rejected children.

Journal: *Journal of School Psychology*, November/December 2002, *40*, 501–522.

Related Research: Kerns, K. A. et al. (1996). Peer relationships and preadolescents' perceptions of security in the child–mother relationship. *Developmental Psychology, 32*, 457–466.

12383

Test Name: SEX-TYPING SCALE FOR CHILDREN'S CHORES

Purpose: To assess sex-typing by parents.

Number of Items: 28

Format: Scales range from 1 (*boy*) to 7 (*girl*).

Reliability: Alpha coefficients ranged from .75 to .85 across subscales.

Validity: Correlations with other variables ranged from –.43 to .59.

Author: Kulik, L.

Article: The impact of family status on gender identity and on sex-role typing of household tasks in Israel.

Journal: *The Journal of Social Psychology*, June 2005, *145*, 299–316.

12384

Test Name: SEXUAL DOMINANCE SCALE

Purpose: To measure the degree to which feelings of power over one's partner motivate sexuality.

Number of Items: 8

Format: Scales range from 1 (*not at all important*) to 4 (*very important*).

Reliability: Alpha coefficients ranged from .86 to .88.

Author: Hall, G. C. N., et al.

Article: Ethnicity, culture, and sexual aggression: Risk and protective factors.

Journal: *Journal of Consulting and Clinical Psychology*, October 2005, *73*, 830–840.

Related Research: Malamuth, N. M., et al. (1995). Using the confluence model of sexual aggression to predict men's conflict with women: A 10-year follow-up study. *Journal of Personality and Social Psychology, 69*, 353–369.

12385

Test Name: SIBLING BEHAVIOR AND FEELINGS QUESTIONNAIRE—MODIFIED

Purpose: To measure children's feelings and behavior toward their siblings.

Number of Items: 20

Format: Includes two subscales: Positive Rapport and Conflict. Responses are made on a 3-point scale ranging from 1 (*not very often*) to 3 (*very often*). Examples are given.

Reliability: Alpha coefficients were .66 and .85.

Author: Howe, N., et al.

Article: "This is a bad dog, you know . . .": Constructing shared meanings during sibling pretend play.

Journal: *Child Development,* July/August 2005, *76,* 783–794.

Related Research: Mendelson, M. J., et al. (1994). Kindergartners' relationships with siblings, peers, and friends. *Merrill-Palmer Quarterly, 40,* 416–435.

12386

Test Name: SIBLING RELATIONSHIP INVENTORY— ADAPTED

Purpose: To rate conflict in the sibling relationship.

Number of Items: 5

Format: Responses are made on a 5-point scale ranging from 1 (*not at all*) to 5 (*very much*). An example is given.

Reliability: Alpha coefficients ranged from .75 to .80.

Author: Feinberg, M. E., et al.

Article: Sibling differentiation: Sibling and parent relationship trajectories in adolescence.

Journal: *Child Development,* September/October 2003, *74,* 1261–1274.

Related Research: Stocker, C. M., & McHale, S. M. (1992). Links between sibling and parent–child

relationships in early adolescence. *Journal of Personal and Social Relationships, 9,* 174–195.

12387

Test Name: SIBLING RELATIONSHIP QUESTIONNAIRE

Purpose: To describe one's relationship with one's closest-in-age sibling.

Number of Items: 39

Format: Includes four factors: warmth, relative status/power, conflicts, and rivalry.

Reliability: Alpha coefficients for the warmth and conflict factors were .92 and .83, respectively.

Author: Lockwood, R. L., et al.

Article: The impact of sibling warmth and conflict on children's social competence with peers.

Journal: *Child Study Journal,* 2001, *31,* 47–69.

Related Research: Furman, W., & Buhrmester, D. (1985). Children's perceptions of the qualities of sibling relationships. *Child Development, 56,* 448–461.

12388

Test Name: SIBLING RELATIONSHIP QUESTIONNAIRE

Purpose: To measure qualitative aspects of the sibling relationship: warmth, rivalry, status/power, and conflict.

Number of Items: 37

Format: Item response scales are anchored by 1 (*hardly at all*) and 5 (*extremely much*). Sample items are presented.

Reliability: Test–retest reliabilities ranged from .58 to .86.

Validity: Correlations with other variables ranged from −.59 to .85.

Author: Moser, R. P., and Jacob, T.

Article: Parental and sibling effects in adolescent outcomes.

Journal: *Psychological Reports,* October 2002, *91,* 463–479.

Related Research: Furman, W., & Buhrmester, D. (1985). Children's perceptions of the qualities of sibling relationships. *Child Development, 56,* 448–461.

12389

Test Name: SIBLING RELATIONSHIP WARMTH SCALE

Purpose: To measure warmth in the sibling relationship.

Number of Items: 8

Format: Responses are made on a 5-point scale ranging from 1 (*not at all*) to 5 (*very much*). An example is given.

Reliability: Alpha coefficients ranged from .78 to .82.

Author: Feinberg, M. E., et al.

Article: Sibling differentiation: Sibling and parent relationship trajectories in adolescence.

Journal: *Child Development,* September/October 2003, *74,* 1261–1274.

Related Research: Blyth, D., et al. (1982). Early adolescents' significant others: Grade and gender differences in perceived relationships with familial and nonfamilial adults and young people. *Journal of Youth and Adolescence, 11,* 425–450.

12390

Test Name: SOCIAL INTIMACY SCALE

Purpose: To assess perceived intimacy in relationships with a spouse and a same-sex friend.

Number of Items: 17

Format: Ten-point scales are used.

Reliability: Alpha coefficients ranged from .86 to .91. Test–retest reliability was .84 (2 months).

Author: Salas, D., and Ketzenberger, K. E.

Article: Associations of sex and type of relationship intimacy.

Journal: *Psychological Reports*, June 2004, *94*, Part 2, 1322–1324.

Related Research: Miller, R. S., & Lefcourt, H. M. (1983). Social intimacy: An important indicator of stressful life events. *American Journal of Community Psychology*, *11*, 127–139.

12391

Test Name: SOCIAL PROVISIONS SCALE—MODIFIED

Purpose: To assess students' perceived availability of family support.

Number of Items: 10

Format: Responses are made on a 5-point scale ranging from 1 (*strongly disagree*) to 5 (*strongly agree*). Sample items are presented.

Validity: Correlations with other variables ranged from −.22 to .46.

Author: Torres, J. B., and Solberg, V. S.

Article: Role of self-efficacy, stress, social integration, and family support in Latino college student persistence and health.

Journal: *Journal of Vocational Behavior*, August 2001, *59*, 53–63.

Related Research: Solberg, V. S., & Villareal, P. (1997). Examination of self-efficacy, social support, and stress as predictors of psychological and physical distress among Hispanic college students. *Hispanic Journal of Behavioral Sciences*, *19*, 182–201.

12392

Test Name: SOCIAL SUPPORT APPRAISALS SCALE

Purpose: To measure extended family support.

Number of Items: 8

Format: Scales range from 1 (*strongly agree*) to 4 (*strongly disagree*).

Reliability: Coefficient alpha was .82.

Validity: Correlations with other variables ranged from −.28 to .06.

Author: Shaffer, M. A., and Harrison, D. A.

Article: Forgotten partners of international assignments: Development and test of a model of spouse adjustment.

Journal: *Journal of Applied Psychology*, April 2001, *86*, 238–254.

Related Research: Vaux, A., et al. (1986). The Social Support Appraisals (SS-A) Scale: Studies of reliability and validity. *American Journal of Community Psychology*, *14*, 195–219.

12393

Test Name: SOCIAL SUPPORT SCALE

Purpose: To assess spousal and family support.

Number of Items: 12

Format: Scales range from 1 (*not at all*) to 4 (*very much*).

Reliability: Coefficient alpha was .85.

Author: Baltes, B. B., and Heydens-Gahir, H. A.

Article: Reduction of work–family conflict through the use of selection, organization, and compensation behaviors.

Journal: *Journal of Applied Psychology*, December 2003, *88*, 1005–1018.

Related Research: Sargent, L. D., & Terry, D. J. (2000). The moderating role of social support in Karasek's job strain model. *Work and Stress*, *14*, 245–261.

12394

Test Name: SOCIAL UNDERMINING SCALE

Purpose: To assess undermining behaviors of marital partners by spouse report.

Number of Items: 7

Format: Scales range from 1 (*never*) to 3 (*always*). Sample items are presented.

Reliability: Alpha coefficients ranged from .76 to .80.

Validity: Correlations with other variables ranged from −.02 to .60.

Author: Westman, M., et al.

Article: Crossover of marital dissatisfaction during military downsizing among Russian army officers and their spouses.

Journal: *Journal of Applied Psychology*, October 2004, *89*, 769–779.

Related Research: Vinokur, A., & van Ryn, M. (1993). Social support and undermining in close relationships: Their independent effects on mental health of unemployed persons. *Journal of Personality and Social Psychology*, *65*, 350–359.

12395

Test Name: SOURCES OF KNOWLEDGE SCALES

Purpose: To identify how parents acquire information about their child's activities, whereabouts, and companions.

Number of Items: 23

Format: Responses are made on 5-point scales ranging from 1 (*almost never*) to 5 (*almost always*). Examples are given.

Reliability: Alpha coefficients ranged from .66 to .85.

Author: Crouter, A. C., et al.

Article: How do parents learn about adolescents' experiences? Implications for parental knowledge and adolescent risky behavior.

Journal: *Child Development*, July/August 2005, *76*, 869–882.

Related Research: Stattin, H., & Kerr, M. (2000). Parental monitoring: A reinterpretation. *Child Development, 71*, 1072–1085.

12396

Test Name: SPOUSE ADJUSTMENT SCALE

Purpose: To measure cultural, interactive, and personal adjustment of expatriate spouses.

Number of Items: 12

Format: Scales range from 1 (*extremely unadjusted*) to 7 (*extremely adjusted*) or from 1 (*strongly disagree*) to 5 (*strongly agree*).

Reliability: Alpha coefficients ranged from .88 and .89 across subscales.

Validity: Correlations with other variables ranged from –.32 to .52.

Author: Shaffer, M. A., and Harrison, D. A.

Article: Forgotten partners of international assignments: Development and test of a model of spouse adjustment.

Journal: *Journal of Applied Psychology*, April 2001, *86*, 238–254.

Related Research: Black, J. S., & Stephens, G. K. (1989). The

influence of the spouse on American expatriate adjustment and intent to stay in Pacific Rim overseas assignments. *Journal of Management, 15*, 529–544.

12397

Test Name: SPOUSE RATING SCALE

Purpose: To assess the global evaluation of another person based on positive and negative personality traits.

Number of Items: 44

Format: Seven-point scales are used.

Reliability: Coefficient alpha was .94.

Author: Sacco, W. P., and Phares, V.

Article: Partner appraisal and marital satisfaction: The role of self-esteem and depression.

Journal: *Journal of Marriage and Family*, May 2001, *63*, 504–513.

Related Research: Sacco, W. P., et al. (1993). Attributional, perceptual, and affective responses to depressed and nondepressed marital partners. *Journal of Consulting and Clinical Psychology, 61*, 1076–1082.

12398

Test Name: STABILITY OF ACTIVITIES IN THE FAMILY ENVIRONMENT SCALE—REVISED

Purpose: To assess family stability during childhood.

Number of Items: 23

Format: Scales range from 0 (*not at all*) to 6 (*extremely or very much*). All items are presented.

Reliability: Alpha coefficients ranged from .84 to .89 across subscales.

Validity: Correlations with other variables ranged from –.22 to .66 across subscales.

Author: Israel, A. C., et al.

Article: A measure of the stability of activities in a family environment.

Journal: *Journal of Psychopathology and Behavioral Assessment*, June 2002, *24*, 85–95.

12399

Test Name: STRESSFUL FAMILY LIFE EVENTS SCALE

Purpose: To assess stressful family life events.

Number of Items: 37

Format: Responses are made on a 4-point scale ranging from 0 (*none*) to 3 (*a great deal*). Examples are given.

Reliability: Test–retest reliability was >.85.

Author: Kertes, D. A., and Gunnar, M. R.

Article: Evening activities as a potential confound in research on the adrenocortical system in children.

Journal: *Child Development*, January/February 2004, *75*, 193–204.

Related Research: Boyce, W. T., et al. (1995). Psychobiologic reactivity to stress and childhood respiratory illnesses: Results of two prospective studies. *Psychosomatic Medicine, 57*, 411–422.

12400

Test Name: SURVEY OF PERCEIVED ORGANIZATIONAL SUPPORT—SHORT VERSION

Purpose: To measure perceived organizational support.

Number of Items: 8

Format: Scales ranged from 1 (*strongly disagree*) to 7 (*strongly agree*). All items are presented.

Reliability: Coefficient alpha was .90.

Validity: Correlations with other variables ranged from −.31 to .65.

Author: Rhoades, L., et al.

Article: Affective commitment to the organization: The contribution of perceived organizational support.

Journal: *Journal of Applied Psychology,* October 2001, *86,* 825–836.

Related Research: Eisenberger, R., et al. (1997). Perceived organizational support, discretionary treatment, and job satisfaction. *Journal of Applied Psychology, 82,* 812–820.

12401

Test Name: SURVEY WORK–HOME INTERFERENCE NIJMEGEN SCALE—MODIFIED

Purpose: To measure the extent to which work is negatively influencing the home situation.

Number of Items: 3

Format: Responses are made on a 5-point scale ranging from 1 (*never*) to 5 (*always*). An example is given.

Reliability: Alpha coefficients ranged from .79 to .83.

Author: Demerouti, E., et al.

Article: The loss spiral of work pressure, work–home interference and exhaustion: Reciprocal relations in a three-wave study.

Journal: *Journal of Vocational Behavior,* February 2004, *64,* 131–149.

Related Research: Wagena, E., & Geurts, S. (2000). SWING: Ontwikkeling en validering van de 'Survey Werk-thuis Interferentie–Nijmegen' [SWING. Development and validation of the 'Survey Work–Home Interference

Nijmegen']. *Gedrag & Gezondheid, 28,* 138–158.

12402

Test Name: TEACHER-REPORT HOME–SCHOOL RELATIONSHIP QUESTIONNAIRE

Purpose: To assess parent involvement in education.

Number of Items: 20

Format: Includes three factors: alliance, general parent involvement, and teacher initiation. Examples are given.

Reliability: Alpha coefficients ranged from .66 to .93.

Author: Hughes, J. N., et al.

Article: Relationship influences on teachers' perceptions of academic competence in academically at-risk minority and majority first grade students.

Journal: *Journal of School Psychology,* October 2005, *43,* 303–320.

Related Research: Kohl, G. O., et al. (2000). Parent involvement in school conceptualizing multiple dimensions and their relations with family and demographic risk factors. *Journal of School Psychology, 38,* 501–523. Vickers, H. S., & Minke, K. M. (1995). Exploring parent–teacher relationships: Joining and communication to others. *School Psychology Quarterly, 10,* 133–150.

12403

Test Name: TODDLER CARE QUESTIONNAIRE

Purpose: To rate parents' self-efficacy in managing tasks related to raising young children.

Number of Items: 38

Format: A Likert format is used.

Reliability: Coefficient alpha was .96.

Author: Gross, D., et al.

Article: Parent training of toddlers in day care in low-income urban communities.

Journal: *Journal of Consulting and Clinical Psychology,* April 2003, *71,* 261–278.

Related Research: Gross, D., et al. (1995). A longitudinal study of maternal depression and preschool children's mental health. *Nursing Research, 44,* 96–101.

12404

Test Name: TRUST AND COMMUNICATION SUBSCALE

Purpose: To assess adolescents' perceptions of the responsiveness, accessibility, and warmth of their mothers.

Number of Items: 6

Format: Responses are made on a 5-point scale ranging from 1 (*never true*) to 5 (*always true*). An example is given.

Reliability: Coefficient alpha was .74.

Author: Coley, L., et al.

Article: Out-of-school care and problem behavior trajectories among low-income adolescents: Individual, family, and neighborhood characteristics as added risks.

Journal: *Child Development,* May/June 2004, *75,* 948–965.

Related Research: Armsden, G. C., & Greenberg, M. T. (1987). The Inventory of Parent and Peer Attachment: Individual differences and their relationship to psychological well-being in adolescence. *Journal of Youth and Adolescence, 16,* 427–454.

12405

Test Name: UTRECHT–GRONINGEN IDENTITY DEVELOPMENT SCALE

Purpose: To measure commitment to the partner.

Number of Items: 6

Format: Responses are made on a 5-point scale ranging from 1 (*completely untrue*) to 5 (*completely true*). An example is given.

Reliability: Alpha coefficients were .86 and .89.

Author: Overbeek, G., et al.

Article: Parental attachment and romantic relationships: Association with emotional disturbance during late adolescence.

Journal: *Journal of Counseling Psychology*, January 2003, *50*, 28–39.

Related Research: Meeus, W. (1996). Studies on identity development in adolescence: An overview of research and some new data. *Journal of Youth and Adolescence, 25*, 569–598.

12406

Test Name: WILLINGNESS TO GRANT AUTONOMY SCALE

Purpose: To measure parents' willingness to grant autonomy to adolescents.

Number of Items: 15

Format: Four-point scales range from 1 (*I want a lot more control*) to 4 (*I want my child to have to have a lot more control*).

Reliability: Coefficient alpha was .88.

Validity: Correlations with other variables ranged from −.37 to .40.

Author: Holmbeck, G. N., et al.

Article: Observed and perceived parental overprotection in relation to psychosocial adjustment in preadolescents with a physical disability: The mediational role of behavioral autonomy.

Journal: *Journal of Consulting and Clinical Psychology*, February 2002, *70*, 96–110.

12407

Test Name: WORK AND FAMILY IMPACT SCALE

Purpose: To measure the impact of work on family and family on work.

Number of Items: 10

Format: Item responses are anchored by 1 (*strongly disagree*) and 7 (*strongly agree*).

Reliability: Alpha was .90.

Validity: Correlations with other variables ranged from .11 to .25.

Author: Sightler, K. W., and Wilson, M. G.

Article: Correlates of the impostor phenomenon among undergraduate entrepreneurs.

Journal: *Psychological Reports*, June 2001, *88*, Part 1, 679–689.

Related Research: Netemeyer, R. G., et al. (1996). The Work–Family Conflict and Family–Work Conflict Scales. *Journal of Applied Psychology, 81*, 400–410.

12408

Test Name: WORK AND FAMILY ORIENTATION SCALE

Purpose: To measure work mastery and competitiveness.

Number of Items: 19

Format: Five-point agreement scales are used. Sample items are presented.

Reliability: Coefficient alpha was .81.

Author: Gable, S. L., et al.

Article: Evidence for bivariate systems: An empirical test of appetition and aversion across domains.

Journal: *Journal of Research in Personality*, October 2003, *37*, 349–372.

Related Research: Spence, J., & Helmrich, R. (1983). Achievement-related motives and behaviors. In J. Spence (Ed.), *Achievement and Achievement Motives: Psychological and Sociological Approaches* (pp. 10–74). San Francisco: Freeman.

12409

Test Name: WORK AND FAMILY SALIENCE SCALE

Purpose: To measure work and family role salience.

Number of Items: 12

Format: Sales range from 1 (*strongly disagree*) to 5 (*strongly agree*). Sample items are presented.

Reliability: Alpha coefficients ranged from .76 to .79.

Validity: Correlations with other variables ranged from −.16 to .27.

Author: Noor, N. M.

Article: Work–family conflict, work- and family-role salience, and women's well-being.

Journal: *The Journal of Social Psychology*, August 2004, *144*, 389–405.

12410

Test Name: WORK–FAMILY AND FAMILY–WORK CONFLICT SCALE

Purpose: To measure family-to-work and work-to-family conflict.

Number of Items: 10

Format: Includes two scales: family-to-work conflict and work-to-family conflict. Responses are made on a 7-point scale ranging from *strongly disagree* to *strongly agree*.

Reliability: Reliabilities ranged from .78 to .92.

Validity: Correlations with other variables ranged from −.53 to .25.

Author: Behson, S. J.

Article: Which dominates? The relative importance of work–family organizational support and general organizational context on employee outcomes.

Journal: *Journal of Vocational Behavior*, August 2002, *61*, 53–72.

Related Research: Netemeyer, R. G., et al. (1996). Development and validation of work–family and family–work conflict scales. *Journal of Applied Psychology, 81*, 400–410.

12411

Test Name: WORK/FAMILY BALANCE MEASURES

Purpose: To measure different facets of work/family balance.

Number of Items: 33

Format: Includes five scales: Role Conflict, Work Satisfaction, Home Satisfaction, Family Functioning, and Employee Citizenship.

Reliability: Alpha coefficients ranged from .78 to .91.

Validity: Correlations with other variables ranged from −.21 to .64.

Author: Clark, S. C.

Article: Work cultures and work/family balance.

Journal: *Journal of Vocational Behavior*, June 2001, *58*, 348–365.

12412

Test Name: WORK–FAMILY BALANCE SCALES

Purpose: To measure work–family conflict and facilitation.

Number of Items: 16

Format: Scales range from 1 (*never*) to 5 (*all the time*). Sample items are presented.

Reliability: Alpha coefficients ranged from .73 to .76 across subscales.

Validity: Correlations with other variables ranged from −.31 to .49.

Author: Aryee, S., et al.

Article: Rhythms of life: Antecedents and outcomes of work–family balance in employed parents.

Journal: *Journal of Applied Psychology*, January 2005, *90*, 132–146.

Related Research: Grzywacz, J. G., & Marks, N. F. (2000). Reconceptualizing the work–family interface: An ecological perspective on the correlates of positive and negative spillover between work and family. *Journal of Occupational Health Psychology, 5*, 111–126.

12413

Test Name: WORK–FAMILY CONFLICT AND SPOUSAL CONCERNS SCALES

Purpose: To measure work–family conflict and spousal concerns about work.

Number of Items: 10

Format: Frequency rating scales range from 1 (*never*) to 5 (*always*). Sample items are presented.

Reliability: Alpha coefficients were .83 (conflict) and .81 (concerns).

Author: Burke, R. J., and Mikkelsen, A.

Article: Benefits to police officers of having a spouse or partner in the profession of police officer.

Journal: *Psychological Reports*, October 2004, *95*, 514–516.

Related Research: Torgen, M., et al. (2001). *Ett harbart arbetsliv foralla aldrar*. Stockholm: Arbetstivsinstitutet.

12414

Test Name: WORK–FAMILY CONFLICT SCALE

Purpose: To measure to what extent work demands interfere with family-role demands.

Number of Items: 11

Format: Scales range from 1 (*strongly disagree*) to 5 (*strongly agree*). Sample items are presented.

Reliability: Coefficient alpha was .94.

Validity: Correlations with other variables ranged from −.23 to .63.

Author: Bolino, M. C., and Turnley, W. H.

Article: The personal costs of citizenship behavior: The relationship between individual initiative and role overload, job stress, and work–family conflict.

Journal: *Journal of Applied Psychology*, July 2005, *90*, 740–748.

Related Research: Carlson, D. S., et al. (2000). Construction and initial validation of a multidimensional measure of work–family conflict. *Journal of Vocational Behavior, 56*, 249–276.

12415

Test Name: WORK–FAMILY CONFLICT SCALE

Purpose: To assess work–family conflict.

Number of Items: 18

Format: Includes six subsections: Work-to-Family Conflict, and Family-to-Work Conflict, each under three dimensions of Time, Strain, and Behavior-Based. Responses are made on a 5-point scale ranging from 1 (*strongly disagree*) to 5 (*strongly agree*). Examples are presented.

Reliability: Alpha coefficients ranged from .76 to .89.

Validity: Correlations with variables ranged from −.43 to .20.

Author: Bruck, C. S., et al.

Article: The relation between work–family conflict and job satisfaction: A finer-grained analysis.

Journal: *Journal of Vocational Behavior*, June 2002, *60*, 336–353.

Related Research: Carlson, D. S., et al. (2000). Construction and initial validation of a multidimensional measure of work–family conflict. *Journal of Vocational Behavior, 56*, 249–276.

12416

Test Name: WORK–FAMILY CONFLICT SCALE

Purpose: To measure work-to-family conflict.

Number of Items: 10

Format: Scales range from 1 (*strongly disagree*) to 5 (*strongly agree*).

Reliability: Alpha coefficients ranged from .87 to .89.

Author: Hammer, L. B., et al.

Article: A longitudinal study of the effects of dual-earner couples' utilization of family-friendly workplace supports on work and family outcomes.

Journal: *Journal of Applied Psychology*, July 2005, *90*, 799–810.

Related Research: Netemeyer, R. G., et al. (1996). Development and validation of work–family conflict and family–work conflict scales. *Journal of Applied Psychology, 81*, 400–410.

12417

Test Name: WORK–FAMILY CONFLICT SCALE

Purpose: To assess the impact of work on family life.

Number of Items: 4

Format: All items are presented.

Reliability: Coefficient alpha was .82.

Validity: Correlations with other variables ranged from −.31 to .55.

Author: Judge, T. A., and Colquitt, J. A.

Article: Organizational justice and stress: The mediating role of work–family conflict.

Journal: *The Journal of Applied Psychology*, June 2004, *89*, 395–404.

Related Research: Gutek, B. R., et al. (1991). Rational versus gender role explanations for work–family conflict. *Journal of Applied Psychology, 76*, 560–568.

12418

Test Name: WORK–FAMILY CONFLICT SCALE

Purpose: To measure work–family conflict.

Number of Items: 10

Format: Includes work interference with family and family interference with work. Examples are presented.

Reliability: Alpha coefficients ranged from .83 to .88.

Validity: Correlations with other variables ranged from −.27 to .40.

Author: Nielson, T. R., et al.

Article: The supportive mentor as a means of reducing work–family conflict.

Journal: *Journal of Vocational Behavior*, December 2001, *59*, 364–381.

Related Research: Gutek, B. et al. (1991). Rational versus gender role explanations for work–family conflict. *Journal of Applied Psychology, 76*, 560–568. Frone, M. R., et al. (1992). Antecedents and outcomes of work–family conflict: Testing a model of the work–family interface. *Journal of Applied Psychology, 77*, 65–78.

12419

Test Name: WORK–FAMILY CONFLICT SCALE

Purpose: To measure work–family and family–work conflict.

Number of Items: 22

Format: Sales range from 1 (*never*) to 4 (*almost always*). Sample items are presented.

Reliability: Alpha coefficients ranged from .81 to .84 across subscales.

Validity: Correlations with other variables ranged from −.30 to .39.

Author: Noor, N. M.

Article: Work–family conflict, work- and family-role salience, and women's well-being.

Journal: *The Journal of Social Psychology*, August 2004, *144*, 389–405.

Related Research: Kelloway, E. K., et al. (1999). The source, nature, and direction of work and family conflict: A longitudinal investigation. *Journal of Occupational Health Psychology, 4*, 337–346.

12420

Test Name: WORK–FAMILY CONFLICT SCALES

Purpose: To assess two directions of work–family conflict.

Number of Items: 6

Format: Includes work-to-family conflict and family-to-work conflict. Responses are made on a 5-point scale ranging from strongly agree to strongly disagree.

Reliability: Alpha coefficients were .56 and .85.

Validity: Correlations with other variables ranged from −.44 to .50.

Author: Greenhaus, J. H., et al.

Article: The relation between work–family balance and quality of life.

Journal: *Journal of Vocational Behavior*, December 2003, *63*, 510–531.

Related Research: Friedman, S. D., & Greenhaus, J. H. (2000). *Work and family—Allies or enemies? What happens when business professionals confront life choices.* New York: Oxford University Press.

12421

Test Name: WORK/FAMILY CONFLICT SCALES

Purpose: To measure work-to-family and family-to-work conflict.

Number of Items: 8

Format: Includes two scales: Work-to-Family Conflict and Family-to-Work Conflict. Responses are made on a 5-point scale ranging from *strongly agree* to *strongly disagree.* Examples are presented.

Reliability: Alpha coefficients were .79 to .81.

Validity: Correlations with other variables ranged from −.14 to .44.

Author: Stoeva, A. Z., et al.

Article: Negative affectivity, role stress, and work–family conflict.

Journal: *Journal of Vocational Behavior*, February 2002, *60*, 1–16.

Related Research: Burley, K. A. (1991). Family–work spillover in dual-career couples: A comparison of two time perspectives. *Psychological Reports, 68*, 471–480. Kopelman, R. E., et al. (1983). A model of work, family, and interrole conflict: A construct validation study. *Organizational Behavior and Human Performance, 32*, 198–215.

12422

Test Name: WORK–FAMILY CULTURE SCALE

Purpose: To measure work–family culture.

Number of Items: 20

Format: Includes three factors: managerial support, career

consequences, and organizational time demands. Responses are made on a 7-point scale ranging from *strongly disagree* to *strongly agree.*

Reliability: Alpha coefficients ranged from .74 to .92.

Validity: Correlations with other variables ranged from −.53 to .69.

Author: Behson, S. J.

Article: Which dominates? The relative importance of work–family organizational support and general organizational context on employee outcomes.

Journal: *Journal of Vocational Behavior*, August 2002, *61*, 53–72.

Related Research: Thompson, C. A., et al. (1999). When work–family benefits are not enough: The influence of work–family culture on benefit utilization, organizational attachment, and work–family conflict. *Journal of Vocational Behavior, 54*, 392–415.

12423

Test Name: WORK–FAMILY LINKAGES QUESTIONNAIRE

Purpose: To measure work–family and family–work spillover, work–family segmentation, and compensatory work–family linkages.

Number of Items: 27

Format: Seven-point scales range from 1 (*strongly disagree*) to 7 (*strongly agree*). All items are presented.

Reliability: Alpha coefficients ranged from .68 to .80.

Validity: Correlations with other variables ranged from −.31 to .53.

Author: Sumer, H. C., and Knight, P. A.

Article: How do people with different attachment styles balance work and family? A personality perspective on work–family linkage.

Journal: *Journal of Applied Psychology*, August 2001, *86*, 653–663.

12424

Test Name: WORK/FAMILY ROLE CONFLICT SCALE

Purpose: To measure work/family conflict.

Number of Items: 10

Format: Sample items are presented. Likert format is used.

Reliability: Coefficient alpha was .86.

Validity: Correlations with other variables ranged from −.29 to .11.

Author: Clark, S. C.

Article: Employees' sense of community, sense of control, and work/family conflict in Native American organizations

Journal: *Journal of Vocational Behavior*, August 2002, *61*, 92–108.

Related Research: Bohen, H. H. & Viceros-Long, A. (1981). *Balancing jobs and family life: Do flexible schedules help?* Philadelphia: Temple University Press.

12425

Test Name: WORK–FAMILY SCALE

Purpose: To assess two directions of work–family influence and two valences.

Number of Items: 16

Format: Includes four dimensions: Work-to-Family, Family-to-Work, Work-to-Family Facilitation, and Work-to-Family Conflict. Responses are made on a 5-point scale ranging from 1 (*all the time*) to 5 (*never*). All items are presented.

Reliability: Alpha coefficients ranged from .68 to .82.

Author: Wayne, J. H., et al.

Article: Considering the rule of personality in the work–family experience: Relationships of the Big Five to work–family conflict and facilitation.

Journal: *Journal of Vocational Behavior*, February 2004, *64*, 108–130.

Related Research: Gutek, B., et al. (1991). Rational versus gender role explanations for work–family conflict. *Journal of Applied Psychology, 76,* 560–568.

12426

Test Name: WORK–HOME INTERFERENCE SCALE

Purpose: To measure work–home interference.

Number of Items: 5

Format: Responses are made on a 4-point scale ranging from 1 (*never*) to 4 (*always*). All items are presented.

Reliability: Alpha coefficients ranged from .72 to .81.

Author: Geurts, S. A. E., et al.

Article: Does work–home interference mediate the relationship between workload and well-being?

Journal: *Journal of Vocational Behavior*, December 2003, *63*, 532–559.

Related Research: Kopelman, R. E., et al. (1983). A model of work, family, and interrole conflict: A construct validation study. *Organizational Behavior and Human Performance, 32,* 198–213.

12427

Test Name: WORK INTERFERENCE WITH FAMILY SCALE

Purpose: To measure how much work demands keep people from home demands.

Number of Items: 6

Format: Scales range from 1 (*strongly disagree*) to 5 (*strongly agree*). A sample item is presented.

Reliability: Coefficient alpha was .94.

Validity: Correlations with other variables ranged from .02 to .50.

Author: Major, V. S., et al.

Article: Work time, work interference with family, and psychological distress.

Journal: *Journal of Applied Psychology*, June 2002, *87*, 427–436.

Related Research: Metemeyer, R. G., et al. (1996). Development and validation of work–family and family–work conflict scales. *Journal of Applied Psychology, 81,* 400–410.

12428

Test Name: WORK TO FAMILY CONFLICT SCALE

Purpose: To measure work to family conflict.

Number of Items: 5

Format: A yes–no format is used. All items are presented.

Reliability: Coefficient alpha was .85.

Validity: Correlations with other variables ranged from −.29 to .63.

Author: Behson, S. J.

Article: The relative contribution of formal and informal organizational work–family support.

Journal: *Journal of Vocational Behavior*, June 2005, *66*, 487–500.

Related Research: Netemeyer, R. G., et al. (1996). Development and validation of work–family and family–work conflict scales. *Journal of Applied Psychology, 81,* 400–410.

12429

Test Name: WORK-TO-FAMILY CONFLICT SCALE

Purpose: To measure work and family conflict.

Number of Items: 8

Format: Responses are made on a 7-point Likert scale.

Reliability: Coefficient alpha was .81.

Validity: Correlations with other variables ranged from −.33 to .47.

Author: Zickar, M. J., et al.

Article: Job attitudes of workers with two jobs.

Journal: *Journal of Vocational Behavior*, February 2004, *64*, 222–235.

Related Research: Rothausen, T. J. (1994). *Expanding the boundaries of job satisfaction: The effects of job facets, life satisfaction, and family situation.* Doctoral dissertation, University of Minnesota.

12430

Test Name: WORK-TO-FAMILY STRESS

Purpose: To measure the degree to which work interferes with personal and family matters.

Number of Items: 6

Format: Scales range from 1 (*never*) to 5 (*very often*). All items are presented.

Reliability: Coefficient alpha was .86.

Validity: Correlations with other variables ranged from −.28 to .48.

Author: Brett, J. M., and Stroh, L. K.

Article: Working 61 plus hours a week: Why do managers do it?

Journal: *Journal of Applied Psychology*, February 2003, *88*, 67–78.

CHAPTER 14

Institutional Information

12431

Test Name: ACADEMIC TENURE JUSTICE SCALES

Purpose: To assess perceived procedural and distributive justice in the tenure process.

Number of Items: 8

Format: Scales range from 1 (*strongly disagree*) to 7 (*strongly agree*). All items are presented.

Reliability: Alpha coefficients ranged from .92 to .99.

Validity: Correlations with other variables ranged from −.56 to .90.

Author: Ambrose, M. L., and Cropanzano, R.

Article: A longitudinal analysis of organizational fairness: An examination of reactions to tenure and promotion decisions.

Journal: *Journal of Applied Psychology*, April 2003, *88*, 266–275.

12432

Test Name: ANTICIPATED ORGANIZATIONAL CHANGE SCALE

Purpose: To measure anticipated organizational change.

Number of Items: 4

Format: Five-point scales are anchored by *very likely* and *very unlikely*.

Validity: Correlations with other variables ranged from −.26 to .59.

Author: Reisel, W. D.

Article: Validation and measurement of perceived environmental threat as an antecedent to job insecurity.

Journal: *Psychological Reports*, October 2003, *93*, 359–364.

Related Research: Ashford, S. J., et al. (1989). Content, causes, and consequences of job insecurity: A theory-based measure and substantive test. *Academy of Management Journal, 32*, 803–829.

12433

Test Name: ARNETT SCALE OF PROVIDER SENSITIVITY

Purpose: To measure the emotional and behavioral relationships between care providers and children in both center- and home-based care arrangements.

Number of Items: 26

Format: Responses are made on a 4-point scale.

Reliability: Coefficient alpha was .94.

Author: Votruba-Drzal, E., et al.

Article: Child care and low-income children's development: Direct and moderated effects.

Journal: *Child Development*, January/February 2004, *75*, 296–312.

Related Research: Arnett, J. (1989). Caregivers in day care centers: Does training matter? *Journal of Applied Developmental Psychology, 10*, 541–552.

12434

Test Name: ASSESSMENT FOR LIVING AND LEARNING SCALE

Purpose: To measure students' perception of the academic climate in residence halls.

Number of Items: 21

Format: Scales range from 1 (*strongly disagree*) to 4 (*strongly agree*). All items are presented.

Reliability: Alpha coefficients for the full scale and subscales exceeded .87.

Validity: Goodness of fit indices exceeded .90 for a two-factor model for a sample most like a public comprehensive Doctoral I institution.

Author: Denzine, G. M., and Kowalski, G. J.

Article: Confirmatory factor analysis of the Assessment for Living and Learning Scale: A cross-validation investigation.

Journal: *Measurement and Evaluation in Counseling and Development*, April 2002, *35*, 14–26.

12435

Test Name: CAMPUS CLIMATE SCALE

Purpose: To measure student perceptions of campus climate, including instructor relations, acceptance, confidence, respect, and safety.

Number of Items: 25

Format: Seven-point scales range from *strongly disagree* to *strongly agree.*

Reliability: Alpha coefficients ranged from .56 to .78. Total alpha was .89.

Author: Tomlinson, M. J., and Fassinger, R. E.

Article: Career development, lesbian identity development, and campus climate among lesbian college students.

Journal: *Journal of College Student Development*, November/December 2003, *44*, 845–860.

Related Research: Fitzgerald, L. F., et al. (1996). *Campus climate at the University of Illinois and Urbana–Champaign: The effects of gender, race/ethnicity, and sexual orientation.* Unpublished manuscript, Psychology Department, University of Illinois at Urbana–Champaign.

12436

Test Name: CAREER BARRIERS INVENTORY—REVISED

Purpose: To assess global career barriers.

Number of Items: 30

Format: Includes six scales: Sex Discrimination, Racial Discrimination, Disapproval by Significant Others, Discouraged From Choosing Nontraditional Careers, Job Market Constraints, and Difficulty With Networking. Responses are made on a 7-point scale ranging from 1 (*not at all likely*) to 7 (*very likely*).

Reliability: Alpha coefficients ranged from .65 to .94.

Validity: Correlations with other variables ranged from −.09 to −.47.

Author: Lent, R. W., et al.

Article: The role of contextual supports and barriers in the choice

of math/science educational options: A test of social cognitive hypotheses.

Journal: *Journal of Counseling Psychology*, October 2001, *48*, 474–483.

Related Research: Swanson, J. L., et al. (1996). Assessing perceptions of career-related barriers: The Career Barriers Inventory. *Journal of Career Assessment, 4,* 219–244.

12437

Test Name: CAREER BARRIERS INVENTORY—REVISED AND MODIFIED

Purpose: To identify barriers to one's career progress.

Number of Items: 49

Format: Includes eight subscales: Sex Discrimination, Lack of Confidence, Multiple Role Conflict, Conflict Between Children and Career Demands, Discouragement From Choosing Nontraditional Careers, Inadequate Preparation, Decision-Making Difficulties, and Dissatisfaction With Careers. Responses are made on a 7-point scale ranging from 1 (*would completely hinder*) to 7 (*would not hinder at all*). Examples are given.

Reliability: Alpha coefficients ranged from .74 to .91.

Validity: Correlations with other variables ranged from −.43 to .24.

Author: Quimby, J. L., and O'Brien, K. M.

Article: Predictors of student and career decision-making self-efficacy among nontraditional college women.

Journal: *The Career Development Quarterly*, June 2004, *52*, 323–339.

Related Research: Swanson, J. L., et al. (1996). Assessing perceptions of career-related barriers: The Career Barriers Inventory. *Journal of Career Assessment, 4,* 219–244.

12438

Test Name: CAREER DIMENSIONS MEASURES

Purpose: To identify career dimensions.

Number of Items: 18

Format: Includes six dimensions: Career Control, Flexibility, Dependence, Task Uncertainty, Interunit Interactions, and Length of Service. Responses are made on 5-point scales. Examples are presented.

Reliability: Alpha coefficients ranged from .68 to .75.

Validity: Correlations with other variables range from −.40 to .52.

Author: Ito, J. K., and Brotheridge, C. M.

Article: An examination of the roles of career uncertainty, flexibility, and control in predicting emotional exhaustion.

Journal: *Journal of Vocational Behavior*, December 2001, *59*, 406–424.

Related Research: London, M. (1993). Relationships between career motivation, empowerment and support for career development. *Journal of Occupational and Organizational Psychology, 66,* 55–69. Van de Van, A. H., & Debecq, A. (1974). A task contingent model of work-unit structure. *Administrative Science Quarterly, 19,* 183–197. Ito, J. K., & Peterson, R. B. (1986). Effects of task difficulty and interdependence on information processing systems. *Academy of Management Journal, 29,* 139–149.

12439

Test Name: CLASSROOM PRACTICES INVENTORY

Purpose: To assess the curricular emphasis and emotional climate of the early childhood classroom.

Number of Items: 26

Format: Includes three subscales: Program Appropriateness, Program Inappropriateness, and Emotional Climate of the Classroom.

Reliability: Alpha coefficients ranged from .92 to .95.

Validity: Correlations with other variables ranged from −.24 to .34.

Author: Mantzicopoulos, P.

Article: Conflictual relationships between kindergarten children and their teachers: Associations with child and classroom context variables.

Journal: *Journal of School Psychology*, November 2005, *43*, 425–442.

Related Research: Hyson, M. C., et al. (1990). The Classroom Practices Inventory: An observation instrument based on NAEYC's guidelines for developmentally appropriate practices for 4- and 5-year-old children. *Early Childhood Research Quarterly, 5,* 475–494.

12440

Test Name: CLIMATE AND WORK ENVIRONMENT SCALES

Purpose: To measure overall climate, supervisory support, and service orientation.

Number of Items: 33

Format: Scales range from 1 (*strongly disagree*) to 5 (*strongly agree*). Sample items are presented.

Reliability: Alpha coefficients ranged from .64 to .88 across subscales.

Validity: Correlations between subscales ranged from .13 to .68.

Author: Ostroff, C., et al.

Article: Substantive and operational issues of response bias across levels of analysis: An example of climate-satisfaction relationships.

Journal: *Journal of Applied Psychology*, April 2002, *87*, 355–368.

12441

Test Name: CLIMATE OF SELF-DETERMINATION SCALE

Purpose: To measure climate of self-determination.

Number of Items: 10

Format: Includes three areas of perceptions: participative management, recognition, and training. Responses are made on 5-point scales ranging from 1 (*strongly disagree*) to 5 (*strongly agree*). One item used a 5-point scale ranging from *Yes, I can count on it* to *No, it would go unnoticed.* All items are included.

Reliability: Alpha coefficients ranged from .75 to .91.

Validity: Correlations with other variables ranged from −.08 to .46.

Author: Wagner, S. H., et al.

Article: Employees that think and act like owners: Effect of ownership beliefs and behaviors on organizational effectiveness.

Journal: *Personnel Psychology*, Winter 2003, *56*, 847–871.

12442

Test Name: CLIMATE STRENGTH SCALES

Purpose: To measure support for work mates' personal problems, innovation, and goals orientation of work-unit members.

Number of Items: 9

Format: Scales range from 1 (*strongly in disagreement*) to 5 (*strongly in agreement*). Sample items are presented.

Reliability: Alpha coefficients ranged from .63 to .86 across subscales.

Validity: Correlations with other variables ranged from .00 to .55 aggregated at the work-unit level.

Author: González-Romá, V., et al.

Article: An examination of the antecedents and moderator influences of climate strength.

Journal: *Journal of Applied Psychology*, June 2002, *87*, 465–473.

12443

Test Name: COLLECTIVE EFFICACY SCALE—REVISED

Purpose: To measure mothers' perceptions of their neighborhoods.

Number of Items: 9

Format: Includes two areas: perceptions of social control and perceptions of neighborhood cohesion and trust. Responses are made on 4- and 5-point scales. Examples are given.

Reliability: Coefficient alpha was .88.

Author: Coley, L., et al.

Article: Out-of-school care and problem behavior trajectories among low-income adolescents: Individual, family, and neighborhood characteristics as added risks.

Journal: *Child Development*, May/June 2004, *75*, 948–965.

Related Research: Sampson, R. J., et al. (1997). Neighborhoods and violent crime: A multilevel study of collective efficacy. *Science, 277,* 918–924.

12444

Test Name: COLLECTIVE EFFICACY SCALE—SHORT TERM

Purpose: To measure the extent to which a faculty believes in its cojoint capability to positively influence student learning.

Number of Items: 12.

Format: A Likert-type format is used. All items are presented.

Reliability: Coefficient alpha was .94.

Author: Goddard, R.

Article: A theoretical and empirical analysis of the measurement of collective efficacy: The development of a short form.

Journal: *Educational and Psychological Measurement*, February 2002, *62*, 97–110.

Related Research: Goddard, R. D. (2001). Collective efficacy: A neglected construct in the study of schools and student achievement. *Journal of Educational Psychology*, *93*, 467–476.

12445

Test Name: COLLECTIVE TEACHER EFFICACY SCALE

Purpose: To measure teachers' belief that the teachers in their school constitute an effective instructional team.

Number of Items: 14

Format: Includes two dimensions: Perceptions of the Task and Perceptions of Teaching Competence. Responses are made on a 6-point Likert-type scale ranging from *strongly disagree* to *strongly agree*.

Validity: Correlations with other variables ranged from .08 to .36.

Author: Ross, J. A.

Article: Effects of running records assessment on early literacy achievement.

Journal: *The Journal of Educational Research*, March/April 2004, *97*, 186–194.

Related Research: Goddard, R. D., et al. (2000). Collective teacher efficacy: Its meaning, measure, and impact on student achievement. *American Education Research Journal*, *37*, 479–507.

12446

Test Name: COMMUNITY DEVIANCE AND SAFETY INVENTORY

Purpose: To measure community deviance and safety.

Number of Items: 10

Format: Deviance scales range from 1 (*not at all a problem*) to 3 (*a big problem*). Safety scales range from 1 (*very safe*) to 4 (*not at all safe*).

Reliability: Total alpha was .70. Coefficient alpha for deviance was .89. Alpha for safety was .60.

Validity: Correlations with other variables ranged from –.76 to .19.

Author: Simons R. L., et al.

Article: Community differences in the association between parenting practices and child conduct problems.

Journal: *Journal of Marriage and Family*, May 2002, *64*, 331–345.

Related Research: Sampson R. J., et al. (1997). Neighborhoods and violent crime: A multilevel study of collective efficacy. *Science*, *277*, 918–924.

12447

Test Name: COMMUNITY SAFETY SCALE

Purpose: To measure social and physical incivilities in communities.

Number of Items: 15

Format: Scales range from 1 (*strongly agree*) to 5 (*strongly disagree*). All items are presented.

Reliability: Alpha coefficients were .84 (social incivility) and .58 (physical incivility).

Validity: The correlation between the two subscales was –.54.

Author: Shoffner, M. F., and Vacc, N. A.

Article: An analysis of the Community Safety Scale: A brief report.

Journal: *Measurement and Evaluation in Counseling and Development*, April 2002, *35*, 49–55.

12448

Test Name: CONSUMER ASSESSMENT OF CARE

Purpose: To measure satisfaction with health services.

Number of Items: 14

Format: Item anchors are 1 (*poor*) and 4 (*excellent*). All items are presented.

Reliability: Coefficient alpha was .91.

Author: Uttaro, T., et al.

Article: Effect of type of survey administrator on Consumer Assessment of Care.

Journal: *Psychological Reports*, June 2004, *94*, Part 2, 1279–1282.

Related Research: Uttaro, T. (2003). The development and administration of the Consumer Assessment of Care by New York State Office of Mental Health downstate facilities. *Evaluation and Program Planning*, *26*, 143–147.

12449

Test Name: COWORKER BEHAVIORS SCALE

Purpose: To measure perceptions of coworkers' behaviors and attitudes within the respondent's department.

Number of Items: 15

Format: Includes three areas: cooperative orientation, innovative orientation, and customer orientation of coworkers. An example is presented.

Reliability: Coefficient alpha was .93.

Validity: Correlations with other variables ranged from −.02 to .53.

Author: Neubert, M. J., and Cady, S. H.

Article: Program commitment: A multistudy longitudinal field investigation of its impact and antecedents.

Journal: *Personnel Psychology,* Summer 2001, *54,* 421–448.

12450

Test Name: DEPARTMENTAL CLIMATE QUESTIONNAIRE

Purpose: To measure doctoral students perceived departmental climate.

Number of Items: 14

Format: Includes three parts: supportive faculty environment, department collegiality, and student scholarly encouragement. All items are presented.

Reliability: Alpha coefficients ranged from .71 to .84.

Validity: Correlations with other variables ranged from −.17 to .46.

Author: Weidman, J. C., and Stein, E. L.

Article: Socialization of doctoral students to academic norms.

Journal: *Research in Higher Education,* December 2003, *44,* 641–656.

12451

Test Name: DIFFERENTIAL TREATMENT SCALE

Purpose: To measure differential treatment in a work unit.

Number of Items: 4

Format: All items are presented along with their 5-point response categories.

Reliability: Alpha was .81.

Validity: Correlations with other variables ranged from −.10 to −.31.

Author: van Breukelen, W., et al.

Article: Effects of LMX and differential treatment on work unit commitment.

Journal: *Psychological Reports,* August 2002, *91,* 220–230.

12452

Test Name: DISPLAY RULE SCALES

Purpose: To measure positive and negative rule demands.

Number of Items: 7

Format: Includes both positive and negative display rule scales. Responses are made on a 5-point Likert scale ranging from 1 (*strongly disagree*) to 5 (*strongly agree*). All items are presented.

Reliability: Alpha coefficients were .73 and .75.

Validity: Correlations with other variables ranged from −.13 to .29.

Author: Diefendorff, J. M., et al.

Article: The dimensionality and antecedents of emotional labor strategies.

Journal: *Journal of Vocational Behavior,* April 2005, *66,* 339–357.

Related Research: Brotheridge, C. M., & Grandey, A. A. (2002). Emotional labor and burnout: Comparing two perspectives of "people work." *Journal of Vocational Behavior, 60,* 17–39. Schaubroeck, J., & Jones, J. R. (2000). Antecedents of workplace emotional labor dimensions and moderators of their effects on physical symptoms. *Journal of Organizational Behavior, 21,* 163–183.

12453

Test Name: DISTRIBUTIVE JUSTICE SCALE FOR TAXATION

Purpose: To measure individual-level justice, grand-level justice, and inclusive-level justice with regard to tax burdens.

Number of Items: 19

Format: Scales for 15 items range from 1 (*much more than their fair share*) to 5 (*much less than their fair share*). All items are presented.

Reliability: Alpha coefficients ranged from .59 to .70.

Author: Wenzel, M.

Article: Social identification as a determinant of concerns about individual-, group-, and inclusive-level justice.

Journal: *Social Psychology Quarterly,* March 2004, *67,* 70–87.

Related Research: Wenzel, M. (2002). The impact of outcome orientation and justice concerns on tax compliance: The role of taxpayers' identity. *Journal of Applied Psychology, 87,* 629–645.

12454

Test Name: DOCTORAL STUDENT SURVEY—REVISED

Purpose: To measure students' perceptions of social support in a doctoral program.

Number of Items: 35

Format: Uses Likert-scaled items. All items are presented.

Reliability: Coefficient alpha was .79.

Author: Williams, K. B.

Article: Minority and majority students' retrospective perceptions of social support in doctoral programs.

Journal: *Perceptual and Motor Skills,* August 2002, *94,* 187–196.

Related Research: Nottles, M. T. (1990). Success in doctoral programs: Experiences of minority and white students. *American Journal of Education, 98,* 494–522.

12455

Test Name: DRUG TESTING DRUG TREATMENT SCALES

Purpose: To assess the general perception of drug treatment, job safety sensitivity, treatment policy fairness, and attractiveness of an organizational treatment policy.

Number of Items: 9

Format: Scales range from 1 (*strongly disagree*) to 5 (*strongly agree*). Sample items are presented.

Reliability: Alpha coefficients ranged from .85 to .90 across subscales.

Author: Paronto, M. E., et al.

Article: Drug testing, drug treatment, and marijuana use: A fairness perspective.

Journal: *Journal of Applied Psychology,* December 2002, *87,* 1159–1166.

Related Research: Tepper, B. (1994). Investigation of general and program-specific attitudes toward corporate drug-testing policies. *Journal of Applied Psychology, 79,* 392–401.

12456

Test Name: EARLY CHILDHOOD CLASSROOM OBSERVATION MEASURE

Purpose: To assess the nature of instruction and the social environment.

Number of Items: 34

Format: Includes two sets of descriptions: T scales (rigid) and C scales (chaotic). Responses are made on a five-point scale ranging from 1 (*low*) to 5 (*high*).

Reliability: Alpha coefficients ranged from .60 to .95.

Author: Valeski, T. N., and Stipek, D. J.

Article: Young children's findings about school

Journal: *Child Development,* July/August 2001, *72,* 1198–1213.

Related Research: Stipek, D., et al. (1998). Good beginnings: What difference does the program make in preparing young children for school? *Journal of Applied Developmental Psychology, 19,* 41–66.

12457

Test Name: EARLY RECRUITMENT PRACTICES MEASURE

Purpose: To identify early recruitment practices.

Number of Items: 13

Format: Includes four components: General Recruitment Ads, Sponsorship, Detailed Recruitment Ads, and Employee Endorsements. Responses are made on a 5-point scale ranging from 1 (*strongly disagree*) to 5 (*strongly agree*). All items are presented.

Reliability: Alpha coefficients ranged from .73 to .75.

Validity: Correlations with other variables ranged from –.07 to .44.

Author: Collins, C. J., and Han, J.

Article: Exploring applicant pool quantity and quality: The effects of early recruitment practice strategies, corporate advertising, and firm reputation.

Journal: *Personnel Psychology,* Autumn 2004, *57,* 685–717.

Related Research: Collins, C. J., & Stevens, C. K. (2002). The relationship between early recruitment and related activities and the application decisions of new labor-market entrants: A brand equity approach to recruitment. *Journal of Applied Psychology, 87,* 1121–1133.

12458

Test Name: EFFECTIVENESS OF PRODUCT INNOVATION SCALE

Purpose: To assess the quality of product development projects.

Number of Items: 4

Format: Item responses are anchored by 4 (*poor*) and 10 (*excellent*). A sample item is presented.

Reliability: Coefficient alpha was .91.

Author: Länsisalmi, H., et al.

Article: Is underutilization of knowledge, skills, and abilities a major barrier to innovation?

Journal: *Psychological Reports,* June 2004, *94,* Part 1, 739–750.

Related Research: Kivimäki, M., et al. (2000). Communication as a determinant of organizational innovation. *Research and Development Management, 30,* 33–42.

12459

Test Name: EMOTION WORK REQUIREMENTS SCALE

Purpose: To measure the level to which employee's reported that their emotional displays were controlled by their jobs.

Number of Items: 7

Format: Includes two factors: display positive emotions and hide negative emotions. Responses are made on a 5-point scale ranging from 1 (*not at all*) to 5 (*always required*). All items all presented.

Reliability: Alpha coefficients ranged from .71 to .99.

Validity: Correlations with other variables ranged from .00 to .47.

Author: Brotheridge, C. M., and Grandey, A. A.

Article: Emotional labor and burnout: Comparing two perspectives of "people work."

Journal: *Journal of Vocational Behavior*, February 2002, *60*, 17–39.

Related Research: Best, R. G., et al. (1997, April). *Incumbent perceptions of emotional work requirements.* Paper presented at the 12th annual conference of the Society for Industrial and Organizational Psychology, St. Louis, MO.

12460

Test Name: ENVIRONMENTAL AND COGNITIVE DETERMINANTS OF COPING STRATEGIES SCALES

Purpose: To measure climate, frequency–duration, and cognitive appraisal of sexual harassment.

Number of Items: 24

Format: Likert scales or dichotomous scales are used. All items are presented.

Reliability: Alpha coefficients ranged from .81 to .94 across subscales.

Validity: Correlations with other variables ranged from −.13 to .55.

Author: Malamut, A. B., and Offermann, L. R.

Article: Coping with sexual harassment: Personal, environmental, and cognitive determinants.

Journal: *Journal of Applied Psychology*, December 2001, *86*, 1152–1166.

12461

Test Name: ENVIRONMENTAL PRESSURE SCALE

Purpose: To measure perceptions of the school atmosphere.

Number of Items: 8

Format: Responses are made on a 6-point scale ranging from 1 (*not at all true*) to 6 (*completely true*).

Reliability: Internal consistency ranged from .68 to .81.

Author: Levesque, C., et al.

Article: Autonomy and competence in German and American university students: A comparative study based on self-determination theory.

Journal: *Journal of Educational Psychology*, March 2004, *96*, 68–84.

Related Research: Deci, E. L., et al. (1989). Self-determination in a work organization. *Journal of Applied Psychology, 74*, 580–590.

12462

Test Name: ERROR CULTURE SCALE

Purpose: To assess error management and error aversion in an organizational setting.

Number of Items: 28

Format: Scales range from 1 (*does not apply at all*) to 5 (*applies completely*). All items are presented.

Reliability: Alpha coefficients ranged from .88 to .92.

Validity: Correlations with other variables ranged from −.23 to .46.

Author: vanDyck, C., et al.

Article: Organizational error management culture and its impact on performance: A two-study replication.

Journal: *Journal of Applied Psychology*, November 2005, *90*, 1228–1240.

12463

Test Name: EXCHANGE IDEOLOGY SCALE—ADAPTED

Purpose: To measure organizational exchange ideology.

Number of Items: 3

Format: Responses are made on a 5-point Likert scale. Examples are presented.

Reliability: Coefficient alpha was .67.

Validity: Correlations with other variables ranged from −.22 to .09.

Author: Andrews, M. C., et al.

Article: The interactive effects of organizational politics and exchange ideology on manager ratings of retention.

Journal: *Journal of Vocational Behavior*, April 2003, *62*, 357–369.

Related Research: Eisenberger, R., et al. (1986). Perceived organizational support. *Journal of Applied Psychology, 71*, 500–507.

12464

Test Name: EXPOSURE TO COMMUNITY VIOLENCE SCALE

Purpose: To measure community violence by asking mothers to report the frequency of their children's exposure to violent incidents.

Number of Items: 10

Format: Responses are 1 (*had*) and 2 (*had not*).

Reliability: Alpha coefficients were .56 (had been victimized) and .74 (witnessed violence).

Author: Ceballo, R., et al.

Article: Inner-city children's exposure to community violence: How much do parents know?

Journal: *Journal of Marriage and Family*, November 2001, *63*, 927–940.

Related Research: Richters, J. E., & Martinez, P. (1993). The NIMH Community Violence Project: I. Children as victims and witnesses to violence. *Psychiatry, 56*, 7–21.

12465

Test Name: FACILITATING CONDITIONS QUESTIONNAIRE—MODIFIED

Purpose: To identify facilitating conditions for school motivation.

Number of Items: 26

Format: Includes seven factors: value, affect, peer positive, peer negative, parent positive, parent negative, and teacher. Responses are made on a 5-point Likert-type scale ranging from 1 (*strongly disagree*) to 5 (*strongly agree*).

Reliability: Alpha coefficients ranged from .68 to .82.

Author: McInerney, D. M., et al.

Article: Facilitating conditions for school motivation: Construct validity and applicability.

Journal: *Educational and Psychological Measurement*, December 2005, *65*, 1046–1066.

Related Research: McInerney, D. M. (1992). Cross-cultural insights into school motivation and decision making. *Journal of Intercultural Studies, 13,* 53–74.

12466

Test Name: FACTUAL AUTONOMY SCALE

Purpose: To measure work autonomy.

Number of Items: 9

Format: Responses are made on a 5-point scale ranging from 1 (*never*) to 5 (*always*). Examples are presented.

Reliability: Alpha coefficients were .81 and .87.

Validity: Correlations with other variables ranged from −.25 to .23 (*N* = 292).

Author: Fox, S., et al.

Article: Counterproductive work behavior (CWB) in response to job stressors and organizational justice: Some mediator and moderator tests for autonomy and emotions.

Journal: *Journal of Vocational Behavior*, December 2001, *59*, 291–309.

Related Research: Fox, S., et al. (1997, April). *Objectivity in the assessment of control at work*. Paper presented at the 12th annual meeting of the Society for Industrial and Organizational Psychology, St. Louis, MO.

12467

Test Name: FEEDBACK ENVIRONMENT SCALE

Purpose: To assess the feedback environment for individual managers and for coworker groups.

Number of Items: 63

Format: Includes seven feedback environment facets. Responses are made on a 7-point Likert-type scale ranging from *strongly disagree* to *strongly agree*. All items are presented.

Reliability: Internal consistency reliability ranged from .74 to .92. Test–retest (5 months) reliability ranged from .26 to .77.

Validity: Correlations with other variables ranged from −.09 to .76.

Author: Steelman, L. A., et al.

Article: The Feedback Environment Scale: Construct definition, measurement, and validation.

Journal: *Educational and Psychological Measurement*, February 2004, *64*, 165–184.

12468

Test Name: FLEXIBIITY SCALE

Purpose: To measure flexibility in work times and places.

Number of Items: 4

Format: All items are presented. A Likert format is used.

Reliability: Correlations with other variables ranged from −.30 to .37.

Author: Clark, S. C.

Article: Employees' sense of community, sense of control, and work/family conflict in Native American organizations.

Journal: *Journal of Vocational Behavior*, August 2002, *61*, 92–108.

Related Research: Clark, S. C. (2001). Work cultures and work/family balance. *Journal of Vocational Behavior, 58,* 348–365.

12469

Test Name: GAY, LESBIAN, BISEXUAL, AND TRANSGENDER STUDENT SURVEY

Purpose: To assess the experiences of GLBT students on a college campus.

Number of Items: 19

Format: Various scales are used. All scales and all items are presented.

Reliability: Alpha coefficients ranged from .75 to .87 on multi-item measures.

Author: Brown, R. D., et al.

Article: Assessing the campus climate for gay, lesbian, bisexual, and transgender (GLBT) students using a multiple perspectives approach.

Journal: *Journal of College Student Development*, January/February 2004, *45*, 8–26.

Related Research: Herek, G. M. (1993). Documenting prejudice against lesbians and gay men on campus: The Yale Sexual Orientation Survey. *Journal of Homosexuality, 25,* 15–30.

12470

Test Name: GENERAL ENVIRONMENT SATISFACTION SCALE

Purpose: To assess satisfaction with public services, consumer products, and other elements of the general environment.

Number of Items: 7

Format: Scales range from 1 (*strongly disagree*) to 5 (*strongly agree*). Sample items are presented.

Reliability: Coefficient alpha was .76.

Validity: Correlations with other variables ranged from −.22 to .44.

Author: Takeuchi, R., et al.

Article: An examination of crossover and spillover effects on spousal and expatriate cross-cultural adjustment on expatriate outcomes.

Journal: *Journal of Applied Psychology*, August 2002, *87*, 655–666.

12471

Test Name: GLOBAL RISK ASSESSMENT MEASURE

Purpose: To measure the potential threats to the overall development and well-being of adolescents in the juvenile justice system. Subscales include Prior Offenses, Family/Parenting, Education/Work, Peer Relationships, Substance Use/Abuse, Personality/Behavior, Attitudes/Orientation, and Leisure.

Number of Items: 113

Time Required: 20 minutes.

Format: All items are presented.

Reliability: Alpha coefficients ranged from .80 to .84 across subscales.

Validity: Correlations between subscales ranged from .33 to .92.

Author: Gauazzi, S. M., et al.

Article: Toward conceptual development and empirical measurement of global risk indicators in the lives of court-involved youth.

Journal: *Psychological Reports*, April 2003, *92*, 599–615.

12472

Test Name: GLOBAL SERVICE CLIMATE SCALE

Purpose: To measure global service climate.

Number of Items: 4

Format: Scales range from 1 (*completely agree*) to 7 (*completely disagree*). All items are presented.

Reliability: Coefficient alpha was .84.

Validity: Correlations with other variables ranged from .15 to .52.

Author: Salanova, M., et al.

Article: Linking organizational resources and work engagement to employee performance and customer loyalty: The mediation of service climate.

Journal: *Journal of Applied Psychology*, November 2005, *90*, 1217–1227.

12473

Test Name: GROUP CLIMATE QUESTIONNAIRE—SHORT FORM

Purpose: To assess individual group members' perceptions of the group's therapeutic environment.

Number of Items: 12

Format: Includes three subscales: Engagement, Avoidance, and Conflict. Responses are made on a 7-point scale ranging from 0 (*not at all*) to 6 (*extremely*).

Reliability: Alpha coefficients ranged from .36 to .94.

Validity: Correlations with other variables ranged from −.62 to .57.

Author: Johnson, J. E., et al.

Article: Group climate, cohesion, alliance, and empathy in group psychotherapy: Multilevel structural equation model.

Journal: *Journal of Counseling Psychology*, July 2005, *52*, 310–321.

Related Research: MacKenzie, K. R. (1983). The clinical application of group measure. In R. R. Dies & K. R. MacKenzie (Eds.), *Advances in group psychotherapy: Integrating research and practice* (pp. 159–170). New York: International Universities Press.

12474

Test Name: GROUP-LEVEL SAFETY CLIMATE SCALE

Purpose: To assess supervisors' commitment to safety.

Number of Items: 16

Format: Rating scales range from 1 (*completely disagree*) to 5 (*completely agree*). All items are presented.

Reliability: Coefficient alpha was .95.

Validity: Correlations with other variables ranged from .11 to .38.

Author: Zohar, D., and Luria, G.

Article: A multilevel model of safety climate: Cross-level relationships between organization and group-level climates.

Journal: *Journal of Applied Psychology*, July 2005, *90*, 616–628.

12475

Test Name: HIGH PERFORMANCE MANAGEMENT PRACTICES SCALE

Purpose: To measure 10 high-performance management practices.

Number of Items: 63

Format: Scales range from 1 (*strongly disagree*) to 5 (*strongly agree*). Sample items are presented.

Reliability: Subscale alpha coefficients ranged from .59 to .83. Total alpha was .89.

Validity: Correlations with other variables ranged from −.26 to .09.

Author: Zacharatos, A., et al.

Article: High-performance work systems and occupational safety.

Journal: *Journal of Applied Psychology*, January 2005, *90*, 77–93.

12476

Test Name: HIGH-PERFORMANCE WORK SYSTEMS SCALE

Purpose: To measure employees' perceptions of the extent to which their employer had adopted human resources practices.

Number of Items: 51

Format: Scales range from 1 (*strongly disagree*) to 5 (*strongly agree*).

Reliability: Subscale alpha coefficients ranged from .68 to .89. Total alpha was .92.

Validity: Correlations with other variables ranged from −.33 to .69.

Author: Zacharatos, A., et al.

Article: High-performance work systems and occupational safety.

Journal: *Journal of Applied Psychology*, January 2005, *90*, 77–93.

12477

Test Name: IMPORTANCE OF JOB ATTRIBUTES SCALES

Purpose: To assess importance of job attributes.

Number of Items: 25

Format: Includes five scales: Information, Job Attributes, Future Employment Prospects, Skill Development, and Willingness to Change Jobs. Responses are made on 5-point scales. Sample items are presented.

Reliability: Alpha coefficients ranged from .78 to .90.

Validity: Correlations with other variables ranged from −.16 to .85.

Author: Ostroff, C., and Clark, M. A.

Article: Maintaining an internal market: Antecedents of willingness to change jobs.

Journal: *Journal of Vocational Behavior*, December 2001, *59*, 425–453.

Related Research: Turban, D. B., et al. (1992). Factors relating to relocation decisions of research and development employees. *Journal of Vocational Behavior, 41*, 183–199.

12478

Test Name: INSTITUTIONALIZED SOCIALIZATION TACTICS SCALE—KOREAN VERSION

Purpose: To measure the degree to which employees experience different socialization tactics.

Number of Items: 26

Format: Scales range from 1 (*strongly disagree*) to 7 (*strongly agree*). Sample items are presented in English.

Reliability: Reported reliability was .86.

Validity: Correlations with other variables ranged from −.20 to .51.

Author: Kim, T.-Y., et al.

Article: Socialization tactics, employee proactivity, and person–organization fit.

Journal: *Journal of Applied Psychology*, March 2005, *90*, 232–241.

Related Research: Jones, G. R. (1986). Socialization tactics, self-efficacy, and newcomers' adjustments to organizations. *Academy of Management Journal, 29*, 262–279.

12479

Test Name: INSTRUCTIONAL AFFECT ASSESSMENT INSTRUMENT

Purpose: To measure student affect toward course content, course behavior, and the instructor.

Number of Items: 24

Format: Seven-point bipolar scales.

Reliability: Coefficient alpha was .86.

Validity: Correlations with other variables ranged from −.33 to .65.

Author: Myers, S. A., and Goodboy, A. K.

Article: A study of grouphate in a course on small group communication.

Journal: *Psychological Reports*, October 2005, *97*, 381–386.

12480

Test Name: INTEGRATIVE EMOTIONAL DISPLAY RULES PERCEPTIONS SCALE

Purpose: To assess perceptions of display rules in an organization.

Number of Items: 7

Format: Scales range from 1 (*strongly disagree*) to 5 (*strongly agree*). A sample item is presented.

Reliability: Coefficient alpha was .77.

Validity: Correlations with other variables ranged from −.02 to .32.

Author: Gosserand, R. H., and Diefendorff, J. M.

Article: Emotional display rules and emotional labor: The moderating role of commitment.

Journal: *Journal of Applied Psychology,* November 2005, *90,* 1256–1264.

12481

Test Name: INTERACTIONAL JUSTICE SCALE

Purpose: To assess supervisors' actions during a layoff.

Number of Items: 4

Format: Scales range from 1 (*strongly disagree*) to 5 (*strongly agree*). Sample items are presented.

Reliability: Coefficient alpha was .86.

Validity: Correlations with other variables ranged from –.52 to .18.

Author: Barclay, L. J., et al.

Article: Exploring the role of emotions in injustice perceptions and retaliation.

Journal: *Journal of Applied Psychology,* July 2005, *90,* 629–643.

Related Research: Moorman, R. H. (1991). Relationship between organizational justice and organizational citizenship behaviors: Do fairness perceptions influence employee citizenship? *Journal of Applied Psychology, 76,* 845–855.

12482

Test Name: INTERNSHIP RESEARCH TRAINING ENVIRONMENT SCALE

Purpose: To assess research training environments found in predoctoral psychology internships.

Number of Items: 23

Format: Includes four content areas: discussing/mentoring, resources, modeling, and recognition/encouragement. Responses are made on a 7-point Likert scale ranging from 1 (*strongly disagree*) to 7 (*strongly agree*). All items are presented.

Reliability: Alpha coefficients ranged from .71 to .92.

Validity: Correlations with other variables ranged from –.03 to .91.

Author: Phillips, J. C., et al.

Article: Preliminary examination and measurement of the internship research training environment.

Journal: *Journal of Counseling Psychology,* April 2004, *51,* 240–248.

12483

Test Name: JOB AUTONOMY SCALE

Purpose: To measure job autonomy.

Number of Items: 4

Format: Scales range from 1 (*not at all*) to 5 (*a great deal*).

Reliability: Alpha coefficients ranged from .72 to .78.

Validity: Correlations with other variables ranged from –.07 to .29.

Author: Parker, S. K.

Article: Longitudinal effects of lean production on employee outcomes and the mediating role of work characteristics.

Journal: *Journal of Applied Psychology,* August 2003, *88,* 620–634.

Related Research: Jackson, P. R., et al. (1993). New measures of job control, cognitive demand, and production responsibility. *Journal of Applied Psychology, 78,* 753–762.

12484

Test Name: JOB AUTONOMY SCALE

Purpose: To assess job autonomy.

Number of Items: 3

Format: Scales range from 1 (*very inaccurate*) to 7 (*very accurate*). All items are presented.

Reliability: Coefficient alpha was .84.

Validity: Correlations with other variables ranged from .29 to .71.

Author: Pierce, J. L., et al.

Article: Work environment structure and psychological ownership: The mediating effects of control.

Journal: *The Journal of Social Psychology,* October 2004, *144,* 507–534.

Related Research: Idaszak, J. R., & Drasgow, F. (1987). A revision of the Job Diagnostic Survey: Elimination of a measurement artifact. *Journal of Applied Psychology, 72,* 69–74.

12485

Test Name: JOB AUTONOMY SCALES

Purpose: To assess the degree of autonomy employees believe is acceptable in their jobs and how much is actually present.

Number of Items: 10

Format: Scales range from 1 (*none at all*) to 5 (*very much*). Sample items are presented.

Reliability: Alpha coefficients were .58 (acceptable) and .74 (present).

Validity: Correlations with other variables ranged from –.25 to .62.

Author: Simmering, M. J., et al.

Article: Conscientiousness, autonomy, fit, and development: A longitudinal study.

Journal: *Journal of Applied Psychology,* October 2003, *88,* 954–963.

Related Research: Pryor, R. G. L. (1988). *Manual for the Work Aspects Preference Scale.* Melbourne, Austrialia: Australian Council for Educational Research.

12486

Test Name: JOB CHARACTERISTICS SCALES

Purpose: To measure method control, time control, situational constraints, and time pressure.

Number of Items: 20

Format: Sample items are presented.

Reliability: Alpha coefficients ranged from .71 to .86 across subscales.

Author: Sonnentag, S.

Article: Recovery, work engagement, and proactive behavior: A new look at the interface between nonwork and work.

Journal: *Journal of Applied Psychology*, June 2003, *88*, 518–528.

Related Research: Semmer, N., et al. (1999). Instrument zur Stressbezogenen Taetigkeitsanalyse (ISTA) [Instruments for stress-oriented task analysis (ITSA)]. In H. Dunckel (Ed.), *Handbuch psychologischer arbeitsanalysevefahren* (pp. 179–204). Zurich, Switzerland: vdf Hochschulverlag an der ETH.

12487

Test Name: JOB COGNITIONS MEASURE

Purpose: To measure intrinsic cognitions, procedural justice, pay cognitions, and work-schedule load.

Number of Items: 40

Format: Scales range from 1 (*strongly disagree*) to 7 (*strongly agree*).

Reliability: Alpha coefficients ranged from .80 to .97 across subscales.

Author: Lee, K., and Allen, N. J.

Article: Organizational citizenship behavior and workplace deviance: The role of affect and cognitions.

Journal: *Journal of Applied Psychology*, February 2002, *87*, 131–142.

Related Research: Brief, A. P., & Robertson, L. (1989). Job attitude organization: An exploratory study. *Journal of Applied Social Psychology*, *19*, 717–727.

12488

Test Name: JOB COMPLEXITY SCALE

Purpose: To measure job complexity.

Number of Items: 6

Format: Scales range from 1 (*almost never*) to 5 (*very often*). A sample item is presented.

Reliability: Coefficient alpha was .78.

Validity: Correlations with other variables ranged from −.16 to .32.

Author: Schaubroeck, J., et al.

Article: Individual differences in utilizing control to cope with job demands: Effects on susceptibility to infectious disease.

Journal: *Journal of Applied Psychology*, April 2001, *86*, 265–278.

Related Research: House, J. S. (1980). *Occupational stress and the physical and mental health of factory workers*. Ann Arbor, MI: Institute for Social Research.

12489

Test Name: JOB CONTROL SCALE

Purpose: To assess the degree of control employees have over various aspects of their job.

Number of Items: 22

Format: Scales range from 1 (*very little*) to 7 (*very much*). A sample item is presented.

Reliability: Alpha coefficients ranged from .88 to .90.

Validity: Correlations with other variables ranged from −.28 to.53.

Author: Bond, F. U., and Bunce, D.

Article: The role of acceptance and job control in mental health, job satisfaction, and work performance.

Journal: *Journal of Applied Psychology*, December 2003, *88*, 1057–1067.

12490

Test Name: JOB CONTROL SCALE

Purpose: To measure a person's freedom to make decisions and carry out work his or her own way.

Number of Items: 2

Format: Four-point scales are anchored by 0 (*never*) and 3 (*very often*).

Reliability: Coefficient alpha was .75.

Author: Torkelson, E., and Muhonen, T.

Article: Coping strategies and health symptoms among women and men in a downsizing organization.

Journal: *Psychological Reports*, June 2003, *92*, Part 1, 899–907.

Related Research: Karasek, R. (1979). Job demands, job decision latitude and mental strain: The implications for job redesign. *Administrative Science Quarterly*, *24*, 285–308.

12491

Test Name: JOB DECISION LATITUDE MEASURE—ADAPTED

Purpose: To assess perceived job control.

Number of Items: 3

Format: Responses are made on a 4-point scale ranging from 1 (*never*) to 4 (*always*).

Reliability: Coefficient alpha was .84.

Validity: Correlations with other variables ranged from −.36 to .30 ($n = 392$).

Author: Boswell, W. R., et al.

Article: Relations between stress and work outcomes: The role of felt challenge, job control, and psychological strain.

Journal: *Journal of Vocational Behavior*, February 2004, *64*, 165–181.

Related Research: Karasek, R. (1989). Control in the workplace and its health-related aspects. In S. L. Sauter et al. (Eds.), *Job control and worker health* (pp. 129–159). New York: Wiley.

12492

Test Name: JOB DEMANDS SCALE

Purpose: To measure employees' job demands.

Number of Items: 6

Format: Seven-point scales range from *strongly disagree* to *strongly agree*. Sample items are presented.

Reliability: Coefficient alpha was .78.

Author: Epitropaki, O., and Martin, R.

Article: From ideal to real: A longitudinal study of the role of implicit leadership theories on leader–member exchange and employee outcomes.

Journal: *Journal of Applied Psychology*, July 2005, *90*, 659–676.

Related Research: Karasek, R. A., Jr., et al. (1998). The Job Content Questionnaire (JCQ): An instrument for internationally comparative assessments of psychosocial job characteristics. *Journal of Occupational Health Psychology, 3*, 322–355.

12493

Test Name: JOB IMPROVEMENT SCALE

Purpose: To assess characteristics of a new job.

Number of Items: 11

Format: Scales range from 1 (*worse than my old job*) to 3 (*better than my old job*). All items are presented.

Reliability: Coefficient alpha was .80.

Validity: Correlations with other variables ranged from −.13 to .12.

Author: Wanberg, C. R., et al.

Article: Predictive validity of a multidisciplinary model of reemployment success.

Journal: *Journal of Applied Psychology*, December 2002, *87*, 1100–1120.

Related Research: Burke, R. J. (1996). Reemployment on a poorer job after a plant closing. *Psychological Reports, 58*, 559–570.

12494

Test Name: JOB INSECURITY SCALE

Purpose: To measure importance of job features, the likelihood of threats to job features, importance of overall job, and likelihood of threat to overall job.

Number of Items: 54

Format: Item responses are anchored by 1 (*strongly agree*) and 5 (*strongly disagree*).

Reliability: Subscale reliabilities ranged from .84 to .93.

Validity: Correlations of total score with other variables ranged from .15 to .78.

Author: Reisel, W. D., and Banai, M.

Article: Comparison of a multidimensional and a global measure of job insecurity: Predicting job attitudes and work behaviors.

Journal: *Psychological Reports*, June 2002, *90*, Part 1, 913–922.

Related Research: Ashford, S. J., et al. (1989). Content, causes, and consequences of job insecurity: A theory-based measure and substantive test. *Academy of Management Journal, 32*, 803–829.

12495

Test Name: JOB QUANTITATIVE OVERLOAD SCALE

Purpose: To measure quantitative work load.

Number of Items: 10

Format: Scales range from 1 (*strongly disagree*) to 7 (*strongly agree*). A sample item is presented.

Reliability: Coefficient alpha was .91.

Validity: Correlations with other variables ranged from −.23 to .54.

Author: Zellars, K. L., and Perrewé, P. L.

Article: Affective personality and the content of emotional social support: Coping in organizations.

Journal: *Journal of Applied Psychology*, June 2001, *86*, 459–467.

12496

Test Name: JOB RESOURCES SCALES

Purpose: To measure four job resources.

Number of Items: 14

Format: Includes four scales: Autonomy, Social Support, Coaching by the Supervisor, and Performance Feedback. Responses are made on 5-point scales ranging from 1 (*never*) to 5 (*always*). Examples are given.

Reliability: Alpha coefficients ranged from .75 to .90.

Validity: Correlations with other variables ranged from −.12 to .23.

Author: Bakker, A. B.

Article: Flow among music teachers and their students: The crossover of peak experiences.

Journal: *Journal of Vocational Behavior*, February 2005, *66*, 26–44.

Related Research: Bakker, A. B., et al. (2003). A multigroup analysis of the job demands–resources model in four home care organizations. *International Journal of Stress Management, 10,* 16–38. Van der Doef, M., & Maes, S. (1999). The job demand–control (–support) model and psychological well-being: A review of 20 years of empirical research. *Work and Stress, 13,* 87–114. LeBlank, P. (1994). De steun van de leiding: Een onderzoek naar het Leader Member Exchange model in de verpleging [Leader's support: A study of the Leader Member Exchange model among nurses]. Amsterdam: Thesis Publishers.

12497

Test Name: JOB ROLE BREADTH SCALE

Purpose: To measure the breadth of tasks in a job.

Number of Items: 94

Format: Scales range from 1 (*task not performed*) to 2 (*task performed*).

Reliability: Internal reliability was .94.

Validity: Correlations with other variables ranged from −.14 to .38.

Author: Morgeson, F. P., et al.

Article: The importance of job autonomy, cognitive ability, and job-related skill for predicting role breadth and job performance.

Journal: *Journal of Applied Psychology*, March 2005, *90*, 399–406.

12498

Test Name: JOB SAFETY CITIZENSHIP ROLE DEFINITIONS SCALE

Purpose: To assess the degree to which team members think safety concerns are part of their job.

Number of Items: 27

Format: Scales range from 1 (*expected part of my job*) to 5 (*definitely above and beyond what is expected for my job*). All items are presented.

Reliability: Coefficient alpha was .98.

Validity: Correlations with other variables ranged from .23 to .35.

Author: Hofmann, D. A., et al.

Article: Climate as a moderator of the relationship between leader–member exchange and content specific citizenship: Safety climate as an exemplar.

Journal: *Journal of Applied Psychology*, February 2003, *88*, 170–178.

12499

Test Name: JUSTICE PERCEPTIONS SCALE

Purpose: To measure procedural and interactional justice.

Number of Items: 13

Format: Scales range from 1 (*strongly disagree*) to 5 (*strongly agree*).

Reliability: Coefficient alpha was .95.

Author: Phillips, J. M., et al.

Article: The role of justice in team member satisfaction with the leader and attachment to the team.

Journal: *Journal of Applied Psychology*, April 2001, *86*, 316–325.

Related Research: Brockner, J., et al. (1997). When trust matters: The moderating effect of outcome favorability. *Administrative Science Quarterly, 42,* 558–583.

12500

Test Name: JUSTICE SCALE

Purpose: To measure distributive, procedural, and interactional justice.

Number of Items: 9

Format: A yes–no format is used. All items are presented.

Validity: Correlations with other variables ranged from .30 to .76.

Author: Martínez-Tur, V., et al.

Article: Relationships among perceived justice, customers' satisfaction, and behavioral intentions: The moderating role of gender.

Journal: *Psychological Reports*, June 2001, *88*, Part 1, 805–811.

Related Research: Tata, J., & Bowes-Sperry, L. (1996). Emphasis on distributive, procedural, and interactional justice: Differential perceptions of men and women. *Psychological Reports, 79,* 1327–1330.

12501

Test Name: JUSTICE SCALES

Purpose: To measure procedural and distributive justice.

Number of Items: 20

Format: Response scales are anchored by 1 (*completely disagree*) and 7 (*completely agree*). All items are presented.

Reliability: Alpha coefficients ranged from .76 to .84.

Author: Flint, D. H., and Cole, N. D.

Article: Decision frame and procedural justice: Interactive effects on perceptions of distributive justice.

Journal: *Psychological Reports,* October 2003, *93,* 631–637.

Related Research: Brockner, J., et al. (1995). Decision frame, procedural justice, and survivors' reactions to job layoffs. *Organizational Behavior and Human Decision Processes, 63,* 59–68.

12502

Test Name: KEPT PROMISE SCALES

Purpose: To assess the extent to which the organizations had kept their promises.

Number of Items: 11

Format: Includes two scales: Facet-Specific and Global. Responses are made on 7-point scales. Sample items are presented.

Reliability: Alpha coefficients were .74 and .81.

Validity: Correlations with other variables ranged from −.14 to .10.

Author: Conway, N., and Briner, R. B.

Article: Full-time versus part-time employees: Understanding the links between work status, the psychological contract, and attitudes.

Journal: *Journal of Vocational Behavior,* October 2002, *61,* 279–301.

Related Research: Robinson, S. L. (1996). Violations of psychological contracts: Impact on employee attitudes. In L. E. Tetrick & J. Barling (Eds.), *Changing employment relations: Behavioral and social perspectives.* Washington, DC: American Psychological Association.

12503

Test Name: LEARNING AND PERFORMANCE ORIENTATIONS IN PHYSICAL EDUCATION CLASSES QUESTIONNAIRE

Purpose: To assess the perceived motivational climate.

Number of Items: 27

Format: Includes five subscales: Teacher Initiated Learning Orientation, Students' Learning Orientation, Students' Competitive Orientation, Student' Worries About Mistakes, and Outcome Orientation Without Effort. Responses are made on a 5-point Likert-type scale ranging from 1 (*strongly disagree*) to 5 (*strongly agree*).

Reliability: Alpha coefficients ranged from .80 to .93.

Author: Ferrier-Caja, E., and Weiss, M. R.

Article: Cross-validation of a model of intrinsic motivation with students enrolled in high school elective courses.

Journal: *Journal of Experimental Education,* Fall 2002, *71,* 41–65.

Related Research: Papaioannou, A. (1994). Development of a questionnaire to measure achievement goal orientations in physical education. *Research Quarterly of Exercise and Sport, 65,* 11–20.

12504

Test Name: LEARNING CLIMATE QUESTIONNAIRE—SHORT FORM

Purpose: To measure student perceptions of the autonomy support provided by their physical education teachers.

Number of Items: 6

Format: Responses are made on a 5-point scale ranging from 1 (*strongly disagree*) to 5 (*strongly agree*).

Reliability: Alpha coefficients were .81 and .96.

Validity: Correlations with other variables ranged from −.26 to .64.

Author: Ntoumanis, N.

Article: A prospective study of participation in optional school physical education using a self-determination theory framework.

Journal: *Journal of Educational Psychology,* August 2005, *97,* 444–453.

Related Research: Williams, G. C., & Deci, E. L. (1996). Internalization of biopsychosocial values by medical students: A test of self-determination theory. *Journal of Personality and Social Psychology, 70,* 767–779.

12505

Test Name: LIKELIHOOD AND FEAR OF FUTURE VIOLENCE AT WORK SCALES

Purpose: To assess the likelihood of future workplace violence and the fear of such violence.

Number of Items: 10

Format: Scales range from 1 (*strongly disagree*) to 7 (*strongly agree*). Sample items are presented.

Reliability: Alpha coefficients were .95.

Validity: Correlations with other variables ranged from −.20 to .74.

Author: LeBlanc, M. M., and Kelloway, E. K.

Article: Predictors and outcomes of workplace violence and aggression.

Journal: *Journal of Applied Psychology,* June 2002, *87,* 444–453.

12506

Test Name: MARKET ORIENTATION QUESTIONNAIRE

Purpose: To measure market orientation of business-school deans as an element in evaluating and promoting their programs. Customer orientation, competitor orientation, interfunctional coordination, and overall market orientation are constructs measured by the scale.

Number of Items: 15

Format: Seven-point scales are anchored by 1 (*not at all*) and 7 (*to an extreme extent*). All items are presented.

Reliability: Reliabilities ranged from .75 to .91.

Validity: Business-school deans scored lower than specialty business managers on all four constructs.

Author: Harmon, H. A., et al.

Article: Pilot study comparing market orientation culture of businesses and schools of business.

Journal: *Psychological Reports,* August 2003, *93,* 241–250.

12507

Test Name: MOTIVATIONAL CLIMATE IN SPORT QUESTIONNAIRE

Purpose: To assess motivational climate.

Number of Items: 28

Format: Includes two climates: mastery climate and performance climate. Responses are made on a 5-point scale ranging from 1 (*never*) to 5 (*always*). All items are presented.

Reliability: Reliability coefficients ranged from .75 to .82.

Validity: Correlations with other variables ranged from .12 to .55.

Author: Skjesol, K., and Halvari, H.

Article: Motivational climate, achievement goals, perceived sport competence, and involvement in physical activity: Structural and mediator models.

Journal: *Perceptual and Motor Skills,* April 2005, *100,* 497–523.

Related Research: Walling, M. D., et al. (1993). The Perceived Motivational Climate in Sport Questionnaire: Construct and predictive validity. *Journal of Sport and Exercise Psychology, 54,* 1063–1070.

12508

Test Name: MULTICULTURAL EDUCATION INDEX

Purpose: To provide a multidimensional index of multicultural education.

Number of Items: 6

Format: Responses are made on a 5-point scale ranging from *strongly agree* to *strongly disagree.* All items are presented.

Reliability: Coefficient alpha was .88.

Author: Asada, H., et al.

Article: The acceptance of a multicultural education among Appalachian college students.

Journal: *Research in Higher Education,* February 2003, *44,* 99–120.

Related Research: Hughes-Miller, M., et al. (1998). Campus racial climate policies: The view from the bottom up. *Race Gender Class, 5,* 139–157.

12509

Test Name: MULTICULTURAL PROGRAM ORGANIZATION ASSESSMENT INSTRUMENT

Purpose: To assess organizational climate supportive of multicultural concerns.

Number of Items: 33

Format: A Likert format is used. All items are presented.

Reliability: Alpha coefficients ranged from .93 to .94.

Author: Longerbeam, S. D., et al.

Article: A multicultural myth: A study of multicultural program organizations at three public research universities.

Journal: *Journal of College Student Development,* January/February 2005, *46,* 88–98.

Related Research: Garcia, M., et al. (2001). *Assessing campus diversity initiatives.* Washington, DC: American Association of Colleges and Universities.

12510

Test Name: MULTIFOCI JUSTICE SCALES

Purpose: To measure organizational and supervisory justice.

Number of Items: 22

Format: Scales range from 1 (*strongly disagree*) to 7 (*strongly agree*). Sample items are presented.

Reliability: Alpha coefficients ranged from .82 to .89 across subscales.

Validity: Correlations with other variables ranged from –.01 to .88.

Author: Liao, H., and Rupp, D. E.

Article: The impact of justice climate and justice orientation on work outcomes: A cross-level multifoci framework.

Journal: *Journal of Applied Psychology,* March 2005, *90,* 242–256.

Related Research: Byrne, Z. S. (1999, April). *How do procedural and interactional justice influence multiple levels of organizational outcomes?* Paper presented at the 14th annual conference of the Society for Industrial and Organizational Psychology, Atlanta, GA.

12511

Test Name: MY CLASS INVENTORY—REVISED

Purpose: To measure elementary school classroom climate.

Number of Items: 18

Time Required: 15 minutes

Format: A yes–no format is used. All items are presented.

Reliability: Alpha coefficients ranged from .65 to .72.

Author: Sink, C., and Spencer, L. R.

Article: My Class Inventory—Short Form as an accountability tool for elementary school counselors to measure classroom climate.

Journal: *Professional School Counseling*, October 2005, *9*(1), 37–48.

Related Research: Fraser, B. J., & Fisher, D. L. (1982). Evaluation studies: Predictive validity of My Class Inventory. *Studies in Educational Evaluation, 8,* 129–140.

12512

Test Name: NEED FOR EMPLOYEES ASSISTANCE PROGRAMS

Purpose: To assess the perceived need for employee assistance: financial, legal, alcohol abuse, drug abuse, mental health, family relationships, marital problems, personal problems, physical health compensation, retirement, performance, promotion, personnel conflicts, career counseling, and discrimination.

Format: Item responses are anchored by 1 (*There is no need for counseling and assistance programs*) and 5 (*There is a strong need for counseling and assistance programs*).

Reliability: Reliabilities ranged from .89 to .92.

Validity: Correlations with other variables ranged from −.20 to .55.

Author: Cohen, A., and Schwartz, H.

Article: An empirical examination among Canadian teachers of determinants of the need for employees' assistance programs.

Journal: *Psychological Reports,* June 2002, *90,* Part 2, 1221–1238.

Related Research: Reed, D. J. (1983). One approach to employee assistance. *Personnel Journal, 77,* 872–874.

12513

Test Name: NEIGHBORHOOD COHESION SCALE

Purpose: To measure neighborhood cohesion.

Number of Items: 5

Format: Responses are made on a 3-point scale ranging from 1 (*strongly agree*) to 3 (*disagree*). All items are presented.

Reliability: Coefficient alpha was .87.

Validity: Correlations with other variables ranged from −.34 to .20.

Author: Kohen, D. E., et al.

Article: Neighborhood income and physical and social disorder in Canada: Associations with young children's competence.

Journal: *Child Development,* November/December 2002, *73,* 1844–1860.

Related Research: Sampson, R. J., et al. (1997). Neighborhoods and violent crime: A multilevel study of collective efficacy. *Science, 277,* 918–924.

12514

Test Name: NEIGHBORHOOD CONTEXT SCALES

Purpose: To assess extent of various acts and problems that exist in the neighborhood.

Number of Items: 13

Format: Includes two scales: Neighborhood Risk Scale and Community Disorganization Scale. Responses are made on 3-point scales.

Reliability: Alpha coefficients were .74 and .90.

Author: Cleveland, M. J., et al.

Article: The impact of parenting on risk cognitions and risk behavior: A study of mediation and moderation in a panel of African American adolescents.

Journal: *Child Development,* July/August 2005, *76,* 900–916.

Related Research: Sampson, R. J., et al. (1997). Neighborhoods and violent crime: A multilevel study of collective efficacy. *Science, 277,* 918–924.

12515

Test Name: NEIGHBORHOOD CRIMINAL EVENTS SCALE

Purpose: To measure perceptions of criminal events.

Number of Items: 12

Format: Scales range from 0 (*never*) to 5 (*daily*). Sample items are presented.

Reliability: Alpha coefficients ranged form .72 to .92.

Validity: Correlations with other variables ranged from −.62 to .31.

Author: Roosa, M. W., et al.

Article: Family and child characteristics linking neighborhood context and child externalizing behavior.

Journal: *Journal of Marriage and Family,* May 2005, *67,* 515–529.

12516

Test Name: NEIGHBORHOOD INFORMAL CONTROL, TRUST, AND COHESION SCALE

Purpose: To measure informal control, trust, and cohesion in a neighborhood.

Number of Items: 12

Format: Four- point scales range from *very likely* or *strongly agree* to *very unlikely* or *strongly disagree*. A sample item is presented.

Reliability: Alpha coefficients ranged from .62 to .85.

Validity: Correlations with other variables ranged from –.41 to .57.

Author: Dorsey, S., and Forehand, R.

Article: The relation of social capital to child psychosocial adjustment difficulties: The role of positive parenting and neighborhood dangerousness.

Journal: *Journal of Psychopathology and Behavioral Assessment*, March 2003, *25*, 11–23.

Related Research: Sampson, R. (1992). Family management and child development: Insights from social disorganization theory. In J. McCord (Ed.), *Advances in criminological theory* (Vol. 3, pp. 63–93). New Brunswick, NJ: Transaction Books.

12517

Test Name: NEIGHBORHOOD PROBLEM SCALE

Purpose: To measure neighborhood stress in economically disadvantaged areas.

Number of Items: 22

Format: Rating scales range from 1 (*not a problem*) to 3 (*a big problem*).

Reliability: Coefficient alpha was .94.

Author: Gross, D., et al.

Article: Parent training of toddlers in day care in low-income urban communities.

Journal: *Journal of Consulting and Clinical Psychology*, April 2003, *71*, 261–278.

Related Research: Elder, G., et al. (1995). Inner-city parents under economic pressure: Perspectives on the strategies of parenting. *Journal of Marriage and the Family, 57*, 771–784.

12518

Test Name: NEIGHBORHOOD QUALITY SCALE

Purpose: To evaluate residents' perceptions of neighborhood quality.

Number of Items: 7

Format: Scales range from 1 (*strongly agree*) to 4 (*strongly disagree*). Sample items are presented.

Reliability: Alpha coefficients ranged from .88 to .90.

Validity: Correlations with other variables ranged from –.62 to –.10.

Author: Roosa, M. W., et al.

Article: Family and child characteristics linking neighborhood context and child externalizing behavior.

Journal: *Journal of Marriage and Family*, May 2005, *67*, 515–529.

12519

Test Name: NEIGHBORHOOD RISK SCALE

Purpose: To measure neighborhood risks associated with danger and violence.

Number of Items: 5

Format: A yes–no format is used.

Reliability: Coefficient alpha was .84.

Validity: Correlations with other variables ranged from -.36 to .53

Author: Dorsey, S., and Forehand, R.

Article: The relation of social capital to child psychosocial

adjustment difficulties: The role of positive parenting and neighborhood dangerousness.

Journal: *Journal of Psychopathology and Behavioral Assessment*, March 2003, *25*, 11–23.

Related Research: Forehand, R., et al. (2000). The role of community risks and resources in the psychosocial adjustment of at-risk children: An examination across two community contexts and two informants. *Behavior Therapy, 31*, 395–414.

12520

Test Name: NEIGHBORHOOD SUPPORT FOR WORK AND PARENTING SCALE

Purpose: To assess mothers' perception of neighborhood social support.

Number of Items: 9

Format: Seven-point scales range from *strongly disagree* to *strongly agree*.

Reliability: Coefficient alpha was .89.

Author: Dorsey, S., and Forehand, R.

Article: The relation of social capital to child psychosocial adjustment difficulties: The role of positive parenting and neighborhood dangerousness.

Journal: *Journal of Psychopathology and Behavioral Assessment*, March 2003, *25*, 11–23.

Related Research: Brody, G. H. (1996). *Neighborhood Support for Work and Parenting Scale*. Unpublished scale, University of Georgia.

12521

Test Name: OCCUPATION SELF-DIRECTION SCALE

Purpose: To measure job characteristics such as autonomy, complexity, routine, closeness of supervision, and control over others.

Number of Items: 20

Format: Scales range from 1 (*very much*) to 4 (*not at all*).

Reliability: Coefficient alpha was .89.

Author: Crouter, A. C., et al.

Article: Implications of overwork and overload for the quality of men's family relationships.

Journal: *Journal of Marriage and Family*, May 2001, *63*, 404–416.

Related Research: Lennon, M. C. (1994). Women, work, and well-being: The importance of work conditions. *Journal of Health and Social Behavior, 35*, 235–247.

12522

Test Name: OLDER WORKER JOB SEARCH CONSTRAINTS SCALE

Purpose: To measure older worker job search constraints.

Number of Items: 4

Format: Includes two dimensions: Perceived Disincentives and Perceived Age Stereotyping. All items are presented.

Reliability: Coefficient alpha was .82.

Validity: Correlations with other variables ranged from –.10 to .51.

Author: Adams, G., and Rau, B.

Article: Job seeking among retirees seeking bridge employment.

Journal: *Personnel Psychology,* Autumn 2004, *57*, 719–744.

Related Research: Allan, P. (1990). Looking for work after forty: Job search experience of older unemployed managers and professionals. *Journal of Employment Counseling, 27*, 113–121. Rife, J., & Kilty, K.

(1989). Job search discouragement and the older worker: Implication for social work practice. *Journal of Applied Social Sciences, 14*, 71–94.

12523

Test Name: ORGANIZATION ATTRACTION SCALE

Purpose: To measure organizational attraction.

Number of Items: 15

Format: Includes three components: general attractiveness, intentions to pursue, and prestige. Responses are made on a 5-point scale ranging from 1 (*strongly disagree*) to 5 (*strongly agree*). All items are presented.

Reliability: Alpha coefficients ranged from .82 to .88.

Author: Highhouse, S., et al.

Article: Measuring attraction to organizations.

Journal: *Education and Psychological Measurement*, December 2003, *63*, 986–1001.

Related Research: Turban, D. B., & Keon, T. L. (1993). Organizational attractiveness: An interactionist perspective. *Journal of Applied Psychology, 78*, 184–193. Ployhart, R. E., & Ryan, A. M. (1998). Applicants' reactions to the fairness of selection procedures: The effects of positive rule violations and time of measurement. *Journal of Applied Psychology, 83*, 3–16. Highhouse, S., et al. (1998). Get'em while they last! Effects of scarcity information in job advertisements. *Journal of Applied Social Psychology, 28*, 779–795.

12524

Test Name: ORGANIZATION-LEVEL SAFETY CLIMATE SCALE

Purpose: To assess top-managements' commitment to safety over competing goals.

Number of Items: 16

Format: Scales range from 1 (*completely disagree*) to 5 (*completely agree*). All items are presented.

Reliability: Coefficient alpha was .92.

Validity: Correlations with other variables ranged from –.02 to .46.

Author: Zohar, D., and Luria, G.

Article: A multilevel model of safety climate: Cross-level relationships between organization and group-level climates.

Journal: *Journal of Applied Psychology*, July 2005, *90*, 616–628.

12525

Test Name: ORGANIZATIONAL ATTRACTIVENESS SCALE

Purpose: To measure perceptions of organizational attractiveness.

Number of Items: 3

Format: Responses to two items are made on a 7-point scale ranging from 1 (*strongly disagree*) to 7 (*strongly agree*). The third item response ranges from 0% to 100%.

Reliability: Coefficient alpha was .89.

Validity: Correlations with other variables ranged from –.04 to .48 ($n = 216$).

Author: Williamson, I. O., et al.

Article: The effect of company recruitment Web site orientation on individuals' perceptions of organizational attractiveness.

Journal: *Journal of Vocational Behavior*, October 2003, *63*, 242–263.

Related Research: Schwoerer, C. E., & Rosen, B. (1989). Effects of employment-at-will policies and compensation policies on corporate image and job pursuit intentions.

Journal of Applied Psychology, 74, 653–656.

12526

Test Name: ORGANIZATIONAL ATTRACTIVENESS SCALE

Purpose: To assess the attractiveness of an organization.

Number of Items: 4

Reliability: Coefficient alpha was .82.

Validity: Correlations with other variables ranged from −.30 to .03.

Author: Avery, D. R.

Article: Reactions to diversity in recruitment advertising—Are differences black and white?

Journal: *Journal of Applied Psychology,* August 2003, *88,* 672–679.

Related Research: Perkins, L. A., et al. (2000). Advertising and recruitment: Marketing to minorities. *Psychology and Marketing, 17,* 235–255.

12527

Test Name: ORGANIZATIONAL ATTRIBUTES SURVEY

Purpose: To measure organizational attributes.

Number of Items: 16

Format: Includes three factors: company image, compensation and job security, and challenging work. Responses are made on a 5-point scale ranging from 1 (*much poorer*) to 5 (*much better*).

Reliability: Alpha coefficients ranged from .83 to .85 (*N*s ranged from 562–569).

Validity: Correlation with other variables ranged from −.15 to .46 (*N*s ranged from 562–569).

Author: Turban, D. B.

Article: Organizational attractiveness as an employer on college campuses: An examination of the applicant population.

Journal: *Journal of Vocational Behavior,* April 2001, *58,* 293–312.

Related Research: Harris, M. M., & Fink, L. S. (1987). A field study of applicant reactions to employment opportunities: Does the recruiter make a difference? *Personnel Psychology, 40,* 765–784. Powell, G. N. (1984). Effects of job attributes and recruiting practices on applicant decisions: A comparison. *Personnel Psychology, 37,* 721–732. Turban, D. B., et al. (1995). Factors related to job acceptance decisions of college recruits. *Journal of Vocational Behavior, 47,* 193–213.

12528

Test Name: ORGANIZATIONAL DEVIANCE MEASURE— ADAPTED

Purpose: To assess perceived organizational deviance.

Number of Items: 6

Format: Responses are made on a 5-point scale ranging from 1 (*never*) to 5 (*once a week or more*). All items are presented.

Reliability: Coefficient alpha was .74.

Validity: Correlations with other variables ranged from −.38 to .52.

Author: Liao, H., et al.

Article: Sticking out like a sore thumb: Employee dissimilarity and deviance at work.

Journal: *Personnel Psychology,* Winter 2004, *57,* 969–1000.

Related Research: Bennett, R. J., & Robinson, S. L. (2000). The development of a measure of workplace deviance. *Journal of Applied Psychology, 85,* 349–360.

12529

Test Name: ORGANIZATIONAL JUSTICE EVALUATION SCALE

Purpose: To measure procedural justice and relational justice.

Number of Items: 9

Format: Scales range from 1 (*totally disagree*) to 5 (*totally agree*).

Reliability: Alpha coefficients were .90 (procedural) and .81 (relational).

Validity: Correlations with other variables ranged from −.01 to .62.

Author: Elovainio, M., et al.

Article: Organizational justice evaluations, job control, and occupational strain.

Journal: *Journal of Applied Psychology,* June 2001, *86,* 418–424.

Related Research: Moorman, R. H. (1991). Relationship between organizational justice and organizational citizenship behaviors: Do fairness perceptions influence employee citizenship? *Journal of Applied Psychology, 76,* 845–855.

12530

Test Name: ORGANIZATIONAL JUSTICE SCALE

Purpose: To measure procedural, distributive, interpersonal, and informational justice.

Number of Items: 20

Format: Scales range from 1 (*to a small extent*) to 5 (*to a large extent*). All items are presented.

Reliability: Alpha coefficients ranged from .90 to .93 across subscales.

Validity: Correlations with other variables ranged from .05 to .46.

Author: Colquitt, J. A.

Article: On the dimensionality of organizational justice: A construct validation measure.

Journal: *Journal of Applied Psychology*, June 2001, *86*, 386–400.

12531

Test Name: ORGANIZATIONAL JUSTICE SCALE

Purpose: To measure organizational justice.

Number of Items: 13

Format: Includes two factors: procedural justice and organizational justice. Responses are made on a 5-point scale ranging from 1 (*totally disagree*) to 5 (*totally agree*).

Reliability: Alpha coefficients were .81 and .90.

Author: Elovainio, M., et al.

Article: Personality as a moderator in the relations between perceptions of organizational justice and sickness absence.

Journal: *Journal of Vocational Behavior*, December 2003, *63*, 379–395.

Related Research: Moorman, R. H. (1991). Relationship between organizational justice and organizational citizenship behaviors: Do fairness perceptions influence employee citizenship? *Journal of Applied Psychology, 76*, 845–855.

12532

Test Name: ORGANIZATIONAL JUSTICE SCALES

Purpose: To measure distributive justice perceptions, procedural justice perceptions, and interactional justice perceptions.

Number of Items: 18

Format: Scales range from 1 (*strongly disagree*) to 7 (*strongly agree*). Sample items are presented.

Reliability: Alpha coefficients ranged from .90 to .96.

Validity: Correlations with other variables ranged from −.23 to .45.

Author: Williams, S., et al.

Article: Justice and organizational citizenship behavior intentions: Fair rewards versus fair treatment.

Journal: *The Journal of Social Psychology*, February 2002, *142*, 33–44.

Related Research: Moorman, R. H. (1991). Relationship between organizational justice and organizational citizenship behaviors: Do fairness perceptions influence employee citizenship? *Journal of Applied Psychology, 76*, 845–855.

12533

Test Name: ORGANIZATIONAL JUSTICE SCALES—SPANISH VERSIONS

Purpose: To measure distributive, procedural, and interactional justice.

Number of Items: 11

Format: Response scales ranged from 1 (*strongly disagree*) to 7 (*strongly agree*). Sample items are presented.

Reliability: Alpha coefficients ranged from .87 to .96.

Validity: Correlations with other variables ranged from −.40 to .17.

Author: Moliner, C., et al.

Article: Linking organizational justice to burnout: Are men and women different?

Journal: *Psychological Reports*, June 2005, *96*, Part 1, 805–816.

12534

Test Name: ORGANIZATIONAL LEARNING SCALE

Purpose: To measure learning capabilities of organizations.

Number of Items: 21

Format: Seven-point scales are anchored by 1 (*strongly disagree*) and 7 (*strongly agree*). All items are presented.

Reliability: Coefficient alpha was .92.

Validity: Subscale correlations ranged from .51 to .74.

Author: Chakrabarty, S., and Rogé, J. N.

Article: An evaluation of the Organizational Learning Scale.

Journal: *Psychological Reports*, December 2002, *91*, Part 2, 1255–1267.

Related Research: Goh, S. C., & Richards, G. (1997, Spring). Benchmarking the learning capability of organizations. *European Management Journal*, 15–22.

12535

Test Name: ORGANIZATIONAL PERCEPTIONS SCALE

Purpose: To assess distributive justice, procedural justice, interpersonal justice, and informational justice.

Number of Items: 20

Format: Sample items are presented.

Reliability: Alpha coefficients ranged from .84 to .96 across subscales.

Validity: Fit indices ranged from .75 to .95.

Author: Judge, T. A., and Colquitt, J. A.

Article: Organizational justice and stress: The mediating role of work–family conflict.

Journal: *Journal of Applied Psychology*, June 2004, *89*, 395–404.

Related Research: Colquitt, J. A. (2001). On the dimensionality of organizational justice. A construct validation of a measure. *Journal of Applied Psychology, 86,* 386–400.

12536

Test Name: ORGANIZATIONAL PERSONALITY SCALE

Purpose: To assess an organization's personality by use of trait adjectives.

Number of Items: 71

Format: Trait adjectives were followed by scales ranging from 1 (*strongly disagree*) to 5 (*strongly agree*). All items are presented.

Reliability: Alpha coefficients ranged from .70 to .88 across subscales.

Validity: Multiple correlation coefficients with other variables ranged from .28 to .38.

Author: Slaughter, J. E., et al.

Article: Personality trait inferences about organizations: Development of a measure and assessment of construct validity.

Journal: *Journal of Applied Psychology,* February 2004, *89,* 85–103.

12537

Test Name: ORGANIZATIONAL POLITICS PERCEPTIONS SCALE

Purpose: To measure organizational politics.

Number of Items: 6

Format: Scales range from 1 (*strongly disagree*) to 7 (*strongly agree*). Sample items are presented.

Reliability: Coefficient alpha was .93.

Author: Treadway, D. C., et al.

Article: The role of age in the perceptions of politics–job

performance relationship: A three-study constructive replication.

Journal: *Journal of Applied Psychology,* September 2005, *90,* 872–881.

Related Research: Hochwarter, W. A., et al. (2003). Perceived organizational support as a mediator of the relationship between politics perceptions and work outcomes. *Journal of Vocational Behavior, 63,* 438–465.

12538

Test Name: ORGANIZATIONAL RECOGNITION AND INCLUSION SCALE

Purpose: To assess the degree to which an employee feels his or her employer fulfills its obligations and to what extent he or she receives recognition from upper management.

Number of Items: 7

Format: Scales range from 1 (*not at all fulfilled* or *much less* or *strongly disagree*) to 5 (*very highly fulfilled* or *much more*). Sample items are presented.

Reliability: Alpha coefficients were .90 (fulfilled obligations) and .87 (recognition).

Validity: Correlations with other variables ranged from −.20 to .72.

Author: Wayne, S. J., et al.

Article: The role of fair treatment and rewards in perceptions of organizational support and leader–member exchange.

Journal: *Journal of Applied Psychology,* June 2002, *87,* 590–598.

12539

Test Name: ORGANIZATIONAL RESOURCES SCALE

Purpose: To measure the importance of training, autonomy, and technology.

Number of Items: 11

Format: Scales range from 1 (*not important*) to 5 (*important*). All items are presented.

Reliability: Alpha coefficients ranged from .84 to .91.

Validity: Correlations with other variables ranged from .06 to .43.

Author: Salanova, M., et al.

Article: Linking organizational resources and work engagement to employee performance and customer loyalty: The mediation of service climate.

Journal: *Journal of Applied Psychology,* November 2005, *90,* 1217–1227.

12540

Test Name: ORGANIZATIONAL REWARDS FOR EMPLOYEE DEVELOPMENT SCALE

Purpose: To assess the extent employees perceived their efforts to develop others were rewarded in the organization.

Number of Items: 4

Format: Responses are made on a 5-point scale ranging from 1 (*strongly disagree*) to 5 (*strongly agree*). An example is given.

Reliability: Coefficient alpha was .88.

Validity: Correlations with other variables ranged from −.23 to .33.

Author: Allen, T. D.

Article: Protégé selection by mentors: Contributing individual and organizational factors.

Journal: *Journal of Vocational Behavior,* December 2004, *65,* 469–483.

12541

Test Name: ORGANIZATIONAL REWARDS SCALE

Purpose: To assess beliefs concerning the favorableness of opportunities for promotion and pay.

Number of Items: 3

Format: Scales range from 1 (*very unfavorable*) to 5 (*very favorable*). All items are presented.

Reliability: Coefficient alpha was .70.

Validity: Correlations with other variables ranged from –.05 to .47.

Author: Rhoades, L., et al.

Article: Affective commitment to the organization: The contribution of perceived organizational support.

Journal: *Journal of Applied Psychology*, October 2001, *86*, 825–836.

Related Research: Eisenberger, R., et al. (1997). Perceived organizational support, discretionary treatment, and job satisfaction. *Journal of Applied Psychology*, *82*, 812–820.

12542

Test Name: ORGANIZATIONAL SAFETY QUESTIONNAIRE

Purpose: To measure safety climate, safety consciousness, safety-related events, and occupational injuries.

Number of Items: 39

Format: Scales range from 1 (*strongly disagree*) to 5 (*strongly agree*) and from 1 (*never*) to 5 (*frequently*). Twenty-nine items are presented.

Reliability: Alpha coefficients ranged from .70 to .92 across subscales.

Validity: Correlations with other variables ranged from –.26 to .55.

Author: Barling, J., et al.

Article: Development and test of a model linking safety-specific

transformational leadership and occupational safety.

Journal: *Journal of Applied Psychology*, June 2002, *87*, 488–496.

Related Research: Zohar, D. (1980). Safety climate in industrial organizations: Theoretical and applied implications. *Journal of Applied Psychology*, *65*, 96–102.

12543

Test Name: ORGANIZATIONAL STRUCTURE MEASURE

Purpose: To assess the degree to which departments reflect mechanistic or organic characteristics.

Number of Items: 7

Format: Seven-point scales assess the degree to which paired statements describe the structure of work. Sample items are presented.

Reliability: Coefficient alpha was .83.

Validity: Correlations with other variables ranged from –.14 to .08.

Author: Ambrose, M. L., and Schminke, M.

Article: Organization structure as a moderator of the relationship between procedural justice, interactional justice, perceived organizational support, and supervisory trust.

Journal: *Journal of Applied Psychology*, April 2003, *88*, 295–305.

Related Research: Khandwalla, P. N. (1976/1977). Some top management styles, their context and performance. *Organization and Administrative Sciences*, *7*, 21–51.

12544

Test Name: ORGANIZATIONAL SUPPORT SCALE

Purpose: To measure organizational support.

Number of Items: 3

Format: A sample item is presented.

Reliability: An estimate of reliability was .82.

Validity: Correlations with other variables ranged from –.33 to .27 (*n* = 226).

Author: Blau, G., et al.

Article: Correlates of professional versus organizational withdrawal cognitions.

Journal: *Journal of Vocational Behavior*, August 2003, *63*, 72–85.

Related Research: Eisenberger, R., et al. (1986). Perceived organizational support. *Journal of Applied Psychology*, *71*, 500–507.

12545

Test Name: ORGANIZATIONAL SUPPORT SCALE

Purpose: To measure employer's respect for workers' nonwork participation.

Number of Items: 4

Format: Item responses are anchored by 1 (*not typical of my organization*) and 5 (*very typical*). Sample items are presented.

Reliability: Cronbach's alpha was .77.

Validity: Correlations with other variables ranged from –.25 to .25.

Author: Cohen, A., and Schwartz, H.

Article: An empirical examination among Canadian teachers of determinants of the need for employees' assistance programs.

Journal: *Psychological Reports*, June 2002, *90*, Part 2, 1221–1238.

Related Research: Kirchmeyer, C. (1993). Managing the work–nonwork boundary: An assessment of organizational responses. *Human Relations, 45,* 775–795.

12546

Test Name: ORGANIZATIONAL SUPPORT SUPPORTIVENESS SCALE

Purpose: To assess support of diversity and gay rights.

Number of Items: 10

Format: Gay rights scales range from 1 (*strongly disagree*) to 7 (*strongly agree*). Diversity support scales range from 1 (*true*) to 2 (*false*). Sample items are presented.

Reliability: Coefficient alpha was .86.

Validity: Correlations with other variables ranged from –.28 to .60.

Author: Griffith, K. H., and Hebl, M. R.

Article: The disclosure dilemma for gay men and lesbians: "Coming out" at work.

Journal: *Journal of Applied Psychology,* December 2002, *87,* 1191–1199.

Related Research: Driscoll, J. M., et al. (1996). Lesbian identity and disclosure in the workplace: Relation to occupational stress and satisfaction. *Journal of Vocational Behavior, 48,* 229–242.

12547

Test Name: ORGANIZATIONAL TOLERANCE FOR SEXUAL HARASSMENT INVENTORY

Purpose: To measure tolerance for sexual harassment in organizations.

Number of Items: 6

Format: Respondents rate vignettes on 5-point scales. Items are described.

Reliability: Coefficient alpha was .90.

Author: Kakuyama, T., et al.

Article: Organizational tolerance as a correlate of sexual harassment of Japanese working women.

Journal: *Psychological Reports,* June 2003, *92,* Part 2, 1268–1270.

Related Research: Hulin, C. L., et al. (1997). Sexual harassment: A preliminary test of an integrative model. *Journal of Applied Social Psychology, 27,* 877–901.

12548

Test Name: ORIGIN CLIMATE QUESTIONNAIRE

Purpose: To assess the degree to which children perceive the teacher and the class to be autonomous.

Number of Items: 24

Format: Includes six subscales: Internal Control, Instrumental Activity, Reality Perception, Personal Responsibility, Self-Confidence, and Goal Setting. Responses are made on a 4-point scale ranging from 1 (*never*) to 4 (*always*). Examples are presented.

Validity: Correlations with other variables ranged from –.27 to .51.

Author: Standage, M., et al.

Article: A model of contextual motivation in physical education: Using constructs from self-determination and achievement goal theories to predict physical activity intentions.

Journal: *Journal of Educational Psychology,* March 2003, *95,* 97–110.

Related Research: de Charms, R. (1976). *Enhancing motivation: Change in the classroom.* New York: Irvington.

12549

Test Name: PERCEIVED CLASSROOM ENVIRONMENT MEASURE

Purpose: To assess perceived classroom environment.

Number of Items: 11

Format: Includes three perceived classroom environment variables: lecture engagement, evaluation focus, and harsh evaluation. Responses are made on a 7-point scale ranging from 1 (*strongly disagree*) to 7 (*strongly agree*). All items are presented.

Reliability: Reliability coefficients ranged from .65 to .91.

Validity: Correlations with other variables ranged from –.22 to .33.

Author: Church, M. A., et al.

Article: Perceptions of classroom environment, achievement goals, and achievement outcomes.

Journal: *Journal of Educational Psychology,* March 2001, *93,* 43–54.

Related Research: Ames, C., & Archer, J. (1988). Achievement goals in the classroom: Student learning strategies and motivation processes. *Journal of Educational Psychology, 80,* 260–267. Frasier, B., & Fisher, D. (1986). Using short forms of classroom climate instruments to assess and improve classroom psychosocial environment. *Journal of Research in Science Teaching, 23,* 387–413. Winston, R., et al. (1994). A measure of college classroom climate. *Journal of College Student Development, 35,* 11–18.

12550

Test Name: PERCEIVED ENVIRONMENT SCALES

Purpose: To measure adolescents' perceptions of specific environmental elements.

Number of Items: 27

Format: Includes six scales: Perceived Parental Support, Perceptions of Friends, Positive School Experiences, Perceptions of Friends' Use of Substances at School, Perceptions of Friends' Positive School Attitudes, and

Perceptions of Friends' Social Support.

Reliability: Alpha coefficients ranged from .59 to .87.

Validity: Bryant, A. L., and Zimmerman, M. A.

Author: Examining the effects of academic beliefs and behaviors on changes in substance use among urban adolescents.

Article: *Journal of Educational Psychology*, September 2002, *94*, 621–637.

Related Research: Eccles, J. S. (1993). *Middle School Family Survey Study*. Boulder: University of Colorado. Procidano, M. E., & Heller, K. (1983). Measure of perceived social support from friends and family: Three validation studies. *American Journal of Community Psychology*, *11*, 1–24

12551

Test Name: PERCEIVED ENVIRONMENTAL SUPPORTS AND BARRIERS SCALES

Purpose: To assess perceived environmental supports and barriers relative to the pursuit of an engineering degree.

Number of Items: 38

Format: Includes two scales: Supports and Barriers. Responses are made on a 5-point scale ranging from 1 (*not at all likely*) to 5 (*extremely likely*). Examples are presented.

Reliability: Alpha coefficients were .92 and .94.

Validity: Correlations with other variables ranged from −.24 to .61 (*N* = 287).

Author: Lent, R. W., et al.

Article: Relation of contextual supports and barriers to choice behavior in engineering majors: Test of alternative social cognitive models.

Journal: *Journal of Counseling Psychology*, October 2003, *50*, 458–465.

Related Research: Lent, R. W., et al. (2001). The role of contextual supports and barriers in the choice of math/science educational options: A test of social cognitive hypotheses. *Journal of Counseling Psychology*, *48*, 474–483.

12552

Test Name: PERCEIVED ENVIRONMENTAL THREAT SCALE

Purpose: To measure environmental sources of threat to an individual's job: job market, mergers and acquisitions, and restructuring.

Number of Items: 10

Format: Five-point scales are anchored by *very concerned* and *very unconcerned*. All items are described.

Reliability: Alpha coefficients ranged from .80 to .90.

Validity: Correlations with other variables ranged from −.52 to .71.

Author: Reisel, W. D.

Article: Validation and measurement of perceived environmental threat as an antecedent to job insecurity.

Journal: *Psychological Reports*, October 2003, *93*, 359–364.

12553

Test Name: PERCEIVED FIRM PERFORMANCE MEASURE

Purpose: To measure perceived firm performance.

Number of Items: 6

Format: Responses are made on a 6-point Likert scale ranging from 1 (*strongly disagree*) to 6 (*strongly agree*). Examples are given.

Reliability: Coefficient alpha was .87.

Validity: Correlations with other variables ranged from −.32 to .17.

Author: Dunford, B., et al.

Article: Out-of-the-money: The impact of underwater stock options on executive job search.

Journal: *Personnel Psychology*, Spring 2005, *58*, 67–101.

Related Research: Chambers, E. G., et al. (1998). The war for talent. *The McKinsey Quarterly*, *3*, 4–57.

12554

Test Name: PERCEIVED JOB CONTROL SCALE

Purpose: To measure perceived job control.

Number of Items: 17

Format: Scales range from 1 (*almost none*) to 5 (*almost total*). A sample item is presented.

Reliability: Coefficient alpha was .88.

Validity: Correlations with other variables ranged from −.41 to .44.

Author: Schaubroeck, J., et al.

Article: Individual differences in utilizing control to cope with job demands: Effects on susceptibility to infectious disease.

Journal: *Journal of Applied Psychology*, April 2001, *86*, 265–278.

Related Research: Smith, C. S., et al. (1997). The measurement of job control. *Journal of Organizational Behavior*, *18*, 225–237.

12555

Test Name: PERCEIVED MOTIVATIONAL CLIMATE IN SPORT QUESTIONNAIRE—2

Purpose: To measure perceptions of mastery- and performance-oriented climate in sport.

Number of Items: 29

Format: Includes six factors: perceptions of cooperative learning, important roles, improvement in the team, punishment for mistakes, unequal recognition, and intrateam rivalry. Responses are made on a 5-point scale ranging from 1 (*strongly disagree*) to 5 (*strongly agree*).

Reliability: Alpha coefficients ranged from .47 to .80.

Validity: Correlations with other variables ranged from −.25 to .41.

Author: Laparidis, K., et al.

Article: Motivational climate, beliefs about the bases of success, and sportsmanship behaviors of professional basketball athletes.

Journal: *Perceptual and Motor Skills*, June 2003, *96*, Part 2, 1144–1151.

Related Research: Newton, M. L., & Duda, J. L. (1993). The Perceived Motivational Climate in Sport Questionnaire—2: Construct and predictive validity. *Journal of Sport and Exercise Psychology*, *15*(Suppl.), S23.

12556

Test Name: PERCEIVED MOTIVATIONAL CLIMATE IN SPORT QUESTIONNAIRE—2 (ADAPTED)

Purpose: To assess participants' perceptions of the motivational climate in their respective activities.

Number of Items: 25

Format: Includes task-involving motivational climate and ego-involving motivational climate. Responses are made on a 5-point Likert-type scale ranging from 1 (*strongly disagree*) to 5 (*strongly agree*). Examples are given.

Reliability: Alpha coefficients were .81 to .89.

Validity: Correlations with other variables ranged from −.16 to .16.

Author: Newton, M., et al.

Article: Relationship between achievement goal constructs and physical self-perceptions in a physical activity setting.

Journal: *Perceptual and Motor Skills*, December 2004, *99*, Part 1, 757–770.

Related Research: Newton, M., et al. (2000). Examination of the psychometric properties of the Perceived Motivational Climate in Sport Questionnaire—2 in a sample of female athletes. *Journal of Sport Sciences*, *18*, 275–290.

12557

Test Name: PERCEIVED MOTIVATIONAL CLIMATE IN SPORT QUESTIONNAIRE— KOREAN VERSION

Purpose: To measure perception of the motivational climate.

Number of Items: 19

Format: Includes performance and mastery items. Responses are made on a 5-point Likert-type scale ranging from 1 (*strongly disagree*) to 5 (*strongly agree*). Sample items are presented.

Reliability: Alpha coefficients are .93 and .94.

Author: Yoo, J.

Article: Motivational climate and perceived competence in anxiety and tennis performance.

Journal: *Perceptual and Motor Skills*, April 2003, *96*, 403–413.

Related Research: Seifriz, J., et al. (1992). The relationship of perceived motivational climate to achievement-related affect and conditions in basketball. *Journal of Sport and Exercise Psychology*, *14*, 375–391.

12558

Test Name: PERCEIVED MOTIVATIONAL CLIMATE SCALE

Purpose: To assess perceived motivational climate.

Number of Items: 18

Format: Includes two higher factors and five lower order factors. Sample items are presented.

Reliability: Alpha coefficients were .88 and .91.

Validity: Correlations with other variables ranged from −.19 to .36.

Author: Cury, F., et al.

Article: Perceptions of competence, implicit theory of ability, perception of motivational climate, and achievement goals: A test of the trichotomous conceptualization of endorsement of achievement motivation in the physical education setting.

Journal: *Perceptual and Motor Skills*, August 2002, *95*, 233–244.

Related Research: Goudas, M., & Biddle, S. J. (1994). Perceived motivational climate and intrinsic motivation in school physical education classes. *European Journal of Psychology and Education*, *9*, 241–250.

12559

Test Name: PERCEIVED ORGANIZATIONAL RESOURCES SCALE

Purpose: To measure sales support, compensation and incentives, administrative support, product, issues, and representative orientation.

Number of Items: 24

Format: Scales range from 1 (*very poor*) to 5 (*excellent*). All items are presented.

Reliability: Alpha coefficients ranged from .70 to .87.

Validity: Correlations with other variables ranged from −.43 to .11.

Author: Brown, S. P., et al.

Article: The attenuating effect of role overload on relationships linking self-efficacy and goal level to work performance.

Journal: *Journal of Applied Psychology*, September 2005, *90*, 972–979.

12560

Test Name: PERCEIVED ORGANIZATIONAL SUPPORT SCALE

Purpose: To measure perceived organizational support.

Number of Items: 7

Reliability: Coefficient alpha was .94.

Validity: Correlations with other variables ranged from −.14 to .61.

Author: Coyle-Shapiro, J. A.-M., and Conway, N.

Article: Exchange relationships: Examining psychological contracts and perceived organizational support.

Journal: *Journal of Applied Psychology*, July 2005, *90*, 774–781.

Related Research: Eisenberger, R., et al. (1986). Perceived organizational support. *Journal of Applied Psychology, 71*, 500–507.

12561

Test Name: PERCEIVED ORGANIZATIONAL SUPPORT SCALE

Purpose: To measure perceived organizational support.

Number of Items: 6

Reliability: Coefficient alpha was .79.

Validity: Correlations with other variables ranged from −.41 to .55 ($n = 309$).

Author: Fortunato, V. J.

Article: A comparison of the construct validity of three measures of negative affectivity.

Journal: *Educational and Psychological Measurement*, April 2004, *64*, 271–289.

Related Research: Eisenberger, R., et al. (1986). Perceived organizational support. *Journal of Applied Psychology, 71*, 500–507.

12562

Test Name: PERCEIVED ORGANIZATIONAL SUPPORT SCALE—SHORT FORM

Purpose: To measure perceived organizational support.

Number of Items: 9

Format: Responses are made on a 7-point scale ranging from 1 (*strongly disagree*) to 7 (*strongly agree*).

Reliability: Coefficient alpha was .92.

Validity: Correlations with other variables ranged from −.21 to .39 ($N = 213$).

Author: Kraimer, M. L., et al.

Article: Sources of support and expatriate performance: The mediating role of expatriate adjustment.

Journal: *Personnel Psychology*, Spring 2001, *54*, 71–99.

Related Research: Eisenberger, R., et al. (1986). Perceived organizational support. *Journal of Applied Psychology, 71*, 500–507.

12563

Test Name: PERCEIVED REWARDS FOR CREATIVITY SCALE

Purpose: To measure the degree to which employees feel they are rewarded for being creative.

Number of Items: 2

Format: Scales range from 1 (*strongly disagree*) to 7 (*strongly agree*). All items are presented.

Reliability: Coefficient alpha was .77.

Validity: Correlations with other variables ranged from −.20 to .45.

Author: George, J. M., and Zhou, J.

Article: Understanding when bad moods foster creativity and good ones don't: The role of context and clarity of feelings.

Journal: *Journal of Applied Psychology*, August 2002, *87*, 687–697.

12564

Test Name: PERCEIVED TREATMENT AND ATTITUDE SCALES

Purpose: To assess students' perceptions of university treatment and perceptions of majority students in an Israeli university.

Number of Items: 24

Format: Seven-point treatment scales and bipolar scales are used.

Reliability: Alpha coefficients ranged from .74 to .87.

Validity: Correlations with other variables ranged from −.25 to .20.

Author: Kurman, J., et al.

Article: Acculturation attitudes, perceived attitudes of the majority, and adjustment of Israeli-Arab and Jewish-Ethiopian students to an Israeli university.

Journal: *The Journal of Social Psychology*, October 2005, *145*, 593–612.

12565

Test Name: PERCEIVED UNION SUPPORT SCALE

Purpose: To measure perceived union support.

Number of Items: 15

Reliability: Coefficient alpha was .94.

Validity: Correlations with other variables ranged from .17 to .79.

Author: Fuller, J. B., Jr., and Hester, K.

Article: A closer look at the relation between justice perceptions and union participation.

Journal: *Journal of Applied Psychology*, December 2001, *86*, 1096–1105.

Related Research: Shore, L. M., et al. (1994). Validation of a measure of perceived union support. *Journal of Applied Psychology, 79*, 971–977.

12566

Test Name: PERCEPTION OF MOTIVATIONAL CLIMATE IN SPORT QUESTIONNAIRE—2 (SPANISH VERSION)

Purpose: To measure students' perception of motivational climate in physical education classes.

Number of Items: 24

Format: Includes two dimensions: Task-Involving Climate and Ego-Involving Climate. Responses are made on a Likert-type scale ranging from 0 (*strongly disagree*) to 100 (*strongly agree*). Examples are given.

Reliability: Alpha coefficients were .81 and .84.

Validity: Correlations with other variables ranged from –.39 to .45.

Author: Cervellô, E. M., et al.

Article: Goal orientations, motivational climate, equality, and discipline of Spanish physical education students.

Journal: *Perceptual and Motor Skills*, August 2004, *99*, 271–283.

Related Research: Balaguer, I., et al. (1997). Análisis de la validez

de constructo y de la validez predictiva del cuestioinario de clima motivacional percibido en el deporte (PMCSQ–2) con tenistas españoles de competición. *Revista de Psicología del Deporte, 11*, 41–57.

12567

Test Name: PERCEPTIONS OF CLASSROOM GOAL STRUCTURES SCALE

Purpose: To report perceptions of the classroom mastery and performance goal structures.

Number of Items: 10

Format: Includes two dimensions: Classroom Mastery Goal Structure and Classroom Performance Goal Structure. Examples are given.

Reliability: Alpha coefficients ranged from .73 to .92.

Author: Bong, M.

Article: Within-grade changes in Korean girls' motivation and perceptions of the learning environment across domains and achievement levels.

Journal: *Journal of Educational Psychology*, November 2005, *97*, 656–672.

Related Research: Roeser, R. W., et al. (1996). Perceptions of the school psychological environment and early adolescents' psychological and behavioral functioning in school: The mediating role of goals and belonging. *Journal of Educational Psychology, 88*, 408–422.

12568

Test Name: PERCEPTIONS OF DISORDER SCALE

Purpose: To measure individual perceptions of physical and social disorder in urban neighborhoods.

Number of Items: 6

Format: Three-point scales range from *a big problem* to *not a problem*.

Reliability: Coefficient alpha was .70.

Author: Sampson, R. J., and Raudenbush, S. W.

Article: Seeing disorder: Neighborhood stigma and the social construction of "broken windows."

Journal: *Social Psychology Quarterly*, December 2004, *67*, 319–342.

Related Research: Skogan, W. (1990). *Disorder and decline: Crime and the spiral of decay in American cities*. Berkeley: University of California Press.

12569

Test Name: PERCEPTIONS OF JOB COMPLEXITY SCALE

Purpose: To assess perceptions of job complexity.

Number of Items: 3

Format: Responses are made on a 5-point Likert-type scale ranging from 1 (*strongly disagree*) to 5 (*strongly agree*). All items are presented.

Reliability: Coefficient alpha was .73.

Author: Shaw, J. D., and Gupta, N.

Article: Job complexity, performance, and well-being: When does supplies–values fit matter?

Journal: *Personnel Psychology*, Winter 2004, *57*, 847–879.

Related Research: Cammann, C., et al. (1983). Assessing the attitudes and perceptions of organizational members. In Seashore, S. E., et al. (Eds.), *Assessing organizational change: A guide to methods, measures, and practices*. New York: Wiley.

12570

Test Name: PERCEPTIONS OF ORGANIZATIONAL POLITICS SCALE

Purpose: To measure perceptions of organizational politics.

Number of Items: 4

Format: Responses are made on a 5-point Likert scale ranging from 1 (*strongly disagree*) to 5 (*strongly agree*). A sample item is given.

Reliability: Coefficient alpha was .74.

Validity: Correlations with other variables ranged from −.23 to .06.

Author: Andrews, M. C., et al.

Article: The interactive effects of organizational politics and exchange ideology on manager ratings of retention.

Journal: *Journal of Vocational Behavior*, April 2003, *62*, 357–369.

Related Research: Kacmar, K. M., & Ferris, G. R. (1991). Perceptions of Organizational Politics Scale (POPS): Development and construct validation. *Educational and Psychological Measurement*, *51*, 193–205.

12571

Test Name: PERCEPTIONS OF ORGANIZATIONAL POLITICS SCALE

Purpose: To measure perceptions of organizational politics.

Number of Items: 15

Format: Scales range from 1 (*strongly disagree*) to 5 (*strongly agree*). A sample item is presented.

Reliability: Coefficient alpha was .88.

Author: Treadway, D. C., et al.

Article: The role of age in the perceptions of politics–job performance relationship: A three-study constructive replication.

Journal: *Journal of Applied Psychology*, September 2005, *90*, 872–881.

Related Research: Kacmar, K. M., & Carlson, D. (1997). Further validation of the Perceptions of Politics Scale (POPS): A multiple sample investigation. *Journal of Management*, 23, 627–658.

12572

Test Name: PERCEPTIONS OF ORGANIZATIONAL POLITICS SCALE

Purpose: To measure perceptions of organizational politics.

Number of Items: 12

Format: Scales range from 1 (*strongly disagree*) to 5 (*strongly agree*). A sample item is presented.

Reliability: Coefficient alpha was .90.

Validity: Correlations with other variables ranged from −.51 to .11.

Author: Valle, M., and Witt, L. A.

Article: The moderating effect of teamwork perceptions on the organizational politics–job satisfaction relationship.

Journal: *The Journal of Social Psychology*, June 2001, *141*, 379–388.

Related Research: Kacmar, K. M., & Ferris, G. R. (1991). Perceptions of Organizational Politics Scale (POPS): Development and construct validation. *Educational and Psychological Measurement*, *51*, 193–205.

12573

Test Name: PERCEPTIONS OF THE DEVELOPMENTAL ENVIRONMENT

Purpose: To assess the perception of how much the workplace environment encourages employee development.

Number of Items: 7

Format: Scales range from 1 (*strongly disagree*) to 5 (*strongly agree*). Sample items are presented.

Validity: Fit coefficients ranged from .90 to .96.

Author: Colbert, A. E., et al.

Article: Interactive effects of personality and perceptions of the work situation on workplace deviance.

Journal: *The Journal of Applied Psychology*, August 2004, *89*, 599–609.

Related Research: The Gallup Organization. (1996). *The Gallop Workplace Audit*. Princeton, NJ: Author.

12574

Test Name: POSITIVE NEIGHBORHOOD PERCEPTION SCALES

Purpose: To measure positive neighborhood perceptions.

Number of Items: 12

Format: Includes three factors: neighborhood aesthetics, neighborhood embarrassment, and neighborhood safety. Examples are presented.

Reliability: Alpha coefficients ranged from .40 to .82.

Validity: Correlation with other variables ranged from −.27 to .24.

Author: Goodyear, R. K., et al.

Article: Pregnant Latina teenagers: Psychosocial and developmental determinants of how they select and perceive the men who father their children.

Journal: *Journal of Counseling Psychology*, April 2002, *49*, 187–201.

Related Research: MacArthur Foundation Research Network on Successful Midlife Development.

(1994). *The Midlife Development Inventory*. Vero Beach, FL: Author.

12575

Test Name: PROCEDURAL CONSIDERATIONS SCALE

Purpose: To assess the degree to which custodial officers treated detainees with respect and consideration.

Number of Items: 6

Format: Various 5-point scales are used. All items and response scales are presented.

Reliability: Coefficient alpha was .86.

Author: Vermunt, R., et al.

Article: Self-esteem and outcome fairness: Differential importance of procedural and outcome considerations.

Journal: *Journal of Applied Psychology*, August 2001, *86*, 621–628.

Related Research: Tyler, T. R., et al. (1996). Understanding why the justice of group procedures matters: A test of the psychological dynamics of the group-value model. *Journal of Personality and Social Psychology, 70*, 913–930.

12576

Test Name: PROCEDURAL FAIRNESS SCALE

Purpose: To measure structural and interactional elements of procedural fairness.

Number of Items: 8

Format: Scales range from 1 (*disagree strongly*) to 7 (*agree strongly*). A sample item is presented.

Reliability: Coefficient alpha was .87.

Validity: Correlations with other variables ranged from .14 to .62.

Author: Siegel, P. A., et al.

Article: The moderating influence of procedural fairness on the relationship between work–life conflict and organizational commitment.

Journal: *Journal of Applied Psychology*, January 2005, *90*, 13–24.

Related Research: Greenberg, J. (1987). Reactions to procedural injustice in payment distributions: Do the ends justify the means? *Journal of Applied Psychology, 72*, 55–61.

12577

Test Name: PROCEDURAL JUSTICE CLIMATE SCALE— ADAPTED

Purpose: To measure procedural justice.

Number of Items: 4

Format: Responses are made on a 5-point scale ranging from 1 (*to a very small extent*) to 5 (*to a great extent*). All items are presented.

Reliability: Coefficient alpha was .95.

Validity: Correlations with other variables ranged from .25 to .72.

Author: Ehrhart, M. G.

Article: Leadership and procedural justice climate as antecedents of unit-level organizational citizenship behavior.

Journal: *Personnel Psychology*, Spring 2004, *57*, 61–94.

Related Research: Colquit, J. A. (2001). On the dimensionality of organizational justice: A construct validation of a measure. *Journal of Applied Psychology, 86*, 386–400.

12578

Test Name: PROCEDURAL JUSTICE PERCEPTIONS SCALE

Purpose: To assess procedural justice and fairness.

Number of Items: 6

Format: Scales range from 1 (*strongly disagree*) to 5 (*strongly agree*). A sample item is presented.

Reliability: Coefficient alpha was .85.

Validity: Correlations with other variables ranged from .06 to .20.

Author: Douthitt, E. A., and Aiello, J. R.

Article: The role of participation and control in the effects of computer monitoring on fairness perceptions, task satisfaction, and performance.

Journal: *Journal of Applied Psychology*, October 2001, *86*, 867–874.

Related Research: Niehoff, B. P., & Moorman, R. H. (1993). Justice as a mediator of the relationship between methods of monitoring and organizational citizenship behavior. *Academy of Management Journal, 36*, 527–556.

12579

Test Name: PROCEDURAL JUSTICE SCALE

Purpose: To assess procedural justice.

Number of Items: 5

Format: Scales range from 1 (*strongly disagree*) to 5 (*strongly agree*). A sample item is presented.

Reliability: Coefficient alpha was .81.

Validity: Correlations with other variables ranged from −.56 to .50.

Author: Alge, B. J.

Article: Effects of computer surveillance on perceptions of privacy and procedural justice.

Journal: *Journal of Applied Psychology*, August 2001, *86*, 797–804.

12580

Test Name: PROCEDURAL JUSTICE SCALE

Purpose: To measure procedural justice.

Number of Items: 7

Format: Responses are made on a 5-point scale ranging from 1 (*to a small extent*) to 5 (*to a large extent*).

Reliability: Coefficient alpha was .97.

Author: Colquitt, J. A., et al.

Article: Justice in terms: Antecedents and consequences of procedural justice climate.

Journal: *Personnel Psychology*, Spring 2002, *55*, 386–400.

Related Research: Colquitt, J. A. (2001). On the dimensionality of organizational justice: A construct validation of a measure. *Journal of Applied Psychology*, *86*, 386–400.

12581

Test Name: PROCEDURAL JUSTICE SCALE

Purpose: To assess perceptions of organizational justice.

Number of Items: 12

Format: Responses are made on a 5-point scale ranging from 1 (*strongly disagree*) to 5 (*strongly agree*).

Reliability: Alpha coefficients ranged from .93 to .96.

Validity: Correlation with other variables ranged from −.44 to .54 (*N* = 292).

Author: Fox, S., et al.

Article: Counterproductive work behavior (CWB) in response to job stressors and organizational justice: Some mediator and moderator tests for autonomy and emotions.

Journal: *Journal of Vocational Behavior*, December 2001, *59*, 291–309.

Related Research: Moorman, R. H., et al. (1998). Does perceived organizational support mediate the relationship between procedural justice and organizational citizenship behavior? *Academy of Management Journal*, *41*, 351–357.

12582

Test Name: PROCEDURAL JUSTICE SCALE

Purpose: To assess the extent to which an employee is kept informed by others and consults with others.

Number of Items: 3

Format: Scales range from 1 (*strongly disagree*) to 7 (*strongly agree*). All items are presented.

Reliability: Coefficient alpha was .62.

Validity: Correlations with other variables ranged from −.01 to .59.

Author: Rhoades, L., et al.

Article: Affective commitment to the organization: The contribution of perceived organizational support.

Journal: *Journal of Applied Psychology*, October 2001, *86*, 825–836.

Related Research: Beehr, T. A., et al. (1976). Relationship of stress to individually and organizationally valued states: Higher order needs as a moderator. *Journal of Applied Psychology*, *61*, 41–47.

12583

Test Name: PROCEDURAL JUSTICE SCALE

Purpose: To measure procedural justice.

Number of Items: 6

Format: Seven-point scales range from 1 (*strongly disagree*) to 7 (*strongly agree*).

Reliability: Coefficient alpha was .88.

Validity: Correlations with other variables ranged from −.20 to .78.

Author: Wayne, S. J., et al.

Article: The role of fair treatment and rewards in perceptions of organizational support and leader–member exchange.

Journal: *Journal of Applied Psychology*, June 2002, *87*, 590–598.

Related Research: Niehof, B. P., & Moorman, R. H. (1993). Justice as a mediator of the relationship between methods of monitoring and organizational citizenship behavior. *Academy of Management Journal*, *36*, 527–556.

12584

Test Name: PROCEDURAL JUSTICE SCALE

Purpose: To measure procedural justice in a blue-collar work setting.

Number of Items: 10

Format: Scales range from 1 (*strongly disagree*) to 7 (*strongly agree*). Sample items are presented.

Reliability: Coefficient alpha was .97.

Validity: Correlations with other variables ranged from −.35 to .41.

Author: Zellars, K. L., et al.

Article: Abusive supervision and subordinates' organizational citizenship behavior.

Journal: *Journal of Applied Psychology*, December 2002, *87*, 1068–1076.

Related Research: Tepper, B. J., et al. (2001). Justice, citizenship, and role definition effects. *Journal of Applied Psychology*, *86*, 789–796.

12585

Test Name: PSYCHOLOGICAL CLIMATE SCALE

Purpose: To measure psychological climate.

Number of Items: 22

Format: Responses are made on a 7-point scale ranging from 1 (*strongly disagree*) to 7 (*strongly agree*). An example is given.

Reliability: Alpha coefficients were .81 and .86 ($n = 139$).

Validity: Correlations with other variables ranged from −.15 to .47 ($n = 139$).

Author: Byrne, Z. S., et al.

Article: The interactive effects of conscientiousness, work effort, and psychological climate on job performance.

Journal: *Journal of Vocational Behavior*, April 2005, *66*, 326–338.

Related Research: Brown, S., & Leigh, T. (1996). A new look at psychological climate and its relationship to job involvement, effort, and performance. *Journal of Applied Psychology, 81*, 358–368.

12586

Test Name: QUESTIONNAIRE ON THE EXPERIENCE AND EVALUATION OF WORK— REVISED

Purpose: To assess workload.

Number of Items: 7

Format: Responses are made on a 4-point scale ranging from 1 (*never*) to 4 (*always*). All items are presented.

Reliability: Alpha coefficients ranged from .71 to .91.

Author: Geurts, S. A. E., et al.

Article: Does work–home interference mediate the relationship between workload and well-being?

Journal: *Journal of Vocational Behavior*, December 2003, *63*, 532–559.

Related Research: Van Veldhoven, M., et al. (1997). *Handleiding VBBA: Onderzoek naar de beleving van psychosociale arbeidsbelasting en werkstress met behulp van de vragenlijst beleving en beoordeling van de arbeid* [Guideline VBBA: Research on the experience of psychosocial workload and job stress with the Questionnaire on the Experience and Evaluation of Work]. Ámsterdam: SKB (Stichting Kwaliteitsbevordering BGZ Nederland).

12587

Test Name: RECRUITMENT ACTIVITIES SURVEY

Purpose: To measure on-campus recruitment activities.

Number of Items: 18

Format: Includes three factors: campus activity, recruitment materials, and recruitment process. Responses are made on a 5-point scale ranging from *much poorer* to *much better*.

Reliability: Alpha coefficients ranged from .83 to .92 (Ns ranged from 531–582).

Validity: Correlations with other variables ranged from −.13 to .43 (Ns ranged from 531–582).

Author: Turban, D. B.

Article: Organizational attractiveness as an employer on college campuses: An examination of the applicant population.

Journal: *Journal of Vocational Behavior*, April 2001, *58*, 293–312.

12588

Test Name: RESEARCH TRAINING ENVIRONMENT SCALE

Purpose: To measure the ingredients of the research training environment.

Number of Items: 45

Format: Evaluates nine ingredients.

Reliability: Test–retest (2–4 weeks) reliabilities ranged from .47 to .84. Internal consistency reliabilities ranged from .24 to .82.

Author: Mallinckrodt, B., and Gelso, C. J.

Article: Impact of research training environment and Holland Personality Type: A 15-year follow-up of research productivity.

Journal: *Journal of Counseling Psychology*, January 2002, *49*, 60–70.

Related Research: Royaty, G. M., et al. (1986). The environment and the student in counseling psychology: Does the research training environment influence graduate students' attitudes toward research? *The Counseling Psychologist, 14*, 9–30.

12589

Test Name: RESEARCH TRAINING ENVIRONMENT SCALE—REVISED (SHORT VERSION)

Purpose: To assess recollection of the academic research training environment.

Number of Items: 18

Format: Responses are made on a 5-point Likert scale ranging from 1 (*disagree*) to 5 (*agree*). Examples are given.

Reliability: Coefficient alpha was .87.

Validity: Correlations with other variables ranged from −.03 to .09.

Author: Phillips, J. C., et al.

Article: Preliminary examination and measurement of the internship research training environment.

Journal: *Journal of Counseling Psychology*, April 2004, *51*, 240–248.

Related Research: Kahn, J. H., & Miller, S. A. (2000). Measuring global perceptions of the research training environment using a short form of the RTES–R. *Measurement Evaluation in Counseling and Development, 33*, 103–119.

12590

Test Name: REVISED JOB DIAGNOSTIC SURVEY

Purpose: To measure intrinsic job characteristics.

Number of Items: 15

Format: Responses are made on a 7-point scale ranging from 1 (*very inaccurate*) to 7 (*very accurate*). An example is given.

Reliability: Alpha coefficients were .79 and .82 (*n* = 195).

Validity: Correlations with other variables ranged from −.24 to .53 (*n* = 195).

Author: Lubbers, R., et al.

Article: Young workers' job self-efficacy and affect: Pathways to health and performance.

Journal: *Journal of Vocational Behavior*, October 2005, *67*, 199–214.

Related Research: Idaszak, J. R., & Drasgow, F. (1987). A revision of the Job Diagnostic Survey: Elimination of a measurement artifact. *Journal of Applied Psychology, 72*, 69–74.

12591

Test Name: ROLE ENHANCEMENT OPPORTUNITY SCALE

Purpose: To measure the extent that one expects to have the chance to take on more complex assignments within the next 2 years.

Number of Items: 7

Format: Responses are made on a 5-point scale ranging from 1 (*strongly disagree*) to 5 (*strongly agree*). All items are presented.

Reliability: Coefficient alpha was .90 (*ns* ranged from 2258–2542).

Validity: Correlations with other variables ranged from .19 to .33.

Author: Prince, J. B.

Article: Career opportunity and organizational attachment in a blue-collar unionized environment.

Journal: *Journal of Vocational Behavior*, August 2003, *63*, 136–150.

Related Research: Kanter, R. M. (1977). *Men and women of the corporation*. New York: Basic Books.

12592

Test Name: SAFETY CLIMATE MEASURE

Purpose: To assess concern for safety in work situations and in the military.

Number of Items: 23

Format: Scales range from 1 (*strongly disagree*) to 5 (*strongly agree*). Sample items are presented.

Reliability: Coefficient alpha was .94.

Validity: Correlations with other variables ranged from .23 to .55.

Author: Hofmann, D. A., et al.

Article: Climate as a moderator of the relationship between leader–member exchange and content specific citizenship: Safety climate as an exemplar.

Journal: *Journal of Applied Psychology*, February 2003, *88*, 170–178.

Related Research: Zohar, D. (1980). Safety climate in industrial organizations: Theoretical and applied implications. *Journal of Applied Psychology, 65*, 96–102.

12593

Test Name: SANDBAGGING SCALE

Purpose: To measure sandbagging behavior in organizations.

Number of Items: 12

Format: Scales range from 1 (*disagree very much*) to 6 (*agree very much*). Sample items are presented.

Reliability: Alpha coefficients ranged from .79 to .88 across subscales.

Author: Lewis, M. A., and Neighbors, C.

Article: Self-determination and the use of self-presentation strategies.

Journal: *The Journal of Social Psychology*, August 2005, *145*, 469–489.

Related Research: Gibson, B., & Sachau, D. (2000). Sandbagging as a self-presentation strategy: Claiming to be less than you are. *Personality and Social Psychology Bulletin, 26*, 56–70.

12594

Test Name: SCALE OF PERCEIVED ORGANIZATIONAL SUPPORT

Purpose: To measure perceived organizational support.

Format: Responses are made on a 7-point scale ranging from *strongly disagree* to *strongly agree*.

Reliability: Coefficient alpha was .93.

Validity: Correlations with other variables ranged from −.29 to .74.

Author: Behson, S. J.

Article: Which dominates? The relative importance of work–family organizational support and general organizational context on employee outcomes.

Journal: *Journal of Vocational Behavior*, August 2002, *61*, 53–72.

Related Research: Eisenberger, R., et al. (1986). Perceived organizational support. *Journal of Applied Psychology, 71*, 500–507.

12595

Test Name: SCHOOL ENVIRONMENTAL CONDITIONS SCALE

Purpose: To obtain student ratings of their school environment.

Number of Items: 4

Format: Scales range from 1 (*strongly disagree*) to 5 (*strongly agree*). All items are presented.

Reliability: Coefficient alpha was .59.

Validity: Correlations with other variables ranged from –.33 to .07.

Author: Lapan, R. T., et al.

Article: Helping seventh graders be safe and successful: A statewide study of the impact of comprehensive guidance and counseling programs.

Journal: *Professional School Counseling*, February 2003, *6*, 186–197.

12596

Test Name: SELECTION, OPTIMIZATION, COMPENSATION SCALE

Purpose: To assess selection, optimization, and compensation.

Format: Analyses are made on a 5-point (0–4) scale. Examples are presented.

Reliability: Alpha coefficients ranged from .47 to .56.

Validity: Correlations with other variables ranged from –.08 to .43.

Author: Wiese, B. S., et al.

Article: Subjective career success and emotional well-being:

Longitudinal predictive power of selection, optimization, and compensation.

Journal: *Journal of Vocational Behavior*, June 2002, *60*, 321–335.

Related Research: Baltes, P. B., et al. (1999). *The measure of selection, optimization, and compensation (SOC) by self-report: Technical Report 1999.* Berlin, Germany: Max Planck Institute for Human Development.

12597

Test Name: SIEGEL SCALE OF SUPPORT FOR INNOVATION

Purpose: To measure support for innovation in schools.

Number of Items: 61

Format: Scales range from 1 (*disagree strongly*) to 6 (*agree strongly*).

Reliability: Split-half reliability coefficients ranged from .86 to .94.

Author: Dee, J. R., et al.

Article: Support for innovation in site-based-managed schools: Developing a climate for change.

Journal: *Educational Research Quarterly*, June 2002, *25*, 36–49.

Related Research: Siegel, S., & Kaemmerer, W. (1978). Measuring perceived support for innovation in organizations. *Journal of Applied Psychology, 63*, 553–562.

12598

Test Name: SKILL UTILIZATION INVENTORY—HEBREW

Purpose: To measure the extent to which an occupation affords an individual opportunities to perform or display personally perceived skills.

Number of Items: 4

Format: Responses are made on a 5-point scale. An example is given.

Reliability: Internal consistency reliabilities were .77 and .78.

Validity: Correlations with other variables ranged from –.20 to .70.

Author: Meir, E. I., and Melamed, S.

Article: Occupational specialty congruence: New data and future directions.

Journal: *Journal of Vocational Behavior*, August 2005, *67*, 21–34.

Related Research: Caplan, R. D., et al. (1975). *Job demands and worker health: Main effects and occupational differences* (HEW Pub. No. NIOSH 75–160). Washington, DC: National Institute for Occupational Safety and Health.

12599

Test Name: SOCIAL EXPECTATIONS SCALE

Purpose: To measure instrumental and expressive social expectations in work settings.

Number of Items: 16

Format: Scales range from 1 (*They don't at all want/expect me to be that way*) to 7 (*They very much want/expect me to be that way*). Sample items are presented.

Reliability: Alpha coefficients were .82 (expressiveness) and .74 (instrumentally).

Validity: Correlations with other variables ranged from .00 to .75.

Author: Wise, D., and Stake, J. E.

Article: The moderating roles of personal and social resources on the relationship between dual expectations (for instrumentality and expressiveness) and well-being.

Journal: *The Journal of Social Psychology*, February 2002, *142*, 109–119.

Related Research: Stake, J. E., et al. (1996). The relation of instrumentality and expressiveness to self-concept and adjustment: A social context perspective. *Journal of Social and Clinical Psychology,* *15,* 167–190.

12600

Test Name: SPORT CLIMATE QUESTIONNAIRE—MODIFIED

Purpose: To measure perceived autonomy support during physical education.

Number of Items: 6

Format: Responses are made on a 7-point scale ranging from 1 (*strongly disagree*) to 7 (*strongly agree*).

Reliability: Coefficient alpha was .93.

Validity: Correlations with other variables ranged from −.09 to .38.

Author: Hagger, M. S., et al.

Article: The processes by which perceived autonomy support in physical education promotes leisure-time physical activity intentions and behavior: A trans-contextual model.

Journal: *Journal of Educational Psychology,* December 2003, *95,* 784–795.

Related Research: Baard, P. P., et al. (2000). *Intrinsic need satisfaction as a motivational basis of performance and well-being at work.* Unpublished manuscript, Fordham University, New York.

12601

Test Name: SPORT ORGANIZATIONAL EFFECTIVENESS SCALE

Purpose: To assess the effectiveness of sport organizations.

Number of Items: 33

Format: Item anchors range from 1 (*strongly disagree*) to 5 (*strongly agree*).

Reliability: Alpha coefficients ranged from .78 to .95.

Validity: Correlations between subscales ranged from .71 to .89.

Author: Karteroliotis, K., and Papadimitrou, D.

Article: Confirmatory factor analysis of the Sport Organizational Effectiveness Scale.

Journal: *Psychological Reports,* August 2004, *95,* 366–370.

12602

Test Name: STANDARD-BASED PRACTICES SCALE

Purpose: To measure standard-based practices.

Number of Items: 32

Format: Includes four subscales: Cross-Content Area, Literacy Instruction, Literacy Application and Analysis, and Numeracy. Responses are made on a 7-point scale ranging from 1 (*never*) to 7 (*daily*).

Reliability: Alpha coefficients ranged from .67 to .93.

Author: Seitsinger, A. M.

Article: Service learning and standards-based instruction in middle schools.

Journal: *Journal of Educational Research,* September/October 2005, *99,* 19–30.

Related Research: Shim, M., et al. (1999). *Standards-based instructional practices: Factor analyses.* Kingston, RI: National Center on Public Education and Social Policy at the University of Rhode Island.

12603

Test Name: STRESSFUL EVENTS SUBSCALE

Purpose: To measure children's exposure to neighborhood violence.

Number of Items: 4 or 5

Format: Responses to each item are either 0 (*no*) or 1 (*yes*). All items are presented.

Reliability: Internal consistency was .61.

Author: Guerra, N. G., et al.

Article: Community violence exposure, social cognition, and aggression among urban elementary school children.

Journal: *Child Development,* September/October 2003, *74,* 1561–1576.

Related Research: Attar, B. K., et al. (1994). Neighborhood disadvantage, stressful life events, and adjustment in urban elementary-school children. *Journal of Clinical Child Psychology, 23,* 391–400.

12604

Test Name: SUPPORT SCALES

Purpose: To measure supervisory and coworker support.

Number of Items: 15

Format: Includes two scales: Supervisory Support and Coworker Support. Responses are made on 7-point scales. A sample item is presented.

Reliability: Alpha coefficients were .87 and .94.

Validity: Correlations with other variables ranged from −.26 to .32 (*N* = 600).

Author: Ito, J. K., and Brotheridge, C. M.

Article: Resources, coping strategies, and emotional exhaustion: A conservation of resources perspective.

Journal: *Journal of Vocational Behavior,* December 2003, *63,* 490–509.

Related Research: Leiter, M. P., & Maslach, C. (1986). *Job stress and social involvement among nurses.* Paper presented at the annual conference of the International Network for Social Network Analysis, Santa Barbara, CA.

12605

Test Name: SURVEY OF PERCEIVED ORGANIZATIONAL SUPPORT

Purpose: To measure perceptions students have of support from the university they attend (the university in general, current and former professors, and professors in their majors).

Number of Items: 30

Format: Item responses are anchored by 0 (*strongly disagree*) and 6 (*strongly agree*).

Reliability: Alphas ranged from .74 to .95 on scales containing similar items.

Validity: Correlations with other variables ranged from –.47 to .57.

Author: LaMastro, V.

Article: Influence of perceived institutional and faculty support on college students' attitudes and behavioral intentions.

Journal: *Psychological Reports*, April 2001, *88*, 567–580.

Related Research: Eisenberger, R., et al. (1986). Perceived organizational support. *Journal of Applied Psychology*, *71*, 500–507.

12606

Test Name: SURVEY OF PERCEIVED ORGANIZATIONAL SUPPORT—ADAPTED

Purpose: To measure perceived organizational support.

Number of Items: 9

Format: A sample item is presented.

Reliability: Coefficient alpha was .87 (*N* = 267).

Validity: Correlations with other variables ranged from –.09 to .62 (*N* = 267).

Author: Erdogan, B., et al.

Article: Work value congruence and intrinsic career success: The compensatory roles of leader–member exchange and perceived organizational support.

Journal: *Personnel Psychology*, Summer 2004, *57*, 305–332.

Related Research: Eisenberger, R., et al. (1986). Perceived organizational support. *Journal of Applied Psychology*, *71*, 500–507.

12607

Test Name: SURVEY OF PERCEIVED ORGANIZATIONAL SUPPORT SCALE—SHORT VERSION

Purpose: To assess perceived organizational support.

Number of Items: 8

Format: Responses are made on a 7-point Likert scale ranging from 1 (*strongly disagree*) to 7 (*strongly agree*).

Reliability: Coefficient alpha was .91.

Validity: Correlations with other variables ranged from –.22 to .65.

Author: Liao, H., et al.

Article: Sticking out like a sore thumb: Employee dissimilarity and deviance at work.

Journal: *Personnel Psychology*, Winter 2004, *57*, 969–1000.

Related Research: Eisenberger, R., et al. (1997). Perceived organizational support, discretionary treatment, and job satisfaction. *Journal of Applied Psychology*, *82*, 812–820.

12608

Test Name: TASK COMPLEXITY SCALE

Purpose: To measure task complexity.

Number of Items: 5

Format: Responses are made on 5-point scales. An example is given.

Reliability: Coefficient alpha was .77.

Validity: Correlations with other variables ranged from –.16 to .35 (*N* = 600).

Author: Ito, J. K., and Brotheridge, C. M.

Article: Resources, coping strategies, and emotional exhaustion: A conservation of resources perspective.

Journal: *Journal of Vocational Behavior*, December 2003, *63*, 490–509.

Related Research: Ito, J. K., & Peterson, R. B. (1986). Effects of task difficulty and interunit interdependence on information processing systems. *Academy of Management Journal*, *29*, 139–149.

12609

Test Name: TEACHER–CLASSROOM ENVIRONMENT MEASURE—ADAPTED

Purpose: To assess teacher fairness and modeling of teacher motivation.

Number of Items: 6

Format: Responses are made on a 4-point scale ranging from 1 (*not very often*) to 4 (*very often*). Sample items are presented.

Reliability: Alpha coefficients were .60 and .68.

Validity: Correlations with other variables ranged from –.43 to .45.

Author: Wentzel, K. R.

Article: Are effective teachers like good parents? Teaching styles and student adjustment in early adolescence.

Journal: *Child Development*, January/February 2002, *73*, 287–301.

Related Research: Feldlaufer, H., et al. (1988). Student, teacher, and observer perceptions of the classroom before and after the transition to junior high school. *Journal of Early Adolescence, 8,* 133–156.

12610

Test Name: TEACHING AUTONOMY SCALE

Purpose: To measure the degree of perceived autonomy of teachers in their jobs.

Number of Items: 18

Format: Scales range from 1 (*definitely false*) to 4 (*definitely true*).

Reliability: Reliability coefficients were .80 and .83.

Author: Pearson, L. C., and Moomaw, W.

Article: The relationship between teacher autonomy and stress, work satisfaction, empowerment, and professionalism.

Journal: *Educational Research Quarterly*, September 2005, *29,* 37–53.

Related Research: Pearson, L. C., & Hall, B. C. (1993). Initial construct validation of the Teaching Autonomy Scale. *Journal of Educational Research, 86,* 172–177.

12611

Test Name: TEAM CLIMATE INVENTORY—SWEDISH VERSION

Purpose: To measure team climate in four dimensions: Vision, Participative Safety, Task Orientation, and Support for Innovation.

Number of Items: 38

Format: Five-point agreement scales.

Reliability: Cronbach's alpha was .95.

Validity: The correlation between inventory scores and observer ratings was .48.

Author: Dackert, I., and Brenner, S.-O.

Article: Team Climate Inventory with a merged organization.

Journal: *Psychological Reports,* October 2002, *91,* 651–656.

Related Research: Agrell, A., & Gustafson, R. (1994). The Team Climate Inventory (TCI) and group innovation. *Journal of Occupational and Organizational Psychology, 67,* 143–151.

12612

Test Name: TEAM EFFECTIVENESS SCALE

Purpose: To measure the effectiveness of trauma care teams.

Number of Items: 12

Format: Scales range from 1 (*strongly disagree*) to 5 (*strongly agree*). All items are presented.

Reliability: Alpha coefficients ranged from .92 to .96 across two subscales.

Author: Yun, S., et al.

Article: Contingent leadership and effectiveness of trauma resuscitation teams.

Journal: *Journal of Applied Psychology,* November 2005, *90,* 1288–1296.

Related Research: Pearce, C. L., & Sims, H. P., Jr. (2002). Vertical vs. shared leadership as predictors of the effectiveness of change management teams: An examination of aversive, directive, transactional, transformational, and empowering leader behaviors. *Group Dynamics: Theory, Research, and Practice, 6,* 172–197.

12613

Test Name: TOP MANAGEMENT SUPPORT FOR QUALITY SCALE

Purpose: To measure top management support for quality.

Number of Items: 5

Format: Responses are made on a 7-point scale ranging from 7 (*strongly agree*) to 1 (*strongly disagree*). Sample items are presented.

Reliability: Coefficient alpha was .79.

Validity: Correlations with other variables ranged from −.03 to .45.

Author: Coyle-Shapiro, J. A.-M., and Morrow, P. C.

Article: The role of individual differences in employee adoption of TQM orientation.

Journal: *Journal of Vocational Behavior,* April 2003, *62,* 320–340.

12614

Test Name: TRADITIONAL JOB SEARCH CONSTRAINTS SCALE

Purpose: To measure traditional job search constraints.

Number of Items: 6

Format: Examples are presented.

Reliability: Coefficient alpha was .80.

Validity: Correlations with other variables ranged from −.05 to .51.

Author: Adams, G., and Rau, B.

Article: Job seeking among retirees seeking bridge employment.

Journal: *Personnel Psychology,* Autumn 2004, *57,* 719–744.

Related Research: Wanberg, C. R., et al. (1999). Unemployed individuals: Motives, job-search competencies, and job-search constraints as predictors of job seeking and reemployment. *Journal of Applied Psychology, 84,* 897–910.

12615

Test Name: TRANSACTIVE MEMORY SYSTEM SCALE

Purpose: To measure the extent to which team members' expertise is leveraged in terms of specialization, credibility, and coordination of member activities.

Number of Items: 15

Format: Scales range from 1 (*strongly disagree*) to 5 (*strongly agree*). All items are presented.

Reliability: Alpha coefficients ranged from .80 to .84 across subscales.

Validity: Correlations with other variables ranged from −.76 to .89.

Author: Lewis, K.

Article: Measuring transactive memory systems in the field: Scale development and validation.

Journal: *Journal of Applied Psychology*, August 2003, *88*, 587–604.

12616

Test Name: TRUST IN MANAGEMENT SCALES— MODIFIED

Purpose: To measure trust in management.

Number of Items: 15

Format: Includes three subscales: Perceived Benevolence of Management, Perceived Integrity of Management, and Perceived Trustworthiness of Management. Responses are made on a seven-point scale ranging from *strongly disagree* to *strongly agree*.

Reliability: Reliability coefficients ranged from .59 to .96.

Validity: Correlations with other variables ranged from −.22 to .74.

Author: Behson, S. J.

Article: Which dominates? The relative importance of work–family organizational support and general organizational context on employee outcomes.

Journal: *Journal of Vocational Behavior*, August 2002, *61*, 53–72.

Related Research: Mayer, R. C., & Davis, J. H. (1999). The effect of the performance appraisal system on trust for management: A field quasi-experiment. *Journal of Applied Psychology, 84,* 123–136.

12617

Test Name: TRUST IN ORGANIZATION SCALE

Purpose: To measure trust in organization.

Number of Items: 7

Format: Responses are made on a 7-point scale ranging from 1 (*strongly disagree*) to 7 (*strongly agree*). Examples are given.

Reliability: Coefficient alpha was .93.

Validity: Correlations with other variables ranged from .25 to .67 (*n* = 186).

Author: Chen, Z. X., et al.

Article: Test of a mediation model of perceived organizational support.

Journal: *Journal of Vocational Behavior*, June 2005, *66*, 457–470.

12618

Test Name: UNCLEAR ENDS AND MEANS SCALE

Purpose: To measure the clarity of job expectations.

Number of Items: 9

Format: Scales range from 1 (*to no extent*) to 5 (*to a great extent*). All items are presented.

Reliability: Coefficient alpha was .68 (ends) and .74 (means).

Validity: Correlations with other variables ranged from −.30 to .22.

Author: George, J. M., and Zhou, J.

Article: When openness to experience and conscientiousness are related to creative behavior: An interactional approach.

Journal: *Journal of Applied Psychology*, June 2001, *86*, 513–524.

12619

Test Name: UNDERUTILIZATION OF PERSONNEL SCALE

Purpose: To measure the underutilization of knowledge, skills, and abilities of personnel.

Number of Items: 7

Format: Item responses are anchored by 1 (*very little*) and 5 (*to a great extent*). A sample item is presented.

Reliability: Coefficient alpha was .79.

Validity: Correlations with other variables ranged from .19 to .63.

Author: Länsisalmi, H., et al.

Article: Is underutilization of knowledge, skills, and abilities a major barrier to innovation?

Journal: *Psychological Reports*, June 2004, *94*, Part 1, 739–750.

Related Research: Kivimäki, M., et al. (2000). Communication as a determinant of organizational innovation. *Research and Development Management, 30,* 33–42.

12620

Test Name: UNIMPORTANCE OF INNOVATIVE ACTIVITIES SCALE

Purpose: To assess the perceived importance of innovative activities in an organization.

Number of Items: 4

Format: Responses are anchored by 1 (*strongly disagree*) and 5 (*strongly agree*). A sample item is presented.

Reliability: Coefficient alpha was .69.

Validity: Correlations with other variables ranged from .22 to .68.

Author: Länsisalmi, H., et al.

Article: Is underutilization of knowledge, skills, and abilities a major barrier to innovation?

Journal: *Psychological Reports*, June 2004, *94*, Part 1, 739–750.

Related Research: Kivimäki, M., et al. (2000). Communication as a determinant of organizational innovation. *Research and Development Management, 30*, 33–42.

12621

Test Name: UNION INSTRUMENTALITY SCALE

Purpose: To measure how good a job one's union is doing in improving one's job.

Number of Items: 9

Format: Scales range from 1 (*not at all good*) to 5 (*very good*). Sample items are presented.

Reliability: Coefficient alpha was .97.

Validity: Correlations with other variables ranged from −.29 to .62.

Author: Aryee, S., and Chay, Y. W.

Article: Workplace justice, citizenship behavior, and turnover intentions in a union context: Examining the mediating role of perceived union support and union instrumentality.

Journal: *Journal of Applied Psychology*, February 2001, *86*, 154–160.

Related Research: Chacko, T. I. (1985). Member participation in union activities: Perceptions of union priorities, performance, and satisfaction. *Journal of Labor Research, 6*, 363–373.

12622

Test Name: UNION INSTRUMENTALITY SCALE

Purpose: To measure how well one's union is improving job conditions and benefits.

Number of Items: 10

Format: Scales range from 1 (*not at all good*) to 5 (*very good*). Sample items are presented.

Reliability: Coefficient alpha was .94.

Validity: Correlations with other variables ranged from .41 to .67.

Author: Tan, H. H., and Aryee, S.

Article: Antecedents and outcomes of union loyalty: A constructive replication and an extension.

Journal: *Journal of Applied Psychology*, August 2002, *87*, 715–722.

Related Research: Chacko, T. I. (1985). Member participation in union activities: Perceptions of union priorities, performance, and satisfaction. *Journal of Labor Research, 6*, 363–373.

12623

Test Name: UNIVERSITY ENVIRONMENT SCALE

Purpose: To assess students' perceptions of the university environment.

Number of Items: 14

Format: Scales range from 1 (*strongly disagree*) to 4 (*strongly agree*). A sample item is presented.

Reliability: Alpha coefficients ranged from .74 to .80.

Validity: Correlations with other variables ranged from .12 to .50.

Author: Gloria, A. M., et al.

Article: Relationships of cultural congruity and perceptions of the university environment to help-seeking attitudes by sociorace and gender.

Journal: *Journal of College Student Development*, November/December 2001, *42*, 545–562.

Related Research: Gloria, A. M., & Robinson-Kurpius, S. E. (1996). The validation of the Cultural Congruity Scale and the University Environment Scale with Chicano/a students. *Hispanic Journal of Behavioral Sciences, 18*, 533–549.

12624

Test Name: VIOLENCE FROM COWORKERS AND FROM THE PUBLIC SCALES

Purpose: To assess the frequency of violence from coworkers and from the public.

Number of Items: 5

Format: Scales range from 0 (*never*) to 4 (*four or more times*). A sample item is presented.

Reliability: Alpha coefficients were .90 (public) and .17 (coworkers).

Validity: Correlations between violence from the public and other variables ranged from −.08 to .74.

Author: LeBlanc, M. M., and Kelloway, E. K.

Article: Predictors and outcomes of workplace violence and aggression.

Journal: *Journal of Applied Psychology*, June 2002, *87*, 444–453.

Related Research: Rogers, K. A., & Kelloway, E. K. (1997). Violence at work: Personal and organizational outcomes. *Journal of Occupational Health Psychology, 1*, 63–71.

12625

Test Name: WEBSITE DESIGN SCALE

Purpose: To measure the personableness, informativeness, attractiveness, and intent to respond to a website.

Number of Items: 18

Format: Item anchors are 1 (*strongly agree*) and 5 (*strongly disagree*).

Reliability: Alpha coefficients ranged from .79 to .90 across subscales.

Validity: Correlations between subscales ranged from .43 to .67.

Author: Thoms, P., et al.

Article: Designing personable and informative job recruiting Web sites: Testing the effect of the design on attractiveness and intent to apply.

Journal: *Psychological Reports*, June 2004, *94*, Part 1, 1031–1042.

12626

Test Name: WOMEN AS MANAGERS SCALE

Purpose: To measure acceptance of women as managers, barriers to female managers, and traits necessary for success as a manager.

Number of Items: 21

Format: Scales range from 1 (*strongly disagree*) to 7 (*strongly agree*).

Reliability: Alpha coefficients ranged from .46 to .83.

Author: Cordano, M., et al.

Article: Dimensionality of the Women as Managers Scale: Factor congruency among three samples.

Journal: *The Journal of Social Psychology*, February 2003, *143*, 141–143.

Related Research: Crino, M. D., et al. (1981). A comment on the dimensionality and reliability of the Women as Managers Scale (WAMS). *Academy of Management Journal*, *24*, 866–876.

12627

Test Name: WORK CONDITIONS MEASURE

Purpose: To assess decision latitude and substantive complexity of work conditions.

Number of Items: 8

Format: Scales range from 1 (*strongly disagree*) to 4 (*strongly agree*).

Reliability: Alpha coefficients ranged from .76 to .85 across subscales.

Author: Erickson, R. J., and Ritter, C.

Article: Emotional labor, burnout, and inauthenticity: Does gender matter?

Journal: *Social Psychology Quarterly*, June 2001, *64*, 146–163.

Related Research: Karasek, R. A. (1979). Job demands, decision latitude, and mental strain: Implications for job redesign. *Administrative Science Quarterly*, *24*, 285–308.

12628

Test Name: WORK CONDITIONS MEASURE

Purpose: To measure autonomy, control over others, organizational control, routine, and closeness of supervision.

Number of Items: 20

Format: Scales range from *not at all* to *very much*.

Reliability: Alpha coefficients were .84 (wives) and .89 (husbands).

Author: Klute, M. M., et al.

Article: Occupational self-direction, values, and egalitarian relationships: A study of dual-earner couples.

Journal: *Journal of Marriage and Family*, February 2004, *64*, 139–151.

Related Research: Lennon, M. C. (1994). Women, work, and well-being. *Journal of Health and Social Behavior*, *35*, 235–247.

12629

Test Name: WORK CULTURE SCALES

Purpose: To measure participants' reported workplace temporal flexibility, operational flexibility, and supportive supervision.

Number of Items: 13

Format: Includes three factors: temporal flexibility, operational flexibility, and supportive supervision.

Reliability: Alpha coefficients ranged from .83 to .86.

Validity: Correlations with other variables ranged from −.21 to .64.

Author: Clark, S. C.

Article: Work culture and work/family balance.

Journal: *Journal of Vocational Behavior*, June 2001, *58*, 348–365.

12630

Test Name: WORK NORMS SCALE

Purpose: To assess organizational rewards and expectations.

Number of Items: 10

Format: Scales range from 1 (*strongly disagree*) to 5 (*strongly agree*). Sample items are presented.

Reliability: Alpha coefficients were .67 (expectations) and .86 (rewards).

Validity: Correlations with other variables ranged from −.28 to .44.

Author: Major, V. S., et al.

Article: Work time, work interference with family, and psychological distress.

Journal: *Journal of Applied Psychology*, June 2002, *87*, 427–436.

12631

Test Name: WORK QUESTIONNAIRE

Purpose: To assess the extent of creative work involved in respondents' jobs.

Number of Items: 20

Format: Includes five sections: Demographics, Current & Recent Jobs, Work Activities, Work Environment, and Job Satisfaction. Responses are made on 6-point scales for sections 3, 4, and 5.

Reliability: Alpha coefficients ranged from .78 to .86.

Validity: Correlations with other variables ranged from −.58 to .74.

Author: Clapham, M. M., et al.

Article: Predicting work activities with divergent thinking tests: A longitudinal study.

Journal: *The Journal of Creative Behavior,* Third Quarter 2005, *39*(3), 149–167.

12632

Test Name: WORK-RELATED VALUES SURVEY MODULE

Purpose: To measure masculinity and individualism in the job setting.

Number of Items: 7

Format: Item responses were anchored by 1 (*very little or no importance*) and 5 (*utmost importance*). Sample items are presented.

Reliability: Internal consistencies were .64 (individualism) and .61 (masculinity).

Author: Hirokawa, K., et al.

Article: Comparison of French and Japanese individuals with reference to Hofstede's comments of individualism and masculinity.

Journal: *Psychological Reports,* October 2001, *89,* 243–251.

Related Research: Hofstede, G. (1994). *Value Survey Module, 1994 manual.* Maastricht, The Netherlands Institute for Research in International Cooperation, University of Limburg. Vannieuwenhuyse, B., et al. (1998). L'influence de la culture nationale

sur les interactions professionnelles entre Japonais et Français: Considérations méthodologiques sur l'utilisation des model de G. Hofstede [The influence of national culture on professional interactions between Japanese and French individuals: Methodological considerations regarding the use of Hofstede's model]. *Annuaire de le Societé Japono-Francaise de Sociologie, 8,* 1–19. [in French]

12633

Test Name: WORKGROUP CHARACTERISTICS INVENTORY

Purpose: To measure perceptions of job design, interdependence, team composition, work context, and group processes.

Number of Items: 51

Format: Scales range from 1 (*strongly disagree*) to 5 (*strongly agree*). Sample items are presented.

Reliability: Alpha coefficients ranged from .55 to .91.

Author: Forrester, W. R., and Tashchian, A.

Article: Characteristics of work groups and their relationship with social and task cohesion in student teams.

Journal: *Psychological Reports,* August 2004, *95,* 207–214.

Related Research: Campion, M. A., et al. (1993). Relations between work group characteristics and effectiveness: Implications for designing effective work groups. *Personnel Psychology, 46,* 823–847.

12634

Test Name: WORKPLACE AGGRESSION SCALE

Purpose: To measure the incidence of workplace aggression and antisocial behavior.

Number of Items: 13

Format: Five-point scales are used. Sample items are presented.

Reliability: Alpha coefficients ranged from .92 to .93.

Validity: Correlations with other variables ranged from −.11 to .68.

Author: Douglas, S. C., and Martinko, M. J.

Article: Exploring the role of individual differences in the prediction of workplace aggression.

Journal: *Journal of Applied Psychology,* August 2001, *86,* 547–559.

Related Research: O'Leary-Kelley, A. M., et al. (1996). Organization-motivated aggression: A research framework. *Academy of Management Journal, 21,* 225–253.

12635

Test Name: WORKPLACE BEHAVIOR QUESTIONNAIRE

Purpose: To measure admissions of dishonesty in the workplace.

Number of Items: 6

Format: Seven-point agreement scales are used.

Reliability: Internal consistency was .77.

Validity: Correlations with other variables ranged from −.67 to .67.

Author: Nicol, A. A. M., and Paunonen, S. V.

Article: Overt honesty measures predicting admissions: An index of validity or reliability.

Journal: *Psychological Reports,* February 2002, *90,* 105–115.

Related Research: Ashton, M. C. (1998). Personality and job performance: The importance of narrow traits. *Journal of Organizational Behavior, 19,* 289–303.

12636

Test Name: WORKPLACE HETEROSEXIST EXPERIENCES QUESTIONNAIRE

Purpose: To measure workplace heterosexism.

Number of Items: 22

Format: Responses are made on a 5-point scale ranging from 0 (*never*) to 4 (*most of the time*). Examples are given.

Reliability: Coefficient alpha was .92.

Validity: Correlations with other variables ranged from −.35 to .73 (*N* = 97).

Author: Smith, N. G., and Ingram, K. M.

Article: Workplace heterosexism and adjustment among lesbian, gay, and bisexual individuals: The role of unsupportive social interactions.

Journal: *Journal of Counseling Psychology*, January 2004, *51*, 57–67.

Related Research: Waldo, C. R. (1999). Working in a majority context: A structural model of heterosexism as minority stress in the workplace. *Journal of Counseling Psychology, 46,* 218–232.

12637

Test Name: WORKPLACE INCIVILITY SCALE

Purpose: To measure the frequency of rudeness, disrespect, and condescension in the workplace.

Number of Items: 4

Format: Scales range from 0 (*never*) to 4 (*most of the time*). Sample items are presented.

Reliability: Coefficient alpha was .85.

Validity: Correlations with other variables ranged from −.38 to .96.

Author: Lim, S., and Cortina, L. M.

Article: Impersonal mistreatment in the workplace: The interface and impact of general incivility and sexual harassment.

Journal: *Journal of Applied Psychology*, May 2005, *90*, 483–496.

Related Research: Cortina, L. M., et al. (2001). Incivility at the workplace: Incidence and impact. *Journal of Occupational Health Psychology, 6,* 64–80.

12638

Test Name: WORKPLACE JUSTICE SCALE

Purpose: To measure distributive and procedural justice in the workplace.

Number of Items: 13

Format: Scales range from 1 (*strongly disagree*) to 5 (*strongly agree*). A sample item is presented.

Reliability: Alpha coefficients were .75 (procedural justice) and .76 (distributive justice).

Validity: Correlations with other variables ranged from −.21 to .60.

Author: Aryee, S., and Chay, Y. W.

Article: Workplace justice, citizenship behavior, and turnover intentions in a union context: Examining the mediating role of perceived union support and union instrumentality.

Journal: *Journal of Applied Psychology*, February 2001, *86*, 154–160.

Related Research: Fryxell, G., & Gordon, M. (1989). Workplace justice and job satisfaction as predictors of satisfaction with union and management. *Academy of Management Journal, 32,* 851–866.

12639

Test Name: WORKPLACE PRODUCTIVITY QUESTIONNAIRE

Purpose: To measure honesty in the workplace.

Number of Items: 72

Format: Seven-point agreement scales are used.

Reliability: Total internal reliability was .90. Reliabilities of all subscales exceeded .70.

Validity: Correlations were .34 (theft) and .19 (cheating).

Author: Nicol, A. A. M., and Paunonen, S. V.

Article: Overt honesty measures predicting admissions: An index of validity or reliability.

Journal: *Psychological Reports*, February 2002, *90*, 105–115.

Related Research: Nicol, A. A. M. (1999). *A measure of workplace honesty.* Unpublished doctoral dissertation, University of Western London, Ontario, Canada.

12640

Test Name: WORLD ASSUMPTIONS SCALE

Purpose: To assess cognitive schemes about individuals and their world.

Number of Items: 32

Format: Scales range from 1 (*strongly disagree*) to 6 (*strongly agree*).

Reliability: Coefficient alpha was .76.

Author: Dekel, R., et al.

Article: World assumptions and combat-related posttraumatic stress disorder.

Journal: *The Journal of Social Psychology*, August 2004, *144*, 407–420.

Related Research: Janoff-Bulman, R. (1989). Assumptive worlds and the stress of traumatic events: Applications of the schema construct. *Social Cognition, 7,* 113–136.

CHAPTER 15

Motivation

12641

Test Name: ACADEMIC MOTIVATION SCALE

Purpose: To measure intrinsic and extrinsic motivation.

Number of Items: 7

Format: Scales range from 1 (*not at all true*) to 7 (*very true*). Sample items are presented.

Reliability: Alpha coefficients ranged from .70 to .75 across subscales.

Validity: Correlations with other variables ranged from −.27 to .30.

Author: Chu, A. H. C., and Choi, J. N.

Article: Rethinking procrastination: Positive effects of "active" procrastination behavior on attitude and performance.

Journal: *The Journal of Social Psychology*, June 2005, *145*, 245–264.

Related Research: Shia, R. M. (1998). *Assessing academic intrinsic motivation: A look at student goals and personal strategy.* Unpublished thesis, Wheeling Jesuit University, Wheeling, WV. Available at http://www.cet.edu/research/papers /motivation/motivation.pdf

12642

Test Name: ACADEMIC MOTIVATION SCALE

Purpose: To measure intrinsic and extrinsic motivation and also a motivation.

Number of Items: 28

Format: Scales range from 1 (*does not correspond at all*) to 7 (*corresponds exactly*). Samples items are presented.

Reliability: Alpha coefficients ranged from .70 to .86 across subscales.

Validity: Correlations with other variables ranged from −.47 to .39.

Author: Cokley, K. O., et al.

Article: A psychometric investigation of the Academic Motivation Scale using a United States sample.

Journal: *Measurement and Evaluation in Counseling and Development*, July 2001, *34*, 109–119.

Related Research: Vallerand, R. J., et al. (1992). The Academic Motivation Scale: A measure of intrinsic, extrinsic, and a motivation in education. *Educational and Psychological Measurement*, *52*, 1003–1017.

12643

Test Name: ACADEMIC MOTIVATION SCALE

Purpose: To assess reasons students hold for pursuing their studies.

Number of Items: 20

Format: Includes five dimensions of reasons. Responses are made on a 7-point scale.

Reliability: Internal consistencies ranged from .75 to .95.

Author: Ratelle, C. F., et al.

Article: Family correlates of trajectories of academic motivation during a school transition: A semiparametric group-based approach.

Journal: *Journal of Educational Psychology*, December 2004, *96*, 743–754.

Related Research: Vallerand, R. J., et al. (1993). On the assessment of intrinsic, extrinsic, and a motivation in education: Evidence on the concurrent and construct validity of the Academic Motivation Scale. *Educational and Psychological Measurement*, *53*, 159–172.

12644

Test Name: ACADEMIC SELF-REGULATION QUESTIONNAIRE

Purpose: To assess self-determined academic motivation.

Number of Items: 15

Format: Responses are made on a scale of 1 to 7. Examples are given.

Reliability: Alpha coefficients ranged from .66 to .87.

Author: Hardre, P. L., and Reeve, J.

Article: A motivational model of rural students' intentions to persist in, versus drop out of, high school.

Journal: *Journal of Educational Psychology*, June 2003, *95*, 347–356.

Related Research: Ryan, R. M., & Connell, J. P. (1989). Perceived locus of causality and internalization: Examining reasons for acting in two domains. *Journal of Personality of Social Psychology, 57*, 749–761.

12645

Test Name: ACHIEVEMENT GOAL QUESTIONNAIRE— JAPANESE VERSION

Purpose: To assess high school students' adoption of mastery, performance-approach, and performance-avoidance goals.

Number of Items: 16

Format: All items are presented in English, but no response categories are reported.

Reliability: Alphas ranged from .82 to .87 across subscales.

Validity: Adjusted goodness of fit was .77. Correlations with other variables ranged from .08 to .70.

Author: Tanaka, A., and Yamauchi, H.

Article: A model for achievement motives, goal orientations, intrinsic interest, and academic achievement.

Journal: *Psychological Reports,* February 2001, *88*, 123–135.

Related Research: Elliot, A. J., & Church, M. A. (1977). A hierarchical model of approach and avoidance achievement motivation. *Journal of Personality and Social Psychology, 70*, 461–475.

12646

Test Name: ACHIEVEMENT GOAL QUESTIONNAIRE— MODIFIED

Purpose: To measure goal orientation for the current semester.

Number of Items: 12

Format: Includes four goal orientations: performance

approach, performance avoidance, mastery avoidance, and mastery approach. Responses are made on a 7-point scale ranging from 1 (*not at all true of me*) to 7 (*very true of me*). All items are presented.

Reliability: Alpha coefficients ranged from .68 to .88.

Author: Finney, S. J., et al.

Article: Examining the psychometric properties of the Achievement Goal Questionnaire in a general academic context.

Journal: *Educational and Psychological Measurement*, April 2004, *64*, 365–382.

Related Research: Elliot, A., & McGregor, H. A. (2001). A 2x2 achievement goal framework. *Journal of Personality and Social Psychology, 80*, 501–519.

12647

Test Name: ACHIEVEMENT GOALS QUESTIONNAIRE

Purpose: To assess students' goal orientations.

Number of Items: 18

Format: Includes three scales: Mastery, Performance Approach, and Performance Avoidance. Responses are made on a 5-point scale ranging from 1 (*not at all true of me*) to 5 (*very true of me*). Sample items are given.

Reliability: Alpha coefficients ranged from .67 to .91.

Validity: Correlations with other variables ranged from –.25 to .70.

Author: Shih, S.-S.

Article: Role of achievement goals in children's learning in Taiwan.

Journal: *Journal of Educational Research*, May/June 2005, *98*, 310–319.

Related Research: Elliot, A. J., & Church, M. A. (1997). A hierarchical model of approach and avoidance achievement motivation.

Journal of Personality and Social Psychology, 72, 218–232.

12648

Test Name: ACHIEVEMENT GOALS SCALE

Purpose: To assess students' mastery, performance-approach, performance-avoidance, and work-avoidance goals.

Number of Items: 22

Format: Includes four scales: Mastery Goals, Performance-Approach Goals, Performance-Avoidance Goals, and Work-Avoidance Goals. All items are presented.

Reliability: Alpha coefficients ranged from .56 to .90.

Validity: Correlations with other variables ranged from –.48 to .64 ($N = 131$).

Author: Tanaka, A., et al.

Article: Achievement motives, cognitive and social competence, and achievement goals in the classroom.

Journal: *Perceptual and Motor Skills*, October 2002, *95*, 445–458.

Related Research: Elliot, A. J., & Church, M. A. (1997). A hierarchical model of approach and avoidance achievement motivation. *Journal of Personality and Social Psychology, 72*, 218–232.

12649

Test Name: ACHIEVEMENT MOTIVES SCALE

Purpose: To assess students' motive to achieve success and their motive to avoid failure.

Number of Items: 9

Format: Includes two factors: Motive to Achieve Success and Motive to Avoid Failure. All items are presented.

Reliability: Alpha coefficients were .84 to .79.

Validity: Correlations with other variables ranged from −.48 to .64 (N = 131).

Author: Tanaka, A., et al.

Article: Achievement motives, cognitive and social competence, and achievement goals in the classroom.

Journal: *Perceptual and Motor Skills*, October 2002, *95*, 445–458.

Related Research: Gjesme, T., & Nygard, R. (1970). *The Achievement Motives Scales (AMS).* Unpublished report, University of Oslo, Oslo, Norway.

12650

Test Name: ACHIEVEMENT MOTIVES SCALES—JAPANESE VERSION

Purpose: To assess a student's motive to achieve success and avoid failure.

Number of Items: 10

Format: All items are presented in English without response categories.

Reliability: Alphas were .79 (avoid failure) and .83 (achieve success).

Validity: Adjusted goodness of fit was .80. Correlations with other variables ranged from .07 to .70.

Author: Tanaka, A., and Yamauchi, H.

Article: A model for achievement motives, goal orientations, intrinsic interest, and academic achievement.

Journal: *Psychological Reports*, February 2001, *88*, 123–135.

Related Research: Gjesme, T., & Nygard, R. (1970). *The achievement Motives Scale (AMS)* Unpublished report, University of Oslo, Oslo, Norway.

12651

Test Name: ACHIEVEMENT-RELATED MOTIVATIONAL BELIEFS AND VALUES SCALES

Purpose: To measure achievement-related motivational beliefs and values

Number of Items: 18

Format: Includes five factors: importance of school grades, value of school experiences, academic self-efficacy, school bonding, and college plans.

Reliability: Alpha coefficients ranged from .62 to .80.

Author: Bryant, A. L., and Zimmerman, M. A.

Article: Examining the effects of academic beliefs and behaviors on changes in substance use among urban adolescents.

Journal: *Journal of Educational Psychology*, September 2002, *94*, 621–637.

Related Research: Eccles, J. S. (1993). *Middle School family survey study.* Boulder: University of Colorado. Hawkins, J. D., et al. (1997). Exploring the effects of age of alcohol use initiation and psychosocial risk factors on subsequent alcohol misuse. *Journal of Studies on Alcohol, 58,* 280–290.

12652

Test Name: ACHIEVEMENT STRIVING SCALE

Purpose: To measure achievement striving.

Number of Items: 6

Format: Responses are made on a 5-point scale. All items are presented.

Reliability: Alpha coefficients were .80 and .87.

Validity: Correlations with other variables ranged from .07 to .57.

Author: Nonis, S. A., and Wright, D.

Article: Moderating effects of achievement striving and situational optimism on the relationship between ability and performance outcomes of college students.

Journal: *Research in Higher Education*, June 2003, *44,* 327–346.

Related Research: Spence, J. T., et al. (1987). Impatience versus achievement striving in the Type A behavior pattern: Differential effects on students' health and academic achievement. *Journal of Applied Psychology, 72,* 522–528.

12653

Test Name: ACHIEVING TENDENCY SCALE

Purpose: To assess individual characteristics associated with achievement.

Number of Items: 36

Format: Nine-point agreement scales are used.

Reliability: Coefficient alpha was .90.

Validity: Correlations with other variables ranged from −.15 to .31.

Author: Klibert, J. J., et al.

Article: Adaptive and maladaptive aspects of self-oriented versus socially prescribed perfectionism.

Journal: *Journal of College Student Development*, March/April 2005, *46,* 141–156.

Related Research: Mehrabian, A. (1994). Individual differences in achieving tendency: Review of evidence bearing on a questionnaire measure. *Current Psychology: Developmental, Learning, Personality, Social, 13,* 351–364.

12654

Test Name: ACTIVE JOB-SEARCH SCALE—ADAPTED

Purpose: To assess job-search intensity.

Number of Items: 5

Format: Responses are made on a 5-point scale ranging from 1 (*never*) to 5 (*very frequently*). An example is given.

Reliability: Alpha coefficients were .78 and .84.

Validity: Correlations with other variables ranged from −.11 to .52.

Author: Crossley, C. D., and Stanton, J. M.

Article: Negative affect and job search: Further examination of the reverse causation hypothesis.

Journal: *Journal of Vocational Behavior*, June 2005, *66*, 549–560.

Related Research: Blau, G. (1993). Further exploring the relationship between job search and voluntary individual turnover. *Personnel Psychology, 46*, 213–330.

12655

Test Name: ADOLESCENT RESILIENCE SCALE

Purpose: To assess novelty-seeking, emotional regulation, and positive future orientation.

Number of Items: 21

Format: Item response categories are anchored by 5 (*definitely yes*) and 1 (*definitely no*). All items are presented.

Reliability: Alpha coefficients ranged from .77 to .85.

Validity: Correlations with other variables ranged from −.49 to −.03.

Author: Oshio, A., et al.

Article: Construct validity of the Adolescent Resilience Scale.

Journal: *Psychological Reports*, December 2003, *93*, Part 2, 1217–1222.

12656

Test Name: AGE-UNIVERSAL I/E SCALE

Purpose: To measure explicit identification with extrinsic and intrinsic motivations for pursuing religion.

Number of Items: 12

Time Required: 5 minutes.

Format: Scales range from 1 (*strongly disagree*) to 5 (*strongly agree*).

Author: Wenger, J. L., and Yarbrough, T. D.

Article: Religious individuals: Evaluating their intrinsic and extrinsic motivations at the implicit level of awareness.

Journal: *The Journal of Social Psychology*, February 2005, *145*, 5–16.

Related Research: Maltby, J. (1999). The internal structure of a derived, revised, and amended measure of the Religious Orientation Scale: The Age-Universal I/E Scale—12. *Social Behavior and Personality, 27*, 407–412.

12657

Test Name: ASPIRATIONS INDEX

Purpose: To assess three intrinsic and three extrinsic value domains.

Number of Items: 30

Format: Scales range from 1 (*not at all important*) to 5 (*very important*). Sample items are presented.

Reliability: Alpha coefficients ranged from .76 to .93.

Validity: Correlations with other variables ranged from −.14 to .43.

Author: Sheldon, K. M.

Article: Positive value change during college: Normative trends and individual differences.

Journal: *Journal of Research in Personality*, April 2005, *39*, 209–223.

Related Research: Kasser, T., & Ryan, R. M. (2001). Be careful what you wish for: Optimal functioning and the relative attainment of intrinsic and extrinsic goals. *Personality and Social Psychology Bulletin, 22*, 281–288.

12658

Test Name: BLAIS WORK MOTIVATION INVENTORY—SHORT VERSION

Purpose: To assess work self-determination.

Number of Items: 18

Format: Includes six motivational dimensions: Toward Accomplishment, Toward Knowledge, Identified Regulation, Introjected Regulation, External Regulation, and a motivation. Responses are made on a 7-point scale ranging from 1 (*do not agree at all*) to 7 (*agree completely*). Examples are given.

Reliability: Alpha coefficients were .57 and .86.

Author: Fernet, C., et al.

Article: Adjusting to job demands: The role of work self-determination and job control in predicting burnout.

Journal: *Journal of Vocational Behavior*, August 2004, *65*, 39–56.

Related Research: Blais, M. R., et al. (1993). L'inventaire des motivations au travail de Blais. [Blais Work Motivation Inventory.] *Revue Québécoise de Psychologie, 14*, 185–215.

12659

Test Name: CAREER DAY SURVEYS

Purpose: To identify science–mathematics educational and career goals of seventh grade through high school female students.

Number of Items: 21 and 28

Format: Includes two questionnaires: one administered in 7th grade, the other administered in 12th grade. All items are presented.

Reliability: Test–retest reliability coefficients ranged from .74 to .88.

Author: Van Leuvan, P.

Article: Young women's science/mathematics career goals from seventh grade to high school graduation.

Journal: *Journal of Educational Research*, May/June 2004, *97*, 248–267.

Related Research: Davis, B. G., & Humphreys, S. (1985). *Evaluating intervention programs: Applications for women's programs in math and science.* New York: Teachers College Press, Columbia University.

12660

Test Name: CAREER MOTIVATION SCALE

Purpose: To measure career motivation.

Number of Items: 21

Format: Includes three parts: Career Insight, Career Resilience, and Career Identity. All items are presented.

Reliability: Coefficient alpha was .84.

Author: Day, R., and Allen, T. D.

Article: The relationship between career motivation and self-efficacy with protégé career success.

Journal: *Journal of Vocational Behavior*, February 2004, *64*, 72–91.

Related Research: London, M. (1993). Relationships between career motivation, empowerment and support for career development. *Journal of Occupational and Organizational Psychology, 66,* 55–69. Noe, R. A., et al. (1990). An investigation of correlates of career motivation. *Journal of Vocational Behavior, 37,* 340–356.

12661

Test Name: CAREER-RELATED MOTIVATION SCALE

Purpose: To measure career-related motivation.

Number of Items: 7

Format: Responses are made on a 5-point scale ranging from 1 (*does not apply at all*) to 5 (*applies fully*). Examples are presented.

Reliability: Coefficient alpha was .75.

Validity: Correlations with other variables ranged from −.24 to .39 ($n = 391$).

Author: Pinquart, M., et al.

Article: Self-efficacy and successful school-to-work transition: A longitudinal study.

Journal: *Journal of Vocational Behavior*, December 2003, *63*, 329–346.

Related Research: Vinokur, A. D., et al. (2000). Two years after a job loss: Long-term impact of the JOBS program on reemployment and mental health. *Journal of Occupational Health Psychology, 5,* 32–47.

12662

Test Name: CITIZENSHIP MOTIVES SCALE

Purpose: To measure organizational concern, prosocial values, and impression management as elements of organizational citizenship behavior.

Number of Items: 30

Format: Rating scales range from 1 (*not at all important*) to 6 (*extremely important*). All items are presented.

Reliability: Alpha coefficients ranged from .84 to .94 across subscales.

Validity: Extensive correlations between the subscales and organizational citizenship measures are presented.

Author: Rioux, S. M., and Penner, L. A.

Article: The causes of organizational citizenship behavior: A motivational analysis.

Journal: *Journal of Applied Psychology*, December 2001, *86*, 1306–1314.

12663

Test Name: CLASSROOM GOAL-ORIENTATION SCALE

Purpose: To measure academic motivation.

Number of Items: 21

Format: Responses are made on a 5-point Likert-type scale ranging from *strongly agree* to *strongly disagree*. An example is given.

Reliability: Coefficient alpha was .77.

Author: Powell, C. L., and Arriola, K. R. J.

Article: Relationship between psychosocial factors and academic achievement among African American students.

Journal: *Journal of Educational Research*, January/February 2003, *96*, 175–181.

Related Research: Duda, J. L., & Nicholls, J. G. (1992). Dimensions of achievement motivation in schoolwork and sport. *Journal of Educational Psychology, 84,* 290–299.

12664

Test Name: COMMITMENT TO DISPLAY RULES SCALE

Purpose: To assess employee commitment to organizational display rules.

Number of Items: 5

Format: Scales range from 1 (*strongly disagree*) to 5 (*strongly agree*). A sample item is presented.

Reliability: Coefficient alpha was .69.

Validity: Correlations with other variables ranged from −.33 to .32.

Author: Gosserand, R. H., and Diefendorff, J. M.

Article: Emotional display rules and emotional labor: The moderating role of commitment.

Journal: *Journal of Applied Psychology*, November 2005, *90*, 1256–1264.

12665

Test Name: COMPETITIVENESS INDEX—REVISED

Purpose: To measure the desire to win in interpersonal situations.

Number of Items: 14

Format: Scales range from 1 (*strongly disagree*) to 5 (*strongly agree*). Sample items are presented.

Reliability: Coefficient alpha was .87. Subscale alphas were .74 and .90.

Author: Houston, J. M., et al.

Article: Competitiveness among Japanese, Chinese, and American undergraduate students.

Journal: *Psychological Reports*, August 2005, *97*, 205–212.

Related Research: Houston, J. M. (2002). Revising the Competitiveness Index. *Psychological Reports, 90,* 31–34.

12666

Test Name: COMPSCALE

Purpose: To assess selected dimensions of motivation and self-regulatory behavior.

Number of Items: 9

Format: Includes two parts: Teacher-Rated Motivation and Teacher-Rated Self-Regulation. Ratings are made on a 4-point Likert-type scale ranging from 1 (*strongly agree*) to 4 (*strongly disagree*). All items are presented.

Reliability: Alpha coefficients were .67 and .86. Test–retest (6 weeks) reliability was .86.

Validity: Correlations with other variables ranged from .08 to .51.

Author: Howse, R. B., et al.

Article: Motivation and self-regulation as predictors of achievement in economically disadvantaged young children.

Journal: *The Journal of Experimental Education*, Winter 2003, *71*, 151–174.

Related Research: Adler, F., & Lange, G. (1997, April). *Children's mastery orientations and school achievement in the elementary grades.* Poster presented at the biennial meeting of the Society for Research in Child Development, Washington, DC.

12667

Test Name: CURIOSITY AND EXPLORATION INVENTORY

Purpose: To measure curiosity.

Number of Items: 7

Format: Includes two factors: exploration and absorption. Responses are made on a 7-point Likert scale ranging from 1 (*strongly disagree*) to 7 (*strongly agree*). All items are presented.

Reliability: Alpha coefficients ranged from .63 to .80.

Validity: Correlations with other variables ranged from −.43 to .71.

Author: Kashdan, T. B., et al.

Article: Curiosity and exploration: Facilitating positive subjective experiences and personal growth opportunities.

Journal: *Journal of Personality Assessment*, June 2004, *82*, 291–305.

12668

Test Name: CURIOSITY QUESTIONNAIRE

Purpose: To assess both epistemic and perceptual curiosity.

Number of Items: 56

Format: Includes two dimensions: Epistemic Curiosity and Perceptual Curiosity. Responses are made on a 4-point scale ranging from 1 (*almost never*) to 4 (*almost always*). All items are presented.

Reliability: Alpha coefficients ranged from .81 to .87.

Author: Litman, J. A., and Spielberger, C. D.

Article: Measuring epistemic curiosity and its diversive and specific components.

Journal: *Journal of Personality Assessment*, February 2003, *80*, 75–86.

Related Research: Collins, R. P. (1996). *Identification of perceptual curiosity as a psychological construct: Development of the Perceptual Curiosity Scale.* Unpublished master's thesis, University of South Florida, Tampa.

12669

Test Name: DAILY GOAL ATTAINMENT SCALE

Purpose: To assess daily attainment of major personal goals.

Number of Items: 5

Format: Responses are made on a 4-point scale ranging from 1 (*not at all*) to 4 (*all day*). Examples are given.

Reliability: Coefficient alpha was .77.

Validity: Correlations with other variables ranged from −.23 to .51.

Author: Daniels, K., and Harris, C.

Article: A daily diary study of coping in the context of the job demands–control–support model.

Journal: *Journal of Vocational Behavior*, April 2005, *66*, 219–237.

Related Research: Harris, C., et al. (2003). A daily diary study of goals and affective well-being at work. *Journal of Occupational and Organizational Psychology, 76,* 401–410.

12670

Test Name: DRINKING MOTIVES QUESTIONNAIRE

Purpose: To measure motivations to drink as enhancement motives, social motives, and coping motives.

Number of Items: 15

Reliability: Alpha coefficients ranged from .77 to .85.

Validity: Correlations with other variables ranged from −.20 to .01.

Author: Daugherty, T. K., and McLarty, L. M.

Article: Religious coping, drinking motivation, and sex.

Journal: *Psychological Reports,* April 2003, *92,* 643–647.

Related Research: Cooper, L., et al. (1992). Development and validation of a three-dimensional measure of drinking motives. *Psychological Assessment, 4,* 123–132.

12671

Test Name: EFFORT AND ENJOYMENT SCALE

Purpose: To assess motivational responses.

Number of Items: 9

Format: Includes two subscales: Effort and Enjoyment. Responses are made on a 4-point Likert scale ranging from 1 (*strongly agree*) to 4 (*strongly disagree*). Examples are given.

Reliability: Alpha coefficients were .79 and .87.

Validity: Correlations with other variables ranged from .29 to .60.

Author: Wright, P. M., et al.

Article: Relations of perceived physical self-efficacy and

motivational responses toward physical activity by urban high school students.

Journal: *Perceptual and Motor Skills,* October 2005, *101,* 651–656.

Related Research: Duda, J., & Nicholls, J. (1992). Dimensions of achievement-motivation in schoolwork and sport. *Journal of Educational Psychology, 84,* 290–299.

12672

Test Name: ENTREPRENEURIAL INTENTION SCALE

Purpose: To measure the intention to engage in entrepreneurial activities.

Number of Items: 4

Format: Scales range from 1 (*very little*) to 5 (*a great deal*).

Reliability: Coefficient alpha was .85.

Validity: Correlations with other variables ranged from −.28 to .43.

Author: Zhao, H., et al.

Article: The mediating role of self-efficacy in the development of entrepreneurial intentions.

Journal: *Journal of Applied Psychology,* November 2005, *90,* 1265–1272.

12673

Test Name: ENTREPRENEURIAL MOTIVATION SCALES

Purpose: To measure perceived passion for work, tenacity, and resource acquisition skills.

Number of Items: 15

Format: Scales range from 1 (*strongly disagree*) to 5 (*strongly agree*). Sample items are presented.

Reliability: Composite reliability coefficients ranged from .83 to .94 across subscales.

Validity: Correlations with other variables ranged from .02 to .24.

Author: Baum, J. R., and Locke, E. A.

Article: The relationship of entrepreneurial traits, skill, and motivation to subsequent venture growth.

Journal: *Journal of Applied Psychology,* August 2004, *89,* 587–598.

12674

Test Name: ENTREPRENEURIAL ORIENTATION SCALE— ADAPTED

Purpose: To measure entrepreneurial orientation.

Number of Items: 5

Format: Responses are made on a 5-point scale ranging from 1 (*strongly disagree*) to 5 (*strongly agree*). Examples are given.

Reliability: Internal consistency was .65.

Validity: Correlations with other variables ranged from −.06 to .22.

Author: Davis, M. A.

Article: Factors related to bridge employment participation among private sector early retirees.

Journal: *Journal of Vocational Behavior,* August 2003, *63,* 55–71.

Related Research: Robinson, P. B., et al. (1991). An attitude approach to the prediction of entrepreneur-ship.*Entrepreneurship Theory and Practice, 15*(4), 13–31.

12675

Test Name: ENTREPRENEURIAL POTENTIAL QUESTIONNAIRE

Purpose: To measure need for achievement, locus of control, problem-solving orientation, risk-taking propensity, and manipulation.

Number of Items: 35

Format: A forced-choice format is used. A sample item is presented.

Reliability: Internal consistency coefficients ranged from .60 to .79. Test–retest reliabilities ranged from .62 to .77.

Validity: Correlations with other variables ranged from .41 to .45.

Author: Mueller, G. F., and Gappisch, C.

Article: Personality types of entrepreneurs.

Journal: *Psychological Reports*, June 2005, *96*, Part 1, 737–746.

Related Research: King, A. S. (1985). Self-analysis and assessment of entrepreneurial potential. *Simulation and Games, 16,* 399–416.

12676

Test Name: FEELINGS ABOUT SCHOOL—MODIFIED

Purpose: To assess young children's motivational propensities.

Format: Includes four parts: Worry, Perceived Competence at School, Attitude, and Preference-for-Challenge Task.

Reliability: Alpha coefficients ranged from .47 to .74. Test–retest reliabilities ranged from .41 to .65.

Validity: Correlations with other variables ranged from −.45 to .39.

Author: Howse, R. B., et al.

Article: Motivation and self-regulation as predictors of achievement in economically disadvantaged young children.

Journal: *Journal of Experimental Education*, Winter 2003, *71*, 151–174.

Related Research: Stipek, D., et al. (1995). Effects of different approaches on young children's achievement and motivation. *Child Development, 66*, 209–223.

12677

Test Name: FLEXIBLE GOAL ADJUSTMENT SCALE

Purpose: To measure accommodative flexibility.

Number of Items: 15

Format: Responses are made on a 5-point Likert-type scale ranging from *strongly disagree* to *strongly agree.*

Reliability: Alpha coefficients ranged from .74 to .83.

Validity: Correlations with other variables ranged from −.46 to .45.

Author: Mueller, D. J., and Kim, K.

Article: The Tenacious Goal Pursuit and Flexible Goal Adjustment scales: Examination of their validity.

Journal: *Educational and Psychological Measurement*, February 2004, *64*, 120–142.

Related Research: Brandtstädter, J., & Renner, G. (1990). Tenacious goal pursuit and flexible goal adjustment: Explication and age-related analysis of assimilative and accommodative strategies of coping. *Psychology and Aging, 5,* 58–67.

12678

Test Name: GAMBLING MOTIVATION SCALE

Purpose: To measure motivation to gamble.

Number of Items: 28

Format: Scales range from 1 (*does not correspond at all*) to 7 (*corresponds exactly*). Sample items are presented.

Reliability: Alpha coefficients ranged from .69 to .90.

Author: Clarke, D.

Article: Motivational differences between slot machine and lottery players.

Journal: *Psychological Reports*, June 2005, *96*, Part 1, 843–848.

Related Research: Chantal, Y., et al. (1994). [On the development and validation of the Gambling Motivation Scale (GMS)]. *Society and Leisure, 17,* 189–212.

12679

Test Name: GENERAL LEARNING AND PERFORMANCE SCALES

Purpose: To assess overall orientations assumed to generalize across different activities.

Number of Items: 16

Format: Includes two scales: General Learning Goal and General Performance Goal. Responses are made on a 7-point scale ranging from 1 (*strongly disagree*) to 7 (*strongly agree*).

Reliability: Alpha coefficients were .85 and .87.

Validity: Correlations with other variables ranged from −.35 to .52.

Author: Jagacinski, C. M., and Duda, J. L.

Article: A comparative analysis of contemporary achievement goal orientation measures.

Journal: *Education and Psychological Measurement*, December 2001, *61*, 1013–1039.

Related Research: Button, S. B., et al. (1976). Goal orientation in organizational research: A conceptual and empirical foundation. *Organizational Behavior and Human Decision Processes, 67*, 26–48.

12680

Test Name: GOAL IMPORTANCE SCALE

Purpose: To measure the importance of motivational goals such as security, safety, and social order.

Number of Items: 24

Format: Scales range from 1 (*not at all important*) to 9 (*extremely important*).

Reliability: Alpha coefficients ranged from .75 to .86.

Author: Nelissen, R. M. A., et al.

Article: Limitations of semantic priming procedures for automatic goal activation.

Journal: *Psychological Reports*, December 2005, *97*, 675–689.

Related Research: Schwartz, S. H. (1992). Universals in the structure and content of values: Theoretical advances and empirical tests in 20 countries. *Advances in Experimental Social Psychology, 25*, 1–65.

12681

Test Name: GOAL INSTABILITY SCALE

Purpose: To assess a person's lack of goal directedness and inhibition in work.

Number of Items: 10

Format: Responses are made on a 6-point Likert scale. Examples are given.

Reliability: Test–retest (2 weeks) reliability was .75. Internal consistency estimates ranged from .80 to .90.

Validity: Correlations with other variables ranged from −.63 to .61.

Author: Heppner, M. J., et al.

Article: The role of problem-solving appraisal in the process and outcome of career counseling.

Journal: *Journal of Vocational Behavior*, October 2004, *65*, 217–238.

Related Research: Robbins, S. B., & Patton, M. J. (1985). Self-psychology in career development: Construction of the superiority and goal instability scales. *Journal of*

Counseling Psychology, 32, 221–231.

12682

Test Name: GOAL ORIENTATION QUESTIONNAIRE

Purpose: To measure goal orientation specifically to mathematics-learning situations.

Number of Items: 21

Format: Includes four subscales: Task Orientation, Error Frustration, Self-Enhancing Ego Orientation, and Self-Defeating Ego Orientation. Responses are made on a 4-point scale ranging from 1 (*never*) to 4 (*always*). Examples are given.

Reliability: Alpha coefficients ranged from .68 to .80.

Validity: Correlations with other variables ranged from −.24 to .36 ($N = 541$).

Author: Seegers, G., et al.

Article: Effects of causal attributions following mathematics tasks on student cognitions about a subsequent task.

Journal: *The Journal of Experimental Education*, Summer 2004, *72*, 307–328.

Related Research: Seegers, G., et al. (2002). Goal orientation, perceived task outcome and task demands in mathematics tasks: Effects on students' attitude in actual task settings. *British Journal of Educational Psychology, 72*, 365–384.

12683

Test Name: GOAL ORIENTATION QUESTIONNAIRE

Purpose: To assess students' mastery and performance orientations.

Number of Items: 14

Format: Includes three subscales: Performance-Avoidance Orientation,

Performance-Approach Orientation, and Mastery Orientation. Responses are made on a 5-point scale ranging from 1 (*completely disagree*) to 5 (*completely agree*). Examples are given.

Reliability: Alpha coefficients ranged from .93 to .97.

Validity: Correlations with other variables ranged from −.63 to .41.

Author: Vansteenkiste, M., et al.

Article: Less is sometimes more: Goal content matters.

Journal: *Journal of Educational Psychology*, December 2004, *96*, 755–764.

Related Research: Midgley, C., et al. (1997). *Patterns of Adaptive Learning Survey (PALS)*. Ann Arbor: University of Michigan Press.

12684

Test Name: GOAL ORIENTATION SCALE

Purpose: To measure a learning goal orientation, a performance-prone orientation, and an avoid-performance orientation.

Number of Items: 13

Format: Scales range from 1 (*strongly disagree*) to 7 (*strongly agree*).

Reliability: Alpha coefficients ranged from .69 to .84 across subscales.

Validity: Correlations with other variables ranged from −.24 to .17.

Author: Brett, J. F., and Atwater, L. E.

Article: 360° feedback: Accuracy, reactions, and perceptions of usefulness.

Journal: *Journal of Applied Psychology*, October 2001, *86*, 930–942.

Related Research: VandeWalle, D. (1997). Development and validation of a work domain goal orientation instrument. *Educational and Psychological Measurement*, 57, 995–1015.

12685

Test Name: GOAL ORIENTATION SCALE

Purpose: To assess goal orientations.

Number of Items: 8

Format: Includes two goal orientations: mastery goal orientation and performance goal orientation. Responses are made on a 4-point scale ranging from *strongly agree* to *strongly disagree*. Sample items are presented.

Reliability: Alpha coefficients were .74 to .62.

Validity: Correlations with other variables ranged from −.33 to .28 ($N = 71$).

Author: Brown, K. G. B.

Article: Using computers to deliver training: Which employees learn and why?

Journal: *Personnel Psychology*, Summer 2001, 54, 271–296.

Related Research: Button, S. B., et al. (1996). The development and psychometric evaluation of measures of learning goal and performance goal orientation. *Organizational Behavior and Human Decision Processes*, 67, 26–48.

12686

Test Name: GOAL ORIENTATION SCALE

Purpose: To measure learning and performance orientation related to work tasks.

Number of Items: 16

Format: Scales range from 1 (*strongly disagree*) to 5 (*strongly agree*). Sample items are presented.

Reliability: Alpha coefficients ranged from .73 to .74.

Validity: Correlations with other variables ranged from −.15 to .27.

Author: Porter, C. O. L. H.

Article: Goal orientation effects on backing up behavior, performance, efficacy, and commitment in teams.

Journal: *Journal of Applied Psychology*, July 2005, 90, 811–818.

12687

Test Name: GOAL ORIENTATION SCALE

Purpose: To assess goal orientation.

Number of Items: 15

Format: Includes three factors: trait mastery, performance approach, and performance avoidance. Responses are made on a 5-point scale ranging from *strongly disagree* to *strongly agree*. Sample items are presented.

Reliability: Alpha coefficients ranged from .75 to .88.

Validity: Correlations with other variables ranged from −.35 to .38.

Author: Schmidt, A. M., and Ford, J. K.

Article: Learning within a learner control training environment: The interactive effects of goal orientation and metacognitive instruction on learning outcomes.

Journal: *Personnel Psychology*, Summer 2003, 56, 405–429.

Related Research: Horvath, M., et al. (2001, April). *Goal orientation: Integrating theory and measurement*. Paper presented at the 16th annual conference of the Society for Industrial and Organizational Psychology, San Diego, CA.

12688

Test Name: GOAL SELF-CONCORDANCE SCALE

Purpose: To assess the external, introjected, identified, and intrinsic reasons why people pursue goals.

Number of Items: 4 items per goal.

Format: Scales range from 1 (*not at all for this reason*) to 9 (*completely for this reason*). Sample items are presented.

Reliability: Coefficient alpha was .68

Author: Ong, A. D., and Phinney, J. S.

Article: Personal goals and depression among Vietnamese American and European American young adults: A mediational analysis.

Journal: *The Journal of Social Psychology*, February 2002, 142, 97–108.

Related Research: Emmons, R. A. (1986). Personal striving: An approach to personal and subjective well-being. *Journal of Personality and Social Psychology*, 51, 1058–1068.

12689

Test Name: GOALS IN LIFE SCALE

Purpose: To measure the importance placed on life goals and relationship possibilities and which has a higher priority if in conflict.

Number of Items: All items are described.

Format: Item formats varied and are described.

Reliability: Coefficient alpha was .73.

Author: Fleming, R. M., and Zucker, E. L.

Article: Influences of type of high school attended and current life relationship status on life goal ratings of college women.

Journal: *Psychological Reports*, December 2002, 91, Part 1, 989–993.

Related Research: Hammersla, J. F., & Frease-McMahan, L. (1990). University students' priorities: Life goals vs. relationships. *Sex Roles, 23,* 1–14.

12690

Test Name: GOALS INVENTORY

Purpose: To measure goal orientation.

Number of Items: 25

Format: Includes two factors: learning and performance. Responses are made on a 5-point Likert scale. Examples are presented.

Reliability: Test–retest (2 weeks) reliability was .73 and .76. Alpha coefficients ranged from .72 to .80.

Author: Bandalos, D. L., et al.

Article: A model of statistics performance based on achievement goal theory.

Journal: *Journal of Educational Psychology,* September 2003, *95,* 604–616.

Related Research: Roedel, T. D., et al. (1994). Validation of a measure of learning and performance orientations. *Educational and Psychological Measurement, 54,* 1013–1021.

12691

Test Name: GOALS INVENTORY

Purpose: To measure mastery and performance.

Number of Items: 17

Format: Scales range from 1 (*strongly disagree*) to 5 (*strongly agree*). Sample items are presented.

Reliability: Coefficient alpha was .76 for each subscale.

Validity: Correlations with other variables ranged from –.07 to .28.

Author: Towler, A. J., and Dipboye, R. L.

Article: Effects of trainer expressiveness, organization, and trainee goal orientation on training outcomes.

Journal: *Journal of Applied Psychology,* August 2001, *86,* 664–673.

Related Research: Roedel-Debacker, T., et al. (1994). Validation of a measure of learning and performance goal orientations. *Educational and Psychological Measurement, 54,* 1013–1021.

12692

Test Name: HONG PSYCHOLOGICAL REACTANCE SCALE

Purpose: To assess the motivational force to react when freedoms are reduced or eliminated.

Number of Items: 11

Format: Scales range from 1 (*disagree completely*) to 5 (*agree completely*). All items are presented.

Reliability: Coefficient alpha was .76.

Author: Thomas, A., et al.

Article: The Hong Psychological Reactance Scale: A confirmatory factor analysis.

Journal: *Measurement and Evaluation in Counseling and Development,* April 2001, *34,* 2–13.

Related Research: Hong, S.-M., & Page, S. (1989). The Psychological Reactance Scale: Development, factor structure, and reliability. *Psychological Reports, 64,* 1323–1326.

12693

Test Name: HYPERCOMPETITIVE ATTITUDE SCALE

Purpose: To assess the need to compete and win at any cost as a measure of maintaining or enhancing feelings of self-worth.

Number of Items: 26.

Format: Responses are made on a 5-point scale ranging from 1 (*never true of me*) to 5 (*always true of me*). Sample items are presented.

Reliability: Internal consistency coefficients were .85 and .91.

Validity: Correlations with other variables ranged from –.18 to .66.

Author: Houston, J. M., et al.

Article: A factorial analysis of scales measuring competitiveness.

Journal: *Educational and Psychological Measurement,* April 2002, *62,* 284–298.

Related Research: Ryckman, R. M., et al. (1990). Construction of a hypercompetitive attitude scale. *Journal of Personality Assessment, 55,* 630–639.

12694

Test Name: INDIVIDUAL INITIATIVE SCALE

Purpose: To measure individual initiative among white-collar workers with a college degree.

Number of Items: 15

Format: All items are presented.

Reliability: Coefficient alpha was .91.

Validity: Correlations with other variables ranged from –.39 to .51.

Author: Bolino, M. C., and Turnley, W. H.

Article: The personal costs of citizenship behavior: The relationship between individual initiative and role overload, job stress, and work–family conflict.

Journal: *Journal of Applied Psychology,* July 2005, *90,* 740–748.

12695

Test Name: INTENTIONS TO SEEK COUNSELING INVENTORY

Purpose: To measure intentions to seek counseling.

Number of Items: 17

Format: Includes three subscales: Interpersonal Problems, Academic Problems, and Drug/Alcohol Problems. Responses are made on a 4-point scale ranging from 1 (*very unlikely*) to 4 (*very likely*).

Reliability: Internal consistency coefficients ranged from .69 to .90.

Validity: Correlations with other variables ranged from −.20 to .56 ($N = 354$).

Author: Vogel, D. L., et al.

Article: The role of outcome expectations and attitudes on decisions to seek professional help.

Journal: *Journal of Counseling Psychology*, October 2005, *52*, 459–470.

Related Research: Cash, T. F., et al. (1975). When counselors are heard but not seen: Initial impact of physical attractiveness. *Journal of Counseling Psychology, 22,* 273–279.

12696

Test Name: INTERNAL AND EXTERNAL MOTIVATION TO RESPOND WITHOUT PREJUDICE SCALES

Purpose: To assess internal and external motivation to respond without prejudice.

Number of Items: 10

Format: Includes two scales: Internal Motivation and External Motivation. Responses are made on 9-point Likert scales ranging from 1 (*strongly disagree*) to 9 (*strongly agree*). Examples are given.

Reliability: Reliability coefficients ranged from .75 to .85.

Validity: Correlations with other variables ranged from −.43 to .33.

Author: Gushue, G. V.

Article: Race, colorblind racial attitudes, and judgments about mental health: A shifting of standards perspective.

Journal: *Journal of Counseling Psychology*, October 2004, *51*, 398–407.

Related Research: Plant, E. A., & Devine, P. G. (1998). Internal and external motivation to respond without prejudice. *Journal of Personality and Social Psychology, 75,* 811–832.

12697

Test Name: INTERPERSONAL COMPETITIVENESS SUBSCALE

Purpose: To measure the desire to win over others.

Number of Items: 8

Format: Responses are made on a 5-point Likert-type scale. Examples are presented.

Reliability: Coefficient alpha .76.

Author: Houston, J. M., et al.

Article: A factorial analysis of scales measuring competitiveness.

Journal: *Educational and Psychological Measurement*, April 2002, *62*, 284–298.

Related Research: Griffin-Pierson, S. (1990). The Competitiveness Questionnaire: A measure of two components of competitiveness. *Measurement and Evaluation in Counseling and Development, 23,* 108–115.

12698

Test Name: INTERVIEW MOTIVATION SCALE

Purpose: To measure how motivated interviewees are to do well in an employment interview.

Number of Items: 6

Format: Scales range from 1 (*strongly disagree*) to 5 (*strongly agree*). A sample item is presented.

Reliability: Coefficient alpha was .85.

Validity: Correlations with other variables ranged from .03 to .49.

Author: Maurer, T. J., et al.

Article: Interviewee coaching, preparation strategies, and response strategies in relation to performance in situational employment interviews: An extension of Maurer, Solamon, and Troxtel (1988).

Journal: *Journal of Applied Psychology*, August 2001, *86*, 709–717.

12699

Test Name: INTRINSIC ACADEMIC MOTIVATION SCALE

Purpose: To measure intrinsic academic motivation.

Number of Items: 5

Format: Responses are made on a 5-point Likert scale ranging from 1 (*strongly disagree*) to 5 (*strongly agree*). Sample items are presented.

Reliability: Coefficient alpha was .77. Test–retest (5 months) reliability was .69.

Validity: Correlations with other variables ranged from −.29 to .63.

Author: Perry, R. P., et al.

Article: Academic control and action control in the achievement of college students: A longitudinal field study.

Journal: *Journal of Educational Psychology*, December 2001, *93*, 776–789.

12700

Test Name: INTRINSIC–EXTRINSIC MOTIVATION RATING SCALE

Purpose: To measure sport motivation.

Number of Items: 40

Format: Includes nine factors: expression of self, mental enrichment, social reinforcements, self-enhancement, proving oneself, social benefits, external forces, sense of accomplishment, and fame and fortune. Responses are made on 7-point scales. All items are presented.

Reliability: Alpha coefficients ranged from .65 to .77.

Author: Pedersen, D. M.

Article: Intrinsic–extrinsic factors in sport motivation.

Journal: *Perceptual and Motor Skills*, October 2002, *95*, 459–476.

Related Research: Pedersen, D. M. (1994). Identification of levels of self-identity. *Perceptual and Motor Skills*, *78*, 1155–1167.

12701

Test Name: INTRINSIC–EXTRINSIC MOTIVATION SUBSCALES

Purpose: To measure intrinsic, identified, introjected, and external regulation.

Number of Items: 15

Format: Sample items are presented.

Reliability: Alpha coefficients ranged from .69 to .79 across subscales.

Validity: Correlations with other variables ranged from −.20 to .49.

Author: Yamauchi, H.

Article: An approach to the hierarchical model of motivation in the classroom: A reply to Rousseau and Vallerand.

Journal: *Psychological Reports*, February 2002, *90*, 273–278.

Related Research: Deci, E. L., & Ryan, R. M. (1985). *Intrinsic motivation and self-determination in human behavior.* New York: Plenum Press.

12702

Test Name: INTRINSIC INTEREST SCALE—JAPANESE VERSION

Purpose: To assess intrinsic interest in learning.

Number of Items: 4

Format: All items are presented in English without response categories

Reliability: Coefficient alpha was .91.

Validity: Adjusted goodness of fit was .92. Correlations with other variables ranged from .07 to .48.

Author: Tanaka, A., and Yamauchi, H.

Article: A model for achievement motives, goal orientations, intrinsic interest, and academic achievement.

Journal: *Psychological Reports*, February 2001, *88*, 123–135.

12703

Test Name: INTRINSIC MOTIVATION INVENTORY

Purpose: To measure physical education intrinsic motivation.

Number of Items: 12

Format: Includes three subscales: Enjoyment/Interest, Effort/Importance, and Pressure/Tension. Responses are made on a 5-point scale ranging from 1 (*strongly disagree*) to 5 (*strongly agree*). Examples are given.

Reliability: Coefficient alpha was .88.

Author: Goudas, M., and Dermitzaki, I.

Article: Participation motives in physical education: An expectancy-value approach.

Journal: *Perceptual and Motor Skills*, December 2004, *99*, Part 2, 1168–1170.

Related Research: Ryan, R. M. (1982). Control and information in the intrapersonal sphere: An extension of cognitive evaluation theory. *Journal of Personality and Social Psychology*, *43*, 450–461.

12704

Test Name: INTRINSIC MOTIVATION INVENTORY

Purpose: To measure enjoyment–interest, effort–importance, competence, and pressure–tension.

Number of Items: 16

Format: Item responses are anchored by 1 (*strongly disagree*) and 5 (*strongly agree*). Sample items are presented.

Reliability: Coefficient alpha was .81.

Author: Goudas, M., et al.

Article: Motivation in physical education is correlated with participation in sports after school.

Journal: *Psychological Reports*, April 2001, *88*, 491–496.

Related Research: Ryan, R. M. (1982). Control and information in the intrapersonal sphere: An extension of cognitive evaluation theory. *Journal of Personality and Social Psychology*, *43*, 450–461.

12705

Test Name: INTRINSIC MOTIVATION INVENTORY

Purpose: To measure an individual's intrinsic motivation for a specific achievement activity.

Number of Items: 20

Format: Includes five dimensions: Enjoyment/Interest, Perceived Competence, Effort/Importance, Tension/Pressure, and Perceived Choice. Responses are made on a

7-point scale ranging from 1 (*strongly disagree*) to 7 (*strongly agree*). Examples are given.

Reliability: Reliability estimates ranged from .73 to .89.

Validity: Correlations with other variables ranged from –.24 to .46.

Author: Ryska, T. A.

Article: Enjoyment of evaluative physical activity among young participants: The role of self-handicapping and intrinsic motivation.

Journal: *Child Study Journal*, 2003, *33*, 213–234.

Related Research: McAuley, E., et al. (1989). Psychometric properties of the Intrinsic Motivation Inventory in a competitive sport setting: A confirmatory factor analysis. *Research Quarterly for Exercise and Sport, 60*, 48–58.

12706

Test Name: INTRINSIC MOTIVATION INVENTORY— GREEK VERSION

Purpose: To assess four dimensions of intrinsic motivation.

Number of Items: 20

Format: Includes four dimensions: Enjoyment/Interest, Effort/Importance, Perceived Competence, and Pressure/Tension.

Reliability: Alpha coefficients ranged from .70 to .81.

Author: Papacharisis, V., and Goudas, M.

Article: Perceptions about exercise and intrinsic motivation of students attending a health-related physical education program.

Journal: *Perceptual and Motor Skills*, December 2003, *97*, Part 1, 689–696.

Related Research: Ryan, R. M. (1982). Control and information in the interpersonal sphere: An extension of cognitive evaluation theory. *Journal of Personality and Social Psychology, 43*, 450–461.

12707

Test Name: INTRINSIC MOTIVATION INVENTORY— GREEK VERSION (ADAPTED)

Purpose: To assess intrinsic motivation.

Number of Items: 18

Format: Includes Perceived Competence, Interest or Enjoyment, Effort or Importance, and Pressure or Tension. Responses are made on a 7-point Likert-type scale ranging from 1 (*strongly disagree*) to 7 (*strongly agree*).

Reliability: Alpha coefficients ranged from .66 to .84.

Author: Tsigilis, N., and Theodosiou, A.

Article: Temporal stability of the Intrinsic Motivation Inventory.

Journal: *Perceptual and Motor Skills*, August 2003, *97*, 271–280.

Related Research: McAuley, E., et al. (1989). Psychometric properties of the Intrinsic Motivation Inventory in a competitive sport setting: A confirmatory factor analysis. *Research Quarterly for Exercise and Sport, 60*, 48–58.

12708

Test Name: INTRINSIC MOTIVATION SCALE

Purpose: To measure intrinsic motivation.

Number of Items: 7

Format: Scales range from 1 (*not at all*) to 7 (*to a large degree*) on four items. Three items are 7-point semantic differential scales.

Reliability: Coefficient alpha was .94.

Author: Debowski, S., et al.

Article: Impact of guided exploration and enactive exploration on self-regulatory mechanisms and information acquisition through electronic search.

Journal: *Journal of Applied Psychology*, December 2001, *86*, 1129–1141.

Related Research: Mossholder, K. W. (1980). Effects of externally mediated goal setting on intrinsic motivation: A laboratory experiment. *Journal of Applied Psychology, 65*, 202–210.

12709

Test Name: INTRINSIC MOTIVATION SCALE

Purpose: To assess intrinsic motivation.

Number of Items: 14

Format: Responses are made on a 4-point Likert-type scale ranging from 1 (*strongly disagree*) to 4 (*strongly agree*).

Reliability: Alpha coefficients were .84 and .91.

Validity: Correlations with other variables ranged from .04 to .60.

Author: Ferrer-Caja, E., and Weiss, M. R.

Article: Cross-validation of a model of intrinsic motivation with students enrolled in high school elective courses.

Journal: *The Journal of Experimental Education*, Fall 2002, *71*, 41–65.

Related Research: Goudas, M. (1994). Perceived locus of causality, goal orientations, and perceived competence in school physical education classes. *British Journal of Educational Psychology, 64*, 453–463.

12710

Test Name: INTRINSIC VERSUS EXTRINSIC ASPIRATIONS SCALE

Purpose: To identify and rate personal future goals.

Number of Items: 57

Format: Scales range from 1 (*not at all*) to 9 (*extremely*).

Reliability: Alpha coefficients ranged from .67 to .79.

Author: Kim, Y., et al.

Article: Self-concept, aspirations, and well-being in South Korea and the United States.

Journal: *The Journal of Social Psychology*, June 2003, *143*, 277–290.

Related Research: Kasser, T., & Ryan, R. M. (1996). Further examining the American dream: Well-being correlates of intrinsic and extrinsic goals. *Personality and Social Psychology Bulletin, 22*, 281–288.

12711

Test Name: LEADERSHIP ASPIRATIONS SCALE

Purpose: To measure leadership aspirations.

Number of Items: 6

Format: Scales range from 0 (*not at all true of me*) to 4 (*very true of me*). Sample items are presented.

Reliability: Reliability coefficients ranged from .79 to .82.

Validity: Correlations with other variables ranged from –.21 to .19.

Author: Boatwright, K. J., and Egidio, R. K.

Article: Psychological predictors of college women's leadership aspirations.

Journal: *Journal of College Student Development*, September/October 2003, *44*, 653–669.

Related Research: O'Brien, K. M., et al. (1966, August). *The operationalization of women's career choices: The Career Aspiration Scale (CAS).* Paper presented at the meeting of the American Psychological Association, Toronto, Ontario, Canada.

12712

Test Name: LEARNING GOAL ORIENTATION

Purpose: To measure mentors' and protégés' learning goal orientation.

Number of Items: 8

Format: Responses are made on a 5-point scale ranging from 1 (*disagree strongly*) to 5 (*agree strongly*). A sample item is presented.

Reliability: Coefficient alpha was .86.

Validity: Correlations with other variables ranged from –.11 to .34.

Author: Godshalk, V. M., and Sosik, J. J.

Article: Aiming for career success: The role of learning goal orientation in mentoring relationships.

Journal: *Journal of Vocational Behavior*, December 2003, *63*, 417–437.

Related Research: Button, S. B., et al. (1996). Goal orientation in organizational research: A conceptual and empirical foundation. *Organizational Behavior and Human Decision Processes, 67*, 26–48.

12713

Test Name: LOGO II

Purpose: To measure intrinsic and extrinsic orientation of undergraduate college students.

Number of Items: 32

Format: Half of the items describe attitudes, the other half describe behaviors. Responses are made on 5-point scales. Examples are given.

Validity: Correlations with other variables ranged from –.22 to .55.

Author: Rettinger, D. A., et al.

Article: Evaluating the motivation of other students to cheat: A vignette experiment.

Journal: *Research in Higher Education*, December 2004, *45*, 873–890.

Related Research: Eison, J. A., et al. (1986). Educational and personal characteristics of four different types of learning-and grade-oriented students. *Contemporary Educational Psychology, 11*, 54–67.

12714

Test Name: MANAGERIAL CAREER ASPIRATIONS SCALES

Purpose: To assess managerial career aspirations and career satisfaction outcomes for protégés.

Number of Items: 27

Format: Includes three scales: Desired Managerial Aspirations, Enacted Managerial Aspirations, and Career Satisfaction. Responses are made on 5-point scales. Sample items are presented.

Reliability: Alpha coefficients ranged from .74 to .91.

Validity: Correlations with other variables ranged from –.15 to .34.

Author: Godshalk, V. M., and Sosik, J. J.

Article: Aiming for career success: The role of learning goal orientation in mentoring relationships.

Journal: *Journal of Vocational Behavior*, December 2003, *63*, 417–437.

Related Research: Tharenou, P., & Terry, D. J. (1998). Reliability and validity of scores on scales to measure managerial aspirations. *Educational and Psychological*

Measurement, 58, 475–493.
Greenhaus, J. H., et al. (1990).
Effects of race on organizational
experiences, job performance
evaluations, and career outcomes.
*Academy of Management Journal,
33,* 64–86.

12715

Test Name: MANIFEST NEEDS
QUESTIONNAIRE

Purpose: To measure need for
achievement

Number of Items: 5

Format: Responses are made on a
7-point scale. Examples are
provided.

Reliability: Coefficient alpha
was .61.

Validity: Correlations with other
variables ranged from –.08 to .20.

Author: Goulet, L. R., and
Singh, P.

Article: Career commitment: A
reexamination and an extension.

Journal: *Journal of Vocational
Behavior,* August 2002, *61,* 73–91.

Related Research: Steers, R. M., &
Braunstein, D. N. (1976). A
behaviorally-based measure of
manifest needs in work settings.
Journal of Vocational Behavior, 9,
251–266.

12716

Test Name: MARIJUANA
CESSATION SELF-EFFICACY
QUESTIONNAIRE

Purpose: To measure the ability to
resist using marijuana in social
situations.

Number of Items: 20

Format: Seven-point confidence
scales are used.

Reliability: Coefficient alpha
was .90.

Author: Litt, M. D., et al.

Article: Coping and self-efficacy in
marijuana treatment: Results from
the Marijuana Treatment Project.

Journal: *Journal of Consulting and
Clinical Psychology,* December
2005, *73,* 1015–1025.

Related Research: Curry, S. J.,
et al. (1988). A comparison of
alternative theoretical approaches
to smoking cessation and relapse.
Health Psychology, 7, 545–556.

12717

Test Name: MASTERY GOAL
ORIENTATION SCALE

Purpose: To assess mastery goal
orientation.

Number of Items: 6

Format: Responses are made on a
5-point scale ranging from 1 (*yes*) to
5 (*no*). A sample item is presented.

Reliability: Coefficient alpha
was .82.

Validity: Correlations with other
variables ranged from –.20 to .47.

Author: Wentzel, K. R.

Article: Are effective teachers like
good parents? Teaching styles and
student adjustment in early
adolescence.

Journal: *Child Development,*
January/February 2002, *73,*
287–301.

Related Research: Nicholls, J. G.,
et al. (1990). Students' theories
about mathematics and their
mathematical knowledge: Multiple
dimensions of assessment
(pp. 137–154). In G. Kulin (Ed.),
*Assessing higher order thinking in
mathematics.* Washington, DC:
American Association of the
Advancement of Science.

12718

Test Name: MASTERY,
PERFORMANCE-APPROACH
GOAL, AND PERFORMANCE-
AVOIDANCE GOAL MEASURES

Purpose: To measure mastery,
performance-approach goal, and
performance-avoidance goal.

Number of Items: 6

Format: Includes three measures:
Mastery, Performance-Approach
Goal, and Performance-Avoidance
Goal. All responses are made on a
7-point scale ranging from 1 (*not at
all true of me*) to 7 (*very true of me*).

Reliability: Alpha coefficients
ranged from .79 to .90.

Validity: Correlations with other
variables ranged from –.24 to .67.

Author: Senko, C., and
Harackiewicz, J. M.

Article: Regulation of achievement
goals: The role of competence
feedback.

Journal: *Journal of Educational
Psychology,* August 2005, *97,*
320–336.

Related Research: Harackiewicz,
J. M., et al. (2000). Short-term and
long-term consequences of
achievement goals in college:
Predicting continued interest and
performance over time. *Journal of
Educational Psychology, 92,*
316–320. Elliott, A. J., & Church,
M. A. (1997). A hierarchical model
of approach and avoidance
achievement motivation. *Journal of
Personality and Social Psychology,
72,* 218–232.

12719

Test Name: MENTOR MOTIVES
SCALE

Purpose: To assess motives for
mentoring others.

Number of Items: 11

Format: Includes three factors: self-
enhancement, intrinsic satisfaction,
and benefit others. Responses are
made on a 5-point scale ranging
from 1 (*no extent*) to 5 (*great
extent*). Examples are given.

Reliability: Alpha coefficients
ranged from .66 to .82.

Validity: Correlations with other variables ranged from –.24 to .33.

Author: Allen, T. D.

Article: Protégé selection by mentors: Contributing individual and organizational factors.

Journal: *Journal of Vocational Behavior*, December 2004, *65*, 469–483.

Related Research: Allen, T. D. (2003). Mentoring others: A dispositional and motivational approach. *Journal of Vocational Behavior, 62*, 134–154.

12720

Test Name: METAMOTIVATIONAL STATES AND AROUSAL PREFERENCE SCALE

Purpose: To assess the telic, paratelic, negativistic, conformist, arousal seeking, and arousal avoidance states.

Number of Items: 12

Format: Includes three subscales. Responses are made on 6-point response scales.

Reliability: Alpha coefficients ranged from .75 to .86.

Author: Thatcher, J., et al.

Article: Motivation, stress, and cortisol responses in skydiving.

Journal: *Perceptual and Motor Skills*, December 2003, *97*, Part 1, 995–1002.

Related Research: Cook, M. R., et al. (1993). Instruments for the assessment of reversal theory states. *Patient Education and Counseling, 22*, 99–106.

12721

Test Name: MOTIVATED STRATEGIES FOR LEARNING QUESTIONNAIRE—PERSIAN VERSION

Purpose: To measure motivational beliefs and self-regulated learning.

Number of Items: 54

Format: Item anchors are 1 (*not at all true of me*) and 5 (*very true of me*).

Reliability: Alpha coefficients ranged from .60 to .84. Test–retest reliability was .89 (21 days).

Author: Ostovar, S., and Khayyer, M.

Article: Relations of motivational beliefs and self-regulated learning outcomes for Iranian college students.

Journal: *Psychological Reports*, June 2004, *94*, Part 2, 1202–1204.

Related Research: Pintrich, P. R., & DeGroot, E. (1990). Motivational and self-regulated learning component of classroom academic performance. *Journal of Educational Psychology, 82*, 33–40.

12722

Test Name: MOTIVATION FOR READING QUESTIONNAIRE— ABBREVIATED

Purpose: To measure reading motivation.

Number of Items: 18

Format: Includes two dimensions: Self-Efficacy for Reading and Intrinsic Motivation. Responses are made on a 4-point scale ranging from 1 (*very different from me*) to 4 (*a lot like me*). Examples are given.

Reliability: Coefficient alpha was .75.

Author: Guthrie, J. T., et al.

Article: Increasing reading comprehension and engagement through concept-oriented reading instruction.

Journal: *Journal of Educational Psychology*, September 2004, *96*, 403–423.

Related Research: Wigfield, A., & Guthrie, J. T. (1997). Relations of children's motivation for reading to the amount and breadth of their reading. *Journal of Educational Psychology, 89*, 420–432.

12723

Test Name: MOTIVATION SCALE

Purpose: To measure the reasons for being in a relationship.

Number of Items: 6

Format: Scales range from 0 (*plays no role at all*) to 8 (*plays a major role*).

Reliability: Coefficient alpha was .75.

Author: Kurdek, L. A.

Article: Gender and marital satisfaction in early marriage: A growth curve approach.

Journal: *Journal of Marriage and Family*, February 2005, *67*, 68–84.

Related Research: Remple, J. K., et al. (1985). Trust in close relationships. *Journal of Personality and Social Psychology, 49*, 95–112.

12724

Test Name: MOTIVATION SOURCES INVENTORY

Purpose: To measure intrinsic process, instrumental, External Self-Concept, Internal Self-Concept, and goal internalization.

Number of Items: 30

Format: Sample items are presented.

Reliability: Alpha coefficients ranged from .61 to .72.

Validity: Correlations with other variables ranged from –.11 to .77.

Author: Moss, J. A., and Barbuto, J. E., Jr.

Article: Machiavellianism's association with sources of

motivation and downward influence strategies.

Journal: *Psychological Reports*, June 2004, *94*, Part 1, 933–943.

Related Research: Barbuto, J. E., Jr., & Scholl, R. W. (1988). Motivation Sources Inventory: Development and validation of new scales to measure an integrative taxonomy of motivation. *Psychological Reports, 82*, 1011–1022.

12725

Test Name: MOTIVATION TO HIDE RACISM SCALE

Purpose: To measure motivation to hide racial prejudice in an organization in order to conform to societal norms.

Number of Items: 5

Format: Nine-point scales are used. A sample item is presented.

Reliability: Coefficient alpha was .77.

Validity: Correlations with other variables ranged from –.17 to .07.

Author: Ziegert, J. C., and Hanges, P. J.

Article: Employment discrimination: The role of implicit attitudes, motivation, and a climate for racial bias.

Journal: *Journal of Applied Psychology*, May 2005, *90*, 553–562.

Related Research: Plant, E. A., & Devine, P. G. (1998). Internal and external motivation to respond without prejudice. *Journal of Personality and Social Psychology, 75*, 811–832.

12726

Test Name: MOTIVATION TO LEAD MEASURE

Purpose: To measure motivation to lead in three dimensions: Affective-Identity, Noncalculative, and Social-Normative.

Number of Items: 27

Format: All items are presented.

Reliability: Alpha coefficients ranged from .65 and .91 across subscales.

Validity: Correlations with other variables ranged from –.33 to .70 in a U.S. student sample.

Author: Chan, K.-Y., and Drasgow, F.

Article: Toward a theory of individual differences and leadership: Understanding the motivation to lead.

Journal: *Journal of Applied Psychology*, June 2001, *86*, 481–498.

12727

Test Name: MOTIVATION TO LEARN SCALE

Purpose: To measure motivation to learn.

Number of Items: 10

Format: Five-point Likert scales are used. A sample item is presented.

Reliability: Scale reliability was .91.

Validity: Correlations with other variables ranged from –.24 to .38.

Author: Towler, A. J., and Dipboye, R. L.

Article: Effects of trainer expressiveness, organization, and trainee goal orientation on training outcomes.

Journal: *Journal of Applied Psychology*, August 2001, *86*, 664–673.

12728

Test Name: MOTIVATION TO PROMOTE INCLUSION AND SOCIAL JUSTICE SCALE

Purpose: To measure the likelihood that one will act to promote inclusion and social justice.

Number of Items: 7

Format: Scales range from 1 (*very unlikely*) to 4 (*very likely*).

Reliability: Coefficient alpha was .87.

Author: Zúñiga, X., et al.

Article: Action-oriented democratic outcomes: The impact of student involvement with campus diversity.

Journal: *Journal of College Student Development*, November/December 2005, *46*, 660–678.

Related Research: Nagda, B. A., et al. (2004). Learning about difference, learning to connect, learning to transgress. *Journal of Social Issues, 60*, 195–214.

12729

Test Name: MOTIVATION TO REDUCE ONE'S OWN PREJUDICES SCALE

Purpose: To measure the perceived likelihood that a person will act to reduce his or her prejudices.

Number of Items: 4

Format: Scales range from 1 (*very unlikely*) to 4 (*very likely*).

Reliability: Coefficient alpha was .82.

Author: Zúñiga, X., et al.

Article: Action-oriented democratic outcomes: The impact of student involvement with campus diversity.

Journal: *Journal of College Student Development*, November/December 2005, *46*, 660–678.

Related Research: Nagda, B. A., et al. (2004). Learning about difference, learning to connect, learning to transgress. *Journal of Social Issues, 60*, 195–214.

12730

Test Name: MOTIVATIONAL ENGAGEMENT SCALES

Purpose: To measure students' motivational engagement.

Number of Items: 17

Format: Includes four scales: Choice, Effort, Persistence, and Procrastination. Examples are given.

Reliability: Alpha coefficients ranged from .73 to .84.

Validity: Correlations with other variables ranged from −.48 to .66 (*N* = 525).

Author: Wolters, C. A.

Article: Advancing achievement goal theory: Using goal structures and goal orientations to predict students' motivation, cognition, and achievement.

Journal: *Journal of Educational Psychology,* June 2004, *96,* 236–250.

Related Research: Wolters, C. (1999). The relation between high school students' motivational regulation and their use of learning strategies, effort, and classroom performance. *Learning and Individual Differences, 11,* 281–299. Wolters, C. (2003). Understanding procrastination from a self-regulated learning perspective. *Journal of Educational Psychology, 95,* 179–187.

12731

Test Name: MOTIVATIONAL ORIENTATION INVENTORY

Purpose: To measure communion striving, status striving, and accomplishment striving.

Number of Items: 31

Format: Scales range from 1 (*strongly agree*) to 5 (*strongly disagree*). All items are presented.

Reliability: Alpha coefficients ranged from .76 to .91.

Validity: Correlations with other variables ranged from −.11 to .48.

Author: Barrick, M. R., et al.

Article: Personality and job performance: Test of the mediating effects of motivation among sales representatives.

Journal: *Journal of Applied Psychology,* February 2002, *87,* 43–51.

12732

Test Name: MOTIVATIONAL ORIENTATION SCALE

Purpose: To measure trait motivation.

Number of Items: 7

Format: Scales range from 1 (*very untrue of me*) to 6 (*very true of me*).

Reliability: Coefficient alpha was .80.

Validity: Correlations with other variables ranged from .06 to .15.

Author: Caldwell, S. D., et al.

Article: Toward an understanding of the relationships among organizational change, individual differences, and changes in person–environment fit: A cross-level study.

Journal: *Journal of Applied Psychology,* October 2004, *89,* 868–882.

Related Research: Heggestad, E. D., & Kanfer, R. (2000). Individual differences in trait motivation: Development of the Motivational Trait Questionnaire. *International Journal of Educational Research, 33,* 751–776.

12733

Test Name: MOTIVATIONS FOR ACCEPTING CONTINGENT EMPLOYMENT SCALE

Purpose: To measure motivation for accepting temporary positions.

Number of Items: 3

Format: Responses are made on a 5-point Likert scale ranging from 1

(*strongly disagree*) to 5 (*strongly agree*). All items are presented.

Validity: Correlations with other variables ranged from −.41 to .44.

Author: Feldman, D. C., and Turnley, W. H.

Article: Contingent employment in academic careers: Relative deprivation among adjunct faculty.

Journal: *Journal of Vocational Behavior,* April 2004, *64,* 284–307.

Related Research: Ellingson, J. E., et al. (1998). Factors related to the satisfaction and performance of temporary employees. *Journal of Applied Psychology, 83,* 913–921.

12734

Test Name: MOTIVATIONS FOR ATTENDING UNIVERSITY SCALE—REVISED

Purpose: To measure motivations to attend college among first-generation minority students.

Number of Items: 15

Format: Scales range from 1 (*strongly disagree*) to 5 (*strongly agree*). Sample items are presented.

Reliability: Alpha coefficients ranged from .75 to .77 across subscales.

Validity: Correlations with other variables ranged from −.16 to .49.

Author: Dennis, J. M., et al.

Article: The role of motivation, parental support, and peer support in the academic success of ethnic minority first-generation college students.

Journal: *Journal of College Student Development,* May/June 2005, *46,* 223–236.

12735

Test Name: MOTIVATIONS TO EAT SCALE

Purpose: To measure motivations to eat as coping, social, compliance, and pleasure.

Number of Items: 20

Format: Scales range from 1 (*almost never/never*) to 5 (*almost always/always*). All items are presented.

Reliability: Alpha coefficients ranged from .82 to .88 across subscales.

Validity: Correlations with other variables ranged from .02 to .72.

Author: Jackson, B., et al.

Article: Motivations to eat: Scale development and validation.

Journal: *Journal of Research in Personality*, August 2003, *37*, 297–318.

12736

Test Name: MOTIVES FOR MONEY SCALE

Purpose: To measure ten motives for money: security, family support, market worth, pride, leisure, charity, freedom, impulse, overcoming self-doubt, and social comparison.

Number of Items: 30

Format: Ten-point scales are anchored by 1 (*totally unimportant*) and 10 (*extremely important*).

Reliability: Alpha coefficients ranged from .49 to .88 across subscales.

Author: Burke, R. J.

Article: Workaholism, self-esteem, and motives for money.

Journal: *Psychological Reports*, April 2004, *94*, 457–463.

Related Research: Srivastava, A., et al. (2002). Money and subjective well-being: It's not the money, it's the motives. *Journal of Personality and Social Psychology, 80,* 271–284.

12737

Test Name: MOTIVES TO STUDY SCALE

Purpose: To measure the scholastic, instrumental, and collegiate motives to study.

Number of Items: 9

Format: Scales range from 1 (*not important at all*) to 6 (*very important*). All items are presented.

Reliability: Alpha coefficients ranged from .76 to .81 across subscales.

Author: Bogler, R., and Somech, A.

Article: Motives to study and socialization tactics among university students.

Journal: *The Journal of Social Psychology*, April 2002, *142*, 233–248.

Related Research: Shapira, R., & Etzioni-Halevey, E. (1973). *Mi ata ha-student ha Yisraeli?* [Who is the Israeli student?]. Tel Aviv, Israel: Am Oved.

12738

Test Name: NONSEXUAL EXPERIENCE-SEEKING SCALE

Purpose: To measure brief general sensation seeking.

Number of Items: 11

Format: Responses are made on a 4-point scale ranging from 1 (*not at all like me*) to 4 (*very much like me*).

Reliability: Coefficient alpha was .81.

Validity: Correlations with the Sexual Sensation Seeking Scale were .35 (women) and .42 (men).

Author: Gaither, G. A., and Sellbom, M.

Article: The Sexual Sensation Seeking Scale: Reliability and validity within a heterosexual college student sample.

Journal: *Journal of Personality Assessment*, October 2003, *81*, 157–167.

Related Research: Kalichman, S. C., & Rompa, D. (1995). Sexual Sensation Seeking and Sexual Compulsivity Scales: Reliability, validity, and predicting HIV-risk behavior. *Journal of Personality Assessment, 65,* 586–601.

12739

Test Name: NOVELTY EXPERIENCING SCALE

Purpose: To measure the tendency to approach or to avoid novel stimuli.

Number of Items: 80

Format: Includes four subscales: External Sensation, Internal Sensation, External Cognition, and Internal Cognition.

Reliability: Kinder–Richardson indexes ranged from .76 to .87.

Author: Litman, J. A., and Spielberger, C. D.

Article: Measuring epistemic curiosity and its diversive and specific components.

Journal: *Journal of Personality Assessment*, February 2003, 80, 75–86.

Related Research: Pearson, P. H. (1970). Relationships between global and specified measures of novelty seeking. *Journal of Consulting and Clinical Psychology, 34,* 199–204.

12740

Test Name: ONLINE MOTIVATION QUESTIONNAIRE

Purpose: To obtain learners' judgments about relevant aspects of the learning situation when confronted with an actual learning task.

Number of Items: 17

Format: Includes four constructs: Subjective Competence, Task Relevance, Task Attraction, and Willingness to Invest Effort. Examples are given.

Reliability: Alpha coefficients ranged from .72 to .88.

Author: Seegers, G., et al.

Article: Effects of causal attributions following mathematics tasks on student cognitions about a subsequent task.

Journal: *The Journal of Experimental Education*, Summer 2004, *72*, 307–328.

Related Research: Boekaerts, M. (2002). The Online Motivation Questionnaire: A self-report instrument to assess students' context sensitivity. In P. R. Pintrich & M. L. Maehr (Eds.), *Advances in motivation and achievement: Vol. 12. New directions in measures and methods* (pp. 77–120). New York: JAI.

12741

Test Name: PARENT MOTIVATION INVENTORY

Purpose: To measure parent motivation for therapy.

Number of Items: 25

Format: Scales range from 1 (*strongly disagree*) to 5 (*strongly agree*). Sample items are presented.

Reliability: Alpha coefficients ranged from .77 to .96.

Author: Nock, M. K., and Kazdin, A. E.

Article: Randomized controlled trial of a brief intervention for increasing participation in parent management training.

Journal: *Journal of Consulting and Clinical Psychology*, October 2005, *73*, 872–879.

Related Research: Nock, M. K., & Photos, V. (2006). Parent motivation to participate in

treatment: Assessment and prediction of subsequent participation. *Journal of Child and Family Studies*, *15*, 333–346.

12742

Test Name: PARTICIPATION MOTIVATION INVENTORY— MODIFIED FOR SWIMMING (SPANISH VERSION)

Purpose: To measure swimming participation motivation.

Number of Items: 35

Format: Includes seven factors: health/fitness, fun/friendship, competition/skills, significant others, affiliation, status, and energy release. Responses are made on a 5-point scale ranging from 1 (*not at all important*) to 5 (*extremely important*). All items are presented.

Reliability: Alpha coefficients ranged from .67 to .82. Test–retest reliability coefficients ranged from .69 to .88.

Author: Salguero, A., et al.

Article: Development of a Spanish version of the Participation Motivation Inventory for young swimmers

Journal: *Perceptual and Motor Skills*, April 2003, *96*, 637–646.

Related Research: Gould, D., et al. (1985). Motives for participation in competitive youth swimming. *International Journal of Sport Psychology*, *16*, 126–140.

12743

Test Name: PERCEPTION OF SUCCESS QUESTIONNAIRE— SPANISH VERSION

Purpose: To measure students' dispositional goal orientations in physical education classes.

Number of Items: 12

Format: Includes task orientation and ego orientation. Responses are

made on a Likert-type scale ranging from 0 (*strongly disagree*) to 100 (*strongly agree*). Examples are presented.

Reliability: Alpha coefficients were .73 and .88.

Validity: Correlationo with other variables ranged from –.15 to .41.

Author: Cervelló, E. M., et al.

Article: Goal orientations, motivational climate, equality, and discipline of Spanish physical education students.

Journal: *Perceptual and Motor Skills*, August 2004, *99*, 271–283.

Related Research: Roberts, G. C., et al. (1998). Achievement goals in sport: The development and validation of the Perception of Success Questionnaire. *Journal of Sport Sciences*, *16*, 337–347.

12744

Test Name: PERCEPTIONS OF STUDENTS' MOTIVATION SCALE

Purpose: To measure teachers' perceptions of students' level of motivation toward school.

Number of Items: 16

Format: Includes four subscales: Intrinsic Motivation, Extrinsic Motivation by Identified Regulation, Extrinsic Motivation by Introjected Regulation, and Extrinsic Motivation by External Regulation. Responses are made on a 7-point scale ranging from 1 (*does not correspond at all*) to 7 (*corresponds exactly*). Examples are presented.

Reliability: Coefficient alpha was .78.

Author: Pelletier, L. G., et al.

Article: Pressure from above and pressure from below as determinants of teachers' motivation and teaching behaviors.

Journal: *Journal of Educational Psychology*, March 2002, *94*, 186–196.

Related Research: Vallerand, R. J., et al. (1993). On the assessment of intrinsic, extrinsic, and a motivation in education: Evidence on the concurrent and construct validity of the Academic Motivation Scale. *Educational and Psychological Measurement, 53*, 159–172.

12745

Test Name: PERFORMANCE GOAL ORIENTATION SCALE

Purpose: To measure learning, proving, and avoiding dimensions of performance goal orientation.

Number of Items: 13

Format: Scales range from 1 (*strongly disagree*) to 7 (*strongly agree*). Sample items are presented.

Reliability: Alpha coefficients ranged from .77 to .84 across subscales.

Validity: Correlations with other variables ranged from –.31 to .43.

Author: VandeWalle, D., et al.

Article: The role of goal orientation following performance feedback.

Journal: *Journal of Applied Psychology*, August 2001, *86*, 629–640.

Related Research: VandeWalle, D. (1996, August). *Are our students trying to prove or improve their ability? Development and validation of an instrument to measure academic goal orientation.* Paper presented at the national meeting of the Academy of Management, Cincinnati, OH.

12746

Test Name: PERSONAL GOALS SCALE

Purpose: To assess the attainability, stress, and control over personal goals.

Number of Items: 6

Format: Scales range from 1 (*not difficult at all*) to 7 (*very difficult*). All items are presented.

Reliability: Alpha coefficients ranged from .60 to .82 across subscales.

Validity: Correlations with other variables ranged from –.40 to .48.

Author: Jokisaari, M.

Article: Regret appraisals, age, and subjective well-being.

Journal: *Journal of Research in Personality*, December 2003, *37*, 487–503.

12747

Test Name: PERSONAL GROWTH INITIATIVE SCALE

Purpose: To measure personal growth initiative.

Number of Items: 9

Format: Responses are made on a Likert-type scale ranging from 0 (*definitely disagree*) to 5 (*definitely agree*). All items are presented.

Reliability: Internal consistency estimates ranged from .78 to .88. Test–retest (8 weeks) reliability was .74.

Validity: Correlations with other variables ranged from –.28 to .42.

Author: Robitschek, C.

Article: Validity of Personal Growth Initiative Scale scores with a Mexican American college student population.

Journal: *Journal of Counseling Psychology*, October 2003, *50*, 496–502.

Related Research: Robitschek, C. (1999). Further validation of the Personal Growth Initiative Scale. *Measurement and Evaluation in Counseling and Evaluation, 31*, 197–210.

12748

Test Name: PROBLEMS IN SCHOOLS QUESTIONNAIRE

Purpose: To assess teachers' motivating style.

Number of Items: 32

Format: Includes four subscales: Highly Controlling, Moderately Controlling, Moderately Autonomous, and Highly Autonomous. Responses are made on a 7-point scale.

Reliability: Alpha coefficients ranged from .63 to .76. Test–retest (2 months) reliability was .70.

Author: d'Ailly, H.

Article: Children's autonomy and perceived control in learning: A model of motivation and achievement in Taiwan.

Journal: *Journal of Educational Psychology*, March 2003, *95*, 84–96.

Related Research: Deci, E. L., et al. (1981). An instrument to assess adults' orientations toward control versus autonomy with children: Reflections on intrinsic motivation and perceived competence. *Journal of Educational Psychology, 73*, 642–650.

12749

Test Name: PURSUIT OF EXCELLENCE, COMPETITIVENESS, AND MASTERY SUBSCALES

Purpose: To assess the need for achievement.

Number of Items: 21

Format: Scales range from 1 (*strongly disagree*) to 6 (*strongly agree*).

Reliability: Alpha coefficients ranged from .55 to .67 across subscales.

Validity: Correlations with other variables ranged from –.32 to .42.

Author: Kirk, A. K., and Brown, D. F.

Article: Latent constructs of proximal and distal motivation predicting performance under maximum test conditions.

Journal: *Journal of Applied Psychology*, February 2003, *88*, 40–49.

Related Research: Cassidy, T., & Lynn, R. (1989). A multifactorial approach to achievement motivation: The development of a comprehensive measure. *Journal of Occupational Psychology, 62*, 301–312.

12750

Test Name: RELIGIOUS MOTIVATION SCALE

Purpose: To measure one's level of religiousness and the extent to which their religiousness is related to intrinsic or extrinsic factors.

Number of Items: 42

Format: Includes four subscales: Intrinsic Religiousness, Extrinsic Religiousness—Social, Extrinsic Religiousness—Personal, and Extrinsic Religiousness—Moral.

Reliability: Internal consistency reliability coefficients ranged from .57 to .89.

Validity: Correlations with other variables ranged from −.20 to .65.

Author: Duffy, R. D., and Blustein, D. L.

Article: The relationship between spirituality, religiousness, and career adaptability.

Journal: *Journal of Vocational Behavior*, December 2005, *67*, 429–440.

Related Research: Gorsuch, R. L., & McPherson, S. E. (1989). Intrinsic/extrinsic measurement: I/E–Revised and single-item scales. *Journal for the Scientific Study of Religion, 28*, 348–354.

12751

Test Name: REVISED AESTHETIC EXPERIENCE SCALE

Purpose: To measure cognitive synergies and elaboration, emotional closeness, experiential emotional distancing, paratelic mode, and expressive perception.

Number of Items: 28

Format: Item responses are anchored by 1 (*never*) and 5 (*very often*). All items are presented.

Reliability: Alpha coefficients ranged from .63 to .75 across subscales.

Validity: Correlations with other variables ranged from .27 to .50.

Author: Stamatopoulou, D.

Article: Integrating the philosophy and psychology of aesthetic experience: Development of the Aesthetic Experience Scale.

Journal: *Psychological Reports*, October 2004, *95*, 673–695.

12752

Test Name: REVISED MARTIN–LARSEN APPROVAL MOTIVATION SCALE

Purpose: To assess the desire to receive positive evaluations and social approval as well as the need to avoid negative evaluation and social criticism.

Number of Items: 20

Format: Responses are made on a 5-point scale ranging from 1 (*disagree strongly*) to 5 (*agree strongly*). An example is given.

Reliability: Coefficient alpha was .75.

Validity: Correlations with other variables ranged from −.45 to .69 ($n = 425$).

Author: Wei, M., et al.

Article: Adult attachment, depressive symptoms, and validation from self versus others.

Journal: *Journal of Counseling Psychology*, July 2005, *52*, 368–377.

Related Research: Martin, H. J. (1984). A revised measure of approval motivation and its relationship to social desirability. *Journal of Personality Assessment, 48*, 508–519.

12753

Test Name: SCHOOL MOTIVATION SCALE

Purpose: To assess students' general interest in classroom activities

Number of Items: 10

Format: Responses are made on a 5-point scale ranging from 1 (*false*) to 5 (*true*). Sample items are presented.

Reliability: Coefficient alpha was .84.

Validity: Correlations with other variables ranged from −.30 to .49.

Author: Wentzel, K. R.

Article: Are effective teachers like good parents? Teaching styles and student adjustment in early adolescence.

Journal: *Child Development*, January/February 2002, *73*, 287–301.

Related Research: Ford, M. E., & Tisak, M. (1982, April). *Evaluation of an educational intervention to enhance social–cognitive skills.* Paper presented at the annual meeting of the American Educational Research Association, New York.

12754

Test Name: SELF-DETERMINATION SCALE

Purpose: To assess self-determination.

Number of Items: 5

Format: Responses are made on a 5-point Likert-type scale ranging from 1 (*strongly disagree*) to 5 (*strongly agree*). Sample items are presented.

Reliability: Alpha coefficients were .73 and .75.

Validity: Correlations with other variables ranged from –.14 to .48.

Author: Ferrer-Caja, E., and Weiss, M. R.

Article: Cross-validation of a model of intrinsic motivation with students enrolled in high school elective courses.

Journal: *Journal of Experimental Education*, Fall 2002, *71*, 41–65.

Related Research: McAuley, E., et al. (1989). Psychometric properties of the intrinsic motivation inventory in a competitive sport setting: A confirmatory factor analysis. *Research Quarterly of Exercise and Sport*, *60*, 48–58. Stein, G. L., & Scanlan, T. K. (1992). Goal attainment and nongoal occurrences as underlying mechanisms to an athlete's sources of enjoyment. *Pediatric Exercise Science*, *4*, 150–165.

12755

Test Name: SELF-DETERMINATION SCALE OF POLITICAL MOTIVATION

Purpose: To measure four reasons (motivations) for following politics: intrinsic motivation, identification, introjection, and a motivation.

Number of Items: 12

Format: Scales range from 1 (*doesn't correspond to me at all*) to 7 (*corresponds exactly to me*). All items are partially described.

Reliability: Alpha coefficients ranged from .77 to .90 across subscales. Test–retest correlations ranged from .63 to .79 (5 weeks).

Validity: Correlations between subscales ranged from –.67 to .42. Other validity data are presented.

Author: Losier, G. F., et al.

Article: Examining individual differences in the internalization of political values: Validation of the Self-Determination Scale of Political Motivation.

Journal: *Journal of Research in Personality*, March 2001, *35*, 41–61.

12756

Test Name: SELF-MOTIVATION INVENTORY

Purpose: To assess motivation to comply with assigned physical therapy treatment.

Number of Items: 40

Format: Item responses are anchored by 1 (*very unlike me*) and 5 (*very much like me*). Sample items are presented.

Reliability: Alpha was .86. Test–retest reliabilities ranged from .92 (1 month) to .86 (20 weeks).

Author: Annesi, J. J.

Article: Preliminary comparison of treatments of shoulder injuries using the FitLinxx™ computer feedback system and standard physical therapy.

Journal: *Psychological Reports*, June 2001, *88*, Part 2, 989–995.

Related Research: Dishman, R. K., et al. (1980). Self-motivation and adherence to habitual physical activity. *Journal of Applied Social Psychology*, *10*, 469–474.

12757

Test Name: SELF-REGULATION QUESTIONNAIRE

Purpose: To measure motivational regulation.

Number of Items: 28

Format: Includes four subscales. Responses are made on a 4-point scale ranging from *very true* to *not true at all*. Examples are given.

Reliability: Alpha coefficients ranged from .77 to .94.

Validity: Correlations with other variables ranged from –.11 to .47.

Author: Bagoien, T. E., and Halvari, H.

Article: Autonomous motivation: Involvement in physical activity, and perceived sport competence: Structural and mediator models.

Journal: *Perceptual and Motor Skills*, February 2005, *100*, 3–21.

Related Research: Ryan, R. M., & Connell, J. P. (1989). Perceived locus of causality and internalization: Examining reasons for acting in two domains. *Journal of Personality and Social Psychology*, *57*, 749–761.

12758

Test Name: SELF-REGULATION QUESTIONNAIRE—ACADEMICS (ADAPTED)

Purpose: To measure motivation for studying English.

Number of Items: 16

Format: Includes four subscales: External Regulation, Introjected Regulation, Identified Regulation, and Intrinsic Motivation. Responses are made on a 5-point scale ranging from 1 (*totally disagree*) to 5 (*totally agree*). Examples are given.

Reliability: Alpha coefficients were .60 and .85.

Validity: Correlations with other variables ranged from –.49 to .74 ($N = 112$).

Author: Vansteenkiste, M., et al.

Article: Experiences of autonomy and control among Chinese learners: Vitalizing or immobilizing.

Journal: *Journal of Educational Psychology*, August 2005, *97*, 468–483.

Related Research: Ryan, R. M., & Connell, J. P. (1989). Perceived locus of causality and internalization: Examining reasons for acting in two domains. *Journal of Personality and Social Psychology, 57,* 749–761.

12759

Test Name: SENSATION SEEKING SCALE

Purpose: To assess individual difference in the tendency to seek novel sensory stimulation.

Number of Items: 40

Format: Includes four subscales: Thrill and Adventure, Experience Seeking, Disinhibition, and Boredom Susceptibility.

Reliability: Internal consistency reliabilities ranged from .56 to .86. Test–retest stability coefficient was .94.

Author: Litman, J. A., and Spielberger, C. D.

Article: Measuring epistemic curiosity and its diversive and specific components.

Journal: *Journal of Personality Assessment,* February 2003, *80,* 75–86.

Related Research: Zuckerman, M., et al. (1964). Development of a sensation-seeking scale. *Journal of Consulting Psychology, 28,* 477–482.

12760

Test Name: SENSATION SEEKING SCALE—FORM V (CROATIAN TRANSLATION)

Purpose: To measure four sensation seeking factors.

Number of Items: 40

Format: Includes four factors: thrill and adventure seeking, experience seeking, disinhibition, and boredom susceptibility.

Reliability: Alpha coefficients ranged from .50 to .87.

Author: Butkovi, A., and Bratko, D.

Article: Generation and sex differences in sensation seeking: Results of the family study.

Journal: *Perceptual and Motor Skills,* December 2003, *97,* Part 1, 965–970.

Related Research: Zuckerman, M., et al. (1978). Sensation seeking in England and America: Cross-cultural, age, and sex comparisons. *Journal of Consulting and Clinical Psychology, 46,* 139–149.

12761

Test Name: SENSATION SEEKING SCALE —SPANISH VERSION

Purpose: To measure thrill and adventure seeking, experience seeking, disinhibition, and boredom susceptibility.

Number of Items: 40

Format: A yes–no format is used. All items are presented in English.

Reliability: Alpha coefficients ranged from .62 to .82.

Author: Aluja, A., and Garcia, O.

Article: Exploring the structure of Zuckerman's Sensation Seeking Scale Form V in a Spanish sample.

Journal: *Psychological Reports,* August 2004, *95,* 338–344.

Related Research: Zuckerman, M., et al. (1964). Development of a sensation seeking scale. *Journal of Consulting and Clinical Psychology, 28,* 477–482.

12762

Test Name: SENSATION SEEKING—SCALE V

Purpose: To measure sensation-seeking.

Number of Items: 31

Format: Scales range from 1 (*strongly disagree*) to 5 (*strongly agree*).

Reliability: Coefficient alpha was .84.

Author: Hall, A.

Article: Sensation seeking and the use and selection of media materials.

Journal: *Psychological Reports,* August 2005, *97,* 236–244.

Related Research: Zuckerman, M. (1979). *Sensation seeking: Beyond the optimal level of arousal.* Hillsdale, NJ: Erlbaum.

12763

Test Name: SENSATION SEEKING—SCALE V

Purpose: To measure individual differences in stimulation and arousal needs.

Number of Items: 40

Format: Includes four factors: thrill and adventure seeking, experience seeking, disinhibition, and boredom susceptibility.

Reliability: Alpha coefficients ranged from .75 to .80.

Validity: Correlations with the Zuckerman–Kuhlman Personality Questionnaire Impulsive Sensation Seeking subscale ranged from .43 to .61.

Author: Roberti, J. W., et al.

Article: Further psychometric support for the Sensation Seeking Scale—Form V.

Journal: *Journal of Personality Assessment,* December 2003, *81,* 291–292.

Related Research: Zuckerman, M. (1994). *Behavioral expressions and biosocial bases of sensation seeking.* New York: Cambridge University Press.

12764

Test Name: SEXUAL SENSATION SEEKING SCALE

Purpose: To measure the propensity to seek out novel or risky sexual stimulation.

Number of Items: 11

Format: Responses are made on a 4-point scale ranging from 1 (*not at all like me*) to 4 (*very much like me*). All items are presented.

Reliability: Alpha coefficients ranged from .79 to .85.

Validity: Correlations with other variables ranged from –.32 to .60.

Author: Gaither, G. A., and Sellbom, M.

Article: The Sexual Sensation Seeking Scale: Reliability and validity within a heterosexual college student sample.

Journal: *Journal of Personality Assessment*, October 2003, *81*, 157–167.

Related Research: Kalichman, S. C., & Rompa, D. (1995). Sexual Sensation Seeking and Sexual Compulsivity Scales: Reliability, validity, and predicting HIV-risk behavior. *Journal of Personality Assessment*, *65*, 586–601.

12765

Test Name: SHORT INDEX OF SELF-DIRECTEDNESS

Purpose: To assess the extent to which people are hopeful in response to rewards and resourceful in the face of punishment.

Number of Items: 10

Format: Scales range from 1 (*strongly disagree*) to 5 (*strongly agree*). Sample items are presented.

Reliability: Coefficient alpha was .87. Test–retest reliability was .86 (7 days).

Validity: Correlations with the parent scales was .77 and .45. Correlations with other variables ranged from –.31 to .45.

Author: Prosnick, K. P., et al.

Article: Development and psychometric properties of scores from the Short Index of Self-Directedness.

Journal: *Measurement and Evaluation in Counseling and Development*, July 2003, *36*, 76–82.

Related Research: Cloninger, C. R. (1992). *The Temperament and Character Inventory—125 (TCI–125, Version I)*. St. Louis, MO: Washington University, Center for Psychobiology of Personality.

12766

Test Name: SOCIAL GOAL PURSUIT SCALES

Purpose: To assess prosocial goals and responsibility goal pursuit.

Number of Items: 6

Format: Includes prosocial goals and responsibility goal pursuit. Responses are made on a 6-point scale ranging from 1 (*rarely*) to 6 (*almost always*). Examples are presented.

Reliability: Alpha coefficients were .74 and .81.

Validity: Correlations with other variables ranged from –.30 to .47.

Author: Wentzel, K. R.

Article: Are effective teachers like good parents? Teaching styles and student adjustment in early adolescence.

Journal: *Child Development*, January/February 2002, *73*, 287–301.

Related Research: Wentzel, K. R. (1993). Social and academic goals at school: Motivation and achievement in early adolescence. *Journal of Early Adolescence*, *13*, 4–20.

12767

Test Name: SPORT ACHIEVEMENT ORIENTATION QUESTIONNAIRE

Purpose: To assess achievement orientation in sport for Japanese athletes.

Number of Items: 42

Format: Includes three factors: top level orientation, demonstrating ability orientation, and win orientation. Responses are made on a 5-point Likert scale ranging from 1 (*strongly disagree*) to 5 (*strongly agree*). All items are presented.

Reliability: Alpha coefficients ranged from .76 to .90.

Validity: Correlations with other variables ranged from –.05 to .02.

Author: Wakayama, H., et al.

Article: Development of the Sport Achievement Orientation Questionnaire for Japanese athletes by exploratory factor analysis.

Journal: *Perceptual and Motor Skills*, April 2004, *98*, 533–541.

12768

Test Name: SPORT MOTIVATION SCALE FOR CHILDREN— MODIFIED

Purpose: To assess motivation at the contextual level.

Number of Items: 28

Format: Includes three types of motivation: intrinsic, extrinsic, and amotivation. Responses are made on a 7-point Likert scale ranging from 1 (*totally disagree*) to 7 (*totally agree*).

Reliability: Alpha coefficients ranged from .60 to .76. Test–retest (30 days) reliabilities ranged from .66 to .74.

Validity: Correlations with other variables ranged from –.51 to .47 ($n = 452$).

Author: Zahariadis, P. N., et al.

Article: The Sport Motivation Scale for Children: Preliminary analysis in physical education classes.

Journal: *Perceptual and Motor Skills*, August 2005, *101*, 43–54.

Related Research: Pelletier, L. G., et al. (1995). Leisure and mental health: Relationship between leisure involvement and psychological well-being. *Canadian Journal of Behavioral Science, 27*, 214–225.

12769

Test Name: SPORT ORIENTATION QUESTIONNAIRE

Purpose: To measure sport orientation.

Number of Items: 25

Format: Includes three subscales: Competitiveness, Goal Orientation, and Win Orientation. Responses are made on a 5-point Likert-type scale ranging from 1 (*strongly disagree*) to 5 (*strongly agree*).

Reliability: Alpha coefficients ranged from .59 to .96.

Author: Skordilis, E. K., et al.

Article: Comparison of sport achievement orientation of male professional, amateur, and wheelchair basketball athletes.

Journal: *Perceptual and Motor Skills*, October 2003, *97*, 483–490.

Related Research: Gill, D., & Deeter, T. (1988). Development of the Sport Orientation Questionnaire. *Research Quarterly for Exercise and Sport, 59*, 191–202.

12770

Test Name: SPORT ORIENTATION QUESTIONNAIRE—REVISED (JAPANESE VERSION)

Purpose: To measure sport orientation.

Number of Items: 24

Format: Includes four factors: goal, participation, success, and win. Responses are made on a 5-point

Likert scale ranging from 1 (*strongly disagree*) to 5 (*strongly agree*). All items are presented.

Reliability: Alpha coefficients ranged from .72 to .86.

Author: Wakayama, H., et al.

Article: Exploratory factor analysis of the Sport Orientation Questionnaire and the Task and Ego Orientation in Sport Questionnaire in a Japanese sport setting.

Journal: *Perceptual and Motor Skills*, December 2002, *95*, Part 2, 1179–1186.

Related Research: Gill, D. L., & Deeter, T. E. (1988). Development of the Sport Orientation Questionnaire. *Research Quarterly for Exercise and Sport, 59*, 191–202.

12771

Test Name: SPORTS ORIENTATION QUESTIONNAIRE

Purpose: To assess the desire to win in sports competition.

Number of Items: 13

Format: Responses are made on a 5-point Likert-type scale. Examples are presented.

Reliability: Coefficient alpha was .94.

Validity: Correlations with other variables ranged from .07 to .75.

Author: Houston, J. M., et al.

Article: A factorial analysis of scales measuring competitiveness.

Journal: *Educational and Psychological Measurement*, April 2002, *62*, 284–298.

Related Research: Gill, D. L., & Deeter, T. E. (1988). Development of the Sport Orientation Questionnaire. *Research Quarterly for Exercise and Sport, 59*, 191–202.

12772

Test Name: STUDENT ACHIEVEMENT MOTIVATION SCALES

Purpose: To assess students' achievement motivation profiles in terms of perseverance, task involvement, and teacher rapport.

Number of Items: 11

Format: Scales range from 1 (*strongly disagree*) to 5 (*strongly agree*). All items are presented.

Reliability: Alpha coefficients ranged from .71 to .73.

Validity: Correlations with other variables ranged from –.20 to –.06.

Author: Strage, A., et al.

Article: What every student affairs professional should know: Student study activities and beliefs associated with academic success.

Journal: *Journal of College Student Development*, March/April 2002, *43*, 246–266.

12773

Test Name: STUDENT ATHLETES' MOTIVATION TOWARD SPORTS AND ACADEMICS QUESTIONNAIRE

Purpose: To measure academic and athletic motivation of college students.

Number of Items: 30

Format: Scales range from 1 (*very strongly disagree*) to 6 (*very strongly agree*). All items are presented.

Reliability: Alpha coefficients ranged from .79 to .86 across subscales.

Author: Gaston-Gayles, J. L.

Article: The factor structure and reliability of the Student Athletes' Motivation Toward Sports and Academics Questionnaire (SAMSAQ).

Journal: *Journal of College Student Development*, May/June 2005, *46*, 317–327.

Related Research: Gaston, J. L. (2002). *A study of student athletes' motivation toward sports and academics.* Unpublished doctoral dissertation, The Ohio State University, Columbus.

12774

Test Name: STUDENT'S INTRINSIC MOTIVATION SCALE

Purpose: To measure student's intrinsic motivation.

Number of Items: 6

Format: Assesses interest and enjoyment. Examples are presented.

Reliability: Coefficient alpha was .93.

Author: Reeve, J., et al.

Article: Testing models of the experience of self-determination in intrinsic motivation and the conundrum of choice.

Journal: *Journal of Educational Psychology*, June 2003, *95*, 375–392.

Related Research: Reeve, J. (1989). The interest–enjoyment distinction in intrinsic motivation. *Motivation and Emotion, 13,* 83–103.

12775

Test Name: TASK AND EGO ORIENTATION IN PHYSICAL EDUCATION QUESTIONNAIRE

Purpose: To assess individuals' disposition for ego orientation and task orientation.

Number of Items: 16

Format: Includes two scales: Ego Orientation and Task Orientation. Responses are made on a 5-point scale ranging from 1 (*strongly disagree*) to 5 (*strongly agree*). Examples are given.

Reliability: Alpha coefficients ranged from .81 to .92.

Author: Bortoli, L., and Robazza, C.

Article: Italian version of the Task and Ego Orientation in Physical Education Questionnaire.

Journal: *Perceptual and Motor Skills*, December 2005, *101*, 901–910.

Related Research: Walling, M. D., & Duda, J. L. (1995). Goals and their associations with beliefs about success in and perceptions of the purposes of physical education. *Journal of Teaching in Physical Education, 14,* 140–156.

12776

Test Name: TASK AND EGO ORIENTATION IN SPORT QUESTIONNAIRE

Purpose: To measure participants' goal orientations.

Number of Items: 13

Format: Includes task orientation and ego orientation. Responses are made on a 5-point Likert-type scale ranging from 1 (*strongly disagree*) to 5 (strongly agree). Examples are given.

Reliability: Alpha coefficients were both .85.

Validity: Correlations with other variables ranged from −.18 to .37.

Author: Newton, M., et al.

Article: Relationship between achievement goal constructs and physical self-perceptions in a physical activity setting.

Journal: *Perceptual and Motor Skills*, December 2004, *99*, Part 1, 757–770.

Related Research: Duda, J. L., et al. (1991). The relationship of task and ego orientations to sportsmanship attitudes and the perceived legitimacy of injurious acts. *Research Quarterly for Exercise and Sport, 62,* 79–87.

12777

Test Name: TASK AND EGO ORIENTATION IN SPORT QUESTIONNAIRE—REVISED (JAPANESE VERSION)

Purpose: To measure task and ego orientation in sport.

Number of Items: 14.

Format: Includes three factors: task, ego—Type 1, and ego—Type 2. All items are presented.

Reliability: Alpha coefficients ranged from .75 to .84.

Author: Wakayama, H., et al.

Article: Exploratory factor analysis of the Sport Orientation Questionnaire and the Task and Ego Orientation in Sport Questionnaire in a Japanese sport setting.

Journal: *Perceptual and Motor Skills*, December 2002, 95, Part 2, 1179–1186.

Related Research: Duda, J. L. (1989). Relationship between task and ego orientation and the perceived purpose of sport among high school athletes. *Journal of Sport and Exercise Psychology, 11,* 318–335.

12778

Test Name: TASK AND EGO SUBSCALES OF THE MOTIVATIONAL ORIENTATION SCALES

Purpose: To measure task and ego motivational orientation.

Number of Items: 16

Format: Includes two subscales: Task and Ego. Responses are made on a 5-point Likert-type scale ranging from 1 (*strongly disagree*) to 5 (*strongly agree*).

Reliability: Alpha coefficients were .82 and .88.

Validity: Correlations with other variables ranged from .22 to .70.

Author: Jagacinski, C. M., and Duda, J. L.

Article: A comparative analysis of contemporary achievement goal orientation measures.

Journal: *Education and Psychological Measurement,* December 2001, *61,* 1013–1039.

Related Research: Duda, J. L., & Nicholls, J. G. (1992). Dimensions of achievement motivation in school work and sport. *Journal of Educational Psychology, 84,* 290–299.

12779

Test Name: TASK INVOLVEMENT MEASURE

Purpose: To assess participants' absorption while studying.

Number of Items: 7

Format: Responses are made on a 7-point scale ranging from 1 (*strongly disagree*) to 7 (*strongly agree*). An example is given.

Reliability: Coefficient alpha was .75.

Validity: Correlations with other variables ranged from −.53 to .29.

Author: McGregor, H. A., and Elliot, A. J.

Article: Achievement goals as predictors of achievement-relevant processes prior to task engagement.

Journal: *Journal of Educational Psychology,* June 2002, *94,* 381–395.

Related Research: Elliot, A., & Harackiewiez, J. (1996). Approach and avoidance achievement goals and intrinsic motivation: A mediational analysis. *Journal of Personality and Social Psychology, 70,* 461–475.

12780

Test Name: TEACHER RATING OF ACADEMIC ACHIEVEMENT MOTIVATION MEASURE

Purpose: To enable teachers to rate students' effort and persistence.

Number of Items: 5

Format: Responses are made on a 5-point Likert-type scale ranging from 1 (*strongly disagree*) to 5 (*strongly agree*).

Reliability: Alpha coefficients were .85 and .92.

Validity: Correlations with other variables ranged from −.14 to .27.

Author: Ferrer-Caja, E., and Weiss, M. R.

Article: Cross-validation of a model of intrinsic motivation with students enrolled in high school elective courses.

Journal: *The Journal of Experimental Education,* Fall 2002, *71,* 41–65.

Related Research: Stinnett, T. A., et al. (1991). Development of the Teacher Rating of Academic Achievement Motivation: TRAAM. *School Psychology Review, 20,* 609–622.

12781

Test Name: TENACIOUS GOAL PURSUIT SCALE

Purpose: To measure assimilative tenacity.

Number of Items: 15

Format: Responses are made on a 5-point Likert-type scale ranging from *strongly disagree* to *strongly agree*. All items are presented.

Reliability: Alpha coefficients ranged from .72 to .82.

Validity: Correlations with other variables ranged from −.22 to .40.

Author: Mueller, D. J., and Kim, K.

Article: The Tenacious Goal Pursuit and Flexible Goal Adjustment scales: Examination of their validity.

Journal: *Educational and Psychological Measurement,* February 2004, *64,* 120–142.

Related Research: Brandtstädter, J., & Renner, G. (1990). Tenacious goal pursuit and flexible goal adjustment: Explication and age-related analysis of assimilative and accommodative strategies of coping. *Psychology and Aging, 5,* 58–67.

12782

Test Name: TRAIT PROACTIVE BEHAVIOR SCALE

Purpose: To measure personal initiative and pursuit of learning.

Number of Items: 12

Format: Scales range from 1 (*not true at all*) to 5 (*very true*). Sample items are presented.

Reliability: Coefficient alpha was .86.

Author: Sonnentag, S.

Article: Recovery, work engagement, and proactive behavior: A new look at the interface between nonwork and work.

Journal: *Journal of Applied Psychology,* June 2003, *88,* 518–528.

Related Research: Frese, M., et al. (1997). The concept of personal initiative: Operationalization, reliability and validity in two German samples. *Journal of Occupational and Organizational Psychology, 70,* 139–161.

12783

Test Name: TRANSGRESSION-RELATED INTERPERSONAL MOTIVATION INVENTORY

Purpose: To measure a victim's motivation to seek revenge against or to avoid an offender.

Number of Items: 12

Format: Includes two subscales: Revenge and Avoidance. Responses are made on a 5-point Likert-type scale ranging from 1 (*strongly disagree*) to 5 (*strongly agree*).

Reliability: Alpha coefficients for the revenge subscale ranged from .83 to .94.

Author: Worthington, E. L., Jr., et al.

Article: The Religious Commitment Inventory—10: Development, refinement, and validation of a brief scale for research and counseling.

Journal: *Journal of Counseling Psychology*, January 2003, *50*, 84–96.

Related Research: McCullough, M. E., et al. (1998). Mental health. In D. B. Larson et al. (Eds.), *Scientific research on spirituality and health: A consensus report* (pp. 55–67). Baltimore: National Institute for Healthcare Research.

12784

Test Name: VOLUNTEER FUNCTIONS INVENTORY

Purpose: To measure motivations for volunteering: social motives, value motives, career motives, need to understand, protective motives, and enhancement motives.

Number of Items: 30

Format: Seven-point scales are anchored by 1 (*least important or accurate*) and 7 (*most important or accurate*).

Reliability: Alpha coefficients were greater than .80.

Author: Gerstein, L. H., et al.

Article: Differences in motivations of paid versus nonpaid volunteers.

Journal: *Psychological Reports*, February 2004, *94*, 163–175.

Related research: Clary, E. G., et al. (1992). Volunteers' motivations: A functional strategy for the recruitment, placement, and retention of volunteers. *Nonprofit Management and Leadership, 2*, 333–350.

12785

Test Name: WISCONSIN INVENTORY OF SMOKING DEPENDENCE MOTIVES

Purpose: To measure thirteen motives for smoking.

Number of Items: 68

Format: Item responses range from 1 (*not true of me at all*) to 7 (*extremely true of me*). All items are presented.

Reliability: Alpha coefficients exceeded .80 on all subscales.

Validity: Correlations with other variables ranged from .15 to .79.

Author: Piper M. E., et al.

Article: A multiple motives approach to tobacco dependence: The Wisconsin Inventory of Smoking Dependence Motives (WISDM-68).

Journal: *Journal of Consulting and Clinical Psychology*, April 2004, 72, 139–154

12786

Test Name: WORK DOMAIN TRAIT GOAL ORIENTATION INSTRUMENT

Purpose: To measure equal orientation.

Number of Items: 13

Format: Includes three dimensions: Learning Goal Orientation, Prove Goal Orientation, and Avoidance Goal Orientation. Responses are made on a 5-point Likert scale ranging from 1 (*strongly disagree*) to 5 (*strongly agree*). Sample items are presented.

Reliability: Alpha coefficients ranged from .62 to .85.

Validity: Correlations with other variables ranged from −.08 to .25.

Author: Heimbeck, D., et al.

Article: Integrating errors into the training process: The function of error management instructions and the role of goal orientation.

Journal: *Personnel Psychology,* Summer 2003, 56, 333–361.

Related Research: VandeWalle, D. (1997). Development and validation of a work domain goal orientation instrument. *Educational and Psychological Measurement*, 57, 995–1015.

12787

Test Name: WORK MOTIVATION SCALE

Purpose: To measure work motivation.

Number of Items: 8

Format: Responses are made on a 5-point scale ranging from 1 (*strongly disagree*) to 5 (*strongly agree*).

Reliability: Coefficient alpha was .65.

Validity: Correlations with other variables ranged from −.23 to .44 ($n = 178$).

Author: Lim, V. K. G., and Loo, G. L.

Article: Effects of parental job insecurity and parenting behaviors on youth's self-efficacy and work attitudes.

Journal: *Journal of Vocational Behavior*, August 2003, *63*, 86–98.

Related Research: Stern, D., et al. (1990). Quality of student's work experience and orientation toward work. *Youth and Society, 22*, 263–282.

12788

Test Name: WORK PREFERENCE INVENTORY—CHINESE VERSION

Purpose: To measure intrinsic and extrinsic motivations.

Number of Items: 18

Format: Scales range from 1 (*never or almost never true of me*) to 4 (*always or almost always true of me*). All items are presented in English.

Reliability: Alpha coefficients ranged from .66 to .72 across primary and secondary scales.

Validity: Correlations with other variables ranged from −.42 to .63.

Author: Moneta, G. B., and Siu, C. M. Y.

Article: Trait intrinsic and extrinsic motivations, academic performance, and creativity in Hong Kong college students.

Journal: *Journal of College Student Development*, September/October 2002, *43*, 664–683.

Related Research: Amabile, T. M., et al. (1994). The Work Preference Inventory: Assessing intrinsic and extrinsic motivational orientations. *Journal of Personality and Social Psychology, 66*, 950–967.

12789

Test Name: WORK PREFERENCE INVENTORY—STUDENT FORM

Purpose: To assess intrinsic and extrinsic motives to work and, secondarily, challenge, enjoyment, outward, and compensation.

Number of Items: 30

Format: Scales range from 1 (*never or almost never true of you*) to 4 (*always or almost always true of you*). A sample item is presented.

Reliability: Alpha coefficients ranged from .60 to .79 across subscales and across sex.

Validity: Correlations with social desirability ranged from −.37 to .26. Correlations with several values scales ranged from −.20 to .50.

Author: Loo, R.

Article: Motivational orientations to work: An evaluation of the Work Preference Inventory (Student Form).

Journal: *Measurement and Evaluation in Counseling and Development*, January 2001, *33*, 222–233.

Related Research: Amabile, T. M., et al. (1994). The Work Preference Inventory: Assessing intrinsic and extrinsic motivational orientations. *Journal of Personality and Social Psychology, 66*, 950–967.

CHAPTER 16
Perception

12790

Test Name: ACADEMIC OUTCOME EXPECTATIONS SCALE

Purpose: To assess beliefs regarding the relevance of educational performance to future career options and success.

Number of Items: 5

Format: Responses are made on a 5-point Likert scale.

Reliability: Alpha coefficients were .64 and .77.

Validity: Correlations with other variables ranged from –.07 to .35.

Author: Wettersten, K. B., et al.

Article: Predicting educational and vocational attitudes among rural high school students.

Journal: *Journal of Counseling Psychology*, October 2005, *52*, 658–663.

Related Research: Betz, N. E., & Voyten, K. K. (1997). Efficacy and outcome expectations influence career exploration and decidedness. *Career Development Quarterly, 46,* 179–189.

12791

Test Name: ACADEMIC SELF-CONCEPT SCALE

Purpose: To measure college students' academic self-concept.

Number of Items: 40

Format: Responses are made on a 4-point Likert-type scale ranging from 1 (*strongly disagree*) to 4

(*strongly agree*). Items are presented.

Reliability: Alpha coefficients ranged from .57 to .88.

Author: Cokley, K., et al.

Article: Ethnic difference in the measurement of academic self-concept in a sample of African American and European American college students.

Journal: *Educational and Psychological Measurement,* August 2003, *63,* 707–722.

Related Research: Reynolds, W. M., et al. (1980). Initial development and validation of the Academic Self-Concept Scale. *Educational and Psychological Measurement, 40,* 1013–1016.

12792

Test Name: ACADEMIC SELF-CONCEPT SCALE

Purpose: To assess academic self-concept in mathematics.

Number of Items: 3

Format: Responses are made on a 6-point scale. All items are presented.

Reliability: Coefficient alpha was .78.

Author: Dresel, M., et al.

Article: Nothing more than dimensions? Evidence for a surplus meaning of specific attributions.

Journal: *The Journal of Educational Research,* September/October 2005, *99,* 31–44.

Related Research: Dweck, C. S. (1999). *Self-theories: Their role in motivation, personality, and development.* Philadelphia: Psychology Press.

12793

Test Name: ACADEMIC SELF-EFFICACY MEASURE

Purpose: To measure respondents' confidence in their ability to perform well academically.

Number of Items: 8

Format: Responses are made on a 7-point Likert scale.

Reliability: Coefficient alpha was .81.

Validity: Correlations with other variables ranged from –.20 to .51.

Author: Chemers, M. M., et al.

Article: Academic self-efficacy and first-year college student performance and adjustment.

Journal: *Journal of Educational Psychology,* March 2001, *93,* 55–64.

Related Research: Bandura, A. (1997). *Self-efficacy: The exercise of control.* New York: Freeman.

12794

Test Name: ACADEMIC SELF-EFFICACY SCALE

Purpose: To measure the extent to which students believe that they are able to successfully perform in school.

Number of Items: 8

Format: Responses are made on a 6-point scale ranging from *strongly disagree* to *strongly agree*.

Reliability: Coefficient alpha was .77.

Validity: Correlations with other variables ranged from −.30 to .42.

Author: Finn, K. V., and Frone, M. R.

Article: Academic performance and cheating: Moderating role of school identification and self-efficacy.

Journal: *The Journal of Educational Research*, January/February 2004, *97*, 115–122.

Related Research: Riggs, M. L., et al. (1994). Development and validation of self-efficacy and outcome expectancy scales for job-related applications. *Educational and Psychological Measurement*, *54*, 793–802.

12795

Test Name: ACADEMIC SELF-EFFICACY SCALE

Purpose: To measure academic self-efficacy.

Number of Items: 4

Format: Item responses are anchored by 1 (*no confidence at all*) and 2 (*100% confident*). All items are presented.

Reliability: Alpha was .76.

Validity: Correlations with other variables ranged from −.02 to .10.

Author: Lane, J., and Lane, A. M.

Article: Predictive validity of variables used to select students for postgraduate management courses.

Journal: *Psychological Reports*, June 2002, *90*, Part 2, 1239–1247.

12796

Test Name: ACADEMIC SELF-EFFICACY SCALE

Purpose: To measure academic self-efficacy.

Number of Items: 17

Format: Scales range from 1 (*never*) to 5 (*always*).

Reliability: Coefficient alpha was .88.

Validity: Correlations with other variables ranged from .29 to .51.

Author: Poyrazli, S., et al.

Article: Relation between assertiveness, academic self-efficacy, and psychosocial adjustment among international graduate students.

Journal: *Journal of College Student Development*, September/October 2002, *43*, 632–642.

Related Research: Sherer, M., & Maddux, J. E. (1982). The Self-Efficacy Scale: Construction and validation. *Psychological Reports*, *51*, 663–671.

12797

Test Name: ACADEMIC SELF-EFFICACY SCALE

Purpose: To measure level of academic self-efficacy.

Number of Items: 14

Format: Includes two scales: Self-Efficacy for Self-Regulated Learning Scale and Student Academic Self-Efficacy Scale.

Reliability: Alpha coefficients ranged from .76 to .87.

Validity: Correlations with other variables ranged from −.31 to .46.

Author: Wettersten, K. B., et al.

Article: Predicting educational and vocational attitudes among rural high school students.

Journal: *Journal of Counseling Psychology*, October 2005, *52*, 658–663.

Related Research: Pajares, F., & Giovanni, V. (2002). Students'

self-efficacy in their self-regulated learning strategies: A developmental perspective. *Psychologia: An International Journal of Psychology in the Orient*, *45*, 211–221. Valiante, G., & Pajares, F. (1999). The Inviting/Disinviting Index: Instrument validation and relation to motivation and achievement. *Journal of Invitational Theory and Practice*, *6*, 28–47.

12798

Test Name: ACCEPTABILITY OF CHEATING SCALE

Purpose: To assess students' perceptions of the acceptability of cheating.

Number of Items: 7

Format: Includes two factors: morality of cheating and justifiability of cheating.

Reliability: Internal consistency estimates were .75 and .86.

Validity: Correlations with other variables ranged from −.60 to .73.

Author: Murdock, T. B., et al.

Article: Effects of classroom context variables on high schools students' judgments of the acceptability and likelihood of cheating.

Journal: *Journal of Educational Psychology*, December 2004, *96*, 765–777.

Related Research: Anderman, E. M., et al. (1998). Motivation and cheating during early adolescence. *Journal of Educational Psychology*, *90*, 84–93.

12799

Test Name: ACTIVITY–FEELING STATES SCALE—PERCEIVED COMPETENCE SUBSCALE

Purpose: To assess perceived competence.

Number of Items: 3

Reliability: Coefficient alpha was .79.

Validity: Correlations with other variables ranged from −.22 to .47.

Author: Hardre, P. L., and Reeve, J.

Article: A motivational model of rural students' intentions to persist in, versus drop out of, high school.

Journal: *Journal of Educational Psychology*, June 2003, *95*, 347–356.

Related Research: Reeve, J., & Sickenius. B. (1994). Development and validation of a brief measure of the three psychological needs underlying intrinsic motivation: The AFS scales. *Educational and Psychological Measurement, 54,* 506–515.

12800

Test Name: ADOLESCENT SELF-EFFICACY BELIEFS SCALE

Purpose: To measure adolescent self-efficacy beliefs.

Number of Items: 10

Format: Employs a Likert scale. Sample items are presented.

Reliability: Average coefficient alpha was .68. One year stability was .59. An additional average coefficient alpha was .84.

Validity: Correlation with the School-Related Self-Efficacy Scale was .50.

Author: Pinquart, M., et al.

Article: Self-efficacy and successful school-to-work transition: A longitudinal study.

Journal: *Journal of Vocational Behavior*, December 2003, *63*, 329–346.

Related Research: Jerusalem, M., & Satow, L. (1999). Schulbezogene Selbstwirksamkeitserwartung [School-related self-efficacy]. In R. Schwarzer & M. Jerusalem (Eds.), *Skalen zur Erfassung von Lehrer-und Schülermerkmalen* (pp. 15–16). Berlin, Germany: Free University.

12801

Test Name: ADOLESCENTS' HOSTILE ATTRIBUTIONAL STYLES TOWARD PEERS SCALE

Purpose: To assess adolescents' social cognitive processes.

Number of Items: 6

Format: Subjects choose 1 of 4 possible causal attributions.

Reliability: Coefficient alpha was .72.

Author: Brookmeyer, K. A., et al.

Article: Adolescents who witness community violence: Can parent support and prosocial cognitions protect them from committing violence?

Journal: *Child Development*, July/August 2005, *76*, 917–929.

Related Research: Albet, J. L., et al. (2003). Developmental trajectories toward violence in middle childhood: Course, demographic differences, and response to school-based intervention. *Developmental Psychology, 39,* 324–348.

12802

Test Name: ANTECEDENTS OF AFFECTIVE COMMITMENT SCALE

Purpose: To measure work attitude/perception variables as antecedents of affective commitment.

Number of Items: 22

Format: Includes 11 work attitude/perception variables: job challenge, role clarity, goal clarity, goal difficulty, management receptiveness, peer cohesion, organizational dependability, equity, personal importance, feedback, and participation. Responses are made on a 7-point scale ranging from *strongly disagree* to *strongly agree*.

Reliability: Alpha coefficients ranged from .31 to .89.

Author: Cheng, Y., and Stockdale, M. S.

Article: The validity of the three-component model of organizational commitment in a Chinese context.

Journal: *Journal of Vocational Behavior*, June 2003, *62*, 465–489.

Related Research: Allen, N. J., & Meyer, J. P. (1990). The measurement and antecedents of affective, continuance and normative commitment to the organization. *Journal of Occupational Psychology, 63,* 1–18.

12803

Test Name: ANTICIPATION OF JOB LOSS SCALE

Purpose: To assess the degree to which an employee expects an employer to cease doing business.

Number of Items: 4

Format: Scales range from 1 (*strongly agree*) to 5 (*strongly disagree*). A sample item is presented.

Reliability: Coefficient alpha was .84.

Author: Prussia, G. E., et al.

Article: Explication of the coping goal construct: Implications for coping and reemployment.

Journal: *Journal of Applied Psychology*, December 2001, *86*, 1179–1190.

Related Research: Kinicki, A. J. (1985). Personal consequences of plant closings: A model and preliminary test. *Human Relations, 38,* 197–212.

12804

Test Name: APPROACH AND AVOIDANCE ACHIEVEMENT IN SPORT QUESTIONNAIRE

Purpose: To measure how much individuals identify with mastery, performance-approach, and performance-avoidance goals.

Number of Items: 15

Format: Includes three goals: mastery, performance-approach, and performance-avoidance. Responses are made on a 5-point rating scale ranging from 1 (*don't agree at all*) to 5 (*agree completely*). Examples are presented.

Reliability: Alpha coefficient ranged from .81 to .92.

Validity: Correlations with other variables ranged from −.37 to .36.

Author: Cury, F., et al.

Article: Perceptions of competence, implicit theory of ability, perception of motivational climate, and achievement goals: A test of the trichotomous conceptualization of endorsement of achievement motivational in the physical education setting.

Journal: *Perceptual and Motor Skills*, August 2002, 95, 233–244.

Related Research: Elliott, A. J., & Church, M. A. (1997). An hierarchical model of approach and avoidance motivation. *Journal of Personality and Social Psychology*, 72, 218–232.

12805

Test Name: ARTHRITIS SELF-EFFICACY SCALE

Purpose: To measure general feelings of self-efficacy about performance capabilities.

Format: Ten-point scales range from 1 (*very uncertain*) to 10 (*very certain*). Sample items are presented.

Reliability: Coefficient alpha was .87.

Validity: Correlations with other variables ranged from −.38 to .44.

Author: Abraído-Lanza, A. F., et al.

Article: En las manos de Dios [In God's hands]: Religious and other forms of coping among Latinos with arthritis.

Journal: *Journal of Consulting and Clinical Psychology*, February 2004, 72, 91–102.

Related Research: Lorig, K., et al. (1989). Development and evaluation of a scale to measure the perceived self-efficacy in people with arthritis. *Arthritis and Rheumatism, 32,* 37–44.

12806

Test Name: ASPECTS OF IDENTITY QUESTIONNAIRE

Purpose: To measure personal identity, collective identity, and social identity.

Number of Items: 35

Format: Scales range from 1 (*not important to my sense of who I am*) to 5 (*extremely important to my sense of who I am*).

Reliability: Alpha coefficients ranged from .70 to .81 across subscales.

Author: Yeh, C., et al.

Article: Self and coping among college students in Japan.

Journal: *Journal of College Student Development*, May/June 2001, 42, 242–254.

Related Research: Cheek, J. M., & Tropp, L. R. (1997). *The Aspects of Identity Questionnaire.* Available at *http://www.wellesley.edu/Psychology/Cheek/identity.html*

12807

Test Name: ATHLETIC IDENTITY SCALE

Purpose: To measure student athletes' athletic identity.

Number of Items: 10

Format: Scales range from 1 (*strongly disagree*) to 7 (*strongly agree*). Sample items are presented.

Reliability: Coefficient alpha was .86.

Validity: Correlations with other variables ranged from −.28 to .38.

Author: Settles, I. H., et al.

Article: One role or two? The function of psychological separation in role conflict.

Journal: *Journal of Applied Psychology*, June 2002, 87, 574–582.

Related Research: Brewer, B. W., et al. (1993). Athletic identity: Hercules' muscles or Achilles heel? *International Journal of Sport Psychology, 24,* 237–254.

12808

Test Name: ATTRIBUTION OF PROBLEM CAUSE AND SOLUTION SCALE

Purpose: To measure helping and coping orientations.

Number of Items: 44

Format: Includes two dimensions of responsibility: Cause and Solution. Responses are made on a 7-point Likert-type scale ranging from 1 (*very strongly disagree*) to 7 (*very strongly agree*). All items are presented.

Reliability: Alpha coefficients were .92 and .95.

Validity: Correlations with other variables ranged from −.39 to .62.

Author: Stepleman, L. M., et al.

Article: Helping and coping attributions: Development of the Attributions of Problem Cause and Solution Scale.

Journal: *Educational and Psychological Measurement*, June 2005, *65*, 525–542.

Related Research: Brickman, P., et al. (1982). Models of helping and coping. *American Psychologist, 37*, 363–384.

12809

Test Name: ATTRIBUTIONAL STYLE QUESTIONNAIRE—JAPANESE SHORT FORM

Purpose: To measure individual differences in the causal explanation for negative events.

Number of Items: 6

Format: Seven-point rating scales are presented for internality, stability, and globality.

Validity: Correlations with other variables ranged from −.08 to .49.

Author: Sonoda, A.

Article: Optimistic bias and pessimistic realism in judgments of contingency with aversive or rewarding outcomes.

Journal: *Psychological Reports*, October 2002, *91*, 445–456.

Related Research: Sonoda, A., & Tunan, K. (1995). [*A short form of the Japanese edition of the Attributional (Explanatory) Style Questionnaire (ASQ-E)*]. [*Annual Reports of Liberal Arts and Sciences, University of Shizuoka*], *8*, 121–125. [in Japanese with English abstract]

12810

Test Name: ATTRIBUTIONS OF BLAME SCALE

Purpose: To assess employee attribution of blame for a layoff.

Number of Items: 3

Format: Scales range from 1 (*strongly disagree*) to 5 (*strongly agree*). Sample items are presented.

Reliability: Coefficient alpha was .83.

Author: Barclay, L. J., et al.

Article: Exploring the role of emotions in injustice perceptions and retaliation.

Journal: *Journal of Applied Psychology*, July 2005, *90*, 629–643.

Related Research: Konovsky, M. A., & Folger, R. (1991). The effects of procedures, social accounts, and benefits level on victims' layoff reactions. *Journal of Applied Social Psychology, 21*, 630–650.

12811

Test Name: AWARENESS SCALES

Purpose: To assess self-awareness and environment awareness.

Number of Items: 12

Format: Includes two scales: Self-Awareness and Environment Awareness. Responses are made on a 5-point scale ranging from *strongly disagree* to *strongly agree*. Examples are given.

Reliability: Alpha coefficients were .71 and .83.

Validity: Correlations with other variables ranged from −.17 to .29.

Author: Singh, R., and Greenhaus, J. H.

Article: The relation between career decision-making strategies and person–job fit: A study of job changers.

Journal: *Journal of Vocational Behavior*, February 2004, *64*, 198–221.

Related Research: Callanan, G. A. (1989). *The career indecision of managers and professionals: Development of a scale and test of a model.* Unpublished doctoral dissertation, Drexel University, Philadelphia.

12812

Test Name: BEHAVIOR EVALUATION SCALE

Purpose: To measure the extent to which people view a specific behavior they exhibit as pathological.

Number of Items: 24

Format: Five-point scales are anchored by *strongly disagree* and *strongly agree*. Sample items are presented.

Reliability: Coefficient alpha was .90. One-month test–retest reliability was .85.

Author: Akillas, E.

Article: Behavior Evaluation Scale: Validity in studies of social anxiety.

Journal: *Psychological Reports*, December 2002, *91*, Part 1, 979–987.

Related Research: Akillas, E. (1998). *The Behavior Evaluation Scale.* Unpublished scale and raw data, Kutztown University of Pennsylvania, Kutztown.

12813

Test Name: BETTS' QUESTIONNAIRE UPON MENTAL IMAGERY—SPANISH VERSION

Purpose: To measure imaging.

Number of Items: 35

Format: Scales range from 1 (*perfectly clear and as vivid as the actual experience*) to 7 (*no image present at all; you only know that you are thinking of the object*).

Reliability: Coefficient alpha was .92.

Validity: Correlations with other variables ranged from −.34 to .58.

Author: Campos, A., and Pérez-Fabello, M. J.

Article: The Spanish Version of Betts' Questionnaire Upon Mental Imagery.

Journal: *Psychological Reports,* February 2005, *96,* 51–56.

Related Research: Sheehan, P. W. (1967). A shortened form of Betts' Questionnaire Upon Mental Imagery. *Journal of Clinical Psychology, 23,* 386–389.

12814

Test Name: BODY-ESTEEM SCALE—CANADIAN FRENCH VERSION

Purpose: To assess participants' evaluations about their body or appearance.

Number of Items: 23

Format: Includes three body-esteem subscales: Appearance, Attribution, and Weight. Responses are made on a 5-point scale ranging from 0 (*never*) to 4 (*always*). Examples are given.

Reliability: Alphas ranged from .77 to .92.

Author: Ferrand, C., et al.

Article: Body-esteem, body mass index, and risk for disordered eating among adolescents in synchronized swimming.

Journal: *Perceptual and Motor Skills,* December 2005, *101,* 877–884.

Related Research: Beaudoin, C., et al. (2001). Traduction et validation canadienne-française d'une échelle portant sur l'estrine de son corps. *Avante, 9,* 15–20.

12815

Test Name: BODY-IMAGE QUESTIONNAIRE

Purpose: To measure body image

Number of Items: 20

Format: Responses are made on a 3-point scale ranging from 1 (*agree*) to 3 (*disagree*).

Reliability: Test–retest (6 weeks) reliability was .96. Coefficient alpha was .74

Author: Duncan, M. J., et al.

Article: Relationship between body image and percent body fat among British school children.

Journal: *Perceptual and Motor Skills,* February 2002, *94,* 197–203.

Related Research: Huddy, D. C., et al. (1993). Relationship between body image and percent body fat among college male varsity athletes and nonathletes. *Perceptual and Motor Skills, 77,* 851–857.

12816

Test Name: BODY-IMAGE QUESTIONNAIRE

Purpose: To explore the dimensionality of perceptions, feelings, and attitudes expressed towards one's body.

Number of Items: 19

Format: Responses are made on a 5-point scale. All items are presented.

Reliability: Alpha coefficients ranged from .82 to .85.

Author: Koleck, M., et al.

Article: The Body-Image Questionnaire: An extension.

Journal: *Perceptual and Motor Skills,* February 2002, *94,* 189–196.

Related Research: Bruchon-Schweitzer, M. (1987). Dimensionality of the body image: The Body-Image Questionnaire. *Perceptual and Motor Skills, 65,* 887–892.

12817

Test Name: BODY PARTS SATISFACTION SCALE— REVISED

Purpose: To measure the strength of feelings toward various body parts and the dimensionality of their body image.

Number of Items: 17

Format: Responses are made on a 4-point scale ranging from 1 (*very dissatisfied*) to 4 (*very satisfied*).

Reliability: Coefficient alpha was .86.

Author: Fung, M. S. C., and Yuen, M.

Article: Body image and eating attitudes among adolescent Chinese girls in Hong Kong.

Journal: *Perceptual and Motor Skills,* February 2003, *96,* 57–66.

Related Research: Chan, S. C. (1995). *Body image concerns and their psychological correlates among Chinese adolescents in Hong Kong.* Unpublished master's thesis, Chinese University of Hong Kong.

12818

Test Name: CANCER LOCUS OF CONTROL SCALE

Purpose: To assess the degree of perceived control expressed by cancer patients.

Number of Items: 17

Format: Scales range from 1 (*not at all in agreement*) to 4 (*full agreement*). All items are presented.

Reliability: Alpha coefficients ranged from .72 to .76 across subscales.

Validity: Correlations with other variables ranged from –.29 to .46.

Author: Cousson-Gélie, F., et al.

Article: Dimensions of Cancer Locus of Control Scale as predictors of psychological adjustment and survival in breast cancer patients.

Journal: *Psychological Reports,* December 2005, *97,* 699–711.

Related Research: Watson, M., et al. (1990). Locus of control and adjustment to cancer. *Psychological Reports, 66,* 39–48.

12819

Test Name: CANCER LOCUS OF CONTROL SCALE—MODIFIED

Purpose: To measure cancer locus of control.

Number of Items: 14

Format: Includes three factors: course, cause, and religious control. Responses are made on 5-point Likert-type scale ranging from 1 (*strongly disagree*) to 5 (*strongly agree*). All items are presented.

Reliability: Alpha coefficients ranged from .71 to .77.

Author: Henderson, J. W., et al.

Article: Confirmatory factor analysis of the Cancer Locus of Control Scale.

Journal: *Educational and Psychological Measurement*, December 2002, *62*, 995–1005.

Related Research: Watson, M., et al. (1990). Locus of control and adjustment to cancer. *Psychological Reports, 66*, 39–48.

12820

Test Name: CAREER BARRIERS INVENTORY—REVISED

Purpose: To measure perceived career barriers.

Format: Scales range from 1 (*would completely hinder*) to 7 (*would not hinder at all*). Sample items are presented.

Reliability: Alpha coefficients ranged from .75 to .86 across subscales.

Validity: Correlations with other variables ranged from −.32 to .24.

Author: Quimby, J. L., and O'Brien, K. M.

Article: Predictors of student and career decision-making self-efficacy among nontraditional college women.

Journal: *The Career Development Quarterly*, June 2004, *54*, 323–339.

Related Research: Swanson, J. L., et al. (1996). Assessing perceptions of career-related barriers: The

Career Barriers Inventory. *Journal of Career Assessment, 4*, 219–244.

12821

Test Name: CAREER BARRIERS INVENTORY—REVISED

Purpose: To identify career barriers for nontraditional college women.

Number of Items: 49

Format: Includes eight subscales: Sex Discrimination, Lack of Confidence, Multiple-Role Conflict, Conflict Between Children and Career Demands, Discouragement From Choosing Nontraditional Careers, Inadequate Preparation, Decision-Making Difficulties, and Dissatisfaction With Careers. Responses are made on a 7-point scale ranging from 1 (*would completely hinder*) to 7 (*would not hinder at all*). Examples are given.

Reliability: Alpha coefficients ranged from .74 to .90.

Validity: Correlations with other variables ranged from −.43 to .24.

Author: Quimby, J. L., and O'Brien, K. M.

Article: Predictors of student and career decision-making self-efficacy among nontraditional college women.

Journal: *The Career Development Quarterly*, June 2004, *52*, 323–339.

Related Research: Swanson, J. L., et al. (1996). Assessing perceptions of career related barriers: The Career Barriers Inventory. *Journal of Career Assessment, 4*, 219–244.

12822

Test Name: CAREER COUNSELING SELF-EFFICACY QUESTIONNAIRE

Purpose: To measure career counseling self-efficacy.

Number of Items: 27

Format: Scales range from 1 (*not at all sure*) to 7 (*very sure*). Sample items are presented in English.

Reliability: Alpha coefficients ranged from .79 to .91 across subscales. Test–retest correlations ranged from .78 to .89 (1 month).

Author: Soresi, S., et al.

Article: Relation of type and amount of training to career counseling self-efficacy in Italy.

Journal: *The Career Development Quarterly*, March 2004, *52*, 194–201.

Related Research: Nota, L., & Soresi, S. (2000). *Autoefficacia nelle scelte* [Self-efficacy and choice]. Firenze, Italy: Giunti-Organizzazioni Speciali.

12823

Test Name: CAREER DECISION MAKING SELF-EFFICACY SCALE—SHORT FORM

Purpose: To measure accurate self-appraisal, gathering information, goal selection, making future plans, and problem solving.

Number of Items: 25

Format: Scales range from 0 (*no confidence*) to 9 (*complete confidence*).

Reliability: Coefficient alpha was .94.

Validity: Correlations with other variables ranged from −.16 to .26.

Author: Kornspan, A. S., and Etzel, E. F.

Article: The relationship of demographic and psychological variables to career maturity of junior college student-athletes.

Journal: *Journal of College Student Development*, March/April 2001, *42*, 122–132.

Related Research: Betz, N. E., et al. (1996). Evaluation of a short form of the Career Decision-Making

Self-Efficacy Scale. *Journal of Career Assessment, 4,* 47–57.

12824

Test Name: CAREER DECISION SELF-EFFICACY SCALE— SHORT FORM

Purpose: To measure self-efficacy expectations for successfully completing tasks requisite to making good career decisions.

Number of Items: 25

Format: Includes five career choice competencies: Self-Appraisal, Gathering Occupational Information, Goal Selection, Planning, and Problem-Solving. Responses are made on a 5-point scale ranging from 1 (*no confidence at all*) to 5 (*complete confidence*).

Reliability: Internal consistency reliabilities ranged from .73 to .94.

Validity: Correlations with other variables ranged from .35 to .59.

Author: Paulsen, A. M., and Betz, N. E.

Article: Basic confidence predictors of career decision-making self-efficacy.

Journal: *The Career Development Quarterly,* June 2004, *52,* 354–362.

Related Research: Betz, N. E., et al. (1996). Evaluation of a short form of the Career Decision-Making Self-Efficacy Scale. *Journal of Career Assessment, 4,* 47–57.

12825

Test Name: CAREER DEVELOPMENT LOCUS OF CONTROL SCALE

Purpose: To measure career-related locus of control.

Number of Items: 18

Format: A true–false format is used.

Reliability: Test–retest reliability was .93. K-R 20 reliability ranged from .81 to .89.

Validity: Correlations with other variables ranged from −.43 to .18.

Author: Kornspan, A. S., and Etzel, E. F.

Article: The relationship of demographic and psychological variables to career maturity of junior college student-athletes.

Journal: *Journal of College Student Development,* March/April 2001, *42,* 122–132.

Related Research: Trice, A. D., et al. (1989). A career locus of control scale for undergraduate students. *Perceptual and Motor Skills, 69,* 555–561.

12826

Test Name: CAREER EXPECTATIONS SCALE

Purpose: To measure perceptions of likelihood to advance in the organization.

Number of Items: 6

Format: Responses are made on a 5-point scale ranging from 1 (*strongly disagree*) to 5 (*strongly agree*). A sample item is presented.

Reliability: Coefficient alpha was .76.

Validity: Correlations with other variables ranged from −.07 to .47.

Author: Scandura, T. A., and Williams, E. A.

Article: Mentoring and transformational leadership: The role of supervisory career mentoring.

Journal: *Journal of Vocational Behavior,* December 2004, *65,* 448–468.

Related Research: Scandura, T. A., & Schriesheim, C. A. (1991). Effects of structural characteristics of mentoring dyads on protégé outcomes. In *Proceedings of the Southern Management Association Meeting,* 206–208.

12827

Test Name: CAREER SELF-EFFICACY SCALE

Purpose: To measure confidence in accomplishing work activities successfully.

Number of Items: 10

Format: Item anchors range from 1 (*no confidence*) to 5 (*complete confidence*). Sample items are presented.

Reliability: Alpha coefficients ranged from .88 to .95.

Validity: Correlations with other variables ranged from −.17 to .63.

Author: Adachi, T.

Article: Career self-efficacy, career outcome expectations and vocational interests among Japanese university students.

Journal: *Psychological Reports,* August 2004, *95,* 89–100.

Related Research: Matsi, T., & Tsukamoto, S. (1991). Relation between career self-efficacy measures based on occupational titles and Holland codes and model environments: A methodological contribution. *Journal of Occupational Behavior, 38,* 78–91.

12828

Test Name: CAREER SELF-EFFICACY SCALE

Purpose: To assess career self-efficacy.

Number of Items: 11

Format: Responses are made on a 5-point Likert-type scale. A sample item is presented.

Reliability: Coefficient alpha was .81.

Author: Day, R., and Allen, T. D.

Article: The relationship between career motivation and self-efficacy with protégé career success.

Journal: *Journal of Vocational Behavior*, February 2004, *64*, 72–91.

Related Research: Kossek, E. E., et al. (1998). Career self-management: A quasi-experimental assessment of the effects of a training intervention. *Personnel Psychology*, *51*, 935–962.

12829

Test Name: CATEGORIES OF EXPERIENCE SCALE

Purpose: To measure subjective experiences of life such as time.

Number of Items: 15

Format: Seven-point scales are anchored by *completely agree* and *completely disagree*. A sample item is presented.

Reliability: Internal reliability was .78.

Author: Creed, P. A., and Machin, M. A.

Article: Access to the latent benefits of employment for unemployed and underemployed individuals.

Journal: *Psychological Reports*, June 2002, *90*, Part 2, 1208–1210.

Related Research: Evans, T. S. (1986). *Variations in activity and psychological well-being in employed young adults*. Unpublished doctoral dissertation, University of Manchester, Manchester, England.

12830

Test Name: CAUSAL ATTRIBUTION SCALE

Purpose: To measure controllability and stability attributions.

Number of Items: 6

Format: Scales range from 1 (*controllable by you or other people*) to 9 (*uncontrollable by you or other people*).

Reliability: Alpha coefficients were .59 (controllability) and .76 (stability).

Validity: Correlations with other variables ranged from −.22 to .36.

Author: Donovan, J. J., and Williams, K. J.

Article: Missing the mark: Effects of time and causal attributions on goal revision in response to goal performance discrepancies.

Journal: *Journal of Applied Psychology*, June 2003, *88*, 379–390.

Related Research: Russell, D. W. (1982). The Causal Dimension Scale: A measure of how individuals perceive causes. *Journal of Personality and Social Psychology*, *32*, 1137–1145.

12831

Test Name: CAUSAL DIMENSION SCALE II

Purpose: To measure attributions focusing on responsibility for cause.

Number of Items: 12

Format: Includes four dimensions: Locus of Causality, Stability, External Control, and Personal Control. Responses are made on a 9-point scale.

Reliability: Alpha coefficients ranged from .67 to .89.

Validity: Correlations with other variables ranged from −.39 to .62.

Author: Stepleman, L. M., et al.

Article: Helping and coping attributions: Development of the Attributions of Problem Cause and Solution Scale.

Journal: *Educational and Psychological Measurement*, June 2005, *65*, 525–542.

Related Research: McAuley, E., et al. (1992). Measuring causal attributions: The revised Causal Dimension Scale (CDSII).

Personality and Social Psychology Bulletin, 18, 566–573.

12832

Test Name: CAUSAL DIMENSION SCALE—REVISED

Purpose: To measure attributions of others' behavior as locus of control, stability, externality, and internality.

Number of Items: 8

Format: Various 9-point scales are used. All are described. Sample items are presented.

Reliability: Alpha coefficients ranged from .70 to .82.

Validity: Correlations with other variables ranged from −.51 to .50.

Author: Takaku, S.

Article: The effects of apology and perspective taking on interpersonal forgiveness: A dissonance-attribution model of interpersonal forgiveness.

Journal: *The Journal of Social Psychology*, August 2001, *141*, 494–508.

Related Research: McAuley, E., & Shaffer, S. (1993). Affective responses to externally and personally controllable attributions. *Basic and Applied Social Psychology*, *14*, 475–485.

12833

Test Name: CAUSAL UNCERTAINTY SCALE

Purpose: To measure chronic individual differences in the strength of causal certainty.

Number of Items: 14

Format: Scales range from 1 (*strongly disagree*) to 6 (*strongly agree*). A sample item is presented.

Reliability: Coefficient alpha was .76 (for the one subscale used in the study).

Author: Edwards, J. A.

Article: The interactive effects of processing preference and motivation on information processing: Causal uncertainty and the MBTI in a persuasion context.

Journal: *Journal of Research in Personality*, April 2003, *37*, 89–99.

Related Research: Weary, G., & Edwards, J. A. (1994). Individual differences in causal uncertainty. *Journal of Personality and Social Psychology*, *67*, 308–318.

12834

Test Name: CAUSES OF SUCCESS AND FAILURE SCALE

Purpose: To measure the locus of causality, stability, and controllability of causes of success and failure.

Number of Items: 17

Format: Three-point response scales are used. All items are presented.

Reliability: Alpha coefficients ranged from .77 to .87. Test–retest reliabilities ranged from .47 to .50 (one month).

Author: Faria, L.

Article: Dimensions of causality as a function of socioeconomic status in a sample of Portuguese adolescents.

Journal: *Psychological Reports*, June 2004, *94*, Part 1, 827–832.

Related Research: Russell, D. (1982). The Causal Dimension Scale: A measure of how individuals perceive causes. *Journal of Personality and Social Psychology*, *42*, 1137–1145.

12835

Test Name: CHALLENGE AND THREAT CONSTRUAL MEASURE

Purpose: To measure challenge and threat construal.

Number of Items: 10

Format: Includes two factors: challenge construal and threat construal. Responses are made on a 7-point scale ranging from 1 (*not at all true of me*) to 7 (*very true of me*). Examples are given.

Reliability: Alpha coefficients ranged from .80 to .91.

Validity: Correlations with other variables ranged from –.25 to .79

Author: McGregor, H. A., and Elliot, A. J.

Article: Achievement goals as predictors of achievement-relevant processes prior to task engagement.

Journal: *Journal of Educational Psychology*, June 2002, *94*, 381–385.

Related Research: Ptacek, J., et al. (1994). Gender differences in coping with stress: When stressor and appraisals do not differ. *Personality and Social Psychology Bulletin*, *20*, 421–430.

12836

Test Name: CHANGE EFFICACY SCALE

Purpose: To measure an individual's confidence in adapting generally to change.

Number of Items: 3

Format: A sample item is presented.

Reliability: Mean coefficient alpha was .73.

Validity: Correlations with other variables ranged from –.15 to .38.

Author: Neubert, M. J., and Cady, S. H.

Article: Program commitment: A multistudy longitudinal field investigation of its impact and antecedents.

Journal: *Personnel Psychology*, Summer 2001, *54*, 421–448.

Related Research: Noe, R. A., & Wilk, S. L. (1993). Investigation of the factors that influence employees' participation in development activities. *Journal of Applied Psychology*, *78*, 311–328.

12837

Test Name: CHARACTER EDUCATION EFFICACY BELIEF INSTRUMENT

Purpose: To measure teacher efficacy.

Number of Items: 24

Format: Includes two dimensions: Personal Teaching Efficacy and General Teaching Efficacy. Responses are made on a 5-point Likert-type scale. All items are presented.

Reliability: Alpha coefficients were .83 and .61.

Author: Milson, A. J., and Mehlig, L. M.

Article: Elementary school teachers' sense of efficacy for character education.

Journal: *Journal of Educational Research*, September/October 2002, *96*, 47–53.

Related Research: Gibson, S., & Dembo, M. H. (1984). Teacher efficacy: A construct validation. *Journal of Educational Psychology*, *76*, 569–582.

12838

Test Name: CHILDREN AND YOUTH PHYSICAL SELF-PERCEPTION PROFILE

Purpose: To assess how competent young people view themselves in a variety of physical domains.

Number of Items: 36

Format: Includes six subscales: Sport/Athletic Competence, Attractive Body Adequacy, Condition/Stamina, Strength,

Physical Self-Worth, and Global Self-Worth.

Reliability: Alpha coefficients ranged from .48 to .61

Author: Daley, A. J. and Hunter, B.

Article: Comparison of male and female junior athletes' self-perceptions and body image.

Journal: *Perceptual and Motor Skills*, December 2001, *93*, 626–630

Related Research: Fox, K. R., & Corbin, C. B. (1989). The Physical Self-Perception Profile: Development and preliminary validation. *Journal of Sport & Exercise Psychology, 11,* 408–430.

12839

Test Name: CHILDREN'S ATTRIBUTIONAL STYLE QUESTIONNAIRE

Purpose: To measure attributional style.

Number of Items: 48

Format: Forced choice format. A sample item is presented.

Reliability: Internal consistency coefficients ranged from .19 to .73.

Author: Cunningham, E. G.

Article: Psychometric properties of the Children's Attributional Style Questionnaire.

Journal: *Psychological Reports*, October 2003, *93*, 481–485.

Related Research: Seligman, M. E. P., et al. (1984). Attributional style and depressive symptoms among children. *Journal of Abnormal Psychology, 93,* 235–238.

12840

Test Name: CHILDREN'S PERCEIVED CONTROL SUBSCALES

Purpose: To assess three aspects of perceived control.

Number of Items: 12

Format: Includes three aspects of perceived control: unknown, powerful others, and internal. Examples are given.

Reliability: Alpha coefficients ranged from .64 to .66.

Validity: Correlation with other variables ranged from −.27 to .24.

Author: Wentzel, K. R.

Article: Are effective teachers like good parents? Teaching styles and student adjustment in early adolescence.

Journal: *Child Development*, January/February 2002, *73*, 287–301.

Related Research: Nicholls, J. G., et al. (1990). Students' theories about mathematics and their mathematical knowledge: Multiple dimensions of assessment. In G. Kulin (Ed.), *Assessing higher order thinking in mathematics* (pp. 137–154). Washington, DC: American Association of the Advancement of Science.

12841

Test Name: CHILDREN'S PERCEIVED OCCUPATIONAL SELF-EFFICACY

Purpose: To measure perceived occupational self-efficacy.

Number of Items: 69

Format: Includes six factors: science–technology efficacy, educational–medical efficacy, literature–art efficacy, social services–managerial efficacy, military–police efficacy, and agriculture–horticulture efficacy. Responses are made on a 6-point scale.

Reliability: Reliabilities ranged from .81 to .89.

Validity: Correlations with other variables ranged from −.26 to .57.

Author: Bandura, A., et al.

Article: Self-efficacy beliefs as shapers of children's aspirations and career trajectories.

Journal: *Child Development*, January/February 2001, *72*, 187–206.

12842

Test Name: CHILDREN'S PERCEIVED SELF-CONTROL SCALE

Purpose: To measure children's impressions of their self-control.

Number of Items: 11

Format: Two-point scales range from *usually yes* to *usually no.*

Reliability: Reliability coefficients ranged from .52 to .71.

Author: Vera, E. M., et al.

Article: Conflict resolution styles, self-efficacy, self-control, and future orientation of urban adolescents.

Journal: *Professional School Counseling*, October 2004, *8*, 73–80.

Related Research: Humphrey, L. L. (1984). Children's self-control in relation to perceived social environment. *Journal of Personality and Social Psychology, 46,* 178–188.

12843

Test Name: CHILDREN'S PERCEIVED SELF-EFFICACY SCALE

Purpose: To measure children's beliefs in their perceived self-efficacy.

Number of Items: 37

Format: Includes three domains: Perceived Academic Self-Efficacy, Perceived Social Self-Efficacy, and Perceived Self-Regulatory Efficacy.

Reliability: Estimated reliabilities ranged from .76 to .89.

Author: Bandura, A., et al.

Article: Self-efficacy beliefs as shapers of children's aspirations and career trajectories.

Journal: *Child Development,* January/February 2001, *72,* 187–206.

Related Research: Bandura, A., et al. (1996). Multifaceted impact of self-efficacy beliefs on academic functioning. *Child Development, 67,* 1206–1222.

12844

Test Name: CHILDREN'S PERCEPTION OF MOTOR COMPETENCE SCALE

Purpose: To assess perceived motor competence in young children ages 4 to 6 years old.

Number of Items: 22

Format: Includes two subscales: Perceived Gross Motor Competence and Perceived Fine Motor Competence. Examples are given.

Reliability: Alpha coefficients ranged from .65 to .81.

Validity: Correlations with other variables ranged from .03 to .31.

Author: Pérez, L. M. R., and Sanz, J. L. G.

Article: New measure of perceived motor competence for children ages 4 to 6 years.

Journal: *Perceptual and Motor Skills,* August 2005, *101,* 131–148.

12845

Test Name: CHILDREN'S PHYSICAL SELF-PERCEPTION PROFILE

Purpose: To assess perceptions of sport competence, physical conditioning, strength, body attractiveness, and general physical self-worth.

Format: Includes four subdomains: sport, condition, body, and strength.

Reliability: Alpha coefficients ranged from .75 to .82.

Validity: Correlations with other variable ranged from −.40 to .56.

Author: Raudsepp, L., and Liblik, R.

Article: Relationship of perceived and actual motor competence in children.

Journal: *Perceptual and Motor Skills,* June 2002, *94,* Part 2, 1059–1070.

Related Research: Whitehead, J. R. (1995). A study of children's physical self-perceptions using an adapted physical self-perception profile questionnaire. *Pediatric Exercise Science, 7,* 132–151.

12846

Test Name: CHILDREN'S SELF-CONTROL SCALE—ADJUSTED

Purpose: To assess child self-regulation.

Number of Items: 10

Format: Include two subscales: Self-Control and Lack of Self-Control. Responses are made on a 5-point scale. Sample items are presented.

Reliability: Alpha coefficients were .85 (self-control) and .87 (lack of self-control).

Validity: Correlations with other variables ranged from −.44 and .45.

Author: Brody, G. H., et al.

Article: Longitudinal pathways to competence and psychological adjustment among African American children living in rural single-parent households.

Journal: *Child Development,* September/October 2002, *73,* 1505–1516.

Related Research: Humphrey, L. L. (1982). Children's and teachers' perspectives on children's self-control: The development of two rating scales. *Journal of Consulting and Clinical Psychology, 50,* 624–633.

12847

Test Name: CHILDREN'S SELF-PERCEPTIONS OF COMPETENCE SCALE

Purpose: To assess children's self-perceptions of competence

Number of Items: 12 (Grades 4–6) and 8 (Grade 7)

Format: Includes four school subjects: language arts, social studies, math, and science. Responses are made a 7-point scale ranging from 1 (not at all good) to 7 (very good).

Reliability: Alpha coefficients ranged from .81 to .93

Author: Pomerantz, E. M., et al.

Article: Making the grade but feeling distressed: Gender differences in academic performance and internal distress.

Journal: *Journal of Educational Psychology,* June 2002, *94,* 396–404.

Related Research: Wigfield, A., et al. (1991). Transitions during adolescence: Changes in children's domain-specific self-perceptions and general self-esteem across the transition to junior high school. *Developmental Psychology, 27,* 552–565.

12848

Test Name: CHINESE SELF-EFFICACY SCALE

Purpose: To measure general self-efficacy.

Number of Items: 10

Format: Scales range from 1 (*not at all true*) to 4 (*exactly true*).

Reliability: Coefficient alpha was .92.

Validity: Correlations with other variables ranged from −.28 to −.14.

Author: Ho, M. Y. S., et al.

Article: Fear of severe acute respiratory syndrome (SARS) among health care workers.

Journal: *Journal of Consulting and Clinical Psychology*, April 2005, *73*, 344–349.

Related Research: Zhang, J. X., & Schwarzer, R. (1995). Measuring optimistic self-beliefs: A Chinese adaptation of the General Self-Efficacy Scale. *Psychologia: An International Journal of Psychology in the Orient*, *38*, 174–181.

12849

Test Name: CLOSE MONITORING SCALE

Purpose: To measure close monitoring.

Number of Items: 6

Format: Scales range from 1 (*strongly disagree*) to 7 (*strongly agree*). All items are presented.

Reliability: Coefficient alpha was .69.

Validity: Correlations with other variables ranged from −.34 to .29.

Author: George, J. M., and Zhou, J.

Article: When openness to experience and conscientiousness are related to creative behavior: An interactional approach.

Journal: *Journal of Applied Psychology*, June 2001, *86*, 513–524.

12850

Test Name: COACHING EFFICACY SCALE

Purpose: To assess coaching efficacy.

Number of Items: 24

Format: Includes four dimensions: Motivation, Strategy, Technique, and Character Building. Items are scored on a 10-point scale ranging from 0 (*not at all true*) to 9 (*extremely confident*). All items are presented.

Reliability: Reliabilities ranged from .93 to .98.

Author: Fung, L.

Article: Task familiarity and task efficacy: A study of sports coaches.

Journal: *Perceptual and Motor Skills*, October 2002, *95*, 367–372.

Related Research: Feltz, D., et al. (1999). A conceptual model of coaching efficacy: Preliminary investigation and instrument development. *Journal of Educational Psychology*, *91*, 675–776.

12851

Test Name: COGNITIVE ENGAGEMENT SCALES

Purpose: To measure both quality and quantity of self-regulation.

Number of Items: 9

Format: Includes two scales: Quality of Self-Regulation and Quantity of Self-Regulation. Examples are given.

Reliability: Alpha coefficients ranged from .60 to .76.

Validity: Correlations with other variables ranged from −.41 to .59.

Author: Linnenbrink, E. A.

Article: The dilemma of performance approach goals: The use of multiple goal contexts to promote students' motivation and learning.

Journal: *Journal of Educational Psychology*, May 2005, *96*, 197–213.

12852

Test Name: COLLECTIVE EFFICACY SCALE

Purpose: To measure collective efficacy.

Number of Items: 9

Format: A sample item is presented.

Reliability: Coefficient alpha was .87.

Validity: Correlations with other variables ranged from −.06 to .51.

Author: Kark, R., et al.

Article: The two faces of transformational leadership: Empowerment and dependency.

Journal: *Journal of Applied Psychology*, April 2003, *88*, 246–255.

Related Research: Guzzo, R. A., et al. (1993). Potency in groups: Articulating a construct. *British Journal of Social Psychology*, *32*, 87–106.

12853

Test Name: COLLECTIVE SELF-ESTEEM SCALE

Purpose: To measure collective self-esteem.

Number of Items: 16

Format: Includes four subscales: Membership, Private Collective, Public Collective, and Importance to Identity. Responses are made on a 7-point scale ranging from 1 (*strongly disagree*) to 7 (*strongly agree*). Sample items are given.

Reliability: Alpha coefficients ranged from .72 to .86.

Validity: Correlations with other variables ranged from −.16 to .40.

Author: Kim, B. S. K., and Omizo, M. M.

Article: Asian and European American cultural values, collective self-esteem, acculturative stress, cognitive flexibility, and general self-efficacy among Asian American college students.

Journal: *Journal of Counseling Psychology*, July 2005, *52*, 412–419.

Related Research: Luhtanen, R., & Crocker, J. (1992). A collective self-esteem scale: Self-evaluation of one's social identity. *Personality and Social Psychology Bulletin, 18*, 302–318.

12854

Test Name: COLLEGE SELF-EFFICACY INVENTORY

Purpose: To measure confidence in performing academic tasks related to college success.

Number of Items: 20

Format: Includes three factors: course self-efficacy, roommate course self-efficacy, and social efficacy. Responses are made on a 10-point scale ranging from 0 (*not at all confident*) to 9 (*very confident*). Examples are presented.

Reliability: Alpha coefficients were .88 and .93.

Validity: Correlations with other variables ranged from −.27 to .49.

Author: Torres, J. B., and Solberg, V. S.

Article: Role of self-efficacy, stress, social integration, and family support in Latino college student persistence and health.

Journal: *Journal of Vocational Behavior*, August 2001, *59*, 53–63.

Related Research: Solberg, V. S., et al. (1993). Self-Efficacy and Hispanic college students: Validation of the College Self-Efficacy Inventory. *Hispanic Journal of the Behavioral Sciences, 15*, 80–95.

12855

Test Name: COLLEGE STUDENTS' PERCEPTIONS OF EDUCATIONAL IMPACT

Purpose: To measure college students' perceptions of educational impact.

Number of Items: 6

Format: Includes three factors: intellectual ability, social ability, and civic interest. Responses are made on 5-point and 4-point scales. All items are presented.

Reliability: Alpha coefficients ranged from .62 to .72.

Author: Chang, M. J., et al.

Article: Cross-racial interaction among undergraduates: Some consequences, causes, and patterns.

Journal: *Research in Higher Education*, August 2004, *45*, 529–553.

Related Research: Astin, A. W. (1993). *What matters in college: Four critical years revisited*. San Francisco: Jossey-Bass.

12856

Test Name: COMPETENCE EXPECTANCY MEASURE

Purpose: To assess participants' competence expectancies for the class.

Number of Items: 2

Format: Responses are made on a 7-point scale ranging from 1 (*strongly disagree*) to 7 (*strongly agree*). Both items are presented.

Reliability: Coefficient alpha was .88.

Author: McGregor, H. A., and Elliot, A. J.

Article: Achievement goals as predictors of achievement-relevant processes prior to task engagement.

Journal: *Journal of Educational Psychology*, June 2002, *94*, 381–395.

Related Research: Elliot, A., & Church, M. A.(1997). A hierarchical model of approach and avoidance achievement motivation. *Journal of*

Personality and Social Psychology, 72, 218–232.

12857

Test Name: COMPREHENSIVE EFFECTS OF ALCOHOL QUESTIONNAIRE

Purpose: To assess the perceived likelihood and desirability of the positive and negative consequences of drinking.

Number of Items: 38

Format: Scales range from 1 (*disagree*) to 4 (*agree*). Sample items are presented.

Reliability: Alpha coefficients ranged from .75 to .89.

Author: Kuther, T. L., and Timoshin, A.

Article: A comparison of social cognitive and psychosocial predictors of alcohol use by college students.

Journal: *Journal of College Student Development*, March/April 2003, *44*, 143–154.

Related Research: Fromme, K., et al. (1993). Comprehensive effects of alcohol: Development and psychometric assessment of a new questionnaire. *Psychological Assessment, 5*, 19–26.

12858

Test Name: COMPREHENSIVE EFFECTS OF ALCOHOL QUESTIONNAIRE—BRIEF VERSION

Purpose: To measure perceived effects of drinking and if the effects are good or bad.

Number of Items: 15

Format: Effect scales range from 1 (*disagree*) to 5 (*agree*). Valuation scales range from 1 (*bad*) to 5 (*good*).

Reliability: Alpha coefficients ranged from .60 to .81 across subscales.

Author: Ham, L. S., et al.

Article: Psychometric assessment of the Comprehensive Effects of Alcohol Questionnaire: Comparing a brief version to the original full scale.

Journal: *Journal of Psychopathology and Behavioral Assessment,* September 2005, 27, 141–158.

Related Research: Fromme, K., et al. (1993). Comprehensive effects of alcohol: Development and psychometric assessment of a new expectancy questionnaire. *Psychological Assessment, 5,* 19–26.

12859

Test Name: COMPUTER AVERSION SCALE

Purpose: To measure perceived competence and comfort with computers.

Number of Items: 30

Format: Items responses are made on Likert-type scales.

Reliability: Alpha coefficients ranged from .77 to .87 across subscales.

Author: Compton, D. M., et al.

Article: No sex difference in perceived competence of computer use among male and female college students in 2002.

Journal: *Psychological Reports,* April 2003, *92,* 503–511.

Related Research: Meier, S. T. (1990). *Construct validity of an instrument designed to measure computer aversion.* Paper presented at the annual convention of the American Psychological Association, Boston.

12860

Test Name: COMPUTER SELF-EFFICACY SCALE

Purpose: To assess computer self-efficacy.

Number of Items: 5

Format: Sample items are given.

Reliability: Coefficient alpha was .67.

Validity: Correlations with other variables ranged from −.22 to .56.

Author: Potosky, D., and Bobko, P.

Article: Selection testing via the Internet: Practical considerations and exploratory empirical findings.

Journal: *Personnel Psychology,* Winter 2004, *57,* 1003–1034.

Related Research: Hill, T., et al. (1987). Role of efficacy expectations in predicting the decision to use advanced technologies: The case of computers. *Journal of Applied Psychology, 72,* 307–313.

12861

Test Name: CONCEPTIONS OF ABILITY AS STABLE TO EXTERNAL FORCES MEASURE

Purpose: To assess conceptions of ability as stable to external forces.

Number of Items: 32

Format: Includes two domains: Academic and Social. Five-point scales are employed.

Reliability: Internal reliability ranged from .71 to .83. Stability over time ranged from .40 to .61.

Author: Pomerantz, E. M., and Saxon, J. L.

Article: Conceptions of ability as stable and self-evaluative processes: A longitudinal examination.

Journal: *Child Development,* January/February 2001, 72, 152–173.

Related Research: Pomerantz, E. M., & Ruble, D. N. (1997). Distinguishing multiple dimensions of conceptions of ability: Implications for self-evaluation. *Child Development, 68,* 1165–1180.

12862

Test Name: CONCEPTIONS OF MATHEMATICS QUESTIONNAIRE

Purpose: To measure university students' conceptions of mathematics

Number of Items: 18

Format: Includes two scales: Fragmented Conceptions Scale and Cohesive Conceptions Scale. Responses are made on a 5-point scale ranging from 1 (*strongly disagree*) to 5 (*strongly agree*). Examples are presented.

Reliability: Alpha coefficients were .82 and .91.

Author: Alkhateeb, H. M.

Article: Correlations for scores on conceptions of mathematics and approaches to learning mathematics.

Journal: *Perceptual and Motor Skills,* December 2002, 95, Part 2, 1251–1254.

Related Research: Crawford, K., et al. (1998). University mathematics students' conceptions of mathematics. *Studies in Higher Education, 23,* 87–94.

12863

Test Name: CONSIDERATION OF FUTURE CONSEQUENCES SCALE

Purpose: To measure future time perspective.

Number of Items: 12

Format: Scales range from 1 (*extremely uncharacteristic*) to 5 (*extremely characteristic*). Sample items are presented.

Reliability: Coefficient alpha was .82.

Validity: Fit indices suggest an 8-item scale may be a better instrument.

Author: Petrocelli, J. V.

Article: Factor validation of the Consideration of Future Consequences Scale: Evidence for a short version.

Journal: *The Journal of Social Psychology*, August 2003, *143*, 405–413.

Related Research: Strathman, A., et al. (1994). The consideration of future consequences: Weighing immediate and distant outcomes of behavior. *Journal of Personality and Social Psychology, 66*, 742–752.

12864

Test Name: CONTROLLABILITY SCALE

Purpose: To measure perceived control of a situation.

Number of Items: 6

Format: Scales range from 1 (*not at all*) to 5 (*very much*). All items are presented.

Reliability: Intra-item reliability was .88. Test–retest reliability was .79.

Author: Puente-Diaz, R., and Anshel, M. H.

Article: Sources of acute stress, cognitive appraisal, and coping strategies among highly skilled Mexican and U.S. competitive tennis players.

Journal: *The Journal of Social Psychology*, August 2005, *145*, 429–446.

Related Research: Terry, D. J. (1991). Coping resources and situational appraisals as predictors of coping behavior. *Journal of Personality and Individual Differences, 12*, 1031–1047.

12865

Test Name: COPING EFFICACY SCALE

Purpose: To assess barrier-coping efficacy.

Number of Items: 18

Format: Responses are made on a 10-point scale ranging from 0 (*no confidence*) to 9 (*complete confidence*).

Reliability: Coefficient alpha was .94.

Validity: Correlations with other variables ranged from –.42 to .63.

Author: Lent, R. W., et al.

Article: The role of contextual supports and barriers in the choice of math/science educational options: A test of social cognitive hypotheses.

Journal: *Journal of Counseling Psychology*, October 2001, *48*, 474–483.

12866

Test Name: CORE SELF-EVALUATIONS SCALE

Purpose: To assess core traits of self-esteem, generalized self-efficacy, emotional stability, and locus of control.

Number of Items: 12

Format: Scales range from 1 (*strongly disagree*) to 5 (*strongly agree*).

Reliability: Coefficient alpha was .86.

Author: Wanberg, C. R., et al.

Article: Job-search persistence during unemployment: A 10-wave longitudinal study.

Journal: *Journal of Applied Psychology*, May 2005, *90*, 411–430.

Related Research: Judge, T. A., et al. (2003). The Core Self-Evaluation Scale: Development of a measure. *Personnel Psychology, 56*, 303–331.

12867

Test Name: COUNSELING ROLE OUTCOME EXPECTATIONS SCALE

Purpose: To measure outcome expectations.

Number of Items: 12

Format: Responses are made on a 5-point scale ranging from 1 (*strongly disagree*) to 5 (*strongly agree*). Examples are provided.

Reliability: Coefficient alpha was .90.

Author: Lent, R. W., et al.

Article: Development and validation of the Counselor Activity Self-Efficacy Scales.

Journal: *Journal of Counseling Psychology*, January 2003, *50*, 97–108.

Related Research: Larson, L. M., & Daniels, J. A. (1998). Review of the counseling self-efficacy literature. *The Counseling Psychologist, 26*, 179–218.

12868

Test Name: COUNSELING SELF-ESTIMATE INVENTORY

Purpose: To measure counseling self-efficacy.

Number of Items: 37

Format: Includes five skill domains: Microskills, Counseling Process, Difficult Client Behaviors, Cultural Competence, and Awareness of Values. Responses are made on a 6-point scale ranging from 1 (*strongly disagree*) to 6 (*strongly agree*). An example is presented.

Reliability: Alpha coefficients ranged from .45 to .93. Test–retest (3 weeks) correlations ranged from .68 to .87.

Author: Lent, R. W., et al.

Article: Development and validation of the Counselor Activity Self-Efficacy Scales.

Journal: *Journal of Counseling Psychology*, January 2003, *50*, 97–108.

Related Research: Larson, L. M., et al. (1992). Development and validation of the Counseling Self-Estimate Inventory. *Journal of Counseling Psychology, 39,* 105–120.

12869

Test Name: COUNSELING SELF-ESTIMATE INVENTORY

Purpose: To measure one's self-efficacy estimates for counseling activities.

Number of Items: 37

Format: Includes five factors: microskills, process, difficult client behaviors, cultural competence, and awareness of values. Responses are made on a 6-point Likert scale ranging from 1 (*strongly disagree*) to 6 (*strongly agree*). Examples are presented.

Reliability: Internal consistencies ranged from .62 to .94. Test–retest (3 weeks) reliability ranged from .68 to .83.

Validity: Correlations with other variables ranged from .08 to .66.

Author: Dillon, F. R., and Worthington, R. L.

Article: The Lesbian, Gay, and Bisexual Affirmative Counseling Self-Efficacy Inventory (LGB-CSI): Development, validation, and training implications.

Journal: *Journal of Counseling Psychology,* April 2003, *50,* 235–251.

Related Research: Larson, L. M., et al. (1992). Development and validation of the Counseling Self-Estimate Inventory. *Journal of Counseling Psychology, 1,* 105–120.

12870

Test Name: CREDIBILITY MEASURE

Purpose: To measure credibility.

Number of Items: 6

Format: Responses are made on a 5-point scale ranging from 1 (*strongly disagree*) to 5 (*strongly agree*). All items are presented.

Reliability: Coefficient alpha was .84 ($N = 989$).

Validity: Correlations with other variables ranged from .02 to .42 ($N = 989$).

Author: Allen, D. G, et al.

Article: Recruitment communication media: Impact on prehire outcomes.

Journal: *Personnel Psychology,* Spring 2004, *57,* 143–171.

Related Research: McCroskey, J. C., & Young, T. J. (1981). Ethos and credibility: The construct and its measurement after decades. *Central States Speech Journal, 32,* 24–34.

12871

Test Name: CREDIBILITY OF TREATMENT QUESTIONNAIRE

Purpose: To assess how credible treatment appears to be and how successful a patient expects it to be.

Number of Items: 4

Format: Six-point scales are used.

Reliability: Alpha coefficients ranged from .87 to .97. Test–retest reliability was .68.

Author: Barrowclough, C., et al.

Article: A randomized trial of the effectiveness of cognitive–behavioral therapy and supportive counseling for anxiety symptoms in older adults.

Journal: *Journal of Consulting and Clinical Psychology,* October 2001, *69,* 756–762.

Related Research: Tarrier, N., et al. (1999). A randomized trial of cognitive therapy and imaginal exposure in the treatment of chronic posttraumatic stress disorder. *Journal of Consulting and Clinical Psychology, 67,* 13–18.

12872

Test Name: DEVELOPMENT SKILLS SELF-EFFICACY

Purpose: To measure relative and absolute self-efficacy related to employee development activity.

Number of Items: 20

Format: Scales range from 1 (*worse than most*) to 5 (*better than most*). A sample item is presented.

Reliability: Alpha coefficients were .88 (absolute) and .93 (relative).

Validity: Correlations with other variables ranged from −.22 to .58.

Author: Maurer, T. J., et al.

Article: A model of involvement in work-related learning and development activity: The effects of individual, situational, motivational, and age variables.

Journal: *Journal of Applied Psychology,* August 2003, *88,* 707–724.

Related Research: Fletcher, W., et al. (1992). Assessing occupational self-efficacy among middle-aged and older adults. *Journal of Applied Gerontology, 11,* 489–501.

12873

Test Name: DIMINISHED SENSE OF SELF-EXISTENCE SCALE

Purpose: To assess diminished sense of self-existence in terms of self, others, and time.

Number of Items: 38

Format: Items are anchored by 1 (*strongly disagree*) and 5 (*strongly agree*).

Reliability: Alpha coefficients ranged from .85 to .87 across subscales.

Validity: Correlations with other variables ranged from −.44 to .39.

Author: Yukawa, S.

Article: Diminished sense of self-existence and self-reported aggression among Japanese students.

Journal: *Psychological Reports*, April 2002, *90*, 634–638.

12874

Test Name: DISCLOSURE EXPECTATIONS SCALE

Purpose: To assess participants' expectations about the utility and the risks associated with talking about an emotional problem with a counselor.

Number of Items: 8

Format: Includes two subscales: Anticipated Utility and Anticipated Risk. Responses are made on a 5-point scale ranging from 1 (*not at all*) to 5 (*very*). Examples are given.

Reliability: Internal consistencies ranged from .74 to .83.

Validity: Correlations with other variables ranged from −.25 to .57.

Author: Vogel, D. L., et al.

Article: The role of outcome expectations and attitudes on decisions to seek professional help.

Journal: *Journal of Counseling Psychology*, October 2005, *52*, 459–470.

Related Research: Vogel, D. L., & Wester, S. R. (2003). To seek or not to seek help: The risks of self-disclosure. *Journal of Counseling Psychology, 50*, 351–361.

12875

Test Name: EATING SELF-EFFICACY SCALE

Purpose: To measure two hypothetical dimensions of self-efficacy in situations related to eating management.

Number of Items: 25

Format: Includes two dimensions: Negative Affect and Socially Acceptable Circumstances. Responses are made a 7-point scale ranging from 1 (*no difficulty controlling eating*) to 7 (*the greatest difficulty in controlling eating*).

Validity: Correlations with the Weight Efficacy Lifestyle Questionnaire ranged from −.30 to −.77.

Author: Ruiz, V. M., et al.

Article: Factor analysis of the Spanish version of the Weight Efficacy Lifestyle Questionnaire.

Journal: *Educational and Psychological Measurement*, June 2002, *62*, 539–555.

Related Research: Glynn, S. M., & Ruderman, A. J. (1986). The development and validation of an Eating Self-Efficacy Scale. *Cognitive Therapy and Research, 10*, 403–420.

12876

Test Name: ECOSCALE

Purpose: To measure ecological (environmental) awareness.

Number of Items: 22

Format: Item responses are anchored by 1 (*strongly disagree or never*) and 5 (*strongly agree or always*).

Reliability: Alpha coefficients ranged from .78 to .93.

Author: Clump, M., et al.

Article: Differences in Schwartz's value survey between high and low scores on the ECOSCALE.

Journal: *Psychological Reports*, June 2002, *90*, Part 2, 1174–1178.

Related Research: Stone, G., et al. (1995). ECOSCALE: A scale for environmentally responsible consumers. *Psychology & Marketing, 12*, 595–612.

12877

Test Name: EDUCATIONAL AND VOCATIONAL DEVELOPMENT SCALES

Purpose: To measure career planning and exploration self-efficacy, knowledge of self and others, and educational and vocational development self-efficacy.

Number of Items: 62

Format: Scales range from 1 (*low efficacy*) to 7 (*high efficacy*).

Reliability: Alpha coefficients ranged from .79 to .96 across subscales.

Author: Alliman-Brissett, A. E., et al.

Article: Parent support and African American adolescents' career self-efficacy.

Journal: *Professional School Counseling*, February 2004, *7*, 124–132.

Related Research: Gysbers, N. C., et al. (1992). *Missouri Comprehensive Guidance Survey*. Jefferson City: Missouri Department of Elementary and Secondary Education.

12878

Test Name: EFFICACY BELIEFS SCALES

Purpose: To measure self-efficacy and collective efficacy.

Number of Items: 8

Format: Scales range from 1 (*strongly disagree*) to 5 (*strongly agree*). Sample items are presented.

Reliability: Alpha coefficients were .70 (self-efficacy) and .81 (collective efficacy).

Validity: Correlations with other variables ranged from −.27 to .65.

Author: Chen, G., and Bliese, P. D.

Article: The role of different levels of leadership in predicting self- and collective efficacy: Evidence for discontinuity.

Journal: *Journal of Applied Psychology*, June 2002, *87*, 549–556.

Related Research: Jex, S. M., & Bliese, P. D. (1999). Efficacy beliefs as a moderator of the impact of work-related stressors: A multilevel study. *Journal of Applied Psychology, 84*, 349–361.

12879

Test Name: EMPLOYMENT OPPORTUNITY INDEX

Purpose: To measure job market perceptions as ease of movement, desirability of movement, networking, crystallization of alternatives, and mobility.

Number of Items: 14

Format: Scales range from 1 (*strongly disagree*) to 5 (*strongly agree*). All items are presented.

Reliability: Alpha coefficients ranged from .66 to .85 across subscales.

Validity: Correlations between subscales ranged from –.03 to .44. Correlations with other variables ranged from –.38 to .59.

Author: Griffeth, R. W., et al.

Article: The development of a multidimensional measure of job market cognitions: The Employment Opportunity Index (EOI).

Journal: *Journal of Applied Psychology*, March 2005, *90*, 335–349.

12880

Test Name: ENGINEERING OUTCOME EXPECTATIONS MEASURE

Purpose: To identify positive outcomes resulting from earning a bachelor's degree in engineering.

Number of Items: 10

Format: Responses are made on a 10-point scale ranging from 0 (*strongly disagree*) to 9 (*strongly agree*). Examples are given.

Reliability: Alpha coefficients were .89 and .91.

Validity: Correlations with other variables ranged from –.15 to .48 ($n = 472$).

Author: Lent, R. W., et al.

Article: Social cognitive predictors of academic interests and goals in engineering: Utility for women and students at historically Black universities.

Journal: *Journal of Counseling Psychology*, January 2005, *52*, 84–92.

Related Research: Lent, R. W., et al. (2003). Relation of contextual supports and barriers to choice behavior in engineering majors: Test of alternative social cognitive models. *Journal of Counseling Psychology, 50*, 458–465.

12881

Test Name: ENTREPRENEURIAL SELF-EFFICACY SCALE

Purpose: To measure self-efficacy expectations in identifying entrepreneurial opportunities.

Number of Items: 4

Format: Scales range from 1 (*no confidence*) to 5 (*complete confidence*).

Reliability: Coefficient alpha was .78.

Validity: Correlations with other variables ranged from –.06 to .44.

Author: Zhao, H., et al.

Article: The mediating role of self-efficacy in the development of entrepreneurial intentions.

Journal: *Journal of Applied Psychology*, November 2005, *90*, 1265–1272.

12882

Test Name: ENVIRONMENTAL MASTERY SCALE

Purpose: To measure a sense of perceived control in one's life and one's environment.

Number of Items: 20

Format: Responses are made on a 6-point Likert-type scale ranging from 1 (*strongly agree*) to 6 (*strongly disagree*).

Reliability: Alpha coefficients were .85 and .90. Test–retest (6 weeks) reliability was .81.

Validity: Correlations with other variables ranged from –.55 to .69.

Author: Moradi, B., and Hasan, N. T.

Article: Arab American persons' reported experiences of discrimination and mental health: The mediating role of personal control.

Journal: *Journal of Counseling Psychology*, October 2004, *51*, 418–428.

Related Research: Ryff, C. D. (1989). Happiness is everything, or is it? Explorations on the meaning of psychological well-being. *Journal of Personality and Social Psychology, 57*, 1069–1081.

12883

Test Name: EVENT PROBABILITY QUESTIONNAIRE

Purpose: To assess judgment of risk.

Number of Items: 25

Format: Nine-point Likert scales range from 0 (*not at all likely*) to 8 (*extremely likely*).

Validity: Correlations with other variables ranged from .16 to .32.

Author: Nortje, C., et al.

Article: Judgment of risk in traumatized and nontraumatized emergency medical service personnel.

Journal: *Psychological Reports*, December 2004, *95*, Part 2, 1119–1128.

Related Research: Butler, G., & Mathews, A. (1987). Anticipatory anxiety and risk perception. *Therapy and Research*, *11*, 551–565.

12884

Test Name: EXERCISE SELF-EFFICACY SCALE FOR CHILDREN

Purpose: To assess exercise self-efficacy.

Number of Items: 10

Format: Responses are made on a 5-point scale ranging from 1 (*not at all confident*) to 5 (*definitely confident*).

Reliability: Internal consistency was .81 to .85. Test–retest (1 week) reliability was .79.

Author: Annesi, J. J.

Article: Relationship between self-efficacy and changes in rated tension and depression for 9- to 12-year-old children enrolled in a 12-week after-school physical activity program.

Journal: *Perceptual and Motor Skills*, August 2004, *99*, 191–194.

Related Research: Annesi, J. J., et al. (2004). *Effects of a physical activity program delivered by YMCA after-school counselors (Youth Fit for Life) on physiological and psychological changes in 5- to 12-year-old boys and girls.* Unpublished manuscript, YMCA of Metropolitan Atlanta, GA.

12885

Test Name: EXPANDED ATTRIBUTION STYLE QUESTIONNAIRE

Purpose: To measure negative attributional style.

Number of Items: 24

Format: Responses are made on a 7-point Likert-type scale.

Reliability: Alpha coefficients ranged from .74 to .87.

Validity: Correlations with other variables ranged from –.21 to .51.

Author: Chang, E. C., and Sanna, L. J.

Article: Negative attributional style as a moderator of the link between perfectionism and depressive symptoms: Preliminary evidence for an integrative model.

Journal: *Journal of Counseling Psychology*, October 2001, *48*, 490–495.

Related Research: Peterson, C., & Villanova, P. (1988). An expanded Attributional Style Questionnaire. *Journal of Abnormal Psychology*, *97*, 87–89.

12886

Test Name: EXPANDED SKILLS CONFIDENCE INVENTORY

Purpose: To measure self-efficacy or confidence.

Number of Items: 60

Format: Includes six scales: Mathematics, Science, Writing, Using Technology, Leadership, and Cultural Sensitivity. Responses are made on a 5-point scale ranging from 1 (*no confidence*) to 5 (*complete confidence*). Examples are given.

Reliability: Alpha coefficients ranged from .80 to .94.

Validity: Correlations with the Career Decision Self-Efficacy Scale—Short Form ranged from .35 to .59.

Author: Paulsen, A. M., and Betz, N. E.

Article: Basic confidence predictors of career decision-making self-efficacy.

Journal: *The Career Development Quarterly*, June 2004, *52*, 354–362.

Related Research: Betz, N. E., et al. (2003). The Expanded Skills Confidence Inventory: Measuring basic domains of vocational activity. *Journal of Vocational Behavior*, *67*, 76–100.

12887

Test Name: EXPECTANCY OF SUCCESS SCALE

Purpose: To assess student expectations of their success with future challenges in mathematics.

Number of Items: 5

Format: Responses are made on a 6-point Likert-type scale ranging from 1 (*absolutely disagree*) to 6 (*agree completely*). All items are presented.

Reliability: Coefficient alpha was .71.

Author: Dresel, M., et al.

Article: Nothing more than dimensions? Evidence for a surplus meaning of specific attributions.

Journal: *Journal of Educational Research*, September/October 2005, *99*, 31–44.

Related Research: Pintrich, P. (2000). An achievement goal theory perspective on issues in motivation terminology, theory, and research. *Contemporary Educational Psychology*, *25*, 92–104.

12888

Test Name: EXPECTATIONS ABOUT COUNSELING—BRIEF FORM

Purpose: To measure expectations about counseling.

Number of Items: 53

Format: Includes four general areas: client attitudes and behaviors, counselor attitudes and behaviors, counselor characteristics, and counseling process and outcomes. Responses are made on a 7-point scale ranging from *not true* to *definitely true.*

Reliability: Alpha coefficients ranged form .69 to .82. Test–retest (2 months) reliability ranged from .47 to .87.

Validity: Correlations with other variables ranged from −.04 to .33.

Author: Rose, E. M., et al.

Article: Spiritual issues in counseling: Clients' beliefs and preferences.

Journal: *Journal of Counseling Psychology,* January 2001, *48,* 61–71.

Related Research: Tinsley, H. E. A., et al. (1980). Factor analysis of the domain of client expectancies about counseling. *Journal of Counseling Psychology,* 27, 561–570.

12889

Test Name: EXPECTATIONS ABOUT COUNSELING—BRIEF FORM

Purpose: To measure expectations about counseling as personal commitment, facilitative conditions, counselor experience, and nurturance.

Number of Items: 66

Format: Scales range from 1 (*not true*) to 7 (*definitely true*).

Reliability: Alpha coefficients ranged from .72 to .97.

Author: Watson, J. C.

Article: College student-athletes' attitudes toward help-seeking behavior and expectations of counseling services.

Journal: *Journal of College Student Development,* July/August 2005, *46,* 442–449.

Related Research: Tinsley, H., et al. (1980). Factor analysis of the domain of client expectations about counseling. *Journal of Counseling Psychology,* 27, 561–570.

12890

Test Name: EXPECTATIONS FOR COUNSELING SUCCESS MEASURE

Purpose: To measure client expectation for counseling success.

Number of Items: 5

Format: Responses are made on a 4-point scale ranging from 1 (*strongly disagree*) to 4 (*strongly agree*). All items are presented.

Reliability: Coefficient alpha was .84.

Validity: Correlations with other variables ranged from −.08 to .20.

Author: Kim, B. S. K., et al.

Article: Effects of client expectation for counseling success, client–counselor worldview match, and client adherence to Asian and European American cultural values on counseling process with Asian Americans.

Journal: *Journal of Counseling Psychology,* January 2005, *52,* 67–76.

12891

Test Name: EXPERIENCE QUESTIONNAIRE

Purpose: To measure sense of presence and flow during an experience.

Number of Items: 10

Format: Four-point scales are anchored by 1 (*not true of my experience*) and 4 (*very true of my experience*). Sample items are presented.

Reliability: Alpha coefficients ranged from .47 to .76.

Validity: Correlations between scales ranged from −.02 to .67.

Author: Fontaine, G.

Article: A sense of presence and self-reported performance in international teams.

Journal: *Psychological Reports,* August 2004, *95,* 154–158.

12892

Test Name: FEMINIST IDENTITY SCALE

Purpose: To assess stage of feminist identity development a woman has reached in terms of passive acceptance, revelation, embeddedness–emanation, and synthesis.

Number of Items: 37

Format: Item responses are anchored by 1 (*strongly disagree*) and 5 (*strongly agree*).

Reliability: Alpha coefficients ranged from .55 to .72. Test–retest reliabilities ranged from .61 to .79 over four months.

Validity: Correlations with other variables ranged from −.21 to 41.

Author: Witte, T. H., and Sherman, M. F.

Article: Silencing the self and feminist identity development.

Journal: *Psychological Reports,* June 2002, *90,* Part 2, 1075–1083.

Related Research: Rickard, K. M. (1989). The relationship of self-monitored dating behaviors to the level of feminist identity on the Feminist Identity Scale. *Sex Roles,* 20, 213–226.

12893

Test Name: FINANCIAL NEEDS SCALE

Purpose: To measure how dependent a subject is on his/her personal income.

Number of Items: 7

Format: Scales range from 1 (*strongly disagree*) to 5 (*strongly agree*). A sample item is presented.

Reliability: Coefficient alpha was .84.

Validity: Correlations with other variables ranged from –.11 to .23.

Author: Major, V. S., et al.

Article: Work time, work interference with family, and psychological distress.

Journal: *Journal of Applied Psychology*, June 2002, 87, 427–436.

12894

Test Name: FUNCTIONAL AND DYSFUNCTIONAL SELF-CONSCIOUSNESS SCALES

Purpose: To measure functional and dysfunctional aspects of self-consciousness.

Number of Items: 4

Format: All items are presented.

Reliability: Alpha coefficients ranged from .60 to .67.

Validity: Correlations with other variables ranged from .09 to .46.

Author: Schneider, J. F.

Article: Relations among self-talk, self-consciousness, and self-knowledge.

Journal: *Psychological Reports*, December 2002, 91, Part 1, 807–812.

Related Research: Hoyer, J. (2000). Der Fragebogen zur Dysfunktionalen Selbstaufmerksamkeit (DFS): Theoretisches Konzept und Befunde zur Reliabilität und Validität [Questionnaire of Dysfunctional and Functional Self-Consciousness (DFS):

Theoretical concept, reliability and validity]. *Diagnostica, 46,* 140–148.

12895

Test Name: FUNCTIONAL SELF-KNOWLEDGE SCALE—GERMAN VERSION

Purpose: To measure functional self-knowledge.

Number of Items: 15

Format: Scales range from 1 (*completely false*) to 6 (*completely true*). Sample items are presented in English.

Reliability: Coefficient alpha was .88.

Validity: Correlations with other variables ranged from –.32 to .56.

Author: Schneider, J. F., et al.

Article: Does self-consciousness mediate the relation between self-talk and self-knowledge?

Journal: *Psychological Reports*, April 2005, 96, 387–396.

Related Research: Westbrook, B. W., et al. (1985). Predictive and construct validity of six experimental measures of career maturity. *Journal of Vocational Behavior, 27,* 338–355.

12896

Test Name: FUTURE CAREER RATING SCALES

Purpose: To assess an employee's perception of his/her career future.

Number of Items: 5

Format: Five-point scales are used.

Reliability: Coefficient alpha was .82.

Author: Shore, L. M., et al.

Article: Work attitudes and decisions as a function of manager age and employee age.

Journal: *Journal of Applied Psychology*, June 2003, 88, 529–537.

Related Research: Smith, F. J. (1976). Index of Organizational Reactions (IOR). *JSAS Catalog of Selected Documents in Psychology, 6,* 54.

12897

Test Name: FUTURE CONSEQUENCES SCALE

Purpose: To measure the tendency to take into account future consequences of one's behavior.

Number of Items: 12

Format: Scales range from 1 (*extremely uncharacteristic*) to 7 (*extremely characteristic*).

Reliability: Coefficient alpha was .84.

Validity: Correlations with other variables ranged from –.26 to .29.

Author: Peters, B. R., et al.

Article: Individual differences in the Consideration of Future Consequences Scale correlate with sleep habits, sleep quality, and GPA in university students.

Journal: *Psychological Reports*, June 2005, 96, Part 1, 817–824.

Related Research: Strathman, A., et al. (1994). The consideration of future consequences: Weighing immediate and distant outcomes of behavior. *Journal of Personality and Social Psychology, 66,* 742–752.

12898

Test Name: GAY AND LESBIAN RECOGNITION INDEX

Purpose: To measure the ability of gays and lesbians to recognize other gay men and lesbians in predominately heterosexual settings.

Number of Items: 2

Format: All items are presented with their 5-point response scales.

Reliability: Alpha was .85.

Author: Carroll, L., and Gilroy, P. J.

Article: Role of appearance and nonverbal behaviors in the perception of sexual orientation among lesbians and gay men.

Journal: *Psychological Reports,* August 2002, *91,* 115–122.

Related Research: Albright, L., et al. (1988). Consensus in personality judgments at zero acquaintance. *Journal of Personality and Social Psychology,* 55, 387–395.

12899

Test Name: GENDER DISCRIMINATION SCALE

Purpose: To measure gender discrimination.

Number of Items: 3

Format: Responses are made on a 4-point scale ranging from 1 (*strongly disagree*) to 4 (*strongly disagree*). A sample item is presented.

Reliability: Reliability estimate was .84.

Validity: Correlations with other variables ranged from −.21 to .25.

Author: Blau, G., et al.

Article: Correlates of professional versus organizational withdrawal cognitions.

Journal: *Journal of Vocational Behavior,* August 2003, *63,* 72–95.

Related Research: Blau, G., & Tatum, D. (2000). Correlates of perceived gender discrimination for female versus male medical technologists. *Sex Roles, 43,* 105–118.

12900

Test Name: GENERAL CAUSALITY ORIENTATIONS SCALE

Purpose: To measure three causality orientations: autonomy, control and amotivated.

Number of Items: 12

Format: Vignettes are followed by three responses that subjects rate from 1 (*not at all likely*) to 5 (*extremely likely*). A sample item is presented.

Reliability: Alpha coefficients ranged from .60 to .77 across subscales.

Validity: Correlations with other variables ranged from −.34 to .46.

Author: Lee, F. K., et al.

Article: Personality and the goal-striving process: The influence of achievement goal patterns, goal level, and mental focus on performance and enjoyment.

Journal: *Journal of Applied Psychology,* April 2003, *88,* 256–265.

Related Research: Deci, E. L., & Ryan, R. M. (1985). The General Causality Orientation Scale: Self-determination in personality. *Journal of Research in Personality, 19,* 109–134.

12901

Test Name: GENERAL CAUSALITY ORIENTATIONS SCALE—REVISED

Purpose: To assess self-determination.

Number of Items: 17

Format: Scenarios are rated by scales ranging from 1 (*very unlikely*) to 7 (*very likely*). A sample item is presented.

Reliability: Alpha coefficients ranged from .80 to .86.

Author: Lewis, M. A., and Neighbors, C.

Article: Self-determination and the use of self-presentation strategies.

Journal: *The Journal of Social Psychology,* August 2005, *145,* 469–489.

Related Research: Hodgins, H. S., et al. (1996). On the compatability of autonomy and relatedness. *Personality and Social Psychology Bulletin, 22,* 227–237.

12902

Test Name: GENERAL SELF-EFFICACY SCALE

Purpose: To measure the belief that one can deal with stressful life events.

Number of Items: 10

Format: Items are anchored by 1 (*not at all true of me*) and 4 (*exactly true of me*).

Reliability: Internal consistency measures ranged from .75 to .90.

Validity: Correlations with other variables ranged from −.35 to .59.

Author: Sachs, J.

Article: Psychometric properties of the Proactive Attitude Scale in students at the University of Hong Kong.

Journal: *Psychological Reports,* December 2003, *93,* Part 1, 805–815.

Related Research: Jerusalem, M., & Schwarzer, R. (1992). Self-efficacy as a resource factor in stress appraisal processes. In R. Schwarzer (Ed.), *Self-efficacy: Thought control of action* (pp. 195–213). Washington, DC: Hemisphere Publication Services.

12903

Test Name: GENERAL SELF-EFFICACY SUBSCALE

Purpose: To measure general self-efficacy.

Number of Items: 17

Format: Responses are made on a 5-point scale ranging from

1 (*strongly disagree*) to 5 (*strongly agree*). A sample item is given.

Reliability: Alpha coefficients ranged from .84 to .88.

Validity: Correlations with other variables ranged from .01 to .55.

Author: Kim, B. S. K., and Omizo, M. M.

Article: Asian and European American cultural values, collective self-esteem, acculturative stress, cognitive flexibility, and general self-efficacy among Asian American college students.

Journal: *Journal of Counseling Psychology*, July 2005, *52*, 412–419.

Related Research: Sherer, M., & Adams, C. H. (1983). Construct validation of the Self-Efficacy Scale. *Psychological Reports*, *53*, 899–902.

12904

Test Name: GENERALIZED SELF-EFFICACY SCALE

Purpose: To measure generalized self-efficacy.

Number of Items: 7

Format: Scales range from 1 (*strongly disagree*) to 5 (*strongly agree*). Sample items are presented.

Reliability: Reported reliability was .85.

Validity: Correlations with other variables ranged from −.49 to .73.

Author: Judge, T. A., et al.

Article: Core self-evaluations and job and life satisfaction: The role of self-concordance and goal attainment.

Journal: *Journal of Applied Psychology*, March 2005, *90*, 257–268.

12905

Test Name: GLOBAL RISK TAKING SCALE

Purpose: To assess global risk taking.

Number of Items: 5

Format: Scales range from 1 (*strongly disagree*) to 5 (*strongly agree*). All items are presented.

Reliability: Coefficient alpha was .74.

Validity: Correlations with other variables ranged from −.19 to .33.

Author: Westaby, J. D., and Lowe, K.

Article: Risk-taking orientation and injury among youth workers: Examining the social influence of supervisors, coworkers, and parents.

Journal: *Journal of Applied Psychology*, September 2005, *90*, 1027–1035.

12906

Test Name: GLOBAL SELF-WORTH SCALE—ABBREVIATED

Purpose: To assess children's perceptions of global self-worth.

Number of Items: 5

Format: Children are asked which of two types they are more like and then they indicate if the description is *sort of true* or *really true* of them.

Reliability: Alpha coefficients ranged from .80 to .84.

Author: Pomerantz, E. M., et al.

Article: Making the grade but feeling distressed: Gender differences in academic performance and internal distress.

Journal: *Journal of Educational Psychology*, June 2002, *94*, 396–404

Related Research: Harter, S. (1982). The Perceived Competence Scale for Children. *Child Development*, *53*, 87–97.

12907

Test Name: GOAL EVALUATION AND SELF-EFFICACY SCALES

Purpose: To measure goal evaluation and goal self-efficacy.

Number of Items: 8

Format: Scales range from 0 (*not at all accurate*) to 3 (*extremely accurate*). Sample items are presented.

Reliability: Alpha coefficients ranged from .82 to .94.

Author: Affleck, G., et al.

Article: Women's pursuit of personal goals in daily life with fibromyalgia: A value–expectancy analysis.

Journal: *Journal of Consulting and Clinical Psychology*, August 2001, *69*, 587–596.

Related Research: Karoly, P., & Ruehlman, L. (1995). Goal cognition and its clinical implications: Development and preliminary validation of four motivational instruments. *Assessment*, *2*, 113–129.

12908

Test Name: GOALS PERCEPTION SCALE

Purpose: To assess perceptions of cooperative, competitive, and unrelated organizational goals.

Number of Items: 14

Format: Scales range from 1 (*strongly disagree*) to 5 (*strongly agree*). All items are presented.

Reliability: Alpha coefficients ranged from .67 to .82.

Validity: Correlations with other variables ranged from −.43 to .50.

Author: Wong, A., et al.

Article: Organizational partnerships in China: Self-interest, goal interdependence, and opportunism.

Journal: *Journal of Applied Psychology*, July 2005, *90*, 782–791.

12909

Test Name: GORDON TEST OF VISUAL IMAGERY CONTROL— SPANISH VERSION

Purpose: To measure the ability to manipulate and control mental images.

Number of Items: 12

Format: Item anchors are 0 (*no*) and 2 (*yes*). All items are presented in Spanish.

Reliability: Coefficient alpha was .69.

Validity: Correlations with other variables ranged from −.40 to .05.

Author: Pérez-Fabello, M. J., and Campos, A.

Article: Factor structure and internal consistency of the Spanish version of the Gordon Test of Visual Imagery Control.

Journal: *Psychological Reports*, June 2004, *94*, Part 1, 761–766.

Related Research: Gordon, R. (1949). An investigation into some of the factors that favour the formation of stereotyped images. *British Journal of Psychology*, *39*, 156–167.

12910

Test Name: GRIEF COGNITIONS QUESTIONNAIRE

Purpose: To assess grief cognitions.

Number of Items: 38

Format: Scales range from 0 (*disagree strongly*) to 5 (*agree strongly*). All items are presented.

Reliability: Alpha coefficients ranged from .81 to .95 across subscales. Total alpha was .96.

Validity: Correlations of total score with other variables ranged from −.64 to .80.

Author: Boelen, P. A., and Lensvelt-Mulders, J. L. M.

Article: Psychometric properties of the Grief Cognitions Questionnaire (GCQ).

Journal: *Journal of Psychopathology and Behavioral Assessment*, December 2005, *27*, 291–303.

12911

Test Name: HARVEY IMPOSTER PHENOMENON SCALE

Purpose: To measure a unidimensional construct of excessive, subjective feelings of phoniness.

Number of Items: 14

Format: Responses are made on a 7-point Likert-type scale. All items are presented.

Reliability: Coefficient alpha was .70.

Author: Hellman, C. M., and Caselman, T. D.

Article: A psychometric evaluation of the Harvey Imposter Phenomenon Scale.

Journal: *Journal of Personality Assessment*, October 2004, *83*, 161–166.

Related Research: Harvey, J. C. (1981). *The imposter phenomenon and achievement: A failure to internalize success.* Unpublished doctoral dissertation, Temple University, Philadelphia.

12912

Test Name: HELP-SEEKING SCALES

Purpose: To measure the threat to self-esteem related to asking for help and the tendency to engage in help-seeking behavior.

Number of Items: 25

Format: Threat scales range from 1 (*strongly disagree*) to 4 (*strongly agree*). Behavior scales range from

0 (*not at all likely*) to 6 (*definitely*). Sample items are presented.

Reliability: Alpha coefficients ranged from .74 to .80.

Validity: Correlations with other variables ranged from −.25 to .38.

Author: Alexitch, L. R.

Article: The role of help-seeking attitudes and tendencies in students' preferences for academic advising.

Journal: *Journal of College Student Development*, January/February 2002, *43*, 5–19.

Related Research: Karabenick, S. A., & Knapp, J. R. (1991). Relationship of academic help-seeking to the use of learning strategies and other instrumental achievement behavior in college students. *Journal of Educational Psychology*, *83*, 221–230.

12913

Test Name: HOPE SCALE

Purpose: To measure an individual's perception of meeting goals.

Number of Items: 8

Format: Includes two subscales: Agency and Pathways. Responses are made on a 4-point scale ranging from 1 (*definitely false*) to 4 (*definitely true*).

Reliability: Coefficient alpha was .68.

Validity: Correlations with other variables ranged from −.52 to .74.

Author: Steed, L. G.

Article: A psychometric comparison of four measures of hope and optimism.

Journal: *Educational and Psychological Measurement*, June 2002, *62*, 466–482

Related Research: Snyder, C. R., et al. (1991). The will and the ways: Development and validation of an individual-differences measure of hope. *Journal of Personality and Social Psychology, 60,* 570–585.

12914

Test Name: HOSTILITY TOWARD WOMEN SCALE—REVISED

Purpose: To assess perceptions of women.

Number of Items: 10

Format: Scales ranged from 1 (*strongly disagree*) to 7 (*strongly agree*). A sample item is presented.

Reliability: Alpha coefficients ranged from .81 to .86.

Author: Hall, G. C. N., et al.

Article: Ethnicity, culture, and sexual aggression: Risk and protective factors.

Journal: *Journal of Consulting and Clinical Psychology,* October 2005, 73, 830–840.

Related Research: Lonsway, K. A., & Fitzgerald, L. F. (1995). Attitudinal antecedents of rape myth acceptance: A theoretical and empirical reexamination. *Journal of Personality and Social Psychology, 68,* 704–711.

12915

Test Name: HOW IMPORTANT THESE THINGS ARE SCALE—ACADEMIC SUBSCALE—MODIFIED

Purpose: To assess adolescents' perceptions of the importance of math/science schoolwork.

Number of Items: 5

Format: Sample items are given.

Reliability: Coefficient alpha was .73.

Validity: Correlations with other variables ranged from .01 to .51.

Author: Bouchey, H. A., and Harter, S.

Article: Reflected appraisals, academic self-perceptions, and math/science performance during early adolescence.

Journal: *Journal of Educational Psychology,* November 2005, *97,* 673–686.

Related Research: Harter, S. (1988). *The Self-Perception Profile for Adolescents.* Unpublished manuscript, University of Denver, Denver, CO.

12916

Test Name: HOW IMPORTANT THINGS ARE SCALE—ADAPTED

Purpose: To assess adolescents' perceptions of significant others' beliefs regarding how important it was for them to do well in math/science.

Number of Items: 7

Format: Responses are made on a 4-point scale ranging from *very true* to *not at all true.* Examples are given.

Reliability: Alpha coefficients ranged from .72 to .84.

Validity: Correlations with other variables ranged from −.11 to .43.

Author: Bouchey, H. A., and Harter, S.

Article: Reflected appraisals, academic self-perceptions, and math/science performance during early adolescence.

Journal: *Journal of Educational Psychology,* November 2005, *97,* 673–686.

Related Research: Harter, S. (1988). *The Self-Perception Profile for Adolescents.* Unpublished manuscript, University of Denver, Denver, CO.

12917

Test Name: IDENTIFICATION WITH SCHOOL QUESTIONNAIRE

Purpose: To assess student identification.

Number of Items: 16

Format: Includes two factors: belonging and values. Responses are made on a 4-point Likert scale ranging from 1 (*strongly agree*) to 4 (*strongly disagree*).

Reliability: Alpha coefficients ranged from .78 to .84.

Validity: Correlations with other variables ranged from −.16 to .49.

Author: Wettersten, K. B., et al.

Article: Predicting educational and vocational attitudes among rural high school students.

Journal: *Journal of Counseling Psychology,* October 2005, *52,* 658–663.

Related Research: Voelkl, K. E. (1996). Measuring students' identification with school. *Educational and Psychological Measurement, 56,* 760–770.

12918

Test Name: IMAGE OF AGING SCALE

Purpose: To measure both positive and negative perceptions individuals hold of old people.

Number of Items: 18

Format: Includes two items in each of nine categories: activity, appearance, cognition, death, dependence, personality, physical health, relationships, and will to live. Responses are made on a 0 to 6 scale. All items are presented.

Reliability: Test–retest (1 week) reliabilities were .79 and .92. Alpha coefficients were .82 and .84.

Author: Levy, B., et al.

Article: Image of Aging Scale.

Journal: *Perceptual and Motor Skills,* August 2004, *99,* 208–210.

Related Research: Levy, B., & Langer, E. (1994). Aging free from negative stereotypes: Successful memory among the American deaf and in China. *Journal of Personality and Social Psychology, 66*, 935–943.

12919

Test Name: IMMIGRATION PORTRAYAL SCALE

Purpose: To assess the perceived political, social, and cultural themes people entertain about a specified immigrant group.

Number of Items: 6

Format: Various 10-point scales are and presented. Items are presented to subjects following a vignette.

Reliability: Coefficient alpha was .84.

Validity: The scale represented one factor with a eigen value of 3.36.

Author: Short, R., and Magaña, L.

Article: Political rhetoric, immigration attitudes, and contemporary prejudice: A Mexican American dilemma.

Journal: *The Journal of Social Psychology*, December 2002, *142*, 701–712.

12920

Test Name: IMPOSTOR PHENOMENON SCALE

Purpose: To measure a person's self-attribution of success in life to luck in spite of external validation to the contrary.

Number of Items: 20

Format: Item responses are anchored by 1 (*not true at all*) and 5 (*very true*).

Reliability: Alpha was .78.

Author: Sightler, K. W., and Wilson, M. G.

Article: Correlates of the impostor phenomenon among undergraduate entrepreneurs.

Journal: *Psychological Reports*, June 2001, *88*, Part 1, 679–689.

Related Research: Clance, P. R. (1985). *The impostor phenomenon: Overcoming the fear that haunts your success.* Atlanta, GA: Peachtree.

12921

Test Name: IMPRESSION RATING SCALES FOR CHRONIC DISEASE

Purpose: To measure the perceived competence, dependence, depression, moral worth, and morbidity of people with cancer, HIV/AIDS, and heart disease.

Number of Items: 17

Format: Seven-point bipolar adjective rating scales.

Reliability: Median reliabilities ranged from .45 to .71 across subscales.

Author: Hayes, R. A., et al.

Article: Stigma directed toward chronic illness is resistant to change through education and exposure.

Journal: *Psychological Reports*, June 2002, *90*, Part 2, 1161–1173.

Related Research: Katz, I., et al. (1987). Lay people's and health care personnel's perceptions of cancer, AIDS, cardiac, and diabetes patients. *Psychological Reports, 60*, 615–629.

12922

Test Name: INFERENCES ABOUT UNKNOWN ORGANIZATIONAL CHARACTERISTICS QUESTIONNAIRE

Purpose: To assess both socio-emotional inferences about the organization and task-related inferences about the organization.

Number of Items: 16

Format: Items concern relationship between employees, organization's

treatment of employees, the challenge of working in the organization, and the organization's reputation. Responses are made on a 5-point scale ranging from 1 (*strongly disagree*) to 5 (*strongly agree*). All items are presented.

Reliability: Alpha coefficients ranged from .65 to .75.

Author: Kim, S. S., and Gelfand, M. J.

Article: The influence of ethnic identity on perceptions of organizational recruitment.

Journal: *Journal of Vocational Behavior*, December 2003, *63*, 396–416.

Related Research: Barber, A. E., & Roehling, M. V. (1993). Job postings and the decision to interview: A verbal protocol analysis. *Journal of Applied Psychology, 78*, 845–856. Goltz, S. M., & Giannantonio, C. M. (1995). Recruiter friendliness and attraction to the job: The mediating role of inferences about the organization. *Journal of Vocational Behavior, 46*, 109–118. Thorsteinson, T. J., et al. (1998, April). *Specificity in job advertisements as signals of unknown organizational characteristics.* Poster presented at the 13th Annual Conference of the Society for Industrial and Organizational Psychology, Dallas, TX.

12923

Test Name: INFLUENCE OF OTHERS ON ACADEMIC AND CAREER DECISION MAKING SCALE

Purpose: To assess participants' perceptions of the amount and types of career role model influence and support from others.

Number of Items: 15

Format: Includes two areas: support/guidance and inspiration/modeling. Responses are made on a 5-point Likert-type scale ranging from 1 (*strongly disagree*) to 5 (*strongly agree*). Examples are presented.

Reliability: Alpha coefficients ranged from .85 to .94.

Author: Nauta, M. M., et al.

Article: Interpersonal influence on students' academic and career decisions: The impact of sexual orientation.

Journal: *The Career Development Quarterly*, June 2001, *49*, 352–362.

Related Research: Nauta, M. M., & Kokaly, M. L. (2001). Assessing role model influences on students' academic and vocational decisions. *Journal of Career Assessment, 9*, 81–99.

12924

Test Name: INSTRUCTIONAL STRATEGIES SCALE

Purpose: To measure teacher perceptions regarding the acceptability of instructional practices identified as related to effective teaching and successful mainstreaming.

Number of Items: 59

Format: Includes seven subscales: Individualized Differentiated Instruction, Assessment for Instruction, Behavior Management, Communication With Parents, Communication With School Professionals, Communication With Principal, and Communication With Students. Responses are made on a 5-point scale ranging from 1 (*not at all*) to 5 (*very frequently or very effective*). Examples are presented.

Reliability: Alpha coefficients ranged from .69 to .94.

Author: Wertheim, C., and Leyser, Y.

Article: Efficacy beliefs, background variables, and differentiated instruction of Israeli prospective teachers.

Journal: *Journal of Educational Research*, September/October 2002, *96*, 54–63.

Related Research: Daniels, V. I., & Vaughn, S. (1999). A tool to encourage the "best practices" in full inclusion. *Teaching Exceptional Children, 31*, 48–55.

12925

Test Name: INTERNET SELF-EFFICACY SCALE

Purpose: To assess Internet self-efficacy.

Number of Items: 8

Format: Responses are made on a 7-point scale ranging from 1 (*not at all confident*) to 7 (*totally confident*). Sample items are presented.

Reliability: Coefficient alpha was .90.

Validity: Correlations with other variables ranged from .03 to .28 ($n = 216$).

Author: Williamson, I. O., et al.

Article: The effect of company recruitment Web site orientation on individuals' perceptions of organizational attractiveness.

Journal: *Journal of Vocational Behavior*, October 2003, *63*, 242–263.

Related Research: Compeau, D. R., & Higgins, C. A. (1995). Computer self-efficacy: Development of a measure and initial test. *MIS Quarterly, 19*, 189–211.

12926

Test Name: INTERPERSONAL LOCUS OF CONTROL SCALE

Purpose: To measure locus of control.

Number of Items: 10

Format: Scales range from 1 (*strongly disagree*) to 7 (*strongly agree*). A sample item is presented.

Reliability: Coefficient alpha was .72.

Validity: Correlations with other variables ranged from −.32 to .17.

Author: Noor, N. M.

Article: Work–family conflict, locus of control, and women's well-being: Tests of alternative pathways.

Journal: *The Journal of Social Psychology*, October 2002, *142*, 645–662.

Related Research: Paulhus, D. (1983). Sphere-specific measures of perceived control. *Journal of Personality and Social Psychology, 44*, 1253–1265.

12927

Test Name: INTERVIEW QUESTIONNAIRE

Purpose: To measure the perceived fairness of a job interview, its difficulty, and the expectancy of a favorable outcome.

Number of Items: 13

Format: Scales range from 1 (*strongly disagree*) to 7 (*strongly agree*). All items are presented.

Reliability: Alpha coefficients ranged from .70 to .82.

Validity: Correlations with other variables ranged from .00 to .16.

Author: Chapman, D. S., et al.

Article: Applicant reactions to face-to-face and technology-mediated interviews: A field investigation.

Journal: *Journal of Applied Psychology*, October 2003, *88*, 944–953.

12928

Test Name: INVENTORY OF CHILDREN'S ACTIVITIES—REVISED

Purpose: To identify interests and perceptions of competence of activities.

Number of Items: 71

Format: Includes two sections: interests and competence perceptions. Responses are made on 5-point scales.

Reliability: Internal consistency ranged from .53 to .86. Stability estimates over 2 weeks were .69 and .71.

Author: Tracy, T. J. G., and Darcy, M.

Article: An idiothetic examination of vocational interests and their relation to career decidedness.

Journal: *Journal of Counseling Psychology*, October 2002, *49*, 420–427.

Related Research: Tracey, T. J. G., & Ward, C. C. (1998). The structure of children's interests and competence perceptions. *Journal of Counseling Psychology, 45,* 290–303.

12929

Test Name: JACKSON–TIMBERLAKE REACTION SCALE

Purpose: To measure the reactions to the Jackson–Timberlake 2004 Super Bowl incident.

Number of Items: 23

Format: Seven-point scales are used. All items are presented.

Reliability: Alpha coefficients ranged from .86 to .91.

Validity: Correlations with other variables ranged from .17 to .39.

Author: Forbes, G. B., et al.

Article: Perceptions of the Jackson–Timberlake Super Bowl incident: The role of sexism and erotophobia.

Journal: *Psychological Reports*, June 2005, *96*, Part 1, 730–732.

12930

Test Name: JANIS–FIELD FEELINGS OF INADEQUACY SCALE

Purpose: To measure self-esteem.

Number of Items: 26

Format: Scales range from 1 (*never/not at all*) to 7 (*always/very much*).

Reliability: Coefficient alpha was .93.

Author: Brown, R. P., and Ziegler-Hill, V.

Article: Narcissism and the nonequivalence of self-esteem measures: A matter of dominance?

Journal: *Journal of Research in Personality*, December 2004, *38*, 585–592.

Related Research: Fleming, J. S., & Courtney, B. E. (1984). The dimensionality of self-esteem: II. Hierarchical facet model for revised measurement scales. *Journal of Personality and Social Psychology, 46,* 404–421.

12931

Test Name: JOB PERCEPTIONS SURVEY

Purpose: To measure job security perceptions, threat perceptions and benefit perceptions.

Number of Items: 21

Format: Scales range from 1 (*strongly disagree*) to 7 (*strongly agree*). All items are presented.

Reliability: Alpha coefficients ranged from .70 to .90.

Validity: Correlations with other variables ranged from −.22 to .28.

Author: Kraimer, M. L., et al.

Article: The role of job security in understanding the relationship between employees' perceptions of temporary workers and employees' performance.

Journal: *Journal of Applied Psychology*, March 2005, *90*, 389–398.

12932

Test Name: JOB-RELATED AFFECTIVE WELL-BEING SCALE—ADAPTED

Purpose: To measure job-related affect.

Number of Items: 20

Format: Responses are made on a 5-point scale ranging from 1 (*never*) to 5 (*extremely often*). An example is given.

Reliability: Coefficient alpha was .90 ($n = 195$).

Validity: Correlations with other variables ranged from −.40 to .51 ($n = 195$).

Author: Lubbers, R., et al.

Article: Young workers' job self-efficacy and affect: Pathways to health and performance.

Journal: *Journal of Vocational Behavior*, October 2005, *67*, 199–214.

Related Research: Van Katwyk, P. T., et al. (2000). Using the Job-Related Affective Well-Being Scale (JAWS) to investigate responses to work stressors. *Journal of Occupational Health Psychology, 5,* 219–230.

12933

Test Name: JOB SEARCH PREDICTORS SCALES

Purpose: To assess job search predictors.

Number of Items: 13

Format: Includes three scales: Personal Job Search Attitude, Perceived Social Pressure, and Job Search Self-Efficacy.

Reliability: Alpha coefficients ranged from .70 to .87.

Validity: Correlations with other variables ranged from −.31 to .58.

Author: Van Hooft, E. A. J., et al.

Article: Predictors and outcomes of job search behavior: The moderating effects of gender and family situation.

Journal: *Journal of Vocational Behavior*, October 2005, *67*, 133–152.

Related Research: Van Ryn, M., & Vinokur, A. D. (1992). How did it work? An examination of the mechanisms through which an intervention for the unemployed promoted job-search behavior. *American Journal of Community Psychology, 20*, 577–597.

12934

Test Name: JOB SEARCH SELF-EFFICACY SCALE

Purpose: To measure job search self-efficacy.

Number of Items: 10

Format: Responses are given on a 5-point scale ranging from 1 (*not at all confident*) to 5 (*totally confident*). An example is given.

Reliability: Coefficient alpha was .86.

Validity: Correlations with other variables ranged from −.29 to .53.

Author: Crossley, C. D., and Stanton, J. M.

Article: Negative affect and job search: Further examination of the reverse causation hypothesis.

Journal: *Journal of Vocational Behavior*, June 2005, *66*, 549–560.

Related Research: Saks, A. M., & Ashforth, B. E. (1999). Effects of individual differences and job search behaviors on the employment status of recent university graduates. *Journal of Vocational Behavior, 54*, 335–349.

12935

Test Name: JOB SEEKING SELF-EFFICACY SCALE

Purpose: To measure job seeking self-efficacy.

Number of Items: 7

Format: Sample items are presented.

Reliability: Coefficient alpha was .93.

Validity: Correlations with other variables ranged from −.06 to .29.

Author: Adams, G., and Rau, B.

Article: Job seeking among retirees seeking bridge employment.

Journal: *Personnel Psychology*, Autumn 2004, *57*, 719–744.

Related Research: Wanberg, C. R., et al. (1996). Individuals without jobs: An empirical study of job-seeking behavior and reemployment. *Journal of Applied Psychology, 81*, 76–87.

12936

Test Name: JOB SELF-EFFICACY SCALE

Purpose: To measure job self-efficacy.

Number of Items: 3

Format: Scales range from 1 (*strongly disagree*) to 5 (*strongly agree*). All items are presented.

Reliability: Coefficient alpha was .89.

Validity: Correlations with other variables ranged from −.24 to .19.

Author: Wilk, S. L., and Moynihan, L. M.

Article: Display rule "regulators": The relationship between supervisors and worker emotional exhaustion.

Journal: *Journal of Applied Psychology*, September 2005, *90*, 917–927.

Related Research: Jones, J. R. (1986). Socialization tactics, self-efficacy, and newcomers' adjustment to organizations. *Academy of Management Journal, 29*, 262–279.

12937

Test Name: LAY THEORIES ABOUT THE MALLEABILITY OF HUMAN TRAITS MEASURE

Purpose: To assess children's theories about traits.

Number of Items: 4

Format: Responses are made on a 6-point scale ranging from 1 (*very strongly disagree*) to 6 (*very strongly agree*). All items are presented.

Reliability: Coefficient alpha was .79.

Validity: Correlations with other variables ranged from −.05 to .44.

Author: Karafantis, D. M., and Levy, S. R.

Article: The role of children's lay theories about the malleability of human attributes in beliefs about and volunteering for disadvantaged groups.

Journal: *Child Development*, January/February 2004, *75*, 236–250.

Related Research: Levy, S. R., & Dweck, C. S. (1999). The impact of children's static versus dynamic conceptions of people on stereotype formation. *Child Development, 70*, 1163–1180.

12938

Test Name: LEARNING CLIMATE QUESTIONNAIRE—MODIFIED

Purpose: To assess perceived teacher autonomy support.

Number of Items: 8

Format: All items are presented.

Reliability: Coefficient alpha was .92.

Validity: Correlations with other variables ranged from −.28 to .49.

Author: Hardre, P. L., and Reeve, J.

Article: A motivational model of rural students' intentions to persist in, versus drop out of, high school.

Journal: *Journal of Educational Psychology*, June 2003, *95*, 347–356.

Related Research: Williams, G. C., & Deci, E. L. (1996). Internalization of biopsychological values by medical students: A test of self-determination theory. *Journal of Personality and Social Psychology, 70*, 767–779.

12939

Test Name: LEARNING PREPAREDNESS AND CAREER DEVELOPMENT SCALES

Purpose: To assess training anxiety, perceived decline in mental abilities, beliefs about processing learning qualities, self-perceived need for training, perceived relative intelligence, and career insight.

Number of Items: 29

Reliability: Alpha coefficients ranged from .73 to .93.

Author: Maurer, T. J., et al.

Article: A model of involvement in work-related learning and development activity: The effects of individual, situational, motivational, and age variables.

Journal: *Journal of Applied Psychology*, August 2003, *88*, 707–724.

Related Research: Bailey, R., & Mettetal, G. (1977). Sex differences in the congruency of perceived intelligence. *Journal of Genetic Psychology, 131*, 29–36. Dixon, R., & Hultsch, D. (1984). The Metamemory in Adulthood (MIA)

Instrument. *Psychological Documents, 14*, 3. Maurer, T., & Tarulli, B. (1994). Perceived environment, perceived outcome, and person variables in relationship to voluntary development activity by employees. *Journal of Applied Psychology, 79*, 3–14. Lodahl, T., & Kejner, M. (1965). The definition and measurement of job involvement. *Journal of Applied Psychology, 49*, 24–33.

12940

Test Name: LEARNING SELF-EFFICACY SCALE

Purpose: To measure self-efficacy.

Number of Items: 3

Format: A sample item is presented.

Reliability: Coefficient alpha was .75.

Validity: Correlations with other variables ranged from −.11 to .28 ($N = 71$).

Author: Brown, K. G. B.

Article: Using computers to deliver training: Which employees learn and why?

Journal: *Personnel Psychology*, Summer 2001, *54*, 271–296.

Related Research: Ford, J. K., et al. (1998). Relationships of goal orientation, metacognitive activity, and practice strategies with learning outcomes and transfer. *Journal of Applied Psychology, 83*, 218–233.

12941

Test Name: LESBIAN, GAY, AND BISEXUAL AFFIRMATIVE COUNSELING SELF-EFFICACY INVENTORY

Purpose: To assess counselor self-efficacy to perform lesbian, gay, and bisexual affirmative counseling behaviors.

Number of Items: 32

Format: Includes five subscales: Advocacy Skills, Assessment, Awareness, Relationship, and Knowledge. Responses are made on a 6-point scale ranging from 1 (*not at all confident*) to 6 (*highly confident*). All items are presented.

Reliability: Alpha coefficients ranged from .70 to .97.

Validity: Correlations with other variables ranged from −.13 to .66.

Author: Dillon, F. R., and Worthington, R. L.

Article: The Lesbian, Gay, and Bisexual Affirmative Counseling Self-Efficacy Inventory (LGB-CSI): Development, validation, and training implications.

Journal: *Journal of Counseling Psychology*, April 2003, *50*, 235–251.

12942

Test Name: LESBIAN IDENTITY VOCATIONAL DEVELOPMENT PROBLEM SCALE

Purpose: To assess the influence of lesbian identity on career development.

Number of Items: 4

Format: Four-point scales range from *not at all true* to *completely true*. All items are presented.

Reliability: Coefficient alpha was .71.

Author: Tomlinson, M. J., and Fassinger, R. E.

Article: Career development, lesbian identity development, and campus climate among lesbian college students.

Journal: *Journal of College Student Development*, November/December 2003, *44*, 845–860.

Related Research: Boatwright, K. J., et al. (1996). Impact of identity development upon career trajectory: Listening to the voices of lesbian women. *Journal of Vocational Behavior, 48*, 210–228.

12943

Test Name: LEVELS OF EMOTIONAL AWARENESS SCALE—PERSIAN VERSION

Purpose: To measure emotional awareness as emotion of the self and emotion of others.

Number of Items: 20 (scenarios)

Format: Raters score responses to scenarios on a 5-point scale.

Reliability: Alpha coefficients ranged from .72 to .76.

Validity: The correlation between self and other scores was .70.

Author: Yousefi, F.

Article: Levels of Emotional Awareness Scale among Iranian gifted and nongifted high school students.

Journal: *Psychological Reports,* October 2004, *95*, 504–506.

Related Research: Lane, R. D., et al. (1990). The Levels of Emotional Wellness Scale: A cognitive–developmental measure of emotion. *Journal of Personality Assessment, 55*, 124–134.

12944

Test Name: LIPSITT'S SELF-CONCEPT SCALE FOR CHILDREN

Purpose: To measure children's feelings about themselves.

Number of Items: 22

Format: Responses are made on a 5-point scale ranging from 1 (*not at all*) to 5 (*all of the time*).

Reliability: Test–retest reliability ranged from .73 to .91. Coefficient alpha was .81.

Validity: Correlations with other variables ranged from –.08 to .35.

Author: Dwairy, M.

Article: Parenting styles and mental health of Arab gifted adolescents.

Journal: *Gifted Child Quarterly,* Fall 2004, *48*, 275–286.

Related Research: Lipsitt, L. P. (1958). A self-concept scale for children and its relationship to the children's form of the Manifest Anxiety Scale. *Child Development, 29*, 463–472.

12945

Test Name: LOCUS OF CONTROL OF BEHAVIOR SCALE

Purpose: To assess locus of control.

Number of Items: 17

Format: Responses are made on a 6-point scale ranging from 0 (*strongly disagree*) to 5 (*strongly agree*).

Reliability: Test–retest (1 week) reliability was .90. Test–retest (6 months) reliability was .73. Coefficient alpha was .79.

Validity: Correlations with other variables ranged from .20 to .70.

Author: Bright, J. E. H., et al.

Article: The role of chance events in career decision making.

Journal: *Journal of Vocational Behavior,* June 2005, *66*, 561–576.

Related Research: Craig, A. R., et al. (1984). A scale to measure locus of control of behaviour. *British Journal of Medical Psychology, 57*, 173–180.

12946

Test Name: LOCUS OF CONTROL SCALE

Purpose: To measure locus of control.

Number of Items: 7

Format: Responses are made on a 5-point Likert-type scale ranging from 1 (*strongly disagree*) to 5 (*strongly agree*). Sample items are given.

Reliability: Coefficient alpha was .87 (*N* = 221).

Validity: Correlations with other variables ranged from –.07 to .19 (*N* = 221).

Author: Andrews, M. C., and Kacmar, K. M.

Article: Impression management by association: Construction and validation of a scale.

Journal: *Journal of Vocational Behavior,* February 2001, *58*, 142–161.

Related Research: Spector, P. E. (1988). Development of the World Locus of Control Scale. *Journal of Occupational Psychology, 61*, 335–340.

12947

Test Name: LOCUS OF CONTROL SCALE

Purpose: To measure locus of control.

Number of Items: 6

Format: Items are scored 0 or 1. Sample items are presented.

Reliability: Coefficient alpha was .62.

Validity: Correlations with other variables ranged from –.26 to .24 (*N* = 600).

Author: Ito, J. K., and Brotheridge, C. M.

Article: Resources, coping strategies, and emotional exhaustion: A conservation of resources perspective.

Journal: *Journal of Vocational Behavior,* December 2003, *63*, 490–509.

Related Research: Rotter, J. B. (1966). Generalized expectancies for internal versus external control of reinforcement. *Psychological Monographs, 80*(Whole No. 609).

12948

Test Name: LOCUS OF CONTROL SCALE

Purpose: To measure locus of control on three loci.

Number of Items: 24

Format: Includes three subscales measuring different loci of control: Internal, Powerful Others, and Chance.

Reliability: Internal consistency ranged from .64 to .78. Test–retest (1 week) reliabilities were .64 (internal) and .78 (chance).

Validity: Correlations of internal and chance with other variables ranged from –.30 to .51.

Author: Robitschek, C.

Article: Validity of Personal Growth Initiative Scale scores with a Mexican American college student population.

Journal: *Journal of Counseling Psychology*, October 2003, *50*, 496–502.

Related Research: Levenson, H. (1974). Activism and powerful others: Distinctions within the concept of internal–external control. *Journal of Personality Assessment, 38*, 377–383.

12949

Test Name: LOCUS OF CONTROL SCALE—ADAPTED

Purpose: To measure locus of control.

Number of Items: 18

Format: Includes three components: difficult-world belief, predictable-world belief, and just-world belief.

Reliability: Alpha coefficients were .64 and .73.

Author: Matters, G., and Burnett, P. C.

Article: Psychological predictors of the propensity to omit short-response items on a high-stakes achievement test.

Journal: *Educational and Psychological Measurement*, April 2003, *63*, 239–256.

Related Research: Collins, B. E. (1974). Four components of the Rotter Internal–External Scale: Belief in a difficult world, a just world, a predictable world, and a politically responsive world. *Journal of Personality and Social Psychology, 29*, 381–391.

12950

Test Name: MANIPULATION OF FUTURE PERFORMANCE EXPECTATIONS MEASURE

Purpose: To assess the manipulation of future performance expectations.

Number of Items: 5

Format: Responses are made on a 7-point scale ranging from 1 (*strongly disagree*) to 7 (*strongly agree*). Sample items are presented.

Reliability: Coefficients alpha was .83.

Author: Alge, B. J., et al.

Article: Remote control: Predictors of electronic monitoring intensity and secrecy.

Journal: *Personnel Psychology*, Summer 2004, *57*, 377–410.

Related Research: McAllister, D. J. (1995). Affect- and cognition-based trust as foundations for interpersonal cooperation in organizations. *Academy of Management Journal, 38*, 24–59.

12951

Test Name: MASTERY INDEX

Purpose: To assess the sense of mastery.

Number of Items: 7

Format: Scales range from 1 (*strongly agree*) to 5 (*strongly disagree*). All items are presented.

Reliability: Coefficient alpha was .74.

Validity: Correlations with other variables ranged from –.09 to .18.

Author: Schieman, S., et al.

Article: Religiosity, socioeconomic status, and the sense of mastery.

Journal: *Social Psychology Quarterly*, September 2003, *66*, 202–221.

Related Research: Ellison, C. G., et al. (2001). Religious involvement, stress, and mental health: Findings from the 1995 Detroit Area Study. *Social Forces, 80*, 215–249.

12952

Test Name: MASTERY SCALE

Purpose: To assess one's generalized sense of perceived control.

Number of Items: 4

Format: Responses are made on 5-point Likert scale ranging from 5 (*strongly agree*) to 1 (*strongly disagree*). All items are presented.

Reliability: Reliabilities ranged from .46 to .67.

Validity: Correlations with other variables ranged from –.29 to .44.

Author: Fugate, M., et al.

Article: Coping with an organizational merger over four stages.

Journal: *Personnel Psychology*, Winter 2002, *55*, 905–928.

Related Research: Pearlin, L., & Schooler, C. (1978). The structure of coping. *Journal of Health and Social Behavior, 19*, 2–21.

12953

Test Name: MASTERY SCALE

Purpose: To measure the extent to which individuals can successfully affect their environment.

Number of Items: 7

Format: Four-point scales range from 1 (*strongly agree*) to 4 (*strongly disagree*). A sample item is presented.

Reliability: Coefficient alpha was .68.

Validity: Correlations with other variables ranged from −.27 to .34.

Author: Hobfoll, S. E., et al.

Article: The impact of perceived child physical and sexual abuse history on Native American women's psychological well-being and AIDS risk.

Journal: *Journal of Consulting and Clinical Psychology*, February 2002, *70*, 252–257.

Related Research: Pearlin, L. I., et al. (1981). The stress process. *Journal of Health and Social Behavior, 22*, 337–356.

12954

Test Name: MATH SELF-CONCEPT SCALE

Purpose: To measure self-concept in math.

Number of Items: 6

Format: Responses are made on a 0 to 10 scale. Examples are presented.

Reliability: Alpha coefficients ranged from .88 to .95.

Validity: Correlations with other variables ranged from .29 to .66.

Author: Klassen, R. M.

Article: A cross-cultural investigation of the efficacy beliefs of South Asian immigrant and Anglo Canadian nonimmigrant early adolescents.

Journal: *Journal of Educational Psychology*, December 2004, *96*, 731–742.

Related Research: Marsh, H. W. (1990). The structure of academic self-concept: The Marsh/Shavelson

model. *Journal of Educational Psychology, 82*, 623–636.

12955

Test Name: MATHEMATICS COURSE SELF-EFFICACY SCALE

Purpose: To measure confidence in students' ability to complete each of 16 math-related college courses with a grade of B or better.

Number of Items: 16

Format: Responses are made on a 10-point scale ranging from 0 (*no confidence*) to 9 (*complete confidence*).

Reliability: Alpha coefficients were .91 and .93. Test–retest (2 weeks) reliability was .94.

Validity: Correlations with other variables ranged from −.19 to .57.

Author: Lent, R. W., et al.

Article: The role of contextual supports and barriers in the choice of math/science educational options: A test of social cognitive hypotheses.

Journal: *Journal of Counseling Psychology*, October 2001, *48*, 474–483.

Related Research: Betz, N. E., & Hackett, G. (1983). The relationship of mathematics self-efficacy expectations to the selection of science-based college majors. *Journal of Vocational Behavior, 23*, 329–345.

12956

Test Name: MATHEMATICS COURSE SELF-EFFICACY SCALE—MODIFIED

Purpose: To enable students to rate their ability to earn a grade of B or better in each of 23 math and science courses.

Number of Items: 23

Format: Responses are made on a 10-point scale ranging from 1 (*no*

confidence at all) to 10 (*complete confidence*). Examples are given.

Reliability: Coefficient alpha was .96.

Author: Nauta, M. M., and Epperson, D. L.

Article: A longitudinal examination of the social–cognitive model applied to high school girls' choices of nontraditional college majors and aspirations.

Journal: *Journal of Counseling Psychology*, October 2003, *50*, 448–457.

Related Research: Gainor, K. A., & Lent, R. W. (1998). Social cognitive expectations and racial identity attitudes in predicting the math choice intentions of Black college students. *Journal of Counseling Psychology, 45*, 403–413.

12957

Test Name: MATHEMATICS PERFORMANCE TEST

Purpose: To measure mathematics performance.

Number of Items: 20

Format: Items were similar to the items on a mathematics self-efficacy instrument.

Reliability: K-R 20 reliability coefficients ranged from .78 to .92.

Author: Stevens, T., et al.

Article: Role of mathematics self-efficacy and motivation in mathematics performance across ethnicity.

Journal: *Journal of Educational Research*, March/April 2004, *97*, 208–221.

Related Research: Pajares, F., & Graham, L. (1999). Self-efficacy, motivation constructs, and mathematics performance of entering middle school students. *Contemporary Educational Psychology, 24*, 124–139.

12958

Test Name: MATHEMATICS SELF-CONCEPT SCALE

Purpose: To measure mathematics self-concept.

Number of Items: 8

Format: Five-point scales are anchored by 1 (*false*) and 5 (*true*). Sample items are presented.

Reliability: Coefficient alpha was .94.

Author: Alkhateeb, H. M., and Taha, N.

Article: Mathematics self-concept and mathematics anxiety of undergraduate majors in education.

Journal: *Psychological Reports,* December 2002, *91,* Part 2, 1273–1275.

Related Research: Marsh, H. W., et al. (1983). Preadolescent self-concept: Its relation to academic ability. *British Journal of Educational Psychology, 53,* 60–78.

12959

Test Name: MATHEMATICS SELF-EFFICACY SCALE

Purpose: To assess students' mathematics self-efficacy.

Number of Items: 20

Format: Responses are made on an 8-point scale ranging from *not confident at all* to *completely confident.* An example is given.

Reliability: Alpha coefficients ranged from .87 to .95.

Author: Stevens, T., et al.

Article: Role of mathematics self-efficacy and motivation in mathematics performance across ethnicity.

Journal: *Journal of Educational Research,* March/April 2004, *97,* 208–221.

Related Research: Pajares, F., & Graham, L. (1999). Self-efficacy,

motivation constructs, and mathematics performance of entering middle school students. *Contemporary Educational Psychology, 24,* 124–139.

12960

Test Name: MATHEMATICS TEACHING EFFICACY BELIEFS SCALE

Purpose: To measure personal mathematics teaching efficacy and teaching outcome expectancies among education majors.

Number of Items: 21

Format: Five-point rating scales. Sample items are presented.

Reliability: Alpha coefficients ranged from .74 to .86.

Author: Alkhateed, H. M., and Abed, A. S.

Article: A mathematics content course and teaching efficacy beliefs of undergraduate majors in education.

Journal: *Psychological Reports,* October 2003, *93,* 475–478.

Related Research: Enochs, L. G., et al. (2000). Establishing factorial validity of the Mathematics Teaching Efficacy Beliefs Instrument. *Social Science and Mathematics, 100,* 194–202.

12961

Test Name: MBA LEARNING PERCEPTIONS SCALE

Purpose: To measure how much students learn in an MBA program.

Number of Items: 4

Format: Scales range from 1 (*very little*) to 5 (*a great deal*).

Reliability: Coefficient alpha was .79.

Validity: Correlations with other variables ranged from .02 to .44.

Author: Zhao, H., et al.

Article: The mediating role of self-efficacy in the development of entrepreneurial intentions.

Journal: *Journal of Applied Psychology,* November 2005, *90,* 1265–1272.

12962

Test Name: MIDDLE SCHOOL CAREER DECISION-MAKING SCALES

Purpose: To measure career decision-making self-efficacy and outcome expectations.

Number of Items: 24

Format: Scales range from 1 (*strongly disagree*) to 5 (*strongly agree*). Sample items are presented.

Reliability: Alpha coefficients ranged from .74 to .88 across samples and subscales.

Validity: Correlations with other variables ranged from .26 to .59.

Author: Turner, S. L., et al.

Article: The Career-Related Parent Support Scale.

Journal: *Measurement and Evaluation in Counseling and Development,* July 2003, *36,* 83–94.

Related Research: Fouad, N. A., et al. (1997). Reliability and validity evidence for the Middle School Self-Efficacy Scale. *Measurement and Evaluation in Counseling and Development, 30,* 17–31.

12963

Test Name: MIROWSKY–ROSS PERSONAL CONTROL SCALE

Purpose: To measure the sense of personal control.

Number of Items: 8

Format: Five-point agreement scales are used. All items are presented.

Reliability: Alpha coefficients ranged from .68 to .71.

Author: Ross, C. E., and Mirowsky, J.

Article: Age and the gender gap in the sense of personal control.

Journal: *Social Psychology Quarterly*, June 2002, *65*, 125–145.

Related Research: Mirowsky, J., & Ross, C. E. (1991). Eliminating defense and agreement bias from measures of the sense of control: A 2x2 Index. *Social Psychology Quarterly, 54*, 127–145.

12964

Test Name: MONEY INADEQUACY SCALE

Purpose: To measure the extent to which respondents feel that their income is adequate.

Number of Items: 5

Format: Responses are made on a 6-point Likert scale ranging from 1 (*strongly disagree*) to 6 (*strongly agree*). Examples are presented.

Reliability: Coefficient alpha was .70.

Validity: Correlations with other variables ranged from −.04 to .25.

Author: Dunford, B., et al.

Article: Out-of-the-money: The impact of underwater stock options on executive job search.

Journal: *Personnel Psychology*, Spring 2005, *58*, 67–101.

Related Research: Furnham, A., & Argyle, M. (1998). *The psychology of money.* London: Routledge.

12965

Test Name: MULTIDIMENSIONAL LOCUS OF CONTROL SCALE— PERSIAN VERSION

Purpose: To measure perceived internal control, powerful others, and the role of chance.

Number of Items: 24

Format: Scales range from 0 (*strongly disagree*) to 4 (*strongly agree*).

Reliability: Alpha coefficients ranged from .59 to .75 across subscales.

Validity: Correlations with other variables ranged from −.35 to .29.

Author: Ghorbani, N., et al.

Article: Private self-consciousness factors: Relationships with need for cognition, locus of control, and obsessive thinking in Iran and the United States.

Journal: *The Journal of Social Psychology*, August 2004, *144*, 359–372.

Related Research: Levenson, H. (1973). Multidimensional locus of control in psychiatric patients. *Journal of Consulting and Clinical Psychology, 41*, 397–404.

12966

Test Name: MULTIDIMENSIONAL MULTIATTRIBUTIONAL CAUSALITY SCALE

Purpose: To assess students' internality.

Format: Includes four subscales: Effort, Ability, Task Difficulty, and Luck.

Reliability: K-R 20 reliability estimates ranged from .53 to .75. Split-half reliability was .77.

Validity: Correlations with other variables ranged from −.16 to .23.

Author: Schoenwetter, D. J., et al.

Article: Content familiarity: Differential impact of effective teaching on student achievement outcomes.

Journal: *Research in Higher Education*, December 2002, *43*, 625–655.

Related Research: Lefourt, H. M., et al. (1979). The multidimensional–multiattributional causality scale: The development of

a goal specific locus of control scale. *Canadian Journal of Behavioural Science, 11*, 286–304.

12967

Test Name: MULTIDIMENSIONAL SCALES OF PERCEIVED SELF-EFFICACY

Purpose: To measure self-efficacy.

Number of Items: 20

Format: Includes two subscales: Self-Efficacy for Self-Regulated Learning and Self-Efficacy for Academic Achievements. Responses are made on a 7-point scale ranging from 1 (*not good*) to 7 (*very good*). Examples are given.

Reliability: Internal consistency coefficients ranged from .70 to .87.

Author: Shechtman, Z., and Pastor, R.

Article: Cognitive–behavioral and humanistic group treatment for children with learning disabilities: A comparison of outcomes and process.

Journal: *Journal of Counseling Psychology*, July 2005, *52*, 322–336.

Related Research: Bandura, A. (1989). *Multidimensional scales of perceived self-efficacy.* Unpublished test, Stanford University, Palo Alto, CA.

12968

Test Name: NEGATIVE ACADEMIC AFFECT SCALE

Purpose: To assess students' perceptions of the frequency of negative affect they experience while engaged in school-related tasks.

Number of Items: 39

Format: Responses are made on a 5-point scale ranging from 1 (*never*) to 5 (*always*). An example is given.

Reliability: Coefficient alpha was .93.

Validity: Correlations with other variables ranged from −.51 to .23.

Author: Gumora, G., and Arsenio, W. F.

Article: Emotionality, emotion regulation, and school performance in middle school children.

Journal: *Journal of School Psychology*, September/October 2002, *40*, 395–413.

Related Research: Gumora, G. (1993). *The construction of the Negative Academic Affect Scale (NAAS)*. Unpublished manuscript.

12969

Test Name: NEGATIVE SELF-DIRECTED AFFECT SCALE

Purpose: To measure negative self-directed affect.

Number of Items: 5

Format: Scales range from 0 (*not that much*) to 5 (*very much*). All items are presented.

Reliability: Coefficient alpha was .91.

Author: Costarelli, S., and Colloca, P.

Article: Intergroup conflict, out-group derogation, and self-directed negative affect among Italian South Tyroleans.

Journal: *The Journal of Social Psychology*, April 2004, *144*, 181–189.

Related Research: Devine, P. G., et al. (1991). Prejudice with and without compunction. *Journal of Personality and Social Psychology, 60*, 817–830.

12970

Test Name: NEWCASTLE ALCOHOL PROBLEMS SCALE

Purpose: To measure perceived consequences of one's own or another person's use of alcohol.

Number of Items: 19

Format: Item responses are anchored by *never* and *often*.

Reliability: K-R 20 reliability was .80.

Author: Dear, G. E., et al.

Article: Perceptions of another person's heavy drinking as a function of one's relationship to the drinker: A pilot study.

Journal: *Psychological Reports*, April 2002, *90*, 426–430.

Related Research: Rydon, R. (1991). *Detection of alcohol problems in general practice: Development of the Newcastle Alcohol-Related Problems Scale*. Unpublished doctoral dissertation, University of Newcastle, Australia.

12971

Test Name: 9/11 FLASHBULB MEMORY SCALES

Purpose: To assess reactions to the 9/11 New York City attack.

Number of Items: 43

Format: Formats vary. All are described.

Reliability: Alpha coefficients ranged from .45 to .82 across subscales.

Author: Luminet, O., et al.

Article: The cognitive, emotional, and social impacts of the September 11 attacks: Group differences in memory for the reception context and the determinants of flashbulb memory.

Journal: *The Journal of General Psychology*, July 2004, *131*, 197–224.

Related Research: Curci, A., et al. (2001). Flashbulb memories in social groups: A comparative test–retest study of the memory of French President Mitterrand's death in a French and Belgian group. *Memory, 9*, 81–101.

12972

Test Name: OBJECTIFIED BODY CONSCIOUSNESS SCALE

Purpose: To assess the degree to which a woman has adopted an externalized view when relating to her own body.

Format: Includes three subscales: Body Surveillance, Body Shame, and Control Beliefs. Responses are made on a 7-point scale ranging from 1 (*strongly disagree*) to 7 (*strongly agree*). Examples are given.

Reliability: Alpha coefficients ranged from .70 to .84.

Validity: Correlations with other variables ranged from .22 to .65.

Author: Piran, N., and Cormier, H. C.

Article: The social construction of women and disordered eating patterns.

Journal: *Journal of Counseling Psychology*, October 2005, *52*, 549–558.

Related Research: McKinley, N. M., & Hyde, J. S. (1996). The Objectified Body Consciousness Scale. *Psychology of Women Quarterly, 20*, 181–215.

12973

Test Name: OFF-TASK ATTENTION MEASURE

Purpose: To measure the extent to which trainees thought about issues unrelated to course content.

Number of Items: 6

Format: A sample item is presented.

Reliability: Coefficient alpha was .73.

Validity: Correlations with other variables ranged from −.33 to .21 ($N = 71$).

Author: Brown, K. G. B.

Article: Using computers to deliver training: Which employees learn and why?

Journal: *Personnel Psychology,* Summer 2001, *54,* 271–296.

Related Research: Kanfer, R., & Ackerman, P. L. (1989). Motivation and cognitive abilities: An integrative aptitude treatment interaction approach to skill acquisition [Monograph]. *Journal of Applied Psychology, 74,* 657–690.

12974

Test Name: ORGANIZATION-BASED SELF-ESTEEM SCALE

Purpose: To measure organization-based self-esteem.

Number of Items: 10

Format: Responses are made on a 7-point scale ranging from 1 (*strongly disagree*) to 7 (*strongly agree*). Examples are given.

Reliability: Coefficient alpha was .91.

Validity: Correlations with other variables ranged from .27 to .60.

Author: Chen, Z. X., et al.

Article: Test of a mediation model of perceived organizational support.

Journal: *Journal of Vocational Behavior,* June 2005, *66,* 457–470.

Related Research: Pierce, J. L., et al. (1989). Organization-based self-esteem: Construct definition, measurement, and validation. *Academy of Management Journal, 32,* 622–648.

12975

Test Name: OUTCOME EXPECTANCY MEASURES

Purpose: To measure work and family outcome of expectancies.

Number of Items: 8

Format: Includes work outcome expectancies and family outcome expectancies. Responses are made on a 5-point scale ranging from 1

(*strongly disagree*) to 5 (*strongly agree*). Examples are given.

Reliability: Alpha coefficients were .81 and .83.

Validity: Correlations with other variables ranged from −.22 to .30.

Author: Butler, A., et al.

Article: A social–cognitive perspective on using family-friendly benefits.

Journal: *Journal of Vocational Behavior,* August 2004, *65,* 57–70.

Related Research: Judiesch, M. K., & Lyness, K. S. (1999). Left behind? The impact of leaves of absence on managers' career success. *Academy of Management Journal, 42,* 641–651. Bridges, J. S., & Etaugh, C. (1996). Black and White college women's maternal employment outcome expectations and their desired timing of maternal employment. *Sex Roles, 35,* 543–562.

12976

Test Name: OUTCOME EXPECTANCY SCALE

Purpose: To assess outcome expectancy.

Number of Items: 4

Format: Responses are made on a 7-point scale ranging from 1 (*strongly disagree*) to 7 (*strongly agree*). All items are presented.

Reliability: Coefficient alpha was .92.

Validity: Correlations with other variables ranged from .03 to .30 (*n* = 216).

Author: Williamson, I. O., et al.

Article: The effect of company recruitment web site orientation on individuals' perceptions of organizational attractiveness.

Journal: *Journal of Vocational Behavior,* October 2003, *63,* 242–263.

12977

Test Name: OUTCOME EXPECTATION SCALE

Purpose: To assess career expectations.

Number of Items: 6

Format: Responses are made on a 4-point Likert scale ranging from 1 (*strongly disagree*) to 4 (*strongly agree*). Examples are given.

Reliability: Alpha coefficients were .83 and .84. Test–retest (9 weeks) reliability was .59 (*N* = 95).

Validity: Correlations with other variables ranged from −.26 to .35.

Author: Kenny, M. E., and Bledsoe, M.

Article: Contributions of the relational context to career adaptability among urban adolescents.

Journal: *Journal of Vocational Behavior,* April 2005, *66,* 257–272.

Related Research: McWhirter, E. H., et al. (2000). The effects of high school career education on social–cognitive variables. *Journal of Counseling Psychology, 47,* 330–341.

12978

Test Name: OUTCOME EXPECTATIONS SCALE— REVISED

Purpose: To assess science, mathematics, and engineering outcome expectations as a result of taking math/science courses.

Number of Items: 19

Format: Responses are made on a 10-point Likert-type scale. Examples are given.

Reliability: Alpha coefficients ranged from .86 to .88.

Validity: Correlations with other variables ranged from <.01 to .55 (*N* = 204).

Author: Nauta, M. M., and Epperson, D. L.

Article: A longitudinal examination of the social–cognitive model applied to high school girls' choices of nontraditional college majors and aspirations.

Journal: *Journal of Counseling Psychology*, October 2003, *50*, 448–457.

Related Research: Schaefers, K. G., et al. (1997). Women's career development: Can theoretically derived variables predict persistence in engineering majors? *Journal of Counseling Psychology*, *44*, 173–183.

12979

Test Name: OUTNESS INVENTORY

Purpose: To provide indicators of the latent construct of public outness.

Format: Responses are made on a 7-point scale ranging from 1 (*Person definitely does not know about your sexual orientation status*) to 7 (*Person definitely knows about your sexual orientation status and it is openly talked about*).

Reliability: Internal consistency was .79.

Validity: Correlations with other variables ranged from −.43 to .22.

Author: Mohr, J. J., and Fassinger, R. E.

Article: Self-acceptance and self-disclosure of sexual orientation in lesbians, gay and bisexual adults: An attachment perspective.

Journal: *Journal of Counseling Psychology*, October 2003, *50*, 482–495

Related Research: Mohr, J. J., & Fassinger, R. E. (2000). Measuring dimensions of lesbian and gay male experience. *Measurement and Evaluation in Counseling and Development*, *33*, 66–90.

12980

Test Name: PARENTAL LOCUS OF CONTROL—SHORT FORM

Purpose: To measure parent's locus of control as control, fate–chance, and responsibility.

Number of Items: 25

Format: Item anchors range from 1 (*strongly agree*) to 5 (*strongly disagree*).

Reliability: Coefficient alpha was .77.

Validity: Correlation with the long form of the scale was .90.

Author: MacNaughton, K. L., and Rodrique, J. R.

Article: Predicting adherence to recommendations by parents of clinic-referred children.

Journal: *Journal of Consulting and Clinical Psychology*, April 2001, *69*, 262–270.

Related Research: Rayfield, A., et al. (1995, November). *Development and validation of the Parental Locus of Control—Short Form.* Paper presented at the annual meeting of the Association for the Advancement of Behavior Therapy Preconference on Social Learning and the Family, Washington, DC.

12981

Test Name: PARENTS' PERCEPTIONS OF STUDENT INVITATIONS SCALE

Purpose: To assess parents' perceptions of student invitations in the academic and social domains.

Number of Items: 9

Format: Includes two domains: academic and social. Responses are made on a 6-point Likert-type scale ranging from 1 (*disagree very strongly*) to 6 (*agree very strongly*). Examples are given.

Reliability: Alpha coefficients were .71 and .79.

Author: Deslandes, R., and Bertrand, R.

Article: Motivation of parent involvement in secondary-level schooling.

Journal: *Journal of Educational Research*, January/February 2005, *98*(3), 164–175.

Related Research: Deslandes, R., & Cloutier, R. (2002). Adolescents' perception of parent–school involvement. *School Psychology International*, *23*, 220–232.

12982

Test Name: PARENTS' PERCEPTIONS OF TEACHER INVITATIONS SCALE

Purpose: To assess parents' perceptions of teacher invitations to become involved in their adolescents' schooling at home.

Number of Items: 4

Format: Responses are made on a 6-point scale ranging from 1 (*never*) to 6 (*once or more per week*). An example is given.

Reliability: Coefficient alpha was .70.

Author: Deslandes, R., and Bertrand, R.

Article: Motivation of parent involvement in secondary-level schooling.

Journal: *Journal of Educational Research*, January/February 2005, *98*, 164–175.

Related Research: Jones, K., et al. (2000). *"Sharing the Dream" Parent Questionnaire.* Retrieved from http://www.Vanderbilt.edu/ Peabody/family-school

12983

Test Name: PARENTS' SELF-EFFICACY FOR HELPING ADOLESCENTS SUCCEED IN SCHOOL SCALE

Purpose: To assess parents' self-efficacy for helping adolescents succeed in school.

Number of Items: 9

Format: Includes two factors: relative parent influence and impact of parent efforts. Responses are made on a 6-point scale ranging from 1 (*disagree very strongly*) to 6 (*agree very strongly*). Examples are given.

Reliability: Alpha coefficients were .63 and .68.

Author: Deslandes, R., and Bertrand, R.

Article: Motivation of parent involvement in secondary-level schooling.

Journal: *Journal of Educational Research*, January/February 2005, *98*, 164–175.

Related Research: Jones, K., et al. (2000). *"Sharing the Dream" Parent Questionnaire.* Retrieved from http://www.vanderbilt.edu/peabody/family-school/

12984

Test Name: PARENTS' SELF-ESTEEM AND EXPECTANCY QUESTIONNAIRE

Purpose: To measure parents' self-esteem and expectancies as perceived by adolescents.

Number of Items: 32

Format: A yes–no format is used.

Reliability: Test–retest reliability was .78 (2 weeks). Alpha coefficients ranged from .70 to .72.

Author: Salimi, S.-H., et al.

Article: Association of parental self-esteem and expectations with adolescents' anxiety about career and education.

Journal: *Psychological Reports*, June 2005, *96*, Part 1, 569–578.

Related Research: Fathi-Ashtiani, A. (1997). [A developmental survey on psychological aspects of Iranian students]. [*Journal of Psychology*], *1*, 75–94.

12985

Test Name: PASTOR PERCEPTION SCALE

Purpose: To assess pastoral success.

Number of Items: 4

Time Required: 10 minutes

Format: Scales range from 1 (*strongly agree*) to 6 (*strongly disagree*). All items are presented.

Reliability: Coefficient alpha was .91.

Author: Degelman, D., and Smith, A. J.

Article: Perceived gender of a pastor's name and ratings of vocational success.

Journal: *Psychological Reports*, April 2005, *96*, 457–463.

Related Research: Eagly, A. H., & Steffen, V. J. (1984). Gender stereotypes stem from the distribution of women and men into social roles. *Journal of Personality and Social Psychology*, *46*, 735–754.

12986

Test Name: PEER BELIEF INVENTORY—MODIFIED

Purpose: To measure children's perceptions of their schoolmates.

Number of Items: 13

Format: Includes three areas: trustworthiness, prosocial, and antisocial. Responses are made on a 5-point scale ranging from 1 (*not very true*) to 5 (*very true*).

Reliability: Coefficient alpha was .81.

Author: Troop-Gordon, W., and Ladd, G. W.

Article: Trajectories of peer victimization and perceptions of the self and schoolmates: Precursors to internalizing and externalizing problems.

Journal: *Child Development*, September/October 2005, *76*, 1072–1091.

Related Research: Rabiner, D. L., et al. (1993). Children's beliefs about familiar and unfamiliar peers in relation to their sociometric status. *Developmental Psychology*, *29*, 236–243.

12987

Test Name: PEER INTERPERSONAL ASSESSMENTS

Purpose: To determine classmates' perceptions of peers' social and behavioral characteristics.

Number of Items: 9

Format: Items include cooperative, disruptive, acts shy, starts fights, leader, gets in trouble, good student, and cool. Examples are given.

Reliability: Test–retest correlations ranged from .72 to .93 (*n* = .65).

Author: Farmer, T. W., et al.

Article: Deviant or diverse peer groups? The peer affiliation of aggressive elementary students.

Journal: *Journal of Educational Psychology*, September 2002, *94*, 611–620.

Related Research: Coie, J. D. et al. (1982). Dimensions and types of social status: A cross-age perspective. *Developmental Psychology*, *18*, 557–571.

12988

Test Name: PERCEIVED ACADEMIC CONTROL SCALE

Purpose: To measure perceived academic control.

Number of Items: 8

Format: Responses are made on a 5-point scale ranging from 1 (*strongly disagree*) to 5 (*strongly agree*).

Reliability: Coefficient alpha was .80. Test–retest reliability (5 months) was .59.

Validity: Correlations with other variables ranged from –.13 to .23.

Author: Perry, R. P., et al.

Article: Perceived academic control and failure in college students: A three-year study of scholastic attainment.

Journal: *Research in Higher Education,* August 2005, *46,* 535–569.

Related Research: Perry, R. P., et al. (2001). Action control and perceived control in the academic achievement of college students: A longitudinal field study. *Journal of Educational Psychology, 93,* 776–789.

12989

Test Name: PERCEIVED ALTERNATIVE EMPLOYMENT OPPORTUNITIES SCALE

Purpose: To measure perceived alternative employment opportunities.

Number of Items: 6

Format: Scales range from 1 (*strongly disagree*) to 7 (*strongly agree*). A sample item is presented.

Reliability: Scale reliability was .79.

Validity: Correlations with other variables ranged from –.02 to .45.

Author: Allen, D. G., and Griffeth, R. W.

Article: Test of a mediated performance-turnover relationship highlighting the moderating roles of visibility and reward contingency.

Journal: *Journal of Applied Psychology,* October 2001, *86,* 1014–1021.

Related Research: Griffeth, R. W., & Steel, R. P. (1992, August). *Turnover decision models: An exploratory investigation toward the development of a multidimensional measure of labor market cognition.* Paper presented at the annual meeting of the Academy of Management, Las Vegas, NV.

12990

Test Name: PERCEIVED AUTONOMY SUPPORT IN PE SCALE

Purpose: To provide a measure of perceived autonomy support in physical education.

Number of Items: 15

Format: Responses are made on a 7-point Likert-type scale ranging from 1 (*strongly disagree*) to 7 (*strongly agree*). An example is given.

Reliability: Alpha coefficients ranged from .82 to .95.

Validity: Correlations with other variables ranged from –.11 to .42.

Author: Hagger, M. S., et al.

Article: Perceived autonomy support in physical education and leisure-time physical activity: A cross-cultural evaluation of the trans-contextual model.

Journal: *Journal of Educational Psychology,* August 2005, *97,* 376–390.

Related Research: Hagger, M. S., et al. (2003). The processes by which perceived autonomy support in physical education promotes leisure-time physical activity intentions and behavior: A trans-contextual model. *Journal of Educational Psychology, 95,* 784–795.

12991

Test Name: PERCEIVED BEHAVIORAL CONTROL MEASURES

Purpose: To measure perceived personal control over internal and external resources.

Number of Items: 16

Format: Includes two components: perceived personal control over internal resources and that of external resources. Responses are made on a 5-point Likert scale ranging from 1 (*strongly disagree*) to 5 (*strongly agree*). Examples are given.

Reliability: Alpha coefficients were .65 and .81.

Validity: Correlations with other variables ranged from –.22 to .56.

Author: van Hooft, E. A. J., et al.

Article: Bridging the gap between intentions and behavior: Implementation intentions, action control, and procrastination.

Journal: *Journal of Vocational Behavior,* April 2005, *66,* 238–256.

Related Research: Armitage, C. J., & Conner, M. (1999). The theory of planned behavior: Assessment of predictive validity and "perceived control." *British Journal of Social Psychology, 38,* 35–54.

12992

Test Name: PERCEIVED BEHAVIORAL CONTROL SCALE

Purpose: To measure control beliefs concerning participation in physical activities.

Number of Items: 3

Format: Responses are made on 7-point scales. All items are given.

Reliability: Alpha coefficients were .78 and .83.

Validity: Correlations with other variables ranged from .05 to .70.

Author: Tsorbatzoudis, H.

Article: Evaluation of a school-based intervention programme to promote physical activity: An application of the theory of planned behavior.

Journal: *Perceptual and Motor Skills*, December 2005, *101*, 787–802.

12993

Test Name: PERCEIVED BEHAVIORAL CONTROL SCALE

Purpose: To assess behavioral control.

Number of Items: 15

Format: Includes three statements for each of five moral behaviors. Responses are made on 7-point scales. All items are presented.

Reliability: Alpha coefficients ranged from .77 to .92.

Validity: Correlations with other variables ranged from .43 to .67.

Author: Tsorbatzoudis, H., and Emmanouilidou, M.

Article: Predicting moral behavior in physical education classes: An application of the theory of planned behavior.

Journal: *Perceptual and Motor Skills*, June 2005, *100*, Part 2, 1055–1065.

12994

Test Name: PERCEIVED BEHAVIORAL CONTROL SCALE

Purpose: To measure self-efficacy concerning job search behavior.

Number of Items: 8

Format: Sample items are presented.

Reliability: Alpha coefficients were .68 and .78.

Validity: Correlations with other variables ranged from −.19 to .39.

Author: van Hooft, E. A. J., et al.

Article: Job search and the theory of planned behavior: Minority–majority group differences in The Netherlands.

Journal: *Journal of Vocational Behavior*, December 2004, *65*, 366–390.

Related Research: Caska, B. A. (1998). The search for employment: Motivation to engage in a coping behavior. *Journal of Applied Social Psychology, 28*, 206–224.

12995

Test Name: PERCEIVED BENEFITS OF HELP-SEEKING SCALE

Purpose: To measure perceived benefits of help seeking.

Number of Items: 7

Format: Responses are made on an 8-point scale. All items are presented.

Validity: Correlations with other variables ranged from −.44 to .41.

Author: Pajares, F., et al.

Article: Psychometric analysis of computer science help-seeking scales.

Journal: *Educational and Psychological Measurement*, June 2004, *64*, 496–513.

Related Research: Newman, R. S. (1990). Children's help-seeking in the classroom: The role of motivational factors and attitudes. *Journal of Educational Psychology, 82*, 71–80. Ryan, A. M., & Pintrich, P. R. (1997). "Should I ask for help?" The role of motivation and attitudes in adolescents help-seeking in math class. *Journal of Educational Psychology, 89*, 329–341.

12996

Test Name: PERCEIVED COMPETENCE SCALE

Purpose: To measure the extent to which one feels competent in the academic domain.

Number of Items: 6

Format: Responses are made on a 6-point scale ranging from 1 (*not at all true*) to 6 (*completely true*). An example is given.

Reliability: Alpha coefficients ranged from .80 to .91.

Author: Levesque, C., et al.

Article: Autonomy and competence in German and American university students: A comparative study based on self-determination theory.

Journal: *Journal of Educational Psychology*, March 2004, *96*, 68–84.

Related Research: Pelletier, L. G., & Vallerand, R. J. (1996). Supervisors' beliefs and subordinates' intrinsic motivation: A behavioral confirmation analysis. *Journal of Personality and Social Psychology, 71*, 331–340.

12997

Test Name: PERCEIVED COMPETENCE SCALE FOR CHILDREN—MODIFIED

Purpose: To measure child competence.

Number of Items: 14

Format: Includes two subscales: Cognitive and Social. Responses are made on a 4-point scale ranging from 1 (*not at all*) to 4 (*always*).

Reliability: Alpha coefficients were .88 (social) and .92 (cognitive).

Validity: Correlations with other variables ranged from −.55 to .40.

Author: Brody, G. H., et al.

Article: Longitudinal pathways to competence and psychological adjustment among African American children living in rural single-parent households.

Journal: *Child Development*, September/October 2002, *73*, 1505–1516.

Related Research: Harter, S. (1982). The Perceived Competence Scale for Children. *Child Development, 53,* 87–97.

12998

Test Name: PERCEIVED COMPETENCE SCALE— PERSIAN VERSION

Purpose: To assess cognitive competence, social competence, physical competence, and general self-worth.

Number of Items: 28

Format: Four-point rating scales are used. All items are presented in English.

Reliability: Alpha coefficients ranged from .74 to .89 across subscales. Total alpha was .91.

Author: Shahim, S.

Article: Self-perception of competence by Iranian children.

Journal: *Psychological Reports,* June 2004, *94,* Part 1, 872–876.

Related Research: Harter, S. (1982). The Perceived Competence Scale for Children. *Child Development, 53,* 87–97.

12999

Test Name: PERCEIVED CONTINGENCY SCALE

Purpose: To measure children's beliefs about the degree of contingency between specific behaviors and outcomes.

Number of Items: 30

Format: Four-point scales are used. A sample item is presented.

Reliability: Alpha coefficients ranged from .53 to .78 across subscales. Total alpha was .85. Test–retest reliabilities ranged from .46 to .68.

Validity: Correlations with other variables ranged from −.04 to .71.

Author: Han, S. S., et al.

Article: Specificity of relations between children's control-related beliefs and internalizing and externalizing psychopathology.

Journal: *Journal of Consulting and Clinical Psychology,* April 2001, *69,* 240–251.

Related Research: Weisz, J. R., et al. (1991). *The Perceived Contingency Scale for Children: Development and validation.* Unpublished manuscript, University of California at Los Angeles.

13000

Test Name: PERCEIVED CONTROL SCALE

Purpose: To measure participants' perceived ease or difficulty in doing leisure-time physical activities.

Number of Items: 3

Format: Responses are made on 7-point scales. An example is given.

Reliability: Coefficient alpha was .81.

Validity: Correlations with other variables ranged from −.04 to .28.

Author: Kerner, M. S., and Kurrant, A. B.

Article: Psychosocial correlates to high school girls' leisure-time physical activity: A test of the theory of planned behavior.

Journal: *Perceptual and Motor Skills,* December 2003, *97,* Part 2, 1175–1183.

13001

Test Name: PERCEIVED CONTROL SCALE

Purpose: To measure perceived control over work and job environment.

Number of Items: 22

Format: Scales range from 1 (*very little*) to 7 (*very much*). Sample items are presented.

Reliability: Coefficient alpha was .92.

Validity: Correlations with other variables ranged from .39 to .52.

Author: Pierce, J. L., et al.

Article: Work environment structure and psychological ownership: The mediating effects of control.

Journal: *The Journal of Social Psychology,* October 2004, *144,* 507–534.

Related Research: Dwyer, D. J., & Ganster, D. C. (1991). The effects of job demands and control on employee attendance and satisfaction. *Journal of Organizational Behavior, 12,* 595–608.

13002

Test Name: PERCEIVED CONTROL SCALE

Purpose: To assess perceived control of personal matters among older people.

Number of Items: 14

Format: Scales range from 1 (*never*) to 7 (*always*). Sample items are presented.

Reliability: Coefficient alpha was .77.

Author: Sinha, S. P., et al.

Article: Social support and self-control as variables in attitude toward life and perceived control among older people in India.

Journal: *The Journal of Social Psychology,* August 2002, *142,* 527–540.

Related Research: Nayyar, P. (1993). *Crowding, stress and environmental perception of the* *elderly: The role of self-control and social support.* Unpublished doctoral dissertation, Dayalbagh Educational Institute, Agra, India.

13003

Test Name: PERCEIVED CONTROL SCALE FOR CHILDREN

Purpose: To measure children's perceptions of personal control.

Number of Items: 24

Format: Four-point rating scales are used. A sample item is presented.

Reliability: Alpha coefficients ranged from .74 to .80 across subscales. Total alpha was .88. Test–retest reliabilities ranged from .51 to .58 across subscales.

Validity: Correlations with other variables ranged from −.01 to .54.

Author: Han, S. S., et al.

Article: Specificity of relations between children's control-related beliefs and internalizing and externalizing psychopathology.

Journal: *Journal of Consulting and Clinical Psychology,* April 2001, *69,* 240–251.

Related Research: Weisz, J. R. (1991). *The Perceived Control Scale for Children.* Unpublished manuscript, University of California, Los Angeles.

13004

Test Name: PERCEIVED CONTROLLEDNESS SCALE

Purpose: To measure perceived controlledness.

Number of Items: 4

Format: Responses are made on a 7-point scale ranging from 1 (*not at all true of me*) to 7 (*very true of me*).

Reliability: Alpha reliabilities were .70 and .72

Validity: Correlations with other variables ranged from −.53 to .43.

Author: McGregor, H. A., and Elliot, A. J.

Article: Achievement goals as predictors of achievement-relevant processes prior to task engagement.

Journal: *Journal of Educational Psychology,* June 2002, *94,* 381–395.

13005

Test Name: PERCEIVED EMPLOYMENT ALTERNATIVES MEASURE

Purpose: To measure perceived employment offers.

Number of Items: 3

Format: Responses are made on 5-point scales. All items are presented.

Reliability: Coefficient alpha was .67.

Validity: Correlations with other variables ranged from −.16 to .17.

Author: Dunford, B., et al.

Article: Out-of-the-money: The impact of underwater stock options on executive job search.

Journal: *Personnel Psychology,* Spring 2005, *58,* 67–101.

Related Research: Martin, T. N. (1980). Modeling the turnover process. *Journal of Management Studies, 17,* 261–274.

13006

Test Name: PERCEIVED ETHNIC SIMILARITY SCALE

Purpose: To determine the client's perception of the counselor's ethnicity.

Number of Items: 3

Format: Responses are made on a 7-point scale ranging from 1 (*not at all*) to 7 (*completely*). All items are presented.

Reliability: Coefficient alpha was .89.

Validity: Correlations with other variables ranged from −.16 to .71.

Author: Kim., B. S. K., and Atkinson, D. R.

Article: Asian American client adherence to Asian cultural values, counselor expression of cultural values, counselor ethnicity, and career counseling process.

Journal: *Journal of Counseling Psychology,* January 2002, *49,* 3–13.

13007

Test Name: PERCEIVED LOCUS OF CAUSALITY IN A LEISURE-TIME PHYSICAL ACTIVITY MEASURE

Purpose: To measure perceived locus of causality in a leisure-time physical activity.

Number of Items: 15

Format: Includes four perceived loci of causality constructs: external regulation, introjected regulation, identified regulation, and intrinsic motivation. Responses are made on a 7-point scale ranging from 1 (*not true at all*) to 7 (*very true*). Examples are presented.

Reliability: Alpha coefficients ranged from .75 to 85.

Validity: Correlations with other variables ranged from −.39 to .49.

Author: Hagger, M. S., et al.

Article: The processes by which perceived autonomy support in physical education promotes leisure-time physical activity intentions and behavior: A trans-contextual model.

Journal: *Journal of Educational Psychology,* December 2003, *95,* 784–795.

Related Research: Mullan, E., et al. (1997). A graded conceptualization of self-determination in the regulation of exercise behavior: Development of a measure using confirmatory factor analysis. *Personality and Individual Differences, 23*, 745–752.

13008

Test Name: PERCEIVED LOCUS OF CAUSALITY IN PHYSICAL EDUCATION MEASURE

Purpose: To measure perceived locus of causality in physical education.

Number of Items: 8

Format: Includes four perceived loci of causality constructs: external regulation, introjected regulation, identified regulation, and intrinsic motivation. Responses are made on a 4-point scale ranging from 1 (*very true*) to 4 (*not true at all*). Examples are given.

Reliability: Alpha coefficients ranged from .66 to .87.

Validity: Correlations with other variables ranged from –.10 to .44.

Author: Hagger, M. S., et al.

Article: The processes by which perceived autonomy support in physical education promotes leisure-time physical activity intentions and behavior: A trans-contextual model.

Journal: *Journal of Educational Psychology*, December 2003, *95*, 784–795.

Related Research: Ryan, R. M., & Connell, J. P. (1989). Perceived locus of causality and internalization. *Journal of Personality and Social Psychology, 5*, 749–761.

13009

Test Name: PERCEIVED ORGANIZATIONAL LEARNING OUTCOMES MEASURE

Purpose: To measure perceived organizational learning outcomes.

Number of Items: 9

Format: Responses are made on a 5-point scale ranging from 5 (*strongly agree*) to 1 (*strongly disagree*). Sample items are presented.

Reliability: Coefficient alpha was .89.

Validity: Correlations with other variables ranged from –.06 to .61.

Author: Mebane, D. J., and Galassi, J. P.

Article: Variables affecting collaborative research and learning in a professional development school partnership.

Journal: *Journal of Educational Research*, May/June 2003, *96*, 259–268.

13010

Test Name: PERCEIVED PARENT EDUCATIONAL ATTITUDES AND BEHAVIORS SCALE

Purpose: To measure students' perceptions of the frequency with which their parent(s) express or are engaged in certain education-facilitative behaviors.

Number of Items: 10

Format: Responses are made on a 5-point Likert scale.

Reliability: Coefficient alpha was .82. Test–retest reliability was .85.

Validity: Correlations with other variables ranged from –.11 to .50.

Author: Wettersten, K. B., et al.

Article: Predicting educational and vocational attitudes among rural high school students.

Journal: *Journal of Counseling Psychology*, October 2005, *52*, 658–663.

13011

Test Name: PERCEIVED PARENTAL VALUE OF ACADEMICS SCALE

Purpose: To measure students' perceptions of their parents' value of academic success.

Number of Items: 6

Format: Responses were made on a 0 to 10 scale. Sample items are presented.

Reliability: Alpha coefficients were .76 and .81.

Validity: Correlations with other variables ranged from .00 to .58.

Author: Klassen, R. M.

Article: A cross-cultural investigation of the efficacy beliefs of South Asian immigrant and Anglo Canadian nonimmigrant early adolescents.

Journal: *Journal of Educational Psychology*, December 2004, *96*, 731–742.

Related Research: Fulgini, A. J. (1997). The academic achievement of adolescents from immigrant families: The roles of family background, attitudes, and behavior. *Child Development, 68*, 351–363.

13012

Test Name: PERCEIVED PEER VALUING OF BEHAVIOR MISCONDUCT SCALE

Purpose: To assess adolescents' perceptions of their peers' values toward the types of behavioral misconduct around which peer pressure frequently occurs.

Number of Items: 8

Reliability: Coefficient alpha was .75.

Validity: Correlations with other variables ranged from –.14 to .49.

Author: Allen, J. P., et al.

Article: The two faces of adolescents' success with peers: Adolescent popularity, social adaptation, and deviant behavior.

Journal: *Child Development,* May/June 2005, 76, 747–760.

Related Research: Clasen, D. R., & Brown, B. B. (1985). The multidimensionality of peer pressure in adolescence. *Journal of Youth and Adolescence, 14,* 451–468.

13013

Test Name: PERCEIVED PHYSICAL EDUCATION COMPETENCE SUBSCALE

Purpose: To assess perceived physical educational competence.

Number of Items: 5

Format: Responses are made on a 5-point scale ranging from 1 (*don't agree at all*) to 5 (*agree completely*). An example is given.

Reliability: Coefficient alpha was .93.

Validity: Correlations with other variables ranged from −.37 to .35.

Author: Cury, F., et al.

Article: Perceptions of competence, implicit theory of ability, perceptions of motivational climate, and achievement goals: A test of the trichotomous conceptualization of endorsement of achievement motivation in the physical education setting.

Journal: *Perceptual and Motor Skills,* August 2002, 95, 233–244.

Related Research: Curry, F., et al. (1996). Personal and situational factors influencing intrinsic interest of adolescent girls in school physical education: A structural equation modeling analysis. *Educational Psychology, 16,* 305–315.

13014

Test Name: PERCEIVED PHYSICAL FITNESS SCALE

Purpose: To assess self-reported physical fitness.

Number of Items: 12

Format: Includes four subdomains: aerobic endurance, flexibility, muscular strength, and body composition. Responses are made on a 5-pont scale. All items are presented.

Reliability: Test–retest (7 to 10 days) reliability coefficient was .92.

Author: Schuler, P. B., and Marzilli, T. S.

Article: Use of self-reports of physical fitness as substitutes for performance-based measures of physical fitness in older adults.

Journal: *Perceptual and Motor Skills,* April 2003, 96, 414–420.

Related Research: Abadie, B. R. (1988). Construction and validation of a Perceived Physical Fitness Scale. *Perceptual and Motor Skills, 67,* 887–892.

13015

Test Name: PERCEIVED SIMILARITY IN VALUES AND PROBLEM-SOLVING SCALE

Purpose: To measure perceived similarity in values and problem-solving style.

Number of Items: 5

Format: Responses are made on a 7-point Likert-type scale ranging from 1 (*strongly disagree*) to 7 (*strongly agree*). Examples are given.

Reliability: Alpha coefficients were .87 and .93.

Validity: Correlations with other variables ranged from −.14 to .76.

Author: Ortiz-Walters, R., and Gilson, L. L.

Article: Mentoring in academia: An examination of the experiences of protégés of color.

Journal: *Journal of Vocational Behavior,* December 2005, 67, 459–475.

Related Research: Ensher, E. A., & Murphy, S. E. (1997). Effects of race, gender, perceived similarity, and contact on mentor relationships. *Journal of Vocational Behavior, 50,* 460–481.

13016

Test Name: PERCEIVED SIMILARITY SCALE

Purpose: To measure doctoral students' perceived similarity to their advisors.

Number of Items: 5

Format: Responses are made on a 7-point scale.

Reliability: Coefficient alpha was .87.

Author: Turban, D. B., et al.

Article: Gender, race, and perceived similarity effects in developmental relationships: The moderating role of relationship duration.

Journal: *Journal of Vocation Behavior,* October 2002, 61, 240–262.

Related Research: Turban, D. B., & Jones, A. P. (1988). Supervisor–subordinate similarity: Types, effects, and mechanisms. *Journal of Applied Psychology, 73,* 228–234.

13017

Test Name: PERCEIVED SOCIAL INEQUITY SCALE—WOMEN'S FORM

Purpose: To measure a woman's perception of her personal experiences of gender-related discrimination.

Number of Items: 26

Format: Includes six factors: physical appearance, career encouragement, academic role models, harassment/assault, career competence, and multiple roles. Responses are made on a 6-point scale ranging from 1 (*not at all*) to 6 (*very much*).

Reliability: Temporal stability (1 and 4 month intervals) was .88.

Author: Corning, A. F.

Article: Self-esteem as a moderator between perceived discrimination and psychological distress among women.

Journal: *Journal of Counseling Psychology*, January 2002, *49*, 117–126.

Related Research: Corning, A. F. (2000). Assessing perceived social inequity: A relative deprivation framework. *Journal of Personality and Social Psychology, 78,* 463–477.

13018

Test Name: PERCEIVED SOCIAL SELF-EFFICACY SCALE

Purpose: To measure social self-efficacy.

Number of Items: 25

Format: Responses are made on a 5-point scale ranging from 1 (*no confidence at all*) to 5 (*complete confidence*). Sample items are presented.

Reliability: Coefficient alpha was .94. Test–retest (3 weeks) reliability was .82.

Validity: Correlation with other variables ranged from –.80 to .62.

Author: Smith, H. M., and Betz, N. E.

Article: An examination of efficacy and esteem pathways to depression in young adulthood.

Journal: *Journal of Counseling Psychology*, October 2002, *49*, 438–448

Related Research: Smith, H. M., & Betz, N. E. (2000). Development and validation of a scale of perceived social self-efficacy. *Journal of Career Assessment, 8,* 283–301.

13019

Test Name: PERCEIVED SOCIOCULTURAL PRESSURE SCALE

Purpose: To measure women's reported pressure for thinness from significant others and the media.

Number of Items: 8

Format: One of three responses is recorded for each item: no pressure, some pressure, or a lot of pressure.

Reliability: Coefficient alpha was .87. Stability over 2 weeks was .93.

Validity: Correlations with other variables ranged from –.30 to –.67.

Author: Tylka, T. L., and Subich, L. M.

Article: Examining a multidimensional model of eating disorder symptomatology among college women.

Journal: *Journal of Counseling Psychology*, July 2004, *51*, 314–328.

Related Research: Stice, E., et al. (1996). The dual pathway model differentiates bulimics, subclinical bulimics, and controls: Testing the continuity hypothesis. *Behavior Therapy, 27,* 531–549.

13020

Test Name: PERCEIVED SYSTEM KNOWLEDGE SCALE

Purpose: To measure employee perceptions of how well they understand the performance appraisal system.

Number of Items: 11

Format: Responses are made on a 5-point Likert scale ranging from *strongly disagree* to *strongly agree*. Sample items are presented.

Reliability: Coefficient alpha was .88.

Validity: Correlations with other variables ranged from .18 to .48.

Author: Haworth, C. L., and Levy, P. E.

Article: The importance of instrumentality beliefs in the prediction of organizational citizenship behaviors.

Journal: *Journal of Vocational Behavior,* August 2001, *59,* 64–75.

Related Research: Levy, P. E., & Williams, J. R. (1998). The role of perceived system knowledge in predicting appraisal reactions, job satisfaction, and organizational commitment. *Journal of Organizational Behavior, 19,* 53–65.

13021

Test Name: PERCEIVED THREAT SCALE

Purpose: To measure perceptions of intergroup threat.

Number of Items: 15

Format: Scales range from 1 (*threatening*) to 7 (*enriching*). Sample items are presented.

Reliability: Coefficient alpha was .93.

Validity: Correlations with other variables ranged from –.66 to .59.

Author: Florack, A., et al.

Article: Perceived intergroup threat and attitudes of host community members toward immigrant acculturation.

Journal: *The Journal of Social Psychology*, October 2003, *143*, 633–648.

13022

Test Name: PERCEIVED UNION SUPPORT SCALE

Purpose: To measure perceived union support.

Number of Items: 8

Format: Scales range from 1 (*strongly disagree*) to 5 (*strongly agree*). Sample items are presented.

Reliability: Coefficient alpha was .86.

Validity: Correlations with other variables ranged from −.29 to .65.

Author: Aryee, S., and Chay, Y. W.

Article: Workplace justice, citizenship behavior, and turnover intentions in a union context: Examining the mediating role of perceived union support and union instrumentality.

Journal: *Journal of Applied Psychology*, February 2001, *86*, 154–160.

Related Research: Shore, L. M., et al. (1994). Validation of a measure of perceived union support. *Journal of Applied Psychology, 79*, 971–977.

13023

Test Name: PERCEIVED WELLNESS SURVEY

Purpose: To assess the degree to which adolescents and adults perceive themselves to be functioning across six life dimensions.

Number of Items: 36

Format: Includes six dimensions: Emotional, Intellectual, Physical, Psychological, Social, and Spiritual. Responses are made on a 6-point scale ranging from 1 (*very strongly disagree*) to 6 (*very strongly agree*). All items are presented.

Reliability: Reliability estimates ranged from .73 to .81 over 2 to 4 weeks.

Author: Harari, M. J., et al.

Article: An empirical investigation of a theoretical based measure of perceived wellness.

Journal: *Journal of Counseling Psychology*, January 2005, *52*, 93–103.

Related Research: Adams, T., et al. (1997). The conceptualization and

measurement of perceived wellness: Integrating balance across and within dimensions. *American Journal of Health Promotion, 11*, 208–218.

13024

Test Name: PERCEPTION OF POWER SCALE

Purpose: To measure coercive, legitimate, and expert power.

Number of Items: 15

Format: Response scales range from 1 (*most strongly agree*) to 15 (*strongly disagree*).

Reliability: Alpha coefficients ranged from .71 to .75.

Author: Ross, A., and Barker, K.

Article: Cell phones, clothing, and sex: First impressions of power using older African Americans as stimuli.

Journal: *Psychological Reports*, December 2003, *93*, Part 1, 879–882.

Related Research: Temple, L. E., & Loewen, K. R. (1993). Perception of power: First impressions of a woman wearing a jacket. *Perceptual and Motor Skills, 76*, 339–348.

13025

Test Name: PERCEPTION OF TATTOOS SCALE

Purpose: To measure perception of tattoos.

Number of Items: 5

Format: Item responses are anchored by *strongly agree* and *strongly disagree*. All items are presented.

Reliability: Alpha was .72.

Validity: Correlations with other variables ranged from −.33 to .72.

Author: Lin, Y.

Article: Age, sex, education, religion and perceptions of tattoos.

Journal: *Psychological Reports*, April 2002, *90*, 654–658.

13026

Test Name: PERCEPTIONS OF BARRIERS SCALE

Purpose: To assess junior and senior high school students' perceptions of the likelihood that they will experience specific barriers to career and educational goals.

Number of Items: 24

Format: Responses are made on a 5-point Likert scale ranging from 1 (*strongly disagree*) to 5 (*strongly agree*).

Reliability: Alpha coefficients were .86 and .87.

Validity: Correlations with other variables ranged from −.02 to −.29.

Author: Kenny, M. E., et al.

Article: The role of perceived barriers and relational support in the educational and vocational lives of urban high school students.

Journal: *Journal of Counseling Psychology*, April 2003, *50*, 142–155.

Related Research: McWhirter, E. H. (1997). Perceived barriers to education and career: Ethnic and gender difference. *Journal of Vocational Behavior, 50*, 124–140.

13027

Test Name: PERCEPTIONS OF EDUCATIONAL BARRIERS SCALE

Purpose: To assess the likelihood of encountering barriers to educational achievement as perceived by high school students.

Number of Items: 28

Format: Includes three areas: individual student characteristics, school and college characteristics, and social group characteristics. Responses are made on a 4-point scale ranging from 1 (*not at all likely*) to 4 (*definitely*).

Reliability: Alpha coefficients were .88 and .89.

Validity: Correlations with other variables ranged from −.10 to −.28.

Author: Kenny, M. E., and Bledsoe, M.

Article: Contributions of the relational context to career adaptability among urban adolescents.

Journal: *Journal of Vocational Behavior*, April 2005, *66*, 257–272.

Related Research: McWhirter, E. H., et al. (2000). The effects of high school career education on social–cognitive variables. *Journal of Counseling Psychology, 47,* 330–341.

13028

Test Name: PERCEPTIONS OF EDUCATIONAL BARRIERS SCALE

Purpose: To assess three dimensions of possible barriers to the pursuit of postsecondary education.

Number of Items: 84

Format: Includes three dimensions of possible barriers: Likelihood of Occurrence, Magnitude of Potential Barrier, and Estimated Difficulty in Overcoming. Responses are made on a 4-point Likert-type scale.

Reliability: Alpha coefficients were .89 and .96. Test–retest reliability was .57.

Validity: Correlations with other variables ranged from −.07 to −.31.

Author: Wettersten, K. B., et al.

Article: Predicting educational and vocational attitudes among rural high school students.

Journal: *Journal of Counseling Psychology*, October 2005, *52*, 658–663.

Related Research: McWhirter, E. H., et al. (2000). The effects of high school career education on social–cognitive variables. *Journal of Counseling Psychology, 47,* 330–341.

13029

Test Name: PERFORMANCE EXPECTATIONS SCALE

Purpose: To assess performance expectations.

Number of Items: 3

Format: Responses are made on a 7-point scale ranging from 1 (*poor performance*) to 7 (*excellent performance*).

Reliability: Coefficient alpha was .79.

Validity: Correlations with other variables ranged from −.29 to .59.

Author: Taggar, S., and Neubert, M.

Article: The impact of poor performers on team outcomes: An empirical examination of attribution theory.

Journal: *Personnel Psychology*, Winter 2004, *57*, 935–968.

Related Research: Struthers, C. W., et al. (1998). Effects of causal attributions on personnel decisions: A social motivation perspective. *Basic and Applied Social Psychology, 20,* 155–166.

13030

Test Name: PERSONAL EFFICACY BELIEFS SCALE

Purpose: To measure job self-efficacy.

Number of Items: 10

Format: Scales range from 1 (*very inaccurate*) to 5 (*very accurate*). A sample item is presented.

Reliability: Coefficient alpha was .74.

Validity: Correlations with other variables ranged from −.38 to .25.

Author: Schaubroeck, J., et al.

Article: Individual differences in utilizing control to cope with job demands: Effects on susceptibility to infectious disease.

Journal: *Journal of Applied Psychology*, April 2001, *86*, 265–278.

Related Research: Riggs, M. L., et al. (1994). Development and validation of self-efficacy and outcome expectancy scales for job-related applications. *Educational and Psychological Measurement, 54,* 793–802.

13031

Test Name: PERSONAL EFFICACY BELIEFS SCALE— ADAPTED

Purpose: To assess job self-efficacy.

Number of Items: 9

Format: Responses are made on a 6-point Likert scale ranging from 1 (*strongly disagree*) to 6 (*strongly agree*). An example is given.

Reliability: Alpha coefficients were .80 and .82 ($n = 195$).

Validity: Correlations with other variables ranged from −.18 to .44 ($n = 195$).

Author: Lubbers, R., et al.

Article: Young workers' job self-efficacy and affect: Pathways to health and performance.

Journal: *Journal of Vocational Behavior*, October 2005, *67*, 199–214.

Related Research: Riggs, M. L., et al. (1994). Development and validation of self-efficacy and outcome expectancy scales for job-related applications. *Educational and Psychological Measurement, 54,* 793–802.

13032

Test Name: PERSONAL EFFICACY SUBSCALE

Purpose: To assess perceptions relevant to goal achievement and personal control.

Number of Items: 10

Format: Responses are made on a 7-pont Likert-type scale ranging from 1 (*disagree*) to 7 (*agree*). An example is given.

Reliability: Alpha coefficients ranged from .36 to .75. Test–retest (4 weeks) coefficient was above 90.

Author: Robinson, B. S., et al.

Article: Motivational attributes of occupational possible selves for low-income rural women.

Journal: *Journal of Counseling Psychology*, April 2003, *50*, 156–164.

Related Research: Paulhus, D., & Christie, R. (1981). Spheres of control: An interactionist approach to assessment of perceived control. In H. M. Defcourt (Ed.), *Research with the locus of control construct* (Vol. 1, pp. 161–185). New York: Academic Press.

13033

Test Name: PERSONAL FOCUS SCALE

Purpose: To measure personal focus.

Number of Items: 5

Format: Responses are made of a 5-point scale ranging from 1 (*strongly disagree*) to 5 (*strongly agree*). All items are presented.

Reliability: Coefficient alpha was .78 (*N* = 989).

Validity: Correlations with other variables ranged from .07 to .52 (*N* = 989).

Author: Allen, D. G., et al.

Article: Recruitment communication media: Impact on prehire outcomes.

Journal: *Personnel Psychology*, Spring 2004, *57*, 143–171.

Related Research: Short, J., et al. (1976). *The social psychology of communications*. London: Wiley.

13034

Test Name: PERSONAL IDENTITY SCALE

Purpose: To measure the psychological state reflecting self-knowledge and a firm, consistent set of personal values.

Number of Items: 25

Format: Sample items are presented.

Reliability: Alpha was .90.

Validity: Correlations with other variables ranged from .23 to .45.

Author: Goldman, B. M., et al.

Article: Goal-directedness and personal identity as correlates of life outcomes.

Journal: *Psychological Reports*, August 2002, *91*, 153–166.

Related Research: Heath, D. H. (1991). *Fulfilling lives: Paths to maturity and success*. San Francisco: Jossey-Bass.

13035

Test Name: PERSONAL NEED FOR STRUCTURE SCALE— ADAPTED CHINESE VERSION

Purpose: To measure stable individual differences in the desire to construe the world in simple structures.

Number of Items: 6

Format: Responses are made on a 6-point scale ranging from 1 (*strongly disagree*) to 6 (*strongly agree*).

Reliability: Alpha coefficients ranged from .73 to .81 (*n* = 239).

Validity: Correlations with other variables ranged from −.09 to .82 (*n* = 239).

Author: Moneta, G. B., and Yip, P. P. Y.

Article: Construct validity of the scores of the Chinese version of the Need for Closure Scale.

Journal: *Educational and Psychological Measurement*, June 2004, *64*, 531–548.

Related Research: Neuberg, S. L., et al. (1997). What the Need for Closure Scale measures and what it does not: Toward differentiating among related epistemic motives. *Journal of Personality and Social Psychology*, *72*, 1396–1412.

13036

Test Name: PHYSICAL SELF-DESCRIPTION QUESTIONNAIRE

Purpose: To measure adolescents' physical self-concept.

Number of Items: 70

Format: Includes 11 subscales: Strength, Body Fat, Physical Activity, Endurance/Fitness, Sports Competence, Coordination, Health, Appearance, Flexibility, General Physical Self-Concept, and Self-Esteem. Responses are made on a 6-point scale ranging from *false* to *true*.

Reliability: Alpha coefficients ranged from .82 to .94.

Author: Fletcher, R., and Hattie, J.

Article: Gender differences in physical self-concept: A multidimensional differential item functioning analysis.

Journal: *Educational and Psychological Measurement*, August 2005, *65*, 657–667.

Related Research: Marsh, H. W., et al. (1994). Physical Self-Description Questionnaire: Psychometric properties and a multitrait-multimethod analysis of relations with existing instruments. *Journal of Sport and Exercise Psychology, 15,* 270–305.

13037

Test Name: PHYSICAL SELF-EFFICACY SCALE

Purpose: To assess confidence in performing physical tasks, confidence in displaying physical skills, and confidence in being evaluated in physical skills.

Number of Items: 22

Format: Includes two subscales: Perceived Physical Ability and Physical Self-Presentation Confidence. Responses are made on a 6-point Likert scale ranging from 1 (*strongly disagree*) to 6 (*strongly agree*). Examples are given.

Reliability: Alpha coefficients were .68 and .77.

Validity: Correlations with other variables ranged from .29 to .60.

Author: Wright, P. M., et al.

Article: Relations of perceived physical self-efficacy and motivational responses toward physical activity by urban high school students.

Journal: *Perceptual and Motor Skills,* October 2005, *101,* 651–656.

Related Research: Ryckman, R., et al. (1982). Development and validation of a physical self-efficacy scale. *Journal of Personality and Social Psychology, 42,* 891–900.

13038

Test Name: PHYSICAL SELF-PERCEPTION PROFILE

Purpose: To assess general physical self-worth and physical self-perceptions.

Number of Items: 30

Format: Includes physical self-worth, body attractiveness, sport competence, strength competence,

and physical conditioning. Uses a 4-point structured alternative format.

Reliability: Alpha coefficients ranged from .85 to .89.

Validity: Correlations with other variables ranged from −.18 to .37.

Author: Newton, M., et al.

Article: Relationship between achievement goal constructs and physical self-perceptions in a physical activity setting.

Journal: *Perceptual and Motor Skills,* December 2004, *99,* Part 1, 757–770.

Related Research: Fox, K. R., & Corbin, C. B. (1989). The Physical Self-Perception Profile: Development and preliminary validation. *Journal of Sport and Exercise Psychology, 11,* 408–430.

13039

Test Name: PHYSICAL SELF-PERCEPTION PROFILE FOR CHILDREN

Purpose: To measure children's physical self-perceptions.

Number of Items: 36

Format: Includes six factors: sports competence, physical condition, body attractiveness, physical strength, general physical self-concept, and global self-concept.

Reliability: Reliability coefficients ranged from .80 to .92.

Author: Hagger, M. S., et al.

Article: Physical self-concept in adolescence: Generalizability of a multidimensional, hierarchical model across gender and grade.

Journal: *Educational and Psychological Measurement,* April 2005, *65,* 297–322.

Related Research: Whitehead, J. R. (1995). A study of children's physical self-perceptions using an adapted Physical Self-Perception

Profile Questionnaire. *Pediatric Exercise Science, 7,* 132–151.

13040

Test Name: PHYSICAL SELF-PERCEPTION PROFILE—JAPANESE SHORT VERSION

Purpose: To assess physical self-perception.

Number of Items: 15

Format: Includes Physical Self-Worth and four subdomains: Sports Competence, Physical Condition, Attractive Body, and Physical Strength. Responses are made on a 4-point Likert scale ranging from 1 (*strongly disagree*) to 4 (*strongly agree*).

Reliability: Alpha coefficients ranged from .74 to .82.

Author: Uchida, W., et al.

Article: Examination of the hierarchical self-esteem model in adults with physical disabilities.

Journal: *Perceptual and Motor Skills,* June 2005, *100,* Part 2, 1161–1170.

Related Research: Minouchi, Y. (1999). [Development of the Physical Self-Perception Profile, Japanese short version]. In [*50th of Japanese Society of Physical Education Proceedings*] (p. 334). [in Japanese]

13041

Test Name: PLURALISM SCALE

Purpose: To measure the plurality of the self.

Number of Items: 10

Format: A yes–no format is used.

Reliability: Coefficient alpha was .79.

Validity: Correlation with Taoist orientation was .47.

Author: Lester, D.

Article: The plural self.

Journal: *Perceptual and Motor Skills*, April 2003, *96*, 370.

Related Research: Altrocchi, J. (1999) Individual differences in pluralism in self-structure. In J. Rowan & M. Cooper (Eds.), *The plural self* (pp. 168–182). London: Sage.

13042

Test Name: POLITICS PERCEPTIONS SCALE

Purpose: To tap politics perceptions at work.

Number of Items: 6

Format: Items examined three organizational levels. Responses are made on a 5-point scale ranging from 1 (*never true*) to 5 (*always true*). All items are presented.

Validity: Correlations with other variables ranged from .31 to −.64 (*n* = 311).

Author: Hochwarter, W. A., et al.

Article: Perceived organizational support as a mediator of the relationship between politics perceptions and work outcomes.

Journal: *Journal of Vocational Behavior*, December 2003, *63*, 438–456.

Related Research: Cropanzano, R. S., et al. (1995). Organizational politics, justice, and support: Their differences and similarities. In R. S. Cropanzano & K. M. Kacmar (Eds.), *Organizational politics, justice, and support: Managing the social climate of the workplace* (pp. 2–18). Westport, CT: Quorum Books.

13043

Test Name: PREENTRY KNOWLEDGE TEST

Purpose: To measure the general perception that new employees understood their new jobs.

Number of Items: 5

Format: Scales range from 1 (*strongly disagree*) to 5 (*strongly agree*). A sample item is presented.

Reliability: Coefficient alpha was .85.

Validity: Correlations with other variables ranged from −.13 to .34.

Author: Kammeyer-Mueller, J. D., and Wanberg, C. R.

Article: Unwrapping the organizational entry process: Disentangling multiple antecedents and their pathways to adjustment.

Journal: *Journal of Applied Psychology*, October 2003, *88*, 779–794.

Related Research: Breaugh, J. A., & Mann, R. B. (1984). Recruiting source effects: A test of two alternative explanations. *Journal of Occupational Psychology*, *57*, 261–267.

13044

Test Name: PRIVATE SELF-CONSCIOUSNESS SCALE

Purpose: To measure consciousness of and reflection upon one's own feelings, motives, and ideas.

Number of Items: 10

Format: Responses are made on a 5-point scale ranging from 0 (*extremely uncharacteristic/not at all like me*) to 4 (*extremely characteristic/very much like me*).

Reliability: Alpha coefficients were .60 and .75. Test–retest (10 weeks) reliability was .69.

Author: Schomburg, A. M., and Tokar, D. M.

Article: The moderating effect of private self-consciousness on the stability of vocational interests.

Journal: *Journal of Vocational Behavior*, December 2003, *63*, 368–378.

Related Research: Fenigstein, A., et al. (1975). Public and private self-consciousness: Assessment and

theory. *Journal of Consulting and Clinical Psychology*, *43*, 522–527.

13045

Test Name: PRIVATE SELF-CONSCIOUSNESS SCALE—HEBREW VERSION

Purpose: To measure the dispositional tendency to focus on the private aspects of the self.

Number of Items: 10

Format: Responses are made on a 5-point scale ranging from 0 (*extremely uncharacteristic*) to 4 (*extremely characteristic*).

Reliability: Test–retest (2 weeks) reliability was .79. Coefficient alpha ranged from .63 to .76.

Author: Ben-Artzi, E.

Article: Factor structure of the Private Self-Consciousness Scale: Role of item wording.

Journal: *Journal of Personality Assessment*, December 2003, *81*, 256–264.

Related Research: Fenigstein, A., et al. (1975). Public and private self-consciousness: Assessment and theory. *Journal of Consulting and Clinical Psychology*, *43*, 522–527.

13046

Test Name: PRIVATE SELF-CONSCIOUSNESS SCALE—PERSIAN VERSION

Purpose: To assess internal state awareness and self-reflectiveness.

Number of Items: 8

Format: Scales ranged from 0 (*strongly disagree*) to 4 (*strongly agree*).

Reliability: Alpha coefficients ranged from .53 to .60.

Validity: Correlations with other variables ranged from −.24 to .41.

Author: Ghorbani, N., et al.

Article: Private self-consciousness factors: Relationships with need for cognition, locus of control, and obsessive thinking in Iran and the United States.

Journal: *The Journal of Social Psychology*, August 2004, *144*, 359–372.

Related Research: Mittal, B., & Balasubramian, S. K. (1997). Testing the dimensionality of the self-consciousness scales. *Journal of Personality Assessment, 51*, 53–68.

13047

Test Name: PSYCHOLOGICAL CONTRACT SCALES

Purpose: To assess the degree to which employees believe employers should meet certain obligations and the degree to which employers actually meet those obligations.

Number of Items: 12

Format: Five-point scales are used. All items and response categories are presented.

Reliability: Alpha coefficients ranged from .83 to .95.

Validity: Correlations with other variables ranged from –.06 to .36.

Author: Coyle-Shapiro, J. A.-M., and Conway, N.

Article: Exchange relationships: Examining psychological contracts and perceived organizational support.

Journal: *Journal of Applied Psychology*, July 2005, *90*, 774–781.

13048

Test Name: PSYCHOLOGICAL ENTITLEMENT SCALE

Purpose: To measure psychological entitlement.

Number of Items: 9

Format: Responses are made on a 7-point scale ranging from 1 (*strong disagreement*) to 7 (*strong*

agreement). All items are presented.

Reliability: Alpha coefficients were .85 and .87. Test–retest (1 month) reliability was .72. Test–retest (2 months) reliability was .70.

Validity: Correlations with other variables ranged from –.43 to .54.

Author: Campbell, W. K., et al.

Article: Psychological entitlement: Interpersonal consequences and validation of a self-report measure.

Journal: *Journal of Personality Assessment*, August 2004, *83*, 29–45.

13049

Test Name: PSYCHOLOGICAL OWNERSHIP OF JOB SCALES

Purpose: To measure employee psychological ownership of organization and job.

Number of Items: 12

Format: Scales range from 1 (*strongly disagree*) to 7 (*strongly agree*). Sample items are presented.

Reliability: Alpha coefficients ranged from .92 to .93.

Validity: Correlations with other variables ranged from .31 to .52.

Author: Pierce, J. L., et al.

Article: Work environment structure and psychological ownership: The mediating effects of control.

Journal: *The Journal of Social Psychology*, October 2004, *144*, 507–534.

Related Research: Pierce, J. L., et al. (1992). Psychological ownership: A conceptual and operational exploration. In *Southern Management Association Proceedings*, 203–211.

13050

Test Name: PSYCHOLOGY AS A SCIENCE SCALE

Purpose: To assess perceptions of psychology as a science.

Number of Items: 15

Format: Scales range from 1 (*strongly disagree*) to 7 (*strongly agree*). All items are presented.

Reliability: Coefficient alpha was .58.

Author: Bartoszeck, A. B., et al.

Article: Perception of students in the south of Brazil of status of psychology as a science.

Journal: *Psychological Reports*, December 2005, *97*, 750–756.

Related Research: Friedrich, J. (1996). Assessing students' perceptions of psychology as a science: Validation of a self-report measure. *Teaching of Psychology, 23*, 6–13.

13051

Test Name: RAPE ATTRIBUTION QUESTIONNAIRE

Purpose: To assess behavioral and characterological self-blame and external blame.

Number of Items: 21

Format: Five-point scales are anchored by *never* and *very often*. Sample items are presented.

Reliability: Alpha coefficients ranged from .76 to .83 across subscales.

Author: Koss, M. P., et al.

Article: Cognitive mediation of rape's mental, physical, and social health impact: Tests of four models in cross-sectional data.

Journal: *Journal of Consulting and Clinical Psychology*, August 2002, *70*, 926–941.

Related Research: Frazier, P. (2000). The role of attributions and perceived control in recovery from rape. *Journal of Personal and Interpersonal Loss, 5*, 203–225.

13052

Test Name: RAPE ATTRIBUTION QUESTIONNAIRE

Purpose: To assess the extent to which assault victims attributed their assault to their past behaviors, felt they had control over their recovery, and engaged in behavior to avoid further assaults.

Number of Items: 16

Format: Response categories range from 1 (*never or strongly disagree*) to 5 (*very often or strongly agree*). Sample items are presented.

Reliability: Alphas averaged .83 to .87 over subscales and over four time periods.

Author: Frazier, P., et al.

Article: Correlates of levels and patterns of positive life changes following sexual assault.

Journal: *Journal of Consulting and Clinical Psychology*, February 2004, 72, 19–30.

Related Research: Frazier, P. A. (2002). *Rape Attribution Questionnaire*. Unpublished manuscript, University of Minnesota.

13053

Test Name: RAPE ATTRIBUTION QUESTIONNAIRE

Purpose: To assess the extent to which survivors attributed the assault to their past behaviors and felt control over the recovery process.

Number of Items: 10

Format: Responses are made on 5-point scales.

Reliability: Alpha coefficients ranged from .71 to .90. Test–retest (4 months) reliability coefficients were .64 and .65.

Author: Frazier, P. A., et al.

Article: Coping strategies as mediators of the relations among

perceived control and distress in sexual assault survivors.

Journal: *Journal of Counseling Psychology*, July 2005, 52, 267–278.

Related Research: Frazier, P. A. (2003). Perceived control and distress following sexual assault: A longitudinal test of a new model. *Journal of Personality and Social Psychology*, 84, 1257–1269.

13054

Test Name: RAPE ATTRIBUTION QUESTIONNAIRE

Purpose: To assess behavioral self-blame, characterological self-blame, and external blame.

Number of Items: 21

Format: Five-point scales range from *never* to *very often*.

Reliability: Alpha coefficients ranged from .76 to .83.

Author: Koss, M. P., and Figueredo, A. J.

Article: Change in cognitive mediators of rape's impact on psychosocial health across 2 years of recovery.

Journal: *Journal of Consulting and Clinical Psychology*, December 2004, 72, 1063–1072.

Related Research: Frazier, P. A. (2000). The role of attributions and perceived control in recovery from rape. *Journal of Personal and Interpersonal Loss*, 5, 203–225.

13055

Test Name: REEMPLOYMENT CONSTRAINT SCALE

Purpose: To assess the perceived barriers to reemployment.

Number of Items: 6

Format: Subjects respond with *agree* or *disagree*. All items are presented.

Reliability: Coefficient alpha was .75.

Validity: Correlations with other variables ranged from −.15 to .18.

Author: Wanberg, C. R., et al.

Article: Predictive validity of a multidisciplinary model of reemployment success.

Journal: *Journal of Applied Psychology*, December 2002, 87, 1100–1120.

Related Research: Brooks, M. G., & Buckner, J. C. (1996). Work and welfare: Job histories, barriers to employment, and predictors of work among low-income single mothers. *American Journal of Orthopsychiatry*, 66, 526–537.

13056

Test Name: RELAPSE SITUATION EFFICACY QUESTIONNAIRE (RSEQ)

Purpose: To measure a person's confidence in their ability to resist temptations to smoke in a wide variety of contexts.

Number of Items: 43

Format: Four-point scales range from 1 (*not confident at all*) to 4 (*extremely confident*). All items are presented.

Reliability: Alpha coefficients ranged from .77 to .91.

Author: Gwaltney, C. J., et al.

Article: Does smoking abstinence self-efficacy vary across situations? Identifying context specificity within the Relapse Situation Efficacy Questionnaire.

Journal: *Journal of Consulting and Clinical Psychology*, June 2001, 69, 516–527.

Related Research: Shiffman, S. (1982). Relapse following smoking cessation: A situational analysis. *Journal of Consulting and Clinical Psychology*, 50, 71–86.

13057

Test Name: RELATIONAL SELF-CONSTRUAL SCALE

Purpose: To measure the extent to which the construal of self is linked to others.

Number of Items: 11

Format: Scales range from 1 (*strongly disagree*) to 7 (*strongly agree*).

Reliability: Scales range from .84 to .94.

Validity: Correlations with other variables ranged from −.11 to .24.

Author: Ma, P.-W. W., and Yeh, C. J.

Article: Factors influencing the career decision status of Chinese American youth.

Journal: *The Career Development Quarterly*, June 2005, *53*, 337–347.

Related Research: Cross, S. E., et al. (2000). The relational-interdependent self-construal and relationships. *Journal of Personality and Social Psychology*, *78*, 791–808.

13058

Test Name: RESEARCH OUTCOME EXPECTATIONS QUESTIONNAIRE

Purpose: To measure students' expected consequences of conducting research.

Number of Items: 17

Format: Responses are made on a 5-point Likert scale ranging from 1 (*strongly disagree*) to 5 (*strongly agree*).

Reliability: Alpha coefficients ranged from .88 to .90.

Validity: Correlations with other variables ranged from −.22 to .74 (*N* = 149).

Author: Kahn, J. H.

Article: Predicting the scholarly activity of counseling psychology students: A refinement and extension.

Journal: *Journal of Counseling Psychology*, July 2001, *48*, 344–354.

Related Research: Bishop, R. M., & Bieschke, K. J. (1998). Applying social cognitive theory to interest in research among counseling psychology doctoral students: A path analysis. *Journal of Counseling Psychology*, *45*, 182–188.

13059

Test Name: RESEARCH OUTCOMES EXPECTATIONS QUESTIONNAIRE

Purpose: To assess research outcome expectations.

Number of Items: 8

Format: Responses are made on a 5-point Likert scale ranging from 1 (*strongly disagree*) to 5 (*strongly agree*). Examples are given.

Reliability: Coefficient alpha was .90.

Author: Phillips, J. C., et al.

Article: Preliminary examination and measurement of the internship research training environment.

Journal: *Journal of Counseling Psychology*, April 2004, *51*, 240–248.

Related Research: Bieschke, K. J. (2000). Factor structure of the Research Outcome Expectations Scale. *Journal of Career Assessment*, *8*, 303–313.

13060

Test Name: REVISED MULTIDIMENSIONAL HEALTH LOCUS OF CONTROL SCALE

Purpose: To measure locus of control.

Number of Items: 27

Format: Scales range from 1 (*disagree a lot*) to 6 (*agree a lot*). Sample items are presented.

Reliability: Alpha coefficients ranged from .66 to .96.

Author: Ayalon, L., and Young, M. A.

Article: Racial group differences in help-seeking behaviors.

Journal: *The Journal of Social Psychology*, August 2005, *145*, 391–403.

Related Research: Bekhuis, T., et al. (1995). Ethnicity, church affiliation and beliefs about the causal agents of health: A comparative study employing a multivariate analysis of covariance. *Health Education Research*, *10*, 73–82.

13061

Test Name: REVISED SELF-MONITORING SCALE

Purpose: To assess self-monitoring and concern for social appropriateness.

Number of Items: 33

Format: Includes two subscales: Self-Monitoring and Concern for Social Appropriateness. Responses are made on a 6-point scale ranging from 0 (*certainly, always false*) to 5 (*certainly, always true*).

Reliability: Alpha coefficients were .77 and .80.

Validity: Correlations with other variables ranged from −.54 to .48 (*n* = 211).

Author: Livingstone, H. A., and Day, A. L.

Article: Comparing the construct and criterion-related validity of ability-based and mixed-model measures of emotional intelligence.

Journal: *Educational and Psychological Measurement*, October 2005, *65*, 851–873.

Related Research: Lennox, R. D., & Wolfe, R. N. (1984). Revision of the Self-Monitoring Scale. *Journal of Personality and Social Psychology, 46,* 1349–1364.

13062

Test Name: RISKY SITUATION SELF-EFFICACY SCALE

Purpose: To assess self-efficacy beliefs in situations of conflict and peer pressure.

Number of Items: 10

Format: Five-point scales range from *always true* to *always false.*

Reliability: Internal consistency reliability was .77.

Author: Vera, E. M., et al.

Article: Conflict resolution styles, self-efficacy, self-control, and future orientation of urban adolescents.

Journal: *Professional School Counseling,* October 2004, *8,* 73–80.

Related Research: Reese, L. E. & Vera, E. M. (1995). *The Risk Situation Self-Efficacy Scale.* Unpublished manuscript.

13063

Test Name: ROLE AMBIGUITY AND ROLE CONFLICT SCALE

Purpose: To measure role ambiguity and role conflict.

Number of Items: 14

Format: Scales range from 1 (*very false*) to 7 (*very true*).

Reliability: Alpha coefficients were .81 (ambiguity) and .84 (conflict).

Author: Zellars, K. L., and Perrewé, P. L.

Article: Affective personality and the content of emotional social support: Coping in organizations.

Journal: *Journal of Applied Psychology,* June 2001, *86,* 59–467.

Related Research: Rizzo, J. R., et al. (1970). Role conflict and ambiguity in complex organizations. *Administrative Science Quarterly, 15,* 150–163.

13064

Test Name: ROLE AMBIGUITY AND ROLE CONFLICT SCALES— FRENCH VERSION ADAPTED

Purpose: To assess role ambiguity and role conflict.

Number of Items: 12

Format: Includes two scales: Role Ambiguity and Role Conflict. Responses are made on a 7-point scale ranging from 1 (*definitively false*) to 7 (*definitively true*). Examples are given.

Reliability: Alpha coefficients were .69 and .80.

Author: Fernet, C., et al.

Article: Adjusting to job demands: The role of work self-determination and job control in predicting burnout.

Journal: *Journal of Vocational Behavior,* August 2004, *65,* 39–56.

Related Research: Lachance, L., et al. (1997). Validation canadienne-française de la mesure de conflit et d'ambiguité derôle de Rizzo et al. [French-Canadian validation of the Rizzo et al.'s role conflict and role ambiguity scale.] (1970). *Revue Canadienne des Sciences du Comportement, 29,* 283–287.

13065

Test Name: ROLE BREADTH SELF-EFFICACY SCALE

Purpose: To assess an employee's confidence in carrying out a range of tasks to improve their work.

Number of Items: 4

Format: Scales range from 1 (*not at all confident*) to 5 (*very confident*). Sample items are described.

Reliability: Alpha coefficients ranged from .86 to .89.

Validity: Correlations with other variables ranged from –.02 to .34.

Author: Parker, S. K.

Article: Longitudinal effects of lean production on employee outcomes and the mediating role of work characteristics.

Journal: *Journal of Applied Psychology,* August 2003, *88,* 620–634.

Related Research: Parker, S. K. (1998). Role breadth self-efficacy: Relationships with work enrichment and other organizational practices. *Journal of Applied Psychology, 83,* 835–852.

13066

Test Name: ROLE CLARITY SCALE

Purpose: To measure role clarity.

Number of Items: 8

Format: Scales range from 1 (*very uncertain*) to 7 (*very certain*).

Reliability: Coefficient alpha was .92.

Validity: Correlations with other variables ranged from –.03 to .64.

Author: Brown, S. P., et al.

Article: Self-efficacy as a moderator of information-seeking effectiveness.

Journal: *Journal of Applied Psychology,* October 2001, *86,* 1043–1051.

Related Research: Singh, J., & Rhoads, G. K. (1991). Boundary role ambiguity in marketing-oriented positions: A multidimensional, multifaceted operationalization. *Journal of Marketing Research, 28,* 328–338.

13067

Test Name: ROLE CONFLICT AND ROLE AMBIGUITY INVENTORY

Purpose: To provide an estimate of trainees' perceptions of opposing expectations for their behavior (conflict) and their uncertainty about supervisory expectations for their performance (ambiguity).

Number of Items: 29

Format: Includes two subscales: Role Conflict and Role Ambiguity. Responses are made on a 5-point scale ranging from 1 (*not at all*) to 5 (*very much*). Sample items are presented.

Reliability: Alpha coefficients were .89 and .91.

Author: Nelson, M. L., and Friedlander, M. L.

Article: A close look at conflictual supervisory relationships: The trainee's perspective.

Journal: *Journal of Counseling Psychology*, October 2001, *48*, 384–395.

Related Research: Olk, M. E., & Friedlander, M. L. (1992). Trainees' experiences of role conflict and role ambiguity in supervisory relationships. *Journal of Counseling Psychology, 39*, 389–397.

13068

Test Name: ROLE CONFLICT AND ROLE AMBIGUITY SCALES

Purpose: To measure role conflict and ambiguity.

Number of Items: 14

Format: Seven-point scales are anchored by 1 (*very false*) and 7 (*very true*) for conflict items and by 1 (*very true*) and 7 (*very false*) for ambiguity items.

Reliability: Alpha coefficients were .71 (conflict) and .73 (ambiguity).

Validity: Correlations with other variables ranged from −.56 to .27.

Author: Koustelios, A.

Article: Organizational factors as predictors of teachers' burnout.

Journal: *Psychological Reports*, June 2001, *88*, Part 1, 627–634.

Related Research: Rizzo, J., et al. (1970). Role conflict and ambiguity in complex organizations. *Administrative Science Quarterly, 15*, 150–163.

13069

Test Name: ROLE IDENTITY SCALE

Purpose: To assess role identity.

Number of Items: 3

Format: Responses are made on a 7-point Likert scale ranging from 1 (*disagree*) to 7 (*agree*). All items are presented.

Reliability: Alpha coefficients were .83 and .85.

Validity: Correlations with other variables ranged from .23 to .71.

Author: Tsorbatzoudis, H.

Article: Evaluation of a school-based intervention programme to promote physical activity: An application of the theory of planned behavior.

Journal: *Perceptual and Motor Skills*, December 2005, *101*, 787–802.

13070

Test Name: ROSENBERG SELF-ESTEEM SCALE

Purpose: To measure self-esteem.

Number of Items: 10

Format: Item responses ranged from 1 (*disagree very much*) to 5 (*agree very much*).

Reliability: Coefficient alpha was .82.

Author: Giri, V. N.

Article: Associations of self-esteem with communication style.

Journal: *Psychological Reports*, June 2003, *92*, Part 2, 1089–1090.

Related Research: Rosenberg, M. (1989). *Society and the adolescent self-image*. Middletown, CT: Weslyan Press.

13071

Test Name: RUNNING SELF-EFFICACY SCALE

Purpose: To assess perceived ability to complete successive 10-minute increments of running on a treadmill at a moderately fast pace.

Number of Items: 8

Format: Responses are made on a 0 to 100% confidence scale.

Reliability: Internal consistency exceeded .92.

Author: Butki, B. D., et al.

Article: Self-efficacy, state anxiety, and cortisol responses to treadmill running.

Journal: *Perceptual and Motor Skills*, June 2001, *92*, Part 2, 1129–1138.

Related Research: Rudolph, D. L., & McAuley, E. (1995). Self-efficacy and salivary cortisol responses to acute exercise in physically active and less active adults. *Journal of Sports and Exercise Psychology, 17*, 206–213.

13072

Test Name: SCALE OF INTRINSIC VERSUS EXTRINSIC ORIENTATION IN THE CLASSROOM

Purpose: To assess five dimensions of classroom learning.

Number of Items: 30

Format: Includes five subscales: Challenge, Curiosity, Mastery, Independent Judgment, and Internal Criteria.

Reliability: Alpha coefficients ranged from .68 to .84.

Author: d'Ailly, H.

Article: Children's autonomy and perceived control in learning: A model of motivation and achievement in Taiwan

Journal: *Journal of Educational Psychology*, March 2003, *95*, 84–96.

Related Research: Harter, S. (1981). A new self-report scale of intrinsic versus extrinsic orientation in the classroom: Motivational and informational components. *Developmental Psychology, 17,* 300–312.

13073

Test Name: SCALE OF PERCEIVED SOCIAL SELF-EFFICACY

Purpose: To measure social self-efficacy.

Number of Items: 25

Format: Responses are made on a 5-point scale ranging from 1 (*no confidence at all*) to 5 (*complete confidence*).

Reliability: Alpha coefficients were .94 to .95. Test–retest (3 weeks) reliability was .82.

Validity: Correlations with other variables ranged from –.80 to .62.

Author: Smith, H. M., and Betz, N. E.

Article: An examination of efficacy and esteem pathways to depression in young adulthood.

Journal: *Journal of Counseling Psychology*, October 2002, *49,* 438–448.

Related Research: Smith, H. M., & Betz, N. E. (2000). Development and validation of a scale of perceived social self-efficacy. *Journal of Career Assessment, 8,* 283–301.

13074

Test Name: SCHOOL COMPETENCY SUBSCALE

Purpose: To measure self-ratings of individual abilities and skills in physics.

Number of Items: 8

Format: Responses are made on a 3-point scale ranging from *true* to *not true at all.*

Reliability: Coefficient alpha was .74.

Author: Ziegler, A., et al.

Article: Predictors of learned helplessness among average and mildly gifted girls and boys attending initial high school physics instruction in Germany.

Journal: *Gifted Child Quarterly,* Winter 2005, *49,* 7–18.

Related Research: Wünsche, P., & Schneewind, K. A. (1989). Entwicklung eines fragebogens zur erfassung von selbst-und kompetenzeinschätz ungen bei kindern (FSK-K) [The development of a questionnaire to assess self-estimations and confidence estimations among children]. *Diagnostica, 35,* 217–235.

13075

Test Name: SCHOOL READINESS BELIEFS SCALE

Purpose: To assess parents' perceptions of the importance of preacademic activity for entry into kindergarten.

Number of Items: 7

Format: Scales range from 1 (*not at all important*) to 5 (*essential*).

Reliability: Coefficient alpha was .81.

Author: Kim, J., et al.

Article: Investigation of parents' beliefs about readiness for kindergarten: An examination of the National Household Education Survey.

Journal: *Educational Research Quarterly,* December 2005, *29,* 3–17.

Related Research: West, J., et al. (1993). *Readiness for kindergarten: Parent and teacher beliefs* (NCES 93–257). Washington, DC: Department of Education, Office of Educational Research and Improvement.

13076

Test Name: SCIENCE TEACHING EFFICACY BELIEF INVENTORY

Purpose: To assess a teacher's confidence in being able to influence student learning.

Number of Items: 25

Format: Five-point rating scales are anchored by 1 (*strongly disagree*) and 5 (*strongly agree*). All items are presented.

Reliability: Coefficient alpha was .87.

Author: Mji, A., and Kiviet, A. M.

Article: Psychometric characteristics of the Science Teaching Efficacy Belief Inventory in South Africa.

Journal: *Psychological Reports,* February 2003, *92,* 325–332.

Related Research: Riggs, I. M., & Enochs, L. G. (1990). Toward the development of an elementary teacher's science teaching efficacy instrument. *Science Education, 74,* 625–637.

13077

Test Name: SELF-ACCEPTANCE SCALE

Purpose: To assess the degree to which a person holds positive views of oneself and his /her accomplishments.

Number of Items: 4

Format: Five-point scales range from *strongly agree* to *strongly disagree.* All items are presented.

Reliability: Coefficient alpha was .68.

Author: Carr, D.

Article: "My daughter has a career: I just raised babies": The psychological consequences of women's intergenerational social comparisons.

Journal: *Social Psychology Quarterly*, June 2004, *67*, 132–154.

Related Research: Ryff, C. D. (1989). Happiness is everything, or is it? Explorations on the meaning of psychological well-being. *Journal of Personality and Social Psychology, 57*, 1069–1081.

13078

Test Name: SELF-ACCEPTANCE SCALE

Purpose: To measure self-acceptance.

Number of Items: 9

Format: A 6-point response format is employed. All items are presented.

Reliability: Coefficient alpha was .82.

Validity: Correlations with other variables ranged from .10 to .63.

Author: Mueller, D. J., and Kim, K.

Article: The Tenacious Goal Pursuit and Flexible Goal Adjustment Scales: Examination of their validity.

Journal: *Educational and Psychological Measurement*, February 2004, *64*, 120–142.

Related Research: Ryff, C. (1989). Happiness is everything, or is it? Explorations on the meaning of psychological well-being. *Journal of Personality and Social Psychology, 57*, 1069–1081.

13079

Test Name: SELF-ACTUALIZATION SCALE

Purpose: To measure self-actualization.

Number of Items: 15

Format: Nine-point scales are used.

Reliability: Coefficient alpha was .64.

Author: Kim, Y., et al.

Article: Self-concept, aspirations, and well-being in South Korea and the United States.

Journal: *The Journal of Social Psychology*, June 2003, *143*, 277–290.

Related Research: Jones, A., & Crandall, R. (1986). Validation of a short index of self-actualization. *Personality and Social Psychology Bulletin, 12*, 63–73.

13080

Test Name: SELF-ASSESSMENT QUESTIONNAIRE

Purpose: To measure perceptions of domain-general and domain-specific cognitive and motivational constructs.

Number of Items: 48

Format: Includes four domain-general areas of views about ability, perceptions of own effort expenditure, general self-efficacy, and cognitive strategy use; four domain-specific areas of perceptions of own math ability, perceived effort exerted in math tasks, perceived value of math, and perceived math self-efficacy. Responses are made on a 4-point scale ranging from 1 (*not at all*) to 4 (*very much so*). Examples are presented.

Reliability: Alpha coefficients ranged from .62 to .93.

Author: Hong, E., and Aqui, Y.

Article: Cognitive and motivational characteristics of adolescents gifted in mathematics: Comparisons among students with different types of giftedness.

Journal: *Gifted Child Quarterly*, Summer 2004, *48*, 191–201.

Related Research: Hong, E. (2001). *Self-Assessment Questionnaire.* Unpublished document, College of Education, University of Nevada, Las Vegas.

13081

Test Name: SELF-ATTRIBUTES QUESTIONNAIRE

Purpose: To measure a person's beliefs about themselves relative to others of the same age and sex.

Number of Items: 8

Format: Rating scales range from 10% (*way below average*) to 100% (*way above average*). All items are presented.

Reliability: Coefficient alpha was .80.

Author: Brown, R. P., and Ziegler-Hill, V.

Article: Narcissism and the nonequivalence of self-esteem measures: A matter of dominance?

Journal: *Journal of Research in Personality*, December 2004, *38*, 585–592.

Related Research: Pelham, B. W., & Swann, W. B., Jr. (1989). From self-conceptions to self-worth: On the sources and structure of global self-esteem. *Journal of Personality and Social Psychology, 57*, 672–680.

13082

Test Name: SELF ATTRIBUTION SCALE

Purpose: To assess a client's responsibility for a problem, control over a problem, ability to avoid a problem, create a solution to a problem, and to deal with a problem alone.

Number of Items: 6

Format: Scales range from 0 (*not at all*) to 6 (*very much*).

Reliability: Alpha coefficients range from .63 to .87.

Author: Redmond, T., and Slaney, R. B.

Article: The influence of information and race on counselors' attributions.

Journal: *Journal of College Student Development*, November/December 2002, *43*, 851–861.

Related Research: Karuza, J., et al. (1990). Models of helping and coping, responsibility attributions, and well-being in community elderly and their helpers. *Psychology and Aging, 5*, 194–208.

13083

Test Name: SELF-CONCEPT CLARITY SCALE—GERMAN VERSION

Purpose: To assess consistency and temporal stability of self-beliefs.

Number of Items: 12

Format: Scales range from 1 (*completely false*) to 6 (*completely true*).

Reliability: Coefficient alpha was .85.

Validity: Correlations with other variables ranged from –.50 to .56.

Author: Schneider, J. F., et al.

Article: Does self-consciousness mediate the relation between self-talk and self-knowledge?

Journal: *Psychological Reports*, April 2005, *96*, 387–396.

Related Research: Campbell, J. D., et al. (1996). Self-concept clarity: Measurement, personality correlates, and cultural boundaries. *Journal of Personality and Social Psychology, 70*, 141–156.

13084

Test Name: SELF-CONCEPT OF MATHEMATICS ABILITY

QUESTIONNAIRE—DUTCH VERSION

Purpose: To measure self-concept of mathematics ability.

Number of Items: 8

Format: Responses are made on a 5-point scale ranging from *very good* to *not good at all*.

Reliability: Internal consistency was .81.

Validity: Correlations with other variables ranged from .06 to .66 (*N* = 541).

Author: Seegers, G., et al.

Article: Effects of causal attributions following mathematics tasks on student cognitions about a subsequent task.

Journal: *Journal of Experimental Education*, Summer 2004, *72*, 307–328.

Related Research: Seegers, G., et al. (2002). Goal orientation, perceived task outcome and task demands in mathematics tasks: Effects on students' attitude in actual task settings. *British Journal of Educational Psychology, 72*, 365–384.

13085

Test Name: SELF-CONCEPT QUESTIONNAIRE

Purpose: To measure self-concept.

Number of Items: 52

Format: A true–false format is used.

Reliability: Alpha was .80.

Validity: Correlations with other variables ranged from .23 to .70.

Author: Mocke, L. M., et al.

Article: Aspects of the construct validity of a preliminary self-concept questionnaire.

Journal: *Psychological Reports*, February 2002, *90*, 165–172.

Related Research: Greefe, A. P. (1988). [*A correlational study with three self-concept questionnaires and the development of a preliminary questionnaire*]. Unpublished master's thesis, University of Stellenbusch, Stellenbusch, South Africa.

13086

Test Name: SELF-CONCORDANCE SCALE

Purpose: To measure goal-based self-concordance.

Format: Scales range from 1 (*not at all for this reason*) to 9 (*completely for this reason*). Scoring methods are described.

Reliability: Reported reliability was .83.

Validity: Correlations with other variables ranged from –.81 to .62.

Author: Judge, T. A., et al.

Article: Core self-evaluations and job and life satisfaction: The role of self-concordance and goal attainment.

Journal: *Journal of Applied Psychology*, March 2005, *90*, 257–268.

Related Research: Sheldon, K. M., & Elliot, A. J. (1998). Not all personal goals are personal: Comparing autonomous and controlled reasons for goals as predictors of effort and attainment. *Personality and Social Psychology Bulletin, 24*, 546–557.

13087

Test Name: SELF-CONFIDENCE AND DECISIVENESS SCALES

Purpose: To measure self-confidence and decisiveness.

Number of Items: 13

Format: Scales range from 1 (*strongly disagree*) to 5 (*strongly agree*).

Reliability: Alpha coefficients ranged from .73 to .87.

Author: Barrick, M. R., and Zimmerman, R. D.

Article: Reducing voluntary, avoidable turnover through selection.

Journal: *Journal of Applied Psychology*, January 2005, *90*, 159–166.

Related Research: Lee, T. W., et al. (1992). Commitment propensity, organizational commitment, and voluntary turnover: A longitudinal study of organizational entry processes. *Journal of Management*, *10*, 15–32.

13088

Test Name: SELF-CONFIDENCE IN MATHEMATICS SCALE

Purpose: To measure self-confidence in mathematics.

Number of Items: 5

Format: Scales range from 1 (*not at all true*) to 5 (*very true*). Sample items are presented in English.

Reliability: Coefficient alpha was .92.

Author: Keller, C.

Article: Effect of teachers' stereotyping on students' stereotyping of mathematics as a male domain.

Journal: *The Journal of Social Psychology*, April 2001, *141*, 165–173.

Related Research: Moser, U., et al. (1989). Fragebogen zur Erfassung von Dimensionen der Integration von Schuelern (FDI 4-6) [Questionnaire for Investigating Dimensions of the Integration of Students (FDI 4-6)]. *Psychologie in Erziehung und Unterricht*, *36*, 19–26.

13089

Test Name: SELF-CONSCIOUSNESS SCALE

Purpose: To measure self-consciousness.

Number of Items: 23

Format: Includes three subscales: Private Self-Consciousness, Public Self-Consciousness, and Social Anxiety. Responses are made on a 5-point scale ranging from 0 (*extremely uncharacteristic of myself*) to 4 (*extremely characteristic of myself*).

Reliability: Test–retest and coefficient alpha reliabilities ranged from .63 to .81.

Author: Lindwall, M.

Article: Factorial structure and invariance across gender of the Swedish Self-Consciousness Scale.

Journal: *Journal of Personality Assessment*, April 2004, *82*, 233–240.

Related Research: Fenigstein, A., et al. (1975). Public and private self-consciousness: Assessment and theory. *Journal of Consulting and Clinical Psychology*, *43*, 522–527.

13090

Test Name: SELF-CONSTRUAL SCALE

Purpose: To measure independent and interdependent self-construals.

Number of Items: 24

Format: Scales range from 1 (*disagree strongly*) to 7 (*agree strongly*). All items are presented.

Reliability: Alpha coefficients ranged from .68 to .72 across subscales.

Validity: Correlations with other variables ranged from −.89 to .23 across two subscales.

Author: Grace, S. L., and Cramer, K. L.

Article: The elusive nature of self-measurement: The Self-Construal Scale and the Twenty Statements Test.

Journal: *The Journal of Social Psychology*, October 2003, *143*, 649–668.

Related Research: Singelis, T. M. (1994). The measurement of independent and interdependent self-construals. *Personality and Social Psychology Bulletin*, *20*, 580–591.

13091

Test Name: SELF CONSTRUAL SCALE

Purpose: To measure an individual's independent and interdependent self-construals.

Number of Items: 30

Format: Includes two scales: Independence and Interdependence. Responses are made on a 7-point Likert scale ranging from 1 (*strongly disagree*) to 5 (*strongly agree*). Examples are presented.

Reliability: Alpha coefficients ranged from .61 to .73.

Author: Hardin, E. E., et al.

Article: Cultural relativity in the conceptualization of career maturity.

Journal: *Journal of Vocational Behavior*, February 2001, *58*, 36–52.

Related Research: Singelis, T. M. (1994). The measurement of independent and interdependent self-construals. *Personality and Social Psychology Bulletin*, *20*, 580–591.

13092

Test Name: SELF-CONTROL SUBSCALE

Purpose: To assess self-regulation.

Number of Items: 5

Format: Responses by mothers and teachers are made on a 5-point scale. All items are presented.

Reliability: Alpha coefficients were .85 (mothers) and .87 (teachers).

Validity: Correlations with other variables ranged from –.26 to .43 ($N = 277$).

Author: Brody, G. H., et al.

Article: Unique and protective contributions of parenting and classroom processes to the adjustment of African American children living in single-parent families.

Journal: *Child Development,* January/February 2002, *73,* 274–286.

Related Research: Humphrey, L. L. (1982). Children's and teachers' perspectives on children's self-control: The development of two rating scales. *Journal of Consulting and Clinical Psychology, 50,* 624–633.

13093

Test Name: SELF-DECEPTION SCALE

Purpose: To assess self-deception.

Number of Items: 20

Format: Scales range from 1 (*not true*) to 7 (*very true*). A sample item is presented.

Reliability: Coefficient alpha was .61.

Author: Lee, S., and Klein, H. J.

Article: Relationships between conscientiousness, self-efficacy, self-deception, and learning over time.

Journal: *Journal of Applied Psychology,* December 2002, *87,* 1175–1182.

Related Research: Paulhus, D. L. (1991). Measurement and control of response bias. In K. P. Robinson, et al. (Eds.), *Measures of personality and social psychological attitudes* (pp. 17–59). San Diego, CA: Academic Press.

13094

Test Name: SELF-DESCRIPTION INVENTORY FOR AFRICAN STUDENTS

Purpose: To assess several aspects of self-concept.

Number of Items: 50

Format: Scales range from 1 (*I disagree very much*) to 5 (*I agree very much*).

Reliability: Alpha coefficients ranged from .65 to .85 across subscales.

Author: Majoribanks, K., and Mboya, M. M.

Article: Age and gender differences in self-concept of South African students.

Journal: *The Journal of Social Psychology,* February 2001, *141,* 148–149.

Related Research: Majoribanks, K., & Mboya, M. M. (1998). Factors affecting the self-concepts of South African students. *The Journal of Social Psychology, 138,* 572–580.

13095

Test Name: SELF-DESCRIPTION QUESTIONNAIRE—AFRIKAANS VERSION

Purpose: To measure self-concept.

Number of Items: 62

Format: Five-point true–false scales are used.

Reliability: Alpha was .75.

Validity: Correlations with other variables ranged from .51 to .70.

Author: Mocke, L. M., et al.

Article: Aspects of the construct validity of a preliminary self-concept questionnaire.

Journal: *Psychological Reports,* February 2002, *90,* 165–172.

Related Research: Marsh, H. W., et al. (1983). Multitrait-multimethod analysis of the Self-Description Questionnaire: Student–teacher agreement on multidimensional ratings of student self-concept. *American Educational Research Journal, 20,* 333–357.

13096

Test Name: SELF-DETERMINATION SCALE

Purpose: To rate self-evaluations of self-determination.

Number of Items: 10

Format: Subject reads two statements and responds on a scale ranging from 1 (*only the first statement seems true*) to 3 (*only the second statement seems true*). A sample item-set is presented.

Reliability: Alpha coefficients ranged from .69 to .78.

Validity: Correlations with other variables ranged from –.11 to .41.

Author: Sheldon, K. M.

Article: Positive value change during college: Normative trends and individual differences.

Journal: *Journal of Research in Personality,* April 2005, *39,* 209–223.

13097

Test Name: SELF-EFFICACY AND SELF-ESTEEM SCALE

Purpose: To measure self-esteem and self-efficacy beliefs related to school achievement in linguistic–literary, logical–mathematical, and technical–practical topics.

Number of Items: 24

Time Required: 15 minutes.

Format: Response scales are anchored by 1 (*low*) and 4 (*high*). All items are presented.

Reliability: Alpha coefficients were .67 (self-esteem) and .80 (self-efficacy). Subscale alphas ranged from .58 to .78.

Validity: Correlations with scholastic performance ranged from −.07 to .85.

Author: D'Amico, A., and Cardaci, M.

Article: Relations among perceived self-efficacy, self-esteem, and school achievement.

Journal: *Psychological Reports*, June 2003, *92*, Part 1, 745–754.

13098

Test Name: SELF-EFFICACY FOR ACADEMIC MILESTONES SCALE

Purpose: To enable students to rate their confidence in their ability to succeed.

Number of Items: 10

Format: Responses are made on a 10-point scale ranging from 1 (*completely unsure*) to 10 (*completely sure*). An example is given.

Reliability: Coefficient alpha was .96.

Author: Nauta, M. M., and Epperson, D. L.

Article: A longitudinal examination of the social–cognitive model applied to high school girls' choices of nontraditional college majors and aspirations.

Journal: *Journal of Counseling Psychology*, October 2003, *50*, 448–457.

Related Research: Nauta, M. M., et al. (1998). A multiple-groups analysis of predictors of higher level career aspirations among women in mathematics, science, and engineering majors. *Journal of Counseling Psychology, 45,* 483–496.

13099

Test Name: SELF-EFFICACY FOR BROAD ACADEMIC MILESTONES SCALE

Purpose: To measure students' confidence in ability to complete a variety of core academic requirements and achievement behaviors common to all students at a given university.

Number of Items: 12

Format: Responses are made on a 10-scale ranging from 0 (*no confidence at all*) 9 (*complete confidence*) Examples are given.

Reliability: Alpha coefficients were .92 and .94.

Author: Kahn, J. H., and Nauta, M. M.

Article: Social–cognitive predictors of first-year college persistence: The importance of proximal assessment.

Journal: *Research in Higher Education*, December 2001, *42*, 633–652.

Related Research: Lent, R. W., et al. (1997). Discriminant and predictive validity of academic self-concept, academic self-efficacy, and mathematics-specific self-efficacy. *Journal of Counseling Psychology, 44,* 307–315.

13100

Test Name: SELF-EFFICACY FOR CHILDREN

Purpose: To measure social self-efficacy, academic self-efficacy, and emotional self-efficacy.

Number of Items: 21

Format: Scales range from 1 (*not at all*) to 5 (*very well*). All items are presented.

Reliability: Total alpha was .88. Alpha coefficients ranged from .85 to .88 across subscales.

Validity: Correlations with depression ranged from −.53 to −.01.

Author: Muris, P.

Article: A brief questionnaire for measuring self-efficacy in youths.

Journal: *Journal of Psychopathology and Behavioral Assessment*, September 2001, *23*, 145–149.

13101

Test Name: SELF-EFFICACY FOR CREATING WEB PAGES SCALE

Purpose: To assess trainees' self-efficacy for creating web pages.

Number of Items: 7

Format: Responses are made on a 5-point scale ranging from 1 (*strongly disagree*) to 5 (*strongly agree*). A sample item is presented.

Reliability: Coefficient alpha was .95.

Validity: Correlations with other variables ranged from −.24 to .56.

Author: Schmidt, A. M., and Ford, J. K.

Article: Learning within a learner control training environment: The interactive effects of goal orientation and metacognitive instruction on learning outcomes.

Journal: *Personnel Psychology*, Summer 2003, *56*, 405–429.

Related Research: Kozlowski, S. W., et al. (2001). Effects of training goals and goal orientation traits on multidimensional training outcomes and performance adaptability. *Organizational Behavior and Human Decision Processes, 85,* 1–31.

13102

Test Name: SELF-EFFICACY FOR LEARNING SCALE

Purpose: To measure self-efficacy beliefs.

Number of Items: 11

Format: Responses are made on a 4-point scale.

Reliability: Coefficient alpha was .87.

Author: Hampton, N. Z., and Mason, E.

Article: Learning disabilities, gender, sources of efficacy, self-efficacy beliefs, and academic achievement in high school students.

Journal: *Journal of School Psychology*, March/April 2003, *41*, 101–112.

Related Research: Zimmerman, B. J., et al. (1992). Self-motivation for academic attainment: The role of self-efficacy beliefs and personal goal setting. *American Educational Research Journal, 29*, 663–676.

13103

Test Name: SELF-EFFICACY FOR REHABILITATION OUTCOME SCALE

Purpose: To assess participants' beliefs about their ability to perform behaviors typical in physical rehabilitation for knee and hip surgery.

Number of Items: 12

Format: Responses are made on an 11-point scale ranging from 0 (*I cannot do*) to 10 (*certain I can do*). Examples are presented.

Reliability: Coefficient alpha was .94.

Validity: Correlations with other variables ranged from −.32 to .47 (*N* = 102).

Author: Waldrop, D., et al.

Article: Self-efficacy, optimism, health competence, and recovery from orthopedic surgery.

Journal: *Journal of Counseling Psychology*, April 2001, *48*, 233–238.

13104

Test Name: SELF-EFFICACY FOR TECHNICAL / SCIENCE FIELDS MEASURE—ADAPTED

Purpose: To assess students' confidence that they could complete each of 10 engineering majors with an overall grade point average of B or better.

Number of Items: 10

Format: Responses are made on a 10-point scale ranging from 0 (*no confidence*) to 9 (*complete confidence*).

Reliability: Coefficient alpha was .94.

Validity: Correlations with other variables ranged from −.15 to .47 (*N* = 287).

Author: Lent, R. W., et al.

Article: Relation of contextual supports and barriers to choice behavior in engineering majors: Test of alternative social cognitive models.

Journal: *Journal of Counseling Psychology*, October 2003, *50*, 458–465.

Related Research: Lent, R. W., et al. (1984). Relation of self-efficacy expectations to academic achievement and persistence. *Journal of Counseling Psychology, 31*, 356–362.

13105

Test Name: SELF-EFFICACY FOR TECHNICAL/SCIENTIFIC FIELDS—ABBREVIATED

Purpose: To assess an individual's science self-efficacy.

Number of Items: 15

Format: Includes two subscales: Educational Requirements—Level and Educational Requirements—Strength. Responses are made on 10-point scales ranging from 1 (*completely unsure*) to 10 (*completely sure*).

Reliability: Test–retest (8 weeks) reliabilities were .76 and .89. Alpha coefficients ranged from .79 to .93.

Author: Scott, A. B., and Mallinckrodt, B.

Article: Parental emotional support, science self-efficacy, and choice of science major in undergraduate women.

Journal: *The Career Development Quarterly*, March 2005, *53*, 263–273.

Related Research: Lent, R. W., et al. (1984). Relation of self-efficacy expectations to academic achievement and persistence. *Journal of Counseling Psychology, 31*, 356–362.

13106

Test Name: SELF-EFFICACY IN PERSONAL RELATIONSHIPS SCALE

Purpose: To assess tendencies linked to self-efficacy in personal relationships: self-confidence in personal relationships, trust in friends, and trust by friends.

Number of Items: 31

Format: Response scales are anchored by 1 (*not at all true of me*) and 4 (*very strongly true of me*). All items are presented.

Reliability: Alpha coefficients ranged from .87 to .90 across subscales.

Validity: Correlations with other variables ranged from −.53 to .60.

Author: Matsushima, R., and Shiomi, K.

Article: Developing a scale of self-efficacy in personal relationships for adolescents.

Journal: *Psychological Reports*, February 2003, *92*, 177–184.

13107

Test Name: SELF-EFFICACY IN RESEARCH MEASURE—BRIEF VERSION

Purpose: To assess research self-efficacy.

Number of Items: 12

Format: Responses are made on a 9-point Likert scale ranging from 1 (*no confidence*) to 9 (*total confidence*). Examples are given.

Reliability: Alpha coefficients were .89 and .90.

Author: Phillips, J. C., et al.

Article: Preliminary examination and measurement of the internship research training environment.

Journal: *Journal of Counseling Psychology*, April 2004, *51*, 240–248.

Related Research: Kahn, J. H., & Scott, N. A. (1997). Predictors of research productivity and science-related career goals among counseling psychology doctoral students. *The Counseling Psychologist, 25*, 38–67.

13108

Test Name: SELF-EFFICACY INDEX

Purpose: To measure job self-efficacy.

Number of Items: 5

Format: Scales range from 1 (*strongly disagree*) to 5 (*strongly agree*). All items are presented.

Reliability: Coefficient alpha was .64.

Author: Yoon, J.

Article: The role of structure and motivation for workplace empowerment: The case of Korean employees.

Journal: *Social Psychology Quarterly*, June 2001, *64*, 195–206.

Related Research: Riggs, M. L., & Knight, P. A. (1994). The impact of perceived group success failure on motivational beliefs and attitudes: A causal model. *Journal of Applied Psychology, 79*, 755–766.

13109

Test Name: SELF-EFFICACY INVENTORY

Purpose: To provide self-report appraisal of trainees' perceptions of their self-efficacy anticipations or belief in their ability to perform specific counseling-related activities.

Number of Items: 21

Format: Includes five domains: completion of academic requirements, assessment, individual psychotherapy, group and family intervention, and case management. Responses are made on a 10-point scale ranging from 0 (*not confident*) to 9 (*completely confident*).

Reliability: Internal consistencies were .88 and .93.

Validity: Correlations with other variables ranged from –.01 to .65.

Author: Lehrman-Waterman, D., and Ladany, N.

Article: Development and validation of the Evaluation Process within Supervision Inventory.

Journal: *Journal of Counseling Psychology*, April 2001, *48*, 168–177.

Related Research: Friedlander, M. L., & Snyder, J. (1983). Trainees' expectations for the supervisory process: Testing a developmental model. *Counselor Education and Supervision, 22*, 342–348.

13110

Test Name: SELF-EFFICACY QUESTIONNAIRE

Purpose: To enable participants to rate their confidence in their ability to successfully learn to perform the job.

Number of Items: 31

Format: Responses are made on a 4-point scale ranging from 1 (*very unsure*) to 4 (*very sure*).

Reliability: Internal consistency was .95.

Author: Flores, L. Y., and O'Brien, K. M.

Article: The career development of Mexican American adolescent women: A test of social cognitive career theory.

Journal: *Journal of Counseling Psychology*, January 2002, *49*, 14–27.

Related Research: Church, A. T., et al. (1992). Self-efficacy for careers and occupational consideration in minority high school equivalency students. *Journal of Counseling Psychology, 39*, 498–508.

13111

Test Name: SELF-EFFICACY QUESTIONNAIRE—GERMAN VERSION

Purpose: To assess self-efficacy expectancies.

Number of Items: 5

Format: Item anchors are 1 (*never*) and 3 (*regularly*).

Reliability: Coefficient alpha was .83.

Validity: Correlations with other variables ranged from –.44 to .28.

Author: Schneider, J. F.

Article: Prayer and inner speech: Is there a connection?

Journal: *Psychological Reports*, June 2004, *94*, Part 2, 1382–1384.

13112

Test Name: SELF-EFFICACY RATING SCALE

Purpose: To rate the certainty of performing behaviors specific to sexual situations that could resist sexual advances.

Number of Items: 7

Format: Seven-point Likert scales are used.

Validity: Correlations with other variables ranged from −.25 to .30.

Author: Marx, B. P., et al.

Article: Sexual revictimization prevention: An outcome evaluation.

Journal: *Journal of Consulting and Clinical Psychology*, February 2001, *69*, 25–32.

Related Research: Hall, R. L. (1989). Self-efficacy ratings. In D. R. Laws (Ed.), *Relapse prevention with sex offenders* (pp. 137–146). New York: Guilford Press.

13113

Test Name: SELF-EFFICACY SCALE

Purpose: To measure the magnitude and strength of self-efficacy.

Number of Items: 10

Format: A yes–no format is used. Items and scoring are described.

Reliability: Alpha coefficients ranged from .96 to .97.

Validity: Correlations with other variables ranged from −.28 to .13.

Author: Cellar, D. F., et al.

Article: Relationships between five factor personality variables, workplace accidents, and self-efficacy.

Journal: *Psychological Reports*, June 2004, *94*, Part 2, 1437–1441.

Related Research: Wood, R. S., & Locke, E. A. (1987). The relation of

self-efficacy and grade goals to academic performance. *Educational and Psychological Measurement, 47*, 1013–1024.

13114

Test Name: SELF-EFFICACY SCALE

Purpose: To measure general and social self-efficacy.

Number of Items: 30

Format: A 5-point Likert format is used. All items are presented.

Reliability: Alpha coefficients ranged from .69 to .86.

Validity: Correlations with other variables ranged from .13 to .52.

Author: Choi, N.

Article: Further examination of the Self-Efficacy Scale.

Journal: *Psychological Reports*, April 2003, *92*, 473–480.

Related Research: Sherer, M., et al. (1982). The Self-Efficacy Scale: Construction and validation. *Psychological Reports, 51*, 663–671.

13115

Test Name: SELF-EFFICACY SCALE

Purpose: To measure self-efficacy.

Number of Items: 10

Format: Scales range from 1 (*strongly disagree*) to 5 (*strongly agree*).

Reliability: Coefficient alpha was .92.

Validity: Correlations with other variables ranged from −.04 to .45.

Author: Gully, S. M., et al.

Article: The impact of error training and individual differences on training outcomes: An attribute–treatment interaction perspective.

Journal: *Journal of Applied Psychology*, February 2002, *87*, 143–155.

13116

Test Name: SELF-EFFICACY SCALE

Purpose: To measure individual-level self-efficacy.

Number of Items: 5

Format: Scales range from 1 (*strongly disagree*) to 5 (*strongly agree*).

Reliability: Coefficient alpha was .83.

Validity: Correlations with other variables ranged from −.23 to .66.

Author: Jex, S. M., et al.

Article: The impact of self-efficacy on stressor–strain relations: Coping style as an exploratory mechanism.

Journal: *Journal of Applied Psychology*, June 2001, *86*, 401–409.

Related Research: Jones, G. R. (1986). Socialization tactics, self-efficacy, and newcomers' adjustments to organizations. *Academy of Management Journal, 29*, 262–279.

13117

Test Name: SELF-EFFICACY SCALE

Purpose: To measure the persistence and life skills self-efficacy of public assistance clients seeking work.

Number of Items: 4

Format: Responses are made on a 5-point scale ranging from 1 (*strongly agree*) to 5 (*strongly disagree*). All items are presented.

Reliability: Reliability was .74.

Author: Kossek, E. E., et al.

Article: Sustaining work force inclusion and well-being of mothers on public assistance: Individual deficit and social ecology perspectives.

Journal: *Journal of Vocational Behavior*, February 2003, *62*, 155–175.

Related Research: Bandura, A. (1986). The explanatory and predictive scope of self-efficacy theory. *Journal of Social and Clinical Psychology, 4*, 359–373.

13118

Test Name: SELF-EFFICACY SCALE

Purpose: To assess expectancies of general self-efficacy.

Number of Items: 17

Format: Responses are made on a 7-point Likert scale ranging from 1 (*strongly agree*) to 7 (*strongly disagree*).

Reliability: Alpha coefficients were .81 (207) and .87 ($N = 205$). Test–retest (1 year) reliability was .76.

Validity: Correlations with other variables ranged from –.40 to .40.

Author: Morris, J. E., and Long, B. C.

Article: Female clerical workers' occupational stress: The role of person and social resources, negative affectivity, and stress appraisals

Journal: *Journal of Counseling Psychology*, October 2002, *49*, 395–410.

Related Research: Sherer, M., et al. (1982). The Self-Efficacy Scale: Construction and validation. *Psychological Reports, 51*, 663–671.

13119

Test Name: SELF-EFFICACY SCALE

Purpose: To measure self-efficacy reflecting a respondent's beliefs in capability to continue exercising when faced with potential barriers.

Number of Items: 5

Format: Responses are made on a 7-point rating ranging from 1 (*not at all competent*) to 7 (*very competent*).

Reliability: Alpha coefficients were .71 and .81.

Author: Rhodes, R. E., et al.

Article: Temporal relationships of self-efficacy and social support as predictors of adherence in a 6-month strength-training program for older women.

Journal: *Perceptual and Motor Skills*, December 2001, *93*, 693–703.

Related Research: Marcus, B., et al. (1992). Self-efficacy and the stages of exercise behavior change. *Research Quarterly for Exercise and Sport, 63*, 60–66.

13120

Test Name: SELF-EFFICACY SCALE

Purpose: To measure self-efficacy.

Number of Items: 23

Format: Scales range from 1 (*strongly disagree*) to 5 (*strongly agree*).

Reliability: Alpha coefficients range from .77 to .90 across two subscales.

Validity: Correlations with other variables range from –.28 to .25.

Author: Shaffer, M. A., and Harrison, D. A.

Article: Forgotten partners of international assignments: Development and test of a model of spouse adjustment.

Journal: *Journal of Applied Psychology*, April 2001, *86*, 238–254.

Related Research: Sherer, M., et al. (1982). The Self-Efficacy Scale: Construction and validation. *Psychological Reports, 51*, 663–671.

13121

Test Name: SELF-EFFICACY SCALE—GERMAN VERSION

Purpose: To measure self-efficacy.

Number of Items: 5

Format: Scales range from 1 (*completely false*) to 6 (*completely true*).

Reliability: Coefficient alpha was .84.

Validity: Correlations with other variables ranged from –.30 to .59.

Author: Schneider, J. F., et al.

Article: Does self-consciousness mediate the relation between self-talk and self-knowledge?

Journal: *Psychological Reports*, April 2005, *96*, 387–396.

Related Research: Scholler, G., et al. (1999). Fragebogen zu selbstwirksomkeit, optimismus und pessimismus, rekonstraktion, item selektion, and validierung eines instruments an untersuchungen klinischer stichproben [Questionnaire for self-efficacy, optimism, and pessimism: Reconstruction, selection of times, and validation of an instrument by means of examinations of clinical samples.] *Psychotherapie, Psychosomatik, Medizinische Psychologie, 49*, 275–283.

13122

Test Name: SELF-EFFICACY SCALE: SOCIAL SELF-EFFICACY SUBSCALE

Purpose: To measure social self-efficacy.

Number of Items: 6

Format: Responses are made on a 5-point scale ranging from 1 (*strongly disagree*) to 5 (*strongly agree*).

Reliability: Coefficient alpha was .73.

Validity: Correlations with other variables ranged from –.49 to .56 (*n* = 430).

Author: Mallinckrodt, B., and Wei, M.

Article: Attachment, social competencies, social support, and psychological distress.

Journal: *Journal of Counseling Psychology,* July 2005, *52,* 358–367.

Related Research: Sherer, M., et al. (1982). The Self-Efficacy Scale: Construction and validation. *Psychological Reports, 51,* 663–671.

13123

Test Name: SELF-EFFICACY SCALE—TEACHER AND STUDENT VERSIONS

Purpose: To assess children's self-efficacy by teacher ratings.

Number of Items: 9

Format: Scales range from *like the child* to *not like the child.* All items are presented for teachers. Sample items are presented for students.

Reliability: Coefficient alpha was .94 for the teacher version and .64 for the student version.

Validity: The correlation between the teacher and student versions was .28.

Author: Fall, M., and McLeod, E. H.

Article: Identifying and assisting children with low self-efficacy.

Journal: *Professional School Counseling,* June 2001, *4,* 334–341.

13124

Test Name: SELF-ESTEEM MEASURE

Purpose: To measure self-esteem of elderly persons.

Number of Items: 10

Format: Responses are made on a 5-point Likert-type scale.

Reliability: Coefficient alpha was .84.

Author: Chowdhary, U., and Ryan, L.

Article: Self-esteem and apparel satisfaction with appropriate clothing: Value of product attributes and support groups for mastectomy survivors.

Journal: *Perceptual and Motor Skills,* August 2003, *97,* 35–44.

Related Research: Chowdhary, U. (1993). Self-perceived somatotypes and clothing-related behavior of older men and women. *Perceptual and Motor Skills, 86,* 819–826.

13125

Test Name: SELF-ESTEEM SCALE

Purpose: To measure self-esteem.

Number of Items: 5

Format: Responses are made on 10-point scales. All items are presented.

Reliability: Coefficient alpha was .88.

Author: Peterson, S. E., and Miller, J. A.

Article: Comparing the quality of students' experiences during cooperative learning and large-group instruction.

Journal: *Journal of Educational Research,* January/February 2004, *97,* 123–133.

Related Research: Csikszentmihalyi, M., et al. (1993). *Talented teenagers: The roots of success and failure.* New York: Cambridge University Press.

13126

Test Name: SELF-ESTEEM SCALE

Purpose: To measure self-esteem.

Number of Items: 7

Format: Item anchors are 1 (*strongly disagree*) and 5 (*strongly agree*).

Reliability: Coefficient alpha was .83.

Author: Pinto, M. B., et al.

Article: Relationship of credit attitude and debt to self-esteem and locus of control in college-age consumers.

Journal: *Psychological Reports,* June 2004, *94,* Part 2, 1405–1418.

Related Research: Yabiku, S. T., et al. (1999). Family integration and children's self-esteem. *American Journal of Sociology, 104,* 1494–1524.

13127

Test Name: SELF-ESTEEM SUBSCALE

Purpose: To assess overall perceptions of self-worth.

Number of Items: 8

Format: Responses are made on a 4-point scale ranging from *strongly disagree* to *strongly agree.* Examples are given.

Reliability: Alpha coefficients ranged from .82 to .84.

Author: Fredriksen, K., et al.

Article: Sleepless in Chicago: Tracking the effects of adolescent sleep loss during the middle school years.

Journal: *Child Development,* January/February 2004, *75,* 84–95.

Related Research: DuBois, D. L., et al. (1996). Early adolescent self-esteem: A developmental–ecological framework and assessment strategy. *Journal of*

Research on Adolescence, 6,
543–579.

13128

Test Name: SELF-IMAGE
QUESTIONNAIRE FOR YOUNG
ADOLESCENTS

Purpose: To assess positive
adjustment.

Number of Items: 20

Format: Includes two subscales:
Mastery and Coping, and Superior
Adjustment. Responses are made on
a 6-point scale ranging from
describes me very well to *does not
describe me at all.* Examples are
given.

Reliability: Alpha coefficients were
.67 and .77.

Validity: The correlation with self-
esteem was in the .60s.

Author: Dixon, F. A., et al.

Article: An empirical typology of
perfectionism in gifted adolescents.

Journal: *Gifted Child Quarterly,*
Spring 2004, *48,* 95–106.

Related Research: Peterson, A. C.,
et al. (1984). A self-image
questionnaire for young adolescents
(SIQYA): Reliability and validity
studies. *Journal of Youth and
Adolescence, 13,* 93–109.

13129

Test Name: SELF-KNOWLEDGE
SCALE—GERMAN VERSION

Purpose: To assess self-knowledge.

Number of Items: 9

Format: Scales range from 1
(*completely false*) to 6 (*completely
true*).

Reliability: Coefficient alpha
was .82.

Validity: Correlations with other
variables ranged from .01 to .51.

Author: Schneider, J. F., et al.

Article: Does self-consciousness
mediate the relation between self-
talk and self-knowledge?

Journal: *Psychological Reports,*
April 2005, *96,* 387–396.

Related Research: Eckert-Nowack,
M. (1988). *Sethstkenntnis: Etikett
fuer die kontrollierbare person?
[Self-knowledge as a determinant
of how a person is perceived: A
neglected analogy to a favorite
concept].* Unpublished doctoral
dissertation, Abteilung Psychologie,
Universitaet Bielefeld, Bielefeld,
Germany.

13130

Test Name: SELF-LIKING AND
COMPETENCE SCALE—
REVISED

Purpose: To measure global self-
regard.

Number of Items: 16

Format: Scales range from 1
(*strongly disagree*) to 5 (*strongly
agree*).

Reliability: Coefficient alpha was
.81 for self-confidence and .92 for
self-liking.

Author: Brown, R. P., and Ziegler-Hill, V.

Article: Narcissism and the
nonequivalence of self-esteem
measures: A matter of dominance?

Journal: *Journal of Research in
Personality,* December 2004, *38,*
585–592.

Related Research: Tafarodi, R. W.,
& Swann, W. B., Jr. (2001). Two-
dimensional self-esteem: Theory
and measurement. *Personality and
Individual Differences, 31,*
653–673.

13131

Test Name: SELF-MONITORING
OF EXPRESSIVE BEHAVIOR
SCALE

Purpose: To provide self-
monitoring of expressive behavior.

Number of Items: 25

Format: A true–false format is used.
An example is given.

Reliability: Kuder–Richardson 20
coefficient was .70. Coefficient
alpha was .64. Test–retest reliability
was .83.

Validity: Correlations with
other variables ranged from –.20
to .39.

Author: Hoyt, W. T.

Article: Bias in participant
ratings of psychotherapy
process: An initial generalizability
study.

Journal: *Journal of Counseling
Psychology,* January 2002, *49,*
35–46.

Related Research: Snyder, M.
(1974). Self-monitoring of
expressive behavior. *Journal of
Personality and Social Psychology,
30,* 526–537.

13132

Test Name: SELF-MONITORING
QUESTIONNAIRE

Purpose: To measure
self-monitoring.

Number of Items: 13

Format: Scales range from *never* to
always. Sample items are
presented.

Reliability: Reliability was .75.

Author: Pallier, G., et al.

Article: The role of individual
differences in the accuracy of
confidence judgments.

Journal: *The Journal of General
Psychology,* July 2002, *129,*
257–299.

Related Research: Cutler, B., &
Wolfe, R. (1989). Self-monitoring
and the association between
confidence and accuracy. *Journal
of Research in Personality, 23,*
410–420.

13133

Test Name: SELF-MONITORING SCALE

Purpose: To measure the respondents' self-monitoring ability.

Number of Items: 25

Format: Responses are made on a 5-point Likert scale ranging from 1 (*strongly disagree*) to 5 (*strongly agree*). Examples are presented.

Reliability: Internal consistency reliability was .75 (*N* = 221).

Validity: Correlations with other variables ranged from .02 to .37 (*N* = 221).

Author: Andrews, M. C., and Kacmar, K. M.

Article: Impression management by association: Construction and validation of a scale.

Journal: *Journal of Vocational Behavior*, February 2001, *58*, 142–161.

Related Research: Synder, M. (1974). Self-monitoring of expressive behavior. *Journal of Personality and Social Psychology, 4*, 526–537.

13134

Test Name: SELF-MONITORING SCALE

Purpose: To measure self-monitoring.

Number of Items: 18

Format: Responses are made on a 5-point Likert scale ranging from 1 (*strongly disagree*) to 5 (*strongly agree*). Sample items are given.

Reliability: Coefficient alpha was .85.

Validity: Correlations with other variables ranged from −.24 to .31 (*n* = 102).

Author: Barrick, M. R., et al.

Article: Self-monitoring as a moderator of the relationships

between personality traits and performance.

Journal: *Personnel Psychology,* Autumn 2005, *58*, 745–767.

Related Research: Snyder, M., & Gangestad, S. (1986). On the nature of self-monitoring: Matters of assessment, matters of validity. *Journal of Personality and Social Psychology, 51*, 125–139.

13135

Test Name: SELF-MONITORING SCALE

Purpose: To assess self-monitoring.

Number of Items: 18

Format: A true–false format is used.

Reliability: Coefficient alpha was .72.

Validity: Correlations with other variables ranged from −.25 to .60.

Author: Edwards, W. R., and Schleicher, D. J.

Article: On selecting psychology graduate students: Validity evidence for a test of tacit knowledge.

Journal: *Journal of Educational Psychology*, September 2004, *96*, 592–602.

Related Research: Snyder, M. (1987). *Public appearances/ private realities: The psychology of self-monitoring.* New York: Freeman.

13136

Test Name: SELF-MONITORING SCALE

Purpose: To measure sensitivity to the expressive behavior of others and the ability to modify self-presentations in response to them.

Number of Items: 13

Format: Scales range from 1 (*certainly, always false*) to 6 (*certainly, always true*). Sample items are presented.

Reliability: Alpha coefficients exceeded .69.

Author: Schutte, N. S., et al.

Article: Emotional intelligence and interpersonal relations.

Journal: *The Journal of Social Psychology* August 2001, *141*, 523–536.

Related Research: Lennox, R. D., & Wolfe, R. N. (1984). Revision of the Self-Monitoring Scale. *Journal of Personality and Social Psychology, 46*, 1349–1364.

13137

Test Name: SELF-MONITORING SCALE

Purpose: To measure self-monitoring as stage presence, other-directed self-presentation, and expressive self-control.

Number of Items: 21

Format: A true–false format is used. Sample items are presented.

Reliability: K-R 20 reliability was .75.

Validity: Correlations with other variables ranged from −.29 to .23.

Author: Sosik, J. J., et al.

Article: Adaptive self-regulation: Meeting others' expectations of leadership and performance.

Journal: *The Journal of Social Psychology*, April 2002, *142*, 211–232.

Related Research: Snyder, M. (1974). The self-monitoring of expressive behavior. *Journal of Personality and Social Psychology, 30*, 526–537.

13138

Test Name: SELF-MONITORING SCALE—REVISED

Purpose: To assess self-monitoring.

Number of Items: 16

Format: Responses are made on a 5-point scale ranging from 1 (*not at all true*) to 5 (*very true*).

Reliability: Coefficient alpha was .70.

Validity: Correlations with other variables ranged from −.09 to .41.

Author: Diefendorff, J. M., et al.

Article: The dimensionality and antecedents of emotional labor strategies.

Journal: *Journal of Vocational Behavior*, April 2005, *66*, 339–357.

Related Research: Snyder, M. (1974). Self-monitoring of expressive behavior. *Journal of Personality and Social Psychology, 30*, 526–537.

13139

Test Name: SELF-PERCEIVED COMPETENCE SCALE

Purpose: To assess self-perceived competence.

Number of Items: 5

Format: Responses are made on an 8-point scale ranging from 1 (*agree*) to 8 (*disagree*).

Reliability: Alpha coefficients were above .75.

Author: Möller, J., and Köller, O.

Article: Dimensional comparisons: An experimental approach to the internal/external frame of reference model.

Journal: *Journal of Educational Psychology*, December 2001, *93*, 826–835.

Related Research: Möller, J., & Köller, O. (2001). Frame of reference effects following the announcement of exam results. *Contemporary Educational Psychology, 26*, 277–287.

13140

Test Name: SELF-PERCEIVED GIFTEDNESS SCALE—CHINESE

Purpose: To assess self-perceived giftedness in academic skills, creativity, and leadership.

Number of Items: 9

Format: Includes three areas: Academic Skills, Creativity, and Leadership. Responses are made on a 5-point scale ranging from 1 (*strongly disagree*) to 5 (*strongly agree*).

Reliability: Alpha coefficients ranged from .63 to .79.

Author: Chan, D. W.

Article: Family environment and talent development of Chinese gifted students in Hong Kong.

Journal: *Gifted Child Quarterly*, Summer 2005, *49*, 211–221.

Related Research: Chan, D. W. (2000). Exploring identification procedures of gifted students by teacher ratings: Parent ratings and student self-reports in Hong Kong. *High Ability Studies, 11*, 69–82.

13141

Test Name: SELF-PERCEPTION PROFILE

Purpose: To measure personal and academic competence.

Number of Items: 36

Format: Respondents select between paired items the one that describes them best and then rates that item on a 4-point scale. A sample item is presented.

Reliability: Reliabilities among scale items ranged from .71 to .86.

Author: Vandiver, T.

Article: Children's social competence, academic competence, and aggressiveness as related to ability to make judgments of fairness.

Journal: *Psychological Reports*, August 2001, *89*, 111–121.

Related Research: Harter, S. (1982). The Perceived Competence Scale for Children. *Child Development, 51*, 87–97.

13142

Test Name: SELF-PERCEPTION PROFILE FOR CHILDREN

Purpose: To measure children's perceptions of their personal competence and self-adequacy in academics, conduct, and social acceptance.

Number of Items: 18

Format: Four-point scales are used. A sample item is presented.

Reliability: Alpha coefficients ranged from .73 to .78. Test–retest reliabilities ranged from .55 to .66.

Author: Han, S. S., et al.

Article: Specificity of relations between children's control-related beliefs and internalizing and externalizing psychopathology.

Journal: *Journal of Consulting and Clinical Psychology*, April 2001, *69*, 240–251.

Related Research: Harter, S. (1985). *Manual for the Self-Perception Profile for Children*. Denver, CO: University of Denver.

13143

Test Name: SELF-PERCEPTION PROFILE FOR CHILDREN

Purpose: To measure self-concept.

Number of Items: 36

Reliability: Mean alpha coefficients ranged from .72 to .79.

Validity: Correlations with other variables ranged from −.65 to .01.

Author: Holmbeck, G. N., et al.

Article: Observed and perceived parental overprotection in relation to psychosocial adjustment in preadolescents with a physical disability: The mediational role of behavioral autonomy.

Journal: *Journal of Consulting and Clinical Psychology*, February 2002, *70*, 96–110.

Related Research: Harter, S. (1985). *Manual for the Self-Perception Profile for Children: Revision of the Perceived Competence Scale for Children*. Denver, CO: University of Denver.

13144

Test Name: SELF-PERCEPTION PROFILE FOR CHILDREN—ADAPTED

Purpose: To measure social self-acceptance.

Number of Items: 12

Format: Includes two subscales: Perceived Social Acceptance and Global Self-Esteem.

Reliability: Alpha coefficients were greater than .80.

Author: Troop-Gordon, W., and Ladd, G. W.

Article: Trajectories of peer victimization and perceptions of the self and schoolmates: Precursors to internalizing and externalizing problems.

Journal: *Child Development*, September/October 2005, *76*, 1072–1091.

Related Research: Harter, S. (1985). *The Self-Perception Profile for Children*. Unpublished manual, University of Denver, Denver, CO.

13145

Test Name: SELF-PERCEPTIONS OF ACADEMIC ABILITY SCALE

Purpose: To assess self-perceptions of academic ability.

Number of Items: 3

Format: Includes three areas: math, science, and English. Responses are made on 7-point scales. All items are presented.

Reliability: Internal consistency estimates ranged from .89 to .97.

Author: Silverthorn, N., et al.

Article: Self-perceptions of ability and achievement across the high school transition: Investigation of a state-trait model.

Journal: *Journal of Experimental Education*, Spring 2005, *73*, 191–218.

Related Research: Parsons, J. E., et al. (1980). *Self-perceptions, task perceptions, and academic choice: Origins and change*. Washington, DC: National Institute of Education. (ERIC Document Reproduction Service No. ED186477)

13146

Test Name: SELF-PLURALISM SCALE

Purpose: To measure the perception that one behaves and feels different in different times and places.

Number of Items: 30

Format: A true–false format is used.

Reliability: Coefficient alpha was .90.

Validity: Correlations with dissociative experiences ranged from .28 to .54.

Author: Suszek, H.

Article: Self-pluralism and dissociation.

Journal: *Psychological Reports*, February 2005, *96*, 181–182.

Related Research: McReynolds, P., & Altrocchi, J. (2000). Self-pluralism: Assessment and relations to adjustment, life changes, and age. *Journal of Personality*, *68*, 347–381.

13147

Test Name: SELF-REFERENT MONITORING THOUGHTS

Purpose: To assess positive and negative self-reactions in regard to tasks performed.

Number of Items: 6

Format: Scales range from 1 (*never*) to 8 (*constantly*). A sample item is presented.

Reliability: Alpha coefficients ranged from .70 to .78.

Author: Gohm, C. L., et al.

Article: Personality in extreme situations: Thinking (or not) under acute stress.

Journal: *Journal of Research in Personality*, September 2001, *35*, 388–399.

Related Research: Kanfer, R., & Ackerman, P. L. (1989). Motivation and cognitive abilities: An integrative aptitude–treatment interaction approach to skill acquisition. *Journal of Applied Psychology*, *74*, 657–690.

13148

Test Name: SELF-REFLECTIVENESS AND SELF-KNOWLEDGE SCALES

Purpose: To measure the general tendency to self-reflect and to measure the self-attributed self-knowledge.

Number of Items: 14

Reliability: Alpha coefficients ranged from .85 to .87.

Validity: Correlations with other variables ranged from .09 to .46.

Author: Schneider, J. F.

Article: Relations among self-talk, self-consciousness, and self-knowledge.

Journal: *Psychological Reports*, December 2002, *91*, Part 1, 807–812.

Related Research: Burnkrant, R. E., & Page, T. J. (1984). A modification of the Fenigstein,

Sheier, and Buss Self-Consciousness Scales. *Journal of Personality Assessment, 48,* 629–637.

13149

Test Name: SELF-REFLECTIVENESS SCALE—GERMAN VERSION

Purpose: To assess the general tendency to self-reflect.

Number of Items: 5

Format: Scales range from 1 (*completely false*) to 6 (*completely true*).

Reliability: Coefficient alpha was .82.

Validity: Correlations with other variables ranged from −.13 to .56.

Author: Schneider, J. F., et al.

Article: Does self-consciousness mediate the relation between self-talk and self-knowledge?

Journal: *Psychological Reports,* April 2005, *96,* 387–396.

Related Research: Merz, J. (1986). SAF: Fragebogen zur messung disposition eller selbstaufmerksamkeit [Questionnaire for the measurement of dispositional self-consciousness]. *Diagnostica, 32,* 142–152.

13150

Test Name: SELF-REGARD SCALE

Purpose: To assess global self-esteem.

Number of Items: 7

Format: Seven-point response scales are used. A sample item is presented.

Reliability: Coefficient alpha was .88.

Author: MacDonald, G., et al.

Article: Social approval and trait self-esteem.

Journal: *Journal of Research in Personality,* April 2003, *37,* 23–40.

Related Research: Flemming, J. S., & Courtney, B. E. (1984). The dimensionality of self-esteem: II.

Hierarchical facet model for revised measurement scales. *Journal of Personality and Social Psychology, 46,* 404–421.

13151

Test Name: SELF-SPLITTING INDEX

Purpose: To assess the ego defense of seeing oneself as all good or all bad.

Number of Items: 24

Format: Scales range from 1 (*strongly disagree*) to 5 (*strongly agree*). Sample items are presented.

Reliability: Coefficient alpha was .90.

Validity: Correlations with other variables ranged from −.63 to .61.

Author: Lopez, F. G., and Hsu, P.-C.

Article: Further validation of a measure of parent–adult attachment style.

Journal: *Measurement and Evaluation in Counseling and Development,* January 2002, *34,* 223–237.

Related Research: Gould, J. R., et al. (1996). The Splitting Index: Construction of a scale measuring the defense mechanism of splitting. *Journal of Personality Assessment, 66,* 414–430.

13152

Test Name: SENSE OF COHERENCE SCALE

Purpose: To measure the sense of coherence in the areas of comprehensibility, manageability, and meaningfulness.

Number of Items: 29

Format: Responses are made on 7-point scales. Examples are presented.

Reliability: Alpha coefficients ranged from .86 to .95.

Validity: Correlations with other variables ranged from −.29 to −.37.

Author: Lustig, D. C., and Strauser, D. R.

Article: The relationship between sense of coherence and career thought.

Journal: *The Career Development Quarterly,* September 2002, *51,* 2–11.

Related Research: Antonovsky, A. (1987). *Unraveling the mystery of health.* San Francisco: Jossey-Bass.

13153

Test Name: SENSE OF COHERENCE SCALE

Purpose: To measure sense of coherence.

Number of Items: 13

Format: Seven-point semantic differential format.

Reliability: Coefficient alpha was .83.

Validity: Correlations with other variables ranged from −.08 to .47.

Author: Toppinen-Tanner, S., and Kalimo, R.

Article: Psychological symptoms and competence at three organizational levels of industrial design: The main and moderating role of sense of coherence.

Journal: *Psychological Reports,* April 2003, *92,* 667–682.

Related Research: Antonovsky, A. (1993). The structure and properties of the Sense of Coherence Scale. *Social Science and Medicine, 36,* 725–733.

13154

Test Name: SENSE OF CONTROL TEST

Purpose: To measure sense of control.

Number of Items: 8

Format: A Likert format is used. All items are presented.

Reliability: Item Kappas ranged from .38 to .66.

Author: Wolinsky, F. D., et al.

Article: Test–retest reliability of the Mirowsky–Ross 2×2 Index of the Sense of Control.

Journal: *Psychological Reports,* April 2004, *94*, 725–732.

Related Research: Mirowsky, J., & Ross, E. E. (1991). Eliminating defense and agreement bias from measures of the Sense of Control: A 2×2 index. *Social Psychology Quarterly, 54,* 127–145.

13155

Test Name: SENSE OF IDENTITY SCALE

Purpose: To measure sense of identity among early, middle, and late adolescence.

Number of Items: 8

Format: Scales range from 1 (*strongly disagree*) to 5 (*strongly agree*). All items are presented.

Reliability: Coefficient alpha was .84.

Validity: Correlations with other variables ranged from .13 to .43.

Author: Lounsbury, J. W., et al.

Article: Sense of identity and collegiate academic achievement.

Journal: *Journal of College Student Development,* September/October 2005, *46,* 501–514.

13156

Test Name: SEXUAL SELF-CONCEPTS SCALE

Purpose: To assess body image and sexual–social comparison.

Number of Items: 14

Format: Scales range from 1 (*does not describe me at all*) to 4

(*describes me very well*). Sample items are presented.

Reliability: Alpha coefficients ranged from .57 to .70.

Validity: Correlations with other variables ranged from −.09 to .46.

Author: Murry, V. M., et al.

Article: Parental involvement promotes rural African American youths' self-pride and sexual self-concepts.

Journal: *Journal of Marriage and Family,* August 2005, *67,* 627–642.

13157

Test Name: SHORT INDEX OF SELF-ACTUALIZATION

Purpose: To measure self-actualization.

Number of Items: 15

Format: Seven-point scales are anchored by 1 (*strongly disagree*) and 7 (*strongly agree*). Sample items are presented.

Reliability: Alpha coefficients ranged in .40s.

Validity: Correlations with other variables ranged from −.24 to .32.

Author: Lee, S. A., and Chard, K. M.

Article: Variables related to graduate students' willingness to forgive a job-related transgression.

Journal: *Psychological Reports,* December 2003, *93,* Part 1, 955–960.

Related Research: Jones, A., & Crandall, R. (1986). Validation of a Short Index of Self-Actualization. *Personality and Social Psychology Bulletin, 12,* 63–73.

13158

Test Name: SITUATION-SPECIFIC COLLECTIVE SELF-ESTEEM SCALE

Purpose: To measure collective self-esteem in a university setting.

Number of Items: 3

Format: Scales range from 1 (*not at all*) to 7 (*very much*). All items are presented.

Reliability: Coefficient alpha was .88.

Author: DeCremer, D.

Article: Relations of self-esteem concerns, group identifications, and self-stereotyping to in-group favoritism.

Journal: *The Journal of Social Psychology,* June 2001, *141,* 389–400.

Related Research: Luhtanen, R., & Crocker, J. (1992). A collective self-esteem scale: Self-evaluation of one's social identity. *Personality and Social Psychology Bulletin, 18,* 302–318.

13159

Test Name: SITUATIONAL JUDGMENT TEST

Purpose: To measure situational judgment of college students' success.

Number of Items: 23

Format: An example is presented.

Reliability: Internal consistency reliabilities were .48 and .62.

Validity: Correlations with other variables ranged from −.10 to .48.

Author: Peeters, H., and Lievens, F.

Article: Situational judgment tests and their predictiveness of college students' success: The influence of faking.

Journal: *Educational and Psychological Measurement,* February 2005, *65,* 70–89.

Related Research: Bess, T. L., & Mullins, M. E. (2002, April). *Exploring a dimensionality of situational judgment: Task and*

contextual knowledge. Paper presented at the 17th annual conference of the Society for Industrial and Organizational Psychology, Toronto, Canada.

13160

Test Name: SITUATIONAL SELF-HANDICAPPING WITHIN YOUTH SPORT

Purpose: To identify self-handicaps that would impede sport performance.

Number of Items: 12

Format: Responses are made on a 7-point scale ranging from 1 (*not at all*) to 7 (*very much*). Examples are given.

Reliability: Internal consistency was .77.

Validity: Correlations with other variables ranged from −.24 to .37.

Author: Ryska, T. A.

Article: Enjoyment of evaluative physical activity among young participants: The role of self-handicapping and intrinsic motivation.

Journal: *Child Study Journal,* 2003, *33,* 213–234.

Related Research: Ryska, T. A., et al. (1999). The role of dispositional goal orientation and team climate on situational self-handicapping among young athletes. *Journal of Sport Behavior, 22,* 410–425.

13161

Test Name: SOCIAL INSECURITY SCALE

Purpose: To measure lack of self-esteem.

Number of Items: 3

Format: Scales range from 1 (*not at all*) to 7 (*very much*). All items are presented.

Reliability: Coefficient alpha was .65.

Author: Barreto, M., and Ellemers, N.

Article: The perils of political correctness: Men's and women's responses to old-fashioned and modern sexist views.

Journal: *Social Psychology Quarterly,* March 2005, *68,* 75–88.

Related Research: Heatherton, T. F., & Polny, J. (1991). Development and validation of a scale for measuring self-esteem. *Journal of Personality and Social Psychology, 60,* 895–910.

13162

Test Name: SOCIAL PRESENCE SCALE

Purpose: To measure social presence.

Number of Items: 4

Format: Responses are made of a 7-point semantic differential scale. All items are presented.

Reliability: Coefficient alpha was .85 (*N* = 989).

Validity: Correlations with other variables ranged from .01 to .40 (*N* = 989).

Author: Allen, D. G., et al.

Article: Recruitment communication media: Impact on prehire outcomes.

Journal: *Personnel Psychology,* Spring 2004, 57, 143–171.

Related Research: Short, J., et al. (1976). *The social psychology of communications.* London: Wiley.

13163

Test Name: SOCIAL SELF-EFFICACY SUBSCALE

Purpose: To measure efficacy beliefs regarding social interactions.

Number of Items: 6

Format: Responses are on a 5-point Likert scale ranging from 1 (*strongly disagree*) to 5 (*strongly agree*). An example is given.

Reliability: Alpha coefficients were .69 to .71.

Author: Anderson, S. L., and Betz, N. E.

Article: Sources of social self-efficacy expectations: Their measurement and relation to career development.

Journal: *Journal of Vocational Behavior,* February 2001, *58,* 98–117.

Related Research: Sherer, M., et al. (1982). The Self-Efficacy Scale: Construction and validation. *Psychological Reports, 51,* 663–671.

13164

Test Name: SOURCE CREDIBILITY SCALE

Purpose: To measure competence, character, sociability, extroversion, and composure.

Number of Items: 15

Format: A 7-point Likert format is used.

Reliability: Alpha coefficients ranged from .70 to .75 across subscales.

Author: Seiter, J. S., and Hatch, S.

Article: Effect of tattoos on perceptions of credibility and attractiveness.

Journal: *Psychological Reports,* June 2005, *96,* Part 2, 1113–1120.

Related Research: Rubin, R. B., et al. (1994). *Communication research measures: A sourcebook.* New York: Guilford.

13165

Test Name: SOURCE OF ACADEMIC SELF-EFFICACY SCALE

Purpose: To measure four primary sources of self-efficacy.

Format: Includes five subscales: Personal Performance Accomplishments, Vicarious Learning, Social Persuasion, and Emotional Arousal.

Reliability: Alpha coefficients ranged from .79 to .91.

Validity: Correlations with other scales ranged from .45 to .57.

Author: Hampton, N. Z., and Mason, E.

Article: Learning disabilities, gender, sources of efficacy, self-efficacy beliefs, and academic achievement in high school students.

Journal: *Journal of School Psychology*, March/April 2003, *41*, 101–112.

Related Research: Hampton, N. Z. (1998). Sources of Academic Self-Efficacy Scale: An assessment tool for rehabilitation counselors. *Rehabilitation Counseling Bulletin, 41*, 260–277.

13166

Test Name: SOURCES OF SELF-EFFICACY SCALE

Purpose: To measure sources of self-efficacy.

Number of Items: 15

Format: Includes three sources: vicarious experience, social persuasion, and emotional arousal. Responses are made on a 0 to 10 scale.

Reliability: Alpha coefficients ranged from .70 to .87.

Validity: Correlations with other variables ranged from .21 to .64.

Author: Klassen, R. M.

Article: A cross-cultural investigation of the efficacy beliefs of South Asian immigrant and Anglo Canadian nonimmigrant early adolescents.

Journal: *Journal of Educational Psychology*, December 2004, *96*, 731–742.

Related Research: Matsui, T., et al. (1990). Mechanisms underlying math self-efficacy learning of college students. *Journal of Vocational Behavior, 37*, 225–238.

13167

Test Name: SPHERES OF CONTROL SCALE

Purpose: To measure perceived personal and interpersonal efficacy.

Format: Seven-point Likert scales are used.

Reliability: Alpha coefficients ranged from .62 to .81.

Validity: Correlations with other variables ranged from −.28 to .45.

Author: Leonardi, A., and Kiosseoglou, G.

Article: Parental psychological control and attachment in late adolescents and young adults.

Journal: *Psychological Reports*, June 2002, *90*, Part 1, 1015–1030.

Related Research: Paulhus, D. (1983). Sphere-specific measures of perceived control. *Journal of Personality and Social Psychology, 44*, 1253–1265.

13168

Test Name: SPLITTING INDEX—DEPERSONALIZATION/SELF-FRAGMENTATION SUBSCALE

Purpose: To assess experience of depersonalization and self-fragmentation.

Number of Items: 8

Format: Responses are made on a 5-point scale ranging from 1 (*strongly disagree*) to 5 (*strongly agree*). An example is given.

Reliability: Alpha coefficients were .89 and .90.

Validity: Correlations with other variables ranged from −.58 to .66.

Author: Lopez, F. G., et al.

Article: Adult attachment orientation and college student distress: Test of a mediational model.

Journal: *Journal of Counseling Psychology*, October 2002, *49*, 460–467.

Related Research: Gould, J. R., et al. (1996). The Splitting Index: Construction of a scale measuring the defense mechanism of splitting. *Journal of Personality Assessment, 66*, 414–430.

13169

Test Name: SPORTS SELF-CONCEPT AND VALUE SCALE

Purpose: To indicate adolescents' self-concept of their athletic ability and the value of sports.

Number of Items: 3

Format: Responses are made on 7-point scales. All items are presented.

Reliability: Coefficient alpha was .88.

Validity: Correlations with other variables ranged from −.03 to .45.

Author: Jodl, K. M., et al.

Article: Parents' roles in shaping early adolescents' occupational aspirations.

Journal: *Child Development*, July/August 2001, *72*, 1247–1265.

Related Research: Eccles, J. S. (1993). School and family effects on the ontogeny of children's interests, self-perceptions, and activity choices. In R. Dienstbier & J. E. Jacobs (Eds.), *Developmental perspectives on motivation* (Vol. 40, pp. 145–208). Lincoln: University of Nebraska Press.

13170

Test Name: STABILITY OF SELF SCALE

Purpose: To assess the stability of self-concept.

Number of Items: 5

Format: Sample items are presented.

Reliability: Guttman coefficient of reproducibility was .94 and scalability was .77.

Validity: Correlations with other variables ranged from −.44 to .34.

Author: Szymanski, D. M., et al.

Article: Psychosocial correlates of internalized homophobia in lesbians.

Journal: *Measurement and Evaluation in Counseling and Development*, April 2001, *34*, 27–38.

Related Research: Rosenberg, M. (1965). *Society and the adolescent self-image*. Princeton, NJ: Princeton University Press.

13171

Test Name: STATE SELF-ESTEEM SCALE

Purpose: To measure self-esteem and confidence about abilities and performance.

Number of Items: 7

Format: Scales range from 1 (*not at all*) to 5 (*extremely*). Sample items are presented.

Reliability: Alpha coefficients exceeded .83.

Author: Neighbors, C., and Knee, C. R.

Article: Self-determination and the consequences of social comparison.

Journal: *Journal of Research in Personality*, December 2003, *37*, 529–546.

Related Research: Heatherton, T. F., & Polivy, J. (1991). Development and validation of a scale for measuring state self-esteem. *Journal of Personality and Social Psychology, 60,* 895–910.

13172

Test Name: STIGMA CONSCIOUSNESS SCALE

Purpose: To measure consciousness of being stereotyped.

Number of Items: 10

Format: Scales ranged from 1 (*strongly disagree*) to 5 (*strongly agree*).

Reliability: Alpha coefficients ranged from .57 to .71.

Author: Hall, G. C. N., et al.

Article: Ethnicity, culture, and sexual aggression: Risk and protective factors.

Journal: *Journal of Consulting and Clinical Psychology*, October 2005, *73*, 830–840.

Related Research: Pinel, E. C. (1999). Stigma consciousness: The psychological legacy of social stereotypes. *Journal of Personality and Social Psychology, 76,* 114–128.

13173

Test Name: STIGMA SCALE

Purpose: To assess expectations of rejection and discrimination regarding homosexuality.

Number of Items: 11

Format: Scales range from 1 (*strongly disagree*) to 6 (*strongly agree*). A sample item is presented.

Reliability: Coefficient alpha was .89.

Validity: Correlations with other variables ranged from −.30 to .27.

Author: Kimmel, S. B., and Mahalik, J. R.

Article: Body image concerns of gay men: The roles of minority stress and conformity to masculine norms.

Journal: *Journal of Consulting and Clinical Psychology*, December 2005, *73*, 1185–1190.

13174

Test Name: STIGMA SCALE FOR RECEIVING PSYCHOLOGICAL HELP

Purpose: To assess perceptions of the stigma associated with seeking professional help.

Number of Items: 5

Format: Responses are made on a 4-point scale ranging from 1 (*strongly disagree*) to 4 (*strongly agree*). A sample item is given.

Reliability: Alpha coefficients were .73 and .78.

Validity: Correlations with other variables ranged from −.31 to .28 ($n = 354$).

Author: Vogel, D. L., et al.

Article: The role of outcome expectations and attitudes on decisions to seek professional help.

Journal: *Journal of Counseling Psychology*, October 2005, *52*, 459–470.

Related Research: Komiya, N., et al. (2000). Emotional openness as a predictor of college students' attitudes toward seeking psychological help. *Journal of Counseling Psychology, 47,* 138–143.

13175

Test Name: STIGMATIZATION SCALE

Purpose: To measure the perception that one is stigmatized.

Number of Items: 18

Format: Scales range from 1 (*strongly disagree*) to 5 (*strongly agree*). All items are presented.

Reliability: Coefficient alpha was .94.

Validity: Correlations with other variables ranged from −.61 to .75.

Author: Harvey, R. D.

Article: Individual differences in the phenomenological impact of social stigma.

Journal: *The Journal of Social Psychology*, April 2001, *141*, 174–189.

13176

Test Name: STUDENT ATHLETE ROLE CONFLICT SCALE

Purpose: To measure the conflict between athlete and student roles and how separate these roles are perceived to be.

Number of Items: 16

Format: Scales range from 1 (*not really true of me*) to 5 (*really true of me*). All items are presented.

Reliability: Alpha coefficients were .84 (conflict) and .54 (separation).

Validity: Correlations with other variables ranged from −.31 to .34.

Author: Settles, I. H., et al.

Article: One role or two? The function of psychological separation in role conflict.

Journal: *Journal of Applied Psychology*, June 2002, *87*, 574–582.

13177

Test Name: STUDENT BELIEFS AND PERCEPTIONS ABOUT CHEATING SCALES

Purpose: To measure student beliefs about cheating and their perceptions of faculty beliefs about cheating.

Number of Items: 34

Format: Scales range from 1 (*strongly disagree*) to 5 (*strongly agree*). All items are presented.

Reliability: Alpha coefficients ranged from .93 to .95.

Author: Cummings, K., and Romano, J.

Article: Effect of an honor code on perceptions of university instructor affinity-seeking behavior.

Journal: *Journal of College Student Development*, November/December 2002, *43*, 862–875.

Related Research: Graham, M. A., et al. (1994). Cheating at small colleges: An examination of student and faculty attitudes and behavior. *Journal of College Student Development, 35*, 255–260.

13178

Test Name: STUDENT SELF-BELIEFS TOWARD READING

Purpose: To assess student self-beliefs toward reading.

Number of Items: 7

Format: Includes two scales: Student Attitudes About Reading and Self-Perceptions of Reading Ability. All items are presented.

Validity: Correlations with reading achievement ranged from −.37 to .33.

Author: House, J. D.

Article: Self-beliefs and reading achievement of elementary school students in Hong Kong and the United States: Results from the PIRLS 2001 Assessment.

Journal: *Child Study Journal*, 2003, *33*, 195–212.

Related Research: Alfassi, M. (2003). Promoting the will and skill of students at academic risk: An evaluation of an instructional design geared to foster achievement, self-efficacy, and motivation. *Journal of Instructional Psychology, 30*, 28–40.

13179

Test Name: STUDENT SELF-EFFICACY SCALE

Purpose: To assess participants' belief in their ability to successfully manage the tasks related to the student role.

Number of Items: 12

Format: Responses are made on a 10-point scale ranging from 0 (*no confidence*) to 9 (*complete confidence*). An example is provided.

Reliability: Alpha coefficients were .91 and .94.

Validity: Correlations with other variables ranged from −.43 to .43.

Author: Quimby, J. L., and O'Brien, K. M.

Article: Predictors of student and career decision-making self-efficacy among nontraditional college women.

Journal: *The Career Development Quarterly*, June 2004, *52*, 323–339.

Related Research: Lefcourt, L. A. (1995). *The Self-Efficacy Expectations for Role Management Measure (SEERM) and its relationship with self-concept constructs and efficacy sources for career women.* Unpublished doctoral dissertation, University of Illinois, Urbana–Champaign.

13180

Test Name: STUDENT'S SELF-DETERMINATION SCALE

Purpose: To measure qualities of perceived self-determination.

Number of Items: 9

Format: Includes three qualities of perceived self-determination: perceived locus of causality, volition, and perceived choice. Responses are made on a 7-point scale ranging from *not at all true* to *very much true*.

Reliability: Alpha coefficients ranged from .81 to .85.

Author: Reeve, J., et al.

Article: Testing models of the experience of self-determination in intrinsic motivation and the conundrum of choice.

Journal: *Journal of Educational Psychology*, June 2003, *95*, 375–392.

Related Research: Judd, C. M., et al. (1986). Structural equation models and personality research. *Journal of Personality, 54*, 149–198.

13181

Test Name: SUBJECTIVE CAREER SUCCESS SCALE

Purpose: To measure subjective career success.

Number of Items: 7

Format: Includes four domains: job success, hierarchical success, financial success, and interpersonal success. Responses are made on a 5-point scale ranging from 1 (*completely disagree*) to 5 (*completely agree*). Examples are presented.

Reliability: Coefficient alpha was .70.

Author: Bozionelos, N.

Article: Mentoring provided: Relation to mentor's career success, personality, and mentoring received.

Journal: *Journal of Vocational Behavior*, February 2004, *64*, 24–46.

Related Research: Gattiker, U. E., & Larwood, L. (1986). Subjective career success: A study of managers and support personnel. *Journal of Business and Psychology, 1*, 78–94.

13182

Test Name: SUBJECTIVE CAREER SUCCESS SCALE

Purpose: To assess subjective career success.

Number of Items: 4.

Format: Responses are made on a 5-point Likert scale ranging from 1

(*strongly disagree*) to 5 (*strongly agree*). An example is given.

Reliability: Alpha coefficients were .83 to .87.

Author: Day, R., and Allen, T. D.

Article: The relationship between career motivation and self-efficacy with protégé career success.

Journal: *Journal of Vocational Behavior*, February 2004, *64*, 72–91.

Related Research: Turban, D., & Dougherty, T. (1994). Role of protégé personality in receipt of mentoring and career success. *Academy of Management Journal*, *37*, 688–702.

13183

Test Name: SURVEY OF PERCEIVED ORGANIZATIONAL SUPPORT—SHORT VERSION

Purpose: To measure perceived organizational support.

Number of Items: 9

Format: Responses are made on a 5-point scale ranging from 1 (*strongly disagree*) to 5 (*strongly agree*). Examples are given.

Reliability: Alpha coefficients were .91 and .92.

Validity: Correlations with other variables ranged from .30 to .64 ($n = 186$).

Author: Chen, Z. X., et al.

Article: Test of a mediation model of perceived organizational support.

Journal: *Journal of Vocational Behavior*, June 2005, *66*, 457–470.

Related Research: Wayne, S. J., et al. (2002). The role of fair treatment and rewards in perceptions of organizational support and leader–member exchange. *Journal of Applied Psychology*, *87*, 590–598.

13184

Test Name: TASK COMPETENCE SCALES

Purpose: To assess inferences about a teammate's view of one's own competence, one's views of one's own competence, and one's feelings while performing a task.

Format: Nine-point rating scales and 9-point semantic differential scales are used. Sample items are presented.

Reliability: Alpha coefficients ranged from .86 to .91 across subscales.

Validity: Correlations between subscales ranged from .01 to .68.

Author: Heilman, M. E., and Alcott, V. B.

Article: What I think you think of me: Women's reactions to being viewed as beneficiaries of preferential selection.

Journal: *Journal of Applied Psychology*, August 2001, *86*, 574–582.

13185

Test Name: TEACHER EFFICACY SCALE FOR WRITING

Purpose: To measure teachers' sense of efficacy in the area of composition instruction.

Number of Items: 16

Format: Includes two factors: personal teaching efficacy and general teaching efficacy. Responses are made on a 6-point Likert-type scale. Examples are presented.

Reliability: Internal consistency reliability coefficients were .69 and .84.

Author: Graham, S., et al.

Article: Primary grade teachers' instructional adaptations for struggling writers: A national survey.

Journal: *Journal of Educational Psychology*, June 2003, *95*, 279–292.

Related Research: Graham, S., et al. (2001). Teacher efficacy in writing: A construct validation with primary grade teachers. *Scientific Study of Reading, 5*, 177–202.

13186

Test Name: TEACHER EFFICACY SCALE—FRENCH CANADIAN VERSION

Purpose: To measure teacher self-efficacy.

Number of Items: 15

Format: Item responses are rated on a scale anchored by 1 (*strongly disagree*) and 6 (*strongly agree*). Sample items are presented in English.

Reliability: Alpha was .63.

Validity: Correlations with other variables ranged from –.25 to .72.

Author: Dussault, M., and Deaudelin, C.

Article: Loneliness and self-efficacy in education majors.

Journal: *Psychological Reports*, October 2001, *89*, 285–289.

Related Research: Dembo, M. H., & Gibson, S. (1985). Teachers' sense of efficacy: An important factor in school improvement. *The Elementary School Journal, 86*, 173–184.

13187

Test Name: TEACHER EFFICACY SCALE—REVISED

Purpose: To measure teaching efficacy.

Number of Items: 18

Format: Includes two dimensions: Personal teaching efficacy and general teaching efficacy. All items are presented.

Reliability: Alpha coefficients ranged from .54 to .79.

Author: Lin, H.-L., et al.

Article: Influence of culture and education on U.S. and Taiwan preservice teachers' efficacy beliefs.

Journal: *Journal of Educational Research*, September/October 2002, *96*, 37–47

Related Research: Gibson, S., & Dembo, M. H. (1984). Teacher efficacy: A construct validation. *Journal of Educational Psychology, 76*, 569–582.

13188

Test Name: TEACHER INTERPERSONAL SELF-EFFICACY SCALE

Purpose: To assess teachers' confidence in their abilities to manage classroom student behavior and elicit support from colleagues and school principals.

Number of Items: 24

Format: Includes three subscales: Perceived Self-Efficacy in Classroom Management, Perceived Self-Efficacy to Elicit Support from Colleagues, and Perceived Self-Efficacy to Elicit Support From Principals. Responses are made on a 6-point Likert-type scale ranging from *strongly agree* to *strongly disagree*.

Reliability: Alpha coefficients ranged from .90 to .95.

Author: Brouwers, A., and Tomic, W.

Article: The factorial validity of scores on the Teacher Interpersonal Self-Efficacy Scale

Journal: *Educational and Psychological Measurement*, June 2001, *61*, 433–445.

Related Research: Emmer, E. T., & Hickman, J. (1991). Teacher efficacy in classroom management and discipline. *Educational and Psychological Measurement, 51*, 755–765.

13189

Test Name: TEACHER OCCUPATIONAL PERCEPTION SCALE

Purpose: To measure a teacher's perception of teaching.

Number of Items: 28

Format: Scales range from 1 (*strongly disagree*) to 5 (*strongly agree*). Sample items are presented.

Reliability: Alpha coefficients ranged from .54 to .93 across subscales.

Author: Bogler, R.

Article: Satisfaction of Jewish and Arab teachers in Israel.

Journal: *The Journal of Social Psychology*, February 2005, *145*, 19–33.

Related Research: Yaniv, B. (1982). *Revealing factors that contribute to teacher dropout*. Unpublished master's thesis, University of Haifa, Haifa, Israel.

13190

Test Name: TEACHER SELF-EFFICACY SCALE—HEBREW VERSION

Purpose: To measure teacher self-efficacy.

Number of Items: 25

Format: Includes two factors: Personal Teaching Efficacy and Teaching Efficacy. Responses are made on a 5-point Likert-type scale ranging from 1 (*strongly disagree*) to 5 (*strongly agree*).

Reliability: Alpha coefficients were .72 and .74.

Author: Wertheim, C., and Leyser, Y.

Article: Efficacy beliefs, background variables, and differentiated instruction of Israeli prospective teachers.

Journal: *Journal of Educational Research*, September/October 2002, *96*, 54–63.

Related Research: Gibson, S., & Dembo, M. H. (1984). Teacher efficacy: A construct validation. *Journal of Educational Psychology, 76*, 569–582.

13191

Test Name: TEACHER SELF-EFFICACY SCALE—MODIFIED

Purpose: To measure self-efficacy.

Number of Items: 10

Format: Responses are made on a 5-point scale ranging from 1 (*totally disagree*) to 5 (*totally agree*). An example is given.

Reliability: Internal consistencies were .76 and .81.

Validity: Correlations with other variables ranged from –.36 to .17.

Author: Shechtman, Z., et al.

Article: Impact of life skills training on teachers' perceived environment and self-efficacy.

Journal: *Journal of Educational Research*, January/February 2005, *98*, 144–153.

Related Research: Woolfolk, A. E., & Hoy, W. K. (1990). Perspective teachers' sense of efficacy and beliefs about control. *Journal of Educational Psychology, 82*, 81–98.

13192

Test Name: TEACHER TREATMENT INVENTORY

Purpose: To measure children's perceptions of 30 teacher behaviors toward hypothetical high- and low-achieving students.

Number of Items: 30

Format: Includes three scales: Negative Feedback; Work and Rule Orientation; and High Expectations, Opportunity, and Choice. Responses are made on a 4-point scale ranging from 1 (*never*) to 4 (*always*).

Reliability: Internal consistency coefficients ranged from .58 to .84.

Author: Kuklinski, M. R., and Weinstein, R. S.

Article: Classroom and developmental differences in a path model of teacher expectancy effects.

Journal: *Child Development*, September/October, 2001, *72*, 1554–1578.

Related Research: Weinstein, R. S., et al. (1987). Pygmalion and the student: Age and classroom differences in children's awareness of teacher expectations. *Child Development, 58*, 1079–1093.

13193

Test Name: TEACHERS' EFFICACY TOWARD INTEGRATION OF INFORMATION TECHNOLOGIES IN THE CLASSROOM—FRENCH VERSION

Purpose: To measure efficacy expectation and outcome expectation toward integration of information technologies in the classroom.

Number of Items: 25

Format: Item anchors are 1 (*strongly disagree*) and 4 (*strongly agree*). All items are presented in English.

Reliability: Alpha coefficients ranged from .84 to .93. Test–retest reliability was .72 (3 weeks).

Validity: Correlations with other variables ranged from .21 to .36.

Author: Dussault, M., et al.

Article: Teachers' instructional efficacy and teachers' efficacy toward integration of information technologies in the classroom.

Journal: *Psychological Reports*, June 2004, *94*, Part 2, 1375–1381.

13194

Test Name: TEACHERS' SELF-EFFICACY SCALE—FRENCH VERSION

Purpose: To measure personal and general teaching efficacy.

Number of Items: 15

Format: Item anchors are 1 (*strongly disagree*) and 6 (*strongly agree*). Sample items are presented in English.

Reliability: Alpha coefficients ranged from .70 to .73. Test–retest reliabilities ranged from .73 to .83 (4 weeks).

Validity: Correlations with other variables ranged from .21 to .36.

Author: Dussault, M., et al.

Article: Teachers' instructional efficacy and teachers' efficacy toward integration of information technologies in the classroom.

Journal: *Psychological Reports*, June 2004, *94*, Part 2, 1375–1381.

Related Research: Dussault, M., et al. (2001). L'Echelle d'Auto-Efficacité des Enseignants (EAEE): Validation canadienne-francaise du Teacher Efficacy Scale. *Revue des Sciences de l'Education, 27*, 181–194.

13195

Test Name: TEAM LEARNING SURVEY—MODIFIED

Purpose: To measure perceived team and organizational learning.

Number of Items: 11

Format: Responses are made on a 5-point scale ranging from 5 (*strongly agree*) to 1 (*strongly disagree*). Sample items are presented.

Reliability: Coefficient alpha was .89.

Validity: Correlations with other variables ranged from –.06 to .64.

Author: Mebane, D. J., and Galassi, J. P.

Article: Variables affecting collaborative research and learning in a professional development school partnership.

Journal: *Journal of Educational Research*, May/June 2003, *96*, 259–268.

Related Research: Dechant, K., et al. (1993). Toward a model of team learning. *Studies of Continuing Education, 15*, 1–13.

13196

Test Name: TEAMWORK IMPORTANCE SCALE

Purpose: To assess perceptions of the value of teamwork within an organization.

Number of Items: 3

Format: Scales range from 1 (*strongly disagree*) to 5 (*strongly agree*). All items are presented.

Reliability: Coefficient alpha was .64.

Validity: Correlations with other variables ranged from –.16 to .40.

Author: Valle, M., and Witt, L. A.

Article: The moderating effect of teamwork perceptions on the organizational politics–job satisfaction relationship.

Journal: *The Journal of Social Psychology*, June 2001, *141*, 379–388.

13197

Test Name: TELECOMMUTER SELF-EFFICACY SCALE

Purpose: To measure self-efficacy.

Number of Items: 3

Format: Responses are made on a 7-point scale ranging from 1 (*strongly disagree*) to 7 (*strongly agree*). A sample item is presented.

Reliability: Coefficient alpha was .83.

Validity: Correlations with other variables ranged from –.05 to .34.

Author: Raghuram, S., et al.

Article: Technology enabled work: The role of self-efficacy in determining telecommuter adjustment and structuring behavior.

Journal: *Journal of Vocational Behavior*, October 2003, *63*, 180–198.

Related Research: Sherer, M., et al. (1982). The Self-Efficacy Scale: Construction and validation. *Psychological Reports, 51*, 663–671.

13198

Test Name: TIME QUESTIONNAIRE

Purpose: To measure the structure of time use, perceptions of time control, and the purposive use of time.

Number of Items: 8

Format: Scales range from 1 (*not at all true*) to 7 (*very true*).

Reliability: Alpha coefficients ranged from .66 to .73 across subscales.

Validity: Correlations with other variables ranged from –.56 to .46.

Author: Chu, A. H. C., and Choi, J. N.

Article: Rethinking procrastination: Positive effects of "active" procrastination behavior on attitudes and performance.

Journal: *The Journal of Social Psychology*, June 2005, *145*, 245–264.

Related Research: Bond, M. J., & Feather, N. T. (1988). Some correlates of structure and purpose in the use of time. *Journal of Personality and Social Psychology, 55*, 321–329.

13199

Test Name: TIME URGENCY SCALE—HEBREW VERSION

Purpose: To assess the degree to which people feel pressed for time.

Number of Items: 33

Format: Scales range from 1 (*strongly agree*) to 5 (*strongly disagree*). Sample items are presented in English.

Reliability: Coefficient alpha was .85.

Author: Dishon-Berkovits, M., and Koslowsky, M.

Article: Determinants of employee punctuality.

Journal: *The Journal of Social Psychology*, December 2002, *142*, 723–739.

Related Research: Landy, F. J., et al. (1991). Time urgency: The construct and its measurement. *Journal of Applied Psychology, 76*, 644–657.

13200

Test Name: UNCONDITIONAL SELF-REGARD SCALE

Purpose: To measure global self-esteem.

Number of Items: 20

Format: Responses are made on a 5-point Likert scale ranging from 1 (*strongly disagree*) to 5 (*strongly agree*).

Reliability: Alpha coefficients ranged from .84 to .92.

Validity: Correlations with other variables ranged from –.68 to .53.

Author: Smith, H. M., and Betz, N. E.

Article: An examination of efficacy and esteem pathways to depression in young adulthood.

Journal: *Journal of Counseling Psychology*, October 2002, *49*, 438–448.

Related Research: Betz, N. E., et al. (1995). Evaluation of a measure of self-esteem based on the concept of unconditional self-regard. *Journal of Counseling Development, 74,* 76–83.

13201

Test Name: UNDEREMPLOYMENT SCALE

Purpose: To assess the degree to which employees perceive themselves to be underemployed.

Number of Items: 4

Format: Scales range from 1 (*strongly agree*) to 5 (*strongly disagree*).

Reliability: Coefficient alpha was .60.

Validity: Correlations with other variables ranged from –.38 to .50.

Author: Holtom, B. C., et al.

Article: The relationship between work status congruence and work-related attitudes and behavior.

Journal: *Journal of Applied Psychology,* October 2002, *87,* 903–915.

13202

Test Name: UNION INSTRUMENTALITY SCALE

Purpose: To measure perceived union instrumentality.

Number of Items: 7 item-pairs

Format: Scales range from 1 (*very unimportant to me*) to 7 (*very important to me*). Scoring procedures are described.

Reliability: Coefficient alpha was .93.

Validity: Correlations with other variables ranged from –.26 to .52.

Author: Redman, T., and Snape, E.

Article: Exchange ideology and member–union relationships: An evaluation of moderation effects.

Journal: *Journal of Applied Psychology,* July 2005, *90,* 765–773.

13203

Test Name: USEFULNESS OF MATHEMATICS SCALE

Purpose: To measure outcome expectations.

Number of Items: 10

Format: Responses are made on a 5-point scale ranging from 1 (*strongly disagree*) to 5 (*strongly agree*).

Reliability: Alpha coefficients were .89 and .92.

Author: Lent, R. W., et al.

Article: The role of contextual supports and barriers in the choice of math/science educational options: A test of social cognitive hypotheses.

Journal: *Journal of Counseling Psychology,* October 2001, *48,* 474–483.

Related Research: Fennema, E., & Sherman, J. A. (1976). Fennema–Sherman Mathematics Attitude Scales: Instruments designed to measure attitudes toward the learning of mathematics by females and males. *JSAS Catalog of Selected Documents in Psychology, 6,* 31.

13204

Test Name: VIVIDNESS OF VISUAL IMAGERY QUESTIONNAIRE

Purpose: To measure the vividness of mental imagery.

Number of Items: 16

Format: Respondents rate images on 5-point scales anchored by 1 (*image is perfectly clear and as vivid as the actual experience*) and 5 (*no image is present at all*).

Reliability: Test–retest reliability was .74. Alpha was .82.

Validity: Correlations with other variables ranged from .12 to .24.

Author: Roberts, D. S. L., and MacDonald, B. E.

Article: Relations of imagery, creativity, and socio-economic status with performance on a stock market e-trading game.

Journal: *Psychological Reports,* June 2001, *88,* Part 1, 734–740.

Related Research: Marks, D. E. (1989). Bibliography of research utilizing the Vividness of Visual Imagery Questionnaire. *Perceptual and Motor Skills, 69,* 707–718.

13205

Test Name: VIVIDNESS OF VISUAL IMAGERY QUESTIONNAIRE—SPANISH VERSION

Purpose: To assess imaging capacity.

Number of Items: 16

Format: Item responses are anchored by 1 (*perfectly clear and as vivid as normal vision*) and 5 (*no image at all, you only know you are thinking of the skill*).

Reliability: Cronbach alpha was .88.

Validity: All items formed a single factor.

Author: Campos, A., et al.

Article: The Spanish Version of the Vividness of Visual Imagery Questionnaire: Factor structure and internal consistency reliability.

Journal: *Psychological Reports,* April 2002, *90,* 503–506.

Related Research: Marks, D. F. (1973). Visual imagery differences in the recall of pictures. *British Journal of Psychology, 64,* 17–24.

13206

Test Name: VOCATIONAL RATING SCALE

Purpose: To provide a global measure of vocational self-concept crystallization.

Number of Items: 40

Format: Responses are made on a 5-point scale ranging from 1 (*completely false*) to 5 (*completely true*).

Reliability: An internal consistency reliability estimate was .94. Test–retest (2 weeks) reliability was .76.

Validity: Correlations with other variables ranged from −.86 to .28.

Author: Tokar, D. M., et al.

Article: Psychological separation, attachment security, vocational self-concept crystallization, and career indecision: A structural equation analysis.

Journal: *Journal of Counseling Psychology*, January 2003, *50*, 3–19.

Related Research: Barrett, T. C., & Tinsley, H. E. A. (1977). Measuring self-concept crystallization. *Journal of Vocational Behavior, 11*, 305–313.

13207

Test Name: VOLUNTEER IDENTITY MEASURES

Purpose: To measure importance of volunteer identity and volunteer expectations of others.

Number of Items: 6

Format: All items are presented. Seven-point agreement scales are used.

Reliability: Alpha coefficients ranged from .78 to .82.

Author: Hiltin, S.

Article: Values as the core of personal identity: Drawing links between two theories of self.

Journal: *Social Psychology Quarterly*, June 2003, *66*, 118–137.

Related Research: Grube, J. A., & Piliavin, J. A. (2000). Role identity, organizational experiences, and the volunteer performance. *Personality and Social Psychology Bulletin, 26*, 1108–1119.

13208

Test Name: WEIGHT EFFICACY LIFE-STYLE QUESTIONNAIRE

Purpose: To measure self-efficacy in relation to food intake.

Number of Items: 12

Format: Includes three factors: negative emotion, social pressure, and physical discomfort. Responses are made on a 10-point scale ranging from 0 (*not confident*) to 9 (*very confident*). All items are presented.

Reliability: Alpha coefficients ranged from .68 to .94

Validity: Correlations with other variables ranged from −.77 to .29.

Author: Ruiz, V. M., et al.

Article: Factor analysis of the Spanish version of the Weight Efficacy Life-Style Questionnaire.

Journal: *Educational and Psychological Measurement*, June 2002, *62*, 539–555.

Related Research: Clark, M. M., et al. (1991). Self-efficacy in weight management. *Journal of Consulting and Clinical Psychology, 59*, 739–744.

13209

Test Name: WHAT I AM LIKE SUBSCALE—ADAPTED

Purpose: To enable adolescents to assess significant others' beliefs about their academic competence.

Number of Items: 5

Format: Sample items are given.

Reliability: Alpha coefficients ranged from .69 to .75.

Validity: Correlations with other variables ranged from −.05 to .62.

Author: Bouchey, H. A., and Harter, S.

Article: Reflected appraisals, academic self-perceptions, and

math/science performance during early adolescence.

Journal: *Journal of Educational Psychology*, November 2005, *97*, 673–686.

Related Research: Harter, S. (1988). *The Self-Perception Profile for Adolescents*. Unpublished manuscript, University of Denver, Denver, CO.

13210

Test Name: WHITE STEREOTYPE SCALE

Purpose: To measure the stereotypes African Americans hold of Whites.

Number of Items: 10

Format: Scales range from 1 (*not all typical of White people*) to 5 (*very typical of White people*). Sample items are presented.

Reliability: Coefficient alpha was .72.

Author: Heaven, P. C. L., and Greene, R. L.

Article: African Americans' stereotypes of Whites: Relationships with social dominance orientation, right-wing authoritarianism, and group identity.

Journal: *The Journal of Social Psychology*, February 2001, *141*, 141–143.

Related Research: Karlins, M., et al. (1969). On the fading of social stereotypes: Studies in three generations of college students. *Journal of Personality and Social Psychology, 13*, 1–16.

13211

Test Name: WORK-DOMAIN SELF-EFFICACY SCALE

Purpose: To measure self-efficacy at work.

Number of Items: 4

Format: A sample item is presented.

Reliability: Coefficient alpha was .76.

Validity: Correlations with other variables ranged from –.12 to .55.

Author: Kark, R., et al.

Article: The two faces of transformational leadership: Empowerment and dependency.

Journal: *Journal of Applied Psychology*, April 2003, *88*, 246–255.

Related Research: Riggs, M. L., & Knight, P. A. (1994). The impact of perceived group success–failure on motivational beliefs and attitudes. *Journal of Applied Psychology, 79,* 755–766.

13212

Test Name: WORK-DOMAIN SELF-EFFICACY SCALE

Purpose: To measure work-domain self-efficacy.

Number of Items: 11

Format: Scales range from 1 (*strongly disagree*) to 6 (*strongly agree*). Sample items are presented.

Validity: Correlations with other variables ranged from –.25 to .43.

Author: Kirk, A. K., and Brown, D. F.

Article: Latent constructs of proximal and distal motivation predicting performance under maximum test conditions.

Journal: *Journal of Applied Psychology*, February 2003, *88*, 40–49.

Related Research: Sherer, M., et al. (1982). The Self-Efficacy Scale: Construction and validation. *Psychological Reports, 51,* 663–671.

13213

Test Name: WORK–FAMILY SELF-EFFICIENCY SCALE

Purpose: To measure perceived self-efficacy to cope with work–family conflicts.

Number of Items: 5

Format: Responses are made on a 5-point scale ranging from 1 (*strongly disagree*) to 5 (*strongly agree*). Sample items are presented.

Reliability: Coefficient alpha was .79.

Validity: Correlations with other variables ranged from –.35 to .20.

Author: Butler, A., et al.

Article: A social–cognitive perspective on using family-friendly benefits.

Journal: *Journal of Vocational Behavior*, August 2004, *65*, 57–70.

Related Research: Wanberg, C. R., & Banas, J. T. (2000). Predictors and outcomes of openness to changes in a reorganizing workplace. *Journal of Applied Psychology, 85,* 132–142.

13214

Test Name: WORK LOCUS OF CONTROL SCALE

Purpose: To measure locus of control at work.

Number of Items: 16

Format: Scales range from 1 (*disagree very much*) to 6 (*agree very much*).

Reliability: Alpha coefficients ranged from .73 to .77.

Validity: Correlations with other variables ranged from –.44 to .23.

Author: Bond, F. U. and Bunce, D.

Article: The role of acceptance and job control in mental health, job satisfaction, and work performance.

Journal: *The Journal of Applied Psychology*, December 2003, *88*, 1057–1067.

Related Research: Spector, P. E. (1988). Development of the work locus of control scale. *Journal of Occupational Psychology, 61,* 335–340.

13215

Test Name: WORK ROLE IDENTITY SCALE

Purpose: To measure psychological identification.

Number of Items: 6

Format: Includes two formats: one measures work role identity and one measures family identity. Responses are made on a 7-point Likert scale ranging from 1 (*strongly disagree*) to 7 (*strongly agree*).

Reliability: Alpha coefficients were .77 and .78 ($N = 623$).

Validity: Correlations with other variables ranged from –.15 to .35. ($N = 623$).

Author: Rothbard, N. P., and Edwards, J. R.

Article: Investment in work and family roles: A test of identity and utilitarian motives.

Journal: *Personnel Psychology*, Autumn 2003, *56*, 699–729.

Related Research: Kanungo, R. N. (1982). Measurement of job and work involvement. *Journal of Applied Psychology, 67,* 341–349.

CHAPTER 17

Personality

13216

Test Name: ADJECTIVE CHECKLIST

Purpose: To measure agreeableness, conscientiousness, emotional stability, surgency, and intellect.

Number of Items: 96

Format: Includes five scales: Agreeableness, Conscientiousness, Emotional Stability, Surgency, and Intellect.

Reliability: Alpha coefficients ranged from .87 to .90.

Author: Zickar, M. J., and Ury, K. L.

Article: Developing an interpretation of item parameters for personality items: Content correlates of parameter estimates.

Journal: *Education and Psychological Measurement*, February 2002, *62*, 19–31.

Related Research: Goldberg, L. R. (1992). The development of markers for the Big-Five factor structure. *Psychological Assessment*, *4*, 26–42.

13217

Test Name: ADOLESCENT PERSONAL STYLE INVENTORY

Purpose: To measure personality.

Number of Items: 118

Format: Includes 12 traits. Responses are made on a 5-point Likert scale ranging from 1 (*strongly disagree*) to 5 (*strongly agree*).

Reliability: Alpha coefficients ranged from .74 to .91.

Validity: Correlations with other variables ranged from –.20 to .60.

Author: Lounsbury, J. W., et al.

Article: An investigation of broad and narrow personality traits in relation to general and domain-specific life satisfaction of college students.

Journal: *Research in Higher Education*, September 2005, *46*, 707–729.

Related Research: Lounsbury, J. W., et al. (2004). The development of a personological measure of work drive. *Journal of Business and Psychology*, *18*, 347–371.

13218

Test Name: AFFECT INTENSITY MEASURE

Purpose: To assess the intensity with which one typically experiences emotions.

Number of Items: 40

Format: Responses are made on a 6-point scale.

Reliability: Test–retest correlations of .80 (1 month), .81 (2 months), and .81 (3 months). Alpha coefficients ranged from .90 to .94.

Author: Crust, L., et al.

Article: Influence of music and distraction on visual search performance of participants with high and low affect intensity.

Journal: *Perceptual and Motor Skills*, June 2004, *98*, Part 1, 888–896.

Related Research: Larsen, R. J., et al. (1986). Affect intensity and reactions to daily life events. *Journal of Personality and Social Psychology*, *51*, 803–814.

13219

Test Name: AFFECTIVE AUTONOMY SCALE

Purpose: To measure affective autonomy.

Number of Items: 6

Format: Items are bipolar. Items are presented.

Reliability: Reliability was .87.

Author: Cameron, J., et al.

Article: Achievement-based rewards and intrinsic motivation: A test of cognitive mediators.

Journal: *Journal of Educational Psychology*, November 2005, *97*, 641–655.

Related Research: Houlfort, N., et al. (2002). The impact of performance-contingent rewards on perceived autonomy and competence. *Motivation and Emotion*, *26*, 279–295.

13220

Test Name: ALTRUISM SCALE FOR ADULTS

Purpose: To measure altruism.

Number of Items: 28

Format: Items are anchored by *true* or *false* responses.

Reliability: Coefficient alpha was .89. Test–retest reliabilities were .90 (1 week) and .80 (5 weeks).

Validity: Correlations with other variables ranged from –.48 to .66.

Author: Lee, D. Y., et al.

Article: Development and validation of an altruism scale for adults.

Journal: *Psychological Reports*, April 2003, *92*, 555–561.

Related Research: Wrightsman, L. (1964). Measurement of philosophies of human nature. *Psychological Reports, 14*, 743–751.

13221

Test Name: AMBIGUITY TOLERANCE SCALE

Purpose: To measure tolerance of ambiguity.

Number of Items: 20

Format: Six-point agreement–disagreement scales are used.

Reliability: Split-half reliability was .86. Six-month test–retest reliability was .63.

Author: Van Hook, C. W., and Steele, C.

Article: Individual personality characteristics related to suggestibility.

Journal: *Psychological Reports*, December 2002, *91*, Part 1, 1007–1010.

Related Research: Rydell, S. T. (1966). Tolerance of ambiguity and semantic differential ratings. *Psychological Reports, 19*, 1303–1312.

13222

Test Name: ANGER AND CONTROL MEASURE

Purpose: To assess child temperament by parent report.

Number of Items: 22

Format: Sample items are presented.

Reliability: Alpha coefficients ranged from .74 (anger) and .80 (control).

Validity: Correlations with other variables ranged from –.64 to .42.

Author: Morris, A. S., et al.

Article: Temperamental vulnerability and negative parenting as interacting predictors of child adjustment.

Journal: *Journal of Marriage and Family*, May 2002, *64*, 461–471.

Related Research: Askan, N., et al. (1999). Derivation and prediction of temperamental types among preschoolers. *Developmental Psychology, 35*, 958–971.

13223

Test Name: ANTILL TRAIT QUESTIONNAIRE

Purpose: To measure girls' gendered personality.

Number of Items: 12

Format: Responses are made on a 5-point scale.

Reliability: Alpha coefficients ranged from .60 to .79.

Author: McHale, S. M., et al.

Article: Developmental and individual differences in girls' sex-typed activities in middle childhood and adolescence.

Journal: *Child Development*, September/October 2004, *75*, 1575–1593.

Related Research: Antill, J. (1993). Measures of children's sex-typing in middle childhood. *Australian Journal of Psychology, 45*, 25–33.

13224

Test Name: ATTENTION AND MONITORING SCALES

Purpose: To measure the extent to which one attends to and values one's feelings.

Number of Items: 18

Format: Scales range from 1 (*strongly disagree*) to 5 (*strongly agree*). Sample items are presented.

Reliability: Alpha coefficients were .84 (attention) and .84 (monitoring).

Validity: Correlations with other variables ranged from –.16 to .54.

Author: Gohm, C. L., et al.

Article: Personality in extreme situations: Thinking (or not) under acute stress.

Journal: *Journal of Research in Personality*, September 2001, *35*, 388–399.

13225

Test Name: AUTONOMY SCALE

Purpose: To measure autonomy.

Number of Items: 3

Format: Responses are made on 5-point scales. An example is given.

Reliability: Coefficient alpha was .73.

Validity: Correlations with other variables ranged from –.25 to .35 ($N = 600$).

Author: Ito, J. K., and Brotheridge, C. M.

Article: Resources, coping strategies, and emotional exhaustion: A conservation of resources perspective.

Journal: *Journal of Vocational Behavior*, December 2003, *63*, 490–509.

13226

Test Name: AUTONOMY SCALE

Purpose: To assess the assertion of autonomy.

Number of Items: 3

Format: Five-point scales are used. All items are presented.

Reliability: Coefficient alpha was .74.

Author: Van Gundy, K.

Article: Gender, the assertion of autonomy, and the stress process in young adulthood.

Journal: *Social Psychology Quarterly*, December 2002, *64*, 346–363.

Related Research: Hirschfeld, R. M. A., et al. (1977). A measure of interpersonal dependency. *Journal of Personality Assessment, 41,* 610–618.

13227

Test Name: BASIC NEED SATISFACTION SCALE— MODIFIED

Purpose: To assess need satisfaction in physical education.

Number of Items: 21

Format: Includes three areas: autonomy, relatedness, and competence. Responses are made on a 7-point scale ranging from 1 (*not at all true*) to 7 (*very true*). Examples are given.

Reliability: Alpha coefficients ranged from .57 to .84.

Validity: Correlations with other variables ranged from −.36 to .69.

Author: Ntoumanis, N.

Article: A prospective study of participation in optional school physical education using a self-determination theory framework.

Journal: *Journal of Educational Psychology*, August 2005, *97,* 444–453.

Related Research: Deci, E. L., et al. (2001). Need satisfaction,

motivation, and well-being in the work organizations of a former Eastern Bloc country. *Personality and Social Psychology Bulletin, 27,* 930–942.

13228

Test Name: BERKELEY EXPRESSIVITY QUESTIONNAIRE

Purpose: To measure dispositional expressivity.

Number of Items: 16

Format: Includes three subscales: Positive Expressivity, Negative Expressivity, and Impulse Strength.

Reliability: Alpha coefficients ranged from .62 to .78.

Author: Okazaki, S.

Article: Self–other agreement on affective distress scales in Asian Americans and White Americans.

Journal: *Journal of Counseling Psychology*, October 2002, *49,* 428–437.

Related Research: Gross, J. J., & John, O. P. (1995). Facets of emotional expressivity: Three self-report factors and their correlates. *Personality and Individual Differences, 19,* 555–568.

13229

Test Name: BIG FIVE INVENTORY

Purpose: To assess the Big Five personality dimensions.

Number of Items: 44

Format: Scales range from 1 (*strongly disagree*) to 5 (*strongly agree*).

Reliability: Alpha coefficients ranged from .78 to .83.

Author: Robins, R. W., et al.

Article: Personality correlates of self-esteem.

Journal: *Journal of Research in Personality*, December 2001, *35,* 463–482.

Related Research: John, O. P., & Srivastava, S. (1999). The Big Five trait taxonomy: History, measurement, and theoretical perspectives. In L. A. Pervin & O. P. John (Eds.), *Handbook of personality: Theory and research.* (2nd ed., pp. 102–138). New York: Guilford Press.

13230

Test Name: BIG FIVE PERSONALITY MEASURE

Purpose: To measure the Big Five personality factors.

Number of Items: 40

Format: Includes the Big Five traits. Responses are made on a 5-point Likert scale ranging from 1 (*strongly disagree*) to 5 (*strongly agree*).

Reliability: Alpha coefficients ranged from .69 to .84.

Validity: Correlations with other variables ranged from −.31 to .41.

Author: Diefendorff, J. M., et al.

Article: The dimensionality and antecedents of emotional labor strategies.

Journal: *Journal of Vocational Behavior*, April 2005, *66,* 339–357.

Related Research: Saucier, G. (1994). Mini-markers: A brief version of Goldberg's unipolar Big-Five markers. *Journal of Personality and Assessment, 63,* 506–516.

13231

Test Name: BORDERLINE PERSONALITY ORGANIZATION SCALE

Purpose: To assess experiences, behaviors, and beliefs common among individuals with borderline personality disorder.

Number of Items: 30

Reliability: Alpha coefficients ranged from .84 to .92 across subscales.

Validity: Correlations with other variables ranged from .35 to .79.

Author: Gratz, K. L.

Article: Measurement of deliberate self-harm: Preliminary data on the Deliberate Self-Harm Inventory.

Journal: *Journal of Psychopathology and Behavioral Assessment*, December 2001, *23*, 253–263.

Related Research: Oldham, J., et al. (1985). A self-report measure for borderline personality organization. In T. H. McGlashan (Ed.), *The borderline: Current Empirical research.* Washington, DC: American Psychiatric Press.

13232

Test Name: CALIFORNIA CHILD Q-SET

Purpose: To obtain material ratings of personality.

Number of Items: 100

Format: Items are sorted into nine categories ranging from 1 (*extremely uncharacteristic*) to 9 (*most characteristic*).

Reliability: Alpha coefficients ranged from .58 to .70.

Author: Abe, J. A. A.

Article: The predictive validity of the five-factor model of personality with preschool age children: A nine-year follow-up study.

Journal: *Journal of Research in Personality*, August 2005, *39*, 423–442.

Related Research: Block, J. H., & Block, J. (1980). The role of ego-control and ego-resiliency in the organization of behavior. In W. A. Collins (Ed.), *Minnesota symposia on child psychology* (Vol. 13, pp. 38–101). Hillsdale, NJ: Erlbaum.

13233

Test Name: CHILDREN'S BEHAVIOR QUESTIONNAIRE

Purpose: To measure temperament characteristics of 3- to 7-year-old children.

Number of Items: 98

Format: Includes 16 scales: Activity Level, Anger/Frustration, Approach/Positive Anticipation, Attention Focusing, Attention Shifting, Discomfort, Soothability, Fear, High-Intensity Pleasure, Impulsivity, Inhibitory Control, Low-Intensity Pleasure, Perceptual Sensitivity, Sadness, Shyness, and Smiling Laughter. Responses are made on a 7-point scale ranging from 1 (*extremely untrue*) to 7 (*extremely true*).

Reliability: Alpha coefficients ranged from .64 to .92.

Author: Chang, F., and Burns, B. M.

Article: Attention in preschoolers: Associations with effortful control and motivation.

Journal: *Child Development*, January/February 2005, *76*, 247–263.

Related Research: Putnam, S. P., & Rothbart, M. K. (2003). *Development of short and very short forms of the Children's Behavior Questionnaire.* Unpublished manuscript.

13234

Test Name: CHILDREN'S BEHAVIOR QUESTIONNAIRE

Purpose: To measure temperament.

Format: Includes eight scales: Activity Level, Anger, Approach, Attentional Focusing, Fear, Inhibility Control, Sadness, and Shyness. Responses are made on a 7-point scale. An example is given.

Reliability: Alpha coefficients ranged from .67 to .89.

Validity: Correlation with other variables ranged from −.58 to .44.

Author: Lamery, K., et al.

Article: Revealing the relation between temperament and behavior problem symptoms by eliminating measurement confounding: Expert ratings and factor analyses.

Journal: *Child Development*, May/June 2002, *73*, 867–882.

Related Research: Rothbart, M. K., et al. (1994). Temperament and social behavior in children. *Merrill-Palmer Quarterly, 40*, 21–39.

13235

Test Name: CHINESE PERSONALITY ASSESSMENT INVENTORY

Purpose: To assess personality.

Number of Items: 510

Format: Includes 22 personality scales, 12 clinical scales, and 3 validity indexes. A true–false format is used.

Reliability: Alpha coefficients ranged from .69 to .78.

Validity: Correlations with other variables ranged from −.60 to .68.

Author: Cheung, F. M., et al.

Article: Convergent validity of the Chinese Personality Assessment Inventory and the Minnesota Multiphasic Personality Inventory—2: Preliminary findings with a normative sample.

Journal: *Journal of Personality Assessment*, February 2004, *82*, 92–103.

Related Research: Cheung, F. M., et al. (1996). Development of the Chinese Personality Assessment

Inventory. *Journal of Cross-Cultural Psychology, 27,* 143–164.

13236

Test Name: CHINESE PERSONALITY ASSESSMENT INVENTORY

Purpose: To assess a wide spectrum of personality traits relevant to the Chinese cultural context.

Number of Items: 352

Format: Includes 22 personality and 3 validity scales. A true–false format is used.

Reliability: Coefficient alpha was .70. Test–retest (1 week and 1 month) reliabilities ranged from .59 to .94.

Author: Kwong, J. Y. Y., and Cheung, F. M.

Article: Prediction of performance facets using specific personality traits in the Chinese context.

Journal: *Journal of Vocational Behavior,* August 2003, *63,* 99–110.

Related Research: Cheung, F. M., & Leung, K. (1998). Indigenous personality measures: Chinese examples. *Journal of Cross-Cultural Psychology, 29,* 233–248.

13237

Test Name: COLLECTIVE PERSONALITY SCALE

Purpose: To measure agreeableness, conscientiousness, emotional stability, extraversion, and openness.

Number of Items: 50

Format: Scales range from 1 (*to a very small extent*) to 5 (*to a great extent*). All items are presented.

Reliability: Alpha coefficients ranged from .67 to .89 across subscales.

Validity: Correlations between subscales ranged from .02 to .90.

Author: Hoffman, D. A., and Jones, L. M.

Article: Leadership, collective personality, and performance.

Journal: *Journal of Applied Psychology,* May 2005, *90,* 509–522.

Related Research: Goldberg, L. R. (1992). The development of markers for the Big-Five factor structure. *Psychological Assessment, 4,* 26–42.

13238

Test Name: CREATIVE PERSONALITY SCALE

Purpose: To measure creative personality.

Number of Items: 19

Format: A check mark is placed by each adjective in the list that the respondents feel describe them.

Reliability: Coefficient alpha was .73.

Author: Zhou, J., and Oldham, G. R.

Article: Enhancing creative performance: Effects of expected developmental assessment strategies and creative personality.

Journal: *The Journal of Creative Behavior,* Third Quarter 2001, *35*(3), 151–167.

Related Research: Geough, H. G. (1979). A Creative Personality Scale for the Adjective Check List. *Journal of Personality and Social Psychology, 37,* 1398–1405.

13239

Test Name: DESIRABILITY OF CONTROL SCALE

Purpose: To measure need for control and control preferences in various domains.

Number of Items: 20

Format: Scales range from 1 (*This sentence does not characterize me*) to 7 (*This sentence greatly characterizes me*). Sample items are presented.

Reliability: Reliability coefficients exceeded .74.

Author: Keinan, G., and Sivan, D.

Article: The effects of stress and desire for control on the formation of causal attributions.

Journal: *Journal of Research in Personality,* June 2001, *35,* 127–137.

Related Research: Burger, J. M., & Cooper, H. M. (1979). The desirability of control. *Motivation and Emotion, 3,* 381–393.

13240

Test Name: DIFFERENTIAL EMOTIONS SCALE—IV

Purpose: To measure differential emotions.

Number of Items: 36

Format: Includes 12 scales. Responses are made on a 5-point scale ranging from *rarely or never* to *very often.*

Reliability: Alpha coefficients ranged from −.23 to .95 ($n = 30$).

Author: Youngstrom, E. A., and Green, K. W.

Article: Reliability generalization of self-report of emotions when using the Differential Emotions Scale.

Journal: *Educational and Psychological Measurement,* April 2003, *63,* 279–295.

Related Research: Izard, C. E., et al. (1993). Stability of emotion experiences and their relations to traits of personality. *Journal of Personality and Social Psychology, 64,* 847–860.

13241

Test Name: DIMENSIONS OF TEMPERAMENT SURVEY

Purpose: To assess child temperament.

Number of Items: 34

Format: Includes five dimensions: Activity Level, Attention Span/Distractivity, Adaptability/Approach–Withdrawal, Rhythmicity, and Reactivity.

Reliability: Alpha coefficients ranged from .43 to .73.

Author: Bingham, C. R., et al.

Article: Parental ratings of son's behavior problems in high risk families: Convergent validity, internal structure, and interparent agreement.

Journal: *Journal of Personality Assessment*, June 2003, *80*, 237–251.

Related Research: Lerner, R. M., et al. (1982). Assessing the dimensions of temperamental individuality across the lifespan: The Dimensions of Temperament Survey (DOTS). *Child Development, 52*, 149–159.

13242

Test Name: EARLY INFANCY TEMPERAMENT QUESTIONNAIRE

Purpose: To measure child temperament.

Number of Items: 14

Format: Scales range from 1 (*almost never*) to 6 (*almost always*). A sample item is presented.

Reliability: Alpha coefficients ranged from .67 to .81 at different time periods.

Author: Mulsow, M., et al.

Article: Multilevel factors influencing maternal stress during the first three years.

Journal: *Journal of Marriage and Family*, November 2002, *64*, 944–956.

Related Research: Medoff-Cooper, B., et al. (1993). Early Infancy Temperament Questionnaire. *Canadian Journal of Behavioural Science, 31*, 92–106.

13243

Test Name: EGO UNDER CONTROL AND EGO-RESILIENCY SCALES

Purpose: To assess impulsivity and the tendency to control impulsivity.

Number of Items: 51

Format: Scales range from 1 (*disagree very strongly*) and 4 (*agree very strongly*). All items are presented.

Reliability: Alpha coefficients ranged from .53 to .76 across samples.

Author: Letzring, T. D., et al.

Article: Ego-control and ego-resiliency: Generalization of self-report scales based on personality descriptions from acquaintances, clinicians, and the self.

Journal: *Journal of Research in Personality*, August 2005, *39*, 395–422.

Related Research: Block, J., & Kremen, A. M. (2006). IQ and ego-resiliency: Conceptual and empirical connections and separateness. *Journal of Personality and Social Psychology, 70*, 349–361.

13244

Test Name: EMOTIONAL EXPRESSIVITY SCALE

Purpose: To measure emotional expressivity.

Number of Items: 17

Format: Responses are made on a 5-point scale ranging from 1 (*never true*) to 5 (*always true*).

Reliability: Coefficient alpha was .92.

Validity: Correlations with other variables ranged from −.14 to .39.

Author: Diefendorff, J. M., et al.

Article: The dimensionality and antecedents of emotional labor strategies.

Journal: *Journal of Vocational Behavior*, April 2005, *66*, 339–357.

Related Research: Kring, A. M., et al. (1994). Individual differences in dispositional expressiveness: Development and validation of the Emotional Expressivity Scale. *Journal of Personality and Social Psychology, 66*, 934–949.

13245

Test Name: EMOTIONAL EXPRESSIVITY SCALE

Purpose: To measure the propensity to display emotions outwardly.

Number of Items: 17

Format: Scales range from 1 (*never*) to 6 (*always*). Sample items are presented.

Reliability: Coefficient alpha was .87.

Validity: Correlations with other variables ranged from −.02 to .03.

Author: Quartana, P. J., et al.

Article: Gender, neuroticism, and emotional expressivity: Effects on spousal constraints among individuals with cancer.

Journal: *Journal of Consulting and Clinical Psychology*, August 2005, *73*, 769–776.

13246

Test Name: EMOTIONALITY, ACTIVITY, AND SOCIABILITY TEMPERAMENT SURVEY

Purpose: To assess temperament.

Number of Items: 20

Format: Includes five dimensions: Sociability, Activity, Fearfulness,

Anger, and Distress. Responses are made on a 5-point scale ranging from 1 (*not characteristic or typical of yourself*) to 5 (*very characteristic or typical of yourself*). All items are presented.

Reliability: Alpha coefficients ranged from .53 to .75. Test–retest reliabilities ranged from .61 to .76.

Author: Naerde, A., et al.

Article: Temperament in adults— Reliability, stability, and factor structure of the EAS Temperament Survey.

Journal: *Journal of Personality Assessment*, February 2004, *82*, 71–79.

Related Research: Buss, A. H., & Plomin, R. (1984). *Temperament: Early developing personality traits.* Hillsdale, NJ: Erlbaum.

13247

Test Name: EMOTIONALITY–ACTIVITY– SOCIABILITY SCALE

Purpose: To enable parents to rate children's temperament.

Number of Items: 20

Format: Includes emotionality, activity level, sociability, and shyness. Responses are made on a 5-point scale ranging from 1 (*not at all like this child*) to 5 (*a lot like this child*).

Reliability: Alpha coefficients ranged from .73 to .84.

Author: O'Connor, T. G., & Croft, C. M.

Article: A twin study of attachment in preschool children.

Journal: *Child Development*, September/October 2001, *72*, 1501–1511.

Related Research: Buss, A. H., & Plomin, R. (1984). *Temperament: Early developing personality traits.* Hillsdale, NJ: Erlbaum.

13248

Test Name: ENTREPRENEURIAL PERSONALITY QUESTIONNAIRE—GERMAN VERSION

Purpose: To assess the Big Five personality traits.

Number of Items: 45

Format: Items consist of bipolar adjective pairs along a 6-point scale.

Validity: Correlations with other variables ranged from −.24 to .48.

Author: Schmitt-Rodermund, E.

Article: Pathways to successful entrepreneurship: Parenting, personality, early entrepreneurial competence, and interests.

Journal: *Journal of Vocational Behavior*, December 2004, *65*, 498–518.

Related Research: Ostendorf, F. (1990). *Sprache und persönlichkeitsstruktur: Zur validität des Fünf-Faktoren Modells der Persönlichkeit* [Language and personality structure: On the validity of the five-factor model of personality]. Regensburg: Roederer Verlag.

13249

Test Name: EXPERIENTIAL SHAME SCALE

Purpose: To assess students' real-time shame reactions in a nonintrusive manner.

Number of Items: 11

Format: Includes three components: physical, emotional, and social. All items are semantic differential items. One additional item employs a 7-point scale ranging from 1 (*strongly disagree*) to 7 (*strongly agree*). Sample items are presented.

Reliability: Coefficient alpha was .86.

Validity: Correlations with other variables ranged from −.26 to .31.

Author: Turner, J. E., and Schallert, D. L.

Article: Expectancy-value relationships of shame reactions and shame resiliency.

Journal: *Journal of Educational Psychology*, June 2001, *93*, 320–329.

Related Research: Turner, J. E. (1998). *An investigation of shame reactions, motivation and achievement in a difficult college course.* Unpublished doctoral dissertation, University of Texas, Austin.

13250

Test Name: EXTENDED OBJECTIVE MEASURE OF EGO IDENTITY STATUS

Purpose: To assess presence of crisis and commitment in personally relevant domains.

Number of Items: 64

Format: A Likert format is used.

Reliability: Alpha coefficients ranged from .58 to .87.

Validity: Correlations with other variables ranged from −.43 to .50.

Author: Milville, M. L., et al.

Article: Integrating identities: The relationships of racial, gender, and ego identities among White college students.

Journal: *Journal of College Student Development*, March/April 2005, *46*, 157–175.

13251

Test Name: HEXACO PERSONALITY INVENTORY

Purpose: To measure six lexically derived personality constructs.

Number of Items: 108

Format: Includes six factors: honesty–humility, emotionality, extroversion, agreeableness, conscientiousness, and openness to experience. Responses are made on a 5-point scale ranging from 1 (*strongly disagree*) to 5 (*strongly agree*).

Reliability: Alpha coefficients ranged from .75 to .88.

Validity: Correlations with other variables ranged from −.61 to .85.

Author: Boies, K., et al.

Article: Psychometric properties of scores on the French and Korean versions of the HEXACO Personality Inventory.

Journal: *Educational and Psychological Measurement,* December 2004, *64,* 992–1006.

13252

Test Name: HIGHER ORDER NEED STRENGTH SCALE

Purpose: To measure higher order need strength.

Number of Items: 5

Format: Responses are made on a 7-point scale ranging from 1 (*not at all important*) to 7 (*extremely important*).

Reliability: Alpha coefficients ranged from .82 to .91.

Validity: Correlations with other variables ranged from −.15 to .43.

Author: Coyle-Shapiro, J. A.-M., and Morrow, P. C.

Article: The role of individual differences in employee adoption of TQM orientation.

Journal: *Journal of Vocational Behavior,* April 2003, *62,* 320–340.

Related Research: Warr, P., et al. (1979). Scales for the measurement of some work attitudes and aspects of psychological well-being. *Journal of Occupational Psychology, 52,* 129–148.

13253

Test Name: HYPOMANIC PERSONALITY SCALE

Purpose: To measure hypomanic personality.

Number of Items: 48

Format: A true–false format is used.

Reliability: Coefficient alpha was ≥ .87. Test–retest reliability was .77 (7 months) and .81 (15 weeks).

Validity: Correlations with other variables ranged from −.09 to .64.

Author: Meyer, T. D., and Hofmann, B. U.

Article: Assessing the dysregulation of the behavioral activation system: The Hypomanic Personality Scale and the BIS-BAS Scales.

Journal: *Journal of Personality Assessment,* December 2005, *85,* 318–324.

Related Research: Eckblad, M., & Chapman, L. J. (1986). Development and validation of a scale for hypomanic personality. *Journal of Abnormal Psychology, 95,* 214–222.

13254

Test Name: IDENTITY STYLE INVENTORY

Purpose: To measure identity styles.

Number of Items: 40

Format: Includes three identity styles: informational, normative, and diffuse/avoidant.

Reliability: Alpha coefficients ranged from .50 to .79.

Author: Cheek, C., and Jones, R. M.

Article: Identity style and employment histories among women receiving public assistance.

Journal: *Journal of Vocational Behavior,* August 2001, *59,* 76–88.

Related Research: Berzonsky, M. D. (1992). Identity style and coping strategies. *Journal of Personality, 60,* 771–788.

13255

Test Name: INFANT CHARACTERISTICS QUESTIONNAIRE

Purpose: To assess perceived infant temperament.

Number of Items: 24

Format: Includes four subscales: Fussy/Difficult, Unadaptable, Dull, and Unpredictable.

Reliability: Alpha coefficients for the Fussy/Difficult scale were .82 and .85.

Author: Bokhorst, C. L., et al.

Article: The importance of shared environment in mother–infant attachment security: A behavioral genetic study.

Journal: *Child Development,* November/December 2003, *74,* 1769–1782.

Related Research: Bates, J. E., et al. (1979). Measurement of infant difficultness. *Child Development, 50,* 794–803.

13256

Test Name: INFANT TEMPERAMENT QUESTIONNAIRE

Purpose: To assess temperament.

Number of Items: 55

Reliability: Coefficient alpha was .81.

Validity: Correlations with other variables ranged from −.10 to .10.

Author: NICHD Early Child Care Research Network.

Article: Child care and children's peer interaction at 24 and 36 months: The NICHD study of early child care.

Journal: *Child Development,* September/October 2001, *72,* 1478–1491.

Related Research: Medoff-Cooper, B., et al. (1993). The Early Infancy Temperament Questionnaire. *Journal of Developmental and Behavioral Pediatrics, 14,* 230–235.

13257

Test Name: INFANT TEMPERAMENT QUESTIONNAIRE—ADAPTED

Purpose: To measure difficult temperament.

Number of Items: 55

Format: Includes approach, activity, intensity, mood, and adaptability.

Reliability: Coefficient alpha was .81.

Author: Fearon, R. M. P., and Belsky, J.

Article: Attachment and attention: Protection in relation to gender and cumulative social–contextual adversity.

Journal: *Child Development,* November/December 2004, *75,* 1677–1693.

Related Research: McDevitt, S. C., & Carey, W. B. (1978). The measurement of temperament in 3–7 year old children. *Journal of Child Psychology and Psychiatry and Allied Disciplines, 19,* 245–253.

13258

Test Name: INTERNATIONAL PERSONALITY ITEM POOL SCALE

Purpose: To assess extraversion, agreeableness, and neuroticism.

Number of Items: 30

Format: Includes three areas: extraversion, agreeableness, and neuroticism. Responses are made on a 7-point agreement scale.

Reliability: Alpha coefficients ranged from .75 to .86.

Validity: Correlations with other variables ranged from −.22 to .34.

Author: Bowling, N. A., et al.

Article: Giving and receiving social support at work: The roles of personality and reciprocity.

Journal: *Journal of Vocational Behavior,* December 2005, *67,* 476–489.

Related Research: Goldberg, L. R. (1999). A broad-bandwidth, public domain, personality inventory measuring the lower-level facets of several five-factor models. In I. Mervielde et al. (Eds.), *Personality psychology in Europe* (Vol. 7, pp. 7–28). Tilburg, the Netherlands: Tilburg University Press.

13259

Test Name: INTERPERSONAL ADJECTIVE SCALES—REVISED

Purpose: To measure interpersonal styles, for example, dominance.

Number of Items: 64

Format: Adjective rating scales range from 1 (*extremely inaccurate*) to 8 (*extremely accurate*).

Reliability: Coefficient alpha was .89.

Validity: Correlations with other variables ranged from .29 to .69.

Author: Brown, R. P., and Ziegler-Hill, V.

Article: Narcissism and the nonequivalence of self-esteem measures: A matter of dominance?

Journal: *Journal of Research in Personality,* December 2004, *38,* 585–592.

Related Research: Wiggins, J. S., et al. (1988). Psychometric and geometric characteristics of the revised Interpersonal Adjective Scales (IAS–R). *Multivariate Behavioral Research, 23,* 517–530.

13260

Test Name: IOWA PERSONALITY INVENTORY

Purpose: To measure several dimensions of personality measured by the longer Multidimensional Personality Questionnaire (MPQ).

Number of Items: 42

Format: Five-point scales are used. All items are presented.

Reliability: Alpha coefficients ranged from .42 to .75.

Validity: Correlations with the MPQ ranged from .49 to .77.

Author: Donnellan, M. B., et al.

Article: Criterion-rated validity, self–other agreement, and longitudinal analyses for the Iowa Personality Inventory: A short alternative for the MPQ.

Journal: *Journal of Research in Personality,* August 2005, *39,* 458–485.

13261

Test Name: KAROLINSKA SCALES OF PERSONALITY

Purpose: To measure personality.

Number of Items: 135

Format: Includes 15 scales: Impulsiveness, Monotony Avoidance, Detachment, Socialization, Social Desirability, Psychic Anxiety, Somatic Anxiety, Muscular Tension, Psychosthenia, Inhibition of Aggression, Verbal Aggression, Indirect Aggression, Irritability, Suspicion, and Guilt. Responses are made on a 4-point scale ranging from 1 (*agree*) to 4 (*disagree*).

Validity: Correlations with the Sense of Coherence Scale ranged from −.49 to .35.

Author: Runeson, R., and Norbäck, D.

Article: Associations among sick building syndrome, psychosocial factors, and personality traits.

Journal: *Perceptual and Motor Skills*, June 2005, *100*, Part 1, 747–759.

Related Research: Klinteberg, B., et al. (1986). *Self-report assessment of personality traits: Data from the KSP Inventory on a representative sample of normal male and female subjects within a developmental project.* (Reports from the project Individual Development and Adjustment 64). Stockholm: Department of Psychology, Stockholm University.

13262

Test Name: LAW ENFORCEMENT PERSONALITY INVENTORY

Purpose: To measure dependability, cooperativeness, emotional stability, initiative, integrity, and prudence.

Number of Items: 63

Format: Scales range from 1 (*strongly agree*) to 5 (*strongly disagree*). Item stems are presented.

Reliability: Alpha coefficients ranged from .62 to .79.

Validity: Correlations with other variables ranged from −.65 to .71.

Author: Vasilopoulos, N. L., et al.

Article: Do warnings of response verification moderate the relationship between personality and cognitive ability?

Journal: *Journal of Applied Psychology*, March 2005, *90*, 306–322.

13263

Test Name: MANIFEST NEED SCALES

Purpose: To measure manifest needs.

Number of Items: 18

Format: Includes three scales: Need for Dominance, Need for Achievement, and Need for Affiliation. Responses are made on a 5-point scale ranging from *almost never* to *always*. Sample items are presented.

Reliability: Internal consistency reliabilities ranged from .66 to .85.

Author: Mael, F. A., et al.

Article: From scientific work to organizational leadership: Predictors of management aspiration among technical personnel.

Journal: *Journal of Vocational Behavior*, August 2001, *59*, 132–148.

Related Research: Steers, R. M., & Braunstein, D. N. (1976). A behaviorally-based measure of manifest needs in work settings. *Journal of Vocational Behavior, 9*, 251–266.

13264

Test Name: MANIFEST NEEDS QUESTIONNAIRE

Purpose: To measure need for power.

Number of Items: 5

Format: A sample item is given.

Reliability: Internal consistency was .71.

Validity: Correlations with other variables ranged from −.38 to .24.

Author: Kacmar, K. M., et al.

Article: Situational and dispositional factors as antecedents of ingratiatory behaviors in organizational settings.

Journal: *Journal of Vocational Behavior*, October 2004, *65*, 309–331.

Related Research: Steers, R. M., & Braunstein, D. N. (1976). A behaviorally-based measure of manifest needs in work settings. *Journal of Vocational Behavior, 9*, 251–266.

13265

Test Name: MANIFEST NEEDS QUESTIONNAIRE

Purpose: To measure need for power.

Number of Items: 5

Format: Responses are made on a 5-point scale ranging from 1 (*never*) to 5 (*always*). Sample items are given.

Reliability: Coefficient alpha was .73 (*N* = 221).

Validity: Correlation with other variables ranged from −.04 to .37 (*N* = 221).

Author: Andrews, M. C., and Kacmar, K. M.

Article: Impression management by association: Construction and validation of a scale.

Journal: *Journal of Vocational Behavior*, February 2001, *58*, 142–161.

Related Research: Steers, R. M., & Braunstein, D. N. (1976). A behaviorally-based measure of manifest needs in work settings. *Journal of Vocational Behavior, 9*, 251–266.

13266

Test Name: MANIFEST NEEDS QUESTIONNAIRE

Purpose: To measure manifest needs.

Number of Items: 20

Format: Includes four needs: Achievement, Affliction, Autonomy, and Dominance. Responses are made on a 7-point scale ranging from *always* to *never*.

Reliability: Alpha and test–retest (2 weeks) coefficients ranged from .56 to .86.

Validity: Correlations with other variables ranged from –.35 to .43.

Author: Miller, M. J., et al.

Article: The meaning and measurement of work ethic: Construction and initial validation of a multidimensional inventory.

Journal: *Journal of Vocational Behavior*, June 2002, *60*, 451–489.

Related Research: Steers, R. M., & Braunstein, D. N. (1976). A behaviorally-based measure of manifest needs in work settings. *Journal of Vocational Behavior, 9*, 251–266.

13267

Test Name: MINI-MARKERS SCALE

Purpose: To measure conscientiousness and openness to experience.

Number of Items: 16

Format: Accuracy scales for descriptive adjectives range from 1 (*very inaccurate*) to 5 (*very accurate*).

Reliability: Coefficient alpha was .83 for conscientiousness and .78 for openness to experience.

Author: Gully, S. M., et al.

Article: The impact of error training and individual differences on training outcomes: An attribute–treatment interaction perspective.

Journal: *Journal of Applied Psychology*, February 2002, *87*, 143–155.

Related Research: Saucier, G. (1994). Mini-markers: A brief version of Goldberg's unipolar Big-

Five markers. *Journal of Personality Assessment, 63,* 506–516.

13268

Test Name: MULTIDIMENSIONAL PERSONALITY QUESTIONNAIRE

Purpose: To provide a multidimensional measure of personality.

Number of Items: 300

Format: A true–false format is used.

Reliability: Reliabilities exceed .80.

Author: Roberts, B. W., et al.

Article: The structure of conscientiousness: An empirical investigation based on seven major personality questionnaires.

Journal: *Personnel Psychology*, Spring 2005, *58*, 103–139

Related Research: Tellegen, A. (1982). *A brief manual for the Multidimensional Personality Questionnaire*. Unpublished manuscript, University of Minnesota.

13269

Test Name: MULTIDIMENSIONAL SEXUALITY QUESTIONNAIRE

Purpose: To measure many dimensions of sexuality.

Number of Items: 60

Format: Includes 12 subscales: Sexual Esteem, Sexual Preoccupation, Internal Sexual Control, Sexual Consciousness, Sexual Motivation, Sexual Anxiety, Sexual Assertiveness, Sexual Depression, External Sexual Control, Self-Monitoring, Fear of Sex, and Sexual Satisfaction. Responses are made on a 5-point scale ranging from 0 (*not at all characteristic of me*) to 4 (*very characteristic of me*).

Reliability: Alpha coefficients ranged from .38 to .89.

Author: Gaither, G. A., and Sellbom, M.

Article: The Sexual Sensation Seeking Scale: Reliability and validity within a heterosexual college student sample.

Journal: *Journal of Personality Assessment*, October 2003, *81*, 157–167.

Related Research: Snell, W. E., et al. (1993). The Multidimensional Sexuality Questionnaire: An objective self-report measure of psychological tendencies associated with human sexuality. *Annals of Sex Research, 6*, 27–55.

13270

Test Name: NARCISSISTIC PERSONALITY INVENTORY

Purpose: To measure the components of narcissism: authority, exhibitionism, superiority, entitlement, exploitiveness, self-sufficiency, and vanity.

Number of Items: 40

Format: Subjects choose 1 of 2 statements in a series of 40 statement pairs.

Reliability: Alpha coefficients ranged from .78 to .80 across subscales.

Author: Witte, T. H., et al.

Article: Narcissism and anger: An exploration of underlying correlates.

Journal: *Psychological Reports*, June 2002, *90*, Part 1, 871–875.

Related Research: Raskin, R., & Hall, C. S. (1979). A Narcissistic Personality Inventory. *Psychological Reports, 45*, 590.

13271

Test Name: NARCISSISTIC PERSONALITY INVENTORY— SHORT VERSION

Purpose: To measure need for praise and attention, sense of superiority and competence, and self-assertion.

Number of Items: 30

Format: Five-point scales are anchored by 1 (*no*) and 5 (*yes*). Sample items are presented.

Reliability: Alpha coefficients ranged from .82 to .87.

Validity: Correlations with other variables ranged from .04 to .48.

Author: Oashi, O.

Article: Relation of Type A behavior and multidimensionally measured narcissistic personalelty of Japanese university students.

Journal: *Psychological Reports*, February 2004, *94*, 51–54.

Related Research: Raskin, R. N., & Terry, H. (1988). A principal–components analysis of the Narcissistic Personality Inventory and further evidence of its construct validity. *Journal of Personality and Social Psychology*, *54*, 890–902.

13272

Test Name: NEED FOR APPROVAL SCALE

Purpose: To assess the degree to which one strives to present oneself in a favorable light.

Number of Items: 33

Format: A true–false format is used.

Validity: Correlations with the Relationship Profile Test ranged from –.31 to .32.

Author: Bornstein, R. F., et al.

Article: Construct validity of the Relationship Profile Test: A self-report measure of dependency–detachment.

Journal: *Journal of Personality Assessment*, February 2003, *80*, 64–74.

Related Research: Crowne, D. P., & Marlowe, D. (1964). *The approval motive*. New York: Wiley.

13273

Test Name: NEED FOR CLOSURE SCALE—ADAPTED CHINESE VERSION

Purpose: To measure one's need for closure.

Number of Items: 42

Format: Responses are made on a 6-point scale ranging from 1 (*strongly disagree*) to 6 (*strongly agree*).

Reliability: Alpha coefficients ranged from .44 to .77 ($n = 239$).

Validity: Correlations with other variables ranged from –.67 to .82 ($n = 239$).

Author: Moneta, G. B., and Yip, P. P. Y.

Article: Construct validity of the scores of the Chinese version of the Need for Closure Scale.

Journal: *Educational and Psychological Measurement*, June 2004, *64*, 531–548.

Related Research: Webster, D. M., & Kruglanski, A. W. (1994). Individual differences in need for cognitive closure. *Journal of Personality and Social Psychology*, *67*, 1049–1062.

13274

Test Name: NEED FOR COGNITION SCALE

Purpose: To measure enjoyment from thinking and problem solving.

Number of Items: 18

Format: Scales range from 1 (*extremely uncharacteristic*) to 5 (*extremely characteristic*). Sample items are presented.

Reliability: Coefficient alpha was .91.

Validity: Correlations with other variables ranged from –.30 to .20.

Author: Hogan, D. E., and Mallott, M.

Article: Changing racial prejudice through diversity education.

Journal: *Journal of College Student Development*, March/April 2005, *46*, 115–125.

Related Research: Cacioppo, J. T., & Perry, R. E. (1982). The need for cognition. *Journal of Personality and Social Psychology*, *42*, 116–131.

13275

Test Name: NEED FOR COGNITION SCALE—PERSIAN VERSION

Purpose: To assess active cognitive processing.

Number of Items: 18

Format: Scales range from 0 (*strongly disagree*) to 4 (*strongly agree*).

Reliability: Coefficient alpha was .83.

Validity: Correlations with other variables ranged from –.35 to .29.

Author: Ghorbani, N., et al.

Article: Private self-consciousness factors: Relationships with need for cognition, locus of control, and obsessive thinking in Iran and the United States.

Journal: *The Journal of Social Psychology*, August 2004, *144*, 359–372.

Related Research: Cacioppo, J. T., et al. (1996). Dispositional differences in cognitive motivation: The life and times of individuals varying in need for cognition. *Psychological Bulletin*, *119*, 197–253.

13276

Test Name: NEED FOR UNIQUENESS SCALE

Purpose: To measure need for uniqueness.

Number of Items: 32

Format: Responses are made on a 5-point scale. A sample item is presented.

Reliability: Internal consistency ranged from .68 to .84. Test–retest (2 months) reliability was .91 and (4 months) was .68.

Author: Dollinger, S. J.

Article: Need for uniqueness, need for cognition, and creativity.

Journal: *The Journal of Creative Behavior*, Second Quarter 2003, *37*(2), 99–116.

Related Research: Snyder, C. R., & Fromkin, H. L. (1980). *Uniqueness: The human pursuit of difference.* New York: Plenum Press.

13277

Test Name: NEEDS FOR ACHIEVEMENT, POWER, AFFILIATION, AND AUTONOMY SCALE

Purpose: To measure manifest needs.

Number of Items: 14

Format: Forced-choice format.

Reliability: Alphas ranged from .04 to .17 across subscales.

Author: Sightler, K. W., and Wilson, M. G.

Article: Correlates of the impostor phenomenon among undergraduate entrepreneurs.

Journal: *Psychological Reports*, June 2001, *88*, Part 1, 679–689.

Related Research: Marcie, D. (1998). Manifest needs. In D. Marcie & J. Seltzer (Eds.), *Organizational behavior: Experiences and cases* (pp. 69–71). Cincinnati, OH: Southwestern College.

13278

Test Name: NEO-FFI INDEX FOR PREADOLESCENTS

Purpose: To assess personality by mother's report and preadolescent self-report.

Number of Items: 60

Format: Five-point Likert scales are used.

Reliability: Alpha coefficients ranged from .51 to .90.

Validity: Correlations between self-ratings and mothers' ratings ranged from .23 to .46.

Author: Markey, P. M., et al.

Article: A preliminary validation of preadolescents' self-reports using the five-factor model of personality.

Journal: *Journal of Research in Personality*, April 2002, *36*, 173–181.

13279

Test Name: PERSONALITY FEELINGS QUESTIONNAIRE

Purpose: To measure guilt and shame.

Number of Items: 16

Format: Adjective checklist format. Items are anchored by 0 (*never experience the feeling*) and 4 (*experience feeling continuously or almost continuously*).

Reliability: Coefficient alpha was .93 on the Shame scale.

Author: Tibbetts, S. G.

Article: Self-conscious emotions and criminal offending.

Journal: *Psychological Reports*, August 2003, *93*, 101–126.

Related Research: Harder, D. W., & Zalma, A. (1990). Two promising Shame and Guilt scales: A construct validity comparison. *Journal of Personality Assessment, 55*, 729–745.

13280

Test Name: PERSONALITY QUESTIONNAIRE

Purpose: To assess personality.

Number of Items: 25

Format: Includes five factors: extraversion, attachment, controlling, emotionality, and playfulness.

Validity: Correlations with other variables ranged from −.16 to .72

Author: Kojima, M., and Ikeda, Y.

Article: Relationships between self-regulation and personality scores of persons with Down syndrome.

Journal: *Perceptual and Motor Skills*, December 2001, *93*, 705–708.

Related Research: Tsuji, H., et al. (1997). [Five factor model of personality: Concept, structure, and measurement of personality traits]. [*Japanese Psychological Review*], *4*, 239–299. [In Japanese]

13281

Test Name: PERSONALITY SCALE

Purpose: To measure extroversion, agreeableness, conscientiousness, neuroticism, and openness to new experience.

Number of Items: 50

Format: Scales range from 1 (*very inaccurate*) to 5 (*very accurate*).

Reliability: Alpha coefficients ranged from .74 to .82 across subscales.

Validity: Correlations with other variables ranged from −.31 to .50.

Author: Lim, B. C., and Ployhart, R. E.

Article: Transformational leadership: Relations to the five-factor model and team performance in typical and maximum contexts.

Journal: *Journal of Applied Psychology*, August 2004, *89*, 610–621.

Related Research: Goldberg, L. R. (1998). *International Personality Item Pool: A scientific collaboratory for the development of advanced measures of personality and other individual differences.* Available at http://ipip.ori.org/ipip/ipip.html.

13282

Test Name: PERSONALITY SCALE

Purpose: To measure openness to experience, conscientiousness, introversion, neuroticism, and agreeableness.

Number of Items: 15

Format: Item anchors range from 1 (*strongly disagree*) to 5 (*strongly agree*). All items are presented.

Reliability: Alpha coefficients ranged from .71 to .87 across subscales.

Validity: Correlations with other variables ranged from −.35 to .26.

Author: vanEmmerik, I. J. H., et al.

Article: The relationship between personality and discretionary helping behaviors.

Journal: *Psychological Reports*, August 2004, *95*, 355–365.

Related Research: Mowen, J. C. (2000). *The 3M model of motivation and personality: Theory and empirical applications to consumer behavior.* Boston: Kluwer Academic.

13283

Test Name: PRESCHOOL PERSONALITY QUESTIONNAIRE—IRANIAN VERSION

Purpose: To measure preschool personality.

Number of Items: 200

Format: Items have a number of different two-category response choices. Sample items are presented in English.

Reliability: Alpha coefficients ranged from .86 to .99 across 14 factors.

Validity: Identifying items and their weights are presented for factors deemed to be the same in the U.S. and Iran.

Author: Etemadi, A., and Dreger, R. M.

Article: Factor structure of the Preschool Personality Questionnaire in Iran.

Journal: *Psychological Reports*, October 2002, *91*, 591–606.

Related Research: Lichtenstein, D., et al. (1986). Factor structure and standardization of the Preschool Personality Inventory. *Journal of Social Behavior and Personality, 1,* 165–182.

13284

Test Name: PROACTIVE PERSONALITY MEASURE

Purpose: To measure proactive personality.

Number of Items: 10

Format: Responses are made on a 7-point scale ranging from 1 (*strongly disagree*) to 7 (*strongly agree*). An example is given.

Reliability: Reliability coefficients were .77 and .90.

Validity: Correlations with other variables ranged from −.21 to .44.

Author: Erdogan, B., and Bauer, T. N.

Article: Enhancing career benefits of employee proactive personality: The role of fit with jobs and organizations.

Journal: *Personnel Psychology*, Winter 2005, *58*, 859–891.

Related Research: Seibert, S. E., et al. (1999). Proactive personality and career success. *Journal of Applied Psychology, 84,* 416–427.

13285

Test Name: PROACTIVE PERSONALITY SCALE

Purpose: To measure proactive personality relevant to organizational behavior.

Number of Items: 8

Format: Scales range from 1 (*strongly disagree*) to 5 (*strongly agree*). Sample items are presented.

Reliability: Coefficient alpha was .82.

Validity: Correlations with other variables ranged from −.31 to .42.

Author: Aryee, S., et al.

Article: Rhythms of life: Antecedents and outcomes of work–family balance in employed parents.

Journal: *Journal of Applied Psychology*, January 2005, *90*, 132–146.

Related Research: Bateman, T. S., & Crant, J. M. (1993). The proactive component of organizational behavior: A measure and correlates. *Journal of Occupational Behavior, 14,* 103–118.

13286

Test Name: PROACTIVE PERSONALITY SCALE

Purpose: To measure proactive personality.

Number of Items: 10

Format: Scales range from 1 (*very strongly disagree*) to 7 (*very strongly agree*). A sample item is presented.

Reliability: Coefficient alpha was .87.

Validity: Correlations with other variables ranged from .19 to .23.

Author: Thompson, J. A.

Article: Proactive personality and job performance: A social capital perspective.

Journal: *Journal of Applied Psychology*, September 2005, *90*, 1011–1017.

13287

Test Name: PROACTIVE PERSONALITY SCALE—SHORT VERSION

Purpose: To assess proactive personality.

Number of Items: 10

Format: Responses are made on a 7-point scale ranging from 1 (*strongly disagree*) to 7 (*strongly agree*). All items are presented.

Reliability: Coefficient alpha was .85.

Validity: Correlations with other variables ranged from .05 to .27 (*N* = 180).

Author: Seibert, S. E., et al.

Article: What do proactive people do? A longitudinal model linking proactive personality and career success.

Journal: *Personnel Psychology*, Winter 2001, *54*, 845–874.

Related Research: Bateman, T. S., & Crant, J. M. (1993). The proactive component of organizational behavior: A measure and correlates. *Journal of Organizational Behavior*, *14*, 103–118.

13288

Test Name: PROACTIVITY INDEX

Purpose: To measure the tendency to be proactive at work.

Number of Items: 5

Format: Scales range from 1 (*strongly disagree*) to 5 (*strongly agree*). All items are presented.

Reliability: Coefficient alpha was .71.

Author: Yoon, J.

Article: The role of structure and motivation for workplace empowerment: The case of Korean employees.

Journal: *Social Psychology Quarterly*, June 2001, *64*, 195–206.

Related Research: Bateman, T. S., & Crant, J. M. (1993). The proactive component of organizational behavior: A measure and correlates. *Journal of Organizational Behavior, 14*, 103–118.

13289

Test Name: PSYCHOPATHIC PERSONALITY INVENTORY

Purpose: To measure psychopathy.

Number of Items: 187

Format: Includes eight subscales: Machiavellian Egocentricity, Social Potency, Cold-Heartedness, Carefree Nonplanfulness, Fearlessness, Blame Externalization, Impulsive Nonconformity, and Stress Immunity. Responses are made on a 4-point scale ranging from 1 (*false*) to 4 (*true*).

Reliability: Alpha coefficients ranged from .71 to .88.

Validity: Correlations with MMPI–2 scales ranged from –.60 to .56.

Author: Sellbom, M., et al.

Article: Assessing psychopathic personality traits with the MMPI–2.

Journal: *Journal of Personality Assessment*, December 2005, *85*, 334–343.

Related Research: Lilienfeld, S. O., & Andrews, B. P. (1996). Development and preliminary validation of a self-report measure of psychopathic personality traits in noncriminal populations. *Journal of Personality Assessment, 66*, 488–524.

13290

Test Name: PSYCHOPATHIC PERSONALITY INVENTORY— SHORT FORM

Purpose: To assess characteristics of psychopathy in nonclinical samples. Characteristics assessed include Machiavellian egocentricity, social potency, cold-heartedness, fearlessness, impulsive nonconformity, blame externalization, carefree nonplayfulness, and stress immunity.

Number of Items: 56

Format: Four-point Likert scales are used. Sample items are presented.

Reliability: Coefficient alpha was .85 for the total scale. Subscale alphas ranged from .64 to .85.

Validity: The correlation with the full form was .90.

Author: Lilienfeld, S. O., and Hess, T. H.

Article: Psychopathic personality traits and somatization: Sex differences and the mediating role of negative emotionality.

Journal: *Journal of Psychopathology and Behavioral Assessment*, March 2001, *23*, 11–24.

Related Research: Lilienfeld, S. O. (1990). *Development and preliminary validation of a self-report measure of psychopathic personality.* Unpublished doctoral dissertation, University of Minnesota, Minneapolis.

13291

Test Name: RESISTANCE TO CHANGE SCALE

Purpose: To measure an individual's dispositional inclination to resist change.

Number of Items: 21

Format: Scales range from 1 (*strongly disagree*) to 6 (*strongly agree*). All items are presented.

Reliability: Alpha coefficients ranged from .68 to .89 across subscales.

Validity: Correlations with other variables ranged from −.58 to .47.

Author: Oreg, S.

Article: Resistance to change: Developing an individual differences measure.

Journal: *Journal of Applied Psychology*, August 2003, *88*, 680–693.

13292

Test Name: RICHNESS SCALES

Purpose: To measure trait richness and strategy richness.

Number of Items: 5

Format: Scales range from 1 (*strongly disagree*) to 7 (*strongly agree*). All items are presented.

Reliability: Alpha coefficients were .78 (trait richness) and .71 (strategy richness).

Validity: Correlations with other variables ranged from .03 to .50.

Author: Bettencourt, L. A., et al.

Article: A comparison of attitude, personality, and knowledge predictors of service-oriented organizational citizenship behaviors.

Journal: *Journal of Applied Psychology*, February 2001, *86*, 29–41.

Related Research: Sujan, H., et al. (1988). Knowledge structure differences between more effective and less effective salespeople. *Journal of Marketing Research*, *25*, 81–86.

13293

Test Name: SENSE OF COHERENCE SCALE

Purpose: To measure personality attributes.

Number of Items: 29

Format: Responses are made on a 7-point scale ranging from 1 (*seldom*) to 7 (*often*).

Validity: Correlations with other variables ranged from −.49 to .35.

Author: Runeson, R., and Norbäck, D.

Article: Associations among sick building syndrome, psychosocial factors, and personality traits.

Journal: *Perceptual and Motor Skills*, June 2005, *100*, Part 1, 747–759.

Related Research: Antonovsky, A. (1993). The structure and properties of the Sense of Coherence Scale. *Social Science and Medicine*, *36*, 725–733.

13294

Test Name: SEXUAL COMPULSIVITY SCALE

Purpose: To measure pathological sexual preoccupation.

Number of Items: 10

Format: Responses are made on a 4-point scale ranging from 1 (*not at all like me*) to 4 (*very much like me*).

Reliability: Coefficient alpha was .84.

Validity: Correlations with the Sexual Sensation Seeking Scale were .52 (women) and .59 (men).

Author: Gaither, G. A., and Sellbom, M.

Article: The Sexual Sensation Seeking Scale: Reliability and validity within a heterosexual college student sample.

Journal: *Journal of Personality Assessment*, October 2003, *81*, 157–167.

Related Research: Kalichman, S. C., & Rompa, D. (1995). Sexual Sensation Seeking and Sexual Compulsivity Scales: Reliability, validity, and predicting HIV-risk behavior. *Journal of Personality Assessment*, *65*, 586–601.

13295

Test Name: SHAME AND GUILT SCALES

Purpose: To measure shame and guilt.

Number of Items: 6

Format: Five-point scales range from *never or hardly ever* to *very often*. Sample items are presented.

Reliability: Alpha coefficients were .81 (guilt) and .87 (shame).

Validity: Correlations with other variables ranged from −.41 to .09.

Author: Abe, J. A.

Article: Shame, guilt, and personality judgment.

Journal: *Journal of Research in Personality*, April 2004, *38*, 85–104.

Related Research: Izard, C. E., et al. (1993). Stability of emotion experiences and their relations to traits of personality. *Journal of Personality and Social Psychology*, *64*, 847–860.

13296

Test Name: SHAME AND GUILT SCALES

Purpose: To measure shame and guilt.

Number of Items: 16

Reliability: Alpha coefficients ranged from .67 to .78.

Validity: Correlations with other variables ranged from .07 to .26.

Author: Klibert, J. J., et al.

Article: Adaptive and maladaptive aspects of self-oriented versus socially prescribed perfectionism.

Journal: *Journal of College Student Development*, March/April 2005, *46*, 141–156.

Related Research: Harder, D. W., & Zalma, A. (1990). Two promising Shame and Guilt scales: A construct validity comparison. *Journal of Personality Assessment, 55,* 729–745.

13297

Test Name: SHAME–GUILT PRONENESS SCALE

Purpose: To assess proneness to shame and guilt.

Number of Items: 46

Format: Item anchors are 0 (*not at all characteristic of me*) and 4 (*extremely characteristic of me*). All items are presented.

Validity: Correlations with a narcissism scale ranged from –.36 to .30.

Author: Montebarocci, O., et al.

Article: Narcissism versus proneness to shame and guilt.

Journal: *Psychological Reports,* June 2004, *94,* Part 1, 883–887.

Related Research: Battacchi, M. W., et al. (2001). [Toward the evaluation of susceptibility to shame and sense of guilt: The Shame–Guilt Propensity Scale]. *Bollettino di Psicologia Applicata, 233,* 19–31.

13298

Test Name: SHAME-PRONENESS SCALE

Purpose: To measure shame proneness.

Number of Items: 35

Format: Five-point scales are used.

Reliability: Coefficient alpha was .76.

Author: Tibbetts, S. G.

Article: Self-conscious emotions and criminal offending.

Journal: *Psychological Reports,* August 2003, *93,* 101–126.

Related Research: Tibbetts, S. G. (1997). Shame and rational choice in offending decisions. *Criminal Justice and Behavior, 24,* 234–255.

13299

Test Name: SHORT-FORM PROSOCIAL PERSONALITY BATTERY

Purpose: To measure other-oriented empathy and helpfulness.

Number of Items: 38

Format: Responses are made on a 5-point scale. Sample items are given.

Reliability: Alpha coefficients were .70 and .83.

Author: Allen, T. D.

Article: Mentoring others: A dispositional and motivational approach.

Journal: *Journal of Vocational Behavior,* February 2003, *62,* 134–154.

Related Research: Penner, L. A., et al. (1995). Measuring the prosocial personality. In J. Butcher & C. D. Spielberger (Eds.), *Advances in personality assessment* (Vol.10, pp. 147–163). Hillsdale, NJ: Erlbaum.

13300

Test Name: SOCIOTROPY–AUTONOMY SCALE

Purpose: To measure sociotropy and autonomy (solitude and independence).

Number of Items: 58

Format: Five-point frequency scales range from 0 (*0%*) to 4 (*100%*). Sample items are presented.

Reliability: Alpha coefficients ranged from .70 to .87.

Author: Sato, T., et al.

Article: Sociotropy–autonomy and situation-specific autonomy.

Journal: *Psychological Reports,* February 2004, *94,* 67–76.

Related Research: Clark, D. A., et al. (1995). Psychometric characteristics of the revised sociotropy and autonomy scales in college students. *Behavior Research and Therapy, 33,* 325–334.

13301

Test Name: TEACHER-RATED EMOTIONALITY SCALE

Purpose: To enable teachers to rate children's temperament.

Number of Items: 24

Format: Includes Negative Affect and Emotional Intensity. Sample items are presented.

Reliability: Alpha coefficients were .78 and .85.

Author: Smith, M., & Walden, T.

Article: An exploration of African American preschool-aged children's behavioral regulations in emotionally arousing situations.

Journal: *Child Study Journal,* 2001, *31,* 13–43.

Related Research: Eisenberg, N., et al. (1994). The relations of emotionality and regulation to children's anger-related reactions. *Child Development, 65,* 109–128. Derryberry, D., & Rothbart, M. (1988). Arousal, affect, and attribution as components of temperament. *Journal of Personality and Social Psychology, 55,* 958–966. Larson, R., & Diener, E. (1987). Affect intensity as an individual difference characteristic: A review. *Journal of Research in Personality, 21,* 1–39.

13302

Test Name: TEMPERAMENT AND CHARACTER INVENTORY

Purpose: To measure temperament and character: novelty-seeking, harm avoidance, reward dependence, persistence, self-directedness, cooperativeness, and self-transcendence.

Number of Items: 240

Format: A yes–no format is used.

Reliability: Alpha coefficients ranged from .64 to .85.

Validity: Correlations with other variables ranged from −.43 to .24.

Author: Tomotake, M., et al.

Article: Temperament, character and eating attitudes in Japanese college women.

Journal: *Psychological Reports*, June 2003, 92, Part 2, 1162–1168.

Related Research: Clonginger, C. R., et al. (1993). A psychological model of temperament and character. *Archives of General Psychiatry, 50*, 975–990.

13303

Test Name: TEN-ITEM PERSONALITY INVENTORY

Purpose: To measure the Big Five personality domains.

Number of Items: 10

Format: Scales range from 1 (*disagree strongly*) to 7 (*agree strongly*). All items are presented.

Reliability: Alpha coefficients ranged from .62 to .77 across the five domains.

Validity: Convergent correlations between the BFI and the 10-item inventory ranged from .65 to .87.

Author: Gosling, S. D., et al.

Article: A very brief measure of the Big Five personality domains.

Journal: *Journal of Research in Personality*, December 2003, 37, 504–528.

13304

Test Name: TEST OF SELF-CONSCIOUS AFFECT

Purpose: To measure shame and guilt.

Number of Items: 10

Format: Ten scenarios are followed by a "shame" response and a "guilt" response. Subjects choose one of them. A sample item is presented.

Reliability: Alpha coefficients were .80 (shame) and .61 (guilt).

Validity: Correlations with other variables ranged from −.34 to .24.

Author: Abe, J. A.

Article: Shame, guilt, and personality judgment.

Journal: *Journal of Research in Personality*, April 2004, 38, 85–104.

Related Research: Tangney, J. P., et al. (1984). *The Test of Self-Conscious Affect.* Fairfax, VA: George Mason University.

13305

Test Name: TEST OF SELF-CONSCIOUS AFFECT

Purpose: To measure several self-conscious emotions.

Number of Items: 15

Format: Five-point scales are used. Items are anchored by 1 (*not likely*) and 5 (*very likely*).

Reliability: Coefficient alpha for the shame-proneness scale was .79.

Author: Tibbetts, S. G.

Article: Self-conscious emotions and criminal offending.

Journal: *Psychological Reports*, August 2003, 93, 101–126.

Related Research: Tangney, J. P., et al. (1989). *The Test of Self-Conscious Affect.* Fairfax, VA: George Mason University.

13306

Test Name: TODDLER BEHAVIOR ASSESSMENT QUESTIONNAIRE

Purpose: To characterize children along five dimensions of temperament.

Number of Items: 108

Format: Includes five dimensions: Activity Level, Pleasure, Social Fearfulness, Anger Proneness, and Interest/Persistence. Responses are made on a 7-point scale. Examples are presented.

Reliability: Alpha coefficients ranged from .77 to .88.

Validity: Correlations ranged from −.26 to .30.

Author: Van Bakel, H. J. A., and Riksen-Walraven, J. M.

Article: Parenting and development of one-year-olds: Links with parental, contextual, and child characteristics.

Journal: *Child Development*, January/February 2002, 73, 256–273.

Related Research: Goldsmith, H. H. (1994). *The Toddler Behavior Assessment Questionnaire: Preliminary manual.* Unpublished manuscript, University of Oregon, Eugene.

13307

Test Name: TOLERANCE FOR AMBIGUITY SCALE

Purpose: To measure tolerance for ambiguity.

Number of Items: 15

Format: Item responses are anchored by 1 (*completely disagree*) and 7 (*completely agree*).

Reliability: Coefficient alpha was .55.

Validity: Correlations with other variables ranged from −.36 to .11.

Author: Sightler, K. W., and Wilson, M. G.

Article: Correlates of the impostor phenomenon among undergraduate entrepreneurs.

Journal: *Psychological Reports,* June 2001, *88,* Part 1, 679–689.

Related Research: Budner, S. (1962). Intolerance of ambiguity as a personality variable. *Journal of Personality, 30,* 34.

13308

Test Name: TOLERANCE FOR AMBIGUITY SCALE

Purpose: To measure tolerance for ambiguity.

Number of Items: 16

Format: Item responses are 7-point rating scales.

Reliability: Cronbach's alpha was .90.

Author: Yurtsever, G.

Article: Tolerance of ambiguity, information, and negotiation.

Journal: *Psychological Reports,* August 2001, *89,* 57–64.

Related Research: Budner, S. (1962). Intolerance of ambiguity as a personality variable. *Journal of Personality, 30,* 29–50.

13309

Test Name: TORONTO ALEXITHYMIA SCALE

Purpose: To assess a person's difficulty in identifying and describing his or her emotions.

Number of Items: 20

Format: Five-point scales range from *strongly disagree* to *strongly agree.* Sample items are presented.

Reliability: Internal consistency reliability exceeded .79.

Validity: Correlations with other variables ranged from –.13 to .43.

Author: Kerr, S., et al.

Article: Predicting adjustment during the transition to college: Alexithymia, perceived stress, and psychological symptoms.

Journal: *Journal of College Student Development,* November/December 2004, *45,* 593–611.

Related Research: Bagby, R. M., et al. (1994). The twenty-item Toronto Alexithymia Scale: I. Item selection and cross-validation of the factor structure. *Journal of Psychosomatic Research, 38,* 23–32.

13310

Test Name: TORONTO ALEXITHYMIA SCALE—20: DIFFICULTY IDENTIFYING FEELINGS SUBSCALE

Purpose: To assess poor introspective awareness.

Number of Items: 7

Format: Responses are made on a 5-point scale ranging from 1 (*strongly disagree*) to 5 (*strongly agree*). An example is given.

Reliability: Alpha coefficients ranged from .78 to .86. Stability over 3 weeks was .77.

Validity: Correlation with other variables ranged from –.38 to .78.

Author: Tylka, T. L., and Subich, L. M.

Article: Examining a multidimensional model of eating disorder symptomatology among college women.

Journal: *Journal of Counseling Psychology,* July 2004, *51,* 314–328.

Related Research: Bagby, R. M., et al. (1994). The twenty-item Toronto Alexithymia Scale: I. Item selection and cross-validation of the factor structure. *Journal of Psychosomatic Research, 38,* 23–32.

13311

Test Name: TRANSGRESSION NARRATIVE TEST OF FORGIVINGNESS

Purpose: To assess the disposition to forgive transgressions across situations and over time.

Number of Items: 5

Format: Responses are made on a 5-point scale ranging from 1 (*definitely not forgive*) to 5 (*definitely forgive*).

Reliability: Alpha coefficients ranged from .78 to .83. Test–retest (8 weeks) stability was estimated at .69.

Validity: Correlations with other variables ranged from –.45 to .73.

Author: Berry, J. W., & Worthington, E. L., Jr.

Article: Forgiveness, relationship quality, stress while imagining relationship events, and physical and mental health.

Journal: *Journal of Counseling Psychology,* October 2001, *48,* 447–455.

13312

Test Name: ZUCKERMAN–KUHLMAN PERSONALITY QUESTIONNAIRE

Purpose: To measure five dimensions of personality.

Number of Items: 99

Format: A true–false format is used.

Reliability: Coefficient alpha was .80 for the Impulsive Sensation Seeking subscale.

Validity: Correlations of the Impulsive Sensation-Seeking subscale with the Sensation Seeking Scale—V ranged from .43 to .61.

Author: Roberti, J. W., et al.

Article: Further psychometric support for the Sensation Seeking Scale—Form V.

Journal: *Journal of Personality Assessment*, December 2003, *81*, 291–292.

Related Research: Zuckerman, M., et al. (1993). A comparison of three structural models for personality: The Big Three, the Big Five, and the Alternative Five. *Journal of Personality and Social Psychology, 65*, 757–768.

13313

Test Name: ZUCKERMAN-KUHLMAN PERSONALITY QUESTIONNAIRE—ITALIAN VERSION

Purpose: To assess the dimensions of personality.

Number of Items: 75

Format: All items are presented.

Reliability: Alpha coefficients ranged from .70 to .86 across subscales.

Validity: Correlations between subscales ranged from −.16 to .39. Correlations with other variables ranged from −.40 to .68.

Author: De Pascalis, V., and Russo, P. M.

Article: Zuckerman–Kuhlman Personality Questionnaire:

Preliminary results of the Italian version.

Journal: *Psychological Reports*, June 2003, *92*, Part 1, 965–974.

Related Research: Zuckerman, M., et al. (1988). What lies beyond E and N? Factor analyses of scales believed to measure basic dimensions of personality. *Journal of Personality and Social Psychology, 54*, 96–107.

CHAPTER 18
Preference

13314

Test Name: ATHLETIC IDENTITY MEASUREMENT SCALE

Purpose: To assess to what extent people identify with an athletic role.

Number of Items: 10

Format: Seven-point scales range from *strongly disagree* to *strongly agree*.

Reliability: Coefficient alpha was .93.

Validity: Correlations with other variables ranged from –.26 to .83.

Author: Kornspan, A. S., and Etzel, E. F.

Article: The relationship of demographic and psychological variables to career maturity of junior college student-athletes.

Journal: *Journal of College Student Development*, March/April 2001, *42*, 122–132.

Related Research: Brewer, B. W., et al. (1993). Athletic identity: Hercules' muscles or Achilles' heel? *International Journal of Sport Psychology*, *24*, 237–254.

13315

Test Name: ATHLETIC IDENTITY MEASUREMENT SCALE

Purpose: To assess the manner in which participants personally identify with their role as a high school athlete.

Number of Items: 9

Format: Includes three dimensions: Social Identity, Exclusivity, and Negative Affectivity. Responses are made on a 7-point scale ranging from 1 (*strongly disagree*) to 7 (*strongly agree*). Examples are presented.

Validity: Correlations with other variables ranged from –.35 to .44.

Author: Ryska, T. A.

Article: The effects of athletic identity and motivation goals on global competence perceptions of student-athletes.

Journal: *Child Study Journal*, 2002, *32*, 109–129.

Related Research: Brewer, B. W., et al. (1993). Athletic identity: Hercules' muscles or Achilles' heel? *International Journal of Sport Psychology*, *24*, 237–254.

13316

Test Name: AUSTRALIAN SEX-ROLE SCALE, FORM A

Purpose: To measure masculinity and femininity.

Number of Items: 50

Format: Scales range from 1 (*never or almost never true*) to 7 (*always or almost always true*).

Reliability: Alpha coefficients ranged from .67 to .68.

Author: McCabe, M. P., and Hardman, L.

Article: Attitudes and perceptions of workers to sexual harassment.

Journal: *The Journal of Social Psychology*, December 2005, *145*, 719–740.

Related Research: Antill, J. K., et al. (1981). An Australian sex role scale. *Australian Journal of Psychology*, *33*, 169–183.

13317

Test Name: CD PURCHASE SCALES—CHINESE VERSION

Purpose: To assess correlates of CD purchases.

Number of Items: 17

Format: Five-point scales are used. All items are presented in English.

Reliability: Alpha coefficients ranged from .81 to .94 across subscales.

Author: Chiou, J.-S., et al.

Article: Antecedents of Taiwanese adolescents' purchase intention toward the merchandise of a celebrity: The moderating effect of celebrity adoration.

Journal: *The Journal of Social Psychology*, June 2005, *145*, 317–332.

Related Research: Taylor, S., & Todd, P. (1995). Decomposition and crossover effects in the theory of planned behavior: A study of consumer adoption decisions. *International Journal of Research in Marketing*, *12*, 137–156.

13318

Test Name: CONFORMITY TO MASCULINE NORMS INVENTORY

Purpose: To measure conformity to masculine norms in the dominant culture of U.S. society.

Number of Items: 94

Format: Scales range from 0 (*strongly disagree*) to 3 (*strongly agree*).

Reliability: Coefficient alpha was .91.

Validity: Correlations with other variables ranged from −.25 to .24.

Author: Kimmel, S. B., and Mahalik, J. R.

Article: Body image concerns of gay men: The roles of minority stress and conformity to masculine norms.

Journal: *Journal of Consulting and Clinical Psychology*, December 2005, *73*, 1185–1190.

Related Research: Mahalik, J. R., et al. (2003). Development of the Conformity to Masculine Norms Inventory. *Psychology of Men and Masculinity, 4*, 3–25.

13319

Test Name: CUSTOMER LOYALTY SCALE

Purpose: To measure likelihood of customers returning.

Number of Items: 3

Format: Scales range from 1 (*strongly disagree*) to 7 (*strongly agree*). All items are presented.

Reliability: Coefficient alpha was .87.

Validity: Correlations with other variables ranged from .10 to .67.

Author: Salanova, M., et al.

Article: Linking organizational resources and work engagement to employee performance and customer loyalty: The mediation of service climate.

Journal: *Journal of Applied Psychology*, November 2005, *90*, 1217–1227.

13320

Test Name: CUSTOMER RETURN INTENTIONS SCALE

Purpose: To measure the customers' degree of willingness to return to a store and recommend it to others.

Number of Items: 6

Format: Five-point Likert scales are used. Sample items are presented.

Reliability: Coefficient alpha was .84.

Validity: Correlations with other variables ranged from .04 to .40.

Author: Tsai, W.-C., and Huang, Y.-M.

Article: Mechanisms linking employee affective delivery and customer behavioral intentions.

Journal: *Journal of Applied Psychology*, October 2002, *87*, 1001–1008.

Related Research: Tsai, W. C. (2001). Determinants and consequences of employee displayed emotions. *Journal of Management, 27*, 497–512.

13321

Test Name: DESIRE FOR CHILDREN SCALE

Purpose: To assess desire for genetically related children.

Number of Items: 22

Format: Response scales range from 1 (*I definitely disagree*) to 5 (*I definitely agree*). All items are presented.

Reliability: Internal consistency was .86.

Validity: Correlations with other variables ranged from −.37 to .40.

Author: Mathes, E. W.

Article: Men's desire for children carrying their genes and sexual jealousy: A test of paternity

uncertainty as an explanation of male sexual jealousy.

Journal: *Psychological Reports*, June 2005, *96*, Part 1, 791–798.

13322

Test Name: DESIRE-FOR-CONTROL SCALE

Purpose: To measure the degree to which individuals want control in a testing situation.

Number of Items: 13

Format: Responses are made on a 5-point scale ranging from *never applies to me* to *always applies to me*. An example is given.

Reliability: Alpha coefficients were .80 and .82.

Author: Flowerday, T., and Schraw, G.

Article: Effect of choice on cognitive and affective engagement.

Journal: *The Journal of Educational Research*, March/April 2003, *96*, 207–215.

Related Research: Wise, S. L., et al. (1996). The development and validation of a scale measuring desire for control on examinations. *Educational and Psychological Measurement, 56*, 710–718.

13323

Test Name: DESIRE TO DRINK SCALE

Purpose: To measure desire to drink.

Number of Items: 3

Format: Scales range from 1 (*definitely false*) to 8 (*definitely true*). All items are presented.

Reliability: Coefficient alpha was .81.

Author: Kranzler, H. R., et al.

Article: Targeted naltrexone treatment moderates the relations between mood and drinking behavior among problem drinkers.

Journal: *Journal of Consulting and Clinical Psychology*, April 2004, *72*, 317–327.

Related Research: Bohn, M. J., et al. (1995). Development and validation of an initial measure of drinking urges in abstinent alcoholics. *Alcoholism: Clinical and Experimental Research*, *19*, 600–606.

13324

Test Name: FAMILY PLANS SCALE

Purpose: To assess one's ideal and expected age of marriage and age of having children.

Number of Items: 4

Format: Responses are made on a 6-point scale ranging from 1 (*younger than 20*), 2 (*21–25*), 3 (*26–30*), 4 (*31–35*), 5 (*36–40*), and 6 (*older than 40*).

Reliability: Coefficient alpha was .83.

Validity: Correlations with other variables ranged from −.23 to .10 ($n = 324$).

Author: Barnett, R. C., et al.

Article: Planning ahead: College seniors' concerns about career–marriage conflict.

Journal: *Journal of Vocational Behavior*, April 2003, *62*, 305–319.

13325

Test Name: FASHION PRICE SENSITIVITY SCALE

Purpose: To assess the degree to which a consumer is willing to pay a high price for new fashion items.

Number of Items: 6

Format: All items are presented in English and Korean.

Reliability: Coefficient alpha was .83.

Validity: Correlations with other variables ranged from −.54 to .17.

Author: Goldsmith, R. E., et al.

Article: Price sensitivity and innovativeness for fashion among Korean consumers.

Journal: *The Journal of Social Psychology*, October 2005, *145*, 501–508.

13326

Test Name: FEEDBACK STYLE QUESTIONNAIRE

Purpose: To identify high school athletes' preferences for feedback styles.

Number of Items: 12

Format: Responses are made on a 9-point Likert scale ranging from 1 (*strongly agree*) to 9 (*strongly disagree*). All items are presented.

Reliability: Test–retest (one week) reliability was .81.

Author: Chen, D. D., and Rikll, R. E.

Article: Survey of preferences for feedback style in high school athletes.

Journal: *Perceptual and Motor Skills*, December 2003, *97*, Part 1, 770–776.

Related Research: Magill, R. A. (2001). Augmented feedback in motor skill acquisition. In R. N. Singer, H. A. Hausenblas, & C. M. Janelle (Eds.), *Handbook of sport psychology* (2nd ed., pp. 86–114). New York: Wiley.

13327

Test Name: FIGURE COMPLEXITY PREFERENCE TASK

Purpose: To measure preference for complex visual figures.

Number of Items: 12

Format: Subjects choose their three most preferred shapes.

Reliability: Test–retest (one month) reliability was .78.

Validity: Correlations with other variables ranged from −.01 to .55.

Author: Dollinger, S. J.

Article: Need for uniqueness, need for cognition, and creativity.

Journal: *The Journal of Creative Behavior*, Second Quarter 2003, *37*(2), 99–116.

Related Research: Eisenman, R. (1992). Creativity, social and political attitudes, and liking or disliking David Duke. *Bulletin of the Psychometric Society*, *30*, 19–22.

13328

Test Name: GENDER IDENTITY MEASURE

Purpose: To assess gender identity.

Number of Items: 10

Format: Responses are made on a 4-point agree/disagree scale. Examples are given.

Reliability: Alpha coefficients ranged from .73 to .80.

Validity: Correlations with other variables ranged from −.13 to .28 ($N = 349$).

Author: Du Bois, D. L., et al.

Article: Race and gender influences on adjustment in early adolescence: Investigation of an integrative model.

Journal: *Child Development*, September/October 2002, *73*, 1573–1592.

Related Research: Michaelieu, Q. (1997). *Female identity: Reports of parenting and adolescent women's self-esteem*. Unpublished doctoral dissertation, University of California at Santa Cruz.

13329

Test Name: GENDER IDEOLOGY SCALE

Purpose: To measure an individual's gender ideology.

Number of Items: 9

Format: All items are presented.

Reliability: Omega reliabilities ranged from .88 to .91.

Author: Cast, A. D., and Bird, S. R.

Article: Participation in household and paid labor: Effects on perceptions of role-taking ability.

Journal: *Social Psychology Quarterly*, June 2005, *68*, 143–159.

Related Research: Spence, J. T., & Helmreich, R. T. (1972). The Attitudes Toward Women Scale: An objective instrument to measure attitudes toward rights and roles of women in contemporary society. *Catalog of Selected Documents in Psychology, 2*, 66–67.

13330

Test Name: GENDER IDEOLOGY SCALE

Purpose: To measure masculine and feminine expectations.

Number of Items: 10

Format: Scales range from *strongly disagree* to *strongly agree*. All items are presented.

Reliability: Alpha coefficients were .82 (men) and .73 (women).

Author: Stevens, D., et al.

Article: Working hard and hardly working: Domestic labor and marital satisfaction among dual-earner couples.

Journal: *Journal of Marriage and Family*, May 2001, *63*, 514–526.

Related Research: Spence, J. T., & Helmreich, R. L. (1978). *Masculinity and Femininity*. Austin: University Texas Press.

13331

Test Name: GENDER ROLE CONFLICT SCALE

Purpose: To measure gender role conflicts.

Number of Items: 37

Format: Includes four subscales: Success, power, and competition; restrictive emotionality; restrictive affectionate behavior between men; and conflict between work and family relations. Responses are made on a 6-point scale ranging from 1 (*strongly disagree*) to 6 (*strongly agree*).

Reliability: Internal consistency correlations ranged from .76 to .87. Test–retest (4 weeks) reliabilities ranged from .72 to .86.

Validity: Correlations with other variables ranged from –.50 to .50.

Author: Breiding, M. J.

Article: Observed hostility and dominance as mediators of the relationship between husbands' gender role conflict and wives' outcomes.

Journal: *Journal of Counseling Psychology*, October 2004, *51*, 429–436.

Related Research: O'Neil, J. M., et al. (1986). Gender Role Conflict Scale: College men's fear of femininity. *Sex Roles, 14*, 335–350.

13332

Test Name: GENDER ROLE CONFLICT SCALE—MODIFIED (SEX-SPECIFIC)

Purpose: To assess conflict with one's gender roles.

Number of Items: 20

Format: Scales range from 1 (*strongly disagree*) to 6 (*strongly agree*).

Reliability: Alpha coefficients ranged from .71 to .90.

Author: Korcuska, J. S., and Thombs, D. L.

Article: Gender role conflict and sex-specific drinking norms: Relationships to alcohol use in undergraduate men and women.

Journal: *Journal of College Student Development*, March/April 2003, *44*, 204–216.

Related Research: O'Neil, J. M., et al. (1986). Gender Role Conflict Scale: College men's fear of femininity. *Sex Roles, 14*, 335–350.

13333

Test Name: GENDER ROLE IDEOLOGY SCALE

Purpose: To measure the degree of appropriateness of specific behaviors for men and women.

Number of Items: 12

Format: Four-point appropriateness scales are used.

Reliability: Coefficient alpha was .75 (.65 for women and .66 for men).

Author: Brennan, R. T., et al.

Article: When she earns more than he does: A longitudinal study of dual-earner couples.

Journal: *Journal of Marriage and Family*, February 2001, *63*, 168–182.

Related Research: Mason, K. O., & Bumpass, L. I. (1975). Change in U.S. women's sex role attitudes. *Journal of Sociology, 80*, n1212–1219.

13334

Test Name: HOFFMAN GENDER SCALE

Purpose: To measure gender self-confidence in terms of gender self-definition and gender self-acceptance.

Number of Items: 28

Format: Scales range from 1 (*strongly disagree*) to 6 (*strongly agree*).

Reliability: Alpha coefficients ranged from .88 to .95.

Validity: Correlations with other variables ranged from −.30 to .43.

Author: Worthington, R. L., and Dillon, F. R.

Article: The Theoretical Orientation Profile Scale—Revised: A validation study.

Journal: *Measurement and Evaluation in Counseling and Development*, July 2003, *36*, 95–105.

Related Research: Hoffman, R. M., et al. (2000). Reconceptualizing femininity and masculinity: From gender roles to gender self-confidence. *Journal of Social Behavior and Personality, 15,* 475–503.

13335

Test Name: IDEAL GENDER IMAGE SCALE

Purpose: To measure mother image, female image, father image, and male image.

Number of Items: 9

Format: Item anchors are 0 (*strongly disagree*) and 6 (*strongly agree*).

Reliability: Alpha coefficients ranged from .39 to .79 across national samples.

Author: Shimoda, H., and Keskinen, S.

Article: Ideal gender identity related to parent images and locus of control: Jungian and social learning perspectives.

Journal: *Psychological Reports,* June 2004, *94,* Part 2, 1187–1201.

Related Research: Yamaguchi, R. (1989). [Two aspects of

masculinity–femininity]. *Shinrigaku Kenkyu, 59,* 350–356.

13336

Test Name: INNER-OTHER SOCIAL PREFERENCE SCALE

Purpose: To measure inner- and other-directedness.

Number of Items: 36

Format: A forced-choice format is used.

Reliability: Test–retest reliability was .85.

Author: Chattergee, A., and Hunt, J. M.

Article: The relationship of character structure to persuasive communication in advertising.

Journal: *Psychological Reports,* February 2005, *96,* 215–221.

Related Research: Kassarjian, W. M. (1962). A study of Riesman's theory of social character. *Sociometry, 25,* 213–230.

13337

Test Name: INTEREST IN RESEARCH QUESTIONNAIRE

Purpose: To measure students' interest in research activities.

Number of Items: 16

Format: Responses are made on a 5-point scale ranging from 1 (*very disinterested*) to 5 (*very interested*).

Reliability: Alpha coefficients ranged from .89 to .91.

Validity: Correlations with other variables ranged from −.26 to .74 ($N = 149$).

Author: Kahn, J. H.

Article: Predicting the scholarly activity of counseling psychology students: A refinement and extension.

Journal: *Journal of Counseling Psychology,* July 2001, *48,* 344–354.

Related Research: Bishop, R. M., & Bieschke, K. J. (1998). Applying social cognitive theory to interest in research among counseling psychology doctoral students: A path analysis. *Journal of Counseling Psychology, 45,* 182–188.

13338

Test Name: INTEREST IN RESEARCH QUESTIONNAIRE

Purpose: To assess research interest.

Number of Items: 14

Format: Responses are made on a 5-point scale ranging from 1 (*very disinterested*) to 5 (*very interested*). Examples are given.

Reliability: Alpha coefficients were .89 and .93.

Author: Phillips, J. C., et al.

Article: Preliminary examination and measurement of the internship research training environment.

Journal: *Journal of Counseling Psychology,* April 2004, *51,* 240–248.

Related Research: Bishop, R. M., & Bieschke, K. J. (1998). Applying social cognitive theory to interest in research among counseling psychology doctoral students: A path analysis. *Journal of Counseling Psychology, 45,* 182–188.

13339

Test Name: LESBIAN AND GAY IDENTITY SCALE

Purpose: To measure the latent construct of negative lesbian, gay, and bisexual identity.

Number of Items: 15

Format: Includes three subscales: Need for acceptance, internalized homonegativity, and difficult process. Responses are made on a 7-point Likert scale ranging from 1 (*disagree strongly*) to 7 (*agree strongly*). Examples are given.

Reliability: Alpha coefficients ranged from .75 to .79.

Author: Mohr, J. J., and Fassinger, R. E.

Article: Self-acceptance and self-disclosure of sexual orientation in lesbians, gay and bisexual adults: An attachment perspective.

Journal: *Journal of Counseling Psychology*, October 2003, *50*, 482–495

Related Research: Mohr, J. J., & Fassinger, R. E. (2000). Measuring dimensions of lesbian and gay male experience. *Measurement and Evaluation in Counseling and Development*, 33, 66–90.

13340

Test Name: LESBIAN IDENTITY QUESTIONNAIRE

Purpose: To measure individual sexual identity and group membership identity.

Number of Items: 40

Format: Scales range from 1 (*disagree strongly*) to 7 (*agree strongly*).

Reliability: Alpha coefficients ranged from .53 to .88 across subscales and across versions of the scale (original and revised).

Author: Tomlinson, M. J., and Fassinger, R. E.

Article: Career development, lesbian identity development, and campus climate among lesbian college students.

Journal: *Journal of College Student Development*, November/December 2003, *44*, 845–860.

Related Research: Fassinger, R. E. (1988). *Lesbian Identity Questionnaire* (Rev. ed.).

Unpublished instrument. University of Maryland, College Park.

13341

Test Name: LIFE ROLE SALIENCE SCALES

Purpose: To measure life role salience.

Number of Items: 11

Format: Includes three subscales: career role, partner role, and parental role.

Reliability: Alpha coefficients ranged from .69 to .91.

Validity: Correlations with other variables ranged from −.26 to .40.

Author: van der Velde, M. E. G., et al.

Article: Gender differences in the determinants of the willingness to accept an international assignment.

Journal: *Journal of Vocational Behavior*, February 2005, *66*, 81–103.

Related Research: Amatea, E., et al. (1986). Assessing the work and family role expectations of career-oriented men and women: The Life Role Salience Scales. *Journal of Marriage and the Family*, 48, 831–838.

13342

Test Name: MALE–FEMALE RELATIONS QUESTIONNAIRE

Purpose: To measure gender role orientations.

Number of Items: 40

Format: Scales range from 1 (*strongly agree*) to 5 (*strongly disagree*).

Reliability: Alpha coefficients were .87 for men and .80 for women.

Author: Scherer, R. F., and Patrick, J. A.

Article: The effects of gender role orientation on team schema: A

multivariate analysis of indicators in a U.S. federal health care organization.

Journal: *The Journal of Social Psychology*, February 2001, *141*, 7–22.

Related Research: Spence, J. T., et al. (1980). The Male–Female Relations Questionnaire: A self-report inventory of sex role behaviors and preferences and its relationships to masculine and feminine personality traits, sex role attitudes, and other measures [Ms. No. 2123]. *JSAS Selected Documents in Psychology*, 10 (No. 87).

13343

Test Name: MALE ROLE NORMS SCALE

Purpose: To measure men's endorsement of traditional male gender role norms.

Number of Items: 26

Format: Includes four subscales: Status/rationality, violent toughness, antifemininity, and tough image.

Reliability: Alpha coefficients ranged from .51 to .91.

Author: Hill, M. S., & Fischer, A. R.

Article: Does entitlement mediate the link between masculinity and rape-related variables?

Journal: *Journal of Counseling Psychology*, January 2001, *48*, 39–50.

Related Research: Brannon, R., & Juni, S. (1984). A scale for measuring attitudes about masculinity. *Psychological Documents*, 14, 6–7.

13344

Test Name: MATH/SCIENCE INTERESTS SCALE

Purpose: To measure degree of interest in studying eight topics or in doing seven activities related to math and science.

Number of Items: 15

Format: Responses are made on a 5-point scale ranging from 1 (*strongly dislike*) to 5 (*strongly like*).

Reliability: Coefficient alpha was .84.

Author: Lent, R. W., et al.

Article: The role of contextual supports and barriers in the choice of math/science educational options: A test of social cognitive hypotheses.

Journal: *Journal of Counseling Psychology*, October 2001, *48*, 474–483.

Related Research: Lopez, F. G., & Lent, R. W. (1992). Sources of mathematics self-efficacy in high school students. *The Career Development Quarterly, 41,* 3–12.

13345

Test Name: MATHEMATICS INTEREST INVENTORY

Purpose: To measure interest in mathematics.

Number of Items: 27

Format: Scales range from 1 (*describes me not at all*) to 7 (*describes me extremely well*). All items are presented.

Reliability: Coefficient alpha was .87.

Validity: Correlations with mathematics grades ranged from .32 to .60.

Author: Stevens, T., and Olivárez, A., Jr.

Article: Development and evaluation of the Mathematics Interest Inventory.

Journal: *Measurement and Evaluation in Counseling and Development*, October 2005, *38*, 141–152.

13346

Test Name: MEN IDENTITY ATTITUDE SCALE

Purpose: To measure gender identity.

Number of Items: 55

Format: A Likert format is used.

Reliability: Alpha coefficients ranged from .62 to .71.

Validity: Correlations with other variables ranged from –.20 to .50.

Author: Milville, M. L., et al.

Article: Integrating identities: The relationships of racial, gender, and ego identities among White college students.

Journal: *Journal of College Student Development*, March/April 2005, *46*, 157–175.

Related Research: Milville, M. L., & Helms, J. E. (1996, August). *Exploring relationships of cultural, gender, and personal identity among Latinos/as.* Poster presentation at the annual meeting of the American Psychological Association, Toronto, Ontario, Canada.

13347

Test Name: MULTIDIMENSIONAL AVERSION TO WOMEN WHO WORK SCALE

Purpose: To measure traditional gender roles and negative views about women's occupational abilities.

Number of Items: 10

Format: Response categories are anchored by 1 (*strongly disagree*) and 4 (*strongly agree*). All items are presented.

Reliability: Coefficient alpha was .88. Subscale alpha coefficients ranged from .82 to .85.

Author: Valentine, S.

Article: Confirmatory examination of the Multidimensional Aversion to Women Who Work Scale.

Journal: *Psychological Reports*, June 2003, *92*, Part 1, 757–762.

Related Research: Valentine, S. (2001). Development of a brief Multidimensional Aversion to Women Who Work Scale. *Sex Roles: A Journal of Research, 44,* 773–787.

13348

Test Name: NEED FOR COGNITIVE CLOSURE SCALE— CROATIAN AND POLISH VERSIONS

Purpose: To measure preference for order and predictability, discomfort with ambiguity, and closed-mindedness.

Number of Items: 35

Format: Scales range from 1 (*completely disagree*) to 5 (*completely agree*). Sample items are presented in English.

Reliability: Coefficient alpha was .83.

Author: Kosic, A.

Article: Acculturation attitudes, need for cognitive closure, and adaptation of immigrants.

Journal: *The Journal of Social Psychology*, April 2002, *142*, 179–201.

Related Research: Webster, M. D., & Kruglanski, W. A. (1994). Individual differences in need for cognitive closure. *Journal of Personality and Social Psychology, 67,* 1049–1062.

13349

Test Name: PERSONAL ATTRIBUTES QUESTIONNAIRE

Purpose: To assess gender role identity.

Number of Items: 24

Format: Includes three scales: Expressive, Instrumentality, and M–F. Responses are made on a 5-point scale ranging from 1 (*never cries*) to 5 (*cries easily*).

Reliability: Alpha coefficients ranged from .67 to .80.

Author: Caldera, Y. M., et al.

Article: Intrapersonal, familial, and cultural factors in the commitment to a career choice of Mexican American and non-Hispanic White college women.

Journal: *Journal of Counseling Psychology*, July 2003, *50*, 309–323.

Related Research: Spence, J. T., et al. (1974). The Personal Attributes Questionnaire: A measure of sex role stereotypes and masculinity–femininity. *Catalog of Selected Documents in Psychology*, *4*, 43–44.

13350

Test Name: PERSONAL ATTRIBUTES QUESTIONNAIRE

Purpose: To measure gender-typing as feminine/expressive and masculine/instrumental.

Number of Items: 16

Format: Seven-point scales are used.

Reliability: Alpha coefficients ranged from .70 to .81.

Author: Forbes, G. B., et al.

Article: Perceptions of the social and personal characteristics of hypermuscular women and the men who love them.

Journal: *The Journal of Social Psychology*, October 2004, *144*, 487–506.

Related Research: Spence, J. T., & Helmreich, R. L. (1978). *Masculinity and femininity: Their dimensions, correlates, and antecedents*. Austin: University of Texas Press.

13351

Test Name: PERSONAL PREFERENCES SELF-DESCRIPTION QUESTIONNAIRE

Purpose: To measure Jungian personality preferences.

Format: Includes four scales: Extraversion–Interversion, Sensing–Intuition, Thinking–Feeling, and Judging–Perceiver.

Reliability: Alpha coefficients ranged from .87 to .92.

Validity: Correlations with the Learning and Studies Strategies Inventory ranged from –.44 to .24.

Author: Melancon, J. G.

Article: Reliability, structure, and correlates of Learning and Study Strategies Inventory scores.

Journal: *Educational and Psychological Measurement*, December 2002, *62*, 1020–1070.

Related Research: Arnau, R. C., et al. (1999). Alternative measures of Jungian personality constructs. *Measurement and Evaluation in Counseling and Development*, *32*, 90–104.

13352

Test Name: POSTREADING SITUATIONAL INTEREST INVENTORY

Purpose: To measure postreading situational interest.

Number of Items: 10

Format: Responses are made on a 5-point rating scale ranging from 1 (*strongly disagree*) to 5 (*strongly agree*). Examples are presented.

Reliability: Coefficient alpha was .83.

Validity: Correlations with other variables ranged from .04 to .76.

Author: Flowerday, T., et al.

Article: The role of choice and interest in reader engagement.

Journal: *The Journal of Experimental Education*, Winter 2004, *72*, 93–114.

Related Research: Schraw, G., et al (1995). Sources of situational interest. *Journal of Reading Behavior*, *27*, 1–17.

13353

Test Name: PREFERENCE FOR CONSISTENCY SCALE

Purpose: To measure the desire for consistency.

Number of Items: 9

Format: Scales range from 1 (*strongly disagree*) to 9 (*strongly agree*). Sample items are presented.

Reliability: Coefficient alpha was .89.

Validity: Correlations with other variables ranged from –.03 to .24.

Author: Brown, S. L., et al.

Article: Evidence of a positive relationship between age and preference for consistency.

Journal: *Journal of Research in Personality*, October 2005, *39*, 517–533.

Related Research: Cialdini, R. B., et al. (1995). Preference for consistency: The development of a valid measure and the discovery of surprising behavioral implications. *Journal of Personality and Social Psychology*, *69*, 318–329.

13354

Test Name: REVISED PRODUCT INVOLVEMENT INVENTORY

Purpose: To measure the importance and interest in products.

Number of Items: 9

Format: Seven-point Likert scales are used.

Reliability: Coefficient alpha was .92.

Author: Chebat, J.-C., et al.

Article: Drama advertisements: Moderating effects of self-relevance on the relations among empathy, information processing, and attitudes.

Journal: *Psychological Reports,* June 2003, *92,* Part 1, 997–1014.

Related Research: McQuarrie, E. F., & Munson, J. M. (1992). A revised product involvement inventory: Improved usability and validity. *Advances in Consumer Research, 19,* 108–115.

13355

Test Name: ROLE-TAKING SCALE

Purpose: To measure role-taking.

Number of Items: 5

Format: Scales range from 1 (*never*) to 5 (*often*). All items are presented.

Reliability: Omega reliabilities ranged from .76 to .81.

Author: Cast, A. D.

Article: Role-taking and interaction.

Journal: *Social Psychology Quarterly,* September 2004, *67,* 296–309.

Related Research: Stets, J. (1993). Control in dating relationships. *Journal of Marriage and the Family, 55,* 673–685.

13356

Test Name: SEXUAL ORIENTATION IDENTITY MEASURE

Purpose: To assess the centrality of one's sexual orientation, self-acceptance of sexual orientation, and the degree one is "out" to others.

Number of Items: 11

Format: Various formats are used. All are presented with sample items.

Reliability: Alpha coefficients ranged from .67 to .68.

Author: Griffith, K. H., and Hebl, M. R.

Article: The disclosure dilemma for gay men and lesbians: "Coming out" at work.

Journal: *Journal of Applied Psychology,* December 2002, *87,* 1191–1199.

Related Research: Waldo, C. R. (1999). Working in a majority context: A structural model of heterosexism as minority stress in the workplace. *Journal of Counseling Psychology, 46,* 218–232.

13357

Test Name: SOCIAL STUDIES INTEREST INVENTORY— INTEREST IN READING MATERIALS

Purpose: To assess student interest in reading materials related to social studies.

Number of Items: 15

Format: Includes three factors: Textbook materials, creative materials, and news materials. Responses are made on a 5-point scale ranging from 1 (*strongly disagree*) to 5 (*strongly agree*). All items are presented.

Reliability: Reliability coefficients ranged from .60 to .86.

Author: Ataya, R. L., and Kulikowich, J. M.

Article: Measuring interest in reading social studies materials.

Journal: *Educational and Psychological Measurement,* December 2002, *62,* 1028–1041.

Related Research: Alexander, P. A. (1997). Mapping the multidimensional nature of domain learning: The interplay of cognitive, motivational, and strategic forces. In M. L. Maehr & P. R. Pintrich (Eds.), *Advances in motivation and achievement* (Vol. 10, pp. 213–250). Greenwich, CT: JAI.

13358

Test Name: SPORT SPECTATOR IDENTIFICATION SCALE

Purpose: To assess attachment to a sports team.

Number of Items: 7

Format: Scales range from 1 (*low identification*) to 8 (*high identification*).

Reliability: Coefficient alpha was .92.

Author: Wann, D. L., and Grieve, F. G.

Article: Biased evaluations of in-group and out-group spectator behavior at sporting events: The importance of team identification and threats to social identity.

Journal: *The Journal of Social Psychology,* October 2005, *145,* 531–545.

Related Research: Wann, D. L., & Branscombe, N. R. (1993). Sports fans: Measuring degree of identification with the team. *International Journal of Sport Psychology, 24,* 1–17.

13359

Test Name: TEACHING AND LEARNING PREFERENCES INVENTORY

Purpose: To measure teaching and learning activities in higher education: concrete activities, reflective activities, conceptual activities and application activities.

Number of Items: 19

Format: Seven-point rating scales are anchored by 1 (This is vital for my learning) and 7 (I do not find this at all useful for my learning).

Reliability: Alpha coefficients ranged from .72 to .88.

Validity: Correlations with other variables ranged from −.24 to .12.

Author: Cockerton, T., et al.

Article: Factorial validity and internal reliability of Honey and Mumford's Learning Styles Questionnaire.

Journal: *Psychological Reports*, October 2002, *91*, 503–519.

Related Research: Fung, Y. H., et al. (1993). Reliability and validity of the Learning Styles Questionnaire. *British Journal of Educational Technology, 24*, 12–21.

13360

Test Name: TEAMWORK ORIENTATION SCALE

Purpose: To measure an individual's preference for working independently or collectively.

Number of Items: 3

Format: A sample item is presented.

Reliability: Mean coefficient alpha was .75.

Validity: Correlations with other variables ranged from –.04 to .58.

Author: Neubert, M. J., and Cady, S. H.

Article: Program commitment: A multistudy longitudinal field investigation of its impact and antecedents.

Journal: *Personnel Psychology*, Summer 2001, *54*, 421–448.

Related Research: Moorman, R. H., & Blakely, G. L. (1995). Individualism–collectivism as an individual difference predictor of organizational citizenship behavior. *Journal of Organizational Behavior, 16*, 127–142.

CHAPTER 19
Problem Solving and Reasoning

13361

Test Name: APPROACHES TO LEARNING MATHEMATICS SCALE

Purpose: To measure surface and deep approaches to learning mathematics.

Number of Items: 28

Format: Five-point scales range from 1 (*only rarely*) to 5 (*almost always true*).

Reliability: Alpha coefficients ranged from .77 to .88.

Author: Alkhateeb, H. M.

Article: University students approach to learning first-year mathematics.

Journal: *Psychological Reports*, December 2003, *93*, Part 1, 851–854.

Related Research: Crawford, K., et al. (1998). Qualitatively different experiences of learning mathematics at university. *Learning and Instruction, 8*, 445–468.

13362

Test Name: COGNITIVE EFFICACY SCALE

Purpose: To measure cognitive efficacy.

Number of Items: 3

Format: Responses are made on a 10-point scale. All items are presented.

Reliability: Alpha coefficients were .46 and .55.

Author: Peterson, S. E., and Miller, J. A.

Article: Comparing the quality of students' experiences during cooperative learning and large group instruction.

Journal: *Journal of Educational Research*, January/February 2004, *97*, 123–133.

Related Research: Csikszentmihalyi, M., et al. (1993). *Talented teenagers: The roots of success and failure.* New York: Cambridge University Press.

13363

Test Name: COGNITIVE FLEXIBILITY SCALE

Purpose: To measure cognitive flexibility.

Number of Items: 12

Format: Responses are made on a 6-point scale ranging from 1 (*strongly disagree*) to 6 (*strongly agree*). An example is given.

Reliability: Alpha coefficients ranged from .76 to .84. Test–retest (1 week) reliability coefficient was .83.

Validity: Correlations with other variables ranged from –.15 to .55.

Author: Kim, B. S. K., and Omizo, M. M.

Article: Asian and European American cultural values, collective self-esteem, acculturative stress, cognitive flexibility, and general self-efficacy among Asian American college students.

Journal: *Journal of Counseling Psychology*, July 2005, *52*, 412–419.

Related Research: Martin, M. M., & Rubin, R. B. (1995). A new measure of cognitive flexibility. *Psychological Reports, 76*, 623–626.

13364

Test Name: COGNITIVE/METACOGNITIVE STRATEGIES, INTRINSIC VALUE, AND TEST ANXIETY SCALES

Purpose: To measure cognitive/metacognitive strategies, intrinsic value, and test anxiety.

Number of Items: 35

Format: Includes cognitive strategy, metacognitive strategy, intrinsic value, and test anxiety. Responses are made on a 5-point scale ranging from 1 (*not at all true of me*) to 5 (*very true of me*). Examples are given.

Reliability: Alpha coefficients ranged from .68 to .90.

Validity: Correlations with other variables ranged from –.25 to .70.

Author: Shih, S.-S.

Article: Role of achievement goals in children's learning in Taiwan.

Journal: *The Journal of Educational Research*, May/June 2005, *98*, 310–319.

Related Research: Pintrich, P. R., & De Groot, E. V. (1990). Motivational and self-regulated learning components of classroom academic performance. *Journal of Educational Psychology, 82*, 33–40.

13365

Test Name: COGNITIVE STYLE ANALYSIS

Purpose: To provide an objective measure of cognitive style.

Number of Items: 88

Format: A computer-applied measure of three subtests: One assesses verbal-imagery and two assess the holistic-analytic dimension.

Reliability: Test–retest reliabilities were around .20 and .30. Parallel form reliability was less than .36. Split-half reliabilities less than .32 and less than .63.

Author: Rawal, A., and Wilson, R.

Article: An exploratory study of cognitive style in performance on matched and unmatched tasks.

Journal: *Perceptual and Motor Skills*, April 2005, *100*, 451–462.

Related Research: Riding, R. (1991). *Cognitive Styles Analysis— Research administration*. Birmingham, England: Learning and Training Technology.

13366

Test Name: COGNITIVE TESTING BATTERY

Purpose: To measure remote personal memory, fund of information, orientation, attention, new learning, construction, language, frontal systems, abstraction and problem-solving, and delayed recall.

Time Required: 45 to 60 minutes

Format: Scaling is based on a 1 to 10 metric. Each subscale is described.

Reliability: Alpha coefficients were .80 or higher.

Validity: Correlations between subscales and total scale ranged from .60 to .88.

Author: Hyer, L., et al.

Article: Cognitive Testing Battery: Differences among groups with dementia, Huntington's disease, and controls.

Journal: *Psychological Reports*, October 2003, *93*, 497–504.

13367

Test Name: COMPOSITE GESTALT COMPLETION TEST

Purpose: To identify and label fragmented or incomplete drawings of objects, animals, or figures.

Number of Items: 21

Format: Free-response format.

Reliability: Coefficient alpha was .82.

Author: Rawal, A., and Wilson, R.

Article: An exploratory study of cognitive style in performance on matched and unmatched tasks.

Journal: *Perceptual and Motor Skills*, April 2005, *100*, 451–462.

Related Research: Eliot, J., & Czarnolewski, M. (1999). A composite gestalt completion test. *Perceptual and Motor Skills*, *89*, 294–300.

13368

Test Name: CONSTRUCTIVE THINKING INVENTORY— PERSIAN VERSION

Purpose: To measure functional and destructive thinking.

Number of Items: 108

Format: Scales range from 0 (*definitely false*) to 4 (*definitely true*).

Reliability: Alpha coefficients ranged from .45 to .85 across subscales.

Validity: Correlations with other variables ranged from −.60 to .63.

Author: Ghorbani, N., and Ghramaleki, F.

Article: Constructive Thinking Inventory: Evidence of validity among Iranian managers.

Journal: *Psychological Reports*, February 2005, *96*, 115–121.

Related Research: Epstein, S. (1998). *Constructive thinking*. Westport, CT: Praeger.

13369

Test Name: HOMEWORK MANAGEMENT STRATEGIES SCALES

Purpose: To identify reasons for doing homework.

Number of Items: 8

Format: Responses are made on a 4-point Likert-type scale ranging from 1 (*strongly agree*) to 4 (*strongly disagree*). All items are given.

Reliability: Alpha coefficients were .80 and .84.

Author: Xu, J.

Article: Purposes for doing homework reported by middle and high school students.

Journal: *The Journal of Educational Research*, September/October 2005, *99*, 46–55.

Related Research: Xu, J., & Corno, L. (2003). Family help and homework management reported by middle school students. *Elementary School Journal*, *103*, 503–518.

13370

Test Name: HOMEWORK MANAGEMENT STRATEGIES SCALES

Purpose: To identify homework management strategies that students might use to aid homework completion.

Number of Items: 23

Format: Includes five features: Arranging Environment, Managing Time, Focusing Attention, Monitoring Motivation, and Monitoring and Controlling Emotion. Responses are made on a 5-point scale ranging from 1 (*routinely*) to 5 (*never*).

Reliability: Alpha coefficients ranged from .61 to .84.

Author: Xu, J.

Article: Purposes for doing homework reported by middle and high school students.

Journal: *The Journal of Educational Research*, September/October 2005, *99*, 46–55.

Related Research: Xu, J., & Corno, L. (2003). Family help and homework management reported by middle school students. *Elementary School Journal*, *103*, 503–518.

13371

Test Name: IMMEDIATE TRANSFER PROBLEM-SOLVING MEASURE

Purpose: To measure immediate transfer problem–solving.

Number of Items: 10

Format: Each item is a word problem in the style of problems used for problem–solution method instruction but with novel cover stories. An example is given.

Reliability: Coefficient alpha was .95.

Validity: Correlation with the Terra Nova was .58.

Author: Fuchs, L. S., et al.

Article: Enhancing mathematical problem solving among third-grade students with schema-based instruction.

Journal: *Journal of Educational Psychology*, December 2004, *96*, 635–647.

13372

Test Name: INVENTORY OF LEARNING PROCESSES

Purpose: To measure learning styles.

Number of Items: 62

Format: A true–false format is used.

Reliability: Alpha coefficients ranged from .58 to .91.

Author: Gadzella, B. M.

Article: Reliability of the Inventory of Learning Processes.

Journal: *Psychological Reports*, June 2003, *92*, Part 1, 1029–1030.

Related Research: Schmeck, R. R., et al. (1977). Development of self-report inventory for assessing individual differences in learning processes. *Applied Psychological Measurement*, *1*, 413–431.

13373

Test Name: INVENTORY OF LEARNING STYLES—ARABIC VERSION

Purpose: To assess methodological study, elaborative processing, deep processing, and fact retention.

Number of Items: 48

Reliability: Alpha coefficients ranged from .51 to .75 across subscales.

Validity: Male and female scores are similar on all subscales.

Author: Kadiem, S.

Article: Confirmation of factor structure for an inventory of learning styles among university students in Jordan.

Journal: *Psychological Reports*, June 2005, *96*, Part 1, 733–736.

Related Research: Schmeck, R. R., et al. (1977). Development of a self-report inventory for assessing individual differences in learning processes. *Applied Psychological Measurement*, *1*, 413–431.

13374

Test Name: LEARNING STRATEGIES SCALE

Purpose: To assess deep processing, surface processing, and self-handicapping.

Number of Items: 15

Format: Sample items are presented.

Reliability: Alpha coefficients ranged from .63 to .69 across subscales.

Validity: Correlations with other variables ranged from −.40 to .50.

Author: Yamauchi, H.

Article: An approach to the hierarchical model of motivation in the classroom: A reply to Rousseau and Vallerand.

Journal: *Psychological Reports*, February 2002, *90*, 273–278.

Related Research: Yamauchi, H., & Tanaka, K. (1998). Relations of autonomy, self-referenced beliefs, and self-regulated learning among Japanese children. *Psychological Reports*, *82*, 803–816.

13375

Test Name: LEARNING STRATEGY USE SCALES

Purpose: To assess students' use of different learning strategies.

Number of Items: 17

Format: Includes two scales: Cognitive Strategies and Metacognitive Strategies. All items are presented.

Reliability: Alpha coefficients were .78 and .82.

Validity: Correlations with other variables ranged from −.34 to .53.

Author: Wolters, C. A.

Article: Advancing achievement goal theory: Using goal structures and goal orientations to predict students' motivation, cognition, and achievement.

Journal: *Journal of Educational Psychology*, June 2004, *96*, 236–250.

Related Research: Pintrich, P., et al. (1993). Predictive validity and reliability of the Motivated Strategies for Learning Questionnaire. *Educational and Psychological Measurement, 53,* 801–813.

13376

Test Name: LEARNING STYLES QUESTIONNAIRE

Purpose: To measure activist, theorist, pragmatist, and reflector learning styles.

Number of Items: 80

Reliability: Internal reliabilities ranged from .46 to .71.

Validity: Correlations with other variables ranged from –.24 to .12.

Author: Cockerton, T., et al.

Article: Factorial validity and internal reliability of Honey and Mumford's Learning Styles Questionnaire.

Journal: *Psychological Reports*, October 2002, *91*, 503–519.

Related Research: Honey, P., & Mumford, A. (1992). *The manual of learning styles*, (3rd ed.) Berkshire, England: Peter Honey.

13377

Test Name: MAGICAL IDEATION SCALE

Purpose: To measure uncommon beliefs and unusual information processing and reasoning.

Number of Items: 30

Format: A true–false format is used.

Reliability: Alpha coefficients were .82 and .85.

Author: Kelly, W. E., and Daughtry, D.

Article: Relationship between magical ideation and noctcaelador.

Journal: *Perceptual and Motor Skills*, October 2005, *101*, 373–374.

Related Research: Eckblad, M., & Chapman, L. J. (1983). Magical ideation as an indicator of schizotypy. *Journal of Consulting and Clinical Psychology, 51,* 215–225.

13378

Test Name: MENTAL SELF-GOVERNMENT THINKING STYLES INVENTORY

Purpose: To measure thinking styles.

Number of Items: 21

Format: Responses are measured on a 7-point scale ranging from 1 (*not at all well*) to 7 (*extremely well*). Examples are presented.

Reliability: Reliabilities ranged from .56 to .88.

Author: Kaufman, J. C.

Article: Narrative and paradigmatic thinking styles in creative writing and journalism students.

Journal: *The Journal of Creative Behavior*, Third Quarter 2002, *36*(3), 201–219.

Related Research: Sternberg, R. J., & Wagner, R. K. (1991). *Mental Self Government Thinking Styles Inventory.* Unpublished test. Dai, D. Y., & Feldhusen, J. F. (1999). A validation study of the Thinking Styles Inventory: Implications for gifted education. *Roeper Review, 21,* 302–307.

13379

Test Name: METACOGNITIVE AWARENESS OF READING STRATEGIES INVENTORY

Purpose: To assess adolescent and adult readers' metacognitive awareness and perceived use of reading strategies while reading academic or school-related materials.

Number of Items: 30.

Format: Includes three factors: global reading strategies, problem-solving strategies, and support reading strategies. Responses are made on a 5-point scale ranging from 1 (*I never or almost never do this*) to 5 (*I always or almost always do this*).

Reliability: Alpha coefficients ranged from .86 to .93.

Author: Mokhtari, K., and Reichard, C. A.

Article: Assessing students' metacognitive awareness of reading strategies.

Journal: *Journal of Educational Psychology*, June 2002, *94*, 249–259.

Related Research: Alexander, P. A., & Jetton, T. L. (2000). Learning from text: A multidimensional and developmental perspective. In M. Kamil, et al. (Eds.), *Handbook of Reading Research* (Vol. 3, pp. 285–310). Mahwah, NJ: Erlbaum.

13380

Test Name: MINNESOTA TEST OF CRITICAL THINKING

Purpose: To measure six dimensions of critical thinking: interpretation, analysis, evaluation, inference, explanation, and self-regulation.

Number of Items: 125

Format: Item anchors are 1 (*not important at all*) and 5 (*extremely important*). A sample item is presented with scoring procedures.

Reliability: Alpha coefficients ranged from .29 to .64 across subscales. Total alpha was .78.

Validity: Correlations between subscales ranged from .05 to .67.

Author: Edman, L. R. O., et al.

Article: Psychometric analysis of the Minnesota Test of Critical Thinking.

Journal: *Psychological Reports*, August 2004, *95*, 3–9.

13381

Test Name: NEAR TRANSFER PROBLEM-SOLVING MEASURE

Purpose: To measure near transfer problem-solving.

Number of Items: 7

Format: Items include a shopping list problem with a novel format, one shopping list problem with a novel question, a buying bags problem with a different key word, a buying bags problem with a novel question, a half problem with unfamiliar vocabulary, and one pictograph problem with a novel question. An example is given.

Reliability: Coefficient alpha was .94.

Validity: Correlation with the Terra Nova was .55.

Author: Fuchs, L. S., et al.

Article: Enhancing mathematical problem solving among third-grade students with schema-based instruction.

Journal: *Journal of Educational Psychology*, December 2004, *96*, 635–647.

13382

Test Name: NOCTCAELADOR INVENTORY

Purpose: To measure psychological attachment to the night-sky.

Number of Items: 10

Format: Responses are made on a 5-point Likert scale ranging from 1 (*strongly disagree*) to 5 (*strongly agree*). Sample items are given.

Reliability: Coefficient alpha was .92. Test–retest (1 month) reliability coefficient was .88.

Author: Kelly, W. E., and Daughtry, D.

Article: Relationship between magical ideation and noctcaelador.

Journal: *Perceptual and Motor Skills*, October 2005, *101*, 373–374.

Related Research: Kelly, W. E. (2004). Development of an instrument to measure noctcaelador: Psychological attachment to the night-sky. *College Student Journal*, *38*, 100–102.

13383

Test Name: PREFERENCE FOR NUMERICAL INFORMATION SCALE

Purpose: To measure the proclivity toward using numerical information thinking with numerical information.

Number of Items: 20

Format: Item anchors range from 1 (*strongly disagree*) to 7 (*strongly agree*).

Reliability: Coefficient alpha was .91.

Validity: The correlation with academic achievement was .27.

Author: Smith, W. I., and Drumming, S. T.

Article: Preference for numerical information and academic achievement of African-American students.

Journal: *Psychological Reports*, October 2004, *95*, 631–636.

Related Research: Viswanathan, M. (1993). Measurement of individual differences in preference for numerical information. *Journal of Applied Psychology, 78*, 741–752.

13384

Test Name: QUESTIONNAIRE OF COGNITIVE STYLES

Purpose: To measure imagery and verbal preferences for thinking.

Number of Items: 85

Format: A true–false format is used. Sample items are presented.

Reliability: Cross-sample congruence was .97 (verbal) and .94 (imagery).

Author: Neils-Strunjas, J., et al.

Article: The influence of learning style and cognitive ability on recall of names and faces in an older population.

Journal: *The Journal of General Psychology*, December 2001, *128*, 433–445.

Related Research: Paivio, A., & Harshman, R. (1983). Factor analysis of a questionnaire on imagery and verbal habits and skills. *Canadian Journal of Psychology, 37*, 461–483.

13385

Test Name: REFLECTION SCALE

Purpose: To measure the extent to which people think through possible processes and outcomes associated with future performances.

Number of Items: 8

Reliability: Coefficient alpha was .81.

Validity: Correlations with other variables ranged from .11 to .27.

Author: Feldman, G., and Hayes, A.

Article: Preparing for problems: A measure of mental anticipatory processes.

Journal: *Journal of Research in Personality*, October 2005, *39*, 487–516.

Related Research: Norem, J. K. (2001). Defensive pessimism, optimism, and pessimism. In E. C. Chang (Ed.), *Optimism and pessimism: Implications for theory, research, and practice* (pp. 77–100). Washington, DC: American Psychological Association.

13386

Test Name: SOCIAL PROBLEM-SOLVING ABILITIES—REVISED

Purpose: To measure social problem-solving abilities.

Number of Items: 52

Format: Includes five scales: Positive Problem Orientation, Negative Problem Orientation, Rational Problem Solving, Impulsivity and Carelessness Style, and Avoidance Style. Responses are made on a 5-point scale ranging from 0 (*not very true of me*) to 4 (*extremely true of me*). Examples are presented.

Reliability: Alphas ranged from .76 to .92. Test–retest (3 weeks) reliability ranged from .72 to .88.

Validity: Correlations with other variables ranged from −.40 to .65.

Author: Elliott, T. R., et al.

Article: Family caregiver social problem-solving abilities and adjustment during the initial year of the caregiving role.

Journal: *Journal of Counseling Psychology*, April 2001, *48*, 223–232.

Related Research: Maydeu-Olivares, A., & D'Zurilla, T. J. (1996). A factor-analytic study of the social problem solving inventory: An integration of theory and data. *Cognitive Therapy and Research, 20,* 115–133.

13387

Test Name: STRATEGY INVENTORY FOR LANGUAGE LEARNING—CHINESE VERSION

Purpose: To measure frequency of strategy use, knowledge, effectiveness, anxiety, and difficulty in using a strategy to learning a language.

Number of Items: 50

Reliability: Coefficient alpha was .95.

Validity: Correlations with frequency of use ranged from −.74 to .81.

Author: Hsiao, T.-Y.

Article: Testing a social psychological model of strategy use with students of English as a foreign language.

Journal: *Psychological Reports,* December 2004, *95*, Part 1, 1059–1071.

Related Research: Oxford, R. L. (1990). *Learning language strategies: What every teacher should know.* Boston: Heinle.

13388

Test Name: STYLE OF PROCESSING SCALE

Purpose: To determine habitual use of verbal and visual representations.

Number of Items: 20

Format: Provides separate Verbal and Visual subscores or an overall Verbal–Visual score. Responses are made on a 5-point scale. Examples are provided.

Reliability: Internal reliability was .78. Test–retest (6 months) reliability was .81.

Validity: Correlations with other variables ranged from −.20 to .12.

Author: Ong, Y. W., and Milech, D.

Article: Comparison of the Cognitive Styles Analysis and the Style of Processing Scale.

Journal: *Perceptual and Motor Skills*, August 2004, *99*, 155–162.

Related Research: Heckler, S. E., et al. (1993). On the construct validity of the SOP Scale. *Journal of Mental Imagery, 17,* 119–132.

13389

Test Name: TEST OF EVERYDAY ATTENTION

Purpose: To assess everyday aspects of a person's attention.

Format: Includes eight subtests.

Reliability: Test–retest reliability coefficients ranged from .41 to .90.

Validity: Convergent validity with other attention measures ranged from .42 to .63.

Author: Groth-Marnat, G., and Baker, S.

Article: Digit span as a measure of everyday attention: A study of ecological validity.

Journal: *Perceptual and Motor Skills*, December 2003, *97*, Part 2, 1209–1218.

Related Research: Robertson, I. H., et al. (1996). The structure of normal human attention: The Test of Everyday Attention. *Journal of International Neuropsychological Society, 2,* 525–534.

13390

Test Name: THINKING STYLE INVENTORY

Purpose: To measure three dimensions of cognitive style.

Number of Items: 48

Format: Includes three dimensions: Scope, Level, and Learning. Responses are made on a 7- point Likert-type scale ranging from

1 (*strongly disagree*) to 7 (*strongly agree*). Sample items are presented.

Reliability: Alpha coefficients ranged from .95 to .97.

Validity: Correlations with other variables ranged from −.45 to .68.

Author: Workman, M., et al.

Article: The effects of cognitive style and media richness on commitment to telework and virtual teams.

Journal: *Journal of Vocational Behavior*, October 2003, *63*, 199–219.

Related Research: Sternberg, R. J. (1997). *Thinking styles.* New York: Cambridge University Press.

13391

Test Name: THINKING STYLES INVENTORY

Purpose: To measure thinking styles.

Number of Items: 65

Format: Seven-point scales are anchored by 1 (*does not at all describe the way that participants carry out their tasks*) and 7 (*characterizes extremely well the way they normally carry out their tasks*).

Reliability: Alpha coefficients ranged from .48 to .80.

Validity: Correlations with other variables ranged from −.21 to .39.

Author: Zhang, L.-F.

Article: Contributions of thinking styles to vocational purpose beyond self-rated abilities.

Journal: *Psychological Reports*, April 2004, *94*, 697–714.

Related Research: Sternberg, R. J., & Wagner, R. K. (1992). *Thinking Styles Inventory.* Unpublished test, Yale University, New Haven, CT.

13392

Test Name: THINKING STYLES INVENTORY—CHINESE VERSION

Purpose: To measure 11 thinking styles.

Number of Items: 65

Format: Response scales are anchored by 1 (*does not represent the way I think*) and 7 (*describes extremely well*). Sample items are presented.

Reliability: Alpha coefficients ranged from .41 to .82.

Validity: Correlations with other variables ranged from −.14 to .38.

Author: Zhang, L.-F.

Article: Are parents' and children's thinking styles related?

Journal: *Psychological Reports*, October 2003, *93*, 617–630.

Related Research: Sternberg, R. J., & Wagner, R. K. (1992). *Thinking Styles Inventory.* Unpublished test, Yale University, New Haven, CT.

13393

Test Name: VERBALIZER–VISUALIZER QUESTIONNAIRE—MODIFIED

Purpose: To assess the degree to which people use verbal or visual modes of thinking.

Number of Items: 15

Format: Responses are made on a 7-point Likert-type scale ranging from 1 (*strongly agree*) to 7 (*strongly disagree*).

Validity: Correlations with other variables ranged from −.27 to .46.

Author: Mayer, R. E., and Massa, L. J.

Article: Three facets of visual and verbal learners: Cognitive ability, cognitive style, and learning preference.

Journal: *Journal of Educational Psychology*, December 2003, *95*, 833–846.

Related Research: Richardson, A. (1977). Verbalization–visualizer: A cognitive style dimension. *Journal of Mental Imagery, 1*, 109–126.

13394

Test Name: VERBALIZER–VISUALIZER QUESTIONNAIRE—SPANISH VERSION

Purpose: To measure differences on the verbal–visual dimension of cognitive style.

Number of Items: 15

Format: A true–false format is used. All items are presented in English.

Reliability: Coefficient alpha was .30.

Author: Campos, A., et al.

Article: Imagery factors in the Spanish version of the Verbalizer–Visualizer Questionnaire.

Journal: *Psychological Reports*, June 2004, *94*, Part 2, 1149–1154.

Related Research: Richardson, A. (1977). Verbalizer–Visualizer: A cognitive style dimension. *Journal of Mental Imagery, 1*, 109–126.

13395

Test Name: VIVIDNESS OF VISUAL IMAGERY QUESTIONNAIRE

Purpose: To provide a test of imagery.

Number of Items: 16

Format: Responses are made on a 5-point scale ranging from 1 (*perfectly clear and vivid*) to 5 (*no image at all*).

Reliability: Alpha coefficients ranged from .78 to .83.

Validity: Correlations with other variables ranged from −.29 to .32.

Author: Berry, J. W., and Worthington, E. L., Jr.

Article: Forgiveness, relationship quality, stress while imagining relationship events, and physical and mental health.

Journal: *Journal of Counseling Psychology*, October 2001, *48*, 447–455.

Related Research: Marks, D. F. (1973). Visual imagery differences in the recall of pictures. *British Journal of Psychology, 64,* 17–24.

13396

Test Name: WAY-FINDING STRATEGY SCALE

Purpose: To identify way-finding strategies.

Number of Items: 14

Format: Includes two sections: Orientation Strategies (9 items) and Route Strategies (5 items). Responses are made on a 5-point scale ranging from 1 (*not at all typical of me*) to 5 (*extremely typical of me*).

Reliability: Alpha coefficients were .65 to .73.

Author: Devlin, A. S.

Article: Sailing experience and sex as correlates of spatial ability.

Journal: *Perceptual and Motor Skills,* June 2004, *98,* Part 2, 1409–1421.

Related Research: Lawton, C. A. (1994). Gender differences in way-finding strategies: Relationship to spatial ability and spatial anxiety. *Sex Roles, 20,* 765–779.

CHAPTER 20
Status

13397

Test Name: STATUS CONSUMPTION SCALE

Purpose: To measure the degree to which consumption is motivated by status concerns.

Number of Items: 3

Format: Seven-point agreement scales are used. A sample item is presented.

Reliability: Alpha was .86.

Author: Jusoh, W. J. W., et al.

Article: Self-ratings of materialism and status consumption in a Malaysian sample: Effects of answering during an assumed recession versus economic growth.

Journal: *Psychological Reports,* June 2001, *88,* Part 2, 1142–1144.

Related Research: Eastman, J. K., et al. (1999). Status consumption in consumer behavior: Scale development and validation. *Journal of Marketing Theory and Practice, 7,* 41–51.

13398

Test Name: WORK SOCIAL STATUS SCALE

Purpose: To assess how valuable, how influential, and how well-respected a coworker is.

Number of Items: 3

Format: Seven-point scales are used. All items and response scales are presented.

Reliability: Alpha coefficients were .91 (givers) and .84 (receivers).

Author: Flynn, F. J., and Brockner, J.

Article: It's different to give than to receive: Predictions of givers' and receivers' reactions to favor exchange.

Journal: *Journal of Applied Psychology,* December 2003, *88,* 1034–1045.

Related Research: Anderson, C., et al. (2001). Who attains social status? Effects of personality and attractiveness in social groups. *Journal of Personality and Social Psychology, 81,* 116–132.

CHAPTER 21
Trait Measurement

13399

Test Name:
ADAPTIVE/MALADAPTIVE
PERFECTIONISM SCALE FOR
CHILDREN

Purpose: To measure perfectionism in children in terms of sensitivity to mistakes, contingent self-esteem, compulsiveness, and need for admiration.

Number of Items: 27

Format: Scales range from 1 (*really unlike me*) to 4 (*really like me.*) All items are presented.

Reliability: Alpha coefficients ranged from .73 to .90 across subscales.

Validity: Correlations between subscales ranged from −.36 to .42.

Author: Rice, K. G., and Preusser, K. J.

Article: The Adaptive/Maladaptive Perfectionism Scale.

Journal: *Measurement and Evaluation in Counseling and Development*, January 2002, *34*, 210–222.

13400

Test Name: ADVERTISEMENT EMPATHY SCALE

Purpose: To measure empathy with characters in an advertisement.

Number of Items: 5

Format: A 7-point Likert format is used. All items are presented.

Reliability: Coefficient alpha was .84.

Author: Chebat, J.-C., et al.

Article: Drama advertisements: Moderating effects of self-relevance on the relations among empathy, information processing, and attitudes.

Journal: *Psychological Reports*, June 2003, *92*, Part 1, 997–1014.

Related Research: Coulson, J. S. (1998). An investigation of mood commercials. In P. Cafferata & A. M. Tybout (Eds.), *Cognitive and affective responses to advertising* (pp. 21–30). Lexington, MA: Lexington Books.

13401

Test Name: AGGRESSION QUESTIONNAIRE—DUTCH VERSION

Purpose: To assess overall aggression and its components: physical aggression, anger, verbal aggression, and hostility.

Number of Items: 29

Format: Item responses are anchored by 1 (*extremely like me*) and 5 (*extremely unlike me.*)

Reliability: Total alpha was .86. Subscale alphas ranged from .70 to .76.

Author: Meesters, C., and Muris, P.

Article: Attachment style and self-reported aggression.

Journal: *Psychological Reports*, February 2002, *90*, 231–235.

Related Research: Buss, A. H., & Perry, M. (1992). The Aggression Questionnaire. *Journal of*

Personality and Social Psychology, 63, 452–459.

13402

Test Name: ALMOST PERFECT SCALE—REVISED

Purpose: To measure perfectionism.

Number of Items: 23

Format: Includes three subscales: High Standards, Order, and Discrepancy. Responses are made on a 7-point Likert scale ranging from 1 (*strongly disagree*) to 7 (*strongly agree.*) Sample items are presented.

Reliability: Alpha coefficients ranged from .75 to .92.

Validity: Correlations with other variables ranged from −.55 to .58 ($N = 251$).

Author: Mobley, M., et al.

Article: Cultural validity of the Almost Perfect Scale—Revised for African American college students.

Journal: *Journal of Counseling Psychology*, October 2005, *52*, 629–639.

Related Research: Slaney, R. B., et al. (1996). *The Almost Perfect Scale—Revised.* Unpublished manuscript, Pennsylvania State University, University Park.

13403

Test Name: ANGER AROUSAL AND LENGTHINESS SCALE— JAPANESE VERSION

Purpose: To measure the tendency to be angry.

Number of Items: 13

Format: Scales range from 1 (*strongly disagree*) to 5 (*strongly agree*.) Sample items are presented.

Reliability: Coefficient alpha was .86.

Author: Yukawa, S.

Article: Sex differences in relationships among anger, depression, and coping strategies of Japanese students.

Journal: *Psychological Reports*, December 2005, *97*, 769–776.

Related Research: Wanatabe, S., & Kodama, M. (2001). [Assessment of anger arousal and anger lengthiness]. [*The Japanese Journal of Health Psychology*], *14*, 32–39.

13404

Test Name: APATHY EVALUATION SCALE

Purpose: To typify and quantify apathy by self-report.

Number of Items: 18

Format: Respondents rate items on a 4-point scale anchored by *not at all* and *a lot*.

Reliability: Alpha coefficients ranged from .86 to .94. Test–retest reliabilities ranged from .76 to .94.

Validity: Correlations with other variables ranged from .63 to .74.

Author: Ramirez, S. M., et al.

Article: Relationship of numbing to alexithymia, apathy, and depression

Journal: *Psychological Reports*, February 2001, *88*, 189–200.

Related Research: Marin, R. S., et al. (1991). Reliability and validity of the Apathy Evaluation Scale. *Psychiatry Research, 38,* 143–162.

13405

Test Name: ARGUMENTATIVENESS SCALE

Purpose: To measure an individual's predisposition to argue.

Number of Items: 20

Format: Likert-type items are anchored by 1 (*almost never true*) and 5 (*almost always true*.)

Reliability: Coefficient alpha was .91.

Validity: Correlations with other variables ranged from –.53 to –.59.

Author: Simmons, D., et al.

Article: Correlations among applicants' communication apprehension, argumentativeness, and verbal aggressiveness in selection interviews.

Journal: *Psychological Reports*, June 2003, *92*, Part 1, 804–808.

Related Research: Infante, D. A., & Rancer, A. S. (1982). A conceptualization and measure of argumentativeness. *Journal of Personality Assessment, 46,* 72–80.

13406

Test Name: ASSERTION INVENTORY

Purpose: To measure assertiveness.

Number of Items: 40

Format: Scales range from 1 (*none*) to 5 (*very much*) as a ratio of the discomfort for each assertive act. Five-point scales also rate the likelihood of engaging in the behavior.

Reliability: Alpha coefficients ranged from .90 to .95 across subscales.

Validity: Correlations with other variables ranged from .11 to .40.

Author: Beck, J. G., and Davila, J.

Article: Development of an interview for anxiety-relevant

interpersonal styles: Preliminary support for convergent and discriminant validity.

Journal: *Journal of Psychopathology and Behavioral Assessment*, March 2003, *25*, 1–9.

Related Research: Gambrill, E. D., & Richey, C. A. (1975). An assertion inventory for use in assessment and research. *Behavior Theory, 6,* 550–561.

13407

Test Name: ASSERTIVENESS INVENTORY

Purpose: To assess two dimensions of assertiveness: Independence and Directiveness.

Number of Items: 8

Format: Six-point Likert scales are used. Sample items are presented.

Reliability: Alpha coefficients were .69 (independence) and .76 (directiveness).

Author: Smith-Jentsch, K. A., et al.

Article: To transfer or not to transfer? Investigating the combined effects of trainee characteristics, team leader support, and team climate.

Journal: *Journal of Applied Psychology*, April 2001, *86*, 279–292.

Related Research: Lorr, M., & Moore, W. (1980). Four dimensions of assertiveness. *Multivariate Behavioral Research, 15,* 127–138.

13408

Test Name: ASSERTIVENESS SELF-REPORT INVENTORY

Purpose: To measure the behavioral and affective dimensions of assertiveness.

Number of Items: 25

Format: A true–false format is used.

Reliability: Coefficient alpha was .53.

Validity: Correlations with other variables ranged from −.43 to .37.

Author: Kuther, T. L., and Timoshin, A.

Article: A comparison of social cognitive and psychosocial predictors of alcohol use by college students.

Journal: *Journal of College Student Development*, March/April 2003, *44*, 143–154.

Related Research: Herzberger, S. D., et al. (1984). The development of an assertiveness self-report inventory. *Journal of Personality Assessment*, *48*, 317–323.

13409

Test Name: ASSERTIVENESS SUBSCALE—REVISED

Purpose: To measure assertiveness.

Number of Items: 6

Format: Responses are made on a 5-point scale ranging from 1 (*never do it*) to 5 (*nearly always do it*). Examples are presented.

Reliability: Internal consistency reliability was .78 ($N = 221$).

Validity: Correlations with other variables ranged from −.07 to .40 ($N = 221$).

Author: Andrews, M. C., and Kacmar, K. M.

Article: Impression management by association: Construction and validation of a scale.

Journal: *Journal of Vocational Behavior*, February 2001, *58*, 142–161.

Related Research: Schriesheim, C. A., & Hinkin, T. R. (1990). Influence tactics used by subordinates: A theoretical and empirical analysis and refinement of the Kipnis, Schmidt, and

Wilkinson subscales. *Journal of Applied Psychology, 75*, 246–257.

13410

Test Name: BALANCED EMOTIONAL EMPATHY SCALE

Purpose: To measure affective or emotional empathy.

Number of Items: 30

Format: Scales range from –4 (*very strong disagreement*) to +4 (*very strong agreement*).

Reliability: Alpha coefficients ranged from .83 to .87.

Author: Toussaint, L., and Webb, J. R.

Article: Gender differences in the relationship between empathy and forgiveness.

Journal: *The Journal of Social Psychology*, December 2005, *145*, 673–685.

Related Research: Mehrabian, A. (1966). *Manual for the Balanced Emotional Empathy Scale*. Monterey, CA: Author.

13411

Test Name: BARRATT IMPULSIVENESS SCALE— VERSION II

Purpose: To measure impulsiveness in three dimensions: Attentional, Motor, and Nonplanning.

Number of Items: 30

Format: Four-point scales range from *rarely/never* to *almost always/always*.

Reliability: Coefficient alpha was .82.

Validity: Correlations with several behavior scales ranged from −.04 to .51.

Author: Wu, K. D., and Clark, L. A.

Article: Relations between personality traits and self-reports of daily behavior.

Journal: *Journal of Research in Personality*, August 2003, *37*, 231–256.

Related Research: Patton, J. H. E., et al. (1995). Factor structure of the Barratt Impulsiveness Scale. *Journal of Clinical Psychology, 51*, 768–774.

13412

Test Name: BATSON'S EMPATHY ADJECTIVES

Purpose: To measure empathy for the robber.

Number of Items: 8

Format: Eight words describing emotions are rated on a 6-point scale ranging from 1 (*not at all*) to 6 (*extremely*).

Reliability: Alpha coefficients ranged from .79 to .95.

Author: Worthington, E. L., Jr., et al.

Article: The Religious Commitment Inventory–10: Development, refinement, and validation of a brief scale for research and counseling.

Journal: *Journal of Counseling Psychology*, January 2003, *50*, 84–96.

Related Research: Batson, C. C., et al. (1983). Self-reported distress and empathy and egoistic versus altruistic motivation for helping. *Journal of Personality and Social Psychology, 45*, 706–718.

13413

Test Name: BURNS PERFECTIONISM SCALE— JAPANESE VERSION

Purpose: To asses neurotic perfectionism thinking.

Number of Items: 10

Format: A sample item is presented.

Reliability: Cronbach's alpha was .62.

Validity: Correlations with other variables ranged from −.29 to .41.

Author: Sumi, K., et al.

Article: Neurotic perfectionism, perceived stress, and self-esteem among Japanese men: A prospective study.

Journal: *Psychological Reports*, February 2001, *88*, 19–22.

Related Research: Burns, D. D. (1983). The spouse who is a perfectionist. *Medical Aspects of Human Sexuality*, *17*, 219–230.

13414

Test Name: CHILDREN'S INVENTORY OF ANGER

Purpose: To measure children's experience of anger.

Number of Items: 71

Format: Responses are made on a 4-point pictorial scale. Examples are given.

Reliability: Internal consistency was .96. Test–retest reliability ranged from .63 to .90.

Author: Dilworth, J. E., et al.

Article: The efficacy of a video-based teamwork-building series with urban elementary school students: A pilot investigation.

Journal: *Journal of School Psychology*, July/August 2002, *40*, 329–349.

Related Research: Nelson, W., et al. (1993). Anger in children: A cognitive behavioral view of the assessment–therapy connection. *Journal of Rational Emotive and Cognitive Behavioral Therapy*, *11*, 135–150.

13415

Test Name: CLARITY AND LABELING SCALES

Purpose: To measure trait clarity.

Number of Items: 16

Format: Scales range from 1 (*strongly disagree*) to 5 (*strongly agree*). Sample items are presented.

Reliability: Alpha coefficients were .78 (clarity) and .70 (labeling).

Validity: Correlations with other variables ranged from −.44 to .70.

Author: Gohm, C. L., et al.

Article: Personality in extreme situations: Thinking (or not) under acute stress.

Journal: *Journal of Research in Personality*, September 2001, *35*, 388–399.

Related Research: Swinkels, A., & Giuliano, T. A. (1995). The measurement and conceptualization of mood awareness: Monitoring and labeling one's mood states. *Personality of Social Psychology Bulletin*, *21*, 934–949.

13416

Test Name: CONSCIENTIOUSNESS SCALE

Purpose: To measure conscientiousness.

Number of Items: 10

Format: Responses are made on a 5-point scale ranging from 1 (*very inaccurate*) to 5 (*very accurate*).

Reliability: Alpha coefficients were .79 and .81.

Validity: Correlations with other variables ranged form −.04 to .52.

Author: Bajor, J. K., and Baltes, B. B.

Article: The relationship between selection optimization with compensation, conscientiousness, motivation, and performance.

Journal: *Journal of Vocational Behavior*, December 2003, *63*, 347–367.

Related Research: Goldberg, L. R. (2001, January). *The development of five-factor domain scales from the IPIP item pool.* Available at http://ipip.ori.org/ipip/memo.htm

13417

Test Name: CREATIVE PERSONALITY TRAITS QUESTIONNAIRE

Purpose: To collect data on creative personality traits.

Number of Items: 42

Format: Responses are made on a 5-point scale ranging from 1 (*not at all*) to 5 (*extremely well*). Samples are presented.

Reliability: Coefficient alpha was .91.

Author: Cheung, C.-K., et al.

Article: Creativity of university students: What is the impact of field and year of study?

Journal: *The Journal of Creative Behavior*, First Quarter 2003, *37*, 42–63.

Related Research: Rudowicz, E., & Hui, A. (1997). The creative personality: Hong Kong perspective. *Journal of Social Behavior and Personality*, *12*, 139–157.

13418

Test Name: DOGMATISM SCALE

Purpose: To measure the extent to which people are relatively unchangeable and unjustifiably certain.

Number of Items: 20

Format: Nine-point scales are used. All items are presented.

Reliability: Coefficient alpha was .90.

Validity: Correlations with other variables ranged from −.51 to .65.

Author: Altemeyer, B.

Article: Dogmatic behavior among students: Testing a new measure of dogmatism.

Journal: *The Journal of Social Psychology*, December 2002, *142*, 713–721.

13419

Test Name: EMOTIONAL REACTION QUESTIONNAIRE

Purpose: To measure sympathy and anger affects toward victims.

Number of Items: 6

Format: Nine-point scales anchor each item. A sample item is presented.

Reliability: Alpha was .92 (sympathy) and .67 (anger).

Author: Heater, J., et al.

Article: Sex and attributions on reactions toward alleged spousal abuse victims.

Journal: *Psychological Reports*, August 2002, *91*, 243–254.

Related Research: Dooley, P. (1995). Perceptions of the onset controllability of AIDS and helping judgments: An attributional analysis. *Journal of Applied Social Psychology, 25*, 858–869.

13420

Test Name: EMPATHY INDEX FOR CHILDREN AND ADOLESCENTS—SPANISH VERSION

Purpose: To measure empathy.

Number of Items: 22

Format: Item anchors range from 1 (*low empathy*) to 5 (*high empathy*). All items are presented in English.

Reliability: Alpha coefficients ranged from .72 to .78.

Author: del Barrio, V., and Aluja, A.

Article: Bryant's Empathy Index for Children and Adolescents: Psychometric properties in the Spanish language.

Journal: *Psychological Reports*, August 2004, *95*, 257–262.

Related Research: Bryant, B. K. (1982). An index of empathy for children and adolescents. *Child Development, 53*, 413–425.

13421

Test Name: EMPATHY SCALE

Purpose: To measure cognitive and affective empathy.

Number of Items: 7

Format: Scales range from 1 (*strongly disagree*) to 7 (*strongly agree*). All items are presented.

Reliability: Alpha coefficients were .74 (cognitive empathy) and .84 (affective empathy).

Validity: Correlations with other variables ranged from −.02 to .44.

Author: Bettencourt, L. A., et al.

Article: A comparison of attitude, personality, and knowledge predictors of service-oriented organizational citizenship behaviors.

Journal: *Journal of Applied Psychology*, February 2001, *86*, 29–41.

Related Research: Davis, M. H. (1983). Measuring individual difference in empathy: Evidence for a multidimensional approach. *Journal of Personality and Social Psychology, 44*, 113–126.

13422

Test Name: EMPATHY SCALE

Purpose: To assess client-perceived counselor empathy.

Number of Items: 10

Format: Responses are made on a 4-point scale ranging from 1 (*not at all*) to 4 (*a lot*). Examples are presented.

Reliability: Alpha coefficients were .70 and .72.

Validity: Correlations with other variables ranged from .08 to .71.

Author: Kim, B. S. K., et al.

Article: Counselor self-disclosure, East Asian American client adherence to Asian cultural values, and counseling process.

Journal: *Journal of Counseling Psychology*, July 2003, *50*, 324–332.

Related Research: Persons, J. B., & Burns, D. D. (1985). Mechanisms of action of cognitive therapy: The relative contributions of technical and interpersonal interventions. *Cognitive Therapy and Research, 9*, 539–551.

13423

Test Name: EMPATHY SCALE

Purpose: To measure empathy.

Number of Items: 6

Format: Responses are made on a 5-point scale ranging from 1 (*does not at all describe how I feel*) to 5 (*describes how I feel extremely well*).

Validity: Correlation with perspective-taking was .14, and correlation with helping was .10.

Author: Oswald, P. A.

Article: Does the Interpersonal Reactivity Index Perspective-Taking Scale predict who will volunteer time to counsel adults entering college?

Journal: *Perceptual and Motor Skills*, December 2003, *97*, Part 2, 1184–1186.

Related Research: Fultz, J., et al. (1986). Social evaluation and the empathy–altruism hypothesis. *Journal of Personality and Social Psychology, 50*, 761–769.

13424

Test Name: EYSENCK IMPULSIVENESS SCALE

Purpose: To measure four components of impulsiveness.

Number of Items: 43

Format: A yes–no format is used. Sample items are presented.

Reliability: Internal consistency reliabilities were .83 and .87.

Validity: Correlations with other variables ranged from −.29 to .53.

Author: Lightsey, O. R., Jr., and Hulsey, C. D.

Article: Impulsivity, coping, stress, and problem gambling among university students.

Journal: *Journal of Counseling Psychology*, April 2002, *49*, 202–211.

Related Research: Eysenck, S. B., & Eysenck, H. J. (1977). The place of impulsiveness in a dimensional system of personality description. *British Journal of Social and Clinical Psychology, 16*, 57–68.

13425

Test Name: HEWITT MULTIDIMENSIONAL PERFECTIONISM SCALE

Purpose: To measure perfectionism.

Number of Items: 45

Reliability: Alpha coefficients ranged from .82 to .91 across subscales.

Validity: Correlations with other variables ranged from .04 to .25.

Author: Bieling, P. J., et al.

Article: Perfectionism as an explanatory construct in comorbidity of Axis I disorders.

Journal: *Journal of Psychopathology and Behavioral Assessment*, September 2004, *26*, 193–201.

Related Research: Hewitt, P. L., et al. (1991). The Multidimensional Perfectionism Scale: Reliability, validity, and psychometric properties in a psychiatric sample. *Psychological Assessment, 3*, 464–468.

13426

Test Name: IMPULSIVITY SCALE

Purpose: To measure impulsivity.

Number of Items: 13

Format: Scales range from 1 (*absolutely not true of me*) to 4 (*absolutely true of me*). A sample item is presented.

Reliability: Coefficient alpha was .81.

Author: Kirkeby, B. S., and Robinson, M. D.

Article: Impulsive behavior and stimulus–response variability in choice reaction time.

Journal: *Journal of Research in Personality*, April 2005, *39*, 263–277.

Related Research: Eysenck, S. B., & Eysenck, H. J. (1977). The place of impulsiveness in a dimensional system of personality description. *British Journal of Social and Clinical Psychology, 16*, 57–68.

13427

Test Name: INTERPERSONAL ADJECTIVE SCALES

Purpose: To measure interpersonal traits.

Number of Items: 128

Format: Includes eight scales: Ambitions–Dominant, Arrogant–Calculating, Cold–Quarrelsome, Aloof–Introverted, Lazy–Submissive, Unassuming–Ingenuous, Warm–Agreeable, and Gregarious–Extraverted. Responses made on an 8-point scale ranging from 1 (*very inaccurate*) to 8 (*very accurate*).

Reliability: Alpha coefficients ranged from .74 to .92.

Author: Acton, G. S., and Revelle, W.

Article: Interpersonal personality measures show circumplex structure based on new psychometric criteria.

Journal: *Journal of Personality Assessment*, December 2002, *79*, 446–471.

Related Research: Wiggins, J. S. (1979). A psychological taxonomy of trait-descriptive terms: The interpersonal domain. *Journal of Personality and Social Psychology, 37*, 395–412.

13428

Test Name: INTERPERSONAL ADJECTIVE SCALES—REVISED

Purpose: To measure interpersonal traits.

Number of Items: 64

Format: Includes eight scales: Assured–Dominant, Arrogant–Calculating, Cold–Hearted, Aloof–Introverted, Unassured–Submissive, Unassuming–Ingenious, Warm–Agreeable, and Gregarious–Extraverted. Responses are made on an 8-point scales ranging from 1 (*very inaccurate*) to 8 (*very accurate*).

Reliability: Alpha coefficients ranged from .59 to .81.

Author: Acton, G. S., and Revelle, W.

Article: Interpersonal personality measures show circumplex structure based on new psychometric criteria.

Journal: *Journal of Personality Assessment*, December 2002, *79*, 446–471.

Related Research: Wiggins, J. S., et al. (1989). Circular reasoning about interpersonal behavior: Evidence concerning some untested assumptions underlying diagnostic classification. *Journal of Personality and Social Psychology, 56*, 296–305.

13429

Test Name: INTERPERSONAL REACTIVITY INDEX

Purpose: To measure empathy.

Number of Items: 28

Format: Scales range from 0 (*does not describe me well*) to 4 (*describes me very well*).

Reliability: Coefficient alpha was .78 for the full scale. Subscale alphas ranged from .68 to .77.

Validity: Correlations with other variables ranged from −.23 to .44.

Author: Constantine, M. G.

Article: Theoretical orientation, empathy, and multicultural counseling competence in school counselor trainees.

Journal: *Professional School Counseling*, June 2001, 4(5), 342–348.

Related Research: Davis, M. H. (1980). A multidimensional approach to individual differences in empathy. *JSAS Catalog of Selected Documents in Psychology, 10*, 85.

13430

Test Name: INTERPERSONAL REACTIVITY INDEX—ADAPTED

Purpose: To measure empathy.

Number of Items: 14

Format: Includes two subscales: Perspective Taking and Empathic Concern. Responses are made on a 5-point scale ranging from 0 (*does not describe me well*) to 4 (*describes me very well*). Examples are given.

Reliability: Alpha coefficients ranged from .71 to .80. Test–retest reliabilities ranged from .62 to .71.

Validity: Correlations with other variables ranged from .18 to .54.

Author: Wang, Y.-W., et al.

Article: The Scale of Ethnocultural Empathy: Development, validation, and reliability.

Journal: *Journal of Counseling Psychology*, April 2003, 50, 221–234.

Related Research: Davis, M. H. (1983). Measuring individual differences in empathy: Evidence for a multidimensional approach. *Journal of Personality and Social Psychology, 44*, 113–126.

13431

Test Name: INTERPERSONAL REACTIVITY SCALE—ADAPTED

Purpose: To assess empathy-related characteristics.

Number of Items: 10

Format: Includes two subscales: Sympathy and Perspective Taking. Responses are made on a 7-point scale. Examples are presented.

Reliability: Coefficient alpha was .70.

Author: Eisenberg, N., et al.

Article: Brazilian adolescents' prosocial moral judgment and behavior: Relations to sympathy, perspective taking, gender-role orientation, and demographic characteristics.

Journal: *Child Development*, March/April 2001, 72, 518–534.

Related Research: Davis, M. H. (1983). Measuring individual differences in empathy: Evidence for a multidimensional approach. *Journal of Personality and Social Psychology, 44*, 113–126.

13432

Test Name: LEARNING AND PERFORMANCE ORIENTATIONS SCALE

Purpose: To measure trait learning and performance orientations.

Number of Items: 16

Format: Scales range from 1 (*strongly disagree*) to 5 (*strongly agree*). Sample items are presented.

Reliability: Alpha coefficients were .77 (learning orientation) and .73 (performance orientation).

Validity: Correlations with other variables ranged from −.16 to .27.

Author: Bell, B. S., and Kozlowski, W. J.

Article: Goal orientation and ability: Interactive effects on self-efficacy, performance, and knowledge.

Journal: *Journal of Applied Psychology*, June 2002, 87, 497–505.

Related Research: Button, S. B., et al. (1996). Goal orientation in organizational research: A conceptual and empirical foundation. *Organizational Behavior and Human Decision Processes, 67*, 26–48. Yeo, G. B., & Neal, A. (2004). A multilevel analysis of effort, practice, and performance: Effects of ability, conscientiousness, and goal orientation. *Journal of Applied Psychology, 89*, 231–247.

13433

Test Name: MACH IV SCALE

Purpose: To measure Machiavellianism.

Number of Items: 20

Format: Item responses are anchored by 1 (*strongly agree*) and 7 (*strongly disagree*).

Validity: Correlations with other variables ranged from −.40 and .46.

Author: Özer, M., et al.

Article: Relation between Machiavellianism and job satisfaction in a sample of Turkish physicians.

Journal: *Psychological Reports*, June 2003, 92, Part 2, 1169–1175.

Related Research: Christie, R., & Geis, F. L. (1970). *Studies in Machiavellianism*. New York: Academic Press.

13434

Test Name: MULTIDIMENSIONAL PERFECTIONISM SCALE— ADAPTED

Purpose: To measure perfectionism.

Number of Items: 13

Format: Includes only two of the six subscales: Concern Over Mistakes and Doubts About Actions. Responses are made on a 5-point scale ranging from 1 (*disagree strongly*) to 5 (*agree strongly*).

Reliability: Alpha coefficients were .74 and .89.

Validity: Correlations with other variables ranged from −.14 to .61.

Author: Wei, M., et al.

Article: Maladaptive perfectionism as a mediator and moderator between adult attachment and depressive mood.

Journal: *Journal of Counseling Psychology*, April 2004, *51*, 201–212.

Related Research: Frost, R. O., et al. (1990). The dimensions of perfectionism. *Cognitive Therapy and Research, 14,* 449–468.

13435

Test Name: MULTIDIMENSIONAL PERFECTIONISM SCALE— FRENCH VERSION

Purpose: To assess perfectionism.

Number of Items: 45

Format: Includes three forms of perfectionism: self-oriented, other-oriented, and socially prescribed. Responses are made on a 7-point scale ranging from 1 (*disagree*) to 7 (*agree*). Examples are given.

Reliability: Alpha coefficients ranged from .70 to .83.

Validity: Correlations with other variables ranged from .38 to .42.

Author: Ferrand, C., and Brunet, E.

Article: Perfectionism and risk for disordered eating among young French male cyclists of high performance.

Journal: *Perceptual and Motor Skills*, December 2004, *99*, Part 1, 959–967.

Related Research: Hewitt, P. L., & Flett, G. L. (1991). Perfectionism in the self and social context: Conceptualization, assessment, and association with psychopathology. *Journal of Personality and Social Psychology, 60,* 456–470.

13436

Test Name: MULTIDIMENSIONAL PERFECTIONISM SCALE— FROST

Purpose: To measure perfectionism.

Number of Items: 35

Format: Includes six subscales: Concern Over Mistakes, Doubts About Actions, Parental Criticism, Parental Expectations, Personal Standards, and Organization. Responses are made on a 5-point scale ranging from 1 (*strongly disagree*) to 5 (*strongly agree*).

Reliability: Alpha coefficients ranged from .77 to .93.

Validity: Correlations with Perfection Inventory Scales ranged from −.03 to .89.

Author: Hill, R. W., et al.

Article: A new measure of perfectionism: The Perfectionism Inventory.

Journal: *Journal of Personality Assessment*, February 2004, *82*, 80–91.

Related Research: Frost, R. O., et al. (1990). The dimensions of perfectionism. *Cognitive Therapy and Research, 14,* 449–468.

13437

Test Name: MULTIDIMENSIONAL PERFECTIONISM SCALE— HEWITT AND FLETT

Purpose: To measure perfectionism.

Number of Items: 45

Format: Includes three subscales: Self-Oriented Perfectionism, Other-Oriented Perfectionism, and Socially-Prescribed Perfectionism. Responses are made on a 7-point rating scale ranging from 1 (*disagree*) to 7 (*agree*).

Reliability: Alpha coefficients ranged from .79 to .89.

Validity: Correlations with other variables ranged from .14 to .79.

Author: Hill, R. W., et al.

Article: A new measure of perfectionism: The Perfectionism Inventory.

Journal: *Journal of Personality Assessment*, February 2004, *82*, 80–91.

Related Research: Hewitt, P. L., & Flett, G. L. (1991). Perfection in the self and social contexts: Conceptionalization, assessment, and association with psychopathology. *Journal of Personality and Social Psychology, 60,* 456–470.

13438

Test Name: MULTIDIMENSIONAL PERFECTIONISM SCALE— JAPANESE VERSION

Purpose: To measure perfectionism.

Number of Items: 35

Format: Scales range from 1 (*strongly disagree*) to 5 (*strongly agree*).

Reliability: Alpha coefficients ranged from .78 to .84.

Validity: Correlations with an obsessive–compulsive scale ranged from .14 to .56.

Author: Suzuki, T.

Article: Relationship between two aspects of perfectionism and obsessive–compulsive symptoms.

Journal: *Psychological Reports,* April 2005, *96,* 299–305.

Related Research: Frost, R. O., et al. (1990). The dimensions of perfectionism. *Cognitive Therapy and Research, 14,* 449–468.

13439

Test Name: NARCISSISTIC PERSONALITY INVENTORY

Purpose: To measure narcissism.

Number of Items: 37

Format: A true–false format is used. Sample items are presented.

Reliability: Coefficient alpha exceeded .70.

Validity: Correlations with other variables ranged from .08 to .34.

Author: Brown, R. P.

Article: Vengeance is mine: Narcissism, vengeance, and the tendency to forgive.

Journal: *Journal of Research in Personality,* December 2004, *38,* 576–584.

Related Research: Emmons, R. A. (1987). Narcissism: Theory and measurement. *Journal of Personality and Social Psychology, 52,* 11–17.

13440

Test Name: PERFECTIONISM INVENTORY

Purpose: To measure perfectionism.

Number of Items: 59

Format: Includes eight subscales: Organization, Striving for Excellence, Planfulness, High Standards for Others, Concern Over Mistakes, Need for Approval, Rumination, and Perceived Parental Pressure.

Reliability: Alpha coefficients ranged from .83 to .91. Test–retest

(3 to 6 weeks) reliabilities ranged from .71 to .91.

Validity: Correlations with other variables ranged from −.18 to .89.

Author: Hill, R. W., et al.

Article: A new measure of perfectionism: The Perfectionism Inventory.

Journal: *Journal of Personality Assessment,* February 2004, *82,* 80–91.

13441

Test Name: PERFECTIONISM SCALE

Purpose: To measure self-oriented, socially prescribed, and other-directed perfectionism.

Number of Items: 45

Format: Seven-point agreement scales are used. Sample items are presented.

Reliability: Alpha coefficients ranged from .78 to .90 across subscales.

Validity: Correlations with other variables ranged from −.63 to .17.

Author: Haring, M., et al.

Article: Perfectionism, coping, and quality of intimate relationships.

Journal: *Journal of Marriage and Family,* February 2003, *65,* 143–158.

Related Research: Hewitt, P. L., & Flett, G. L. (1991). Dimensions of perfectionism in unipolar depression. *Journal of Abnormal Psychology, 100,* 98–101.

13442

Test Name: PERSONALITY TRAIT MEASURES

Purpose: To measure three personality traits.

Number of Items: 11

Format: Includes three scales: Internal Locus of Control, Work Involvement, and Negative Affectivity.

Reliability: Alpha coefficients ranged from .62 to .70.

Validity: Correlations with other variables ranged from −.50 to .43.

Author: Wallace, J. E.

Article: The benefits of mentoring for female lawyers.

Journal: *Journal of Vocational Behavior,* June 2001, *58,* 366–391.

Related Research: Levenson, H. (1973). Multidimensional locus of control in psychiatric patients. *Journal of Consulting and Clinical Psychology, 41,* 397–404. Kanungo, R. N. (1982). Measurement of job and work involvement. *Journal of Applied Psychology, 67,* 341–349. Watson, D., & Clark, L. A. (1984). Negative affectivity: The disposition to experience aversive emotional states. *Psychological Bulletin, 96,* 465–490.

13443

Test Name: POSITIVE AND NEGATIVE PERFECTIONISM SCALE

Purpose: To measure positive and negative perfectionism.

Number of Items: 40

Format: Item responses are anchored by 1 (*strongly disagree*) and 5 (*strongly agree*). Sample items are presented.

Reliability: Alpha coefficients ranged from .83 to .88.

Author: Besharat, M. A.

Article: Parental perfectionism and children's test anxiety.

Journal: *Psychological Reports,* December 2003, *93,* Part 2, 1049–1055.

Related Research: Terry-Short, L. A., et al. (1995). Positive and negative perfectionism. *Personality and Individual Differences, 18,* 663–668.

13444

Test Name: POSITIVE AND NEGATIVE PERFECTIONISM SCALE—FARSI VERSION

Purpose: To measure perfectionism.

Number of Items: 40

Format: Response scales range from 1 (*strongly disagree*) to 5 (*strongly agree*). All items are presented in English.

Reliability: Alpha coefficients exceeded .86. Test–retest reliabilities (1 month) exceeded .86.

Validity: Correlations with other variables ranged from −.58 to .63.

Author: Besharat, M. A.

Article: Evaluating psychometric properties of Farsi version of the Positive and Negative Perfectionism Scale.

Journal: *Psychological Reports,* August 2005, *97,* 33–42.

Related Research: Terry-Short, L. A., et al. (1995). Positive and negative perfectionism. *Personality and Individual Differences, 18,* 663–668.

13445

Test Name: RAPE EMPATHY SCALE

Purpose: To measure respondent empathy and attributions of responsibility for victim and rapist in a rape situation.

Number of Items: 19

Format: Responses are made on a 7-point scale.

Reliability: Alpha coefficients were .82 and .84.

Author: Jimenez, J. A., and Abreu, J. M.

Article: Race and sex effects on attitudinal perceptions of acquaintance rape.

Journal: *Journal of Counseling Psychology,* April 2003, *50,* 252–256.

Related Research: Deitz, S. R., et al. (1982). Measurement of empathy toward rape victims and rapists. *Journal of Personality and Social Psychology, 43,* 372–384.

13446

Test Name: RATHUS ASSERTIVENESS SCHEDULE

Purpose: To measure assertiveness.

Number of Items: 30

Format: Responses are made on a 6-point scale ranging from −3 (*very uncharacteristic of me, extremely nondescriptive*) to 3 (*very characteristic of me, extremely descriptive*).

Reliability: Alpha coefficients were .77 and .87. Test–retest (8 weeks) reliability was .79.

Validity: Correlations with other variables ranged from −.23 to .70.

Author: Robitschek, C.

Article: Validity of personal growth initiative scale scores with a Mexican American college student population.

Journal: *Journal of Counseling Psychology,* October 2003, *50,* 496–502.

Related Research: Rathus, S. A. (1973). A 30-item schedule for assessing assertive behavior. *Behavior Therapy, 4,* 398–406.

13447

Test Name: RIGHT-WING AUTHORITARIANISM SCALE

Purpose: To measure authoritarianism.

Number of Items: 10

Reliability: Coefficient alpha was .75.

Validity: The correlation with the full scale was .90.

Author: Kemmelmeier, M.

Article: Private self-consciousness as a moderator of the relationship between value orientations and attitudes.

Journal: *The Journal of Social Psychology,* February 2001, *141,* 61–74.

Related Research: Altemeyer, B. (1988). *Enemies of Freedom: Understanding right-wing authoritarianism.* San Francisco: Jossey-Bass.

13448

Test Name: RISK PROPENSITY SCALE

Purpose: To measure risk propensity as a personality trait.

Number of Items: 6

Format: Scales range from 1 (*disagree completely*) to 5 (*agree completely*). Sample items are presented.

Reliability: Coefficient alpha was .68.

Validity: Correlations with other variables ranged from −.16 to .43.

Author: Zhao, H., et al.

Article: The mediating role of self-efficacy in the development of entrepreneurial intentions.

Journal: *Journal of Applied Psychology,* November 2005, *90,* 1265–1272.

13449

Test Name: SCALE OF ETHNOCULTURAL EMPATHY

Purpose: To measure empathy toward people of racial and ethnic backgrounds different from one's own.

Number of Items: 31

Format: Contains four factors: empathic feeling and expression, empathic perspective taking, acceptance of cultural differences, and empathic awareness. All items are presented.

Reliability: Alpha coefficients ranged from .71 to .91.

Validity: Correlations with other variables ranged from .07 to .70.

Author: Wang, Y.-W., et al.

Article: The Scale of Ethnocultural Empathy: Development, validation, and reliability.

Journal: *Journal of Counseling Psychology*, April 2003, *50*, 221–234.

13450

Test Name: SELF-CONSCIOUSNESS SCALE—FRENCH CANADIAN VERSION

Purpose: To assess trait self-consciousness.

Number of Items: 22

Format: Scales range from 0 (*extremely uncharacteristic*) to 3 (*extremely characteristic*). Sample items are presented in English.

Reliability: Alpha coefficients ranged from .66 to .79 across subscales.

Author: Ferrand, C., et al.

Article: Relations between female students' personality traits and reported handicaps to rhythmic gymnastics performance.

Journal: *Psychological Reports*, April 2005, *96*, 361–373.

Related Research: Pelletier, L., & Vallerand, R. J. (1990). Translation and French Canadian validation of

the Revised Self-Consciousness Scale. *Canadian Journal of Behavioral Science, 22,* 191–206.

13451

Test Name: SELF-DYADIC PERSPECTIVE-TAKING SCALE

Purpose: To assess empathy as perspective-taking and awareness.

Number of Items: 13

Format: Five-point scales are used. Sample items are presented.

Reliability: Alpha coefficients ranged from .73 to .87.

Author: Scott, K. L., and Wolfe, D. A.

Article: Readiness to change as a predictor of outcome in batterer treatment.

Journal: *Journal of Consulting and Clinical Psychology*, October 2003, *71*, 879–889.

Related Research: Long, E. J. C. (1990). Measuring dyadic perspective-taking: Two scales for assessing perspective-taking in marriage and similar dyads. *Educational and Psychological Measurement, 50,* 91–103.

13452

Test Name: SHYNESS SCALE

Purpose: To enable parents and teachers to rate children in shyness.

Number of Items: 13

Format: Responses are made on a 7-point scale.

Reliability: Alpha coefficients ranged from .79 to .91.

Validity: Correlations with other variables ranged from −.32 to .35.

Author: Eisenberg, N., et al.

Article: The relation of regulation and negative emotionality in Indonesian children's social functioning.

Journal: *Child Development*, November/December 2001, *72*, 1747–1763.

Related Research: Rothbart, M. K., et al. (1994). Temperament and social behavior in childhood. *Merrill-Palmer Quarterly, 40,* 21–39.

13453

Test Name: SHYNESS SCALE

Purpose: To measure shyness.

Number of Items: 6

Format: A sample item is given.

Reliability: Internal reliability estimate was .75.

Validity: Correlations with other variables ranged from −.38 to .18.

Author: Kacmar, K. M., et al.

Article: Situational and dispositional factors as antecedents of ingratiatory behaviors in organizational settings.

Journal: *Journal of Vocational Behavior*, October 2004, *65*, 309–331.

Related Research: Scheier, M. R., & Carver, C. S. (1985). The Self-Consciousness Scale—A revised version for use with general populations. *Journal of Applied Social Psychology, 15,* 687–699.

13454

Test Name: SHYNESS SCALE—REVISED

Purpose: To assess shyness.

Number of Items: 13

Format: Responses are made on a 5-point scale ranging from 1 (*very uncharacteristic or untrue*) to 5 (*extremely characteristic or true*). Examples are presented.

Reliability: Alpha coefficients are .86 to .90. Test–retest (45 days) reliability was .88.

Validity: Correlations with other variables ranged from −.80 to .30.

Author: Smith, H. M., and Betz, N. E.

Article: An examination of efficacy and esteem pathways to depression in young adulthood.

Journal: *Journal of Counseling Psychology*, October 2002, *49*, 438–448.

Related Research: Cheek, J. M. (1983). The Revised Cheek and Buss Shyness Scale. Unpublished manuscript, Wellesley College, Wellesley, MA.

13455

Test Name: SOCIAL COMPETENCE SCALES

Purpose: To assess dating competence and assertiveness.

Number of Items: 9

Format: Includes two scales: Dating Competence and Assertiveness. Responses are made on a 5-point scale ranging from 1 (*never*) to 5 (*always*). Examples are presented.

Reliability: Alpha coefficients were .84 (dating competence) and .82 (assertiveness).

Validity: Correlation with other variables ranged from −.38 to .21.

Author: Goodyear, R. K., et al.

Article: Pregnant Latina teenagers: Psychosocial and developmental determinants of how they select and perceive the men who father their children.

Journal: *Journal of Counseling Psychology*, April 2002, *49*, 187–201.

Related Research: Levenson, R. W., & Gottman, J. M. (1978). Toward the assessment of social competence. *Journal of Consulting and Clinical Psychology, 46*, 453–462.

13456

Test Name: STATE EMPATHY SCALE

Purpose: To measure empathy.

Number of Items: 6

Format: Scales range from 1 (*strongly disagree*) to 7 (*strongly agree*). All items are presented.

Reliability: Coefficient alpha was .91.

Author: Nezlek, J. B., et al.

Article: Day-to-day variability in empathy as a function of daily events and moods.

Journal: *Journal of Research in Personality*, December 2001, *35*, 401–423.

Related Research: Mehrabian, A. (1996). *Manual for the Balanced Emotional Empathy Scale* (*BEES*). [Available from A. Mehrabian, 1130 Alta Mesa Rd., Monterey, CA 93440.]

13457

Test Name: THE ALMOST PERFECT SCALE—REVISED

Purpose: To measure perfectionism in both its positive and negative dimensions.

Number of Items: 23

Format: All items are presented.

Reliability: Alpha coefficients ranged from .82 to .91 across subscales.

Validity: Correlations between subscales ranged from −.19 to .47. Correlations with other variables ranged from −.44 to .64.

Author: Slaney, R. B., et al.

Article: The Revised Almost Perfect Scale.

Journal: *Measurement and Evaluation in Counseling and Development*, October 2001, *34*, 130–145.

13458

Test Name: TOUGHNESS NORM SCALE

Purpose: To assess adherence to toughness norms.

Number of Items: 8

Format: Responses are made on a 7-point scale ranging from 1 (*strongly disagree*) to 7 (*strongly agree*). A sample item is presented.

Reliability: Alpha coefficients were .74 and .76.

Validity: Correlations with other variables ranged from −.19 to .31.

Author: Bruch, M. A.

Article: Shyness and toughness: Unique and moderated relations with men's emotional inexpression.

Journal: *Journal of Counseling Psychology*, January 2002, *49*, 28–34.

Related Research: Brannon, R. (1976). The male sex role: One culture's blueprint for manhood and what it's done for us lately. In D. David and R. Brannon (Eds.), *The forty-nine percent majority: The male sex role* (pp. 1–48). Reading, MA: Addison-Wesley.

13459

Test Name: TRAIT AFFECT SCALE

Purpose: To measure affective well-being at work.

Number of Items: 15

Format: Responses are made on a 6-point scale ranging from 1 (*never*) to 6 (*all of the time*). Examples are given.

Reliability: Coefficient alpha was .91.

Validity: Correlations with other variables ranged from .77 to .96.

Author: Daniels, K., and Harris, C.

Article: A daily diary study of coping in the context of the job demands-control-support model.

Journal: *Journal of Vocational Behavior*, April 2005, *66*, 219–237.

Related Research: Daniels, K. (2000). Measures of five aspects of affective well-being at work. *Human Relations*, *53*, 275–294.

13460

Test Name: TRAIT EXPRESSIVENESS SCALE

Purpose: To measure trait expressiveness.

Number of Items: 8

Format: Five-point Likert scales are used.

Reliability: Alpha coefficients exceeded .71.

Author: Miller, P. J. E., et al.

Article: Trait expressiveness and marital satisfaction: The role idealization process.

Journal: *Journal of Marriage and Family*, November 2003, *65*, 978–995.

Related Research: Spence, J. T., et al. (1974). The Personal Attributes Questionnaire: A measure of sex-role stereotypes and masculinity–femininity. *JSAS Catalog of Selected Documents in Psychology*, *4*, 127.

13461

Test Name: TRAIT META-MOOD SCALE

Purpose: To measure mood clarity/emotional intelligence.

Number of Items: 10

Format: Scales range from 1 (*strongly disagree*) to 5 (*strongly agree*). Sample items are presented.

Reliability: Coefficient alpha was .77.

Author: Zautra, A., et al.

Article: Examinations of chronic pain and affect relationships: Applications of a dynamic model of affect.

Journal: *Journal of Consulting and Clinical Psychology*, October 2001, *69*, 786–795.

Related Research: Salovey, P., et al. (1995). Emotional attention, clarity, and repair: Exploring emotional intelligence using the Trait Meta-Mood Scale. In J. W. Pennebaker (Ed.), *Emotion, disclosure, and health* (pp. 125–154). Washington, DC: American Psychological Association.

13462

Test Name: TRAIT META-MOOD SCALE—SPANISH VERSION

Purpose: To measure perceived emotional intelligence as an individual's beliefs about their own intelligence.

Number of Items: 24

Format: Item anchors are 1 (*strongly disagree*) and 5 (*strongly agree*).

Reliability: Alpha coefficients ranged from .86 to .90.

Validity: Correlations with other variables ranged from −.33 to .41.

Author: Fernandez-Berrocal, P., et al.

Article: Validity and reliability of the Spanish modified version of the Trait Meta-Mood Scale.

Journal: *Psychological Reports*, June 2004, *94*, Part 1, 751–755.

Related Research: Salovey, P., et al. (1995). Emotional attention, clarity, and repair: Exploring emotional intelligence using the Trait Meta-Mood Scale. In J. W. Pennebaker (Ed.), *Emotion, disclosure, and health*. Washington, DC: American Psychological Association.

13463

Test Name: TRAIT PROCRASTINATION SCALE

Purpose: To measure trait procrastination.

Number of Items: 9

Format: Responses are made on a 5-point Likert scale ranging from 1 (*strongly disagree*) to 5 (*strongly agree*). Sample items are given.

Reliability: Coefficient alpha was .78.

Validity: Correlations with other variables ranged from −.01 to −.58.

Author: van Hooft, E. A. J., et al.

Article: Bridging the gap between intentions and behavior: Implementation intentions, action control, and procrastination.

Journal: *Journal of Vocational Behavior*, April 2005, *66*, 238–256.

Related Research: Lay, C. H. (1986). At last, my research article on procrastination. *Journal of Research in Personality*, *20*, 474–495.

13464

Test Name: TRAIT SPORT CONFIDENCE INVENTORY

Purpose: To measure one's feeling of confidence when competing in sports compared to the most confident athlete one knows.

Number of Items: 13

Format: Responses are made on a 9-point scale ranging from 1 (*low*) to 9 (*high*).

Reliability: Coefficient alpha was .93. Test–retest reliabilities ranged from .83 to .89.

Validity: Correlations with other variables ranged from −.09 to .83.

Author: Cresswell, S., and Hodge, K.

Article: Coping skills: Role of trait sport confidence and trait anxiety.

Journal: *Perceptual and Motor Skills*, April 2004, *98*, 433–438.

Related Research: Vealy, R. S. (1988). Sport confidence and competitive orientation: An addendum on scoring procedures and gender differences. *Journal of Sport and Exercise Psychology, 10*, 471–478.

13465

Test Name: TRAIT UNFORGIVENESS— FORGIVENESS SCALE

Purpose: To assess the disposition to forgive.

Number of Items: 15

Format: Responses are made on a 5-point scale ranging from 1 (*strongly disagree*) to 5 (*strongly agree*).

Reliability: Coefficient alpha was .80.

Validity: Correlations with other variables ranged from −.66 to .73.

Author: Berry, J. W., and Worthington, E. L., Jr.

Article: Forgiveness, relationship quality, stress while imagining relationship events, and physical and mental health.

Journal: *Journal of Counseling Psychology*, October 2001, *48*, 447–455.

13466

Test Name: VERBAL AGGRESSIVENESS SCALE

Purpose: To measure trait verbal aggressiveness.

Number of Items: 20

Format: Items are anchored by 1 (*almost never true*) and 5 (*almost always true*).

Reliability: Coefficient alpha was .92.

Validity: Correlations with other variables ranged from −.59 to .42.

Author: Simmons, D., et al.

Article: Correlations among applicants' communication apprehension, argumentativeness, and verbal aggressiveness in selection interviews.

Journal: *Psychological Reports*, June 2003, *92*, Part 1, 804–808.

Related Research: Infante, D. A., & Wigley, C. J. (1986). Verbal aggressiveness: An interpersonal model and measure. *Communication Monographs, 53*, 61–69.

CHAPTER 22

Values

13467

Test Name: ACCEPTANCE AND ACTION QUESTIONNAIRE

Purpose: To assess people's willingness to accept their undesirable thoughts while acting in a way that is congruent with their values.

Number of Items: 16

Format: Scales range from 1 (*never true*) to 7 (*always true*). All items are presented.

Reliability: Alpha coefficients ranged from .72 to .79.

Validity: Correlations with other variables ranged from –.61 to.26.

Author: Bond, F. U., and Bunce, D.

Article: The role of acceptance and job control in mental health, job satisfaction, and work performance.

Journal: *Journal of Applied Psychology*, December 2003, *88*, 1057–1067.

13468

Test Name: ACT/ACTOR DISCRIMINATION ABILITY TEST

Purpose: To measure children's ability to make moral judgments about an act on the basis of aspects of the act rather than on liking and preconceived ideas about the actor.

Number of Items: 8

Format: Items are cartoons. Children respond on a 7-point scale ranging from –3 to +3.

Reliability: Alpha coefficients were .87 and .89.

Validity: Correlations with other variables ranged from .30 to .55.

Author: Bjorkqvist, K., and Osterman, K.

Article: At what age do children learn to discriminate between act and actor?

Journal: *Perceptual and Motor Skills*, February 2001, *92*, 171–176.

13469

Test Name: ACTIVITY SCALE

Purpose: To measure social justice advocacy.

Number of Items: 24

Format: Cumulative frequency scales are used.

Reliability: Alpha coefficients ranged from .74 to .92.

Validity: Correlations with other variables ranged from –.16 to .51.

Author: Nilsson, J. E., and Schmidt, C. K.

Article: Social justice advocacy among graduate students in counseling: An initial exploration.

Journal: *Journal of College Student Development*, May/June 2005, *46*, 267–279.

Related Research: Kerpelman, L. C. (1969). Student political activism and ideology: Comparative characteristics of activists and nonactivists. *Journal of Counseling Psychology, 16*, 8–13.

13470

Test Name: ANTIEGALITARIANISM SCALE

Purpose: To measure the degree to which an individual supports or rejects social equality.

Number of Items: 4

Format: Scales range from 1 (*strongly agree*) to 7 (*strongly disagree*).

Reliability: Alpha coefficients ranged from .63 to .77.

Author: Sidanius, J., and Peña, Y.

Article: The gendered nature of family structure and group-based antiegalitarianism: A cross-national analysis.

Journal: *The Journal of Social Psychology*, April 2003, *143*, 243–251.

Related Research: Pratto, F., et al. (1994). Social dominance orientation: A personality variable predicting social and political attitudes. *Journal of Personality and Social Psychology, 67*, 741–763.

13471

Test Name: ASIAN VALUES SCALE

Purpose: To assess a person's adherence to Asian cultural values.

Number of Items: 25

Format: Scales range from 1 (*strongly disagree*) to 4 (*strongly agree*). All items are presented.

Reliability: Person separation reliability was .80.

Author: Kim, B. S. K., and Hong, S.

Article: A psychometric revision of the Asian Values Scale using the Rasch model.

Journal: *Measurement and Evaluation in Counseling and Development*, April 2004, *37*, 15–27.

Related Research: Gim Chung, R., et al. (2004). Asian American Multidimensional Acculturation Scale: Development, factor analysis, reliability, and validity. *Cultural Diversity and Ethnic Minority Psychology*, *10*, 66–80.

13472

Test Name: ASIAN VALUES SCALE

Purpose: To measure adherence to Asian values.

Number of Items: 36

Format: Includes six major Asian values: conformity to norms, collectivism, humility, family recognition through achievement, emotional control, and filial piety. Responses are made on a 7-point scale ranging from 1 (*strongly disagree*) to 7 (*strongly agree*).

Reliability: Coefficient alpha was .78. Test–retest (2 weeks) reliability was .83.

Validity: Correlations with other variables ranged from −.34 to .16.

Author: Liao, H.-Y., et al.

Article: A test of Cramer's (1999) help-seeking model and acculturation effects with Asian and Asian American college students.

Journal: *Journal of Counseling Psychology*, July 2005, *52*, 400–411.

Related Research: Kim, B. S. K., et al. (1999). The Asian Values Scale: Development, factor analysis, validation, and reliability.

Journal of Counseling Psychology, *46*, 342–352.

13473

Test Name: AWARENESS OF VALUES—SUBSCALE

Purpose: To assess the degree to which counselors believe they can avoid imposing their biases and values on their clients.

Number of Items: 4

Format: Responses are made on a 5-point scale ranging 1 (*strongly disagree*) to 5 (*strongly agree*). An example is presented.

Reliability: Internal consistency reliability was .55 and .62.

Validity: Correlations with other variables ranged from −.32 to .48.

Author: Mohr, J. J., et al.

Article: Counselors' attitudes regarding bisexuality as predictors of counselors' clinical responses: An analogue study of a female bisexual client.

Journal: *Journal of Counseling Psychology*, April 2001, *48*, 212–222.

Related Research: Larson, L. M., et al. (1992). Development and validation of the counseling self-estimate inventory. *Journal of Counseling Psychology*, *39*, 105–120.

13474

Test Name: BUSINESS ETHICS SCALES

Purpose: To measure business ethics.

Number of Items: 15

Format: Item response scales ranged from 1 (*strongly agree*) to 5 (*strongly disagree*).

Reliability: Alpha coefficients ranged from .71 to .80.

Author: Matsui, T., et al.

Article: Effects of situational conditions on students' views of business ethics.

Journal: *Psychological Reports*, December 2003, *93*, Part 2, 1135–1140.

Related Research: Froelich, K., & Kottke, J. (1991). Measuring individual beliefs about organizational ethics. *Educational and Psychological Measurement*, *51*, 378–383.

13475

Test Name: CHINESE VALUES SCALE

Purpose: To measure traditional Chinese values.

Number of Items: 40

Format: Scales range from 1 (*of very little importance*) to 5 (*of ultimate importance*). Sample items are presented.

Reliability: Alpha coefficients exceeded .85.

Validity: Correlations with other variables ranged from −.09 to .35.

Author: Lu, L., et al.

Article: Cultural values and happiness: An East–West dialogue.

Journal: *The Journal of Social Psychology*, August 2001, *141*, 477–493.

Related Research: The Chinese Cultural Connection. (1987). Chinese values and the search for culture-free dimensions of culture. *Journal of Cross-Cultural Psychology*, *18*, 143–164.

13476

Test Name: COLLECTIVISM SCALE

Purpose: To measure collectivism.

Number of Items: 8

Format: Scales range from 1 (*strongly disagree*) to 9 (*strongly agree*). A sample item is presented.

Reliability: Coefficient alpha was .76.

Author: Killian, T., and Ganong, L. H.

Article: Ideology, context, and obligations to assist older persons.

Journal: *Journal of Marriage and Family*, November 2002, *64*, 1080–1088.

Related Research: Triandis, H. C. (1995). *Individualism and Collectivism*. Boulder, CO: Westview.

13477

Test Name: COMMITMENT TO SOCIAL JUSTICE SCALE

Purpose: To assess sense of personal responsibility to serve others.

Number of Items: 4

Format: Scales range from 0 (*not at all or never true of me*) to 4 (*definitely or always true of me*).

Reliability: Coefficient alpha was .83.

Validity: Correlations with other variables ranged from –.20 to –.19.

Author: Fenzel, L. M.

Article: Multivariate analysis of predictors of heavy episodic drinking and drinking-related problems among college students.

Journal: *Journal of College Student Development*, March/April 2005, *46*, 126–140.

13478

Test Name: CONCEPTS OF NATURE SCALE

Purpose: To measure the positive evaluation of nature and the

rejection of manipulation of human life.

Number of Items: 20

Format: Scales range from 1 (*strongly disagree*) to 5 (*strongly agree*). All items are presented.

Validity: Correlations with other variables ranged from –.20 to .40.

Author: Iwata, O.

Article: Relationships between proenvironmental attitudes and concepts of nature.

Journal: *The Journal of Social Psychology*, February 2001, *141*, 75–83.

Related Research: Iwata, O. (1996). The relationship of personality to environmental vulnerability and proenvironmental orientation. *Progress in Experimental Personality Research*, *14*, 165–203.

13479

Test Name: CULTURAL AND ECONOMIC CONSERVATISM SCALE

Purpose: To measure cultural and economic conservatism.

Number of Items: 24

Format: Items are anchored by response scales ranging from 1 (*certainly disagree*) to 5 (*certainly agree*). Sample items are presented.

Reliability: Alpha coefficients ranged from .70 to .86.

Validity: Correlations with other variables ranged from –.80 to .44.

Author: Duriez, B.

Article: Religiosity and conservatism revisited: Relating a new religiosity measure to the two main conservative political ideologies.

Journal: *Psychological Reports*, April 2003, *92*, 533–539.

Related Research: Duriez, B., et al. (2002). The importance of religiosity and values in predicting political attitudes: Evidence for the continuing importance of religion in Flanders (Belgium). *Mental Health, Religion and Culture*, *5*, 35–54.

13480

Test Name: CULTURAL CONGRUITY SCALE

Purpose: To measure the cultural fit of individual and environmental values.

Number of Items: 13

Format: Scales range from 1 (*strongly disagree*) to 4 (*strongly agree*). Sample items are presented.

Reliability: Reliability coefficients ranged from .76 to .88.

Validity: Correlations with other variables ranged from .12 to .50.

Author: Gloria, A. M., et al.

Article: Relationships of cultural congruity and perceptions of the university environment to help-seeking attitudes by sociorace and gender.

Journal: *Journal of College Student Development*, November/December 2001, *42*, 545–562.

Related Research: Gloria, A. M., & Robinson-Kurpius, S. E. (1996). The validation of the Cultural Congruity Scale and the University Environment Scale with Chicano/a students. *Hispanic Journal of Behavioral Sciences*, *18*, 533–549.

13481

Test Name: DEMOCRATIC VALUES SCALE

Purpose: To assess support for democratic values.

Number of Items: 44.

Format: A yes–no format is used. A sample item is presented.

Reliability: Coefficient alpha was .89.

Validity: Correlations with other variables ranged from −.66 to −.40.

Author: Hastings, B. M., and Shaffer, B. A.

Article: Authoritarianism and sociopolitical attitudes in response to threats of terror.

Journal: *Psychological Reports*, October 2005, *97*, 623–630.

13482

Test Name: DUKE RELIGION INDEX

Purpose: To measure religiosity in terms of organizational and intrinsic dimensions.

Number of Items: 5

Format: Six-point frequency scales for organizational items are anchored by 1 (*never*) and 6 (*several times a week*). Intrinsic items are anchored by 1 (*minimal*) and 6 (*high*).

Reliability: Alphas ranged from .70 to .75.

Author: Storch, E. A., and Storch, J. B.

Article: Organizational, nonorganizational, and intrinsic religiosity and academic dishonesty.

Journal: *Psychological Reports*, April 2001, *88*, 548–552.

Related Research: Koenig, H. G., et al. (1997). Religion index for psychiatric research. *American Journal of Psychiatry, 153*, 885–886.

13483

Test Name: EQUITY SENSITIVITY INSTRUMENT—SPANISH VERSION

Purpose: To measure how closely individuals adhere to the norm of equity.

Number of Items: 5

Format: Forced-choice format. Respondents allocate 10 points between a benevolent and an entitled response. All items are presented in Spanish.

Reliability: Coefficient alpha was .86.

Validity: Interitem correlations ranged from .36 to .71.

Author: Mintu-Wimsatt, A.

Article: King and Miles' Equity Sensitivity Instrument: A cross-cultural validation.

Journal: *Psychological Reports*, February 2003, *92*, 23–26.

Related Research: King, W. C., & Miles, E. W. (1994). The measurement of equity sensitivity. *Journal of Occupational and Organizational Psychology, 67*, 133–142.

13484

Test Name: ETHICS POSITION QUESTIONNAIRE

Purpose: To measure idealism and relativism.

Number of Items: 19

Format: Scales range from 1 (*strongly disagree*) to 7 (*strongly agree*). Sample items are presented.

Reliability: Alpha coefficients ranged from .75 to .79.

Validity: Correlations with other variables ranged from −.40 to .32.

Author: Wilson, M. S.

Article: Social dominance and ethical ideology: The end justifies the means?

Journal: *The Journal of Social Psychology*, October 2003, *143*, 549–558.

Related Research: Forsyth, D. R. (1980). A taxonomy of ethical ideologies. *Journal of Personality and Social Psychology, 39*, 175–184.

13485

Test Name: ETHICS POSITION QUOTIENT

Purpose: To measure ethical values with regard to idealism and relativism.

Number of Items: 20

Format: Response scales range from 1 (*strongly disagree*) to 7 (*strongly agree*).

Reliability: Alpha coefficients ranged from .81 to .85.

Author: Venable, B. T., and Wagner, J.

Article: An exploratory study of ethical values in nonprofit fundraising: Survey of fundraising executives.

Journal: *Psychological Reports*, October 2005, *97*, 527–537.

Related Research: Forsyth, D. R. (1980). A taxonomy of ethical ideologies. *Journal of Personality and Social Psychology, 39*, 175–184.

13486

Test Name: EUROPEAN AMERICAN VALUES SCALE FOR ASIAN AMERICANS—REVISED

Purpose: To measure adherence to European American cultural values.

Number of Items: 25

Format: Responses are made on a 4-point scale ranging from 1 (*strongly disagree*) to 4 (*strongly agree*). Examples are given.

Reliability: Coefficient alpha was .63.

Validity: Correlations with other variables ranged from −.09 to .45.

Author: Kim, B. S. K., and Omizo, M. M.

Article: Asian and European American cultural values, collective self-esteem, acculturative stress, cognitive flexibility, and general self-efficacy among Asian American college students.

Journal: *Journal of Counseling Psychology*, July 2005, *52*, 412–419.

Related Research: Hong, S., et al. (2005). A psychometric revision of the European American Values Scale for Asian Americans using the Rasch model. *Measurement and Evaluation in Counseling and Development*, *37*, 194–207.

13487

Test Name: EXPRESSIONS OF SPIRITUALITY INVENTORY

Purpose: To measure spirituality in terms of cognitive orientation, experiential states, existential well-being, paranormal beliefs, and religiousness.

Number of Items: 98

Format: Five-point response scales are anchored by 0 (*strongly disagree*) and 4 (*strongly agree*).

Reliability: Alpha coefficients ranged from .85 to .97 across subscales.

Validity: Correlations with partial epileptic-like signs ranged from −.16 to .41.

Author: MacDonald, D. A., and Holland, D.

Article: Spirituality and complex partial epileptic-like signs.

Journal: *Psychological Reports*, December 2002, *91*, Part 1, 785–792.

Related Research: MacDonald, D. A. (2000). Spirituality: Description, measurement, and relation to the Five-Factor Model of personality. *Journal of Personality*, *68*, 153–197.

13488

Test Name: FAITH IN HUMANITY SCALE

Purpose: To measure faith in humanity.

Number of Items: 5

Format: Responses are made on a 6-point scale ranging from 1 (*strongly disagree*) to 6 (*strongly agree*). Examples are given.

Reliability: Alpha coefficients were .73 and .86.

Validity: Correlations with other variables ranged from −.15 to .32.

Author: Linnehan, F., et al.

Article: African American students' early trust beliefs in work-based mentors.

Journal: *Journal of Vocational Behavior*, June 2005, *66*, 501–515.

Related Research: McKnight, D. H., et al. (1998). Initial trust formation in new organizational relationships. *Academy of Management Review*, *22*, 473–490.

13489

Test Name: FAITH MATURITY SCALE

Purpose: To measure Protestant personal religiosity.

Number of Items: 12

Format: All items are presented.

Reliability: Coefficient alpha was .93. Subscale alphas ranged from .77 to .88.

Validity: Correlations with an orthodoxy scale ranged from .19 to .39.

Author: Ji, C.-H. C.

Article: Faith maturity and doctrinal orthodoxy: A validity study of the Faith Maturity Scale.

Journal: *Psychological Reports*, December 2004, *95*, Part 1, 993–998.

Related Research: Benson, P. L., et al. (1993). The Faith Maturity Scale: Conceptualization, measurement, and empirical validation. *Research in the Social Scientific Study of Religion*, *5*, 1–26.

13490

Test Name: FAMILISM SCALE

Purpose: To assess the degree to which families should be valued.

Number of Items: 15

Format: Four-point agreement scales are used. A sample item is presented.

Reliability: Coefficient alpha was .80.

Author: Killian, T., and Ganong, L. H.

Article: Ideology, context, and obligations to assist older persons.

Journal: *Journal of Marriage and Family*, November 2002, *64*, 1080–1088.

Related Research: Heller, P. L. (1976). Familism Scale: Revalidation and revision. *Journal of Marriage and Family*, *38*, 423–429.

13491

Test Name: GENERATIVITY SCALE

Purpose: To measure adult concern for and commitment to the well-being of youth and future generations.

Number of Items: 20.

Format: Scales range from 0 (*Statement never applies to you*) to 3 (*Statement very often or nearly always applies to you*). Sample items are presented.

Reliability: Coefficient alpha was .83.

Validity: Correlations with other variables ranged from .13 to .38.

Author: Hart, H. M., et al.

Article: Generativity and social involvement among African Americans and White adults.

Journal: *Journal of Research in Personality*, June 2001, *35*, 208–230.

Related Research: McAdams, D. P., et al. (1998). The anatomy of generativity. In D. P. McAdams & E. de St. Aubin (Eds.), *Generativity and adult development: How and why we care for the next generation* (pp. 7–43). Washington, DC: American Psychological Association.

13492

Test Name: GOD-IMAGE SCALE

Purpose: To measure presence, challenge, and acceptance of God.

Number of Items: 36

Format: Response scales are anchored by 1 (*strongly agree*) and 4 (*strongly disagree*). Sample items are presented.

Reliability: Alpha coefficients ranged from .86 to .94 across subscales.

Validity: Correlations with other variables ranged from –.25 to .55.

Author: Buchko, K. J., and Witzig, T. F., Jr.

Article: Relationship between God-image and religious behaviors.

Journal: *Psychological Reports*, December 2003, *93*, Part 2, 1141–1148.

Related Research: Lawrence, R. T. (1997). Measuring the image of God: The God Image Inventory and the God-Image Scale. *Journal of Psychology and Theology, 25*, 214–226.

13493

Test Name: HEALTH VALUE SCALE

Purpose: To measure the value participants place on their health.

Number of Items: 4

Format: Responses are made on a 7-point Likert scale ranging from 1 (*strongly disagree*) to 7 (*strongly agree*). A sample item is presented.

Reliability: Alpha coefficients were .62 and .67. Test–retest (6 weeks) was .78.

Validity: Correlations with other variables ranged from –.14 to .08.

Author: Waldrop, D., et al.

Article: Self-efficacy, optimism, health compliance, and recovery from orthopedic surgery.

Journal: *Journal of Counseling Psychology*, April 2001, *48*, 233–238.

Related Research: Lau, R. R., et al. (1986). Health as a value: Methodological and theoretical considerations. *Health Psychology, 5*, 25–43.

13494

Test Name: HORIZONTAL INDIVIDUALISM SCALE

Purpose: To measure individualism.

Number of Items: 7

Format: Scales range from 1 (*strongly disagree*) to 9 (*strongly agree*). A sample item is presented.

Reliability: Coefficient alpha was .60.

Author: Killian, T., and Ganong, L. H.

Article: Ideology, context, and obligations to assist older persons.

Journal: *Journal of Marriage and Family*, November 2002, *64*, 1080–1088.

Related Research: Triandis, H. C. (1995). *Individualism and Collectivism*. Boulder, CO: Westview.

13495

Test Name: INDIVIDUALISM–COLLECTIVISM SCALE

Purpose: To measure the cultural orientations of individualism and collectivism.

Number of Items: 32

Format: Scales range from 1 (*strongly disagree*) to 10 (*strongly agree*).

Reliability: Alpha coefficients ranged from .67 to .78.

Author: Le, T. N., and Levenson, M. R.

Article: Wisdom as self-transcendence: What's love (& individualism) got to do with it?

Journal: *Journal of Research in Personality*, August 2005, *39*, 443–457.

Related Research: Singelis, T. A., et al. (1995). Horizontal and vertical dimensions of individualism and collectivism: A theoretical and measurement refinement. *Cross-Cultural Research, 29*, 240–275.

13496

Test Name: INDIVIDUALISM–COLLECTIVISM SCALE

Purpose: To measure individualist and collectivist tendencies.

Number of Items: 21

Reliability: Alpha coefficients were .68 (individualism) and .72 (collectivism).

Validity: The correlation between collectivism and individualism was –.06 (orthogonal dimensions).

Author: Kemmelmeier, M.

Article: Private self-consciousness as a moderator of the relationship between value orientations and attitudes.

Journal: *The Journal of Social Psychology*, February 2001, *141*, 61–74.

Related Research: Oyserman, D., (1993). The lens of personhood:

Viewing the self, others and conflict in a multicultural society. *Journal of Personality and Social Psychology, 65,* 993–1009.

13497

Test Name: INDIVIDUALISM–COLLECTIVISM SCALE

Purpose: To measure individualism and collectivism.

Number of Items: 29

Format: Scales are anchored by 1 (*very strongly disagree*) and 10 (*very strongly agree*). Sample items are presented.

Reliability: Alpha coefficients ranged from .74 to .82.

Author: Santiago, J. H., and Tarantino, S. J.

Article: Individualism and collectivism: Cultural orientation in locus of control and moral attribution under conditions of social change.

Journal: *Psychological Reports,* December 2002, *91,* Part 2, 1155–1168.

Related Research: Singelis, T. M., et al. (1995). Horizontal and vertical dimensions of individualism and collectivism: A theoretical and measurement refinement. *Cross-Cultural Research, 29,* 240–275.

13498

Test Name: INDIVIDUALISM/COLLECTIVISM SCALE

Purpose: To measure individualism–collectivism.

Number of Items: 16

Format: Includes four dimensions: Vertical and Horizontal Individualism and Vertical and Horizontal Collectivism. Responses are made on a 0 to 10 scale. Examples are given.

Reliability: Alpha coefficients ranged from .57 to .80.

Author: Klassen, R. M.

Article: A cross-cultural investigation of the efficacy beliefs of South Asian immigrant and Anglo Canadian nonimmigrant early adolescents.

Journal: *Journal of Educational Psychology,* December 2004, *96,* 731–742.

Related Research: Triandis, H. C., & Gelfand, M. J. (1998). Converging measurement of horizontal and vertical individualism and collectivism. *Journal of Personality and Social Psychology, 74,* 118–128.

13499

Test Name: INDIVIDUALISM–COLLECTIVISM SCALE—SPANISH VERSION

Purpose: To measure the horizontal and vertical dimensions of individualism and collectivism.

Number of Items: 32

Format: Scales ranged from 1 (*strongly disagree*) to 9 (*strongly agree*). Sample items are presented in English.

Reliability: Alpha coefficients ranged from .67 to .78 across factorial models.

Validity: Correlations with other variables ranged from –.18 to .40.

Author: Gouveia, V. V., et al.

Article: The horizontal and vertical attributes of individualism and collectivism in a Spanish population.

Journal: *The Journal of Social Psychology,* February 2003, *143,* 43–63.

Related Research: Singelis, T. M., et al. (1995). Horizontal and vertical dimensions of individualism and collectivism: A theoretical and

measurement refinement. *Cross-Cultural Research, 29,* 240–275.

13500

Test Name: INSPIRIT—REVISED

Purpose: To provide an index of spiritual experience.

Number of Items: 7

Reliability: Test–retest (10 week) reliability was .90.

Validity: Correlations with other variables ranged form –.32 to .65.

Author: Rose, E. M., et al.

Article: Spiritual issues in counseling: Clients' beliefs and preferences.

Journal: *Journal of Counseling Psychology,* January 2001, *48,* 61–71.

Related Research: Kass, J. D., et al. (1991). Health outcomes and a new index of spiritual experience. *Journal of the Scientific Study of Religion, 30,* 203–211.

13501

Test Name: INTERNALIZATION SCALE

Purpose: To assess how much an individual accepts and internalizes societal standards of beauty.

Number of Items: 8

Format: Responses are made on a 5-point Likert-type scale ranging from 1 (*completely disagree*) to 5 (*completely agree*). Examples are given.

Reliability: Alpha coefficients were .85 and .88.

Validity: Correlations with other variables ranged from .25 to .58.

Author: Moradi, B., et al.

Article: Roles of sexual objectification experiences and internalization of standards of beauty in eating disorder symptomatology: A test and extension of objectification theory.

Journal: *Journal of Counseling Psychology*, July 2005, 52, 420–428.

Related Research: Heinberg, L. J., et al. (1995). Development and validation of the Sociocultural Attitudes Towards Appearance Questionnaire. *International Journal of Eating Disorders*, 17, 81–89.

13502

Test Name: INTRINSIC RELIGIOSITY SCALE

Purpose: To assess internal commitment to personal religious beliefs.

Number of Items: 3

Format: Five-point scales are anchored by 1 (*definitely not true*) and 5 (*definitely true*). A sample item is presented.

Reliability: Coefficient alpha was .90.

Validity: Correlations with other variables ranged from –.22 to –.16.

Author: Storch, E. A., and Storch, J. B.

Article: Intrinsic religiosity and aggression in a sample of intercollegiate athletes.

Journal: *Psychological Reports*, December 2002, 91, Part 2, 1041–1042.

Related Research: Koenig, H. G., et al. (1997). Religion index for psychiatric research. *American Journal of Psychiatry*, 153, 885–886.

13503

Test Name: INTRINSIC RELIGIOUS MOTIVATION SCALE

Purpose: To measure intrinsic religiousness.

Number of Items: 10

Format: Scales range from 1 (*strongly disagree*) to 4 (*strongly agree*).

Reliability: Coefficient alpha was .87.

Author: Rye, M. S., et al.

Article: Can group interventions facilitate forgiveness of an ex-spouse? A randomized clinical trial.

Journal: *Journal of Consulting and Clinical Psychology*, October 2005, 73, 880–892.

Related Research: Hoge, D. R. (1972). A validated intrinsic religious motivation scale. *Journal for the Scientific Study of Religion*, 11, 369–376.

13504

Test Name: INTRINSIC RELIGIOUS ORIENTATION SUBSCALE

Purpose: To measure intrinsic religious orientation.

Number of Items: 8

Format: Responses are made on a 5-point scale. Examples are given.

Reliability: Coefficient alpha was .77.

Validity: Correlations with other variables ranged from –.07 to .76 (*n* = 583).

Author: Lease, S. H., et al.

Article: Affirming faith experiences and psychological health for Caucasian lesbian, gay, and bisexual individuals.

Journal: *Journal of Counseling Psychology*, July 2005, 52, 378–388.

Related Research: Gorsuch, R., & McPherson, S. E. (1989). Intrinsic/extrinsic measurement: I/E–Revised and single-item scales. *Journal for the Scientific Study of Religion, 28*, 348–354.

13505

Test Name: INTRINSIC VALUE OF THE WORK

Purpose: To measure intrinsic value of work.

Number of Items: 4

Format: All items are presented. Likert format is used.

Reliability: Coefficient alpha was .87.

Validity: Correlations with other variables ranged from –.29 to .57.

Author: Clark, S. C.

Article: Employees' sense of community, sense of control, and work/family conflict in Native American organizations

Journal: *Journal of Vocational Behavior*, August 2002, *61*, 92–108

13506

Test Name: INVASION OF PRIVACY SCALE

Purpose: To measure invasion of privacy.

Number of Items: 13

Format: Scales ranged from 1 (*strongly disagree*) to 5 (*strongly agree*). A sample item is presented.

Reliability: Coefficient alpha was .96.

Validity: Correlations with other variables ranged from –.56 to –.01.

Author: Alge, B. J.

Article: Effects of computer surveillance on perceptions of privacy and procedural justice.

Journal: *Journal of Applied Psychology*, August 2001, *86*, 797–804.

Related Research: Eddy, E. R., et al. (1999). The effects of information management policies on reactions to human resource information systems: An integration of privacy and procedural justice perspectives. *Personnel Psychology, 52,* 335–358.

13507

Test Name: JUSTICE ORIENTATION SCALE

Purpose: To measure to what extent individuals internalize justice as a moral virtue and the extent to which they are cognizant of fairness issues around them.

Number of Items: 16

Format: Scales range from 1 (*strongly disagree*) to 7 (*strongly agree*). A sample item is presented.

Reliability: Coefficient alpha was .85.

Validity: Correlations with other variables ranged from –.04 to .14.

Author: Liao, H., and Rupp, D. E.

Article: The impact of justice climate and justice orientation on work outcomes: A cross-level multifoci framework.

Journal: *Journal of Applied Psychology,* March 2005, *90,* 242–256.

Related Research: Rupp, D. E., et al. (2003, April). *Justice orientation and its measurement: Extending the deontological model.* Paper presented at the 18th Annual Conference of the Society for Industrial and Organizational Psychology, Orlando, FL.

13508

Test Name: MEASURE OF SPIRITUALITY

Purpose: To measure spiritual beliefs and actions.

Number of Items: 58

Format: Scales range from 1 (*strongly disagree*) to 5 (*strongly agree*). Sample items are presented.

Reliability: Alpha coefficients ranged from .71 to .95.

Validity: Correlations with other variables ranged from –.29 to .83.

Author: Berkel, L. A., et al.

Article: Gender role attitudes, religion, and spirituality as predictors of domestic violence attitudes in White college students.

Journal: *Journal of College Student Development,* March/April 2004, *45,* 119–133.

Related Research: Armstrong, T. D. (1996). Exploring spirituality: The development of the Armstrong Measure of Spirituality. In R. Jones (Ed.), *Handbook of tests and measurements for Black populations* (pp. 105–115). Hampton, VA: Cobb & Henry.

13509

Test Name: MILITARY PROFESSIONAL VALUES SCALE

Purpose: To measure military values: military dedication, integrity, job commitment, and military bearing.

Number of Items: 15

Format: Item anchors ranged from 0 (*not at all important*) to 6 (*extremely important*). All items are presented.

Reliability: Alpha coefficients ranged from .83 to .88 across subscales.

Validity: Correlations with other variables ranged from –.12 to .38.

Author: Schumm, W. R., et al.

Article: Dimensionality of military professional values items: An exploratory factor analysis of data from the Spring 1996 sample of military personnel.

Journal: *Psychological Reports,* June 2003, *92,* Part 1, 831–841.

13510

Test Name: MIVILLE-GUZMAN UNIVERSALITY–DIVERSITY SCALE

Purpose: To assess a universal-diverse orientation.

Number of Items: 15

Format: Includes three subscales: Diversity of Contact, Relativistic Appreciation, and Comfort with Differences. Responses are made on a 7-point Likert-type scale ranging from 1 (*strongly disagree*) to 7 (*strongly agree*).

Reliability: Internal consistency and test–retest reliabilities ranged from .75 to .95.

Validity: Correlations with other variables ranged from .05 to .70.

Author: Wang, Y.-W., et al.

Article: The Scale of Ethnocultural Empathy: Development, validation, and reliability.

Journal: *Journal of Counseling Psychology,* April 2003, *50,* 221–234.

Related Research: Miville, M. L., et al (1999). Appreciating similarities and valuing differences: The Miville-Guzman Universality–Diversity Scale. *Journal of Counseling Psychology, 46,* 291–307.

13511

Test Name: MONEY SUCCESS SCALE

Purpose: To measure the extent to which individuals perceive money as a symbol of success.

Number of Items: 8

Format: Responses are made on a 6-point Likert scale ranging from 1 (*strongly disagree*) to 6 (*strongly agree*).

Reliability: Coefficient alpha was .85.

Validity: Correlations with other variables ranged from −.07 to .25.

Author: Dunford, B., et al.

Article: Out-of-the-money: The impact of underwater stock options on executive job search.

Journal: *Personnel Psychology,* Spring 2005, *58,* 67–101.

Related Research: Tang, D., & Singh, G. (2003). Executive compensation: A comparison of the United States and Japan. *Compensation and Benefits Review, 35,* 68–78.

13512

Test Name: MORAL INTENSITY SCALE

Purpose: To measure the dimensions of moral intensity in marketing decisions.

Number of Items: 6

Format: Seven-point rating scales are anchored by 1 (*completely disagree*) and 7 (*completely agree*). All items are presented.

Reliability: Alpha was .90.

Author: Valentine, S., and Silver, L.

Article: Assessing the dimensionality of the Singhapakdi, Vitell, and Kraft measure of moral intensity.

Journal: *Psychological Reports,* February 2001, *88,* 291–294.

Related Research: Singhapakdi, A., et al. (1996). Moral intensity and ethical decision-making of marketing professionals. *Journal of Business Research, 36,* 245–255.

13513

Test Name: MULTIDIMENSIONAL MEASURE OF RELIGIOUS INVOLVEMENT FOR AFRICAN AMERICANS

Purpose: To measure religious involvement.

Number of Items: 12

Format: Includes three dimensions of religiosity: Organizational, Nonorganizational, and Subjective. Responses are made on 4- and 5-point scales.

Reliability: Alpha coefficients ranged from .59 to .85.

Validity: Correlations with other variables ranged from −.05 to .43 (*N* = 86).

Author: Frazier, C., et al.

Article: A multidimensional look at religious involvement and psychological well-being among urban elderly African Americans.

Journal: *Journal of Counseling Psychology,* October 2005, *52,* 583–590.

Related Research: Chatters, L. M., et al. (1992). Antecedents and dimensions of religious involvement among older Black adults. *Journal of Gerontology: Social Sciences, 47,* S269–S278.

13514

Test Name: MULTIDIMENSIONAL WORK ETHIC PROFILE

Purpose: To measure one's work ethic.

Number of Items: 65

Format: Includes seven subscales: Leisure, Centrality of Work, Wasted Time, Hard Work, Self-Reliance, Delay of Gratification, and Morality/Ethics. Responses are made on a 5-point Likert scale ranging from 1 (*strongly disagree*) to 5 (*strongly agree*). Sample items are presented.

Reliability: Alpha coefficients ranged from .78 to .92.

Author: Pogson, C. E., et al.

Article: Differences in self-reported work ethic across three career stages.

Journal: *Journal of Vocational Behavior,* February 2003, *62,* 189–201.

Related Research: Miller, M. J., et al. (2002). The meaning and measurement of work ethic: Construction and initial validation of a multidimensional inventory [Monograph]. *Journal of Vocational Behavior, 60,* 451–489.

13515

Test Name: PADUA SCALE OF MORAL JUDGMENT

Purpose: To measure moral judgment.

Number of Items: 28

Format: Four-point scales are anchored by 1 (*not at all*) and 4 (*very much*). Sample items are presented in English.

Reliability: Coefficient alpha was .81. Test–retest reliability was .71 (4 weeks).

Validity: The correlation with a moral reflection measure was .35.

Author: Comunian, A. L.

Article: Construction of a scale for measuring development of moral judgment.

Journal: *Psychological Reports,* April 2004, *94,* 613–618.

13516

Test Name: PARENTS' VALUES, BELIEFS, AND EXPECTATIONS SCALE

Purpose: To measure mothers' and fathers' values and beliefs in the academic domain.

Number of Items: 9

Format: Responses are made on 5-point and 7-point scales. All items are presented.

Reliability: Alpha coefficients ranged from .73 to .90.

Author: Jodl, K. M., et al.

Article: Parents' roles in shaping early adolescents' occupational aspirations.

Journal: *Child Development*, July/August 2001, 72, 1247–1265.

Related Research: Eccles, J. S., et al. (1989). Self-concepts, domain values, and self-esteem: Relations and changes at early adolescence. *Journal of Personality*, 57, 283–310.

13517

Test Name: PERSONAL BELIEF IN A JUST WORLD SCALE

Purpose: To measure the personal justice motive.

Number of Items: 7

Reliability: Coefficient alpha was .86.

Validity: Correlations with other variables ranged from –.34 to .46.

Author: Otto, K., and Dalbert, C.

Article: Belief in a just world and its functions for young prisoners.

Journal: *Journal of Research in Personality*, December 2005, 39, 559–573.

Related Research: Dalbert, C. (1999). The world is more just for me than generally: About the personal belief in a just world scale's validity. *Social Justice Research*, 12, 79–98.

13518

Test Name: PERSONAL FAITH INVOLVEMENT SCALE

Purpose: To assess the extent to which prayer and faith in God is incorporated into one's personal life in times of need.

Number of Items: 6

Format: Scales range from 0 (*not at all or never true of me*) to 4 (*definitely or always true of me*).

Reliability: Coefficient alpha was .93.

Validity: Correlations with other variables ranged from –.19 to –.14.

Author: Fenzel, L. M.

Article: Multivariate analysis of predictors of heavy episodic drinking and drinking-related problems among college students.

Journal: *Journal of College Student Development*, March/April 2005, 46, 126–140.

Related Research: Benson, P. L., et al. (1993). The Faith Maturity Scale. *Research in the Social Scientific Study of Religion*, 5, 1–26.

13519

Test Name: PERSONAL VALUES SCALE

Purpose: To assess values.

Number of Items: 64

Format: Scales range from 1 (*strongly disagree*) to 5 (*strongly agree*).

Reliability: Alpha coefficients ranged from .57 to .81.

Author: Giberson, T. R., et al.

Article: Embedding leader characteristics: An examination of homogeneity of personality and values in organizations.

Journal: *Journal of Applied Psychology*, September 2005, 90, 1002–1010.

Related Research: Smith, D. B., et al. (2002). *Development and validation of a new measure of personal values* [Working paper]. Houston, TX: Rice University.

13520

Test Name: PORTRAIT VALUES QUESTIONNAIRE—ADAPTED

Purpose: To measure basic values.

Number of Items: 30

Format: Responses are made on a 6-point scale ranging from 1 (*not like me at all*) to 6 (*very much like me*). Examples are given.

Validity: Correlations with other variables ranged from .45 to .78.

Author: Lindeman, M., and Verkasalo, M.

Article: Measuring values with the Short Schwartz's Value Survey.

Journal: *Journal of Personality Assessment*, October 2005, 85, 170–178.

Related Research: Schwartz, S., et al. (2001). Extending the cross-cultural validity of the theory of basic human values with a different method of measurement. *Journal of Cross-Cultural Psychology*, 32, 519–542.

13521

Test Name: POST CRITICAL BELIEF SCALE

Purpose: To measure exclusion versus inclusion of transcendence and literal versus symbolic interpretation of religious expression.

Number of Items: 33

Format: Seven-point scales are anchored by *certainly disagree* and *certainly agree*.

Validity: Correlations with other variables ranged from –.80 to .44.

Author: Duriez, B.

Article: Religiosity and conservatism revisited: Relating a new religiosity measure to the two main conservative political ideologies.

Journal: *Psychological Reports*, April 2003, 92, 533–539.

Related Research: Fontaine, J. R. J., et al. (2003). The internal structure of the Post-Critical Belief Scale. *Personality and Individual Differences*, 35, 501–518.

13522

Test Name: PROSOCIAL REASONING OBJECTIVE MEASURE—ADAPTED

Purpose: To measure adolescents' level of prosocial moral reasoning.

Number of Items: 36

Format: Consists of six stories, each of which includes six items.

Reliability: Alpha coefficients ranged from .59 to .84.

Author: Eisenberg, N., et al.

Article: Brazilian adolescents' prosocial moral judgment and behavior: Relations to sympathy, perspective taking, gender-role orientation, and demographic characteristics.

Journal: *Child Development*, March/April 2001, *72*, 518–534.

Related Research: Carlo, G., et al. (1992). An objective measure of adolescents' prosocial moral reasoning. *Journal of Research on Adolescence, 2,* 331–349.

13523

Test Name: PROTESTANT ETHIC SCALE—ADAPTED

Purpose: To measure work ethic.

Number of Items: 4

Format: All items are presented.

Reliability: Coefficient alpha was .78.

Validity: Correlations with other variables ranged from −.13 to .24.

Author: Adams, G., and Rau, B.

Article: Job seeking among retirees seeking bridge employment.

Journal: *Personnel Psychology*, Autumn 2004, *57*, 719–744.

Related Research: Blood, M. R. (1969). Work values and job satisfaction. *Journal of Applied Psychology, 53,* 456–459.

13524

Test Name: PROTESTANT WORK ETHIC

Purpose: To measure belief in the importance of hard work and frugality.

Number of Items: 19

Format: Responses are made on a 7-point scale. Examples are given.

Reliability: Coefficient alpha was .76.

Validity: Correlations with other variables ranged from −.18 to .27.

Author: Goulet, L. R., and Singh, P.

Article: Career commitment: A reexamination and an extension.

Journal: *Journal of Vocational Behavior*, August 2002, *61*, 73–91.

Related Research: Mirels, H., & Garrett, J. (1971). Protestant ethic as a personality variable. *Journal of Consulting and Clinical Psychology, 36,* 40–44.

13525

Test Name: RELIGIOSITY SCALE

Purpose: To measure religious beliefs and practices of college students.

Number of Items: 8

Format: Various 5-point scales are used. All items are presented.

Reliability: Alpha coefficients exceeded .87.

Author: Buchko, K. J.

Article: Religious beliefs and practices of college women as compared to college men.

Journal: *Journal of College Student Development*, January/February 2004, *45*, 89–96.

Related Research: Rohrbaugh, J., & Jessor, R. (1975). Religiosity in youth: A personal control against deviant behavior. *Journal of Personality, 43,* 136–155.

13526

Test Name: RELIGIOSITY SCALE

Purpose: To measure religiosity.

Number of Items: 3

Format: All items are presented. Three different frequency scales are used.

Reliability: Cronbach's alpha was .74. Split-half reliability was .72.

Author: Peltzer, K., et al.

Article: Sociodemographic factors, religiosity, academic performance, and substance abuse among first-year university students in South Africa.

Journal: *Psychological Reports*, August 2002, *91*, 105–113.

Related Research: Pargament, K. I., et al. (1988). Religion and the problem-solving process: Three styles of coping. *Journal for the Scientific Study of Religion, 27,* 90–104.

13527

Test Name: RELIGIOSITY SCALE

Purpose: To measure religiosity.

Number of Items: 4

Format: Various response categories are used. All items and scales are presented.

Reliability: Interitem correlations ranged from .45 to .62.

Validity: Correlations with other variables ranged from −.33 to .18.

Author: Schieman, S., et al.

Article: Religiosity, socioeconomic status, and the sense of mastery.

Journal: *Social Psychology Quarterly*, September 2003, *66*, 202–221.

13528

Test Name: RELIGIOUS COMMITMENT INVENTORY—17

Purpose: To measure religious commitment.

Number of Items: 17

Reliability: Coefficient alpha was .94. Test–retest (3 weeks) reliability coefficient was .87 ($n = 119$).

Validity: Correlations with other variables ranged from –.13 to .96.

Author: Worthington, E. L., Jr., et al.

Article: The Religious Commitment Inventory–10: Development, refinement, and validation of a brief scale for research and counseling.

Journal: *Journal of Counseling Psychology*, January 2003, *50*, 84–96.

Related Research: McCullough, M. E., et al. (1997). Gender in the context of supportive and challenging religious counseling interventions. *Journal of Counseling Psychology, 44*, 80–88.

13529

Test Name: RELIGIOUS ORIENTATION SCALE

Purpose: To measure extrinsic and intrinsic religious orientations.

Number of Items: 17

Reliability: Alpha coefficients ranged from .70 to .87 across subscales.

Validity: Correlations with other variables ranged from –.15 to .83.

Author: Berkel, L. A., et al.

Article: Gender role attitudes, religion, and spirituality as predictors of domestic violence attitudes in White college students.

Journal: *Journal of College Student Development*, March/April 2004, *45*, 119–133.

Related Research: Allport, G., & Ross, J. M. (1967). Personal religious orientation and prejudice. *Journal of Personality and Social Psychology, 5*, 432–433.

13530

Test Name: RELIGIOUSNESS SCALE

Purpose: To assess religiousness.

Number of Items: 16

Format: Includes four sections: Organizational Religiousness, Private Practices Religiousness, Daily Spiritual Experience Beliefs, and Self-Ranked Religiousness. Responses are made on 4- and 5-point scales.

Reliability: Alpha coefficients ranged from .65 to .88.

Validity: Correlations with other variables ranged from –.12 to .27.

Author: Pearce, M. J., et al.

Article: The protective effects of religiousness and parent involvement on the development of conduct problems among youth exposed to violence.

Journal: *Child Development*, November/December 2003, *74*, 1682–1696.

13531

Test Name: ROLE VALUE INVENTORY

Purpose: To assess career and family values.

Number of Items: 19

Format: Includes two subscales: Career Value and Family Value. Responses are made on a 7-point scale ranging from 1 (*strongly agree*) to 7 (*strongly disagree*). Sample items are given.

Reliability: Test–retest (2 weeks) reliabilities were .84 and .92. Alpha coefficients ranged from .58 to .80.

Author: Meinster, M. O., and Rose, K. C.

Article: Longitudinal influences of educational aspirations and romantic relationships on

adolescent women's vocational interests.

Journal: *Journal of Vocational Behavior*, June 2001, *58*, 313–327.

Related Research: Farmer, H. S. (1983). Career and homemaking plans for high school youth. *Journal of Counseling Psychology, 30*, 40–45.

13532

Test Name: SANTA CLARA STRENGTH OF RELIGIOUS FAITH QUESTIONNAIRE

Purpose: To measure strength of faith.

Number of Items: 10

Format: Responses are made on a 5-point scale ranging from 1 (*strongly disagree*) to 5 (*strongly agree*).

Reliability: Alpha coefficients were .89 and .95 ($n = 583$). Split-half reliability was .92.

Author: Lease, S. H., et al.

Article: Affirming faith experiences and psychological health for Caucasian lesbian, gay, and bisexual individuals.

Journal: *Journal of Counseling Psychology*, July 2005, *52*, 378–388.

Related Research: Plante, T. G., & Boccaccini, M. (1997). Reliability and validity of the Santa Clara Strength of Religious Faith Questionnaire. *Pastoral Psychology, 45*, 429–437.

13533

Test Name: SCALE OF REJECTION OF CHRISTIANITY

Purpose: To measure rejection of Christianity.

Number of Items: 20

Format: Scales are anchored by 5 (*agree strongly*) and 1 (*disagree*

strongly). Sample items are presented.

Reliability: Alpha coefficients ranged from .94 to .95.

Author: Robbins, M., et al.

Article: Reliability and construct validity for Scale of Rejection of Christianity.

Journal: *Psychological Reports*, February 2003, *92*, 65–66.

Related Research: Greer, J. E., & Francis, L. J. (1992). Measuring 'rejection of Christianity' and 14–16-year-old adolescents in Catholic and Protestant schools in Northern Ireland. *Personality and Individual Differences*, *13*, 1345–1348.

13534

Test Name: SCALE TO ASSESS WORLD VIEWS

Purpose: To measure beliefs and values of world views.

Number of Items: 45

Format: Scales range from 1 (*strongly disagree*) to 5 (*strongly agree*).

Reliability: One subscale had an alpha of .60.

Validity: Correlations with other variables ranged from –.31 to .34.

Author: Nilsson, J. E., and Schmidt, C. K.

Article: Social justice advocacy among graduate students in counseling: An initial exploration.

Journal: *Journal of College Student Development*, May/June 2005, *46*, 267–279.

Related Research: Ibrahim, F. A., & Kahn, H. (1987). Assessment of world views. *Psychological Reports*, *60*, 163–176.

13535

Test Name: SCHWARTZ VALUE SURVEY

Purpose: To measure values.

Number of Items: 56

Format: Includes 10 value constructs: power, achievement, hedonism, stimulation, self-direction, universalism, benevolence, tradition, conformity, and security. Responses are made on a scale ranging from 7 (*supreme importance*) to –1 (*opposed to my values*).

Reliability: Internal consistency coefficients ranged from the low .50s to the high .70s.

Validity: Correlations with other variables ranged from –.28 to .36.

Author: Mumford, M. D., et al.

Article: Alternative approaches for measuring values: Direct and indirect assessments in performance prediction.

Journal: *Journal of Vocational Behavior*, October 2002, *61*, 348–373.

Related Research: Schwartz, S. H. (1994). Are there universal aspects in the structure and contents of human values? *Journal of Social Issues*, *50*, 19–45.

13536

Test Name: SCHWARTZ'S VALUE SURVEY

Purpose: To measure 10 general values.

Number of Items: 52

Format: Scales range from –1 (*I am opposed to this value*) to 7 (*This value is of supreme importance to me*).

Reliability: Alpha coefficients ranged from .54 to .82 across subscales.

Validity: Correlations with social desirability ranged from –.14 to .07.

Author: Ryckman, R. M., and Houston, D. M.

Article: Value priorities in American and British female and male university students.

Journal: *The Journal of Social Psychology*, February 2003, *143*, 127–138.

Related Research: Schwartz, S. H. (1994). Are there universal aspects in the structure and contents of human values? *Journal of Social Issues*, *50*, 19–45.

13537

Test Name: SHORT SCHWARTZ'S VALUE SURVEY

Purpose: To measure values.

Number of Items: 10

Format: Responses are made on a 9-point scale ranging from 0 (*opposed to my principles*) to 8 (*of supreme importance*). Examples are given.

Reliability: Test–retest (2 weeks) reliability ranged from .34 to .78.

Author: Lindeman, M., and Verkasalo, M.

Article: Measuring values with the Short Schwartz's Value Survey.

Journal: *Journal of Personality Assessment*, October 2005, *85*, 170–178.

Related Research: Schwartz, S. (1996). Value priorities and behavior: Applying a theory of integrated value systems. In C. Seligman, et al. (Eds.), *The psychology of values* (pp. 1–24). Hillsdale, NJ: Erlbaum.

13538

Test Name: SOCIAL CONFORMITY SCALE

Purpose: To assess conformity as law abidance, conservatism, and religious commitment.

Number of Items: 12

Format: A semantic differential format is used. Sample items are presented.

Reliability: Period-free reliability ranged from .55 to .83 across subscales.

Author: Galaif, E. R., et al.

Article: Prospective relationships between drug problems and work adjustment in a community sample of adults.

Journal: *Journal of Applied Psychology*, April 2001, *86*, 337–350.

Related Research: Stein, J. A., et al. (1986). Stability and change in personality: A longitudinal study from early adolescence to young adulthood. *Journal of Research in Personality, 20*, 276–291.

13539

Test Name: SOCIAL INTEREST SCALE

Purpose: To measure interest in and concern for the welfare of others.

Number of Items: 15

Format: A forced-choice format is used.

Reliability: Coefficient alpha was .82.

Validity: Correlations with other variables ranged from –.16 to .44.

Author: Nilsson, J. E., and Schmidt, C. K.

Article: Social justice advocacy among graduate students in counseling: An initial exploration.

Journal: *Journal of College Student Development*, May/June 2005, *46*, 267–279.

Related Research: Crandall, J. E. (1975). A scale for social interest. *Journal of Individual Psychology, 31*, 187–195.

13540

Test Name: SPIRITUAL ASSESSMENT INVENTORY

Purpose: To measure individual awareness of God in the person's life and the quality of that relationship.

Number of Items: 54

Format: Includes six subscales: Awareness of God, Realistic Acceptance, Disappointment in God, Spiritual Grandiosity, Spiritual Instability, and Impression Management.

Reliability: Internal consistency reliability coefficients ranged from .61 to .97.

Author: Duffy, R. D., and Blustein, D. L.

Article: The relationship between spirituality, religiousness, and career adaptability.

Journal: *Journal of Vocational Behavior*, December 2005, *67*, 429–440.

Related Research: Hall, T. W., & Edwards, K. J. (1996). The initial development and factor analysis of the Spiritual Assessment Inventory. *Journal of Psychology and Theology, 24*, 233–246.

13541

Test Name: SPIRITUAL INVOLVEMENT AND BELIEFS SCALE

Purpose: To assess aspects of spirituality applicable to individuals of different religious backgrounds and to assess both spiritual beliefs and activity.

Number of Items: 25

Format: Responses are made on a 5-point scale ranging from 1 (*strongly agree*) to 5 (*strongly disagree*).

Reliability: Coefficient alpha was .75.

Validity: Correlations with other variables ranged from –.13 to .62 (*n* = 583).

Author: Lease, S. H., et al.

Article: Affirming faith experiences and psychological health for Caucasian lesbian, gay, and bisexual individuals.

Journal: *Journal of Counseling Psychology*, July 2005, *52*, 378–388.

Related Research: Hatch, R., et al. (1998). The Spiritual Involvement and Beliefs Scale: Development and testing of a new instrument. *Journal of Family Practice, 46*, 476–486.

13542

Test Name: SPIRITUAL SUPPORT SCALE

Purpose: To measure religiosity.

Number of Items: 13

Format: Scales range from 1 (*strongly disagree*) to 5 (*strongly agree*). Sample items are presented.

Reliability: Coefficient alpha was .97.

Author: Wilkinson, W. W., and Roys, A. C.

Article: The components of sexual orientation, religiosity, and heterosexuals' impressions of gay men and lesbians.

Journal: *The Journal of Social Psychology*, February 2005, *145*, 65–83.

Related Research: Genia, V. (1997). The Spiritual Experience Index: Revision and reformulation. *Review of Religious Research, 38*, 344–361.

13543

Test Name: SPIRITUAL WELL-BEING SCALE

Purpose: To measure religious and existential well-being.

Number of Items: 20

Format: Seven-point scales range from 1 (*strongly agree*) to 7 (*strongly disagree*).

Reliability: Alpha coefficients ranged from .78 to .94.

Validity: Correlations with other variables ranged from –.66 to .82.

Author: Pollard, L. J., and Bates, L. W.

Article: Religion and perceived stress among undergraduates during Fall 2001 final examinations.

Journal: *Psychological Reports,* December 2004, *95,* Part 1, 999–1007.

Related Research: Ellison, C. W. (1983). Spiritual well-being: Conceptualization and measurement. *Journal of Psychology and Theology, 11,* 330–340.

13544

Test Name: SPIRITUALITY SCALE

Purpose: To measure spirituality: self-effacing altruism, blissful transcendence, religiosity/sacredness, and loving connection.

Number of Items: 79

Format: Five-point scales are anchored by 1 (*definitely not spiritual*) and 5 (*definitely spiritual*). Sample items (words) are presented.

Reliability: Alpha coefficients ranged from .75 to .91 across subscales.

Author: Greenwald, D. F., and Harder, D. W.

Article: The dimensions of spirituality.

Journal: *Psychological Reports,* June 2003, *92,* Part 1, 975–980.

Related Research: MacDonald, D. A. (2000). Spirituality: Description, measurement, and relation to the Five Factor Model of personality. *Journal of Personality, 68,* 153–197.

13545

Test Name: SPIRITUALITY SCALE

Purpose: To assess intrinsic spirituality.

Number of Items: 13

Format: Taps both dispositions and behaviors. Examples are presented.

Reliability: Coefficient alpha was .91.

Validity: Correlations with other variables ranged from −.16 to .34 (*N* = 230).

Author: Simoni, J. M.

Article: Spirituality and psychological adaptation among women with HIV/AIDS: Implications for counseling.

Journal: *Journal of Counseling Psychology,* April 2002, *49,* 139–147.

Related Research: Somlai, A. M., et al. (1996). An empirical investigation of the relationship between spirituality, coping, and emotional distress in people living with HIV infection and AIDS. *Journal of Pastoral Counseling, 50,* 171–179.

13546

Test Name: SPIRITUALITY SCALE

Purpose: To assess the spiritual and behavioral dimensions of spirituality.

Number of Items: 25

Format: Scales range from 1 (*completely false*) to 6 (*completely true*). Sample items are presented.

Reliability: Alpha coefficients ranged from .77 to .85.

Validity: Correlations with other variables ranged from −.73 to .64.

Author: Constantine, M. G., et al.

Article: Religious participation, spirituality, and coping among African American college students.

Journal: *Journal of College Student Development,* September/October 2002, *43,* 605–613.

Related Research: Jagers, R. J., & Smith, P. (1996). Further examination of the Spirituality Scale. *Journal of Black Psychology, 22,* 429–442.

13547

Test Name: SUBTLE AND BLATANT PREJUDICE SCALES

Purpose: To measure defense of individualist values (subtle prejudice) and derogatory out group attitudes (blatant prejudice).

Number of Items: 20

Format: Six-point scales are anchored by 1 (*disagree absolutely*) and 6 (*I agree absolutely*), and 5-point scales by 1 (*never*) and 5 (*very often*). All items are presented.

Reliability: Alpha coefficients were .69 (subtle) and .80 (blatant).

Validity: Correlations with social desirability ranged from −.01 to .10.

Author: Rattazzi, A. M. M., and Volpato, C.

Article: Social desirability of Subtle and Blatant Prejudice Scales.

Journal: *Psychological Reports,* February 2003, *92,* 241–250.

Related Research: Pettigrew, T. F., & Meertens, R. W. (1995). Subtle and blatant prejudice in Western Europe. *European Journal of Social Psychology, 25,* 57–75.

13548

Test Name: TAOIST-ORIENTATION SCALE

Purpose: To measure the extent to which individuals have a Taoist orientation to life.

Number of Items: 20

Format: A true–false format is used.

Reliability: Cronbach's alpha was .69 (Kuwaiti sample) and .80 (American sample).

Validity: Factor identified in the two samples did not match.

Author: Lester, D., and Abdel-Khalek, A.

Article: Reliability and factorial structure of the Taoist-Orientation Scale for samples of Kuwaiti and American students.

Journal: *Psychological Reports*, August 2002, *91*, 114.

Related Research: Knoblauch, D. L., & Falconer, J. A. (1986). The relationship of a measured Taoist orientation to Western personality dimensions. *Journal of Transpersonal Psychology, 18*, 73–83.

13549

Test Name: THE INTRINSIC/EXTRINSIC RELIGIOSITY SCALE—REVISED

Purpose: To measure religiosity.

Number of Items: 14

Format: Five-point Likert format.

Reliability: Alpha coefficients ranged from .64 to .78.

Validity: Correlations with job involvement ranged from –.35 to .62.

Author: Knotts, T. L.

Article: Relation between employees' religiosity and job involvement.

Journal: *Psychological Reports*, December 2003, *93*, Part 1, 867–875.

Related Research: Gorsuch, R. L., & McPherson, S. E. (1989). Intrinsic/Extrinsic Measurement: I/E–Revised and single-item scales. *Journal for the Scientific Study of Religion, 28*, 348–354.

13550

Test Name: THE THREE DIMENSIONAL MEASURE OF RELIGIOUS ORIENTATION— SIMPLIFIED PROCEDURE

Purpose: To measure religious orientation.

Number of Items: 32

Format: Scales range from 1 (*strongly agree*) to 9 (*strongly disagree*).

Reliability: Alpha coefficients ranged from .68 to .83 across subscales.

Author: Sanchez, D., and Carter, R. T.

Article: Exploring the relationship between racial identity and religious orientation among African American college students.

Journal: *Journal of College Student Development*, May/June 2005, *46*, 280–295.

Related Research: Batson, C. D., & Ventis, W. L. (1982). *The religious experience: A social psychological perspective*. New York: Oxford University Press.

13551

Test Name: THEORIES OF REALITY QUESTIONNAIRE

Purpose: To assess an individual's theories about the world, reality, and morality.

Number of Items: 9

Format: Scales range from 1 (*strongly agree*) to 7 (*strongly disagree*). Sample items are presented.

Reliability: Coefficient alpha was .70.

Author: Bèjue, L., and Apostolidis, T.

Article: Implicit theories of reality and differentiation from gay people.

Journal: *The Journal of Social Psychology*, February 2001, *141*, 132–134.

Related Research: Chiu, C. Y., et al. (1997). Implicit theories and conceptions of morality. *Journal of Personality and Social Psychology, 73*, 923–940.

13552

Test Name: V DIFFER SCALE

Purpose: To measure the explicit value set upon behavioral differentiation.

Number of Items: 32

Format: Each item is a pair of adjectives from which the respondents choose the one that they would rather have be true of them.

Reliability: Internal consistency was in the .78 range.

Validity: Correlations with other variables ranged from .05 to .31.

Author: Joy, S.

Article: The need to be different predicts divergent production: Toward a social learning model of originality.

Journal: *The Journal of Creative Behavior*, First Quarter 2001, *35*(1), 51–64.

Related Research: Joy, S. (1998, May). *Needing to be different: Development and validation of an innovation motivation inventory*. Poster presented at the annual convention of the American Psychological Society, Washington, DC.

13553

Test Name: VALUE DOMAIN SCALE—TURKISH VERSION

Purpose: To assess values of Turkish adults.

Number of Items: 43

Format: Scales range from 1 (*not important to me at all as a value*) to 7 (*extremely important to me as a value*). All items are presented in English.

Reliability: Alpha coefficients ranged from .66 to .84 across value domain subscales.

Validity: Correlations between subscales ranged from –.08 to .51.

Author: Aygun, Z. K., and Imamoglu, E. O.

Article: Value domains of Turkish adults and university students.

Journal: *The Journal of Social Psychology*, June 2002, *142*, 333–351.

13554

Test Name: VALUE EPISTEMOLOGICAL BELIEFS SCALE

Purpose: To measure beliefs about the source of values of religion, science, and truth/faith.

Number of Items: 12

Format: Item anchors range from 1 (*strongly disagree*) to 7 (*strongly agree*). All items are presented.

Reliability: Alpha coefficients ranged from .70 to .80 across subscales.

Validity: Correlations with other variables ranged from –.49 to .68.

Author: Latifian, M., and Bashash, L.

Article: Relation of Value Epistemological Beliefs Scale and judgments of two similar scenarios attributed to two different authorities.

Journal: *Psychological Reports*, October 2004, *95*, 371–385.

13555

Test Name: VALUE PRIORITIES SCALES

Purpose: To assess openness to change, conservation, achievement, and power.

Number of Items: 44

Format: Scales range from –1 (*opposed to my values*) to 7 (*of supreme importance*).

Reliability: Alpha coefficients ranged from .69 to .83.

Author: Gaunt, R.

Article: The role of value priorities in paternal and maternal involvement in child care.

Journal: *Journal of Marriage and Family*, August 2005, *67*, 643–655.

Related Research: Struch, N., et al. (2002). Meanings of basic values for women and men: A cross-cultural analysis. *Personality and Social Psychology Bulletin, 28*, 16–28.

13556

Test Name: VALUE SCALE

Purpose: To rate values as a guiding principle in life.

Number of Items: 56

Format: Item responses are anchored by 1 (*not of importance*) and 8 (*of supreme importance*).

Reliability: Alpha coefficients ranged from .54 to .83.

Author: Clump, M., et al.

Article: Differences in Schwartz's Value Survey between high and low scores on the ECOSCALE.

Journal: *Psychological Reports*, June 2002, *90*, Part 2, 1174–1178.

Related Research: Schwartz, S. H., & Bilsky, W. (1987). Toward a universal psychological structure of human values. *Journal of Personality and Social Psychology, 53*, 550–562.

13557

Test Name: VALUES INVENTORY

Purpose: To measure the extent to which a value is a guiding principle in a person's life.

Number of Items: 56

Format: Scales range from 0 (*of little importance*) to 7 (*of supreme importance*). Scoring is described briefly.

Reliability: Reliabilities ranged from .60 to .75 for second-order values.

Validity: Correlations between post materialism and values ranged from –.38 to 27.

Author: Wilson, M. S.

Article: A social-value analysis of postmaterialism.

Journal: *The Journal of Social Psychology*, April 2005, *145*, 209–224.

Related Research: Schwartz, S. H. (1992). Universals in the content and structure of values: Theoretical advances and empirical texts in 20 countries. *Advances in Experimental Social Psychology, 25*, 1–65.

13558

Test Name: VALUING OF EDUCATION SCALE

Purpose: To measure one's valuing of a graduate education.

Number of Items: 51

Format: Responses are made on a 5-point scale ranging from *strongly agree* to *strongly disagree*. All items are presented.

Reliability: Alpha coefficients ranged from .60 to .96.

Author: Battle, A., and Wigfield, A.

Article: College women's value orientations toward family, career, and graduate school.

Journal: *Journal of Vocational Behavior*, February 2003, *62*, 56–57.

Related Research: Eccles (Parsons), J., et al. (1983). Expectancies, values, and academic behaviors. In J. T. Spence (Ed.), *Achievement and achievement motives* (pp. 75–145). San Francisco: Freeman.

13559

Test Name: VISIONS OF EVERYDAY MORALITY SCALE—REVISED

Purpose: To measure everyday morality.

Number of Items: 21

Format: Includes three morality domains: private, interpersonal, and social.

Reliability: Mean alpha coefficient was .78.

Validity: Correlations with other variables ranged from −.02 to .27.

Author: Worthington, E. L., Jr., et al.

Article: The Religious Commitment Inventory—10: Development, refinement, and validation of a brief scale for research and counseling.

Journal: *Journal of Counseling Psychology*, January 2003, *50*, 84–96.

Related Research: Shelton, C. M., & McAdams, D. P. (1990). In search of an everyday morality: The development of a measure. *Adolescence, 25,* 923–943.

13560

Test Name: YOUTHS' VALUES, BELIEFS, AND EXPECTATIONS SCALES

Purpose: To measure adolescents' values, beliefs, and expectations in the academic domain.

Number of Items: 11

Format: Includes three self-report scales: Values, Beliefs, and Expectations. All items are presented.

Reliability: Alpha coefficients ranged from .69 to .83.

Author: Jodl, K. M., et al.

Article: Parents' roles in shaping early adolescents' occupational aspirations.

Journal: *Child Development,* July/August 2001, *72,* 1247–1265.

Related Research: Eccles, J. S. (1993). School and family effects on the ontogeny of children's interests, self-perceptions, and activity choices. In R. Dienstbier & J. E. Jacobs (Eds.), *Developmental perspectives on motivation* (Vol. 40, pp. 145–208). Lincoln: University of Nebraska Press.

13561

Test Name: WORK ETHIC SCALE

Purpose: To measure work ethic.

Number of Items: 11

Format: Responses are made on a 5-point Likert scale. All items are presented.

Reliability: Alpha coefficients were .86 and .88.

Author: ter Bogt, T., et al.

Article: Socialization and development of the work ethic among adolescents and young adults.

Journal: *Journal of Vocational Behavior,* June 2005, *66,* 420–437.

Related Research: Raaijmakers, Q. (1987). The work ethic of Dutch adolescents. In J. L. Hazekamp, et al. (Eds.), *Europlan contributions to youth research* (pp. 117–130). Amsterdam: Free University Press.

CHAPTER 23
Vocational Evaluation

13562

Test Name: ABUSIVE SUPERVISION SCALE

Purpose: To measure abusive supervision.

Number of Items: 15

Format: Scales range from 1 (*I cannot remember him/her using this behavior with me*) to 5 (*He/She uses this behavior very often with me*). Sample items are presented.

Reliability: Coefficient alpha was .95.

Validity: Correlations with other variables ranged from −.53 to −.20.

Author: Tepper, B. J., et al.

Article: Moderators of the relationships between coworkers' organizational citizenship behavior and fellow employees' attitudes.

Journal: *Journal of Applied Psychology*, June 2004, *89*, 455–465.

Related Research: Tepper, B. J. (2000). Consequences of abusive supervision. *Academy of Management Journal, 43*, 178–190.

13563

Test Name: ACADEMIC DEPARTMENT CHAIRPERSON LEADERSHIP ACTIVITIES MEASURE

Purpose: To measure academic department chairperson leadership activities.

Number of Items: 34

Format: Includes four factors: coordination, balanced oversight, external sensing, and evaluation. Responses are made on 5-point scales. All items are presented.

Reliability: Internal consistency ranged from .70 to .85.

Author: Stark, J. S.

Article: Testing a model of program curriculum leadership

Journal: *Research in Higher Education*, February 2002, *43*, 59–82.

Related Research: Stark, J. S., and Lattuca, L. R. (1997). Shaping the college curriculum: Academic plans in action. Needlum Heights, MA: Allyn & Bacon.

13564

Test Name: ACADEMIC MENTORING BEHAVIOR SCALE—ADAPTED

Purpose: To identify the interpersonal aspects of the mentoring relationship.

Number of Items: 6

Format: Only two subscales were used: Self-Disclosure and Comfort With Proximity.

Reliability: Alpha coefficients ranged from .61 to .83.

Author: Bernier, A., et al.

Article: Academic mentoring in college: The interactive role of student's and mentor's interpersonal dispositions.

Journal: *Research in Higher Education*, February 2005, *46*, 29–51.

Related Research: Larose, S., et al. (2001). Parental representations and attachment style as predictors of support-seeking behaviors and perceptions of support in an academic counseling relationship. *Personal Relationships, 8*, 93–113.

13565

Test Name: ADVISORY WORKING ALLIANCE INVENTORY

Purpose: To measure the graduate advising relationship from the student's perspective.

Number of Items: 48

Format: Responses are made on a 5-point Likert scale ranging from 1 (*strongly disagree*) to 5 (*strongly agree*). Examples are presented.

Reliability: Alpha coefficients ranged from .57 to .95. Test–retest (2 weeks) reliability coefficients ranged from .75 to .92.

Author: Schlosser, L. Z., & Gelso, C. J.

Article: Measuring the working alliance in advisor–advisee relationships in graduate school.

Journal: *Journal of Counseling Psychology*, April 2001, *48*, 157–167.

Related Research: Efstation, J. F., et al. (1990). Measuring the working alliance in counselor supervision.

Journal of Counseling Psychology, 37, 322–329.

13566

Test Name: ADVISORY WORKING ALLIANCE INVENTORY—ADVISOR VERSION

Purpose: To assess the advisory working alliance in graduate school from the advisor's perspective.

Number of Items: 31

Format: Includes three components: rapport, apprenticeship, and task focus. Responses are made on a 5-point Likert scale ranging from 1 (*strongly disagree*) to 5 (*strongly agree*). All items are presented.

Reliability: Alpha coefficients ranged from .60 to .90. Test–retest (2 weeks) reliabilities ranged from .78 to .88.

Validity: Correlations with other variables ranged from −.44 to .60.

Author: Schlosser, L. Z., and Gelso, C. J.

Article: The Advisory Working Alliance Inventory—Advisor Version: Scale development and validation.

Journal: *Journal of Counseling Psychology,* October 2005, 52, 650–654.

13567

Test Name: AGNEW RELATIONSHIP MEASURE—ADAPTED

Purpose: To measure client-related alliance.

Number of Items: 17

Format: Includes three scales: Bond, Partnership, and Confidence.

Reliability: Coefficient alpha was .93.

Author: Stiles, W. B., et al.

Article: Patterns of alliance development and the rupture–repair hypothesis: Are productive relationships U-shaped or V-shaped?

Journal: *Journal of Counseling Psychology,* January 2004, 51, 81–92.

Related Research: Agnew-Davies, R., et al. (1998). Alliance structure assessed by the Agnew Relationship Measure (ARM). *British Journal of Clinical Psychology,* 37, 155–172.

13568

Test Name: CALIFORNIA PSYCHOTHERAPY ALLIANCE SCALES

Purpose: To measure patient commitment, patient working capacity, working strategies consensus, and therapist understanding and involvement.

Number of Items: 12

Format: Scales range from 1 (*not very much*) to 7 (*very much so*).

Reliability: Alpha coefficients ranged from .27 to .78 across subscales. Total alpha was .84.

Author: Hardy, G. E., et al.

Article: Client interpersonal and cognitive styles as predictors of response to time-limited cognitive therapy for depression.

Journal: *Journal of Consulting and Clinical Psychology,* October 2001, 69, 841–845.

Related Research: Gaston, L., & Marmar, C. R. (1994). The California Psychotherapy Alliance Scales. In A. O. Horvath & L. S. Greenberg (Eds.), *The working alliance: Theory, research, and practice* (pp. 85–108). New York: Wiley.

13569

Test Name: CAREER COUNSELING SELF-EFFICACY QUESTIONNAIRE

Purpose: To measure career counseling self-efficacy.

Number of Items: 27

Format: Includes four factors: problem understanding, educational counseling, career indecision/choice, and career information. Responses are made on a 7-point scale ranging from 1 (*not at all sure*) to 7 (*very sure*). Examples are presented.

Reliability: Alpha coefficients ranged from .79 to .94. Test–retest (1 month) correlations ranged from .78 to .89.

Author: Soresi, S., et al.

Article: Relation of type and amount of training to career counseling self-efficacy in Italy.

Journal: *The Career Development Quarterly,* March 2004, 52, 194–201.

Related Research: Nota, L., & Soresi, S. (2000). *Autoefficacia nelle scelte* [*Self-efficacy and choice*]. Firenze, Italy: Giunti-Organizzazioni Speciali.

13570

Test Name: CAREER MENTORING SCALE

Purpose: To measure career mentoring.

Number of Items: 7

Format: Responses are made on a 5-point scale ranging from 1 (*strongly disagree*) to 5 (*strongly agree*). A sample item is given.

Reliability: Coefficient alpha was .87.

Validity: Correlations with other variables ranged from .10 to .29.

Author: Scandura, T. A., and Williams, E. A.

Article: Mentoring and transformational leadership: The role of supervisory career mentoring.

Journal: *Journal of Vocational Behavior*, December 2004, *65*, 448–468.

Related Research: Scandura, T. A. (1992). Mentorship and career mobility: An empirical investigation. *Journal of Organizational Behavior, 13*, 169–174.

13571

Test Name: CAUSE AND SOLUTION SCALES

Purpose: To assess clinician attributions of client responsibility for the cause of and solution to a problem.

Number of Items: 6

Format: Includes two scales: Cause and Solution. Responses are made on a 7-point Likert scale ranging from 1 (*not at all*) to 7 (*very much*).

Reliability: Alpha coefficients ranged from .63 to .79. Test–retest (2 weeks) reliabilities were .70 to .86.

Validity: Correlations with other variables ranged from –.01 to .21.

Author: Burkard, A. W., and Knox, S.

Article: Effect of therapist color-blindness on empathy and attributions in cross-cultural counseling.

Journal: *Journal of Counseling Psychology*, October 2004, *51*, 387–397.

Related Research: Karuza, J., et al. (1990). Models of helping and coping, responsibility attributions, and well-being in community elderly and their helpers. *Psychology and Aging, 5*, 194–208.

13572

Test Name: CLASSROOM INSTRUCTIONAL PRACTICE SCALE

Purpose: To assess teachers' classroom instructional practices.

Number of Items: 82

Format: Includes 16 subscales. Responses are made on a 7-point scale ranging from 1 (*never*) to 7 (*daily*).

Reliability: Alpha coefficients were greater than .95.

Author: Seitsinger, A. M.

Article: Service-learning and standards-based instruction in middle schools.

Journal: *Journal of Educational Research*, September/October 2005, *99*, 19–30.

Related Research: Shim, M., et al. (2000, April). Consistency within schools in the implementation of instructional practices: Implications for the assessment of common national recommendations for middle school reform. In R. D. Felner (Chair), *The project on high performance learning communities: Longitudinal studies of foundation-based efforts to create networks of schools engaged in comprehensive middle school transformation.* Symposium conducted at the annual meeting of the American Education Research Association, New Orleans, LA.

13573

Test Name: CLASSROOM INSTRUCTIONAL PRACTICES SCALE

Purpose: To measure how teachers organize their classrooms in adapting for learner differences.

Number of Items: 27

Format: Includes five areas: content, rate, rate with assessment, environment, and performance. All items are presented.

Reliability: Interrater reliability was .92.

Author: Johnson, S. K., et al.

Article: Changing general education classroom practices to adapt for gifted students.

Journal: *Gifted Child Quarterly*, Winter 2002, *46*, 45–63.

Related Research: Johnsen, S. K. (1992). *Classroom Instructional Practices Scale.* Unpublished manuscript, Baylor University, Waco, TX.

13574

Test Name: CLIENT ATTACHMENT TO THERAPIST SCALE

Purpose: To measure clients' perceptions of their relationships with their therapist from an attachment theory perspective.

Number of Items: 36

Format: Includes three subscales: Secure, Preoccupied–Merger, and Avoidant–Fearful. Responses are made on a 6-point scale ranging from 1 (*strongly disagree*) to 6 (*strongly agree*). Examples are presented.

Reliability: Alpha coefficients ranged from .63 to .84. Test–retest coefficients ranged from .72 to .86.

Validity: Correlations with other variables ranged from –.31 to .49.

Author: Woodhouse, S. S., et al.

Article: Client attachment to therapist: Relations to transference and client recollections of parental caregiving.

Journal: *Journal of Counseling Psychology*, October 2003, *50*, 395–408.

Related Research: Mallinckrodt, B., et al. (1995). Attachment patterns in the psychotherapy relationship: Development of the Client Attachment to Therapist Scale. *Journal of Counseling Psychology, 42*, 307–317.

13575

Test Name: CLIENT SESSION SATISFACTION

Purpose: To assess global client satisfaction.

Number of Items: 5

Format: Responses are made on a 7-point scale ranging from 1 (*very strongly disagree*) to 7 (*very strongly agree*). Examples are given.

Reliability: Alpha coefficients ranged from .71 to .94. Test–retest (1 week) reliability was .64.

Validity: Correlations with other variables ranged from −.05 to .67.

Author: Lichtenberg, J. W., and Tracey, T. J. G.

Article: Interaction rules and strategies in psychotherapy.

Journal: *Journal of Counseling Psychology*, July 2003, *50*, 267–275.

Related Research: Tracey, T. J. (1989). Client and therapist session satisfaction over the course of psychotherapy. *Psychotherapy, 26*, 177–182.

13576

Test Name: COMBINED ALLIANCE SHORT FORM— PATIENT VERSION

Purpose: To provide a patient-rated alliance measure.

Number of Items: 20

Format: Responses are made on a 7-point scale ranging from 1 (*never*) to 7 (*always*).

Reliability: Alpha coefficients were .91 to .93.

Author: Hilsenroth, M. J., et al.

Article: The development of therapeutic alliance during psychological assessment: Patient and therapist perspectives across treatment.

Journal: *Journal of Personality Assessment*, December 2004, *83*, 332–344.

Related Research: Hatcher, R. L., & Barends, A. W. (1996). Patient's view of the alliance in psychotherapy: Exploratory factor analysis of three alliance measures. *Journal of Consulting and Clinical Psychology, 64*, 1326–1336.

13577

Test Name: COMMITMENT TO PROTÉGÉ SCALE

Purpose: To measure mentor's commitment to protégé.

Number of Items: 4

Format: All items are given.

Reliability: Coefficient alpha was .83.

Validity: Correlations with other variables ranged from −.10 to .73.

Author: Ortiz-Walters, R., and Gilson, L. L.

Article: Mentoring in academia: An examination of the experiences of protégés of color.

Journal: *Journal of Vocational Behavior*, December 2005, *67*, 459–475.

Related Research: Rusbult, C. E., et al. (1999). The Investment Model Scale: Measuring commitment level, satisfaction level, quality alternatives, and investment size. *Personal Relationships, 5*, 357–392.

13578

Test Name: COMPETENCIES SCALES

Purpose: To assess three areas of competence.

Number of Items: 20

Format: Includes three areas of competence: general management, knowledge, and analytical.

Reliability: Alpha coefficients ranged from .70 to .90.

Author: Baruch, Y., et al.

Article: Generalist and specialist graduate business degrees: Tangible and intangible value.

Journal: *Journal of Vocational Behavior*, August 2005, *67*, 51–68.

Related Research: Baruch, Y., & Peiperi, M. A. (2000). The impact of an MBA on graduate careers. *Human Resource Management Journal, 10*, 69–90.

13579

Test Name: CONSULTANT EVALUATION FORM

Purpose: To assess consultee satisfaction.

Number of Items: 12

Format: Responses are made on a 7-point Likert scale.

Reliability: Alpha coefficients ranged from .83 to .95.

Author: Sheridan, S. M., et al.

Article: The effects of conjoint behavioral consultation results of a 4-year investigation.

Journal: *Journal of School Psychology*, September/October 2001, *39*, 361–385.

Related Research: Erchul, W. P. (1987). A relational communication analysis of control in school consultation. *Professional School Psychology, 2*, 113–124.

13580

Test Name: CONTEXTUAL PERFORMANCE SCALE

Purpose: To provide the contextual performance of individual team members.

Number of Items: 9

Format: Responses are made on a 5-point scale. All items are included.

Reliability: Internal consistency was .98.

Validity: Correlations with other variables ranged from −.17 to .89 (*n* = 90).

Author: Morgeson, F. P., et al.

Article: Selecting individuals in team settings: The importance of social skills, personality characteristics, and teamwork knowledge.

Journal: *Personnel Psychology,* Autumn 2005, *58*, 583–611.

Related Research: Moorman, R. H., & Blakely, G. L. (1995). Individualism as an individual difference predictor of organizational citizenship. *Journal of Organizational Behavior, 16*, 127–142. Van Scotter, J. R., & Motowidlo, S. J. (1996). Interpersonal facilitation and job dedication as separate facets of contextual performance. *Journal of Applied Psychology, 81*, 525–531.

13581

Test Name: COUNSELING SELF-ESTIMATE INVENTORY

Purpose: To measure an individual's confidence in his or her ability to counsel effectively in the future or in the past.

Number of Items: 37

Format: Six-point scales are used. Sample items are presented.

Reliability: Alpha coefficients ranged from .90 to .97.

Validity: Correlations with other variables ranged from −.31 to −.17.

Author: Larson, L. M., et al.

Article: Developing a supervisor feedback rating scale: A brief report.

Journal: *Measurement and Evaluation in Counseling and Development*, January 2003, *35*, 230–238.

Related Research: Larson, L. M., et al. (1992). The development and validation of the Counseling Self-Estimate Inventory. *Journal of Counseling Psychology, 39*, 105–120.

13582

Test Name: COUNSELOR EFFECTIVENESS RATING SCALE

Purpose: To measure client-perceived counselor credibility.

Number of Items: 10

Format: Includes four dimensions: Expertness, Attractiveness, Trustworthiness, and Utility. Responses are made on a 7-point scale ranging from 1 (*bad*) to 7 (*good*).

Reliability: Coefficient alpha was .90.

Validity: Correlations with other variables ranged from .71 to .80.

Author: Kim, B. S. K., et al.

Article: Counselor self-disclosure, East Asian American client adherence to Asian cultural values, and counseling process.

Journal: *Journal of Counseling Psychology*, July 2003, *50*, 324–332.

Related Research: Atkinson, D. R., & Carskaddon, G. (1975). A prestigious introduction, psychological jargon, and perceived counselor credibility. *Journal of Counseling Psychology, 22*, 180–186.

13583

Test Name: COUNSELOR PERCEPTION SCALE

Purpose: To assess an observer's perceptions of counselors.

Number of Items: 8

Format: Item anchors are 1 (*low or poor*) and 7 (*high or good*). All items are described.

Reliability: Coefficient alpha was .84.

Author: Lee, D. Y., et al.

Article: Does sex of client affect counselors' evaluation?

Journal: *Psychological Reports,* June 2004, *94*, Part 2, 1205–1211.

Related Research: Lee, D. Y., et al. (1999). Forming clinical impressions during the first five minutes of the counseling interview. *Psychological Reports, 85*, 835–844.

13584

Test Name: COUNSELOR RATING FORM—SHORT

Purpose: To provide a client-rated measure of therapist credibility.

Number of Items: 12

Format: Includes three dimensions: Expertness, Attractiveness, and Trustworthiness. Responses are made on a 7-point scale ranging from 1 (*not very*) to 7 (*very*).

Reliability: Internal consistency reliabilities ranged from .82 to .96.

Validity: Correlations with other variables ranged from −.05 to .78.

Author: Hoyt, W. T.

Article: Bias in participant ratings of psychotherapy process: An initial generalizability study.

Journal: *Journal of Counseling Psychology*, January 2002, *49*, 35–46.

Related Research: Corrigan, J. D., & Schmidt, L. D. (1983). Development and validation of revisions in the Counselor Rating Form. *Journal of Counseling Psychology, 30*, 64–75.

13585

Test Name: COUNSELOR'S COUNSELING STYLE QUESTIONNAIRE

Purpose: To measure the client's perception of the counselor's counseling style.

Number of Items: 10

Format: Includes two subscales: Directive and Nondirective. Responses are made on a 7-point Likert-type scale ranging from 1 (*strongly disagree*) to 7 (*strongly agree*). Examples are given.

Reliability: Alpha coefficients were .51 and .72.

Validity: Correlations for only the nondirective subscale with other variables ranged from −.26 to .44.

Author: Li, L. C., and Kim, B. S. K.

Article: Effects of counseling style and client adherence to Asian cultural values on counseling process with Asian American college students.

Journal: *Journal of Counseling Psychology*, April 2004, *51*, 158–167.

13586

Test Name: COUNTERTRANSFERENCE BEHAVIOR MEASURE

Purpose: To assess supervisors' perceptions of countertransference behavior in their supervisees.

Number of Items: 10

Format: Includes three subscales: Dominant Countertransference Behavior, Distant Countertransference Behavior, and Hostile Countertransference Behavior. Responses are made on a 5-point scale ranging from 1 (*to no extent*) to 5 (*to a great extent*). All items are presented.

Reliability: Alpha coefficients ranged from .82 to .89.

Author: Mohr, J. J., et al.

Article: Client and counselor trainee attachment as predictors of session evaluation and countertransference behavior in first counseling sessions.

Journal: *Journal of Counseling Psychology*, July 2005, *52*, 298–309.

Related Research: Friedman, S. M., & Gelso, C. J. (2000). The development of the Inventory of Countertransference Behavior. *Journal of Clinical Psychology, 56*, 1221–1235.

13587

Test Name: CROSS-CULTURAL COUNSELING INVENTORY— REVISED

Purpose: To assess client-perceived counselor cross-cultural competence.

Number of Items: 20

Format: Responses are made on a 6-point Likert-type scale ranging from 1 (*strongly disagree*) to 6 (*strongly agree*). An example is given.

Reliability: Alpha coefficients ranged from .89 to .95.

Validity: Correlations with other variables ranged from −.12 to .72.

Author: Li, L. C., and Kim, B. S. K.

Article: Effects of counseling style and client adherence to Asian cultural values on counseling process with Asian American college students.

Journal: *Journal of Counseling Psychology*, April 2004, *51*, 158–167.

Related Research: LaFromboise, T. D., et al. (1991). Development and factor structure of the cross-cultural counseling inventory— Revised. *Professional Psychology: Research and Practice, 22*, 380–388.

13588

Test Name: CROSS-SPORT ATHLETIC PERFORMANCE RATING SCALE

Purpose: To compare the characteristics of successful athletes across sports.

Number of Items: 37

Format: Includes five factors: self-motivation, self-confidence, emotional stability, athletic ability, and character. Responses are made on a 5-point scale ranging from 1 (*considerably below average*) to 5 (*considerably above average*). All items are presented.

Reliability: Alpha coefficients ranged from .83 to .97.

Author: Pedersen, D. M., and Manning, C. L.

Article: A cross-sport athletic performance rating scale.

Journal: *Perceptual and Motor Skills*, December 2003, *97*, Part 2, 1128–1132.

Related Research: Privette, G., & Bundrick, C. M. (1997). Psychological processes of peak, average, and failing performance in sport. *International Journal of Sport Psychology, 28*, 323–334.

13589

Test Name: DEPTH SCALE

Purpose: To assess client perception of session depth.

Number of Items: 6

Format: Bipolar adjectives are rated on a 7-point scale.

Reliability: Alpha coefficients ranged from .84 to .91.

Validity: Correlations with other variables ranged from −.17 to .79.

Author: Li, L. C., and Kim, B. S. K.

Article: Effects of counseling style and client adherence to Asian cultural values on counseling process with Asian American college students.

Journal: *Journal of Counseling Psychology*, April 2004, *51*, 158–167.

Related Research: Stiles, W. B., & Snow, J. S. (1984). Dimensions of psychotherapy session impact across sessions and across clients. *British Journal of Clinical Psychology*, *23*, 59–63.

13590

Test Name: EMPATHIC UNDERSTANDING SUBSCALE

Purpose: To assess level of client-perceived counselor empathic understanding.

Number of Items: 16

Format: Responses are made on a 7-point endorsement scale ranging from –3 (*I strongly feel that it is not true*) to 3 (*I strongly feel that it is true*). Sample items are presented.

Reliability: Alpha coefficients ranged from .81 to .89.

Validity: Correlation with other variables ranged from –.08 to .66.

Author: Kim., B. S. K., and Atkinson, D. R.

Article: Asian American client adherence to Asian cultural values, counselor expression of cultural values, counselor ethnicity, and career counseling process.

Journal: *Journal of Counseling Psychology*, January 2002, *49*, 3–13.

Related Research: Barrett-Lennard, G. T. (1962). Dimensions of therapist response as causal factors in therapeutic change. *Psychological Monographs*, *76*, (43, No. 562).

13591

Test Name: EMPLOYABILITY SCALE

Purpose: To assess employability.

Number of Items: 3

Format: Includes flexibility and adaptability, proficiency in current job, and appearance. Ratings are made on a 3 (*low*), 4 (*average*), or 5 (*high*) scale.

Reliability: Reliability was .68.

Validity: Correlations with other variables ranged from –.13 to .22 ($n = 818$).

Author: Boudreau, J. W., et al.

Article: Effects of personality on executive career success in the United States and Europe.

Journal: *Journal of Vocational Behavior*, February 2001, *58*, 53–81.

13592

Test Name: EMPLOYEE FIT SCALES

Purpose: To measure person–organization fit, needs–supplies fit, and demands–abilities fit.

Number of Items: 10

Reliability: Alpha coefficients ranged from .89 to .93 across subscales.

Validity: Correlations with other variables ranged from –.02 to .61.

Author: Cable, D. M., and DeRue, D. S.

Article: The convergent and discriminant validity of subjective fit perceptions.

Journal: *Journal of Applied Psychology*, October 2002, *87*, 875–884.

Related Research: Cable, D. M., & Judge, T. A. (1997). Interviewers' perceptions of person–organization fit and organizational selection decisions. *Journal of Applied Psychology*, *82*, 546–561.

13593

Test Name: EVALUATION PROCESS WITHIN SUPERVISION INVENTORY

Purpose: To assess the degree to which trainees thought their supervision was characterized by effective goal setting and feedback.

Number of Items: 21

Format: Includes two subscales: Goal Setting and Feedback. Responses are made on a 7-point Likert-type scale ranging from 1 (*strongly disagree*) to 7 (*strongly agree*).

Reliability: Alpha coefficients were .69 (feedback) and .89 (goal setting).

Validity: Correlations with other variables ranged from –.02 to .78.

Author: Lehrman-Waterman, D., and Ladany, N.

Article: Development and validation of the Evaluation Process Within Supervision Inventory.

Journal: *Journal of Counseling Psychology*, April 2001, *48*, 168–177.

13594

Test Name: EVALUATIVE JUDGMENT SCALES

Purpose: To measure participants' evaluations of the hiree.

Number of Items: 5

Format: Includes two scales: Job Performance and Career Progression. Responses are made on a 9-point scale ranging from 1 (*not at all competently/not at all effective*) to 9 (*very competently/very effective*). All items are presented.

Reliability: Coefficient alpha was .84.

Validity: Correlations with other variables ranged from –.25 to .68.

Author: Aquino, K., et al.

Article: How social dominance orientation and job status influence perceptions of African American affirmative action beneficiaries.

Journal: *Personnel Psychology,* Autumn 2005, *58,* 703–744.

Related Research: Heilman, M. E., et al. (1992). Presumed incompetent? Stigmatization and affirmative action efforts. *Journal of Applied Psychology, 77,* 536–544.

13595

Test Name: EXERCISE INSTRUCTOR STYLES

Purpose: To measure three types of instructors' responses.

Number of Items: 16

Format: Includes three parts: instructor-mastery, instructor-performance, and instructor-support. Responses are made on a 5-point Likert scale ranging from 1 (*strongly disagree*) to 5 (*strongly agree*). Examples are presented.

Reliability: Test–retest (4 weeks) reliabilities ranged from .57 to .64. Alpha coefficients ranged from .61 to .88.

Author: Harju, B. L., et al.

Article: Relations of women exercisers' mastery and performance goals to traits, fitness, and preferred styles of instructors.

Journal: *Perceptual and Motor Skills,* December 2003, *97,* Part 1, 939–950.

Related Research: Harju, B. L., & Stroebele, N. (2002). *Motivation, preferred instructor styles, and health habits of novice and experienced exercisers.* Unpublished paper, East Carolina University.

13596

Test Name: EXPECTATIONS ABOUT COUNSELORS'

MULTICULTURAL COMPETENCE SCALE

Purpose: To assess college students' expectations about the multicultural competence of a mental health counselor they might see.

Number of Items: 20

Format: Scales range from 1 (*strongly disagree*) to 6 (*strongly agree*).

Reliability: Coefficient alpha was .88.

Validity: Correlations with other variables ranged from .15 to .36.

Author: Constantine, M. G., and Arorash, T. J.

Article: Universal-diverse orientation and general expectations about counseling: Their relation to college students' multicultural counseling expectations.

Journal: *Journal of College Student Development,* November/December 2001, *42,* 535–544.

13597

Test Name: EXPERIENCES IN CLOSE RELATIONSHIPS SCALE

Purpose: To assess adult attachment in clients and counselor trainees.

Number of Items: 36

Format: Includes two subscales: Avoidance and Anxiety. Responses are made on 7-point scales ranging from 1 (*disagree strongly*) to 7 (*agree strongly*). Examples are given.

Reliability: Consistency coefficients ranged from .90 to .94.

Author: Mohr, J. J., et al.

Article: Client and counselor trainee attachment as predictors of session evaluation and countertransference behavior in first counseling sessions.

Journal: *Journal of Counseling Psychology,* July 2005, *52,* 298–309.

Related Research: Brennan, K. A., et al. (1998). Self-report measurement of adult attachment: An integrative overview. In J. A. Simpson & W. S. Rholes (Eds.), *Attachment theory and close relationships* (pp. 46–77). New York: Guilford Press.

13598

Test Name: GAINS FROM DREAM INTERPRETATIONS— MODIFIED

Purpose: To assess specific gains that clients report from dream work sessions.

Number of Items: 12

Format: Includes two subscales: Exploration–Insight Gains and Action Gains. Responses are made on a 9-point scale. Examples are given.

Reliability: Alpha coefficients ranged .82 to .84.

Validity: Correlations with other variables ranged −.22 to .86 ($N = 94$).

Author: Hill, C. E., et al.

Article: Working with dreams using the Hill cognitive–experiential model: A comparison of computer-assisted, therapist empathy, and therapist empathy + input conditions.

Journal: *Journal of Counseling Psychology,* April 2003, *50,* 211–220.

Related Research: Heatton, K. J., et al. (1998). A comparison of therapist-facilitated and self-guided dream work sessions. *Journal of Counseling Psychology, 45,* 115–121.

13599

Test Name: GLOBAL SATISFACTION WITH THERAPY SCALE

Purpose: To measure global satisfaction with therapy.

Number of Items: 3

Format: Responses are made on a 7-point scale ranging from 1 (*not very*) to 7 (*very*). All items are presented.

Reliability: Internal consistency reliability was .94.

Validity: Correlations with other variables ranged from −.08 to .78.

Author: Hoyt, W. T.

Article: Bias in participant ratings of psychotherapy process: An initial generalizability study.

Journal: *Journal of Counseling Psychology*, January 2002, *49*, 35–46.

13600

Test Name: HELPING ALLIANCE QUESTIONNAIRE

Purpose: To measure the quality of the therapeutic alliance from the patient's perspective.

Number of Items: 11

Format: Scales range from 3 (*I feel strongly it is true*) to −3 (*I feel strongly it is not true*). Sample items are presented.

Validity: Correlations with other variables ranged from −.27 to .40.

Author: Constantino, M. J., et al.

Article: The association between patient characteristics and the therapeutic alliance in cognitive–behavioral and interpersonal therapy for bulimia nervosa.

Journal: *Journal of Consulting and Clinical Psychology*, April 2005, *73*, 203–211.

Related Research: Alexander, L. B., & Luborsky, L. (1986). The Penn Helping Alliance Scales. In L. S. Greenberg & W. M. Pinshof (Eds.), *The psychotherapeutic process: A research handbook* (pp. 325–366). New York: Guilford Press.

13601

Test Name: HUMAN CAPITAL SCALES

Purpose: To measure four areas of human capital.

Number of Items: 12

Format: Includes four types of capital: scholastic, cultural, social, and inner-value. Responses are made on a 7-point scale ranging from 1 (*very low*) to 7 (*very high*). Examples are given.

Reliability: Alpha coefficients ranged from .80 to .87.

Validity: Correlations with other variables ranged from −.16 to .27.

Author: Baruch, Y., et al.

Article: Generalist and specialist graduate business degrees: Tangible and intangible value.

Journal: *Journal of Vocational Behavior*, August 2005, *67*, 51–68.

13602

Test Name: IDEAL MENTOR SCALE

Purpose: To assess the importance of various attributes to each student's concept of the ideal mentor.

Number of Items: 34

Format: Includes three subscales: Integrity, Guidance, and Relationship. Responses are made on a 5-point scale ranging from 1 (*not at all important*) to 5 (*extremely important*).

Reliability: Alpha coefficients ranged from .79 to .90.

Author: Rose, G. L.

Article: Group differences in graduate students' concepts of the ideal mentor.

Journal: *Research in Higher Education*, February 2005, *46*, 53–80.

Related Research: Rose, G. L. (2003). Enhancement of mentor selection using the Ideal Mentor Scale. *Research in Higher Education, 44*, 473–494.

13603

Test Name: IMMEDIATE SUPERVISOR SATISFACTION SCALE

Purpose: To measure supervisory satisfaction.

Number of Items: 13

Format: Scales range from 1 (*strongly disagree*) to 7 (*strongly agree*). A sample item is presented.

Reliability: Coefficient alpha was .93.

Validity: Correlations with other variables ranged from .14 to .67.

Author: Liao, H., and Rupp, D. E.

Article: The impact of justice climate and justice orientation on work outcomes: A cross-level multifoci framework.

Journal: *Journal of Applied Psychology*, March 2005, *90*, 242–256.

Related Research: Warr, P. B., & Routledge, T. (1969). An opinion scale for the measurement of managers' job satisfaction. *Occupational Psychology, 43*, 95–109.

13604

Test Name: IMPLICIT LEADERSHIP THEORY SCALE— REVISED

Purpose: To rate characteristics of a business leader: sensitivity, dedication, tyranny, masculinity, intelligence, and dynamism.

Number of Items: 21

Format: Scales range from 1 (*not at all*) to 9 (*extremely characteristic*).

Reliability: Alpha coefficients ranged from .70 to .88 across subscales.

Author: Epitropaki, O., and Martin, R.

Article: Implicit leadership theories in applied settings: Factor structure, generalizability, and stability over time.

Journal: *Journal of Applied Psychology*, April 2004, *89*, 293–310.

Related Research: Offermann, L. R., et al. (1994). Implicit leadership theories: Content, structure, and generalizability. *Leadership Quarterly, 5*, 43–58.

13605

Test Name: IN-ROLE BEHAVIOR SCALE

Purpose: To measure performance effectiveness.

Number of Items: 7

Format: Responses are made on a 5-point scale ranging from 1 (*ineffective*) to 5 (*highly effective*). An example is given.

Reliability: Alpha coefficients ranged from .90 to .95.

Author: Day, R., and Allen, T. D.

Article: The relationship between career motivation and self-efficacy with protégé career success.

Journal: *Journal of Vocational Behavior*, February 2004, *64*, 72–91.

Related Research: Williams, L. J., & Anderson, S. E. (1991). Job satisfaction and organizational commitment as predictors of organizational citizenship and in-role behaviors. *Journal of Management, 17*, 601–617.

13606

Test Name: IN-ROLE PERFORMANCE SCALE

Purpose: To measure in-role performance.

Number of Items: 4

Format: Responses are made on a 7-point scale ranging from 1 (*strongly disagree*) to 7 (*strongly agree*). Examples are given.

Reliability: Coefficient alpha was .87.

Validity: Correlations with other variables ranged from .31 to .67 (*n* = 186).

Author: Chen, Z. X., et al.

Article: Test of a mediation model of perceived organizational support.

Journal: *Journal of Vocational Behavior*, June 2005, *66*, 457–470.

Related Research: Farh, J. L., & Cheng, B. S. (1999). An investigation of modesty bias in self-ratings of work performance among Taiwan workers. *Chinese Journal of Psychology, 39*, 103–118. [In Chinese]

13607

Test Name: INTERPERSONAL FACILITATION SCALE

Purpose: To assess interpersonal job effectiveness by supervisor rating.

Number of Items: 5

Format: Scales range from 1 (*weak or bottom 10%*) to 5 (*best or top 10%*). All items are presented.

Reliability: Alpha coefficients ranged from .75 to .77.

Validity: Correlations with other variables ranged from −.04 to .25.

Author: Witt, L. A., and Ferris, G. R.

Article: Social skill as moderator of the conscientiousness–performance relationship: Convergent results across four studies.

Journal: *Journal of Applied Psychology*, October 2003, *88*, 809–820.

13608

Test Name: JEFFERSON SCALE OF PHYSICIAN EMPATHY

Purpose: To measure physician empathy.

Number of Items: 20

Format: Responses are made on a 7-point scale ranging from 1 (*strongly disagree*) to 7 (*strongly agree*). All items are presented.

Reliability: Alpha coefficients were .87 and .89.

Validity: Correlations with other variables ranged from −.05 to .56.

Author: Hojat, M., et al.

Article: The Jefferson Scale of Physician Empathy: Development and preliminary psychometric data.

Journal: *Educational and Psychological Measurement*, April 2001, *61*, 349–365.

13609

Test Name: JOB PERFORMANCE RATING SCALE

Purpose: To rate job performance.

Number of Items: 6

Format: Includes two factors: Task Performance and Contextual Performance. Responses are made on a 7-point scale ranging from 1 (*very poor*) to 7 (*outstanding*).

Reliability: Coefficient alpha was .81.

Validity: Correlations with other variables ranged from −.25 to .26.

Author: Kraimer, M. L., et al.

Article: Sources of support and expatriate performance: The mediating role of expatriate adjustment.

Journal: *Personnel Psychology*, Spring 2001, *54*, 71–99.

13610

Test Name: JOB PERFORMANCE SCALE

Purpose: To assess job performance.

Number of Items: 4

Reliability: Coefficient alpha was .92.

Validity: Correlations with other variables ranged from −.04 to .29.

Author: Cable, D. M., and DeRue, D. S.

Article: The convergent and discriminant validity of subjective fit perceptions.

Journal: *Journal of Applied Psychology*, October 2002, *87*, 875–884.

Related Research: Van Dyne, L., & LePine, J. A. (1998). Helping and voice extra-role behaviors: Evidence of construct and predictive validity. *Academy of Management Journal, 41*, 108–119.

13611

Test Name: JOB PERFORMANCE SCALE

Purpose: To measure job performance.

Number of Items: 30

Format: Includes three dimensions: Technical Performance, Communication Competency, and Management and Leadership Skills. Responses are made on a 5-point scale ranging from 1 (*very poor*) to 5 (*excellent*). Examples are given.

Reliability: Alpha coefficients were .89 and .90.

Validity: Correlations with other variables ranged from −.36 to .37 (*n* = 133).

Author: Takeuchi, R., et al.

Article: Antecedents and consequences of psychological workplace strain during expatriation: A cross-sectional and longitudinal investigation.

Journal: *Personnel Psychology,* Winter 2005, *58*, 925–948.

13612

Test Name: LEADERSHIP CLIMATE SCALE

Purpose: To assess leadership of military officers.

Number of Items: 5

Format: Scales range from 1 (*strongly disagree*) to 5 (*strongly agree*). Sample items are presented.

Reliability: Alpha coefficients ranged from .89 to .90.

Validity: Correlations with other variables ranged from −.09 to .65.

Author: Chen, G., and Bliese, P. D.

Article: The role of different levels of leadership in predicting self- and collective efficacy: Evidence for discontinuity.

Journal: *Journal of Applied Psychology,* June 2002, *87*, 549–556.

Related Research: Marlowe, D. H. (1986). *New manning system field evaluation* (Tech. Rep. No. 1, DTIC # ADA 162087). Washington, DC: Walter Reed Army Institute of Research.

13613

Test Name: LEADERSHIP SURVEY SCALE

Purpose: To enable subordinates to rate their managers.

Number of Items: 31

Format: Responses are made on a 5-point Likert-type scale ranging from 1 (*strongly agree*) to 5 (*strongly disagree*). All items are presented.

Reliability: Coefficient alpha was .98.

Validity: Correlations with other variables ranged from −.32 to .19.

Author: Smither, J. W., et al.

Article: An examination of the equivalence of web-based versus paper-and-pencil upward feedback ratings: Rater- and ratee-level analyses.

Journal: *Educational and Psychological Measurement,* February 2004, *64*, 40–61.

13614

Test Name: MANAGERIAL PERFORMANCE SCALE

Purpose: To assess managerial performance of the focal manager.

Number of Items: 5

Format: Responses are made on a 5-point scale ranging from 1 (*never*) to 5 (*almost always*).

Reliability: Coefficient alpha was .91.

Validity: Correlations with other variables ranged from −.06 to .79 (*N* = 3217).

Author: Ostroff, C., et al.

Article: Understanding self-other agreement: A look at rater and ratee characteristics, context, and outcomes.

Journal: *Personnel Psychology,* Summer 2004, *57*, 333–375.

13615

Test Name: MENTOR FUNCTIONS SCALES— ADAPTED

Purpose: To assess career and psychosocial mentoring functions.

Number of Items: 17

Format: Includes career mentoring and psychosocial mentoring items. Responses are made on a 5-point scale ranging from 1 (*no extent*) to 5 (*great extent*). Examples are given.

Reliability: Alpha coefficients were .76 and .84.

Validity: Correlations with other variables ranged from −.21 to .38.

Author: Allen, T. D.

Article: Mentoring others: A dispositional and motivational approach.

Journal: *Journal of Vocational Behavior,* February 2003, *62,* 134–154.

Related Research: Kram, K. E. (1985). *Mentoring at work: Developmental relationships in organizational life.* Glenview, IL: Scott Foresman.

13616

Test Name: MENTOR/PROTÉGÉ MENTORING RELATIONSHIP SATISFACTION SCALE

Purpose: To assess mentor–protégé satisfaction with the mentoring relationship.

Number of Items: 4

Format: Examples are given.

Reliability: Alpha coefficients were .75 and .92.

Validity: Correlations with other variables ranged from −.07 to .81.

Author: Ortiz-Walters, R., and Gilson, L. L.

Article: Mentoring in academia: An examination of the experiences of protégés of color.

Journal: *Journal of Vocational Behavior,* December 2005, *67,* 459–475.

Related Research: Ragins, B. R., et al. (2000). Marginal mentoring: The effects of type of mentor, quality of relationship, and program design on work and career attitudes. *Academy of Management Journal, 43,* 1177–1194.

13617

Test Name: MENTOR SUPPORT SCALE

Purpose: To assess mentor's support of one's efforts to balance work and family demands.

Number of Items: 8

Format: Responses are made on a 5-point scale ranging from 1 (*strongly disagree*) to 5 (*strongly agree*). All items are presented.

Reliability: Reliability coefficient was .77.

Validity: Correlations with other variables ranged from −.27 to .51.

Author: Nielson, T. R., et al.

Article: The supportive mentor as a means of reducing work–family conflict.

Journal: *Journal of Vocational Behavior,* December 2001, *59,* 364–381.

Related Research: Thomas, L. T., & Ganster, D. C. (1995). Impact of family-supportive work variables on work–family conflict and strain: A control perspective. *Journal of Applied Psychology, 80,* 6–15.

13618

Test Name: MENTORING AND COMMUNICATIONS SUPPORT SCALE

Purpose: To measure task support, career mentoring, coaching mentoring, and collegial social support.

Number of Items: 15

Format: Scales range from 1 (*strongly disagree*) to 5 (*strongly agree*).

Reliability: Alpha coefficients ranged from .75 to .89.

Validity: Correlations with other variables ranged from −.12 to .29.

Author: Harris, J. I., et al.

Article: The comparative contributions of congruence and social support in career outcomes.

Journal: *The Career Development Quarterly,* June 2001, *49,* 314–323.

Related Research: Hill, S. E. K., et al. (1989). Mentoring and other communication support in the academic setting. *Group and Organization Studies, 14,* 355–368.

13619

Test Name: MENTORING FUNCTIONS QUESTIONNAIRE

Purpose: To measure mentoring functions.

Number of Items: 9

Format: Includes three areas: vocational support, psychosocial support, and role modeling. Responses are made on a 5-point scale ranging from 1 (*strongly disagree*) to 5 (*strongly agree*). All items are presented.

Reliability: Alpha coefficients ranged from .71 to .88.

Validity: Correlations with other variables ranged from .48 to .78.

Author: Pellegrini, E. K., and Scandura, T. A.

Article: Construct equivalence across groups: An unexplored issue in mentoring research.

Journal: *Educational and Psychological Measurement,* April 2005, *65,* 323–335.

Related Research: Castro, S. L., & Scandura, T. A. (2004, November). *The tale of two measures: Evaluation and comparison of Scandura's (1992) and Ragins and McFarlin's (1990) mentoring measures.* Paper presented at the Southern Management Association Meeting, San Antonio, TX.

13620

Test Name: MENTORING FUNCTIONS SCALE

Purpose: To measure mentoring functions.

Number of Items: 21

Format: Includes two types of items: career function and psychosocial. Examples are presented.

Reliability: Alpha coefficients ranged from .79 to .94.

Author: Day, R., and Allen, T. D.

Article: The relationship between career motivation and self-efficacy with protégé career success.

Journal: *Journal of Vocational Behavior,* February 2004, *64,* 72–91.

Related Research: Noe, R. A. (1988). An investigation of the determinants of successful assigned mentoring relationships. *Personnel Psychology, 41,* 457–479.

13621

Test Name: MENTORING FUNCTIONS SCALE

Purpose: To measure mentoring functions.

Number of Items: 22

Format: Includes two scales: one pertaining to the mentor and one pertaining to the protégé. Responses are made on a 5-point scale ranging from 1 (*strongly disagree*) to 5 (*strongly agree*).

Reliability: Alpha coefficients ranged from .69 to .87.

Author: Lankau, M. J., et al.

Article: The effects of similarity and liking in formal relationships between mentors and protégés.

Journal: *Journal of Vocational Behavior,* October 2005, *67,* 252–265.

Related Research: Scandura, T. A., & Ragins, B. R. (1993). The effects of sex and gender role orientation on mentorship in male-dominated occupations. *Journal of Vocational Behavior, 43,* 251–265.

13622

Test Name: MENTORING FUNCTIONS SCALE

Purpose: To measure amount of mentoring one received.

Number of Items: 15

Format: Includes three subscales: Career Development, Psychosocial Support, and Role Modeling. Examples are presented.

Reliability: Alpha coefficients ranged from .80 to .85.

Validity: Correlations with other variables ranged from –.20 to .43.

Author: Nielson, T. R., et al.

Article: The supportive mentor as a means of reducing work–family conflict.

Journal: *Journal of Vocational Behavior,* December 2001, *59,* 364–381.

Related Research: Scandura, T. A. (1992). Mentorship and career mobility: An empirical investigation. *Journal of Organizational Behavior, 13,* 169–174.

13623

Test Name: MENTORING FUNCTIONS SCALE—REVISED

Purpose: To assess students' perceptions of the adequacy of their relationship with their mentor.

Number of Items: 10

Format: Responses are made on a 5-point scale ranging from 1 (*to a very slight extent*) to 5 (*to a very large extent*).

Reliability: Internal consistency was .88.

Validity: Correlations with other variables ranged from –.01 to .35 (*N* = 149).

Author: Kahn, J. H.

Article: Predicting the scholarly activity of counseling psychology students: A refinement and extension.

Journal: *Journal of Counseling Psychology,* July 2001, *48,* 344–354.

Related Research: Noe, R. A. (1988). An investigation of the determinants of successful assigned mentoring relationships. *Personnel Psychology, 41,* 457–479.

13624

Test Name: MENTORING FUNCTIONS SCALE— REVISED

Purpose: To measure mentoring functions.

Number of Items: 17

Format: Includes three scales: Vocational Support, Psychosocial Support, and Role Modeling. Responses are made on a 5-point scale ranging from 1 (*strongly agree*) to 5 (*strongly disagree*). Sample items are presented.

Author: Scandura, T. A., and Williams, E. A.

Article: An investigation of the moderating effects of gender on the relationships between mentorship initiation and protégé perceptions of mentoring functions.

Journal: *Journal of Vocational Behavior,* December 2001, *59,* 342–363.

Related Research: Scandura, T. A. (1992). Mentorship and career mobility: An empirical investigation. *Journal of Organizational Behavior, 13,* 169–174.

13625

Test Name: MENTORING FUNCTIONS SCALES

Purpose: To assess the degree of mentoring received by the protégé.

Number of Items: 17

Format: Includes two scales: Career Development and Psychosocial Support. Sample items are presented.

Reliability: Alpha coefficients were .86 and .87.

Validity: Correlations with other variables ranged from −.22 to .69.

Author: Godshalk, V. M., and Sosik, J. J.

Article: Aiming for career success: The role of learning goal orientation in mentoring relationships.

Journal: *Journal of Vocational Behavior*, December 2003, *63*, 417–437.

Related Research: Noe, R. (1988). An investigation of the determinants of successful assigned mentoring relationships. *Personnel Psychology, 41*, 457–479.

13626

Test Name: MENTORING PROVIDED SCALE

Purpose: To assess mentoring provided.

Number of Items: 6

Format: Responses are made on a 5-point scale ranging from 1 (*not at all*) to 5 (*to a great extent*).

Reliability: Coefficient alpha was .87.

Author: Bozionelos, N.

Article: Mentoring provided: Relation to mentor's career success, personality, and mentoring received.

Journal: *Journal of Vocational Behavior*, February 2004, *64*, 24–46.

Related Research: Kram, K. E. (1985). *Mentoring at work: Developmental relationships in organizational life.* Glenview, IL: Scott Foresman.

13627

Test Name: MENTORING RECEIVED SCALE

Purpose: To assess mentoring received.

Number of Items: 7

Format: Responses are made on a 5-point scale ranging from 1 (*not at all*) to 5 (*to a great extent*).

Reliability: Coefficient alpha was .88.

Author: Bozionelos, N.

Article: Mentoring provided: Relation to mentor's career success, personality, and mentoring received.

Journal: *Journal of Vocational Behavior*, February 2004, *64*, 24–46.

Related Research: Dreher, G. F., & Ash, R. A. (1990). A comparative study of mentoring among men and women in managerial, professional, and technical positions. *Journal of Applied Psychology, 75*, 539–546.

13628

Test Name: MENTORING RECEIVED SCALE

Purpose: To provide a comprehensive measure of mentoring.

Number of Items: 24

Format: Includes four factors: psychosocial mentoring, exposure/visibility and sponsorship, challenging assignments, and protection and assistance. All items are presented.

Reliability: Alpha coefficients ranged from .83 to .96.

Validity: Correlations with other variables ranged from −.21 to .73.

Author: Turban, D. B., et al.

Article: Gender, race, and perceived similarity effects in developmental relationships: The moderating role of relationship duration.

Journal: *Journal of Vocational Behavior*, October 2002, *61*, 240–262.

Related Research: Kram, K. (1985). *Mentoring at work: Developmental relationships in organizational life.* Glenview, IL: Scott Foresman.

13629

Test Name: MENTORING SUPPORT SCALE

Purpose: To measure psychosocial, instrumental, and networking support.

Number of Items: 19

Format: Includes three factors: psychosocial, instrumental, and networking. Responses are made on a 7-point scale ranging from 1 (*not at all*) to 7 (*a great deal*). Examples are given.

Reliability: Alpha coefficients were .92 and .93 with the two items of the networking factor correlating at .76.

Validity: Correlations with other variables ranged from −.02 to .78.

Author: Ortiz-Walters, R., and Gilson, L. L.

Article: Mentoring in academia: An examination of the experiences of protégés of color.

Journal: *Journal of Vocational Behavior*, December 2005, *67*, 459–475.

Related Research: Tenenbaum, H. R., et al. (2001). Mentoring relationships in graduate school. *Journal of Vocational Behavior, 59*, 326–341.

13630

Test Name: MISSOURI IDENTIFYING TRANSFERENCE SCALE

Purpose: To enable the therapist to evaluate client transference reactions during the most recent session.

Number of Items: 37

Format: Includes two subscales: Negative Transference and Positive Transference. Responses are made on a 5-point scale ranging from 1 (*not evident*) to 5 (*very evident*). Examples are given.

Reliability: Alpha coefficients ranged from .84 to .96

Validity: Correlations with other variables ranged from −.39 to .53.

Author: Woodhouse, S. S., et al.

Article: Client attachment to therapist: Relations to transference and client recollections of parental caregiving.

Journal: *Journal of Counseling Psychology*, October 2003, *50*, 395–408.

Related Research: Multon, K. D., et al. (1996). Development of the Missouri Identifying Transference Scale. *Journal of Counseling Psychology, 43,* 243–252.

13631

Test Name: MULTICULTURAL AWARENESS, KNOWLEDGE, AND SKILLS SURVEY— COUNSELOR EDITION REVISED

Purpose: To measure counseling awareness, knowledge, and skills.

Number of Items: 33

Format: Scales range from 1 (*very limited/strongly disagree*) to 4 (*very aware/good/strongly agree*). All items are presented.

Reliability: Subscales alpha coefficients ranged from .82 to .87.

Validity: Correlations with other variables ranged from .01 to .80.

Author: Kim, B. S. K., et al.

Article: A revision of the Multicultural Awareness, Knowledge, and Skills Survey— Counselor Edition.

Journal: *Measurement and Evaluation in Counseling and Development*, October 2003, *36*, 161–180.

Related Research: D'Andrea, M., et al. (1991). Evaluating the impact of multicultural counseling training. *Journal of Counseling and Development, 70,* 143–150.

13632

Test Name: MULTICULTURAL COMPETENCE IN STUDENT AFFAIRS SCALE

Purpose: To assess cultural competence of student affairs professionals.

Number of Items: 34

Format: Scales range from 1 (*not at all accurate*) to 7 (*very accurate*).

Reliability: Coefficient alpha was .94.

Author: Pope, R. L., and Mueller, J. A.

Article: Faculty and curriculum: Examining multicultural competence and inclusion.

Journal: *Journal of College Student Development*, November/December 2005, *46*, 679–688.

Related Research: Pope, R. L., & Mueller, J. A. (2000). Development and initial validation of the Multicultural Competence in Student Affairs—Preliminary 2 Scale. *Journal of College Student Development, 41,* 599–608.

13633

Test Name: MULTICULTURAL COUNSELING COMPETENCE AND TRAINING SURVEY

Purpose: To measure the perceived multicultural competence of counselors.

Number of Items: 32

Format: All items are presented. Four-point scales range from 1 (*not competent*) to 4 (*extremely competent*).

Reliability: Alpha coefficients ranged from .66 to .92 across subscales.

Author: Holcomb-McCoy, C. C.

Article: Investigating school counselors' perceived multicultural competence.

Journal: *Professional School Counseling*, June 2005, *8*, 414–423.

Related Research: Holcomb-McCoy, C. (2001). Exploring the self-perceived multicultural counseling competence of elementary school counselors. *Professional School Counseling, 4,* 195–201.

13634

Test Name: MULTICULTURAL COUNSELING INVENTORY

Purpose: To provide a self-report measure of multicultural competencies.

Number of Items: 40

Format: Includes four subscales: Awareness, Knowledge, Skills, and Relationship. Responses are made on a 4-point scale ranging from 1 (*very inaccurate*) to 4 (*very accurate*).

Reliability: Alpha coefficients ranged from .68 to .89.

Validity: Correlations with other variables ranged from −.09 to .35.

Author: Constantine, M. G.

Article: Predictors of observer ratings of multicultural counseling competence in Black, Latino, and White American trainees.

Journal: *Journal of Counseling Psychology*, October 2001, *48*, 456–462.

Related Research: Sodowsky, G. R., et al. (1994). Development of the Multicultural Counseling Inventory: A self-report measure of multicultural competencies. *Journal of Counseling Psychology*, *41*, 137–148.

13635

Test Name: MULTICULTURAL KNOWLEDGE AND AWARENESS SCALE

Purpose: To measure multicultural counseling competence.

Number of Items: 32

Format: Scale range from 1 (*not at all true*) to 7 (*totally true*).

Reliability: Alpha coefficients ranged from .85 to .90 across subscales.

Validity: Correlations with other variables ranged from −.22 to .67.

Author: Kim, B. S. K., et al.

Article: A revision of the Multicultural Awareness, Knowledge, and Skills Survey—Counselor Edition.

Journal: *Measurement and Evaluation in Counseling and Development*, October 2003, *36*, 161–180.

Related Research: Ponterontto, J. G., et al. (2002). A revision of the Multicultural Counseling Awareness Scale. *Journal Multicultural Counseling and Development*, *30*, 153–180.

13636

Test Name: NEGATIVE APPRAISALS SCALE

Purpose: To measure negative appraisals.

Number of Items: 2

Format: Responses are made on a 5-point Likert scale ranging from 5 (*strongly agree*) to 1 (*strongly disagree*). Both items are presented.

Reliability: Alpha coefficients were .83 and .92. Test–retest reliability was .56.

Validity: Correlations with other variable ranged from −.14 to .57.

Author: Fugate, M., et al.

Article: Coping with an organizational merger over four stages.

Journal: *Personnel Psychology*, Winter 2002, *55*, 905–928.

Related Research: MacNair, R. R., & Elliot, T. R. (1992). Self-perceived problem-solving ability, stress appraisal, and coping over time. *Journal of Research in Personality*, *26*, 150–164.

13637

Test Name: NEGATIVE MENTORING EXPERIENCES MEASURE

Purpose: To measure negative mentoring experiences.

Number of Items: 42

Format: Includes five factors: mismatch within the dyad, distancing behavior, manipulative behavior, lack of mentor expertise, and general dysfuntionality. Responses are made on 5-point scales ranging from 1 (*strongly disagree*) to 5 (*strongly agree*). All items are presented.

Reliability: Alpha coefficients ranged from .87 to 94.

Validity: Correlations with other variables ranged from −.64 to .58.

Author: Eby, L., et al.

Article: Proteges' negative mentoring experiences: Construct development and nomological validation.

Journal: *Personnel Psychology*, Summer 2004, *57*, 411–447.

13638

Test Name: OUTCOME QUESTIONNAIRE

Purpose: To measure client changes occurring throughout the course of mental health treatments.

Number of Items: 45

Format: Includes three subscales: Symptom Distress, Interpersonal Relations, and Social Role. Responses are made on a 5-point scale ranging from 0 (*never*) to 4 (*almost always*). Examples are given.

Reliability: Test–retest (3 weeks) reliability was .84. Alpha coefficients ranged from .66 to .93.

Author: Vermeersch, D. A., et al.

Article: Outcome Questionnaire: Is it sensitive to changes in counseling center clients?

Journal: *Journal of Counseling Psychology*, January 2004, *51*, 38–49.

Related Research: Lambert, M. J., et al. (1996). The reliability and validity of the Outcome Questionnaire. *Clinical Psychology and Psychotherapy*, *3*, 249–258.

13639

Test Name: PATIENT SATISFACTION SCALE

Purpose: To measure patient perceptions of physician behavior.

Number of Items: 26

Format: A Likert format is used.

Reliability: Coefficient alpha was .97.

Author: Aruguete, M. S., and Roberts, C. A.

Article: Participants' ratings of male physicians who vary in race and communication style.

Journal: *Psychological Reports*, December 2002, *91*, Part 1, 793–806.

Related Research: Wolfe, M. H., et al. (1978). The Medical Interview Satisfaction Scale: Development of a scale to measure patient perceptions of physician behavior. *Journal of Behavioral Medicine, 1*, 391–401.

13640

Test Name: PENNEBAKER INVENTORY OF LIMBIC LANGUIDNESS SCALE

Purpose: To assess caregiver health complaints.

Number of Items: 54

Format: A yes–no format is used.

Reliability: Internal consistency was .88. Test–retest reliability ranged from .51 to .84.

Validity: Correlations with other variables ranged from −.08 to .75.

Author: Elliott, T. R., et al.

Article: Family caregiver social problem-solving abilities and adjustment during the initial year of the caregiving role.

Journal: *Journal of Counseling Psychology*, April 2001, *48*, 223–232.

Related Research: Pennebaker, J. W. (1982). *The psychology of physical symptoms.* New York: Springer-Verlag.

13641

Test Name: PERCEIVED AUTHORITATIVE TEACHING SCALE

Purpose: To measure perceived authoritative teaching style.

Number of Items: 9

Format: Responses are made on a 5-point scale ranging from 0 (*not at all true of our teacher*) to 4 (*very much true of our teacher*). Sample items are presented.

Reliability: Alpha coefficients were .87 and .93.

Validity: Correlations with other variables ranged from −.03 to .28.

Author: Chang, L., et al.

Article: Mediating teacher liking and moderating authoritative teaching on Chinese adolescents' perceptions of antisocial and prosocial behaviors.

Journal: *Journal of Educational Psychology*, June 2004, *96*, 369–380.

Related Research: Paulson, S. E., et al. (1998). Early adolescents' perceptions of patterns of parenting, teaching, and school atmosphere: Implications for achievement. *Journal of Early Adolescence, 18*, 5–26.

13642

Test Name: PERCEIVED COMPETENCE, INTEGRITY, AND RISK SCALES

Purpose: To assess perception of job applicants' competence, integrity, and willingness to take risks.

Number of Items: 3

Format: Scales range from 1 (*strongly disagree*) to 7 (*strongly agree*). All items are presented.

Reliability: Alpha coefficients ranged from .69 to .84.

Validity: Correlations with other variables ranged from .28 to .66.

Author: Kim, P. H., et al.

Article: Removing the shadow of suspicion: The effects of apology versus denial for repairing competence- versus integrity-based trust violations.

Journal: *Journal of Applied Psychology*, February 2004, *89*, 104–118.

Related Research: Mayer, R. C., & Davis, J. H. (1999). The effect of the performance appraisal system on trust for management: A field quasi-experiment. *Journal of Applied Psychology, 84*, 123–136.

13643

Test Name: PERCEIVED PERSON–JOB FIT SCALE

Purpose: To measure perceived person–job fit.

Number of Items: 5

Format: Responses are made on a 7-point Likert scale ranging from *strongly disagree* to *strongly agree*. Examples are presented.

Reliability: Coefficient alpha was .79.

Validity: Correlations with other variables ranged from −.31 to .46.

Author: Lauver, K. L., and Kristof-Brown, A.

Article: Distinguishing between employees' perceptions of person–job and person–organization fit.

Journal: *Journal of Vocational Behavior*, December 2001, *59*, 454–470.

Related Research: Edwards, J. R. (1991). Person–job fit: A conceptual integration, literature review, and methodological critique. *International Review of Industrial and Organizational Psychology, 6*, 283–357.

13644

Test Name: PERCEIVED PERSON–ORGANIZATION FIT SCALE

Purpose: To assess employees' perceived person–organization fit.

Number of Items: 3

Format: Responses are made on a 7-point Likert scale ranging from *strongly disagree* to *strongly agree*. All items are included.

Reliability: Coefficient alpha was .83.

Validity: Correlations with other variables ranged from –.53 to .47.

Author: Lauver, K. L., and Kristof-Brown, A.

Article: Distinguishing between employees' perceptions of person–job and person–organization fit.

Journal: *Journal of Vocational Behavior*, December 2001, *59*, 454–470.

Related Research: Cable, D. M., & Judge, T. A. (1996). Person–organization fit, job choice decisions, and organizational entry. *Organizational Behavior and Human Decision Processes*, *67*, 294–311.

13645

Test Name: PERCEIVED SUPERVISOR SUPPORT SCALE

Purpose: To assess to what degree a supervisor shows concern for those who work for him or her.

Number of Items: 4

Format: Scales range from 1 (*strongly disagree*) to 7 (*strongly agree*). All items are presented.

Reliability: Coefficient alpha was .90.

Validity: Correlations with other variables ranged from –.12 to .65.

Author: Rhoades, L., et al.

Article: Affective commitment to the organization: The contribution of perceived organizational support.

Journal: *Journal of Applied Psychology*, October 2001, *86*, 825–836.

13646

Test Name: PERCEIVED TEACHER SUPPORT FOR MUTUAL RESPECT SCALE

Purpose: To measure students' perceptions of the extent to which the teachers in their teams promoted mutual respect among classmates in the context of instruction.

Number of Items: 7

Format: An example is given.

Reliability: Coefficient alpha was .78.

Validity: Correlations with other variables ranged from .14 to .65 (*n* = 599).

Author: Anderman, L. H.

Article: Academic and social perceptions as predictors of change in middle school students' sense of school belonging.

Journal: *Journal of Experimental Education*, Fall 2003, *72*, 5–22.

Related Research: Ryan, A. M., & Patrick, H. (2001). The classroom social environment and changes in adolescents' motivation and engagement during middle school. *American Educational Research Journal*, *38*, 437–460.

13647

Test Name: PERCEPTION OF EQUALITY/DISCRIMINATION IN PHYSICAL EDUCATION QUESTIONNAIRE—REVISED

Purpose: To assess whether pupils perceive that their teacher carries out sex-equitable physical education sessions.

Number of Items: 17

Format: Includes two factors: equality and discrimination. Responses are made on a Likert-type scale ranging from 0 (*total disagreement*) to 100 (*total agreement*). Examples are given.

Reliability: Alpha coefficients were .78 and .82.

Validity: Correlations with other variables ranged from –.37 to .45.

Author: Cervelló, E. M., et al.

Article: Goal orientations, motivational climate, equality, and discipline of Spanish physical education students.

Journal: *Perceptual and Motor Skills*, August 2004, *99*, 271–283.

13648

Test Name: PERCEPTIONS OF EFFECTIVE DELIVERY SCALE

Purpose: To evaluate a speaker on effectiveness of delivery.

Number of Items: 13

Format: Bipolar adjectives are rated on a 7-point scale.

Reliability: Coefficient alpha was .92.

Author: Towler, A. J.

Article: Effects of charismatic influence training on attitudes, behavior, and performance.

Journal: *Personal Psychology*, Summer 2003, *56*, 363–381.

Related Research: Holladay, S. J., & Coombs, W. T. (1993). Communicating visions: An exploration of the role of delivery in the creation of leader charisma. *Management Communication Quarterly*, *6*, 405–427.

13649

Test Name: PERFORMANCE MEASURES

Purpose: To measure performance.

Number of Items: 8

Format: Includes two scales: Task Performance and Interpersonal Performance. Responses are made on a 6-point scale ranging from 1 (*somewhat below requirements*) to 6 (*consistently exceeds requirements*). Examples are given.

Reliability: Coefficient alpha was .84.

Validity: Correlations with other variables ranged from –.15 to .20 (*n* = 102).

Author: Barrick, M. R., et al.

Article: Self-monitoring as a moderator of the relationships between personality traits and performance.

Journal: *Personnel Psychology*, Autumn 2005, *58*, 745–767.

Related Research: Campbell, J. P. (1991). Modeling the performance prediction problem in industrial and organizational psychology. In Dunnette, M. D., & Hough, L. M. (Eds.), *Handbook of industrial and organizational psychology* (2nd ed., Vol. 1, pp. 687–732). Palo Alto, CA: Consulting Psychologists Press.

13650

Test Name: PERSON–JOB AND PERSON–ORGANIZATION FIT SCALES

Purpose: To assess how employees fit their organizational environment.

Number of Items: 4

Format: Scales range from 1 (*strongly disagree*) to 5 (*strongly agree*). All items are presented.

Reliability: Alpha coefficients exceeded .81.

Validity: Correlations with other variables ranged from –.13 to .09.

Author: Caldwell, S. D.

Article: Toward an understanding of the relationships among organizational change, individual differences, and changes in person–environment fit: A cross-level study.

Journal: *Journal of Applied Psychology*, October 2004, *89*, 868–882.

13651

Test Name: PERSON–JOB AND PERSON–ORGANIZATION FIT SCALES

Purpose: To assess perceptions of how well a person will fit a job and an organization.

Number of Items: 8

Format: Scales range from 1 (*to a very little extent*) to 5 (*to a very large extent*). All items are presented.

Reliability: Alpha coefficients ranged from .84 to .90.

Validity: Correlations with other variables ranged from –.70 to .77.

Author: Saks, A. M., and Ashforth, B. E.

Article: Is job search related to employment quality? It all depends on the fit.

Journal: *Journal of Applied Psychology*, August 2002, *87*, 646–654.

13652

Test Name: PERSON–JOB FIT MEASURE

Purpose: To measure person–job fit.

Number of Items: 3

Format: Responses are made on a 7-point scale ranging from 1 (*strongly disagree*) to 7 (*strongly agree*). An example is given.

Reliability: Reliability coefficients were .71 and .93.

Validity: Correlations with other variables ranged from –.20 to .67.

Author: Erdogan, B., and Bauer, T. N.

Article: Enhancing career benefits of employee proactive personality: The role of fit with jobs and organizations.

Journal: *Personnel Psychology*, Winter 2005, *58*, 859–891.

Related Research: Cable, D. M., & DeRue, D. S. (2002). The convergent and discriminant validity of subjective fit perceptions. *Journal of Applied Psychology*, *87*, 875–884.

13653

Test Name: PERSON–JOB FIT SCALE

Purpose: To provide a global assessment of person–job fit.

Number of Items: 3

Format: Responses are made on a 5-point scale ranging from *strongly disagree* to *strongly agree*. All items are presented.

Reliability: Coefficient alpha was .85.

Validity: Correlations with other variables ranged from –.16 to .46.

Author: Singh, R., and Greenhaus, J. H.

Article: The relation between career decision-making strategies and person–job fit: A study of job changers.

Journal: *Journal of Vocational Behavior*, February 2004, *64*, 198–221.

Related Research: Bretz, R. D., & Judge, T. A. (1994). Person–organization fit and the theory of work adjustment: Implications for satisfaction, tenure, and career success. *Journal of Vocational Behavior*, *44*, 32–54.

13654

Test Name: PERSON–ORGANIZATION FIT SCALE—KOREAN VERSION

Purpose: To measure person–organization fit.

Number of Items: 3

Format: Scales range from 1 (*strongly disagree*) to 7 (*strongly agree*). All items are presented in English.

Reliability: Reported reliability was .91.

Validity: Correlations with other variables ranged from –.20 to .51.

Author: Kim, T.-Y., et al.

Article: Socialization tactics, employee proactivity, and person–organization fit.

Journal: *Journal of Applied Psychology*, March 2005, *90*, 232–241.

Related Research: Cable, D. M., & DeRue, D.S. (2002). The convergent, and discriminant validity of subjective fit perceptions. *Journal of Applied Psychology, 87*, 875–884.

13655

Test Name: POLITICAL SKILL INVENTORY

Purpose: To assess level of political skill.

Number of Items: 6

Format: Responses are made on a 7-point scale ranging from 1 (*strongly disagree*) to 7 (*strongly agree*). All items are presented.

Reliability: Coefficient alpha was .74.

Validity: Correlations with other variables ranged from –.15 to .48.

Author: Kolodinsky, R. W., et al.

Article: Nonlinearity in the relationship between political skill and work outcomes: Convergent evidence from three studies.

Journal: *Journal of Vocational Behavior*, October 2004, *65*, 294–308.

Related Research: Ferris, G. R., et al. (1999). *Development and initial validation of the Political Skill Inventory.* Paper presented at the 59th annual national meeting of the Academy of Management, Chicago.

13656

Test Name: PREMARITAL COUNSELING SCALES

Purpose: To measure pastoral competence, counseling quality, and counseling value.

Number of Items: 13

Format: Five-point agreement scales are used. All items are presented.

Reliability: Alpha coefficients ranged from .61 to .87 across subscales.

Validity: Correlations with other variables ranged from –.27 to .17.

Author: Schumm, W. R., and West, D. R.

Article: Development of three new scales for assessing clients' perspectives on premarital counseling.

Journal: *Psychological Reports*, June 2001, *88*, Part 2, 1071–1074.

13657

Test Name: PRIMARY ADVISER HELP SCALE

Purpose: To measure primary adviser's psychosocial, instrumental, and networking help.

Number of Items: 19

Format: Includes three factors: psychosocial, instrumental, and networking. All items are presented.

Reliability: Alpha coefficients ranged from .80 to .93.

Author: Tenenbaum, H. R., et al.

Article: Mentoring relationships in graduate school.

Journal: *Journal of Vocational Behavior*, December 2001, *59*, 326–341.

Related Research: Dreher, G. F., & Ash, R. (1990). A comparative study of mentoring among men and women in managerial, professional, and technical positions. *Journal of Applied Psychology, 75*, 539–546.

13658

Test Name: PRINCIPAL'S LEADERSHIP SCALES

Purpose: To assess transformational and transactional leadership in school principals.

Number of Items: 27

Format: Scales range from 1 (*not at all typical*) to 5 (*very typical*). Sample items are presented.

Reliability: Alpha coefficients ranged from .70 to .94.

Author: Bogler, R.

Article: Satisfaction of Jewish and Arab teachers in Israel.

Journal: *The Journal of Social Psychology*, February 2005, *145*, 19–33.

Related Research: Bass, B. M. (1985). *Leadership and performance beyond expectations.* New York: Free Press.

13659

Test Name: PRODUCTIVITY MAINTENANCE SCALE

Purpose: To measure productivity maintenance.

Number of Items: 5

Format: Responses are made on a 5-point Likert scale ranging from *strongly disagree* to *strongly agree*. All items are presented.

Reliability: Internal consistency reliability was .71.

Validity: Correlations with other variables ranged from –.10 to .17.

Author: Parker, L., and Allen, T. D.

Article: Work/family benefits: Variables related to employees' fairness perceptions.

Journal: *Journal of Vocational Behavior*, June 2001, *58*, 453–468.

13660

Test Name: PROTÉGÉ SATISFACTION SCALE

Purpose: To measure protégé satisfaction with the mentoring relationship.

Number of Items: 4

Format: Responses are made on a 7-point scale ranging from 1 (*strongly disagree*) to 7 (*strongly agree*). A sample item is given.

Reliability: Coefficient alpha was .79.

Validity: Correlations with other variables ranged from .48 to .78.

Author: Pellegrini, E. K., and Scandura, T. A.

Article: Construct equivalence across groups: An unexplored issue in mentoring research.

Journal: *Educational and Psychological Measurement*, April 2005, *65*, 323–335.

Related Research: Ragins, B. R., & Cotton, J. L. (1999). Mentor functions and outcomes: A comparison of men and women in formal and informal mentoring relationships. *Journal of Applied Psychology, 84*, 529–550.

13661

Test Name: PROTÉGÉ SATISFACTION WITH THE MENTOR SCALE

Purpose: To measure protégé satisfaction with the mentor.

Number of Items: 6

Format: Responses are made on a 7-point scale ranging from 1 (*strongly disagree*) to 7 (*strongly agree*). Examples are presented.

Reliability: Alpha coefficients ranged from .83 to .89.

Author: Linnehan, F.

Article: A longitudinal study of work-based, adult–youth mentoring.

Journal: *Journal of Vocational Behavior*, August 2003, *63*, 40–54.

Related Research: Ragins, B. R., & Cotton, J. L. (1999). Mentor functions and outcomes: A comparison of men and women in formal and informal mentoring relationships. *Journal of Applied Psychology, 84*, 529–550.

13662

Test Name: PROTÉGÉ SELECTION CHARACTERISTICS SCALE

Purpose: To identify the importance of mentoring protégé characteristics.

Number of Items: 8

Format: Include two factors: ability and willingness to learn. Responses are made on a 5-point scale ranging from 1 (*not at all important*) to 5 (*extremely important*).

Reliability: Alpha coefficients were .70 and .76.

Validity: Correlations with other variables ranged from –.03 to .31.

Author: Allen, T. D.

Article: Protégé selection by mentors: Contributing individual and organizational factors.

Journal: *Journal of Vocational Behavior*, December 2004, *65*, 469–483.

Related Research: Allen, T. D., et al. (1997). The mentor's perspective: A qualitative inquiry and agenda for future research. *Journal of Vocational Behavior, 51*, 70–89.

13663

Test Name: REAL RELATIONSHIP INVENTORY— THERAPIST FORM

Purpose: To measure the relationship between therapist and client.

Number of Items: 24

Format: Includes two subscales: Realism and Genuineness.

Responses are made on a 5-point Likert scale ranging from 1 (*strongly disagree*) to 5 (*strongly agree*). All items are presented.

Reliability: Alpha coefficients ranged from .72 to .93.

Validity: Correlations with other variables ranged from –.29 to .55.

Author: Gelso, C. J., et al.

Article: Measuring the real relationship in psychotherapy: Initial validation of the Therapist Form.

Journal: *Journal of Counseling Psychology*, October 2005, *52*, 640–649.

13664

Test Name: RELATIONAL HEALTH INDICES

Purpose: To measure relationship quality in peer and mentor relationships in terms of engagement, authenticity, and empowerment.

Number of Items: 37

Format: Five-point Likert scales are used. All items are presented.

Reliability: Alpha coefficients ranged from .73 to .91.

Validity: Correlations between subscales ranged from .07 to .37.

Author: Frey, L. L., et al.

Article: The Relational Health Indices: Reanalysis of a measure of relational quality.

Journal: *Measurement and Evaluation in Counseling and Development*, October 2005, *38*, 153–164.

Related Research: Liang, B., et al. (2002). The Relational Health Indices: A study of women's relationships. *Psychology of Women Quarterly, 26*, 25–35.

13665

Test Name: RELATIONSHIP QUALITY SCALE

Purpose: To assess perceptions employees have of their supervisors' understanding of problems and needs.

Number of Items: 7

Format: Scales range from 1 (*strongly disagree*) to 5 (*strongly agree*). A sample item is presented.

Reliability: Coefficient alpha was .87.

Validity: Correlations with other variables ranged from −.14 to .47.

Author: Kacmar, K. M., et al.

Article: The interactive effects of leader–member exchange and communication frequency on performance ratings.

Journal: *Journal of Applied Psychology*, August 2003, *88*, 764–772.

Related Research: Scandura, T. A., et al. (1986). When managers decide not to decide autocratically: An investigation of leader–member exchange and decision influence. *Journal of Applied Psychology, 71*, 579–585.

13666

Test Name: RELATIONSHIP SCALE

Purpose: To assess client-perceived strength of the therapeutic relationship.

Number of Items: 4

Format: Responses are made on a 4-point scale ranging from 1 (*strongly disagree*) to 4 (*strongly agree*). All items are presented.

Reliability: Alpha coefficients ranged from .72 to .81.

Validity: Correlations with other variables ranged from .51 to .77.

Author: Kim, B. S. K., et al.

Article: Counselor self-disclosure, East Asian American client adherence to Asian cultural values, and counseling process.

Journal: *Journal of Counseling Psychology*, July 2003, *50*, 324–332.

Related Research: Hill, C. E., & Kellems, I. S. (2002). Development and use of the Helping Skills Measure to assess client perceptions of the effects of training and of helping skills in sessions. *Journal of Counseling Psychology, 49*, 264–272.

13667

Test Name: REVISED HELPING ALLIANCE QUESTIONNAIRE

Purpose: To measure the alliance between client and therapist.

Number of Items: 19

Reliability: Alpha coefficients were .84 and .90. Test–retest reliability was .78

Validity: Correlations with the California Psychotherapy Alliance Scales ranged from .59 to .71.

Author: Whipple, J. L., et al.

Article: Improving the effects of psychotherapy: The use of early identification of treatment failure and problem-solving strategies in routine practice.

Journal: *Journal of Counseling Psychology*, January 2003, *50*, 59–68.

Related Research: Luborsky, L., et al. (1996). The revised Helping Alliance Questionnaire (HAq–II). *Journal of Psychotherapy Practice and Research, 5*, 260–271.

13668

Test Name: ROLE-BASED JOB PERFORMANCE SCALE

Purpose: To assess job performance.

Number of Items: 4

Format: Responses are made on a 5-point scale ranging from 1 (*needs much improvement*) to 5 (*excellent*). Examples are given.

Reliability: Coefficient alpha was .76 (*n* = 195).

Validity: Correlations with other variables ranged from −.21 to .44 (*n* = 195).

Author: Lubbers, R., et al.

Article: Young workers' job self-efficacy and affect: Pathways to health and performance.

Journal: *Journal of Vocational Behavior*, October 2005, *67*, 199–214.

Related Research: Welbourne, T. M., et al. (1998). The Role-Based Performance Scale: Validity analysis of a theory-based measure. *Academy of Management Journal, 41*, 540–555.

13669

Test Name: SALES ROLE PERFORMANCE SCALES

Purpose: To measure in-role performance dealing with customers and extra-role performance in dealing with others.

Number of Items: 27

Format: Scales range from 1 (*totally disagree*) to 7 (*totally agree*). All items are presented.

Reliability: Alpha coefficients ranged from .72 to .92.

Validity: Correlations with other variables ranged from −.36 to .69.

Author: Bagozzi, R. P., et al.

Article: Culture moderates the self-regulation of shame and its effects on performance: The case of salespersons in the Netherlands and the Philippines.

Journal: *Journal of Applied Psychology*, April 2003, *88*, 219–233.

13670

Test Name: SATISFACTION WITH SUPERVISOR SCALE

Purpose: To measure subordinate's satisfaction with supervisor.

Number of Items: 9

Format: A yes–no format is used.

Reliability: Coefficient alpha was .84.

Validity: Correlations with other variables ranged from –.19 to .20.

Author: Glomb, T. M., and Welsh, E. T.

Article: Can opposites attract? Personality heterogeneity in supervisor–subordinate dyads as a predictor of subordinate outcomes.

Journal: *Journal of Applied Psychology*, July 2005, *90*, 749–757.

13671

Test Name: SATISFACTION WITH THE LEADER SCALE

Purpose: To measure satisfaction with a team leader.

Number of Items: 7

Format: Scales range from 1 (*strongly disagree*) to 5 (*strongly agree*).

Reliability: Coefficient alpha was .94.

Author: Phillips, J. M., et al.

Article: The role of justice in team member satisfaction with the leader and attachment to the team.

Journal: *Journal of Applied Psychology*, April 2001, *86*, 316–325.

Related Research: Seashore, S. E., et al. (1982). *Observing and measuring organizational change: A guide to field practice.* New York: Wiley.

13672

Test Name: SCALE OF ATHLETE SATISFACTION—GREEK VERSION

Purpose: To measure athlete's satisfaction.

Number of Items: 10

Format: Responses are made on a 7-point scale ranging from 1 (*extremely dissatisfied*) to 7 (*extremely satisfied*). Includes two factors: leadership and personal outcome. All items are presented.

Reliability: Alpha coefficients were .74 and .90.

Author: Bebetsos, E., and Theodorakis, N.

Article: Athletes' satisfaction among team handball players in Greece.

Journal: *Perceptual and Motor Skills*, December 2003, *97*, Part 2, 1203–1208.

Related Research: Chelladurai, P., et al. (1988). Sport leadership in a cross-national setting: The case of Japanese and Canadian university athletes. *Journal of Sport & Exercise Psychology, 10,* 374–389.

13673

Test Name: SCALE OF PHYSICIAN EMPATHY

Purpose: To measure physician empathy toward patients.

Number of Items: 20

Format: Scales range from 1 (*strongly disagree*) to 7 (*strongly agree*). A sample item is presented.

Reliability: Coefficient alpha was in the .80s.

Validity: Correlations with other variables ranged from .24 to .56.

Author: Hojat, M., et al.

Article: Empathy scores in medical school and ratings of empathic behavior in residency training 3 years later.

Journal: *The Journal of Social Psychology*, December 2005, *145*, 663–672.

13674

Test Name: SCHOOL COUNSELING STANDARDS QUESTIONNAIRE

Purpose: To assess the perceived importance of counseling standards set forth by the Council for the Accreditation of Counseling and Related Educational Programs.

Number of Items: 38

Format: Scales range from 0 (*not important*) to 4 (*very highly important*). All items are presented.

Reliability: Total alpha was .89. Subscale alphas ranged from .33 to .91.

Author: Holcomb-McCoy, C., and Rahill, S.

Article: Importance of the CACREP School Counseling Standards: School counselors' perceptions.

Journal: *Professional School Counseling*, December 2002, *6*(2), 112–118.

Related Research: CACREP (2001). *Accreditation procedures manual and application.* Alexandria, VA: Author.

13675

Test Name: SCHOOL COUNSELOR SELF-EFFICACY SCALE

Purpose: To measure school counselor self-efficacy.

Number of Items: 43

Format: Importance rating scales are used. All items are presented.

Reliability: Coefficient alpha was .96.

Validity: Correlations with other variables ranged from –.42 to .49.

Author: Bodenhorn, N., and Skaggs, G.

Article: Development of the School Counselor Self-Efficacy Scale.

Journal: *Measurement and Evaluation in Counseling and Development*, April 2005, *38*, 14–28.

13676

Test Name: SCHOOL VIOLENCE QUESTIONNAIRE

Purpose: To assess school psychologists' role in the prevention of school violence.

Number of Items: 5

Format: A 7-point Likert format is used. All items are presented.

Reliability: Coefficient alpha was .76.

Author: Dean, V. J., and Burns, M. K.

Article: Practicing school psychologists' perceived role in prevention of school violence.

Journal: *Psychological Reports*, February 2004, *94*, 243–250.

Related Research: Furlong, M., et al. (1996). Factors associated with school psychologists' perception of campus violence. *Psychology in the Schools, 33*, 28–37.

13677

Test Name: SESSION EVALUATION QUESTIONNAIRE

Purpose: To measure clients' perceptions of session depth, smoothness, positivity, and arousal.

Number of Items: 24

Format: Includes four subscales: Depth, Smoothness, Positivity, and Arousal. Responses are made on a 7-point semantic differential scale.

Reliability: Alpha coefficients ranged from .80 to .90.

Validity: Correlations with other variables ranged from –.24 to .67.

Author: Kim, B. S. K., and Atkinson, D. R.

Article: Asian American client adherence to Asian cultural values, counselor expression of cultural values, counselor ethnicity, and career counseling process.

Journal: *Journal of Counseling Psychology*, January 2002, *49*, 3–13.

Related Research: Stiles, W. B., & Snow, J. S. (1984). Dimensions of psychotherapy session impact across sessions and across clients. *British Journal of Clinical Psychology, 23*, 59–63.

13678

Test Name: SESSION EVALUATION QUESTIONNAIRE—ADAPTED

Purpose: To measure session outcome.

Format: Includes two subscales: Depth and Smoothness. Responses are made on a 7-point semantic differential scale.

Reliability: Alpha coefficients were .82 and .83.

Validity: Correlations with other variables ranged from –.35 to .43.

Author: Gelso, C. J., et al.

Article: Measuring the real relationship in psychotherapy: Initial validation of the Therapist Form.

Journal: *Journal of Counseling Psychology*, October 2005, *52*, 640–649.

Related Research: Stiles, W. B., & Snow, J. S. (1984). Counseling session impact as viewed by novice counselors and their clients. *British Journal of Clinical Psychology, 23*, 59–63.

13679

Test Name: SESSION EVALUATION QUESTIONNAIRE—DEPTH SUBSCALE

Purpose: To provide a client-rated measure of the quality of sessions.

Number of Items: 5

Format: The adjective-anchored items include valuable–worthless, full–empty, special–ordinary, powerful–weak, and deep–shallow.

Reliability: Alpha coefficients were .86 and .87.

Validity: Correlations with other variables ranged from .01 to .66 (*N* = 94).

Author: Hill, C. E., et al.

Article: Working with dreams using the Hill cognitive–experiential model: A comparison of computer-assisted, therapist empathy, and therapist empathy + input conditions.

Journal: *Journal of Clinical Psychology*, April 2003, *23*, 59–63.

Related Research: Stiles, W. B., & Snow, J. S. (1984). Dimensions of psychotherapy session impact across sessions and across clients. *British Journal of Clinical Psychology, 23*, 59–63.

13680

Test Name: SESSION EVALUATION QUESTIONNAIRE—SMOOTHNESS AND DEPTH SUBSCALES

Purpose: To measure the extent to which a session is perceived to be deep, valuable, comfortable, and pleasant.

Number of Items: 10

Format: Includes two subscales: Smoothness and Depth.

Reliability: Internal consistency estimates ranged from .78 to .91.

Author: Mohr, J. J., et al.

Article: Client and counselor trainee attachment as predictors of session evaluation and countertransference behavior in first counseling sessions.

Journal: *Journal of Counseling Psychology*, July 2005, *52*, 298–309.

Related Research: Stiles, W. B., & Snow, J. S. (1984). Counseling session impact as viewed by novice counselors and their clients. *Journal of Counseling Psychology, 31*, 3–12.

13681

Test Name: SESSION EVALUATION SCALE

Purpose: To provide an assessment of client perceptions of session quality.

Number of Items: 4

Format: Responses are made on a 7-point scale ranging from 1 (*strongly disagree*) to 7 (*strongly agree*). All items are presented.

Reliability: Alpha coefficients ranged from .87 to .91.

Validity: Correlations with other variables ranged from –.07 to .87 (*N* = 94).

Author: Hill, C. E., et al.

Article: Working with dreams using the Hill cognitive–experiential model: A comparison of computer-assisted, therapist empathy, and therapist empathy + input conditions.

Journal: *Journal of Counseling Psychology*, April 2003, *50*, 211–220.

Related Research: Stiles, W. B., & Snow, J. S. (1984). Dimensions of psychotherapy session impact across sessions and across clients. *British Journal of Clinical Psychology, 23*, 59–63.

13682

Test Name: SESSION EVALUATION SCALE

Purpose: To assess client-perceived session quality.

Number of Items: 4

Format: Responses are made on a 5-point scale ranging from 1 (*strongly disagree*) to 5 (*strongly agree*). All items are presented.

Reliability: Alpha coefficients ranged from .87 to .89.

Validity: Correlations with other variables ranged from .04 to .73.

Author: Kim, B. S. K., et al.

Article: Counselor self-disclosure, East Asian American client adherence to Asian cultural values, and counseling process.

Journal: *Journal of Counseling Psychology*, July 2003, *50*, 324–332.

Related Research: Hill, C. E., & Kellems, I. S. (2002). Development and use of the Helping Skills Measure to assess client perceptions of the effects of training and of helping skills in sessions. *Journal of Counseling Psychology, 49*, 264–272.

13683

Test Name: SESSION IMPACTS SCALE

Purpose: To assess clients' perceptions in presenting their problems, the therapist, and the therapy relationship.

Number of Items: 17

Format: Responses are made on a 5-point scale ranging from 1 (*not at all*) to 5 (*very much*).

Reliability: Coefficient alpha was approximately .90.

Author: Fauth, J., and Williams, E. N.

Article: The in-session self-awareness of therapist-trainees: Hindering or helpful?

Journal: *Journal of Counseling Psychology*, July 2005, *52*, 443–447.

Related Research: Elliott, R., & Wexler, M. M. (1994). Measuring the impact of sessions in process-experiential therapy depression:

The Session Impacts Scale. *Journal of Counseling Psychology, 41*, 166–174.

13684

Test Name: STRUCTURED TELEPHONE REFERENCE CHECK MEASURE

Purpose: To predict job performance.

Number of Items: 16

Format: Includes three dimensions: Commitment/Reliability, Teamwork/Team Communication, and Customer Service. Responses are made on a 5-point scale ranging from 1 (*below average*) to 5 (*outstanding*).

Validity: Correlations with job performance ratings ranged from .18 to .26.

Author: Taylor, P. J., et al.

Article: Dimensionality and validity of a structured telephone reference check procedure.

Journal: *Personnel Psychology*, Autumn 2004, *57*, 745–772.

Related Research: Goldberg, L. R. (1992). The development of markers for the Big Five factor structure. *Psychological Assessment, 4*, 26–42. Goff, B. G., et al. (1997). The influence of salesperson selling behaviors on customer satisfaction with products. *Journal of Retailing, 73*, 171–183.

13685

Test Name: STUDENT–TEACHER RELATIONSHIP SCALE— SHORTENED VERSION

Purpose: To enable kindergarten teachers to rate the quality of their relationship with the target child.

Number of Items: 10

Format: Includes two scales: Closeness Scale and Conflict Scale. Responses are made on a 5-point scale ranging from 1 (*definitely does not apply*) to 5 (*definitely does apply*).

Reliability: Internal consistencies were .83 and .87.

Author: Silver, R. B., et al.

Article: Trajectories of classroom externalizing behavior: Contributions of child characteristics, family characteristics, and teacher–child relationship during the school transition.

Journal: *Journal of School Psychology*, January/February 2005, *43*, 39–60.

Related Research: Pianta, R. C., et al. (1995). The first two years of school: Teacher–child relationships and deflections in children's classroom adjustment. *Development and Psychopathology*, *7*, 295–312.

13686

Test Name: STUDENTS' EVALUATION OF EDUCATIONAL QUALITY QUESTIONNAIRE

Purpose: To provide a measure of students' evaluations of teaching.

Number of Items: 35

Format: Includes nine factors: learning/value, instructor enthusiasm, organization/clarity, group interaction, individual rapport, breadth of coverage, examination/grading, assignments/readings, and workload/difficulty.

Reliability: Alpha coefficients ranged from .64 to .98.

Validity: Correlations with other variables ranged from .13 to .76.

Author: Toland, M. D., and De Ayala, R. J.

Article: A multilevel factor analysis of students' evaluations of teaching.

Journal: *Educational and Psychological Measurement*, April 2005, *65*, 272–296.

Related Research: Marsh, H. W. (1987). Students' evaluations of university teaching: Research findings, methodological issues, and directions for future research. *International Journal of Educational Research*, *11*, 253–288.

13687

Test Name: STUDENTS' EVALUATION OF TEACHING EFFECTIVENESS RATING SCALE

Purpose: To provide a measure of students' evaluations of teaching.

Number of Items: 25

Format: Includes three factors: instructor's delivery of course information, instructor/student interactions, and regulating student learning. Responses are made on a 5-point scale ranging from 1 (*strongly disagree*) to 5 (*strongly agree*). All items are presented.

Reliability: Alpha coefficients ranged from .82 to .94.

Validity: Correlations with other variables ranged from .13 to .76.

Author: Toland, M. D., and De Ayala, R. J.

Article: A multilevel factor analysis of students' evaluations of teaching.

Journal: *Educational and Psychological Measurement*, April 2005, *65*, 272–296.

13688

Test Name: SUBSTITUTES FOR LEADERSHIP SCALES

Purpose: To measure professionalism, indifference toward rewards, no control of rewards, spatial distance, and task variability.

Number of Items: 15

Format: Scales range from 1 (*strongly disagree*) to 5 (*strongly*

agree) and from 1 (*very seldom*) to 5 (*very often*). Sample items are presented.

Reliability: Alpha coefficients ranged from .65 to .81.

Author: Dionne, S. D., et al.

Article: Neutralizing substitutes for leadership theory: Leadership effects and common-source bias.

Journal: *Journal of Applied Psychology*, June 2002, *87*, 454–464.

Related Research: Podsakoff, P. M., et al. (1993). Substitutes for leadership and the management of professionals. *Leadership Quarterly*, *4*, 1–44.

13689

Test Name: SUPERVISION SATISFACTION QUESTIONNAIRE

Purpose: To measure participants' satisfaction with various aspects of supervision.

Number of Items: 8

Format: Responses are made on a 4-point scale ranging from 1 (*low*) to 4 (*high*).

Reliability: Internal consistency ranged from .96 to .97.

Validity: Correlations with other variables ranged from .02 to .81.

Author: Lehrman-Waterman, D., and Ladany, N.

Article: Development and validation of the Evaluation Process Within Supervision Inventory.

Journal: *Journal of Counseling Psychology*, April 2001, *48*, 168–177.

Related Research: Ladany, N., & Lehrman-Waterman, D. (1999). The content and frequency of supervisor self-disclosure and the relationship to supervisory working alliance and satisfaction with supervision. *Counselor Education and Supervision*, *38*, 143–160.

13690

Test Name: SUPERVISOR CLOSE MONITORING SCALE

Purpose: To assess the extent to which supervisors monitor a person while on the job.

Number of Items: 5

Format: Scales range from 1 (*strongly disagree*) to 7 (*strongly agree*). A sample item is presented.

Reliability: Coefficient alpha was .87.

Validity: Correlations with other variables ranged from −.22 to .10.

Author: Zhou, J.

Article: When the presence of creative coworkers is related to creativity: Role of supervisor close monitoring, developmental feedback, and creative personality.

Journal: *Journal of Applied Psychology*, June 2003, *88*, 413–422.

13691

Test Name: SUPERVISOR EMPHASIS FORM—REVISED (FORM SG)

Purpose: To measure the general emphasis taken by the supervisor with a first or second practicum-level doctoral student.

Number of Items: 15

Format: Includes four scales: Professional Behavior, Process Skills, Personalization Skills, and Conceptualization Skills.

Reliability: Alpha coefficients ranged from .68 to .80.

Author: Dennin, M. K., and Ellis, M. V.

Article: Effects of a method of self-supervision for counselor trainees.

Journal: *Journal of Counseling Psychology*, January 2003, *50*, 69–83.

Related Research: Laning, W., & Freeman, B. (1994). The Supervisor Emphasis Rating Form—Revised. *Counselor Education and Supervision, 33,* 294–304.

13692

Test Name: SUPERVISOR FEEDBACK RATING SCALE

Purpose: To assess supervisor feedback by the reports of trained observers. Positive, negative, constructive, and specificity are assessed.

Format: Scales range from 1 (*absence of the dimension*) to 4 (*a large amount of the dimension*). Sample items are presented.

Reliability: Interrater reliabilities ranged from .74 to .95.

Validity: Correlations with other variables ranged from −.31 to .92.

Author: Larson, L. M., et al.

Article: Developing a supervisor feedback rating scale: A brief report.

Journal: *Measurement and Evaluation in Counseling and Development*, January 2003, *35*, 230–238.

13693

Test Name: SUPERVISOR SUPPORT SCALE

Purpose: To assess supervisor support.

Number of Items: 9

Format: Responses are made on a 5-point scale ranging from 1 (*never*) to 5 (*very often*). A sample item is presented.

Reliability: Coefficient alpha was .80.

Validity: Correlations with other variables ranged from −.33 to .62.

Author: Allen, T. D.

Article: Family-supportive work environments: The role of organizational perceptions.

Journal: *Journal of Vocational Behavior*, June 2001, *58*, 414–435.

Related Research: Shin, M., et al. (1989). Promoting the well-being of working parents: Coping, social support, and flexible job schedules. *American Journal of Community Psychology, 17,* 31–55.

13694

Test Name: SUPERVISOR SUPPORT SCALE

Purpose: To measure supervisor support.

Number of Items: 5

Format: Scales range from 1 (*strongly agree*) to 5 (*strongly disagree*).

Reliability: Coefficient alpha was .94.

Author: Baltes, B. B., and Heydens-Gahir, H. A.

Article: Reduction of work–family conflict through the use of selection, organization, and compensation behaviors.

Journal: *Journal of Applied Psychology*, December 2003, *88*, 1005–1018.

Related Research: Kossek, E. E. (1990). *Findings from the June–October 1990 data collection of the productivity impact of Mercy Health Center's Child Development Center.* East Lansing: School of Labor and Industrial Relations, Michigan State University.

13695

Test Name: SUPERVISOR SUPPORT SCALE

Purpose: To assess worker's perception of immediate work supervisor's quality of social support.

Number of Items: 4

Format: Responses are made on a 4-point scale ranging from 1 (*not at all*) to 4 (*very much*).

Reliability: Alpha coefficients were .83 and .88.

Validity: Correlations with other variables ranged from −.46 to .49.

Author: Schirmer, L. L., and Lopez, F. G.

Article: Probing the social support and work strain relationship among adult workers: Contributions of adult attachment orientations.

Journal: *Journal of Vocational Behavior*, August 2001, *59*, 17–33.

Related Research: Caplan, R. D., et al. (1975). *Job demands and worker health* (U.S. Department of Health, Education, and Welfare Pub. No. 175-160): U.S. Government Printing Office. Washington, D.C.

13696

Test Name: SUPERVISOR TREATMENT SCALE

Purpose: To measure interactional justice.

Number of Items: 11

Format: A yes–no format was used.

Reliability: Coefficient alpha was .89.

Validity: Correlations with other variables ranged from −.29 to .55.

Author: Marcus, B., and Shuler, H.

Article: Antecedents of counterproductive behavior at work: A general perspective.

Journal: *Journal of Applied Psychology*, August 2004, *89*, 647–660.

Related Research: Donovan, M. A., et al. (1998). Perceptions of Fair Interpersonal Treatment Scale: Development and validation of a measure of interpersonal treatment in the workplace. *Journal of Applied Psychology, 83*, 683–692.

13697

Test Name: SUPERVISORY REINFORCEMENT OF QUALITY AND IMPROVEMENT SCALE

Purpose: To assess one's perception of the degree to which one's immediate supervisor displayed commitment to quality and improvement.

Number of Items: 6

Format: Responses to each item indicate the extent of agreement or disagreement. Sample items are presented.

Reliability: Coefficient alpha was .89.

Validity: Correlations with other variables ranged from −.01 to .45.

Author: Coyle-Shapiro, J. A.-M., and Morrow, P. C.

Article: The role of individual differences in employee adoption of TQM orientation.

Journal: *Journal of Vocational Behavior*, April 2003, *62*, 320–340.

13698

Test Name: SUPERVISORY SATISFACTION QUESTIONNAIRE

Purpose: To enable supervisees to rate their satisfaction with various aspects of supervision.

Number of Items: 8

Format: Responses are made on a 4-point scale ranging from 1 (*quite dissatisfied*) to 4 (*very satisfied*).

Reliability: Alpha coefficients were .96 and .97.

Author: Gray, L. A., et al.

Article: Psychotherapy trainees' experience of counterproductive events in supervision.

Journal: *Journal of Counseling Psychology*, October 2001, *48*, 371–383.

Related Research: Ladany, N., et al. (1996). Nature, extent, and importance of what psychotherapy trainees do not disclose to their supervisors. *Journal of Counseling Psychology, 43*, 10–24.

13699

Test Name: SUPERVISORY STYLE AND INITIATION OF STRUCTURE SCALES

Purpose: To assess a respectful and trusting leadership style and the extent to which a leader specifies assignment of tasks.

Number of Items: 11

Format: Scales range from 1 (*very false*) to 7 (*very true*).

Reliability: Alpha coefficients ranged from .70 to .84 across subscales.

Author: Brown, S. P., et al.

Article: Self-efficacy as a moderator of information-seeking effectiveness.

Journal: *Journal of Applied Psychology*, October 2001, *86*, 1043–1051.

Related Research: House, R. J., & Dessler, G. (1974). The path goal theory of leadership: Some post hoc and a priori tests. In J. G. Hunt & L. L. Larson (Eds.), *Contingency approaches to leadership* (pp. 29–55). Carbondale: Southern Illinois University Press.

13700

Test Name: SUPERVISORY STYLES INVENTORY

Purpose: To measure perceptions of the supervisor's characteristic approach to supervision.

Number of Items: 33

Format: Includes three dimensions: Attractive, Interpersonally Sensitive, and Oriented.

Reliability: Alpha coefficients ranged from .70 to .84.

Author: Dennin, M. K., and Ellis, M. V.

Article: Effects of a method of self-supervision for counselor trainees.

Journal: *Journal of Counseling Psychology*, January 2003, *50*, 69–83.

Related Research: Friedlander, M. L., & Ward, L. G. (1984). Development and validation of the Supervisory Styles Inventory. *Journal of Counseling Psychology*, *31*, 541–557.

13701

Test Name: SUPERVISORY STYLES INVENTORY

Purpose: To provide an estimate of the trainee's perception of the supervisor's approach or style.

Number of Items: 25

Format: Includes three subscales: Attractive, Interpersonally Sensitive, and Task Oriented. Responses are made on a 7-point scale ranging from 1 (*not very*) to 7 (*very*).

Reliability: Alpha coefficients ranged from .76 to .93.

Author: Nelson, M. L., & Friedlander, M. L.

Article: A close look at conflictual supervisory relationships: The trainee's perspective.

Journal: *Journal of Counseling Psychology*, October 2001, *48*, 384–395.

Related Research: Friedlander, M. L., & Ward, L. G. (1984). Development and validation of the Supervisory Styles Inventory. *Journal of Counseling Psychology*, *31*, 541–557.

13702

Test Name: SUPERVISORY TRUST SCALE

Purpose: To assess trust with a supervisor.

Number of Items: 11

Format: Seven-point Likert scales are used. Sample items are presented.

Reliability: Coefficient alpha was .92.

Validity: Correlations with other variables ranged from .01 to .66.

Author: Ambrose, M. L., and Schminke, M.

Article: Organization structure as a moderator of the relationship between procedural justice, interactional justice, perceived organizational support, and supervisory trust.

Journal: *Journal of Applied Psychology*, April 2003, *88*, 295–305.

Related Research: McAllister, D. (1995). Affect- and cognition-based trust as foundations for interpersonal cooperation in organizations. *Academy of Management Journal*, *38*, 24–59.

13703

Test Name: SURVEY OF PERCEIVED ORGANIZATIONAL SUPPORT

Purpose: To measure perceived organizational support.

Number of Items: 8

Format: Responses are made on a 7-point scale ranging from 1 (*strongly disagree*) to 7 (*strongly agree*). All items are presented.

Validity: Correlations with other variables ranged from −.68 to .68 ($n = 311$).

Author: Hochwarter, W. A., et al.

Article: Perceived organizational support as a mediator of the relationship between politics perceptions and work outcomes.

Journal: *Journal of Vocational Behavior*, December 2003, *63*, 428–456.

Related Research: Eisenberger, R., et al. (1990). Effects of perceived organizational support on employee diligence, innovation, and commitment. *Journal of Applied Psychology*, *53*, 51–59.

13704

Test Name: TEACHER DIRECTIVENESS OF TEACHER–STUDENT INTERACTION MEASURE—ADAPTED

Purpose: To assess teaching style.

Number of Items: 5

Format: Responses are made on a 4-point ranging from 1 (*low nondirectiveness*) to 4 (*high nondirectiveness*).

Reliability: Alpha coefficients were .56 and .62.

Author: Ferrer-Caja, E., and Weiss, M. R.

Article: Cross-validation of a model of intrinsic motivation with students enrolled in high school elective courses.

Journal: *The Journal of Experimental Education*, Fall 2002, *71*, 41–65.

Related Research: Tuckman, B. W. (1985). *Evaluating instructional programs* (2nd ed.). Boston: Allyn & Bacon.

13705

Test Name: TEACHER TREATMENT INVENTORY—ADAPTED

Purpose: To assess high expectations and nurturance.

Number of Items: 20

Format: Responses are made on a 4-point scale ranging from 1 (*always*) to 4 (*never*). Sample items are presented.

Reliability: Alpha coefficients were .70 and .78.

Author: Wentzel, K. R.

Article: Are effective teachers like good parents? Teaching styles and student adjustment in early adolescence.

Journal: *Child Development*, January/February 2002, *73*, 287–301.

Related Research: Weinstein, R. S., & Marshall, H. H. (1984). Ecology of students' achievement expectations. *Review of Educational Research*, *54*, 301–325.

13706

Test Name: TEACHERS' RELATIONSHIPS WITH INDIVIDUAL CHILDREN SCALE

Purpose: To enable teachers to note the quality of their relationships with individual children.

Number of Items: 10

Format: Includes closeness and conflict items. Examples are presented.

Reliability: Alpha coefficients ranged from .79 to .91.

Author: Valeski, T. N., and Stipek, D. J.

Article: Young children's findings about school.

Journal: *Child Development*, July/August 2001, *72*, 1198–1213.

Related Research: Pianta, R. (1994). Patterns of relationships between children and kindergarten teachers. *Journal of School Psychology*, *32*, 15–31.

13707

Test Name: THEORETICAL ORIENTATION PROFILE SCALE—REVISED

Purpose: To measure theoretical orientation among counselors and trainees.

Number of Items: 18

Format: Scales range from 1 (*never*) to 10 (*always*). All items are presented.

Reliability: Alpha coefficients ranged from .92 to .97 across subscales.

Validity: Correlations with other variables ranged from −.33 to .49.

Author: Worthington, R. L., and Dillon, F. R.

Article: The Theoretical Orientation Profile Scale—Revised: A validation study.

Journal: *Measurement and Evaluation in Counseling and Development*, July 2003, *36*, 95–105.

13708

Test Name: THERAPEUTIC FACTORS INVENTORY— COHESION SUBSCALE

Purpose: To measure group members' perception of cohesion.

Number of Items: 9

Format: Responses are made on a 7-point scale ranging from 1 (*strongly disagree*) to 7 (*strongly agree*).

Reliability: Test–retest (1 week) reliability was .93. Coefficient alpha was .90.

Validity: Correlations with other variables ranged from −.62 to .89.

Author: Johnson, J. E., et al.

Article: Group climate, cohesion, alliance, and empathy in group psychotherapy: Multilevel structural equation models.

Journal: *Journal of Counseling Psychology*, July 2005, *52*, 310–321.

Related Research: Lese, K. P., & MacNair-Semands, R. R. (2000). The Therapeutic Factors Inventory:

Development of a scale. *Group, 24*, 303–317.

13709

Test Name: THERAPIST DIRECTIVENESS SCALE

Purpose: To rate therapists' directiveness by viewing videotaped sessions.

Number of Items: 6

Format: Five-point scales are used.

Reliability: Interrater reliability was .75. Coefficient alpha was .77. Interitem correlations ranged from .18 to .32.

Author: Karno, M. P., and Longabaugh, R.

Article: Less directiveness by therapists improves drinking outcomes of reactant clients in alcoholism treatment.

Journal: *Journal of Consulting and Clinical Psychology*, April 2005, *73*, 262–267.

Related Research: Fisher, D., et al. (1995). *Systematic Treatment Selection Therapy Rating Scale manual*. Unpublished manuscript, University of California, Santa Barbara.

13710

Test Name: THERAPIST PERSONAL REACTION QUESTIONNAIRE

Purpose: To measure the positivity of trainees' anticipated reaction to clinical work with a fictional client.

Number of Items: 15

Format: Responses are made on a 5-point scale ranging from 1 (*strongly disagree*) to 5 (*strongly agree*). Sample items are presented.

Reliability: Internal consistency was .77.

Validity: Correlations with other variables ranged from −.26 to .48.

Author: Mohr, J. J., et al.

Article: Counselors' attitudes regarding bisexuality as predictors of counselors' clinical responses: An analogue study of a female bisexual client.

Journal: *Journal of Counseling Psychology*, April 2001, *48*, 212–222.

Related Research: Tryon, G. S. (1989). The Therapist Personal Reaction Questionnaire: A cluster analysis. *Measurement and Evaluation in Counseling and Development, 21*, 149–156.

13711

Test Name: THERAPIST SESSION SATISFACTION

Purpose: To measure global therapist satisfaction.

Number of Items: 7

Format: Responses are made on a 7-point scale ranging from 1 (*very strongly disagree*) to 7 (*very strongly agree*). Examples are given.

Reliability: Alpha coefficients ranged from .80 to .93. Test–retest (1 week) reliability was .55.

Validity: Correlations with other variables ranged from –.33 to .77.

Author: Lichtenberg, J. W., and Tracey, T. J. G.

Article: Interaction rules and strategies in psychotherapy.

Journal: *Journal of Counseling Psychology*, July 2003, *50*, 267–275.

Related Research: Tracey, T. J. (1989). Client and therapist session satisfaction over the course of psychotherapy. *Psychotherapy, 26*, 177–182.

13712

Test Name: THERAPY PROCESS OBSERVATIONAL CODING SYSTEM—ALLIANCE SCALE

Purpose: To rate child–therapist and parent–therapist alliance by observer report.

Number of Items: 9

Format: Scales range from 0 (*not at all*) to 5 (a *great deal*). All items are presented.

Reliability: Alpha coefficients ranged from .54 to .95.

Validity: Correlations between child and parent forms ranged from .58 to .71. Correlations with other variables ranged from .24 to .53.

Author: McLeod, B. D., and Weisz, J. R.

Article: The Therapy Process Observational Coding System— Alliance Scale: Measure characteristics and prediction of outcome in usual clinical practice.

Journal: *Journal of Consulting and Clinical Psychology*, April 2005, *73*, 323–333.

13713

Test Name: TRAUMA VICTIM INTERACTION SCALE

Purpose: To measure the willingness of a helping professional to trust and interact with victims of trauma.

Number of Items: 12

Format: Scales range from 1 (*strongly agree*) to 6 (*strongly disagree*). All items are presented.

Reliability: Coefficient alpha was .86.

Author: Liebkind, K., and Eränen, L.

Article: Attitudes of future human service professionals: The effects of victim and helper qualities.

Journal: *The Journal of Social Psychology*, August 2001, *141*, 457–475.

Related Research: Link, B. G. (1987). Understanding labeling effects in the area of mental disorders: An assessment of the effects of expectations of rejection. *American Sociological Review, 52*, 96–112.

13714

Test Name: TREATMENT CREDIBILITY QUESTIONNAIRE

Purpose: To measure the credibility of analogue therapy rationales.

Number of Items: 6

Format: Seven-point Likert scales are used. All items are presented.

Reliability: Coefficient alpha was .86.

Author: Addis, M. E., et al.

Article: Effectiveness of cognitive-behavioral treatment for panic disorder versus treatment as usual in a managed care setting.

Journal: *Journal of Consulting and Clinical Psychology*, August 2004, *72*, 625–635.

Related Research: Borkovec, T. D., & Nau, S. D. (1972). Credibility of analogue therapy rationales. *Journal of Behavior Therapy and Experimental Psychiatry, 3*, 257–260.

13715

Test Name: TREATMENT EVALUATION INVENTORY

Purpose: To measure the acceptability of psychological treatment interventions.

Number of Items: 19

Format: A Likert format is used. All items are presented.

Reliability: Coefficient alpha was .96.

Author: Newton, J. T., and Sturmey, P.

Article: Development of a short form of the Treatment Evaluation Inventory for acceptability of psychological interventions.

Journal: *Psychological Reports*, April 2004, *94*, 475–481.

Related Research: Kazdin, A. E. (1984). Acceptability of aversive procedures and medication or treatment alternatives for child deviant behavior. *Journal of Abnormal Psychology, 12*, 289–301.

13716

Test Name: TREATMENT EVALUATION SCALE

Purpose: To assess whether couples learned anything new about cancer treatment after couple-focused intervention.

Number of Items: 20

Format: Scales range from 1 (*not at all*) to 5 (*a great deal*).

Reliability: Coefficient alpha was .94.

Author: Manne, S. L., et al.

Article: Couple-focused group intervention for women with early stage breast cancer.

Journal: *Journal of Consulting and Clinical Psychology*, August 2005, *73*, 634–646.

Related Research: Borkovec, T. D., & Nau, S. (1972). Credibility of analogue therapy rationales. *Journal of Behavior Therapy and Experimental Psychiatry, 3*, 117–126.

13717

Test Name: TRUST IN PHYSICIAN SCALE

Purpose: To assess interpersonal trust in patient–physician relationships.

Number of Items: 11

Format: A Likert format is used.

Reliability: Coefficient alpha was .90.

Author: Aruguete, M. S., and Roberts, C. A.

Article: Participants' ratings of male physicians who vary in race and communication style.

Journal: *Psychological Reports*, December 2002, *91*, Part 1, 793–806.

Related Research: Anderson, L. A., & Dedrick, R. F. (1990). Development of the Trust in Physician Scale: A measure to assess interpersonal trust in patient–physician relationships. *Psychological Reports, 67*, 1092–1100.

13718

Test Name: TRUST IN PHYSICIAN SCALE

Purpose: To measure a person's trust in his or her physician.

Number of Items: 4

Format: Scales range from *strongly disagree* to *strongly agree*. All items are presented.

Reliability: Coefficient alpha was .62.

Author: Schnittker, J.

Article: Social distance in the clinical encounter: Interactional and sociodemographic foundations for mistrust in physicians.

Journal: *Social Psychology Quarterly*, September 2004, *67*, 217–235.

Related Research: Anderson, L. A., & Dedrick, R. F. (1990). Development of the Trust in Physician Scale: A measure to assess interpersonal trust in patient–physician relationships. *Psychological Reports, 67*, 1091–1100.

13719

Test Name: VANDERBILT THERAPEUTIC ALLIANCE SCALE

Purpose: To rate the therapeutic alliance by observer report.

Number of Items: 24

Format: Six-point Likert scales are used. Sample items are presented.

Reliability: Coefficient alpha was .93.

Author: Shelef, K., et al.

Article: Adolescent and parent alliance and treatment outcome in multidimensional family therapy.

Journal: *Journal of Consulting and Clinical Psychology*, August 2005, *73*, 689–698.

Related Research: Diamond, G. M., et al. (1996). *Revised version of the Vanderbilt Therapeutic Alliance Scale*. Unpublished manuscript, Temple University, Philadelphia.

13720

Test Name: WILLINGNESS TO MENTOR SCALE

Purpose: To measure willingness to mentor others.

Number of Items: 4

Format: Responses are made on a 5-point scale ranging from 1 (*strongly disagree*) to 5 (*strongly agree*). An example is provided.

Reliability: Internal consistency was .80.

Author: Allen, T. D.

Article: Mentoring others: A dispositional and motivational approach.

Journal: *Journal of Vocational Behavior*, February 2003, *62*, 134–154.

Related Research: Ragins, B. R., & Scandura, T. A. (1994). Gender differences in expected outcomes of mentoring. *Academy of Management Journal, 37*, 957–971.

13721

Test Name: WORKING ALLIANCE INVENTORY

Purpose: To measure the client–therapist working alliance.

Number of Items: 36 (client); 12 (therapist)

Format: Seven-point Likert scales are used.

Reliability: Alpha coefficients ranged from .92 to .98.

Validity: Correlations between client and therapist forms ranged from .35 to .45.

Author: Taft, C. T., et al.

Article: Process and treatment adherence factors in group cognitive–behavioral therapy for partner violent men.

Journal: *Journal of Consulting and Clinical Psychology*, August 2003, *71*, 812–820.

Related Research: Horvath, A. O., & Greenberg, L. S. (1986). The development of the Working Alliance Inventory. In L. S. Greenberg & W. M. Pinshof (Eds.), *The psychotherapeutic process: A research handbook* (pp. 529–556). New York: Guilford Press.

13722

Test Name: WORKING ALLIANCE INVENTORY— SHORT FORM

Purpose: To assess the constructs of bond, task, and goal.

Number of Items: 12

Format: Responses are made on a 7-point scale ranging from 1 (*never*) to 7 (*always*). Includes two parallel forms: one for the counselor and one for the client.

Reliability: Alpha coefficients ranged from .87 to .93.

Validity: Correlations with other variables ranged from −.22 to .30.

Author: Heppner, M. J., et al.

Article: The role of problem-solving appraisal in the process and outcome of career counseling.

Journal: *Journal of Vocational Behavior*, October 2004, *65*, 217–238.

Related Research: Horvath, A. O., & Greenberg, L. S. (1989). Development and validation of the Working Alliance Inventory. *Journal of Counseling Psychology*, *36*, 223–232.

13723

Test Name: WORKLOAD SHARING SCALE

Purpose: To rate one another on workload sharing.

Number of Items: 5

Format: Responses are made on a 7-point scale ranging from 1 (*strongly disagree*) to 7 (*strongly agree*). All items are presented.

Reliability: Alpha coefficients were .89 to .91.

Validity: Correlations with other variables ranged from .41 to .75.

Author: Erez, A., et al.

Article: Effects of rotated leadership and peer evaluations on the functioning and effectiveness of self-managed teams: A quasi-experiment.

Journal: *Personnel Psychology*, Winter 2002, *55*, 929–948.

13724

Test Name: YOUNG CHILDREN'S APPRAISALS OF TEACHER SUPPORT

Purpose: To assess Head Start children's appraisals of teacher support.

Number of Items: 27

Format: Includes three factors: warmth, conflict, and autonomy. The child either agrees or disagrees with each statement. All items are presented.

Reliability: Alpha coefficients ranged from .57 to .85.

Validity: Correlations with other variables ranged from −.34 to .25.

Author: Mantzicopoulos, P., and Neuharth-Pritchett, S.

Article: Development and validation of a measure to assess Head Start children's appraisals of teacher support.

Journal: *Journal of School Psychology*, November/December 2003, *41*, 431–451.

CHAPTER 24
Vocational Interest

13725

Test Name: AFFECTIVE AND CONTINUANCE COMMITMENT SCALES

Purpose: To assess commitment.

Number of Items: 12

Format: Includes affective and continuance measure. Responses are made on a 7-point scale ranging from 1 (*strongly disagree*) to 7 (*strongly agree*).

Reliability: Alpha coefficients were .71 and .83.

Validity: Correlations with other variables ranged from −.32 to .61.

Author: Conway, N., and Briner, R. B.

Article: Full-time versus part-time employees: Understanding the links between work status, the psychological contract, and attitudes.

Journal: *Journal of Vocational Behavior*, October 2002, *61*, 279–301.

Related Research: Meyer, J. P., et al. (1993). Commitment to organizations and occupations: Extension and test of a three-component conceptualization. *Journal of Applied Psychology, 78,* 538–551.

13726

Test Name: AFFECTIVE COMMITMENT SCALE

Purpose: To measure liking for, pride in, and valuation of institutional commitment.

Number of Items: 9

Format: Item responses are anchored by 0 (*strongly disagree*) and 6 (*strongly agree*). All items are presented.

Reliability: Coefficient alpha was .80.

Validity: Correlations with other variables ranged from −.53 to .57.

Author: LaMastro, V.

Article: Influence of perceived institutional and faculty support on college students' attitudes and behavioral intentions.

Journal: *Psychological Reports*, April 2001, *88*, 567–580.

Related Research: Meyer, J. P., & Allen, N. J. (1984). Testing the "side bet theory" of organizational commitment: Some methodological considerations. *Journal of Applied Psychology, 69,* 372–378.

13727

Test Name: AFFECTIVE COMMITMENT SCALE

Purpose: To measure organizational commitment.

Number of Items: 8

Reliability: Coefficient alpha was .82.

Validity: Correlations with other variables ranged from .01 to .52.

Author: Liao, H., and Rupp, D. E.

Article: The impact of justice climate and justice orientation on work outcomes: A cross-level multifoci framework.

Journal: *Journal of Applied Psychology*, March 2005, *90*, 242–256.

Related Research: Allen, M. W., & Meyer, J. P. (1999). The measurement and antecedents of affective, continuance, and normative commitment to the organization. *Journal of Occupational Psychology, 63,* 1–18.

13728

Test Name: AFFECTIVE COMMITMENT SCALE

Purpose: To measure employee affective commitment by manager report.

Number of Items: 4

Format: Scales range from 1 (*disagree completely*) to 5 (*agree completely*).

Reliability: Coefficient alpha was .85.

Validity: Correlations with other variables ranged from −.11 to .57.

Author: Shore, L. M., et al.

Article: Work attitudes and decisions as a function of manager age and employee age.

Journal: *Journal of Applied Psychology*, June 2003, *88*, 529–537.

Related Research: Shore, L. M., et al. (1995). Managerial perceptions of employee commitment to the organization. *Academy of Management Journal, 38,* 1593–1615.

13729

Test Name: AFFECTIVE COMMITMENT SCALE— REVISED

Purpose: To measure commitment to the organization.

Number of Items: 12

Format: Includes two areas: commitment to the supervisor and commitment to the work group. Responses are made on a 5-point Likert-type scale ranging from 1 (*strongly disagree*) to 5 (*strongly agree*).

Reliability: Reliability was .82.

Author: Vandenberghe, C., et al.

Article: Affective commitment to the organization, supervisor, and work group: Antecedents and outcomes.

Journal: *Journal of Vocational Behavior*, February 2004, *64*, 47–71.

Related Research: Meyer, J. P., et al. (1993). Commitment to organizations and occupations: Extension and test of a three-component conceptualization. *Journal of Applied Psychology, 78*, 538–551.

13730

Test Name: AFFECTIVE COMMITMENT SCALES

Purpose: To measure organization affective commitment (with main revisions to measure department and work group affective commitments).

Number of Items: 8 (for each scale).

Format: Responses are made on a 7-point Likert-type scale ranging from 1 (*strongly disagree*) to 7 (*strongly agree*).

Reliability: Alpha coefficients ranged from .83 to .85. (*N* ranged from 150–154).

Validity: Correlations with other variables ranged from –.04 to .66 (*N* ranged from 150–154).

Author: Heffner, T. S., and Rentsch, J. R.

Article: Organizational commitment and social interaction: A multiple constituencies approach.

Journal: *Journal of Vocation Behavior*, December 2001, *59*, 471–490.

Related Research: Meyer, J. P., & Allen, N. J. (1984). Testing the "side-bet theory" of organizational commitment: Some methodological considerations. *Journal of Applied Psychology, 69*, 372–378.

13731

Test Name: AFFECTIVE, CONTINUANCE, AND NORMATIVE ORGANIZATIONAL COMMITMENT SCALES

Purpose: To measure organizational commitment.

Number of Items: 21

Format: Includes the following subscales: Affective Commitment, Normative Commitment, Continuance Commitment: High Sacrifice, and Continuance Commitment: Low Alternatives. Responses are made on a 7-point scale ranging from 1 (*strongly disagree*) to 7 (*strongly agree*). Several items are presented.

Reliability: Alpha coefficients ranged from .81 to .89.

Validity: Correlations with other variables ranged from –.49 to .64.

Author: Powell, D. M., and Meyer, J. P.

Article: Side-bet theory and the three-component model of organizational commitment.

Journal: *Journal of Vocational Behavior*, August 2004, *65*, 157–177.

Related Research: Meyer, J. P., et al. (1996). *Revised measures of affective, continuance, and normative commitment to organizations*. Unpublished measure, University of Western Ontario, London, Ontario, Canada.

13732

Test Name: AFFECTIVE ORGANIZATIONAL COMMITMENT SCALE

Purpose: To measure an employee's emotional attachment to the organization.

Number of Items: 4

Format: Five-point agreement scales are used. A sample item is presented.

Reliability: Alpha coefficients ranged from .86 to .87.

Validity: Correlations with other variables ranged from –.55 to .33.

Author: Parker, S. K.

Article: Longitudinal effects of lean production on employee outcomes and the mediating role of work characteristics.

Journal: *Journal of Applied Psychology*, August 2003, *88*, 620–634.

Related Research: Cook, J., & Wall, T. D. (1980). New work attitude measures of trust, organizational commitment and personal need fulfillment. *Journal of Occupational Psychology, 53*, 39–52.

13733

Test Name: AFFECTIVE ORGANIZATIONAL COMMITMENT SCALE

Purpose: To measure affective organizational commitment and pride in organizational membership.

Number of Items: 6

Format: Scales range from 1 (*strongly disagree*) to 7 (*strongly agree*). All items are presented.

Reliability: Coefficient alpha was .85.

Validity: Correlations with other variables ranged from –.22 to .63.

Author: Rhoades, L., et al.

Article: Affective commitment to the organization: The contribution of perceived organizational support.

Journal: *Journal of Applied Psychology,* October 2001, *86,* 825–836.

Related Research: Meyer, J. P., & Allen, N. J. (1997). *Commitment in the workplace: Theory, research, and application.* Thousand Oaks, CA: Sage.

13734

Test Name: AFFECTIVE ORGANIZATIONAL COMMITMENT SCALE

Purpose: To assess affective organizational commitment.

Number of Items: 8

Format: Responses are made on a 5-point Likert scale. An example is given.

Reliability: Alpha coefficients were .80 and .82.

Validity: Correlations with other variables ranged from –.27 to .66.

Author: Zickar, M. J., et al.

Article: Job attitudes of workers with two jobs.

Journal: *Journal of Vocational Behavior,* February 2004, *64,* 222–235.

Related Research: Meyer, J. P., et al. (1993). Commitment to organizations and occupations: Extension and test of a three-component conceptualization. *Journal of Applied Psychology, 78,* 538–551.

13735

Test Name: AFFECTIVE ORGANIZATIONAL COMMITMENT (SUB)SCALE

Purpose: To assess the extent to which an employee feels emotionally attached to an organization.

Number of Items: 6

Format: Scales range from 1 (*strongly disagree*) to 5 (*strongly agree*). Sample items are presented.

Reliability: Coefficient alpha was .79.

Validity: Correlations with other variables ranged from –.33 to .71.

Author: Tepper, B. J., et al.

Article: Moderators of the relationships between coworkers' organizational citizenship behavior and fellow employees' attitudes.

Journal: *Journal of Applied Psychology,* June 2004, *89,* 455–465.

Related Research: Meyer, J. P., et al. (1993). Commitment to organizations and occupations: Extension and test of a three-component model. *Journal of Applied Psychology, 78,* 538–551.

13736

Test Name: APPLICANT ATTRACTION SCALE

Purpose: To measure applicant's interest in pursuing employment opportunities with the company.

Number of Items: 5

Format: Responses are made on a 5-point Likert scale ranging from 1 (*strongly disagree*) to 5 (*strongly agree*). All items are presented.

Reliability: Coefficient alpha was .96.

Author: Rau, B. L., and Hyland, M. M.

Article: Role conflicts and flexible work arrangements: The effects on applicant attraction.

Journal: *Personnel Psychology,* Spring 2002, *55,* 111–136.

Related Research: Cable, D. M., & Judge, T. A. (1994). Pay preferences and job search decision: A person–organization fit perspective. *Personnel Psychology, 47,* 317–348. Honeycutt, T. L., & Rosen, B. (1997). Family friendly human resource policies, salary levels, and salient identity as predictors of organization attraction. *Journal of Vocational Behavior, 50,* 271–290. Schwoerer, C., & Rosen, B. (1989). Effects of employment-at-will policies and compensation policies on corporate image and job pursuit intentions. *Journal of Applied Psychology, 74,* 653–656.

13737

Test Name: ASSESSMENT OF CAREER NEEDS INVENTORY

Purpose: To measure the core elements of career development: self-assessment data needs, occupational–educational information needs and general employability information needs.

Number of Items: 30

Format: Item responses are anchored by 1 (*no need*) and 4 (*a great need*). All items are presented.

Reliability: Test–retest reliability was .71.

Author: Peng, H.

Article: Taiwanese junior college students' needs for and perceptions of a career planning course.

Journal: *Psychological Reports,* February 2004, *94,* 131–138.

Related Research: Peng, H., & Herr, E. L. (1999). The impact of career education courses on career beliefs and career decision making among business college students in Taiwan. *Journal of Career Development, 25,* 3.

13738

Test Name: ATTRACTION TO THE FIRM SCALE

Purpose: To measure attraction to the firm.

Number of Items: 3

Format: Responses are made on a 5-point scale ranging from *strongly disagree* to *strongly agree*. All items are given.

Reliability: Coefficient alpha was .88 ($N = 684$).

Validity: Correlations with other variables ranged from −.25 to .46 ($N = 684$).

Author: Turban, D. B.

Article: Organizational attractiveness as an employer on college campuses: An examination of the application population.

Journal: *Journal of Vocational Behavior*, April 2001, *58*, 293–312.

13739

Test Name: BEHAVIORAL PROFESSIONAL COMMITMENT

Purpose: To measure behavioral professional commitment.

Number of Items: 7

Format: Responses are made on a 3-point scale ranging from 1 (*never*) to 3 (*frequently, 4 or more times*). Sample items are presented.

Reliability: Reliability estimate was .75.

Validity: Correlations with other variables ranged from −.11 to .16.

Author: Blau, G., et al.

Article: Correlates of professional versus organizational withdrawal cognitions.

Journal: *Journal of Vocational Behavior*, August 2003, *63*, 72–85.

Related Research: Summers, S., et al. (2000). Professional development activities of medical technologists: Management implications for allied health. *Journal of Allied Health, 29,* 214–219.

13740

Test Name: BEHAVIORAL SUPPORT FOR CHANGE SCALE

Purpose: To assess behavioral support for organizational change initiatives.

Number of Items: 17

Format: Scales range from 1 (*strongly disagree*) to 5 (*strongly agree*). Sample items are presented.

Reliability: Alpha coefficients ranged from .49 to .90 across subscales.

Validity: Correlations with other variables ranged from −.18 to .70.

Author: Herscovitch, L., and Meyer, J. P.

Article: Commitment to organizational change: Extension of a three-component model.

Journal: *Journal of Applied Psychology*, June 2002, *87*, 474–487.

13741

Test Name: CAREER ASPIRATION SCALE

Purpose: To assess participants' aspirations to become leaders in their career fields.

Number of Items: 10

Format: Responses are made on a 5-point scale ranging from 1 (*not at all true of me*) to 5 (*very true of me*). An example is given.

Reliability: Alpha coefficients ranged from .72 to .80.

Validity: Correlations with other variables ranged from −.08 to .35 ($N = 204$).

Author: Nauta, M. M., and Epperson, D. L.

Article: A longitudinal examination of the social–cognitive model applied to high school girls' choices of nontraditional college majors and aspirations.

Journal: *Journal of Counseling Psychology*, October 2003, *50*, 448–457.

Related Research: O'Brien, K. M. (1996). The influence of psychological separation and parental attachment on the career development of adolescent women. *Journal of Vocational Behavior, 48,* 257–274.

13742

Test Name: CAREER COMMITMENT SCALE

Purpose: To measure career commitment.

Number of Items: 8

Format: Responses are made on a 5-point scale ranging from *strongly agree* to *strongly disagree*. Examples are presented.

Reliability: Coefficient alpha was .82.

Validity: Correlations with other variables ranged from −.15 to .57.

Author: Goulet, L. R., and Singh, P.

Article: Career commitment: A reexamination and an extension.

Journal: *Journal of Vocational Behavior*, August 2002, *61*, 73–91.

Related Research: Blau, G. (1985). The measurement and prediction of career commitment. *Journal of Occupational Psychology, 58,* 277–288.

13743

Test Name: CAREER DECISION-MAKING AUTONOMOUS SCALE

Purpose: To assess motivational constructs posited by self-determination theory.

Number of Items: 32

Format: Responses are made on a 7-point scale ranging from 1 (*does not correspond at all*) to 7 (*corresponds completely*).

Reliability: Alpha coefficients ranged from .91 to .94.

Author: Guay, F., et al.

Article: Predicting career indecision: A self-determination theory perspective.

Journal: *Journal of Counseling Psychology*, April 2003, *50*, 165–177.

Related Research: Guay, F. (2001). *The Career Decision-Making Autonomy Scales.* Unpublished manuscript, Laval University, Quebec, Canada.

13744

Test Name: CAREER DECISION-MAKING DIFFICULTIES QUESTIONNAIRE—INTERNET VERSION

Purpose: To measure lack of readiness, lack of information, and inconsistent information.

Number of Items: 34

Time Required: 5 minutes.

Reliability: Alpha coefficients ranged from .55 to .90 across subscales and across two versions (Hebrew and English).

Validity: Goodness of fit indexes ranged from .94 to .96.

Author: Kleiman, T., and Gati, I.

Article: Challenges of internet-based assessment: Measuring career decision-making difficulties.

Journal: *Measurement and Evaluation in Counseling and Development*, April 2004, *37*, 41–55.

13745

Test Name: CAREER DECISION-MAKING DIFFICULTY QUESTIONNAIRE

Purpose: To measure career decision-making difficulties.

Number of Items: 44

Format: Includes 10 subscales. Responses are made on a 9-point scale ranging from 1 (*does not describe me at all*) to 9 (*describes me well*).

Reliability: Median alpha coefficients were .77 and .78. Test–retest (2 days) reliabilities ranged from .67 to .80.

Author: Mau, W.-C. J.

Article: Cultural dimensions of career decision-making difficulties.

Journal: *The Career Development Quarterly*, September 2004, *53*, 67–77.

Related Research: Gati, I., et al. (1996). A taxonomy of difficulties in career decision making. *Journal of Counseling Psychology*, *43*, 510–526.

13746

Test Name: CAREER DECISION-MAKING DIFFICULTY QUESTIONNAIRE—HIGH SCHOOL (ADAPTED)

Purpose: To measure high school students career decision-making difficulties.

Number of Items: 35

Format: Includes three subscales: Lack of Readiness, Lack of Information, and Inconsistent Information. Responses are made on a 7-point scale ranging from 1 (*does not describe me at all*) to 7 (*describes me well*).

Reliability: Alpha coefficients ranged from .60 to .91.

Author: Mau, W.-C. J.

Article: Cultural dimensions of career decision-making difficulties.

Journal: *The Career Development Quarterly*, September 2004, *53*, 67–77.

Related Research: Gati, I., & Saka, N. (2001). High school students' career-related decision-making difficulties. *Journal of Counseling and Development*, *79*, 331–340.

13747

Test Name: CAREER DECISION-MAKING DIFFICULTY SCALE

Purpose: To assess lack of readiness, lack of information, and inconsistent information as elements of career decision-making difficulty.

Number of Items: 35

Format: Scales range from 1 (*does not describe me at all*) to 7 (*describes me well*).

Reliability: Coefficient alpha for the total scale was .91. Subscale alphas ranged from .60 to .91.

Author: Mau, W.-C. J.

Article: Cultural dimensions of career decision-making difficulties.

Journal: *The Career Development Quarterly*, September 2004, *53*, 67–77.

Related Research: Gati, I., & Saka, N. (2001). High school students' career-related decision-making difficulties. *Journal of Counseling and Development*, *79*, 331–340.

13748

Test Name: CAREER DECISION-MAKING DIFFICULTIES SCALE—ARABIC VERSION

Purpose: To measure lack of readiness, lack of information, and inconsistent information in career decisions.

Number of Items: 36

Time Required: 30 to 45 minutes.

Format: Scales range from 1 (*doesn't describe me at all*) to 9 (*describes me well*).

Reliability: Alpha coefficients ranged from .44 to .79 across subscales.

Validity: Goodness of fit measures ranged from .94 to .97.

Author: Hijazi, Y., et al.

Article: Career decision-making difficulties among Israeli and Palestinian Arab high school seniors.

Journal: *Professional School Counseling*, October 2004, *8*(1), 64–72.

Related Research: Gati, I., & Saka N. (2001). High school students' career-related decision-making difficulties. *Journal of Counseling and Development*, *79*, 331–340.

13749

Test Name: CAREER DECISION-MAKING SELF-EFFICACY SCALE—SHORT FORM

Purpose: To assess confidence in the ability to successfully make career decisions.

Number of Items: 25

Format: Scales range from 0 (*no confidence*) to 9 (*complete confidence*).

Reliability: Coefficient alpha was .94. Test–retest reliability was .83 (6 weeks).

Author: Maples, M. R., and Luzzo, D. A.

Article: Evaluating DISCOVERS's effectiveness in enhancing college students' social cognitive career development.

Journal: *The Career Development Quarterly*, March 2005, *53*, 263–273.

Related Research: Betz, N. E., et al. (1996). Evaluation of a short form of the Career Decision-Making Self-Efficacy Scale. *Journal of Career Assessment, 4*, 47–57.

13750

Test Name: CAREER DECISION-MAKING STRATEGIES SCALE

Purpose: To assess career decision-making strategies.

Number of Items: 24

Format: Includes three areas: rational decision making, intuitive decision making, and dependent decision making.

Reliability: Alpha coefficients ranged from .75 to .85.

Validity: Correlations with other variables ranged from –.19 to .20.

Author: Singh, R., and Greenhaus, J. H.

Article: The relation between career decision-making strategies and person–job fit: A study of job changers.

Journal: *Journal of Vocational Behavior*, February 2004, *64*, 198–221.

Related Research: Harren, V. A. (1979). A model of career decision-making for college students. *Journal of Vocational Behavior, 14*, 119–133. Scott, S. G., & Bruce, R. A. (1995). Decision-making style: The development and assessment of a new measure. *Educational and Psychological Measurement, 55*, 818–831.

13751

Test Name: CAREER DECISION PROFILE

Purpose: To assess how decided individuals are and how comfortable they are with their decisions and career decision needs.

Number of Items: 16

Format: Includes six factors: decidedness, comfort, self-clarity, knowledge about occupations, decisiveness, and career importance. Responses are made on an 8-point Likert scale ranging from

1 (*strongly disagree*) to 8 (*strongly agree*).

Reliability: Internal consistency ranged from .73 to .89. Test–retest (3 weeks) correlation coefficients ranged from .66 to .80.

Validity: Correlations with other variables ranged from –.54 to .48.

Author: Heppner, M. J., et al.

Article: The role of problem-solving appraisal in the process and outcome of career counseling.

Journal: *Journal of Vocational Behavior*, October 2004, *65*, 217–238.

Related Research: Jones, L. K. (1989). Measuring a three-dimensional construct of career indecision among college students: A revision of the Vocational Decision Scale—The Career Decision Profile. *Journal of Counseling Psychology, 36*, 477–486.

13752

Test Name: CAREER IDENTITY SCALE

Purpose: To measure identification with one's career.

Number of Items: 3

Format: Scales range from 1 (*strongly disagree*) to 5 (*strongly agree*). All items are presented.

Reliability: Coefficient alpha was .74.

Validity: Correlations with other variables ranged from –.33 to .20.

Author: Wilk, S. L., and Moynihan, L. M.

Article: Display rule "regulators": The relationship between supervisors and worker emotional exhaustion.

Journal: *Journal of Applied Psychology*, September 2005, *90*, 917–927.

Related Research: Carson, K. D., & Bedeian, A. G. (1994). Career commitment: Construction of a measure and examination of its psychometric properties. *Journal of Vocational Behavior, 44*, 237–262.

13753

Test Name: CAREER INVOLVEMENT SCALE

Purpose: To assess career involvement.

Number of Items: 3

Format: Responses are made on a 5-point scale ranging from *strongly disagree* to *strongly agree*. An example is presented.

Reliability: Coefficient alpha was .77.

Author: Greenhaus, J. H., et al.

Article: The relation between work–family balance and quality of life.

Journal: *Journal of Vocational Behavior*, December 2003, *63*, 510–531.

Related Research: Lodahl, T. M., & Kejner, M. (1965). Definition and measurement of job involvement. *Journal of Applied Psychology, 49*, 24–33.

13754

Test Name: CAREER OUTCOME MEASURES

Purpose: To measure four career outcomes.

Number of Items: 9

Format: Employed 5-point Likert scales ranging from 1 (*strongly disagree*) to 5 (*strongly agree*) and the natural logarithm of total annual earnings. Includes measures of Earnings, Promotional Opportunities, Procedural Justice, and Social Interaction.

Reliability: Reliabilities ranged from .77 to .91.

Validity: Correlations with other variables ranged from –.25 to .46.

Author: Wallance, J. E.

Article: The benefits of mentoring for female lawyers.

Journal: *Journal of Vocational Behavior*, June 2001, *58*, 366–391.

Related Research: Price, J. L., & Mueller, C. W. (1986). *Absenteeism and turnover of hospital employees.* Greenwich, CT: JAI Press. Mueller, C. W., & Wallace, J. E. (1996). Justice and the paradox of the contented female worker. *Social Psychology Quarterly, 59*, 338–349.

13755

Test Name: CAREER SALIENCE SCALE—SHORT FORM

Purpose: To assess the respondent's perceived importance of work or career, including planning and general attitudes about work.

Number of Items: 6

Format: Responses are made on a 5-point scale. An example is given.

Reliability: Alpha coefficients were .56 and .83.

Validity: Correlations with other variables ranged from –.08 to .20.

Author: Wettersten, K. B., et al.

Article: Predicting educational and vocational attitudes among rural high school students.

Journal: *Journal of Counseling Psychology*, October 2005, *52*, 658–663.

Related Research: Greenhaus, J., & Simon, W. (1977). Career salience, work values, and vocational indecision. *Journal of Vocational Behavior, 10*, 104–110.

13756

Test Name: CAREER SATISFACTION MEASURE

Purpose: To measure career satisfaction.

Number of Items: 4

Format: All items are presented.

Reliability: Coefficient alpha was .88 (*N* = 267).

Validity: Correlations with other variables ranged from .18 to .63 (*N* = 267).

Author: Erdogan, B., et al.

Article: Work value congruence and intrinsic career success: The compensatory roles of leader–member exchange and perceived organizational support.

Journal: *Personnel Psychology*, Summer 2004, *57*, 305–332.

Related Research: Greenhaus, J. H., et al. (1990). Effects of race on organizational experiences, job performance evaluations, and career outcomes. *Academy of Management Journal, 33*, 64–86.

13757

Test Name: CAREER SATISFACTION SCALE

Purpose: To measure career satisfaction.

Number of Items: 5

Format: Responses are made on a 5-point scale ranging from 1 (*strongly disagree*) to 5 (*strongly agree*). Examples are given.

Reliability: Alpha coefficients ranged from .68 to .88.

Validity: Correlations with other variables ranged for –.18 to .36.

Author: van der Velde, M. E. G., et al.

Article: Gender differences in the determinants of the willingness to accept an international assignment.

Journal: *Journal of Vocational Behavior*, February 2005, *66*, 81–103.

Related Research: Greenhaus, J. H., et al. (1990). Effects of race on organizational experience, job performance evaluations, and career outcomes. *Academy of Management Journal, 33,* 64–96.

13758

Test Name: CAREER TRANSITIONS INVENTORY

Purpose: To assess the psychological resources and barriers of adults in career transition.

Number of Items: 40

Format: Includes five factors: readiness, confidence, control, support, and decision independence. Responses are made on a 6-point scale ranging from 1 (*strongly disagree*) to 6 (*strongly agree*).

Reliability: Internal consistency ranged from .66 to .88. Temporal stability (3 weeks) was .84.

Validity: Correlations with other variables ranged from −.63 to .48.

Author: Heppner, M. J., et al.

Article: The role of problem-solving appraisal in the process and outcome of career counseling.

Journal: *Journal of Vocational Behavior,* October 2004, *65,* 217–238.

Related Research: Heppner, M. J. (1991). *The Career Transitions Inventory.* (Available from M. J. Heppner, Department of Educational and Counseling Psychology, 16 Hill Hall, University of Missouri, Columbia, MO 65211)

13759

Test Name: COMMITMENT SCALES

Purpose: To measure organizational commitment.

Number of Items: 17

Format: Includes three scales: Affective Commitment, Continuance Commitment, and Normative Commitment. Responses are made on a 7-point scale ranging from 1 (*strongly disagree*) to 7 (*strongly agree*).

Reliability: Alpha coefficients ranged from .61 to .82.

Validity: Correlations with other variables ranged from −.59 to .47.

Author: Wasti, S. A.

Article: Commitment profiles: Combinations of organizational commitment forms and job outcomes.

Journal: *Journal of Vocational Behavior,* October 2005, *67,* 290–308.

Related Research: Meyer, J. P., et al. (1993). Commitment to organizations and occupations: Extension and test of a three-component conceptualization. *Journal of Applied Psychology, 78,* 538–551.

13760

Test Name: COMMITMENT TO CAREER CHOICES SCALE

Purpose: To measure commitment to career choices.

Number of Items: 28

Format: Includes two subscales: Vocational Exploration and Commitment, and Tendency to Foreclose.

Reliability: Reliability coefficients were .82 and .85.

Validity: Correlations with other variables ranged from −.20 to .30.

Author: Duffy, R. D., and Blustein, D. L.

Article: The relationship between spirituality, religiousness, and career adaptability.

Journal: *Journal of Vocational Behavior,* December 2005, *67,* 429–440.

Related Research: Blustein, D. L. (1989). The role of career exploration in the career decision making of college students. *Journal of College Student Development, 30,* 111–117.

13761

Test Name: COMMITMENT TO CHANGE SCALE

Purpose: To measure affective, continuance, and normative commitment to change.

Number of Items: 18

Format: Scales range from 1 (*strongly disagree*) to 5 (*strongly agree*). All items are presented.

Reliability: Alpha coefficients ranged from .71 to .94 across subscales.

Validity: Correlations with other variables ranged from −.25 to .61.

Author: Herscovitch, L., and Meyer, J. P.

Article: Commitment to organizational change: Extension of a three-component model.

Journal: *Journal of Applied Psychology,* June 2002, *87,* 474–487.

13762

Test Name: COMMITMENT TO THE PROFESSION SCALE

Purpose: To measure individuals' commitment to their profession.

Number of Items: 4

Format: Responses are made on a 5-point scale ranging from 1 (*strongly disagree*) to 5 (*strongly agree*). A sample item is given.

Reliability: Coefficient alpha was .79.

Validity: Correlations with other variables ranged from −.50 to .43.

Author: Feldman, D. C., and Turnley, W. H.

Article: Contingent employment in academic careers: Relative deprivation among adjunct faculty.

Journal: *Journal of Vocational Behavior*, April 2004, *64*, 284–307.

Related Research: O'Reilly, C., & Chatman, J. (1986). Organizational commitment and psychological attachment: The effects of compliance, identification, and internalization on prosocial behavior. *Journal of Applied Psychology*, *71*, 492–499.

13763

Test Name: COMPANY LOYALTY SCALE

Purpose: To measure an employee's loyalty to his or her employer.

Number of Items: 3

Format: Scales range from 1 (*strongly disagree*) to 5 (*strongly agree*). A sample item is presented.

Reliability: Coefficient alpha was .65.

Validity: Correlations with other variables ranged from −.38 to .20.

Author: Olson-Buchanan, J. B., and Boswell, W. R.

Article: The role of employee loyalty and formality in voicing discontent.

Journal: *Journal of Applied Psychology*, December 2002, *87*, 1167–1174.

Related Research: Boroff, K. E., & Lewin, D. (1997). Loyalty, voice, and intent to exit a union firm: A conceptual and empirical analysis. *Industrial and Labor Relations Review*, *51*, 50–63.

13764

Test Name: CONTINUANCE COMMITMENT SCALES

Purpose: To measure organization continuance commitment (with minor revisions to measure

department and work group continuance commitment).

Number of Items: 8 (for each scale).

Format: Responses are made on a 7-point Likert-type scale ranging from 1 (*strongly disagree*) to 7 (*strongly agree*).

Reliability: Alpha coefficients ranged from .80 to .90 (*N* ranged from 150–154).

Validity: Correlations with other variables ranged from −.16 to .29 (*N* ranged from 150–154).

Author: Heffner, T. S., and Rentsch, J. R.

Article: Organizational commitment and social interaction: A multiple constituencies approach.

Journal: *Journal of Vocational Behavior*, December 2001, *59*, 471–490.

Related Research: Meyer, J. P., & Allen, N. J. (1984). Testing the "side-bet theory" of organizational commitment: Some methodological considerations. *Journal of Applied Psychology*, *69*, 372–378.

13765

Test Name: CONTINUANCE ORGANIZATIONAL COMMITMENT SCALE

Purpose: To assess continuance organizational commitment.

Number of Items: 8

Format: Responses are made on a 5-point Likert scale. An example is given.

Reliability: Alpha coefficients were .79 and .82.

Validity: Correlations with other variables ranged from −.30 to .37.

Author: Zickar, M. J., et al.

Article: Job attitudes of workers with two jobs.

Journal: *Journal of Vocational Behavior*, February 2004, *64*, 222–235.

Related Research: Meyer, J. P., et al. (1993). Commitment to organizations and occupations: Extension and test of a three-component conceptualization. *Journal of Applied Psychology*, *78*, 538–551.

13766

Test Name: DECISIONAL PROCESS INVENTORY

Purpose: To measure level of contact and resistance related to the career decision-making process.

Number of Items: 25

Format: Includes three factors: readiness, action, and resistance. Responses are made on a 5-point scale. An example is presented.

Reliability: Alpha coefficients ranged from .79 to .93.

Author: Marco, C. D., et al.

Article: Validity of the Decisional Process Inventory.

Journal: *Journal of Vocational Behavior*, August 2003, *63*, 1–19.

Related Research: Hartung, P. J. (1994). *Decisional Process Inventory*. Unpublished test, Northeastern Ohio Universities College of Medicine, Rootstown, OH.

13767

Test Name: ENGINEERING EDUCATIONAL GOALS SCALE

Purpose: To assess engineering academic goal intentions.

Number of Items: 4

Format: Responses are made on a 5-point scale ranging from 1 (*strongly disagree*) to 5 (*strongly agree*). Examples are given.

Reliability: Coefficient alpha was .95.

Validity: Correlations with other variables ranged from −.20 to .53 (N = 287).

Author: Lent, R. W., et al.

Article: Relation of contextual supports and barriers to choice behavior in engineering majors: Test of alternative social cognitive models.

Journal: *Journal of Counseling Psychology*, October 2003, *50*, 458–465.

Related Research: Lapan, R. T., et al. (1996). Efficacy expectations and vocational interest as mediators between sex and choice of math/science college majors: A longitudinal study. *Journal of Vocational Behavior, 49*, 277–291.

13768

Test Name: GENERAL INDECISIVENESS SCALE

Purpose: To measure general indecisiveness.

Number of Items: 22

Format: Responses are made on a 7-point scale ranging from (*strongly disagree*) to 6 (*strongly agree*). All items are given.

Reliability: Coefficient alpha was .91.

Author: Germeijs, V., and DeBoeck, P.

Article: Career indecision: Three factors from decision theory.

Journal: *Journal of Vocational Behavior*, February 2003, *62*, 11–25.

Related Research: Germeijs, V., & DeBoeck, P. (2002). A measurement scale for indecisiveness and its relationship to career indecision and other types of indecision. *European Journal of Psychological Assessment, 18*, 113–122.

13769

Test Name: JOB ASPIRATIONS SCALE

Purpose: To measure job aspirations.

Number of Items: 8

Format: Responses are made on a 5-point scale ranging from 1 (*not at all important*) to 5 (*very important*). An example is given.

Reliability: Coefficient alpha was .72.

Validity: Correlations with other variables ranged from −.11 to .39 (n = 391).

Author: Pinquart, M., et al.

Article: Self-efficacy and successful school-to-work transition: A longitudinal study.

Journal: *Journal of Vocational Behavior*, December 2003, *63*, 329–346.

Related Research: O'Brien, K. M., et al. (2000). Attachment, separation, and women's vocational development: A longitudinal analysis. *Journal of Counseling Psychology, 47*, 301–315.

13770

Test Name: JOB DESIRABILITY SCALE

Purpose: To measure desire for job.

Number of Items: 7

Format: Scales range from 1 (*strongly disagree*) to 5 (*strongly agree*).

Reliability: Alpha coefficients ranged from .76 to .82.

Validity: Correlations with other variables ranged from −.17 to .47.

Author: Barrick, M. R., and Zimmerman, R. D.

Article: Reducing voluntary, avoidable turnover through selection.

Journal: *Journal of Applied Psychology*, January 2005, *90*, 159–166.

Related Research: Lee, T. W., et al. (1992). Commitment propensity, organizational commitment, and voluntary turnover: A longitudinal study of organizational entry processes. *Journal of Management, 10*, 15–32.

13771

Test Name: JOB INVOLVEMENT SCALE

Purpose: To measure the centrality of a person's job.

Number of Items: 3

Format: Scales range from 1 (*strongly agree*) to 5 (*strongly disagree*). All items are presented.

Reliability: Coefficient alpha was .68.

Validity: Correlations with other variables ranged from −.16 to .39.

Author: Brett, J. M., and Stroh, L. K.

Article: Working 61 plus hours a week: Why do managers do it?

Journal: *Journal of Applied Psychology*, February 2003, *88*, 67–78.

13772

Test Name: JOB INVOLVEMENT SCALE

Purpose: To measure job involvement.

Number of Items: 3

Format: An example is given.

Reliability: Internal reliability was .71.

Validity: Correlations with other variables ranged from −.10 to .34.

Author: Kacmar, K. M., et al.

Article: Situational and dispositional factors as antecedents of ingratiatory behaviors in organizational settings.

Journal: *Journal of Vocational Behavior*, October 2004, *65*, 309–331.

Related Research: Buchanan, B. (1964). Building organizational commitment: The socialization of managers in work organizations. *Administrative Science Quarterly, 19*, 533–546.

13773

Test Name: JOB INVOLVEMENT SCALE

Purpose: To measure job involvement.

Number of Items: 9

Format: Responses are made on a 5-point scale. Examples are given.

Reliability: Coefficient alpha was .86.

Validity: Correlations with other variables ranged from –.10 to .57.

Author: Goulet, L. R., and Singh, P.

Article: Career commitment: A reexamination and an extension.

Journal: *Journal of Vocational Behavior*, August 2002, *61*, 73–91.

Related Research: Kanugo, R. (1982). *Work alienation: An integrative approach.* New York: Praeger Publishers.

13774

Test Name: JOB INVOLVEMENT SCALE—KUWAITI VERSION

Purpose: To measure job involvement.

Number of Items: 20

Format: Response categories are anchored by 1 (*strongly disagree*) and 5 (*strongly agree*).

Reliability: Coefficient alpha was .80.

Validity: Correlation with a meaning of work scale was .65.

Author: Hasan, H.

Article: Meaning of work among a sample of Kuwaiti workers.

Journal: *Psychological Reports*, February 2004, *94*, 195–207.

Related Research: Lodahl, T. M., & Kejner, M. (1965). The definition and measurement of job involvement. *Journal of Applied Psychology, 49*, 24–33.

13775

Test Name: JOB SEARCH SCALE

Purpose: To measure job search.

Number of Items: 4

Format: Responses are made on a 5-point scale ranging from 1 (*strongly disagree*) to 5 (*strongly agree*).

Reliability: Coefficient alpha was .85.

Validity: Correlations with other variables ranged from –.56 to .79.

Author: Feldman, D. C., and Turnley, W. H.

Article: Contingent employment in academic careers: Relative deprivation among adjunct faculty.

Journal: *Journal of Vocational Behavior*, April 2004, *64*, 284–307.

Related Research: Feldman, D. C., & Turnley, W. H. (1995). Underemployment among recent college graduates. *Journal of Organizational Behavior, 16*, 691–706.

13776

Test Name: MAPPING VOCATIONAL CHALLENGES

Purpose: To assess occupational interests, career self-efficacy expectations, parent support, and gender-typing.

Number of Items: 90

Format: Sample items and various response scales are presented.

Reliability: Alpha coefficients ranged from .70 to .91.

Author: Turner, S., and Lapan, R. T.

Article: Career self-efficacy and perceptions of parent support in adolescent career development.

Journal: *The Career Development Quarterly*, September 2002, *51*, 44–55.

Related Research: Lapan, R. T., & Turner, S. L. (1997). *Mapping Vocational Challenges.* Unpublished assessment instrument. (Available from first author.)

13777

Test Name: MOBILITY OPPORTUNITY SCALE

Purpose: To measure mobility opportunity.

Number of Items: 5

Format: Responses are made on a 5-point scale ranging from 1 (*strongly disagree*) to 5 (*strongly agree*). All items are presented.

Reliability: Coefficient alpha was .82.

Validity: Correlations with other variables ranged from –.07 to .33.

Author: Prince, J. B.

Article: Career opportunity and organizational attachment in a blue-collar unionized environment.

Journal: *Journal of Vocational Behavior*, August 2003, *63*, 136–150.

Related Research: Prince, J. B. (1984). *Allocative and opportunity structures and their interaction with career orientation.* Unpublished doctoral dissertation, University of Southern California, Los Angeles.

13778

Test Name: OCCUPATIONAL COMMITMENT SCALE

Purpose: To measure identification, affiliation and moral involvement as components of affective attachment to the organization.

Format: Item responses are anchored by 1 (*strongly disagree*) and 7 (*strongly agree*). Sample items are presented.

Reliability: Cronbach's alpha was .77.

Validity: Correlations with other variables ranged from −.26 to .35.

Author: Cohen, A., and Schwartz, H.

Article: An empirical examination among Canadian teachers of determinants of the need for employees' assistance programs.

Journal: *Psychological Reports*, June 2002, *90*, Part 2, 1221–1238.

Related Research: Cohen, A. (1993). Work commitment in relations to withdrawal intentions and union effectiveness. *Journal of Business Research, 26*, 75–90.

13779

Test Name: ORGANIZATIONAL CITIZENSHIP BEHAVIOR QUESTIONNAIRE

Purpose: To measure altruism, conscientiousness, and sportsmanship.

Number of Items: 18

Reliability: Internal consistency ranged from .72 to .83 across scales.

Validity: Correlations with other variables ranged from −.13 to .38.

Author: Lowery, C. M., et al.

Article: Note on the relationships among job satisfaction, organizational commitment, and organizational citizenship behavior.

Journal: *Psychological Reports*, October 2002, *91*, 607–617.

Related Research: Smith, A. C., et al. (1983). Organizational citizenship behavior: Its nature and

antecedents. *Journal of Applied Psychology, 68*, 653–663.

MacKenzie, S. B., et al. (1991). Organizational citizenship behavior and objective productivity as determinants of managerial evaluations of salespersons' performance. *Organizational Behavior and Human Decision Processes, 50*, 123–150.

13780

Test Name: ORGANIZATIONAL CITIZENSHIP BEHAVIOR ROLE SCALE

Purpose: To assess the perception employees have of expected citizenship behavior.

Number of Items: 20

Format: Scales range from 1 (*definitely exceeds my job requirements*) to 2 (*definitely part of my job*). Sample items are presented.

Reliability: Coefficient alpha was .92.

Validity: Correlations with other variables ranged from −.03 to .19.

Author: Zellars, K. L., et al.

Article: Abusive supervision and subordinates' organizational citizenship behavior.

Journal: *Journal of Applied Psychology*, December 2002, 87, 1068–1076.

Related Research: Podsakoff, P. M., et al. (1990). Transformational leader behaviors and their effects on followers' trust in leader, satisfaction, and organizational citizenship behavior. *Leadership Quarterly, 1*, 107–142.

13781

Test Name: ORGANIZATIONAL CITIZENSHIP BEHAVIOR SCALE

Purpose: To measure contextual job performance by supervisors' ratings.

Number of Items: 13

Format: Scales range from 1 (*weak or bottom 10%*) to 5 (*best or top 10%*).

Reliability: Coefficient alpha was .89.

Validity: Correlations with other variables ranged from −.39 to .68.

Author: Witt, L. A., and Ferris, G. R.

Article: Social skill as moderator of the conscientiousness–performance relationship: Convergent results across four studies.

Journal: *Journal of Applied Psychology*, October 2003, *88*, 809–820.

13782

Test Name: ORGANIZATIONAL CITIZENSHIP BEHAVIORS SCALE

Purpose: To measure altruism, courtesy, sportsmanship, conscientiousness, and civic virtue.

Number of Items: 20

Format: Items are anchored by 1 (*strongly disagree*) and 5 (*strongly agree*).

Reliability: Alpha coefficients ranged from .69 to .88.

Validity: Correlations with other variables ranged from .06 to .25.

Author: Charbonneau, D., and Nicol, A. A. M.

Article: Emotional intelligence and prosocial behaviors in adolescents.

Journal: *Psychological Reports*, April 2002, *90*, 361–370.

Related Research: Niehoff, B. P., & Moorman, R. H. (1993). Justice as a mediator of the relationship between methods of monitoring and organizational citizenship behavior. *Academy of Management Journal, 36*, 526–556.

13783

Test Name: ORGANIZATIONAL COMMITMENT

Purpose: To measure organizational commitment.

Number of Items: 4

Format: Responses are made on a 5-point scale ranging from 1 (*strongly disagree*) to 5 (*strongly agree*). All items are presented.

Reliability: Coefficient alpha was .80.

Validity: Correlations with other variables ranged from −.07 to .50.

Author: Prince, J. B.

Article: Career opportunity and organizational attachment in a blue-collar unionized environment.

Journal: *Journal of Vocational Behavior*, August 2003, *63*, 136–150.

Related Research: Mowday, R., et al. (1979). The measurement of organizational commitment. *Journal of Vocational Behavior, 14*, 224–247.

13784

Test Name: ORGANIZATIONAL COMMITMENT QUESTIONNAIRE

Purpose: To measure organizational commitment.

Number of Items: 15

Format: Responses are made on a 5-point scale. Sample items are presented.

Reliability: Coefficient alpha was .91.

Validity: Correlations with other variables ranged from −.14 to .59.

Author: Goulet, L. R., and Singh, P.

Article: Career commitment: A reexamination and an extension.

Journal: *Journal of Vocational Behavior*, August 2002, *61*, 73–91.

Related Research: Mowday, R. T., et al. (1979). The measurement of organizational commitment.

Journal of Vocational Behavior, 14, 224–247.

13785

Test Name: ORGANIZATIONAL COMMITMENT QUESTIONNAIRE—ADAPTED

Purpose: To measure commitment to telework and to virtual teams.

Number of Items: 15

Format: Includes two formats: one for telework and one for virtual teams. Responses are made on a 7-point Likert-type scale ranging from 1 (*strongly disagree*) to 7 (*strongly agree*).

Reliability: Alpha coefficients were .94 to .96.

Validity: Correlations with other variables ranged from −.45 to .68.

Author: Workman, M., et al.

Article: The effects of cognitive style and media richness on commitment to telework and virtual teams.

Journal: *Journal of Vocational Behavior*, October 2003, *63*, 199–219.

Related Research: Mowday, R. T., et al. (1978). The measurement of organizational commitment. *Journal of Vocational Behavior, 14,* 224–247.

13786

Test Name: ORGANIZATIONAL COMMITMENT QUESTIONNAIRE—HEBREW VERSION

Purpose: To measure organizational commitment.

Number of Items: 15

Format: Scales range from 1 (*strongly disagree*) to 7 (*strongly agree*).

Reliability: Coefficient alpha was .75.

Author: Dishon-Berkovits, M., and Koslowsky, M.

Article: Determinants of employee punctuality.

Journal: *The Journal of Social Psychology*, December 2002, *142*, 723–739.

Related Research: Porter, L. W., et al. (1974). Organizational commitment, job satisfaction, and turnover among psychiatric technicians. *Journal of Applied Psychology, 59*, 603–609.

13787

Test Name: ORGANIZATIONAL COMMITMENT QUESTIONNAIRE—SHORT VERSION

Purpose: To measure organizational commitment.

Number of Items: 9

Format: Responses are made on a 7-point scale ranging from *strongly disagree* to *strongly agree*. An example is given.

Reliability: Coefficient alpha was .93.

Validity: Correlations with other variables ranged from −.34 to .64.

Author: Liao, H., et al.

Article: Sticking out like a sore thumb: Employee dissimilarity and deviance at work.

Journal: *Personnel Psychology*, Winter 2004, *57*, 969–1000.

Related Research: Mowday, R. T., et al. (1979). The measurement of organizational commitment. *Journal of Vocational Behavior, 14,* 224–247.

13788

Test Name: ORGANIZATIONAL COMMITMENT SCALE

Purpose: To measure organizational commitment.

Number of Items: 6

Format: Scales range from 1 (*strongly disagree*) to 5 (*strongly agree*). Sample items are presented.

Reliability: Coefficient alpha was .86.

Validity: Correlations with other variables ranged from −.34 to .41.

Author: Aryee, S., et al.

Article: Rhythms of life: Antecedents and outcomes of work–family balance in employed parents.

Journal: *Journal of Applied Psychology*, January 2005, *90*, 132–146.

Related Research: Meyer, J. P., et al. (1993). Commitment to organizations and occupations: Extension and a test of a three-component conceptualization. *Journal of Applied Psychology, 78*, 538–551.

13789

Test Name: ORGANIZATIONAL COMMITMENT SCALE

Purpose: To measure organizational commitment.

Format: Includes three dimensions: Affective Commitment, Normative Commitment, and Continuance Commitment. Responses are made on a 5-point scale ranging from 1 (*not at all*) to 5 (*to a large extent*). Sample items are presented.

Reliability: Alpha coefficients ranged from .87 to .90.

Validity: Correlations with other variables ranged from −.32 to .46 (*n* = 214).

Author: Bakker, A. B., et al.

Article: Job demands and job resources as predictors of absence duration and frequency.

Journal: *Journal of Vocational Behavior*, April 2003, *62*, 341–356.

Related Research: Meyer, J. P., & Allen, N. J. (1991). A three-component conceptualization of

organizational commitment. *Human Resource Management Review, 1*, 61–98.

13790

Test Name: ORGANIZATIONAL COMMITMENT SCALE

Purpose: To measure organizational commitment.

Number of Items: 6

Format: Scales range from 1 (*strongly agree*) to 6 (*strongly disagree*). All items are presented.

Reliability: Coefficient alpha was .76.

Author: Clay-Warner, J., et al.

Article: Procedural justice, distributive justice: How experiences with downsizing condition their impact on organizational commitment.

Journal: *Social Psychology Quarterly*, March 2005, *68*, 89–102.

Related Research: Lincoln, J. R., & Kalleberg, A. L. (1990). *Culture, control, and commitment: A study of work organization and work attitudes in the United States and Japan.* Cambridge, England: Cambridge University Press.

13791

Test Name: ORGANIZATIONAL COMMITMENT SCALE

Purpose: To measure organizational commitment.

Number of Items: 6

Format: Responses are made on a 7-point scale ranging from *strongly agree* to *strongly disagree*.

Reliability: Alpha coefficients ranged from .76 to .87.

Validity: Correlations with other variables ranged from −.04 to .36.

Author: Coyle-Shapiro, J. A.-M., and Morrow, P. C.

Article: The role of individual differences in employee adoption of TQM orientation.

Journal: *Journal of Vocational Behavior*, April 2003, *62*, 320–340.

Related Research: Cook, J., & Wall, T. (1980). New work attitude measures of trust, organizational commitment and personal need non-fulfillment. *Journal of Occupational Psychology, 53*, 39–52.

13792

Test Name: ORGANIZATIONAL COMMITMENT SCALE

Purpose: To measure organizational commitment.

Number of Items: 3

Format: Scales range from 1 (*strongly in disagreement*) to 5 (*strongly in agreement*). A sample item is presented.

Reliability: Coefficient alpha was .91.

Validity: Correlations with other variables ranged from .00 to .60 aggregated at the work-unit level.

Author: González-Romá, V., et al.

Article: An examination of the antecedents and moderator influences of climate strength.

Journal: *Journal of Applied Psychology*, June 2002, *87*, 465–473.

13793

Test Name: ORGANIZATIONAL COMMITMENT SCALE

Purpose: To measure affective, continuance, and normative commitment.

Number of Items: 28

Format: Scales range from 1 (*strongly disagree*) to 7 (*strongly agree*).

Reliability: Alpha coefficients ranged from .87 to .91 across subscales.

Validity: Correlations with other variables ranged from −.21 to .41.

Author: Herscovitch, L., and Meyer, J. P.

Article: Commitment to organizational change: Extension of a three-component model.

Journal: *Journal of Applied Psychology*, June 2002, *87*, 474–487.

Related Research: Allen, N. J., & Meyer, J. P. (1996). Affective, continuance, and normative commitment to the organization: An examination of construct validity. *Journal of Vocational Behavior, 49*, 252–276.

13794

Test Name: ORGANIZATIONAL COMMITMENT SCALE

Purpose: To measure organizational commitment.

Number of Items: 6

Format: Responses are made on a 5-point scale ranging from 1 (*fully disagree*) to 5 (*fully agree*). Examples are given.

Reliability: Alpha coefficients ranged from .82 to .86.

Validity: Correlations with other variables ranged from −.19 to .48.

Author: van der Velde, M. E. G., et al.

Article: Gender differences in the determinants of the willingness to accept an international assignment.

Journal: *Journal of Vocational Behavior*, February 2005, *66*, 81–103.

Related Research: Blau, G., et al. (1993). On developing a general index of work commitment. *Journal of Vocational Behavior, 42*, 298–314.

13795

Test Name: ORGANIZATIONAL COMMITMENT SCALE— ADAPTED

Purpose: To measure the affective commitment aspect of organizational commitment.

Number of Items: 8

Format: Responses are made on a 7-point scale ranging from 1 (*strongly disagree*) to 7 (*strongly agree*). Sample items are given.

Reliability: Coefficient alpha was .87.

Validity: Correlations with other variables ranged from .23 to .67 ($n = 186$).

Author: Chen, Z. X., et al.

Article: Test of a mediation model of perceived organizational support.

Journal: *Journal of Vocational Behavior*, June 2005, *66*, 457–470.

Related Research: Allen, N. J., & Meyer, J. P. (1990). The measurement and antecedents of affective, continuance, and normative commitment to the organization. *Journal of Occupational Psychology, 63*, 1–18.

13796

Test Name: ORGANIZATIONAL COMMITMENT SCALE— FRENCH VERSION

Purpose: To measure organizational commitment.

Number of Items: 18

Format: Scales range from 1 (*strongly disagree*) to 5 (*strongly agree*).

Reliability: Alpha coefficients ranged from .74 to .92.

Validity: Correlations with other variables ranged from −.42 to .14.

Author: Bentein, K., et al.

Article: The role of change in the relationship between commitment

and turnover: A latent growth modeling approach.

Journal: *Journal of Applied Psychology*, May 2005, *90*, 468–482.

Related Research: Meyer, J. P., et al. (1993). Commitment to organizations and occupations: Extension and test of a three-component conceptualization. *Journal of Applied Psychology, 78*, 538–551.

13797

Test Name: ORGANIZATIONAL COMMITMENT SCALES

Purpose: To measure three dimensions of organizational commitment.

Number of Items: 24

Format: Includes three commitment scales: Affective, Normative, and Continuance. Responses are made on a 5-point Likert scale ranging from 1 (*strongly disagree*) to 5 (*strongly agree*).

Reliability: Internal reliability coefficients ranged from .77 to .84.

Author: Kondratuk, T. B., et al.

Article: Linking career mobility with corporate loyalty: How does job change relate to organizational commitment?

Journal: *Journal of Vocational Behavior*, October 2004, *65*, 332–349.

Related Research: Allen, N. J., & Meyer, J. P. (1990). The measurement and antecedents of affective, continuance, and normative commitment to the organization. *Journal of Occupational Psychology, 63*, 1–18.

13798

Test Name: ORGANIZATIONAL COMMITMENT SCALES— KOREAN VERSIONS

Purpose: To measure organizational commitment.

Number of Items: 26

Reliability: Alpha coefficients ranged from .57 to .88.

Validity: Correlations between scales ranged from .36 to .70.

Author: Lee, J. A., and Yang, C.

Article: Factor structure of organizational commitment: Differences between U.S. and South Korean samples.

Journal: *Psychological Reports,* June 2005, *96,* Part 1, 595–602.

Related Research: Mowday, R. T., et al. (1979). The measurement of organizational commitment. *Journal of Vocational Behavior, 14,* 224–247. Allen, N. J., & Meyer, J. P. (1990). The measurement and antecedents of affective, continuance, and normative commitment to the organization. *Journal of Occupational Psychology, 63,* 1–18.

13799

Test Name: ORGANIZATIONAL IDENTIFICATION SCALE

Purpose: To measure a person's perception of oneness felt toward a focal unity.

Number of Items: 5- and 6-item versions.

Format: Two identification scales: Organization and Profession.

Reliability: Reliability coefficients were .82 to .84.

Author: Mael, F. A., et al.

Article: From scientific work to organizational leadership: Predictors of management aspiration among technical personnel.

Journal: *Journal of Vocational Behavior,* August 2001, *59,* 132–148.

Related Research: Mael, F. A., & Alderks, C. E. (1993). Leadership

team cohesion and subordinate work unity morale and performance. *Military Psychology, 5,* 141–158. Mael, F. A., & Ashfarth, B. E. (1995). Loyal from day one: Biodata, organizational identification, and turnover among new members. *Personnel Psychology, 48,* 309–333. Mael, F. A., & Tetrick, L. E. (1992). Identifying organizational identification. *Educational and Psychological Measurement, 52,* 813–824.

13800

Test Name: PERSONAL GLOBE INVENTORY

Purpose: To examine Irish students' vocational interests and competence perceptions.

Number of Items: 108 (per form)

Format: Includes two forms: One form measures liking each occupation; the other form measures liking each activity and rating perceived competence to perform the activity. Seven-point scales are used.

Reliability: Alpha coefficients were above .80.

Author: Darcy, M. U. A.

Article: Examination of the structure of Irish students' vocational interests and competence perceptions.

Journal: *Journal of Vocational Behavior,* October 2005, *67,* 321–333.

Related Research: Tracey, T. J. G. (2002). Personal Globe Inventory: Measurement of the spherical model of interests and competence beliefs. *Journal of Vocational Behavior, 60,* 113–172.

13801

Test Name: SCIENTIST–PRACTITIONER INVENTORY—20

Purpose: To measure interest in scientific and practitioner activities in psychology.

Number of Items: 20

Format: Responses are made on a 5-point scale ranging from 1 (*very low interest*) to 5 (*very high interest*).

Reliability: Internal consistencies ranged from .82 to .90.

Author: Schlosser, L. Z., and Gelso, C. J.

Article: The Advisory Working Alliance Inventory—Advisor Version: Scale development and validation.

Journal: *Journal of Counseling Psychology,* October 2005, *52,* 650–654.

Related Research: Leong, F. T. L., & Zachar, P. (1993). Presenting two brief versions of the Scientist Practitioner Inventory. *Journal of Career Assessment, 1,* 162–170.

13802

Test Name: SPORTS INTEREST SCALE

Purpose: To measure interest in sports.

Number of Items: 7

Format: Item anchors are 1 (*strongly disagree*) and 4 (*strongly agree*). All items are presented.

Reliability: Coefficient alpha was .84.

Validity: Correlations with other variables ranged from .00 to .34.

Author: McClearn, D. G.

Article: Interest in sports and belief in sports superstitions.

Journal: *Psychological Reports,* June 2004, *94,* Part 1, 1043–1047.

13803

Test Name: TECHNICAL INTERESTS MEASURE

Purpose: To determine interest in performing seven engineering-related activities.

Number of Items: 7

Format: Responses are made on a 5-point scale ranging from 1 (*very low interest*) to 5 (*very high interest*). Examples are given.

Reliability: Alpha coefficients were .80 and .83.

Validity: Correlations with other variables ranged from −.10 to .48 (*n* = 472).

Author: Lent, R. W., et al.

Article: Social cognitive predictors of academic interests and goals in engineering: Utility for women and students at historically Black universities.

Journal: *Journal of Counseling Psychology*, January 2005, *52*, 84–92.

Related Research: Lent, R. W., et al. (2003). Relation of contextual supports and barriers to choice behavior in engineering majors: Test of alternative social cognitive models. *Journal of Counseling Psychology, 50*, 458–465.

13804

Test Name: THERAPY ACTIVITIES SCALE

Purpose: To measure students' interest in performing a variety of activities associated with the therapist or counselor role.

Number of Items: 13

Format: Responses are made on a 5-point scale ranging from 1 (*very low interest*) to 5 (*very high interest*). An example is presented.

Reliability: Alpha coefficients were .89 and .96.

Author: Lent, R. W., et al.

Article: Development and validation of the Counselor Activity Self-Efficacy Scales.

Journal: *Journal of Counseling Psychology*, January 2003, *50*, 97–108.

Related Research: Leong, F. T. L., & Zachar, P. (1991). Development and validation of the Scientist–Practitioner Inventory for Psychology. *Journal of Counseling Psychology, 38*, 331–341.

13805

Test Name: UNION COMMITMENT SCALE

Purpose: To assess union loyalty, responsibility to the union, and willingness to work for the union.

Number of Items: 13

Reliability: Alpha coefficients exceeded .76.

Validity: Correlations with other variables ranged from .02 to .69.

Author: Fullagar, C. J., et al.

Article: Union commitment and participation: A 10-year longitudinal study.

Journal: *Journal of Applied Psychology*, August 2004, *89*, 730–737.

Related Research: Kelloway, E. K., et al. (1992). Construct validity of union commitment: Development and dimensionality of a shorter scale. *Journal of Occupational and Organizational Psychology, 65*, 197–211.

13806

Test Name: UNION COMMITMENT SCALE

Purpose: To measure commitment to one's labor union.

Number of Items: 6

Reliability: Coefficient alpha was .78.

Validity: Correlations with other variables ranged from −.37 to .54.

Author: Redman, T., and Snape, E.

Article: Exchange ideology and member–union relationships: An evaluation of moderation effects.

Journal: *Journal of Applied Psychology*, July 2005, *90*, 765–773.

Related Research: Meyer, J. P., & Allen, N. J. (1997). *Commitment in the workplace: Theory, research, and application.* Thousand Oaks, CA: Sage.

13807

Test Name: UTRECHT WORK ENTHUSIASM SCALE

Purpose: To measure how enthusiastically people are engaged in their work.

Number of Items: 16

Format: Scales range from 1 (*never*) to 7 (*every day*). Sample items are presented.

Reliability: Coefficient alpha was .91.

Author: Sonnentag, S.

Article: Recovery, work engagement, and proactive behavior: A new look at the interface between nonwork and work.

Journal: *Journal of Applied Psychology*, June 2003, *88*, 518–528.

Related Research: Schaufeli, W. B., et al. (2002). The measurement of engagement and burnout: A two sample confirmatory factor analytic approach. *Journal of Happiness Studies, 3*, 71–92.

13808

Test Name: WITHIN-SOFTWARE INTERESTS INVENTORY

Purpose: To measure level of interest in each of six core function dimensions characterizing computer software specialties.

Number of Items: 42

Format: Includes six core function dimensions: Planning and Design, Development, Support, Management, Quality Control, and Training.

Reliability: Split-half reliability coefficients ranged from .71 and .88.

Validity: Correlations with other variables ranged from −.19 to .60.

Author: Meir, E. I., and Melamed, S.

Article: Occupational specialty congruence: New data and future directions.

Journal: *Journal of Vocational Behavior*, August 2005, *67*, 21–34.

Related Research: Meir, E. I., & Erez, M. (1981). Fostering a career in engineering. *Journal of Vocational Behavior, 18*, 115–120.

13809

Test Name: WORK COMMITMENT MEASURES

Purpose: To measure six aspects of work commitment.

Number of Items: 39

Format: Includes six scales: Organizational Commitment, Occupational Commitment, Job Involvement, Work Involvement, Organizational Withdrawal Intentions, and Occupational Withdrawal Intentions. Responses are made on a 5-point and 7-point scales. Sample items are presented.

Reliability: Alpha coefficients ranged from .77 to .91.

Validity: Correlations with other variables ranged from −.28 to .15.

Author: Hackett, R. D., et al

Article: Understanding the links between work commitment constructs.

Journal: *Journal of Vocational Behavior*, June 2001, *58*, 392–413.

Related Research: Mowday, R. T., et al. (1979). The measurement of organizational commitment. *Journal of Vocational Behavior, 14*, 224–247. Blau, G. J. (1985). The measurement and prediction of career commitment. *Journal of Occupational Psychology, 58*, 277–288. Landy, F. J., & Gvion, R. M. (1970). Development of scales for the measurement of work motivation. *Organizational Behavior and Human Performance, 5*, 93–103. Kanungo, R. (1982). *Work alienation: An integrative approach*. New York: Praeger Publishers. Mobley, W. (1977). Intermediate linkages in the relationship between job satisfaction and employee turnover. *Journal of Applied Psychology, 62*, 237–240.

13810

Test Name: WORK EFFORT SCALE

Purpose: To measure work effort.

Number of Items: 5

Format: Responses are made on a 7-point scale ranging from 1 (*strongly disagree*) to 7 (*strongly agree*). An example is given.

Reliability: Coefficient alpha was .91 ($n = 139$).

Validity: Correlations with other variables ranged from −.19 to .47 ($n = 139$).

Author: Byrne, Z. S., et al.

Article: The interactive effects of conscientiousness, work effort, and psychological climate on job performance.

Journal: *Journal of Vocational Behavior*, April 2005, *66*, 326–338.

Related Research: Chung, Y., & Ding, C. (2002). Development of the Sales Locus of Control Scale. *Journal of Occupational and Organizational Psychology, 75*, 233–246.

13811

Test Name: WORK ENGAGEMENT SCALE

Purpose: To measure the engagement to work as vigor, dedication, and absorption.

Number of Items: 15

Format: Seven-point scales range from 0 (*never*) to 6 (*daily*).

Reliability: Alpha coefficients ranged from .81 to .85 across subscales.

Validity: Subscale correlations with other variables ranged from .20 to .36.

Author: Duran, A., et al.

Article: Self-reported emotional intelligence, burnout, and engagement among staff services for people with intellectual disabilities.

Journal: *Psychological Reports*, October 2004, *95*, 386–390.

Related Research: Salanova, M., et al. (2000). Desde el "burnout" al "engagement": Una nueva perspectiva? [From burnout to engagement: A new perspective?] *Revista de Psicología del Trabajo y de las Organizaciones, 16*, 117–134.

13812

Test Name: WORK INVOLVEMENT SCALE

Purpose: To assess work involvement.

Number of Items: 6

Format: Responses are made on a 5-point scale ranging from 1 (*strongly disagree*) to 5 (*strongly agree*).

Reliability: Coefficient alpha was .83.

Validity: Correlations with other variables ranged from −.22 to .32 ($n = 178$).

Author: Lim, V. K. G., and Loo, G. L.

Article: Effects of parental job insecurity and parenting behaviors on youth's self-efficacy and work attitudes.

Journal: *Journal of Vocational Behavior,* August 2003, *63*, 86–98.

Related Research: Kanungo, R. N. (1982). *Work alienation: An integrative approach.* New York: Praeger Publishers.

13813

Test Name: WORK INVOLVEMENT SCALE

Purpose: To measure work involvement.

Number of Items: 4

Format: Responses are made on a 4-point scale ranging from 1 (*strongly disagree*) to 5 (*strongly agree*). All items are presented.

Reliability: Coefficient alpha was .62.

Validity: Correlations with other variables ranged from .07 to .50.

Author: Prince, J. B.

Article: Career opportunity and organizational attachment in a blue-collar unionized environment.

Journal: *Journal of Vocational Behavior,* August 2003, *63*, 136–150.

Related Research: Lodahl, T., & Kejner, M. (1965). The definition and measurement of job involvement. *Journal of Applied Psychology, 49*, 24–33.

13814

Test Name: WORK UNIT COMMITMENT SCALE

Purpose: To measure work unit commitment.

Number of Items: 3

Format: Five-point scales are anchored by 1 (*strongly disagree*) and 5 (*strongly agree*). Sample items are presented.

Reliability: Cronbach's alpha was .74.

Validity: Correlations with other variables ranged from −.10 to .40.

Author: van Breukelen, W., et al.

Article: Effects of LMX and differential treatment on work unit commitment.

Journal: *Psychological Reports,* August 2002, *91*, 220–230.

Author Index

Thompson, K. L., 10238, 10525, 11448, 11915, 12075

Thompson, M. P., 12215

Thoms, P., 12625

Tibbetts, S. G., 11693, 11926, 11928, 13279, 13298, 13305

Tiegreen, S. B., 12121

Tillema, H. H., 11991

Timmerman, A., 11708

Timoshin, A., 10468, 11663, 12364, 12857, 13408

Ting, L., 12000

Tischner, E. C., 11647

Titone, D., 11378

Tokar, D. M., 10303, 10901, 12368, 13044, 13206

Toland, M. D., 13686, 13687

Tomás-Sábado, J., 10473, 10474,10476, 10859

Tomic, W., 13188

Tomlinson, M. J., 12435, 12942, 13340

Tomoda, A., 10794

Tomotake, M., 11494, 13302

Toner, B. B., 11443

Toppinen-Tanner, S., 10445, 13153

Torf, B., 11484

Torkelson, E., 10462, 12490

Torres, J. B., 10283, 10284, 10334, 12391, 12854

Totterdell, P., 11168, 11241, 11263

Toussaint, L., 13410

Towler, A. J., 11346, 12691, 12727, 13648

Tracey, T. J. G., 11815, 12928, 13575, 13711

Treadway, D. C., 12537, 12571

Trickett, E. J., 11017, 11737, 12363

Trombini, E., 10915, 11575

Troop-Gordon, W., 10313, 11021, 11067, 11117, 11996, 11997, 12986, 13144

Tsai, W.-C., 13320

Tsao, J. C. I., 10428

Tseng, V., 11640

Tsigilis, N., 12707

Tsorbatzoudis, H., 10300, 11402, 11675, 11786, 12992, 12993, 13069

Tuckman, B. W., 12011

Turban, D. B., 12527, 12587, 13016, 13628, 13738

Turner, J. E., 13249

Turner, R. J., 10819

Turner, S., 13776

Turner, S. L., 11503, 12962

Turnipseed, D. L., 10712, 11845

Turnley, W. H., 11287, 11324, 11328, 11471, 11803, 11853, 12045, 12414, 12694, 12733, 13762, 13775

Tylka, T. L., 10406, 10593, 10820, 11075, 11610, 13019, 13310

Tziner, A., 11187

Uchida, W., 13040

Umaña-Taylor, A. J., 10918, 10955, 11427, 12186

Umberson, D., 10703, 10725

Updegraph, K. A., 10919

Urdan, T., 12187

Ury, K. L., 13216

Utsey, S. O., 10905

Uttaro, T., 10396, 12448

Vacc, N. A., 12447

Valentine, S., 13347, 13512

Valeski, T. N., 10279, 12456, 13706

Valk, A., 10963

Valle, M., 12572, 13196

Van Bakel, H. J. A., 12130, 13306

Van Braak, J. P., 11480

van Breukelen, W., 12056, 12451, 13814

Vancouver, J. B., 11647

van de Meerendonk, B., 11426

Vandenberg, B., 10751

Vandenberghe, C., 12058, 13729

van den Bout, J., 10606, 10680

van den Oord, E. J. C. G., 11664

van der Veer, K., 11524

van der Velde, M. E. G., 13341, 13757, 13794

Van der Zee, K. I., 11039

VandeWalle, D., 12745

Vandiver, B. J., 10946

Vandiver, T., 10315, 12109, 13141

vanDyck, C., 12462

vanEmmerik, I. J. H., 13282

Van Gundy, K., 13226

van Hooft, E. A. J., 11646, 11791, 11818, 11819, 11823, 12933, 12991, 12994, 13463

Van Hook, C. W., 13221

van Knippenberg, B., 11830

van Knippenberg, D., 11830

Van Leuvan, P., 12659

Van Oudenhoven, J. P., 11039

Vansteenkiste, M., 12683, 12758

van Velzen, J. H., 11991

Vardi, Y., 11861

Vasilopoulos, N. L., 13262

Venable, B. T., 13485

Vera, E. M., 10580, 12842, 13062

Verkasalo, M., 13520, 13537

Vermeersch, D. A., 13638

Vermunt, R., 12575

Vernon-Feagons, L., 12107, 12290

Verschueren, K., 12382

Vidal, L. A., 11530

Vignoli, E., 12289, 12347

Vinokurov, A., 10331, 10470, 10897

Vitaro, F., 11573, 11862

Vittengl, J. R., 10603

Vogel, D. L., 10584, 10861, 11437, 11439, 11810, 12034, 12038, 12039, 12073, 12695, 12874, 13174

Volling, B. L, 12222

Volpato, C., 13547

Vondracek, F. W., 10267

Votruba-Drzal, E., 12433

Wade, S. L., 10467

Wagner, J., 13485

Wagner, S. H., 11571, 11864, 12441

Wakayama, H., 12767, 12770, 12777

Walden, T., 11080, 12180, 12264, 13301

Waldrop. D., 10542, 10623, 13103, 13493

Walker, J. S., 10436

Walker-Barnes, C. J., 11780, 11868, 12136

Walkup, J., 11140

Wallace, J. E., 10247, 13442, 13754

Wallace, J. G., 10408, 10442, 11656

Walton, P. D., 10247, 10257

Wanberg, C. R., 11319, 11337, 11822, 12020, 12493, 12866, 13043, 13055

Wang, Y.-W., 13430, 13449, 13510

Wann, D. L., 13358

Wanous, J. P., 11218

Warburton, E. C., 11484

Wardrop, J. L., 10632

Wasti, S. A., 11291, 11339, 11859, 12021, 13759

Watamura, S. E., 11798, 12008

Waters, L., 11321

Watson, D., 12370

Watson, J. C., 12889

Watt, M. C., 12166

Watt, S. K., 11637

Wayne, J. H., 12425

Wayne, S. J., 12538, 12583

Webb, J. R., 13410

Weertman, A., 10534

Wegner, S. H., 11390

Wei, M., 10393, 10410, 10519, 10541, 10579, 10707, 10734, 10795, 10971, 11155, 11388, 12752, 13434

Subject Index

About the Authors

Bert A. Goldman, EdD, is a professor in the School of Education at the University of North Carolina at Greensboro. He has edited nine volumes of the *Directory of Unpublished Experimental Mental Measures* and has authored over 50 journal articles concerning a variety of educational and psychological topics. His latest research deals with factors in college student retention.

David F. Mitchell, PhD, is an assistant professor of sociology at the University of North Carolina at Greensboro. He is the author of several papers about attitudes toward fertility and child rearing, parent–child relationships, intraurban migration, and the empirical dimensions of ethnicity.